Encyclopedia of

Library and Information Sciences, Fourth Edition

Volume 5

Encyclopedia of

Library and Information Sciences, Fourth Edition

Volume 5

From: *Library Science in the United States: Early History* To: *Philosophy of Science*

Encyclopedia Edited By

John D. McDonald

and

Michael Levine-Clark

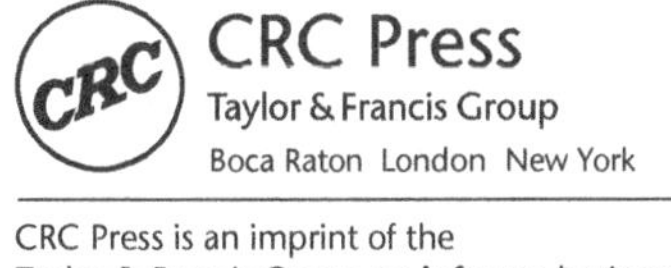

CRC Press is an imprint of the
Taylor & Francis Group, an **informa** business

First published 2018 by CRC Press

Published 2019 by CRC Press
Taylor & Francis Group
6000 Broken Sound Parkway NW, Suite 300
Boca Raton, FL 33487-2742

First issued in paperback 2020

CRC Press is an imprint of the Taylor & Francis Group, an informa business

ISBN-13: 978-1-4665-5259-3 (HB Set)
ISBN-13: 978-0-8153-8629-2 (Vol. 5) (hbk)

ISBN-13: 978-0-3675-7010-1 (PB Set)
ISBN-13: 978-0-3675-7020-0 (Vol. 5) (pbk)

Visit the Taylor & Francis Web site at
http://www.taylorandfrancis.com

and the CRC Press Web site at
http://www.crcpress.com

Encyclopedia of Library and Information Sciences, Fourth Edition

Brief Contents

Volume I

Volume I (cont'd.)

Volume I (cont'd.)

Volume II

Volume II (cont'd.)

Volume III

Volume III (cont'd.)

Volume III (cont'd.)

Volume IV

Volume IV (cont'd.)

Volume V

Volume V (cont'd.)

Volume V (cont'd.)

Volume VI

Volume VI (cont'd.)

Volume VII

Volume VII (cont'd.)

Volume VII (cont'd.)

Encyclopedia of Library and Information Sciences, Fourth Edition

Editors-in-Chief

John D. McDonald
Analytics and Assessment, EBSCO Information Services
Michael Levine-Clark
University of Denver Libraries, Denver, Colorado

Editorial Advisory Board

Contributors

June Abbas / *School of Library and Information Studies, University of Oklahoma, Norman, Oklahoma, U.S.A.*
Richard Abel / *Portland, Oregon, U.S.A.*
Eileen G. Abels / *College of Information Science and Technology, Drexel University, Philadelphia, Pennsylvania, U.S.A.*
Tia Abner / *American Medical Informatics Association (AMIA), Bethesda, Maryland, U.S.A.*
Donald C. Adcock / *Dominican University, River Forest, Illinois, U.S.A.*
Kendra S. Albright / *School of Library and Information Science, University of South Carolina, Columbia, South Carolina, U.S.A.*
Mikael Alexandersson / *University of Gothenburg, Gothenburg, Sweden*
Joan M. Aliprand / *Cupertino, California, U.S.A.*
Jacqueline Allen / *Dallas Museum of Art, Dallas, Texas, U.S.A.*
Romano Stephen Almagno / *International College of St. Bonaventure, Rome, Italy*
Connie J. Anderson-Cahoon / *Southern Oregon University Library, Ashland, Oregon, U.S.A.*
Karen Anderson / *Archives and Information Science, Mid Sweden University, ITM, Härnösand, Sweden*
Rick Anderson / *University of Utah, Salt Lake City, Utah, U.S.A.*
Silviu Andrieş-Tabac / *Institute of Cultural Heritage, Moldova Academy of Sciences, Chişinău, Republic of Moldova*
Peng Hwa Ang / *Wee Kim Wee School of Communication and Information, Nanyang Technological University, Singapore*
Hermina G.B. Anghelescu / *School of Library and Information Science, Wayne State University, Detroit, Michigan, U.S.A.*
Leah Arroyo / *American Association of Museums, Washington, District of Columbia, U.S.A.*
Terry Asla / *Senior Lifestyles Researcher, Seattle, U.S.A.*
Shiferaw Assefa / *University of Kansas, Lawrence, Kansas, U.S.A.*
Ilse Assmann / *Radio Broadcast Facilities, SABC, Johannesburg, South Africa*
Maija-Leena Aulikki Huotari / *University of Oulu, Oulu, Finland*
Henriette D. Avram / *Library of Congress, Washington, District of Columbia, U.S.A.*
Sven Axsäter / *Department of Industrial Management and Logistics, Lund University, Lund, Sweden*
Murtha Baca / *Getty Research Institute, Los Angeles, California, U.S.A.*
Roger S. Bagnall / *Institute for the Study of the Ancient World, New York University, New York, New York, U.S.A.*
Nestor Bamidis / *GSA-Archives of Macedonia, Thessaloniki, Greece*
Franz Barachini / *Business Innovation Consulting—Austria, Langenzersdorf, Austria*
Rebecca O. Barclay / *Rensselaer Polytechnic Institute, Troy, New York, U.S.A.*
Judit Bar-Ilan / *Department of Information Science, Bar-Ilan University, Ramat Gan, Israel*
Alex W. Barker / *Museum of Art and Archaeology, University of Missouri, Columbia, Missouri, U.S.A.*
John A. Bateman / *University of Bremen, Bremen, Germany*

Marcia J. Bates / *Department of Information Studies, Graduate School of Education and Information Studies, University of California, Los Angeles (UCLA), Los Angeles, California, U.S.A.*
Philippe Baumard / *School of Engineering, Stanford University, Stanford, California, U.S.A., and University Paul Cézanne, Aix-en-Provence, France*
David Bawden / *City, University of London, London, U.K.*
Jennifer Bawden / *Museum Studies Program, Faculty of Information Studies, University of Toronto, Toronto, Ontario, Canada*
David Bearman / *Archives & Museum Informatics, Toronto, Ontario, Canada*
William K. Beatty / *Northwestern University Medical School, Chicago, Illinois, U.S.A.*
A.R. Bednarek / *University of Florida, Gainesville, Florida, U.S.A.*
Clare Beghtol / *Faculty of Information Studies, University of Toronto, Toronto, Ontario, Canada*
Lori Bell / *Alliance Library System, East Peoria, Illinois, U.S.A.*
Danna Bell-Russel / *Library of Congress, Washington, District of Columbia, U.S.A.*
William Benedon / *Benedon & Associates, Encino, California, U.S.A.*
Anna Bergaliyeva / *Kazakhstan Institute of Management, Economics and Strategic Research (KIMEP), Almaty, Kazakhstan*
Sidney E. Berger / *Phillips Library, Peabody Essex Museum, Salem, Massachusetts, U.S.A.*
Andrew J. Berner / *University Club of New York, New York, New York, U.S.A.*
Sean F. Berrigan / *Policy, Library and Archives Canada, Ottawa, Ontario, Canada*
John W. Berry / *NILRC: Network of Illinois Learning Resources in Community Colleges, Dominican University, River Forest, Illinois, U.S.A.*
Michael W. Berry / *Department of Electrical Engineering and Computer Science, University of Tennessee, Knoxville, Tennessee, U.S.A.*
Suresh K. Bhavnani / *Center for Computational Medicine and Bioinformatics, University of Michigan, Ann Arbor, Michigan, U.S.A.*
Tamara Biggs / *Chicago History Museum, Chicago, Illinois, U.S.A.*
Frank Birkebæk / *Roskilde Museum, Roskilde, Denmark*
Ann P. Bishop / *Graduate School of Library and Information Science, University of Illinois at Urbana-Champaign, Urbana, Illinois, U.S.A.*
Julia Blixrud / *Association of Research Libraries, Washington, District of Columbia, U.S.A.*
Gloria Bordogna / *Italian National Research Council, Institute for the Dynamics of Environmental Processes, Dalmine, Italy*
Steve Bosch / *Administration Department, University of Arizona, Tucson, Arizona, U.S.A.*
Kimberly S. Bostwick / *Ecology and Evolutionary Biology, Cornell University Museum of Vertebrates, Ithaca, New York, U.S.A.*
Natalia T. Bowdoin / *University of South Carolina Aiken, Aiken, South Carolina, U.S.A.*
Patrick J. Boylan / *Department of Cultural Policy and Management, City University, London, U.K.*
Amy E. Brand / *CrossRef, Lynnfield, Massachusetts, U.S.A.*
Judy Brooker / *Australian Library and Information Association, Deakin, Australian Capital Territory, Australia*
Terrence Brooks / *iSchool, University of Washington, Seattle, Washington, U.S.A.*
Vanda Broughton / *School of Library, Archive and Information Studies, University College London, London, U.K.*
Cecelia Brown / *School of Library and Information Studies, University of Oklahoma, Norman, Oklahoma, U.S.A.*

Jos de Bruijn / *Digital Enterprise Research Institute, University of Innsbruck, Innsbruck, Austria*
Steve Bryant / *BFI National Archive, Herts, U.K.*
Alan Bryden / *International Organization for Standardization, Geneva, Switzerland*
Jeff E. Bullard / *Free Library of Philadelphia, Philadelphia, Pennsylvania, U.S.A.*
Kathleen Burns / *Beinecke Rare Book and Manuscript Library, Yale University, New Haven, Connecticut, U.S.A.*
Brenda A. Burton / *Library, Kirkland & Ellis LLP, Chicago, IL, U.S.A.*
E. Burton Swanson / *Anderson School of Management, University of California, Los Angeles, Los Angeles, California, U.S.A.*
Donald I. Butcher / *Canadian Library Association, Ottawa, Ontario, Canada*
Kevin Butterfield / *Wolf Law Library, College of William and Mary, Williamsburg, Virginia, U.S.A.*
Alex Byrne / *University of Technology, Sydney—Sydney, New South Wales, Australia*
Brian Byrne / *Discipline of Psychology, School of Behavioural, Cognitive and Social Sciences, University of New England, Armidale, New South Wales, Australia, Australian Research Council Centre of Excellence in Cognition and its Disorder, Australia, and National Health and Medical Research Council Centre of Research Excellence in Twin Research, Australia*
Bernadette G. Callery / *School of Information Sciences, University of Pittsburgh, Pittsburgh, Pennsylvania, U.S.A.*
Paul D. Callister / *Leon E. Bloch Law Library, University of Missouri-Kansas City School of Law, Kansas City, Missouri, U.S.A.*
Perrine Canavaggio / *International Council on Archives, Paris, France*
Sarah R. Canino / *Dickinson Music Library, Vassar College, Poughkeepsie, New York, U.S.A.*
Robert Capra / *School of Information and Library Science, University of North Carolina, Chapel Hill, North Carolina, U.S.A.*
Nicholas Carroll / *Hastings Research, Inc., Las Vegas, Nevada, U.S.A.*
Ben Carterette / *Department of Computer and Information Sciences, University of Delaware, Newark, Delaware, U.S.A.*
Vittorio Castelli / *T.J. Watson Research Center, IBM, Yorktown Heights, New York, U.S.A.*
Jane Rosetta Virginia Caulton / *Library of Congress, Washington, District of Columbia, U.S.A.*
Richard Cave / *Formerly at the Public Library of Science, San Francisco, California, U.S.A.*
Roderick Cave / *Loughborough University, Loughborough, U.K.*
Marcel Caya / *Department of History, University of Quebec at Montreal (UQAM), Montreal, Quebec, Canada*
Frank Cervone / *Purdue University Calumet, Hammond, Indiana, U.S.A.*
Leslie Champeny / *Alaska Resources Library and Information Services (ARLIS), Anchorage, Alaska, U.S.A.*
Lois Mai Chan / *School of Library and Information Science, University of Kentucky, Lexington, Kentucky, U.S.A.*
Sergio Chaparro-Univazo / *Graduate School of Library and Information Science, Simmons College, Boston, Massachusetts, U.S.A.*
Mary K. Chelton / *Graduate School of Library and Information Studies, Queens College Flushing, New York, U.S.A.*

Hsinchun Chen / *Department of Management Information Systems, University of Arizona, Tucson, Arizona, U.S.A.*
Jianhua Chen / *Computer Science Department, Louisiana State University, Baton Rouge, Louisiana, U.S.A.*
Eric R. Childress / *OCLC, Dublin, Ohio, U.S.A.*
Michael A. Chilton / *Department of Management, Kansas State University, Manhattan, Kansas, U.S.A.*
TzeHuey Chiou-Peng / *Spurlock Museum, University of Illinois at Urbana-Champaign, Urbana, Illinois, U.S.A.*
Hyun-Yang Cho / *Department of Library and Information Science, Kyonggi University, Suwon, South Korea*
Jae-Hwang Choi / *Department of Library and Information Science, Kyungpook National University, Daegu, South Korea*
Carol E.B. Choksy / *School of Library and Information Science, Indiana University, Bloomington, Indiana, U.S.A.*
Su Kim Chung / *University Libraries, University of Nevada–Las Vegas, Las Vegas, Nevada, U.S.A.*
James Church / *University Libraries, University of California, Berkeley, Berkeley, California, U.S.A.*
Barbara H. Clubb / *Ottawa Public Library, Ottawa, Ontario, Canada*
Arlene Cohen / *Pacific Islands Library Consultant, Seattle, Washington, U.S.A.*
Barbara Cohen-Stratyner / *New York Public Library for the Performing Arts, New York, U.S.A.*
Edward T. Cokely / *Center for Adaptive Behavior and Cognition, Max Planck Institute for Human Development, Berlin, Germany*
Arthur H. Cole / *Harvard University, Cambridge, Massachusetts, U.S.A.*
John Y. Cole / *Center for the Book, Library of Congress, Washington, District of Columbia, U.S.A.*
Patrick Tod Colegrove / *DeLaMare Science & Engineering Library, University Libraries, University of Nevada, Reno, Reno, Nevada, U.S.A.*
Edwin T. Coman, Jr. / *University of California, Riverside, California, U.S.A.*
Nora T. Corley / *Arctic Institute of North America, Montreal, Quebec, Canada*
Sheila Corrall / *Department of Information Studies, University of Sheffield, Sheffield, U.K.*
Erica Cosijn / *Department of Information Science, University of Pretoria, Pretoria, South Africa*
Richard J. Cox / *School of Computing and Information, University of Pittsburgh, Pittsburgh, Pennsylvania, U.S.A.*
Barbara M. Cross / *Records and Information Management, Sony Pictures Entertainment, Culver City, California, U.S.A.*
Kevin Crowston / *School of Information Studies, Syracuse University, Syracuse, New York, U.S.A.*
Adrian Cunningham / *National Archives of Australia (NAA), Canberra, Australian Capital Territory, Australia*
Judith N. Currano / *University of Pennsylvania, Philadelphia, Pennsylvania, U.S.A.*
Susan Curzon / *University Library, California State University–Northridge, Northridge, California, U.S.A.*
Ingetraut Dahlberg / *Bad Koenig, Germany*

Nan Christian Ploug Dahlkild / *Royal School of Library and Information Science, Copenhagen, Denmark*
Jay E. Daily / *University of Pittsburgh, Pittsburgh, Pennsylvania, U.S.A.*
Kimiz Dalkir / *Graduate School of Library and Information Studies, McGill University, Montreal, Quebec, Canada*
Prudence W. Dalrymple / *Drexel University College of Computing & Informatics, Philadelphia, Pennsylvania, U.S.A.*
Marcel Danesi / *Department of Anthropology, University of Toronto, Toronto, Ontario, Canada*
Xuan Hong Dang / *Computer Vision and Image Understanding, Institute for Infocomm, A* STAR, Singapore*
Yan Dang / *Department of Management Information Systems, University of Arizona, Tucson, Arizona, U.S.A.*
Evelyn Daniel / *School of Information and Library Science, University of North Carolina at Chapel Hill, Chapel Hill, North Carolina, U.S.A.*
Richard A. Danner / *School of Law, Duke University, Durham, North Carolina, U.S.A.*
Regina Dantas / *Museu Nacional, HCTE, Universidade Federal do Rio de Janeiro, Rio de Janeiro, Brazil*
Daniel C. Danzig / *Consultant, Pasadena, California, U.S.A.*
Robert Allen Daugherty / *University Library, University of Illinois at Chicago, Chicago, Illinois, U.S.A.*
Charles H. Davis / *Indiana University, Bloomington, IN, U.S.A., and School of Library and Information Science, Indiana University, Bloomington, Indiana, U.S.A.*
Gordon B. Davis / *Carlson School of Management, University of Minnesota, Minneapolis, Minnesota, U.S.A.*
Mary Ellen Davis / *American Library Association, Chicago, Illinois, U.S.A.*
Peter Davis / *International Centre for Cultural and Heritage Studies, Newcastle University, Newcastle upon Tyne, U.K.*
Sheryl Davis / *University Library, University of California, Riverside, Riverside, California, U.S.A.*
Ronald E. Day / *School of Library and Information Science, Indiana University, Bloomington, Indiana, U.S.A.*
Cheryl Dee / *School of Library and Information Science, University of South Florida, Tampa, Florida, U.S.A.*
Robert DeHart / *Department of History, Middle Tennessee State University, Murfreesboro, Tennessee, U.S.A.*
Brenda Dervin / *School of Communication, Ohio State University, Columbus, Ohio, U.S.A.*
Brian Detlor / *Information Systems, McMaster University, Hamilton, Ontario, Canada*
Don E. Detmer / *American Medical Informatics Association (AMIA), Bethesda, Maryland, U.S.A.*
Stella G. Dextre Clarke / *Information Consultant, Oxfordshire, U.K.*
Catherine Dhérent / *National Library of France, Paris, France*
Anne R. Diekema / *Gerald R. Sherratt Library, Southern Utah University, Cedar City, Utah, U.S.A.*
Susan S. DiMattia / *DiMattia Associates, Stamford, Connecticut, U.S.A.*
Gloria Dinerman / *The Library Co-Op, Inc., Edison, New Jersey, U.S.A.*
Jesse David Dinneen / *School of Information Studies, McGill University, Montreal, Quebec, Canada*

Bernard Dione / *School of Librarianship, Archivists Information Science (EBAD), Cheikh Anta Diop University, Dakar, Senegal*
Dieyi Diouf / *Central Library, Cheikh Anta Diop University of Dakar, Dakar, Senegal*
Keith Donohue / *National Historical Publications and Records Commission, Washington, District of Columbia, U.S.A.*
Ann Doyle / *X̱wi7x̱wa Library, First Nations House of Learning, University of British Columbia, Vancouver, British Columbia, Canada*
Carol D. Doyle / *Government Documents Department and Map Library, California State University, Fresno, California, U.S.A.*
Marek J. Druzdzel / *School of Information Sciences and Intelligent Systems Program, University of Pittsburgh, Pittsburgh, Pennsylvania, U.S.A., and Faculty of Computer Science, Bialystok Technical University, Bialystok, Poland*
Kathel Dunn / *National Library of Medicine, Bethesda, Maryland, U.S.A.*
Luciana Duranti / *School of Library, Archival and Information Studies, University of British Columbia, Vancouver, British Columbia, Canada*
Joan C. Durrance / *School of Information, University of Michigan, Ann Arbor, Michigan, U.S.A.*
Maria Economou / *Department of Communication and Cultural Technology, University of the Aegean, Mytilini, Greece*
Gary Edson / *Center for Advanced Study in Museum Science and Heritage Management, Museum of Texas Tech University, Lubbock, Texas, U.S.A.*
Mary B. Eggert / *Library, Kirkland & Ellis LLP, Chicago, IL, U.S.A.*
Daniel Eisenberg / *Florida State University, Tallahassee, Florida, U.S.A.*
Innocent I. Ekoja / *University Library, University of Abuja, Abuja, Nigeria*
Sarah Elliott / *International Centre for Cultural and Heritage Studies, Newcastle University, Newcastle upon Tyne, U.K.*
David Ellis / *Department of Information Studies, Aberystwyth University, Wales, U.K.*
Jill Emery / *Portland State University Library, Portland, Oregon, U.S.A.*
Zorana Ercegovac / *InfoEN Associates, Los Angeles, California, U.S.A.*
Timothy L. Ericson / *School of Information Science, University of Wisconsin-Milwaukee, Milwaukee, Wisconsin, U.S.A.*
Elena Escolano Rodríguez / *National Library of Spain, Madrid, Spain*
Leigh S. Estabrook / *Graduate School of Library and Information Science, University of Illinois at Urbana- / Champaign, Champaign, Illinois, U.S.A.*
Mark E. Estes / *Alameda County Law Library, Oakland, California, U.S.A.*
Beth Evans / *Library, Brooklyn College, City University of New York, Brooklyn, New York, U.S.A.*
Joanne Evans / *Centre for Organisational and Social Informatics, Monash University, Melbourne, Victoria, Australia*
Dominic J. Farace / *Grey Literature Network Service, TextRelease/GreyNet, Amsterdam, The Netherlands*
David Farneth / *Special Collections and Institutional Records, Getty Research Institute, Los Angeles, California, U.S.A.*
Sharon Fawcett / *Office of Presidential Libraries, National Archives and Records Administration, College Park, Maryland, U.S.A.*
Dieter Fensel / *Institute of Computer Science, University of Innsbruck, Innsbruck, Austria, and National University of Ireland, Galway, Galway, Ireland*
Thomas L. Findley / *Leo A. Daly/Architects & Engineers, Omaha, Nebraska, U.S.A.*

Karen E. Fisher / *Information School, University of Washington, Seattle, Washington, U.S.A.*
Nancy Fjällbrant / *Chalmers University of Technology Library, International Association of Technological University Libraries, Gothenburg, Sweden*
Julia Flanders / *Brown University, Providence, Rhode Island, U.S.A.*
Nancy Flury Carlson / *Westinghouse Electric Corporation, Pittsburgh, Pennsylvania, U.S.A.*
Roger R. Flynn / *School of Information Sciences and Intelligent Systems Program, University of Pittsburgh, Pittsburgh, Pennsylvania, U.S.A.*
Helen Forde / *Department of Information Studies, University College London, London, U.K.*
Douglas J. Foskett / *University of London, London, U.K.*
Susan Foutz / *Institute for Learning Innovation, Edgewater, Maryland, U.S.A.*
Christopher Fox / *Department of Computer Science, James Madison University, Harrisonburg, Virginia, U.S.A.*
Carl Franklin / *Consultant, Columbus, Ohio, U.S.A.*
Jonathan A. Franklin / *Gallagher Law Library, University of Washington, Seattle, Washington, U.S.A.*
Thomas J. Froehlich / *School of Library and Information Science, Kent State University, Kent, Ohio, U.S.A.*
Steve Fuller / *Department of Sociology, University of Warwick, Coventry, U.K.*
Crystal Fulton / *School of Information and Communication Studies, University College Dublin, Dublin, Ireland*
Carla J. Funk / *Medical Library Association, Chicago, Illinois, U.S.A.*
Jonathan Furner / *Department of Information Studies University of California, Los Angeles, Los Angeles, California, U.S.A.*
Dennis Galletta / *Katz Graduate School of Business, University of Pittsburgh, Pittsburgh, Pennsylvania, U.S.A.*
D. Linda Garcia / *Communication Culture and Technology, Georgetown University, Washington, District of Columbia, U.S.A.*
Holly Gardinier / *Honnold/Mudd Library, Libraries of The Claremont Colleges, Claremont, California, U.S.A.*
Sally Gardner Reed / *Association of Library Trustees, Advocates, Friends and Foundations (ALTAFF), Philadelphia, Pennsylvania, U.S.A.*
Janifer Gatenby / *Online Computer Library Center (OCLC), Leiden, The Netherlands*
Ramesh C. Gaur / *Kalanidhi Division, Indira Gandhi National Centre for the Arts (IGNCA), New Delhi, India*
Lee Anne George / *Association of Research Libraries, Washington, District of Columbia, U.S.A.*
David E. Gerard / *College of Librarianship Wales, Cardiganshire, Wales, U.K.*
Malcolm Getz / *Department of Economics, Vanderbilt University, Nashville, Tennessee, U.S.A.*
Mary W. Ghikas / *American Library Association, Chicago, Illinois, U.S.A.*
Nicholas Gibbins / *School of Electronics and Computer Science, University of Southampton, Southampton, U.K.*
Gerd Gigerenzer / *Center for Adaptive Behavior and Cognition, Max Planck Institute for Human Development, Berlin, Germany*
Tommaso Giordano / *Library, European University Institute, Florence, Italy*
Lilian Gisesa / *Kenya National Archives, Nairobi, Kenya*
Edward A. Goedeken / *Iowa State University, Ames, Iowa, U.S.A.*
Warren R. Goldmann / *National Technical Institute for the Deaf, Rochester Institute of Technology, Rochester, New York, U.S.A.*

David Gordon / *Milwaukee Art Museum, Milwaukee, Wisconsin, U.S.A.*
David B. Gracy II / *School of Information, University of Texas at Austin, Austin, Texas, U.S.A.*
Karen F. Gracy / *School of Library and Information Science, Kent State University, Kent, Ohio, U.S.A.*
Renny Granda / *Universidad Central de Venezuela, Caracas, Venezuela*
Paul Gray / *School of Information Systems and Technology, Claremont Graduate University, Claremont, California, U.S.A.*
Jane Greenberg / *Metadata Research Center, School of Information and Library Science, University of North Carolina at Chapel Hill, Chapel Hill, North Carolina, U.S.A.*
Karen Greenwood / *American Medical Informatics Association (AMIA), Bethesda, Maryland, U.S.A.*
Jill E. Grogg / *Libraries, University of Alabama, Tuscaloosa, Alabama, U.S.A.*
Melissa Gross / *School of Information, Florida State University, Tallahassee, Florida, U.S.A.*
Andrew Grove / *Guest Faculty, Information School, University of Washington, Seattle, Washington, U.S.A.*
Dinesh K. Gupta / *Department of Library and Information Science, Vardhaman Mahaveer Open University, 3 Kota, India*
Laurel L. Haak / *Open Researcher and Contributor ID, Inc. (ORCID), U.S.A.*
Kate Hagan / *American Association of Law Libraries, Chicago, Illinois, U.S.A.*
Kathleen Hall / *Leon E. Bloch Law Library, University of Missouri-Kansas City School of Law, Kansas City, Missouri, U.S.A.*
Virginia M.G. Hall / *Center for Educational Resources, The Sheridan Libraries, Johns Hopkins University, Baltimore, Maryland, U.S.A.*
Wendy Hall / *Intelligence, Agents, Multimedia Group, University of Southampton, Southampton, U.K.*
Stuart Hamilton / *International Federation of Library Associations and Institutions, The Hague, The Netherlands*
Maureen L. Hammer / *Knowledge Management, Batelle Memorial Institute, Charlottesville, Virginia, U.S.A.*
Jong-Yup Han / *Research Information Team, KORDI, Seoul, South Korea*
Debra Gold Hansen / *School of Library and Information Science, San Jose State University, Yorba Linda, California, U.S.A.*
Derek L. Hansen / *University of Maryland, College Park, Maryland, U.S.A.*
Eugene R. Hanson / *Shippensburg State College, Shippensburg, Pennsylvania, U.S.A.*
Jane Hardy / *Australian Library and Information Association, Deakin, Australian Capital Territory, Australia*
Julie Hart / *American Association of Museums, Washington, District of Columbia, U.S.A.*
Hiroyuki Hatano / *Surugadai University, Saitama, Japan*
Robert M. Hayes / *Department of Information Studies, University of California, Los Angeles, Los Angeles, California, U.S.A.*
Caroline Haythornthwaite / *Graduate School of Library and Information Science, University of Illinois at Urbana- / Champaign, Champaign, Illinois, U.S.A.*
Penny Hazelton / *Gallagher Law Library, University of Washington, Seattle, Washington, U.S.A.*
P. Bryan Heidorn / *Graduate School of Library and Information Science, University of Illinois at Urbana-Champaign, Champaign, Illinois, U.S.A.*
Helen Heinrich / *Collection Access and Management Services, California State University–Northridge, Northridge, California, U.S.A.*

Doris S. Helfer / *Collection Access and Management Services, California State University–Northridge, Northridge, California, U.S.A.*
Markus Helfert / *School of Computing, Dublin City University, Dublin, Ireland*
Jean Henefer / *School of Information and Communication Studies, University College Dublin, Dublin, Ireland*
Steven L. Hensen / *Rare Book, Manuscript and Special Collections Library, Duke University, Durham, North Carolina, U.S.A.*
Pamela M. Henson / *Archives, Smithsonian Institution, Washington, District of Columbia, U.S.A.*
Peter Hernon / *Graduate School of Library and Information Science, Simmons College, Boston, Massachusetts, U.S.A.*
Dorothy H. Hertzel / *Case Western Reserve University, Cleveland, Ohio, U.S.A.*
Francis Heylighen / *Free University of Brussels, Brussels, Belgium*
Randolph Hock / *Online Strategies, Annapolis, Maryland, U.S.A.*
Theodora L. Hodges / *Berkeley, California, U.S.A.*
Sara S. Hodson / *Huntington Library, San Marino, California, U.S.A.*
Judy C. Holoviak / *American Geophysical Union, Washington, District of Columbia, U.S.A.*
Aleksandra Horvat / *Faculty of Philosophy, University of Zagreb, Zagreb, Croatia*
Ali Houissa / *Olin Library, Cornell University, Ithaca, New York, U.S.A.*
Pamela Howard-Reguindin / *Library of Congress Office, Nairobi, Kenya*
Han-Yin Huang / *International Centre for Cultural and Heritage Studies, Newcastle University, Newcastle upon Tyne, U.K.*
Kathleen Hughes / *American Library Association, Chicago, Illinois, U.S.A.*
Betsy L. Humphreys / *National Library of Medicine, Bethesda, Maryland, U.S.A.*
Charlene S. Hurt / *University Library, Georgia State University, Atlanta, Georgia, U.S.A.*
Sue Hutley / *Australian Library and Information Association, Deakin, Australian Capital Territory, Australia*
John P. Immroth / *University of Pittsburgh, Pittsburgh, Pennsylvania, U.S.A.*
Peter Ingwersen / *Royal School of Library and Information Science, University of Copenhagen, Copenhagen, Denmark*
Vanessa Irvin / *Library and Information Science Program, Information and Computer Sciences Department, University of Hawaii at Mānoa, Honolulu, Hawaii, U.S.A.*
Karla Irwin / *University Libraries, University of Nevada–Las Vegas, Las Vegas, Nevada, U.S.A.*
October R. Ivins / *Ivins eContent Solutions, Sharon, Massachusetts, U.S.A.*
Kalervo Järvelin / *School of Information Science, University of Tampere, Tampere, Finland*
Jean Frédéric Jauslin / *Federal Department of Home Affairs (FDHA), Swiss Federal Office of Culture, Bern, Switzerland*
V. Jeyaraj / *Hepzibah Institute of Conversion, Chennai, India*
Scott Johnston / *McPherson Library, University of Victoria, Victoria, British Columbia, Canada*
Trevor Jones / *Mountain Heritage Center, Western Carolina University, Cullowhee, North Carolina, U.S.A.*
William Jones / *Information School, University of Washington, Seattle, Washington, U.S.A.*
Jay Jordan / *OCLC Online Computer Library Center, Inc., Dublin, Ohio, U.S.A.*
Corinne Jörgensen / *School of Information Studies, Florida State University, Tallahassee, Florida, U.S.A.*
Gene Joseph / *Aboriginal Library Consultant, Langley, British Columbia, Canada*

Daniel N. Joudrey / *School of Library and Information Science, Simmons College, Boston, Massachusetts, U.S.A.*
Heidi Julien / *Library and Information Studies, State University of New York–Buffalo, Buffalo, New York, U.S.A.*
Janet Kaaya / *Department of Information Studies, University of California, Los Angeles, California, U.S.A.*
Philomena Kagwiria Mwirigi / *Kenya National Library Service (KNLS), Nairobi, Kenya*
Athanase B. Kanamugire / *Library Consultant, Dhahran, Saudi Arabia*
Paul B. Kantor / *School of Communication and Information, Rutgers University, New Brunswick, New Jersey, U.S.A.*
Sofia Kapnisi / *International Federation of Library Associations and Institutions, The Hague, the Netherlands*
Nelson Otieno Karilus / *Kenya National Library Service (KNLS), Nairobi, Kenya*
Amy M. Kautzman / *University of California, Berkeley, Berkeley, California, U.S.A.*
Karalyn Kavanaugh / *Account Services Manager, EBSCO Information Services, Birmingham, Alabama, U.S.A.*
Caroline Kayoro / *Kenya National Library Service (KNLS), Nairobi, Kenya*
Andreas Kellerhals / *Federal Department of Home Affairs (FDHA), Swiss Federal Archives, Bern, Switzerland*
John M. Kennedy / *Indiana University, Bloomington, Indiana, U.S.A.*
Kristen Kern / *Portland State University, Portland, Oregon, U.S.A.*
Christopher S.G. Khoo / *School of Communication and Information, Nanyang Technological University, Singapore*
Tapan Khopkar / *University of Michigan, Ann Arbor, Michigan, U.S.A.*
Irene Muthoni Kibandi / *Kenya National Library Service (KNLS), Nairobi, Kenya*
Ruth E. Kifer / *Dr. Martin Luther King, Jr. Library, San Jose State University, San Jose, California, U.S.A.*
Seong Hee Kim / *Department of Library and Information Science, Chung-Ang University, Seoul, South Korea*
Pancras Kimaru / *Kenya National Library Service (KNLS), Nairobi, Kenya*
Karen E. King / *Washington, District of Columbia, U.S.A.*
William R. King / *University of Pittsburgh, Pittsburgh, Pennsylvania, U.S.A.*
Susan K. Kinnell / *Consultant, Santa Barbara, California, U.S.A.*
Laurence J. Kipp / *Harvard University, Cambridge, Massachusetts, U.S.A.*
Thomas G. Kirk, Jr. / *Earlham College Libraries, Earlham College, Richmond, Indiana, U.S.A.*
Breanne A. Kirsch / *Library, Emerging Technologies, University of South Carolina Upstate, Spartanburg, South Carolina, U.S.A.*
Vernon N. Kisling, Jr. / *Marston Science Library, University of Florida, Gainesville, Florida, U.S.A.*
Adam D. Knowles / *San Diego, California, U.S.A.*
Rebecca Knuth / *Library and Information Science Program, University of Hawaii, Honolulu, Hawaii, U.S.A.*
Michael Koenig / *College of Information and Computer Science, Long Island University, Brookville, New York, U.S.A.*
Jesse Koennecke / *Cornell University Library, Cornell University College of Arts and Sciences, Ithaca, New York, U.S.A.*
Jes Koepfler / *Museum Studies Program, Faculty of Information Studies, University of Toronto, Toronto, Ontario, Canada*

Amelia Koford / *Blumberg Memorial Library, Texas Lutheran University, Seguin, Texas, U.S.A.*
Toru Koizumi / *Library, Rikkyo University, Tokyo, Japan*
Josip Kolanović / *Croatian State Archives, Zagreb, Croatia*
Sjoerd Koopman / *International Federation of Library Associations and Institutions, The Hague, the Netherlands*
Donald Kraft / *Department of Computer Science, U.S. Air Force Academy, Colorado Springs, Colorado, U.S.A.*
Allison Krebs / *University of Arizona, Tucson, Arizona, U.S.A.*
Judith F. Krug / *Office for Intellectual Freedom, American Library Association, Chicago, Illinois, U.S.A.*
D.W. Krummel / *Emeritus, Graduate School of Library and Information Science, University of Illinois at Urbana-Champaign, Champaign, Illinois, U.S.A.*
Carol Collier Kuhlthau / *Department of Library and Information Science, Rutgers University, New Brunswick, New Jersey, U.S.A.*
Krishan Kumar / *Former Head, Department of Library and Information Science, University of Delhi, New Delhi, India*
Sanna Kumpulainen / *Library, Tampere University of Technology, Tampere, Finland*
Michael J. Kurtz / *National Archives at College Park, U.S. National Archives and Records Administration, College Park, Maryland, U.S.A.*
Zhenhua Lai / *Department of Management Information Systems, University of Arizona, Tucson, Arizona, U.S.A.*
Mounia Lalmas / *Department of Computing Science, University of Glasgow, Glasgow, U.K.*
Heather M. Lamond / *Massey University Library, Palmerston North, New Zealand*
F.W. Lancaster / *Graduate School of Library and Information Science, University of Illinois at Urbana-Champaign, Urbana, Illinois, U.S.A.*
Ronald L. Larsen / *School of Information Sciences, University of Pittsburgh, Pittsburgh, Pennsylvania, U.S.A.*
Ray R. Larson / *School of Information, University of California—Berkeley, Berkeley, California, U.S.A.*
Jesús Lau / *Library Services Unit USBI Veracruz (USBI VER), University of Veracruz, Veracruz, Mexico*
Judith V. Lechner / *Department of Educational Foundations, Leadership, and Technology, Auburn University, Auburn, Alabama, U.S.A.*
Christopher A. Lee / *School of Information and Library Science, University of North Carolina at Chapel Hill, Chapel Hill, North Carolina, U.S.A.*
Janet Lee / *University of Denver, Denver, Colorado, U.S.A, and Regis University, Denver, Colorado, U.S.A.*
Catherine Leekam / *Museum Studies Program, Faculty of Information Studies, University of Toronto, Toronto, Ontario, Canada*
Kjell Lemström / *Department of Computer Science, University of Helsinki, Helsinki, Finland*
Timothy F. Leslie / *Department of Geography and Geoinformation Science, George Mason University, Fairfax, Virginia, U.S.A.*
Noémie Lesquins / *Scientific Mission (DSR), National Library of France, Paris, France*
Rosalind K. Lett / *Information-2-Knowledge, Atlanta, Georgia, U.S.A.*
Allison V. Level / *Colorado State University, Fort Collins, Colorado, U.S.A.*
Michael Levine-Clark / *Penrose Library, University of Denver, Denver, Colorado, U.S.A.*
Anany Levitin / *Department of Computing Sciences, Villanova University, Villanova, Pennsylvania, U.S.A.*

Marjorie Lewis / *Canaan, New York, U.S.A.*
Elizabeth D. Liddy / *School of Information Studies, Syracuse University, Syracuse, New York, U.S.A.*
Silje C. Lier / *Software & Information Industry Association, Washington, District of Columbia, U.S.A.*
Jane E. Light / *Dr. Martin Luther King, Jr. Library, San Jose Public Library, San Jose, California, U.S.A.*
Paul M. Lima / *Canadian Heritage Information Network (CHIN), Gatineau, Quebec, Canada*
Louise Limberg / *Swedish School of Library and Information Science, University of Borås and University of Gothenburg, Borås, Sweden*
Shin-jeng Lin / *Department of Business Administration, Le Moyne College, Syracuse, New York, U.S.A.*
Sarah Lippincott / *Educopia Institute, Atlanta, Georgia, U.S.A.*
Peter Johan Lor / *School of Information Studies, University of Wisconsin-Milwaukee, Milwaukee, Wisconsin, U.S.A., and Department of Information Science, University of Pretoria, Pretoria, South Africa*
Beth Luey / *Fairhaven, Massachusetts, U.S.A.*
Joseph Luke / *Kazakhstan Institute of Management, Economics and Strategic Research (KIMEP), Almaty, Kazakhstan*
Claudia Lux / *Central and Regional Library of Berlin (ZLB), Berlin, Germany*
Marianne Lykke / *Information Interaction and Architecture, Royal School of Library and Information Science, Aalborg, Denmark*
Elena Macevičiūtė / *Faculty of Communication, Vilnius University, Vilnius, Lithuania, and Swedish School of Library and Information Science, University of Borås, Borås, Sweden*
Juan D. Machin-Mastromatteo / *Universidad Central de Venezuela, Caracas, Venezuela*
Barbara A. Macikas / *American Library Association, Chicago, Illinois, U.S.A.*
Leslie Madsen-Brooks / *Boise State University, Boise, Idaho, U.S.A.*
William J. Maher / *Archives, University of Illinois at Urbana-Champaign, Urbana, Illinois, U.S.A.*
Thomas Mann / *Library of Congress, Washington, District of Columbia, U.S.A.*
Sylva Natalie Manoogian / *Department of Information Studies, University of California, Los Angeles, Los Angeles, California, U.S.A.*
Daniel Marcu / *Information Sciences Institute, University of Southern California, Marina del Rey, California, U.S.A.*
James W. Marcum / *Fairleigh Dickinson University, Madison, New Jersey, U.S.A.*
Francesca Marini / *School of Library, Archival and Information Studies, University of British Columbia, Vancouver, British Columbia, Canada*
Johan Marklund / *Department of Industrial Management and Logistics, Lund University, Lund, Sweden*
Dian I. Martin / *Small Bear Technical Consulting, LLC, Thorn Hill, Tennessee, U.S.A.*
Susan K. Martin / *Lauinger Library, Georgetown University, Washington, District of Columbia, U.S.A.*
Paul F. Marty / *College of Communication and Information, Florida State University, Tallahassee, Florida, U.S.A.*
Dan Marwit / *Lee H. Skolnick Architecture + Design Partnership, New York, New York, U.S.A.*
Laura Matzer / *Arizona Museum for Youth, Mesa, Arizona, U.S.A.*

Robert L. Maxwell / *Special Collections and Metadata Catalog Department, Brigham Young University, Provo, Utah, U.S.A.*
Hope Mayo / *Houghton Library, Harvard University, Cambridge, Massachusetts, U.S.A.*
Sally H. McCallum / *Network Development and MARC Standards Office, Library of Congress, Washington, District of Columbia, U.S.A.*
Gavan McCarthy / *eScholarship Research Centre, University of Melbourne, Melbourne, Victoria, Australia*
Ian McGowan / *Former Librarian, National Library of Scotland, Edinburgh, U.K.*
Roger McHaney / *Department of Management, Kansas State University, Manhattan, Kansas, U.S.A.*
I.C. McIlwaine / *University College London, School of Library, Archive and Information Studies, London, U.K.*
Sue McKemmish / *Centre for Organisational and Social Informatics, Monash University, Melbourne, Victoria, Australia*
Marie E. McVeigh / *JCR and Bibliographic Policy, Thomson Reuters - Scientific, Philadelphia, Pennsylvania, U.S.A.*
Linda Mboya / *National Museums of Kenya, Nairobi, Kenya*
Judith Adams Meadows / *State Law Library of Montana, Helena, Montana, U.S.A.*
K. van der Meer / *Faculty of Electrical Engineering, Mathematics and Computer Science, Delft University, the Netherlands; Information and Library Science, IOIW, Antwerp University, Belgium; and D-CIS, Delft, The Netherlands*
Bharat Mehra / *School of Information Sciences, University of Tennessee, Knoxville, Tennessee, U.S.A.*
Margaret Ann Mellinger / *OSU Libraries & Press, Oregon State University, Corvallis, Oregon, U.S.A.*
Elizabeth E. Merritt / *American Association of Museums, Washington, District of Columbia, U.S.A.*
David Millman / *Academic Information Systems, Columbia University, New York, U.S.A.*
Jack Mills / *North-Western Polytechnic, London, U.K.*
Kevin L. Mills / *National Institute of Standards and Technology, Gaithersburg, Maryland, U.S.A.*
Staša Milojević / *Department of Information Studies, University of California, Los Angeles, Los Angeles, California, U.S.A.*
Marla Misunas / *Collections Information and Access, San Francisco Museum of Modern Art, San Francisco, California, U.S.A.*
Joan S. Mitchell / *OCLC Online Computer Library Center, Inc., Dublin, Ohio, U.S.A.*
Yoriko Miyabe / *Rikkyo University, Tokyo, Japan*
Diane Mizrachi / *University Libraries, University of California–Los Angeles, Los Angeles, California, U.S.A.*
William Moen / *Texas Center for Digital Knowledge, University of North Texas, Denton, Texas, U.S.A.*
Abdul Moid / *University of Karachi, Karachi, Pakistan*
Hermann Moisl / *Center for Research in Linguistics, University of Newcastle upon Tyne, Newcastle upon Tyne, U.K.*
Ole Magnus Mølbak Andersen / *Danish State Archives, Copenhagen, Denmark*
Mavis B. Molto / *Utah State University, Logan, Utah, U.S.A.*
Philip Mooney / *Heritage Communications, Coca-Cola Company, Atlanta, Georgia, U.S.A.*
Reagan W. Moore / *San Diego Supercomputer Center, University of North Carolina at Chapel Hill, Chapel Hill, North Carolina, U.S.A.*

Mersini Moreleli-Cacouris / *Department of Library Science and Information Systems, Technological Educational Institute (TEI) of Thessaloniki, Sindos, Greece*
Paul K. Moser / *Department of Philosophy, Loyola University Chicago, Chicago, Illinois, U.S.A.*
Clara C. Mosquera / *Library, Kirkland & Ellis LLP, Chicago, IL, U.S.A.*
David J. Muddiman / *Leeds Metropolitan University, Leeds, U.K.*
Nancy C. Mulvany / *Bayside Indexing Service, Fort Collins, Colorado, U.S.A.*
Sue Myburgh / *School of Communication, University of South Australia, Adelaide, South Australia, Australia*
Elli Mylonas / *Brown University, Providence, Rhode Island, U.S.A.*
Jeremy Myntti / *J. Willard Marriott Library, Salt Lake City, Utah, U.S.A.*
Jacob Nadal / *ReCAP: The Research Collections and Preservation Consortium, Princeton, New Jersey, U.S.A.*
Diane Nahl / *Information and Computer Sciences Department, University of Hawaii, Honolulu, Hawaii, U.S.A.*
Robert Nardini / *Vice President, Library Services, ProQuest Books, La Vergne, Tennessee, U.S.A.*
Arnold vander Nat / *Department of Philosophy, Loyola University Chicago, Chicago, Illinois, U.S.A.*
Charles M. Naumer / *Information School, University of Washington, Seattle, Washington, U.S.A.*
Sophie Ndegwa / *Kenya National Library Service (KNLS), Nairobi, Kenya*
Dixie Neilson / *University of Florida, Gainesville, Florida, U.S.A.*
Sarah Beth Nelson / *School of Information and Library Sciences, University of North Carolina at Chapel Hill, Chapel Hill, North Carolina, U.S.A.*
Stuart J. Nelson / *National Library of Medicine, Bethesda, Maryland, U.S.A.*
Stephanie Nemcsok / *Museum Studies Program, Faculty of Information Studies, University of Toronto, Toronto, Ontario, Canada*
Ken Neveroski / *College of Information and Computer Science, Long Island University, Brookville, New York, U.S.A.*
Jennifer Ng / *Museum Studies Program, Faculty of Information Studies, University of Toronto, Toronto, Ontario, Canada*
Melissa Niiya / *Portland Public Schools, Portland, Oregon, U.S.A.*
Angela Noseworthy / *Museum Studies Program, Faculty of Information Studies, University of Toronto, Toronto, Ontario, Canada*
Barbara E. Nye / *Ictus Consulting, LLC, Pasadena, California, U.S.A.*
Charles Nzivo / *Kenya National Library Service (KNLS), Nairobi, Kenya*
Dennis O'Brien / *Maps and Wayfinding, LLC, Mystic, Connecticut, U.S.A.*
Karen Lynn O'Brien / *American Library Association, Chicago, Illinois, U.S.A.*
Kieron O'Hara / *Intelligence, Agents, Multimedia Group, University of Southampton, Southampton, U.K.*
Elizabeth O'Keefe / *Morgan Library and Museum, New York, U.S.A.*
Denise I. O'Shea / *Fairleigh Dickinson University, Teaneck, New Jersey, U.S.A.*
Douglas W. Oard / *College of Information Studies, University of Maryland, College Park, Maryland, U.S.A.*
Maria Oldal / *Morgan Library and Museum, New York, U.S.A.*
Lorne Olfman / *School of Information Systems and Technology, Claremont Graduate University, Claremont, California, U.S.A.*

Bette W. Oliver / *Austin, Texas, U.S.A.*
Annette Olson / *Biological Resources Division, U.S. Geological Survey, Reston, Virginia, U.S.A.*
Hope A. Olson / *School of Information Studies, University of Wisconsin-Milwaukee, Milwaukee, Wisconsin, U.S.A.*
Lawrence J. Olszewski / *OCLC Library, Dublin, Ohio, U.S.A.*
Kok-Leong Ong / *School of Information Technology, Deakin University, Burwood, Victoria, Australia*
Tim Owen / *Chartered Institute of Library and Information Professionals (CILIP), London, U.K.*
John C. Paolillo / *School of Informatics and School of Library and Information Science, Indiana University, Bloomington, Indiana, U.S.A.*
Eun Bong Park / *Library Service Department, National Library of Korea, Seoul, South Korea*
Soyeon Park / *Department of Library and Information Science, Duksung Womens University, Seoul, South Korea*
Gabriella Pasi / *Department of Informatics, Systems and Communication, University of Studies of Milano Bicocca, Milan, Italy*
Norman Paskin / *Tertius Ltd., Oxford, U.K.*
Christiane Paul / *Whitney Museum of American Art, New York, U.S.A.*
Ellen Pearlstein / *Information Studies and UCLA / Getty Program in the Conservation of Ethnographic and Archaeological Materials, University of California, Los Angeles, Los Angeles, California, U.S.A.*
Kathleen de la Peña McCook / *School of Library and Information Science, University of South Florida, Tampa, Florida, U.S.A.*
Steve Pepper / *Department of Linguistics, University of Oslo, Oslo, Norway*
Manuel A. Pérez-Quiñones / *Department of Software and Information Systems, University of North Carolina, Charlotte, North Carolina, U.S.A.*
Paul Evan Peters / *University of Pittsburgh, Pittsburgh, Pennsylvania, U.S.A.*
Jakob Heide Petersen / *Danish Agency for Libraries and Media, Copenhagen, Denmark*
Mary Jane Petrowski / *American Library Association, Chicago, Illinois, U.S.A.*
Katharine J. Phenix / *Northglenn Branch, Rangeview Library District, Northglenn, Colorado, U.S.A.*
Robert B. Pickering / *Gilcrease Museum, and Museum Science and Management Program, University of Tulsa, Tulsa, Oklahoma, U.S.A.*
Janice T. Pilch / *Rutgers University Libraries, Rutgers University, New Brunswick, New Jersey, U.S.A.*
Thomas E. Pinelli / *Langley Research Center, National Aeronautics and Space Administration (NASA) Hampton, Virginia, U.S.A.*
Daniel Pitti / *Alderman Library, Institute for Advanced Technology in the Humanities, University of Virginia, Charlottesville, Virginia, U.S.A.*
Elena Ploşniţă / *Science Department, National Museum of Archaeology and History of Moldova, Chisinau, Republic of Moldova*
Gabriela Podušelová / *Slovak National Museum, Bratislava, Slovak Republic*
Danny C.C. Poo / *School of Computing, Department of Information Systems, National University of Singapore, Singapore*
Martine Poulain / *Department of Libraries and Documentation, National Institute for the History of Art (INHA), Paris, France*
Tammy Powell / *National Library of Medicine, Bethesda, Maryland, U.S.A.*
Stephen Prine / *Library of Congress, Washington, District of Columbia, U.S.A.*

Mary Jo Pugh / *Editor, American Archivist, Walnut Creek, California, U.S.A.*
Ajit K. Pyati / *University of Western Ontario, London, Ontario, Canada*
Aimée C. Quinn / *Government Publications Services, Brooks Library, Central Washington University, Ellensburg, Washington, U.S.A.*
Jennie Quiñónez-Skinner / *University Library, California State University–Northridge, Northridge, California, U.S.A.*
Debbie Rabina / *School of Library and Information Science, Pratt Institute, New York, New York, U.S.A.*
Katalin Radics / *Research Library, University of California—Los Angeles, Los Angeles, California, U.S.A.*
Carl Rahkonen / *Harold S. Orendorff Music Library, Indiana University of Pennsylvania, Indiana, Pennsylvania, U.S.A.*
Jocelyn Rankin / *Centers for Disease Control and Prevention Library, Atlanta, Georgia, U.S.A.*
Samuel J. Redman / *Department of History, University of California, Berkeley, Berkeley, California, U.S.A.*
Thomas C. Redman / *Navesink Consulting Group, Little Silver, New Jersey, U.S.A.*
Barbara Reed / *Recordkeeping Innovation, Sydney, New South Wales, Australia*
Marcia Reed / *Getty Research Institute, Los Angeles, CA, U.S.A.*
CarrieLynn D. Reinhard / *Department of Communication, Business, and Information Technologies, Roskilde University, Roskilde, Denmark*
Harold C. Relyea / *Congressional Research Service, Library of Congress, Washington, District of Columbia, U.S.A.*
Steve Ricci / *Department of Information Studies/Film and Television, University of California–Los Angeles, Los Angeles, California, U.S.A.*
Ronald E. Rice / *Department of Communication, University of California–Santa Barbara, Santa Barbara, California, U.S.A.*
John V. Richardson, Jr. / *Department of Information Studies, University of California, Los Angeles, Los Angeles, California, U.S.A.*
Soo Young Rieh / *School of Information, University of Michigan, Ann Arbor, Michigan, U.S.A.*
Kevin S. Rioux / *Division of Library and Information Science, St. John's University, Queens, New York, U.S.A.*
Julian Roberts / *Wolfson College, University of Oxford, Oxford, U.K.*
Lyn Robinson / *City, University of London, London, U.K.*
Diane Robson / *University Libraries, Media Library, University of North Texas, Denton, Texas, U.S.A.*
Michael Rodriguez / *Michigan State University Libraries, East Lansin, Michigan, U.S.A.*
Juraj Roháč / *Department of Archival Science and Auxiliary Historical Sciences, Comenius University in, Bratislava, Slovak Republic*
Mark Roosa / *Pepperdine University, Malibu, California, U.S.A.*
Jonathan Rose / *Department of History, Drew University, Madison, New Jersey, U.S.A.*
Howard Rosenbaum / *School of Library and Information Science, Indiana University, Bloomington, Indiana, U.S.A.*
Catherine Sheldrick Ross / *Faculty of Information and Media Studies, University of Western Ontario, London, Ontario, Canada*
Shannon Ross / *Canadian Heritage Information Network (CHIN), Gatineau, Quebec, Canada*

Richard Rubin / *School of Library and Information Science, Kent State University, Kent, Ohio, U.S.A.*
Lynne M. Rudasill / *University of Illinois at Urbana-Champaign, Champaign, Illinois, U.S.A.*
Michael Rush / *Beinecke Rare Book and Manuscript Library, Yale University, New Haven, Connecticut, U.S.A.*
Mariza Russo / *Faculty of Administration and Accounting Sciences (FACC), Federal University of Rio de Janeiro, Rio de Janeiro, Brazil*
Athena Salaba / *Kent State University, Kent, Ohio, U.S.A.*
Romelia Salinas / *California State University, Los Angeles, Los Angeles, California, U.S.A.*
Airi Salminen / *Department of Computer Science and Information Systems, University of Jyväskylä, Jyväskylä, Finland*
Michael J. Salvo / *Department of English, Purdue University, West Lafayette, Indiana, U.S.A.*
Robert J. Sandusky / *University Library, University of Illinois at Chicago, Chicago, Illinois, U.S.A.*
Tefko Saracevic / *School of Communication and Information, Rutgers University, New Brunswick, New Jersey, U.S.A.*
Chris Sauer / *Said Business School, University of Oxford, Oxford, U.K.*
Rejéan Savard / *School of Library and Information Science, University of Montreal, Montreal, Quebec, Canada*
Reijo Savolainen / *School of Information Sciences, University of Tampere, Tampere, Finland*
Barbara Schaefer / *Geneseo, New York, U.S.A.*
Silvia Schenkolewski-Kroll / *Department of Information Science, Bar-Ilan University, Ramat Gan, Israel*
Lael J. Schooler / *Center for Adaptive Behavior and Cognition, Max Planck Institute for Human Development, Berlin, Germany*
Joachim Schöpfel / *Department of Library and Information Sciences (IDIST), GERiico Laboratory Charles de Gaulle University Lille 3, Villeneuve d'Ascq, France*
Catherine F. Schryer / *Department of English Language and Literature, University of Waterloo, Waterloo, Ontario, Canada*
Marjorie Schwarzer / *Museum Studies Department, John F. Kennedy University, Berkeley, California, U.S.A.*
Jo Ann Secor / *Lee H. Skolnick Architecture + Design Partnership, New York, New York, U.S.A.*
Sara Selwood / *Department of Cultural Policy and Management, City University, London, U.K.*
Frank B. Sessa / *University of Pittsburgh, Pittsburgh, Pennsylvania, U.S.A.*
Mark Sgambettera / *Bronx County Historical Society, Bronx, New York, U.S.A.*
Ayman Shabana / International Institute, University of California, Los Angeles, Los Angeles, California, U.S.A.
Nigel Shadbolt / *School of Electronics and Computer Science, University of Southampton, Southampton, U.K.*
Kalpana Shankar / *School of Informatics, Indiana University, Bloomington, Indiana, U.S.A.*
Debora Shaw / *School of Library and Information Science, Indiana University, Bloomington, Indiana, U.S.A.*
Conrad Shayo / *Department of Information and Decision Sciences, California State University—San Bernardino, San Bernardino, California, U.S.A.*
Elizabeth Shepherd / *Department of Information Studies, University College London, London, U.K.*
Beverly K. Sheppard / *Institute for Learning Innovation, Edgewater, Maryland, U.S.A.*
Ross Shimmon / *Faversham, U.K.*

Snunith Shoham / *Department of Information Science, Bar-Ilan University, Ramat Gan, Israel*
Lyudmila Shpilevaya / *New York Public Library, New York, New York, U.S.A.*
David Shumaker / *School of Library and Information Science, Catholic University of America, Washington, District of Columbia, U.S.A.*
Judith A. Siess / *Information Bridges International, Inc., Champaign, Illinois, U.S.A.*
John Edward Simmons / *Museologica, Bellefonte, Pennsylvania, U.S.A.*
Anestis Sitas / *Aristotle University of Thessaloniki, Thessaloniki, Greece*
Roswitha Skare / *Institute of Culture and Literature, UiT The Arctic University of Norway, Tromsø, Norway*
Katherine Skinner / *Educopia Institute, Atlanta, Georgia, U.S.A.*
Lee H. Skolnick / *Lee H. Skolnick Architecture + Design Partnership, New York, New York, U.S.A.*
Mette Skov / *Department of Communication and Psychology, Aalborg University, Aalborg, Denmark*
Bobby Smiley / *Vanderbilt University, Heard Libraries, Nashville, Tennessee, U.S.A.*
Linda C. Smith / *School of Information Sciences, University of Illinois at Urbana-Champaign, Champaign, Illinois, U.S.A.*
Lois Smith / *Human Factors and Ergonomics Society, Santa Monica, California, U.S.A.*
Lori Smith / *Linus A. Sims Memorial Library, Southeastern Louisiana University, Hammond, Louisiana, U.S.A.*
Patricia A. Smith / *Colorado State University, Fort Collins, Colorado, U.S.A.*
Scott A. Smith / *Langlois Public Library, Langlois, Oregon, U.S.A.*
A. Patricia Smith-Hunt / *Science Library, Preservation Services, University of California, Riverside, Riverside, California, U.S.A.*
Karen Smith-Yoshimura / *Online Computer Library Center (OCLC), San Mateo, California, U.S.A.*
Diane H. Sonnenwald / *University College Dublin, Dublin, Ireland*
Nour Soufi / *Library Cataloging and Metadata Center, University of California, Los Angeles, Los Angeles, California, U.S.A.*
Barbara M. Spiegelman / *Churchill Associates, Pittsburgh, Pennsylvania, U.S.A.*
Robert P. Spindler / *Department of Archives and Manuscripts, Arizona State University, Tempe, Arizona, U.S.A.*
Joie Springer / *Information Society Division, UNESCO, Paris, France*
Suresh Srinivasan / *National Library of Medicine, Bethesda, Maryland, U.S.A.*
Guy St. Clair / *Knowledge Management and Learning, SMR International, New York, New York, U.S.A.*
Cheryl L. Stadel-Bevans / *National Archives and Records Administration, College Park, Maryland, U.S.A.*
Jill Stein / *Institute for Learning Innovation, Edgewater, Maryland, U.S.A.*
Marcia K. Stein / *Museum of Fine Arts, Houston, Houston, Texas, U.S.A.*
Jela Steinerová / *Department of Library and Information Science, Comenius University in, Bratislava, Slovak Republic*
Dick Stenmark / *Department of Applied IT, IT University of Gothenburg, Gothenburg, Sweden*
Andy Stephens / *OBE, Board Secretary, Head of International Engagement, The British Library, London, U.K.*
Margaret Stieg Dalton / *School of Library and Information Studies, University of Alabama, Tuscaloosa, Alabama, U.S.A.*

Katina Strauch / *Addlestone Library, College of Charleston, Charleston, South Carolina, U.S.A.*
Robert D. Stueart / *Graduate School of Library and Information Science, Simmons College, Boston, Massachusetts, U.S.A.*
Paul F. Stuehrenberg / *Yale Divinity Library, New Haven, Connecticut, U.S.A.*
Brian William Sturm / *School of Information and Library Sciences, University of North Carolina at Chapel Hill, Chapel Hill, North Carolina, U.S.A.*
Anna Suorsa / *University of Oulu, Oulu, Finland*
Brett Sutton / *Aurora University, Aurora, Illinois, U.S.A.*
Sarah Sutton / *Mary and Jeff Bell Library, Texas A&M University-Corpus Christi, Corpus Christi, Texas, U.S.A.*
Destinee Kae Swanson / *Adams Museum & House, Inc., Deadwood, South Dakota, U.S.A.*
H.L. Swanson / *GSOE, University of California, Riverside, California, U.S.A.*
Miriam E. Sweeney / *School of Library and Information Studies, University of Alabama, Tuscaloosa, Alabama, U.S.A.*
Shelley Sweeney / *University of Manitoba, Winnipeg, Manitoba, Canada*
Jean Tague-Sutcliffe / *Graduate School of Library and Information Science, University of Western Ontario, London, Ontario, Canada*
Masaya Takayama / *National Archives of Japan, Tokyo, Japan*
Sanna Talja / *Department of Information Studies and Interactive Media, University of Tampere, Tampere, Finland*
G. Thomas Tanselle / *Vice President, John Simon Guggenheim Memorial Foundation, New York, New York, U.S.A.*
Ivan Tanzer / *Museum Studies Program, Faculty of Information Studies, University of Toronto, Toronto, Ontario, Canada*
Melissa Terras / *UCL Department of Information Studies, UCL Centre for Digital Humanities, University College London, London, U.K.*
Mike Thelwall / *School of Computing and Information Technology, University of Wolverhampton, Wolverhampton, U.K.*
Lynne M. Thomas / *Rare Books and Special Collections, Northern Illinois University, DeKalb, Illinois, U.S.A.*
Lawrence S. Thompson / *University of Kentucky, Lexington, Kentucky, U.S.A.*
Jens Thorhauge / *Danish Agency for Libraries and Media, Copenhagen, Denmark*
Anne Thurston / *International Records Management Trust, London, U.K.*
Michael Tiemann / *Open Source Initiative, Chapel Hill, North Carolina, U.S.A.*
Christinger Tomer / *School of Information Sciences, University of Pittsburgh, Pittsburgh, Pennsylvania, U.S.A.*
Elaine G. Toms / *Faculty of Management, Dalhousie University, Halifax, Nova Scotia, Canada*
Jack Toolin / *Whitney Museum of American Art, New York, U.S.A.*
Jennifer Trant / *Archives & Museum Informatics, Toronto, Ontario, Canada*
Barry Trott / *Williamsburg Regional Library, Williamsburg, Virginia, U.S.A.*
Alice Trussell / *Hale Library, Kansas State University, Manhattan, Kansas, U.S.A.*
John Mark Tucker / *Abilene Christian University, Abilene, Texas, U.S.A.*
James M. Turner / *School of Library and Information Sciences, University of Montreal, Montreal, Quebec, Canada*
Louise Tythacott / *Centre for Museology, University of Manchester, Manchester, U.K.*

George Tzanetakis / *Department of Computer Science, University of Victoria, Victoria, British Columbia, Canada*
Franklyn Herbert Upward / *Centre for Organisational and Social Informatics, Monash University, Melbourne, Victoria, Australia*
Richard Urban / *Graduate School of Library and Information Science, University of Illinois, Champaign, Illinois, U.S.A.*
Rachel E. Vacek / *University of Michigan, Ann Arbor, Michigan, U.S.A.*
Ron Van den Branden / *Centre for Scholarly Editing and Document Studies, Royal Academy of Dutch Language and Literature, Gent, Belgium*
Sydney C. Van Nort / *The City College of New York, The City University of New York, New York, U.S.A.*
Edward Vanhoutte / *Centre for Scholarly Editing and Document Studies, Royal Academy of Dutch Language and Literature, Gent, Belgium*
Rebecca Vargha / *Information and Library Science Library, University of North Carolina at Chapel Hill, Chapel Hill, North Carolina, U.S.A.*
Jana Varlejs / *School of Communication, Information and Library Studies, Rutgers University, New Brunswick, New Jersey, U.S.A.*
Jason Vaughan / *Library Technologies, University of Nevada, Las Vegas University Libraries, Las Vegas, Nevada, U.S.A.*
Dale J. Vidmar / *Southern Oregon University Library, Ashland, Oregon, U.S.A.*
Diane Vizine-Goetz / *OCLC Online Computer Library Center, Inc., Dublin, Ohio, U.S.A.*
Ellen M. Voorhees / *Information Technology Laboratory, National Institute of Standards and Technology, Gaithersburg, Maryland, U.S.A.*
Sharon L. Walbridge / *Libraries Washington State University, Pullman, Washington, U.S.A.*
Stephanie Walker / *Brooklyn College, City University of New York, Brooklyn, New York, U.S.A.*
Virginia A. Walter / *Department of Information Studies, University of California, Los Angeles, Los Angeles, California, U.S.A.*
Mark Warschauer / *School of Education, University of California, Irvine, CA, U.S.A.*
Nigel M. Waters / *Department of Geography and Geoinformation Science, George Mason University, Fairfax, Virginia, U.S.A.*
Kathryn M. Wayne / *Art History/Classics Library, University of California, Berkeley, California, U.S.A.*
Frank Webster / *City University, London, U.K.*
Jeff Weddle / *School of Library and Information Studies, University of Alabama, Tuscaloosa, Alabama, U.S.A.*
Judith Weedman / *School of Library and Information Science, San Jose State University, Fullerton, California, U.S.A.*
Stuart L. Weibel / *Office of Research and Special Projects, OCLC Research, Dublin, Ohio, U.S.A.*
Jennifer Weil Arns / *School of Library and Information Science, University of South Carolina, Columbia, South Carolina, U.S.A.*
Bella Hass Weinberg / *Division of Library and Information Science, St. John's University, Queens, New York, New York, U.S.A.*
Volker M. Welter / *Department of the History of Art and Architecture, University of California, Santa Barbara, Santa Barbara, California, U.S.A.*
Caryn Wesner-Early / *ASRC Aerospace & Defense, US Patent & Trademark Office, Alexandria, Virginia, U.S.A.*
Lynn Westbrook / *School of Information, University of Texas at Austin, Austin, Texas, U.S.A.*

Howard D. White / *College of Computing and Informatics, Drexel University, Philadelphia, PA, U.S.A., and College of Information Science and Technology, Drexel University, Philadelphia, Pennsylvania, U.S.A.*
Layna White / *San Francisco Museum of Modern Art, San Francisco, California, U.S.A.*
Michael J. White / *Engineering and Science Library, Queen's University, Kingston, Ontario, Canada*
Sarah K. Wiant / *School of Law, Washington and Lee University, Lexington, Virginia, U.S.A.*
Stephen E. Wiberley, Jr. / *University of Illinois at Chicago, Chicago, Illinois, U.S.A.*
Gunilla Widén-Wulff / *Information Studies, Åbo Akademi University, Åbo, Finland*
Bradley J. Wiles / *Hill Memorial Library, Louisiana State University, Baton Rouge, Louisiana, U.S.A.*
Mary I. Wilke / *Center for Research Libraries, Chicago, Illinois, U.S.A.*
Barratt Wilkins / *Retired State Librarian of Florida, Tallahassee, Florida, U.S.A.*
Peter Willett / *Department of Information Studies, University of Sheffield, Sheffield, U.K.*
Kate Williams / *University of Illinois at Urbana-Champaign, Champaign, Illinois, U.S.A.*
Kirsty Williamson / *Caulfield School of IT, Monash University, Caulfield, Victoria, Australia and School of Information Studies, Charles Sturt University, Wagga Wagga, New South Wales, Australia*
Concepción S. Wilson / *School of Information Systems, Technology and Management, University of New South Wales, Sydney, New South Wales, Australia*
Ian E. Wilson / *Librarian and Archivist of Canada 2004–2009, Ottawa, Ontario, Canada*
Kristen Wilson / *North Carolina State University Libraries, Raleigh, North Carolina, U.S.A.*
Thomas D. Wilson / *Publisher/Editor in Chief, Information Research, U.K.*
Catherine C. Wilt / *PALINET, Philadelphia, Pennsylvania, U.S.A.*
Charles Wilt / *Association for Library Collections and Technical Services (ALCTS), Chicago, Illinois, U.S.A.*
Niels Windfeld Lund / *Institute of Culture and Literature, UiT The Arctic University of Norway, Troms , Norway*
Michael F. Winter / *Shields Library, University of California, Davis, California, U.S.A.*
Erica Wiseman / *Graduate School of Library and Information Studies, McGill University, Montreal, Quebec, Canada*
Steve W. Witt / *University of Illinois at Urbana-Champaign, Champaign, Illinois, U.S.A.*
Blanche Woolls / *iSchool, San Jose State University, San Jose, California, U.S.A.*
Louisa Worthington / *Public Library Association, Chicago, Illinois, U.S.A.*
Jadwiga Woźniak-Kasperek / *Institute of Information and Book Studies, University of Warsaw, Warsaw, Poland*
Judith Wusteman / *School of Information and Communication Studies, University College Dublin, Dublin, Ireland*
Iris Xie / *School of Information Studies, University of Wisconsin–Milwaukee, Milwaukee, Wisconsin, U.S.A.*
Yiyu Yao / *Department of Computer Science, University of Regina, Regina, Saskatchewan, Canada, and International WIC Institute, Beijing University of Technology, Beijing, China*
Janis L. Young / *Library of Congress, Washington, District of Columbia, U.S.A.*
Priscilla C. Yu / *University Library, University of Illinois at Urbana-Champaign, Urbana, Illinois, U.S.A.*
Jana Zabinski / *American National Standards Institute, New York, New York, U.S.A.*
Lisl Zach / *iSchool, Drexel University, Philadelphia, Pennsylvania, U.S.A.*
Olga Zaitseva / *Kazakhstan Institute of Management, Economics and Strategic Research (KIMEP), Almaty, Kazakhstan*

Marcia Lei Zeng / *School of Library and Information Science, Kent State University, Kent, Ohio, U.S.A.*
Yi Zeng / *International WIC Institute, Beijing University of Technology, Beijing, China*
Višnja Zgaga / *Museum Documentation Center, Zagreb, Croatia*
Jun Zhang / *Pitney Bowes, Shelton, Connecticut, U.S.A.*
Yulei Zhang / *Department of Management Information Systems, University of Arizona, Tucson, Arizona, U.S.A.*
Kai Zheng / *Department of Health Management and Policy, University of Michigan, Ann Arbor, Michigan, U.S.A.*
Ning Zhong / *Department of Life Science and Informatics, Maebashi Institute of Technology, Maebashi-City, Japan, and International WIC Institute, Beijing University of Technology, Beijing, China*
Maja Žumer / *University of Ljubljana, Slovenia*
Vladimir Zwass / *Computer Science and Management Information Systems, Fairleigh Dickinson University, Teaneck, New Jersey, U.S.A.*

Encyclopedia of Library and Information Sciences, Fourth Edition

Contents

Volume I

Volume I (*cont'd.*)

Volume I (*cont'd.*)

Volume II

Volume II (*cont'd.*)

Volume III

Volume III (*cont'd.*)

Volume III (*cont'd.*)

Volume IV

Volume IV (*cont'd.*)

Volume V

Volume V (*cont'd.*)

Volume VI

Volume VI *(cont'd.)*

Volume VI (*cont'd.*)

Volume VII

Volume VII (*cont'd.*)

Introduction to the Encyclopedia of Library and Information Sciences, Fourth Edition

How to Use This Encyclopedia

Entries are arranged alphabetically in this encyclopedia (see end papers for alphabetical list). The editors of this edition (ELIS-4) have decided to forego the Topical Table of Contents that was provided in ELIS-3 by editors Marcia Bates and Mary Niles Maack. At the time of publication of ELIS-3, the Topical TOC was crucial for readers to get a sense of how subjects were grouped and an understanding of the field or subfield through the clustering of categorical entries in the print edition. ELIS-4 is envisioned as a primarily online reference work where a Topical TOC does not serve the same purpose. The print edition is served well by the main TOC as well as the detailed index, while entries in the online version are easily discoverable through title, author, keyword, and full text searches.
In sum, relevant entries can be found by

1. Entry title (alphabetical arrangement of entries in the encyclopedia or listing in the end papers)
2. Specific name or keyword, including the index at the end of each volume

If the first name or keyword searched is not found, try several more variations—either different words or a different order of words. Most topics are described in several ways in the literature of a discipline, and the first term or phrase that comes to mind may not be the one used here.

Scope of the Encyclopedia

The title of the third edition, *Encyclopedia of Library and Information Sciences*, ended with the letter "s" because the encyclopedia was broadened to cover a spectrum of related and newly emerging information disciplines, including archival science, document theory, informatics, and records management, among others. The fourth edition continues this trend but with an extensive focus on the aspects of library and information sciences that have been heavily impacted by the adoption and reliance on online information distribution. This focus is reflected in the inclusion of numerous new entries such as digital preservation, altmetrics, web-scale discovery services, demand-driven acquisitions, and global open knowledgebases. Alongside these entries based on entirely new topics, the expanded use of the Internet for information has led to new treatment of traditional LIS topics such as resource description and access (RDA) that reflects the adoption of new standards for cataloging.

ELIS-4 also seeks to build upon the description of professional practice to round out the theoretical perspective that previous editions covered very well. Both current editors are academic research librarians and thus, focused heavily on addressing gaps in the encyclopedia related to academic research information while still relying heavily on the structure established by editors of ELIS-3. For example, ELIS-3 introduced country profiles and ELIS-4 builds upon that with new entries for New Zealand and a third on Brazil, in addition to revisions for Slovakia, Netherlands, Canada, Belarus, Kazakhstan, and Brazil among others. This edition also expands the number of entries for named cultural and information entities that did not appear in previous editions, such as the National Library of Medicine, North American Serials Interest Group (NASIG), the International Association of Scientific, Technical and Medical Publishers (STM), and ASLIB, as well as entities like the HathiTrust that have been established since the last edition was published. A number of new entries describing important information conferences such as the Acquisitions Institute at Timberline, the Charleston Conference, and Electronic Resources in Libraries (ER&L) also help round out the encyclopedia and further the description of the current state of academic research librarianship.

ELIS-4 also continues the tradition of designating important entries of historical or theoretical importance as "ELIS Classics." These are entries by major figures in the library and information sciences or those that describe core concepts in LIS theory, practice, or education that appeared in earlier editions of the encyclopedia. The current editors preserved the approximately 40 previous "ELIS Classics" and designated 13 previous entries as new "ELIS Classics."

There are more than 550 entries, of which more than 20 are new, another 93 are revisions to prior entries that have been brought up to date by their authors or by new authors, about 30 are ELIS Classics, and about 400 are reprinted from an earlier edition since they have remained relevant to the present. It is important to note that the editors also had to make some choices related to retiring entries that were no longer relevant—due to the passage of time and the development of the field, the technologies and theories described in those entries were deemed to be out of scope for the new edition and thus not revised or reprinted.

Encyclopedia Authors

As in past editions, the authors writing for the encyclopedia are major researchers, librarians and practitioners, and leaders in the fields and subfields in the disciplines in which they are writing. Noted scholars are well represented, and a number of authors are former leaders in LIS associations, including the American Library Association (ALA), the Association for College and Research Libraries (ACRL), the International Federation of Library Associations and Institutions (IFLA), the American Society for Information Science and Technology (ASIS&T), and the American Association of Library and Information Science Education (ALISE). In addition, there are many contributors who are current or former directors of major institutions. As in past editions, the editors are very proud of the range and diversity of authors who have written these entries for the encyclopedia and we thank them for sharing their expertise with the current and future readers and researchers in the field.

Finally, the editors for ELIS-4 have grappled with the challenges of entry generation that was noted by previous editors in nearly every edition: that not all ideas, topics, and potential entries were able to be completed for publication in this edition. While we made a valiant attempt to include entries identified by ELIS-3 editors but not secured for publication in that edition, we sometimes could not find authors willing to take those topics on. Similarly, we were sometimes unable to secure revisions to entries from new authors when previous authors were unable to perform that task. To the greatest extent possible, we endeavored to replace authors when entries were deemed important enough to appear in ELIS-4 but initial or previous authors had to decline or defaulted. No doubt, the editors of ELIS-5 will also pick up the mantle and attempt to round out the encyclopedia with entries for anything that ELIS-4 missed. As noted by editors Bates and Niles Maack in ELIS-3, this problem of missing topics was also acknowledged by Allen Kent, editor of the first edition of ELIS. Kent stated in 1973, "I have prepared this presentation to make sure the lessons of Diderot-d'Alembert are recalled in terms of encyclopedia-making as an exercise in the art of the possible."

Background and Development of the Encyclopedia

The first edition of ELIS, under the editorship principally of Allen Kent and Harold Lancour, was published between 1968 and 1982. The 33 volumes of the first edition were published in alphabetical sequence during those years. After the "Z" volume appeared in 1982, a number of supplements were published at roughly the rate of two per year, up to and including volume 73, which appeared in 2003. Miriam Drake was appointed editor for the second edition, which appeared in 2003, both online and in paper. The second edition came out at one time in four large-format volumes, with a supplement in 2005 [3]. Kent and Lancour covered a wide range of librarianship, information science, and some computer science topics. Drake, an academic library director, emphasized academic libraries, and the ELIS-2 volumes contained many profiles of major academic libraries and professional library associations.

The third edition, under the editorship of Marcia Bates and Mary Niles Maack, reflected a growing convergence among the several disciplines that concern themselves with information and the cultural record. As information science educators and noted researchers in the field, their focus was on growing the encyclopedia in the theoretical fields of information sciences as well as drawing together the associated information and cultural disciplines such as archival sciences and museum studies within the overall field of LIS.

For this edition, we have focused on developing the encyclopedia to reflect the changing nature of information production and consumption through online and digital forms. We have also endeavored to fill in gaps in the description of important people, places, and theories in the information sciences, and further enhanced the description of important concepts related to the provision of research information and the field's major institutions.

We continue to see the audience for the encyclopedia just as previous editors have: as principally consisting of 1) the educated lay person interested in one or more of its topics, 2) students learning about a topic, and 3) professionals and researchers in the several fields who want to learn about something new, or to be refreshed on a familiar topic.

We honored the previous editors by reengaging their superb Editorial Advisory Board with significant new additions of experts known to the current editors. (See listing in the front matter.) These leaders and experts from as many disciplines as are in the encyclopedia provided excellent guidance and feedback for the editors as they began the process of new topic generation, evaluation of previous entries, and offering to author or review numerous entries throughout the process of publication.

All new and revised entries were reviewed by one or more outside expert reviewer as well as one or more of the editors. Referees provided invaluable feedback to authors, including noting errors or omissions as well as making suggestions on additional aspects of the topic to cover. While we made every reasonable attempt through this process to check the accuracy of every entry and every fact, undoubtedly readers will find some topics explained more thoroughly or accurately than others. Indeed, due to the time frame from the beginning of the generation of the fourth edition and the time of publication, readers will reasonably note that some topics have been quickly superseded due to this passage of time, so the date of acceptance of the entry will be noted on each entry since several years may have passed since the writing of the entry and the publication of this edition.

Acknowledgments

This edition of the encyclopedia was possible only through the countless hours that the editors, John McDonald and Michael Levine-Clark, spent reviewing the previous encyclopedia entries, outlining the topics that were missing or that were newly emerging in the field, and identifying appropriate expert authors to write those new entries. In addition, the editors devoted extensive time to corresponding with previous authors encouraging them to revise their entries, and finding replacement authors for important entries that needed revisions but whose original authors were unavailable.

Both editors wish to acknowledge the expertise of each other and their knowledge of our field, their extensive network of contacts, and their ability to work closely together to ensure the success of this encyclopedia. Neither of them could have completed this project alone.

They acknowledge and thank the Taylor & Francis Group editors, Claire Miller and Rich O'Hanley, as well as Susan Lee, who passed away at the early stages of the preparation of this edition, and more recently, Alexandra Torres, who supported and kept the editors and authors on track over the course of the years of work on this edition of the encyclopedia.

The editors thank the authors who wrote and revised entries, and the huge number of reviewers who refereed the entries. Without their dedication, expertise, and willingness to share their knowledge with others, there would be no encyclopedia. They also wish to thank the Editorial Advisory Board for their advice, suggestions of topics and authors, their hours spent writing or reviewing for the final edition. They also wish to thank the previous editors, Marcia Bates and Mary Niles Maack, whose organization and structure for ELIS-3 provided an excellent blueprint for ELIS-4.

Encyclopedia of Library and Information Sciences, Fourth Edition

Volume 5

Pages 2909–3636

Library Science–Management
Managing–Metamarkup
Mexico–Museum Informatics
Museum Management–Music Information
Music Librarianship–Natural Language
Network–Online Library
Online Public–Organizational
Pacific–Philosophy

Library Science in the United States: Early History

John V. Richardson, Jr.
Department of Information Studies, University of California, Los Angeles, Los Angeles, California, U.S.A.

Abstract
The narrow purpose of this entry is threefold: 1) to identify the key events and players in the origin and early development of the discipline of library science in the United States (and perhaps North America more generally, but certainly not Europe, much less India, other than to mention its origins in Germany); 2) to describe the intellectual foundations and history for the discipline of library science as developed at the University of Chicago's GLS; and 3) to briefly identify the knowledge and skills as well as values associated with this emergent field. Strictly speaking, therefore, it is not a discourse on computer science, informatics, information science, information studies, or for that matter, the history of librarianship nor books and libraries; neither is it a history of literary endeavors, printing, writing, or scholarly communication per se, but rather it is an introductory orientation to a highly specialized field of knowledge.

INTRODUCTION

Library science has its origins in early nineteenth century Germany, notably as *bibliothekswissenschaft*. Despite the fact that thousands of Americans studied in Germany before the World War I, Schrettinger[1] and Schmidt[2] are unknown or forgotten today; elsewhere, someone might answer the provocative question: "whereas Germany hugely influenced US universities, almost all disciplines, and university research, what was the German influence on library science in the United States?"[3] The narrow purpose of this entry is threefold: 1) to identify the key events and players in the origin and early development of the discipline of library science in the United States (and perhaps North America more generally, but certainly not Europe, much less India, other than to mention its origins in Germany); 2) to describe the intellectual foundations and history for the discipline of library science as developed at the University of Chicago's GLS; and 3) to briefly identify the knowledge and skills as well as values associated with this emergent field. For a detailed chronology of significant events in education for librarianship rather than a discussion of three major thematic elements, see Appendix A.

In other words, the scope of this entry covers only the field as it developed in the United States: as the profession of library economy first, with a strong emphasis on efficiency in library techniques due to the influence of Melvil Dewey at the New York State Library in Albany. In the later nineteenth century and into the first quarter of the twentieth century, the field also adopted certain overtones of the Social Gospel movement as librarians viewed themselves as "apostles of culture"[4] and the field embraced the cult of efficient and scientific management under the influence of F. W. Taylor and Charles McCarthy.[5] Importantly, though, the outdated nineteenth century natural history worldview based upon Enlightenment ideas: "Let's see what's there and we'll record it," did not survive as the principal means of knowing, but that heritage or genealogy is still occasionally present and or at least lamented in some quarters.

In what I wish to call its protohistory, library science then, evolved out of a library apprenticeship or a silent reading on one's own like the early study of law. Indeed, many practitioners adopted a kind of intuitive approach until Melvil Dewey's school at Columbia College appeared on the scene in the last decades of the nineteenth century Wiegand[6]—as a side note, most early programs of librarianship were affiliated with academic or public libraries and provided their students with firsthand, practical experience with, and knowledge of, these library collections; given this American pragmatism (i.e., the practical problem solving orientation of their teachers and their students), it is not surprising that these programs produced little, if any, research per se, unless the compilation of descriptive, annotated bibliographies counts as research.

Certainly, this early kind of "library science," with its emphasis on applied workability and scientific knowledge, was based on a notion of American exceptionalism, which is "the idea that America occupies an exceptional place in history, based on her republican government and wide economic opportunity" Ross.[7] In other words, library science then was one of those rather American social sciences which began coalescing in the late nineteenth and early twentieth centuries as part of the move to professionalize vocational activities and as such would include dairy science, management science, military science, mortuary science, political science, and even creation science/intelligent design today. In the early twenty-

Encyclopedia of Library and Information Sciences, Fourth Edition DOI: 10.1081/E-ELIS4-120043738

first century, the term is still used interchangeably with librarianship, library and information science, and perhaps even information science, but there are important semantic differences. So, this entry will define what library science meant to a group of practitioners and professors after the turn of the twentieth century.

In Chicago during the late 1920s, a group of local librarians rallied for something more substantive than the existing institutionally based library programs after the appearance of the highly influential C. C. Williamson Report of 1923, which argued for dividing library clerical tasks from professional ones. Education for the latter, Williamson argued, should take place in universities where instructors would hold higher academic degrees and have had prior teaching experience. Hence, a so-called advanced or "Graduate Library School" was established at the University of Chicago to meet the Association of American Universities' standards, and which imbued a more exact meaning to this previous hollow phrase.

By "library science," they now meant the scientific study of the intersection of books and people.[8] In other words, attention shifted away from a library economy and its focus on institutional structures and processes to the user of the library—as an aside, American glossaries may have dropped the phrase "library economy" in the late 1920s, but bibliothécomie remained in French with its equivalents in other Romance languages.

Notably, the first Graduate Library School faculty at Chicago, under the leadership of George Works, embraced the twin concepts of original, independent research and promoted the publication of the results of their investigations (notably, diffusion via books in the "Studies in Library Science" series and in refereed articles in journals such as the *Library Quarterly*). Carleton B. Joeckel's *The Government of the American Public Library* of 1935, part of this SLS series, is particularly noteworthy for drawing upon political science for its theoretical orientation; according to some international reviewers, this work "at once placed American library research on a higher plane... [and, as a result, it] received the James Terry White Award in 1938 for 'notable published writing.'"[8]

In January 1931, the school published the first issue of *The Library Quarterly*, a double blind refereed "journal of investigation and discussion in the field of library science," edited by William M. Randall, who was assisted by a distinguished international advisory board. Rather than serve as a news magazine like the extant publications, the *LQ* was intended to strengthen the scientific underpinnings of the profession by stressing the social significance of the library rather than its internal operations and by publishing "exploratory rather than merely descriptive articles."[8] To understand this new conception of research, one need only read the lead article: C. C. Williamson's "The Place of Research in Library Service."[9]

The journal was edited at the University of Chicago until Stephen Harter (PhD, Chicago) at Indiana University took over in October 1990; John Richardson at UCLA served as editor from 1994 to 2003; next, Wayne Wiegand and John Bertot of Florida State University served as coeditors from 2003 to 2008; and from October 2008 to the present, John Carlo Bertot and Paul T. Jaeger serve as coeditors.

LQ, though still respected, has long since lost its absolute preeminence in the field with the rise of such scholarly journals as *College and Research Libraries* (1939), *Journal of Documentation* (1945), and the *Journal of the American Society for Information Science and Technology* (formerly *American Documentation*, 1950). Nonetheless, to understand more fully the role and contribution of the journal over time, one should consult Arthur P. Young's 2006 *LQ* article which identifies *LQ*'s leading contributors (i.e., Howard Winger and Lawrence Thompson), the most cited authors (i.e., Don Swanson and Abe Bookstein), and the most cited articles (see his top thirty list presented as table five) between 1956 and 2004.[10]

KNOWLEDGE AND SKILLS (OBJECTS OF STUDY)

The essential skill provided by librarians, curators, archivists, and others is the provision of information, especially via organized collections of reading materials. Hence, how one might best provide this information is the main problem. Concomitantly, the dual mission of this field is to ensure the preservation of such materials (thus, the leading intellectual question is: what should you save, if you can't save everything?) and then delivering access to these materials (hence, the main intellectual question is: how to best do so, given the variety of formats and technologies?). Therefore, these are the two primary theoretical questions which one must answer.

Historically, these skills demanded a knowledge set related to bibliographical access control: 1) bibliographical description (aka rules for cataloging) and 2) bibliographical arrangement (aka systems for classification) as well as infrastructural concerns (such as the proper administration and management of complex institutions); furthermore, the desire for more scholarly librarians, ones capable of creating new knowledge about the interaction of books and people, required the use of statistical techniques and interpretive models (drawn from history or cultural anthropology, in particular).

Once highly valued by bibliographers and librarians in the nineteenth century, the compilation of bibliographies (even rigorous or systematic annotated ones) came to be viewed as merely the parent of real research, as merely the first step prior to solving a research problem. At Chicago, Waples' graduate courses in research methods drew upon interdisciplinary sources including history (i.e., of books, libraries, and printing), psychology (i.e., of the patron, reader, or user's information seeking behavior), and sociology (i.e., a rigorous and systematic community analysis or needs profiling is necessary prior to building diverse, useful or viable collections of materials for library users). Now the classic methods textbook, Waples' 1939 *Investigating Library Problems*, with its emphasis upon the validity and reliability of evidence, served several generations of graduate students. In essence, this text and his course inspired the confidence of young researchers to conduct research independently; to communicate and thereby share their findings; pursue adaptive, critical, and reflective thinking; undertake logical problem solving; and respect for the diversity of opinions. Library science would not develop its own unique methodologies until the introduction of a kind of statistical bibliography, also known as bibliometrics or citation counting, until the 1950s. And even so, that is still debated by some writers who attribute its true origins to psychologists in the early 1900s; clearly, though. E. Wyndham Hulme coined the phrase "statistical bibliography" in 1922–1923 and such work appeared in the Bulletin of the International Institute of Bibliography as early as 1911. This point is important to those who hold that to be considered a discipline, library science must have its own unique methods.

To achieve what Harvard University had done for law and what Johns Hopkins University had done for medicine, then a true "library science" would have to be offered at the graduate level. There would be no place for the holder of a high school degree or some mere technical/trade school curricular orientated worker (which would produce a technician who knew how to do something, rather than a professional who also knew why do something in the first place by investigating the philosophical underpinnings of such actions). In other words, what some graduate educators sought was a diagnostician of professional tasks, not a mere mechanic suited to routine library clerical tasks.

So, in the mid-1920s onward, the American Library Association's Board of Education for Librarianship, influenced by the Williamson Report, mandated a set of admissions requirements to accredited programs of librarianship. One of the explicitly, stated entrance requirements now included a college degree (commonly held in English literature, American history, or a western European foreign language—a social science major, if present, was rather more common than the natural or physical science backgrounds of the small remainder of applicants). This stance is well articulated in Pierce Butler's *Introduction to Library Science* and Douglas Waples' *Investigating Library Problems* which taken together, established an epistemological stance toward our activities—with a good science and good practice, things should take care of themselves.

As expressed in Butler's *Introduction*, the scope of library science covered the sociological problem (e.g., the role of books in society), the psychological problem (e.g., the psychological motive for reading among individuals or the effect of reading on the reader), and the historical problem (e.g., the literary history of scholarship). By the 1990s, increased interest was paid to the distinction between tacit and implicit knowledge as well as the difference between declarative (i.e., know what) and procedural (i.e., know how) knowledge.

The relationship between the empirical knowledge as generated by GLS faculty and its doctoral graduate students and the practical knowledge which could be applied by practitioners is most clearly demonstrated in their Annual Library Institutes beginning in 1936. Topics are those of pragmatic interest to practitioners and cover such topics as book selection (1939), acquisition and cataloging (1940), and reference service (1943). For more thematic issues, one can consult the list of these annual institutes through 1951 in Appendix B.

TYPES OF LIBRARIES (INSTITUTIONAL INFRASTRUCTURES)

Early education for librarianship in the late nineteenth century possessed a strong applied or pragmatic work orientation due to its being situated within the institutional framework of a local public or academic library. At the University of Chicago, the new appointed faculty members, except for Pierce Butler who came from the Newberry Library and Harriet E. Howe, a peace offering to American Library Association, were not library practitioners. Rather they held degrees in various academic disciplines including education (Howe and Works), educational psychology (Waples), ecclesiastical history (Butler), linguistics (Randall), and philological studies (Wilson). Nonetheless, they continued to teach about types of libraries: college (Randall and Wilson); public (Wilson and Joeckel), and school (Waples).

GLS graduates also played an important role in shaping American education for librarianship, as they became deans and directors there and in the other leading programs across the nation: Bernard R. Berelson at the University of Chicago; J. Periam Danton at UC, Berkeley; Raynard Swank at UC, Berkeley; Jesse Shera at Case Western Reserve University; and Ralph Shaw of Rutgers University.

Later in the 1950s, library science programs, such as those at the University of Michigan and the University of Illinois, downstate at Urbana-Champaign (and populated with GLS alumni including Thelma Eaton, Herbert Goldhor, Rose Phelps, and Mary A. Lohrer), would shift their curricular emphasis from types of libraries to library services (which would include functional activities such as abstracting and indexing, acquisitions, cataloging and classification, collection development, outreach to underserved populations, programming, reader's advisory, and reference work). Most recently, the curriculum has shifted yet again, this time to the role of information in society.

VALUES

As articulated in Butler's *Introduction*,

> a scientist always selects the field of his observation. In his eyes not all facts are of equal importance. He does not devote his days to the endless multiplication of his sensual perceptions in the hope that perhaps something new will come to his notice. . .His professional ambition would prefer that his name should be used to designate a new theory than any number of previously unrecorded species. His concern is, first of all, functional significance. He has also a perverse curiosity about the unexplained.[11]

In the narrowest institutional terms, Butler's classic work helped the library profession understand the mission of an Advanced, Graduate Library School, serving as an aspirational document of what the GLS's goals and objectives were. Concomitantly, Waples research methods textbook is a companion piece on how to undertaking reliable and valid social science research. Waples recommends that a would-be researcher focus on stating a research problem, examine the validity of evidence, draw an adequate sample to ensure reliability, and pay attention to sources of evidence.[12] Basically, Waples' text offered readers a structured way of thinking about the field of library science.

Many thoughtful writers today suggest that library science has been shaped by an instrumental, positivistic social science during its Chicago years. Despite later claims of being value-free or neutral (which necessarily arise when talking about the need to build balanced collections of library materials, at least if one wishes to be respectful of the diversity of different points of view and provide these different perspectives on socially controversial matters), a complex constellation of values exists (namely, the perceived need for preservation and the concomitant access services for library users and their right to know as well as equity of access; literacy is foundational for the preceding, but not numeracy per se; rights to privacy and free speech, contextualized inside a democratic society, often associated with a liberal or advanced capitalism). In short, many of us believe that it is better to be informed than ignorant because access to information reduces social inequities.

One of the best examples is the *Public Library Inquiry* of 1949[13] which posits the American public library as a democratic institution, responsible for social equalization. Many librarians would agree with the following belief statement (aka articles of the Library Faith): that the act of silent reading of nonfiction as well as fiction is desirable; libraries should avoid censorship and support intellectual freedom by offering a balanced or unbiased collection of authoritative or at least credible materials, be public, free of direct use fees; furthermore, these cultural nonprofits are good or desirable while large, for-profit companies are bad (if not, lazy or even evil)—or simply put, many librarians would respect intellectual property rights (but support the notion of fair use within the bundle of copyrights), yet oppose the increasing "commodification" of information, a term which dates to the 1970s.

Controversy exists about the proper role of pure versus applied problem solving; see, for example, Works' cooperative research agenda proposal.[14] Likewise, Butler initially argued for a strongly interdisciplinary approach, drawing upon the three academic disciplines of history, sociology and psychology.[11]

Like other research university disciplines, though, original, independent research in the form of a dissertation or thesis is still expected, if not valued, as is the desirableness of seminars, or scholars' workshops, over large classroom lectures (although popular, asynchronous online courses as offered by some LIS programs may be cited as a counterexample). Despite some antagonism at the outset and continuing today because one's research agenda may be set by the agency or philanthropic organization, nonetheless, the role of extramural funding is significant in research universities (note that the Chicago GLS got its start from the Carnegie Corporation with a one million dollar grant); and in situ, may explain, at least partially, the rise of the I-school movement.[15] Perhaps someone else should write on its origins in the research university because it is out of scope for this entry on library science. Certainly, a recent tension has emerged between two models—the scholarly professor and the research professor. Early on, the former model, aka the "lone wolf" model (i.e., an independent scholar working alone in the library/archives writing a monographic volume, published by a leading university press) dominated the discipline of library science. Later, the field witnessed a shift to the other model, which may have begun with the introduction of information science into the more traditional library service programs in the 1960s and 1970s. At this time, another group of individuals, largely from mathematics (such as Robert M. Hayes) and the physical sciences (such as Don R. Swanson) were hired into library science programs, and with them came an interest in extramural funding, a strong sense of the need for collaboration, a major role for microfilm and computer technology including punch cards, and a rather ahistorical approach to the profession. They called themselves information scientists (note that one rarely encounters a library scientist).

Perhaps the rise of superior Soviet technology in the late 1950s (notably, the successful launch of Sputnik, the first man into space, as well as the first ICBM), caused the U.S. Congress to pass the National Defense Education Act of 1958 and in turn caused the federal government to spend even more on competitive research grants in higher education, benefiting the information science types in library programs; certainly, there is also evidence of the Cold War, the National Science Foundation, and Big

Science before these events, however, which could also explain the large-scale U.S. federal grant making.

Doug Raber's *The Problem of Information: An Introduction to Information Science*[16] brings a strongly humanistic orientation to the discussion of representation of information, relevance, and the value of semiotics. Likewise, the library science field has embraced the inclusion of archival sciences in the 1980s and informatics (not to be confused with computer science) in the 1990s. Since computer science focuses on algorithmic solutions to improving the speed and space domain of computation, library science stresses the more humanistic interests (or, the people aspects) in the intersection of science, technology and society.

Philosophically speaking, library science researchers believe that things can be measured; on the other hand, that may well beg the more fundamental question of what cannot be measured. The differing methodological orientations have caused the discipline to divide into two camps at times: the "quals" versus the "quants." The desire for universalistic abstraction (rather than mere descriptive chronologies of the local library[17] can be cited as a model in this regard) has been problematic even in the historically oriented side of the house. In any event, however, the fundamental unity in library science lies in the rigorous, spirit of inquiry as articulated at Chicago. The following example from the 1930s of Leon Carnovsky's spirit of inquiry is illustrative: while walking on the Midway with Wilson, Carnovsky challenged on the vendors hawking an expensive cigarette lighter called the everlasting match. "See here, Mister, there is something wrong with that assumption. If one match is everlasting, why get three?"[8] By the mid-to-late 1930s, Butler had begun to recognize a possibly fatal flaw in the GLS approach mainly that of scientism, the overly narrow focus on only the quantifiable aspects of the field. He wrote on this topic in 1941 and again in 1951; by then, he had become absolutely convinced that

> there was no room for humanistic concerns in this new world view. Although [Butler] believed that the GLS's 'highest intellectual achievement was the establishment of library science on a sound basis in a few areas,' the humanistic side of librarianship had been displaced by practitioners of a narrow objectivity. Librarianship had, in fact, been replaced by a pseudo-science in Butler's opinion. Ideas were supplanted by facts, or even worse, by mere data. The field risked becoming truly anti-intellectual, lost in 'the simplicity of its pragmatism.'[11]

CONCLUSIONS

"Within the recent past, librarianship had placed a heavy emphasis upon tradition and custom as a way of doing things."[11] Yet, many of these earlier works by bibliographers and librarians were viewed as "too practical and obvious to merit" attention in a research-oriented environment like the American university,[8] nonetheless the introduction of a library economy, similar to hone economics or domestic science, by Melvil Dewey and other events in 1876 are two of the important watershed events in the history of library science. In addition, the establishment of the Graduate Library School at Chicago was a pivot watershed event in the establishment of a real library science in the United States and the subsequent professionalization of education for librarianship. At Chicago, early writers

> described library science 'as the science of the care and use of books both for the control of knowledge already in existence and for the discovery of new knowledge through researches in books themselves or with books in connection with other sources of information'. . ..Waples, as acting dean, in 1931 defined research in library science as 'extending the existing body of knowledge concerning the values and practices of libraries in their many aspects, and including the development of methods of investigation whereby significant data are obtained, tested, and applied.'[8]

The affiliation of a program with a research oriented university like the University of Chicago imparted a more theoretical dimension to librarianship; the key players and staunch supporters of this movement include the early GLS faculty such as George Works, William M. Randall, Douglas Waples, and Pierce Butler (at least until near the end of his life, when he began to have grave doubts). GLS alumni, such as Herbert Goldhor, also played a role in the adoption of social science research methodologies.[19] In short, I have argued that the American notion of library science is largely a creation of the GLS at Chicago. I have not intentionally ignored other library science programs, or Shera's foundation of a new kind of school at Case Western Reserve University, where the introduction of graduate studies in what became known as documentation led eventually to the idea of an information science. Simply, these ideas are out of scope for the purposes of this entry.

More recently, writers, notably John Budd,[20] have remained optimistic about the role of hermeneutical phenomenology ("which combines a kind of realism with understanding of the dynamics of human action and perception") which brings a sense of intersubjectivity to combat the repressive aspects of scientism in library science.

> Whether 'books' was too narrowly understood [at Chicago] to mean the codex rather than the 'generic book,' thus ignoring scientific report literature and giving rise to the new intellectual discipline of information science, is outside the scope of this article (although there appears to be evidence for this hypothesis).[8]

The introduction of library automation in the 1960s buoyed the field.

Likewise, information studies (a recently emergent dimension) seems to offer the softer intersection of information resources, information technology processes, and user needs. Yet, the recent discussions of a humanistic I-school seem strongly reminiscent of this library science as understood by the University of Chicago and their being situated in large research universities will influence much of their research agenda. Of course, only time will tell if this "school of thought" holds up. Certainly, the intellectual history of specific programs is yet to be written; a notable one would look at the aggressive expansionism at Berkeley by Danton followed by the underestimated intelligence and strategic shrewdness of Ray Swank.[3]

More than ten years ago, a fellow encyclopedist observed that

> although research in library science has come a long way, it still has not reached the maturity of other disciplines... [and struggles with] an academically imposed inferiority complex and linguistic dilemmas on the meaning of research for an applied and service field[18]

and it is hard to disagree with his assertions. In fact, the continuing relevance of a "library science" to an information society remains an open question and Blaise Cronin has provocatively asserted that "there is, and can be no such thing as 'library science.'"[21]

ACKNOWLEDGMENTS

This work benefited from the comments of two anonymous reviewers as well as one of the editors, Mary Niles Maack. In addition, I greatly appreciate the fact that Larry Olszewski; Boyd Rayward; John Budd; and Michael Buckland answered my questions, contributed ideas as well as took the time to read and comment on an earlier draft of this entry.

APPENDICES

A. CHRONOLOGY OF SIGNIFICANT EVENTS IN EDUCATION FOR LIBRARIANSHIP

1870s

1879, May: Melvil Dewey suggests a "librarians' college" which would be attached to a normal school with a considerable library.

1880s

1883, August: Dewey proposes school of library economy at Columbia College.

1886, July: Dewey announces his school will open in October at Columbia College.

1887, 5 January: First class in library economy offered at Columbia College.

1888: Dewey argues for correspondence courses in special library and small library services (hence, first distance education program).

1889: First class graduates from Columbia College; school transferred to New York State Library in Albany on 1 April; August: Annie C. Moore argues for special training of children's librarians.

1890s

1890, June: Pratt Institute, Brooklyn offers its first class in cataloging followed by library economy courses.

1891: Drexel Institute started offering library economy courses.

1893, September: Armour Institute Library Class first term under direction of Katharine L. Sharp in Chicago.

1895: First separate course in government publications offered by F. Jackson at Armour Institute.

1897: Transfer of the Armour Institute to University of Illinois, Urbana.

1898, August: New York State Library's Library School offers specialized instruction for law, medical, education, and engineering librarians.

1900s

1901: Carnegie Library of Pittsburgh establishes Training School for Children's Librarians; Western Reserve proposes library school.

1902, August: Four year library training class announced by Simmons College, Boston.

1903: New York Public Library establishes training class; Western Reserve receives endowment for library school from Andrew Carnegie; American Library Association's Committee on Library Training recommends correspondence work offerings

1905: Melvil Dewey suggests that only three schools are needed: one at Albany, one in Midwest, and another at the University of California; University of Washington offers their first annual summer school for library training; Syracuse University establishes Library School; Andrew Carnegie tells library school class serve that "nowadays professionally trained people are needed."

1906, June 16: First MLS *(honoris causa)* degree conferred at SLS, Albany.

1907: Library School faculty from various schools met for the first time at Asheville, NC, American Library Association Convention (ALA).

1910s

1911: Roundtable of Library School Instructors formed in ALA.

1915: Association of American Library Schools founded.

1919: University of Texas establishes School of Library Science; September: Andrew Keogh (Yale) argues that academic librarians need advanced library training; Charles C. Williamson publishes ground-breaking *Some Present-Day Aspects of Library Training.*

1920s

1922: Charles C. Williamson transmits "Training for Library Work" to Carnegie Corporation.

1923: Williamson's *Training for Library Service* appears in print; ALA's Executive Board appoints Temporary Library Training Board.

1924: ALA establishes Board of Education for Librarianship with Carnegie Corporation assistance.

1925: Tse-Chien Tai's "Professional Education for Librarianship," PhD dissertation, University of Iowa.

1926: Carnegie Corporation funds the first Graduate Library School at the University of Chicago, which offers first summer institute for Library Science; the Albany Library School and NYPL Library School merge and transferred to Columbia University.

1927: GLS at Chicago appoints George Works first dean; ALA launches Curriculum Study under the direction of W.W. Charters.

1928, Fall: GLS at Chicago admits students working toward PhD degree.

1929, April 12: George Works resigns as Dean of Chicago GLS.

1930s

1930: First PhD in library science: Eleanor Upton's "A Guide to 17th Century Materials in the Reports of the Historical Manuscripts Commission of Great Britain to Date" at University of Chicago.

1932: Louis Round Wilson appointed dean of Chicago GLS.

1933: Publication of Pierce Butler's *An Introduction to Library Science;* ALA Board of Education for Librarianship establishes qualitative Minimum Requirements for library schools.

1936: Two major studies appear: Ralph Munn's *Conditions and Trends in Education for Librarianship* and Ernest J. Reece's *The Curriculum in Library Schools.*

1940s

1942: Louis Round Wilson retires as Dean of Chicago GLS.

1943: Publication of Metcalf, Osborn, and Russell's *Program of Instruction in Library Schools.*

1946: Publication of Joseph L. Wheeler's *Progress and Problems in Education for Librarianship* and J. Periam Danton's *Education for Librarianship;* ALA Council establishes Library Education Division.

1947: Harriet E. Howe moves the University of Denver program from a BLS to a one year MLS degree; Florida State University sends library science educators throughout the state in automobiles.

1948, 1 August: ALA's BEL suspends accreditation of library schools; University of Illinois and University of Michigan offer PhD program in library science.

1949: Twenty-seven of the thirty-two accredited schools adopt the new MLS degree (or in process of doing so); publication of Bernard Berelson's *Education for Librarianship.*

1950s

1951, July: ALA adopts new *Standards of Accreditation* making MLS entry level degree.

1952: Columbia University offers Doctor of Library Science.

1956: Western Reserve University offers PhD degree.

1959: Robert M. Hayes at UCLA teaches first course ever on information storage and retrieval; University of California at Berkeley offers PhD degree; ALA Council adopts Standards and Guidelines for Undergraduate Programs in Library Science.

1960s

1960: Rutgers University offers PhD degree.

1961: *Journal of Education for Librarianship* established; publication of Sarah Vann's *Education for Librarianship Before* 1923.

1962: ALA appoints Commission on a National Plan for Library Education.

1965: U.S. Office of Education establishes position of Library Education Specialist; NDEA Institute funds made available for school librarianship; HEA, Title II Part B provides funds for institutes and fellowships.

1966: ALA establishes Office for Library Education; UCLA establishes two year MSIS degree program.

1968: ALA's COA establishes subcommittees on undergraduate and graduate standards for accreditation.

1970s

1970: ALA Council adopts Library Education and Manpower policy (so-called Asheim statement); Publication of Hal Borko and Robert Hayes' *Education for Information Science* and C. Edward Carroll's *The Professionalization of Education for Librarianship.*

1972: ALA's COA establishes revised *Standards for Accreditation*; Jesse Shera's Foundations of Education for Librarianship; UCLA establishes two-year MLS degree incorporating MSIS degree.

1974, School of Information Studies, Syracuse University, established.

1975: Publication of Charles Churchwell's *The Shaping of American Library Education.*

1980s

1980: Publication of *The Conant Report: A Study of the Education of Librarians.*

1982: Publication of Richardson's *The Spirit of Inquiry, the GLS at Chicago, 1921–1951.*

1983: AALS changes name to Association for Library and Information Science Education.

1986: ALISE and ALA celebrates 100 years of education for librarianship in New York City.

1988: ALA executive Board endorses joining the National Council on Accreditation of Teacher Education as a specialty organization for the purpose of accrediting first professional degrees for school library media specialists.

1989: Library and Information Science Distance Education Consortium formed; Graduate Library School, University of Chicago, closes.

1990s

1990: ALA Executive Board appoints a Special Committee on Library Closings.

1992: *Standards for Accreditation*, 1992, adopted by the Council of the American Library Association; ALA president-elect, Marilyn Miller, announces Project Century 21, a major research and study project for the development of library and information science education.

1993: Columbia University, echoing its 1889 action, once again closes its School of Library Service.

1996, School of Information, University of Michigan, established.

2000s

2001, iSchool, University of Michigan, established.

2002, School of Information, University of Texas at Austin, established.

2005, First conference of i-School Community at Pennsylvania State University.

Sources: Updating John V. Richardson Jr. et al., *Chronology of Significant Events in Education for Librarianship, 1879–1986* (Chicago, IL: American Library Association Standing Committee on Library Education, 1987); John V. Richardson Jr. with Jane B. Robbins, reprint ed., In *Education for the Library/Information Professions: Strategies for the Mid-1990s*, edited by Patricia G. Reeling (Jefferson, NC: McFarland Publishing, 1993), pp. 73–76.

B. Annual Library Institutes Held in the GLS at Chicago, 1936–1951

Volume Number	Title of Institute	Dates of Institute	Volume Editor	Publication Date
1	Library Trends	3–15 August 1936	Louis R. Wilson	March 1937
2	The Role of the Library in Adult Education	2–13 August 1937	Louis R. Wilson	December 1937
3	Current Issues in Library Administration	1–12 August 1938	Carleton B. Joeckel	April 1939
4	The Practice of Book Selection	31 July–13 August 1939	Louis R. Wilson	February 1940
5	The Acquisition and Cataloging of Books	29 July–9 August 1940	William M. Randall	December 1940
6	Print, Radio, and Film in a Democracy	4–9 August 1941	Douglas Waples	February 1942
7	Reference Function of the Library	29 June – 10 July 1942	Pierce Butler	1943
8	The Library in the Community	23–28 August 1943	Leon Carnovsky and Lowell Martin	June 1944
9	Library Extension: Problems and Solutions	21–26 August 1944	Carleton B. Joeckel	1944
10	Personnel Management in Libraries	27 August–1 September 1945	Lowell Martin	1946
11	Library Buildings for Library Service	5–10 August 1946	Herman H. Fussler	1947
12	Youth, Communication, and Libraries	11–16 August 1947	Frances Henne, Alice Brooks, and Ruth Ersted	1949
13	Education for Librarianship	16–21 August 1948	Bernard Berelson	1949
14	A Forum on the Public Library Inquiry	1949	Lester Asheim	1950
15	Bibliographic Organization	24–29 July 1950	Jesse J. Shera and Margaret E. Egan	1951
16	Librarians, Scholars, and Booksellers at Mid-Century	1951.	Pierce Butler	1953

Source: John V. Richardson Jr., *The Spirit of Inquiry: The GLS at Chicago, 1921–1951.* Foreword by Jesse Shera, ACRL Publications in Librarianship, No. 42, American Library Association, Chicago, IL, 1982, p. 173.[8]

REFERENCES

1. Schrettinger, M.W. *Versuch eines vollständigen Lehrbuchs der Bibliothek-Wissenschaft, oder Anleitung zur vollkommenen Geschäftsführung eines Bibliothekärs*; Verlag des Verfasser and J. Lindauersche: München, Germany, 1808–1829.
2. Schmidt, J.A.F. *Handbuch der Bibliothekswissenschaft, der literatur-und buücherkunde*; Weimar: B.F. Voigt, 1840.
3. Michael Buckland to John Richardson, August 11, 2007.
4. Garrison, D. *Apostles of Culture: The Public Librarian and American Society, 1876–1920*. Foreword by Christine Pawley. Print Culture History in Modern America. University of Wisconsin Press: Madison, WI, 2003.
5. Casey, M.; McCarthy, C. *Librarianship and Reform*; American Library Association: Chicago, IL, 1981.
6. Wiegand, W.A. *Irrepressible Reformer: A Biography of Melvil Dewey*; American Library Association: Chicago, IL, 1996.
7. Ross, D. *The Origins of American Social Science*; Ideas in Context, No. 19. Cambridge University Press: Cambridge, MA, 1992.
8. Richardson, J.V. Jr. *The Spirit of Inquiry: The GLS at Chicago, 1921–1951*. Foreword by Jesse Shera. ACRL Publications in Librarianship, No. 42. American Library Association: Chicago, IL, 1982.
9. Williamson, C.C. The place of research in library service. Libr. Q. January **1931**, *1*, 1–17.
10. Young, A.P. Library Quarterly, 1956–2004: An exploratory bibliometric analysis. Libr. Q. January **2006**, *76*, 10–18.
11. Butler, P. *Introduction to Library Science*; University of Chicago: Chicago, IL, 1933; reprint ed., Richardson, J.V. Jr., *The Gospel of Scholarship: Pierce Butler and a Critique of American Librarianship*; Scarecrow Press: Metuchen, NJ, 1992.
12. Waples, D. *Investigating Library Problems*; University of Chicago Press: Chicago, IL, 1939.
13. Raber, D. *Librarianship and legitimacy: The ideology of the Public Library Inquiry*. Contributions in Librarianship and Information Science, no. 90 Greenwood Press: Westport, CT, 1997.
14. Richardson, J.V. Jr., George Alan Works (1877–1957): Seeking neither fame nor fortune, J. Libr. Hist. Spring **1984**, *19*, 298–304; reprint ed., Supplement to the Dictionary of American Library Biography. Libraries Unlimited: Littleton, CO, 1990.
15. Geiger, R.L. *To Advance Knowledge: The Growth of the American Research University*; Oxford University Press: Oxford, U.K., 1986.
16. Raber, D. *The Problem of Information: An Introduction to Information Science*; Scarecrow Press: Lanham, MD, 2003.
17. Shera, J.H. *Foundations of the Public Library: The Origins of the Public Library Movement in New England, 1629–1855*; University of Chicago Press: Chicago, IL, 1949.
18. Stielow, F.J. Library and Information Science Research. In *Encyclopedia of Library History*; Wiegand, W.A., Davis, D.G. Jr., Eds.; Garland Publishing Inc.: New York, 1994.
19. Goldhor, H. *An Introduction to Scientific Research in Librarianship*, Monograph number 12. Graduate School of Library Science: Urbana, IL, 1972.
20. Budd, J.M. *Knowledge and Knowing in Library and Information Science: A Philosophical Framework*; Scarecrow Press: Lanham, MD, 2001.
21. Cronin, B. Pierce Butler's An introduction to library science: A tract for our times? A review article. J. Libr. Inform. Sci. December **2004**, *36*, 183–188.

Library Technical Services

Doris S. Helfer
Helen Heinrich
Collection Access and Management Services, California State University–Northridge, Northridge, California, U.S.A.

Abstract
The entry describes the key functions of library's technical services (TS) components. It traces the history and the major developments that affected the evolution of TS. The entry highlights the progression of cataloging-related standards and the way technology impacts the current workflow and expectations for staff expertise.

INTRODUCTION

Technical services (TS) usually refers to the combination of the acquisitions, cataloging, and collections management functions of a library into one unit or department. Acquisitions are used to refer to the functional department responsible for all aspects of obtaining materials libraries acquire for their collections. Cataloging is used to refer to the functional department responsible for all aspects of describing, assigning subject headings, and classifying to ensure that users can find the materials they need. Cataloging also encompasses authority control or the process of authorizing and verifying author/title/subject headings contained in bibliographic records and ascertaining their usage in the established form. Collections management entails physical processing and preservation of the materials libraries have obtained and cataloged.

While "the technical services are as old as libraries, the technical services unit is a development of the past forty years"[1] and that places the development of Technical Services Departments in the 1930s. Donald Coney presented the first published examination of the unit organization of technical processes in 1938.[2] The isolation of TS in a separate division is a function of size more than a change in attitude toward the services—first a separate unit is established to handle cataloging, then one for acquisitions, later serials, and, finally, all of them together as a separate division with its specialist head.[1]

ACQUISITIONS

As libraries grew in size, so did the need to ensure that the materials could be acquired and then found by the libraries' patrons. Historically, the acquisitions decisions were done by the Head Librarian and the actual ordering done by the clerical staff, but with the ever-increasing size of the collections and budgets, this became impractical and a specialized department in libraries was established. The unit was often originally called the order department, but that name was gradually replaced by acquisitions to reflect the broadening duties that could often include gifts, exchanges, mail services for the entire library, bindery, serials check-in and control, government documents, budget and financial control, and purchasing of all types of equipment for the library. With the advent of electronic resources, many purchase decisions are often negotiated through purchasing consortiums formed to help individual libraries obtain the best possible prices for their member libraries.

The organization of acquisitions unit varies greatly depending on the size and scope and mission of the library. In special libraries and very small specialized schools or colleges, the acquisitions unit typically collects in great depth only in the area of specialization of the organization, school, college, or business the library supports.[3] Special libraries generally do not have sufficient financial or space resources to collect or retain vast collections of materials but instead buy or borrow materials as needed to support the research needs of the organization at that moment, which may frequently change and evolve rapidly and therefore have smaller acquisitions units. As most purchasing/accounting organizations, they also adhere to standard accounting practices developed by the American Institute for Certified Public Accountants (AICPA), which insist that ordering, receiving, and payment functions are done by separate individuals in the organization to help avoid fraud, theft, or embezzlement.

In academic libraries, acquisitions units are often organized by the material types to be ordered, usually breaking into either a monographs units, a serials or continuations unit, and/or periodicals or journals unit and further subdivided by the country or region of the world where the materials being requested originate from and can be obtained if the library collects in a large number of languages. In addition to the Head Librarian who

Encyclopedia of Library and Information Sciences, Fourth Edition DOI: 10.1081/E-EISA-120053430

originally made collection decisions, faculty members were consulted regularly to give input on purchase requests of materials in their specific subject areas of expertise. With the growth in the size of collections, it usually now falls to a team of subject specialist bibliographers to do collection development. The bibliographers determine the scope and nature of what the library collects. Bibliographers then make specific recommendations as new books get published or new subject disciplines added to the area of studies of the academic institution to ensure necessary books and materials are added retrospectively if necessary to support the new curriculum and the research mission of the university. Depending on the library, collection development may not always fall within the TS department. Collection development is sometimes a stand-alone department or even a part of the reference department since there is a strong component of outreach to faculty involved in making collection development decisions. Once materials have been selected by the subject bibliographers, generally acquisitions units order materials also ensuring that they adhere to standard accounting practices of the AICPA. In some organizations, purchasing functions may be part of the larger organizations procurement or accounting departments but with the increased specialization required by the growing electronic nature of library materials; this is not something most procurement or accounting departments are desirous or are capable of handling and the library purchasing functions are generally a part of the library whether they are an academic, public, or special library. Unlike other library departments, acquisitions are often staffed by paraprofessionals with accounting experience. The need for the formerly ubiquitous position of acquisitions librarian is rapidly deteriorating, suggesting the deprofessionalization of acquisitions.[4] With the proliferation of online purchasing tools and software, acquisitions personnel are also expected to be computer savvy and familiar with the software purchasing systems used by the library.

Public libraries purchase materials of general and widespread interest, information, and enlightenment to all people in the communities they serve, and the materials strive to represent a broad range of views to ensure that the communities they serve have access to information to help them know more about themselves and their world; supplement formal study or encourage informal education and reading; improve job-related skills; stimulate participation and interest in world and community affairs; and provide access to variety of opinions. They provide access to materials of varying reading levels and languages depending on the community's needs to generally support educational, civic, and cultural activities.[5]

Public libraries TS departments are usually centralized and offer standardized materials throughout their system and depending on the library system may offer local branch libraries the ability to buy specialized materials in various languages to better serve local populations reading interests.

While very small libraries might be able to handle individual ordering with vendors and publishers, most academic and public libraries deal with vendors who provide book approval plans, such as Baker and Taylor, YBP, among others, and subscription vendors such as EBSCO, WT Cox, and Prenax in addition to direct ordering for titles not handled by these vendors. Subscription agents handle the renewals and any missing issues claims for the thousands of journals and standing orders for the library to ensure the library receives all periodical issues for which it has paid. Libraries use subscription vendors to help them keep track and handle subscription renewals and increasingly complex issues regarding handling electronic journals.

Libraries work with approval plan vendors by setting up a profile indicating the types and categories of materials the library wishes to obtain, and as materials are published meeting those criteria, the approval vendor automatically ships those materials to the library. Those books are reviewed by the subject specialist bibliographers for approval and can be returned to the vendor if the bibliographer does not feel the book is of sufficient quality or subject interest for the library. If libraries cannot afford to collect everything in certain categories, they can sign up with approval plan vendors to have their bibliographers/subject specialist librarians regularly look at the bibliographic information about newly published books either on what were called approval slips or increasingly in an online bibliographic system where they can mark and select only those books the library would like to buy from them, and the approval vendor then sends only the selected books.

As with the other areas of the libraries, acquisitions procedures and processes started changing in the late 1960s and 1970s with the purchase of automated and integrated library systems and the acquisitions processes streamlined and improved by the adoption of automation and standards, which allowed libraries to send orders using electronic data interchange (EDI) and to be billed and to pay vendors electronically in return. While the trend toward computerization of acquisitions records has been strong since the 1970s, many acquisitions procedures were not done online until the advent of the web-based services and electronically available journals and books. In addition, the growth and development of new TS-related products and services from vendors meant the increased need for cataloging and acquisitions to work together in order to make accurate bibliographic information appear on orders transmitted to vendors and thus ensure libraries gets shipped the correct item. The inter-reliant workflow between acquisitions and cataloging signified a trend toward blurring of the traditionally separate cataloging and acquisitions units that made up the TS department of the library.

CATALOGING

Cataloging is the process of describing materials for the purpose of compiling inventories and providing organized access to the collections. Relative to the movement of materials within TS, cataloging usually follows the receipt of ordered books in acquisitions. There are two types of cataloging: original and copy. Original cataloging entails the creation of the bibliographic description from scratch. Cataloging has three components: description, subject analysis and classification, and authority control. Descriptive component includes recording the attributes of an item: its author, title, publisher, the number of pages, its size, etc. This component allows the user to find and identify a book, by the author's name, the title, edition, size, etc. Subject analysis and classification are considered the intellectual elements of cataloging. Subject analysis entails determining the subject matter of the item and assigning corresponding subject headings from a controlled vocabulary, such as Library of Congress Subject Headings, Medical Subject Headings from the National Library of Medicine, or a variety of other thesauri, depending on the cataloging rules of a particular country. Classification of materials is done according to their discipline and topic, and is, therefore, closely tied to subject analysis. There are two main classification schemes in the United States: Dewey Decimal Classification (DDC) and Library of Congress (LCC). The DDC system is primarily used by public libraries, whereas LCC is preferred by academic and research libraries. The cataloger assigns a classification, or call number, in correlation with the subject headings. The call number serves a dual purpose: it determines the place of a book on the shelf and it collocates books on the same topic next to each other.

Authority control is the process that is applied to both descriptive and subject analysis parts of cataloging. It ensures the consistency and correctness of names and subject headings entered into bibliographic description. It also functions as a collocation and disambiguation device in the library catalog. Through authority control, the works written by the same author under different pseudonyms will be gathered in a single search due to behind-the-scenes cross-references; Multilanguage translations of a book or a musical piece will be brought together. By the same token, conflicting entries, such as common names, will be distinguished from each other through specifying information, for example, date of birth, death, etc.

Copy cataloging, which became possible with the practice of shared cataloging, represents the process of using the bibliographic record of an item created by another library to describe the same item held in the local collection.

Most TS departments perform both types of cataloging. However, the ratio between original and copy cataloging depends on the type of the library. Libraries holding a lot of unique materials have a substantial proportion of their cataloging done as original, whereas libraries with mainstream materials rely heavily on copy cataloging.

The distinction between original and copy cataloging determines the requirements for skills and education of personnel. While the relative ease of copy cataloging permits employment of paraprofessional staff, original cataloging is still considered the domain of professional catalogers with a master's degree in Library Science, although shrinking resources and increased workload create a trend of employing cataloging assistants for original cataloging as well.

In addition to cataloging itself, cataloging units also perform database (or catalog) maintenance. This is done in order to keep the catalog accurate by reconciling data conflicts, correcting mistakes, and reflecting changes in regards to cataloging. Larger libraries often have database maintenance as a separate section.

Cataloging has a rich history. Throughout the centuries, it underwent major transformations following changing needs of the society and advances in technology. The earliest known compilation of a catalog of a collection was completed in 1558 and was called the Catalogue of Bretton Monastery Library.[6] In 1759, the Trustees of the British Museum expressed the desirability of a catalog and further suggested in 1807 that a separate alphabetical catalog for each collection be compiled as well as a general classed catalog.[7]

In 1841, one of the founding fathers of modern cataloging Sir Anthony Panizzi, keeper of the printed books at the British Museum, published his *Rules for the Compilation of the Catalogue* where he considered the same problems of choice and form of entry, description, cross-referencing, and filing order that are repeated in codes to the present day. In the United States, Panizzi's ideas were taken up and modified by Charles Coffin Jewett, librarian of the Smithsonian Institution, who needed standardized rules in order to accomplish his plan of collecting bibliographic data and making it available for printing individual library catalogs.[8] He compiled the very first United States' code of cataloging rules that was issued in 1853. In 1876, Charles Cutter's *Rules for a Printed Dictionary Catalog*, the dictionary catalog, was becoming the dominate form.[9] His rules went through four editions between the first in 1876 and 1904, and increased in coverage and were a major influence over later codes.[8]

At the dawn of the twentieth century, the LCC, the principal cataloging agency, began selling library catalog cards. This caused a much greater degree of consistency in library catalogs and ushered in the era of copy cataloging. Up to that moment, libraries were responsible for creating their own original descriptions of the materials in their collections; thereafter, they gained a choice of buying those descriptions from the LCC. In 1908, the *Anglo-American Cataloging Rules* were first published and were called that because of the cooperation between the British and American catalogers, and were the offspring of Cutter, plus accommodation to the LCC practice.[10] Seymour Lubetzky, who was working at the LCC at the time, wrote *Cataloging Rules and Principles*, in which he suggested the requisites of a new code.[11] Within the next 7 years, he also presented two revised codes that eventually became the basis for the AACR.[12,13] In 1967, two versions of the *Anglo-American Cataloguing Rules* were published, a North American text and a British text.[14] Finally, in 1978, the rules were published in one version as *Anglo-American Cataloguing Rules, second edition* (AACR2).[15] The AACR2 was adopted by the LCC, the National Library of Canada, the British Library, and the Australian National Library in January 1981.[16] There were subsequent revisions to the second edition that were published in 1988, 1998, and 2002.[17]

The major developments in the area of cataloging and bibliographic retrieval of the twentieth century can be characterized first of all as a period of growth and development of productivity. The adaptation and use of technology and standards such as machine-readable cataloging (MARC), based on ISBD's (International Standard Bibliographic Description) eight areas of description, has enabled libraries to standardize and share bibliographic records. In addition, with the dawn of the computer and the start of the information age, libraries began to either develop their own internal library software systems or increasingly started buying them from the growing numbers of library software vendors such as GEAC, CLSI, among a number of other early pioneering library software vendors.

The twentieth century was also marked by the development of bibliographic networks, such as Online Computer Library Center (OCLC) and Research Libraries' Network (RLIN). In 1967, the Ohio College Library Center developed a computerized system in which the libraries of Ohio academic institutions could share resources and reduce costs.[18] In 1977, the Ohio members of OCLC adopted changes in the governance structure that enabled libraries outside Ohio to become members. In 1981, the legal name of the corporation became Online Computer Library Center, Inc.[19] RLIN started in 1974 as a competitor to OCLC and was focused primarily on research libraries and specialized research collections, like art, law, etc. The development of these bibliographic utilities contributed to the rapid growth of copy cataloging and resource-sharing among libraries nationwide.

The natural outgrowth of shared cataloging was the establishment of cooperative programs by the LCC. During the 1970s, LC initiated NACO and CONSER programs. NACO stands for the Name Authority Program Component for the Program for Cooperative Cataloging (PCC) that was developed by the LCC in order to share the name authority work previously done only by the LCC. Through this program, participants contribute authority records for names, uniform titles, and series to the LCC Name Authority File. An individual institution may join this program or a group of libraries with a common interest may form a funnel project to contribute records via a coordinator. Participants agree to follow a common set of standards and guidelines when creating or changing authority records in order to maintain the integrity of a large shared authority file. This file helps the global library community work more efficiently and effectively, allowing it to maximize its resources.[20]

CONSER began in the early 1970s as a project to convert manual serial cataloging into machine-readable records and has evolved into an ongoing program to create and maintain high-quality bibliographic records for serials. In keeping with its evolution, the name was changed in 1986 from the CONSER (CONversion of SERials) Project to the CONSER (Cooperative ONline SERials) Program. In October 1997, CONSER became a bibliographic component of the PCC.[21]

Building on the success of NACO and CONSER, in 1995, LC established the PCC that subsumed NACO and CONSER as two of its four components. The primary goal of PCC is to cooperatively enhance the timely availability of bibliographic and authority records by cataloging more items, producing cataloging that is widely available for sharing and use by others, and performing cataloging in a more cost-effective manner.[22]

The third component of PCC deals with contribution of bibliographic records for monographs in all formats and is called BIBCO. The fourth and final component of PCC—Subject Authority Cooperative Program (SACO)—deals with subject authority.

The SACO was established to provide a means for libraries to submit subject headings and classification numbers to the LCC via the PCC.[23]

The emergence of digital materials expanded the field of information standards. In addition to MARC, which was devised for print format, there appeared standards for the description of digital materials, such as Dublin Core, Metadata Encoding and Transmission Standard, and some others. Local Integrated Library Systems (ILS) acquired web interfaces, and library catalogs evolved from being accessible strictly from designated terminals to become available on the Internet.

The beginning of the twenty-first century was marked by a trend toward mergers and acquisitions in the area of TS. In 2006, two major library networks and union catalogs, OCLC and RLIN, merged into one company—OCLC. This move created a single bibliographic database and cemented OCLC's role as the leader in shaping TS practices in acquisitions and cataloging. ILS vendors continued the acquisition trend reducing the library software market to a few major companies. In competition to proprietary systems, emerging on the scene are open-source applications, such as Koha and Evergreen. While integrated library systems have front-end (i.e., public) and back-end (i.e., nonpublic) modules, the implementation of the new ILS and their upgrades, as well as library-wide training and documentation, often rests on TS.

The advent of the Internet in the 1990s had a major impact on the work of library services. It brought on a sharp division of publications into print and online formats with print being quickly replaced by the Internet-based matter, especially in the area of periodicals but increasingly electronic books as well. Cataloging services and tools migrated online and became available through such LCC's instruments as Cataloger's Desktop and Classification Web. However, the exponential growth of electronic resources created a cataloging dilemma for TS. Shrinking library budgets, increased volume of work, and the rising cost of cataloging spurred a trend toward simplification and streamlining of descriptive cataloging rules. The emergence of large online aggregations of electronic books and journals created the alternative to catalog access methods to the resources, for example, A–Z lists and databases, thus raising a national debate about the diminishing role of the catalog and cataloging itself as the conduit to the collections.[24–30]

At the same time vendors, publishers, and intermediaries entered the TS scene offering bulk cataloging, acquisitions services, and outsourcing of authority control. In 2004, in the article entitled "Taking the drudgery out of book acquisitions," which appeared in *Library & Information Update*, talks about the services of a book supplier whose services now include online searching of item record databases; browsing of databases that include sample pages, contents, online ordering using EDI, order management, shelf-ready stock with OPAC-ready records, automated alerts for items that based on your libraries profile may be of interest to your library.[31] Major book vendors, such as YBP, and others began bundling their primary business—the book trade—with cataloging and materials processing, thus offering a replacement for services that traditionally were carried out by library's TS. While providing a faster turnaround time and, in many cases, reducing the cataloging, authority control, and processing costs, outsourcing earned its skeptics. The downside of outsourcing is primarily tied to the quality of services provided by vendors and the need by TS to maintain quality control processes in order to uphold the standards and ensure the accuracy of records. When new libraries are being started, they generally use outsource vendors to provide them with opening day collections to fill the library on their opening day with wide-ranging and popular books available to the public.

With the increasing use of the Internet since the mid-1990s, many journals transitioned to electronic formats. Libraries began offering numerous article databases with varied interfaces, which felt cumbersome to both librarians and users, especially when compared to the relative ease and accuracy of Google searching. In order to resolve this issues, starting in the late 1990s and early 2000s Roy Tennant and others suggested federated searching (also known as metasearching) as the solution.[32] The principle of federated searching, which ultimately proved too limiting and slow,[33,34] was searching multiple sources from a single point. The development of web-based Google Scholar and problems with Federated Searching led to calls for a development of a resource that could compete with Google.[34]

The emergence of online materials introduced a new function to TS—administration and management of electronic collections. Libraries moved from subscribing to individual print journals to subscribing to e-journal aggregations, abstract and indexing services, and article databases. Online materials spurred the development of new technologies, such as tools for linking between the citation and full text via OpenURL or Digital Object Identifier, and for managing electronic resources. The issues of management, access, and licensing of electronic materials created the need for specialized positions on professional and paraprofessional levels. Many libraries introduced the job of an electronic resources librarian, or its variants, and dedicated the support staff to this function. These positions commonly deal with administration of licensing agreements, resolution of access issues, and maintenance of databases at the root of the access tools, such as the knowledge base of a link resolver and an electronic resources management system (ERMS). The principles of ERMS as a management tool for electronic resources were developed by Digital Library Federation. They encompass listing and descriptive; license-related; financial and purchasing; process and status; systems and technical; contact and support; and usage functions.[35] A rapid growth of digital materials encoded in non-MARC metadata created parallel virtual collections and thus separate silos of information for many libraries.

Library information technology developers created the first generation of enterprise Google-like search engines, which became known as discovery interfaces. They began to emerge in 2002 with AquaBrowser from Medialab Solutions, capable of cross-searching the library's diverse collections, such as digital libraries, databases, and the catalog. It was about 2006 when this software genre saw Primo from Ex Libris and Encore from Innovative Interfaces, Inc. launched. In 2007, an open-source option VuFind became available. In 2009, Serials Solutions, EBSCO, OCLC, and Ex Libris all made announcements they would combine the next-generation interface technologies with large bodies of content into one single index[36] allowing access to more results much faster and with better deduplication and relevancy ranking than federated searching.[37,38] Implementation of such systems significantly increased users access to full-text articles as well as to web resources.[32]

The new discovery products provide a more modern, web interface, broader approach to discovery, and access to social networks. Discovery interfaces incorporate newer tools such as tagging, integrated social features, easier search and navigation, and relevancy-ranked results.[36]

The library catalog has been changing with the times as well. Bringing Amazon-like experience to the library, many bibliographic records now have links to the online table of contents, publisher and author information, and reviews. The evolution of the web into an interactive experience with user-generated content left its mark on the public face of the catalog. Main problems with the traditional online catalog was that it did not include the deeper content of its collections such as the contents of its periodical collections, local digital and special collections, which were cataloged using systems outside of the traditional integrated library systems. Library patrons did not understand the entire library's holdings were no longer in the library catalog, and their interfaces were text-based and dated in comparisons to the Internet search engines.

A new generation of catalogs emerged, such as Endeca and OCLC's WorldCat Local, that provide faceted browsing and navigation of results similar to the Internet search engines. Legacy library catalogs became capable of displaying images of book jackets, sending text messages, integrating users' input through book reviews and recommendations, and tagging using non-LCC, community-generated terms.[36]

As the nature of the work changed, the name TS and the units within TS have begun to change as well. Cataloging has changed to names such as Bibliographic Assess, Metadata Services, Metadata and Digital Library Services, while TS name has changed to such things as Collection Support Services, Materials Acquisitions Processing Services, and Collection Access and Management Services.[39]

The opportunities provided by the electronic information exchange increased national and international cooperation between libraries in the arena of shared cataloging.

The report produced by the IFLA Study Group on Functional Requirements for Bibliographic records (FRBR)[40] contains a description of the conceptual model (the entities, relationships, and attributes), a proposed national-level bibliographic record for all types of materials, and user tasks associated with the bibliographic resources described in catalogs, and other bibliographic tools.[41] Aiming to conceptualize the entire bibliographic universe, the FRBR report introduced the new vocabulary to describe bibliographic entities. Such terms as "work, expression, manifestation, item" as well as user tasks defined as "find, identify, select and obtain" influenced the bibliographic lexicon. The next set of cataloging rules, Resource Description and Access (RDA), the successor to AACR2, uses FRBR terminology and its user-centric approach in its contents.[42]

The work on adapting *Anglo-American Cataloging Rules* to the new digital world began in 2004 by Joint Steering Committee, and initially as AACR3, the next revision of AACR2. As the work progressed, it appeared that the existing standard could not accommodate the changes in publication models of the twenty-first century. The cataloging community comments to the early drafts demonstrated that the proposed changes were not sufficient. This led to the shift to a new approach in devising a new cataloging standard, and the new name RDA: Resource Description and Access was adopted in 2005. The scope of RDA is defined as "a set of guidelines and instructions on formulating descriptive data and access point control data to support resource discovery."[43] RDA was conceived as a content standard with the following features: rules that are easy to use and apply; it is designed for an online, networked environment; provides effective bibliographic control for all types of media; presents a logical structure based on internationally agreed principles (e.g., FRBR, FRAD); compatible with other standards, and is of use beyond the library community.[44]

The first draft of RDA, followed by the comments period, was issued in November 2008. The new cataloging standard sparked a dynamic discussion within the profession. The comments provided by the cataloging community reflected a wide range of views: from the appreciation for inclusion of FRBR/FRAD data models and the collaboration with publishing community, to sharp criticism on the lack of clarity and failure to address the needs of special formats' cataloging, such as maps and moving images.[45] The revised text, based on the feedback, was finalized in June 2009. RDA was released as an online subscription product, named the RDA Toolkit, in June 2010[46] Three national libraries—the LCC, the National Library of Medicine, and the National Agricultural Library—as well as the broader constituency, conducted a testing process that ran from October to December of 2010. As the result, the recommendation from the testing group was to continue improvement of RDA and postpone its implementation until 2013.[45] Subsequently, RDA implementation day was set by the LCC for March 31, 2013, when it became the new cataloging standard.

The emergence of RDA with its expanded scope and a new model triggered changes in MARC format, previously designed to support AACR2. In order to accommodate RDA, the number of MARC fields and codes was increased, the rules for mandated, repeatable, and nonrepeatable fields evolved to allow more flexibility, and the terminology was augmented or changed.[47]

MARC has been serving the library community since the 1960s, providing the structure for bibliographic data. However, as a format designed for libraries, MARC became a constraint on the use of bibliographic data interchange between publishers, vendors, and a broader networked community. MARC is principled on the concept of a record, thus making each description a discrete and closed data set, enabling vast duplication of data, and disabling relationship between the entities encoded in the record. In order to break down the insulation of the bibliographic data from the networked information exchange, as well as within MARC corpus itself, in 2011, the LCC announced Bibliographic Framework Initiative to redesign the underlying structure of the data description.[48] The following year (2012), the new data model for bibliographic description, named BIBFRAME, emerged.[49] As described by the LCC, "instead of bundling everything neatly as a 'record' and potentially duplicating information across multiple records, the BIBFRAME Model relies heavily on relationships between resources (Work-to-Work relationships; Work-to-Instance relationships; Work-to-Authority relationships). It manages this by using controlled identifiers for things (people, places, languages, etc.)."[50] A limited number of libraries—among them LCC, Cornell, Princeton, Stanford, and National Library of Medicine—are currently testing the BIBFRAME model. At this point, there is no target date for the implementation of the BIBFRAME environment.[50]

The changes occurring in TS with the advance of technology, network environment, and new standards have altered the requirements for staff skills set. Modern-day catalogers and acquisitions specialists need to understand the mechanics of EDI, know not only the current bibliographic format and other metadata schemes (e.g., Dublin Core for cataloging digital libraries), but be prepared for their replacements in the rapidly changing environment. In addition to technical skills, TS staff need to be flexible, open to change, and be willing to learn.

COLLECTIONS MANAGEMENT

Despite the rapid growth of digital resources since the advent of the Internet, print materials continue to play an important role in library functions. In many libraries, processing, and mending of print resources is in the purview of TS; it is the final step in the acquisition-to-shelf cycle of materials movement. While there are variations in the order of processing steps, a typical workflow is designed as follows: once the books and print periodicals arrive in the library, they are received, cataloged (i.e., an electronic record describing the item's physical and subject attributes has been created in the local system), and then the items go to the materials processing section. There, items are stamped with a property stamp, indicating the ownership of a book, a date due slip is pasted for circulation to note when an item is due back in the library after the checkout, a call number (or classification number) label is affixed so that the item is shelved in the logical order, and, finally, a barcode linking the physical piece with its electronic record in the catalog is attached to the book. Additionally, processing may entail adhering Mylar covers, security beepers, and reinforcement of publisher's binding. Regular binding of periodicals and monographs is usually contracted out to a binding facility.

Collections management, along with other spheres of the library, has been impacted by the technology. In addition to now routine barcodes and security devices, Radio Frequency IDentification (RFID) entered the library scene. While having the potential of replacing barcodes and tattle-tapes by combining their functions, RFID has been slow to spread. Despite the convenience with inventorying, shelving/retrieving items, and detecting and tracking theft, the considerations of patrons' privacy, as well as the cost, prevent this technology from broad adoption by library community.

As electronic information exchange ties the processes of libraries and their book vendors closer, the latter began expanding their services into materials processing, leveraging the information they receive from libraries and bulk cataloging services, such as OCLC WorldCat Cataloging Partners (formerly PromptCat). If a library outsources its materials processing, the books come back with the full set of processing elements, such as classification labels, property stamps, barcodes, etc.

CONCLUSION

Historically, TS have been the behind-the-scenes backbone of the library. Today, more than ever they play a crucial role in the delivery of user services by providing support to information search and retrieval tools and access to online materials.

The current trends in automation, development of new library standards, evolution of the OCLC library network into a major tool for universal bibliographic control that provides access to the collections of libraries, museums, and other cultural institutions worldwide, make the work of individual TS department's part of global information network. In addition, adoption of the native Internet tools, such as faceted browsing, user-created content, and integration of social media, by libraries signifies a continuing trend toward user-centric and interactive interfaces.

TS, especially cataloging departments, are undergoing major changes. The implementation of RDA and development of new data model, BIBFRAME, will test the viability and robustness of the new library standards.

REFERENCES

1. Tuttle, H. From Cutter to computer: Technical services in academic and research libraries 1876–1976. Coll. Res. Libr. **1976**, *37* (5), 421–439.
2. Coney, D. The administration of technical processes. In *Current Issues in Library Administration*, Papers Presented before the Library Institute at the University of Chicago, August 1–12, 1938; Carleton, B.J., Ed.; University of Chicago Press: Chicago, IL, 1939; 163–180.
3. Walsh, H. Acquisitions. In *Encyclopedia of Library and Information Science*, 2nd Ed.; Drake, M., Ed.; Marcel Dekker, Inc.: New York, 2003; 76–81.

4. Deeken, J.; Thomas, D. Technical services job ads: Changes since 1995. Coll. Res. Libr. **2006**, *67* (2), 136–145.
5. Futas, E. *Library Acquisition Policies and Procedures*, 2nd Ed.; Oryx Press: Phoenix, AZ, 1984.
6. Thornton, J.L. *The Chronology of Librarianship: An Introduction to the History of Libraries and Book-Collecting*; Grafton & Co: London, U.K., 1941.
7. Hanson, E.R.; Daily, J.E. Catalogs and cataloging. In *Encyclopedia of Library and Information Science*, 2nd Ed.; Drake, M., Ed.; Marcel Dekker, Inc.: New York, 2003; 431–468.
8. Massonneau, S. Technical services and technology: The bibliographical imperative. In *A Century of Service: Librarianship in the United States and Canada*; Jackson, S.L., Ed.; American Library Association: Chicago, IL, 1976; 192–207.
9. Cutter, C.A. *Rules for a Printed Dictionary Catalogue*, U.S. Bureau of Education; Government Printing Office: Washington, DC, 1876.
10. Hanson, J.C.M. *Catalog Rules: Author and Title Entries*, American Ed.; American Library Association: Chicago, IL, 1908.
11. Lubetzky, S. *Cataloging Rules and Principles: A Critique of the ALA Rules for Entry and a Proposed Design for their Revision*; Library of Congress: Washington, DC, 1953.
12. Lubetzky, S. *Code of Cataloging Rules: Bibliographic Entry and Description. A Partial and Tentative Draft for a New Edition of Bibliographic Cataloging Rules*; American Library Association: Chicago, IL, 1958.
13. Lubetzky, S. *Code of Cataloging Rules: Author and Title Entry*; American Library Association: Chicago, IL, 1960.
14. Spalding, C.S. *Anglo-American Cataloging Rules*; American Library Association: Chicago, IL, 1967.
15. Gorman, M.; Winkler, P.W. *Anglo-American Cataloguing Rules*, 2nd Ed.; American Library Association: Chicago, IL, 1978.
16. Gorman, M. *The Concise AACR 2: Being a Rewritten and Simplified Version of Anglo-American Cataloguing Rules*; American Library Association: Chicago, IL, 1981, [Note: Later revised in line with the 1988 and 1998 revisions of AACR2].
17. Joint Steering Committee for the Development of RDA. In *A Brief history of AACR*. http://www.rda-jsc.org/history.html (accessed November 9, 2014).
18. Tate, E.L. International standards: the road to universal bibliographic control. Libr. Resour. Tech. Serv. **1976**, *20* (1), 16–24.
19. OCLC. *History of OCLC*; 2008, http://www.oclc.org/about/history/default.html (accessed November 9, 2014).
20. Library of Congress. Program for cooperative cataloging. In *NACO—The name authority component of the PCC*; 2008, http://www.loc.gov/aba/pcc/ (accessed November 9, 2014).
21. Library of Congress. Program for cooperative cataloging. In *What is Conser?*; 2008, http://www.loc.gov/aba/pcc/conser/ (accessed November 9, 2014).
22. Library of Congress. Program for cooperative cataloging. In *About the PCC*; 2008, http://www.loc.gov/catdir/pcc/2001pcc.html (accessed December 13, 2008).
23. Library of Congress. Program for cooperative cataloging subject authority cooperative program of the PCC. In *About the SACO Program*; 2008, http://www.loc.gov/aba/pcc/saco/index.html (accessed November 9, 2014).
24. Marcum, D.B. *The Future of Cataloging*; Boston, MA, 2005, Address to the Ebsco Leadership seminar, January 16 2005; Associate Librarian of congress: http://www.loc.gov/library/reports/CatalogingSpeech.pdf (accessed November 9, 2014).
25. Mann, T. *Will Googlens Keyword Searching Eliminate the Need for LC Cataloging and Classification?*; 2005, http://www.guild2910.org/searching.htm (accessed November 9, 2014).
26. Calhoun, K. *The Changing Nature of the Catalog and its Integration with Other Discovery Tools*. Final Report. March 17, 2006. http://www.loc.gov/catdir/calhoun-report-final.pdf (accessed November 9, 2014).
27. Mann, T. *The Changing Nature of the Catalog and Its Integration with Other Discovery Tools*. Prepared for the Library of Congress by Karen Calhoun; A Critical Review by Thomas Mann, April, 4, 2006; Final Report. March 17, 2006. http://guild2910.org/AFSCMECalhounReviewREV.pdf (accessed November 9, 2014).
28. Library of Congress. Working Group on the Future of Bibliographic Control. In *On the Record, Report of the Library of Congress Working Group on the Future of Bibliographic Control*; 2008; 44. (January 9, 2008; p. 44), http://www.loc.gov/bibliographic-future/news/lcwg-ontherecord-jan08-final.pdf (accessed November 9, 2014).
29. Mann, T. Library of Congress, Working Group on the Future of Bibliographic Control. On the Record, Report of the Library of Congress Working Group on the Future of Bibliographic Control..., March, 14, 2008; 38. http://www.guild2910.org/WorkingGrpResponse2008.pdf (accessed November 9, 2014).
30. Marcum, D.B. *Library of Congress Response to "On the Record, Report of the Library of Congress Working Group on the Future of Bibliographic Control,"*; 2008, http://www.loc.gov/bibliographic-future/news/lcwg-ontherecord-jan08-final.pdf (accessed November 9, 2014).
31. Chartered Institute of Library & Information Professionals. Taking the drudgery out of book acquisitions. Libr. Inf. Update **2004**, *3* (7/8), 52–53.
32. Way, D. The impact of web-scale discovery on the use of a library collection. Ser. Rev. **2010**, *7* (2), 214–220.
33. Helfer, D.S.; Wakimoto, J.C. Metasearching, the good, the bad and the ugly of making it work in your library. Searcher **2005**, *13* (2), 40–41.
34. Breeding, M. Plotting a new course for metasearch. Comput. Libr. **2005**, *25* (2), 27–29.
35. Jewell, T.D. *Selection and Presentation of Commercially Available Electronic Resources: Issues and Practices*; 2001, http://www.clir.org/pubs/reports/pub99/pub99.pdf (accessed November 9, 2014).
36. Breeding, M. *Next-Gen Library Catalogs*; Neal-Schuman Publishers, Inc: New York, 2010.
37. Hadro, J. EBSCOhost unveils discovery service. Libr. J. **2009**, *134* (8), 17.
38. Primo Central-More Data for Discovery. Better Service to end users. http://initiatives.exlibrisgroup.com/2009/07/primo-centralmore-data-for-discovery.html (accessed September 26, 2014).

39. Yale University. Library. Task force on vision and directions. Last modified October 26, 2006; http://www.library.yale.edu/~dlovins/vtf/namechange.html (accessed September 26, 2014).
40. Functional Requirements for Bibliographic Records (FRBR). *IFLA Study Group on the Functional Requirements for Bibliographic Records*; K.G. Saur: München, Germany, 1998, Final Report: (UBCIM Publications, New Series; v. 19) http://www.ifla.org/VII/s13/frbr/frbr.htm or http://www.ifla.org/VII/s13/frbr/frbr.pdf (accessed November 9, 2014).
41. Tillett, B. What is FRBR? A conceptual model for the bibliographic universe. Aust. Libr. J. **2005**, *54* (1), 24–30. http://www.loc.gov/cds/downloads/FRBR.PDF (accessed November 9, 2014).
42. Working Group on Functional Requirements and Numbering of Authority Records (FRANAR)-IV. *Division of Bibliographic Control*; 2007, http://www.ifla.org/VII/d4/wg-franar.htm (accessed September 5, 2008).
43. Chapman, A. *RDA: A cataloguing code for the 21st century*; 2008, http://www.cilip.org.uk/publications/updatemagazine/archive/archive2008/september/rdachapman.htm (accessed November 9, 2014).
44. Kiorgaard, D. *Joint Steering Committee for Development of RDA subject: RDA Scope and Structure*; 2007, http://www.rda-jsc.org/docs/5rda-scoperev3.pdf (accessed November 18, 2014).
45. American Library Association. Chartered Institute of Library and Information Professionals. RDA Toolkit; 2014, http://www.rda-jsc.org/docs/5rda-fulldraft-alaresp.pdf (accessed November 18, 2014).
46. American Library Association. Chartered Institute of Library and Information Professionals. RDA Toolkit; 2014, http://www.rdatoolkit.org/ (accessed November 18, 2014).
47. Library of Congress. MARC standards. Last modified July 30, 2014; http://www.loc.gov/marc/RDAinMARC.html (accessed November 18, 2014).
48. Library of Congress. Bibliographic Framework Initiative (BIBFRAME). n.d (no date), http://www.loc.gov/bibframe/news/framework-103111.html (accessed November 18, 2014).
49. Library of Congress. BIBFRAME Primer Document Announced (November 21, 2012), http://www.loc.gov/bibframe/news/bibframe-112112.html (accessed November 18, 2014).
50. Library of Congress. BIBFRAME Frequently Asked Questions. n.d. (no date), http://www.loc.gov/bibframe/faqs/ (accessed November 18, 2014), http://www.loc.gov/bibframe/faqs/#q08 (accessed November 18, 2014).

Linguistics and the Information Sciences

John C. Paolillo
School of Informatics and School of Library and Information Science, Indiana University, Bloomington, Indiana, U.S.A.

Abstract
Linguistics is the scientific study of language which emphasizes language spoken in everyday settings by human beings. It has a long history of interdisciplinarity, both internally and in contribution to other fields, including information science. A linguistic perspective is beneficial in many ways in information science, since it examines the relationship between the forms of meaningful expressions and their social, cognitive, institutional, and communicative context, these being two perspectives on information that are actively studied, to different degrees, in information science. Examples of issues relevant to information science are presented for which the approach taken under a linguistic perspective is illustrated.

INTRODUCTION

Linguistics is the scientific study of language, where language is generally taken to be *natural language*, spoken by human beings and acquired informally from one's parents, siblings, and community. Natural language is contrasted with written language, which must be learned formally; artificial languages, which are intentionally designed for some purpose such as intercultural communication; and formal languages, like those of computer science, mathematics, and logic, which are designed to express abstract meanings in well-defined ways. To the extent that these other types of language resemble natural language in their structure or use, a linguistic perspective may be relevant to understanding them. Linguistics has a long history which can be traced to ancient sources such as the *Ashthadhyayi* of Panini, an Indian grammarian of the fifth century B.C.E., or the invention of the Phoenician and Ugaritic alphabetic orders approximately 1000 B.C.E.,[1] but its modern practice is largely based on the structuralism of Ferdinand de Saussure[2] and Leonard Bloomfield,[3] the anthropological perspective of Edward Sapir,[4] and the formal perspective of Noam Chomsky.[5–7]

Natural language is a highly complex phenomenon, and consequently the field of linguistics has a great deal of internal structure, with largely separate subfields for specific areas of linguistics. At the same time, linguistics has close interactions with fields such as psychology, anthropology, sociology, computer science, education, and communications, thus many applied and "hyphenated" areas of linguistic study are found as well.

The aim of this entry is to explain the organization of linguistics as a field, to identify some of its main points of interaction with the information sciences (broadly construed to include the full spectrum of studies focused on information technology and its uses, from technical research and development to applied social science, including information retrieval, information seeking behavior, information policy, human–computer interaction, etc.), and to provide indications of where and how linguistic approaches might benefit the information sciences. The organization of this entry is as follows. The next section describes the structural subfields of linguistics, describing the questions that each addresses. The third section treats hybrid subfields of linguistics, whose questions are not strictly about language structure but which deeply involve either external context or application of some sort. The fourth section identifies a number of linguistic issues in the information sciences. The final section offers some general conclusions. Computational linguistics, Natural Language Processing (NLP), and information retrieval are not discussed in any depth in this entry. Instead, emphasis is placed on the range of questions addressed in the field of linguistics and their relevance to the information sciences.

STRUCTURAL SUBFIELDS OF LINGUISTICS

Although linguistics is small relative to other fields, in terms of the number of people working within it, linguists tend to specialize, so that their work specifically addresses one or more subfields; few linguists consider themselves "generalists."

A major focus of linguistics is language structure, and linguistics is a largely structuralist field, in the sense that it concerns itself with categories of entities and their relations to one another. Other philosophical orientations exist in the field, notably the Cartesian mentalism of Chomsky which posits innate cognitive structures governing language, but other philosophical movements shared among social science and humanities fields, such as the postmodern turn, have not had a strong impact on linguistics. Moreover, in actual practice, structuralist forms of inquiry and analysis, as laid out by Saussure and Bloomfield, are

Encyclopedia of Library and Information Sciences, Fourth Edition DOI: 10.1081/E-ELIS4-120044491

fundamental to most forms of analysis in the field. In some sense this is inescapable, at least in so far as human languages have regular patterning, and that patterning is shared among different speakers of a language. It is tempting to treat the language as an object unto itself, independent of the speakers or their contexts, however it arises.

Linguistics is typically taught starting from a "core" of its structural subfields, characteristically organized in terms of analytic "levels" of structure (not unlike the "layer-cake" model of the organization of WWW protocols and standards, see below). At the lowest level, linguistics considers the sound structures of human languages: which sounds are possible in a language, and what sequences of sounds are possible, their articulatory mechanisms, acoustic perception and patterns of relationship with other sounds. This is the domain of *phonetics* and *phonology*. One level above this is the structure of words, and the patterns of relationship among word structures that take meaning into account. This is the domain of *morphology* and the study of the *lexicon*. At one level above this, linguists consider the arrangement of words into well-formed utterances (i.e., those accepted as "grammatical" by a native speaker). This is the domain of *syntax*. The study of the meanings of these utterances, how they are built from the meanings of their parts, together with the meanings of words themselves, comprise the study of *semantics*. Beyond this, linguists recognize a level of *linguistic pragmatics*, which deals with the ways in which linguistic expressions are used, such that conventional or contextual meaning can differ from literal meaning.

A characteristic common to all of these levels is a property sometimes called "duality of structure." Originally, this term described Saussure's notion of the arbitrariness of the linguistic sign, i.e., that forms of words in any language have no necessary relationship to their meaning, and that sounds and meaning are arbitrarily associated. The principle is more general than this, however, as it can be seen that units at each level of structure are essentially independent. Lower levels of structure (e.g., sounds) may be referred to in higher levels of structure (e.g., morphemes, words) but the patterns that obtain at each level have no necessary relation to those of the other levels, and a similar arbitrariness of relation between all different levels of language structure can be observed. In the following subsections, the major structural subfields of linguistics are described. The following section details some of the more important hybrid areas of linguistics, ending with its more applied subfields.

Phonetics and Phonology

Phonetics is the study of the sounds of languages, their articulatory and perceptual properties, and patterns of regularity found therein. Phonetics is thus concerned with the material reality of language sounds, and is not concerned with what makes the sounds of languages meaningful. Phonetics makes extensive use of instrumentation, such as audio recording, spectral and other forms of acoustic analysis, and x-ray and video recording. Phonology is the study of the sound systems of languages, where differences in sound that carry meaning in a language are considered. To illustrate the difference in these two levels of analysis, consider the sounds represented by the letter *p* in English words like *pot* and *spot*. In *pot*, where the *p* is the first sound in the syllable, speakers of most dialects of English will produce a short burst of air ("aspiration") immediately after the release of the lips (symbolized [p^h]), whereas in *spot*, no aspiration is produced (symbolized [p]). There is a phonetic distinction between these two sounds or *phones*, but speakers of English nonetheless recognize these as the "same" sound. In another language such as Hindi, a difference between the two phones is enough to yield entirely different words, e.g., [p^hal] "fruit" and [pal] "instant, moment." Hence in Hindi, the phones [p^h] and [p] correspond to distinct phonemes /p^h/ and /p/, whereas in English, both phones correspond to the single phoneme /p/.

Phonetics and phonology illustrate an important principle in linguistics, namely that of *etic* (as in "phonetic") and *emic* (as in "phonemic") levels of description of a phenomenon. The etic level is what is empirically observable in a given instance, whereas the emic level is what is perceived by the native speaker of a language to be distinct. This distinction is maintained most robustly at the level of sound structure, but is found at other levels of structure as well.

Phonology is concerned with matters beyond the existence of categories of sounds used to describe the utterances of languages. It is also concerned with regularities of patterning that exist in sounds. These patterns include *phonotactics*, the sound sequences that can occur in a language (e.g., English permits words like [spat] "spot," but not [vpat] or [fpat], although these may be possible in other languages), and *phonological processes*, in which the juxtaposition of two words may result in a sound sequence that the words would not have exhibited independently (e.g., /kænt/ "can't" + /yu/ "you" yields [kænšu] "can't you"). Phonological processes sometimes depend on the identities of the specific forms to which they are attached, in which case they are referred to as *morphophonemic processes*. Phonological theories sometimes make a distinction between the two types of patterns, such that phonotactic patterns are governed by constraints (extrinsic conditions on what can or cannot occur in a language), whereas phonological processes are handled by *rules*, which are understood as cognitive or descriptive processes that transform one sequence into another. Current phonological theory tends to follow the approach of Optimality Theory[8] in conflating the distinction, regarding both types of patterns as the consequence of a common set of constraints. The reasons for this are somewhat technical, and the interested reader is referred to discussion in the relevant literature for further explanation.

Morphology and Lexicon

Morphology concerns the structure and forms of words, and patterns in their relations to one another. The lexicon is the store of words of a language, hence morphological patterns have a lot to do with the lexicon, but not all patterns in the lexicon are morphological. A morpheme is considered to be the most basic meaningful unit of language: it is a form–meaning pairing which ceases to be meaningful if it is subdivided further. As in sound structure, we may speak of an emic and an etic level in morphology: morphemes are realized as different specific variants (known as "morphs") in one context or another. For example, in English the word *card* is a singular noun referring to a stiff piece of heavy paper, which can be expressed in the plural as *cards*, for multiple stiff pieces of paper; similarly, the noun *winch* refers to a mechanical device for pulling or raising something, also in the singular, whose plural is *winches*. In contrast to these two, the noun *mouse*, meaning a small rodent, has the plural *mice*. All three types of plural exhibit regularity in the sense that there are other exemplars with the same characteristics: *shoe~shoes*, *peach~peaches*, *louse~lice*. All three patterns, adding [-z], adding [-ez] and changing the stem vowel, are alternant morphs of the plural morpheme. Of these, the plural morph in which the stem vowel changes is the less common pattern, and one readily finds examples where it could be expected to occur but does not: *spouse~spouses*. Irregularities in morphology of a language are common, and typically the reasons for it are historical in nature, concerning the evolution of the lexicon and its relation to sound change, etc. The vowel-changing plurals were once the dominant pattern in Old English, for example, but most of the pattern was lost in the Great Vowel Shift between Middle and Modern English (between 1200 and 1600 A.D.) which radically altered the pronunciation of most English vowels.

Languages differ in terms of the kind of morphological patterns they exhibit. On the one hand, languages show morphological *inflection* if words change form based on their grammatical function (subject, object, etc.); Latin, Greek (ancient and modern), and Finnish are three such languages. *Derivational* morphology, on the other hand, derives words of one category (such as nouns) from those of another (such as verbs). Languages may be *analytic*, having separate morphemes for clearly separate functions, or *synthetic*, where a single morpheme may simultaneously serve otherwise unrelated functions. Languages like Turkish tend to be more analytic, while Inuit (an Eskimo language spoken in Nunavit, Canada) and Onondaga (a Native American language of New York State) are more synthetic. Languages whose words are often composed of long sequences of analytic morphemes are said to be *agglutinating*; Turkish and Tamil are examples. Some languages, such as Mandarin Chinese, are said to be nearly entirely lacking in morphology.

Beyond morphology, many other linguistic patterns exist in the lexicon. Relations between languages, via lexical borrowing, are often observable in the lexicon, and sometimes languages borrow from their own past, resulting in entire classes of archaic words. Such lexical items may also systematically differ in *register*, i.e., their appropriateness for formal or informal circumstances; this is common in *diglossic* languages such as Arabic, Greek, Tamil (spoken in South India), and Sinhala (spoken in Sri Lanka), in which spoken and written forms of the language are structurally highly divergent.[9] Other lexical patterns revolve more closely around meaning: homonymy (words with identical meanings, e.g., *bird* and *avian*), antonymy (opposite meanings, e.g., *hot* and *cold*), hypernymy (a similar but more general meaning, e.g., *songbird* and *bird*), and hyponymy (a similar but more specific meaning, e.g., *songbird* and *sparrow*) are some of these patterns.

Syntax, Semantics, and Pragmatics

The arrangement of words into larger units, namely phrases and sentences, is the domain of syntax. Traditionally, morphology and syntax taken together were known as "grammar"; this term is currently dis-preferred by linguists. For several decades, syntax has held a dominant position in linguistics, due largely to the influence of Noam Chomsky and his approach to syntax known as *Generative Grammar*. Basically, the generative approach seeks to explain properties of language as manifestations of *linguistic universals*, which are regarded as properties of a uniquely human language faculty, distinct from other cognitive capacities. Since *Universal Grammar* (UG), as it is sometimes called, is held to be a universal human species characteristic, its effects are expected to be equally manifest in all languages. The differences among languages are regarded as interactions between UG and a child learner's linguistic experience. Variants of this theory are employed by people working in other formal frameworks such as *Lexical-Functional Grammar*,[10] *Relational Grammar*,[11,12] and *Head-Driven Phrase Structure Grammar*.[13,14]

Generative grammar and the theory of UG have been controversial since first being proposed in Chomsky's 1955 dissertation. A number of current alternative theories adopt somewhat different starting assumptions. For example, Cognitive Grammar,[15] while it emerged out of one branch of Generative Grammar in the 1970s,[16] regards properties of language as emergent from more general cognitive principles, such as iconicity,[17] metaphor,[18] and embodiment.[19] Closely allied to this are a range of approaches that can broadly be considered *Functional* approaches to grammar, represented by various authors such as Croft,[20] Fillmore and Kay,[21] Givón,[22] and Hopper and Traugott.[23] As the label suggests, functional approaches to syntax seek to explain the construction of sentences based on their function, e.g., for communication. Functionalism is often contrasted with *formalism*, where by "formal" what is meant is an emphasis on form, as in the sense of formal logic.

Functional accounts of language syntax often make appeals to principles of linguistic semantics and/or pragmatics (such appeals are rarer in the generative literature). Linguistic semantics is the study of the meanings of natural language expressions, while pragmatics refers to the real-world uses of utterances that are often not reflected in their literal meaning. For example, the utterance "Can you pass the salt?" is literally a yes/no question about the addressee's ability to perform an act. A semantic analysis of the sentence would be expected to account for how this meaning is obtained from the component words and their combination into phrases; such analyses tend to emphasize formal, set-theoretic interpretations, which employ various forms of logic to state meanings and their relations to linguistic forms.[24]

Conventionally, the same utterance is used as a request to the addressee that s/he perform an act. A pragmatic analysis must account for how the utterance's conventional meaning differs from its literal meaning in this systematic way. Austin[25] approached this problem from the perspective of *speech acts*, observing that certain types of utterances explicitly perform conventional acts, under the right circumstances (e.g., "I promise to answer," "I sentence you to 5 years in prison") and analyzed all utterances as operating under an implicit "performative" of some kind, even if it is not linguistically present. Grice[26] opted for a different approach, in which he invoked a general *cooperative principle*, according to which people in a conversation assume that others in the same conversation are being cooperative, and they tailor their contributions accordingly. Utterances that are apparently noncooperative on the surface are permitted if they rationally lead to one or more *implicatures*, i.e., nonliteral interpretations that are the real communicative intent of the speaker. Both the speech acts approach and the Gricean approach remain influential in contemporary linguistics.

Discourse Analysis

Linguistic structure does not end with the sentence, but rather, sentences can be seen to be structured at yet higher levels. These are collectively known as "discourse," and the branch of linguistics that addresses structure beyond the sentence is known as Discourse Analysis. Discourse Analysis is characterized by two main foci of interest: longer texts, whether as written texts or oral performances, and dyadic or multiparticipant conversations. The former focus is best represented by *Text Analysis*, while the latter is known as *Conversation Analysis*. Text Analysis primarily addresses how texts function as units, their internal structure in terms of narrative units and/or rhetorical acts, and the role of sentence-level grammar in contributing to that structure (via discourse markers, emphasizing and topicalizing constructions, etc.). Similarly, Conversation Analysis addresses the characteristics of conversations that permit them to function as units, examining turn-taking mechanisms, sequencing of speech acts, and cross-cultural and gender differences in the ways conversation unfolds. A third branch, known as Critical Discourse Analysis, applies the tools of both Text Analysis and Conversation Analysis to social criticism. For example, one might examine the use of passive constructions to mask the agency of powerful actors (e.g., the government, the army, etc.) in the news reportage of war or other political events. This in combination with observation of other linguistic strategies can be used to expose and examine the ideologies of different societal actors as encoded in their communications, and how such ideologies relate to the actors' stakes in the current events of the day.

HYBRID SUBFIELDS OF LINGUISTICS

Historical Linguistics and Language Classification

Modern linguistics is very much shaped by the awareness that languages are not static, and that change in historical time affects language in numerous ways. The study of language change is known as Historical Linguistics. One of its main methods is the *comparative method*, in which languages hypothesized to arise from a common ancestor are compared, typically by comparing words with similar form and meaning in the different languages (called "cognate forms" or "cognates"), to ascertain the degree and nature of relationship among the languages. The outcome of this is typically a language classification, in which groups of languages are said to be related across splits in the language group at different time depths. The best known example of this, and the longest established language family, is the Indo-European language family, members of which are spread over the entire globe, with members as diverse as Albanian, Dutch, English, French, German, Greek, Italian, Russian, Spanish, etc., in the European branch, and Assamese, Bhojpuri, Farsi, Gujarati, Hindi-Urdu, Kashmiri, Marathi, Punjabi, Romani, Sinhala, Tajik, etc. in the Indo-Iranian branch. Subfamilies are also recognized, such as the Germanic languages, represented by Dutch, English, and German in the above list. These share structural properties not shared by the other languages of the Indo-European family, in particular a series of consonant mutations known as "Grimm's Law," in which Proto-Indo-European voiceless stop consonants became fricatives in Germanic, such as the /p/ ~/f/ correspondence in padre (Spanish), pater (Latin) ~ father (English), vater (German).

The genetic groupings provided by the comparative method are the main source of information for most language classifications, such as those used in library cataloging (see the discussion of ISO 639-3, below). A major challenge for the comparative method is lexical borrowing, and most languages with any degree of contact with other languages at all in their history exhibit borrowing to some extent. Some historical linguists see borrowing or *diffusion* of linguistic features as an important mechanism in language change that leads to *areal* features, i.e., linguistic features that are shared among languages in a geographic region, where there may be no common linguistic ancestor.[27,28] Hence, classifications based on geographic distribution sometimes make more sense than genetic ones.

A similar problem for classification is raised by *Pidgin* and *Creole Languages*, which are mixed languages, having structural features of two or more languages, which arise in circumstances of intense and usually deeply unequal contact among speakers of different languages. Most of the creoles known today arose during the colonization of the Americas and other regions by European powers, and hence they tend to be mixed forms of European, African, and indigenous languages of the colonized areas. Pidgin languages are used only as second languages for contact between people who have no other common language, such as the Chinese Pidgin English once used in Hong Kong. Pidgins only tend to exist in the initial stages of contact, but when speakers of the contact community intermarry without having a common first language, a Creole may develop. Many of the Creole languages in existence today, from West Africa to the Caribbean, to Hawaii, and the Indian subcontinent, arose in this way during colonization. The specific challenge for historical linguistics is that the mixed character of Pidgin and Creole languages makes it difficult to assign ancestry as would normally be done in linguistic comparison. Also, it may be difficult to tell when a language has gone through a Pidgin and/or Creole stage in its past. For example, most Pygmy communities in Africa today speak one form of Bantu language or another, but it is unlikely that they originally spoke languages from this family before contact with other speakers of Bantu languages. Hence, some of the differences between the languages spoken by the Pygmy people and other Bantu languages might be attributed to a process of creolization, at some point in their past.

These things being said, "genetic" classifications, that is, classifications based on language ancestry, are the main type of classification of language discussed in linguistics. While areal features of languages (across language families) are sometimes recognized, they are generally treated as secondary to historical, ancestral relationships.

Sociolinguistics and Psycholinguistics

Sociolinguistics is the study of language in its social context, and two general areas are recognized within it: "macrosociolinguistics" and "microsociolinguistics." Macrosociolinguistics is typically concerned with national communities and their composition, and the individual and community-level attitudes and discourses that bear on language policies, whether implicit or explicit; and *language planning*, the employment of governmental or institutional resources to promote certain language uses (e.g., in education, commerce, or the media). Microsociolinguistics is more concerned with phenomena at the individual level, such as linguistic variation across speaking styles, circumstances of use, occupations, ethnicities, and other subnational groups. Within microsociolinguistics, there are two main areas of study: interactional sociolinguistics, which overlaps greatly with conversation analysis, but also includes intercultural communication (at the individual level), and language variation and change, or urban dialectology, which examines contemporary historical patterns in language change, typically on a generational time scale.

Psycholinguistics is the study of language in relation to cognition, the brain, and the mind. Its main areas are speech perception, sentence processing, language deficits, and language acquisition. Of these, the last is probably the dominant area of inquiry, and it is described in a separate subsection below. Speech perception primarily concerns auditory processing. Sentence processing tends to focus on the syntactic parsing and semantic interpretation of sentences by human subjects, to illuminate the cognitive mechanisms involved. Language deficits, such as aphasia (a loss of the ability to produce and/or comprehend language) and anomia (inability to access common words) are studied for similar reasons, as well as for what they reveal about the organization of language processing in the physical material of the brain itself. Written language processing is not studied much within the field of linguistics, for reasons that have to do with the field's emphasis on spoken communication, which is more of a human universal than written communication.

Language Acquisition and Applied Linguistics

While language acquisition has a central place in Generative Grammar and other linguistic theories, its study is specialized and typically requires training in psychology, especially developmental psychology. Two general areas are recognized: acquisition of a first language by children, or *first language acquisition*, and acquisition of a second language by bilinguals, whether adults or children, or *second language acquisition*. First language acquisition is generally studied by developmental psychologists and psycholinguists, and a large literature on this has been generated, both for English and for other languages. Second language acquisition tends to be studied by language educators and psycholinguists. It is a matter of much theoretical debate and empirical study to what extent these two processes can be compared.

Computational Linguistics and NLP

Computational linguistics and NLP, both of which are treated in other entries in this encyclopedia, are considered to be part of linguistics; at the same time, the training of linguists and computational linguists/NLP researchers may have relatively little overlap. Principally this is because, at least historically, computational linguistics is mostly practiced by people with engineering, rather than linguistic, training, and the research agendas are set from within an engineering perspective (e.g., the aim of the European *Verbmobil* project was to build a portable speech-to-speech translation system), rather than from within the goals of linguistic theory (e.g., explaining language acquisition, change, or evolution). More linguists are becoming involved in NLP projects through the development of *language resources*, i.e., dictionaries and text corpora for use in NLP tasks.

LINGUISTIC ISSUES IN THE INFORMATION SCIENCES

Linguistics is relevant to the Information Sciences in a number of ways. On a basic level, much of what we call "information" is encoded in human language of some form: textual documents, audio and video media with spoken language soundtracks, logs of computer-mediated communication, etc. Many of the levels of linguistic structure or interdisciplinary approaches to linguistic analysis could potentially illuminate what is informative about the material artifacts and processes studied in the Information Sciences. Moreover, the material processes by which information is handled, exchanged, archived, etc. share with human language their fundamental patterns of structural arbitrariness along with their embeddedness within a community of users. In this way, informational processes are fundamentally linguistic: whether human languages are involved or artificial languages, whether for encoding sounds, images, or arbitrary sensor data, or for manipulating computers or other automatic systems, all of these systems involve a representation with multiple levels of arbitrary structure, meaning there are potential levels of analysis which parallel those used in linguistics. The observed structures are governed by social conventions, much as the structures of language are.

To make these parallels more explicit, consider the oft-cited "layer cake" for Web technologies. From the lowest level upward, there are various physical media for internetworking (cables, microwave signals, etc.) upon which low-level protocols such as Transmission Control Protocol/ Internet Protocol (TCP/IP, used by most Internet applications) and Asynchronous Transfer Mode (ATM, used in high-speed networks for simultaneous use of voice, video, and data) are operated. On top of these, there are applications protocols such as Hypertext Transfer Protocol (HTTP, used by Web browsers and servers), which is used to transfer Web pages between server and client. The Web page itself is composed in either Hypertext Markup Language (HTML) or eXtensible Markup Language (XML), which is further extended via annotations in the Resource Description Framework (RDF, the metadata definition language for the Semantic Web), etc. Each of these layers represents a level of structure whose organization and interpretation are independent of those of neighboring levels. Hence Web-based communication is structured in the same way as natural language, with relatively independent levels whose operation is nonetheless important to the levels above and below for overall system functionality. Further like linguistic communications, the Web protocols are defined and elaborated by the community structures they are embedded within, much as languages are constituted and developed in the interactions of people in a speech community. Although these protocols may be defined through a formal standards process, yet again as in human language the participants in the process do not exercise equal power to influence the outcomes. The way that the protocols are ultimately used, or what protocols are adopted, is profoundly influenced by the economic and institutional power of large players such as Microsoft, just as language policy and planning outcomes are shaped by populous or economically powerful speaker groups.

A few of the ways in which the circumstances of information technology resemble those involving human language areas are discussed in more specific terms below, focusing on issues that bring language and information-related concerns particularly close together.

Semantics and the Web

The "Semantic Web" is a technology research and development project aimed at addressing information management issues with the current World Wide Web, in which the goals of search, data interoperability, and "intelligent" applications are foregrounded. Central to this project is the development of standard formats for the definition, interchange, and use of metadata, i.e., the data used to describe documents, resources, and other material by describing authors, subject, title date of publication, etc. The Semantic Web metadata formats are characterized as encoding "semantic" information about documents and resources on the Web. Unfortunately for this project, there is a three-way systematic ambiguity in the sense of "semantic" that is intended. The following senses of semantics can be distinguished:

1. *Information retrieval (IR)*. Semantics in IR is focused on the concept of *relevance*, which is generally defined as an aboutness relation that holds of a document and its content. This aboutness relation is generally represented by metadata and/or keywords, whether from a controlled vocabulary or extracted from full text. Document semantics associates a document with its content, with other documents with similar content, and with queries.
2. *Formal logic*. Semantics in formal logic is defined in terms of the *truth conditions* of an expression, i.e., the conditions that need to hold in the world for that expression to be true. Semantics in this sense concerns the propositional content of expressions, their composition from constituent parts of the expression, and the inferences that can be licensed from them logically.
3. *Linguistics*. Semantics in linguistics is concerned with the meanings of natural language most generally. In addition to aboutness, compositionality, and inference, linguistic semantics recognizes and studies the dependence of linguistic meaning on the external social context and the complex historical dialectic between literal meaning and pragmatic inference.

Different technologies developed for the Semantic Web primarily address the first two senses of semantics. The RDF metadata interchange language and its associated syntax RDF/XML most directly address document semantics in the IR sense. They achieve the function of associating documents or resources with metadata labels that are intended to reflect their relevance to queries and other documents. The metadata definition languages RDFS and OWL, as well as the processors defined for them, most directly address the logical sense of semantics, by defining the inferences that are licensed when particular metadata elements are present. As yet, no Semantic Web technology directly addresses the broader linguistic semantics of documents and/or metadata. The Web 2.0 system feature that comes closest to this is "folksonomy" tagging, which is the provision for allowing users to apply uncontrolled metadata items that are not formally differentiated. According to proponents, tagging allows users' own semantics to "emerge" from the contexts in which they apply tags, making formal controlled vocabularies unnecessary.

However, this latter perspective owes more to complex systems than linguistics, and it does not fully engage with the social processes involved in the informal standardization and norming in language. In the complex systems model of emergent behavior, individuals are more or less equivalent agents, and complex collective behaviors are a consequence of these simple actors conforming to simple rules. Linguists would typically recognize the actors' behavior as likely to be heterogeneous and anything but simple. Different people may have different meanings for the same terms, or different meanings for a term in different contexts. Complex self-referential deixis can be involved (e.g., the tag "to read" implicitly references the person who applies the tag), as can cultural, political, and other interpretive frames. People enter into the tagging activity with different levels of knowledge, expertise, power, etc., and consequently are not equivalent actors in the construction of a consensus semantics. Hence, the semantics of a large group of people tagging resources on, e.g., a social book-marking site such as del.icio.us is more likely to involve an averaging or bleaching of individual differences and a predominance of hegemonic meanings than the emergence of complexity envisioned in the "emergent semantics" perspective.

A linguistic perspective on the Semantic Web project would emphasize the social and usage-based aspects of metadata. In terms of the already existing technologies, we could ask to what extent particular RDF vocabularies are used according to their defined intent, or whether their application to particular resources and documents has altered their meaning in some way. For example, the Dublin Core metadata set is widely used in a range of applications, including the import/export of user profiles on social network/journal sites such as LiveJournal. In particular, the dc:title item is used to indicate text labels for a broad range of things, including personal interests, community names, etc., most of which were not envisioned in the original Dublin Core standard. It thus appears that the range of usage available for dc:title has been extended in a way much like the historical extension of word meanings. Note that this has consequences for logical semantics, since the extension affects the inferences one can make based on the content of dc:title. In terms of design recommendations, a linguistic perspective on document semantics would instruct us to anticipate that meanings may depend in complex ways on social and historical context, and to avoid attempting to codify semantics rigidly. A useful area to explore for technical development would be the design of mechanisms that permit meaning to be negotiated on the fly, much as humans are able to negotiate meaning, through comprehension checks and the application of pragmatic inference.

Language Categorization

Another area of linguistics that has special relevance for the Information Sciences is the area of language classification. As mentioned above, the primary classifications used by linguists are historical "genetic" classifications. These classifications do not necessarily reflect other important aspects of a language's ethno-historical background that might be relevant for other purposes, such as its writing system, literary heritage, or available technical vocabulary. A recent development in language classification is the 2006 adoption of a new standard under the auspices of the International Standards Organization

(ISO), ISO 639-3, managed under the registration authority of SIL International, a nongovernmental organization that performs consulting services on linguistic issues, and which is closely associated with various Christian missionary organizations. ISO 639-3 supplements the older ISO 639-1 standard, which provides 180 two-letter codes, and the ISO 639-2 standard, which provides approximately 400 three-letter codes. In contrast, ISO 639-3 has three-letter codes for 7863 known languages. The importance of ISO 639 comes from its targeted adoption in libraries and archives (where ISO 639-2 is now widely used) and Web technologies (where ISO 639-1 is more commonly used) as a means of identifying languages by using fixed codes, where names and other identifications can be ambiguous. The rationale for the revised ISO 639-3 standard is that neither earlier standard can adequately represent the complete range of human languages that might be used either in writing or in spoken media.

The codes in the new standard represent a superset of the earlier 639-2 codes. The largest change in the standard is the addition of more than 7000 languages, based on the entries of the Ethnologue,[29] a publication of SIL International cataloging the world's languages, their locations, linguistic characteristics, and speaker populations. While the Ethnologue is generally regarded as the most respected and complete authority of this type, its selection as the basis of ISO 639-3 is not neutral with regard to certain linguistic issues. Hence, adoption of ISO 639-3 in libraries or other contexts where languages need to be differentiated implies tacit acceptance of the Ethnologue's sometimes controversial language classifications.

At a most basic level, there appears to be little agreement among linguists on the number of living human languages. Estimates vary from a low of 2000 to a high of 8000 or more, and the Ethnologue is positioned toward the high end of this range. A related issue concerns the identification of distinct languages where speakers of those language varieties would not necessarily recognize them as distinct; in these contexts, Ethnologue classifications (and by extension ISO 639-3) tend to be language "splitters," based on a criterion of mutual intelligibility. One case that exemplifies this is that of Quiché (Mayan) in Guatemala, where the Enthologue, and by extension ISO 639-3, counts 69 distinct languages. Quiché speakers on the other hand tend to prefer recognition of a single Quiché language, fearing that recognizing multiple Quichéan languages would fragment their cultural and political identity. A similar situation holds for various Germanic varieties in Germany (e.g., Bavarian, Swabian), which most speakers would probably classify as dialects of German, for reasons of national identification, even though these are linguistically closer to Allemanic and Swiss varieties spoken nearby. Splitting language identities in these and other circumstances is politically charged, hence the maintenance of the ISO 639-3 technical standard is one with a complex political dimension.

In some notable cases, identification goes in the other direction (lumpers), such as in the case of Mandarin Chinese, whose reported 800 million native speakers is a statistical anomaly, being many times larger than the typical language population of 10,000–50,000 native speakers, and several times larger than the nearest large language. This number probably over-reports the native Mandarin-speaking population by insufficiently distinguishing related varieties of Chinese.

The fundamental problem that remains to be addressed in the maintenance of the standard is the potentially inconsistent application of criteria that establish a speech variety as a language, dialect, or other speech variety. In the past the process of modifying language codes in the Ethnologue has been treated as a largely editorial one, whose consequences mainly affected SIL International's book-keeping on its language development projects. Maintenance of ISO 639-3, however, is a formal standards process whose authority is established by international treaties among participating governments, and which is required to be open to submissions from a range of different interests. In the 2007 changes to ISO 639-3, 395 changes were approved, including 76 "retired" codes, 59 new language codes, and 176 updates (meaning name changes, etc.), representing a 5% change in the available codes. It is unclear whether the reasons for addition/retirement of ISO 639-3 codes represent the application of the same linguistic criteria in all cases.

Language in Information Policy

In recent years, language has emerged as an important area in information policy, for a number of reasons. One fairly salient reason is the continued management of the Domain Name System (DNS), under which numerical Internet Protocol addresses are associated with natural language mnemonic identifiers, by the Internet Corporation for Assigned Names and Numbers (ICANN), under contract from the U.S. Commerce Department. This system uses a 7-bit ASCII encoding for names of Internet hosts that natively supports only U.S. English names. Since native-language naming is a central touchstone for Internet governance, numerous governmental and non-governmental organizations pressured ICANN for a number of years to adopt some form of multilingual standard for domain names. This pressure culminated at the United Nations World Summit for the Information Society in Tunis, 2005, where ICANN agreed in principle to open Internet governance to participation by a wider range of organizations, and to consider expansion of the DNS. In 2006, the formal adoption by ICANN of Punycode, a 7-bit variable-width encoding of the Unicode character set, permitted domain name registrars in some domains to begin offering domain names in a broader range of languages, known as Internationalized Domain Names (IDNs). These policies were further expanded in 2008.

The basic function of the DNS is much the same as that of Semantic Web metadata: to disambiguate the reference of certain mnemonic expressions used in an electronic information system. These mnemonics are intended as a human convenience: they are not required for the Internet itself to function, and their only value is that they might mean something to people. Peculiarly, at least from the perspective of human languages, both DNS identifiers and Semantic Web metadata are required to be globally unique, something that is never the case in natural languages. While this requirement is obviously instituted for the convenience of computer processing, in reality, global uniqueness is a fiction that can only be maintained under the closed-world assumption that everything worth reasoning about can be enumerated and contained within one fixed system. This assumption of a Platonic ideal universe rapidly becomes difficult to implement when it is transferred to a shared information network with inputs from multiple sources in multiple social contexts. It also becomes politically oppressive when taken to its logical conclusion, forcing everyone and everything to access the reference of any Internet host or any ordinary expression through a centralized authority. While national governments and other groups often engage in formal efforts to standardize natural languages, such efforts typically have little impact on the native-speaking public. Ordinary language use, a fundamental human experience, and arguably a fundamental human right,[30] needs to be responsive to the changing context and experience of speakers' everyday circumstances. The failure of the DNS to naturally accommodate naming in languages other than English, and the requirement that the reference of names be globally fixed for the system to function, are thus failures of the system design to properly address its human interface goals.

What is at stake in both the DNS and the Semantic Web is actually the extension of property rights to language (the "commodification" of language), a much broader trend encompassing trademarks, copyrights, and other forms of "intellectual property." Requiring global uniqueness creates a property system wherein prospectors can claim potentially valuable territory, and develop it to extract rents or turn a profit, as in the case of certain two-letter domain names (actually ISO 3166-1 country codes), such as .tv (Tuvalu, used for "television"), .ad (Andorra, used for "advertising"), and .cd (Democratic Republic of the Congo, used for "compact disc"). While something like this property system has arguably existed for some time in the case of copyright, trademark, and other forms of intellectual property, the manifestation and interpretation of such intellectual property systems is not the same across cultures,[31] and such an extensive property system has never been created before for reference, a far more basic linguistic function than, e.g., literature or invention. A linguistic agenda for research and development in the DNS would examine the manner in which DNS entries are actually used, the purposes to which they are put, and the dynamic nature of referential meaning in the context of information technology use.

Computer-Mediated Communication

Another area of the study of information in which linguistic approaches have been actively adopted is computer-mediated communication (CMC). Currently, the primary use of the Internet remains human-to-human communication over computer media, most of which involve text. Consequently, most uses of CMC make heavy use of written language, and hence linguistic means of analyzing text and language are relevant to the study of CMC. However, studies of CMC have only slowly gathered acceptance within the field of linguistics, mainly because of the primary status accorded to spoken over written communication. Since many of the initial questions around CMC concerned differences between speaking and writing, or features of spoken language appearing in written CMC, linguists have tended to neglect or disregard linguistic studies of CMC as being less than central to the concerns of the field. At the same time, it is becoming clearer to many researchers that some forms of CMC, such as instant messaging and short-messaging (SMS) via cell phones, communication on Weblogs, and social networking sites, are developing into primary modes of interaction for some purposes. As this awareness develops, and as the full range of linguistic phenomena relevant to CMC become recognized, study of CMC is gradually gaining acceptance within linguistics.

Studies of CMC from a linguistic perspective have focused on a broad range of phenomena, of which four general categories might be recognized: register and genre effects, interactional dynamics, cognitive processing constraints, and language contact phenomena. The earliest CMC studies, e.g.,[32] generally address register and genre effects; these studies tend to consider CMC types such as e-mail, chat, and discussion boards and ask how they differ from writing and/or speech, noting in particular a divergence between informal written CMC modes such as e-mail or chat and that of standard written language. Later studies in this vein[33] have tended to interpret such observations from the perspective of genre theory, rather than as deterministic effects of the medium. Different CMC modes also tend to have different kinds of constraints, e.g., on message length, and may be favored by different communities of users. Consequently there are different structural adaptations that are found in different modes, such as chat (which is exchanged synchronously, when the users are logged in at the same time) and e-mail (which is exchanged asynchronously). Even superficially similar communication modes, such as chat within MUDs or MOOs (a kind of text-based multiplayer game environment) and Internet Relay Chat (a general real-time chat system) can show sharply different structural adaptations of language, because of the different communities of users that frequent those systems.[34]

Within the area of interactional dynamics, probably the first area to receive extensive study was that of gender,[35] although studies of flaming, trolling, and other antisocial behaviors followed. Other aspects of interactional dynamics, such as turn-taking in various CMC modes, the coherence of extended interactions, and social network effects on the distribution of languages or linguistic variants, have also been studied. Building on much of this work is a body of design and experimental work, in which various parameters of CMC are manipulated. In the experimental tradition, the effects of these manipulations are studied in controlled experiments to identify medium effects on task performance in different contexts.

Finally, a group of studies has attempted to address an issue unique to the international context of the Internet, namely the effects of language contact among speakers of different languages using CMC. This contact is perhaps less obvious to speakers of English than it is to speakers of almost any other language, who are typically confronted with English in most of their online activities. At times, speakers of other languages have responded to the perceived dominance of English, e.g., in the case of Brazilian members of the social networking service Orkut who visibly used their Portuguese language in public fora as a political statement, much to the consternation of some English-speaking members. Most studies in this area are individual case studies, often of small-scale settings.[36] There have been a few attempts to survey languages used on the Internet more generally,[37] but this has not been done yet in any comprehensive way.

CONCLUSION

Linguistics is a discipline that inhabits an interdisciplinary problem-space with many points of intersection, realized and unrealized, with the field of information studies. Its primary mode of investigation is structural analysis, although the modern practice of linguistics uses methods informed by many other disciplines. In addition, linguistics has broad applicability to information studies, where it can contribute insights that unite the contextual aspects of information use (e.g., cognitive, social, and cultural context) with concerns about the structural manifestations of information.

ACKNOWLEDGMENT

I am grateful for the assistance of Susan Herring, who read and commented on an earlier version of this entry.

REFERENCES

1. Watt, W.C. The Byblos matrix. J. Near East. Stud. **1987**, *46*(1), 1–14.
2. de Saussure, F. *Course in General Linguistics (Cours de Linguistique Générale)*; Philosophical Library: New York, 1959; (1916).
3. Bloomfield, L. *Language*; Holt: New York, 1933.
4. Sapir, E. *Language: An Introduction to the Study of Speech*; Harcourt Brace: New York, 1921.
5. Chomsky, N. *The Logical Structure of Linguistic Theory*; Plenum: New York, 1975; (1955).
6. Chomsky, N. *Lectures on Government and Binding*; Foris: Dordrecht, 1981.
7. Chomsky, N. *The Minimalist Program*; MIT Press: Cambridge, MA, 1995.
8. Prince, A.; Smolensky, P. *Optimality Theory: Constraint Interaction in Generative Grammar*; Blackwell: Oxford, 2004; Rutgers University and University of Colorado at Boulder, 1993 (technical report).
9. Ferguson, C. Diglossia. Word **1959**, *15*(2), 325–340.
10. Bresnan, J. *Lexical-Functional Syntax*; Blackwell: Oxford, 2000.
11. Perlmutter, D., Ed. *Studies in Relational Grammar 1*; University of Chicago Press: Chicago, IL, 1983.
12. Perlmutter, D.; Rosen, C., Eds. *Studies in Relational Grammar 2*; University of Chicago Press: Chicago, IL, 1984.
13. Pollard, C.; Sag, I. *Information-Based Syntax and Semantics, Volume 1: Fundamentals*; CSLI Publications: Stanford, CA, 1987.
14. Pollard, C.; Sag, I. *Head Driven Phrase Structure Grammar*; University of Chicago Press and CSLI Publications: Chicago, IL, 1994.
15. Langacker, R. *Foundations of Cognitive Grammar: Volume I: Theoretical Perquisites*; Stanford University Press: Stanford, CA, 1999.
16. Harris, R.A. *The Linguistics Wars*; Oxford University Press: Oxford, 1995.
17. Pierce, C.S. *Collected Papers. vol. 2, Elements of Logic*; Harvard University Press: Cambridge, MA, 1932.
18. Lakoff, G.; Johnson, M. *Metaphors We Live By*; University of Chicago Press: Chicago, IL, 1980.
19. Lakoff, G.; Nuñez, R. *Where Mathematics Comes from: How the Embodied Mind Brings Mathematics into Being*; Basic Books: New York, 2001.
20. Croft, W. *Radical Construction Grammar: Syntactic Theory in Typological Perspective*; Oxford University Press: Oxford, 2001.
21. Kay, P.; Fillmore, C.J. Grammatical constructions and linguistic generalizations: The what's X doing Y? Construct. Lang. **1999**, *75* (1), 1–33.
22. Givón, T. *Functionalism and Grammar*; John Benjamins: Philadelphia, PA, 1995.
23. Hopper, P.; Traugott, E. *Grammaticalization*; Cambridge University Press: Cambridge, 2003.
24. Montague, R. The proper treatment of quantification in ordinary English. In *Formal Philosophy: Selected Papers*; R. Thomason, R., Ed.; Yale University Press: New Haven, CT, 1974.

25. Austin, J.L. *How to Do Things with Words*; Oxford University Press: Oxford, 1963.
26. Grice, H.P. Logic and conversation. In *Syntax and Semantics, Volume 3: Speech Acts*; Cole, P.; Morgan, J.L., Eds.; Seminar Press: New York, 1975; 225–242.
27. Dixon, R.M.W. *The Rise and Fall of Languages*; Cambridge University Press: Cambridge, 1997.
28. Muhlhausler, P. *Linguistic Ecology: Language Change and Linguistics Imperialism in the Pacific Region*; Routledge: Oxford, 1996.
29. Gordon, R.G., Jr. *Ethnologue: Languages of the World, Fifteenth Edition*; SIL International: Dallas, TX, 2005.
30. Skutnabb-Kangas, T.; Phillipson, R., Eds. *Linguistic Human Rights: Overcoming Language Discrimination*; Mouton De Gruyter: Berlin, 1995.
31. Scollon, R.; Scollon, S.B.K. *Intercultural Communication: A Discourse Approach*; Blackwell: Oxford, 2001.
32. Ferrara, K.; Brunner, H.; Whittemore, G. Interactive written discourse as an emergent register. Writt. Commun. **1991**, *8* (1), 8–34.
33. Cherny, L. *Community and Conversation: Chat in a Virtual World*; CSLI Publications: Stanford, CA, 1999.
34. Herring, S. Computer-mediated discourse. In *Handbook of Discourse Analysis*; Tannen, D.; Schiffrin, D.; Hamilton, H., Eds.; Blackwell: Oxford, 2001; 612–634.
35. Herring, S. Interactional coherence in CMC. J. Comp. Mediat. Commun. **1999**, *4*, 4.
36. Danet, B.; Herring, S. *The Multilingual Internet: Language, Culture and Communication Online*; Oxford University Press: Oxford, 2007.
37. Paolillo, J.C.; Pimienta, D.; Prado, D. et al. *Measuring Linguistic Diversity on the Internet*; UNESCO: Paris, 2005.

Linked Data

Jeremy Myntti
J. Willard Marriott Library, Salt Lake City, Utah, U.S.A.

Abstract
In the evolving world of data on the World Wide Web, there are many standards that are used to provide better data with more context and meaning in the Semantic Web. Linked Data standards must be followed in order to fully utilize Semantic Web technologies by creating a web of data that can be interpreted by both human and machine. This entry provides an overview of what Linked Data means and the basic best practices for implementing Linked Data, as well as a quick survey of how Linked Data is being used in libraries.

INTRODUCTION

Simply put, Linked Data refers to publishing data on the web that links to other data on the web. In the traditional World Wide Web, documents were linked to other documents, but individual pieces of data were not linked to anything. Linked Data is the mechanism that is used to create links between individual pieces of data in order to provide richer information about things and concepts.

This entry will give an overview of how the Web environment is evolving to allow for the linkage of pieces of data rather than only documents, the basic principles that should be followed to create Linked Data, the benefits of implementing Linked Data, and the ways that Linked Data can be created. It will conclude with a brief overview of some Linked Data projects underway in libraries.

OVERVIEW OF LINKED DATA

Tim Berners-Lee first coined the phrase "Linked Data" in 2006 when talking about the design of the Semantic Web. According to Berners-Lee, "The Semantic Web isn't just about putting data on the web. It is about making links, so that a person or machine can explore the web of data. With Linked Data, when you have some of it, you can find other, related, data."[1] He has also been quoted from the Library of Congress in an overview of the BIBFRAME project as saying:[2]

> The realization [behind creation of the Internet] was, "It isn't the cables, it is the computers which are interesting." The Net was designed to allow the computers to be seen without having to see the cables. The [World Wide Web] increases the power we have as users again. The realization was "It isn't the computers, but the documents which are interesting." Now you could browse around a sea of documents without having to worry about which computer they were stored on. Now, people are making another mental move. There is realization now, "It's not the documents, it is the things they are about which are important."

While they are closely related, Linked Data and the Semantic Web are two separate ideas. To distinguish between the two ideas, it has been said that the "Semantic Web is defined as a 'web of data'; a web created for computers linking data that is structured in such a fashion that computers do most of the linking."[3] Linked Data is the set of standards and technologies that are used to build the relationships between individual pieces of data. Data linked in this fashion can be described as "structured, reusable, machine-actionable, and interrelated."[4]

PRINCIPLES OF LINKED DATA

For many years, data has been published on the web in a human-readable format. Linked Data builds upon this structure by publishing data on the web according to a set of standards that make the data both readable by humans and also formatted in a standardized way for a computer to interpret the meaning and context of the data. This makes it possible for both humans and computers to identify related data on other sites that can provide a wealth of information about a thing or an idea, as well as to disambiguate between data that may share the same name.

Tim Berners-Lee has said that there are four principles that must be followed in order to create Linked Data. These principles are as follows:[1]

- Use URIs (Uniform Resource Identifiers) as names for things.
- Use HTTP (Hypertext Transfer Protocol) URIs so that people can look up those names.
- "When someone looks up a URI, provide useful information, using the standards (RDF*, SPARQL)."
- "Include links to other URIs, so that they can discover more things."

Encyclopedia of Library and Information Sciences, Fourth Edition DOI: 10.1081/E-ELIS4-120049498

All four of these principles need to be followed in order to provide true Linked Data. A majority of information on the web currently follows some of these principles, but not all of them. These principles build upon the general architecture of the World Wide Web by taking web documents and marking them up using common standards in order to provide structured data that is open and reusable by others as well as linked to data housed on other websites.[5]

Use URIs as Names for Things

The first principle of Linked Data is to use a URI to identify individual "things." These URIs are different from URIs that are used to identify documents on the Web since they represent an individual piece of data rather than the location of a full document. Linked Data URIs can not only be used to identify real objects, such as a person, place, or thing, but they can also be used to identify a concept or an idea. Without a unique URI to identify something, it can be difficult for humans and nearly impossible for computers to always disambiguate ideas correctly.

A URI consists of a string of characters identifying a domain name and the unique file path of the item being described. A URI identifies a reference to a resource rather than providing a file name or location of a resource. The location of a resource is denoted by a URL, or Universal Resource Locator, which links to a specific document on the web.

HTTP URIs

Users must be able to look up the data represented by a URI through the HTTP. This protocol is the foundation for communication via the World Wide Web. Other forms of unique identifiers on the Web are to be avoided if they cannot be looked up via HTTP, such as a URN (Uniform Resource Name) or DOI (Digital Object Identifier). There are two main reasons why HTTP URIs are necessary for Linked Data. These are as follows:[5]

1. "They provide a simple way to create globally unique names in a decentralized fashion, as every owner of a domain name, or delegate of a domain name owner, may create new URI references."
2. "They serve not just as a name but also as a means of accessing information describing the identified entity."

Since HTTP URIs can be accessed by both humans and computers, a method of content negotiation is used for the web server to return either an HTML-coded document for a person to read or RDF (Resource Description Framework) data for the computer to interpret. According to the World Wide Web Consortium (W3C), HTTP content negotiation means that the web server is able to make a decision based upon the information available and the Web Client's preferences in order to deliver the type information needed by the user in order to make the data human or computer accessible.[6]

Use Linked Data Standards

The primary standard used to encode Linked Data is RDF in its various forms (e.g., RDF/XML, N3 Triples, Turtle, JSON-LD). These Linked Data sets are then queried through SPARQL (SPARQL Protocol and RDF Query Language). The building block of RDF is the triple, a set of three URIs or literal values denoting a property held by the resource being described. The three parts of a Linked Data or RDF triple can be defined as follows:

1. Subject—a URI identifying the resource to be described
2. Predicate—a URI from a specific domain or vocabulary creating a relationship between the subject and object
3. Object—a URI or literal value (e.g., string, number, date) describing the subject

There are two main types of triples that can be created with this structure: a literal triple or a linked triple. A literal triple will contain a data string, number, or date as the object describing the subject, such as describing the name of a person or the date of an event. A linked triple consists of three URI references relating the subject URI to the object URI through a predicate URI. The URIs for the subject and object can either be in the same domain or different domains. Links to different domains are used in a triple to link multiple websites, which then creates the web of data. A single triple describes one aspect of a resource and many triples linked together describe multiple aspects of a resource. For example, if the object being described is a book, there can be multiple triples linked to the resource describing its title, publishing information, extent, creators, etc.

The information that is provided when a URI is looked up needs to be further information and context in order to disambiguate between different concepts with the same name that can be interpreted by both human and computer. For instance, if the thing that is being represented by a URI is "Mercury," there needs to be other data retrievable from the URI in order to know whether the item is the chemical element, the planet, the automobile, or one of the many corporate bodies with that name.

When data is structured according to the RDF standard, it becomes possible to query that data using SPARQL. When SPARQL was first implemented by the W3C in 2008, it was "designed for use at the scale of the Web, and thus enables queries over distributed data sources, independent of format."[7] This would lead to providing richer results that would cost less since a single query could be used to search multiple data stores.

Link to Other URIs

The final principle of Linked Data is to link to URIs from different domains in order to connect the full web of data. Data is not considered true Linked Data until it has been linked to sites outside of the current domain or web server. These external links are generally used as the predicate and object of an RDF triple. Links like this can be one of three types:[5]

1. "Relationship Links point at related things in other data sources, for instance, other people, places or genes. For example, relationship links enable people to point to background information about the place they live, or to bibliographic data about the publications they have written."
2. "Identity Links point at URI aliases used by other data sources to identify the same real-world object or abstract concept. Identity links enable clients to retrieve further descriptions about an entity from other data sources. Identity links have an important social function as they enable different views of the world to be expressed on the Web of Data."
3. "Vocabulary Links point from data to the definitions of the vocabulary terms that are used to represent the data, as well as from these definitions to the definitions of related terms in other vocabularies. Vocabulary links make data self-descriptive and enable Linked Data applications to understand and integrate data across vocabularies."

BENEFITS OF LINKED DATA

There are many formats that can be used to publish data on the Web. Heath and Bizer say that some of the benefits of using Linked Data for publishing on the Web include the following:[5]

- "A unifying data model. Linked Data relies on RDF as a single, unifying data model. By providing for the globally unique identification of entities and by allowing different schemata to be used in parallel to represent data, the RDF data model has been especially designed for the use case of global data sharing. In contrast, the other methods for publishing data on the Web rely on a wide variety of different data models, and the resulting heterogeneity needs to be bridged in the integration process."
- "A standardized data access mechanism. Linked Data commits itself to a specific pattern of using the HTTP protocol. This agreement allows data sources to be accessed using generic data browsers and enables the complete data space to be crawled by search engines. In contrast, Web APIs are accessed using different proprietary interfaces."
- "Hyperlink-based data discovery. By using URIs as global identifiers for entities, Linked Data allows hyperlinks to be set between entities in different data sources. These data links connect all Linked Data into a single global data space and enable Linked Data applications to discover new data sources at run-time. In contrast, Web APIs as well as data dumps in proprietary formats remain isolated data islands."
- "Self-descriptive data. Linked Data eases the integration of data from different sources by relying on shared vocabularies, making the definitions of these vocabularies [retrievable] and by allowing terms from different vocabularies to be connected to each other by vocabulary links."

Other benefits as described by Lampert and Southwick are as follows:[8]

- "An opportunity to connect distributed sets of structured data about 'things'."
- "The more structured the data are, the more actions that can be performed on the data."
- "Open data relieves the frustration of accessing data that cannot be used due to formatting or restriction in silos [. . .] and it allows the data to not only be discovered on the open Web, it can be delivered for use, reuse, or [. . .] to help bridge applications and systems."
- Data are reusable and break out of their silos.

PUBLISHING LINKED DATA

In order for data providers to understand if they are providing true Linked Data, Tim Berners-Lee created a five star model that can be followed:

- 1 star—"Available on the web (whatever format) but with an open license, to be Open Data"
- 2 stars—"Available as machine-readable structured data (e.g. excel instead of image scan of a table"
- 3 stars—"As[2] plus non-proprietary format (e.g., CSV instead of excel)"
- 4 stars—"All the above plus, Use open standards from W3C (RDF and SPARQL) to identify things, so that people can point at your stuff"
- 5 stars—"All the above, plus: Link your data to other people's data to provide context"[1]

Another way that this five star data model for evaluating data can be understood is as follows:

- 1 star—Data structure
- 2 stars—Licensing
- 3 stars—Format
- 4 stars—Identifiers
- 5 stars—Data linking[9]

Many different methods have been discussed to create Linked Data. A simple process can be described in three steps:[10]

1. "Assign URIs to the entities described by the data set and provide for dereferencing these URIs over the HTTP protocol into RDF representations."
2. "Set RDF links to other data sources on the Web, so that clients can navigate the Web of Data as a whole by following RDF links."
3. "Provide metadata about published data, so that clients can assess the quality of published data and choose between different means of access."

Different checklists for publishing Linked Data have also been created. Some questions that must be answered in order to create Linked Data include the following:[5]

- "Does your data set links to other data sets?"
- "Do you provide provenance metadata?"
- "Do you provide licensing metadata?"
- "Do you use terms from widely deployed vocabularies?"
- "Are the URIs of proprietary vocabulary terms dereferenceable?"
- "Do you map proprietary vocabulary terms to other vocabularies?"
- "Do you provide data set-level metadata?"
- "Do you refer to additional access methods?"

If the answer to all of these questions is "yes," then the data has been created according to all of the Linked Data standards. If one or more of the answers is no, then things must be corrected in order to make the data truly linked.

Creating a Linked Data Application

In order to create a basic Linked Data application for use on a website, there are a few steps that must be completed. First, data sources that contain relevant data about the items to be described need to be identified in order to retrieve useful information to represent the items. Once this data is identified from other sources, it should be downloaded into a local Linked Data RDF store so that it can be used and consumed on a local level. The final step is to query and retrieve this information when needed from the local data store so that it can be displayed for the users of the website.

While that can be a relatively simple way to implement a Linked Data application, the data in the RDF store will need to be updated and refreshed periodically in order to maintain the completeness and accuracy of the data. This can be achieved by crawling the data from the external sources on a regular basis to find new or changed data or an "on-the-fly dereferencing pattern" can be used to dereference URIs at the same time that the Linked Data application requests the information. The latter method will provide the most up-to-date information, but it could also be a slower method since URIs from many different domains would need to be queried when the user requests the data.[5]

LIBRARY LINKED DATA

Some Linked Data initiatives that are underway in libraries worldwide as of this writing include the Library of Congress' Bibliographic Framework Initiative (BIBFRAME – http://bibframe.org/) and the Europeana Linked Open Data Project (http://pro.europeana.eu/linked-open-data). Both of these library-centric initiatives are working to take existing library data and transform it into a Linked Data model that will help library data to be more shareable and accessible on the open web.

The Library of Congress started the BIBFRAME project "to re-envision and, in the long run, implement a new bibliographic environment for libraries that makes 'the network' central and makes interconnectedness commonplace."[2] This model is being explored "to provide a pattern for modeling both future resources and bibliographic assets traditionally encoded in MARC 21."[2] This is said to be achieved by working toward two objectives: "1) enable far more integration of existing bibliographic resources and 2) create a roadmap for moving forward toward refinement, redevelopment or development of alternative approaches."[2]

In addition to the emergence of Linked Data, there is also the movement toward Linked Open Data in libraries, archives, and museums. While there can be restrictions on the use of Linked Data, Linked Open Data is data created with an open license that can be downloaded and repurposed, with or without attribution, depending on the licensing terms in use by the data creator.

The Europeana Linked Open Data Project has been a work in progress for several years, with the first datasets being released as Linked Open Data in February 2012. In a 2011 paper presented at the International Conference on Dublin Core and metadata applications, it was said that:[11]

> With data.europeana.eu we are making a first version of the Europeana metadata set available as Linked Open Data. It includes data from those providers who have opted for their data to be published in the public domain. Anyone can now obtain descriptive metadata about Europeana resources by downloading the dumps, dereferencing HTTP URIs, or executing SPARQL queries against a dataset that follows the Europeana Data Model (EDM). The tools and scripts we developed for this purpose are open source and can freely be re-used or extended by others.

CONCLUSION

Linked Data has the potential to break down data silos by creating methods and best practices for providing data from a host of different sources to users of websites using Linked Data. This will allow for sharing common metadata standards, reutilizing existing controlled vocabularies, and the integration of additional sources of data to a website's existing data source.

With more cultural heritage institutions starting to experiment with Linked Data, metadata in libraries, archives, and museums could vastly change in the future. The vast amount of data that libraries hold can be a great addition to the Linked Data environment, making it possible for other institutions and websites to reuse library data in many different ways.

REFERENCES

1. Berners-Lee, T. Linked Data—Design issues, 2006. Available at: http://www.w3.org/DesignIssues/LinkedData.html (accessed January 16, 2014).
2. Library of Congress. Bibliographic framework as a web of data: Linked Data model and supporting services, 2012. Available at: http://www.loc.gov/bibframe/pdf/marcld-report-11-21-2012.pdf (accessed January 16, 2014).
3. Youse, B.; Perkins, J. Linked open data landscape. J. Libr. Metadata **2013**, *13* (2-3), 197–211.
4. Singer, R. Linked library data now!. J. Electr. Resour. Libr. **2009**, *21* (2), 14–126.
5. Heath, T.; Bizer, C. Linked Data: Evolving the web into a global data space. Synthesis Lectures Semantic Web: Theory Technol. **2011**, *1* (1), 1–136. Morgan & Claypool. Available at: http://linkeddatabook.com/editions/1.0/ (accessed January 16, 2014).
6. Thereaux, O.Content negotiation: Why it is useful, and how to make it work, 2006. Available at: http://www.w3.org/blog/2006/02/content-negotiation/ (accessed January 16, 2014).
7. W3C opens data on the web with SPARQL, 2007. Available at: http://www.w3.org/2007/12/sparql-pressrelease (accessed January 16, 2014).
8. Lampert, C.; Southwick, S. Leading to linking: Introducing Linked Data to academic library digital collections. J. Libr. Metadata **2013**, *13* (2–3), 230–253.
9. Hyvönen, E. In *Publishing and Using Cultural Heritage Linked Data on the Semantic Web: Synthesis Lectures on Semantic Web: Theory and Technology*; Morgan & Claypool, San Rafael, CA, 2012.
10. Bizer, C.; Heath, T.; Berners-Lee, T. Available at: http://tomheath.com/papers/bizer-heath-berners-lee-ijswis-linked-data.pdf (accessed January 16, 2014).
11. Haslhofer, B.; Isaac, A. data.europeana.eu: The Europeana Linked Open Data pilot. *Proceedings of the International Conference on Dublin Core and Metadata Applications*, 2011. Available at: http://dcpapers.dublincore.org/pubs/article/viewFile/3625/1851 (accessed January 16, 2014).

BIBLIOGRAPHY

1. Berners-Lee, T. Giant global graph, 2007. Available at: http://dig.csail.mit.edu/breadcrumbs/node/215 (accessed January 16, 2014).
2. Berners-Lee, T.; Chen, Y.; Chilton, L.; Connolly, D.; Dhanaraj, R.; Hollenbach, J.; Lerer, A.; Sheets, D. Tabulator: Exploring and analyzing linked data on the Semantic Web, 2006. Available at: http://swui.semanticweb.org/swui06/papers/Berners-Lee/Berners-Lee.pdf (accessed January 16, 2014).
3. Berners-Lee, T.; Fischetti, M. In *Weaving the Web: The Past, Present and Future of the World Wide Web by its Inventor*; Texere: London, U.K., 2000.
4. Berners-Lee, T.; Hendler, J.; Lassila, O. The semantic web. Sci. Am. **2001**, *284* (5), 34–43.
5. Berners-Lee, T.; Hollenbach, J.; Lu, K.; Presbrey, J.; Prud'ommeaux, E.; Schraefel, M. Tabulator redux: Browsing and writing linked data, 2008. Available at: http://events.linkeddata.org/ldow2008/papers/11-berners-lee-hollenbach-tabulator-redux.pdf (accessed January 16, 2014).
6. Bizer, C.; Cyganiak, R.; Heath, T. How to publish linked data on the web, 2007. Available at: http://www4.wiwiss.fu-berlin.de/bizer/pub/LinkedDataTutorial/ (accessed January 16, 2014).
7. Cyganiak, R.; Jentzsch, A.The linking open data cloud diagram, Available at: http://lod-cloud.net/ (accessed January 16, 2014).
8. Thereaux, O. Content negotiation: Why it is useful, and how to make it work, 2006, Available at: http://www.w3.org/blog/2006/02/content-negotiation/ (accessed January 16, 2014).
9. W3C opens data on the web with SPARQL. 2007. Available at: http://www.w3.org/2007/12/sparql-pressrelease (accessed January 16, 2014).
10. LODLAM: Linked Open Data in Libraries, Archives, and Museums. Available at: http://lodlam.net/ (accessed August 28, 2017).
11. Europeana Labs. Europeana Linked Open Data. Available at: http://pro.europeana.eu/linked-open-data (accessed August 28, 2017).
12. Berners-Lee, L. et al. Uniform Resource Identifier (URI): Generic Syntax. Available at: http://tools.ietf.org/html/rfc3986 (accessed August 28, 2017).

Lithuania: Libraries and Librarianship

Elena Macevičiūtė
Faculty of Communication, Vilnius University, Vilnius, Lithuania, and Swedish School of Library and Information Science, University of Borås, Borås, Sweden

Abstract

The entry is devoted to the present situation (2001–2006) of libraries in Lithuania, a Baltic state that regained independence from the Soviet Union in 1990. The author describes general features of the historical and modern context that formed and influenced the Lithuanian library sector and presents the characteristic features, achievements, and problems of the public library network, academic and research libraries, and networks of school and special libraries. The institutions educating library and information specialists and conducting research and the professional organizations of librarians are introduced. The entry is a general introduction to modern Lithuanian libraries.

INTRODUCTION

The Republic of Lithuania has a complex political history ranging from a medieval Polish-Lithuanian State to a neglected, nineteenth century province of the Russian Empire. Its cultural history and heritage are equally complex. Its modern cultural and information institutions are the result of this history and of the mixed traditions inherited from different peoples and historical periods.

This entry provides a broad introduction to libraries in Lithuania since 1990 when the independence of the country was restored. These years were rich in events ranging from the Soviet Union blockade (lasted 74 days from April 20 to July 2, 1990, when Soviet Union stopped all provision of oil, fuel and raw materials demanding to revoke the Act of the Re-Establishment of the State of Lithuania from March 11, 1990) to unprecedented economic growth and a changing political and cultural scene.

One of the goals that unites different types of libraries is providing information services to various segments of Lithuanian society and ensuring wide national and international access to information and cultural materials for the sake of the progress and development of a democratic society. Another goal is preserving and making sense of the rich cultural heritage during a period of intensive change in modern Lithuanian society. The range of information and cultural institutions pursuing these goals is broad, but space limitations do not allow us to introduce them all. Therefore, we will confine our discussion to the library sector, leaving out other providers of information products and services.

Definitions

Lithuania—(Lithuanian: *Lietuva*), officially the *Republic of Lithuania* (Lithuanian: *Lietuvos Respublika*), is a northern European country situated along the south-eastern shore of the Baltic Sea, sharing borders with Latvia to the north, Belarus to the southeast, and Poland, and the Russian exclave of the Kaliningrad Oblast (county) to the southwest (see Fig. 1). It has a population of 3,575,439 (2007 estimate); 83.6% are ethnic Lithuanians, with minority groups that include Poles, Russians, and Belarusians.[1]

Library system. The totality of networks of various library types that perform a variety of functions in service of the same local or national community and are governed by unified legislative, economic, and organizational principles.

Library network. A group of libraries that perform the same social functions for a typical group of users, based on the same principles and supported by a professional guidance center.

Library sector. The whole library sector can be treated as a broad social system based on a common legislative foundation, consisting of several interwoven organizational networks pursuing specific but complementary goals and using educational, professional, technological, and research resources provided by other, closely associated, societal systems. The entry will treat all of these components at an introductory level providing a snapshot of the present situation.

HISTORICAL CONTEXT

Discussing East European nations in their historical context is complicated by the changing political, military, economic and ethnic composition of the region. The Lithuanian case is further complicated because ethnic Lithuania has two parts: Lithuania Minor (the left bank of the river Nemunas that was mainly under the control of German states) and Great Lithuania. This division is important for cultural history, because Lithuania Minor played a huge role in the development of Lithuanian

Encyclopedia of Library and Information Sciences, Fourth Edition DOI: 10.1081/E-ELIS4-120043556

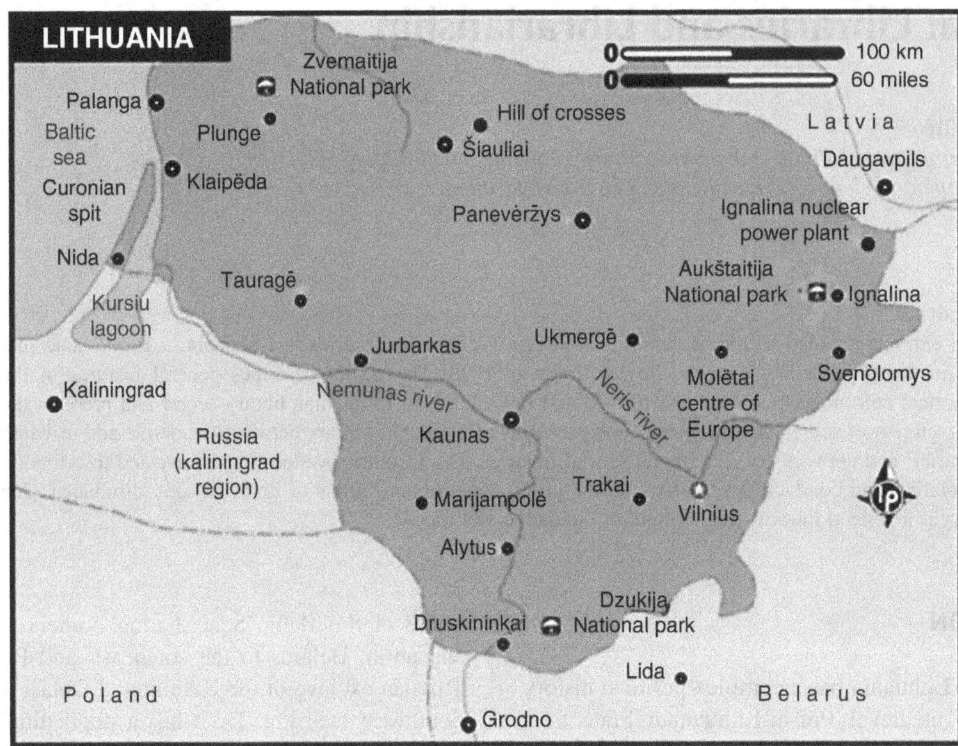

Fig. 1 Map of Lithuania.

culture, literacy, book publishing, and education. Lithuanian history may be divided into the following three periods:

- *Fourteenth to eighteenth century*—formation of the state, its expansion, and decline.
- *End of eighteenth to start of twentieth century*—partition of the state and survival under Tsarist Russia, rise of a national movement.
- *Twentieth to twenty-first century* (since 1918)—first independence period; Soviet period; second independence period.

Each of these periods can also be characterized by specific cultural features and developments in the media, book and library history.

The first period (fourteenth to eighteenth century) is characterized by the formation of the Lithuanian superstate, the late adoption of Christianity at the end of the fourteenth century, the Union with Poland and military conflict in the West (with the Teutonic Order), East (with Russia), North (with Sweden), and South (with Turkey). The militarization of the state and the geopolitical situation inhibited cultural development. However, the first libraries (mainly in monasteries) were established during this period, the first private book collections were built by Lithuanian aristocracy and rulers and the first printing houses were established. Lithuanian script was created and the first Lithuanian book was published in 1547 in Lithuania Minor; subsequently, publishing in the Lithuanian language expanded. The first library for a Lithuanian college at Prague University was created in 1397. Vilnius University Library began in 1579 as a Library of the Jesuit Academy.[2] The eighteenth century saw the development of the libraries of educational institutions and churches and the rise of the first ideas of public access to libraries.

During the second period (eighteenth to twentieth century) the Polish-Lithuanian state, including the Grand Duchy of Lithuania, ceased to exist and was divided among Tsarist Russia, Prussia and the Austro-Hungarian empire (last division in 1795). The largest part of ethnic Lithuania belonged to Tsarist Russia, and Lithuania Minor—to Prussia. Lithuanian libraries suffered great losses together along with the rest of Lithuanian culture. However, there were also developments significant for libraries. Vilnius University played a significant role in the education of Lithuanian authors and scholars writing in different languages, but also in Lithuanian. The first scholarly works related to library work and bibliography were created by a number of scholars of Vilnius University (Groddeck, Lelewel, Bohatkiewicz). The first course in bibliography was taught at Vilnius University in 1828–1831 by Bohatkiewicz. In 1831, after a insurrection against Tsarist rule, Vilnius University was closed, so its library ceased to exist as a university library.

From 1864 to 1904, Lithuanian script was banned, affecting the development of literature, education, publishing, book trade, and other spheres of life. During this period, the role of Lithuania Minor increased, because it served as a source of literature in the Lithuanian language for Great Lithuania. Literature produced there and in other regions was smuggled in and gave rise to a cultural phenomena known as "book carrying." The first communal library was established in Šiauliai (1850–1864); Vilnius Public Library was opened in 1867. Once the ban was lifted, the first legal Lithuanian libraries began to appear in parishes, educational institutions, and societies. Vrublevskis Public Library was opened in 1912 (later included in the Library of the Academy of Science), and the first bibliographies of Lithuanian publications appeared.

The Baltic states emerged from the political turmoil caused by the First World War. The first independence period (1918–1944) was most important for the development of libraries. The National Library of Lithuania (NLL) was founded in 1919 in Kaunas, then the provisional capital of Lithuania, as the Central State Library of Lithuania. The Bibliographic Institute was established at Kaunas University Library and started publishing the national bibliography (1928–1944). The system of public libraries was created, the first courses for librarians were organized and the Lithuanian Librarians' Association was established in 1931. The Law on State Public Libraries was adopted in 1936.

Soviet rule, from 1940 and after World War II, distorted the role of libraries and diverted their natural development to a different direction. Collections were destroyed and their renewal controlled, the functions of libraries changed and the Lithuanian Librarians' Association, which has been closed by the Germans, was not recreated until 1989. The libraries mainly served as ideological institutions; however, the actual needs of life demanded certain services. The Soviet period saw the expansion of mass libraries and the creation of the State System of Information Support for industry and other branches of the economy. The Book Chamber, established in 1945, took over compiling the current state bibliography and started work on a retrospective national bibliography. The State Republican Library performed the role of the main support center for all libraries and functioned as a national library. In 1949, it started the journal *Bibliotekų darbas* (Library Work) (changed title to *Tarp knygų—In the World of Books*—in 1991). In 1949, Vilnius University admitted the first students to the program of library science and bibliography. Despite being under tight ideological control, Lithuanian librarians managed to accomplish significant work in preserving the cultural heritage. Gudauskas[3] has provided a more detailed picture of the history of Lithuanian libraries.

Modern Context

The second independence era, which began in 1990, is as controversial from the point of view of library development as the Soviet period. Rather than having an ideological press, market forces, the problems of a young developing state, and the advent of new information and communication technologies influenced the library system. The factors that have had the greatest impact on library development include

- *A changing market for books and information products:* almost 500 publishers produce more than 4200 titles a year (p. 4–5);[4] information production is more diverse with regard to media and form; local digital information products compete with those produced internationally.
- *A saturated and more competitive mass media and entertainment market.*
- In 2005 *computer penetration* was 31.10% and the *Internet penetration* was 15.45%,[5] but in 2007 it was already 35.9 % (usage growth in 2000–2007, 443.0%).[6]
- *The educational level of Lithuanian population:* 16.1% of the population had higher education; in 2006, more than 199,000 students studied at Lithuanian universities and colleges and more than 514,000 in secondary schools.[7]
- *The policy of successive Lithuanian governments in education, culture, health, and research areas:* expenditure on education per student/pupil is one of the lowest in Europe (pp. 97–98);[8] the same can be said about health and culture.

Since 1992, there has been strong interest in creating an Information Society. The Information Society Development Committee under the Government of Lithuania was established in 2002. It takes care of the development and implementation of information technology and communications and is also concerned with ensuring equal access to the information infrastructure by various social groups, seeking to prevent excluding anyone from participation in information society and providing access by developing the required competence. The Committee also expands the services of e-government and ensures the progress of e-democracy.[9]

THE LIBRARY SYSTEM OF LITHUANIA

Legal Foundations

The legal foundations for access to information and the institutions providing information and ensuring its preservation in various forms are set out in the Constitution of the Republic of Lithuania. Article 25 of the Constitution guarantees that "Human beings must not be hindered from seeking, receiving and imparting information and ideas"; article 42 obliges the State to "support culture and science, and [. . .] take care of the protection of Lithuanian historical, artistic and cultural monuments and other culturally valuable objects."[10] The right to receive information and express oneself is mainly ensured by the *Law on provision of information to the public*[11] that deals mainly with mass media activity. Other public and private institutions are important in guaranteeing these rights and their implementation.

Since 1990 a number of laws have been passed to regulate state and private institutions concerned with the preservation of the cultural heritage and creating or delivering information products and services. Several of these laws deal with library and information service: *the Law on libraries, the Law on documents and archives, the* Law on museums, and the Law on provision of information *to the public*. Another category of laws regulates certain aspects of information activity and has a direct impact on libraries and other information mediators: *the Law on copyright and related rights, the Law on legal protection of personal data, and the Law on the right to get information from the state and municipal institutions and others.*

The rapid development and diffusion of information and communication technologies has stimulated the creation of laws regulating new relations and activities, e.g., *the Law on information society services, the Law on electronic communications, the Law on electronic signature.* These laws apply to libraries as providers of Internet services, creators of digital information and mediators of access to the products created by commercial and public providers.

The *Law on libraries* was adopted in 1995 and revised June 15, 2004. It establishes the system of Lithuanian libraries, relations between libraries, rules of establishment, financing and administration of libraries, building library collections and their structure and principles of service. According to the law, printed matter and any other documents must be accessible to everyone free of charge regardless of their authorship or their political and ideological orientation. A library ensures this accessibility as an institution of culture, education and information.[12] Other laws and legal acts support this role of libraries. For example, the *Law on copyright and related rights* ensures their right to lend copyrighted works (in the case of educational and scientific libraries without remuneration) and to reproduce them for preservation purposes and for the personal needs of their users. The law also defines usage and reproduction of digital (electronic) documents through libraries. To some extent it also regulates the ownership and usage of the databases created by libraries, e.g., electronic catalogs.[13]

Types of Libraries and Their Management

Libraries in Lithuania can be classified according to two main criteria:

1. Foundation and ownership
   a. State libraries (founded by state institutions, local authorities, etc.). Their collections constitute state property and a joint library collection of Lithuania based on the general information system and standards.
   b. Nongovernmental libraries (founded by private companies, political, professional, religious or other nongovernmental organizations or individuals).
2. Functions and community served
   a. General libraries that serve the information needs of the readers of all professions, diverse levels of education, different ages and social or cultural background living within the boundaries of a certain territory. The following libraries belong to the group of general libraries:
      (i) The National Library (the main public research library)
      (ii) County public libraries
      (iii) Municipal public libraries
   b. Special libraries that satisfy the special needs of a certain served community by building specialized collections answering these needs (education, research, manufacturing, etc.)
      (i) Special governmental libraries (serving a specialized sector, e.g., medicine, agriculture, etc.)
      (ii) Libraries of research institutions
      (iii) Academic libraries of higher educational institutions
      (iv) School libraries
      (v) Libraries of other institutions and organizations (hospital, prison, corporate, etc.)[12]

Five libraries with exceptionally valuable collections have the status of "libraries of national significance." They serve as consultation centers for their networks. There is a special line in the budget of the national government to finance the National Library and the libraries of national significance (except Vilnius University Library). These libraries are also officially designated to receive legal deposit copies of documents. According to this decision

> "creators of the public information in 2 days after publication of the print-runs of at least 100 copies of non-secret documents (books, periodicals, microforms, audio and visual, cartographic, video, electronic, and printed in the script for blind) deliver legal deposit copies free of charge"[14]
>
> to

1. National Martynas Mažvydas Library of Lithuania (2 copies)
2. Vilnius University Library (1 copy)
3. The Library of the Academy of Science of Lithuania (1 copy)
4. Lithuanian Library for the Blind (1 copy of all documents for the blind including large print and audio documents)
5. Technical Library of Lithuania (1 copy of standards, technical documentation and patent documents)[13]

Kaunas County Public Library as a second national archive also receives a legal deposit of the same type of materials that are sent to the National Library. Together with other specialized libraries (like the Lithuanian Medical Library and Lithuanian Agricultural Library) they coordinate acquisition and overall Lithuanian library collection-building in specific subjects and document types.

The Ministry of Culture of the Republic of Lithuania is authorized to regulate state administration of all libraries in Lithuania. The Library Council (currently consisting of 11 members delegated by the community of librarians and the Minister of Culture) is an advisory body, which helps to formulate the strategy of library development and library policy, define the principles of library financing, and establish the need for library education and research. The Ministry of Culture manages the NLL and the Library for the Blind and, through the state funding, directly influences the network of public libraries. Other networks of libraries are managed by other governmental departments. Among them is the Ministry of Education and Science, which is responsible for the largest network of school libraries and also takes care of academic libraries.

Martynas Mažvydas National Library of Lithuania

Since May 30, 1989, Martynas Mažvydas National Library of Lithuania has been the principal public and research library of Lithuania, according to the *Law on Libraries*. It performs all the functions of a national library:

- Serves as a national archive of all publications and ensures preservation of Lithuanian printed heritage and Lituanica (publications related to Lithuania and Lithuanians published abroad).
- Is the center of the national bibliography and publishing statistics and the center of coordination of consultation and research on library methods.
- Serves as an information center for social sciences and humanities, the center of allocation of ISBN, ISMN, and ISSN, and the center for the Lithuanian Integrated Library Information System (LIBIS).
- Serves as a Parliamentary Library (since 1991).

The NLL participates in international library activity and belongs to 11 international library associations. It has been a member of International Federation of Library Associations (IFLA) since 1992. It offers a variety of services for different groups of readers: provides the Lithuanian population with access to all its collections and seeks to widen this access through digitization; informs the public about the items in the collections through its Online Public Access Catalog (OPAC) ensures access to Lithuanian and foreign databases; promotes reading, Lithuanian culture and publications. The NLL also serves other Lithuanian libraries: collects library statistics and information about libraries in Lithuania, disseminates this information, participates and supports the union catalog of lithuanian libraries, creates standards for library and information work, publishes library literature and organizes courses of professional development. The performance of these tasks is ensured by 537 employees, including 389 professional librarians.[15]

According to its annual report, in 2006 NLL had a collection of 6,912,266 physical items, 15,845 registered users, 151,116 visitors and circulated 2.2 million documents.[15] A detailed article on Martynas Mažvydas National Library of Lithuania was published in ELIS in 2003.[16] Some of the main functions and new projects (e.g., digitization initiatives, participation in the European Library and TEL-ME-MOR project) of this library are especially important for information policy, publishing activity, development of information services in general as well as for the other libraries in the Republic. A short overview of these functions is presented here.

Production of national bibliography and current information on publications. The NLL has performed the functions of the national bibliographic agency since 1992 when the former Book Chamber of Lithuania was reorganized into a Bibliography and Book Science Centre of the NLL. This Centre is responsible for the accumulation and preservation of the national archive of publications that appear in Lithuania: books, periodicals, printed music, cartography, audiovisual documents (since 1997), and electronic resources. This work is carried out on the basis of legal deposit. The Centre catalogs the legal deposit copies, produces current bibliographies of the documents and their component parts (*Bibliografijos žinios*—The Bibliographical News, *Knygos*—Books, *Straipsniai*—Articles, *Serialiniai leidiniai*—Serials, *Garso dokumentai*—Sound Recording Documents, *Lietuvos bibliografinės priemonės*—Lithuanian Bibliographical Tools), and compiles the database of authority records. Bibliographical records are prepared and accumulated at the National Bibliographic Data Bank, which is available on the Internet (see http://www.libis.lt:8082/). The legal deposit acquisitions also serve as a basis for *Lietuvos spaudos statistika* (Lithuanian Publishing Statistics). The Centre informs the public of new publications in a weekly bulletin and compiles an e-bulletin of forthcoming books. This task is accomplished as part of the activity of Cataloging in Publication (preparation of a cataloging record for forthcoming publications).

The Centre includes the Department of the Retrospective Bibliography of the National Press, which works on the bibliographies of Lithuanian publications from 1547 to 1940 irrespective of the publishing place and on publications in Lithuania irrespective of language. In relation to this work, the Department carries out extensive book research and coordinates its activities with other research libraries in Lithuania. The Retrospective Bibliography consists of several series and databases devoted to Lithuanian books, serials, articles in Lithuanian periodicals, books in other languages published in Lithuania and small press publications.

LIBIS. The NLL started library automation work in 1985 when a special department was established to create and implement computerized library systems. In 1995 the Ministry of Culture and the government began work on the Integrated Library Information System (it was actually launched in 1996), and in 1998, the LIBIS Centre was established to ensure the implementation and development of the system in Lithuanian libraries. The system is based on original LIBIS software, which was designed by Lithuanian company *Sintagma*, and is used to create the National bibliography database and the Union Catalogue of Lithuanian Libraries — which in turn helps to integrate access to the libraries in Lithuania. The system is fully developed with all the functional modules. It is continually upgraded and the Centre helps the libraries maintain and upgrade the system regularly.

At the beginning of 2007, the LIBIS system was used by

- National Lithuanian Library
- Five out of five county libraries
- Sixty out of sixty municipal public libraries
- One university department for educational purposes
- Seven research and special libraries
- Ten museum libraries[17]

The standards developed by the NLL ensure the interoperability of LIBIS and other computerized library systems used by Lithuanian libraries. Since 2002, the users of the libraries operating LIBIS have been issued a unified user's card that allows the user access to library services provided by all LIBIS libraries.

Library statistics. According to the change in the *Law on Libraries* from 2004 (article 8.5.14), the National Library has the function of collecting and analyzing Lithuanian library statistics, a function previously the responsibility of the Ministry of Culture. All libraries have to provide an annual statistical report of their activity for the NLL. The Library Science Centre is directly responsible for this task and uses it for monitoring the library situation, planning the assistance to public and other libraries and disseminating it to policy and decision makers as well as to the libraries. Since 2004, this material has been available electronically through the Web site of the NLL.[15] In 2006, the paper forms of the statistical reports were changed to electronic ones and are available to the libraries through the NLL LIBIS Library Statistics module.[18] On the basis of this data, the NLL publishes statistical reports and reference material about Lithuanian libraries.

Public libraries today

In 2006, the public library network consisted of five county public libraries (governed by the regional administrations) and 60 municipal public libraries with 1312 branches in the towns and villages all over Lithuania (governed by local authorities). Although it is the second largest library network in the country, it reaches the widest public. The achievements and the drawbacks of the development of Lithuanian libraries can best be demonstrated by the present situation of public library system. The following Table 1 shows the number of public libraries and the total number of libraries in recent years.

Table 1 Number of libraries in Lithuania in 2001–2006.

Year	Number of libraries	Public libraries among them
2001	3677	1497
2002	3571	1405
2003	3406	1393
2004	3133	1377
2005	3020	1371
2006	2975	1372

Source: Compiled from the library statistic sources produced by the Ministry of Culture and the NLL.

The number of public libraries in the country is gradually diminishing due to the closure of small branches, integration of school and public libraries and reorganization of library networks. There are 4 public libraries per 10,000 people at present. This density is similar to that of other Baltic states and higher than in other European countries [e.g., 2.5 libraries per 10,000 people in Finland in 2006 (Calculated from Finnish Public Library Statistics at http://tilastot.kirjastot.fi/Default.aspx?pageId¼Statistics/Default&StatisticsTypeId¼1&ScopeTypeId¼101&Years¼2006&ScopeItemIds¼1.)]. However, it seems that the number of public libraries stabilized in 2004–2006. This might be a result of the implementation of the program of modernization of libraries.

In 2002, the government of Lithuania adopted a program of modernization of Lithuanian Libraries for 2003–2013.[19] In 1999, Lithuanian librarians had begun preparing a long-term program for the development of libraries with the intention of changing the attitude towards libraries that had prevailed for a decade while maintaining the existing level of support for libraries (p. 9).[20] The program was developed after carrying out a detailed analysis of library work in the Republic, which proved that the situation of Lithuanian libraries (especially public libraries) was much worse than in the average European country, even in neighboring countries, such as Latvia and Estonia. The library collection was out of date, the services poor, the funding inadequate and the possibilities to develop inhibited by inadequate premises and lack of technology. Despite the adequate number of qualified staff, the libraries could not serve the changing needs of the population. The program of modernization mainly obliges the central and local governments to create adequate conditions for library work and to ensure that the necessary material and economic basis for their activity exists. Its purpose is to develop and renew the Lithuanian

National Library, county and municipal public libraries, and the Lithuanian Library for the Blind, i.e., a group of general libraries in the cultural sector. The following goals are to be achieved in 10 years:

- To ensure Lithuanian inhabitants the possibility of acquiring the knowledge and qualifications that would enable them to adapt to the rapidly changing conditions of life and work and to compete successfully in world markets.
- To eliminate the inequalities within information infrastructures in the cities and provinces and provide equal conditions of information technology usage to all the inhabitants for any social and public needs.
- To create in the libraries the necessary conditions for collecting, preserving and disseminating to the public the objects of national, cultural and scientific heritage and to ensure access to the library collections.

The priorities that needed greatest attention were the renovation of the library collections and acquisition of databases, a vast program for building and renovation of library buildings and intensive computerization of libraries.[19] Another element of this vision was the development of professional competence in libraries.[21] The program not only established goals and priorities, it also included the analysis and calculation of the required investments over 10 years and annually. The program is financed by state and local authorities as well as through different specialized programs and foundations, but it places responsibility on the librarians and library management for reaching these goals.

In addition to this overarching library development program, the following long-term projects were and still are directed towards public libraries: development of LIBIS, "Computerization of Libraries," and "Development of Public Internet Access Points network" (funded through European structural funds and PHARE—EU assistance instrument abbreviation for original name *Poland and Hungary: Assistance for Restructuring their Economies*—especially in rural areas).

Since 2002 when the Program began, there have been gradual improvements in public libraries due to restructuring of the state capital investment with emphasis on the cultural sphere. The most visible changes are related to library buildings and computerization. Eight libraries, among them County public libraries in Klaipėda and Panevėžys (Fig. 2), municipal public libraries in Utena, Šakiai, Radviliškis, Varėna, Šilutė, and others have been built anew or renovated. Many more are undergoing reconstruction. This is a promising start, and some checks are built into the cultural policy that should prevent the cutting of financing, although librarians still fear that new priorities could reverse the present trend.

The progress in computerization of libraries can be expressed in the following figures: in 2004, computers and the access to the Internet were available in one-third (327) of public libraries. As a result of several programs and projects, by 2006, already half of the public libraries (650) offered access to computers and, out of these, 535 were connected to the Internet.[15] Since the beginning of 2006, according to the policy of the Ministry of Culture, access to the Internet in public libraries is to be free of charge. Before that, most of the libraries provided the use of the Internet free of charge for a certain limited time and charged a fee for additional time. Now libraries provide public access not only to the Internet, but also to an increasing number of databases: two national and 11 international in 2006 (the full list can be found on http://www.bibliotekos.lt).[22] Most of the public libraries have created Web sites that provide information about the their services and have also started providing some services online (mainly access to OPACs and "Ask the librarian" service).

However, the situation is not without problems. In many libraries, especially those in cities, hardware and software are old. Eighty-one percent of librarians think that their computer literacy skills are too low, and 68%

Fig. 2 Panevėžys County G. Petkevičaitė-Bitė Public Library: Catalogue terrace. Picture by Virginijus Benašas.
Source: Courtesy of the journal *In the World of Books*.

say their skills are nonexistent. Therefore, they are not able to help or instruct readers. These problems still require serious attention and that will be addressed not only through the ongoing projects but also through a new project prepared by the Ministry of Culture, the National Library, and the Bill and Melinda Gates Foundation "Libraries for Innovation."[23]

The changes in the areas of library collection and readers are more problematic, because their assessment is more controversial. The acquisition of materials is financed partly by the Ministry of Culture (according to the number of inhabitants in the served territory) and partly by municipality ([12], article 6). Although financing is increasing slightly, it is still significantly lower than in neighboring countries and inadequate from any point of view. The allocated resources can buy only one quarter of the new books per 1000 users recommended by IFLA. The budget is secured by law, but its reduction by the authorities on various levels is still a threat.[24]

The increasing funding cannot stop the decrease of the library collection. The discarding of old publications is greater than acquisition of new ones. The decrease in itself is not a great danger since the collections of public libraries inherited from the Soviet period were too large and did not satisfy the new information needs of their communities. However, the inadequate funding, the increasing prices of publications, demand for the new electronic resources and the need to assess and balance the hybrid collections inhibits efforts to raise the quality of the collections (p. 3).[25] More than 80% of collections in peripheral libraries consist of publications older than 10 years.[24] The decreasing and poor collections of the libraries do not provide a great incentive for users, and the number of users is decreasing slowly but surely. However, the number of visitors to all libraries is growing, and the number of visitors to the public libraries is fairly stable (Fig. 3).

This could be the result of the new services and the role of the library as a cultural and public center of the community. On the other hand, the number of users may be diminishing because of the introduction of fees for the unified library card. The introduction of a variety of fees in the libraries is indicated as a reason for the decrease of public library usage in the discussions of the issues (p. 5);[24] (pp. 17–18).[26] Fifty-one percent of the population use libraries. Non-users participating in one of the surveys mentioned that they do not use libraries because of poor collections (23%) and the lack of required information (7%).[27]

A third place is an easily accessible, inexpensive, pleasant place where one feels welcomed and comfortable, meets friends and relaxes. A 2005 study of a library as a third place, conducted among users and non-users in different towns and villages, revealed that libraries are usually compared to a school or university and hospital or clinics. Thus, libraries are treated as places visited because of necessity and obligation. They are not perceived as relaxing spaces for leisure. On the other hand, some of the respondents compared a library to a church or a cathedral, thus, identifying them as spiritual and sacred spaces.[28]

Public libraries are closely involved in the life of the communities. This involvement sets the general attitude towards libraries in the country and ensures that the next generation of users comes to the library. At present, public libraries still face a gigantic task: in Lithuania 35% of inhabitants between 16 and 74 years of age have not read a book, and 2.5% indicate that they do not read newspapers. (This answer may indicate the discontent of serious readers with the contents of Lithuanian newspapers E.M.)[27]

The results of the recent study of public libraries in Lithuania have confirmed that the greatest achievement of the independence period is implementation of a new conception of libraries that equals the best international models of the public library. Future development will be defined by the clear cultural policy and modernization

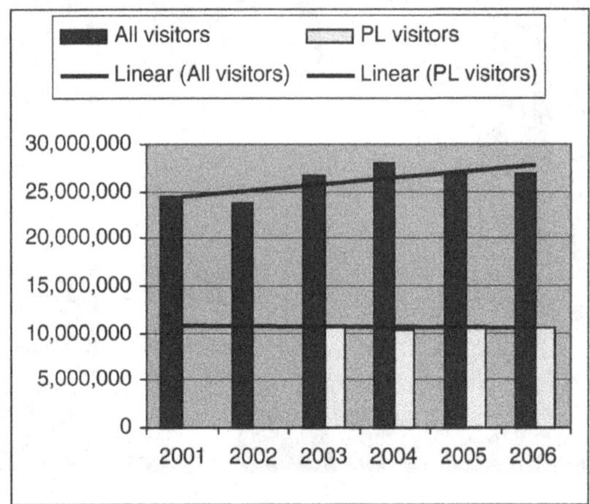

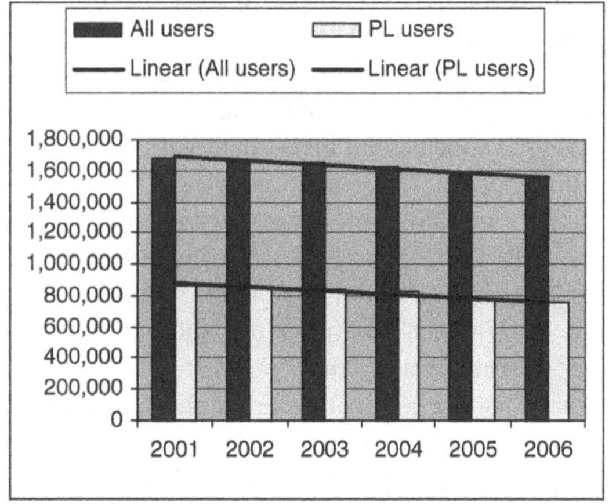

Fig. 3 The numbers of visitors and users to all libraries and public libraries in 2001–2006.
Sources: Statistikos departamentas[7] and *Lietuvos nacionalinė biblioteka*,[15]

strategies of central and local governments. The professional community will influence the governmental decisions, but its greatest role is seen in the development of modern information services, increase of professional competence and cooperation between all types of libraries on international and national levels (pp. 15–16).[20]

School libraries

In 2006, the largest network of libraries (1593) belonged to the Ministry of Education and Science. The category of school libraries includes 1339 primary and secondary school libraries and 76 libraries of professional schools, 41 libraries of higher education institutions (governmental and private), and 137 libraries of other educational institutions.[15] This network has lost 111 libraries since 2005, mainly due to the continuing reorganization of schools. There are also 150 public library branches that are integrated with school libraries.[15]

Service levels and conditions of school libraries throughout Lithuania are very unequal. Some meet the highest standards of library work (e.g., Šiauliai Julius Janonis Gymnasium Library, Library of "Verdenė" school in Panevėžys, Šventupis secondary school library in Šiauliai, A. Brazauskas secondary school in Kaišiadorys, etc.), while others just manage to struggle with basic access to educational literature. This depends on the policy of local authorities and school management and the support they provide. The problems these libraries face are the same as those of other types of libraries: shortage of financing for acquisition, difficulties with provision of access to a range of materials, computers, and electronic resources, unsuitable premises and equipment.

Previously, school libraries that had creative staff could take advantage of the competitions and initiatives started by the Open Society Fund for the development of school libraries. In 1999 and 2000, the Educational Change Fund of the OSF announced a call for applications in the areas of "Modernization of the libraries of educational institutions" and "The dissemination of the work models of a modern library" and financed 50 projects for school libraries.

Many school libraries now actively take part in various projects, such as annual Nordic Library Week organized by the Nordic Council of Ministers (Fig. 4) or "Be Friends with a Book. Discover the Lithuanian Book," initiated in the summer of 2007 by the Ministry of Education and Science in cooperation with the Ministry of Culture.

However, the greatest problem is the lack of professional competence in this sphere. A recent study initiated by librarians and undertaken by the Ministry of Education and Science has shown that 25% of the libraries do not have proper staff (if any). Those employed in school libraries are overworked and underpaid and lack possibilities of professional development as well as guidance and support. Most of them (46.5%) have pedagogical education, 33.9% are educated librarians, and 7% have only

Fig. 4 Nordic Library Week in Šventupis secondary school library.
Source: Courtesy of Šventupis school in Šiauliai.

secondary education.[29] The competence level, and especially computer or information literacy, is recognized as a most important issue in school libraries. In 2002, the Minister of Education and Science approved the Standard of Computer Literacy for School Librarians.[30] At present the competence levels in school libraries are crucial as these libraries are involved in the implementation of MOBIS (The Information System for School Libraries—a part of LIBIS). Special courses for training the staff working with this system are organized by the Centre of Professional Development for Teachers.

Academic and research libraries

In addition to other laws regulating library work, academic and research libraries, like school libraries, are dependent on the legislation relating to education, higher education and research. The reforms of these spheres on the national and European level (Bologna process), the growing international cooperation and the access to European and international financing have influenced their present situation. However, most of the achievements, and especially the problems, are in line with other libraries. Although they have fewer libraries than any other network, these libraries are among the most active participants in advancing librarianship in accordance with modern developments.

The network of academic libraries includes 19 libraries at universities and higher education institutions (16 public and 3 private) and 22 libraries at university colleges. There is also a small group of purely research libraries: the Library of the Academy of Science of Lithuania and eight libraries of research institutes. For a long time, academic and research libraries (except for the small libraries in research institutes) were mainly valued for their collections. One can say that this network is still most burdened with both the worst and the best of the heritage of bygone eras. The Library of the Academy of Science (see http://www.mab.lt/eng/index.html) and Vilnius University Library (see http://www.mb.vu.lt/titulinis) (Fig. 5) have the status of national significance. Both have rich collections of international interest and play important roles in the system of libraries in general. These two libraries are housed in historical buildings that do not correspond to the requirements of modern libraries. The same may be said of most of other academic libraries. Even when housed in newer buildings, they suffer from a lack of space that prevents open access to the collections, so most still operate closed stacks. This is understood by librarians and many parent institutions. The first academic library (in Kaunas University of Medicine) has recently moved into a new building; others plan construction of new premises or renovation (Vilnius University Library, Šiauliai University Library, Klaipėda University Library, Vilnius Pedagogical University Library). However, the costs of library buildings are high, and the progress in this sphere is slow.

Academic and research libraries are taking a multidimensional approach to ensure innovative services for their readers. Academic libraries exploit the possibilities provided by European Union programs, the Open Society Institute (and local OS Fund), Nordinfo, and other funding agencies as well as EU structural funds or governmental projects. In 1997, they established the Lithuanian Academic Library Network (Lietuvos akademinių bibliotekų tinklas—LABT), which is driven and coordinated by Lithuanian Academic Libraries Directors Association (LABA) and Kaunas University of Technology. The LABT is an integral part of the LIBIS, though using different software (namely, ALEPH, Metalib, SFX produced by Ex Libris Group). It also has become a part of a wider program of the Ministry of Education and Science, "Information Technologies for Science and Studies" (for 2001–2006). The Network has grown to 75 participating libraries and has expanded its tasks. At present they are as follows:

- Automation of libraries by uniting them into a solid network.
- Rendering of virtual services.
- Accumulation of e-resource bases.
- Creation of a solid search system with unified user interface.
- Ensuring quality links between library e-catalogs and e-resources.[31]

The LABT develops the multilevel Information System of Lithuanian Research and Studies (publications databases, electronic thesis and dissertations information system) and conducts two big projects financed by EU structural funds: the Lithuanian Virtual Library (see http://www.lvb.lt) and Collection and Presentation of Electronic Documents for Lithuanian Science and Studies.

Academic and research libraries have also created the Lithuanian Research Libraries Consortium (see Professional associations and unions), which negotiates licenses and access to the databases with a variety of providers on behalf of its members. At present all the libraries provide access to the international databases relevant to Lithuanian researchers and students. A full list of databases available to Lithuanian users is found at the site of the Consortium (http://www.lmba.lt/db/angl/eindex.htm).

Despite the rapid development of the infrastructure, increased access to the computers and the Internet provided by the universities and the libraries, and the development of online services, some of the problems persist: academic libraries cannot compete with other organizations offering more attractive work environments and salaries to ambitious professionals (especially, working in the areas of ICT, computers and information systems). Furthermore the funding for acquisition is entirely inadequate, and providing user-centered service is inhibited by old premises and outdated library equipment. Academic libraries are confronting these issues as they look for ways to overcome barriers that inhibit them from becoming more modern and relevant for research and studies.

Fig. 5 Vilnius University Library, Reading Room for Humanities.
Source: Courtesy of Vilnius University Library.

A more detailed account of Lithuanian academic libraries is presented by Pupelienė.[32]

Networks of special libraries

Certain categories of state libraries are classified as specialized libraries. Among them are libraries with delegated responsibility for special library networks:

- Technical Library of Lithuania is responsible for 21 technical libraries and also has its own branches in the largest cities: Kaunas, Klaipėda, Panevėžys, and Šiauliai. It is a library of national significance. (see http://www.tb.lt).
- Lithuanian Library of Medicine is responsible for 38 libraries of health institutions and has six branches in clinics and research centers in Vilnius, Panevėžys, and Klaipėda (see http://www.lmb.lt/).
- Lithuanian Agricultural Library takes care of 8 agricultural libraries. (see http://www.zub.lt/).

These major libraries were established during the Soviet period and have faced significant changes since 1990. The Technical Library of Lithuania (Fig. 6) is one of the largest in the country (it owns 38,554,600 items), and its unique collections are of great importance to the industry and research. It was the first library to create a Business Information Centre (in 1992) and is now building a specialized collection to serve business information needs. It is also a center of information about national and international standards. Since 1999, the Centre of Patent Information (a depository library of Lithuanian, foreign, and international patent documents) has been one of the most important functions of the library. The Technical Library is one of the most active supporters of professional librarians' movements and associations.

Fig. 6 The courtyard of the Technical Library of Lithuania.
Source: Courtesy of the Library.

The Lithuanian Library of Medicine serves the needs of medical researchers, practitioners, and students. It collects medical, biological, psychological, and related literature; some of great historical value. It is a depository library for World Health Organization documentation and a member of the Global Environmental Library Network.

The Lithuanian Agricultural Library "acquires, manages, preserves, and disseminates publications and other documents covering science and technologies of the agricultural sector and related branches of economy." It takes part in the creation of a unified information system for agriculture and an information system for agricultural science. In addition, it functions as a national focal point for AGRIS/CARIS—the system of the International Food and Agriculture Organization.

Among special libraries are 16 museum libraries and 4 libraries of cultural institutions that serve the needs of professional communities in the respective organizations. They fall under the care of the Ministry of Culture.

The Lithuanian Library for the Blind (Lietuvos aklųjų biblioteka—LAB) has a special status as a general public library catering to the needs of people with visual impairments. It also publishes talking books, periodicals and materials in Braille and print. Besides the central library in Vilnius, LAB has five branch libraries in different towns of Lithuania (Kaunas, Klaipėda, Panevėžys, Šiauliai, and Ukmergė) (see http://labiblioteka.lt/english.html).

Though the publics served by these libraries are rather limited from the point of view of numbers and the professional needs served, their information services are of great value to the respective spheres of the economy. They are regulated and financed by ministries or state agencies and also participate in common projects and programs of libraries.

RESEARCH AND EDUCATION FOR INFORMATION

The main institution for LIS research and education is the Faculty of Communication at Vilnius University. It carries on the tradition begun at that University in the nineteenth century by famous scholars of that period—Lelewel, Bohatkiewicz, and others—of teaching and studying bibliographic and library work in the cultural context. This tradition was broken for a long time, and it was not until 1940 that the academic department for LIS-related research opened. It functioned in Kaunas and Vilnius universities led by Vaclovas Biržiška (1884–1956) (Fig. 7), a serious scholar of bibliography, the founder of the current national bibliography. In 1949, Vilnius University started an undergraduate program for librarians. It grew and

Fig. 7 Vaclovas Biržiška.

matured under the leadership of Lev Vladimirov (1912–1999) (Fig. 8), one of the renaissance figures on the landscape of Lithuanian LIS. He was director of Vilnius University Library, director of the Dag Hammarskjold library of the United Nations in New York, author of the only monograph in Lithuanian on universal book history, a reformer of LIS education and a visionary who foresaw the computerized future of information work. In 1991, the departments of Journalism and LIS, previously situated in the Faculty of History, established the Faculty of Communication and developed a number of undergraduate and graduate programs with a common core of communication and information disciplines (see http://www.kf.vu.lt). The Faculty also participates as a leading partner in the professional development of working librarians.

Fig. 8 Levas Vladimirovas.

The Faculty of Communication at Vilnius conducts the only doctoral program in Communication and Information Science in Lithuania. Since 1991, 35 students have received a doctoral degree, of which 30 defended their theses in LIS topics. The Faculty was led by a team of researchers in LIS and cognate disciplines–Audronė Glosienė, Arūnas Augustinaitis, Renaldas Gudauskas and others. Recently, Domas Kaunas, the first correspondent member from the Faculty, was elected to the Academy of Science of the Republic of Lithuania. The Faculty also publishes the scholarly journals in LIS: *Knygotyra* since 1961 and *Informacijos mokslai* since 1990 when Knygotyra was divided into two separate publications catering to two major directions of LIS (and broader Information and Communication Science), one based on a humanities perspective, the other on social science.[33]

LIS research is also conducted by the National Library. Currently, it monitors the general situation of Lithuanian libraries and carries out a number of research projects, such as, *The Public Libraries and Their Image* (2005) and *The Image of a Librarian* (in 2006). It also has a strong tradition in reading research. Other academic and research libraries conduct research in the areas of book science, book and library history and bibliography (Library of the Academy of Science, Vilnius University Library), as well as participate in such projects as TEMPUS (1995–2001), EU DEDICATE on distance education information courses (Library of Kaunas University of Technology in 1998–1999), PERINE, pedagogical and educational research information network (Library of Kaunas University of Technology in 2002),[32] or the EU PHARE project BIBLIONOVA on development of information skills in a learning region (Šiauliai University Library and Klaipėda University Library in 2004).

Library education is also offered at the Department of Librarianship (Faculty of Social Sciences at the Klaipėda University). This department was established in 2001 (studies in Lithuanian Philology and Librarianship started in 1995) to educate librarians for the Northwest regions of Lithuania where the shortage of professionals was felt acutely, especially in school libraries. At present the Department offers several on-campus and distance study options in librarianship (one of them in combination with Lithuanian philology). It also conducts research in the area of academic librarianship, library management, and bibliotherapy.

However, the efforts of LIS departments have not solved the problem of the shortage of professionals. The numbers of librarians graduating with degrees from Vilnius University has diminished and, moreover, young professionals bypass libraries that are not attractive from the point of view of salaries, career, or working environment in comparison to alternatives in the private sector or other fields of the public sector. Broad information and communication competence allows LIS graduates to compete with other specialists on the labor market.

The professional development of librarians is under the auspices of the Lithuanian Centre of Professional Development of Cultural Workers. It organizes courses and seminars for the librarians on relevant topics. In 1999–2004 an Integrated Training Centre for LIS Specialists in Lithuania functioned as part of an initiative on training centers of the Open Society Institute. The Centre was run collectively by the Faculty of Communication (Vilnius University), the National Library, Klaipėda University Library, Vilnius A. Mickevičius County Library, and the Baltic Computer Academy, and it was a successful attempt at cooperation in competence development of professional librarians. In addition, competence development is a part of the most of the projects, that libraries participate in. Librarians also take advantage of possibilities offered by various agencies (Open Society Institute, European Commission, Nordinfo, etc.). In 2006–2007, several university libraries raised the competence of their staff through the Leonardo da Vinci mobility program, "Digital competence and information dissemination in libraries." Library associations and libraries themselves monitor the level of competence of the staff and changes in the environment and seek to address the emerging needs. using various means.

PROFESSIONAL ASSOCIATIONS AND UNIONS

According to library statistics, 6469 librarians worked in Lithuanian libraries in 2006.[15] Their number is decreasing with time, e.g., in 2004, there were 7797 librarians. About half of librarians have professional library education. Professional self-consciousness of librarians was beginning to revive in Soviet Lithuania long before the reestablishment of independence. It manifested itself in the circumvention of ideological limitations and regulations in everyday library work and in attempts to organize the professional community. Discussions of the revival of the librarians' professional organization were started as soon as circumstances permitted, and the Lithuanian Librarians' Association (LLA) was reestablished on June 29, 1989. Since then, the Association has been an integrating force for all librarians. Specific problems and situations in various libraries lead to the formation of other associations (Lithuanian Academic Library Directors' Association, Lithuanian County Public Libraries' Association, Lithuanian Municipal Public Libraries' Association, Lithuanian College Libraries' Association). At present the LLA unites more than one third of librarians (2400), and it is still growing. Its main aims are

- To raise the reputation of librarians in Lithuanian society.
- To represent the social and professional rights of its members.
- To initiate and provide in-service training of librarians.
- To petition Lithuanian government and authorities for better recourses and equipment for libraries.
- To gain experience in the world practice of librarianship.
- To ensure the utmost professionalism in its members.[34]

The Association works through its local chapters in libraries and forms the working groups. In 2005–2007 they were: Library Policy and Fundraising; Continuous Education; School Libraries; Public Libraries; Seniors; Financial Control and Commission of Ethics. The LLA is responsible to its members and organizes the Annual Conference for the members.

The LLA is actively involved in a variety of policy making and lobbying activities: exemptions from copyright for libraries, library renovation and modernization, librarians' salaries, etc. At present it sees collection development as the most acute problem. Therefore, at the end of 2006, together with the Seimas (parliamentary) Committee for Education and Science, it organized a national conference in the Seimas to discuss the problems of acquisition and collection development with MPs, representatives of the President, and Government. Recommendations were drawn up and the initiative to announce the Year of Reading in 2008 emerged from this initiative.[35] Since 2001, the LLA has conducted the annual National Week of Lithuanian Libraries, which aims to make libraries visible in society and communities and to unite librarians from all types of libraries. Since 1993, awards and titles of the Best Librarian of the Year have gone to 15 librarians from different libraries all over Lithuania. The LLA initiates various projects and helps libraries take part in various programs. In 2007, together with Utena A. and M. Miškiniai Public Library, the Lithuanian County Public Libraries' Association, and the Lithuanian Municipal Public Libraries' Association it has won the award for the best project of public relations of Lithuanian public organizations, namely, the portal of Lithuanian Public Libraries (http://www.libraries.lt).

The LLA also actively participates in international projects and develops contacts with similar foreign organizations. In 1990, the LLA was readmitted to IFLA. It cooperates closely with library organizations from other Baltic States, organizing the Congresses of Baltic librarians on a rotational basis (eight so far have been organized). Strong ties with Nordic librarians manifest themselves in common meetings and occasional congresses. Bilateral agreements with library associations from other countries (e.g., Great Britain, Russia, Byelorussia) signify mutual interest in each other's experience. The LLA also takes part in different international projects. Some of these were especially important for lobbying activities and general understanding of entirely new problems for Lithuanian libraries, e.g., copyright for libraries (CECUP—Central and Eastern European Copyright User Platform); licensing of digital resources (CELIP—Central and Eastern European Licensing Information Platform).

Others address the needs of the partners, e.g., the establishment of Martynas Mažvydas library of the Lithuanian community of Sovetsk (Kaliningrad, Russia).

Both directions of LLA activity help achieve the aims of the Association and channel the efforts of librarians to the achievement of common goals.

The Consortium of Lithuanian Research Libraries (see http://www.lmba.lt/) has a different direction, but it also serves the needs of all Lithuanian libraries. Its main aims are

- Promotion of the creation of virtual libraries, preparation and implementation of advanced technology and innovative projects in the libraries.
- Subscription to electronic databases for Consortium members and other libraries.
- Coordination of the acquisition of foreign periodicals among research libraries.

The Consortium has 38 member libraries of various types. It is supported by the Ministry of Culture, the Ministry of Education and Science (the acquisition of databases is partly financed by ministries), Open Society Fund (Lithuania) and Open Society Institute, British Council Lithuania and other agencies. Its main activity is negotiation of licensing agreements with the providers of online databases, organization of their deployment, and control of usage. Its efforts extend beyond its 38 members and benefit other libraries and their users. It organizes seminars and training for librarians, participates in eIFL.net consortium and is a member of EBLIDA (European Bureau of Library, Information and Documentation Associations). It regularly informs the librarians in Lithuania of its activities and news about work with databases.[36] It also disseminates expertise and examples of best practices of licensing and working with digital resources to librarians of other countries (Russia, Georgia, Byelorusia, Kyrgyz, Lebanon, Jordan, etc.)

CONCLUSION

The Lithuanian library sector at present functions as a modern, open, user-oriented and professional system comparable to other library sectors in Europe. In the 17 years since the restoration of independence, there has been a dynamic development of new services, expertise, and models. Equally important are the activities of professionals who participate in shaping the libraries of the future in Lithuania. The catalysts for this transformation include the changing society, the economy, and the arrival of new concepts and technologies, as well as the strong commitment of librarians to fulfill their professional obligations. The international professional community, various funding agencies, and international bodies also supported these changes. The role of funding agencies, especially the Open Society Fund (Lithuania) and the Open Society Institute were essential in stimulating the creativity of librarians and in some cases these agencies also helped by drawing the attention of authorities to the importance of libraries. In addition, international bodies, such as the Nordic Council of Ministers, Nordinfo and the European Commission, helped to create international networks, and taught Lithuanian librarians to work together with partners from other cultures, and adapt their models and experiences to Lithuanian conditions. Close partnerships with librarians from the Nordic countries have influenced the directions of development of Lithuanian libraries. While adopting the best international practice, Lithuanian librarians have also preserved the best local traditions. The community of Lithuanian librarians still needs to go a long way to overcome the inertia of the central and local government, not only in their habit of severely underfunding libraries but also in treating libraries as inefficient and unnecessary appendices to the country's economy. This is an especially difficult but most urgent task. The future of libraries will mainly depend on the policies and strategies adopted and implemented by the government as well as on the energy and attention of librarians devoted to library users' needs and to the development and expansion of innovative, high quality services that span physical buildings and virtual spaces.

ACKNOWLEDGMENTS

I would like to thank my friends and colleagues—Emilija Banionytė, Jūratė Bičkauskienė, Audronė Glosienė, Eduardas Macevičius, Aušra Navickienė, Ramunė Petuchovaitė, Antanas Senkus and others—who have helped me to write the entry by finding required material, reading and commenting on the text and supporting my efforts in other ways.

REFERENCES

1. Lithuania. In *Wikipedia*, 2007. Access through the Internet: http://en.wikipedia.org/wiki/Lithuania.
2. Navickiene, A. Vilnius University Library. In *International Dictionary of Library Histories*; Stam, D.H., Ed.; Fitzroy Dearborn Publishers: Chicago, IL, 2001; Vol. 2, 925–927.
3. Gudauskas, R. Lithuanian Library History. Int. Inform. Libr. Rev. **1994**, *26*(4), 271–287.
4. *Lietuvos spaudos statistika*, LNB: Vilnius, Lithuania, 2006. Available at http://www.lnb.lt/doc/bkc/statistika2005.pdf (accessed June 2007).
5. *Kompiuterių ir interneto skvarba namų ūkiuose 2004 ir 2005 metais*; Tnsgallup: Vilnius, Lithuania, 2006. Available at http://www.infobalt.lt/docs/Kompiuteriai_Internetas_2004_2005.pdf (accessed June 2007).
6. Internet World Stats. *Internet Usage in Europe 2007*; Miniwatts Marketing Group, 2000–2007. Available at http://www.internetworldstats.com/stats4.htm#europe.

7. Statistikos departamentas. Švietimas, kultūra, spauda, Vilnius, 2007. Available at http://www.stat.gov.lt/lt/pages/view/?id=2088 (accessed June 2007).
8. Europe in figures—Eurostat yearbook 2006–07: Educational expenditure 2. Eurostat, 2007. Available at http://epp.eurostat.ec.europa.eu/cache/ITY_OFFPUB/KS-CD-06-001-02/EN/KS-CD-06-001-02-EN.PDF.
9. *Informacinės visuomenės plėtros komitetas prie Lietuvos Respublikos Vyriausybės. 2006 metų veiklos ataskaita*, Vilnius, 2007. Available at http://www.ivpk.lt/dokumentai/ataskaitos/2006_IVPK_ataskaita.pdf (accessed June 2007).
10. Republic of Lithuania. *Constitution of the Republic of Lithuania (Adopted by citizens of the Republic of Lithuania in the Referendum of 25 October 1992)*; Seimas of the Republic of Lithuania: Vilnius, Lithuania. Available at http://www3.lrs.lt/home/Konstitucija/Constitution.htm (accessed May 2007).
11. Republic of Lithuania. *Law on Provision of Information to the Public, 2 July 1996 (revised version on 11 July 2006): Official translation*; Seimas of the Republic of Lithuania: Vilnius, Lithuania. Available at http://www3.lrs.lt/cgi-bin/getfmt?c1=w&c2=170831 (accessed May 2007).
12. Republic of Lithuania. *Law on Libraries*; Seimas of the Republic of Lithuania: Vilnius, Lithuania, June 6, 1995. Available at http://www3.lrs.lt/pls/inter3/dokpaieska.showdoc_e?p_id=29466&p_query=&p_tr2= (accessed May 2007).
13. Republic of Lithuania. *Law on Copyright and Related Rights, May 18, 1999 (Last amended on 12 October 2006): Official translation*; Seimas of the Republic of Lithuania: Vilnius, Lithuania. Available at http://www3.lrs.lt/pls/inter3/dokpaieska.showdoc_e?p_id=291051&p_query=&p_tr2= (accessed May 2007).
14. Lietuvos Respublikos Vyriausybė. Dėl dokumentų privalomųjų egzempliorių skaičiaus ir jų perdavimo bibliotekoms: nutarimas. 1996 m. lapkričio 22 d. Nr. 1389. *Nauja nutarimo redakcija nuo 2006 m. gruodžio 15 d*, Vilnius. Available at http://www3.lrs.lt/pls/inter3/dokpaieska.showdoc_e?p_id=288722&p_query=&p_tr2= (accessed May 2007).
15. *Lietuvos nacionalinė biblioteka. Lietuvos bibliotekų statistika*; LNB: Vilnius, Lithuania, 2006. Available at http://www.lnb.lt/lnb/selectPage.do?docLocator=3AE98A10AA6611D98296746164617373&inlanguage=lt&pathId=67 (accessed June 2007).
16. Bulavas, V. National Library of Lithuania. *In: Encyclopedia of Library and Information Science*; Marcel Dekker, Inc.: New York, 2003; 1991–2001.
17. *LIBIS programinė įranga: diegimo darbai*; LNB: Vilnius, Lithuania, 1997–2006.
18. *Lietuvos nacionalinė biblioteka. Lietuvos bibliotekų statistinės ataskaitos 2006 metais*; LNB: Vilnius, Lithuania, 2006. Available at http://www.lnb.lt/lnb/SelectPage.do?docLocator=0C3352EE722411DAA310746164617373&inlanguage=ltspathid=110 (accessed June 2007).
19. Lietuvos Respublikos Vyriausybė. *Bibliotekų renovacijos ir modernizavimo 2003–2013 metų programa. patvirtinta 2002 m. rugsėjo 17 d. nutarimu Nr. 1454*, Vilnius, 2002. Available at http://www3.lrs.lt/pls/inter3/dokpaieska.showdoc_1?id=184168 (accessed May 2007).
20. Petuchovaitė, R. *Viešųjų bibliotekų paslaugų bendruomenei plėtra: sėkmingos praktikos Lietuvoje ir tarptautinių veiksnių studija*; VUL: Vilnius, Lithuania, 2004.
21. Dovydėnienė, R. Bibliotekų politika: dabartis ir ateitis. Tarp knygų **2003**, *5*, 1–2.
22. *Lietuvos Respublikos Kultūros ministerija. 2006 metų veiklos ataskaita*, Vilnius, 2007. Available at http://www.lrkm.lt/index.php?1032318204 (accessed May 2007).
23. Rutkauskienė, U. Internetas visose Lietuvos VB—per trejus metus. Tarp knygų **2007**, *3*, 1–3.
24. Garunkštytė, V. *LBD ataskaita 2006*; LBD: Vilnius, Lithuania, 2006. Available at http://www.lbd.lt/reng/LBD%20ataskaita%202006.pdf (accessed June 2007).
25. Jaskonienė, D. Savivaldybių viešosios bibliotekos 2005 metais. Tarp knygų **2006**, *7/8*, 1–15.
26. Nemokamas internetas Lietuvos bibliotekose. Tarp knygų **2006**, *6*, 15–20.
27. Kirtiklienė, D.; ir Lapinskienė, A. Kodėl Lietuvos bibliotekos praranda vartotoją? Tarp knygų **2007**, *4*, 1–4.
28. Glosienė, A.; Petuchovaitė, R.; Padaigaitė, G. Biblioteka kaip "trečioji vieta." Informacijos mokslai **2006**, *39*, 32–52.
29. Kryžanauskienė, I. Bendrojo lavinimo mokyklos šiandien. Tarp knygų **2007**, *5*, 9–12.
30. Banionytė, E.; et al. *Mokyklų bibliotekininkų kompiuterinio raštingumo standartas*, LŠMM: Vilnius, Lithuania, 2002. Available at http://www.emokykla.lt/doc/bib1_kompiuterinio_rastingumo_ standartas.pdf (accessed June 2007).
31. *LABT Project Highlights*; LABT: Kaunas, 2003–2007. Available at http://www.labt.lt/index_projektas_en.php?psl=projektas_en.php (access June 2007).
32. Pupeliene, J. Lithuania: the changing image of academic libraries. J. Acad. Libr. **2003**, *30*(1), 80–84.
33. Macevičiūtė, E. Knygotyra: pastovumas ir permainos. Knygotyra **2006**, *47*, 297–306.
34. *Lithuanian Librarians' Association*, Vilnius, 2005. Available at http://www.lbd.lt/lbd/angl/eindex.htm (accessed June 2007).
35. Rimša, V. Lietuvos bibliotekų fondų komplektavimas: realijos ir perspektyvos. Tarp knygų **2007**, *1*, 1–5.
36. Vaškevičienė, A.; ir Banionytė, E. Duomenų bazių, prenumeruojamų tarpininkaujant eIFL.net konsorciumui, naudojimo Lietuvos bibliotekose 2004–2005 metais analizė. Informacijos mokslai **2006**, *38*, 71–89.

Louvre

Bette W. Oliver
Austin, Texas, U.S.A.

Abstract

The Louvre evolved from the castle fortress of Philippe-Auguste in 1190 to a royal residence occupied by French monarchs until Louis XIV moved to Versailles in 1678, and finally in 1793, into the national museum of France. Under both royal and republican governments, the museum has enriched its collections and enhanced its building program culminating in the creation of the Grand Louvre, begun under François Mitterand in the 1980s and finished under Jacques Chirac in 1996. The Louvre is considered the finest example of a universal survey museum in the world and is visited by millions of tourists and scholars annually.

The Louvre evolved from the castle fortress of Philippe-Auguste in 1190 to a royal residence occupied by French monarchs until Louis XIV moved to Versailles in 1678, and finally in 1793, into the national museum of France. Today, considered the finest example of a universal survey museum in the world and visited by millions of tourists and scholars, the Louvre has become what its founders intended when they preserved and enriched its collections during the period of the French Revolution and the First Empire (1789–1815). Under subsequent governments, whether royal or republican, the museum has continued to add to its collections and to enhance its building program, resulting in the realization of the Grand Louvre, which began under Françios Mitterand's presidency in the 1980s and later culminated in Jacques Chirac's presidency in 1996 with the architectural additions designed by I.M. Pei. "The Louvre was the prototypical public art museum," according to art historian Carol Duncan. "By the end of the 19th-century, every western nation would boast at least one important public art museum."[1]

THE EARLY LOUVRE

The evolution of the Louvre has been subject to the changing needs of the French state. First, it served as a square fortress positioned on the right side of the Seine to defend against attacks from the English to the north. Archeological evidence of the original castle and its moat was discovered during construction work for the Grand Louvre. Under the reign of Charles V (1364–1380) and his architect Raymond du Temple, the palace was raised and terraces were added as it was incorporated within the defensive walls of Paris. François I (1515–1547) chose to transform the Louvre into more of an Italian Renaissance palace with additions designed by Pierre Lescot, notably the Hall of the Caryatids. More importantly, François I had amassed a fine collection of paintings at his residence of Fontainbleau including several works by Leonardo da Vinci, who died at Amboise in 1519. Works by Raphael, del Sarto, and Fra Bartolomeo, among others, would form the basis of the collections for the Louvre Museum.

Building continued under François I's successor, Henri II (1547–1559) and his widow Catherine de Medici, who in 1564 ordered the construction of the Palais des Tuileries, which would be joined to the Louvre. Under Henri IV (1568–1610), the first Bourbon king, the Grand Gallery was built and the collections enriched, while artists and craftsmen were invited to live and work in the palace. Under Louis XIII (1610–1643) and his architect Jacques Lemercier, the palace was enlarged and the imposing Tower Clock Pavilion was constructed. During Louis XIII's reign, Cardinal Richelieu added to the royal collections, and upon his death in 1642 his property, the Palais Cardinal, passed to the king and became known as the Palais Royal, situated directly behind the Louvre.

Cardinal Mazarin ruled as regent for Louis XIV until his death in 1661 and worked to enrich the royal collections. When Mazarin died the Louvre became the beneficiary, receiving works by Correggio, Raphael, Veronese, Titian, and Holbein, among others. Louis XIV's astute minister, Jean-Baptiste Colbert, purchased many fine works for the royal collection. The Sun King's architect, Louis Le Vau, was responsible from 1661–1670 for major additions to the Louvre, including completion of the north and south wings of the Cour Carrée, the Cour de la Reine, the Apollo Gallery, the Arts, Marsan, and Marengo pavilions, and with Charles Perrault and Charles LeBrun, the building of the Colonnade. In 1678, when the work on the Cour Carrée had been completed, Louis XIV chose to move himself and his royal court to Versailles, where he would remain until his death in 1715. The Louvre then served as the home of artists and academics, where they

Encyclopedia of Library and Information Sciences, Fourth Edition DOI: 10.1081/E-ELIS4-120044558

would remain until 1793, when the Louvre would become the national museum of France.

The royal collection was no longer centralized after Louis XIV's move to Versailles, but the 1709–1710 inventory listed 2000 paintings. By the time Louis XV (1715–1774) had become king, many paintings from the royal collection were exhibited in the private homes of aristocrats, but in 1725 the Academy of Painting and Sculpture held its first exhibition in the Salon Carrée. These exhibitions at the Louvre would be held annually from 1737 to 1848.[2]

In keeping with Enlightenment ideas on the role of the state in the arts and sciences, a movement developed to transform the Louvre into a great palace of the arts. The Count d'Angiviller, curator of the royal Cabinet des Peintures, sought to increase the royal collection and in 1774, with the ascension of Louis XVI (1774–1793), worked to increase acquisitions for the proposed museum and to undertake architectural improvements. These acquisitions included not only early works from Italy and France but also contemporary French paintings from the annual salons and a large number of seventeenth-century Dutch and Flemish works. D'Angiviller aimed to create a museum that would reflect national pride and royal glory, as well as one that would address the needs of a larger public who were interested in viewing great works of art. The average annual expenditure on the Louvre in the early 1780s was approximately 100,000 livres, while d'Angiviller spent one million livres on increasing the royal collection over a 15-year period.[2,3]

FRENCH REVOLUTION AND NAPOLEONIC ERA

The advent of the French Revolution in 1789 led d'Angiviller, and many others loyal to the king, to flee into exile, but plans for the Louvre Museum escalated, even as the new republican government faced challenges from every side. Decrees were passed by the National Assembly to make the Interior Ministry, under Jean Roland, responsible for safeguarding the national collections, defining the role of the national museum, and creating a commission for the selection of artworks. The confiscations by the republican government of art works that had belonged to the church, the crown, the émigrés, and those who had been imprisoned or executed, amounted to a windfall for the museum. By the time the Louvre Museum opened officially on August 10, 1793, as many as 537 oil paintings and 124 marble and bronze sculptures, and other objects, were displayed in the Grand Gallery, all of which the public could visit three times a week free of charge; the other days were reserved for artists and special guests.[4,5]

As the revolution within France led to the Napoleonic wars with other western European monarchies, the legally decreed confiscations of artworks, as well as books and manuscripts, increased dramatically. The first manifestation of this policy became clear with the arrival in Paris of seven convoys of paintings taken from Belgium in 1794. An inventory of each convoy was made upon its arrival, and each painting was identified. Gilberte Emile-Mâle, who served as head of restoration services for the French national museums from 1971 to 1981, documented in some detail the contents of each of the seven convoys from Belgium, as well as indicating the current location of each painting wherever possible. Included in these works were pieces by Rubens, Van Dyck, Jordaens, Van Eyck, Teniers, de Lairesse, and other lesser-known Dutch and Flemish artists; they had been taken from churches and city halls in Antwerp, Brussels, Bruges, Lille, Dunkerque, and St. Omer.

Later convoys would arrive from Italy, Austria, Germany, and Spain, all heralded by public announcements in the press, so that by the time the artworks arrived in Paris, the public was eager to view them at the museum. For example, the third convoy of Italian artworks in 1798 amounted to a treasure trove of 45 cases of fine art, books and manuscripts, and natural history materials loaded onto wagons, 25 of which contained the cases of paintings and sculptures, and a special wagon to display the bronze horses taken from St. Mark's in Venice. A special song composed for the occasion proclaimed, "Rome is no more in Rome/ it is all in Paris."[3,4]

In addition to the foreign confiscations, artworks from Versailles and from the abolished Royal Academy of Painting and Sculpture were sent to the Louvre. In 1797 the Apollo Gallery was opened, and by 1799 half of the Grand Gallery had been renovated and filled with Flemish and Dutch paintings. By 1801, the Italian works were arranged in the remaining half of the Grand Gallery.[2]

Napoleon's influence became ever more evident, thanks to the careful acquisitions of artworks from conquered countries. Both the Louvre Museum (at that time called the Musée Central des Arts) and the Bibliothèque Nationale had sent experts, armed with lists of items to be confiscated, to accompany the military units engaged in combat. As a result of a plebiscite in 1802, Napoleon was named Consul for life, and in 1804, by another plebiscite, he was made Emperor. The First Empire, which would last until 1814, had begun.

The name of the museum was changed to the Musée Napoleon in 1803 and its first director was Dominique Vivant-Denon, an artist and writer who had participated in Napoleon's Egyptian campaign. Napoleon appointed the architects Charles Percier and Pierre-François Fontaine to make extensive improvements to the museum, including the division of the Grand Gallery into nine sections with skylights installed to enhance viewing, as well as the creation of an imposing new staircase. Under Denon's supervision, the museum's collections continued to increase as acquisitions followed military victories in Germany and Spain.[2]

With Napoleon's final defeat and forced abdication in 1815, many of the artworks exhibited at the museum were returned to their countries of origin. The representatives from those countries, who met at the Congress of Vienna in 1814–1815 to address how best to control Napoleon's power and influence, had decreed this repatriation of valuable cultural items. However, many of the foreign acquisitions remained at the museum due to bureaucratic obstruction and clever diplomacy. For example, of the 506 paintings confiscated from Italy, 249 were returned, 248 remained, and 9 had mysteriously disappeared.[5]

The Napoleonic wars had greatly increased artistic activity across Europe, and spurred the development of subsequent national museums based on the successful model of the Louvre. Just as its founders had intended in 1793, the museum had become a great cultural institution, and Paris had become the art capital of the western world and would remain so until the mid-twentieth century.

NINETEENTH-CENTURY DEVELOPMENTS

The museum, once again renamed the Musée Royal, grew more slowly after the Bourbon Restoration in 1815, because the period of great military glory and acquisitions had ended with Napoleon's downfall. However, under Louis XVIII (1815–1824) and Charles X (1824–1830), both brothers of the executed Louis XVI, Napoleon's building projects continued, including the Rohan Pavilion. Count Forbin replaced Denon as director of the museum in 1816, serving in that position until 1836. Paintings transferred from the Palais du Luxembourg replaced those that had been repatriated in 1815, and three halls of the Grand Gallery were filled with French artworks. During the Restoration period, the Egyptian section of the museum was opened on the first floor of the Cour Carrée and the future Department of Sculptures was inaugurated.[2]

Following the Revolution of 1830 and the ascension of Louis Philippe (1830–1848) of the Orléans branch of the royal family, work on the Assyrian Halls proceeded, but not much more was accomplished until Louis Napoleon gained power through a plebiscite in 1848, much like his uncle had before him. He was named Emperor and ruled as Napoleon III from 1851 to 1870. Under his architects, Joachim Visconti, Hector Lefuel, and Felix Duban, the New Louvre (now called the Musée Imperial) was constructed around the Place Napoléon. The Flore Pavilion and the western section of the Grand Gallery were demolished and reconstructed, while the parallel buildings on the north and south sides of the Carrousel area were built and connected to the new wing on the new rue de Rivoli. The Musée des Souverains was established on the first floor of the Colonnade to display the former splendor of the Valois and Bourbon dynasties.[2,6]

Following the Franco-Prussian War during the period of the Commune in 1871, the Palais des Tuileries was set afire, which destroyed the Marsan Pavilion, the western section of the Galerie Napoléon, and the library. The Tuileries Palace was not rebuilt, but reconstruction of the other areas continued from 1871 to 1878.[2]

With the fall of Napoleon III after the French defeat in the Franco-Prussian War, and the establishment of the Third Republic (1870–1940), a period of relative calm ensued. This hiatus allowed for gradual embellishments to the museum and for the acquisitions of important nineteenth-century artworks. A gallery of living artists was established in 1886 at the Orangerie Museum nearby, which would later contain a large collection of Impressionist paintings. In 1900, the Hall of States, later called the Hall Rubens, was completed. In addition, the Musée des Arts Décoratifs was opened in 1905. In 1914 work began on the second floor of the Mollien Wing, but the advent of World War I necessitated closing the Louvre for the duration of the war. From 1926 to 1939, the director of the museum was Henri Verne, who set about reorganizing exhibitions and restoring artworks. The Impressionist paintings were transferred from the Orangerie and installed on the top floor of the Colonnade, while eighteen new halls were opened on the third floor of the Vieux Louvre.[2]

CHANGES AFTER WORLD WAR II

In anticipation of certain war and a Nazi invasion, a massive exodus of valuable artworks from the Louvre to the provinces began in 1938 and continued into 1939. In preparation, the Department of Paintings, under the direction of René Huyghe, was divided into sectors; each painting in a sector was packed and labeled according to its destination. Five chateaux between Le Mans and Louvigny and eighty warehouses in the provinces had been requisitioned to receive the artworks.[7] Despite the Nazi confiscations of private collections and museums during the Occupation, the paintings from the Louvre were saved and returned in 1945. A number of unclaimed recovered works from private collections also found a temporary home in the Louvre, which assumed responsibility for them as long as they remained unclaimed. In some cases, that could be forever, if there were no living heirs to claim them.[8]

The opening of the Grand Gallery in 1947, featuring some improvements that originally had been advocated by the artist Hubert Robert in 1796, contained artworks from the Italian and Spanish schools. Meanwhile, the Impressionist paintings were moved yet again, this time to the nearby Jeu de Paume, where they would remain until their transfer in 1986 to the new Musée d'Orsay across the Seine.[2,4] The Daru, Mollien, and Denon Halls were reopened in 1949 and, under the new curator for paintings, Germain Bazin, the artworks from the French school were returned from the Petit Palais.[2] The new sculpture rooms in the Flore Wing, which would later be connected to the Grand Gallery, opened in 1960, and in 1968 those collections dated after 1848 were transferred to the Musée d'Orsay. The Richelieu Wing, which had been the home of the Ministry of Finance, was inaugurated as part of the museum in 1981, the same year that President François Mitterand set forth his impressive plans for the Grands Travaux.

Other internal changes were underway as well at the Louvre in the 1980s. In 1987, the director of the Musées de France, Hubert Landais, asked Michel Laclotte, head of the Paintings Department at the Louvre, to assume the role of director of the museum. Three administrators who worked under the supervision of the Musées de France had previously filled that position. With the appointment of Laclotte, the director's position conferred greater decision-making authority and staff support. Pierre Rosenberg, who later became museum director himself, assumed the duties of head of the Paintings Department. Under Laclotte's management, museum personnel would be involved in the changes necessary to transform the old Louvre into the new Grand Louvre.[6,9]

THE GRAND LOUVRE

Mitterand's ambitious building program included the modernization of the Louvre, making it the Grand Louvre, and new buildings for the Bibliothèque Nationale de France, the Opéra de la Bastille, and the great arch of La Defense. The Grand Louvre project, which began in 1982 and was completed during Jacques Chirac's presidency in 1996, amounted to a series of dramatic architectural innovations, the most prominent being that of I.M. Pei's great glass pyramid as the central entrance to the museum. Pei enjoyed a reputation as an innovative architect, and his renovation of the National Gallery in Washington, D.C. offered proof that he could successfully modernize a museum located in an older building, or in the case of the Louvre, an ancient building. The immensity of the Grand Louvre project demanded careful planning, budgeting, and consideration of the urban aspects of the museum, such as parking, situated as it is in the historic heart of Paris. It was a matter of

> conceiving and overseeing the development of the Domaine Nationale du Louvre et des Tuileries in view of creating an original cultural complex of museological character which will be called the Grand Louvre, as well as providing for the integration of this complex into its environment.[6]

Like the Eiffel Tower, Pei's glass pyramid, widely admired now, was a hotly debated topic when it was proposed in the early 1980s. Some critics feared that such a structure would destroy the aesthetic appearance of such a beloved and historic structure as the Louvre. However, the idea of a pyramid was actually appropriate because the museum's Egyptian collection was one of the best known in the world. In addition, the glass tower provided much-needed light into the entrance hall, which is situated directly below it, connected by an escalator. In effect, the pyramid literally opened up the museum and made it a more welcoming venue for its millions of visitors. The large space created beneath the Cour Napoléon allowed for the addition of various shops and services, including a conference hall, an auditorium, a bookstore, and a cafeteria. In 1993, after the Finance Ministry was relocated and the Richelieu Wing became available, it was possible to use one of the glass-covered courtyards to display the famous Marly horses, great marble sculptures that had once graced the gardens of Marly-le-roi under Louis XIV. In addition, the Passage Richelieu was transformed into a public space to link the new section of the Louvre with the Place du Palais-Royal across the street.[2,6] Thus, public access to the museum was facilitated, while at the same time providing an attractive window into the museum.

The traditional boundaries between the seven sections of the museum which housed the collections were maintained, but access to the collections was centralized at the main entrance in the Cour Napoléon. The collections are divided into the archeological sections (antiquities) and the four sections of art ranging from the Middle Ages to mid-nineteenth century (graphic arts, decorative arts, painting, and sculpture).[6] These sections include: Oriental Antiquities, Egyptian Antiquities, Greek Antiquities, Etruscan Antiquities, Roman Antiquities, Arts of Islam, Sculptures, Objects of Art, Paintings, and Graphic Arts.

While it is generally agreed that the Grand Louvre is a grand success, with the number of visitors increasing every year, such good fortune has led to some budgetary problems. The French government spent $1.1 billion between 1987 and 2002 on architectural improvements, which led to greater public access and the necessity of increasing the museum staff. While part of the museum's budget is dependent on the government, other sources of income derive from entrance fees, special exhibitions which draw the largest crowds, and related services within the museum complex. In addition, private funds are raised for specific projects, such as the new Mona Lisa Gallery, financed by Nippon Television of Japan, and the construction of a new wing for the Louvre's large collection of Islamic art, the funds for which were donated by a Saudi prince. Even for those who cannot visit the Louvre in person, it is possible to view its treasures via the Internet (http://www.louvre.fr) and to purchase the excellent scholarly catalogs that accompany special exhibitions.[4]

The Louvre also will exist in other locations outside of Paris. The Louvre-Lens, in the Nord-Pas de Calais region of France, is expected to open in 2010, while the Louvre Abu Dhabi, designed by Jean Nouvel, is scheduled to open in 2012 or soon thereafter. The government of Abu Dhabi is willing to pay France $747 million in exchange for using the "Louvre" name as well as for loans of artworks, special exhibitions, and management advice.[10] The evolution of the Louvre from a fortress to a royal residence and finally to one of the greatest museums in the world is a tribute to the many visionaries who worked to make it such a success. The government of the first French republic took it upon itself to ensure that the national museum would reflect the high ideals of the early days of the Revolution of 1789 and allocated sufficient funds to preserve and enrich its collections. That they did so, while dealing with ongoing conflicts both inside and outside of France, is a tribute to their determination to transform the Louvre into a public symbol of French culture. Other visionaries were needed to have the courage to make radical, if beneficial, changes to what, by the 1980s, had become a hallowed national institution. One of the oldest museums in Europe, the Louvre's collections encompass artworks from the earliest civilizations to those of modern times, truly a universal survey museum of the highest order.

As Carol Duncan has stated: "The importance of the Louvre for other national galleries and as an international training ground for the first community of professional museum men is everywhere recognized."[1] Perhaps President Charles de Gaulle's culture minister, André Malraux, said it best in speaking to the National Assembly on December 14, 1961. Explaining why it was important to appropriate funds for the preservation of France's historical monuments, such as the Louvre, he said that such monuments represented the highest aspirations of their time, that they were "the greatest dreams of France," which would serve to provide hope and courage to future generations of French citizens.[11] The Louvre continues to pursue this mission as it expands to serve an ever-increasing public.

REFERENCES

1. Duncan, C. *Civilizing Rituals: Inside Public Art Museums*; Routledge: London, 1995.
2. Abate, M., Ed. *Great Museums of Europe: The Dream of the Universal Museum*; Skira: Milan, 2002; Translated by Shugar, A.
3. McClellan, A. *Inventing the Louvre: Art, Politics, and the Origins of the Modern Museum in Eighteenth-Century Paris*; Cambridge University Press: New York, 1994.
4. Oliver, B.W. *From Royal to National: The Louvre Museum and the Bibliothèque Nationale*; Lexington Books: Lanham, MD, 2007.
5. Gould, C. *Trophy of Conquest: The Musée Napoléon and the Creation of the Louvre*; Faber and Faber: London, 1965.
6. Bezombes, D., Ed. *The Grand Louvre: History of a Project*; Éditions du Moniteur and Établissement Public du Grand Louvre: Paris, 1994; Translated by Bogin, N.
7. Bazin, G. *L'Exode du Louvre, 1940–1945*; Éditions d'Art Somogy: Paris, 1992.
8. Feliciano, H. *The Lost Museum: The Nazi Conspiracy to Steal the World's Greatest Works of Art*; Basic Books: New York, 1997.
9. Laclotte, M. *A Key to the Louvre: Memoirs of a Curator*; Polizzotti, M., Ed.; Abbeville Press: New York, 2004; Translated by.
10. Riding, A. *The Louvre's Art: Priceless. The Louvre's Name: Expensive*; The New York Times, March 7, 2007.
11. Lantelme, M., Ed. *La Grande Pitié des Monuments de France: André Malraux, Débats parlementaires (1960–1968)*; Presses Universitaires du Septentrion: Paris, 1998.

Machine Readable Cataloging (MARC): 1961–1974 *[ELIS Classic]*

Henriette D. Avram
Library of Congress, Washington, District of Columbia, U.S.A.

Abstract

The MARC Program of the Library of Congress, led during its formative years by the author of this entry, was a landmark in the history of automation. Technical procedures, standards, and formatting for the catalog record were experimented with and developed in modern form in this project. The project began when computers were mainframe, slow, and limited in storage. So little was known then about many aspects of automation of library information resources that the MARC project can be seen as a pioneering effort with immeasurable impact.

—***ELIS Classic***, *from 1975*

INTRODUCTION

Many words have been written on the subject of the Machine-Readable Cataloging (MARC) Program: the events that led to the pilot project, the development of the format, the operational Distribution Service, the influence of MARC on standardization, and the impetus it gave to library automation projects and to the creation of networks here and abroad. This article serves to gather together all aspects of the national and international MARC system.

Much of what follows has been fairly well documented in many published reports, journal articles, etc., and therefore this article relies heavily on that material. A Bibliography based on the article's main headings has been included for those readers who wish to explore any aspect of MARC in greater depth.

BACKGROUND, 1961–1965

The Library of Congress's (LC) investigations of the possibility of using automated techniques for its internal operations began in the late 1950s. As a result of the interest generated by these investigations, the Librarian of Congress requested a grant from the Council on Library Resources (CLR) for a study to determine the feasibility of applying automated techniques to the operations of LC. The study, published in 1963,[1] recommended that a group be established to design and implement the procedures required to automate the cataloging, searching, indexing, and document retrieval functions. A systems staff was assembled in the Office of the Librarian to proceed with the recommendations. During this same period, motivated by the increasing attention given to automation in libraries, CLR awarded a contract for a study of the possible methods of converting the data on LC cards to machine-readable form for the purpose of printing bibliographical products by computer. The report of the study[2] was the subject of a conference held at LC in January 1965, under the sponsorship of LC, the Committee on Automation of the Association of Research Libraries (ARL), and CLR. Participants included representatives from universities, research agencies, government agencies, and private industry. The conferees concluded that:

1. Availability of machine-readable catalog records produced and distributed by LC would help those libraries that have automated systems.
2. The machine-readable record should include all the data presently available on LC's printed card, plus additional information to produce a multipurpose record.
3. Agreement by a broad segment of the library community on the elements to be included in the record was most desirable, and the design of the record at LC was probably the best means of achieving standardization.

Three LC staff members were assigned to the task of analyzing cataloging data from a machine processing point of view. A report,[3] issued in June 1965, was reviewed by over 150 LC staff members and their comments were issued as a supplement to the report. Comments were also elicited from many representatives of the library community.

The report was discussed at a conference supported by CLR and held at LC in November 1965. The enthusiasm generated at this meeting again demonstrated the desirability of LC becoming the distribution source of machine-readable records. As a result, LC sought funds from CLR to conduct a pilot project and in December 1965 received a grant to test the feasibility and utility of the distribution of cataloging data in machine-readable form from LC to user libraries. The project was named MARC, for *ma*chine-*r*eadable *c*ataloging.

Encyclopedia of Library and Information Sciences, Fourth Edition DOI: 10.1081/E-ELIS4-120008993

MARC PILOT PROJECT, 1966–1968

Planning for the pilot project began early in January 1966. CLR funds were used for contractual support: 1) to develop procedures and programs for the conversion, file maintenance, and distribution of MARC data, as well as programs to use the data at the participating libraries; and 2) to assist in the evaluation of the project. Participants in the pilot project were invited by LC, and from the 40 libraries that responded affirmatively, 16 were chosen. Selection was based on type of library (special, government, state, university, public, and school), geographic location, availability of personnel, equipment, funds, proposed use of MARC data, and willingness to evaluate the utility of the data and prepare written reports. It was thought that for the project to provide the most useful information, different types of libraries and geographical areas should be represented. The first (types of libraries) was a valid decision; the second (geographical areas) is questionable.

The participants selected were: Argonne National Laboratory; Georgia Institute of Technology; Harvard University; Indiana University; Montgomery County Public Schools; Nassau (County) Library System; National Agricultural Library; Redstone Scientific Information Center; Rice University; University of California Institute of Library Research, Los Angeles; University of Chicago; University of Florida; University of Missouri; University of Toronto; Washington State Library; and Yale University. By February 1966, the LC staff assigned to the project was prepared to call a conference of the participants for the purpose of describing: 1) the concepts, objectives, schedules, functions, and requirements of the experiment; 2) the operation at LC; 3) the MARC format; 4) the materials to be sent weekly to participants; and 5) the content of the reports expected from the participants. The February meeting was considered the official opening of the pilot project. [The pilot project format, later in the life of the project, was called MARC I to differentiate it from the distribution format (MARC II), which was designed later.]

LC set for itself the herculean task of completing within eight months the design of procedures and computer programs required both for the LC operations and for the participants. The MARC I format had to be stabilized by April 1966 to begin programming. Consequently, the time spent in analysis and design was severely limited and the form of material was restricted to book materials.

The first distribution was to begin in September 1966. Actually, the first test tape was mailed in October and the weekly service began in November.

The months following the initial distribution were hectic for all. The computer programs provided to participating libraries were not, in all cases, error free and had to be modified; the participants were busily engaged in writing their own tailor-made programs; and LC was learning better production methods "on the job" to reduce the large number of incorrectly edited and inadequately verified records. The load on the telephone lines between the participants' locations and Washington, District of Columbia, was heavy from November 1966 through the next several months.

The pilot project had originally been scheduled to end in June 1967. This termination date, however, seemed unrealistic. Setup time had taken longer than anticipated at the participating libraries and, with June as a cutoff date, there could be little operational experience. LC stated at the midwinter meeting of the American Library Association (ALA) in January 1967 that the pilot would be extended. (LC made arrangements to hold MARC meetings during ALA conferences as a vehicle of communications with pilot participants.) During the next six-month period, it became obvious that MARC served a useful purpose and, encouraged by the enthusiasm of the library community, LC announced at the June 1967 ALA/MARC meeting that a full-scale operational MARC Distribution Service was in the planning stages. The pilot project would continue through June 1968 while the operational system was being planned and implemented. The pilot service was extended to four additional participants—California State Library, Illinois State Library, Cornell University, and the State University of New York Biomedical Communications Network.

The participating libraries experimented with card catalog and book catalog production, current awareness listings, filing arrangement by computer, etc. Not all participants were successful in mounting an operational system but, nonetheless, all cooperated to the fullest in reporting back to LC the pros and cons of each aspect of the project. In particular, the need for timely receipt of data and quality of records was stressed.

Part of the rationale for the pilot project was the test of a machine format under operational conditions in order to design a next generation format based on the experience gained. In addition to the substantive evaluation of the MARC I format provided by the participating libraries, an important event occurred during the project which exerted a strong influence on the design of MARC II. The interest expressed by the British National Bibliography (BNB) in mounting a UK/MARC Pilot Project and the many visits from foreign librarians directed thinking toward a standard communications format suitable for interchanging bibliographic data, not only from one organization (LC) to many, but also among organizations, perhaps crossing national boundaries.

The philosophy behind MARC II was the design of one format structure (the physical representation on a machine-readable medium) capable of containing bibliographic information for all forms of material (books, serials, maps, music, journal articles, etc.) and related records (name and subject reference records, etc.). The *structure*, or "empty container," the *content designators* (tags, indicators, and subfield codes) used to explicitly identify or to additionally characterize the data elements, and the *content*, the data itself (author's names, titles, etc.), are the three components of the format. It was recognized that under ideal conditions the universe of material would be studied at one time for a more coordinated approach to the assignment of content designators. However, those responsible knew the magnitude of such a task, the time required, and the need for specialists to be involved. Consequently, to make progress in the near term, it was decided to handle one form of material at a time, beginning with books.[4]

LC staff held many meetings discussing the book format contents and content designators. The intent was to provide a multipurpose record "rich" enough in detail to allow inclusion or exclusion of data elements based on the user's needs. The resultant MARC II format for books reflects the consensus of a large number of librarians and systems personnel.

Another significant outcome of the pilot project was the design of an extended character set for roman alphabet languages. At the onset of the project, a character set was specified based on the work in progress by the Library Typewriter Keyboard Committee of the Resources and Technical Services Division of ALA. Once the pilot was in operation, LC, in consultation with the National Agricultural Library and the National Library of Medicine, turned its attention to the development of an extended character set to cover all the major roman alphabet languages as well as the romanized forms of nonroman alphabets.

In December 1967 a meeting funded by CLR was held at LC for the purpose of discussing the MARC II format and the proposed character set. This meeting was particularly significant since the participants, based on shared experiences in the pilot project, were setting the framework for an operational MARC system that would have wide implications for the entire library community and the future of automated library systems.

At the conclusion of the pilot project in June 1968, LC had distributed approximately 50,000 machine-readable records for English language book materials. All concerned were a little wiser than at the onset of the experience. LC had learned a great deal about the procedures and the funds needed to convert cataloging data to machine-readable form. The participants realized the complexities inherent in applying the computer as a tool for library operations and the requirement for management support, time for implementation, and funds. All organizations were aware of the close cooperation required between computer and library personnel for a successful project.

A project report[5] was published in 1968 describing the experiences of LC and participating organizations, the expanded character set, and the MARC II format.

MARC DISTRIBUTION SERVICE, 1968–

From June 1967 through June 1968, LC staff, in addition to concentrating on the MARC II format design and the expanded character set, were engaged in the redesign of the procedures and programs for the operational MARC Distribution Service. The pilot project was officially terminated in June 1968, and from July through March 1969 LC shifted over to a period of testing the new procedures and programs.

During this practice period, a proposal was written by LC to the Information Science and Automation Division of ALA recommending that a series of workshops (which became known as the MARC Institutes) be held throughout the country for the purpose of briefing library staffs on the MARC II format, LC procedures, and the uses of MARC data by libraries during the pilot project. The first institute was held in Seattle, Washington, in July 1968. This series continued for several years and was attended by over 2000 individuals.

The first *Subscriber's Guide to the MARC Distribution Service* [which later became *Books: A MARC Format*[6]] was published in August 1968 so that institutions planning to subscribe to MARC would have the necessary information for programming. The *Guide* was followed by a test tape in the fall of 1968 to provide the means of checking user programs.

In March 1969 the operational system was launched covering all English-language monographs cataloged by LC including titles acquired through the National Program for Acquisitions and Cataloging (NPAC). (Initially, only United States imprints were distributed but this was rapidly expanded to include all English-language monographs.) The distribution cycle was weekly, and approximately 1000 records appeared on each MARC tape.

Before the actual implementation of the distribution service, a great deal of interest was generated in MARC procedures. Consequently, in 1969, LC issued, through ALA, the first edition of the *MARC Manuals*.[7] This publication contained the *Data Preparation Manual: MARC Editors*, the *Transcription Manual: MARC Typists*, the *Subscriber's Guide to the MARC Distribution Service*, and *Computer and Magnetic Tape Unit Usability Study* (an analysis to determine which computers and peripheral devices could be used to process MARC tapes).

Because of hardware limitations and time and funding constraints, the new MARC system was designed as a batch tape system composed of four subsystems: input, file maintenance, retrieval, and output. The programs within each subsystem were generalized, data independent where possible, table driven where the characteristics of the data were known (i.e., validation of tags across forms of material), and parameterized to the extent possible to allow the specification of unique requirements (e.g., output formatting).

From the beginning of the design phase, LC staff recognized that the system would require updating to use disk as the storage medium and to provide for online correction. (In the LC environment, online input of new records is not desirable but there is a definite need for on-line correction and verification to reduce the volume of paper work and expedite the processing of records). In 1971, work was begun on the Multiple USE MARC System (MUMS) to provide on-line capability and on the redesign of the MARC input and maintenance system.

In accordance with the original plans to specify MARC formats for forms of material other than books, LC published formats for serials[8] and maps[9] in 1970, films[10] in 1971, and manuscripts[11] in 1973. The music and sound recordings format is in draft form at the time this is written and should be published in 1975.[12] In the design of all formats, LC worked with other organizations that had expert knowledge of the material concerned.

The distribution service has been expanded as funding permitted. Distribution of records for films began in 1972, and for serials, maps, and French-language monographs in 1973. The present services represent approximately 105,000 records per year. If the service is expanded to include books in other romance languages and in German late in 1974, the total record count will reach approximately 150,000 annually. As of summer 1974, the database totaled approximately 500,000 records. The present service is available in several forms. These include: 1) all MARC records; 2) books (All) covering records for English-language monographs including titles acquired through NPAC, titles in all languages in the Cataloging in Publication (CIP) Program, and French-language monographs; 3) books (English) as described in books (All) above, but excluding the French-language records; 4) films, covering motion pictures, filmstrips, transparencies, slide sets, and other projected materials, in all languages; 5) maps, covering records for single and multisheet thematic maps, map sets, and maps treated as serials, in roman-alphabet languages; and 6) serials, covering all serials receiving printed card cataloging, including romanized records for titles in nonroman alphabets. Records for books (English) and films can be purchased in annual cumulations. Test tapes for all services are available for experimental purposes.

In 1973, LC suggested to the Resources and Technical Services Division/Reference and Adult Services Division/Information Science and Automation Division (ALA RTSD/RASD/ISAD) Committee on Representation in Machine-Readable Form of Bibliographic Information (MARBI) that a MARC advisory committee be formed to work with LC regarding changes to the various MARC formats. The MARBI committee decided it would be the MARC advisory committee, and LC was asked to prepare a paper[13] proposing how such a committee would operate in relationship to the MARC Development Office (MDO). The LC proposals and recommendations were adopted by the MARBI committee during its meeting at the 1974 ALA midwinter meeting.

The term "change" includes additions, modifications and deletions of content data (in both fixed and variable fields), and content designators made to the format as well as additions, modifications, and deletions made to the tape labels. The changes under consideration fall into five categories: 1) changes resulting from a change in cataloging rules or systems, 2) changes made to satisfy a requirement of LC, 3) changes made to satisfy a subscriber's request, 4) changes to support international standardization, and 5) changes made to expand the MARC program to include additional services.

Guidelines have been established to handle the above categories of changes and a time period set for the MARBI committee, working through the MARC users, to react to a proposed change. LC agreed to notify MARC subscribers two months prior to including any change in the MARC Distribution Service.

LC plans to continue to expand MARC until all of LC cataloging (approximately 250,000 titles annually) is encompassed within the MARC system. (Since LC redistributes all changed records and, in addition, each CIP record is updated at least once to a full MARC record, the actual number of records distributed is significantly larger than the number of titles cataloged and included within the scope of MARC at any time.) In certain nonroman alphabets this extension may mean romanization. Equally as important as the bibliographic records is the availability of name and subject authority records. The procedures to input subject records and to maintain the files have been operational for some time. The design of similar procedures for name records, as well as distribution procedures for name and subject records, began in 1974, and it is hoped that in 1975 the library community will have these records for processing in their local systems.

Although the primary advantage of the distribution service is considered to be the cost savings resulting from centralized cataloging and from centralized editing and transcription of machine-readable records, another by-product of MARC is often overlooked. It is impossible to estimate the resources (people and time) saved by national and international organizations implementing automated systems through the use of MARC publications. The LC language and country codes and character sets have been widely adopted, and the various MARC editorial and transcription manuals adapted to local needs. Thus, through the efforts of a dedicated LC staff, significant cost savings have been effected throughout the world.

RETROSPECTIVE CONVERSION, 1968–

With the assurance of an ongoing MARC Distribution Service, libraries throughout the country began to discuss and, in some instances, to plan the conversion of their existing catalogs. Such uncoordinated conversion activities would result in costly duplication of titles in machine-readable form. Any future amalgamation of the multiple databases into a single unified national database would entail a formidable task of human editing to make the name and subject headings assigned by many libraries consistent with authorized forms.

Since LC was also interested in the conversion of its retrospective records, it appeared timely to investigate the feasibility of a large-scale centralized conversion of retrospective cataloging records and their distribution to the library community.

In 1968 a proposal was submitted to CLR for a feasibility study to be conducted by LC. Recognizing the far-reaching significance of a centralized conversion effort, CLR responded immediately by providing funds. The responsibility for the conduct of the study which was dubbed *Re*trospective *Con*version (RECON) was assigned to a working task force. An advisory committee composed of members of the library profession was appointed to provide guidance for the study. Both groups included representatives from LC as well as from other organizations.

A report[14] published in 1969 described the work performed during the feasibility study and stated the major conclusions reached and recommendations made by the task force. The task force examined in detail: 1) the hardware and software required for a large-scale conversion; 2) existing LC files to select the one most suitable for conversion; 3) the rationale for setting priorities for conversion, and how best to accomplish the job; and 4) the costs of hardware, software, and manpower for a conversion project.

As a result of its investigations, the task force arrived at the following conclusions:[14]

1. The MARC Distribution Service should be expanded to cover all languages and all forms of material as rapidly as resources and technology allow. There should be no conversion of any category of retrospective records until that category is being currently converted.
2. Conversion of some portion of retrospective records to machine-readable form should be an early goal for library automation efforts.
3. Conversion for a national bibliographic database requires standardization of bibliographic content and machine format. Standards for conversion of retrospective records should be the same as those for current records.
4. The highest priority for retrospective conversion should be given to records most likely to be useful to the largest number of libraries. As nearly as possible, subsequent priorities should be determined by the same criteria.
5. Large-scale conversion should be accomplished as a centralized project. Decentralized conversion would be more costly and unlikely to satisfy requirements for standardization. The project should be under the direction of the Library of Congress.

Based on these conclusions, the task force recommended that conversion should take place in reverse chronological order, by language, using the LC Card Division record set, which is arranged in sequence by date. Each record would be compared against the LC Official Catalog for updating purposes.

The order of conversion should be: 1) English-language monograph records issued from 1960 to date, 2) Romance- and German-language monograph records issued from 1960 (this conversion would not begin until MARC had been expanded to include these languages), and 3) English-language monograph records issued from 1898 to 1959. Every effort should be made to convert items 1) and 2) within four years.

An initial method of conversion was prescribed and it was proposed that further studies be initiated to determine: 1) the best means of obtaining standard records for items not represented in the LC Official Catalog to build a complete national bibliographic data store, and 2) the feasibility of establishing a national union catalog by recording holdings of libraries in the data store.

The task force further recommended that an implementation committee be established to investigate sources of funds for a detailed system design for a large-scale conversion effort and the initiation of a pilot project to test the proposed conversion system.

The implementation committee was never formed. However, LC took the initiative and proposals were submitted to CLR and the U.S. Office of Education (OE) to augment the resources committed by LC with additional funds required to support both a pilot project and the continuation of the activities of the working task force. Both CLR and OE responded positively and in August 1969 the RECON Pilot Project was initiated, with the additional funds designated for the studies by the task force and the travel expenses of both the task force and the advisory committee.

The pilot project conducted by LC covered five major areas:

1. Conversion techniques postulated in the RECON feasibility report were tested in an operational environment by converting English-language monographs cataloged in 1968 and 1969 but not included in the MARC Distribution Service. (Many of the 1968 titles were formerly distributed to the participants of the MARC Pilot Project in the MARC I format.)
2. Procedures and programs to implement format recognitioning were developed. (Format recognition is a technique for the automatic assignment of tags, indicators, subfield codes, and fixed fields to machine-readable bibliographic records.)

3. Problems associated with the conversion of records in other languages and cataloged according to other conventions and cataloging rules were analyzed for their effect on a conversion effort.
4. The state of the art of input devices for a large conversion effort was monitored. This included the testing of two devices in a production mode.
5. Microfilming techniques and their associated costs were studied to determine a best method for copying the sections of the LC Card Division record set. Microfilming was suggested because the record set is a "high use" file that cannot be withdrawn in whole or in part for any substantial period of time.

The pilot project continued for two years (August 1969–August 1971) and is fully documented in a report[15] published in 1972. The findings of the project are briefly summarized below.

1. Format recognition applied to unedited records is a practical computer technique, eliminating the need for human editing prior to keying. The costs for keying and proofing for format recognition remain approximately the same as for processing records fully edited by humans. However, applying format recognition in place of human editing does effect a cost reduction of approximately 12% in manpower costs.
2. The magnetic tape selectric typewriter, currently in use, was found to be as cost efficient as any other off-line device given the requirements for easy accommodation of variable length records and an expanded character set. Cathode ray tube terminals were also investigated for use in an on-line mode for corrections. Only one device was available with the expanded character set. The results of testing direct-read optical character readers (OCR) to convert LC cards to machine-readable form were negative; no device could perform adequately.
3. Filming all cards in a given series of the Card Division record set against a form and reproducing hard copy proved to be the most efficient method of producing source documents. The desired subset of records would then be selected for conversion.
4. Processing of older catalog records and those in foreign languages is more complex than processing current English-language records for books, and therefore conversion costs will be higher.
5. The lowest RECON unit cost that can be anticipated for a record processed by format recognition is approximately $3.06. (Projected costs were based on the MARC Pilot and Distribution Service experience because RECON was an experiment rather than a production effort. Time was expanded on testing devices, alternative methods, etc., and consequently there was no basis for determining accurate cost projections.)

Approximately 58,000 records were converted during the pilot project. The 1969 titles were distributed free of charge to MARC subscribers in 1971 and the 1968 titles were made available through sale.

The most significant technical achievement of the pilot project was the development and implementation of the format recognition process. Automatic identification of the data elements of machine-readable records had been tested in other organizations, namely the Institute of Library Research at the University of California, Berkeley, and the Bodleian Library, Oxford. However, LC was the first to attempt to assign the content designators (i.e., tags, indicators, and subfield codes) and the fixed fields for a full MARC II record by program. The cataloging source data are transcribed from left to right and from top to bottom. (The source document is either an LC-printed card or a MARC worksheet.) The data are input as fields, which are detected by the program because each field ends with a carriage return, and each field continuation is indicated by a carriage return and tab. The title paragraph is the only field where the program is given an additional clue in the form of a delimiter (a special character used to separate units of data) separating the title, edition, and imprint. The format recognition program searches first for the collation statement, which is easily located and always present. Once the collation statement is found and identified, the fields preceding and following collation are analyzed and identified separately using a variety of clues, such as first characters present and punctuation. The first pass of the program provides gross identification (in most instances only a partial tag is provided) and the remainder of the process is a reexamination of each field to provide final and complete tags, indicators, and subfield codes. After each variable field is fully identified, the data are scanned for information required to set the fixed fields. Tables of keywords consisting of items such as U.S. cities, foreign cities, geographical names, meetings, and honorary titles associated with personal names are used for matching purposes to aid in the identification of a variable field, or a data element within a field, as well as providing, in some instances, the information needed to fill in a fixed field.

Format recognition is currently used for the processing of English- and French-language monographs. Additional keyword lists will be built for other languages as the MARC service is expanded. The program has been operational since May 1971. RECON records were processed to test the technique in a production environment until January 1972. At that time, satisfied with the results, LC proceeded to use the technique for the processing of current MARC records.

Concurrent with the RECON Pilot Project, the task force considered certain basic issues of retrospective conversion that were of national scope. The studies, with conclusions and recommendations, were reported in a publication[16] in 1973. Underlying all the work performed was the reaffirmation of the importance of a coordinated retrospective conversion activity to keep duplication of effort to a minimum and to achieve a high degree of compatibility among records.

The special studies involved four areas that are described along with the findings of the task force.

1. There have been many attempts made and a great deal of effort expended to determine a subset (hereafter referred to as level) of the MARC format that would still allow a library using it to be part of any future national network. A level of a MARC record can be distinguished by differences in: 1) the data content of a record, and 2) the extent to which its contents are separately identified. Upon agreement as to the use to be made of machine-readable cataloging records, two or more parties can define a level of the MARC format to satisfy that use. The task force was concerned with the creation of machine-readable records for national use, i.e., either the recording of holdings to a national union catalog or the distribution of cataloging information in machine-readable form to library networks, systems, or individual institutions. The task force concluded that level of MARC records can be defined for each of these functions. Since the union catalog function is well defined, a level of less completeness than the full MARC could be determined. However, the record for the distribution function must satisfy the needs of diverse installations and applications and, consequently, must be the fullest MARC record.
2. A large pool of machine-readable bibliographic records exists. Since MARC is still limited in its coverage, there is the potential of using this pool of records to accelerate the building of a national database and to reduce the duplication of input with a resultant cost savings. The task force undertook to investigate representative machine-readable databases and to assess their potential for this purpose. The study indicated that the per record cost of converting non-MARC records to MARC, comparing them with the records in the LC Official Catalog (to ensure consistency and completeness), and updating their contents, approached the per record LC/MARC cost. However, if the record was similar to an LC/MARC record in terms of fullness of catalog entry, format, and character set, i.e., a high potential record, then comparing only its access points with the LC Official Catalog record and updating those access points when required, would result in a conversion cost estimated to be in the order of one-half of present LC/MARC conversion costs.
3. The National Union Catalog (NUC) serves two major functions: the provision of cataloging data and a finding list for the locating of a title. With the advent of LC/MARC and the proliferation of library automation projects, it was logical for the task force to consider the implications of a national union catalog in machine-readable form. On-line access to a national union catalog did not appear to be likely in the near future. Attention was consequently turned to the automatic production of the NUC in book form or microform. This mode of production would relieve humans of the drudgery of preparing the catalogs, make the information more rapidly available, and provide the facility for additional access points to the data. The task force selected the register/index as the optimum format for NUC. This type of catalog is composed of a register of complete bibliographic entries arranged in numeric sequence according to a number assigned to each entry when the register is prepared. The register is never cumulated. The indexes are derived from the register entry and contain a brief bibliographic entry and the register number. The indexes are cumulated at predetermined intervals. This format has the advantage of providing several points of access without having to print the full bibliographic record more than once. The task force concluded that the cost of the automated system with its associated advantages would not exceed the cost of the present manual system, and the cost of producing the quinquennial would be significantly reduced. In addition, the database might eventually form the basis for an on-line network of regional bibliographic centers.
4. Experience in the RECON Pilot Project indicated that a large-scale conversion project as projected in the RECON feasibility study demanded far more resources (staff, space, and funds) than there is hope of obtaining. To convert chronologically by language as recommended in the feasibility study, on a lesser scale, would be too slow to satisfy those libraries requiring machine-readable records for their automation efforts. Therefore, the task force examined alternative strategies, hoping to arrive at a means of more rapidly responding to the needs of libraries, but concluded that there was no perfect solution to the problem, since preferences for languages, dates, and forms of material are dependent on the type and size of library involved. Systematic conversion, i.e., orderly conversion by language and date, has the advantage of allowing the user to predict with reasonable certainty what is in machine-readable form. It has the disadvantage that users may wait for long periods of time before desired records may be available. Conversely, nonsystematic conversion (based on some criterion such as all records in a given bibliography) might have the advantage of more rapidly converting records desired by a larger number of organizations, but it would have the disadvantage that, without querying the database, the user cannot predict which titles are in machine-readable form.

The task force concluded that LC should concentrate on going forward as rapidly as possible to convert all of its current cataloging to machine-readable form and that an agency, established expressly for the purpose of a large-scale retrospective activity, should undertake to convert the retrospective LC records that are most in demand and be responsible for adapting records from libraries other than LC for inclusion in the national database. (Initially, these records might be those ordered from the LC Card Division most frequently.) The task force recommended that since the problem of retrospective conversion is of concern to all of the nation's libraries, the National Commission on Libraries and Information Science (NCLIS) might be the appropriate agency to determine a course of action and explore sources of funding to implement a national program.

To date, no central agency has been established nor has NCLIS taken any express action concerning retrospective conversion. LC, when resources permit, continues to convert retrospective titles selected from the Card Division as well as MARC Pilot records that were not converted during the RECON Pilot Project. (The MARC Editorial Division, responsible for the conversion of MARC records, is geared to peak load conditions. When the volume of records diminishes for any period of time, the gap is filled in by converting retrospective titles.) These records are distributed as part of the MARC service.

There is continuing interest in a centralized conversion activity. The concern of the participants in a series of meetings[17] sponsored by CLR is one manifestation of this interest. The purpose of these meetings is to seek a means of exchanging machine-readable records among organizations until such time as a national service may exist to perform this function centrally. The records under consideration are of two types: 1) records converted from LC cataloging copy not included in the MARC Distribution Service (i.e., either items cataloged prior to the MARC service for a particular language or form of material or records not yet within the scope of MARC), and 2) records representing titles not cataloged by LC. The emphasis here is placed on all records, both retrospective and prospective, being converted by organizations other than LC. As progress is made on the automation projects of individual institutions and as regional networks evolve, it is an accepted fact that institutions will be doing local conversion. The excessive cost of duplicate conversion that will result if machine-readable data are not shared, as well as the problems of an inconsistent data base, can only be resolved if a single organization assumes the responsibility and has the resources for building a national data base.

INFLUENCE OF MARC ON STANDARDIZATION

Libraries acknowledged the importance of standardization long before MARC came into being. Machine systems, however, showed the need for an extra measure of conformity over what had been apparent in the past. What appears in the printed record is human readable, not bit configurations representing characters or codes or explicitly identifying content data. Variations in the placement or the formatting of words, paragraphs, and numbers in the printed record are not too damaging to the initiated, but can be intolerable to efficient machine processing. The interest of libraries in the computer for library operations was increasing in the 1960s. The availability of cataloging data in machine-readable form supplied by LC, the need to input cataloging data locally (data not within the scope of MARC or titles not cataloged by LC), the possibility of sharing these locally generated records, the potential for using computer programs across organizations to reduce the high cost of designing and writing software, and the need for hardware capable of handling large character sets were all factors that put increased emphasis on the establishment of and conformity to standards.

The impetus given to standardization by LC/MARC is doubtless one of its most important results. The establishment of bibliographic standards did not happen chronologically but in many instances overlapped, i.e., the development of a new standard might begin while a proposed standard was in the process of adoption. Consequently, reporting of the standards cannot be made in strict chronological order.

Format for Information Interchange

During the operation of the MARC Pilot Project, BNB personnel visited LC to investigate the possibility of a UK/MARC Pilot Project. At a later date, when BNB decided to proceed with its MARC project, its staff worked with the MARC staff on the MARC II format in an effort to satisfy the requirements of both agencies. This cooperation had long-term effects. Both agencies recognized the future implications of an interchange format and the importance of two major publishing countries agreeing on a standard. No only would it be possible to exchange machine-readable records between the United States and the United Kingdom, but the way would be open for other countries to follow the lead and develop their own MARC projects. This possibility was particularly interesting to LC because of NPAC, where LC uses the descriptive cataloging as given by other countries in the program, adding or modifying main and added name entries, subject headings, etc., to the record as necessary. The entire process is a manual operation using printed records. The potential exists for updating machine-readable records from countries in the program and thus reducing the cost of conversion at LC.

Recognizing the worldwide impact of sharing machine-readable records, LC and BNB, in addition to being active in their respective national standards organizations, in

1969 submitted the then proposed American National Standards Institute (ANSI) format and its equivalent, the proposed British Standards Institute (BSI) format to the International Organization for Standardization (ISO). The MARC projects in the United States and Great Britain and the developing ANSI, BSI, and ISO standards created the environment for many countries (including Australia, Canada, Denmark, France, Germany, Italy, Japan, Latin America, Norway, and Sweden) to begin to plan for and implement their own national MARC system. (In addition to national libraries and bibliographies, many organizations based outside of the United States, such as UNISIST, the International Labor Organization, Information Services in Physics, Electrotechnology, Computers and Control, and the International Atomic Energy Agency, have adopted or recommended adoption of the format structure.)

The MARC format *structure*, as a vehicle for information interchange, was adopted in the United States by the three national libraries, ALA, ARL, the Committee on Scientific and Technical Information (COSATI), the Educational Resources Information Center (ERIC), the Association for Scientific Information Dissemination Centers (ASIDIC), and others. The format structure became an ANSI standard in 1971[18] and an international standard in 1973 [ISO 2709–1973 (E)].[19]

International Standard Bibliographic Description

In 1969 the International Federation of Library Associations (IFLA) convened an International Meeting of Cataloguing Experts. Since the Paris Principles had set the framework for an international cataloging code, it seemed appropriate to call an international meeting to discuss the next step, a standard bibliographic description. A working paper[20] prepared by Michael Gorman of the BNB, with the support of a United Nations Educational and Scientific Organization (UNESCO) grant, demonstrated the difference in the order of data and in punctuation patterns of various national bibliographies (NUC represented the United States bibliography). A working party was selected to draft an international standard bibliographic description for monographs. An international standard bibliographic description would provide a standard set of descriptive elements in a standard order using standard punctuation to separate the elements. Such a description would facilitate: 1) the comprehension of the description in printed form regardless of language, and 2) the automatic recognition of elements of the description for machine identification. The first published draft of the International Standard Bibliographic Description (ISBD) was issued in 1971, followed by the first standard edition in 1974.[21] [A recommended ISBD for serials was also published in 1974.[22]]

Content Designators

The ISBD for monographs, the ISO standard format structure for bibliographic interchange, Kaltwasser's paper[23] concerning universal bibliographic control, and the ever-increasing number of national MARC formats were all positive steps toward international cooperation. Problems remained, however. One of the significant areas of nonstandardization among national MARC formats was in the assignment of content designators to elements of information in the machine-readable records. Accordingly, IFLA established, under the auspices of the Committees on Cataloguing and Mechanization, an international Working Group on Content Designators. The Working Group held its first meeting in Grenoble, France, during the 1973 IFLA conference. Obstacles in the way of agreement on content designators include: 1) diverse functions of the bibliographic agencies, 2) lack of an internationally accepted cataloging code, 3) lack of agreement among different bibliographic communities on organization of data content in machine-readable records, and 4) lack of agreement as to the functions of content designators.

The Working Group realized that the issues concerning data organization and functions of content designators could be resolved (subsequently agreement on these points was reached in a meeting in Brussels in February 1974) but that the lack of an internationally accepted cataloging code and the dissimilarities in the functions of different bibliographic services were areas over which it had no control.

Encouraged by the fact that it has been possible to work around these differences in the formulation of the ISBD, the Working Group proceeded to adopt the concept of a SUPERMARC[24,25] as an international system for exchange, leaving the various national systems as they now exist. Each country would have an agency that would translate its own machine-readable records into the format of the SUPERMARC system; likewise, each agency would translate SUPERMARC records into its own national format.

The international machine-readable record was divided into functional blocks (e.g., intellectual responsibility block, descriptive block, subject block). There was unanimous agreement that the descriptive block would follow the ISBD, and it is this block where agreement on content designators and content is most likely possible.

It is recognized that the content and consequently the content designation of certain blocks is dependent on cataloging codes and practices. Therefore, the best that can be hoped for in the near term is agreement on content designation at a level of specificity less than that presently used by national systems. For example, the intellectual responsibility block contains names of persons and organizations associated with the work described. In national systems, each type of name may be further expanded to multiple levels of subtypes and subfields coded in a variety of ways. In the international record, the expansion may be limited to indicating personal, family, corporate, and conference names; and primary, alternate, and secondary responsibility.

The concept is a record composed of two principal parts: 1) the identification of the item (descriptive block modeled after the ISBD), and 2) all other elements making up the bibliographic record, e.g., headings, subjects, and classification numbers. This will allow the user to accept the descriptive block for inclusion in his system and provide the option of using or discarding the other elements of information.

Work on this international standard is still underway. It is hoped that agreement will be reached on a standard set of content designators by the IFLA meeting in 1975.

Other Activities

The expanded roman-alphabet character set designed by LC was adopted by ALA, has been used in information systems throughout the world, and is the basis for the current work in progress in ISO/TC46/SC4/WG1, Character Sets for Documentation and Bibliographic Use. The acceptance of a character set for bibliographic use, indicating marketability to hardware vendors, led to the manufacture of a typewriter sphere, a print train, and several cathode ray tube terminals.

Country of publication codes and language codes originally established by LC for the MARC Pilot Project and, based on experience, modified for the MARC Distribution Service have also been accepted as the codes for several systems. Although these codes have not been adopted as ANSI or ISO standards, they do have an impact on current standardization activities.

The challenge to the individuals involved in standards setting is great. Much remains to be accomplished. Progress has been made, however, and it appears that "International MARC" may become a reality.

MARC USERS

Use of MARC at the Library of Congress

The main thrust of LC's bibliographic automation program during the years 1966–1970 was the distribution of MARC data. In terms of LC, MARC up to 1974 covered approximately 40% of LC's total cataloging effort.

In 1970, sights began to turn inward, and MDO was established in the Processing Department to concentrate on automating the functions concerned with technical processing. (Before June 1970, staff responsible for MARC, RECON, etc., was part of the Information Systems Office (ISO), organizationally situated in the Office of the Librarian. At the same time that MDO was established, ISO was transferred to the Administrative Department.) An article describing the automation programs of the Processing Department was published in 1972.[26] The program can be considered to have a three-pronged approach: 1) expansion of the MARC Distribution Service, 2) design and implementation of a core bibliographic system,[†] and 3) products and services for LC and the library community. It is principally in item 3) that the MARC data base is used at LC at this time. Several of these projects are briefly described below.

Book Catalogs

1. The Main Reading Room catalog consists of records included in MARC (books and serials) and records input especially for the project. Catalogs have been produced, via computer printer, arranged by call number, author, title, and subject for use in LC. Plans include the general distribution of the catalogs in this form as well as photocomposed issues at a later date.
2. The Science Reading Room file is also composed of MARC records (books and serials) in addition to records input specifically for the project. Computer-printed catalogs have been produced for use in LC.
3. The catalog of *Films and Other Materials for Projection* for the last quarter of 1972 and the first two quarters of 1973 was produced from the MARC films database in 1974. This catalog is issued in two sections in one volume: 1) title main entries and added author entries, and 2) subject added entries. "See" and "see also" references are included.

All machine-produced book catalogs and other bibliographic listings are arranged by means of a program called Library Sort Key Edit (LIBSKED). This program was designed to implement the new LC filing rules[27] formulated by the Technical Processes Research Office of the Processing Department.

Printed Cards

MARC records are input to the Card Division's automated system to compose and print LC cards, complete with overprinted headings, for use in the LC catalogs. On-demand production of cards for film and map titles in response to orders from subscribing libraries or for cards that are out of stock is operational, but on-demand production for all orders (approximately 40,000 per day) for which there is a MARC record cannot be implemented until quantity limitations imposed by the present capabili-

[†]This includes automation of the Order Division functions and the Process Information File (PIF) which are presently in various stages of operation, implementation, and design. The Core Bibliographic System includes the use of LC name and subject authority records to produce book catalogs as well as linking them to MARC records as a cataloging aid. Several ongoing operational projects, such as the building and maintenance of the subject heading file, are modules of this activity.

ties of the offset press and accompanying cutting and collation equipment are resolved. Consequently typeset cards are still being prepared for MARC titles through the Government Printing Office.

MARC Retriever

The MARC database is being used more and more frequently in LC as a bibliographic reference to supplement the card catalogs. The machine-readable records provide access via fields not used as headings in the card catalogs, and the richness of the MARC format offers new possibilities for the retrieval of information.

The MARC Retriever was originally seen as a research tool to promote the use of the MARC data base in new and unexplored ways. This experimental mode is still of interest in LC but, in addition, the system is used operationally for many purposes in LC as well as to provide special searches to outside organizations. The Retriever allows the user to search the contents of any variable field, subfield, or fixed field, as well as any specific tag, indicator, or subfield code value.

Recent searches include: 1) monthly lists of books on Africa, Mainland China, Latin America, Eastern Europe; 2) books in translation; 3) children's books in translation; 4) serials in French published in France, Belgium, and Canada; 5) railroad maps; 6) maps of East Africa, Kenya, Tanzania, and Uganda; 7) CIP records in history, LC class schedules E and F; 8) Festschriften; 9) atlases published in 1972; and 10) books about Africa containing statistical information.

The records retrieved are arranged and printed according to the user's specifications. The sort may be on author, title, subject, classification, date, etc. Output may be printed in card or list form, with the amount of information displayed (short form or full record printout) a user option.

Other Uses in LC

The LC Division for the Blind and Physically Handicapped selects pertinent records from the MARC files for inclusion in its system for the production of bibliographic tools, e.g., printed cards and book catalogs for such items as talking and braille books.

As the scope of MARC expands and as the ongoing projects such as the automation of the PIF become operational, more and more use will be made of MARC at LC, both for technical processing and reference.

MARC is now searchable on-line by LC card number within LC. Access to the file will be expanded to include author/title and title only search keys. Preliminary catalogers will be able to search the MARC file as well as the PIF to determine whether the item in hand is already in the collection or requires cataloging; the Card Division will be able to search for titles for which printed cards were ordered but for which the LC card number was not given; and the Catalog Publication Division will be able to search for items reported by NUC libraries to ascertain if the reporting record is a title already covered by LC cataloging so that holdings can be posted to the proper record.

Plans include making the MARC file accessible by the Reference Department and expanding searching capabilities, as well as the eventual two-way linking between the authority records (name and subject) and each bibliographic record where the name or subject or both were used. This linking will enhance the present book catalog production system as well as provide the means to use the MARC files as a cataloging aid.

Use of MARC by Subscribers

At present (March 1974) there are 74 organizations subscribing to the MARC services. (The last MARC Survey was conducted in the spring of 1972 and the results published later in that year. The subscriber figures cited in this section have been updated to reflect the current situation.) The 74 subscribers purchase the following subscriptions:

MARC, Complete	13
MARC, Books (All)	28
MARC, Books (English)	19
MARC, Films	4
MARC, Serials	12
MARC, Maps	3

This list can be further subdivided within the category MARC, Complete. For example, there are 13 complete subscriptions and three map subscriptions, meaning that 16 map subscriptions are actually in force. Dividing the subscriptions in this manner results in the following:

Books, Foreign	41
Books, English	70
Films	17
Serials	25
Maps	16

Since an organization may order more than one type of service, the actual number of individual subscriptions as given above total 169. The subscribers are made up of 18 commercial enterprises, 23 organizations outside the United States (one of these has been previously counted with the commercial enterprises), and the remainder divided among large research, college and university, state, special, and national libraries and library centers. Institutions are difficult to identify accurately since any one institution may perform the functions of another type, e.g., a university library may act as a center, serving, in addition to itself, several other organizations. Therefore, it is not possible to derive an accurate tally of subscribers by type of library. The subscribers discussed above are considered primary users. All of the commercial vendors and library centers as well as some of the organizations in the other categories of users provide services to other institutions. These latter institutions are considered secondary users of MARC data and, according to LC's best estimates, total approximately 1500.

There are difficulties inherent in any presentation of MARC uses. This difficulty is in part created by the tendency of library functions to overlap. For example, the search/select function is not an end unto itself but instead may be a component of a system to print catalog cards or of an SDI system. There are also various levels of the use of MARC data, depending on the mix of manual and automated processing. MARC records are, in some cases, simply used as a source of bibliographic information with the rest of the processing purely manual, or MARC records become an integral part of an automated system. Some systems are wholly dependent on MARC; in others, MARC is some percentage of the total database. There are systems that are totally batch oriented, others are partially batch oriented and partially on-line, and still others operate principally in an on-line mode. These various differences in systems do not affect the function performed, e. g., looking up a title to find where it is located, regardless of how the system is designed or how the files are organized.

The following discussion of MARC uses attempts to avoid the problems described by addressing MARC uses in general terms and not probing into individual systems.

The majority of uses of MARC data fall into the technical processing area. This is not surprising, since before the reference function can be served adequately, items must be put under bibliographic control. Furthermore, it is in technical processing that the professional librarian needs to be relieved of performing repetitive tasks or supervising others in the performance of such tasks. However, the reference function is somewhat satisfied by SDI services, LC's MARC Retriever, and the searching of index files of author, title, and subject.

Current MARC tapes are used for selection purposes by printing out the records and routing them to persons responsible for selecting materials for acquisition, or by comparing the tapes against stored profiles and printing the records that match. Printed indexes are also prepared from the MARC files (weekly or cumulative) and made available for selection.

To the extent that MARC records are available for items to be ordered, manual bibliographic searching is eliminated, and the MARC records selected are used to produce the orders and associated documents and the records are added to the institution's in-process or master file.

MARC records are used in the production of catalog cards and book form catalogs. Book catalogs have appeared in dictionary form, register/index form, or as separate author, title, and subject catalogs (or any combination thereof). The level of sophistication of catalog production varies greatly. The production forms include computer line printing, photocomposition, and microform.

A bibliography in microform, called *Books in English*, is produced by merging BNB/MARC records with relevant LC/MARC records. A catalog of English-language acquisitions of a university library and affiliated institutions is also produced by selecting appropriate records from these two databases.

Shared cataloging systems with access to LC/MARC and locally input cataloging records by LC card number and/or search keys are also in operation. (The Ohio College Library Center is the most advanced system at this time providing this type of service.) Member libraries search the files for a specific record. If the record is in the file and if the cataloging data is acceptable to the institution, printed cards in the format and quantity desired by the institution are sorted (prearranged in a filing sequence) and prepared off-line for the selected record. If the record is not available, the member library inputs the locally cataloged record that then becomes available to all other participants and the printed cards are prepared from the locally input record. In some systems, records can also be output on tape for any library desiring its cataloging data in machine-readable form. The on-line posting of the locations of the requesting library and the use of this file for interlibrary loan is also in operation.

The production of catalog cards remains the most popular operation, although in many instances card production is not the raison d'être of the system. The production of book preparation materials (bookcards, pockets, and spine labels), as well as circulation cards, is a useful by-product of some systems.

In one system the MARC record is used as a bibliographic source, and agency subject terms, call numbers, etc., are added. The entire MARC file is maintained as a composite database, and a subset of the file relevant to the specialization of the organization is selected by such criteria as LC class numbers or subject headings, added to the records in the system not included in MARC, and both types made available on-line to participating libraries. A full free text search is provided with a modified Key-Word-in-Context (KWIC) display for titles, series names, conference names, corporate names, publishers' names, and subject headings. Additional on-line searching capabilities include other names, LC call numbers, LC card numbers, international standard book numbers, Dewey Decimal numbers, local library card numbers, and local library location indicators. This sophisticated searching capability is in addition to the production of several library products, e.g., current awareness listings and book catalogs.

CONCLUSION

MARC is an assemblage of formats, publications, procedures, people, standards, codes, programs, systems, equipment, etc., that has evolved over the years, stimulating the development of library automation and information networks.

Any discussion about MARC in particular involves discussing library automation in general. Progress in the field is evident. There is a definite advance from the automation of discrete functions toward the automation of modules leading to integrated systems. Emphasis is being placed on the implementation of on-line systems and the use of one system to provide services to many other organizations.

Library automation activities in 1974 appear to fall into the following categories:

1. Institutions are automating their technical processing functions and, as a by-product, providing services, e. g., cards and listings, to other organizations.
2. Institutions are automating a particular aspect of their service, e.g., book catalog production, and as a by-product their procedures and programs are used to produce a like product for another organization.
3. Institutions are creating automated systems designed principally as a bibliographic center to provide services, e.g., printed cards and union catalogs, for other organizations that do not intend to automate.

Libraries have passed through an era of much talk but few results into the 1970s where the automation of library operations is no longer a promise but a demonstrated success. Faced with economic realities, the availability of bibliographic information in machine-readable form and the possibility of sharing these resources through computer technology, there is an increasing awareness that standardization, nationally and internationally, is the sine qua non of the information system.

The benefits that accrue to a library and its clients from the establishment of and the conformity to standards are many. Products from different sources will mesh. Records from different libraries will be interchanged. Machine systems will be more easily developed and shared. Union catalogs will be possible without costly editing for consistency, thus facilitating interlibrary loan. Cost of local changes to catalog records will be minimized. It will be advantageous for vendors to manufacture hardware to handle the requirements of libraries. The process of ordering, cataloging, etc., will be more uniform. Therefore, less searching and bibliographic verification will be necessary and duplication of effort will be avoided. Networking will be facilitated. Various databases will be accessible through the use of standard protocol. Service to the user will be improved, and that is really what MARC is all about.

REFERENCES

1. King, G.W.; et al. *Automation and the Library of Congress; A Survey Sponsored by the Council on Library Resources, Inc.*; Library of Congress: Washington, DC, 1963.
2. Buckland, L.F. *The Recording of Library of Congress Bibliographical Data in Machine Form; A Report Prepared for the Council on Library Resources, Inc.*; Council on Library Resources: Washington, DC, 1965, rev.
3. Avram, H.D.; Freitag, R.S.; Guiles, K.D. *A Proposed Format for a Standardized Machine-Readable Catalog Record; A Preliminary Draft*; June 1965. Reprinted with Index and Appendix, Library of Congress, Washington, DC, 1971. (ISS Planning Memorandum Number 3).
4. Avram, H.D.; Knapp, J.F.; Rather, L.J. *The MARC II Format: A Communications Format for Bibliographic Data*; Information Systems Office, Library of Congress: Washington, DC, January 1968.
5. Avram, H.D. *The MARC Pilot Project: Final Report on a Project Sponsored by the Council on Library Resources, Inc.*; Library of Congress: Washington, DC, 1968.
6. Library of Congress, MARC Development Office *Books: A MARC Format; Specifications for Magnetic Tapes Containing Catalog Records for Books*, 5th Ed.; Library of Congress: Washington, DC, 1972. The 1st through the 3rd editions, 1968–1969, have the title: Subscribers' Guide to the MARC Distribution Service.
7. Library of Congress, Information Systems Office. *MARC Manuals Used by the Library of Congress*, 2nd Ed.; American Library Assoc.: Chicago, IL, 1970; 1 vol.
8. Library of Congress, MARC Development Office. *Serials: A MARC Format; Specifications for Magnetic Tapes Containing Catalog Records for Serials*, 2nd Ed.; 1974. Washington, D.C.
9. Library of Congress, Information Systems Office. *Maps: A MARC Format; Specifications for Magnetic Tapes Containing Catalog Records for Maps*; Library of Congress: Washington, DC, 1970.
10. Library of Congress, MARC Development Office. *Films: A MARC Format; Specifications for Magnetic Tapes Containing Catalog Records for Motion Pictures, Filmstrips, and Other Pictorial Media Intended for Projection*; Library of Congress: Washington, DC, 1970.
11. Library of Congress, MARC Development Office. *Manuscripts: A MARC Format; Specifications for Magnetic Tapes Containing Catalog Records for Single Manuscripts or Manuscript Collections*; 1973. Washington, DC.
12. Library of Congress, MARC Development Office. *Music: A MARC Format; Specifications for Magnetic Tapes Containing Catalog Records for Music Scores and Musical and Non-musical Sound Recordings*; May 1973, Draft.
13. Avram, H.D. The library of congress view on its relationship to the ALA MARC advisory committee. J. Libr. Autom. June **1974**, *7* (2), 119–125. Also published in Libr. Congr. Inf. Bull., 33(9), Appendix II, A60–A64 (March 1, 1974).
14. RECON Working Task Force *Conversion of Retrospective Catalog Records to Machine-Readable Form; A Study of the Feasibility of a National Bibliographic Service*; Library of Congress: Washington, DC, 1969; 10–11.

15. Avram, H.D. *RECON Pilot Project; Final Report on a Project Sponsored by the Library of Congress*; The Council on Library Resources, Inc., and the U.S. Dept. of Health, Education, and Welfare, Office of Education; Library of Congress: Washington, DC, 1972. Progress reports have appeared in J. Libr. Autom. June **1970** *3*(2), 102–114; September **1970** *3*(3), 230–251; March **1971** *4*(1), 38–51; and September **1971** *4*(3), 159–169.
16. RECON Working Task Force. *National Aspects of Creating and Using MARC/RECON Records*; Rather, J.C., Avram, H. D., Eds.; Library of Congress: Washington, DC, 1973. Chapter entitled "Levels of Machine-Readable Records" also appeared in J. Libr. Autom. June **1970** *3*(2), 122–127.
17. Avram, H.D. Sharing machine-readable bibliographic data: A progress report on a series of meetings sponsored by the Council on Library Resources, Inc. J. Libr. Autom. March **1974**, *7* (1), 57–60. Also published in Libr. Congr. Inf. Bull. January 11, **1974** *33*(2), Appendix II, A21–A23.
18. American National Standards Institute. *American National Standard Format for Bibliographic Information Interchange on Magnetic Tape*; 1971. New York (ANSI Z39.2–1971). Draft appeared in J. Libr. Autom. June **1969** *2*(2), 53–95.
19. International Organization for Standardization. *Documentation—Format for Bibliographic Information Interchange on Magnetic Tape*; ISO 2709–1973 (E).
20. Gorman, M. *Bibliographical Data in National Bibliography Entries; A Report on Descriptive Cataloging Made for UNESCO and IFLA*; Provisional Abridged Text.
21. International Federation of Library Associations *ISBD(M) International Standard Bibliographic Description for Monographic Publications*, 1st Ed.; IFLA Committee on Cataloguing: London, U.K., 1974.
22. International Federation of Library Associations. *ISBD(S) International Standard Bibliographic Description for Serials, Recommended by the Joint Working Group on the International Standard Bibliographic Description for Serials Set up by the IFLA Committee on Cataloguing and the IFLA Committee on Serial Publications*; IFLA Committee on Cataloguing: London, U.K., 1974.
23. Kaltwasser, F.G. The quest for universal bibliographical control. UNESCO Bull. Libr. September/October **1971**, *25* (5), 252–259.
24. Coward, R.E. In *MARC: National and International Cooperation*. The Exchange of Bibliographic Data and the MARC Format, International Seminar on the MARC Format and the Exchange of Bibliographic Data in Machine Readable Form, Berlin, 1971; Verlag Dokumentation: München-Pullach, Berlin, Germany, 1972; 17–23.
25. Duchesne, R.M. In *MARC and SUPERMARC*. The Exchange of Bibliographic Data and the MARC Format, International Seminar on the MARC Format and the Exchange of Bibliographic Data in Machine Readable Form, Berlin, 1971; Verlag Dokumentation: München-Pullach, Berlin, Germany, 1972; 37–56.
26. Avram, H.D.; Maruyama, L.S.; Rather, J.C. Automation activities in the Processing Department of the Library of Congress. Libr. Resour. Tech. Serv. **1972**, *16* (2), 195–239.
27. Rather, J.C. Filing arrangement in the Library of Congress catalogs. Libr. Resour. Tech. Serv. **1972**, *16* (2), 240–261.

BIBLIOGRAPHY

Compiledby Josephine S. Pulsifer, MARC Development Office, Library of Congress.

Background, 1961–1965

1. Avram, H.D. The philosophy behind the proposed format for a library of congress machine-readable record. In *Institute on Information Storage and Retrieval*; 2nd Ed.; University of Minnesota, 1965.
2. Avram, H.D. The philosophy behind the proposed format for a library of congress machine-readable record. In *Information Retrieval with Special Reference to the Biomedical Sciences*; 1966; 155–174. Minneapolis.
3. Avram, H.D.; Guiles, K.D.; Meade, G.T. Fields of information on Library of Congress catalog cards: Analysis of a random sample, 1950–1964. Libr. Q. **1967**, *37* (2), 180–192.
4. Curram, A.T.; Avram, H.D. *The Identification of Data Elements in Bibliographic Records: Final Report of the Special Project on Data Elements for the Subcommittee on Machine Input Records (SC–2) of the Sectional Committee on Library Work and Documentation (Z39) of the United States of America Standards Institute (USASI)*; 1967. Needham, MA, 1 vol. (various pagings).
5. Reimers, P.R.; Avram, H.D. Automation and the Library of Congress: 1970. Datamation June **1970**, *16* (6), 138–143.

MARC Pilot Project, 1966–1968

1. Avram, H.D. MARC is a four-letter word: A report on the first year and a half of LC's machine-readable cataloging pilot project. Libr. J. **1968**, *93* (13), 2602–2605.
2. Avram, H.D. The MARC project at the Library of Congress. Drexel Libr. Q. **1968**, *4* (4), 279–309.
3. Avram, H.D. Implications of Project MARC. In *Library Automation: A State of the Art Review*; Salmon, S.R., Ed.; American Library Association: Chicago, IL, 1969; 79–89.
4. Avram, H.D.; Droz, J.R. MARC II and COBOL. J. Libr. Autom. **1968**, *1* (4), 261–272.
5. Avram, H.D.; Markuson, B.E. In *Library Automation and Project MARC: An Experiment in the Distribution of Machine-Readable Cataloging Data*. Brasenose Conference on the Automation of Libraries: Oxford, England, 1966, Proceedings of the Anglo-American Conference on the Mechanization of Library Services, Harrison, J., Laslett, P., Eds.; Mansell: London, U.K., 1967; 97–127.
6. Avram, H.D.; Leach, T.E.; Knapp, J.F.; Rather, L.J.; Simmons, P.A.; Parker, P.E. Project MARC reports. Libr. Resour. Tech. Serv. **1968**, *12* (3), 245–319.

MARC Distribution Service, 1968–

1. Ayres, F.H. The case against MARC: How strong is it? Libr. Assoc. Rec. July **1971**, *73*(7)130–131, 142.

2. Carrington, D.K.; Mangan, E.U. *Data Preparation Manual for the Conversion of Map Cataloging Records to Machine-Readable Form*; Library of Congress: Washington, DC, 1971.
3. Library of Congress, MARC Development Office, *Information on the MARC System*, 4th Ed.; Library of Congress: Washington, DC, 1974.
4. Library of Congress, MARC Development Office, *Serials Data Preparation Manual: MARC Editors*, 2nd Ed.; April 1974.
5. Library of Congress, MARC Development Office, *Serials Editing Guide: MARC Editors*, 2nd Ed.; April 1974.
6. Maruyama, L.S.; Avram, H.D. Cataloging and the computer. Fontis Artis Musicae September/December **1972**, *19* (3), 164–171.
7. Pulsifer, J.S.; Woods, E.W. The MARC serials distribution service. Libr. Congr. Inf. Bull. April 12, **1974**, *33* (15), A81–A84. Appendix.

Retrospective Conversion, 1968–

1. Butler, B. Automatic format recognition of MARC bibliographic elements: A review and projection. J. Libr. Autom. **1974**, *7* (1), 27–42.
2. De Gennaro, R. A national bibliographic data base in machine-readable form: Progress and prospects. Libr. Trends **1970**, *18* (4), 537–550.
3. French, T. Conversion of library card catalogues. Program **1971**, *5* (2), 41–66.
4. Irvine, R. A note on the conversion of existing catalogue records to MARC format. Program **1973**, *7* (2), 96–100.
5. Jeffreys, A.E. *The Conversion of the Catalogue into Machine Readable Form*; Oriel Press: Newcastle upon Tyne, England, 1972. Published for University of Newcastle upon Tyne, University Computing Laboratory and University Library.
6. Library of Congress, Information Systems Office, *Format Recognition Process for MARC Records: A Logical Design*; American Library Association: Chicago, IL, 1970.
7. Maruyama, L.S. Format recognition: A report of a project at the Library of Congress. J. Am. Soc. Inf. Sci. **1971**, *22* (4), 283–287.
8. Port, I. Developing a strategy for retrospective conversion of the card catalog to a machine readable data base in three academic libraries (small, medium, and large): Two alternatives considered. Inf. Storage Retr. **1973**, *9* (5), 267–280.
9. Shoffner, R.M. Some implications of automatic recognition of bibliographic elements. J. Am. Soc. Inf. Sci. **1971**, *22* (4), 275–282.

Influence of MARC on Standardization

1. Anderson, D. International developments in cataloging. Libr. Resour. Tech. Serv. **1973**, *17* (2), 134–143.
2. Anderson, D. International standardization of cataloguing and bibliographical records: The work of the IFLA committee on cataloguing. UNESCO Bull. Libr. **1973**, *27* (2), 66–71.
3. Avram, H.D.; Guiles, K.D. Content designators for machine-readable records: A working paper. J. Libr. Autom. **1972**, *5* (4), 207–216.
4. Avram, H.D.; Pulsifer, J.S. In *Bibliographic Services for a National Network*. Proceedings, Conference on Interlibrary Communications and Information Networks, Airlie House, Warrenton, VA, September 28–October 2, 1970; American Library Association: Chicago, IL, 1971; 92–100.
5. Avram, H.D.; Rather, L.J. Principles of format design. J. Libr. Autom. **1974**, *7*(3).
6. *Bibliografia Nazionale Italiana, Nuova Serie del Bollettino delle Pubblicazioni Italiane Ricevute per Diritto di Stampa*; 1972. Supplementi 3, Firenze, 93.
7. Chauveinc, M. MONOCLE. J. Libr. Autom. **1971**, *4* (3), 113–128.
8. Chauveinc, M. *MONOCLE: Projet de Mise en Ordinateur d'une Notice Catalographique de Livre*, 2nd Ed.; Bibliotheque Interuniversitaire: Grenoble, France, 1972.
9. Coward, R.E. MARC international. J. Libr. Autom. **1969**, *2* (4), 181–186.
10. de Bruin, H. MARC: A review. S. Afr. Libr. **1973**, *40* (4), 214–229.
11. Duchesne, R.M. MARC et SUPERMARC. Bull. Bibl. Fr. **1972**, *17* (4), 153–172.
12. Gorman, M. *Description of the BNB/MARC Record; A Manual of Practice (with the Assistance of John E. Linford)*; Council of the British National Bibliography: London, U.K., 1971.
13. Gorman, M. *Standard Bibliographic Description (for Single Volume and Multi-Volume Monographs) Part 2: The Standard*; 1971. Prepared for the International Meeting of Cataloguing Experts Working Party on the Standard Bibliographic Description.
14. In *The Exchange of Bibliographic Data and the MARC Format*. International Seminar on the MARC Format and the Exchange of Bibliographic Data in Machine Readable Form, Berlin, 1971; Verlag Dokumentation: München-Pullach, Berlin, Germany, 1972.
15. Kilgour, F.G. In *Standardization for Interchange of Cataloging Records—MARC II*. Proceedings, International Congress of Medical Librarianship, 3rd, Amsterdam, May, 5–9, 1969.
16. Livingston, L.G. International standard bibliographic description for serials. Libr. Resour. Tech. Serv. **1973**, *17* (3), 293–298.
17. Livingston, L.G. National bibliographic control: A challenge. Libr. Congr. Inf. Bull. June 21, **1974**, *33* (25), A108–A113. Appendix III.
18. Maltese, D. *Razionalizzazione e Automazione della Biblioteca Nazionale Centrale di Firenze*; Biblioteca Nazionale Centrale: Firenze, 1970.
19. *MARC II Specifications*; Council of the British National Bibliography, 1969.
20. Maruyama, S. Māku II Fōmatto; Subscriber's Guide Yōyaku MARC II Format: A Synopsis of the Subscriber's Guide). In *Toshokan/Gyōmu Kikaika Jumbishitsu*; National Diet Library: Tokyo, 1969.
21. National Library of Australia, *Australian MARC Specifications*; 1973. Canberra.
22. National Library of Canada, *Canadian MARC: A Report of the Activities of the MARC Task Group Resulting in a*

Recommended Canadian MARC Format for Monographs and a Canadian Format for Serials; 1972. Ottawa.

23. National Library of Canada, Research and Planning Branch, Canadian MARC Office, *Canadian MARC Communications Format: Monographs*; 1973. Ottawa, 1 vol.
24. Spaulding, C.S. ISBD: Its origin, rationale, and implications. Libr. J. January 15 **1973**, *98* (2), 121–123.

MARC Users

1. Atherton, P.; Tessier, J. Teaching with MARC tapes. J. Libr. Autom. **1970**, *3* (1), 24–35.
2. Austin, D. An information retrieval language for MARC. Aslib Proc. **1970**, *22* (10), 481–491.
3. Avram, H.D.; et al. MARC program research and development. J. Libr. Autom. **1969**, *2* (4), 242–265.
4. Ayres, F.H. Making the most of MARC: Its use for selection, acquisitions and cataloging. Program **1969**, *3* (1), 30–37.
5. Bierman, K.J.; Blue, B.J. Processing of MARC tapes for cooperative use. J. Libr. Autom. **1970**, *3* (1), 36–64.
6. Bierman, K.J.; Blue, B.J. A MARC based SDI service. J. Libr. Autom. **1970**, *3* (4), 304–319.
7. Buckle, D.G.R.; The Birmingham Libraries' co-operative mechanisation project; Progress report, January 1972–June 1973. Program **1973**, *7* (4), 196–204.
8. Buhr, L.R. Selective dissemination of MARC: A user evaluation. J. Libr. Autom. **1972**, *5* (1), 39–50.
9. Burgis, G.C. A MARC user's seminar. Can. Libr. J. **1970**, *27* (3), 227–229.
10. Burgis, G.C.; Buchinski, E. In *MARC at the University of Saskatchewan. Automation in Libraries; Papers Presented at the C.A.C.U.L. Workshop on Library Automation in a Pre-Conference of CLA*, Hamilton, June, 20–21, 1970; Canadian Association of College and University Libraries: Ottawa, 1970; 62–120.
11. *Business and Economics Book Guide*, Swanson, G.L., Ed. Computext Book Guide Series; Hall: Boston, MA. Issued monthly with annual cumulations.
12. Clinic on Library Applications of Data Processing: MARC Uses and Users, 1970. In *Proceedings*; Henderson, K.L., Ed.; University of Illinois, Graduate School of Library Science: Urbana, 1971.
13. *Conference Publications Guide*; Swanson, G.L., Ed.; Computext Book Guide Series; Hall: Boston. Issued monthly with annual cumulations.
14. Corbett, L.; German, J.A. AMCOS project stage 2; A computer aided integrated system using BNB MARC literature tapes. Program **1972**, *6* (1), 1–35.
15. Corbett, L.; German, J. MARC II based mechanised cataloguing and ordering system offered as a package by AWRE. Program **1970**, *4* (2), 64–67.
16. Dieneman, W. MARC tapes in Trinity College Library. Program **1970**, *4* (2), 70–75.
17. Driver, E.H.C.; et al. The Birmingham Libraries' cooperative mechanisation project; Progress report, June 1970–January 1972. April **1972**, *2* (2), 120–126.
18. Duchesne, R.M.; Donbroski, L. BNB/Brighton public libraries catalogue project—'BRIMARC'. Program **1973**, *7* (4), 205–224.
19. Epstein, A.H.; et al. *Bibliographic Automation of Large Library Operations Using a Time-Sharing System: Phase II, Part 1 (July 1970–June 1972), Final Report*; Stanford University Libraries: Stanford, CA, February 1972.
20. Epstein, A.H.; Veaner, A.B. *A User's View of BALLOTS*; BALLOTS Project, Stanford University: Stanford, CA, June 1972. An earlier version was published in Clinic on Library Applications of Data Processing, Proceedings, 1972.
21. Epstein, H. BALLOTS-MARC Operations at Stanford University. Libr. Congr. Inf. Bull. **1973**, *32* (15), 130–131.
22. Fasana, P.J. *Utilization of MARC Data in the Columbia University Automated Technical Services System*; Columbia University Libraries, Systems Office: New York, November 1970.
23. Gibson, L. BIBCON—A general purpose software system for MARC-based book catalog production. J. Libr. Autom. December **1973**, *6* (4), 237–256.
24. Goldstein, S.; et al. *Development of a Machine Form Union Catalog for the New England Library Information Network (NELINET), Final Report*; New England Board of Higher Education: Wellesley, MA, September 1970.
25. Gorsch, A.N. The Minnesota union list of serials. J. Libr. Autom. **1973**, *6* (3), 167–181.
26. *Government Publications Guide*, Swanson, G.L., Ed.; Computext Book Guide Series; Hall: Boston. Issued monthly with annual cumulations.
27. Heilik, J. Information retrieval and MARC at the National Science Library. Can. Libr. J. **1971**, *28* (2), 120–123.
28. Hennepin County Library, *Multi-Media Catalog*; Technical Services Division: Edina, MN. Issued in a main edition with cumulative supplements.
29. Hopkins, J. The Ohio College Library Center. Libr. Resour. Tech. Serv. **1973**, *17* (3), 308–319.
30. Humphreys, K.W. The utilization of the MARC project in libraries outside the United States and Canada. Libri **1970**, *20* (1,2), 133–134.
31. IDC introduces BIBNET on-line services. J. Libr. Autom. **1974**, *7* (2), 147–148.
32. Kennedy, J.P. File size and the cost of processing MARC records. J. Libr. Autom. **1971**, *4* (1), 1–12.
33. Kilgour, F.G.; et al. The shared cataloging system of the Ohio College Library Center. J. Libr. Autom. **1972**, *5* (3), 157–183.
34. Kniesner, D.L.; Meyer, B.J. On-line computer techniques in shared cataloging. Libr. Resour. Tech. Serv. **1973**, *17* (2), 225–230.
35. *Law Book Guide*; Berelson, P.P., Ed.; Computext Book Guide Series; Hall: Boston. Issued monthly with annual cumulations.
36. Library of Congress. *Library of Congress Catalogs: Films and Other Materials for Projection*; 1974. Combined Issue October 1972–June 1973, Washington, DC.
37. Library of Congress. *Main Reading Room Reference Collection, Subject Catalog*; MARC Development Office and General Reference and Bibliography Division Cooperation: Washington, DC, February 1974.

38. Library of Congress. MARC Development Office, *MARC User Survey, 1972*; Library of Congress: Washington, DC, 1972.
39. Livingston, L. A composite effort to build an on-line national serials data base. J. Libr. Autom. **1974**, *7* (1), 60–64.
40. Lodder, N.M.; Fokker, D.W. An investigation into the possible application of MARC records in South African libraries. S. Afr. Libr. **1973**, *40* (4), 206–213.
41. Logan, T.; Epstein, A.H.; Davison, W. *A User's View of BALLOTS, No. 2, The IPF Module*; BALLOTS Propect, Stanford University Libraries: Stanford, CA, June 1973.
42. Malinconico, S.M.; Rizzolo, J.A. The New York Public Library automated book catalog subsystem. J. Libr. Autom. **1973**, *6* (1), 3–36.
43. Martin, D.H. MARC tape as a selection tool in the medical library. Spec. Libr. **1970**, *61* (4), 190–193.
44. *MASS: MARC-Based Automated Serials System*; Birmingham Libraries Co-operative Mechanisation Project and Loughborough University of Technology Library, December 1960.
45. Massil, S.W. Music in an automated cataloguing system using MARC. Brio **1973**, *10* (1), 1–4.
46. Mauerhoff, G.R. Science-oriented and MARC II tape services. Spec. Libr. **1973**, *64* (3), 135–140.
47. Mauerhoff, G.R.; Smith, R.G. A MARC II-based program for retrieval and dissemination. J. Libr. Autom. **1971**, *4* (3), 141–158.
48. McCabe, C.E. In *Computer Applications in the Library of Congress Science and Technology Division*. American Society for Information Science, Proceedings of the 32nd Annual Meeting, San Francisco, CA, October 1–4, 1969; Greenwood: Westport, CT, 1969; Vol. 6, 63–67.
49. Swanson, G.L., Ed. *Medical Book Guide*; Computext Book Guide Series, Hall: Boston. Issued monthly with annual cumulations.
50. New England Library Information Network. *Demonstration of Cataloging Support Services and MARC II Conversion*; January 2 1969. Prepared by Lawrence F. Buckland, Ann T. Curran, [and] William R. Nugent, Submitted to the New England Board of Higher Education, Final Report, 31.
51. New England Library Information Network. *Computer Programming and Pilot Operation of MARC II Cataloging Support Services*; December 31, 1969. Prepared by Lawrence F. Buckland [and others], Submitted to the New England Board of Higher Education, Final Report, 125.
52. New England Library Information Network. *Transferability of the Ohio College Library Center Computer System to the New England Library Information Network. Final Report, Part 2: A Dynaprobe Validated SCERT Simulation Report to the New England Board of Higher Education*; COMRESS, Inc.: Wellesley, MA, June 1, 1972.
53. New England Library Information Network. *Transferability of the Ohio College Library Center Computer System to the New England Library Information Network. Final Report, Part 1: Introduction, Participants, Events, and Summary*; January 1973. Submitted to the Council on Library Resources by the New England Board of Higher Education, Wellesley, Massachusetts.
54. New York Public Library, Research Libraries. *Dictionary Catalog of the Research Libraries; A Cumulative List of Authors, Titles, and Subjects Representing Books and Book-Like Materials Added to the Collections Since January 1, 1971*; New York Public Library: New York, 1972–.
55. Nixon, R.; Bell, R. The U.C.L.A. Library catalog supplement. Libr. Resour. Tech. Serv. **1973**, *17* (1), 28–31.
56. Ohmes, F.; Jones, J.F. The other half of cataloging. Libr. Resour. Tech. Serv. **1973**, *17* (3), 320–329.
57. Parr, T. Library automation at the New York Public Library and the Association of New York Libraries for Technical Services. LARC Reports **1970**, *3*(3).
58. Payne, C.T.; McGee, R.S. Comparisons of LC proofslips and MARC tape arrival dates at the University of Chicago Library. J. Libr. Autom. **1970**, *3* (2), 115–121.
59. Rather, J.C.; Pennington, J.G. The MARC sort program. J. Libr. Autom. **1969**, *2* (3), 125–138.
60. Ristow, W.W.; Carrington, D.K. Machine-readable map cataloging in the Library of Congress. Spec. Libr. **1971**, *62* (9), 343–352.
61. Roberts, E.G.; Kennedy, J.P. The Georgia Tech Library's microfiche catalog. J. Microgr. **1973**, *6* (6), 245–251.
62. In *Seminar on the U.K. MARC Project, University of Southampton, 1969, In* U.K. MARC Projects: Proceedings of the Seminar on the U.K. MARC Project Organized by the Cataloguing and Indexing Group of the Library Association at the University of Southampton, March 28–30, 1969; Jeffreys, A.E., Wilson, F.D., Eds.; Oriel Press: Newcastle upon Tyne, England, 1970.
63. Southwestern Library Interstate Cooperative Endeavor. *First Annual Report of the Southwestern Library Interstate Cooperative Endeavor (SLICE) Project of the Southwestern Library Association, Covering the Period October 1, 1971 to December 31, 1972 and Final Report for Council on Library Resources Grant No. 529*; December 27, 1972. 1 vol.
64. Swanson, G.L. *Selected Statistics on LC MARC Bibliographic Records; Cumulated Statistics for Vol. 1, Nos. 1–54, March 1969–March 1970*; Columbia University Libraries, Systems Office: New York, September 1970.
65. Swanson, G.L. *Selected Statistics on LC MARC Bibliographic Records; Cumulated Statistics for Vol. 2, Nos. 1–13, April 1970–June 1970*; Columbia University Libraries, Systems Office: New York, October 1970.
66. *Technology Book Guide*; Swanson, G.L., Ed.; Computext Book Guide Series, Hall: Boston. Issued monthly with annual cumulations.
67. Wainwright, J.M. BNB MARC users in the U.K.: A survey. Program **1972**, *6* (4), 271–285.
68. *Washington Library Network Resource Directory*; Washington State Library: Olympia, July 1972–August 1973, 5 vols., Issued in four parts: Register, Authors, Titles, Subjects.

Machine Readable Cataloging (MARC): 1975–2007

Sally H. McCallum
Network Development and MARC Standards Office, Library of Congress, Washington, District of Columbia, U.S.A.

Abstract

This entry describes the development of the MARC Communications format. After a brief overview of the initial 10 years it describes the succeeding phases of development up to the present. This takes the reader through the expansion of the format for all types of bibliographic data and for a multiple character scripts. At the same time a large business community was developing that offered products based on the format to the library community. The introduction of the Internet in the 1990s and the Web technology brought new opportunities and challenges and the format was adapted to this new environment. There has been a great deal of international adoption of the format that has continued into the 2000s. More recently new syntaxes for MARC 21 and models are being explored.

The Machine Readable Cataloging (MARC) format, developed in the late 1960s as an electronic carrier of traditional library cataloging data, became the cornerstone for the transformation of library catalogs from card to computer and for a new era of shared cataloging, union catalogs, and integrated systems in libraries. Today it is used around the world, with new users still joining its data exchange environment, even as the basic structure of the format is being brought forward into new models.

This entry sets the context with a short review of the initial development of MARC, highlighting its innovative design and advanced character set developments. The period of expansion of the format, of character sets, and of implementation options and systems are described. With the 1990s, the Internet, Web, and Unicode presented new challenges for the format's user community with many process changes. The convergence on MARC 21 internationally is described followed by recent developments in syntax variation and modeling. A more detailed history of the format is found in McCallum.[1]

MARC DEVELOPMENT PERIOD

In the early 1960s, libraries in North America and in Europe began to experiment with the application of the computer to library processes. This was at the beginning of the computer explosion which was fueled by the introduction in 1964 of the IBM 360—the machine that brought computers out of the universities and research labs and into the business world. It was an environment of large mainframe machines. It was before the personal computer, and even before common deployment of cathode ray tube terminals and networking of installations. For more detail on the MARC 21 development period see Henriette D. Avram's classic article "Machine-Readable Cataloging (MARC) 1961–1974" reprinted in this edition of the *Encyclopedia of Library and Information Sciences*. It contains an excellent detailed description of the format development process from the 1960s through the early 1970s and an extensive bibliography. The following section is only a brief overview of that period, which provides the context for later developments described in this entry.

MARC Pilot Project

Following several investigations of the potential uses of computers in libraries,[2,3] the MARC project was launched by the Library of Congress in January 1966 with a focus on getting cataloging data that had been typed onto cards for decades, into computers from which multiple forms of access could be provided. The project had to work with several unique characteristics of bibliographic data. One involved lengths. In the 1960s fixed length data formats were standard, yet bibliographic data elements could very considerably in length. Titles alone could be one character to hundreds of characters long; descriptions that might be detailed or brief created great variation in the content size of records; and files of records could be quite large, requiring records for descriptions of millions of items in larger libraries. In addition, flexibility was needed as records were often updated and different subsets of the data in the record were used for different applications that the records had to support—circulation, finding, requesting materials from stacks, acquisitions. At a more microlevel, was the need to accommodate data in many languages, including some transliterated from non-Latin scripts, and that required several special alphabetic characters and many diacritics that were not in the standard Latin alphabet ASCII character set. ASCII is a basic Latin alphabet set. It contains 94 graphic characters including upper and lower case Latin alphabet letters A–Z, numbers 0–9, common punctuation marks, and a few symbols. It

Encyclopedia of Library and Information Sciences, Fourth Edition DOI: 10.1081/E-ELIS4-120044392

was first approved as an American National Standard in 1968.[4]

The MARC pilot project was carried out from 1966–1968, led at the Library of Congress by an early computer expert Henriette D. Avram, who had been a programmer at the National Security Agency where computers were essentially developed in the 1950s. The pilot involved 16 libraries of various types—universities, research institutes, and public. The focus of the pilot was to develop a format for the bibliographic record that would enable the distribution of cataloging data in machine-readable form via magnetic tape from the Library of Congress to libraries across the country.[5] By the end of the pilot, the structure and basic data tagging for an initial MARC format were drafted and testing had begun.[6–8] Within a few years as networks and terminals became viable, several of these early pilot participants and institutions became important figures in advancing library automation using the standard MARC record, including Yale's Frederick Kilgour who moved to Ohio and founded the OCLC bibliographic network, and the Universities of Toronto, Washington, and Columbia that led the founding of the UTLAS, WLN, and RLG networks, respectively. The OCLC was originally named the Ohio College Library Center, but as it became national in the 1980s and global in 1999, changed its name to Online Computer Library Center; RLG was the Research Libraries Group that grew out of a consortium of Harvard, Yale, Columbia University and New York Public Library and was merged with OCLC in 2006; WLN was originally the Washington Library Network in Washington state, which became the Western Library Network as it expanded and was finally absorbed into OCLC in the late 1990s; and UTLAS was originally the University of Toronto Library Automation System, which was purchased in the 1990s by Auto Graphics Canada. Not only was cataloging shared through these networks but large union catalogs were built from the cataloging activities that supported growing national and international interlibrary loan programs.

MARC Character Encoding

The MARC pilot project also spearheaded development of an extended Latin alphabet character set to be used to supplement the standard ASCII characters for MARC data.[9] The set was characterized by its content model that encoded diacritics separately from the base character that they modified, depending on display devices to position the diacritics correctly. Precomposed characters were not feasible for library data since the combinations that occurred in large libraries's multilingual data were both extensive and not always predictable. The Library of Congress worked with the computer industry on devices for displaying and printing the extra characters and diacritics correctly, with mixed success, since most computer devices only handled precomposed alphabetic character and diacritic combinations. The extended Latin character set eventually became an ANSI standard: *Extended Latin Alphabet Coded Character Set for Bibliographic Use* (ANSEL) (ANSI Z39.47).[10]

MARC Features

Briefly, the MARC format structure is composed of a short introductory fixed length (36 byte) segment, called the Leader; followed by a Directory giving the tag, length, and starting character position of each of the record's data content fields; followed by the data content fields themselves. The innovative features of the MARC format structure that supported the characteristics of the MARC record indicated above were the following.

The information in the Leader made the format self-defining. It included the record's length, which meant a record was not constrained to fixed lengths as was common at the time. If record content was brief, the record was brief, thus the size of the total file was no larger than necessary. The Directory was a "table of contents" and avenue into the record that enabled variable length data content fields within the record—a title field for a one character title was only one character long. It allowed easy addition or deletion of fields, and it enabled rapid access to fields needing update or to subsets of fields needed for a specific application.

The data content fields were identified by tags in the Directory and are further defined by two positions at the beginning of each, called indicators, and by subdivision of the data into specifically identified subfields within a field. The tagged fields, indicators, and subfield structures enable the format to be responsive to the need in library applications to carry and identify highly parsed, structured data, show relationships among data, and even assist with sorting. Fields and subfields easily accommodate the many different data elements needed to describe special aspects of diverse types of resources (Fig. 1).

The innovative structure for the MARC record became first an American standard, *Information Interchange Format* (ANSI Z39.2)[11] in 1971, and then an international standard, *Format for Information Exchange* (ISO 2709)[12] in 1973.

The MARC format was developed as an exchange format, without the expectation that it would also serve as an internal format for systems serving end users. Exchange has essentially been its use over the years, but with some qualifications. The way data elements are parsed is important to preserve when passing data to an internal format, so that the parsing can be reconstructed when the data needs to be transformed into MARC again for communication to another system. Therefore internal systems have tended to retain some aspects of the record since data is transferred so frequently. The MARC content designation (tags, subfields, indicators, coded data) also became vocabularies that catalogers learned across the library community,

00669cam##2200217#a#45000010013000000003000400013
005001700017008004100034020001800075040001300093
050002500106082001500131**100**003500146**245**005200181
250001200233**260**004300245300002100288650002600309
655002500335856009100360%##2005044790%DLC%200610
10093126.0%051102s2006####nyu###########000#1#en
g##%##$a9780805080339%##$aDLC$cDLC%00$aPS3615.B4
6$bD74 2006%00$a813/.6$222%**1#$aOberbeck, Elizabe**
th Birkelund.%14$aThe dressmaker /$cElizabeth Bi
rkelund Oberbeck.%##$a1st ed.%##$aNew York :$bHe
**nry Holt and Co.,$c2006.**%##$a306 p. ;$c22 cm.%#0
$aDressmakers$vFiction.%#7$aLove stories.$2gsafd
%42$3Publisher description$uhttp://www.loc.gov/c
atdir/enhancements/fy0624/2005044790-d.html%@

Fig. 1 Record for the book *The dressmaker* by Elizabeth Birkelund Oberbeck, published in New York by Henry Holt, and Co. in 2006. The record has a link (via a URL) to a description of the book supplied by the publisher. Complete MARC 21 record (author, title, edition, and publisher part in bold): (Graphic substitutions: # for blank; $ for subfield identifier; % for end of field character; @ for end of record character).

becoming a *lingua franca* for the discussion of record components. The metadata-rich MARC record contains data to support indexing and other functions, in addition to end-user displays, thus the communications record continued in the terminal and personal computer eras to be important for interchange between systems.

MARC FORMAT FAMILY AND SYSTEM DEVELOPMENT

After the initial implementation period of the 1960s and early 1970s the MARC format underwent dramatic development and up-take in the late 1970s and early 1980s. The advances in the technology for online systems and access were the catalyst. By 1975, roughly 60% of the records produced annually by the Library of Congress were available as MARC records, with the number increasing rapidly as format requirements for new forms of material were implemented.

Family of Formats

By the mid-1970s the MARC Bibliographic format[13] was a suite of coordinated specifications for not just books but also serials, maps, films, music, sound recordings, and manuscripts. The next advance was development of a format for records for the standardized forms of names and for subject thesauri that appear in bibliographic records, the MARC Authority format.[14] Then in the early 1980s, there was interest in integrating holdings and other data into library catalogs. Thus the MARC Holdings,[15] MARC Classification,[16] and MARC Community Information[17] formats were developed by special interest groups. The Holdings format contains sufficient detail to indicate to a user the volumes and issues of a serial held by an institution and to support serial check-in systems that needed to predict expected issues and generate claims for serial issues that are overdue from the publisher. It is a companion to the bibliographic format, and in fact was developed according to a model that allows the holdings data to be contained in separate holdings records or embedded in bibliographic records. The Classification format supports the online transmission and use of common classification schedule files, including the Library of Congress Classification and the Dewey Decimal Classification. The most unusual format was the one for community information data, which allows a library to integrate information about public events and community services into a bibliographic database. It was used in public library settings but Web sites have largely replaced it for that original purpose.

With the auxiliary formats completed, a review of the Bibliographic formats for the various forms of material took place in the late 1980s, when the Bibliographic format had just reached 20 years of use. While the core data elements of each bibliographic type, such as names, titles, and publishers had been kept consistent across the Bibliographic formats, they also contained many data elements that were "form of material specific." After extensive discussion with the user community, the Bibliographic formats were integrated into one, eliminating earlier designations of field validity by type of material. This new freedom and flexibility enabled the format to be more readily responsive to changes in resource media and technology, especially for accommodating the description of electronic and modern multimedia material. At the same time some simplification of the format was attempted, although the main counter to any simplification was and is the persistent need to parse and structure bibliographic data in order to support complex and diverse retrieval options for systems and, ultimately, end users. Libraries serve a varied clientele and while a majority of their end users may not have complex needs, librarians provide services to both the generalists and specialists.[18]

Record Use and System Developments

In the 1970s, with a known data standard and a critical mass of bibliographic records in that standard, libraries first experimented with producing focused automated systems that took the records and used them, for example, for card printing, circulation control, book catalog printing, book preparation (binding labels, book pockets, etc.), or current purchase awareness lists. The bibliographic networks mentioned above, OCLC, RLG, WLN, and UTLAS, were established to facilitate record sharing and build union catalogs that they used to support automated interlibrary loan. The Library of Congress achieved a distribution service for all of its cataloging records and its related subject and name authority files in MARC format, while also developing an internal online catalog. By 1980, several other libraries had developed online catalogs and during the 1980s, the local system development that started in the previous decade led to widespread availability of vendor software for library processing and online catalogs.

The success of a few vendors of bibliographic systems attracted more development, until the marketplace offered large and small systems with a variety of differences and special features—and a broad price range. The MARC communications format provided a record rich with data that system engineers used for innovative applications, retrieval programs, and user interfaces, but it did not dictate internal system design. MARC data within a system will usually be carried in an internal format or configuration that is efficient for the system hardware or platform, but highly compatible with the communications format. Inevitable transitions from a locally developed system to a vendor system or from one vendor system to another would take place over the next decades in libraries, but this migration has been eased by the standard data format all systems could export and import.

As more libraries obtained online catalogs, interest turned to retrospective conversion of older bibliographic data. Libraries wanted to consolidate all holdings in a single online catalog and retire their card catalog. Thus many retrospective conversion projects were undertaken in the 1980s resulting in an explosion of records in the automated bibliographic "universe," and in particular, in union catalogs like OCLC and RLG. Even the Library of Congress undertook the conversion of its retrospective file of over 5 million records, a project that had been explored by the Avram team beginning as early as 1968.[19] While early conversion of the Library of Congress's very large catalog could have been valuable to later conversion projects of the nation's libraries, the bibliographic networks contributed greatly to reducing the cost of later conversions by making the records converted by one library available to other libraries.

Character Set Expansion

In the 1980s, MARC also went beyond the initial Latin character sets when one of the major networks, RLG, developed a MARC-based bibliographic system that allowed input and search of data utilizing standard character sets for Arabic, Cyrillic, Chinese, Greek, Hebrew, Japanese, and Korean scripts (with over 16,000 characters in the Chinese, Japanese, and Korean set).[20,21] The RLG staff did ground breaking work on the Chinese, Japanese, and Korean set—work that predated Unicode by over 10 years, and in turn contributed to the eventual development and refinement of the present day global Unicode set.[22] Extending script capabilities in MARC was followed by the development of non-Latin capability in OCLC and several vendor systems.

INTRODUCTION OF THE INTERNET AND WEB

Since 1990 the technology has made enormous advances that both open new uses for the MARC record data and are pushing MARC into new directions. By 1990, the personal computer (rather than a "dumb" terminal) was well established, as was the development of the infrastructure for the Internet for the United States, supported by the National Science Foundation. Libraries had been using proprietary networks to build and exchange MARC records for two decades but now there was a much easier environment for sharing. Computer specialists rapidly explored the new possibilities by developing protocols that produced Web technology, which took aggressive advantage of the Internet. There were two immediate challenges at first for MARC, one was establishing new exchange patterns that enabled and enhanced the flow of records between systems. The other was the adaptation of the record to accommodate the new forms of materials such as electronic publications and Web sites.

New Interchange Options

One new interchange pattern was the widespread implementation of a search and retrieval protocol, called ISO 23950: "Information Retrieval (Z39.50): Application Service Definition and Protocol Specification."[23] This is a machine-to-machine protocol developed by the library community and originally standardized in the United States as ANSI/NISO Z39.50,[24] then later becoming an ISO standard. It enabled local systems to retrieve records in the MARC communications format from remote sites in response to normal local system searches—records that could be formatted for the local system's end-user displays or immediately used in a variety of ways including incorporation into a MARC-based online catalog. This was a significant improvement over day or longer delays for a download of a MARC record from a bibliographic network. While Z39.50 is still used extensively around the world because of its widespread implementation, the new technologies since 2000 have spawned a simpler, more streamlined version of that protocol, called SRU, *Search/Retrieve via URL*.[25] The SRU has many of the same characteristics of Z39.50 but uses an XML syntax structure.

The new interchange options also meant that in the 1990s, batch distribution of MARC records via physical media such as tape almost completely disappeared. The replacement was the batch electronic transfer protocol FTP (File Transfer Protocol). This simple protocol continues to be heavily used in 2008 for transfer of MARC records. Another simple download protocol with slightly more flexibility became an option in the early 2000s, the Open Archive Initiative's Protocol for Metadata Harvesting (OAI-PMH).[26] This protocol again enables easy exchange of full communications format records, and is used with MARC in its XML forms described below.

Electronic Resources

For the second challenge in the Internet era, the adaptation of the MARC record to accommodate the description of new forms of material such as electronic publications and Web sites, the format has had to address several major issues, the most prominent being the need to provide Internet linking to actual resources from the bibliographic record that described the resource. In 1993, even before the now-common Uniform Resource Locator (URL) addressing scheme was completely defined, a field in the MARC format was detailed to contain pathway components for accessing digital resources from a MARC record. That field eventually became the container for the resource's URL. For several years this linking field was adjusted at least annually as the Internet and Web environment matured and became more standards-based. Partly due to the distrust for the persistence of the URL, the community was cautious about adding the URL subfields to other fields. It was clearly important, however, to begin to link out for information that would expand on or supplement that in the MARC record. Thus a subfield for a URL was added to Bibliographic format fields such as the ones for contents notes, summary notes, citations to Archival Finding Aids, citations to additional forms of items, and bibliographical or historical data notes, among others, and the URL linking subfield continues to be added to other relevant fields as uses are identified. The modern MARC-based catalog is thus able to retrieve material comprehensively, integrating access to descriptions for both physical and electronic resources. For electronic material, it can bring to the end user the resources themselves and related resources from a variety of locations.

Other changes to the MARC format as more electronic material required bibliographic description have been addition and adjustment of coded data for the various electronic formats to assist retrieval, additional data for preservation aspects of digital and digitized material, and the addition of copyright status information to assist with issues when digitizing analog material. Partly to accommodate Web resources, the concept of the serial was redefined resulting in the addition of "integrating" resources as a basic form in the MARC record and date types for creation and modification.

Unicode

In the 1990s, the question of using Unicode (which became the ISO standard ISO 10646, *Universal Multi-Octet Coded Character Set (UCS)*[27]) rather than the original MARC character sets (Latin characters and seven other scripts as described above and commonly referred to as "MARC-8"). The MARC-8 contained over 16,000 characters but the Unicode set that emerged from the computer industry in the 1990s had a global goal to accommodate all scripts and today contains over 100,000 characters. The MARC community therefore elected to cease development of additional scripts for the MARC-8 set and start working toward the implementation of Unicode with MARC. The first step was to map all of the MARC-8 characters to Unicode so that institutions would eventually be able to convert their data. Then rules and conventions for using Unicode in a MARC exchange record were established, such as the use of Unicode's UTF-8 encoding, definition of character counts, and the marking of a record as Unicode encoded. Unicode specifies three encoding forms of which UTF-8 (UCS Transformation Format 8) is one. Unicode characters in UTF-8 can be represented in a single octet or a sequence of two, three, or four octets, depending on the character's code point. The UTF-8 encoding for Unicode was selected for use with MARC 21 records because the characters in the ASCII repertoire part have UTF-8 encoding identical to ASCII encoding. The UTF-8 is also used in many other applications outside the library community for the same compatibility with ASCII. Finally the community turned its attention to enabling use of all Unicode characters yet still preserving interchange with those using only MARC-8. Thus in 2007 two techniques for conversion of full Unicode records to MARC-8 records were established, one that drops unknown Unicode characters when moving data from Unicode to MARC-8, and another that preserves a reference to the characters that do not exist in MARC-8 so that reconversion or suitable substitutions can be made. The development of these techniques was assisted by modern Internet communications that allowed MARC users from around the globe to participate in the discussion. By 2008, systems were implementing Unicode rapidly and cataloging agencies were beginning to look past the scripts supported by MARC-8 to additional scripts such as those found in Southeast Asia and the Indian subcontinent.

INTERNATIONALIZATION

While ISO 2709 provided a fundamental standard for the structure of the MARC format, its flexibility with respect to tagging allowed its use with differently defined sets of data tags as needed according to other data models. For example, ISO 2709 only specifies tags as three character numeric, but does not designate the semantics of any tag number. Therefore a number of similar but different national MARC formats were designed and implemented around the world in the 1970s and 1980s, primarily on a national basis, such as CAN/MARC in Canada, UKMARC from the British National Bibliography, IberMARC from Spain, SWEMARC from Sweden, and FINMARC from Finland, to name a few. Some of these formats were very similar to MARC 21 but adapted data fields to suit their national cataloging norms. All of these formats used ISO 2709 for their structure, choosing the same options within the standard that MARC 21 had used, but they often defined different tags for the data fields and different parsing of the data into subfields.

Some of the questions and issues that either united or divided developers of the emerging MARC formats and created this diversity were the following. Fields chosen and subfields defined might vary depending on the purpose of the tagging—for indexing, for special processing, for display or print, for sorting, even for ISBD punctuation. The *library* functions of the record also influenced content designation; functions such as acquisitions and circulation had special needs. The cataloging rules used by an institution could require different heading structures, for example, or special notes, and the subject heading and classification systems used could have specific parsing requirements. Different organizations used different data models for bibliographic data, preferring, for example, to chain together parts of a total description, creating linked dependent records, rather than putting the parts together in one record, creating independent records as with MARC 21. Attempts were made during this period to bring the different MARC formats together with umbrella formats like the IFLA UNIMARC Format[28] and the UNESCO Common Communications Format[29] that could be used as bridges for international exchange but that model was more suitable to batch environments which began to disappear rapidly in the 1990s with the Internet advances in communications.

Convergence

Several factors encouraged the harmonization of these various national formats.[30] One was the movement to vendor rather than locally developed systems that came about in the 1980s and 1990s. As vendors began to saturate the home markets they started looking for external markets, becoming international companies. The different formats in each country hampered this internationalization, and vendors often responded by limiting format offerings, with MARC 21 being the most prevalent format supported, or charging institutions extra for retooling a system for a different format. This extensive use of MARC 21 occurred partially because a number of the system vendors originated in the United States that used MARC 21 as the national format, or, if the vendor came from another country, it wanted to introduce its system into a MARC 21 market, such as the United States market. The large numbers of libraries, strong standards orientation, common language, and the availability of Library of Congress cataloging in MARC 21 since 1969 made the United States an especially fertile vendor market and country for vendor development. The large networks such as OCLC were another major influence on MARC standardization. In the 1990s, there were several of these large networks in the United States, all MARC 21-based, and they provided services to other countries. With the consolidation of several of these into OCLC, the impetus to use MARC 21 was strengthened.

In the 1990s, the decision by South Africa and Canada to move from national formats to using MARC 21, if appropriate harmonization changes could take place, was an important event. In the case of South Africa, which had used a UNIMARC-like format for almost two decades, a careful cost–benefit study recommended a shift to MARC 21 in order to be able to take advantage of MARC 21-based records and systems and to be able to join international cooperative cataloging programs. For Canada, the Canadian and the United States formats were so similar that it was hard to justify their differences. That harmonization led to the establishment of the name MARC 21 for what was before USMARC and CAN/MARC.

A number of countries have adopted MARC 21 or changed to it from national formats over the last decades; for example, Poland, Switzerland, and Brazil adopted MARC 21, and Australia changed to it from AUSMARC and Sweden from SWEMARC. Since 2000, harmonization processes have taken place between MARC 21 and the British UKMARC and German MAB formats bringing a significant body of users to a common format. International interest in MARC 21 has led to the development of a number of translations of the format, especially of the concise version. The Bibliographic format has been translated into a diverse number of languages, including Arabic, Catalan, Czech, Finnish, French, German, Hungarian, Italian, Korean, Norwegian, Persian, Portuguese, Russian, Serbian, Spanish, and Swedish.

Maintenance

Maintenance of the MARC 21 format was traditionally centered at the Library of Congress, as the agency that led its development. This is still the case but the format changes are in response to the input from the whole community of users. Today any user may submit a proposal for change that is then processed and posted on the MARC 21 Web site[31] for review, and various groups hold discussions and forward their recommendations. The primary review body has become one established under the auspices of the American Library Association, MAchine-Readable Bibliographic Information (MARBI), whose meetings also include representatives from multiple user constituencies, such as several national libraries that use MARC 21, the other United States national libraries, representatives from special material associations and committees, such as music and maps, and representatives from record and system vendor communities. The discussion and votes at these twice-yearly MARC advisory committee meetings and from the Internet provide guidance for the Library of Congress, Library and Archives Canada, and the British Library to make final decisions on changes.

OTHER RECENT DEVELOPMENTS

The MARC 21 format is still being adopted in various countries and by institutions around the world. However, explorations are taking place to leverage the data elements of MARC and the millions of MARC records in the bibliographic universe to new platforms. Current efforts revolve around syntax flexibility, data modeling, and element retagging.[32]

Syntax

An additional development in the 1990s has been the attempt to separate the MARC data elements from the MARC structure (ISO 2709) to enable representations of the highly developed MARC data elements in other syntaxes. The development of the Internet and the Web technology in the early 1990's rapidly increased the real-time interaction of people, institutions, and applications in the computer environment. Computer specialists thus became much more interested in universal data markup standards that have the possibility to be read, understood, and displayed by any computer system. Initially this took the form of markup for display, epitomized by HTML (HyperText Markup Language), which is an implementation of a more generalized structure standard, Standard Generalized Markup Language (SGML).[33] The SGML is a structure with rules for tagging data, roughly comparable to ISO 2709. The SGML, while somewhat complex, seemed to have traction in the computer community by the mid-1990s. The Library of Congress thus convened a small group of MARC experts and SGML experts to investigate using the SGML markup structure as an alternative to ISO 2709 with the MARC data elements. At that time several attempts had already been made to define MARC in SGML so those experiences were a component of the discussion.

The ISO 2709 structure of the MARC record was innovative and forward looking—and carefully adapted to the characteristics of bibliographic data—but it was not adopted outside the library community and is not a suitable markup for full text of documents, such as books. ISO 2709 was optimized for records composed of many shorter variable length data elements to which random access is desirable, whereas SGML initially targeted full text markup, focusing on sequential access to data.

Following guidelines specified by this experts group, the Library of Congress had two MARC in SGML formats written, one that combined the elements from the MARC Bibliographic, Holdings and Community Information formats and another the elements from the Authorities and Classification MARC formats. These SGML formats, called Document Type Definitions (DTD) in the SGML environment, took the approach of including context in the name of each element, which resulted in both long names and a large number of elements—thus very large DTDs. While the DTDs had some significant advantages over the ISO 2709 formats, such as the validation attributes that could be built into the DTD enabling machine-driven "self-validation" of records, by the time experimentation began to take place the computing environment had developed a simpler derivative of SGML, called eXtensible Markup Language (XML).[34] The original MARC SGML DTDs were converted into XML DTDs later. Besides being simpler, XML could also be specified as an "XML schema" in addition to a DTD. While XML schemas do not have the validation attributes of the DTD, they are themselves written in XML which has other processing advantages. XML has achieved broad adoption by the Web and the computing environments, which means many generalized tools that manipulate XML data are available.

Based on the experience with MARC in SGML and several other models for MARC in XML that took a streamlined approach producing a very brief XML schema, the Library of Congress prepared an XML schema for MARC in 2003 that the community has found very useful and timely.[35] This schema, called MARCXML, enables MARC data to be easily translated into an XML structure for manipulation or for exchange using interchange protocols that either require or prefer to carry XML structured data (Fig. 2). For example, the SRU search protocol prefers XML and the OAI-PMH record distribution protocol requires it.

```
<datafield tag="100" ind1="1" ind2=" ">
    <subfield code="a">Oberbeck, Elizabeth Birkelund.</subfield>
</datafield>
<datafield tag="245" ind1="1" ind2="4">
    <subfield code="a">The dressmaker /</subfield>
    <subfield code="c">Elizabeth Birkelund Oberbeck.</subfield>
</datafield>
<datafield tag="250" ind1=" " ind2=" ">
    <subfield code="a">1st ed.</subfield>
</datafield>
<datafield tag="260" ind1=" " ind2=" ">
    <subfield code="a">New York :</subfield>
    <subfield code="b">Henry Holt and Co.,</subfield>
    <subfield code="c">2006.</subfield>
</datafield>
```

Fig. 2 Bold segment of the MARC 21 record in Fig. 1 with MARCXML syntax (author, title, edition, and publisher part only).

A pathway into XML appears not to be single threaded, but the library community will be able to use the new structures for MARC where applicable along with the classic structure until there is a clear way forward. The prior convergence of MARC formats to MARC 21 in the classic structure will be highly useful as MARC evolves into new structures.

While these structures are still under development and adoption, another technique for markup, called RDF (Resource Description Framework) is also being explored. The RDF makes it possible to mix XML data elements from different schemas in one "package," a flexibility that could prove useful to libraries as they interact with the broader cultural community.

Modeling

There has been a strong focus on more rigorous information modeling over the last decade. A conceptual model for bibliographic data was completed by the International Federation of Library Associations and Institutions in 1997 and published as the *Functional Requirements for Bibliographic Records* (FRBR).[36] At a simplified level, FRBR defines a four tier hierarchy for elements of document description—*work* (the most general), *expression*, *manifestation*, and *item*—and identifies the entities and relationships that are appropriate for each. Over the decades, the bibliographic universe has devised various methods to bring together for the library patron different editions, performances, versions in different media, etc., anticipating that the patron is often seeking a work, not necessarily a particular version or manifestation of a work. The FRBR analysis thus supports new approaches for presenting bibliographic search results to users that bring materials of potential interest together, making them easier for the user to peruse. The Library of Congress commissioned a mapping of all the MARC 21 data elements onto the FRBR model, *Functional Analysis of the MARC 21 Bibliographic and Holdings Formats*[37] in order to enable experimentation. This was followed by explorations by various organizations of presenting bibliographic search results in a FRBR form from MARC records.[38]

While the MARC 21 record can accommodate data brought together following a number of models, the record content model that is used almost universally is the unit record that in FRBR terms describes a manifestation. In a unit record, a bibliographic resource is fully described in one record and, while there may be references and linkages to other resources or entities described in other records, a fully understandable presentation can be made from the unit record since the names and titles of related entities are also contained in it. Many internal files hold the MARC-based record data in unit form but others take a more relational approach internally. The focus on the unit record by MARC 21 users also relates to the multiple uses of the bibliographic record. Union databases attach holdings to specific manifestations of a work, and catalogers need to be able to carry out copy cataloging for specific manifestations. Given the advantages to the end user of some aspects of the FRBR model and the expectation that it may be fundamental to newer cataloging rules, investigations will continue to assure that systems are able to use and share FRBR-based entity-relationship analysis.

Related Developments

MARCXML brings some advantages of the XML environment to MARC 21 but leaves the MARC data elements somewhat bound by the same constraints that MARC data now have in the MARC 2709 environment after many years of constant adjustment and augmentation. The MARCXML simply changes the structure, not the fields, indicators, subfields, and coded values of MARC 21. Therefore a next logical step is to remodel and retag the MARC data and explorations have taken place in that area also. In 2003, the Library of Congress introduced for public review the Metadata Object Description Schema (MODS),[39] an XML schema that is much simpler than MARC and repackages some of the MARC data that had become scattered in MARC 21 because of its development over time.[40] MODS has a strong affinity to MARC 21, however, so that for most records little is lost in the transformation from MARCXML to MODS (Fig. 3). The MODS is more oriented toward XML data models so it is especially useful for the descriptive metadata component of "wrapper" formats that bundle together the descriptive

```
<titleInfo>
      <nonSort>The</nonSort><title>dressmaker</title>
</titleInfo>
<name type="personal">
      <namePart>Oberbeck, Elizabeth Birkelund.</namePart>
      <role><roleTerm>creator</roleTerm></role>
</name>
<originInfo>
      <place><placeTerm type="text">New York</placeTerm></place>
      <publisher>Henry Holt and Co.</publisher>
      <dateIssued>2006</dateIssued>
      <edition>1st ed.</edition>
</originInfo>
```

Fig. 3 Bold segment of the MARC 21 record in Fig. 1 with MODS syntax (author, title, edition and publisher part only).

metadata, technical and administrative metadata, and the actual digital resources themselves, such as the Metadata Encoding and Transmission Standard (METS).[41]

SUMMING UP

MARC has achieved worldwide use as a format for the exchange of bibliographic data, and thus served as a facilitator of global library cooperation. It was a key component in the library environment to standardize in order to stimulate, rather than stifle, innovations in the systems for end users and record sharing networks. Today its innovative structure, while still serving in most venues, is beginning to transform into new data structures that take better advantage of the newer Web technologies. Already MARC is available in XML forms and additional syntaxes will be offered for MARC data. However, the enormous body of MARC 21 records and MARC-21-based systems will assure that format interchangeability will remain an important component of new environments.

REFERENCES

1. McCallum, S.H. MARC: Keystone for library automation. IEEE Ann. Hist. Comput. **2002**, *24* (2), 34–49.
2. Licklider, J.C.R. *Libraries of the Future*; MIT Press: Cambridge, MA, 1965.
3. King, G.W. *Automation and the Library of Congress; a Survey Sponsored by the Council on Library Resources, Inc.*; Library of Congress: Washington, DC, 1963.
4. American National Standards Institute *American Standard Code for Information Interchange (ASCII)*; ANSI X3.4; ANSI: New York, 1986.
5. Buckland, L.F. *The Recording of Library of Congress Bibliographical Data in Machine Form; A Report Prepared for the Council on Library Resources, Inc.*; Council on Library Resources: Washington, DC, 1965.
6. Avram, H.D. *The MARC Pilot Project, Final Report*; Library of Congress: Washington, DC, 1968.
7. Avram, H.D.; Knapp, J.F.; Rather, L.J. *The MARC II Format: A Communications Format for Bibliographic Data*; Library of Congress: Washington, DC, January 1968; 167.
8. Avram, H.D. Implications of project MARC. In *Library Automation: A State of the Art Review*, Papers presented at the Preconference Institute on Library Automation held at, San Francisco, CA, June, 22–24, 1967. American Library Association: Chicago, IL, 1969.
9. Rather, L.J. Special characters and diacritical marks used in Roman alphabets. Libr. Resour. Tech. Serv. **1968**, *12* (3), 285–295.
10. American National Standards Institute, *Extended Latin Alphabet Coded Character Set for Bibliographic Use (ANSEL)*; ANSI Z39.47; ANSI: New York, 1998.
11. American National Standards Institute, *Information Interchange Format*; ANSI/NISO Z39.2; ANSI: New York, first published in 1971. http://www.niso.org/standards/index.html (accessed February 2008).
12. International Organization for Standardization *Documentation, Format for Information Interchange*, ISO 2709; ISO: Geneva, first published in 1973.
13. Library of Congress *MARC 21 Format for Bibliographic Data*; 1999 edition and updates, looseleaf; Network Development and MARC Standards Office, Library of Congress: Washington, DC. http://www.loc.gov/marc/bibliographic/ (accessed February 2009).
14. Library of Congress, *MARC 21 Format for Authority Data*; 2000 edition and updates, looseleaf; Network Development and MARC Standards Office, Library of Congress: Washington, DC. http://www.loc.gov/marc/bibliographic/ (accessed February 2009).
15. Library of Congress. *MARC 21 Format for Holdings Data*; 2000 edition and updates, looseleaf; Network Development and MARC Standards Office, Library of Congress: Washington, DC. http://www.loc.gov/marc/holdings/ (accessed February 2009).
16. Library of Congress. *MARC 21 Format for Classification Data*; 2000 edition and updates, looseleaf; Network Development and MARC Standards Office, Library of Congress: Washington, DC. http://www.loc.gov/marc/classification/ (accessed February 2009).
17. Library of Congress. *MARC 21 Format for Community Information Data*; 2000 edition and updates, looseleaf; Network Development and MARC Standards Office, Library of Congress: Washington, DC. http://www.loc.gov/marc/community/ (accessed February 2009).
18. *Format Integration and its Effects on Cataloging, Training, and Systems*; American Library Association: Chicago, IL, 1993.
19. *Recon Pilot Project; Final Report*; Library of Congress: Washington, DC, 1972.
20. Aliprand, J. NonRoman scripts in the bibliographic environment. Inform. Technol. Libr. **1992**, *11* (2), 105–119.
21. Aliprand, J. Linkage in USMARC bibliographic records. Catalog. Classif. Q. **1993**, *18* (1), 5–37.
22. http://unicode.org (accessed February 2009).
23. International Organization for Standardization, *Information and Documentation, Information Retrieval (Z39.50), Application Service Definition and Protocol Specification (ISO 23950)*; ISO: Geneva, Switzerland, 1998.
24. American National Standards Institute. *Information Retrieval: Application Service Definition and Protocol Specification*; ANSI: New York, 1995. http://www.niso.org/standards/index.html (accessed February 2008).
25. http://www.loc.gov/standards/sru (accessed February 2008).
26. http://www.openarchives.org/OAI/openarchivesprotocol.html (accessed February 2008).
27. International Organization for Standardization. *Universal Multi-Octet Coded Character Set (UCS)*; ISO 10646; ISO: Geneva, Switzerland, 2003.
28. International Federation of Library Associations and Institutions, *UNIMARC, Universal MARC Format*; K.G. Saur: Munich, Germany, 1977, revised edition 1994.
29. United National Educational, Scientific and Cultural Organization *CCF: The Common Communications Format*; UNESCO: Paris, France, 1984.
30. McCallum, S.H. International MARC: Past, present, and future. Adv. Libr. **2002**, *26*, 127–148.
31. http://www.loc.gov/marc/ (accessed February 2008).

32. McCallum, S.H. Extending MARC for bibliographic control in the Web environment: challenges and alternatives. In Proceedings of the Bicentennial Conference on Bibliographic Control for the New Millennium: Confronting the Challenges of Networked Resources and the Web, Library of Congress: Washington, DC, 2001; 245–261.
33. International Organization for Standardization. *Information Processing, Text and Office Systems, Standard Generalized Markup Language (SGML)*; ISO 8879; ISO: Geneva, Switzerland, 1986.
34. http://www.w3.org/XML (accessed February 2008).
35. http:www.loc.gov/marcxml (accessed February 2008).
36. International Federation of Library Associations and Institutions, *Functional Requirements for Bibliographic Records, Final Report*; UBCIM Publications, New Series, Vol. 19; K.G. Saur: Munich, 1998. http://www.ifla.org/VII/s13/frbr/frbr.pdf (accessed February 2008).
37. Delsey, T. *Functional Analysis of the MARC 21 Bibliographic and Holdings Formats*; Network Development and MARC Standards Office, Library of Congress: Washington, DC, http://www.loc.gov/marc/marc-functional-analysis/home.html (accessed February 2008).
38. http://www.loc.gov/marc/marc-functional-analysis/tool.html (accessed February 2009).
39. http:www.loc.gov/mods (accessed February 2008).
40. McCallum, S.H. An introduction to the metadata object description schema (MODS). Libr. HiTech **2004**, *22* (1), 82–88.
41. http:www.loc.gov/mets (accessed February 2008).

Makerspaces in Libraries

Patrick Tod Colegrove
DeLaMare Science & Engineering Library, University Libraries, University of Nevada, Reno, Reno, Nevada, U.S.A.

Abstract
From the advent of hackerspaces and Fab Labs to the rise of the maker movement, makerspaces, and their integration with library practice, an underlying societal shift toward embracing the active do-it-yourself culture of "making" seems fundamental to the increase of makerspaces in libraries. This entry explores the concepts of makerspaces generally, building from a historical background to examine theoretical and practical underpinnings of the movement. A timeline is presented tracing early implementations of makerspaces in both public and academic libraries, and rationales for their integration into library practice examined. A seemingly natural combination, makerspace in libraries offers a framework by which shared core library and community values such as equitable access to information, resources, and opportunity for lifelong learning can be reconciled and amplified. Alignment with a number of broader national educational initiatives is enhanced, including efforts focused on closing learning gaps in science, technology, engineering, math, and the arts; support for the active production of knowledge and information products is increased, yielding deep learning and engagement on the part of library users. Adoption and implementation of makerspaces in libraries is widespread and growing, enabling libraries worldwide to realize evermore central roles in their communities.

INTRODUCTION

As libraries around the world evolve to meet changing needs of the communities they serve, the adoption of makerspaces in libraries is increasingly seen as core to library practice. Broad overlap exists between the missions and core values of libraries and makerspaces. Both intrinsically enable and provide equitable access to a diverse set of resources in the service of education, learning, and by extension the greater public good. Libraries and makerspaces are fundamentally about knowledge creation, achieved through a combination of self-directed and peer-to-peer engagement and collaboration around shared resources in an open environment. Consider the long-held mission and core practice of libraries articulated in a way that just as easily describes makerspaces:

> [t]he mission of a library is to improve society through facilitating knowledge creation in the community. ... Good libraries build services (and the collection is one of many). Great libraries build communities.[1]

The following sections explore what is meant by "makerspace" and the root word "maker," examining whether makerspaces in libraries is a natural next step in the practice of librarianship or a radical new departure. Building from a brief historical and theoretical background of the undercurrents driving the adoption and integration of makerspaces in libraries today, the practice is framed against enduring values of librarianship and established with appropriate theoretical underpinnings. Rationales for the potential incorporation of makerspaces in libraries are considered, including the potential for increased alignment and support for K-12 and lifelong learning objectives, innovation and entrepreneurship, and career development. Finally, a number of resources are provided to enable exploration and use in further development of the practice of makerspaces in libraries.

MAKERS, THE MAKER MOVEMENT, AND THE RISE OF MAKERSPACE

In the premiere issue of *Make* magazine, February 2005, founder Dale Dougherty coined the term "maker" as a deliberately generalized way to describe the new publication's customers. Rather than "users" or "patrons," the term "maker" would soon become associated with a sense of curiosity and intellectual adventure. The publication served as a touchstone for the rapidly growing maker subculture: a community of individuals with an interest in *making* things as opposed to merely *consuming*. An extension of do-it-yourself (DIY) culture, in the subsequent year over 22,000 makers converged on the San Francisco Bay Area for the first ever "Maker Faire"—clearly, the public's interest was caught. The following year saw the number of attendees triple over two separate events, and by 2014 Maker Faires attracted a total of 781,000 attendees to 135 designated events worldwide in celebration of making.[2]

The grassroots movement catalyzed around the words "make," "maker," and "making," began to be referred to

Encyclopedia of Library and Information Sciences, Fourth Edition DOI: 10.1081/E-EISA-120053780

as the "maker movement." An "umbrella term for independent inventors, designers and tinkerers,"[3] the phrase refers "broadly to the growing number of people who are engaged in the creative production of artifacts in their daily lives and who find physical and digital forums to share their processes and products with others."[4] The words "maker" and "making" derive from the underlying verb "make" and are themselves literal terms; Roslund and Rodgers explain

> Makers are people who do things to improve the world around them. If something is broken, they try to fix it. They try to find solutions to problems. Someone who likes to build new things or use tools or materials in new ways can be considered a maker. Anyone who has ever had an idea for a new invention and then made that idea a reality is a maker. Makers love to create, tinker, and play with the world and the resources around them. They also love to share their experiences with others.[5]

Makers are fundamentally experiential learners, actively engaged and solving problems, posing questions, and making decisions. In combination with more traditional library resources, such as supporting print and digital resources, the value of makerspaces in libraries becomes clear; whether K-12, higher education, or lifelong, makerspaces directly enable learning. Halverson and Sheridan[4] point out that "educators and researchers have been talking for decades about the role of making in learning," suggesting that Papert's learning theory of constructionism, which places production-based experiences at the core of how people learn, fundamentally undergirds learning and the maker movement generally. Blikstein[6] agrees, adding experiential education and critical pedagogy to comprise three theoretical pillars on which the foundation of digital fabrication and "making" in education is based; going further to point out that "the ideas behind this movement are at least a century old," tracing the root of the idea that education should be more connected to real world objects and experiences back to John Dewey and others.

Making is an overarching term that encompasses a wide range of activity. Prior to the popular use of the terms making and makerspace, broad categories of maker activity grew under the names of "hacking" and "fabbing." The emergence of community "hackerspaces" and "Fab Labs" (Fabrication Laboratory), each a specialized type of makerspace, served growing communities, with one of the first independent hackerspaces, the German *c-base*, opening its doors in 1995.[7] Although the terms hackerspace and Fab Lab are often treated as being synonymous, each refers to distinctly differing constructs despite appeal to often overlapping interests and communities of practice. Each is a type of makerspace, with hackerspaces defined in broad strokes as "community operated physical places where members can meet and work on projects."[8] In practice, membership and activities at hackerspaces tend to be largely focused on repurposing hardware, working on electronics, and programming rather than broad-based fabrication.

The concept of the Fab Lab grew out of a popular class at the Massachusetts Institute of Technology (MIT) named "How To Make (Almost) Anything."[9] In 2001, the Fab Lab program, and eventual international network, began as an educational outreach program funded by the National Science Foundation for the newly established Center for Bits and Atoms at the MIT Media Lab.[10] Rather than repurposing or programming with existing components, a Fab Lab is a space designed specifically around enabling individuals to personally manufacture physical items from source materials. Focused on enabling its users to bring their ideas to life by means of personal digital fabrication, resources are comprised of "off-the-shelf, industrial-grade fabrication and electronics [sic]tools, wrapped in open source software and programs."[11] Typical equipment in a Fab Lab might include laser cutters, computer numerical controlled milling machines and lathes, 3D printers, and other rapid prototyping equipment. With the ability to make almost anything, the perspective of a Fab Lab user quickly changes as recognition begins to dawn: literally *each and everything in the manufactured world around us has in some way been made*. Curiosity piqued, wonder as to exactly how starts to become unavoidable; household items become objects of close scrutiny, reverse engineering, redevelopment, and reuse. Recognizing the potential of the deep project-based learning and engagement enabled by access to such an environment, in 2008 Stanford University started building Fab Labs in cooperation with K-12 schools worldwide as part of the FabLab@Schoolproject.[6]

With hackerspaces numbering today over 1200 worldwide,[12] and Fab Labs in the hundreds,[13] in 2011 Dale Dougherty and Dr. Saul Griffith[14] proposed the audacious *MENTOR Makerspace* program to the Defense Advanced Research Projects Agency of the US federal government. With a goal of "reaching 1000 high schools over 4 years," the program was part of an initiative "aimed at introducing new design tools and collaborative practices of making to high school students." Intended to not only to bring a more diverse group of young people into careers such as scientist, engineer, or programmer, the goal of the proposed program was to address a recognition that "one of the biggest challenges we face as a nation is the decline in our ability to make things."[15] Awarded in 2012, the term "makerspace" quickly became mainstream as "countless museums, schools, community centers, and libraries announced plans to build digital fabrication and 'making' facilities."[6] Across the United States and Europe, technology-oriented makers began to come together to pursue interests including electronics, robotics, and 3D printing, supported by these makerspaces.

As the practice grew, the term "makerspace," a deliberate blend of the word "maker" with "space," quickly became accepted as the broad overarching term—a general term, inclusive of the earlier, more specialized spaces such as Fab Labs and hackerspaces:

> *A makerspace is a physical location where people gather to share resources and knowledge, work on projects, network, and build.* Makerspaces provide tools and space in a community environment—a library, community center, private organization, or campus. Expert advisors may be available some of the time, but often novices get help from other users (emphasis added).[16]

MAKERSPACES IN LIBRARIES: A TIMELINE

In 2011, Lauren Smedley and colleagues, under the direction of Sue Considine, Executive Director at the Fayetteville Free Library (FFL) in New York State, were forging a new path for libraries and the maker movement. Recognizing the dual opportunity of outreach and support for lifelong learning and engagement, the FFL's "Fabulous Laboratory" was launched, making the FFL "Fab Lab" the first makerspace created by a public library.[17] Other public libraries quickly followed suit; first movers and notable early adopters included

- Steve Teeri, in partnership with the local Mt Elliot Makerspace, launched the Detroit Public Library's HYPE (Helping Young People Exel) Makerspace in April 2012. With the goal of supporting the community by creating "interesting, inventive, and productive citizens who make a difference,"[18] the space set out to inspire young adults "through the spirit of invention, creativity, learning, and do-it-yourself (DIY) culture."[19]
- Bill Derry and director Maxine Bleiweis boldly carved out space in the midst of open bookstacks to create the Westport Public Library Makerspace, opening "a place for creation, collaboration, innovation and entrepreneurship"[20] on July 2, 2012.
- Andrea Sàenz, First Deputy Commissioner for the Chicago Public Library, was instrumental building on a successful 2009 launch of its YouMedia teen digital learning space,[21] itself an early form of makerspace in libraries. Based largely on the HOMAGO framework of Muzuki Ito et al., and focused "on art, digital media, making and STEM (science, technology, engineering and math) projects," Chicago's first free and publicly accessible makerspace opened the doors of its Maker Lab July 2013.[22]

At the same time, similar development was ongoing in academic libraries across the United States:

- Lisa Kurt, Emerging Technologies Librarian, and director Tod Colegrove, of the DeLaMare Science & Engineering Library at the University of Nevada, Reno, made news in July 2012 with the launch of 3D printing and scanning as a service of the academic library.[23] Notably, the library went on to be named one of the "Most Interesting Makerspaces in America" in 2014 by *Make* magazine.[24]
- Also in 2012, the library at the University of Mary Washington, in collaboration with their College of Education and Division of Teaching and Learning Technologies,[25] converted an unused classroom into its ThinkLab makerspace: "if you can DREAM it you can MAKE it."[26]
- Adam Rogers, Emerging Technologies Librarian, planned and launched[27] the Hunt Library Makerspace January 2013 on the fourth floor of the James B Hunt Library at North Carolina State University: supporting "students, faculty, and staff in learning about emerging technologies and bringing their creations to life."[28]

A survey of libraries conducted near the end of 2013 indicated that makerspaces had already gained significant and increasing traction in libraries around the world. In response to the question, "Does your library provide a makerspace or similar space?" of 143 respondents across 30 states in the United States and librarians from seven other countries, 42% (58) of the respondents answered yes, with another 36% (51) answering they were planning to do so in the near future. Fully *78% of the respondents indicated they either already provided makerspace or were planning to do in the near future.* The majority of individuals participating in the survey, 51% (73), indicated they were from public libraries, academic libraries as the next largest group at 36% (51). Overall, nearly half indicated their makerspace was less than a year old, with 11% (16) indicating that their space had existed for more than 2 years.[29]

RATIONALE: CORE LIBRARY VALUES, STRATEGIC ALIGNMENT

The membership of a library, much like that of a makerspace, are typically users of a wide range of highly individualized information resources. In addition to directly enabling self-directed learning and innovation, makerspaces in libraries are proving to be hotbeds of collaboration, co-learning, and acquisition of twenty-first-century literacies. Librarians and libraries adopting and integrating makerspaces into practice worldwide need look no further than the Core Values of Librarianship as articulated by the American Library Association to be able to recognize and articulate an underlying rationale for their incorporation and use. Of the 11 values identified, over half appear to resonate in support of makerspaces (emphasis added):[30]

- *Access*: equitable access to information resources *regardless of technology*

- *Democracy*: an informed citizenry *through free and equal access to information* [and by extension, information resources and appropriate technology needed for that access]
- *Diversity*: providing *a full spectrum of resources and services*
- *Education and lifelong learning*: promoting the creation, maintenance, and *enhancement of a learning society*
- *Intellectual freedom*: upholding and *resisting efforts to censor library resources*
- *The public good*: libraries, and the access we provide is *a fundamental institution that should not be outsourced or privatized*
- *Service*: professional development of co-workers as well as community members, *maintaining and enhancing our own knowledge and skills*
- *Social responsibility*: contributing to *solving the critical problems of society*, support for efforts to *help inform and educate the people*

As libraries continue to explore the possibilities and impact of incorporating makerspace in service of their core mission, the potential significance is becoming clear. Makerspace is first and foremost about active and participatory learning, whether self-directed or guided; its incorporation yields potentially immediate improvement in alignment with overarching learning, discovery, and engagement missions of libraries. That potential has been repeatedly identified by the New Media Consortium (NMC) in its annual environmental scan. The *NMC Horizon Report 2015 Library Edition* goes further, stating

> The turn of the 21st century has signaled a *shift in the types of skillsets that have real, applicable value in a rapidly advancing world.* Creativity, design, and engineering, or in a word — invention — has become the hallmark of innovation on campuses across the globe.... During a time when academic libraries are undergoing significant transformation, *the addition of makerspaces is solidifying the library's position as a hub* where students and faculty can access, create, or engage in hands-on projects across departmental lines (emphasis added).[31]

The overall goals and concept of makerspace as described in the *Makerspace Playbook* further amplify the potential:

> By helping schools and communities everywhere establish Makerspaces, we expect to *build your Makerspace users' literacy* in design, science, technology, engineering, art, and math... We see making as *a gateway to deeper engagement in science and engineering but also art and design.*Makerspaces share some aspects of the shop class, home economics class, the art studio and science lab. In effect, a Makerspace is a physical mashup of these different places that allows projects to integrate these different kinds of skills (emphasis added).[32]

Table 1 Top 10 technology/activities most commonly reported in library makerspaces worldwide.

Technology or activity	% of All respondents
Computer workstations	67%
3D printing	46%
Photo editing	45%
Video editing	43%
Computer programming/software	39%
Arts and crafts	37%
Scanning photos to digital	36%
Creating a Website or Online Portfolio	34%
Digital music recording	33%
3D Modeling	31%

Source: From Burke.[29]

Whether "building users' literacies across multiple domains" or serving as "gateway to deeper engagement," the outcomes speak to core library values. With resources and opportunities like those found in a makerspace, the environment is rich with possibility to build user literacies across a wide range of new media. A subset of the findings of a global survey, Table 1 details the top 10 most commonly reported technologies or activities in library makerspaces.[29] Consider the diversity: from computer workstations, photo and video editing, 3D modeling and printing to arts and crafts or music recording. Where else could an individual reasonably expect to access such a breadth of access to technology—complete with opportunity and encouragement to acquire and practice such potentially emergent literacies?

Library support for educational and learning objectives may derive further benefit from an apparently remarkable alignment between makerspaces and a number of broader national educational initiatives. In 2015, a survey conducted by the Maker Education Initiative[33] found at least half of makerspaces surveyed reporting alignment with the following:

- Science, Technology, Engineering, and Mathematics, STEM (as illustrated at ed.gov/stem), 94% of sites indicated alignment
- STEM + Art = STEAM (stemtosteam.org), 89%
- Technology education (ed.gov/connected), 79%
- Media education, 57% (no url provided to illustrate the initiative)
- Twenty-first-century Community Learning Centers (www2.ed.gov/programs/21stcclc), 51%

Given the breadth of access to resources, and alignment with national K-12 and lifelong learning initiatives, it is becoming plain that makerspaces in libraries can provide an environment rich with opportunity. Beyond cultivating interest and engagement across STEAM disciplines among individuals in the K-12 pipeline, the makerspace environment can at the same time enable parents and communities to actively develop life and career skills.

Information, media, and technology skills develop as a direct result of user engagement with makerspaces in libraries. Innovation and entrepreneurship are also proving to be natural outcomes; similarly, creativity, critical thinking, problem solving, communication, and collaboration seem to fall out naturally—top skills and values sought after by employers today. Clearly, the incorporation of makerspaces with libraries offers potential benefit in the strategic alignment of the library with goals and objectives of both the parent organization and the greater community. Further, alignment and affiliation with broader educational initiatives, perhaps in cooperation with community makerspaces external to the library, can benefit the entire community. Arguably, the traditional role of the library has been to encourage and enable the creation of knowledge; rather than conflicting, makerspace in libraries is in direct alignment with traditional roles.

Makerspaces and libraries are clearly distinct entities; their similarities are nevertheless striking.[34] To begin with, makerspaces and libraries are fundamentally constructivist learning spaces; places where members of the community have equitable access to materials and resources that might not otherwise be available to them—indeed, that they may have never even considered to be within reach. A by-product of shared community access, libraries, and makerspaces both serve to reinforce and build community among their membership. One-on-one guidance and mentoring is more the norm than the exception in both libraries and makerspaces; when combined with their fundamentally interdisciplinary nature, an environment alive with creativity and knowledge creation results. Individuals from across a wide range of interests, social backgrounds, and expertise, share access to a limited set of resources in both makerspaces and libraries, including each other. The resulting creative abrasion and collaboration, with appropriate support and encouragement, virtually ensures an environment of continuous and ongoing innovation. Together, makerspaces in libraries can truly be more than the sum of their parts.

CONCLUSION

Throughout history, libraries have adapted and evolved to better meet the needs of their communities, adopting and incorporating technologies along the way. The turn of the twenty-first century finds many libraries embracing an underlying societal shift toward making as opposed to merely consuming, moving away from a largely exclusive focus on the collection of knowledge artifacts that have ranged from papyrus scrolls through the print codex to e-books and other digital resources. As the practice of librarianship continues to evolve, increasing support for the active creation of knowledge and knowledge artifacts—in a word, *making*—by members and communities of the library is becoming standard practice. Examples might include print or electronic documents and databases being actively created and/or accessed by means of computer workstations, software, and printers; photo, video, and 3D scans or models similarly being created, edited, and remixed across a variety of media; or computer programming taking place next to arts and crafts projects. As information becomes increasingly fluid, across not only media but technologies, enabling knowledge creation among individuals and communities of practice becomes an ever more valued and central role of the library.

Implementation of makerspaces in libraries is widespread and increasing, with libraries worldwide realizing an ever more central role in the communities they serve. With the growing number of individuals identifying with DIY "maker" culture finding community in makerspaces around the world, libraries have recognized an opportunity to reconcile the shifts with core library values. Makerspaces in libraries were born and are flourishing, resonating with corresponding values of the organization and greater community. With knowledge creation a by-product of both the consumption and production of information and tangible products, the advent and integration of makerspaces into libraries promises a depth of opportunity—enabling deeply personal learning and engagement even as it transforms the library's support for innovation and entrepreneurship. As libraries continue to explore and develop the practice, makerspaces in libraries is yielding benefits that go beyond strategic alignment: improved support for K-12 and lifelong learning initiatives, transformative opportunity to develop information, media, and technology skills, and enhanced community are all natural outcomes.

ACKNOWLEDGMENTS

The author is deeply grateful for the many and ongoing contributions of colleagues across libraries, museums, and learning facilities actively exploring the possibilities of makerspace and contributing to the conversation. In particular, the Institute of Museum and Library Services is explicitly acknowledged for the critical path role they have taken to convene the conversations and catalyze continued collective development.

REFERENCES

1. Lankes, R.D. *Expect More: Demanding Better Libraries for Today's Complex World*; Riland Publishing: Jamesville, NY, 2012. http://davidlankes.org/wp-content/uploads/2014/01/ExpectMoreOpen.pdf (accessed March 2016).
2. McCracken, H. Maker faire founder dale dougherty on the past, present, and online future of the maker movement. Fast Company, April 29, 2015. http://www.fastcompany.

com/3045505/maker-faire-founder-dale-dougherty-on-the-past-present-and-online-future-of-the-maker-moveme (accessed March 2016).

3. Voight, J. Which big brands are courting the maker movement, and why. AdWeek, March 17, 2014. http://www.adweek.com/news/advertising-branding/which-big-brands-are-courting-maker-movement-and-why-156315 (accessed December 2015).
4. Halverson, E.R.; Sheridan, K.M. The maker movement in education. Harv. Educ. Rev. **2015**, *84* (4), 495–504. 563, 565.
5. Roslund, S.; Rodgers, E.P. What are makers?. In *Makerspaces 21st Century Skills Innovation Library: Makers As Innovators*; Fontichiaro, K., Ed.; Cherry Lake Publishing: Ann Arbor, MI, 2014, 9.
6. Blikstein, P. Digital fabrication and 'making' in education: the democratization of invention, cultural and media studies. In *FabLabs: Of Machines, Makers and Inventors*; Walter-Herrmann, J., Büching, C., Eds.; Transcript Verlag: Bielefeld, Germany, 2014; 203–225.
7. Cavalcanti, G. Is it a Hackerspace, Makerspace, TechShop, or FabLab? Make, May 22, 2013. http://makezine.com/2013/05/22/the-difference-between-hackerspaces-maker spaces-techshops-and-fablabs/ (accessed February 2016).
8. Hackerspaces. On hackerspaces.org. http://hackerspaces.org (accessed March 2016).
9. Anderson, C. The History of the Future. In *Makers: The New Industrial Revolution*; Crown Business: New York, 2012; 33–51.
10. Johnson, L.; Adams Becker, S.; Estrada, V.; Freeman, A. *NMC Horizon Report: 2014 Higher Education Edition*, NMC Horizon Report Series; The New Media Consortium: Austin, TX, 2014; 41.
11. Fab Foundation – What is a Fab Lab?. Fab Foundation, http://www.fabfoundation.org/fab-labs/what-is-a-fab-lab/ (accessed December 2015).
12. Williams, E. Hackers and heroes: rise of the CCC and hackerspaces. Hackaday, January 12, 2016. http://hackaday.com/2016/01/12/hackers-and-heroes-rise-of-ccc-and-hacker spaces/ (accessed February 2016).
13. Fab Foundation – Fab Labs. On Fab Foundation, http://www.fabfoundation.org/fab-labs/ (accessed December 2015).
14. About Us. Otherlab. https://otherlab.com/about (accessed December 2015).
15. Dougherty, D. DARPA mentor award to bring making to education. Make, January 29, 2012. http://makezine.com/2012/01/19/darpa-mentor-award-to-bring-making-to-education/ (accessed March 2016).
16. 7 things you should know about makerspaces. EDUCAUSE Learning Initiative. https://net.educause.edu/ir/library/pdf/eli7095.pdf (accessed December 2015).
17. McCue, T.J. First public library to create a makerspace. Forbes, November 15, 2011. http://www.forbes.com/sites/tjmccue/2011/11/15/first-public-library-to-create-a-maker-space/ (accessed January 2016).
18. HYPE Makerspace. Urban Libraries Council, http://www.urbanlibraries.org/hype-makerspace-pages-322.php (accessed March 2015).
19. HYPE—Detroit Public Library Teen Center. Detroit Public Library. http://www.detroitpubliclibrary.org/hype (accessed December 2015).
20. Untermeyer, L. Library Launches Maker Space. Westport Now, July 2, 2012. http://www.westportnow.com/index.php?/v2_5/comments/library_launches_maker_space/ (accessed January 2016).
21. YOUmedia. Chicago Public Library. http://www.chipublib.org/youmedia/ (accessed December 2015).
22. Programs and Partnerships. Chicago Public Library. http://www.chipublib.org/programs-and-partnerships/ (accessed December 2015).
23. Chin, Y. U. Nevada library offers 3D printing across the board. Libr. J. August 7, 2012. http://lj.libraryjournal.com/2012/08/academic-libraries/u-nevada-library-offers-3d-printing-across-the-board/ (accessed January 2016).
24. Most Interesting Makerspaces in America. Make, July 29, 2014. http://makezine.com/2014/07/29/most-interesting-makerspaces-in-america/ (accessed March 2016).
25. Fisher, E. Makerspaces move into academic libraries. ACRL TechConnect Blog, November 28, 2012. http://acrl.ala.org/techconnect/post/makerspaces-move-into-academic-libraries.
26. Thinklab. University of Mary Washington: Fredericksburg, VA, http://umwthinklab.com (accessed December 2015).
27. Keynote: Adam Rogers. AcadeMAKE. https://academake.wordpress.com/keynote-adam-rogers/ (accessed December 2015).
28. Hunt Library Makerspace. NCSU libraries. http://www.lib.ncsu.edu/spaces/hunt-library-makerspace (accessed March 2016).
29. Burke, J.J. Appendix: makerspaces in libraries survey. In *Makerspaces: A Practical Guide for Librarians*; Rowman& Littlefield: Lanham, MD, 2014; 165–171.
30. American Library Association (ALA). Core values of librarianship. http://www.ala.org/advocacy/intfreedom/statementspols/corevalues (accessed March 2016).
31. Johnson, L.; Adams Becker, S.; Estrada, V.; Freeman, A. *NMC Horizon Report: 2015 Library Edition*, NMC Horizon Report Series; The New Media Consortium: Austin, TX, 2015; 36.
32. Makerspace Playbook. Maker Media, Spring 2013. http://makered.org/wp-content/uploads/2014/09/Makerspace-Playbook-Feb-2013.pdf (accessed January 2016).
33. Peppler, K.; Maltese, A.; Keune, a.; Chang, S.; Regalla, L. Survey of makerspaces, Part II. The Maker Ed Open Portfolio Project. http://makered.org/wp-content/uploads/2015/02/OPP_ResearchBrief7_SurveyofMakerspacesPart2_final.pdf (accessed March 2016).
34. Weisgrau, J. School libraries and makerspaces: can they coexist?. Edutopia, September 24, 2015http://www.edutopia.org/blog/school-libraries-makerspaces-coexist-josh-weisgrau (accessed March 2016).

BIBLIOGRAPHY

1. Doorley, S.; Witthoft, S. *Make Space: How to Set the Stage for Creative Collaboration*; John Wiley & Sons: Hoboken, NJ, 2012.
2. Gershenfeld, N. *Fab: The Coming Revolution on Your Desktop—From Personal Computers to Personal Fabrication*; Basic Books, Inc.: New York, 2007.

3. Gubnitskaia, V.; Smallwood, C., Eds. *How to STEM: Science, Technology, Engineering, and Math Education in Libraries*; The Scarecrow Press, Inc: Plymouth, U.K., 2014.
4. ILEAD USA. Make it @ your library. http://makeitatyourlibrary.org (accessed December 2015).
5. Kemp, A. *The Makerspace Workbench: Tools, Technologies, and Techniques for Making*; Maker Media Inc.: Sebastopol, CA, 2013.
6. Library Makers. {hands-on learning for all ages}. http://librarymakers.blogspot.com (accessed December 2015).
7. Maker Education Initiative. Maker Ed's Resource Library. http://makered.org/resources/ (accessed December 2015).
8. Maker Media, Inc. MakerSpace beta: connect with makers. https://makerspace.com (accessed December 2015).
9. Remake Learning Initiative. http://remakelearning.org (accessed December 2015).
10. Renovated Learning. Building a culture of creativity & discovery in education. http://renovatedlearning.com/makerspace-resources/ (accessed December 2015).
11. Snow, J. Looking to Create a Makerspace in Your Library? Here are some ideas. YALSA Blog, 2015. http://yalsa.ala.org/blog/2015/10/14/looking-to-create-a-makerspace-in-your-library-here-are-some-ideas/ (accessed December 2015).

Management of Very Large Distributed Shared Collections *[ELIS Classic]*

Reagan W. Moore
San Diego Supercomputer Center, University of North Carolina at Chapel Hill, Chapel Hill, North Carolina, U.S.A.

Abstract
Large scientific collections may be managed as data grids for sharing data, digital libraries for publishing data, persistent archives for preserving data, or as real-time data repositories for sensor data. Despite the multiple types of data management objectives, it is possible to build each system from generic software infrastructure. This entry examines the requirements driving the management of large data collections, the concepts on which current data management systems are based, and the current research initiatives for managing distributed data collections.

INTRODUCTION

Scientific data collections are being assembled that contain the digital holdings on which future research is based. The collections are assembled by researchers from multiple institutions, and then accessed by all members of a scientific discipline. The data collections are massive in size, comprising hundreds of terabytes of data (a terabyte is a thousand gigabytes) and tens of millions of files. The software infrastructure that manages these collections must provide not only traditional digital library services, such as indexing, discovery, and presentation, but also preservation services to ensure authenticity and integrity. The types of material in the collections range from digital simulation output generated by scientific applications, to observational data taken by experiments, to real-time sensor data streams from thousands of sensors. Thus the management of scientific data collections requires the integration of capabilities from multiple disparate communities: data grids for sharing data, digital libraries for publishing data, persistent archives for preserving data, and real-time sensor systems for automating the creation of collections.

The challenge is made more difficult by the fact that large data collections are inherently distributed. The collections may reside on multiple storage systems with a copy on disk for interactive access and a backup copy on tape for long-term preservation. Their assembly may involve collaborators from multiple institutions, with both the sources of the collection coming from multiple sites and the users of the collection located at multiple sites. To effectively mitigate risk of data loss, data collections are distributed across multiple types of storage systems located at geographically separated locations. All of these reasons force scientific data collections to build upon software systems that are capable of managing distributed data.

In this entry, we give some examples of large scientific collections, examine the fundamental principles on which distributed shared collections are based, describe data management infrastructure that is in production use today, and close with a description of the next generation of data management software that is currently under development.

SCIENTIFIC DATA COLLECTIONS

Researchers that generate large scientific data collections include seismologists, high-energy physicists, astronomers, and educators. Seismologists manage observational data about the propagation of seismic waves through the earth crust, and generate very large simulation output data sets to predict the effect of earthquakes. An example is the Southern California Earthquake Center (SCEC),[1] which has stored over 165 TB of simulation output, comprising more than 3.5 million files, with more than 70 researchers collaborating on the creation of the SCEC collection.[2] The SCEC project is now proposing the generation of more than a petabyte of data (a petabyte is a thousand terabytes) from higher resolution simulations of seismic waves generated by an earthquake on the San Andreas Fault in Southern California.

The BaBar high-energy physics project[3] replicates experimental data taken at the Stanford Linear Accelerator in Palo Alto, California to researchers in Lyon, France at the Institut National de Physique Nucleaire et de Physique des Particules. The project has replicated more than 700 TB of data, moving up to 5 TBs of data per day between the sites. When the CERN accelerator becomes functional, related high-energy physics projects will generate a petabyte of data per year.[4]

The largest data sets in the future may come from the astronomy community. The Large Synoptic Survey

Encyclopedia of Library and Information Sciences, Fourth Edition DOI: 10.1081/E-ELIS4-120043252

Telescope[5] will take images of the sky every 3 days to detect near-earth objects such as asteroids, starting in 2013. More than 100 PB of images will be archived. Current astronomy sky surveys are measured in the tens of terabytes in size. The 2-Micron All Sky Survey comprises 12 TB of images aggregated across 6 million 2 MB files.[6]

The National Science Digital Library[7] organizes scientific educational material that is posted on Web sites. The URL of each item is registered into a central repository at Cornell University. An archive, comprising over 70 million Web pages, has been assembled by crawling the Web sites. The archived Web pages are aggregated into containers and stored on both tape and disk to provide an alternate retrieval location when the original Web site is not available.

The Real-time Observatories, Applications, and Data management Network (ROADNet)[8] manages real-time sensor data streams from more than 4,000 sensors. Data is streamed from seismic sensors, environmental sensors, coastal lidar systems, remote cameras, and oceanographic sensors into object ring buffers, and then archived for later use. The sensor streams can be queried to identify relevant data, and then correlated with other data streams. The 4,000 sensor data streams come from multiple independent projects, but rely upon common software infrastructure to facilitate use by researchers.

Each of these collections is distributed across multiple storage systems, located at different institutions, with the local infrastructure managed by local administrators. The fundamental underlying principle that is used to manage the data is that of a shared collection. Software infrastructure is installed at each site that makes it possible to name, organize, and access the data as if it were stored on a local resource. The software infrastructure has to provide a uniform name space for identifying the files, manage access controls across multiple independent institutions, manage replication of the files onto multiple types of storage systems, manage checksums to ensure data integrity, manage descriptive information about each file, and provide uniform access mechanisms to data stored on multiple types of storage systems (disk, tape archives, binary large objects in databases, database tables, and object ring buffers for sensor data). The software technology that does this is called a data grid.[9]

DISTRIBUTED DATA MANAGEMENT PRINCIPLES

The preservation community bases their data management on the principles of authenticity and integrity.[10] Authenticity is an assertion that the provenance (attributes about the creation of the data) is preserved. This includes the concept of "chain of custody"; that operations on the data have only been performed by authorized archivists. Integrity is an assertion that the preservation environment has not compromised the data; that the bits have not changed. It is not sufficient to show that the data are uncompromised, one must also show that the data correspond to the original deposition into the collection with an unbroken chain of control, and that the data can be interpreted and manipulated even after the original creating application is gone. The latter implies the need to manage technology evolution. A preservation environment insulates the records from changes occurring in the technology used to support the collection.

The same principles apply when assembling distributed shared collections. The origin of the scientific data must be tracked to assign academic credit, provenance information is needed to guide the use of the data, and the integrity of the data must be maintained. Shared collections use descriptive metadata organized in a central catalog to manage provenance information. However, management of integrity in a distributed environment is much harder. There are multiple risks that must be mitigated: media corruption such as a disk crash or broken tape; operator error such as data overwrites on both disk and tape; systemic vendor error such as bad microcode in a tape drive; natural disaster such as fire or flood; and malicious users. These are compounded by the unavailability of systems due to network outages and remote maintenance periods. Any problem that occurs in the distributed environment is treated as a problem of the data grid, instead of the remote resource.

The additional principle that is needed is the concept of infrastructure independence.[11] The properties of the shared collection are managed independently of the capabilities of the storage systems where the data reside. The three main categories of properties that must be managed for shared collections are data virtualization, trust virtualization, and management virtualization. Data virtualization manages the naming, access, and manipulation of data independently of the type of storage system. Trust virtualization manages authentication and authorization independently of the remote administrative domains. Management virtualization characterizes and automates the application of management policies independently of the remote institutions. Through these three virtualization mechanisms, one can access distributed data, control who is allowed to use the data, and verify that the authenticity and integrity have been preserved even for data located on another continent on a storage system managed by a separate institution. Because the virtualization mechanisms are automated by software infrastructure, very large collections can be maintained with a minimal amount of labor support. The goal is software that can evaluate assessment criteria, track whether each file in the system has been correctly managed, and initiate recovery procedures while maintaining audit trails of all operations applied to each file. Such an environment can institute management policies that mitigate the risk of data loss through replication and synchronization within a data grid, and federation between independent data grids.

Note that infrastructure independence implies the ability to add new technology over time, and migrate a collection from obsolete technology onto new technology. The ability to manage data distributed across multiple types of storage systems is the same ability that is needed to manage technology evolution for preservation environments.

Data Virtualization

Data grids implement logical name spaces that are used to identify not only the files, but also the users of the system and the components of the system. Typically, three name spaces are controlled by data grids:

1. Distinguished name space for users. The identity of the archivists, or curators, or users is managed independently of the remote storage system or administrative domain. Users of the system authenticate their access based upon the authentication system implemented by the data grid.
2. Logical name space for files or digital entities. The digital entities that are registered into the shared collection may be files, binary large objects, database tables, URLs, SQL command strings, or remote directories. Any organization that is imposed on the distributed data is expressed as a structure on the logical file name space such as a collection hierarchy.
3. Logical name space for storage systems. Multiple physical storage systems may be identified through a single logical storage resource name. This makes it feasible to support collective operations across storage systems, such as automated data replication (writing to a logical resource name causes a copy to be made at each of the associated physical storage systems), load leveling (a copy is made at the storage system with the most space left), or caching (a copy is made on a disk cache associated with a tape archive).

Given these three logical name spaces, access controls can be asserted as constraints between the logical user name space, the logical storage name space, and the logical file name space. When data is migrated onto new resources within a data grid, neither the file name nor the access controls change. The data grid associates provenance information with the logical file name, ensuring that authenticity can be preserved. The data grid associates system-level metadata such as checksums, audit trails, replica location, access controls, file size, and creation time with the logical file name, ensuring that integrity can be tracked over time. Data grids use a central metadata catalog to hold both the provenance and system-level metadata.

Data grids are implemented as peer-to-peer software servers, with a software server installed at each storage system where the data reside. The software server manages the mapping from the logical file name to the physical file residing on the storage system for access, and the mapping from the access protocol desired by the user to the access protocol used by the storage system. Part of infrastructure independence is the ability to use your preferred access protocol to retrieve data from legacy systems that are unable to process modern protocols. Data grids support access by C library calls, Unix shell commands, Perl/Python/Windows load libraries, workflow systems, grid portals, Web browsers, digital libraries such as DSpace[12] and Fedora,[13] and Web service description languages (WSDL) across all storage systems where the software servers reside.

Data grids act as middleware, enabling the execution of the file-based and metadata-based operations required by data management applications. It is not sufficient to provide just the POSIX I/O operations supported by disk file systems (open, close, read, write, seek, stat, sync, etc.). Operations required for authenticity and integrity assurance, and network latency management are also needed. Since data grids manage distributed data, multiple levels of aggregation are needed to minimize the impact of the network latency caused by the finite speed of light. This is done by aggregating files before movement over the wide area network, aggregating metadata before movement and loading into a metadata catalog, and aggregating I/O commands into remote procedures that are executed at the remote storage system. In each case, the number of messages that are sent over the wide area network is minimized. This not only improves response time, but also improves scalability, enabling the manipulation of 1000 files at a time.

Trust Virtualization

The management of access controls at remote sites is possible if the data grid owns the data that are stored at each remote site. This means that data are written onto the remote storage system under an account that corresponds to the data grid. Persons accessing the data grid authenticate their identity to the data grid system. The data grid then checks whether they are authorized to perform the desired operation. If so, the data grid accesses the remote storage system on behalf of the user and performs the operation. Thus the data grid software servers must also map from requests made by a user to allowed operations on data that are stored under a data grid account. The trust virtualization mechanisms provide an additional level of authentication beyond the security mechanisms employed at each site. A desired impact is the ability to create a single sign-on environment. Once the user has authenticated their identity to the data grid, they can perform authorized operations on data anywhere within the data grid. They do not need to authenticate their identity at each remote storage system.

The data grid technology used to support each of the above application examples is the Storage Resource Broker (SRB), developed at the San Diego Supercomputer Center (SDSC).[14] Each of the capabilities listed above is supported by the SRB, and is in production use. SRB data grids are typically implemented as federations of multiple independent data grids. Each data grid manages a local metadata catalog and multiple storage systems. Federation is the controlled sharing of name spaces between two or more data grids. A trust relationship is established between two data grids and the data grid administrators decide which of the name spaces will be shared. Different types of federation are then possible:[15]

- Peer-to-peer data grids. None of the name spaces are shared. Instead a person can only access public data within the remote data grid.
- Central archive. Each data grid replicates a copy of their data onto the central archive, including both the files and the provenance metadata.
- Master–slave data grids. All data that reside in a slave data grid are distributed from the master data grid.
- Chained data grids. A data grid administrator pulls data and metadata successively from one data grid in a chain to the next. This is typically used in international collaborations that are managing replicas on different continents.
- Deep archives. The goal is to build a preservation environment that cannot be seen or accessed from a publicly accessible data grid. The approach requires the creation of a staging data grid between the public data grid and the deep archive. The administrator of the staging data grid pulls data from the public data grid to the staging data grid. The administrator of the deep archive then pulls data from the staging data grid into the deep archive. The result is that the identity of the deep archive administrator, the location of the deep archive, and the content of the deep archive cannot be seen from the public data grid.

Management Virtualization

The ability to automate the application of management policies in a distributed environment is critical to the ability to manage very large collections. As the size of collections grow, the validation of integrity and authenticity becomes onerous. Since a data grid is composed of storage systems in which failures might occur at any point in time, both authenticity and integrity must be periodically reassessed, and recovery operations implemented to correct identified problems. Examples include replacement of a replica if a remote storage system crashes, validation of audit trails to prove that only the authorized administrators performed selected operations, and verification of checksums. Each time a problem is identified, the data grid should initiate the required management policy for recovery.

The automation of management policies is an active area of research. The approach taken by the integrated Rule-Oriented Data System (iRODS) under development UNC and UCSD[16] is to differentiate between institutional policies, the management infrastructure needed to implement the policies, and the underlying data grid infrastructure that interacts with the remote storage system.[17] Table 1 shows the additional levels of virtualization that are required.

Each community specifies the assessment criteria they use to validate properties about their data collections. Assessment criteria might be driven by measures of trustworthiness such as those proposed by the Research Libraries Group and the National Archives and Records Administration.[18] The assessment criteria are mapped onto sets of persistent state information that can be compared to desired values. An example is assessment of risk mitigation against data loss, by requiring at least two copies of each file be stored on two different storage systems. The persistent state information for each file would need to include the number of copies and the location of each copy.

Each assessment criterion is maintained by management policies that control what can be done with the files. The management policies are mapped onto sets of rules that control the execution of the remote operations at each storage system. An example is a rule that automatically creates a replica of any file written to a specified collection. The capabilities needed to implement the management policies are mapped onto a set of remote microservices. Each microservice corresponds to a set of operations performed at the remote storage system. The rules are executed by a rule engine, and the resulting persistent state information is stored in a database. Data grid technology provides the infrastructure independence needed to deal with multiple types of databases and storage systems.

The choice of rules to apply is driven by a combination of the identity of the person requesting an operation, the collection that is being manipulated, and the storage

Table 1 Characterization of management policies and corresponding infrastructure

Data management environment	Conserved properties	Control mechanisms	Remote operations
Management functions	Assessment criteria	Management policies	Capabilities
Data management infrastructure	Persistent state	Rules	Remote microservices
Software infrastructure	Database	Rule engine	Storage system

system where the data resides. The ability to apply different rules for each operation means that operations required by the data grid administrator can be controlled independently of the operations that might be performed by a public user. The rules can be applied at the time of the requested operation, or deferred for later execution, or executed periodically to validate an assessment criterion.

Management virtualization requires the definition of three more logical name spaces. Within the iRODS system, logical name spaces are also provided for

- Rules—new versions of rules can be added
- Microservices—new versions of microservices can be added
- Persistent state information—additional persistent state information attributes can be added

By adding simultaneously the triplet of {rule, microservice, persistent state}, it is possible to control the evolution of the rule management system itself. New capabilities can be added and executed in parallel with old capabilities, since each new capability can reference a different set of rules, microservices, and state information. A metarule can be written that controls the migration of a collection from an old set of management policies to a new set of management policies.

A second desired capability is improved control of federations of data grid. Under the SRB data grid, authentication was done by the home data grid, but authorization was done by the remote data grid. In a rule-based environment, when data is replicated onto a second data grid, the controlling rules and microservices can also be replicated, implying that it is possible to build a federation environment in which the home data grid remains in control of how their files may be used, even then they are shared with other data grids.

Rule-based systems are optimized by minimizing the number of rules that are applied. This in turn requires defining the correct level of aggregation of remote operations into microservices, and the correct set of microservices for aggregation into capabilities. Microservices that only implement the basic POSIX I/O operations are too low a level for use by a data grid administrator. The number of commands that would need to be executed for a file-level operation become excessive. Fortunately, the operations supported by data grids provide a strong template for deciding how to aggregate operations. Within the SRB data grid, multiple levels of aggregation are used within each of the logical name spaces:

The SRB data grids support identification of users as an individual entity, as a member of a group, or as a member of a data grid within a federation. Storage resources can be referenced as single storage systems, or as a compound resource such as a disk cache in front of a tape archive, or as a cluster across which load leveling is done. Files can be manipulated as individual files, or after aggregation

• Users	{Single user, group, federation}
• Users	{Single user, group, federation}
• Resources	{Single storage system, compound resource, cluster}
• Files	{Single file, container, directory}
• Metadata	{Single attribute, hierarchical table, collection}
• Management policies	{Single capability, set of capabilities, nested rules}

into a physical container, or recursively in a logical directory hierarchy. Metadata attributes can be manipulated as single attributes defined by a user, or through a hierarchical table structure that implements a snowflake schema, or as a collection containing multiple files. Management policies also have multiple levels of aggregation as rules controlling a single microservice, or a set of microservices, or in a recursive-nested hierarchy of rules and microservices.

By building microservices that manipulate each level of granularity, it becomes easier to map operations within the data grid to management policies. Analyses have been made of the capabilities required for the NARA Electronic Records Archive,[19] and their mapping onto rules that can be implemented in the iRODS environment.[20] The mapping identified over 170 rules that would be used to control either operations on records, or the manipulation of structured information. More than 200 persistent state information attributes were identified that were needed to express the results of applying the rules. A similar mapping has been made of the RLG/NARA assessment criteria for trusted digital repositories to iRODS rules and microservices. The assessment criteria comprised about 105 rules for the tracking of trustworthiness. Together, these two assessments provide a definition of the minimal rule set needed to manage distributed shared collections.

A second approach toward quantifying the required management policies for distributed shared collections is to examine the policies requested by production users of the SRB data grid technology. A generic set of 15 rules were identified that would allow each data grid administrator to implement the specific control policies they desired. These rules are primarily for the management of shared collections and include

- Administration—controlling the creation and deletion of users and collections
- Storage selection—controlling how physical resources are selected within a given logical resource name
- Data access—controlling the additional steps performed when data is read from a collection
- Data write—controlling the additional steps performed when data is added to a collection
- Transport—controlling the number of parallel I/O threads to use when moving data

- Deletion—controlling the operations performed when data is deleted

Thus it is possible to build the simple rule environments that meet the needs of today's production shared collections.

DATA MANAGEMENT TECHNOLOGIES

Many of the multiple data management systems currently under development have made explicit choices for the integration of management policies into their software systems. It is worthwhile to examine how their management policies have been implemented, and whether it is possible to integrate each of the approaches into a common system. Three notable systems are the Logistical Distribution Network,[21] LOCKSS—Lots of Copies Keep Stuff Safe,[22] and the Semantic Grid.[23]

The Logistical Distribution Network uses the Internet Backplane Protocol to manage data at the block level. A file is broken up into multiple blocks, with the blocks distributed to multiple remote storage systems. The blocks are migrated between storage systems based on demand to keep the data close to the user. The blocks can also be replicated to support load balancing. A Logistical Distribution Network is designed to make very efficient use of the network bandwidth, and move data at rates approaching the network bandwidth using a single data stream. An interesting integration effort is the porting of data grid technology on top of a Logistical Distribution Network, with the data grid providing interoperability with archives and databases.

The LOCKSS system replicates data at the file level, assuming an authoritative source for the original ingestion of data into the system. The system is used to support data downloaded from publishers. Access control policies are implemented as modules controlling access for data received from each publisher. Integrity is managed by federating with preferably at least six other sites that have also downloaded the same files. A voting protocol between sites that have downloaded the same material is used to verify that each site's copy is authentic. This minimizes risk that operations by a local administrator have compromised the integrity and authenticity of files in a collection. Again, a research topic is the integration of a LOCKSS system with rule-based systems for automating application of additional management policies.

The Semantic Grid uses logical relationships between semantic terms to reason on inferred attributes about independent data collections. The logical relationships are organized in ontologies for each scientific domain. Semantic Grids apply the reasoning to data stored in multiple data grids to improve discovery of the desired data. An example of this is the integration of inference engines with SRB data grids, in a product called S-SRB.[24]

SUMMARY

Data management systems are rapidly evolving from single site collections into distributed environments in which the data are stored across multiple systems. The initial SRB data grid technology supported shared data collections and provided the essential virtualization mechanisms needed to manage and manipulate distributed data for digital libraries and persistent archives.[25] The next generation of rule-based data management systems will automate the application of management policies, minimizing the amount of labor needed to build and maintain a shared collection. Rule-based systems have the attraction of being able to manage their own evolution, directly associate allowed operations (microservices) with individual files or collections, and apply access controls even in federated environments. Given the expected emergence of data format description languages that will characterize structures in data, rule-based systems will be able to apply access controls on structures within files, enabling the automated redaction of data files. The drive for the creation of rule-based systems is coming from the massive collections that will appear in the next 5–10 years. Without rule-based data management systems, the labor requirements for assessing integrity and authenticity will not be possible to sustain.

ACKNOWLEDGMENT

The principle developers of the SRB and iRODS technology are Michael Wan (UCSD), Arcot Rajasekar (UNC), and Wayne Schroeder (UCSD), of the San Diego Supercomputer Center. This work was supported in part by the NSF ITR grant on Constraint-based Knowledge Systems for Grids, Digital Libraries, and Persistent Archives, the NSF SCI0438741 (National Archives and Records Administration research prototype persistent archive supplement), and the Lawrence Livermore National Laboratory project with UCSD on Scientific Data. The views and conclusions contained in this entry are those of the authors and should not be interpreted as representing the official policies, either expressed or implied, of the National Science Foundation, the National Archives and Records Administration, or the U.S. government.

REFERENCES

1. http://www.scec.org (accessed February 2007).
2. Faerman, M.; Moore, R.; Minster, B.; Maechling, P. Managing large scale data for earthquake simulations. J. Grid Comput. **2007**, *5*(3)295–302.
3. http://www.slac.stanford.edu/BFROOT/ (accessed February 2007).

4. http://public.web.cern.ch/Public/Welcome.html (accessed February 2007).
5. http://www.lsst.org/lsst_home.shtml (accessed February 2007).
6. http://www.ipac.caltech.edu/2mass/ (accessed February 2007).
7. http://nsdl.org/ (accessed February 2007).
8. Rajasekar, A.; Vernon, F.; Lindquist, K.; Orcutt, J.; Lu, S.; Moore, R. Accessing sensor data using meta data: A virtual object ring buffer framework. In *Proceedings of the 2nd International Very Large DataBase Workshop on Data Management for Sensor Networks*, Trondheim, Norway, Europe, August, 29, 2005.
9. Moore, R. Data intensive computing. In *The Grid: Blueprint for a New Computing Infrastructure*; 1st Ed.; Foster, I.; Kesselman, C., Eds.; Morgan Kaufmann: San Francisco, CA, 1999; 105–129.
10. Moore, R. Building preservation environments with data grid technology. Am. Archivist **2006**, *69* (1), 139–158.
11. Moore, R.; Baru, C.; Rajasekar, A.; Ludascher, B.; Marciano, R.; Wan, M.; Schroeder, W.; Gupta, A. *Collection-Based Persistent Digital Archives—Parts 1& 2. D-Lib Magazine*; April/March 2000. http://www.dlib.org/.
12. http://www.dspace.org/ (accessed February 2007).
13. http://www.fedora.info/ (accessed February 2007).
14. http://www.srb.diceresearch.org (accessed February 2007).
15. Rajasekar, A.; Wan, M.; Moore, R.; Schroeder, W. Data grid federation. In *Proceedings of the 2004 International Conference on Parallel and Distributed Processing Techniques and Applications—Special Session on New Trends in Distributed Data Access*, Las Vegas, NV, June, 21–24, 2004.
16. http://irods.diceresearch.org (accessed February 2007).
17. Rajasekar, A.; Wan, M.; Moore, R.; Schroeder, W. http://irods.diceresearch.org A prototype rule-based distributed data management system. In *Proceedings of High Performance Distributed Computing Workshop on Next Generation Distributed Data Management*, Paris, France, June, 20, 2006.
18. http://www.rlg.org/en/pdfs/rlgnara-repositorieschecklist.pdf (accessed February 2006).
19. http://www.archives.gov/era/pdf/requirements-amend0001.pdf (accessed February 2006).
20. Smith, M.; Moore, R. Digital archive policies and trusted digital repositories. In *Proceedings of the 2nd International Digital Curation Conference: Digital Data Curation in Practice*, Glasgow, Scotland, November, 21–22, 2006.
21. http://loci.cs.utk.edu/ (accessed February 2007).
22. http://www.lockss.org/lockss/Home (accessed February 2007).
23. http://www.semanticgrid.org/index.html (accessed February 2007).
24. http://www.itee.uq.edu.au/~eresearch/projects/dart/workpackages/si3.php (accessed February 2007).
25. Moore, R.; Rajasekar, A.; Wan, M. Data grids, digital libraries and persistent archives: An integrated approach to publishing, sharing and archiving data. Proc. IEEE Grid Comput. **2005**, *93* (3), 578–588. [special issue].

Managing an Information Business

Gloria Dinerman
The Library Co-Op, Inc., Edison, New Jersey, U.S.A.

Abstract
This entry provides an outline that may be used to assist an information specialist who is contemplating going into business. It focuses on the management process, as well as emphasizing strategic details that are often overlooked by librarians as they expand their sites into a new dimension.

INTRODUCTION

The skill set required to be a successful entrepreneur is different from the ability to explore the intricacies of scholarly research or the detailed skills of indexing, cataloging, and other technological proficiencies. The librarian in a corporate or academic setting has only to think about the work at hand and the attendant concerns that challenge day-to-day duties, but a librarian in the competition of the business world has to perform many additional tasks that are far removed from the searching and disseminating of information. The realization that mundane duties are an integral part of being self-employed takes on important significance and may require some introspection before changing direction from employee to employer.

The following competencies are vital for success:

1. The ability to schedule time to include office details as well as professional production.
2. The character to develop the mental toughness to withstand adversity.
3. The aptitude to set priorities without getting buried in mundane details.
4. The stamina and the drive to survive the first year in business.
5. The resources to call for assistance, if needed, and the independence to stand alone.

MANAGING TIME

The organization of time should include completion of work on hand, business development, follow-up, technical reading, meetings, networking, social engagements, personal downtime, and the flexibility to ride the tide of the unexpected.

You may want to construct your work week on a calendar, first notating all activities that are preplanned such as meetings, appointments, classes, and research. Allow part of each day for production, preferably allocating the same hours to regulate a schedule. Then fill in the rest of the week with other duties such as clerical, e-mail, telephone responses, etc. Each specific task is then accounted for even though the time spent may change.

Another method of managing time is to set up the week like a budget, but instead of using numbers, use hours as the unit of calculation.

Example—Working a 50-hour week

25 hours—work in progress
5 hours—marketing/business development
5 hours—e-mail, telephone, correspondence etc.
5 hours—meetings
3 hours—professional reading
2 hours—networking
5 hours—clerical (accounts payable, ordering supplies, reviewing mail, billing your accounts, etc.)

Try to keep phone calls short, covering the salient points of the conversation with direct questions or responses, and personal calls should be kept to a minimum. When working with a new client, request the best time to return calls or whether they would prefer to be contacted through e-mail. Many people prefer calls early in the day, others in late afternoon. Keep a profile sheet online with client preferences and, until it is committed to memory, have it open whenever you are on the phone. A good program to use is ACT; it is simple and inexpensive, with all the features built in for ready reference. Becoming overwhelmed with minor details is a common error of the single business owner. As soon as it is economically possible after the business has been opened, consider hiring a part-time person to do the routine clerical work and save your time for the professional duties.

The economic reality of employing a clerical assistant is that it maximizes the value of your production. Professional income may range between $50 and $100 per hour. Clerical wages usually fall between $15 and $25 per hour. The more work an office assistant can accomplish, the more time the professional is free to earn the income commensurate with their skill level.

Encyclopedia of Library and Information Sciences, Fourth Edition DOI: 10.1081/E-ELIS4-120008905

Local centers of education are the best sources for recruiting office personnel because guidance teachers and career instructors are available for references and suggestions. Writing a job description is essential, clearly stating responsibilities, skill level, salary, and hours.

Try to avoid spending time worrying about a business situation over which you have no control. Excessive concern is counterproductive because energy is sapped by negativity. If a contract has been lost to a competitor, get as much information as possible as to the reason for the decision, so that errors become a learning experience.

Vigilantly scrutinize for burnout and loss of creativity. If time gets out of control, step back and reassess the productivity level, paying particular concern to deadlines and job satisfaction.

The business of information is dynamic in its structure, and there will always be changes in the process of building a foundation for success.

UNDERSTANDING PRIORITIES

Setting priorities can be exclusive and personal. At the outset, it would seem that work is scheduled in the order in which it was received, but this logic is not necessarily best for business. If a large and loyal account wants special treatment, that request should be honored. Rush jobs might take priority, particularly if there is extra compensation attached to the task. When a new account that has the potential for continued business asks for a quick turnaround, that request can be honored. Trying to please everyone is impossible, but the ability to please most people comes with experience. Do not be afraid to ask questions that will make your job easier.

Every job requires a reference interview, basic in our profession. When developing a business, is it more profitable to seek one or two large accounts, or should priority be given to the expansion of a large and possibly diverse client base? The decision depends on the comfort level of the owner. Some professionals leave a job only to become a consultant for their former employers and the fact that they have a ready-made client fosters a false sense of security. That company can relocate, hire another associate, restructure their management responsibilities, merge with a competitor, go out of business, or institute a combination of changes that unfortunately do not include their independent consultants. It is a safer business practice to vend your services to a number of different users and cultivate a list of references that can be cited whenever there is a call for services. Rarely should priority status be given to a job as a favor to a friend. You have no friends in business, only professional acquaintances.

The following suggestions summarize considerations for establishing production priorities:

- Which account is most loyal?
- What work is for a new account?
- Which account has consistently come forth with repeat business?
- What requests were on the books first?
- What job is the largest in terms of gross dollars?
- What work will bring in the greatest margin of profit?
- What work will take the longest or shortest time to complete?
- Can any of the work be delegated?

There are other types of priorities that come under consideration when starting a business. The appearance of your workplace demands attention, particularly if you plan to entertain clients. A home office should have the look and feel of an office outside your residence. Surroundings make a difference in how you perceive yourself, and you want to feel like a successful owner. Even if the area is small, or if you have to share space, segregate your furnishings so that the room or part thereof is designated exclusively for business use. If your office is private, adequate file space, seating, and lighting should be in place before the door is open for business.

Setting priorities requires logical thinking, personal preferences, evaluation, and organizational understanding.

WHEN THE CASH FLOW GETS CLOGGED

The definition of cash flow is the money that actually is received in the office. Billing, accounts payable, and contract assignments are all promises of money earned, but until it is in the bank, it cannot pay bills, salaries, utilities, or any of the other expenses that are inherent to running a business.

If \$5000 per month is billed, if ordinary expenses run \$4000 per month, and if \$3500 per month is paid in, there is a negative cash flow of \$500 per month. Simply stated, this is why a reserve is essential.

A small business may often be on the verge of bankruptcy because the owner is not alert to financial planning. Suggestions to help you to maintain solvency are as follows:

- When starting your business, have enough ready cash on hand to sustain your lifestyle for at least 1 year.
- Have enough ready cash to pay basic office expenses for at least 1 year.
- Be aware that most accounts do not pay on time—that is, within 30 days.
- Be aware that even though you might want to add interest to your billing after 30 days, you probably will not be able to collect it.
- Good work and prompt delivery are not always followed by rapid payment. Corporations earn millions of dollars by not paying their bills on time.
- It might be necessary to engage a collection agency. Agencies work on a contingency basis and usually

charge between one-third and one-half of the money collected.

- Never work without a purchase order or an authorization in writing signed by someone in authority. You have no friends in business. The number on the purchase order may be needed to track payments to your company.
- As a nonessential service provider, payment to a library consultant is not a priority for the corporate account. The longer a company keeps its money and invests what it keeps at even a nominal rate of interest, the more money it earns at the expense of the small contractor.

Eventually, however, the payment comes through. To expedite cash flow:

- Bill immediately upon the completion of a job. Make this clerical work a priority.
- Ascertain the recipient of the invoices—phone number and e-mail.
- If payment is a day past 30 days, send a second notice.
- Two weeks later, send a third notice (return receipt requested).
- When you build up a reserve in your corporate account, put any excess that is not needed for monthly expenses into an interest-bearing instrument or a money market account. Do not let it sit without drawing some interest.
- Establish a line of credit with your bank, in case of emergency.
- Pay bills on the last day of the month.
- If possible, save purchases for the end of December or the beginning of January. Most companies clear their payables by the end of the year, and the best buys on equipment and supplies are during the start of the new year.

To expedite the flow of cash into a business account, there are a few strategies that produce results:

- Establish a FedEx account and have clients use your number to send payment.
- Request direct deposits from the client's bank directly into yours.
- If a check has to be mailed, request second-day air delivery.
- Request a wire transfer of funds.
- Pick up the check personally if the location is within easy driving distance.

INVESTMENTS

The disposition of money must be included as a major part of any business plan. However, investing is not to be confused with speculation. Whatever amount is put to work in a safe haven, the principal should be risk-free. Whether interest rates are low or high, the extra earnings can compound into a considerable sum at the end of the year. To maximize earnings, checks should be deposited into a savings account as soon as they come in.

Arrange to transfer funds into a checking account on an "as-needed" basis. The most efficient way to accomplish this transfer is to have both the savings account and checking account in the same bank, making sure to ascertain the length of time needed to be able to use the proceeds.

When there is enough available money in the account to sustain the business for 2 or more months, it is time to purchase other types of investments. Bank Certificates of Deposit yield more interest than a savings account, but if you redeem before maturity there will be a penalty. These short-term instruments have a fixed maturity date and the interest is fixed at the time of purchase.

If you have accumulated $10,000 or more, U.S. treasury bills are safe, readily available, and generally provide a higher yield than Certificates of Deposit. These bills are issued by the U.S. government and can be bought through a commercial bank or brokerage house. The percent of interest given to investors is controlled by the Federal Reserve Open Market Committee, which meets at least once every 3 months. Interest rates are pegged downward, usually by one-quarter of a percentage point at a time, to stimulate the economy and conversely, the rates are increased when there is a danger of inflation.

The manipulation of the prime rate is an economic control that is perceived to work. When interest rates go down, the cost of borrowing becomes cheaper, more projects are expanded, new equipment is purchased, more people are put to work, and as purchases are made, the economy flourishes. When interest rates rise, goods and services become more expensive, buying may be curtailed, and the economy slows.

People have a tendency to think that investing is only for those with high incomes, but even a modest investment is a beginning. Translate earnings into practical purchasing. If you received only $20 the first year, that could buy $20 worth of copy paper, part of a lunch tab with a client, money toward your phone bill, or other purchases of importance. Money earned is working for your benefit.

Federal government securities, such as Federal National Mortgage Association or Government National Mortgage Association, yield more than certificates and bills, and the rate is fixed for a longer period of time. These instruments are safe and pay interest monthly or quarterly, depending on your particular investment and can be readily sold if the invested principal is needed. There is a plethora of advice that is given in the name of "reliable information," and much of it will benefit the sales representative more than it will the investor. Banks or large brokerage houses employ their own researchers to help both customers and representatives, and even though a commission is charged on each transaction the advice that is received is well worth the payment.

MARKETING

Marketing is the strategy and the resultant action of promoting a business. The difference between advertising, selling, and marketing is:

- Advertising is when there is a purchase of airtime, print space, billboards, or other types of promotion to display a product or service.
- Selling involves person-to-person contact. If someone calls about your service, if a casual meeting leads to a work assignment, or if persuasion will increase the scope of a contract, these are the circumstances that create a selling experience.
- Marketing is spreading the word that you are in business and that you are the best at it. Marketing demands confidence. To convince others that the service you provide is essential, you have to truly believe in yourself. Put very simply, when you go to the store and are given a sample of a product, that is marketing. When the person who gave you the product starts a sales talk, that is selling. When you get a coupon for the product, that is advertising.

Asking for a recommendation from a satisfied client is a simple marketing tool, as is giving a lecture or demonstration, or hosting a booth at a conference. Somewhat more difficult is cold calling or using mailing lists. The average positive response is from 2% to 5%, and it takes a tremendous number of contacts to produce a worthwhile return. With electronic communication becoming ever more important to business promotion, developing a website and keeping it current is excellent for marketing a new venture. Business cannot succeed unless your potential clients know about your work.

Professionals often make the mistake of thinking that, because they are lucky enough to start a business with one or two promised accounts, their services will always be needed. In the brokerage business, an often-quoted maxim is "you are only as good as your last trade." To paraphrase the adage, "a good reputation must be constantly renewed."

Marketing takes a lot of time and careful planning. In a niche business, services rendered do not appeal to a huge market. When you plan your campaign, the first workable solution might be the methodology of contacting the obvious customers and most likely users. Then stretch your imagination to explore and identify other markets where competitors have not yet saturated the field.

Networking is essential. There will always be colleagues promoting allied endeavors where you may be able to dovetail your expertise. Talk to people—anyone. Let them know you are in business. Even if they can never become an account, they might have a friend or relative who is waiting to be shown your talent. Talking to seatmates on planes and trains is ideal for this type of conversation.

Try to market every day, even if only one new contact is developed. This effort keeps the name of the company in front of the potential audience so that you will be recognized. Think about brochures and business cards, and how to coordinate the color scheme and legend with your website. Keep it simple, attractive, and uncluttered.

The world of commerce is constantly changing, sometimes for the better and sometimes into stagnation or recession. When you plan for difficult times, the good times take care of themselves. The core of planning is keeping alert to opportunities to spread the word about your services and to follow up on all leads that might be fruitful. Keep a record of names, places, e-mail, and results of every conversation. Rejection will come followed by discouragement, but let discouragement build determination and let that determination become the driving force toward your goal.

Train yourself to be alert to new developments and innovative technologies, not only in the profession of librarianship, but more so in the broader outlook of the global economy. Imagine how you can service new clients by employing the most modern methodology and technical acumen to your work. The more you expand your depth of knowledge, the more prestige you bring to your talent.

HIRING AND FIRING—THE PEOPLE PROBLEM

Unless you expect to be a self-employed solo librarian, the time will come when help will have to be hired, either to take care of some of the routine work, to assist you on special projects, or to add another dimension to the company. When you retain more people, there is always the possibility that you will be forced to fire an employee who has proved to be unsatisfactory. Hiring and firing are both difficult and even traumatic because there are no guarantees that the right decision was made.

Hiring

Have a clear idea of where help is most needed, and write a job description that is detailed and simple to read. Put the duties in priority order according to importance to the company and according to the skill level at which you expect the person to operate. State number of hours per week, hourly or weekly wage, whether the job is temporary or permanent, holidays, vacation time, benefits, and whether you are willing to support working on a flexible schedule. Include training, if any.

Hours of interviewing will not produce the perfect candidate, and a resume is descriptive only of education and experience. Working with someone is the only way to ascertain if each personality blends with the other.

It is recommended that a telephone interview be conducted first to find if your candidate speaks clearly, responds literally, and understands your requirements. Write out questions that are relevant to the job and record the answers for later evaluation. Also grade your overall impression of the applicant. When the phone interview agrees with the personal interview, that person should be strongly considered.

When hiring someone for office detail, the writing of a clear and concise e-mail message takes on new importance. If you are out of the office on an assignment or at a conference, it is essential for client relations to have someone who can be responsive to the needs of your accounts and be able to convey any messages necessary to continue business in your absence.

Training someone with potential may be preferable to hiring someone with experience. As long as the candidate is intelligent, flexible, willing, and has no personality problems that will interfere with performance, honing the skills and teaching priorities will create an adaptive and eager employee. The argument against training is that it takes too long to bring someone up to speed. This is fallacious thinking because the most loyal and dedicated employees are those that come up from the ranks, regardless of the nature of the company.

If possible, hire on a 3-month trial basis. At the end of that time, meet with the candidate and discuss problems or revisions in the job description; then both of you can make a determination if the job and job performance has been satisfactory and whether the relationship should continue.

Many people, especially those who are well educated, become disenchanted with their work because they are not given enough responsibility. If you have hired correctly, there should be a gradual assigning of more difficult duties so that your own workload can be relieved of some managerial obligations. Be secure enough in your own ability to disengage the minor details of running an office.

When you are in a small office, it may be tempting and almost natural to become friends with your co-workers. DON'T. You have only one role—that of boss or supervisor. You are not a buddy, confessor, family counselor, banker, or broker. If you mix up your own job description, the boundaries get blurred and you lose control, discipline, and importance.

Firing

If you find that a mistake has been made in hiring, cut your losses quickly. Letting someone go for cause is most difficult because you have to be cautious not to infringe on the human rights that dominate today's personnel regulations.

Years ago, a person was generally given a week or two to finalize the work at hand before leaving the company, but giving a long notice time builds up more resentment as the days pass. Now, it is preferable to speak in a private conference, explain the reason for the decision, and then say good-bye. Keep it simple. Keep it professional. Above all, do not argue and do not change your mind.

Expect a challenge to your decision and be prepared. Rehearse in your mind what you are going to say and keep to the scenario. Even though you may not have an answer for every possible question, you are still the boss and the buck stops at your desk. Do not be persuaded to award a second chance because in the long run it will not work, the same difficulties will surface and you will be faced with firing the same person twice.

Surprisingly enough, even though a person has been let go, they may give you as a reference when applying for another job. This is a real dilemma. You do not want to compromise your integrity by glossing over inadequacies; yet, you cannot leave yourself open to any legal action. The law only requires you to say that the person worked for you during the time that is stated on the application. After that you do not have to commit to any other information. The standard questions are "Was the work satisfactory?," "Would you hire this person again?," "What was the reason for the separation?," and "Were there any glaring problems?" Be evasive on all the above.

CONTRACTS

Of all the bits of knowledge associated with starting a business, the least familiar to librarians is arguably working with the details of contracts. Many jobs will be sealed with a handshake or even an okay over the phone. Many others will require a contract, defining the scope of work in explicit detail, and some will only need a letter of confirmation.

Whatever the parameters of the job, regardless of the person or corporation who requested the services, each deliverable should be stated in clear language. It should be a policy decision never to work without a purchase order or something in writing authorizing you to proceed. A formal contract may not be necessary, but the authorization should contain at minimum the scope of work, total payment amount, start date, terms of payment, and who will sign off on the work. If the contract is large, it should also state what is not covered (i.e., indexing but not abstracting, research but not a synopsis, editing but not proofreading, copy cataloging but not original cataloging). The services of an attorney might be worthwhile to ensure that you are properly protected.

In spite of careful scrutiny of the terms of the contract, you might be asked to do work that is beyond that to which you originally agreed. At that time, you will have to decide whether to ask for an additional fee. The request could involve nothing more than a small item that will make the deliverable better. Four questions to be answered: "Will the additional work earn more business?," "Is it worth doing for public relations?," "Will there be a sterling recommendation at the completion of the job?," and "Is the account taking advantage of my lack of business experience?"

If there is any doubt about how to proceed, imagine what IBM would do. When you are in business, it is incumbent upon you to conduct your business like a chief financial officer. When figuring the cost of a job, there are several components to be considered before arriving at a total. Estimate the time it will take to complete; add any staff or clerical time; and estimate cost of travel, FedEx, subsistence if going out of your commuting range, overhead, margin of profit and 5% to 10% of the entire cost for contingencies. Whether the charge is 5% or 10% can depend on whether the work is for a new account or one with a prior business history; whether the work is difficult or detailed, where there could be a substantial margin for error; whether there is a strong possibility of hidden expenses; or whether the account have made prior requests for additional work at no cost.

If a contract requires an addendum, you can:

- Prepare the revisions yourself and submit the changes for approval.
- Request that the account write the revisions and submit them to you for approval.
- Submit the change order to your attorney and have the attorney review it for approval.

If you believe that working with contracts will be a large part of your business and if the nature of your business does not vary substantially from job to job, it might be preferable for an attorney to prepare a boilerplate contract for you to use and modify as needed. Then you can be relatively sure that most of the essential points will always be covered.

Government contracts can be the most difficult to understand, and bidding on government jobs is extremely competitive, regardless of the protestations that they want to cater to women and minority vendors. It can take months to get an award and payments are slow. However, government contracts are large, and there is money to be made if you are careful when drawing your estimates. Sometimes an on-site visit is required, and sometimes a bond has to be posted. Proof of insurance is always required. Before you take the time to develop a proposal for any contract, weigh the risk against the rewards. There is no greater personal satisfaction than in growing a successful business. No detailed and difficult assignment that has ever been completed for an employer compares with the gratification you get when that first check is deposited into your own business account. There is no greater thrill than in seeing one of your ideas transform from a thought into a reality—without committees, without meetings, without administrative delays. By working your own business, you may be giving up security and gaining independence. You change from a worker into an entrepreneur, from an "extra" into a star, from one of the crowd to one of a kind.

There will be jealousies and joys, loneliness and laughter, and the worst and the best of the commercial world. It takes courage to be a success.

BIBLIOGRAPHY

1. Adams, B. *Adams Streetwise Small Business Start-Up: Your Comprehensive Guide to Starting and Managing a Business*; Adams Pub.: Holbrook, MA, 1996.
2. Alarid, W. M. *Free Help from Uncle Sam to Start Your Own Business (Or Expand the One You Have)*; Puma Publishing Company: Santa Maria, CA, October 2000.
3. Biech, E. *The Consultant's Quick Start Guide: An Action Plan for Your First Year in Business*; John Wiley & Sons, May 9, 2001.
4. Dinerman, G. Chapter in expanding technologies-expanding careers. In *From Financial Management to Library Managers*; Mount, E., Ed.; SLA, 1997; 97–102.
5. Dinerman, G. Success. Inf. Outlook October **1997**.
6. Eisenberg, R.; Kelly, K. *Guide to Starting and Managing a Business*; Adams Pub.: Holbrook, MA, 1996.
7. Eisenberg, R.; Kelly, K. Organize your start up!: simple methods to help you start the business of your dreams. Hyperion April **2001**.
8. Hall, D. *Jump Start Your Business Brain*; F & W Publications, Inc.: Cincinnati, OH, September 2001.
9. Kamoroff, B. *Stay Out of Trouble*; Bell Springs Publishing, September 2001.
10. Norman, J. *What No One Ever Tells You About Starting Your Own Business: Real Life Start-Up Advice from 101 Successful Entrepreneurs*; Upstart Pub. Co.: Chicago, IL, January 1999.
11. Pakroo, P. *The Small Business Start-Up Kit: A Step-by-Step Legal Guide*, Nolo.com, November 2000.
12. Pinson, L. *Keeping the Books: Basic Recordkeeping and Accounting for the Successful Small Business (Keeping the Books)*, 5th Ed.; Dearborn Trade, January 2001.
13. Pinson, L.; Jinnet, J. *Steps to Small Business Start-Up: Everything You Need to Know to Turn Your Idea into a Successful Business*; Dearborn Trade, January 2000.
14. Reierson, V. Start your business: a beginner's guide. PSI Res. January **1999**.
15. Root, H.; Koenig, S. *The Small Business Start-Up Guide*; Sourcebooks: Naperville, IL, 1995.
16. Severance, T. *Business Start-Up Guide: How to Create, Grow, and Manage Your Own Successful Enterprise*; Tycoon Publishing: Oceanside, CA, February 1998.
17. Sitarz, D. *Partnerships: Small Business Start-Up Kit*; Nova Publishing Company: Carbondale, IL, February 2000.
18. Sitarz, D. *S-Corporations: Small Business Start-Up Kit*; Nova Pub. Co: Carbondale, IL, 2000.

19. Spiegel, R. *Home Business Magazine's Complete Guide to Home Business; Choosing Your Business, Start-Up Planning, Home Business Space, Launch Funding, Fine Tuning, Growth, Exit Strategies*, AMACOM, 1999.
20. Sullivan, R. *The Small Business Start-Up Guide: Practical Advice on Starting and Operating a Small Business*; Information International, January 1998.

Marketing Library and Information Services

Dinesh K. Gupta
Department of Library and Information Science, Vardhaman Mahaveer Open University, 3 Kota, India

Réjean Savard
School of Library and Information Science, University of Montreal, Montreal, Quebec, Canada

Managing–Metamarkup

Abstract

After introductory remarks on the definition of marketing, the evolution of library and information services (LIS) marketing is explained. The authors then describe how marketing was applied to LIS over the years. Marketing is also related to other concepts used in the management of LIS. Finally the role of professional associations in diffusing marketing theory is portrayed and the importance of education addressed. The entry ends with a reflection on the future of marketing for LIS.

INTRODUCTION

It is widely admitted that libraries and archives have for a very long time suffered from their image and visibility problems. This is probably why many librarians and archivists now see marketing as a very important topic; for example, in a survey conducted in Canada in 1997,[1] 84.4% of the respondents answered that marketing is important or very important for library and information services (LIS). Similar results were observed earlier in the United Kingdom.[2]

Many also think that marketing is a new issue for LIS, something that only emerged during the last three decades. Although marketing was more formally introduced in the profession after the 1970s it is interesting to know that in North America at least, librarians adopted marketing techniques as early as 1876, as Kleindl (a marketing professor, illustrated how libraries at this stage were innovative in many marketing strategies: segmenting and targeting clienteles, using publicity, direct mail, streetcar signs, telephone solicitation, banners, etc. The twentieth-century library, the progressive library, would throw its doors open to all and encourage them to come in and join in the building of a community cultural center)[3] and Renberg (who traces history of marketing since 1876 and goes till formal marketing starts taking place in 1970, confirms the occurrences of terms such as, advertising in 1896, management in 1897, outreach in 1903, and extension work in 1909, in library literature, mainly in public libraries)[4] demonstrated in their articles.

However, what is true about marketing in general is the confusion concerning the concept itself. Most people seem to see marketing only as the equivalent to advertising or promotion: they do not see "what's below 'the tip of the iceberg.'" To use this analogy, what is below the surface in marketing theory includes important strategic components such as evaluating the needs of the customer; planning the various elements of the mix in order to answer those needs; and periodically evaluating the results. While this is the most commonly accepted framework of marketing, over the years, marketing activities have expanded from being assigned to one designated "marketing department" to becoming an overall organizational function. This, in turn, requires the involvement of everyone in the organization, and thus it becomes integral to the philosophy of the whole organization.

MARKETING REDEFINED

Marketing has been defined and explained in many ways by different marketing authors. Though the definitions given by the American Marketing Association (AMA) and The Chartered Institute of Marketing (CIM) have been widely accepted over the years, but are redefined time and again. The National Association of Marketing Teachers, a predecessor of the AMA, adopted what seems to be the first official definition of marketing in 1935:[5] "Marketing is the performance of business activities that direct the flow of goods and services from producer to consumers." The AMA adopted the 1935 definition in 1948, and in 1960 when the AMA revisited the definition it was decided not to change it. This original definition stood for 50 years, until it was revised in 1985, as: "Marketing consists of individual and organizational activities that facilitate and expedite exchange relationships in a dynamic environment through the creation, servicing, distribution, promotion and pricing of goods, services, and ideas." Again in 2004, the AMA the definition was revised to read: "Marketing is an organizational function and a set of processes for creating, communicating and delivering value to customers and for managing customer

Encyclopedia of Library and Information Sciences, Fourth Edition DOI: 10.1081/E-ELIS4-120044552

relationships in ways that benefit the organization and its stakeholders."

Examination of these three definitions reveals a change of focus over the time. The first definition of marketing embraced all the business activities involved in getting commodities of all kinds, including services, from the hands of producers and manufacturers into the hands of the final consumers. It focused significant attention on the distribution functions. The 1985 modification of the definition was a significant one, turning attention squarely toward the managerial tasks. The emphasis was put on how the individual organizational processes, marketing and developing the strategic dimensions of marketing activities.

In 2004, while there is still an emphasis on process—that is fundamental to marketing—one can see the transition in the focus areas: the use of the words "value," "managing customer relationships," and "stakeholders" being brought to the center stage in this definition. Gupta[6] contends that this definition sets many new dimensions to marketing concept—the emphasis is on that:

- Marketing serves as the overriding philosophy in conducting marketing task in the organization as a whole.
- It is a set of processes; process involves interactions among people, technology, methods, procedure, environment, and material (information or information sources in case of libraries), by which any offer comes to the customer.
- Value is the basket of benefits or utilities which a user or customer gets while using a product or service. Value is clearly communicated to customers so that it can be understood easily.
- A long-term relationship is developed among customers and marketers through deep understanding, reciprocal dependency, and mutual trust.
- Relationship is substantially beneficial to both the parties. From the organization's point of view, relationship is a tactical issue, but for customers, it is just a communication process.

Thus, the 2004 definition not only extends managerial dynamics but also goes on to delimit marketing to a singular focus on the individual customers, stakeholders, and the organization.

Similarly, CIM defined marketing in 1976, as, "Marketing is the management process which identifies, anticipate and supplies customer requirements efficiently and profitably." CIM proposes to redefine marketing in 2007,[7] as

> The strategic business function that creates value by stimulating, facilitating, and fulfilling customer demand. It does this by building brands, nurturing innovation, developing relationships, creating good customer service and communicating benefits. By operating customer-centrically, marketing brings positive return on investment, satisfies shareholders and stake-holders from business and the community, and contributes to positive behavioural change and a sustainable business future.

While there are differences between the definitions given above it is important to state that definitions of marketing change as a result of environmental changes, or because our knowledge of the subject improves, or indeed through a combination of these two reasons. Marketing as a subject or discipline is therefore evolving as explained by Cooke et al.[8] What is important to remember is the notion of managing the exchange process between an organization and its publics with a view to developing relationships between both the parties is at the heart of marketing. It involves philosophical thinking, strategic outlook, and operational tactics for LIS, thus clearly putting marketing above simple advertising, promotion, or public relations part of marketing.

ORIGIN AND HISTORY OF LIS MARKETING

Early Marketing Efforts in Libraries (Prior to 1920)

Historically, one can easily find the roots of library marketing in the attempts to extend opening hours of libraries in the United States during last quarter of the twentieth century and in efforts to make books available in locations outside the library building. Samuel Swett Green advocated marketing the library through reference services in his article, "Personal Relations between Librarians and Readers,"[9] which appeared in 1876 in the *American Library Journal* (later known simply as *Library Journal*). Green also spread his message through the American Library Association (ALA) conferences and meetings. Somewhat later, portable libraries were introduced in the Light-House Establishment and these were provided to all light vessels and inaccessible offshore light stations in an attempt to meet out the reading needs of the community residing in distant locations. The books were carefully selected from a list of books of a good quality appropriate to the families who would use them.[10] Melvil Dewey and others advocated for traveling libraries which were small rotating collections that provided a means for extending library service to rural areas. These small libraries (usually from 30 to a 100 books) were located in a post office or store with a volunteer acting as the caretaker of the collection.[11] Such initiatives that also took place in other countries (India, Canada, France, etc.) can be considered as concrete marketing efforts.

John Cotton Dana

> was a pioneer in what we now call public relations, marketing, and other promotional activities. He was an early practitioner of needs assessment, defining target

> audiences, goal setting, planning, and evaluation that could be quantified. He saw performance in numbers and in customer satisfaction. If readers liked a service he made sure others knew about it. If he added a new service—like creating separate children's libraries or business libraries—he made sure everyone had an opportunity to learn of it. He used newsletters, pamphlets, posters, flyers, exhibits, newspaper announcements and speeches to groups, and special events to publicize library events and encourage library use. He urged librarians to better understand their institutions from the patron's perspective—to put themselves in the worlds of actual and potential users.[12]

(Reference[12] has bibliography of publications about Dana, important ones include works by John Cotton Dana[13] and Mattson and Eldredge.[14]) He emphasized for specialized libraries for special kind of users and the concept of special libraries came in the beginning of the twentieth century that led to formation of Special Libraries Association (SLA) in 1909. Dana became the founder President of the SLA and later he became President of ALA. ALA started a Public Relations Award in his name in 1946. It is also important to note that to further the idea of outreach, the SLA in cooperation with other library associations organized numerous activities to celebrate "Library Week" during June 26–July 01, 1916.

Thus, during this period, the books themselves were considered the product, and place was emphasized for utilizing library services through space utilities, extended opening hours, and mobile library services. The open access system started which allowed users the freedom to move around the collection and make their own selection of material to consult on the premises or to borrow. Similarly, librarians started using terminologies related to communication, viz., advertising, publicity, and exhibit. Such development was limited to public libraries. Work related to compilation of bibliographies, documentation, and user-based services started taking place in libraries in early twentieth century, as librarians became more proactive and shifted their focus to individuals and their specific information needs.

From Publicity to Promotion (1920–1969)

By the 1920s the library movement had started in many countries. Many national and international professional associations (including IFLA, 1927) came into existence during this period and their work improved the overall situation of libraries and librarianship world over. There is evidence that special libraries, school libraries, and other libraries started taking keen interest in marketing-related activities.

During this period, a series of articles appeared in the SLA's magazine *Special Libraries*. Special library and information professionals themselves started taking interest in marketing their services by highlighting the importance of promotion through exhibitions. In addition to the widespread use of displays, special librarians used public relations to attract help from the authorities and institutions; they also engaged in extension activities and in many other aspects of marketing that served to strengthen library–user relations. Some other themes addressed in *Special Libraries* include Selling the Special Library Idea; how can we sell ourselves to our organization; budgeting; in inside publicity and exhibit and exhibits.

Several books on specific aspects of marketing were also published during this period, including a 1921 manual by W. A. Briscoe entitled "*Library Advertising*: *'Publicity' Methods for Public Libraries, Library-Work with* Children, *Rural Library Schemes;* this book also had a chapter on the cinema and library in 1921.[15] This work foreshadows some of the strategies advocated even today, such as targeting library newsletters at different groups, and having tie-ins with films.

Ranganathan's famous *Five Laws of Library Science*[16] was published in 1931. The Five laws have been discussed in the light of marketing by many authors. Interestingly, these laws can be said to be relatively well aligned to marketing theory. From these laws logical corollaries are derived that can be directly related to marketing. (See Table 1 below.) The reader (sometimes called the customer) is king, and is the focal point of the library; thus the whole organization (resources, services, facilities, rules and regulations, procedures) becomes customer focused. As the table below demonstrates, each of these laws has important implications in regard to basic marketing strategies.[17]

T. D. Wilson finds that although user studies started around 1948 they did not became a hot topic in LIS until the 1960s (Wilson considers that the "starting point of user studies to be the individual information user who, in response to some perceived 'need' engages in information-seeking behaviour.").[18] Although linked to marketing because of the interest in a better customer knowledge, in many cases user studies merely describe information habits and do not explain the decision-making process behind information strategies. In order to evaluate service vis-à-vis outcome performance, new measurement techniques began to be developed in the 1950s. The bibliography by Atkin[19] and the survey by Nobel and Layzellward[20] cover much of the literature published on performance measurement during 1950–1970. However the concept of customer satisfaction broadened and changed by the 1970s.[21] (Nahl mentions that library managers started acquiring an understanding of how the user-centeredness can be embedded in the culture of services via strategic and operational management and summarizes eleven user-centered principles). Prior to this time, it would be fair to say that service provision was professionally determined and system centered rather than customer driven. As a result, the measurement of

Table 1 Five laws and marketing implications.

The law	Actions to be taken	Marketing implications
Books are for use	Optimum use of resources, facilities, and services.	Acquiring appropriate information material and ensuring sufficient resources and services are available for the use of users. Convenient location, effective signage, and longer opening hours; helping hands for using resources and services.
Every reader his/her book	Meeting users need satisfactorily	Collecting and interpreting information, understanding the needs of users, and matching with the organizational resources.
Every book its reader	Reaching out to users	Publicizing value and benefits, promotional campaign, advocacy, public relations, personal communication, etc.
Save the time of user	User benefits and preferences	Repackaging information into appropriate form, availability of information when they need. Ensuring quality of services and offerings.
Library is a growing organism	Adapting to future user needs	Mobilizing resources, dealing with uncertainty about future user needs, new services, new customer groups, new environment, etc.

performance has shifted from input to output: books borrowed, articles photocopied, items consulted, demands met, market penetration, and more subjectively perceived satisfaction.

In conclusion, between the 1920s until the early 1970s, aside from special libraries most libraries, archives, and information services did not see much, if any, need to market their products and services. Most marketing-related documentation in the field of librarianship had been presented under such labels, as user needs, user training, performance measurement, and economics of information, and efforts toward promotion, public relations, selling, and related concepts.

Library Marketing: The Formal Beginning

At the end of the 1960s, the world famous marketing author Philip Kotler and his colleague, Sidney Levy, published a landmark paper entitled: "Broadening the Concept of Marketing"[22] In this 1969 paper Kotler and Levy suggested new avenues for marketing in nonprofit organizations. This marked a change among the marketing specialists who had previously considered marketing mainly as the field of commercial organizations. In the 1970s, marketing in nonprofit organizations and the associated areas of public sector and social marketing received a lot of attention. At the same time, LIS managers witnessed a kind of formalization process concerning the marketing of LIS. Indeed a number of important trends occurred in marketing of LIS during the last three decades.

First, the concept of "marketing mix" emerged and became the most popular concept in LIS marketing. The marketing mix is commonly referred to the four Ps of marketing—product, price, place, and promotion. This is a simple, yet effective means of considering the key elements necessary and the emphasis to be placed on each, in order to effectively implement any marketing strategy. The mix still provides a useful framework for thinking about ways in which an organization's marketing strategy is implemented. Writings related to pricing or charging fees for library services also started to appear, thus the pricing aspect of marketing started getting attention in library and information centers.

Within the last 5 years the library community demonstrated a growing interest in marketing information products and services. Nevertheless, the approach to marketing in the LIS field continues to be characterized by a high degree of fragmentation. Surveys of information needs, wants, use, and satisfaction are important kinds of knowledge for a library and represent an element of marketing. However, the LIS approach has often been limited to disseminating information about library services and programs; this represents only a single aspect of marketing, and ignores product, pricing, and distribution activities. The majority of marketing-related work done in libraries has concentrated on one (or at best a couple), of these elements of marketing, and need to be melded into a coherent marketing program that is integrated into the organizational structure of the library. In 1977, the Library Association of the United Kingdom published the first simplified text which was entitled *Marketing the Library*.[23] In this work, by A. Yorke, he affirms that libraries and marketing are compatible and explains similarities which do exist between a library and most other organizations irrespective of the field of activity in which they are operating; Yorke also attempts to show how the library should try to organize itself and its activities from a marketing point of view and looks into future.

In 1981, Blaise Cronin[24] compiled a famous set of marketing papers for the Association of Special Libraries and Information Bureaux (ASLIB). This book covered topics such as marketing myopia; broadening the concept of marketing; marketing for nonprofit organizations; and strategies for introducing marketing into nonprofit organizations. It also reprinted quality papers published over library marketing during last two decades. It was only in the 1980s that marketing of services started to attract the attention of information professionals. The difference between products and services were repeatedly highlighted and finally the features of the service category (intangibility, inseparability, heterogeneity, and perishability) were established. The new three Ps—people, process, and physical evidence—became equally important;

writers who discuss these new three mix consider a range of aspects concerning marketing of services and also reflect on how they interact with each other. However, there is a continual debate whether the marketing mix is relevant in the present. Sueli Ferreira in her paper "4Ps Concept in LIS Literature"[25] addressed the extension of the marketing mix in library literature during 1975–1995: she concluded that although "the four Ps can be an important tool to help librarians to understand information agencies as a 'business', librarians need to overcome the concept and go out of the four walls of the information agencies to guarantee the future of these organizations."

Another significant trend noted during 1980s is the combining of strategic planning and marketing. In 1983, Wood wrote an article "Strategic Planning and the Marketing Process: Library Applications,"[26] in which she stressed providing programs which support the library's mission. She considered that libraries must consider adopting business concepts, such as marketing and strategic planning, if they were to survive the challenges of the 1980s. In the following years Wood expanded her article into a full-length book *Strategic Marketing for Libraries: A Handbook*.[27] In her introduction, she noted that the combination of marketing and strategic planning "promotes not only strength in the short run, but also the kind of long-term viability needed to work towards each organization's vision of the future." Darlene Weingand also published a monograph entitled *Marketing/Planning Library and Information Services*[28] in which she integrated the ideas of planning and marketing. She emphasized that marketing and planning must be integrated if either is to be effective. Marketing and planning should be integral functions within a library and marketing and planning must be combined in to a "unified whole." Throughout the book, Weingand stressed that "to be effective, the marketer must understand his environment, must design the products and services the environment needs, must monitor and evaluate their use, and then must build on this process for future planning." According to her, marketing is a managerial process that must be carefully formulated and thought out. There are many other works which deal with marketing–planning combination in libraries.

In the 1990s the question of quality services in libraries became an important issue in library literature, a problem intimately linked to marketing. SERVQUAL,[29] a tool to measure quality based on survey methods, became the model for the profit sector but the instrument was not fully applicable in the nonprofit sectors such as LIS. Starting from this model, the American Association of Research Libraries (ARL) developed an adapted instrument called LibQUAL+, and later WebQUAL. The tool was used widely in North American libraries as well as in other contexts, and it has become a useful marketing tool for library managers.

Later librarians began to consider relationship marketing, that is, integrating marketing with customer services and quality into one stream. Relationship marketing is based on a motion of establishing trust and cooperation with known customers. As a library operates routinely with a known set of customers, this concept is seen as very important for the marketing of LIS. A library also operates on trust. Essentially, it is based on the idea that when a client walks into the library, he trusts that the service provider will find the material or information that he needs. The library in turn, trusts that the client will return the items he borrows within the specified borrowing period.

Table 2 gives a cluster of marketing and related themes that have been covered in literature in the last three-and-half decades. The table is not a complete list of terminologies that were first used during a given decade, but is indicative of trends that have occurred and can thus help to understand the scope of marketing and the way it has changed over the years.

With the impact of technologies and other environmental changes, the role and concept of library services is changing very fast. The range of services that take place outside the physical library is expanding due to the new technology, and it is likely to expand further. Additionally, the scope of some services has become nearly unlimited. Some forms of service can be offered almost as easily around the globe as around the town. Libraries serve and will serve far beyond their walls. All business activities may be seen through marketing lenses. Marketing in case of libraries is necessary to offer benefits to users want, reduce barriers to use and access, persuade and inform the users, and carefully plan to satisfy users' needs effectively. "Marketing is so basic that it cannot be considered a separate function within the library. Marketing is a central dimension of the entire library. It is the entirety of the library's operations and services seen from a point of view of its final result, that is, from the customer's point of view."[30]

ROLE OF ASSOCIATIONS

Library associations, both at national and international level have played a vital role in popularizing, promoting role of libraries, their present and potential services, resources, and facilities for the benefit of the community at large. And also in developing their member's marketing skills, and providing them with support.[31] (Reference [31] is an extensive review sponsored by IFLA covering areas such as conceptual framework, LIS marketing practices around the world, role of library associations, education, research and training for library marketing, excellence in marketing, literature review, databases, etc., 47 contributors from more than 40 countries have contributed for the volume.) Rigorous efforts have been made by international, national, and regional associations for popularizing marketing through establishing separate sections,

Table 2 Changes in marketing themes.

1970–1980	1981–1990	1991–2000	2000–
• Product development • User free • Information brokers • User charges • Market analysis • Information economy • Information utilities • Economic modeling • Pricing • User education	• Marketing products and services • Mega trend marketing • New technology and marketing • Segmentation • Marketing communication • Strategic marketing • Marketing planning • Marketing strategy • Online services marketing • Fee-based services • Fund raising • Fee or free • Information • Marketing through physical environment • Global marketing • Environmental scanning • Library identity • Marketing through your story • Mission statement • Marketing audit	• Costing and pricing • Service quality • Market value • Electronic information service marketing • Positioning • Advocacy • Marketing campaign • Marketing library online • Meaning use and value • Information marketplace • Marketing public relations • Marketing services and products • Part-time public relations • Future-driven marketing • Relationship marketing • Marketing 101 • Savvy marketing • Publicity through Web design • Marketing: A total solution • Product designed and testing	• Performance measurement within marketing frame • Marketing your expertise • Marketing yourself • Think like a business act like a library • Visible librarian: Asserting your value with marketing and powerful public relation and advocacy • Designing brochures • Shy librarian: Marketing and PR • Develop and market a winning collection • Develop and market a winning collection • Card campaign • Focus group • @ your library campaign • Virtual reference • Realistic Marketing • Marketing through blogs

e.g., Management and Marketing Section at IFLA, Advertising and Marketing Section at SLA, Public Relations and Marketing Section at ALA, Publicity and Public Relations Section at Chartered Institute of Library and Information Professionals (CILIP). These associations organize various programs and activities, they issue publications, and they recognize the best practices through awards, etc.

In its programs and activities, the Special Library Association (http://www.sla.org) has been giving increased attention to marketing. The SLA Management Division gives training and publishes bibliographies on marketing from time to time, and the SLA Advertising and Marketing Division has a discussion list on the subject (sla-dam@lists.sla.org). Similarly, at the IFLA 2001 Annual Congress in Boston, the ALA launched "@your library"—a new advocacy Campaign for the World's Libraries. Through this bold initiative IFLA and over 25 national library associations who have embraced the campaign are able to make ALA's collective and individual accomplishments better known across the world. ALA has also published many useful texts on marketing area.

In Britain, CILIP's Publicity and Public Relations Group, which was established in 1983, works to make library and information professionals aware of the value of marketing and PR and also offers a platform for sharing ideas and experiences. CILIP has produced various publications and organizes an annual conference with training workshops and other events; it also produces publicity and promotional material, and rewards excellence in libraries through "*Public Relations and Publicity Award*" (recently renamed as the "PPRG Marketing Excellence Awards").

Launched in 1997, the IFLA Marketing and Management Section (http://www.ifla.org/vii/s34/somm) is made up of library professionals who either work actively in marketing and management in their libraries or teach these techniques to future librarians. Members of this section, who come from countries throughout the world, are working to develop a conceptual basis for marketing in libraries; they also formulate guidelines to teach management and marketing, and they aid LIS professionals throughout the world in their efforts to promote the broader acceptance of marketing. The section also organizes annual conferences and training programs, and it issues publications, including a newsletter. In order to recognize best practices in marketing of library and information sector worldwide, the section created the IFLA International Award in 2001. The work of IFLA's Marketing and

Management Section illustrates the internationalization of the concept of marketing LIS.

EDUCATION FOR LIS MARKETING

A large part of being an effective librarian involves being an effective marketer. Many successful librarians concede that, as one climbs the organizational ladder, the relative importance of technical skills declines while that of marketing skills increases. Therefore, library schools have realized the need to add a focus on acquiring marketing skills along with the regular quantitative and technical skills in their course curricula. UNESCO confirmed the importance of education when it published in 1988 the "Guidelines for the teaching of marketing in the training of librarians, documentalists and archivists."[32]

Marketing has been identified as one of the areas of competency that is important for professionals in library and information science in the United States and Canada. However, marketing is not a major area of focus in graduate LIS education. It is certainly the case that library and information science programs must fulfill the role of graduate programs in general, with regard to presenting the theoretical and practical in a range of content areas. In Canada, marketing/advocacy/public relations courses are offered in all seven information science schools. The content of these five LIS marketing courses is comparable to a great extent. However, in regard to objectives, readings, and assignments, there are some distinctive priorities. One course includes an advocacy component affirming the idea that, "advocacy is essentially the marketing of an issue." Finally, an assessment of the state of development of a "public relations and advocacy" course in the seventh LIS school is underway.

In the United Kingdom, management is still strongly represented in the curriculum, with marketing sometimes mentioned as one of the topics covered in a management module. A few specific marketing modules exist. There have been some changes during recent years within the marketing curriculum, reflecting developments in the field. For example, customer relationship management, relationship marketing, and aspects of Internet marketing are now more likely to be taught. CILIP conducts short-term training programs on different aspects of library marketing.

In India, the need for education in marketing LIS was felt in early 1980s. Although marketing was widely discussed in literature, conferences, and many training programs started during 1980s, the inclusion of marketing in the curricula was slow as the University Grants Commission (UGC) Model Curriculum did not lay much emphasis on marketing. Nonetheless some universities and institutions have recognized the need for inclusion of the topic in their syllabi. For example, the University of Bangalore has a full paper on Marketing LIS whereas University of Delhi has half paper on marketing LIS and in the National Institute of Science Communication and Information Resources (NISCAIR), the topic of marketing of information products and services is covered under the paper on Information Products and Services. However, the role of Indian Institute of Management (IIM), Lucknow in training for LIS is significant. It offers short-term courses for top- and middle-level librarians of all kind of libraries.

In Pakistan, only a few large public, special, and university libraries make use of certain public relations tactics. A course on marketing was first introduced in 1995 by the Course revision Committee of the UGC, but prior to 2002 books on LIS marketing were not included in the list of recommended books. In the year 1999, Islamia University implemented the curriculum recommendations. The University of Punjab introduced the elective course in Marketing of LIS and was made a core course in 2002. In 2001, Sindh University of Hyderabad also started Marketing of LIS course as core course in 2001. Another university, Bahaudin Zikriya University in Multan, has adopted the curriculum of University of Pakistan in 2004.

In France, although marketing is present as a topic in the syllabi of most of the universities, little time is devoted to the study of marketing, and lectures are often given by faculty in fields other than library science. However the topic of marketing is not often offered in continuing education programs given to library or documentation professionals. However, at the national school of library and information science in Lyon (ENSSIB: École nationale supérieure des sciences de l'information et des bibliothèques), there is an online course on marketing strategy available for heads of libraries and documentation services.

In Estonia, among the institutions that prepare information professionals, library marketing is currently being taught both in the curricula of Department of Information Science in Tallinn Pedagogical University and the curricula of Department of Librarianship and Information Studies in Viljandi Culture Academy. In Norway, marketing component in library syllabi is different from university to university. There is very less part of "marketing" or "public relations" or "communication" in curriculum.

These examples from several countries demonstrate that education for marketing among library and information professionals is more and more part of the curricula. However, most of the time it remains an option and is not a core, required topic.

CONCLUSION

Although the idea of marketing LIS is not new, and some progress has been made in the past, more efforts have to be made if we want to see better marketing of a wide range of LIS. In recent years there has been a kind of overconfidence in information technologies, and many

LIS professionals believe that these new technologies will provide a way to make LIS more visible. It is true those technologies are important and librarians, archivists, and other information professionals need to make effective use of technology in order to improve the services to users. Library and information managers need to realize that these technologies are broadening the market and therefore provide immense opportunities to them to offer services and products at the global level. To effectively reach this broadened group of potential users, it becomes imperative that positive attitudes toward marketing be part of the organizational culture of libraries. LIS managers must be aware of and sensitive to marketing in every aspect of acquisition, digitization, sharing of resources, access and delivery, and services to the users. Without a marketing orientation, a high-tech library or information service would not necessarily be successful.

REFERENCES

1. Savard, R. La perception du marketing chez les bibliothécaires. In *Adapting Marketing to Libraries in a Changing and World-Wide Environment*; Savard, R., Ed.; K.G. Saur: Munchen, 2000; 12–32.
2. Collins, M.F.; Glyptis, S.A. Marketing public leisure services in the U.K. Libr. Manage. **1992**, *13*(4).
3. Kleindl, B. Marketing practices used by the emerging American Public Library System from inception to 1930. J. Macromarketing **2007**, *27*(1).
4. Renberg, G. Marketing library services: How it all began. In *Adapting Marketing to Libraries in a Changing World-Wide Environment*; Savard, R., Ed.; K.G. Saur: Munchen, 2000; 5–11 Available at http://www.ifla.org/IV/ifla63/63reng.htm (IFLA Publications; 89).
5. AMA Adopts New Definition of Marketing. *Marketing News*, 2004; September 15. Available at http://www.marketingpower.com/content21257.php (accessed January 28, 2008).
6. Gupta, D.K. Broadening LIS marketing. In *Marketing Library and Information Services: International Perspectives*; Dinesh, K.G., Ed.; K G Saur: Munich, 2006; 5–20.
7. CIM definition, Leading Body Calls for a New Definition of Marketing, http://www.creativematch.co.uk/viewnews/?94810.
8. Cooke, E.F.; Rayburn, J.M.; Abercrombie, C.L. The history of marketing thought as reflected in the definitions of marketing. J. Marketing—Theory Practice **1992**, (Fall), 10–20.
9. Green, S.S. Personal relations between librarians and readers. Libr. J. **1876**, October *1*, 74–81.
10. Traveling Library, http://www.michiganlights.com/lhlibrary.htm.
11. Traveling Libraries in Wisconsin, http://www.libraryhistorybuff.org/traveling-wi.htm.
12. About John Cotton Dana, http://www.hwwilson.com/jcdawards/about_jcd.htm.
13. *John Cotton Dana: Libraries, Addresses and Essays*; Books for Libraries Press: Freeport, NY, 1969; 17, 53.
14. Mattson, K.; Eldredge, J. *John Cotton Dana Legacy: Promoting Libraries for Users*.; Wilson Libr. Bull., 1992; April, 66, 48.
15. Briscoe, W.A. *Library Advertising: Publicity Methods for Public Libraries, Library- Work with Children, Rural Library Schemes*; Grafton & Co.: London; The H.W. Wilson Co.: New York, 1921; 127.
16. Ranganathan, S.R. *Five Laws of Library Science*; Madras Library Association: Madras (Now Chennai): India, 1931. Available at http://dlist.sir.arizona.edu/1220/.
17. Gupta, D.K. User-focus approach: Central to Ranganathan's philosophy. Libr. Sci. Slant Document. Inform. Stud. (Now Srels J. Inform. Stud.) **1999**, June *36*(2), 123–128.
18. Wilson, T.D. Information needs and uses: Fifty years of progress?. In *Fifty Years of Information Progress: A Journal of Documentation Review*; Vickery, B., Ed.; ASLIB: London, U.K., 1994; 15–51.
19. Atkin, P. Bibliography of use surveys of public and academic libraries 1950–November 1970. Libr. Inform. Bull. **1971**, *14*, 1–82.
20. Nobel, R.; Layzellword, P. *Performance measures and criteria for libraries*, 1976; PLRG Occasional paper no. 3.
21. Nahl, D. The user-centered evaluation: 1970–1995. In *Encyclopedia of Library and Information Science*; Allen, K., Ed.; Marcel Dekker: New York, 1998; vol.62.
22. Kotler, P.; Levy, S.J. Broadening the concept of marketing. J. Marketing **1969**, January *33*(1), 10–15.
23. Yorke, A. *Marketing the Library Service (Library Association Management Pamphalets-3)*; The Library Association: London, U.K., 1977.
24. In *Marketing of Library and Information Services*; Cronin, B., Ed.; ASLIB: London, U.K., 1981.
25. Angelica do Amaral, S. The four Ps concept in library and information services: A review of literature. In *Marketing Library and Information Services: International Perspectives*; Dinesh, K.G., Ed.; K.G. Saur: Munich, 2006; 398–409.
26. Wood, E.J.S. Strategic planning and the marketing process: Library applications. J. Acad. Librarian **1983**, March *9*(1), 15–20.
27. Wood, E. *Strategic Marketing for Libraries*, Greenwood Press: Westport, CT, 1988.
28. Weigand, D.E. *Marketing/Planning Library and Information Services*, Libraries Unlimited: Littleton, CO, 1987.
29. Berry, L.; Zeithaml, V.; Parasuraman, A. SERVQUAL: A Multiple-item scale for measuring consumer perceptions of service quality. J. Retailing **1988**, *64*, 12–40.
30. Cram, J.K. *Marketing for Non-School Libraries: A Guide to an Essential Management Activity*; Department of Education: Queensland, 1994.
31. In *Marketing Library and Information Services: International Perspectives*; Gupta; D.K., Ed.; K.G. Saur: Munich, 2006.
32. Savard, R. *Principes directeurs pour l'enseignement du marketing dans la formation des bibliothécaires, documentalistes et archivists*; Programme general d'information et UNISIST: Paris, 1988. Available at http://www.unesco.org/webworld/ramp/html/r8801f/r8801f00.htm (The text has been translated in English and Spanish).

Mathematics Literature: History *[ELIS Classic]*

Barbara Schaefer
Geneseo, New York, U.S.A.

Abstract

One of the objectives of the information disciplines is to study the universe of recorded information—that is, to study the documentary products of domains of human activity—and to come to understand such bodies of literature as social and historical phenomena in and of themselves. Schaefer reviews the history of mathematics from ancient times, and discusses the forms of mathematics literature, and their transformations, through time.

—ELIS Classic, from 1976

INTRODUCTION

The investigation of the literature of mathematics may be placed in perspective by relating the development of the literature to the development of mathematics itself. Throughout the long history of mathematics, the records and communications of mathematicians have taken a variety of forms, depending not only upon the state of the art, but also upon the information needs and the technology at a given time. For these reasons, this description of mathematics literature will begin with a brief survey of mathematics history.

For convenience in discussing the subject, mathematics history will be divided into eight chronological periods, from the prehistoric period to about 1940. The period of contemporary mathematics, which began about the time of World War II, and the literature dating from that time will be discussed in detail in the second half of this article. These historical divisions are only approximations, of course, since ideas tend to overlap and intermingle with the passage of time. They are intended simply as an aid in analyzing the characteristics and accomplishments of mathematics at various stages in history.

THE LITERATURE TO 1940

Prehistory

Knowledge about mathematics in prehistoric times is based largely on conjecture. However, it is generally believed that during that time two general concepts began to emerge from the phenomena of the physical world: quantity and form. The concept of quantity is thought to have started from attempts to compare collections of objects by counting and slowly evolved into a variety of primitive number systems. These number systems became more extensive as exchange and barter became important. The concept of form probably began as primitive art, with woven patterns in cloth and ornamentation on pottery and buildings. The mathematical aspects of form did not emerge until later; what we would now call geometric figures were simply decorative designs at the time.

5000 B.C. to 600 B.C.

There are sufficient records extant to provide a picture of the mathematics of the early civilizations of the Near East, since the Babylonians wrote on almost indestructible clay tablets and the Egyptian papyrus stayed well-preserved in the dry climate of northern Africa. The quantitative needs of early societies had increased to the point where it was necessary to develop general methods for calculation and to record these methods for future use. The earliest evidence of organized mathematical knowledge seems to indicate the existence of an Egyptian calendar in 4241 B.C. and possibly a Babylonian one before that. By 3000 B.C. the Sumerians had a workable mercantile arithmetic, and texts from the Third Dynasty of Ur (2100 B.C.) indicate a well-developed number system. Texts from the First Babylonian Dynasty show that by 1950 B.C. an elementary algebra had been established. The Babylonians also had a geometry, consisting of formulas for simple areas and volumes, and including recognition of the rule for triangles that is now called the Pythagorean theorem.

The earliest Egyptian source still in existence is the Ahmes Papyrus, written in 1650 B.C. (This is commonly referred to as the Rhind Papyrus, named after A. Henry Rhind, the nineteenth-century English archaeologist who brought the manuscript to England.) This is a practical handbook containing methods of solving types of linear equations, material on unit fractions, mensuration techniques, and problems in elementary series. It may be considered a compilation of the established mathematical

Encyclopedia of Library and Information Sciences, Fourth Edition DOI: 10.1081/E-ELIS4-120008994

knowledge of that time, since the scribe Ahmes stated that he was copying an earlier work that had been written about 1800 B.C.

Knowledge of early Chinese and Indian mathematics of this period is comparatively poor, since these peoples wrote on bark or bamboo, which was susceptible to decay. The burning of all existing books and the burying alive of all protesting scholars by order of the Emperor Shi Huang-ti of the Ch'in Dynasty in 213 B.C. is another reason why there are so few records from this period in Chinese history. Nevertheless, transcriptions of several ancient treatises have been preserved, among them the "Chou-pei," a dialog concerning astronomy and mathematics. This work, which was written shortly before 110 B.C., contains material on mensurational geometry, the computational principles of the Pythagorean theorem, some elementary trigonometry, and a discussion of instruments for astronomical measurements. Even less is known of Indian mathematics of this period. All that can be said is that there is evidence of a workable number system and an elementary geometry.[1]

The outstanding feature of all pre-Hellenic mathematics is the complete absence of deductive reasoning. Knowledge was derived from trial-and-error methods, and successful results were recorded and passed on to succeeding generations as formulas. Mathematics before 600 B.C. was merely a tool in the form of disconnected, simple rules derived from experience and immediately applicable to daily life. Mathematics as an organized, independent, and reasoned discipline did not exist until the blossoming of Greek civilization.[2]

600 B.C. TO A.D. 400

Thales of Miletus (ca. 640 to ca. 546 B.C.), the founder of the Ionian School, is credited with being the first person to speculate about the rules of mathematics. By demonstrating that certain statements of geometry followed logically from previous ones, he contributed to the third phase in the development of mathematics: a science studied for its own sake.

One of the members of the Ionian School was Pythagoras (ca. 570 to ca. 500 B.C.). He later founded his own school at Crotona, a town of Magna Graecia, that contributed greatly to number theory, the theory of music, astronomy, and geometry. Pythagoras was the first to insist on assumptions (axioms or postulates) as the basis for proof, and he offered the first proof of the theorem about right angles that bears his name.

Another interesting figure of this time was Zeno of Elea, a philosopher of the early fifth century B.C., who taught that motion or change of any kind is only apparent. He posed four paradoxes that could not be solved by using the mathematical tools available in his time. His contribution to mathematics was that he planted an idea that 2000 years later resulted in the development of calculus.[1]

The study of mathematics, through the influence of Plato and Aristotle, achieved the status of a philosophical science second to none. Their development of logical principles and axiomatic methods put mathematics on a foundation that was considered unshakable until the twentieth century. Attempts to solve some of the famous geometric construction problems that arose during this period, and that remained unsolved until modern times, gave rise to a host of new discoveries.

Probably the most famous figure of this period was Euclid (ca. 300 B.C.), whose greatest contribution was the 13-book treatise, the *Elements*. The *Elements* incorporated all the essential accumulated mathematical knowledge of the time, organized into a system logically deduced from a single axiomatic foundation. The works of Euclid were so comprehensive that they superseded all previous writings, and it is probably for this reason that very few pre-Euclidean Greek manuscripts were preserved.[3]

During the Alexandrian period, from about 300 B.C. to A.D. 400, Western civilization underwent a change. Greek culture mingled with that of the Orient, and the mathematical center of the Western world shifted to Alexandria. Greek mathematics reached its peak with the flourishing of the School of Alexandria. Two important figures connected with the school were Archimedes of Syracuse (287 to 212 B.C.) and Apollonius of Perga (ca. 260 to ca. 210 B.C.). Archimedes, an astronomer, physicist, and applied and speculative mathematician, made major contributions to number theory, algebra, and geometry. Apollonius, called "the great geometer" because of his important contributions to synthetic geometry, wrote eight books on conic sections, of which seven have survived intact.

After Apollonius, Greek mathematics began its decline, along with the rest of Greek civilization. For the next 600 years, only two important writers stand out among the minor ones. Ptolemy (Claudius Ptolemaeus, ca. A.D. 85 to ca. 165) wrote a comprehensive treatise on astronomy, the *Almagest*, which extended computational mathematics to plane trigonometry and the beginnings of spherical trigonometry. About a century later, Diophantus of Alexandria (ca. A.D. 275) wrote the *Arithmetica*, a milestone in the development of number theory. This work was a blend of Greek and Oriental mathematics, and six of the books have survived.

A.D. 400 to 1400

With the end of Greek civilization, the center of mathematical activity shifted to India, Central Asia, and the Arabic countries.

The Hindus achieved significant results in algebra and arithmetic, but by far their most important contribution was the development of the numeration system we use today: a place system based on 10 and including a symbol for zero.

Perhaps the greatest contribution of the Moslems was preserving the continuity of mathematical thought. They translated most of the important Greek and Hindu manuscripts into Arabic and spread them in their travels throughout the Arab world. However, two Moslem scholars of this period deserve mention. The first is Mohammed ibn Musa al-Khowârizmî (ca. 825), who wrote two significant books, one on arithmetic and the other on algebra. Only the second still exists in the original Arabic, but both were translated into Latin in the twelfth century. The title of the first in translation is *Algorithmi de numero Indorum* (literally "Al-Khowârizmî on Indian numbers"), which is the source of the term "algorithm." The second book is entitled *Al-jebr al-muqabala* (literally "Restoration and Opposition"), and by latinization the key word in the title became "algebra."

There was no mathematical progress in Europe during this time. Throughout the period of the Roman Empire and until the fifteenth century, the language of instruction in Europe was Latin. Despite their contributions in many other areas, the Romans did not produce any significant mathematics and they had carried to Europe only that of Greek mathematics that had practical applications. The only noteworthy Roman mathematician was Boethius (ca. 475 to 524), whose works included an arithmetic, *Institutis arithmetica*, a geometry, *Geometry*, and a treatise on music (considered to be a part of mathematics at that time). His texts were considered authoritative by the European monastic schools and were widely used until the twelfth century.[1]

It was not until the latter part of the eleventh century that the Greek mathematical classics started to filter into Europe. As trade and travel expanded, the Europeans came into contact with the Arabs of the Mediterranean area and the Near East and with the Byzantines of the eastern Roman Empire, from whom they learned about the Greek works. During the twelfth century the mathematical works that had been translated into Arabic a few centuries before were translated into Latin.

The next few hundred years were a time of absorption of the Greek and Arabic mathematics; mathematical creativity did not resume until the fifteenth century. The emerging European civilization, which had seemed so promising with the founding of the first universities in the thirteenth century, was postponed by the Hundred Years' War (1337 to 1453) and the Black Death (1347 to 1351).[2]

The Fifteenth and Sixteenth Centuries

In response to the increasing demands of astronomy, navigation, trade, and surveying, mathematics of this period was concerned principally with computation. The leading mathematician of the fifteenth century, Johannes Müller (1436–1476), was also an astronomer and he wrote *De triangulis omnimodis*, the first treatise to be devoted solely to trigonometry. The foremost scientist of this age, Leonardo da Vinci (1452–1519), was concerned with the application of geometry to the physical sciences and also to art. His writings on perspective are contained in his *Trattato della pittura* (1651), compiled by some unknown author.

There also occurred during this period two events that laid the groundwork for future mathematical developments: the invention of movable-type printing and the beginning of writing in the vernacular.

The first printed books on mathematics were a commercial arithmetic that appeared in 1478 and a Latin edition of Euclid's *Elements* that appeared in 1482. Of greater mathematical significance was the publication in 1494 of *Summa de Arithmetica*, by Luca Pacioli. This book was written in Italian and was a complete summary of all arithmetic, algebra, and trigonometry known at that time.

Robert Recorde (ca. 1510–1558), called "the father of English mathematics," published four books on mathematics, written in English: *The Ground of Artes*, an arithmetic; *The Castle of Knowledge*, the first English exposition of the Copernican theory in astronomy; *The Pathwaie to Knowledge*, an abridged version of Euclid's *Elements;* and *The Whetstone of Witte*, an algebra, in which the equality sign "=" appears for the first time.

The Seventeenth Century

As part of the scientific explosion of the seventeenth century, mathematics experienced a period of growth unparalleled until modern times. The practical demands of society, the spread of education, and the general intellectual climate of the time contributed to this growth. The number of people engaged in mathematical activity became so large that only a few of the outstanding creative mathematicians and their major works can be mentioned.

John Napier (1550–1617), the Scottish contemporary of Galileo, published *Mirifici Logarithmorum Canonis Descriptio* (1614), in which he set forth the theory of logarithms.

Rene Descartes (1596–1650), the philosopher-scientist, sought to demonstrate that all scientific investigations are related and the key to that relation is mathematics. One of the appendixes to his famous *Discourse on Method* (1537), entitled "La Geometrie," was the first publication of analytic geometry. In it, Descartes applied methods of algebra to geometry, enabling him to settle some previously insoluble classical problems.

Pierre de Fermat (1601–1665) is credited with inventing analytic geometry independently of Descartes, with conceiving the tangential approach to differential calculus before either Newton or Leibniz were born, and with being one of the creators of the mathematical theory of probability. He is probably best known, however, for his work in number theory. Fermat published only a few papers; most of his results are known through letters he wrote to friends and from notes he made in margins of books.

Much of the work of Gerard Desargues (1593–1662) was eclipsed during his lifetime by Descartes' writings. But two centuries after his death his treatise on conics, *Brouillon project d'une atteinte aux événemens des rencontres du cône avec un plan* (1639), was republished and he is considered the founder of modern projective geometry.

Another Frenchman, Blaise Pascal (1623–1662), did work in geometry (*Essay on Conics*, 1640) and also was the cocreator with Fermat of probability theory.

One of the most significant contributions of the seventeenth century was the invention of differential and integral calculus, which led to the development of analysis, one of the three major branches of mathematics. (Algebra and geometry are the other two.) Calculus may be characterized as the gateway between elementary and advanced mathematics; a knowledge of calculus is essential to any real understanding of physics and related branches of technology and a prerequisite to the study of analysis. As is the case so often in mathematical creativity, calculus was developed independently in England by Isaac Newton (1642–1727) and in Germany by Gottfried Wilhelm von Leiniz (1646–1716). This fact engendered one of the most bitter partisan feuds in mathematical history, with admirers of each man hurling charges of plagarism at the other.

Newton's first publication involving his calculus was his famous *Philosophiae Naturalis Principia Mathematica*, 1687 (*The Mathematical Principles of Natural Philosophy*). His later monographs on the subject are: *De Analysi per Aequationes Numero Terminorum Infinitas*, 1669 (*An Analysis by Means of Equations with an Indefinite Number of Terms*); *Methodus Fluxionum et Serierum Infinitarum*, 1671 (*Method of Fluxions and Infinite Series*); and *Tractatus de Quadratura Curvarum*, 1676 (*Quadrature of Curves*).

Leibniz's results, as well as the development of his ideas, are contained in hundreds of pages of notes made from 1673 on, but never published by him. In 1684 he began publishing a few papers on calculus in the journal *Acta Eruditorum* and in 1714 he wrote *Historia et Origo Calculi Differentialis*, in which he gave an account of the development of his own thinking on the subject.

In addition to the expansion of mathematical content and activity, this period is significant for developments that occurred with respect to communication among mathematicians. Prior to the late sixteenth century, mathematics was created by individuals and small groups headed by one or two prominent leaders. The results were communicated orally, through personal correspondence, and occasionally written up in texts-first in manuscript form and later as printed books. As more people began to participate in mathematical research, the desire for exchange of information and for the stimulus of meeting others with the same intellectual interests resulted in the founding of scientific societies. These societies were important not only in making possible direct contact and exchange of ideas, but also because they supported journals, which eventually became the accepted medium for publication of new research results. The oldest mathematical society still in existence is the Mathematische Gesellschaft in Hamburg, Germany, founded in 1690 as the Kunstrechnungsliebende Societät, and continued (1790–1876) as the Gesellschaft zur Verbreitung der Mathematischen Wissenschaften. Its publications were entitled *Jahresbriefe* or *Jahres-Berichte* or *Berichte* from 1723 to 1878 and its current journal is entitled *Mitteilungen*, 1873–.[4]

Another seventeenth century development was the establishment of Royal Academies, subsidized by the rulers of the time. These academies sponsored research and also supported journals, in which they published the results of their research.

Eighteenth Century

Calculus dominated mathematical development in the eighteenth century. Research in this new theory took two directions: extension and application of calculus to other parts of mathematics and to physics, and examination of its logical foundations.

Research during this century was carried on mainly by the Royal Academies. The most prominent academies were at Berlin, London, Paris, and St. Petersburg. Prior to 1800, universities played only a minor role in research and the great mathematicians were attached to the academies.

Leonhard Euler (1707–1783), who was attached to both the Berlin Academy and the St. Petersburg Academy during his career, was the most productive mathematician of the century. He wrote about 900 books and papers, including works on mechanics, music, and astromony, as well as mathematics. Euler is considered the creator of analytic mechanics (as opposed to the older geometrical mechanics), based on his achievements in establishing calculus as a purely analytic theory. His *Mechanica* (1736) is a major contribution to the analytical foundation of mechanics. Euler's texts on mechanics, algebra, mathematical analysis, analytic and differential geometry, and calculus of variations were standard works for a 100 years or more. Three landmark texts in calculus are: *Introductio in Analysin Infinitorum* (1748), the first connected presentation of calculus and elementary analysis; *Institutiones Calculi Differentialis* (1755); and the three-volume *Institutiones Calculi Integralis* (1768–1770).

French mathematics held a position of superiority during the eighteenth century and some of the important works from that country are: *Traité de dynamique* (1743) and *Reflexions sur la cause générale des vents* (1747), by Jean d'Alembert; *Mecanique analytique* (1788) and *Theorie des fonctions analytiques* (1797), by Joseph Louie Lagrange; *Eléments de géométrie* (1794) and *Essai de la théorie des nombres* (1798), by Adrien-Marie Legendre; and *Feuilles d'analyse appliquée à la géométrie* (1795), by Gaspard Monge. An important work which, like its author, bridges two centuries, is the five-volume *Mécanique céleste* (1799–1825), by Pierre Simon Laplace. This work reviewed, unified, and greatly extended all previous work of Newton, d'Alembert, Euler, Lagrange, and Laplace, himself, in the fields of probability and celestial mechanics.

1800 to 1940

The modern area in mathematics is considered to have begun with Carl Friedrich Gauss (1777–1855), the German mathematician who dominated nineteenth century mathematics. He contributed to almost every branch of mathematics, but is perhaps best known for his work in the theory of numbers, represented by his monumental *Disquisitiones Arithmeticae* (1801).

With the beginning of the century, mathematical creativity began to increase exponentially, and by 1900 had produced about five times as much original mathematics as had been accomplished in all previous ages.[1] Every major branch of mathematics underwent profound changes in terms of expansion of subject matter and the opening of new fields as well as the extension of older ones. Consequently, mathematics became so vast a subject that mathematicians were forced to confine their efforts to one major branch: algebra, geometry, or analysis. It has been said that Gauss was one of the last men to know the subject as a whole.

Algebra, which previously was little more than generalized arithmetic, was liberated from its dependence on arithmetic and became abstract, with wider applications, during this period. Early work in this area was done by the Irish mathematician William Rowan Hamilton (1805–1865) and the German mathematician Hermann Grassmann (1809–1877). Important works of Hamilton are *Lectures on Quaternions* (1853) and *Elements of Quaternions* (1866), and of Grassman, *Die Lineale Ausdehnungslehre* (1844). England was the center of this nineteenth-century algebra with its geometric applications under the guidance of Arthur Cayley (1821–1895), the originator of matrix theory, and James Joseph Sylvester (1814–1897). Cayley's writings are found in his *Collected Mathematical Papers*, 13 volumes, Cambridge University Press, 1889–1897. Sylvester, who taught at Johns Hopkins University from 1876 until his return to England in 1884, published in various journals. He is also important for having initiated research in pure mathematics in the United States and for founding the first American mathematics journal, the *American Journal of Mathematics.* Also in the field of algebra, work was done in the theory of groups, notably by Felix Klein (1849–1925) in Germany, and by Marius Sophus Lie (1842–1899) in Norway. Both men published widely in journals and Klein also wrote books on the theory, history, and teaching of mathematics. Two of his books are *Famous Problems of Elementary Geometry* (1895; English translation 1930), and *Elementary Mathematics from an Advanced Standpoint* (2 vols., 1907–1908; English translation 1932–1940). Another man working in algebra at this time was the French mathematician Évariste Galois. One of the more romantic figures in mathematics history, Galois was killed in a duel in 1832, shortly before his twenty-first birthday. His unpublished notes, that were later deciphered and revised, turned out to be the theory of groups, the foundation of modern algebra and modern geometry.[1]

In the field of analysis, three men are acknowledged to be the founders of the theory of complex functions: Augustin Louis Cauchy (France, 1789–1857), Bernhard Riemann (Germany, 1826–1866), and Karl Weirstrass (Germany, 1815–1897). Cauchy was a prolific writer, whose over 700 papers covered all branches of mathematics. His first significant paper in complex function theory was "Mémoire sur la théorie des intégrales définies," read to the Paris Academy in 1814. The paper considered his most important was "Memoire sur les intégrales définies prises entre des limites imaginaires," written in 1825 but not published until 1874. Riemann's doctoral thesis of 1851, "Grundlagen für eine allgemeine Theorie der Functionen einer veränderlichen complexen Grösse," is a basic paper in complex function theory. Weierstrass did not publish his results at the time he first achieved them. His research became known only in the late 1890s when he published his collected *Werke*. Also in analysis, the theory of elliptic functions was developed by Niels Henrik Abel (Norway, 1802–1829) and Carl Gustav Jacob Jacobi (Germany, 1804–1851). The paper that contains Abel's famous theorem was first submitted to the Academy of Sciences in Paris in 1826 for publication in its journal. The manuscript was either disregarded or mislaid, however, and it was not published until after Abel's death, in 1841. A key work in elliptic functions is Jacobi's book *Fundamenta Nova Theoriae Functionum Ellipticarum* (1829).

Developments in geometry affected not only that field, but all the branches of mathematics. Early in the century, three men in different countries all published consistent non-Euclidean systems of geometry, each independently of the other two. In Russia, Nicolai Lobachevsky (1793–1856) published a series of journal articles between 1829 and 1837. In 1840 he published a book in German, *Geometrische Untersuchungen zur Theorie*, in which he lamented the slight interest shown in his writings. His *Pangéométrie*, published in 1855, was a completely new exposition of his geometry. In Hungary, Janos Bolyai (1802–1860) wrote a paper entitled "The Science of Absolute Spaces," which was published in 1832. And in Germany, Bernhard Riemann, in 1886, published "Über die Hypothesen, welche der Geometrie zu Grundeliegen" (On the Hypotheses Which Lie at the Foundation of Geometry). This paper was based on a lecture he had delivered in 1854 to the faculty at Göttingen. These men showed that the axioms of Euclid were not self-evident truths, as had been assumed for centuries, and that consistent geometries built on other axioms were possible. This idea produced fundamental changes in notions of physical and mathematical space, and the axiomatic method that pervades all modern mathematics is one of the consequences of this discovery.[2]

The formalistic treatment of algebra and the abstract axiomatic approach to geometry triggered an interest in logic and foundations of mathematics. This interest was redoubled when George Cantor (1845–1918) first published his controversial theory of sets. Cantor's theory is spread over numerous papers that appeared in *Mathematische Annalen* and the *Journal für Mathematik* from 1874 to 1897. The first significant mathematical studies of logic were *The Mathematical Analysis of Logic* (1847) and *The Laws of Thought* (1854), both by George Boole (1815–1864). In 1884, Gottlob Frege (1848–1925) published *Die Grundlagen der Arithmetik*, which stimulated efforts to unify logic and mathematics.[1]

As mathematics expanded and changed during the nineteenth century, so too did the agencies for the propagation of results. First, the universities participated in research, the writing of textbooks, and the systematic training of mathematicians. The dominance of the royally supported academies began to decline at this time and research became an important function of the universities.[2]

Second, there was a vast increase in the number of journals. The first purely mathematical journal, *Annales de Mathematiques Pures et Appliquees*, was started in France in 1810; it ceased publication in 1831. *Crelle's Journal*, the oldest mathematical journal still in existence, began in 1826. Among the numerous other titles are the *Mathematische Annalen* (Germany, 1868–), the *Acta Mathematica* (Sweden, 1882–), and the *American Journal of Mathematics* (1878–), the first mathematical journal in the United States.

Finally, another type of agency that has promoted mathematical activity since the nineteenth century is the national professional society. With the exception of the Wiskundig Genootschap, founded in Amsterdam in 1778, most national societies did not appear until the second half of the nineteenth century. The oldest of the major national societies is the Moskovskoe Matematicheskoe Obshchestvo (Moscow Mathematical Society), organized in 1864. Some others are the London Mathematical Society (1865), the Societe Mathematique de France (1872), the American Mathematical Society (1894; founded in 1888 as the New York Mathematical Society), and the Deutsche Mathematiker-Vereinigung (1890). These societies hold regular meetings at which papers are presented and each sponsors one or more journals.

Occasional international meetings of mathematicians took place during the nineteenth century, but the first of the present series of international congresses of mathematicians was held in 1897. The congress has met regularly every four years since 1900, except for interruptions caused by the two World Wars. The *Proceedings* of each congress have been published, usually by the mathematical society of the sponsoring country.[4]

In 1900, at the International Congress of Mathematicians assembled in Paris, David Hilbert (1862–1943) lectured on mathematics in the new century. Hilbert, who had just published his now-famous *Grundlagen der Geometrie*, a complete revision of Euclid's *Elements* using modern axiomatic methods, outlined 23 unsolved problems, a challenge for the new century. Hilbert's insight was so accurate that every one of these problems has led to important new results, but even he could not foresee how mathematics would expand in the 1900s.

The phenomenal growth rate that began in the 1800s continued, with mathematical knowledge doubling every 15 or 20 years. Quantity, however, is not the chief feature of twentieth century mathematics. One of the outstanding characteristics of mathematics of the present century is a fundamental trend toward unity; for an abstract axiomatic treatment of mathematics as a whole.[5] As a result of Boole's work and the recognition of formal axiomatics that followed the discovery of non-Euclidean geometries, interest in the logical foundations of mathematics began to spread rapidly. The most notable successor to Boole's initial efforts in mathematical logic is the *Principia Mathematica*, a monumental two-volume work that appeared during the years 1910–1913. In this work the philosopher-mathematicians Bertrand Russell (1872–1970) and Alfred North Whitehead (1861–1947) attempted to express all of mathematics in a universal logical symbolism. This goal of finding a single consistent set of axioms upon which all mathematics could be based was proved unattainable in 1931 when Kurt Gödel (1906–) published "Uber formal unentscheidbare Sätze der *Principia Mathematica* und verwandter Systeme I" (On Formally Undecidable Propositions of *Principia Mathematica* and Related Systems; English translation 1965). Another important book of Gödel's is *The Consistency of the Axiom of Choice and of the Generalized Continuum Hypothesis with the Axioms of Set Theory* (1940; rev. ed. 1951). Gödel demonstrated that in any axiom system broad enough to contain all the formulas of a formalized elementary number theory, there exist theorems (formulas) that can neither be proved nor disproved within the system.[6]

Having accepted the fact that mathematics is not provably consistent from within, mathematicians continued to explore their own branches of the subject. Algebra has become far more general than it has ever been before, and similar tendencies toward abstraction in geometry have led to advances in the field of algebraic geometry and the hybrid field of differential geometry (a synthesis of geometry and parts of analysis). Analysis itself has become more generalized, linked with both algebra and topology. The methods of algebraic topology, which began to be a major field of investigation at the end of the nineteenth century, have become the basis for a newer field, homological algebra.[7]

The desire to consolidate and simplify previous results can be seen throughout mathematical history; Euclid's *Elements* was an example of this tendency. In the twentieth century, another attempt was begun in the 1930s to integrate all contemporary mathematics within a single framework by a group of French mathematicians writing under the name of "Bourbaki." The work of this group will be discussed in the next section of this article.

During and after World War II, mathematical thinking penetrated the sciences and technology at an ever-increasing rate. In the decades since the war the methodological and conceptual tools of mathematics have been utilized by the social sciences as well.

A measure of the growth and volume of the modern world's utilization of mathematics is given by the estimates that show that of all the mathematicians who ever lived, over 80% are alive today. The U.S. Office of Education, which publishes statistics on the number of degrees granted each year, reports 250 doctorates in mathematics in 1955, 660 in 1965, and predicts 1840 in 1975.

More original mathematics has been produced since the end of World War II than in all previous history. Over 1200 journals publish mathematical articles, of which more than 12,000 were reviewed in the first six months of 1975 by *Mathematical Reviews*.[8]

It is this literature-the literature since the end of the War-that is the subject of the following section.

THE CURRENT MATHEMATICS LITERATURE

Introduction

As a working hypothesis for its studies on mathematical information exchange, the American Mathematical Society's Committee to Monitor Problems in Communication considered the current mathematics literature to be publications that are reviewed in *Mathematical Reviews*.[9] This seems to be an acceptable definition for our purposes, also, since *Mathematical Reviews* is the principal abstracting journal of mathematics and covers the world literature in the field. The current literature may be further defined as that which forms the content of graduate education and represents present-day research interests. Mathematics that is studied at the elementary, secondary, and collegiate levels is a consolidation of results and ideas from the earlier periods of mathematical history and, therefore, does not satisfy the definition of current mathematics. The literature of mathematics below the graduate level is found in the form of textbooks and can be easily located in general bibliographies, indexes, and publishers' catalogs.

Another class of materials that will be omitted from our discussion is mathematical literature for the layman: popularizations, mathematical games and recreations, and so forth. Again, the standard bibliographic tools can be used for locating information about this type of literature.

In the discussion that follows, the mathematics literature is divided into two categories: the primary literature and the secondary literature. After a general description of the types of publications in each category, specific titles are cited as illustrations of the various types.

The Primary Mathematics Literature

The current mathematics literature is chiefly serial in nature. The principal medium for the dissemination of mathematical information is the journal, followed by the book series, including series of monographs, proceedings of symposia, and translation series. The least common form of publication is the nonserial book. In this group are found dictionaries, handbooks, mathematical tables, directories, histories, collected papers of individual mathematicians, and Festschriften. Because of the way the nonserial literature is used, it will be dealt with in connection with the secondary literature.

The broad headings used to classify entries in *Mathematical Reviews* gives an indication of the subject coverage of the literature. The current literature reflects a wide variety of research activity, ranging from traditional topics, such as geometry, to more recent topics, such as homological algebra. The increasing penetration of mathematics into other disciplines is evidenced by literature dealing with the biological and behavioral sciences, in addition to the traditional applications in the physical sciences.

While a reading knowledge of French, German, Italian, and Russian is useful to the mathematician, English has recently become the dominant language in world mathematical circles. For example, in the German journal *Mathematische Annalen*, the percentage of papers in English rose from approximately 5% in the mid-1930s to nearly 20% in the mid-1950s, and to 55% in the mid-1960s.[7] Most countries with an academic tradition produce at least one mathematical periodical that is internationally recognized. English language abstracts of many articles from these periodicals appear in *Mathematical Reviews*. (A small number of *Mathematical Reviews* abstracts are still written in French, German, and Italian, however.) The American Mathematical Society also has an active translation program, notably in the area of Russian mathematics, about which more is said later.

Mathematics literature is issued by three general categories of publishers: societies, universities and academies, and commercial houses. All three groups issue both serial and nonserial publications, covering both basic research and applied mathematics. It is not the case in mathematics, as in many subjects, that research is published by institutions and practical applications of the research are reported by the commercial press. There are instances where mathematical societies place their publications in the hands of commercial houses, but this is for the purpose of administrative convenience; Bell of London, for example, is the publisher for the Mathematical Association. Again, unlike the case in other sciences, there are few publications issued by the U.S. government that are of value to mathematicians. The only such publication abstracted in *Mathematical Reviews* is *The Journal of Research of the National Bureau of Standards. Section B: The Mathematical Sciences.*[10] The National Science Foundation does not publish mathematics under its own name, but gives financial support to other mathematical publications, especially for translations of foreign-language works. An interesting example of such cooperative publishing is a three-volume survey of mathematics that was translated from the Russian: *Mathematics: Its Content, Methods, and Meaning*, edited by A.D. Aleksandrov, A.N. Kolmogorov, M.A. Lavrent'ev, and translated by S. H. Gould and T. Bartha (Russian edition 1956; American edition 1963). A National Science Foundation grant enabled the American Mathematical Society to translate and publish this work, which subsequently received wider circulation by being reissued by the M.I.T. Press.

Journals

The history of scientific journals, as noted earlier, began with the formation of scientific societies and academies in the seventeenth century. These first journals, such as the *Philosophical Transactions of the Royal Society* (London, 1665), contained both mathematical and scientific articles. During the eighteenth century, when journals had become the accepted medium for publication of research, they increased in number. By the nineteenth century they had become more specialized. The *Annales de Mathématiques Pures et Appliquées* (France, 1810–1831) was the first journal devoted solely to mathematics. The *Journal für die reine und angewandte Mathematik*, founded in Germany in 1826, and usually referred to as *Crelle's Journal* (after its founder), is the oldest mathematics journal still in existence.

The number of mathematical journals vastly increased with the establishment of national mathematical societies in the second half of the nineteenth century. Today most countries have national societies that publish at least one journal. The oldest and largest U.S. society, the American Mathematical Society, publishes six journals.

In addition to national societies, there are a number of societies of a specialized nature that issue journals. Two examples of this type of society are The Mathematical Association of America and the Society for Industrial and Applied Mathematics.

The Mathematical Association of America is concerned primarily with collegiate-level mathematics and teaching, and publishes three journals: *The American Mathematical Monthly*, a journal containing original and expository articles at the undergraduate and beginning graduate level; *Mathematics Magazine*, which is similar in content to the *Monthly*, but focuses at a somewhat lower level; and *The Two-Year College Mathematics Journal*, established in 1970 by the commercial firm of Prindle, Weber, and Schmidt, but published since the fall of 1974 by the association. This journal features articles, book reviews, and problems of special interest to students and teachers in two-year colleges.

The Society for Industrial and Applied Mathematics (SIAM) publishes eight journals in the area of applied mathematics: *SIAM Journal on Applied Mathematics* (formerly the *SIAM Journal*): *SIAM Journal on Control; SIAM Journal on Theory of Probability and Its Applications*, which is a translation of the Russian journal *Teoriya Veroyatnostei i Ee Primeneniya.*

Universities also began to issue journals in the nineteenth century. The first mathematical journal in the United States was the *American Journal of Mathematics*, founded in 1878 by J.J. Sylvester when he was a professor at Johns Hopkins University. Currently, many universities with strong mathematics programs, in the United States and worldwide, publish journals; some are general in nature and some are specialized. Two examples from the United States are the *Duke Mathematical Journal* (general) and the *Notre Dame Journal of Formal Logic* (specialized).

Until recently, commercial houses have played a more important role in journal publishing in Europe than in the United States. For example, Springer-Verlag of Germany publishes *Mathematische Annalen* and *Mathematische Zeitschrift*, while in England Pergamon Press publishes *Topology, an International Journal of Mathematics.* In 1960, Academic Press of New York inaugurated an impressive program of publishing journals devoted to special areas of mathematics. Currently it issues the following titles: *Journal of Mathematical Analysis and Applications; Journal of Algebra; Journal of Differential Equations; Journal of Combinatorial Theory; Journal of Functional Analysis* (articles in French and English); *Journal of Approximation Theory* (German and English); and, *Journal of Multivariate Analysis* (German, French, and English).

As the foregoing remarks indicate, the current journal literature covers a broad range of topics, is produced by several different types of publishers, and is issued in all of the modern languages, although English has become the dominant language of mathematical research. Many important foreign language journals are now being translated into English on a continuing basis. (The latest index volume of *Mathematical Reviews* lists the journals in translation that are abstracted in that publication.)

In quantitative terms, the journal literature has experienced the same rapid growth that typifies all scientific and technical literature in general. The latest index issue of *Mathematical Reviews* lists approximately 1200 journals that contain mathematical contributions. Since space does not permit describing them all, the journals published by the American Mathematical Society have been selected for discussion. The publications of the society have been chosen as examples because they illustrate the variety of journals that are available. The society not only issues six journals under its own name, but it publishes translations of foreign journals, it has cooperative agreements with other mathematical societies, and it subsidizes several journals published by universities and other organizations. Furthermore, most of the general comments about the society's journals are applicable to the journals of other national societies.

Of the six journals published under the society's name, two are devoted solely to the results of original research. They are: *Transactions of the American Mathematical Society* (1900–) and *Proceedings of the American Mathematical Society* (1950–). Both of these journals, which are issued monthly, cover all areas of pure and applied mathematics. Ordinarily, longer papers are published in the *Transactions* and shorter ones in the *Proceedings*. A strict editor-referee system, which ensures the highest level of excellence of the papers, makes these among the more prestigious journals in which to publish.

The *Bulletin of the American Mathematical Society* (1891–) is the official journal of the society. A bimonthly publication, it contains reports of the meetings, financial reports, and miscellaneous other material of interest to professional mathematicians. It also contains the full texts of many invited addresses at meetings, long survey articles by invited authors, reviews of advanced mathematics books, and a department of research announcements.

Notices of the American Mathematical Society (1954–) is published eight times a year, primarily to transmit the programs of meetings of the society. It contains author abstracts of all contributed papers for meetings, announcements of research in progress, personal notes, and other news items.

Two journals of the society are devoted to research in special areas. They are: *Mathematics of Computation* (formerly *Mathematical Tables and Other Aids to Computation*, 1943–), which is a quarterly devoted to advances in numerical analysis, the application of computational methods, mathematical tables, high-speed calculators, and other aids to computation; and *Journal of Differential Geometry*, a publication that began in 1970.

Three journals of Russian translations are currently published by the society. They are: *Soviet Mathematics-Doklady* (bimonthly), which is a translation of the entire pure mathematics section of the *Doklady Akademii Nauk SSSR*, consisting of short reports of current research in the former Soviet Union. It provides a comprehensive, up-to-date survey of what is going on in Soviet mathematics. *Mathematics of the USSR-Sbornik* (monthly) is a translation of *Matematiceskii Sbornik*, which is published by the Moscow Mathematical Society and the Academy of Sciences of the USSR. It deals with current research in all fields of mathematics. The third journal is *Mathematics of the USSR-Izvestija* (bimonthly), which is a translation of *Izvestija, Mathematiceskaja Serija*, published by the Academy of Sciences of the USSR and dealing with research in pure areas.

The society also published *Chinese Mathematics-Acta*, a translation into English of *Acta Mathematica Sinica*, which was published from 1960 until 1966 by the Academia Sinica, Peking, People's Republic of China. Until the publication is resumed in Peking, the latest available volume is Vol. 9 (1967).

The American Mathematical Society has entered into cooperative agreements with other mathematical societies, both in the United States and abroad. In the United States, one of the forms this cooperation takes is joining in the support and publication of a number of mathematical journals. It shares with the Johns Hopkins University the publication of the *American Journal of Mathematics*, and it assumes responsibility for the technical editing of the *Quarterly of Applied Mathematics* of Brown University. The society also contributes to the financial support of a number of other mathematical journals. These include, at present, the *Canadian Journal of Mathematics* and the *Rocky Mountain Mathematical Journal*. It also provides editorial services for the *Journal of Symbolic Logic*, a publication of the Association for Symbolic Logic.

Book Series

Mathematical Reviews abstracts books as well as journals, so the headings referred to previously give some indication of the subject coverage of this form of literature. However, books generally do not deal with the latest developments on the frontiers of research. The nature of book publishing is such that older, more established topics are dealt with, usually in an expository manner.

As is the case with journals, books are published by societies, universities and academies, and commercial houses, This is true both in the United States and abroad.

Once again, the American Mathematical Society plays an important publishing role. Its several book series are typical of the kinds of material found in this category and provide good examples for discussion. The society publishes 13 book series, including several series of monographs, proceedings of symposia, and translation series.

The society's three monograph series are *Memoirs of the American Mathematical Society, Colloquium Publications*, and *Mathematical Surveys. Memoirs* (1950–) is the longest of the monograph series. It contains research tracts of the same general character as the papers published in the *Transactions. Colloquium Publications*, a monograph series that began in 1905, is the oldest of these series and contains the syntheses of recent and older mathematical work prepared by outstanding research mathematicians. *Mathematical Surveys* covers fields of current interest, each volume giving a brief survey of a subject and an introduction to its recent developments and unsolved problems.

The four series of proceedings are: *Proceedings of Symposia in Pure Mathematics*, which contains lectures from symposia and summer institutes sponsored by the society; *Lectures in Applied Mathematics*, which contains a series of lectures given at the summer seminars sponsored by the society; *SIAM-AMS Proceedings*, which contains lectures from symposia and summer institutes in applied mathematics, sponsored jointly with the Society for Industrial and Applied Mathematics; and *Lectures on Mathematics in the Life Sciences*, a recent series dealing with the mathematical aspects of biology.

Society translations include one monograph series and five translation series. They are: *Translations of Mathematical Monographs*, which is a series translated chiefly from the Russian; *Selected Translations in Mathematical Statistics and Probability*, published by the society for the Institute of Mathematical Statistics; *Translations Series I* and *II*, translated from the Russian and other Eastern European and Oriental langauges; *Proceedings of the Steklov Institute of Mathematics in the Academy of Sciences of the USSR;* and *Transactions of the Moscow Mathematical Society*. These last two series are cover-to-cover translations of two Russian series.

The monographs and other serials of the American Mathematical Society may be characterized as advanced research-level publications. To meet the need for expository presentations at the collegiate and graduate level, The Mathematical Association of America publishes two important series. The *Carus Mathematical Monographs* is a series of books in pure and applied mathematics, each written by an authority in the field. The scope of this series also includes historical and biographical monographs. The *MAA Studies in Mathematics* is a series devoted to recent developments in mathematics. Each volume is a collection of reprints of short papers on a given topic by several authors.

Some important foreign series that should be mentioned are:

Cambridge Tracts in Mathematics and Mathematical Physics, a monograph series published by Cambridge University Press since 1905. The purpose of this series is to provide introductions to modern topics in mathematics. While the books are not intended for specialists, they cannot be considered elementary in the conventional sense.

Ergebnisse der Mathematik und ihrer Grenzbebiete is issued by a commercial publisher, Springer-Verlag of Berlin. Each volume in this monograph series may be described as a state-of-the-art treatment of an individual topic. The treatment of a topic is exhaustive, bringing together and relating results that previously were scattered throughout the literature, primarily the journal literature. Of immeasurable value to the researcher is the extensive bibliography, arranged chronologically, which appears at the end of each volume. German and English are the languages in which these books are published.

Lecture Notes in Mathematics is another Springer publication. This series attempts to report quickly new developments in mathematical research and teaching. The type of material in this series includes preliminary drafts of original papers, lectures on a new field, or presentations of new perspectives on a classical field, and papers from seminars. Each volume is devoted to a single topic and the language may be German, French, or English.

No discussion of the primary mathematics literature would be complete without mention of the works of a nonexistent Frenchman named Bourbaki. Nicolas Bourbaki is the collective pseudonym used by an informal corporation of French mathematicians, numbering from 10 to 20 at any one time. This anonymous society is writing a comprehensive treatise on mathematics, starting with the most general basic principles and to conclude, presumably, with the most specialized application. The treatise, whose general title is *Elémentes de Mathématique*, is a survey of all mathematics from a sophisticated point of view. The Bourbaki presentation of each subject is systematic and thorough, often including an historical review of the subject and a set of exercises. The Bourbaki gadgetry includes inserts constituting a set of directions on the proper use of the treatise, foldout sheets that summarize important definitions and assumptions, and a dictionary for each book that serves also as an index to "Bourbachique" terminology. The project, published by Hermann of Paris, got under way in 1939 and over 30 titles of this monumental work have appeared to date. The number of volumes is somewhat larger, since many of the earlier titles have been revised and issued as second and even third editions. The influence of this series is equalled only by the amount of apocryphal stories about Bourbaki, most of them perpetrated by the members of the group.[11]

The Secondary Mathematics Literature

The secondary mathematics literature is not extensive. Indeed, when compared with the bibliographic tools and services of other sciences, it is somewhat meager and even primitive. Sophisticated information systems, based on computer technology, have been employed by other disciplines for some time. However, the establishment of machine-readable databases, and the use of the computer to assemble and compose indexes, are very recent developments in mathematics. Within the last five years some new tools and services have resulted from the utilization of new technology, and they are discussed later in this paper.

In examining the secondary literature it might be helpful to view it in terms of the information needs of mathematicians: current awareness (what are the latest developments in a particular field of interest?); day-to-day specifics (is there a solution of this problem? what is the meaning of this foreign term?); and retrospective (what has been written on the history of this topic?).

The need to be informed about recent developments and publications is met by the traditional abstracting and reviewing journals and by the newer current awareness services. Day-to-day needs are met by information contained in monographs, treatises, and reference books, such as dictionaries and mathematical tables. Retrospective needs are satisfied by indexes, collections of reviews, and by bibliographies found in monographs and treatises.[12]

Current Awareness Needs

By the middle of the nineteenth century the number of mathematical journals and the scattering of mathematical articles over a number of more general periodicals made it difficult for the individual to keep informed, and in 1868 the first mathematical abstracting journal, *Jahrbuch über die Fortschritte der Mathematik*, was founded. Its success was only partial because of a substantial time lag and it ceased publication in 1934. The literature from that time to the present day is covered by the following abstracting journals: *Zentralblatt für Mathematik*, founded in 1931; *Mathematical Reviews*, founded in 1940; and *Referativyni Zhurnal Matematika*, founded in 1953. A number of specialized abstracting journals have also appeared in recent years: *Statistical Theory and Method Abstracts* and *Computer Abstracts* are two examples.

Mathematical Reviews, published by the American Mathematical Society, is undoubtedly the most valuable English-language publication for locating current mathematical literature. It is international in scope, covering about 1200 journals of every mathematical specialty and every language in which mathematics is written. A special attempt is made to cover the mathematical activities in the USSR and the countries within its sphere of influence. Selected books and other nonserials as well as journals and series are reviewed. Books of a popular nature or below the level of graduate education are not usually included.

Entries from other abstracting and reviewing services are reprinted in *Mathematical Reviews*. They are: *Applied Mechanics Review, Computing Reviews, Electrical and Electronics Abstracts, Mathematics of Computation, Operations Research, Physics Abstracts, Referativnyi Zhurnal Matematika (Mehanika*, etc.), *Statistical Theory and Methods Abstracts*, and *Zentralblatt für Mathematik*.

In addition to the American Mathematical Society, about 30 other national mathematically oriented societies sponsor *Mathematical Reviews*. The publication was initiated in 1940 with funds granted by the Carnegie Corporation of New York, and over the years it has received support from the National Science Foundation, the Rockefeller Foundation, the American Philosophical Society, and the Alfred P. Sloan Foundation. It is presently facing an uncertain future, due to the recent withdrawal of National Science Foundation and private foundation funding.

The reviews are written by approximately 2000 mathematicians who are experts in the subject areas of the original papers. The reviews, which are critical in nature, describe and evaluate the subject content of the original paper, often reproduce factual data and the steps of proofs, and relate the results to previous works.

Mathematical Reviews is published monthly in two annual volumes, with a separate index issue for each volume. The reviews in each volume are numbered consecutively. Some idea of the exhaustiveness of this work is given by the fact that in the first six months of 1975 (Vol. 49), 12,217 reviews were published.

Reviews in the monthly issues are currently arranged under 61 headings, in accordance with a subject classification scheme developed in 1970. Minor revisions are constantly being made in the scheme, based on literary warrant.

The index volumes include: an author index; a reprinting of the subject classification mentioned above; abbreviations of names of journals abstracted; a list of journals in translation; transliteration of Cyrillic employed by *Mathematical Reviews*, the Library of Congress, and selected abstracting journals; errata and addenda; and, since Vol. 45 (January–June 1973), a subject index. This subject index is a classified one, arranged according to the American Mathematical Society subject classification scheme. Briefly, this scheme consists of the main headings used to arrange the reviews in the monthly issues, which have been further subdivided into more specific subheadings, and to which code numbers have been assigned. Each review in the subject index is listed under the classification code numbers that have been assigned to it. The review is listed under the name of the author of the original paper and reference is to the number of the review.

Periodic cumulative author indexes are also published and are discussed later in this paper.

Zentralblatt für Mathematik und ihre Grenzgebiete is published in Berlin by Springer-Verlag, with editorial offices at Deutsche Akademie der Wissenschaften and Heidelberger Akademie der Wissenschafter (both in Berlin). Like *Mathematical Reviews* it is international in scope, has signed abstracts of the literature in various languages (chiefly German and English), is arranged in classified order (using the American Mathematical Society scheme at the present time), and has author indexes. It also has separately published cumulative author indexes.

Since late 1973 *Zentralblatt* has been gradually changing over to the use of author abstracts in an effort to satisfy the demand for more rapid and comprehensive information about mathematical research. This procedure, according to the publisher, is intended to lead to a certain degree of differentiation and complementation between the mathematical reviewing/abstracting journals. The journal has advised authors that an abstract should not be a short summary, but should comply in size and form with a normal review (although criticism is not expected) and may be written in English, French, or German. If authors' abstracts can be published within 10 weeks of receipt, as *Zentralblatt* hopes to do, this will be a great improvement over the time lag of many months that now exists.

Referativyni Zhurnal has been issued since 1953 by the Akademiya Nauk SSSR, Institut Nauchnoi Informatsii, Moscow. It is a major abstracting journal for the world's literature in most branches of science and technology.

Referativyni consists of several series, designated *svodnyi tom* (joint volume), each devoted to an individual branch of science or technology. The number and titles of the series have varied over the years. A series, or joint volume, is made up of chapters that are issued as separate periodicals with their own titles, and designated *vypusk RZh* (section of the *Referativnyi Zhurnal*). The mathematical series is titled *Referativyni Zhurnal Matematika* and consists of three chapters: General. Mathematical logic. Theory of numbers. Algebra. Topology. Geometry.-Mathematical analysis.-Numerical analysis. Probability theory and mathematical statistics. Cybernetics.

Bibliographic information in *Referativyni* is listed in the original languages following the Russian entry. There is a monthly author index.

As the volume of literature has steadily increased, the abstracting and reviewing journals have found it increasingly difficult to remain current. For example, the number of abstracts in *Mathematical Reviews* has been doubling every eight or 10 years, and presently there is a time lag of up to two years before an article or book is reviewed. The active researcher must depend largely on personal communications among members of invisible colleges, according to procedures that differ from those of ancient times only in the media of communication and travel.[12] As noted above, the publisher of *Zentralblatt* is hoping to improve the currency of that journal by the device of authors' abstracts. The American Mathematical Society, as a by-product of converting the database of *Mathematical Reviews* to machine-readable form, was recently able to offer two new current awareness services.

The first service, the Mathematical Title Service, provides lists of titles in all areas of mathematics, based on detailed interest profiles of the subscribers. This service originally started in 1968 as an experiment in automatic dissemination of information, was then called the Mathematical Offprint Service, which supplied offprints of articles. Articles that satisfied the subscriber's interest profile were mailed to him on a continuing basis, along with title listings of articles in which he indicated a peripheral interest. However, this service was discontinued because it could not be made self-supporting, and it was replaced by the Mathematical Title Service.[13]

The second service was a biweekly alerting journal, *Contents of Contemporary Mathematical Journals*, started in 1969, which reprinted the tables of contents of about 240 mathematical journals. In 1972 the title was changed to *Contents of Contemporary Mathematical Journals and New Publications*, when the scope of the journal was enlarged to include books and other separately published materials. (This type of publication had formerly been announced in the *Notices*.) In early 1974 the format of *Contents* was completely revised. It no longer reproduces title pages of journals, but is a listing of the material (articles, books, collections, etc.) that has been received in the editorial offices of *Mathematical Reviews* during a specific period of time and that is to be eventually reviewed. The material is arranged in classified order according to the major sections of the American Mathematical Society subject classification scheme. In each issue there is also an author index and a list of the journals represented in the issue. The increased coverage is an advantage of this new publication, but the information is not as prompt as formerly, since the materials must now be processed before *Contents* is printed. It remains to be seen whether this factor, plus the harder-to-use format will reduce the usefulness of this publication.

Day-to-Day Needs

As noted earlier, the least common form of literature is the nonserial publication. This category includes dictionaries, handbooks, mathematical tables, and directories, which are used to answer specific questions. It also includes indexes, bibliographies, and expository materials (histories, essays, collected papers of mathematicians, etc.), which meet retrospective needs and which are discussed later in this section.

There are relatively few reference books that answer day-to-day specifics. The mathematician is usually required to locate such information in treatises or other nonserial publications. The types of reference books that are available, together with some representative titles, can be dealt with briefly.

The dictionary is one of the more useful types of reference tool available to mathematicians. Mathematical dictionaries are often encyclopedic in nature, presenting condensations of mathematical concepts, not merely word definitions. *Mathematics Dictionary*, by Glenn and Robert James, is an example of this type. Another kind of dictionary is the bilingual or multilingual one, of which the *Russian-English Dictionary of the Mathematical Sciences*, by Lohwater and Gould, is an example. Dictionaries of special terms represent still another type; e.g., *Dictionary of Statistical Terms*, by Kendall and Buckland.

The *Mathematical Handbook for Scientists and Engineers*, by Korn and Korn, *Tables of Series, Products and Integrals*, by Ryshik and Gradstein, and the *Combined Membership List of the American Mathematical Society, The Mathematical Association of America, and the Society for Industrial and Applied Mathematics* are examples of handbooks, mathematical tables, and directories, respectively.

Retrospective Needs

The situation with respect to retrospective needs is similar to that for day-to-day needs. Again, the difficulty lies partly in the lack of adequate reference sources and search systems. Mathematics is substantially behind other sciences not only in the preparation of quick reference materials but also in the compilation of indexes, bibliographies, and expository materials, such as encyclopedias and historical studies. And again, as is the case with respect to day-to-day needs, treatises and monographs are used as supplements to, or substitutes for, reference books. As noted earlier, treatises and monographs usually contain extensive bibliographies, and mathematicians tend to use these sources, rather than more general, separately-published bibliographies.

The American Mathematical Society has again taken the lead in attempting to correct this situation. From time to time it publishes comprehensive indexes and collections of reviews in specialized areas.

The cumulative indexes published by the society are: the *20 Year Author Index of Mathematical Reviews, 1940–1959*, (Vols. 1–20); *Author Index of Mathematical Reviews, 1960–1964*, (Vols. 21–28); and *Author Index of Mathematical Reviews, 1965–1972*, (Vols. 29–44). It is interesting to note that the first two cumulative indexes cover 25 years in four volumes and contain 156,000 reviews. The latest index covers eight years in four volumes and contains 127,000 reviews.

The Index to Translations, (1966) is a cumulative author and subject index to material published in three of the society's translation series: *Translations Series I; Translations Series II;* and *Selected Translations in Mathematical Statistics and Probability*. In 1974 a second volume of the *Index* was published, covering the years 1966 through 1973.

The volumes of reviews published by the society are: *Reviews of Papers in Algebraic and Differential Topology, Topological Groups, and Homological Algebra*, containing reviews that appeared in *Mathematical Reviews* from 1940 through 1967; *Reviews of Papers on Infinite Groups; Reviews of Papers on Finite Groups;* and *Reviews of Papers in Number Theory*. These last three volumes contain reviews that appeared in *Mathematical Reviews* from 1940 through 1973. The reviews in all of the volumes are arranged in classified order and each volume has an author index. Of special interest are the forward citations given at the end of many reviews. These citations take note of any references made to the article at a later date by a review or reviews in the collection. The advantage of a review volume of this type is that it brings together in one location material that previously had to be searched in several volumes. One must bear in mind, however, that only reviews that appear in *Mathematical Reviews* are included.

CONCLUSION

Mathematics has conformed to the general pattern of explosive exponential growth that typifies all of the sciences. The unprecedented demands made upon mathematics by contemporary society have resulted in an increase in the number of mathematicians and a corresponding increase in the mathematics literature. From 1868 (the year the first abstracting journal was founded) until 1966, the literature grew from approximately 40,000 to about 430,000 titles.[14] If the estimated 2.5% annual rate of increase continues, the total should exceed 620,000 by the end of the 1970s.

REFERENCES

1. Berlinghoff, W.P. *Mathematics: The Art of Reason*; Heath: Boston, MA, 1968.
2. Kline, M. *Mathematical Thought from Ancient to Modern Times*; Oxford Univ. Press: New York, 1972.
3. Smith, D.E. *History of Mathematics*; Ginn: Boston, 1923; Vols. 1 and 2.
4. Mathematics, Societies of. In *Encyclopaedia Britannica 1973*; Vol. 14.
5. Dieudonné, J. Recent developments in mathematics. Am. Math. Mon. **1964**, *71*, 239–248.
6. Wilder, R.L. *Introduction to the Foundations of Mathematics*; Wiley: New York, 1952.
7. Committee on Support of Research in the Mathematical Sciences Report of the Committee. In *The Mathematical Sciences*; National Academy of Sciences: Washington, DC, 1968.

8. Saaty, T.L. *The Spirit and the Uses of the Mathematical Sciences*; McGraw-Hill: New York, 1969.
9. Committee to Monitor Problems in Communication Report of the Committee. In *Priorities for Projects in Mathematical Information Exchange and Retrieval*; American Mathematical Society: Providence, 1972.
10. Pemberton, J.A. *How to Find Out in Mathematics*; Pergamon: Oxford, U.K., 1963.
11. Halmos, P.R. Nicolas Bourbaki. In *Mathematics in the Modern World, Readings from Scientific American*; Freeman: San Francisco, CA, 1968; 77–81.
12. May, K.O. Problems of Information Retrieval in Mathematics. In *Proceedings of the Canadian Mathematical Congress*; University of Manitoba: Winnipeg, Manitoba, Canad, 1971; 477–484.
13. Conference Board of the Mathematical Sciences. *Proceedings of a Conference on a National Information System in the Mathematical Sciences*; Washington, DC, 1970.
14. May, K.O. Growth and quality of the mathematical literature. Isis **1969**, *59* (4), 363–371.

Medical Library Association (MLA)

Carla J. Funk
Medical Library Association, Chicago, Illinois, U.S.A.

Abstract
The Medical Library Association (MLA) aspires to be the association of the most visible, valued, and trusted health information experts working to enhance the quality of health care, education and research throughout the world. MLA fulfills its mission and goals through its continuing education, credentialing, professional recognition, research, publications, and international programs. The association also offers career services and advocates on behalf of its members through the association's public relations program and governmental relations programs. This entry explains how MLA serves its members, the profession, and society through its programs and services.

INTRODUCTION

The Medical Library Association (MLA), a 501(c)3 not-for-profit educational association, is a leading advocate for health sciences information professionals worldwide. Through its programs and services, MLA provides life-long educational opportunities, supports a knowledgebase of health information research, and works with a global network of partners. The association also promotes the importance of quality information for improved health to the health care community and the public. The association's organizational structure includes a board of directors, committees, a variety of task forces, sections organized by special subject interests and areas of responsibilities, ad hoc special interest groups (SIGs), representatives to allied organizations such as the National Information Standards Organization, and affiliated chapters representing the United States and parts of Canada. MLA aspires to be the association of the most visible, valued, and trusted health information experts working to enhance the quality of health care, education, and research throughout the world.[1] This entry explains how MLA serves its members, the profession, and society through its programs and services.

PROFESSIONAL AND MEMBERSHIP RECRUITMENT

Founded on May 2, 1898, by four librarians and four physicians, MLA is the second oldest special library association in the United States. The Association of Medical Librarians (as it was known until 1907) was founded "to encourage the improvement and increase of public medical libraries." More than a century later, MLA has grown to a professional organization of about 4000 members including 3300 health sciences librarians and 670 health sciences libraries and institutions in the health information profession. MLA also has international members from 56 countries in addition to the United States and Canada.

Working through its organizational structure (Fig. 1), the association continues to assist librarians with the exchange of health sciences books and periodicals (the MLA Exchange is one of the founders' earliest and most important projects) and to develop a variety of programs and services to serve the needs of health information specialists.

Demographically, MLA is comprised primarily of white females, in their 50s with master of library science (MLS) degrees, who are employed in hospital settings. This description is based upon data from the Hay Group/MLA 2008 Salary Survey.[2] Thirty-nine percent of MLA's members are employed in hospital libraries, 34% in academic medical centers, and 27% in other settings such as pharmaceutical companies. Eighty-nine percent of the membership is white, 3% Asian, 2% African-American, and 3% Hispanic or other backgrounds. In 2008, the median annual salary for a health sciences librarian was \$60,000 and the average annual salary, \$65,796. Between 2002 and 2008, actual wage rates of health sciences librarians were slightly higher than projected by CPI data.

Membership recruitment and retention is becoming more challenging for a variety of reasons for both the national association and affiliated chapters. The majority of health sciences librarians who entered the profession in the 1970s after the passage of the Medical Library Assistance Act are now retiring. Downsizing and consolidation in the health care industry have resulted in fewer health sciences libraries and fewer health sciences librarians. Although a record number of new members have joined MLA since 1997, these members do not offset those who are leaving the association due to retirement or change in profession. The Membership Committee continues to work to recruit members into the association.

Encyclopedia of Library and Information Sciences, Fourth Edition DOI: 10.1081/E-ELIS4-120043943

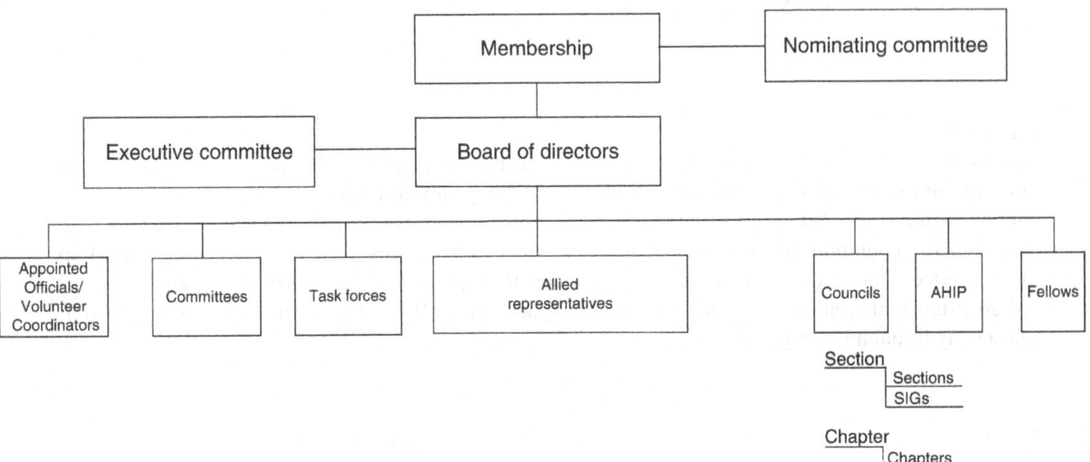

Fig. 1 MLA structure chart.

To meet the challenge of recruiting people into the profession, MLA established the Professional Recruitment and Retention Committee in 2006. The committee has developed initiatives to recruit an increasingly diverse group of people into the profession of health sciences librarianship. Through a series of awards from the National Library of Medicine (NLM) (http://www.nlm.nih.gov) and the South Central Region of National Network of Libraries of Medicine (http://nnlm.gov/scr/), MLA began a program to recruit people from diverse cultural backgrounds into health sciences librarianship. Through the awards, MLA was able to increase the number and stipend amount of GSLIS scholarships and develop career materials, in both English and Spanish, to inform students about opportunities in the profession. MLA is also actively involved with NLM, in the American Library Association's Spectrum Initiative. MLA launched its mentoring Web site (http://www.mlanet.org/mentor/) in 2003, to link people in the profession with interested students and other professionals and developed a "recruitment into the profession" DVD (http://www.mlanet.org/career/career_vid.html).

PROGRAMS AND SERVICES

MLA fulfills its mission and goals through its continuing education, credentialing, professional recognition, research, publications, and international programs. The association also offers career services and advocates on behalf of its members through the association's public relations program and governmental relations programs. In 1994, MLA adopted the Code of Ethics for Health Sciences Librarianship (http://www.mlanet.org/about/ethics.html). The code describes the goals and principles for ethical conduct for its members in relation to society, their clients, their institutions, the profession, and themselves. MLA promulgates practice standards for membership segments such as hospital librarians and chiropractic librarians and promotes research in the provision of information for quality health care.

LIFELONG LEARNING

Medical practice, research, and technology continue to change at a breathtaking pace. Supporting and promoting lifelong learning opportunities for health sciences librarians to meet these future challenges has been a major priority of MLA for almost 50 years. Lifelong learning includes both MLA's continuing education and credentialing programs. These have recently been combined with MLA's research programs to form the Center of Research and Education (CORE) Program. The history of the programs since the 1970s is described in detail in the first edition of the *Encyclopedia of Library and Information Science (ELIS)*[3] and in a supplement published in 1977.[4]

Continuing Education

Major changes occurred in the continuing education (CE) program during the 1990s due to the costs involved in administering the program, the need to more quickly incorporate new trends and topics into the course offerings, and the demand to make educational opportunities more accessible using new technologies. Today, CE courses are no longer designated as core or basic courses and new perspective courses, but are organized by areas of knowledge and skills needed by health sciences librarians as described in the Educational Policy Statement of the MLA: Competencies for Lifelong Learning and Professional Success (http://www.mlanet.org/education/policy/.[5]

Courses are offered at the association's annual meeting and by chapters at their annual meetings. Also, MLA's annual meeting schedule frequently includes symposia on important topics, such as scholarly publishing and leadership development. The course approval process (http://www.mlanet.org/education/cech/cedevelop.html) is a rigorous one, and course evaluations are carefully considered by the Continuing Education Committee (CEC). Contact hours are awarded to course participants based upon the number of hours students are in class.

The MLA CEC and headquarters staff worked together to establish MLA's Educational Clearinghouse (http://cech.mlanet.org), an online listing of continuing-education opportunities, from a variety of sources that support the core competencies deemed necessary and appropriate for health sciences librarians in their professional development. The Educational Clearinghouse has proven to be an effective resource in furthering health sciences librarians' professional development. Currently information about over 200 courses is available through the clearinghouse. MLA is also working with the National Training Center and Clearinghouse (NTCC) (http://nnlm.gov/ntcc), part of the National Network of Libraries of Medicine (NN/LM), to add the NTCC's courses and tutorials to MLA's Educational Clearinghouse.

The kinds of courses offered, both in subject matter and in format, have also changed. The increasing number of courses about Internet applications reflects the tremendous change in the practice of health sciences librarianship over the past 10 years. Courses such as searching the Web for quality health information, developing Web-based CE courses, negotiating licenses for electronic journals and databases, expert searching, and consumer health have been offered. MLA also continues to address the challenge of offering quality and affordable professional development opportunities to people both regionally and at their desktops. MLA's first teleconference in 1996, "The Role of the Library in Accreditation," was received by over 100 sites in the United States and Canada and was seen by about 1300 people. MLA now offers Webcasts to both groups and individuals and provides access to a number of Web-based courses and tutorials on a variety of profession-specific topics.

The demand for Web-based courses continues to increase, and this demand will prove challenging for small associations with few staff and fewer financial resources. To meet this demand, MLA also partners with graduate schools of library and information sciences; supports development of specialty specific Web-based courses; provides access to Web-based courses from other providers; and develops less costly, local opportunities for CE including independent learning opportunities and discussion groups. Success in effectively using new technologies in this area is essential for the continued success of MLA's continuing education program. Since 2008, MLA has provided hosting services for e-learning courses to encourage the development of these important learning formats.

MLA's move into distance education has increased participation in the association's continuing education program over 700% from 1990 (1,245 participants) to 2008 (9,210 participants).[6,7]

Specialist credentials

In 2000, MLA established a specialist program in consumer health (CHIS), developed for health sciences librarians as well as other librarians working in the area of consumer health. The program consists of basic and advanced courses on various aspects of consumer health (http://www.mlanet.org/education/chc/) taught by health sciences librarians. The program was introduced in 2001 at the "The Public Library and Consumer Health" Conference cosponsored by MLA, the Public Library Association, and the National Library of Medicine. By 2008, almost 400 librarians had received the CHIS credential.

Credentialing and the Academy of Health Information Professionals

MLA has the oldest ongoing recognized credentialing program in the library profession. MLA established the Academy of Health Information Professionals (AHIP) (http://www.mlanet.org/academy/) in 1989 to encourage individual professional growth and lifelong learning in health sciences librarianship. The academy replaced a test-based certification program that had been in place since 1973. Since health sciences librarians work with physicians, nurses, and allied health workers who require licenses or certifications and recertifications to continue to practice in their chosen professions, health sciences librarians also felt a need to seek additional credentials beyond the MLS as a way to document their continuing education and demonstrate continued competency in their profession. Today, admission to the Academy is based upon educational qualifications, documented knowledge in established knowledge and skills or competencies areas, and professional contributions through teaching, publishing, or holding leadership positions in the association and its units.

Membership in the Academy is open to both MLA members and nonmembers. Over 1000 health information professionals belong to the academy at one of five levels: provisional, member, senior, distinguished, or emeritus member. Data from the 2008 Hay Group/MLA Salary Survey[2] indicated that academy members were better compensated than nonmembers, but more analysis is needed to establish a cause and effect relationship. MLA, through its Credentialing Committee and mentorship program, continues to simplify the application process to encourage membership in the Academy as part of an individual's lifelong learning program.

ADVOCACY

MLA plays a strong advocacy role on behalf of its members to demonstrate the value of quality health information to society and the role that health information professionals play in producing and managing that information. This is achieved through the association's professional recognition, governmental relations, and public relations programs.

Professional Recognition

The grants and scholarships program (http://www.mlanet.org/awards/grants/) and the awards program (http://www.mlanet.org/awards/) remain strong components of MLA's professional recognition program. At the close of 2008, endowment funds for this purpose represented 44% of the association's total assets.

Grants and scholarships

MLA offers a variety of scholarships and grants administered by the Grants and Scholarships Committee. These stipends assist qualified students, including minorities to attend graduate schools of library and information sciences and enable practicing health sciences librarians to take advantage of opportunities for continuing professional development. This program also enables recipients to attend meetings and conferences and do research important to the practice and progress of the profession.

For example, in 2001, MLA established the Lindberg Research Fellowship, honoring Donald A.B. Lindberg, M.D., director of the National Library of Medicine (NLM), in recognition of his significant national and international achievements at NLM, the world's largest medical library. This research fellowship, given annually, strives to provide a more formal structure for supporting research activities that will benefit the health information sciences by strengthening the knowledge base of information research and improve the practice of health sciences librarianship.

Awards

The awards program, administered by MLA's Awards Committee, honors superior individual achievement in specific areas of health sciences librarianship including hospital librarianship, collection development, history or philosophy of the profession, chapter programs, education, research, governmental relations, and distinguished public service. Named in honor of distinguished health sciences librarians such as Estelle Brodman, Lois Ann Colaianni, Eileen Cunningham, Louise Darling, Janet Doe, and Lucretia McClure (http://www.mlanet.org/awards/honors/fellows/) and honorary members and sponsored by MLA corporate partners important to health sciences libraries, awards are given annually. MLA also honors those who have made outstanding and sustained contributions to the advancement of the purposes of MLA through fellowships and honorary memberships.

Governmental Relations

MLA's governmental relations program (http://www.mlanet.org/government/) addresses national information issues and policies that affect the health sciences library community. The association testifies before Congress on a regular basis on the importance of the National Library of Medicine to the provision of clinical and scientific information that supports medical education, research, and, ultimately, improved patient care. MLA has published position papers on a number of issues including fair use, copyright, scholarly publishing, open access, patient safety, and distance education. The association also works in coalition with the other major library associations such as the American Association of Law Libraries and the Special Libraries Association on issues of mutual concern in copyright and scholarly publishing. MLA will continue to partner with other organizations to address information access issues as they continue to evolve in this very complex digital environment.

Public Relations

MLA began a major public relations effort in 1996 to help promote the association's Centennial Celebration in 1998. Today, the program focuses on assisting MLA members and other health sciences information professionals to market their expertise and services both to their institutions and to outside publics. MLA provides a number of advocacy resources (http://www.mlanet.org/resources/index.html) including posters for librarians to use in their institutions to heighten awareness of the value of the services provided by the medical libraries and librarians. The association has designated October as National Medical Librarians Month (http://www.mlanet.org/resources/nml-month/index.html) to help members promote their services to their institutions and users.

Deciphering MedSpeak publications

The public relations program also aims to create awareness of the health sciences library and information profession through several outreach initiatives to consumers. Distribution of consumer health information such as the

Deciphering Medspeak series, in both English and Spanish (http://www.mlanet.org/resources/medspeak/) provides general and disease specific health and Web site information to the public in a simple format, creating awareness of the profession and assisting the public.

Health information literacy

MLA's health information literacy initiative began in 2003 with the appointment of a Health Information Literacy Task Force that studied how health sciences librarians could put "information" into health literacy initiatives, resulting in a number of resources (http://www.mlanet.org/resources/healthlit/). This work continued through 2008 with a major health information literacy research project funded through a contract with NLM to study health providers' perceptions of health information literacy and develop a curriculum to support these initiatives in the hospital. With the Pew Internet and American Life Project, MLA members also developed a user's guide to finding and evaluating health information on the Web (http://www.mlanet.org/resources/userguide.html) and other consumer resources.

MLA will continue to use its public relations program as an advocacy tool for the profession by addressing the needs of specific membership segments such as hospital librarians or academic medical center librarians. Members increasingly recognize the important role public relations can play in the perceived value of the library and librarian to the institution and to the community.

CREATING AND COMMUNICATING OUR KNOWLEDGE

Research

Part of MLA's mission is to promote research in information management and the profession. Several of the association's grants and scholarships provide stipends for those interested in doing research that will contribute to the profession's body of knowledge. In 2007, MLA published a revision of its research policy statement. The Research Imperative (http://www.mlanet.org/research/policy/policy-ol_toc.html).[8] The revised statement encourages new directions for the association's research program. In 2008, MLA, working through its Research Section, adopted a research agenda to guide the association and its members in research efforts. In addition, MLA sponsors research studies in areas that will help the profession. For example, the MLA Benchmarking Network (http://www.mlanet.org/members/benchmark/) offers hospital, academic, and specialty health libraries an opportunity to learn more about benchmarking, compare data, establish best practices, and identify and work with a benchmarking partner. Hundreds of health sciences libraries nationwide participate. Other studies including MLA's Vital Pathways Project for Hospital Librarians (http://www.mlanet.org/resources/vital/) deal with the compensation, the value of information services to institutions' bottom lines, and new roles for health sciences information professionals (http://www.mlanet.org/research/index.html). MLA also posts presentations and posters presented at the association's annual meetings on MLANET and has developed a member area on the Web site, the CORE Toolbox, where members can exchange ideas, research, and other helpful information. The association will continue to partner with other organizations to provide research data and resources that will assist health sciences librarians and the public.

Publications

The association's publications program, accomplished through the work of the *JMLA* and *MLA News* Editorial Boards and the Books Panel, encourages and publishes research in health sciences librarianship, provides texts for those studying to be health sciences librarians, provides authorship opportunities for health sciences librarians, and provides consumer health materials for the public. The venerable *Journal of the Medical Library Association (JMLA)* (http://www.mlanet.org/publications/jmla/index.html) published almost continually under several names since 1902, was one of MLA's first regular publications. The journal has been made freely available electronically since January 2000 over *PubMed Central (PMC)*, a digital archive of life sciences journal literature developed and managed by the National Center for Biotechnology Information (NCBI) and NLM. In 2006/2007, NLM, working with MLA Headquarters, made the full-text archives of the journal from 1902 freely available online through PMC, putting into practice MLA's support of open access. This is an excellent resource for the study of health information sciences and the management of knowledge-based information.

A Handbook of Medical Library Practice[9] was one of the first texts published by MLA in the association's book publications program and went through four editions over a 40-year period. The handbook was succeeded by *Current Practice in Health Sciences Librarianship*,[10] a multivolume series completed in 2001. Until about 1990, all association publishing was centralized at MLA headquarters. In 1990, MLA began working with a series of copublishers to produce a number of noteworthy books and other resources, adding to the research base of the profession (http://www.mlanet.org/order/index.html). This includes *The Medical Library Association Guide to Managing Health Care Libraries*,[11] recognized as "the new gold standard in health sciences library textbooks."[12]

During the 1990s, MLA expanded its publishing program (http://www.mlanet.org/publications/) to include DocKits and BibKits. These publications are collections of documents or bibliographies of resources about specific topics and are published in-house. MLA also publishes materials in compact disc and digital formats to make information more widely available. Other components in the program are house publications (annual report, Directory, MLA-FOCUS) and *MLA News* (http://www.mlanet.org/publications/mlanews/). Experimentation with alternate formats will continue for the foreseeable future as the association continues to convert print products into electronic ones and develop new digital products and services.

Professional Networking

Since associations were one of the early ways in which people of common interests came together, it is not surprising that associations have adopted an increasing variety of social networking tools for the benefit of their members. The association's Web site, MLANET (http://www.mlanet.org) provides MLA with a global reach and reveals the richness of our resources and the expertise of our members as never before possible. MLANET not only provides organizational information about MLA, the Web site also provides member networking services; acts as a resources gateway; contains career, educational, and recognition information; and provides online access to research, standards, and publications.

For many years, MLA has supported MEDLIB-L (http://www.mlanet.org/discussion/medlib_l_faq.html), a discussion list that has over 2100 member and nonmember participants. The list is used for interlibrary loan, reference, announcements, and other items that help health sciences librarians in their daily work. MLA headquarters staff also support more than 100 discussion lists, blogs, wikis, and other social networking tools for association units and provides space on MLANET for section and chapter Web sites. Most recently the association has supported blogs, wikis, and RSS feeds for various association units to improve communications and collaboration.

MLA's annual meeting (http://www.mlanet.org/am/index.html) (Fig. 2), held annually in May, continues to be the top face-to-face professional networking event for the profession. It is an opportunity to present and discuss papers, posters, applied research, and important issues in health sciences information management. The event gives MLA members and affiliated professionals a chance to share ideas, hear from experts, see the latest products, network, and socialize. MLA has actively begun to push annual meeting content out to members who can't attend through a variety of social media tools.

BUILDING A NETWORK OF GLOBAL PARTNERS

MLA works actively to serve health care providers and the public through a global network of members and partners who share expertise and resources. Some of the programs already mentioned support this goal through collaborations among the association's sections and chapters, other library associations and organizations, and the international library and information community. In the international arena, MLA is a longtime active member of the International Federation of Library Associations and Institutions (IFLA) and supports the International Congress on Medical Librarianship (ICML) held every 4–5 years around the world. MLA's global initiatives are a part of

Fig. 2 MLA's annual meeting is the premier event in the health information sciences profession.

Fig. 3 2007/2008 MLA President Mark E. Funk, AHIP (center, back row), with members of the South African National Health Information Partnership at the 2007 IFLA Conference and Exhibition in Durban, South Africa.

the association's Librarians without Borders ® program (http://www.mlanet.org/resources/global/) that includes a sister library initiative, a world-wide e-library training program, and the T. Mark Hodges International Service Award program. MLA also has bilateral agreements with the Canadian Health Libraries Association/ABSC, the German Working Group, the European Association of Health Information Libraries, the Association for Health Information and Libraries in Africa (AHILA), and the Korean Medical Library Association (KMLA) and connects with health sciences librarians throughout the world (Fig. 3)—a truly global organization.

In 2006, MLA assumed management of the Association for Library and Information Science Education (ALISE) strengthening our ties with the library education community. Founded in 1915 as the Association of American Library Schools, ALISE provides a forum for library educators to share ideas, to discuss issues, and to seek solutions to common problems. MLA members also formally represent MLA at a number of other allied organizations (http://www.mlanet.org/about/leaders/allied.html).

CONCLUSION

MLA continues to work actively to recruit people into the health sciences information profession, to promote and support lifelong learning, to advocate on behalf of the profession, to create and communicate the profession's knowledge, and to build a network of global partners to serve the member, the profession, and society. For example, the association is working on several future challenges for the profession concerning roles of the health sciences librarian, including the Vital Pathways Project for Hospital Librarians and the Health Information Literacy Research project. The association is also furthering the concept of evidence-based medicine through the support of conferences and publications in this area. Future challenges for MLA as for many other associations are in the areas of membership recruitment, technology, finances, outside competition, and environmental impacts. Keeping up with new technologies to provide programs and services is a tremendous challenge for a small association. However, MLA continues to be a vital organization after more than 100 years of operation. One of the major reasons that the association was founded was to provide for an exchange of materials among its membership. Today, the MLA Exchange is transmitted electronically among 900 subscribers and has become just one of many programs and services that MLA provides for its membership. MLANET, MLA's Web site, is the association's face to the world, enabling a librarian in India to teach MLA's health literacy and health information literacy concepts to medical staff and librarians from Australia and Asia to participate in its Web-based courses. There has never been a more exciting or challenging time to be a librarian or a library association staff member.

REFERENCES

1. *Strategic Plan of the Medical Library Association*; MLA: Chicago, IL, 2003, http://www.mlanet.org/about/strategc.html.
2. Hay Group/MLA. *2008 Salary Survey*; Medical Library Association, Incorporated: Chicago, IL, 2008. http://www.mlanet.org/publications/hay_mla_08ss.html (accessed May 2009).
3. Virgo, J.A. Education of medical librarians. In *Encyclopedia of Library and Information Science*; Marcel Dekker: New York, 1976; Vol. 17, 342–378.

4. McClure, L.W. Education for health sciences librarians. In *Encyclopedia of Library and Information Science*; Marcel Dekker: New York, 1977; Vol. 17, Suppl. 23, 65–82.
5. Educational Policy Statement of the Medical Library Association, *Competencies for Lifelong Learning and Professional Success*; Medical Library Association, Incorporated: Chicago, IL, 2007. http://www.mlanet.org/education/policy/ (accessed May 2007).
6. Annual Report, 1995/96. Medical Library Association, Incorporated: Chicago, IL, 1996; i.
7. Annual Report, 2008/2009. Medical Library Association, Incorporated: Chicago, IL, 2009. http://www.mlanet.org/about/annual_report/08_09/index.html (accessed May 2009).
8. The Research Imperative: Research Policy Statement of the Medical Library Association, Incorporated: Chicago, IL, 2007. http://www.mlanet.org/research/policy/policy-ol_toc.html (accessed May 2009).
9. Doe, J., Ed. *A Handbook of Medical Library Practice*; American Library Association: Chicago, IL, 1943.
10. Bunting, A., Ed. *Current Practice in Health Sciences Librarianship*; MLA/Scarecrow Press: Lanham, MD, 1994–2001; 9 vols.
11. Holst, R.; Phillips, S.A., Eds. *The Medical Library Association Guide to Managing Healthcare Libraries*; MLA/Neal-Schuman: New York, 2000.
12. Tomlin, A.C. Professional media (book review). Libr. J 2000, *125* (19), 103.

BIBLIOGRAPHY

1. Association Record- Proceedings. JMLA. Found in first issue of each volume.
2. Connor, J. *Guardians of Medical Knowledge, the Genesis of the Medical Library Association*; MLA/Scarecrow Press: Lanham, MD, 2000.
3. Medical Library Association Web site, http://www.mlanet.org.
4. *MLA News*; Medical Library Association, Incorporated: Chicago, IL.

Medical Literature: History *[ELIS Classic]*

William K. Beatty
Northwestern University Medical School, Chicago, Illinois, U.S.A.

Managing–Metamarkup

Abstract

One of the objectives of the information disciplines is to study the universe of recorded information—that is, to study the documentary products of domains of human activity—and to come to understand such bodies of literature as social and historical phenomena in and of themselves. Beatty discusses the rich history of medical literature from ancient times to the mid-twentieth century. Forms of bibliographic control, such as *Index Medicus*, are also covered.

—ELIS Classic, from 1976

INTRODUCTION

The earliest extant piece of medical literature is a Sumerian clay tablet that contains medical recipes. This tablet, approximately 4 × 7 inches and made of baked red clay, probably dates from about 2100 B.C. It is written in Sumerian cuneiform and contains 15 prescriptions but no supernatural elements. The Code of Hammurabi, from approximately the same time, includes some regulations on medical practice and penalties for failure to produce a cure.

Many of these clay tablets, or rather in most cases fragments of clay tablets, were in the collection of King Assurbanipal of Assyria who lived in the seventh century B.C. The British Museum has over 30,000 of these, several hundred of which are medical. Many drugs, plants, and minerals are referred to in medical prescriptions, and some tablets also contain incantations. One series of these tablets was used for letters from the royal physician, Aradnana, to King Esarhaddon.

The papyri from Egypt, most of which were written around 1500 B.C. (although their contents in some cases include much older material), present interesting examples of the early medical literature. The oldest of these, written about 1900 B.C., was discovered by Sir Flinders Petrie in 1889 at Kahun. The Kahun Papyrus is now at University College in London. A transcript and English translation by F.Ll. Griffith was published in 1898. Three pages in length, this papyrus deals with gynecological material.

A major surgical papyrus, the Edwin Smith, dates from about 1600 B.C. and was obtained at Luxor in 1862 by Edwin Smith, an American. The papyrus itself is at the New York Academy of Medicine; a translation and transliteration of it was published by James H. Breasted in 1930. This roll is a little less than 16 feet long, 1 foot wide, and has writing on both sides. The 17 columns on the front describe 48 cases, most of which involve injuries to the head, chest, or spine. The five columns on the back contain charms unrelated to the material on the front.

The most famous of these medical papyri is the Papyrus Ebers, written about 1550 B.C. This was discovered about 1860 and acquired at Thebes by Georg Ebers in 1873. Most of the material in it comes from a much earlier period, perhaps as far back as 3000 B.C. The Ebers is the only papyrus extant that is complete. The roll was originally 68 feet long, a foot wide, with 108 columns of 20 lines each. It was later cut into pages and bound as a modern book. This is now in the University Library at Leipzig; a translation by Ebbell was published in London in 1937. The text consists primarily of 877 prescriptions, one of which contains 37 ingredients. Frequently occurring items include opium, hellebore, salts of lead and copper, and blood, excreta, and viscera of animals. The last section describes the treatment of tumors.

Also from about 1550 B.C. is the Hearst Medical Papyrus, named for Mrs. Sophie B. Hearst who gave the money for the excavations that produced it. This papyrus is preserved at the University of California. The scroll contains 18 columns and is incomplete. It consists of a formulary (apparently used by a practicing physician) quite similar to parts of the Ebers Papyrus. Both papyri probably came, at least in part, from the same source. The Hearst Papyrus also contains descriptions of three methods for uniting bones. A translation into German and a transliteration by Wreszinski appeared in 1901.

The Berlin Museum has a papyrus of 15 columns dealing with childbirth and infants, which also dates from about 1550 B.C. This was translated into German by Erman in 1912. The British Museum in 1860 purchased the London Medical Papyrus, which was written about 1350 B.C. In 1912, Wreszinski published a German translation of this. Wreszinski also published in 1912 German translations of the Berlin Medical Papyrus and the Brugsch Maior Papyrus. Both of these are preserved in Berlin. They date from about 1300 B.C., and the former contains some 200 prescriptions. The Chester Beatty Papyrus, with eight columns extant, concerns diseases of the anus and

Encyclopedia of Library and Information Sciences, Fourth Edition DOI: 10.1081/E-ELIS4-120008995

was probably written around 1200 B.C. Jonckheere published a French translation in 1947.

The Babylonian Talmud includes considerable material on anatomy and surgery, although this is mostly embedded in statements about the law. Tumors of the lungs, diseases of the liver, and diphtheria are also mentioned. Amputations, trephining, and other surgical procedures are referred to briefly. The Old Testament contains many regulations dealing with public health and hygiene. The isolation and care of individuals with contagious diseases, and the prohibition of certain foods (with logical overtones of preventing sickness) form the bulk of this material.

EARLY GREECE, INDIA, AND CHINA

Items of medical and surgical treatment appear in Homer, mostly in the *Iliad*, but the Greek medical literature itself did not actually begin until Alcmaeon of Crotona, a younger contemporary of Pythagoras and the most famous Greek physician before Hippocrates. Only a few fragments of Alcmaeon exist. He is credited with the discovery of the optic nerve, knowledge of the trachea, and the belief that the brain was the central organ of intellectual activity. Other pre-Hippocratic authors of importance include Anaxagoras, who wrote of the dissection of animals and recognized the lateral ventricles of the brain, Empedocles, who was the first to formulate the theory of the flux and reflux of the blood from and to the heart, and Diogenes of Apollonia, whose small book on the heart became the outstanding anatomical work in the Hippocratic Corpus and exerted considerable influence.

The Hippocratic Corpus is a large collection of medical writings, some credited to Hippocrates but most of which were probably written by pupils or even later authors. These range from medical textbooks and reports of investigations, through lectures for medical students all the way to works obviously intended for laymen. The works that are generally attributed to Hippocrates include the three books of Epidemics; Regimen in Acute Diseases; Airs, Waters, and Places; Fractures; Joints; Wounds of the Head; Ancient Medicine; Prognostics; and Prorrhetics. Hippocrates is best known for his careful clinical observations and for his reporting of his failures as well as his successes. The first printed complete edition of the works of Hippocrates appeared in a folio at Rome in 1525. This Latin text was based on manuscripts in the Vatican. The first Greek edition was published by Aldus in 1526, and is one of the most beautiful productions of Hippocratic material. Other outstanding editions include Froben's printing at Basel in 1538 of Janus Cornarius's carefully edited text, the 1588 Venice edition by the Junta with both Greek and Latin texts, and the beautiful Vienna edition of 1743–1749. The 10-volume edition by Littré, which was originally published in 1839–1861 and reprinted in 1961–1962, is basic. English translations are available by Francis Adams (first printed in 1849 and reprinted in 1964) and by W.H.S. Jones and E.T. Withington, in four volumes, in the Loeb Classical edition (1923–1931). The first French translation was done at Lyons in 1555, the first Spanish one in Madrid in 1757–1770, and the first German edition in Altenburg in 1781–1792.

While the Greek medical literature lies in the main stream of our own heritage, this was not the only area of such activity. India and China both made substantial contributions to the medical literature. Susruta wrote one of the major works in the Sanskrit literature, and one that is especially important in such surgical matters as extraction of cataract, caesarean section, lithotomy, and plastic surgery. Over 760 medicinal plants are mentioned. Charaka, another Hindu writer, produced a medical treatise around 400 B.C. This was translated into Arabic and Persian in the tenth century A.D., and an English translation was published in 1949 (six volumes).

Pien Ch'iao (Ch'in Yüeh), who flourished in the first half of the fifth century B.C., supposedly wrote the *Nan Ching*, a medical treatise of 81 chapters, in which he developed the theory of the pulse. This became one of the most popular Chinese medical works, has had many commentaries, and was translated into German. The *Nan Ching* was based in good part on an even earlier work, the *Huang Ti Nei Ching*, which was probably written about 1000 B.C. Chapters 1 to 34 were translated into English by Ilza Veith in 1949.

Among the Greeks that came after Hippocrates was, of course, Aristotle, whose dissections of animals added much to the basic medical literature. The best edition of his works was a Greek-Latin text in five volumes published in Berlin in 1851–1870. An English translation edited by J.A. Smith and W.D. Ross was published in 12 volumes by Oxford, 1908–1952. A son-in-law of Hippocrates, Polybos, wrote *On the Nature of Men* around 400 B.C., and this became the main source for the theory of the four humors. Diocles of Carystos, called the "second Hippocrates" in Athens, shortly thereafter wrote the first work entitled *Anatomy* and the first work on medical botany.

A pupil of Aristotle, Menon, wrote an important book in verse that summarized the pathological views of the predecessors and contemporaries of Hippocrates. A student's notebook based on this work and dating from about A.D. 150 was found in Egypt and provides an important link to a truer perspective of the Hippocratic doctrines.

Nacandros of Colophon in Ionia used both prose and verse for his works on drugs, poisonous animals, and prognostics. He was the first to speak of the therapeutic use of leeches. Aldus published his *Theriaca et Alexipharmaca* in Greek in 1499. A Latin translation appeared at Cologne in 1531 and a French translation came out in 1568. Another Greek writer on drugs, Servilius Damocrates of Athens (fl. A.D. 60–80), attempted to provide a safety feature in his prescriptions by couching them in iambic trimeters. In this way any careless changes in the numbers made by the copyists could be detected. This can be looked on as an early form of the check digit used in some computer programs.

The works of the Greek medical writers, Erasistratus and Herophilos, of the Alexandrian School (flourished around 300 B.C.) were caught up in the destruction of the Alexandrian Library under Theodosius the Great. Some fragments of their texts and comments on their work have been preserved in the writings of Galen and others. Erasistratus was among the first physicians to discard the humoral theory, and his experimental work has led some to call him the founder of physiology.

Apollonios of Citium, around 100 B.C., wrote a commentary on Hippocrates' *On Articulations* that has survived in a ninth century A.D. manuscript illustrated with figures that probably date from even earlier times.

Specialization occurs in Greek times, and Demosthenes Philalethes (fl. A.D. 60) wrote an important work on ophthalmology that was a major source for many years. Manuscripts were still being made of this in the fourteenth century.

The work of Xenocrates of Aphrodisias appeared around A.D. 70. This was a major source for Pliny's *Natural History*, which had a profound and far-reaching effect in the medical literature as well as in many other areas.

At about this same time Pedacius Dioscorides, a Greek army surgeon, wrote his materia medica, which was to be widely used for 1500 years. This work, describing some 600 medicinal plants, survives in a beautifully illustrated manuscript written about 512 and preserved in the National Library at Vienna. The first Latin edition was printed at Colle in 1478, and Aldus produced the first Greek text in 1499. This is a typically beautiful Aldine production but is of great rarity. An Italian translation was printed in Venice in 1542, German in Frankfurt in 1546, and Spanish in Amsterdam in 1555.

The first major text in obstetrics and gynecology was written by Soranus of Ephesus (A.D. 98–138). His acute observations and excellent teaching ability are evident in his accounts of obstetric manipulations and of infant hygiene and nutrition. His writings were later the sources for Rösslin's *Rosengarten* (1513) and Raynalde's *Byrthe of Mankynde* (1545). Soranus gave sources for his quotations, one of the first writers to do this with any consistency. Most of his works have been lost, although his text on gynecology has survived in Greek and an English translation was made by Temkin in 1956.

LATIN AND GREEK MANUSCRIPTS

The earliest scientific medical work to be written originally in Latin was the *De Re Medicina* of Aurelius Cornelius Celsus, a layman. The eight books making up this compilation were based on Hippocrates. It became one of the most frequently produced medical publications, although it was barely noticed either by Celsus's contemporaries or the medieval commentators. The first printed edition appeared in Florence in 1478. Over 105 editions of Celsus have been printed. In addition to the Florentine, which is quite rare, important editions were produced in Milan in 1481, in Venice in 1524, by the Aldine press in 1525, and by the Elzevirs in 1657. The Loeb Classical Library published a three-volume English translation by Walter George Spencer in 1935–1938.

Pliny produced his *Historia Naturalis* in the first century A.D. Three books of this deal with medicine. Many manuscripts and early printings of this exist. The first printed edition appeared in Venice in 1469.

Galen, second only to Hippocrates among the authors of Greek medical literature, lived from A.D. 130–200. Galen's writings—nine books on anatomy, 17 on physiology, six on pathology, 14 on therapeutics, and 30 on pharmacy—provided standards in medicine for over a thousand years. Much of his work has not been available in English until recently. In fact, his *On Medical Experience* was unknown until 1931 when a manuscript of it was found in Istanbul and translated from the Arabic into English by Walzer (1944). A major English translation was made by Margaret T. May of his *On Usefulness of the Parts of the Body*, which was published in two volumes in 1968. Galen's other major anatomical work, *On Anatomical Procedures*, has been translated in two parts, the first by Singer in 1956 and the second by Duckworth in 1962. Rudolph Siegel has translated substantial portions of Galen's work in his volumes, and Paul W. Harkins translated *On the Passions & Errors of the Soul* in 1964. Much of Galen's work was preserved only through the medium of Arabic translations.

The first Latin edition of Galen's works to be printed was done in 1490 in Venice where the first Greek edition, in five volumes, was printed by Aldus in 1525. Conrad Gesner did a Latin translation in 1562. The best text was the Greek-Latin edition done by Kühn at Leipzig (20 volumes, 1821–1833). A reprinting began in 1964.

China continued to produce medical works of importance. The most famous was the *Shang Han Lun* (*Essay on Typhoid*) published in A.D. 217 and written by Chang Chung-ching, the "Hippocrates of China." Hua T'o (Yüan), ca A.D. 190–265, wrote medical and surgical works that were also translated into Japanese. Huang Fu (Shih An), ca. 215–282, wrote widely, and his most famous treatise, *Chia-i-Ching*, on acupuncture, became the basis for all future works on this subject.

From the fourth through the seventh centuries a number of Greek compilators performed valuable services for the medical literature by gathering many manuscripts and commenting on them. These compilations provide us today with our only knowledge of many writers.

Oribasius (325–403) was the first of these. His two encyclopedias preserved much material that would otherwise be lost. A Latin edition of his works was printed at

Basel in 1557. The best edition is a French translation by Bussemaker and Daremberg (six volumes, Paris, 1851–1876). Oribasius carefully explained Galen's doctrines, preserved many of his writings, and did much to establish the supremacy of Galen in the medical literature for the next thousand years. Oribasius also wrote a four-volume work, *Euporista*, designed to present reliable medical information to the laity.

Aëtius of Amida (502–575) compiled the *Tetrabiblion*, which contains many valuable quotations. Froben printed a Latin translation by Montanus and Cornuarius at Basel (1533–1535, 1542).

Alexander of Tralles (525–605), another compilator, included some of his own observations on worms and vermifuges in his compilations, and so could be called the first parasitologist. The first printed edition appeared at Lyons in 1504. The best text is the Greek-German edition produced by Puschmann at Vienna (1878–1879). This was reprinted at Amsterdam in 1963.

Paul of Aegina (625–690) wrote an *Epitome* in seven books that included many of his own valuable writings on lithotomy, tonsillectomy, amputation of the breast, and the first clear description of lead poisoning. The Aldine Press produced a Greek edition in 1528, and a Latin translation was done in Paris in 1532. Francis Adams, under the auspices of the Sydenham Society, made an English translation in three volumes (1844–1847).

Medical writing appeared in Spain in the seventh century: three books of Isidore of Seville's massive encyclopedia dealt with medical subjects. Shortly thereafter in England the Venerable Bede wrote on bloodletting and the rehabilitation of sufferers from aphasia.

ARABIC WRITINGS, SCHOOL OF SALERNO, AND LATE MANUSCRIPTS

Major developments in the Middle Ages took place in the Arabic literature and at the School of Salerno just south of Naples. The ebb and flow of religious and military struggles had led to the establishment of a medical school at Jundishapur in Persia in the middle of the eighth century. The need for texts produced both translations and original writings. Hunain ibn Isabq Al-Ibadi made translations of Hippocrates, Galen, Oribasius, and others from Greek into Arabic and so helped to preserve the works of these writers during the destructive times that had settled on Europe. Among the Arabic authors to make substantial contributions to the literature were Rhazes (860–932) who gave the first accurate descriptions of smallpox and measles. His major work, the *Al-Hawi* or *Continents*, was compiled posthumously from notes made by his students. The ninth book of this was used as a basis for therapeutics for several centuries; one of the revisions of it was done by first printed edition, by Britannicus at Brescia in 1486, ranks not only as an important work in the history of the medical literature but also as (at 22 pounds) the heaviest of the medical incunabula.

The location of pieces of the medical literature can sometimes come as a surprise. Two leaves of a twelfth-thirteenth century manuscript of Rhazes were found in the twentieth century by J. Christian Bay as he was preparing a sixteenth century volume for rebinding. The Rhazes material had been incorporated in the covers of the newer work.

The "Prince of Physicians," Avicenna (980–1037), included many of his own original observations in his major work that codified all medical knowledge known at that time. This publication, the *Canon*, became the standard text for many years and was used in European and Asian universities for five centuries. The original Arabic version was printed at Rome in 1593, the first of many Latin editions was printed in 1472, and an edition in Hebrew appeared at Naples in 1491. However, much of Avicenna's work has not been printed, and very little is available in English.

The leading textbook of surgery during the Middle Ages was the *Altastrif* written by Albucasis (936–1013), a native of Zahra near Cordova. This was based on the work of Paul of Aegina. An excellent Arabic-Latin edition was done by Channing at Oxford (two volumes, 1778). Portions of this have been translated into English by Spink (1937).

Another major contributor growing from the Arabic conquests was Moses Maimonides (Rabbi Moses ben Maimon) who lived from 1135 to 1204. Born at Cordova, Maimonides became court physician to the sultan at Cairo. Maimonides's *Aphorisms* was his most popular medical work, but he wrote on many subjects including poisons, personal hygiene, and asthma. His list of drug names in Arabic, Greek, Persian, Berber, and Spanish was of great importance. The Arabic manuscript for this list was not discovered until 1932. Maimonides did his writing in Arabic but the books were immediately translated into Hebrew. English translations of his works by Munter, Rosner, and Danby have been appearing since the 1950s.

The preservation of Greek and Latin works in Arabic was an outstanding contribution of this period. The gradual retranslation back into the original languages began as early as the eleventh century. Constantinus Africanus, a native of Carthage working at Salerno and Monte Cassino, translated many of the manuscripts of Hippocrates and Galen out of Arabic and also helped to make the works of Rhazes and Avicenna known to the physicians of Western Europe. Other well-known translators of a slightly later date were Gerard of Cremona and Michael Scotus.

The School of Salerno, which flourished between 1050 and 1200, not only provided a home for many translators such as Constantinus but also itself contributed important works to the literature. The poetic handbook of domestic medicine known as the *Regimen Sanitatis Salernitanum* is the most famous of these; over 100 manuscripts of this exist in European libraries and more than 500 editions have been printed. Many of the major works produced at Salerno are contained in the twelfth-century Breslau Codex, which was discovered in 1837.

A new form of medical literature, "consilia," sprang up in the fourteenth and fifteenth centuries. These took the form of medical casebooks or clinical records. Some of these were written in the form of letters from a physician to his student or colleague. The consilia of Alderotti, a thirteenth-century physician of Bologna, became widely known.

In the three centuries immediately preceding the invention of printing from movable metal type, several manuscript works became especially well known. Lanfranc of Milan completed his major text on surgery in 1296. This was translated into English about 1380 and became the first important surgical work to appear in that language. The first printed version was supposedly done at Venice in 1490 but no copy of it has been found. However, a French translation at Lyons in the same year does exist. An English edition was printed in 1565. Other important surgical works were written by Theodoric, Henri de Mondeville, and Guy de Chauliac. Mondeville incorporated illustrations of separate organs and full-length pictures in his manuscripts.

Mondino de Luzzi of Bologna wrote a practical manual of anatomy that was completed in 1316 and served as the only textbook of anatomy for use in medical schools until well into the next century. The first printed edition appeared at Pavia in 1478. Over three dozen editions and translations of this popular work were eventually published. Charles Singer produced an English translation in 1925.

One of the most popular surgical works of this period was the *Chirurgia Magna* written in 1363 by Guy de Chauliac. The Bibliothèque Nationale alone has 14 manuscript versions; 43 French editions, 16 Latin, five Italian, and four Dutch editions are known. It was also translated into English, German, Italian, Spanish, Hebrew, Provençal, and Catalan.

Major medical writers in England included Gilbertus Anglicus (ca. 1166–1230), who had studied at Salerno, and John of Gaddesden (1280?–1361), who wrote the *Rosa Anglica, Practica Medicina a Capite ad Pedes* in 1314. When this was edited by Nicolaus Scyllatius Siculus in 1492 it became the first printed medical book by an Englishman. Many manuscript and printed versions of the *Rosa* still exist.

The first pharmacopoeia in the modern sense appeared in the middle of the fifteenth century. The *Compendium Aromatorium* by Saladinus de Asculo of Tarento, was used by apothecaries for centuries. It also served as a model for all of the early pharmaceutical textbooks.

EARLY PRINTED WORKS

With the invention of printing from movable metal type in the middle of the fifteenth century the medical literature underwent a rapid and widespread growth, much more so than many other disciplines. The earliest example extant of such printed medical literature is the top half of a purgation calendar printed at Mainz in 1457. These calenders gave the best dates for bleeding and purging, were very popular, and were apparently worn out by their users. The Mainz Kalendar was printed with the same Gutenberg types used for the Thirty-Six Line Bible. It was discovered in 1803 and is now in the Bibliothèque Nationale.

Another popular from of the early printed medical literature was the "Pestblätter." These tracts, giving advice on treatment of the plague, were issued throughout Europe; originals and facsimiles are housed in many current collections. The printed tracts are descended from a manuscript form, one of the earliest representatives of which was written by John of Burgundy in 1365.

A fascinating off-shoot of medical printing, in production approximately from 1493 to 1683, is known as the anatomical fugitive sheet. Manuscripts of a medical nature had gradually been making more use of illustrations in the centuries just before the modern type of printing started. When this much faster method of production became available a flood of these sheets, most of which were designed for the curious layman, poured from presses in many countries. These sheets were generally on good quality soft, rather thick paper, and measured about 30 × 40 cm (some were substantially larger). A central anatomical figure was usually surrounded by a descriptive text and often a decorative border. The illustrations were done either by woodblock or copperplate. The earliest sheets were printed in black; colors were soon introduced. The first texts were generally in Latin, but vernacular versions rapidly appeared. Simple skeletons formed the earliest subjects (frequently in the rather distorted, almost frog-like, patterns of the manuscripts). There were sheets of a single male or female figure, of the "Adam and Eve" plates, and then of the Tabulae originally produced by Vesalius in 1538. The Vesalian sheets were plagiarized and edited at a great rate.

Most of these fugitive sheets were single, although some consisted of two sheets with the second containing most of the descriptive text. The Vesalius set ran to six sheets, and a variation on this by Walter Ryff was composed of 10. Superimposed flaps were used to show different levels of the viscera. A pregnant uterus was frequently one level of these flaps, and the fetus in these representations was often in the cowering "see no evil" position. As this form of publication became more sophisticated, as many as a dozen or more such flaps would be used. These reached their peak in the work of Remmelin in the seventeenth century.

Anatomical illustrations also appeared in the early printed medical books. A major example is found in Johann de Ketham's *Fasciculus Medicinae*. This collection of short treatises was first printed in Venice in 1491 with rather primitive woodcuts. However, the beautiful figures in the 1493 edition were probably done directly from a dissection. Ultimately 33 editions were published, and it was translated into several languages. Singer translated it into English in 1925 and a facsimile of the 1493 edition was printed in 1963.

The book usually referred to as the first printed medical book is really a general encyclopedia with a chapter on medicine. Adolf Rusch of Strassburg printed the *De Sermonum Proprietate, seu de Universo* of Rabanus Maurus probably in 1467. Book 18, Chapter 5, deals with medicine; it was translated into English by Jessup in 1934. The earliest printed medical books included the following titles. The "*Speculum Vitae Humanae*" by Rodericus Zamorensis was printed by Sweynheym and Pannartz at Rome in 1468. Pliny's *Historia Naturalis* was printed by Johannes de Spira in Venice in 1469, and in Rome in 1470 by Sweynheym and Pannartz. Gulielmus de Saliceto, professor of surgery at Bologna in the middle of the thirteenth century, was especially popular in medical incunabula with several of his works appearing in the 1470s. Two editions of his *De Salute Corporis* were printed in 1470. Albucasis' *Liber Servitoris*, translated by Simon Januensis, was printed by Nicolas Jenson in Venice in 1471. In that same year Jenson also printed one of the most popular works from the School of Salerno, Nicholas's *Antidotarium*. The *Opera* of Joannes Mesue, Junior, was produced in two versions by Clemens Patavinus at Venice in 1471.

In April 1472 the first medical work in German, the *Regimen Sanitatis Deutsch*, was printed by Johann Bämler. This was translated into many languages and appeared in about 250 editions. The first printed medical book in Italian was by Gulielmo de Saliceto, *La Ciroxia Vulgarmento Fata*, done by Filip di Pietro at Venice in 1474. This is also very likely the first printed work on surgery. The first French book, as might be expected, was Guy de Chauliac's *Chirurgia Magna*, printed at Lyons in 1478. Pediatrics achieved its first printed work in the form of the *De Infantium Aegritudinibus et Remediis* by Paolo Bagellardi, done at Padua in 1472. The first work in ophthalmology was published a year earlier in Ferrara, *De Oculis Eorumque Aegritudinibus et Curis* by Benvenuto Grassi. Casey Wood translated this into English in 1929.

The first practical medical dictionary to appear in print was the *Aggregator Paduanus de Medicinis* by De Dondis done by Rusch in 1480, although fragments exist from Simone de Cordo's *Synonyma Medicinae seu Clavis Sanationis* printed at Ferrara in 1471 or 1472.

The John Rylands Library in Manchester has the only known copy of the first medical book printed in England. This was written by Canutus (Knutsson), Bishop of Arusiens, and is entitled *A Litil Boke the which Traytied and Reherced many Gode Things necessaries for the...Pestilence*, and published by William Machlinia at London in 1485. Machlinia produced new versions in 1488 and 1490, the latter claiming some fame as being the first English book with a title page. Wynkyn de Worde published an edition of this in 1510. William Caxton printed the second English medical book, *Governayle of Helthe*, in 1489, and de Worde later reprinted this.

The rapid spread and increasing numbers of medical books produced by the development of modern printing makes it necessary from now on to be much more highly selective.

The earliest printed herbal, the grandfather, so to speak, of a major class of medical works, was the *Herbarium* of Apuleius Barbarus (the "Pseudo-Apuleius") printed at Rome in 1481. The contents of this herbal dated back to the fourth century. Gunther produced a modern English translation at Oxford in 1925. A manuscript herbal of considerable interest, written by the Aztec Indian physician Martinus de la Cruz, and translated into Latin by another Aztec, Juannes Badianus, in 1552, is housed in the Vatican Library. A beautiful color facsimile, with translation into English by Emily Walcott Emmart, was published at Baltimore in 1940.

Many intriguing medical works called "olas" were written on the leaves of talipot palms in Ceylon and neighboring areas between 1400 and 1750. Most of these contained prescriptions, some were primarily magical, and a few had illustrations.

THE SIXTEENTH CENTURY

Vesalius was the earliest outstanding contributor to the medical literature after the invention of modern printing. He performed his first public anatomy at Bologna in 1540 (when he was just 26 years old), and the notes made on that occasion by one of his students, Baldasar Heseler (five or six years older than his teacher), were translated into English by Eriksson and published at Stockholm in 1959. Vesalius's major work, *De Humani Corporis Fabrica Libri Septem*, was printed by Oporinus at Basel in 1543. This monumental work, the first scientific text in anatomy, is one of the classics in the development of the medical literature. Vesalius based his work on his own dissections, and questioned many of the statements made by Galen that had been widely accepted and used for almost 1500 years. No English translation of the complete *Fabrica* has yet appeared, although a handsome facsimile was produced at Brussels in 1963. The "muscle men" plates by Calcar, a pupil of Titian, are works of both art and science. An epitome was issued the same year, and a corrected and expanded edition of the *Fabrica* came out in 1555. An English translation of the *Epitome* by Lind was published in New York in 1949.

The Vesalian plates were plagiarized far and wide. Thomas Geminus, both a surgeon and an engraver, persuaded Henry VIII to underwrite the publication of his *Compendiosa*, which was based on Vesalius. The copper plates, engraved by Geminus, marked this as the first illustrated textbook published in England. Nicholas Hyll printed it at London in 1545, an English translation by Nicholas Udall appeared in 1553, and Charles O'Malley produced a facsimile of Udall's translation in 1959.

Important contributions to the publication of anatomical information were made by Eustachius in his *Opuscula Anatomica* printed at Venice in 1564. He had completed 38 copper plates for another book, but was prevented by death from publishing it. These plates disappeared for 150 years; they were finally discovered by Lancisi and published as the *Tabulae Anatomicae* at Rome in 1714.

Eucharius Rösslin, a physician at Worms and Frankfurt-on-Main, compiled the first printed textbook for midwives from the earlier work of Soranus of Ephesus. This *De Swangern Frawen und Hebammen Roszgarten*, illustrated by woodcuts, was printed in 1513 at Strassburg. It became widely used, went through at least 40 editions, and was translated into Dutch, Czech, French, Latin, and English.

The first medical book by a medical man to be originally written and printed in English was the *Breviary of Health* by Andrew Boorde. This was published by Middleton at London in 1547, and five more editions had appeared by the end of the century. The *Breviary* was an important contribution to family medicine despite the facts that Boorde was the model for the term "A Merry Andrew," left as one of his aphorisms the true statement, "Myrth is one of the chiefest thynges in Physicke," and died in the Fleet Prison.

In 1530 appeared the major poetic contribution to the medical literature, Girolamo Fracastoro's *Syphilis, sive Morbus Gallicus*. This was printed by do Sabbio at Verona, and went through over 100 editions, being translated into Italian, English, French, German, Spanish, and Portuguese. Fracastoro's poem recognized the venereal cause of syphilis, gave the disease its name, and referred to mercury as a remedy.

The first major text in physiology, the *De Naturali Parte Medicinae* by Jean Fernel, was printed at Paris in 1542. The original edition is rare but later editions from France and Italy are more common. Fernel also wrote important contributions on pathology and therapeutics, as well as mathematics and astronomy.

An original thinker by the name of Philippus Aureolus Theophrastus Bombastes von Hohenheim, better known as Paracelsus, shot across the medical scene in the first half of the sixteenth century. He did much to change the emphasis in medicine to a more chemically oriented viewpoint, and advanced the availability of the medical literature by writing in his native German rather than Latin. Ambroise Paré, the great surgeon, was increasing his accessibility in the French medical literature. Until medical works became available in the vernacular, the spread of medical knowledge was considerably limited.

A German work holds an important place in the development of the ophthalmological literature. Georg Bartisch, the founder of modern ophthalmology, had his *Ophthalmodouleia, das ist Augendienst* published at Dresden in 1583. This book, well-illustrated with woodcuts, makes use of the overlays found in some of the anatomical fugitive sheets. A facsimile was issued in 1966.

Paré, who made his name as a military surgeon and the royal surgeon to four kings of France, wrote up his discovery of a new method of treating wounds (rather than the previously used boiling oil) in 1545. This went through several editions and was translated into Dutch and English. A handsome folio edition of his complete works appeared at Paris in 1575. A facsimile of the best French edition (Lyons, 1585) was reprinted in 1962. Paré's works were translated into Latin (1582), marking acceptance by the conservatives, and into English, by Thomas Johnson, in 1634. German, Dutch, and Japanese translations were also published. Several of Paré's works contain striking illustrations of surgical instruments and prostheses.

The literature of plastic surgery received its first major contribution from the pen of Gaspare Tagliacozzi of Bologna. His *De Curtorum Chirurgia per Insitionem*, published at Venice by Bindoni in 1597, has become a classic. This was issued in a pirated edition the same year. Despite the importance of Tagliacozzi's work, both Paré and Fallopius spoke out against him, and the Church dug up his body and reburied it in unconsecrated ground.

Although there was an increasing number of original contributions by contemporary authors, the classical writers were not forgotten. The first English translation of Hippocrates, done by Peter Lowe, was published in 1597. An excellent Latin translation of Hippocrates' *Aphorisms* was produced by François Rabelais.

The first book on pediatrics to be written in English was published in 1545 when *The Boke of Children* by Thomas Phaire appeared as an addendum to an English translation Phaire had made of the *Regimen Sanitatis Salerni*. Many later editions of the *Boke* were published, and it was reprinted in 1955.

In bringing the medical literature of the sixteenth century to a close, we may note the earliest medical works printed in America. The first of these, Francisco Bravo's *Opera Medicinalia*, was published in Mexico in 1570. Only three copies of this are now known. The *Summa y Recopilacion de Cirugia* by Alphonso Lopez de Hinozoso, the first important surgical work produced in the Americas, was published in 1578 with a second edition in 1595. The first text in anatomy was Farfan's *Tractado Brebe de Anothomia y Chirurgia*, printed in 1579.

THE SEVENTEENTH CENTURY

The outstanding medical book of the seventeenth century, and one of the classics of all time, was William Harvey's *Exercitatio Anatomica de Motu Cordis et Sanguinis in Animalibus*, often called simply the *De Motu Cordis*. This small volume, in which Harvey announced his discovery of the circulation of the blood, was published by William Fitzer at Frankfort in 1628. A few copies were printed on heavy paper, and these have become top prizes in the book-purchasing efforts of both institutions and individuals. Important editions were produced at Padua in 1643 and 1689; Rotterdam in 1648, 1654, 1660, 1671; London, 1660; Bologna, 1697; Leyden, 1736; Glasgow, 1751; and Edinburgh, 1824. Dutch and English (1653, 1673) translations have been made. A modern translation by Kenneth Franklin came out in 1957. Harvey is one of the few medical authors who has not only had a bibliography of his works compiled (by Geoffrey Keynes) but has had it go into a second edition. Several manuscripts important to Harvey's work have recently been translated and printed by Gweneth Whitteridge, Kenneth Franklin, and others.

The "first of the great English surgeons," Richard Wiseman, had his *A Treatise of Wounds* published in London in 1672. Copies of this are in the British Museum and the National Library of Medicine. Wiseman's *Severall Chirurgicall Treatises*, published in 1676, another important work, went through many editions.

The "English Hippocrates," Thomas Sydenham, emphasized careful and detailed observations. Among his outstanding contributions to the medical literature were his work on gout, *Tractatus de Podagra et Hydrope*, published at London in 1683, and books on hysteria and fevers. His complete works, published in Amsterdam (1683) and London (1685), went through many editions and translations. The best English translation was done by R.G. Latham in 1848–1850. Sydenham's medical notes and observations were printed at Oxford in 1845 as *Anecdota Sydenhamiana*. Sydenham wrote his works in English and had them translated into Latin so that they could achieve a wider circulation. Several of his manuscripts have recently been described and work is continuing on these, especially on the relationships between Sydenham and John Locke.

One of the most fascinating English medical authors of this period was Nicholas Culpeper. His writings were especially popular with apothecaries and laymen although he was a classical scholar. The first, *Pharmacopoeia Londinensis*, was published in 1618 by the College of Physicians (a facsimile was produced in 1944). Since this was in Latin, the information it contained was not accessible to most people. Culpeper translated it into English as *A Physicall Directory* in 1649, and aroused the unforgiving wrath of the College. When the second edition came out in 1650, Culpeper translated it also (1653), and this was rapidly spread both legally and piratically over many countries. An edition printed in Boston in 1720 probably has title to being the first full-length medical work to be produced in the colonies. Culpeper's *A Directory for Midwives*, London, 1651, was so popular that by 1777 it had been reprinted 17 times.

In 1651 Francis Glisson produced his *De Rachitide, sive Morbo Puerili, qui Vulgo The Rickets Dicitur* in London, and Culpeper promptly translated it into English. Culpeper's most famous work was probably his herbal, *The English Physitian*, which appeared in three editions its first year (1652); 14 more came out before 1700, and over 100 editions have been printed.

Culpeper's appeal through his herbal, anti establishment translations, and lively style has been long lasting. As recently as 1910 he was the subject of a story by Rudyard Kipling.

The seventeenth century saw the first major work on vital statistics by John Graunt, Edmund Halley, and Sir William Petty. The Italian, Sanctorio Sanctorius, wrote up his careful studies on the physiology of metabolism based on experiments on himself using a steelyard balance. His *De Statica Medicina*, first published in Leipzig in 1614, went through at least 20 editions and several translations. In his commentary on the first book of Avicenna's *Canon* (1625), Sanctorius described his development and use of a thermometer and a pulse-clock in both text and picture.

The first major work in medical jurisprudence was published in a nine-volume set, 1621–1661, at Rome and Amsterdam. The *Quaestiones Medico-Legales* was written by Paolo Zacchias, a Papal physician, who may be looked on as one of the founders of this field.

Another "founder" of a field was active appeared at the same time. In 1623 the first important work on tropical medicine appeared, the *Tratado de las Siete Enfermedades* by Alexo de Abreu, printed at Lisbon. Abreu's text contained the first accurate descriptions of yellow fever and amebic hepatitis.

Although Francis Glisson had been a member of a committee selected to write a book on rickets, most of the medical literature produced up to this time had been the work of individuals (as Glisson's book eventually turned out to be). In the seventeenth century scientists began to assemble in societies for the purpose of presenting papers and exchanging informatioin. This development had a profound and far-reaching effect on the production of medical literature by giving birth to the concept of important, stable, scientific periodicals.

The Royal Society of London was formally organized in 1660, and began publication of its *Philosophical Transactions* on March 6, 1665. This journal, still being published, has had the honor of printing many substantial contributions to the medical literature by such authors as Lower, Hooke, Leeuwenhoek, Cowper, Cheselden, Priestly, Hunter, and many others, as well as important work by relatively unknown individuals (e.g., smallpox inoculation by Timoni and Pylarini). Over 80 papers printed in the *Philosophical Transactions* have merited a place in the *Garrison-Morton Bibliography* of contributions to the history of medicine.

Other societies in different countries were also formed at this time. The Collegium Naturae Curiosorum was founded in Germany in 1651 and produced the first volume of its *Miscellanea Curiosa sive Ephemeridium Medico Physicorum Germanorum* in 1670.

The earliest periodical with some medical material to be printed in France was the *Journal des Scavans*, which began on January 5, 1665, and is still being published. Nicolas de Blegny's *Nouvelles Découverts sur Toutes les Parties de la Médecine* ran from 1679 to 1683; this was the first medical journal in the vernacular although it had a separate Latin version as well. Early medical periodicals in both the seventeenth and eighteenth centuries were often translated into other languages and had several editions of some or all of their volumes.

The first medical journal in English, *Medicina Curiosa*, had its first issue (of two) out on June 17, 1684. The only other English medical journal of the seventeenth century was the *Hippocrates Ridens*, which was born and died in 1686. The *Acta Medica et Philosphica Hafniensia* was printed in Denmark from 1673 to 1680.

Prior to the appearance of the periodical, current medical information was usually transmitted by letter. One physician would include clinical observations in a letter to a colleague who would then reply with comments and questions. A particularly important letter might be circulated by its recipient among his colleagues so that the information could reach a wider audience. This could in turn provoke additional letters back to the original writer.

Other manuscript sources of medical literature included student notebooks which were often retained by the graduate for later consultation while in practice. This was particularly true of the North American colonists who attended medical school in Great Britain or on the continent and returned to the colonies to practice. Some of these notebooks were indexed for easier location of information.

Manuscript compilations of prescriptions would also serve as medical works, especially in the absence of printed materials. These would sometimes be used both in the clinical work of the practitioner and as a textbook for his apprentices.

The North American colonies, later to become the United States of America, saw the first glimmerings of medical literature in the seventeenth century. The first such document printed in the colonies was *God's Terrible Voice in the City of London* by Thomas Vincent, an account of the plague in London in 1665. This 31-page booklet was printed at Cambridge in 1668 by Marmaduke Johnson. The American Antiquarian Society at Worcester has a copy.

The first piece of medical literature to be written and printed in this country was Thomas Thacher's *A Brief Rule to Guide the Common-People of New-England how to order themselves and theirs in the small pocks or measels*, printed by John Foster at Boston in 1678. This broadside, 17 × 12 5/16 inches, exists in only a single copy, which is at the Massachusetts Historical Society. Benjamin Harris at Boston printed in 1694 a 129-page book by John Olwer entitled *A Present to be Given to Teeming Women*, a copy of which is held by the New York Academy of Medicine Library.

The first medical book published in South America was the *Dos Tratados*...by Francisco Figueroa, which appeared at Lima in 1616. No copy of this is known to exist today.

THE EIGHTEENTH CENTURY

One of the classic works appeared just before the end of the century. On May 14, 1796, Edward Jenner, a pupil of the great John Hunter, performed his first vaccination for smallpox. In June 1798 his classic, *An Inquiry into the Causes and Effects of the Variolae Vaccinae*, was printed in London by Low. Jenner described in it his 23 successful vaccinations, and also presented what is probably the first mention of anaphylaxis. A second edition was published in 1800 and a third in 1801. The book spread with almost the same rapidity as the disease itself. Ashley and Brewer reprinted the second edition at Springfield, Massachusetts, in 1802, and it appeared at Hanover (1799), Vienna (1799), Lyons (1800), Lisbon (1803), Pavia (1800), Haarlem (1801), and Madrid (1801). Later it reached Russia and Australia. Facsimiles have been printed at Milan (1923), Denver (1949), and London (1966). LeFanu produced a biobibliography of Jenner in 1951.

The outstanding English surgeon of this century was John Hunter, who was the one individual primarily responsible for placing the field of surgery on a scientific foundation. Hunter had been a pupil of both Cheselden and Pott, and had also studied with his older brother, William. John Hunter's most important book was his *A Treatise on the Blood, Inflammation and Gunshot Wounds*, first published in 1794 shortly after his death. This appeared in three more editions at London and in three editions at Philadelphia (the first by Thomas Bradford in 1796). French and German translations were produced before the end of the century.

Hunter's *Observations on Certain Parts of the Animal Oeconomy* was first published in 1786 with a second edition in 1813. A German translation appeared the same year. Hunter's detailed work in comparative anatomy and his own skillful operative procedures did much to raise the level of surgery.

His *A Treatise on the Venereal Disease* was published at London in 1786 and was most popular. Many editions and translations were produced.

Hunter not only had an excellent museum at his home but also his own private press, which produced his three most important books. He contributed to the periodical literature by papers in the *Philosophical Transactions*, but despite these publications much of his work was still in manuscript form at his death. His brother-in-law,

Everard Home, used this material for his own lectures and writings and then destroyed many of these valuable items.

John's older brother, William, made a major contribution to the medical literature in the form of the *Anatomia Uteri Gravidi Tabulis Illustrata*, one of the finest anatomical atlases ever published. This was printed by John Baskerville in 1774 with 34 life-size copper plates and text in both Latin and English. The Sydenham Society reprinted it in 1851. Baskerville's only other medical publication had appeared 12 years earlier, *Virtues of Cinnabar and Musk Against the Bite of a Mad Dog* by J. Dalby.

The most outstanding eighteenth century English contribution to anatomy was made by the surgeon-anatomist William Cheselden in 1733 with publication at London of his *Osteographia, or the Anatomy of the Bones*. This covered all human bones as well as many of those in animals. Accuracy in the illustrations was achieved by using a camera obscura, devised by Cheselden. A facsimile of the *Osteographia* was printed in 1968.

Cheselden's *The Anatomy of the Human Body* was first published in 1713 when he was 25. Thirteen editions of this popular work had appeared by 1792; two American editions were published (1795 and 1806) and a German translation appeared in 1790.

Another anatomist who used careful measurements and mechanical assistance in the production of an atlas was Bernhard Siegfried Albinus, a pupil of Boerhaave. According to one report Albinus spent 24,000 florins on the illustrations (by Jan Wandelaer) for his atlases, the most important of which, *Tabulae Sceleti et Musculorum Corporis Humani*, was published at Leyden in 1747 with English editions in London, 1749, and Edinburgh, 1777.

Percival Pott made many substantial contributions to the surgical literature on ruptures, injuries of the head, fistulas, fractures, hydroceles, amputations, and cataract. These monographs frequently appeared in many editions and were often translated. Pott was also known for his work on curvature of the spine, cancer of the scrotum, and tumors.

James Lind produced his classic work, *A Treatise of the Scurvy*, in 1753. He described his experiments with citrus fruit in combatting this major problem for navies, explorers, and commercial sailors. Lind gave credit to previous writers on the subject, but it was his book and continued efforts that ultimately led to the control of this problem. The treatise was reprinted in 1953.

The first English text on dermatology, *De Morbis Cutaneis* by Daniel Turner, was printed in London in 1714. A pharmacological classic, William Withering's *An Account of the Foxglove and some of its Medical Uses*, was published at Birmingham in 1785. A facsimile edition was printed at London in 1949. The first English historian of medicine also appeared in this century, John Freind, whose 2-volume work, *The History of Physick; from the Time of Galen to the beginning of the sixteenth century*, was published at London in 1725–1726. Freind planned out this history while he was in the Tower of London on a charge of high treason.

Another major work in the history of medicine appeared just 4 years later in France. Daniel LeClerc's *Histoire de la Médecine* ranks as the first major work in its field, one that is still consulted today. Although the first edition had appeared in French in 1696 and a translation into English was printed in 1699, the 1729 French edition is the best.

Kurt Sprengel's monumental 5-volume *Versuch einer pragmatischen Geschicte der Arzneikunde* was printed at Halle, 1792–1803. This has been a foundation stone for many later works in the history of medicine.

The outstanding physician of the eighteenth century, Hermann Boerhaave, published many works himself on clinical medicine, physiology, and chemistry, and substantial commentaries were produced by his students, especially Gerard van Swieten. Boerhaave's works, the most important of which were the *Aphorismi et Cognoscendis et Curandis Morbis in Usum Doctrinae Domesticae* (first edition, Leyden, 1709) and the *Elementa Chemiae* (first edition, Leyden, 1732), appeared in many editions and translations.

One of the all-time medical classics was published in 1761 at Venice. This was Giovanni Battista Morgagni's 2-volume *De Sedibus et Causis Morborum per Anatomen Indagatis Libri Quinque*. With this monumental publication Morgagni became the founder of modern pathological anatomy. Morgagni, professor of anatomy at Padua, correlated his findings at autopsy with the clinical records of some 700 patients. An English translation, done by Alexander in 1769, was reprinted in 1960.

A much smaller book, although also a medical classic of considerable proportions, came out the same year at Vienna. This was Leopold Auenbrugger's *Inventum Novum ex Percussione Thoracis Humani ut Signo Abstrusos Interni Pectoris Morbos Detergendi* in which he described his discovery of percussion. The *Inventum Novum* did not catch on until Corvisart produced his French translation in 1808, which led to percussion achieving its role of major importance. Forbes did an English translation in 1824; this was reprinted in 1936.

Medical publication began in earnest in the North American colonies that later became the United States. Pamphlets were an important feature of the early years of the century with the pamphlet war over smallpox inoculation taking place in the 1720s and 1730s and involving such individuals as Cotton Mather, Zabdiel Boylston, William Douglass, and Benjamin Franklin. Pamphlets also appeared on other communicable diseases and medical problems. Much of the early medical literature was printed in newspapers.

Cadwallader Colden wrote many pamphlets and texts, including his *Treatise on Wounds and Fevers* (printed about 1765—no copy is known today), which became a standard authority for many years. Thomas Cadwalader wrote his *Essay on the West-India Dry-Gripes* in 1745. It described lead poisoning from rum. John Lining wrote important papers on metabolism and yellow fever.

In 1765 a classic work in medical education appeared, John Morgan's *A Discourse upon the Institution of Medical Schools in America*. This small book set the pattern for medical education in this country and had a considerable influence in other countries as well.

Four year later Samuel Bard wrote his *A Discourse upon the Duties of a Physician*, the first book on medical ethics in the North American colonies. It preceded Thomas Percival's important contribution by 25 years. Bard also wrote (1771) another major work, *An Enquiry into the Nature, Cause and Cure of the Angina Suffocativa* (one of the earliest accurate descriptions of diphtheria). The first colonial publication on medical history, Peter Middleton's *A Medical Discourse, or an Historical Inquiry into the Ancient and Present State of Medicine*, was published in 1769.

John Jones, drawing heavily on the writings of earlier English surgeons, produced the first surgical book published in the colonies in 1775. His *Plain Concise Practical Remarks on the Treatment of Wounds and Fractures* went through four editions and was the standard guide used during the Revolution.

One of the physicians who signed the Declaration of Independence, Benjamin Rush, was a prolific contributor to the literature of medicine and several other fields. Of importance were his *An Account of the Bilious Remitting Yellow Fever* (1794) and *Directions for Preserving the Health of Soldiers* (1778).

Two major medical works by laymen appeared in the last decade of the century. One of these, Mathew Carey's *A Short Account of the Malignant Fever, lately prevalent in Philadelphia* is an important description of yellow fever that was frequently reprinted and was translated into French and German. The other, a 2-volume set, was Noah Webster's *A Brief History of Epidemic and Pestilential Diseases*, 1799.

The first medical publication in Canada was the *Direction pour la Guerison du Mal de la Braie St. Paul*, published at Quebec in 1785, and the earliest general medical treatise produced in the Americas was Juan Manual Venegras' *Compendio de la Medicina: ó Medicina Practica* from Mexico in 1788.

Books on home medicine were produced in the colonies just as they were in many other areas of the world. The first completely American offering was Dr. John Tennent's *Every Man His Own Doctor: or, the Poor Planter's Physician* (1734), which went through several editions and was widely used. Popular also were colonial reprints of Culpeper's *The English Physician* (Boston, 1708) and William Buchan's *Domestic Medicine* (over 30 American editions between 1771 and 1815).

The physician, in the early days of the United States, who wanted to write an article for publication in a medical journal had to look either outside the country or to a nonmedical journal. England and France were favorites among the foreign countries. In fact it was a translation of a French medical journal, *Journal de Médecine Militaire*, whose first volume was published in New York around 1790 as the *Journal of the Practice of Medicine and Surgery and Pharmacy in the Military Hospitals of France* that has a tenuous claim to being the first medical journal published in the United States. Among the nonmedical journals in the United States favored by physicians for their medical articles were the *Memoirs of the American Academy of Arts and Sciences*, *American Museum*, *Philadelphia Monthly Magazine*, and the *Royal American Magazine*.

The first truly indigenous American medical journal was the *Medical Repository* whose first issue appeared on July 26, 1797. This was printed in New York by T.&J. Swords, and edited by Samuel Latham Mitchill, Edward Miller, and Elihu Hubbard Smith. This quarterly journal, the brainchild of Smith, the youngest of the three, met with immediate success and continued publication through volume 23 for 1824. Important articles that appeared in the *Medical Repository* included John Otto's "An Account of an Hemorrhagic Disposition Existing in Certain Families" [**6**, 1–3, (1803)], the first (American) description of hemophilia, and John Stearn's report of the first use of ergot in childbirth [2d Hexade, **5**, 308–309 (1808)]. Outstanding authors whose articles were printed in these pages also included Philip Syng Physick, Benjamin Rush, Benjamin Waterhouse, and Noah Webster.

Transactions of various medical societies appeared sporadically in Europe. Early British medical journals (strictly speaking) included the *Foreign Medical Review* (1779–1880) and the *London Medical Journal* (1780–1800). The first substantial representative of this group was the *Medical and Physical Journal of London* (a continuation of the *Medical Facts and Observations*), which lived from 1799 to 1814. Much of its content consisted of translations and comments on articles from foreign journals.

The first major French medical journal was *Le Journal de Médecine, Chirurgie et Pharmacie*, which was published from 1754 to 1794 and 1801 to 1817. The *Gazette de Médecine* appeared under a variety of titles from 1761 until 1792. The *Gazette de Santé* began in 1773 and continued until 1829 when it became the *Gazette Medical de Paris*. The *Journal General de Médecine, de Chirurgie et de Pharmacie* ran from 1796 to 1830.

Germany's first medical journal, from Leipzig, was the *Deliciae Medicae et Chirurgicae* which began in 1703 but lasted only until 1705. The *Natur und Medizin Kunst und Literature Geschichte* was published at Breslau from 1717 to 1729. The first major German medical journal was the *Acta Medicorum Berolinensium* which ran from 1717 to 1731. The first surgical journal to appear in Germany was Richter's *Chirurgische Bibliothek* (1771–1797). A semiweekly journal, Hartenkeil's *Salzburger medicinische-chirurgische Zeitung*, had enough material to keep going from 1790 to 1842. The first established journal in medical history was edited by the scholarly Sprengel; the *Beiträge zur Geschichte der Medicin* lasted from 1794 to 1796.

The first major medical journal produced in Italy was the *Giornale per Servire alla Storia Ragionata della Medicina di questo Secole* which was printed in Venice from 1783 to 1790.

THE NINETEENTH CENTURY

Among the English medical books of this century to make a lasting impression on the medical literature must certainly be counted Henry Gray's *Anatomy, Descriptive and Surgical.* The first edition of "Gray's" was published in 1858, just three years before the author's early death from smallpox at 34. John W. Parker & Son published the first two editions (the only ones seen by Gray), and Henry Carter drew the illustrations. The first American edition was published in 1859, and the two countries have regularly produced separate editions since then (current editions, both for 1973, are the thirty-fifth in England and the twenty-ninth in the United States.)

One major feature of the nineteenth century was the appearance of the specific monograph, a trend which has increased in the present. An outstanding example of this was James Parkinson's *An Essay on the Shaking Palsy*; the original account of this eponymous disease was published by Whittingham and Rowland in London in 1817. The American Medical Association printed a facsimile in honor of the book's centennial, and Dawsons printed another facsimile in 1959. This essay has been twice reprinted in the journal literature (1922 and 1937–1938), and a German translation appeared in 1912.

A good example of the growing emphasis on journal publication is presented by the career of Sir James Paget who died in 1899. His name is memorialized in two diseases, and both of the original descriptions appeared not in book form but in journal articles. "On Disease of the Mammary Areola Preceding Cancer of the Mammary Gland" was printed in *St. Bartholomew's Hospital Reports* in 1874. "On a Form of Chronic Inflammation of Bones (Osteitis Deformans)" appeared in the *Medico-Chirurgical Transactions* in two papers (1877 and 1882). The *Reports* from St. Bartholomew's are an outstanding representative of this form of medical literature. Seven volumes of Paget's manuscript casebooks, another important facet of the literature, are in the Medical College Library at Bart's.

The French Revolution held up the publication of Philippe Pinel's *Traité Medico-Philosophique sur l'Aliénation Mentale ou la Manie* from 1792 until 1801. When this classic was finally published it created a great impetus for improvements in the treatment of the insane. An English translation appeared in 1806.

The invention of the stethoscope not only led to Laennec's *De l'Auscultation Mediate* in 1819, one of the most influential books of the century, but it also became the first "give-away" gimmick to accompany the sale of a book. Laennec's set (the first edition was in two volumes) had four more French editions, two printings in Belgium, seven English editions (the first in 1821), four printings in the United States (the first two in 1823), three German editions, and an Italian edition. The original French version was reprinted in 1962.

Claude Bernard, the founder of experimental medicine, published many of his important research reports in the burgeoning journals, but his *Introduction a l'Étude de la Médecine Experimentale*, first published at Paris in 1865, probably ranks as one of the most stimulating works in the medical literature. This edition was reprinted in 1949, and an English translation was produced in 1927.

The founder of scientific medicine in Germany was Johannes Peter Müller who, while primarily a physiologist, also had substantial interests in biology, comparative morphology, and pathology. Müller's two-volume *Handbuch der Physiologie des Menschen für Vorlesungen* (Coblenz, 1834–1840) was translated into both French and English. He founded the *Archiv für Anatomie, Physiologie, und wissenschaftliche Medicin* in 1834, a respected vehicle for many important papers over the years.

The most important German work on the history of medicine yet produced was written by Heinrich Haeser. The first edition of his *Lehrbuch der Geschichte der Medicin und der Volkskrankheiten* was published at Jena in 1845, and a three-volume third edition came out in 1875–1882.

The age of modern medicine was ushered in by *Die Cellularpathologie* of Rudolph Virchow in 1858. This was reprinted in 1966 and was translated into English (1860) and French (1861). Virchow, who was active in politics, anthropology, and history as well as medicine, was the founder of the *Archiv für pathologische Anatomie*, still known as *Virchow's Archiv*.

As a final example of the German medical literature of the nineteenth century the pioneering work of Wilhelm Conrad Röntgen may be cited. Röntgen never even wrote a book on X-rays, and his classic contribution took the form of a 10-page article in a rather obscure journal. Reprints of this article (which first appeared in 1895) are among the most expensive (per page) items in the history of the medical literature.

One of the major Russian contributions to the medical literature, Pavlov's *Lectures on the Work of the Principal Digestive Glands*, was published (in Russian) at St. Petersburg in 1897. A French translation appeared in 1901 and an English version in the following year.

During the nineteenth century medical literature in the United States was blossoming quickly and in many areas. Caspar Wistar wrote the first text in anatomy, the two-volume *System of Anatomy*, which was published in 1811–1814, Robley Dunglison's textbook of physiology came out in 1832. Benjamin Smith Barton's *Elements of Botany* (1812) was the first book on materia medica and therapeutics, and Jacob Bigelow's three-volume *American Medical Botany* (1817–1820) achieved a considerable renown.

The first general pharmacopoeia was produced by the Massachusetts Medical Society in 1808, and 12 years later—also in Boston—appeared the first pharmacopoeia of the United States. The first Dispensatory was published in 1833. The first substantial textbook of surgery was John Syng Dorsey's *Elements of Surgery* which came out in 1813.

Samuel Bard wrote the first textbook in obstetrics, *Compendium of the Theory and Practice of Midwifery*, in 1807. William Dewees has credit for the first United States texts in pediatrics (1825) and gynecology (1826).

The United States produced several classics in the literature of medicine during this century. In 1812 Benjamin Rush wrote his *Medical Inquiries and Observations upon the Diseases of the Mind*, which was not only the first American book in that field but also ranks as a landmark in its subject. In 1833 William Beaumont's *Experiments in Digestion* describing his investigations on Alexis St. Martin, the half-breed who miraculously survived a point-blank gunshot wound, was published. A British edition was published in Edinburgh in 1838. A German translation appeared in 1834. A facsimile of the 1833 edition was produced in 1929. In 1850 and 1854 the two volumes that composed Daniel Drake's *A Systematic Treatise, Historical, Etiological, and Practical, on the Principal Diseases of the Interior Valley of North America* were printed. In 1859 the first of six editions of Samuel David Gross' *A System of Surgery* was published, two volumes that did much to raise the level of American surgery both practically and in the eyes of the rest of the world. Among Gross's several monographs, the *Elements of Pathological Anatomy* and *A Practical Treatise on the Diseases, Injuries and Malformations of the Urinary Bladder, and Prostate Gland, and the Urethra* each went through three editions. William Osler published his *Principles and Practice of Medicine* in 1892, a textbook that set a standard for single-author works of this type. "Osler" went through many editions and was translated into a wide variety of languages.

The first United States medical journal after the *Medical Repository* was the *Philadelphia Medical Museum*, founded by John Redman Coxe, which ran through seven volumes between 1804 and 1811. This form of medical publication spread rapidly with the first medical journal appearing in Massachusetts in 1806 (*Medical and Agricultural Register*), in Maryland in 1808 (*Baltimore Medical and Physical Recorder*), in Ohio in 1822, Connecticut in 1823, and South Carolina in 1825. The first medical journal to appear west of the Mississippi was the *St. Louis Medical and Surgical Journal*, which began in 1843 and continued for many years; and the first on the West Coast appeared in 1856, the *San Francisco Medical Journal*, which lasted for only one issue. The *Pacific Medical and Surgical Journal*, also from San Francisco, began in 1858 and was the first West Coast medical journal to be successful.

David Hosack and John W. Francis edited the *American Medical and Philosophical Register* through its four volumes (1810–1814), producing a second edition of the first volume, a practice that was fairly common at that time.

As medical journals became more accepted by both readers and authors as a means of transmitting medical information, important articles began to appear and important journals began long runs. Ephraim McDowell's report of his classic ovariotomy was printed in the *Eclectic Repertory and Analytical Review* [**7**, 242–244 (1817)]. William Beaumont's first report on his studies of St. Martin's stomach appeared in the *American Medical Recorder* [**8**, 14–19 (1825)]. The author was erroneously given as Joseph Lovell, the surgeon general, but this mistake was corrected later in the same volume.

The *American Journal of Science*, which early contained much material of medical interest, was founded in 1818 by Benjamin Silliman and continues to this day.

The *Philadelphia Journal of the Medical and Physical Sciences* was founded by Nathaniel Chapman in 1820 as a patriotic response to Sydney Smith's slur earlier that year in the *Edinburgh Review*, "In the four quarters of the globe, who reads an American Book? or goes to an American play? or looks at an American picture or statue? What does the world yet owe to American physicians or surgeons?" This quotation appeared on the title page of Chapman's journal for several years, and the journal itself became in 1827 the renowned *American Journal of the Medical Sciences*, still published today. Its first editor, Isaac Hays, was one of the leaders in American medical journalism.

The early American medical journals contained many articles on meteorological conditions, fevers, and surgical procedures. Later, translations of articles (either summarized or complete) from the foreign journals often appeared. News items took up many pages, and editorials—sometimes of a vitriolic nature—showed the use of the medical journal as a platform for individual, institutional, or sectarian controversy.

The *Boston Medical Intelligencer* was founded in 1823 by Jerome F.C. Smith as this country's first weekly medical journal. In 1828 it was merged with the *New England Journal of Medicine and Surgery* (which had begun in 1812) to form the *Boston Medical and Surgical Journal*. This, one of the leading medical journals in the country, changed its title in 1929 to the *New England Journal of Medicine*, and now occupies one of the highest positions in medical journalism throughout the world.

The first sectarian journal, the *Medical Advocate*, was founded by Samuel Thomson in 1827 to promote the Thomsonian (Botanical) System.

Among the important American medical journals that did not have long lives was the *Transylvania Journal of Medicine and the Associate Sciences* which ran from 1828 to 1839 and included many important papers.

The first American homeopathic journal, the *American Journal of Homoeopathia*, began and ended publication in New York in 1835.

The *Journal of the American Medical Association* began its weekly appearances with Volume 1, Number 1, for July 14, 1883. American medical journals were now being published by a wide variety of commercial concerns, specialty and geographical societies, and by hospitals and medical schools.

The first medical journal to be published in Canada began at Quebec in 1826. The *Journal de Médecine de Quebec* was printed in both French and English although the contents of the two sections were different. This quarterly lasted for two years. The first English-language journal was the *Montreal Medical Gazette* which began in 1845. Medical journalism had spread over most of the country by 1911, when the *Canadian Medical Association Journal* came out with its first issue.

English periodical medical literature was roused out of its quiet existence in 1823 by the appearance of Thomas Wakley's *Lancet.* Wakley believed in responsibility and progress in medical practice, education, and journalism, and the *Lancet* provided an effective platform for his often outspoken comments and aggressive approaches. He backed his beliefs by court appearances as both a plaintiff and a defendant. He even carried his programs into Parliament and was able to lead reform movements in several areas. During his controversial career Wakley kept the level of contributions in the *Lancet* high and it became deeply respected not only in Great Britain but also throughout the world. Of the contributions listed in "Garrison-Morton," 117 were printed in the *Lancet.* The authors included such names as Lister, Simpson, Snow, Horsley, and Fleming.

In 1857 saw the beginning of the other major weekly medical journal in England, the *British Medical Journal*, the official publication of the British Medical Association. The "BMJ" has long maintained a worldwide reputation as an outstanding publication. Lister, Tait, Wells, Osler, and Manson are among the authors who wrote the 122 papers listed in "Garrison-Morton."

The *Edinburgh Medical Journal*, under a variety of titles, had a distinguished career for a century and a half. The *Practitioner* has been making important contributions since 1868 and still holds a respectable position. The *Dublin Journal of Medical and Chemical Science* began publication in 1832 and continues today as the *Irish Journal of Medical Science.*

In 1846 the first issue of the *Australian Medical Journal* appeared, although it ceased publication the following year. After several other medical journals entered the field the present *Medical Journal of Australia* was formed by an amalgamation in 1914.

The birth and growth of specialty medical journals has been a phenomenon primarily of the nineteenth and twentieth centuries. They have developed at different rates in different countries and their story is too long and detailed for this article. Accounts and pertinent references will be found in the books cited at the end of this entry.

In France the *Archives de Médecine et de Pharmacie Militaires* had a useful career from 1815 to 1882. The *Archives Generales de Médecine* ran from 1823 to 1914, making notable contributions under the editorship of Trousseau. The *Comptes Rendus* of the Academie des Sciences and the Société de Biologie, beginning in 1835 and 1849, respectively, and are still being published. They have carried many important medical papers.

In addition to the journals founded by Müller and Virchow, Germany was the source of many other important titles. *Pflüger's Archiv für die gesamte Physiologie* began publication in 1868; *Langenbeck's Archiv für klinische Chirurgie* in 1861; *Wiener medizinische Wochenschrift* in 1851; *Münchener medizinische Wochenschrift* in 1854 (as *Arztliches Intelligenz-Blatt*); *Berliner klinische Wochenschrift* in 1864; and *Deutsche medizinische Wochenschrift* in 1875. These journals are all still making worthwhile contributions to the literature.

Among the early major Russian medical journals was the *Moskowkye Medizhinskaja Gazeta* 1866–1878, the *Wojenao Medizinske Journal* (*Military Medical Journal*) 1823–1907, and the *Wratsch* (*Physician*).

THE TWENTIETH CENTURY

The medical literature of the middle twentieth century has become essentially a journal literature. Articles in journals are now the standard method of announcing discoveries, new methods, and even new hypotheses. Speedy publication, wide circulation, and lower cost have all emphasized the journal over the book. This trend was evident toward the end of the previous century, and could be demonstrated in this century by such items as Joseph Goldberger's first major publication on pellagra in 1920. This was a 109-page report that most probably would have been published as a book earlier, but in the twentieth century it appeared as a journal article.

The book portion of the medical literature showed two major trends in the twentieth century. The first was toward the comprehensive and detailed set, of which the German Handbücher are good representatives. The 12-volume *Handbuch der speziellen pathologischen Anatomie und Histologie*, edited by Henke and Lubarsch and published by Springer at Berlin, 1924–1952, was typical. Another facet of this trend is the multiauthored set, such as Duke-

Elder's *System of Ophthalmology* in 15 volumes. This began in 1958 and Volume 14 appeared in 1972.

The second was a continuation of the trend toward the highly specialized monograph. A classic of this century, Felix d'Herelle's *Le Bacteriophage*, published at Paris in 1921, exemplifies this trend. In the first half of the century this type of monograph could have also been represented by a two-volume one-author work such as Henry Head's *Aphasia and Kindred Disorders of Speech*, published by the Cambridge University Press in 1926. This is still in such demand that a reprint was produced in 1963.

Reference works of several varieties were frequent additions to the medical literature of the twentieth century. These could be works that keep reappearing, such as David Bergey's *Manual of Determinative Bacteriology*, first published at Baltimore in 1923 and now in its eighth edition, or a single-appearance publication such as the World Health Organization's (WHO) *Bibliography of Yaws 1905–62*, printed at Geneva in 1963. The publication program of WHO has made many worthwhile contributions to the medical literature.

Popularizations of scientific medical work for the layman, although not new to the medical literature in this century, have been much more frequent. These serve a variety of valuable purposes.

But essentially this has been the century of the medical journal, and the proliferation and variety of these publications has been remarkable. Journals are now dealing with highly specialized subjects, and the rise and fall of research and clinical fashions can be traced in the corresponding births, mutations, and deaths of the journals.

Whether the journal will remain the chief form of the medical literature for the rest of this century and into the next is an unpredictable matter, although some trends at present suggest that it may not. The printing of separate fascicles of a journal for each separate article has been tried experimentally. Related to this trend is the publication of only an abstract or a tightly shortened version of the article with the storage of the full text in a central location to which readers may write for full copies if they are interested. The medical newspaper is another new phenomenon in the literature.

Medical journals have appeared in microfiche rather than the traditional printed form. So far these have not been too successful, but as a new generation of readers comes along this form of publication may spread.

The audio side of the audiovisual approach has also entered the medical literature. More than a few journals are now available on tape. This is true of the digest type of publication as well as the full-length article variety. The audio method seems to have met with more favorable reader acceptance than the visual.

Books, too, are changing their format. The programmed-learning text with its columns, boxes, and variously sized and shaped pages, is a common sight. The next step is already being taken experimentally, the computerized nonprinted text. In this case the text of a book (most logically a multiauthored handbook) is stored in a computer and never printed as a whole. When one of the authors wants to bring his section up to date he displays it on the terminal page by page, makes additions, deletions, or corrections, and sends it back to the storage unit. When a reader wants a more permanent copy than the terminal display, he asks for the page(s) he wants to be printed out and sent to him.

The medical literature is now in a state of flux, even more so than it has been in the past. What shapes it will have in 25, 50, and 100 years no one can predict. The only certainty is that it will continue to exist in some form or forms—because both the readers and the authors need it.

BIBLIOGRAPHIC CONTROL

Within 50 years after the invention of printing from movable metal type the medical literature had grown to the point where a bibliography was felt to be needed. Symphorien Champier accordingly compiled his *De Medicinae Claris Scriptoribus*, which was printed at Lyons in 1506. Champier listed the books in five divisions: ancient medical writers; philosophical medical writers; ecclesiastical writers on medicine; Italian medical writers; and French, German, Spanish, and English medical writers. Dates were infrequently given, and little other information was included beyond author and title. A rough author and subject index was included in the table of contents.

It was 84 years before a bibliographic work showing substantial improvements appeared. (Conrad Gesner never completed the medical volume of his monumental *Bibliotheca Universalis*.) Paschalis Gallus produced his *Bibliotheca Medica* in 1590 at Basel. Again the text was broken down by languages. The bulk of Gallus's text dealt with writers in Latin, and this is a practical annotated list arranged alphabetically by the given name of the author. Gallus's volume was the first general bibliography of medicine arranged by authors with adequate bibliographic information.

The next year Israel Spach published his *Nomenclator Scriptorum Medicorum* at Frankfort. The text was arranged in a minutely classified format with alphabetical subject and author (given names) indexes. The individual entries contained fairly complete bibliographic information.

Johannes-Antonides der Linden made several substantial improvements in the editions of his *De Scriptis Medicis*. These included practical use of type size and spacing for increased legibility and easier location of information. Although he retained the alphabetical arrangement of authors by given names (really a logical contemporary approach because surnames were not yet widely used), Linden added information to his entries and brought his bibliography close to a modern production. The first edition appeared in 1637 at Amsterdam, and two later ones came out in 1651 and 1662.

In 1686 Linden's work was revised and considerably enlarged by Georg Abraham Mercklin, who took an important step by including for the first time some articles from the periodical publications of the learned societies that were just springing into formation.

In 1679 Martinus Lipenius published his *Bibliotheca Realis Medica* at Frankfurt am Main. He was able to include a large amount of material by using a two-column format in a large quarto volume. Lipenius also used letter headings for each column as a guide to the searcher. The text was arranged by subjects with the authors arranged alphabetically by given name. Many cross references (primarily subject, but some author) were given throughout the text. There was an index for authors, commentators, et al.

Further steps were taken by Cornelius à Beughem who, in 1681 at Amsterdam, published his *Bibliographia Medica et Physica Novissima*. This publication circumvented one of the problems brought on by the increasing outpouring of the medical literature by limiting its coverage to material published within a specific time span, roughly 1651 to 1681. The text was arranged by authors.

In 1696, also at Amsterdam, Beughem produced his *Syllabus Recens Exploratorum in Re Medica*, which covered the periodical literature, mostly from the transactions of various learned societies. In both of these pioneering publications Beughem made improvements in accuracy and detail.

The first "giant" in medical bibliography appeared in the eighteenth century. Albrecht von Haller had compiled a nine-volume work, *Elementa Physiologiae Corporis Humani*, at Lausanne, 1757–1782, in which he listed and annotated many of the publications in that broad field. This was, in a sense, a warm-up for his four major bibliographies. The first of these, *Bibliotheca Botanica*, two volumes printed at Zurich in 1771–1772, contained much medical material. The botanical volumes were quickly followed by the *Bibliotheca Chirurgica*, two volumes, Bern, 1774–1775; the *Bibliotheca Anatomica*, two volumes, Zurich, 1774–1777; and the *Bibliotheca Medicinae Practicae*, four volumes, Basel, 1776–1788. These were arranged by broad subject, and then chronologically. Many of the items listed had abstracts. There was an author index.

Wilhelm Gottfried Ploucquet initiated the concept of the cyclical bibliography, and his arguments for and against this solution make interesting reading in the introductions to his publications. His first basic set was the *Initia Bibliothecae Medico-Practica et Chirurgica* in eight volumes, printed at Tübingen (as were all his works) in 1793–1796. A four-volume supplement, *Bibliotheca Medico-Practica et Chirurgica*, was printed in 1799–1803. A combined set, with new material, *Literatura Medica Digesta*, appeared in 1808–1809, in four volumes, and one supplemental volume was produced in 1813, the year before Ploucquet's death. Ploucquet was able to put so much material in the *Literatura* because he used smaller type than previously and a three-column format. All of his works were arranged by subject, and included many journal articles as well as books, pamphlets, and dissertations. Unfortunately, he had no author index.

Between 1830 and 1845 Adolph Carl Peter Callisen produced, at Copenhagen, thirty-three small volumes of his *Medicinisches Schriftsteller Lexicon der jetzt lebenden Aerzte*.... This mammoth undertaking provided an author list of books and journal articles printed roughly between 1750 and 1830. This, the last major one-man medical bibliography, made a useful complement to the work of Ploucquet. Callisen's set was reprinted in 1962–1965.

The next outstanding figure was John Shaw Billings who lived from 1838 to 1913. Billings not only realized the bibliographic needs of the users of the medical literature but was able to work out practical publications to meet these needs and workable methods to produce the publications. The first volume of the *Index-Catalogue of the Library of the Surgeon-General's Office* appeared in 1880. The series was to have 60 more volumes before it ceased in 1961. This set (in five series) covered the books and articles in the collection at the Surgeon-General's Library, providing an author and subject approach to the former and a subject approach to the latter. Using typographic aids and a two-column format, Billings was able to make a vast amount of material easily accessible.

The first series of the *Index-Catalogue* included 16 volumes printed between 1880 and 1895; the second series of 21 volumes ran from 1896 to 1916; and the third series of 10 volumes appeared from 1918 to 1932. The fourth series, which went only through "M," was printed in 11 volumes between 1936 and 1955, and the fifth series of three volumes was printed in 1959–1961. The complete set ranks as a major contribution to the bibliographic control of the medical literature, and will serve as a lasting memorial to Billings's imagination, perseverance, and ability. Lack of money and the rapidly increasing flow of the literature eventually made the approach of the *Index-Catalogue* no longer feasible.

Billings envisioned a frequently appearing series as a current supplement to the foundation of the *Index-Catalogue*. The first monthly issues of this supplement, which was called the *Index Medicus*, were printed in 1879. These issues covered primarily articles from selected medical journals although some other material was also included. The text was classified, and the only indexes were the annual author and subject listings. Robert Fletcher assisted Billings with the production of the *Index Medicus* just as he did with the *Index-Catalogue*. A carefully worked-out team handled the processing of the materials and information.

The *Index Medicus* ran into financial difficulties at the end of the century (Ser. I, Vols. 1–21, 1879–1899), and sufficient income was not generated again until the Carnegie Institute helped out and made possible the continuation of this valuable tool (Ser. II, Vols. 1–18, 1903–1920; Ser. III,

Vols. 1–6, 1921–1927). With the third series the *Index Medicus* became a quarterly and took on a subject arrangement with an annual author index.

The American Medical Association produced a similar index with its *Quarterly Cumulative Index to Current Medical Literature* (Vols. 1–12, 1916–1926). The drain on finances and growing production time led to an amalgamation of this with the *Index Medicus* to form the *Quarterly Cumulative Index Medicus* (Vols. 1–60, 1927–1956) which had authors and subjects arranged in an easy-to-use dictionary format. The Surgeon-General's Library (going through an evolutionary series of names) began a *Current List of Medical Literature* during World War II that continued until 1959 and was particularly useful for the period 1952–1959.

With the demise of the *Index-Catalogue* and the *Quarterly Cumulative Index Medicus* a restructuring of the bibliographic mechanism was needed. The coverage of books was taken care of by the Army Medical Library (now the National Library of Medicine) with a sequence of annual and quinquennial catalogs leading up to the *Current Catalog* which began in 1966. Journals were indexed in the "new" *Index Medicus* which began in 1960. This appears in 12 monthly issues and a bound annual cumulation of several volumes.

The mechanization project at the National Library of Medicine that developed along with the new *Index Medicus* under the direction of Frank B. Rogers led eventually to the computerized MEDLARS (*Med*ical *L*iterature *A*nalysis and *R*etrieval *S*ystem) program, which has speeded up the production of the *Index Medicus* and made computerized searching of the literature a reality, has also led to the development of Medline (the on-line computerized program that provides access to the National Library of Medicine's data banks) and to a variety of related programs. Some of these services have been made available in England, Sweden, and other countries. A greatly enlarged and improved Medlars II program has just been put into operation. An experimental program with the use of a satellite for the communication of medical information has been successfully tried out by the library. The State University of New York has developed a broad computerized program that provides bibliographic control for and access to a vast amount of the medical literature.

Abstract journals have provided another approach to the medical literature. Karl Christian Schmidt initiated *Schmidt's Jahrbücher der in- und ausländischen gesamten Medicin* in 1834. The *Jahrbücher* met such a great need that they continued through 336 volumes until 1922. The Germans developed a network of bibliographic journals based on the Zentralblätter or Berichte in the different subject areas that provided brief abstracts, through their annual compilations (Jahresberichte or Jahrbücher) to the review journals usually titled Ergebnisse. The major English-language abstracting journal is the *Excerpta Medica* series which began in 1947 and has grown considerably. Indexing or abstracting journals are also found in France, Russia, Japan, and many other countries.

CONCLUSION

The bibliographic control of the medical literature in the Americas has been greatly assisted by such works as the *Epitome de la Biblioteca Oriental i Occidental, Nautica i Geografica* of Antonio de Leon published in Madrid in 1629, the *Historia Bibliografica de la Medicina Española* of Antonio Hernandez Morejon (seven volumes, Madrid, 1842–1845; reprinted in 1965), and the *Biblioteca Hispano-Americana* (1493–1810) of Jose Toribio Medina (six volumes, Santiago de Chile, 1898–1907). Francisco Guerra's *American Medical Bibliography 1639–1783* (New York, 1962), which includes newspapers, broadsides, and almanacs as well as books, pamphlets, and journal articles, is a major bibliographic work, and Robert B. Austin's *Early American Medical Imprints: A Guide to Works Printed in the United States 1668–1820* (1961) is invaluable in its area.

SELECTED READINGS AND REFERENCE WORKS

1. Brodman, E. *The Development of Medical Bibliography*; Medical Library Association: Baltimore, MD, 1954.
2. Choulant, L. *History and Bibliography of Anatomic Illustration*; University of Chicago Press: Chicago, IL, 1920. (Mortimer Frank, trans. and ed.).
3. Fulton, J.F. *The Great Medical Bibliographers; A Study in Humanism*; University of Pennsylvania Press: Philadelphia, PA, 1951.
4. Hahn, A., et al., *Histoire de la Médecine et du Livre Medical*; Perrin: Paris, France, 1962.
5. Morton, L.T. *A Medical Bibliography (Garrison and Morton), An Annotated Check-List of Texts Illustrating the History of Medicine*, 3rd Ed.; Lippincott: Philadelphia, PA, 1970.
6. Postell, W.D. *The Development of Medical Literature*; Louisiana State University School of Medicine: New Orleans, n.d.
7. Thornton, J.L. *Medical Books, Libraries and Collectors*, 2nd Ed.; Deutsch: London, U.K., 1966.

Metadata and Digital Information *[ELIS Classic]*

Jane Greenberg
Metadata Research Center, School of Information and Library Science, University of North Carolina at Chapel Hill, Chapel Hill, North Carolina, U.S.A.

Abstract

The range of metadata activity over this last decade is both extensive and astonishing, and substantiates metadata as an integral part of our digital information infrastructure. This entry begins with a brief history of metadata relating to digital information, followed by an overview of different metadata types, functions, and domain-specific definitions. Next, the family of standards comprising a metadata architecture are defined, followed by an overview of metadata generation processes, applications, and people: this latter section gives particular attention to automatic metadata generation approaches. The following section explores four key metadata models. The conclusion summarizes the entry, highlights a number of significant metadata challenges, and notes efforts underway to address metadata challenges in the new millennium.

INTRODUCTION

Today one can hardly talk about digital libraries, data repositories, and many aspects of the library 2.0/web 2.0 environment without mention of *metadata*. This is because metadata is a crucial part of these digital information systems. Metadata describes information and its context and associations; it is integral to the operation and function of any system preserving and supporting discovery, access, and use of information. Metadata is also a necessary component of physical information systems, such as the traditional library card catalog. In this context, bibliographic records (an equivalent of *descriptive metadata*) represent library holdings and facilitate resource discovery and use.

The first article on "metadata" appearing in the *Encyclopedia of Library and Information Science (ELIS)* was published in 2002,[1] under the title, "Metadata and the World Wide Web." This work was revised and republished in 2003.[2] These noted entries define metadata, compare metadata to library cataloging, describe concepts for discussing metadata, and review different methods for generating metadata.

Metadata developments have matured considerably since these first *ELIS* entries were published, and a number of initially ambiguous aspects surrounding the topic are more fully understood. For example, when the term metadata was first being explored in the library community, via digital library and World Wide Web (web) development, there were efforts to distinguish metadata from library catalog data, including MAchine Readable Cataloging (MARC) bibliographic data. Today, library catalogers and digital library professionals generally agree that MARC bibliographic data is metadata, and that the family of MARC formats—bibliographic, authority control, and so forth[3,4]—all have a place within metadata discussions. Another sign of growth is that metadata-related development and inquiry has expanded well beyond National Information Standards Organization (NISO) and the International Standards Organization (ISO) metadata standards to include ontologies,[5,6] the Semantic Web,[7] annotation,[8] and social computing/web 2.0 developments relating to tagging and folksonomy.[9,10] In short, our perception and comprehension of metadata has been influenced by time and the evolution of technology and information practices requiring metadata.

This encyclopedia entry considers the evolution of metadata and presents a fresh perspective on this topic. The rest of the entry is organized by the following section headers: "Metadata: Origin and History" covers the origin and history of metadata relating to digital information; "Defining Metadata" explains the different types and functions of metadata and presents a series of domain-specific definitions for metadata; "Metadata Standards" defines the family of metadata standards that comprise a metadata architecture—these include data structure standards, content value standards, data communication standards, and syntax standards; "Metadata Generation" reviews metadata generation, processes, applications, people—giving focused attention to automatic approaches; "Metadata Models" explores several key metadata models; and the "Conclusion" summarizes the entry, and highlights several significant metadata challenges being faced in this new millennium.

METADATA: ORIGIN AND HISTORY

The etymology of metadata draws from the classical Greek prefix *meta*, which means "after, behind, or higher;"

Encyclopedia of Library and Information Sciences, Fourth Edition DOI: 10.1081/E-ELIS4-120044415

and the from Latin word *data*, plural for datum, which means "a piece of information" or "something given."[11] Metadata is, in essence, a piece of information generated *after* the object of focus has been produced; and the information given is at a higher level (more abstract) than the object.

Metadata, as an information concept, is known to have first been used in the late 1960s by individuals in the statistics/database community, and it has been recollected that it was a standard word by the 1970s, although references are difficult to find. The first known reference appears in *An Infological Approach to Data Bases*, a doctoral dissertation completed in 1973, by Bo Sundgren, at the Statistiska Centralbyren (pp. 104–105).[12] This work also includes the concept of *metainformation* and articulates distinctions between the real-world phenomena; information about phenomena; and data representing the information describing the phenomena; the last conception is referred to as meta-metadata in today's information systems.

The most frequent historical reference given for *metadata* is for a marketing brochure, printed for Jack E. Myers, representing a MetaModel and company products. References credit Meyers with coining the term *metadata* in 1969,[13] and in 1986 METADATA® was registered as an United States trademark for The Metadata Company (http://www.metadata.com/), where Meyers is a principal. Meyers is known to have legally contested the use of term *metadata* by others. However, his ownership claims have been successfully refuted, given the publication of *An Infological Approach to Data Bases* and the longstanding historical use of this term in the statistics community.

Today, the term metadata has been steadfastly integrated into our information culture, and it is generally, although not exclusively, associated with digital information. Evidence of growth includes the increase in people engaged in metadata work in the library and other information intensive environments, such as scientific research centers. As part of this growth we see professional titles like *metadata librarian* and *metadata specialist*. The body of scholarly research on metadata is also expanding; in fact there are two fairly new scholarly journals targeting metadata: *The International Journal of Metadata, Semantics and Ontologies* (http://www.inderscience.com/ijmso) published by Inderscience Publishers, and *Journal of Library Metadata* (http://www.tandf.co.uk/journals/) published by Taylor & Francis. Additionally, the number of books on metadata continues to grow yearly, with very recent notable publications by Riley and Foulonneau,[14] Zeng and Qin,[15] and Liu.[16] Finally, a factor of growth is the Dublin Core Metadata Initiative (DCMI) (http://www.dublincore.org/), which has been flourishing since 1995, promoting the Dublin Core Metadata Element Set (DCMES),[17] an open, interoperable, interdisciplinary metadata standard. The DCMI and metadata initiatives in the education, science, government, industry, and other communities have been a major force bringing metadata issues to the forefront of library and information science, and demonstrate the wide reach and complexity of this topic.

DEFINING METADATA

Definitions for metadata have been influenced by both the objects to which the metadata is being applied, and the functions it is intended to support. The most often uttered and most inclusive definitions for metadata are *data about data* and *information about* information. Although *data* and *information* can have distinct meanings,[18] these terms are frequently used interchangeably, and it is not uncommon for metadata to be also defined as *information about data*, or even *data about information*. What makes these definitions high-level is that the "information" or "data" being described connotes an *abstract object*—that is "anything perceivable or conceivable," as defined in the ISO/IEC (International Organization for Standardization/International Electrotechnical Commission) 11179-1: 2004, Metadata registries (MDR)—Part 1: Framework (p. 4).[19]

The earlier *ELIS* metadata entries give attention to the unbounded nature of an object as "any *entity*, *mode* or *form*" to which metadata can be applied, ranging from "information resources, such as a monograph, newspaper, or photograph—to activities, events, persons, places, structures, transactions, relationships, execution directions, and programmatic applications."[1,2] The ways in which people work with and understand information varies enormously across disciplines, cultures, and societal strata, and it follows that their conception of the information object varies as well.

Library and information science is primarily concerned with metadata for *information resources*—the types of *objects* housed in libraries, repositories, museums, archives, and other types of information centers. In this environment, metadata is frequently defined as "structured data about data."[20,21] The structured metadata is gathered to form a *metadata surrogate*—a "stand in" for the real resource akin to a bibliographic surrogate.

Metadata surrogates are usually comprised of *descriptive metadata*, which is metadata that supports resource discovery. Detailed, more granular metadata definitions, beyond data about data, emphasize types (or classes) of metadata and the associating functional aspects, such as describing, preserving, and contextualizing information (see Table 1).

Although literature confirms there is no single agreed upon typology of metadata types or functions, metadata discussions promote similar and overlapping labels and definitions (pp. 20–22).[22] Further, more granular

Table 1 Examples of metadata types, functions and properties

Type of metadata	Function supported	Metadata property (element)
Descriptive metadata	Resource discovery; selection; access	[a]Creator; title; subject
Preservation metadata	Resource management	Resolution; density; fixity
Provenance metadata	Lifecycle management; authentication	[a]Creator; date created; date modified
Contextual metadata	Awareness; comprehension; interpretation	Date created; temporal data; arrangement (placement of an object in relation to other objects)
Technical metadata	Use; access	System requirements; format
Rights management metadata	Access; reproduction; use/re-use	Rights

[a] A metadata property that can be labeled as more than one *type* of metadata is multifunctional.[22] The Dublin Core property *creator* is identified as "descriptive metadata" because it helps with discovery and "provenance metadata" because it helps with lifecycle tracking; creator is, therefore, a multifunctional property.

definitions are important because they provide insight into the functional aspect of metadata and the way in which different communities work with and understand metadata. The following community-oriented definitions illustrate this point more concretely:

- The *library community* emphasizes *descriptive metadata*; that is "metadata that serves the purposes of discovery (how one finds a resource), identification (how a resource can be distinguished from other, similar resources), and selection (how to determine that a resource fills a particular need, for example, for the DVD version of a video recording)" (pp. 210).[23,24]
- The *digital geospatial and environmental science communities* have consistently stated that "Metadata or 'data about data' describes the content, quality, condition, and other characteristics of data" (p. 1),[25] providing a definition reflecting needs of associated with digital geospatial and similarly related materials.
- The *business community* highlights metadata for *machine processing* and *user activities*, and adheres to two main metadata classes: *technical metadata* describing database information and machine driven tasks; and *business metadata* supporting input/output tasks overseen by humans (p. 12).[26]
- The World Wide Web Consortium (W3C) emphasizes the *computing potential* of metadata for growing the Semantic Web, and defines metadata as "machine understandable information for the web" (W3C Metadata and Resource Description: http://www.w3.org/Metadata/).
- The social networking and web 2.0 environment promotes the use of the term tag/tags/tagging instead of metadata. Definitions for these terms underscore the functional aspect of tags as "keywords" for *describing*, *classifying*, *finding*, and *sharing* information.[27]

These more descriptive definitions show a range of activities and functions metadata supports (e.g., retrieval, preservation, and machine processing). The range of definitions also provides insight into the complexity of this topic, and helps explain why, in many respects, the high-level definition of *data about data* is the accepted unifying definition, despite its generality.

METADATA STANDARDS

Metadata generally involves standards. The degree to which standards apply varies tremendously, depending on the object of interest, available technology, and community overseeing the metadata activity. Metadata activities in the library and information community are supported by a series of standards that comprise a metadata architecture. These include: *data structure standards*, *content value standards*, *communication standards*, and *syntax standards*. Although different aspects of these types of standards are generally integrated in a single metadata package, they are reviewed separately here to emphasize specific functions. Many instances of the standards reviewed here are endorsed by agencies, such as the American National Standards Institute (ANSI), National Information Standards Organization (NISO), International Organization for Standardization (ISO), Internet Engineering Task Force (IETF), and the World Wide Web (W3C), and designated by an identifier often consisting of numbers or numbers and letters.

Data Structure Standards

Data structure standards are the most familiar metadata standard. A data structure is essentially a list or container of explicit properties (elements). A data structure standard names and defines the *semantic categories* representing the information system's metadata. These semantic categories are most often referred to as *metadata elements*, although *metadata facets* are also becoming common. Most recently, the Dublin Core community has been promoting the term *metadata properties* in an effort to align metadata activities with the Semantic Web.

The DCMES, version 1.1 (here after referred to as the Dublin Core) is among the most internationally and interdisciplinary recognized metadata data structure standards. The Dublin Core and is defined as "a vocabulary of 15 properties for use in resource description,"[17] and is endorsed by the ISO (ISO 15836-2003), ANSI/NISO (ANSI/NISO Z39.85-2007), and the IETF via a request for comment (IETF/RFC 5013-2007). Examples of Dublin

Core properties include *creator*, *title*, and *subject*. An example for the property "creator" from the Dublin Core, 1.1, is provided in Example 1.

Example 1: Characteristics for the Dublin Core Metadata Property *Creator*

Term Name: Creator	
URI:	http://purl.org/dc/elements/1.1/creator
Label:	Creator
Definition:	An entity primarily responsible for making the resource.
Comment:	Examples of a Creator include a person, an organization, or a service. Typically, the name of a Creator should be used to indicate the entity.

Data structure standards are fairly equivalent to data dictionaries developed for databases and frequently include additional information about the use and application of metadata properties. For example, a data structure standard may recommend a *public label*; confirm property *cardinality*—if the metadata property is repeatable; declare property *obligation*—is property required, recommended, or optional; and list legal content values or standards for a property.

Data structure standards have been developed for a wide range of domains. Examples include following:

- *Metadata Object Description Schema* (MODS)[28] for digital library resources.
- *Visual Resources Association Core Categories* (VRA Core)[29] for visual resources.
- *Encoded Archival Description* (EAD)[30] for electronic finding aids.
- *Data Document Initiative* (DDI)[31] for social science research data.
- *Federal Geographic Data Committee/Content Standard for Digital Geospatial Metadata* (FGDC/CSDGM)[25] for digital geospatial resources.
- *Ecological Metadata Language* (EML)[32] for ecological research data.
- *Institute of Electrical and Electronics Engineers/Learning Object Metadata* (IEEE/LOM)[33] for digital learning objects.
- *PREservation Metadata: Implementation Strategies* (PREMIS)[23] for preservation information about any digital object.
- *Darwin Core* (DwC)[34] for specimen collections and the geographic occurrence of species.

The immediate above list includes only several of the hundreds, and potentially thousands, of metadata schemes that function as data structures. The widespread availability and increased sharing of schemes represents a maturity in metadata development; and it is simply *best practice* to first consider if a scheme (or schemes) fulfilling project needs has already been developed when embarking on any new initiative requiring metadata. Among incentives for adopting, and potentially modifying, existing metadata schemes are the desire to support interoperability and avoid duplicative efforts. Supporting this trend are *application profiles*,[35] which are data structures composed of defined properties from established standardized schemes. The DCMI has developed the Singapore Framework[36] to standardize the creation and documentation for application profiles.

Content Value Standards

Content value standards contain words, names, and symbols connoting meaning. Common types of content value standards include *subject heading lists*, *thesauri*, *classification systems*, *taxonomies*, *ontologies*, and *name authority files* (for people, places, geographical jurisdictions, and other named entities). Content value systems containing concepts used for topical, domain, or intellectual representation are increasingly referred to as knowledge organization systems (KOS).[37]

Values are drawn from content value standards and paired with properties to complete a metadata record; hence, the common notion of property/value pairs. For example, the Harley–Davidson Web site as *a digital resource* has various properties, such as title, subject, and date. These properties are defined in the Dublin Core, and assigned values to construct a metadata record. Example 2 presents a fragment of a Dublin Core metadata record showing *Library of Congress Subject Headings* (LCSH)[38] values in XML for the Harley–Davidson Web site.

Example 2: Fragment of a Dublin Core metadata record showing *LCSH* values in XML for the Harley-Davidson Web site

```
<dc:subject xsi:type="dcterms:LCSH" >Harley-Davidson motorcycle </dc:subject>
<dc:subject xsi:type="dcterms:LCSH" >Harley-Davidson motorcycle-Collectibles</dc:subject>
```

Content value systems are neither available nor desirable for every property defined in every metadata scheme; and the freedom to create content values via tagging is part of the appeal and success of folksonomies. In fact, one may argue that a folksonomy presents a de facto content value standard via sharing and aggregating agreed upon tags.

Data Communication Standards

Data communication standards are the encoding or markup language that wraps around the property/value pairs in the metadata record. Data communication standards permit metadata records to be stored, searched, retrieved, and exchanged with other information systems. The prescribed system of punctuation that is part of the International Standard Bibliographic Description (ISBD), and the other ISBD formats that have now been consolidated,[39] is an example of a pre-Web data communication standard. Developed in the late 1960s, with the eye toward supporting computer exchange of bibliographic data, the prescribed punctuation separates designated areas of description, such as resource "title" and "statement of responsibility."

Data communication standards commonly used today for encoding metadata include MARC bibliographic format (ISO 2709/ANSI/NISO Z39.2), which incorporates ISBD; eXtensible Hypertext Markup Language (X/HTML; W3C WD-xhtml2-20060726); and XML (W3C REC-xml-20060816). Example 3 presents a MARC bibliographic record with core properties and the XML Dublin Core equivalent for the same metadata.

Example 3: MARC Bibliographic Record and Dublin Core XML Metadata Record for Berners-Lee's book *Weaving the Semantic Web*

MARC Bibliographic record	Dublin Core XML record
100 1 Berners-Lee, Tim.	<dc:creator>Tim Berners-Lee </dc:creator>
245 10 Weaving the Web / $c Tim Berners-Lee with Mark Fischetti.	<dc:title>Weaving the Web </dc:title>
260 [San Francisco]:$b HarperSanFrancisco,$c c1999.	<dc:pulisher>HarperSanFrancisco </dc:pulisher>
300 xi, 226 p.;$c 25 cm.	<dcterms:created >1999</dcterms:created >
650 0 World Wide Web.	<dcterms:extent >xi, 226 p. and 25 cm </dcterms:extent >
700 1 Fischetti, Mark.	<dc:subject xsi:type= "dcterms. LCSH"> World Wide Web </dc:subject> <dc:contributor>Mark Fischetti</dc:contributor>

Syntax Standards

Syntax standards are not stand-alone standards designated by an identifier, rather they are integrated each of the standards reviewed, and guide metadata creation and encoding. For example, syntax standardization may dictate element ordering for data structure standards; value structuring for value content standards; and grammar for communication standards. (The word *element* is used in this section instead of property, given that *property* is not as familiar a concept across all metadata communities.) These aspects of syntax standardization are further explained below:

- *Element ordering*: Data structure standards may include element ordering recommendations or specifications, such as the author/creator element should (or must) always preceded the title element. Familiar bibliography standards, such as the American Psychological Association or the Chicago citation style have an element ordering syntax in the way bibliographies citations are constructed; and these standards integrate a grammar syntax (defined below) via prescribed punctuation. There are many data structures, such as the Dublin Core, that do not have a standardize element ordering protocol; however initiatives using such schemes may determine their own standard approach to organizing metadata elements.
- *Value structuring*: Content value standards may include value structuring requirements. For example, *LCSH* has a protocol for constructing subject heading strings [topic—period subdivision]; or [topic—geographical subdivision]. Similarly, the *Art & Architecture Thesaurus*[40] has a protocol for building faceted strings. The Library of Congress Name Authority Headings (http://authorities.loc.gov/) includes syntaxes for named entities following the *Anglo-American Cataloging Rules*.[41] For example, personal name is structured with the surname, followed by foreman (e.g., Picasso, Pablo). There are also syntax standards to help with content values that may not necessarily be taken from a controlled vocabulary. One example is the W3C Date and Time Formats,[42] a subset of ISO 8601, which recommend the syntax of YYYY-MM-DD for dates and other content syntaxes depending on available date and time information.
- *Grammar syntax*: Communication standards embody a grammar syntax for producing valid encoding. An obvious example is the way in which XML angle brackets are created with a "<" to represent the start of encoding a metadata element, and then use a "/>" to represent closure. Example 3, above, illustrates both MARC and XML encoding syntax. The core of the MARC bibliographic record includes tags (the three digit numbers), delimiters (a dollar sign: $), and delimiter codes (often lower case letters). The Dublin Core metadata record presents an example of XML grammar, with angle brackets as well as prescribed punctuation.

Standards, as reviewed here, are integral to many aspects of metadata. It is useful to keep in mind that metadata standards are discussed and labeled in many ways, and generally "a said standard" includes multiple aspects or types of standards. A case in point is the *Anglo-American Cataloging Rules*,[41] which is often labeled as a *content standard*, integrating aspects of a data structure, content syntax, and encoding syntax (the encoding follows ISBD punctuation). The most important aspect of any standard is that they enable metadata to be used more effectively supporting functions (e.g., resource discovery, management, or authentication); and, at the foundation level, standards guide metadata generation.

METADATA GENERATION

Metadata generation is the act of creating or producing metadata, and can be generated via different processes, applications, and classes of people.[43]

Metadata Generation Processes

Metadata is generated via manual, automatic, or, a combinatory approach. Manual metadata generation necessitates human engagement (e.g., metadata professionals, content creators, and technical assistants); automatic metadata generation involves the use of machine processing; and the combinatory approach integrates both manual and automatic methods.

An overview of metadata generation processes

It is nearly impossible to find an example of metadata produced entirely by manual means, given that metadata is fairly well rooted in the world of electronic and digital information. In fact, it is commonplace that metadata generation activities include some reliance on technology and programmed algorithms. For example, an application requiring manual metadata input may link to external standards and automatically generate and validate encoding. The OpenSource Metadata Framework (OMF) Template (Example 4) for Linux software and software documentation presents an example, with the last button saying "xmlify."

Automatic metadata algorithms are frequently in place recording the date the digital object was created or modified, who created the object or its metadata (depending on login information or work station accessed), and size of the object; although, authors and application users are often unaware of these algorithms. The only example of a purely manual metadata approach is the process of *handwritten* labeling, indexing, or cataloging.

Similarly to the near absence of purely automatic metadata generation, most automatic processes require some human involvement to, at the very least, initiate the operation. At minimum the human may need to point the application to a resource identifier as required with DC-dot (http://www.ukoln.ac.uk/metadata/dcdot/). Humans are frequently involved in some aspect of metadata evaluation when automatic processes are used, given known shortcomings of machine processing (e.g., limited capabilities to disambiguate among concepts).

Automatic metadata generation approaches

Recognizing that metadata generation generally involves a mix of manual and automatic methods has prompted the metadata community to pin-point areas where human engagement is essential, and where automatic processes should dominate. For example, it does not make sense for a human to manually reproduce resource identifier, such as a URL, when it could be automatically harvested from a Webpage; and the automatic approach is less prone to errors than the manual approach. As part of an effort to advance the development of metadata generation applications, the DCMI Tools Community has prepared a glossary [draft][43] defining specific types of automatic metadata generation approaches, which are further articulated here.

- *Derived metadata*: Metadata automatically generated according to system designed (pre-programmed) profiles. For example, a system program may automatically derive metadata values for "date created," "date modified," or "resource size." Profiles can be designed to automatically populate a metadata record with default values, such as "rights access," or "creator" information.
- *Metadata extraction*: Metadata generated by running automatic indexing algorithm against resource content. For example, term frequency algorithms are used to extract and determine subject keywords; and automatic detection of noun phrases may help extract values for other metadata properties, such as "author," "date," and "title." Semi-structured metadata, determined by the fairly consistent placement of metadata values (e.g., title, keywords, and author names) within document content, can also be extracted.
- *Metadata harvesting*: Metadata is automatically gathered from existing metadata sources, regardless of whether it was originally generated via automatic or manual means. Metadata can be harvested from a range of sources (e.g., a resource header, metadata registries, or database). Metadata harvesting is a key aspect of the Open Archives Initiative (OAI) (http://www.openarchives.org/), an electronic pre-print service. Extraction of semi-structured metadata from document content has an element of harvesting.

There are multiple approaches for generating metadata; and the method selected depends on a host of factors. Chief considerations include the type of objects being represented (e.g., online conference proceedings, personal photographs, a scientific data set); the environment where the metadata will be hosted (e.g., a digital library, scientific repository, or personal account on a social networking site); who is creating the metadata; available financial and human resources for the task; and the complexity of and intellectual requirements associated with the underlying schemes and standards used. All of these factors together have a direct bearing on the type of application selected for generating metadata.

Applications

The range of applications supporting metadata is extensive. The previous *ELIS* entry covered this topic by identifying templates, editors, generators, and document editors. Although these intellectual distinctions are still applicable, these concepts are used interchangeably and inconsistently by application developers and users alike. Another way to view the range of metadata applications available is to consider the context in which they are used, including how they are marketed. Four contexts considered here include: 1) tools designated specifically as metadata applications; 2) library management systems (LMS); 3) content management systems (CMS); and 4) daily use applications.

- *Metadata applications*: The growing need for metadata has motivated the development of applications specifically labeled as metadata tools. These applications generally provide templates for manual metadata input, and permit manual editing once the metadata is generated. Many of these applications automatically link to property definitions; list acceptable content value standards or even values for selection; and automatically generate XML or other desired encoding, as illustrated with the "xmlify" button in the OMF

Top of Form

creator

Person or organization primarily responsible for creating the intellectual content of the resource

First Name

Last Name

Email

add creator

maintainer

Person or organization responsible for publishing the resource in its current form

First Name

Last Name

Email

add maintainer

contributor

Person or organization not specified in a CREATOR or MAINTAINER

First Name

Last Name

Email

add contributor

title

The name given to the resource by the CREATOR or MAINTAINER

add title

date

The date on which the resource was made available in its current form

add date

version

A string or number that distinguishes the current revision of the resource from other revisions

Version Identifier

add version

keywords

The topic of the resource. Typically, this element employs keywords that summarize the subject or content of the resource. (one word or phrase per line)

add keywords

Example 4: OpenSource Metadata Framework (OMF) Template

description
A textual description of the content of the resource (e.g., an abstract, contents note)
add description

type
The category of the resource
add type

format
Details about the implementation of the resource
Mime Type
DTD
add format

identifier
A specification of a unique ID by which the resource may be identified and from which the resource may be retrieved. (e.g. a URL or URN)
add identifier

source
A specification of any previous or alternative publication of the resource in its current form (e.g. a larger work from which the resource is extracted, such as a chapter taken from a book). SOURCE may include a URL, ISBN or similar device
add source

language
Language(s) of the intellectual content of the resource
add language

relation
A URL that points to the IDENTIFIER element of another resource. Each instance of RELATION links the resource to other resources of similar domain or style
add relation

coverage
A description of the resource's intellectual scope
Geographic
Distribution
Kernel
Architecture
OS
add coverage

rights
An indication of the copying policy under which the resource is distributed
License Type
License Version
License Holder
First Name
Last Name
Email
add rights

xmlify
Bottom of Form

Template (Example 4). The Berkeley Web Template CGI script for EAD finding aids (http://sunsite3.berkeley.edu/ead/tools/template/), and the hCard Creator (http://microformats.org/code/hcard/creator) for hCard Microformats Wiki 2.0 (http://microformats.org/) (a standard used to represent people, companies, organizations, and places) are examples of these more manually driven metadata applications.

There are metadata applications supporting a greater degree of automatic processing, such as DC-dot and Metatag Extractor (http://www.hooverwebdesign.com/tools/metatags.php). These applications automatically harvest metadata from the resource's source code. Additionally, DC-dot extracts resource content where harvesting proves insufficient and also includes a template for manual editing.

- *Library management systems* (LMS): As libraries have engaged in metadata generation, library software has integrated the support for metadata standards. Examples include Innovative Interfaces Inc.'s MetaData Builder (http://www.iii.com/products/metadata_builder.shtml), which supports the creation for both Dublin Core and the EAD metadata; and CONTENTdm (http://www.contentdm.com/), which supports Dublin Core, VRA Core, and newly created metadata schemes and vocabularies. There are also a number of open source LMS, such as Greenstone Digital Library Software (http://www.greenstone.org/), supporting many of the metadata functions found in commercial products.
- *Content management systems* (CMS): CMS require metadata for content management. Ektron (http://www.ektron.com/web-content-management-solutions.aspx) includes basic metadata properties such a as title, keywords, language; and this software can be programmed to assign default keywords. IBM Lotus Quickr Web (http://www.ibm.com/developerworks/lotus/library/quickr-web-services/) automatically generates date created, last modified timestamps, and identifier metadata to maintain server activities. Similar to LMS, there are many open source CMS that support metadata. Additionally, many CMS integrate taxonomy plug-ins to improve metadata quality. Synaptica® (http://www.synaptica.com/djcs/synaptica/) from Dow Jones Client Solutions is among one of the more popular plug-ins for developing and managing taxonomies.
- *Daily use software*: Although this is rather a "catch-all" category, it is the case that anyone working on any type of computer interfaces with some form of metadata generation software, whether or not they are aware of it. Examples include software people use daily to arrange information captured on their iPods, palms, cell phones, and other mobile devices. The AMeGA Report,[44] produced to address Section 4.2 of the *Library of Congress Bibliographic Control Action Plan*,[45] analyzed metadata generation features and functionalities embedded in software people use to create content daily (e.g., Microsoft Word, Adobe, Dreamweaver, and Moveable Type), and found that several metadata elements supported by these applications easily map to the Dublin Core. Finally, and perhaps the most obvious daily use applications supporting metadata generation underlie social networking activities. For example, Flickr (http://www.flickr.com/) and Delicious (http://delicious.com/) support folksonomic tagging and the generation of metadata, a good portion of which aligns with Dublin Core properties.[10]

Classes of Persons

Among the classes of persons involved in metadata generation, are professional metadata creators, technical metadata creators, content creators, and public metadata creators.

- *Professional metadata creators* include catalogers, indexers, and other individuals who have had formal education or official on-the-job training to learn about metadata standards and issues; and they generally work in libraries, archives, publishing houses, and formal information agencies. This class of persons is known as third-party metadata creators because they produce metadata for content created by other individuals. Professional metadata creators have the intellectual capacity to make sophisticated interpretative metadata-related decisions, work with classificatory systems and other complex content value systems, and have some theoretical understanding of metadata. Given expert knowledge, the professional's greatest contribution may be evaluating metadata, managing metadata generation activities, or helping to develop tools that facilitate effective and expedient metadata production.
- *Technical metadata creators* include data in-putters, paraprofessionals, and other individuals who generally have had basic training, but have not participated in a formal structured or certified educational program. Technical metadata creators are also third-party metadata creators, and generally not assigned the same degree of responsibility as a metadata professional; however, they may take on more sophisticated tasks over the duration of their work-life.
- *Content creators* are individuals creating metadata for intellectual content they have authored. There are many types of content creators—authors of text, photographers, creators of video—amateurs, professionals, and the average citizen.

Authors of scientific publications regularly engaged in metadata generation in the pre-Web environment by writing abstracts, identifying keywords, and even assigning classificatory indicators when submitting their work via peer-review channels. The online peer-review process has maintained these author metadata requirements. An example is the Association of Computing Machinery/Special Interest Group (ACM/SIG) Proceedings Templates (http://www.acm.org/sigs/publications/proceedings-templates), which require authors to select "categories and subject descriptors" from the *ACM Computing Classification Scheme*.[46]

The content creator metadata environment is thriving today via developments such as the OAI, institutional and specialized repositories (e.g., GenBank, http://www.ncbi.nlm.nih.gov/Genbank/, for gene sequences), and social networking sites, where people create metadata to share photographs (e.g., Flickr), bookmarks (e.g., Delicious), news (e.g., Blogs), and news about oneself (e.g., Facebook, http://www.facebook.com/).

- *Public metadata creators* include community or subject enthusiasts who create metadata for a resource authored by other individuals. A subcategory of public metadata creators includes *users*—people creating metadata by annotating content they have used, and sharing their insights.

During the very early years of the Web, 1995–1999, people created lists of hyperlinks for topics they were passionate about (e.g., travel, sports, cooking, pets, politics, and entertainment), resulting in personal subject gateways. These personal undertaking included basic metadata: title, creator, and sometimes an annotation. While these types of Web sites are still visible, public metadata creators have generally turned to social networking cites to share favorite Web sites, tag information, blog, or annotate information.

Public metadata creators help build collective knowledge through their efforts, and are increasingly being accommodated in reputable information systems. For example, WorldCat (http://www.worldcat.org/), a service connecting more than 10,000 libraries worldwide, has introduced a user tagging option. This service allows users to manage bibliographic records and enhance resource discovery for other WorldCat users. The Steve project (http://www.steve.museum/), a partnership between leading museums and the general public, is another important example exploring how social tagging can enhance access to museum collections and further engage visitors.[47]

Professional catalogers and metadata experts are not able to handle the sheer volume of information being generated today; and it is not feasible to ask these highly skilled and paid individuals to create metadata for every digital object, particularly when there are other individuals and applications to help with the process. It is, therefore, encouraging to see the increased functionalities in metadata application and more and more people engaging in metadata generation.

METADATA MODELS

The increase in metadata generation has encouraged the development of metadata models supporting interoperability, data reuse, and more intelligent packaging of metadata. This section reviews four key models gaining acceptance in the metadata community, although there are many additional models.

Arguably the most simplistic model impacting metadata developments is the Resource Description Framework (RDF).[48] RDF is a simple model for rendering metadata instances into simple discrete and explicit statements (Example 5). The overriding goals of RDF are to impose structure, facilitate the unambiguous and consistent expression of semantics, and support more intelligent use of Web data. RDF underlies the Web Ontology Language Overview[49] and Simple Knowledge Organization System[50]—two key specifications for developing the Semantic Web.

RDF statements are frequently referred to as *literals* or *triples*, and include a subject, predicate, and object (Example 5); these statements can be visually represented via RDF graphs (Fig. 1).

Multiple RDF statements can be made about the same object. Additionally, RDF supports an iterative process, whereby an "object" of one RDF statement could be the subject of another RDF statement. A statement illustrating iteration might say that the "subject" *Harley–Davidson motorcycle* (from *LCSH*) (which is the "object" in Figure 1), has a "predicate" *identifier* (the LC control number) with the "object" (meaning the *value*) *85058931* (see Fig. 2).

RDF was initiated as a model that does not necessarily need to be expressed in XML. However, RDF implementation is supported by series of additional specifications addressing the syntax, vocabulary, and semantics for creating RDF/XML statements that permit metadata to be shared. Conceivably, once an RDF statement is made about an object on the Web, that statement (a metadata

Example 5: RDF triple

Subject	Predicate	Object
The **subject** (meaning the resource) http://www.harley-davidson.com	Has a **predicate** (a Dublin Core property) The "dc.subject"	Containing **object** (a value; and in this case an *LCSH* value) "Harley–Davidson motorcycle"

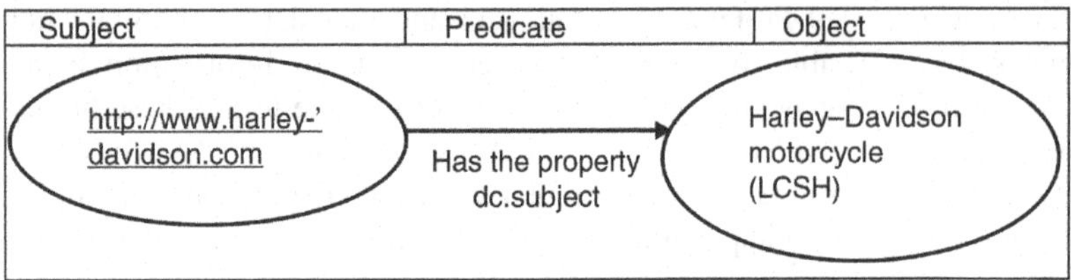

Fig. 1 RDF graphical representation for the triple in Example 5.

instance) can be reused again and again, although more development is needed to truly share and reuse RDF renderings.

Another model increasingly being discussed in the metadata community is the Functional Requirement for Bibliographic Records (FRBR),[51] published by the International Federation of Library Associations and Institutions. A body of research has advanced knowledge about the bibliographic object and the notion of the *work*[52,53] in our online library catalogs. Building on these advancements, the FRBR model includes four entities: *work*, *expression*, *manifestation*, and *item*. The partitioning of bibliographic data (or metadata) following FRBR allows for data reuse; more sophisticated linking of entities; and a richer descriptive environment. The model is still heavily conceptual, although there are instances of FRBR implementations, most notably OCLC's Fiction Finder (http://fictionfinder.oclc.org/).

FRBR's foundation work predates the Web; and, yet, it is extremely applicable to the digital world, where resources are copied and modified rapidly, and the reuse of bibliographic data is an important goal. FRBR presents library users with an opportunity for gaining a greater understanding of the bibliographic universe from where they gather sources; and, in the long run, FRBR could prove extremely cost effective, not only for users making important links among resources, but by eliminating duplicative metadata efforts. These goals have inspired additional FRBR efforts relating to name and subject authority data.

The Metadata Encoding and Transmission Standard (METS)[54] is another model being used in the digital library/repository environment. METS is a framework for packaging descriptive, administrative, and structural metadata within an XML framework, and wrapping that metadata around a digital resource. As digital initiatives began to proliferate toward the end of the 1990s, the need for different types of metadata standards supporting different functions became increasingly evident. This need led to interest in developing a consistent way to package resource metadata drawing from different standards—a goal that was further motivated by the need to enable greater interoperability and reuse of the resource and its associated metadata. The Making of Amercica-2 (MOA-2) (http://sunsite.berkeley.edu/moa2/), a Digital Library Federation project, formalized these ideas and created a XML/document type definition (DTD) for packaging metadata; and these efforts progressed to form what is today METS.

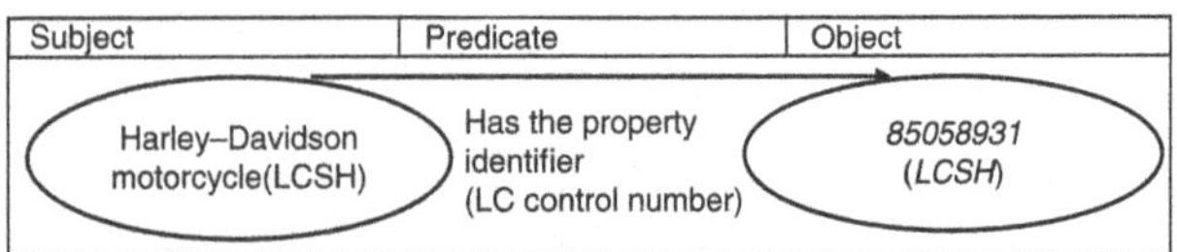

Fig. 2 RDF graphical representation for the "subject" *Harley–Davidson motorcycle* (an *LCSH* heading).

METS has the following seven key sections: 1) *METS header* for describing the object; 2) *descriptive metadata* linking to external metadata (e.g., a MARC bibliographic record or a Dublin Core record, representing the object, but stored elsewhere), and internal descriptive metadata enriching external descriptions; 3) *administrative metadata* documenting creation, source, and rights information both externally and internally; 4) *file section* listing all files comprising the digital object; 5) *structural map* outlining the resource's arrangement and linking to the object's content; 6) *structural links* recording hyperlinks between sections of an object's content; and 7) *behavior* documenting and pointing to executable behaviors associated with the METS object's content, or code for initiating an operation.

The Dublin Core Abstract Model (DCAM)[55] is among the more recent metadata models. The DCAM incorporates RDF and has been developed to advance the metadata development, and to bring metadata activities more in-line with the Semantic Web initiative. Two key principles underlying DCAM are: 1) a resource can be any type of discrete entity (as discussed above in "Defining Metadata" section), and 2) metadata can be created for any object. The DCAM asserts that a metadata record can include one or more metadata statements; and a simple RDF statement is an acceptable metadata record. This approach differs from traditional notions of a bibliographic cataloging, where a metadata record includes multiple property/value pairs. The DCAM is "object centered," and the emphasis is on cataloging objects (e.g., words, numbers, discrete entities) at the most discrete level, so that the object and metadata are reusable. The majority of metadata work is resource centric—with resource referring to an entire Web site, or the types of entities collected by libraries, albeit digital (e.g., books, reports, photographs). Implementing metadata within the

DCAM requires a new, more object-centered perspective for metadata. DCAM is in its infancy, but the approach may transform metadata activities to a new level.

CONCLUSION

Metadata is a dynamic topic and has evolved considerably since the initial *ELIS* metadata entry was published in 2002.[1] This current entry stands as a new article, with fresh coverage of the earlier topics (e.g., the definition of metadata and metadata generation), and greater attention to metadata models. This entry provides new facts uncovered on the history of metadata; presents an overview of different metadata types, functions, and schemes; provides a series of domain-specific definitions for metadata; and discusses the various types of standards comprising metadata architectures.

The remarkable growth in metadata activities has been extremely positive, resulting in greater access to information and better documentation. However, like many developments, this growth has not been without challenges. Determining how to generate metadata (emphasizing an automatic or manual approach), and who to involve in the process (professionals, technical assistants, content creators, the public), presents metadata quality and workflow challenges. Striving for interoperability and sharing metadata can pit local metadata needs against higher level goals. And, perhaps the most exciting challenges stem from the goal of *metadata reuse*. Those engaged in metadata activities debate if metadata should be generated for every discrete object and if a more globally linked Semantic Web is achievable. Efforts underway, such as the Dublin Core Singapore Framework[12] guiding application profile development, and the National Science Digital Library Metadata Registry (http://metadataregistry.org/), for sharing metadata schemes, provide a means for addressing several metadata reuse challenges. These efforts will, no doubt, continue to evolve through evaluation and use. And, as metadata progresses, new challenges will undoubtedly surface, and new solutions will be sought.

It is clear that metadata is an ubiquitous topic and an integral part of our digital information infrastructure. Education, the arts, science, industry, government, and the many humanistic, scientific, and social pursuits that comprise our world have rallied to develop, implement, and adhere to some form of metadata practice. There is ample evidence showing that metadata has touched nearly every discipline and societal sector coming into contact with digital information. The goals are similar across the board—to facilitate the preservation, discovery, access, and sharing of digital output. In closing, the range of metadata activities over this last decade are both extensive and astonishing, and presents an unprecedented opportunity to share information and knowledge as we move forward in this millennium.

REFERENCES

1. Greenberg, J. Metadata and the World Wide Web. In *Encyclopedia of Library and Information Science*; Drake, M., Ed.; Marcel Dekker, Inc.: New York, 2003; 1876–1888.
2. Greenberg, J. Metadata and the World Wide Web. In *Encyclopedia of Library and Information Science*; Marcel Dekker, Inc.: New York, 2002; Vol. 72, 244–261.
3. Crawford, W. *MARC for Library Use: Understanding Integrated USMARC*; GK Hall & Co.: Boston, MA, 1989.
4. Library of Congress—Network Development and MARC Standards Office. MARC Standards, http://www.loc.gov/marc/ (accessed November 2008).
5. Supekar, K.; Musen, M. Ontology metadata to support the building of a library of biomedical ontologies. In AMIA Annual Symposium Proceedings, Washington, D.C., 2005, 1127. PMCID: PMC1560427.
6. Kauppinen, T.; Väätäinen, J.; Hyvönen, E. Creating and using geospatial ontology time series in a semantic cultural heritage portal. In *The Semantic Web: Research and Applications*; Lecture Notes in Computer Science; Springer: Berlin, Heidelberg, Germany, 2008; Vol. 5021, 110–123.
7. Greenberg, J.; Mendez, E. *Knitting the Semantic Web*; Haworth Press, Inc.: Binghamton, New York, 2007.
8. Paul, A.C.; Costache, S.; Nejdl, W; Handschuh, S. P-TAG: Large Scale Automatic Generation of Personalized Annotation Tags for the Web, Proceedings of the 16th International Conference on World Wide Web, Banff, AB, Canada, May 8–12, 2007, 845–854.
9. Mathes, A. Folksonomies—cooperative classification and communication through shared metadata, 2004, http://adammathes.com/academic/computer-mediated-communication/folksonomies.pdf (accessed November 2008).
10. Catarino, M.E.; Baptista, A.A. Relating folksonomies with Dublin core. In *Metadata for Semantic and Social Applications*; International Conference on Dublin Core and Metadata Applications, Berlin, Germany, Sept 22–26, 2008; 14–22.
11. Oxford University Press. AskOxford, http://www.askoxford.com/ (accessed November 2008).
12. Sundgren, B. *An Infological Approach to Data Bases*; Urval, no. 7; Statistiska Centralbyren: Stockholm, Sweden, 1973.
13. Howe, D. Metadata. In *The Free On-line Dictionary of Computing* via Dictionary.com, http://dictionary.reference.com/browse/metadata (accessed November 2008).
14. Riley, J.; Foulonneau, M. *Metadata for Digital Resources: Implementation, Systems Design, and Interoperability*; Chandos: Oxford, U.K., 2008.
15. Zeng, M.L.; Qin, J. *Metadata*; Neal-Schuman: New York, 2008.
16. Liu, J. *Metadata and Its Applications in the Digital Library: Approaches and Practices*; Libraries Unlimited: Westport, CT, 2007.

17. Dublin Core Metadata Element Set, Version 1.1, http://dublincore.org/documents/dces/ (accessed November 2008).
18. Meadow, C.T.; Boyce, B.R.; Kraft, D.H.; Barry, C.L. *Information Retrieval Systems*, 3rd Ed.; Academic Press: New York, 2007; 37–52.
19. ISO/IEC 11179–1:2004. *Information Technology Metadata registries (MDR). Part 1: Framework*, 2nd Ed.; http://standards.iso.org/ittf/PubliclyAvailableStandards/c035343_ISO_IEC_11179–1_2004(E) (accessed November 2008).
20. Duval, E.; Hodgins, W.; Sutton, S.; Weibel, S. Metadata principles and practicalities. D-Libr. Mag. 2002, *8*(4), http://www.dlib.org/dlib/april02/weibel/04weibel.html (accessed November 2008).
21. Woodley, M.S.; Clement, G.; Winn, P. *DCMI Glossary*, http://dublincore.org/documents/2005/11/07/usageguide/glossary.shtml (accessed November 2008).
22. Greenberg, J. Understanding metadata and metadata schemes. Catalog. Classif. Quart. 2005, *40* (3/4), 17–36.
23. PREMIS Editorial Committee. PREMIS Data Dictionary for Preservation Metadata version 2.0, 2008, http://www.loc.gov/standards/premis/v2/premis-2–0.pdf (accessed November 2008).
24. Caplan, P. *Metadata Fundamentals for All Librarians*; ALA Editions: Chicago, IL, 2003.
25. Metadata Ad Hoc Working Group, Federal Geographic Data Committee. Content Standard for Digital Geospatial Metadata (FGDC-STD-001–1998), 1998 http://www.fgdc.gov/standards/projects/FGDC-standards-projects/metadata/base-metadata/v2_0698.pdf (accessed November 1998).
26. Inmon, W.H.; O'Neil, B.K.; Fryman, L. *Business Metadata: Capturing Enterprise Knowledge*; Morgan Kaufmann: New York, 2008.
27. *Digizen Glossary*, http://www.digizen.org/socialnetworking/glossary.aspx (accessed November 2008).
28. Metadata Object Description Schema (MODS), http://www.loc.gov/standards/mods/v3/mods-3–1-outline.html (accessed November 2008).
29. Visual Resources Association Core (VRA-Core), http://www.vraweb.org/projects/vracore4/ (accessed November 2008).
30. Encoded Archival Description (EAD), http://www.loc.gov/ead/ (accessed November 2008).
31. Data Document Initiative (DDI), http://webapp.icpsr.umich.edu/cocoon/DDI-LIBRARY/Version2–1.xsd?section=all (accessed November 2008).
32. Ecological Metadata Language (EML), http://knb.ecoinformatics.org/software/eml/eml-2.0.1/index.html (accessed November 2008).
33. Institute of Electrical and Electronics Engineers/Learning Object Metadata (IEEE/LOM), http://ltsc.ieee.org/wg12/files/LOM_1484_12_1_v1_Final_Draft.pdf (accessed November 2008).
34. Darwin Core (DwC), version 1.21, http://digir.net/schema/conceptual/darwin/manis/1.21/darwin2.xsd (accessed November 2008).
35. Heery, R.; Patel, M. Application profiles: Mixing and matching metadata schemas. Ariadne *25*, 2000, http://www.ariadne.ac.uk/issue25/app-profiles/ (accessed November 2008).
36. Nilsson, M.; Baker, T.; Johnston, P. The Singapore Framework for Dublin Core Application Profiles, 2008, http://dublincore.org/documents/singapore-framework/ (accessed November 2008).
37. Hodge, G. *Systems of Knowledge Organization for Digital Libraries. Beyond Traditional Authority Files*; The Council on Library and Information Resources: Washington, DC, 2000, http://www.clir.org/pubs/reports/pub91/contents.html (accessed November 2008).
38. *Library of Congress Subject Headings*, 30th Ed.; Cataloging Distribution Service: Washington, DC, 2007.
39. International Standard Bibliographic Description (ISBD)/ recommended by the ISBD, Review Group approved by the Standing Committee of the IFLA Cataloguing Section. Preliminary consolidated ed. K.G., Saur: München, Germany, 2007.
40. *Art & Architecture Thesaurus*. online, http://www.getty.edu/research/conducting_research/vocabularies/aat/ (accessed November 2008).
41. *Anglo-American Cataloguing Rules*, 2nd Ed (2002 Revision/2005 Update), American Library Association: Chicago, IL, 2005.
42. Wolf, M.; Wicksteed, C. W3C Date and Time Formats, 1998, http://www.w3.org/TR/NOTE-datetime.
43. Greenberg, J.; Severins, T.DCMI Tools Glossary Draft version, May 6, 2007, http://dublincore.org/groups/tools/glossary.shtml (accessed November 2008).
44. Greenberg, J.; Spurgin, K.; Crystal, A. Final report for the AMeGA (Automatic Metadata Generation Applications) Project, UNC & Library of Congress, 2005, 16, http://www.loc.gov/catdir/bibcontrol/lc_amega_final_report.pdf (accessed November 2008).
45. Bibliographic Control of Web Resources: A Library of Congress Action Plan Last updated: February 23, 2005, http://www.loc.gov/catdir/bibcontrol/actionplan.pdf (accessed November 2008).
46. *ACM Computing Classification Scheme*, http://www.acm.org/class/1998/ (accessed November 2008).
47. Trant, J. Access to Art Museums On-Line: A Role for Social Tagging and Folksonomy? Keynote Presentation at the International Conference on Dublin Core and Metadata Applications, Berlin, Germany, Sept 22–26, 2008, http://conference.archimuse.com/files/steveDC08-trant.pdf (accessed November 2008).
48. Resource Description Framework (RDF), http://www.w3.org/RDF/ (accessed November 2008).
49. OWL Web Ontology Language Overview. W3C Recommendation 10 February 2004, http://www.w3.org/TR/owl-features.
50. SKOS Simple Knowledge Organization System Reference W3C Working Draft 9 June 2008, http://www.w3.org/TR/skos-reference/.
51. IFLA Study Group on the Functional Requirements for Bibliographic Records. Functional Requirements for Bibliographic Records: Final Report, Feb 2008 http://www.ifla.org/VII/s13/frbr/frbr_2008.pdf (accessed November 2008).
52. Smiraglia, R.P. *The Nature of "A Work": Implications for the Organization of Knowledge*; Scarecrow Press: Lanham, MD, 2001; *88–119*; 165.
53. Yee, M.M. What is a work? International Conference on the Principles and Future Development of AACR, Toronto,

ON, Canada, Oct 23–25, 1997, http://repositories.cdlib.org/postprints/3085/ (accessed November 2008).

54. Metadata Encoding and Transmission Standard (METS) Metadata Schema and Documentation, http://www.loc.gov/standards/mets/mets-schemadocs.html (accessed November 2008).
55. Powell, A.; Nilsson, M.; Naeve, A.; Johnston, P.; Baker, T. DCMI Abstract Model, 2007, http://dublincore.org/documents/abstract-model/ (accessed November 2008).

BIBLIOGRAPHY

1. Gill, T.; Gilliland, A.J.; Whalen, M.; Woodley, M.S. *Introduction to Metadata*, Version 3.0, Baca, M., Ed.; Getty Information Institute: Los Angeles, CA, 2008, http://www.getty.edu/research/institute/standards/intrometadata/index.html (accessed November 2008).
2. Hillmann, D.I.; Westbrooks, E.L. *Metadata in Practice*. American Library Association: Chicago, IL, 2004.
3. Riley, J.; Foulonneau, M. *Metadata for Digital Resources: Implementation, Systems Design, and Interoperability*; Chandos: Oxford, U.K., 2008.
4. Smiraglia, R.P. *Metadata: A Cataloger's Primer*; Haworth Press: New York, 2005.
5. *Understanding Metadata*; NISO Press: Bethesda, MD, 2004, http://www.niso.org/standards/resources/Understanding-Metadata.pdf (accessed November 2008).
6. Woodley, M.S.; Clement, G.; Winn, P.DCMI Glossary 2005, http://dublincore.org/documents/2005/11/07/usageguide/glossary.shtml (accessed November 2008).
7. Zeng, M.L.; Qin, J. *Metadata*; Neal-Schuman: New York, 2008.

Metamarkup Languages: SGML and XML

Airi Salminen
Department of Computer Science and Information Systems, University of Jyväskylä, Jyväskylä, Finland

Abstract

Current global communication of people and software applications over the Internet is facilitated by the use of markup languages. This entry introduces the principles and different types of markup, and the history behind the current markup languages. The basis of most of the modern markup languages is the Standard Generalized Markup Language (SGML) or its restricted form Extensible Markup Language (XML). Both of them are metalanguages that are used to define specific markup languages for specific application areas. The entry describes the markup techniques used in SGML and XML, gives examples of their use, and briefly describes some representative SGML and XML applications from different domains. An important factor in the success of XML has been the possibility to reuse markup vocabularies and combine vocabularies originating from different sources. The entry describes the concepts and methods facilitating the reuse of names from earlier defined vocabularies.

INTRODUCTION

Markup languages have become an important means to communicate information on the Internet. On November 2014, Google search `markup language` derived more than 29 million hits, mentioning on the first pages, for example, the following languages:

- Standard Generalized Markup Language (SGML)
- Extensible Markup Language (XML)
- HyperText Markup Language (HTML)
- Emotion Markup Language
- Chemical Markup Language
- Graffiti Markup Language
- Music Markup Language
- Geography Markup Language
- Systems Biology Markup Language
- Theological Markup Language
- Election Markup Language
- Fountain: A markup language for screenwriting

The list clearly shows the diversity of application areas where markup languages have been developed. This diversity is an important reason for the fact that not only information specialists but also many application domain specialists face the need to understand the principles of markup languages. The first two on the list, Standard Generalized Markup Language and Extensible Markup Language, better known by their acronyms SGML and XML, respectively, are not languages for a particular application domain but *metalanguages* that are used as a basis to develop markup languages for various domains. From the languages of the list Emotion Markup Language, Chemical Markup Language, Graffiti Markup Language, Music Markup Language, Geography Markup Language, Systems Biology Markup Language, Theological Markup Language, and Election Markup Language are XML-based languages. HyperText Markup Language instead, also known as HTML, is a markup language older than XML and based on SGML, the "mother language" of XML. The last in the list of languages represents markup languages that are not based on SGML or XML.

The markup techniques in the contemporary markup languages are intended primarily for computers. Markup as a technique to add information to documents is, however, older than computers and originally intended for human use only. This entry first introduces different types of markup and provides a classification of the types. A brief history of SGML[1] is then provided, examples of the most important SGML applications are given, and reasons for the evolution of XML[2] from SGML are described. The markup in SGML and XML is intended to indicate two different structures in documents: a logical structure and a physical structure. The markup techniques to indicate those structures in documents are described and some examples are given. Neither SGML nor XML provides a predefined markup vocabulary, instead they include a definition capability to describe markup vocabularies for particular application areas. The vocabularies carry semantic information to the human users of the languages. The definition mechanism is introduced briefly, the topic is covered more extensively in another entry of the Encyclopedia. XML-based languages have been developed for various domains. This sectoral development has been facilitated not only by XML but also by the XML family of languages developed at the World Wide Web Consortium (W3C), the organization coordinating web technology development. At the end of the entry, a

Encyclopedia of Library and Information Sciences, Fourth Edition DOI: 10.1081/E-ELIS4-120053525

classification of the XML family of languages is introduced and some representative languages are briefly described.

MARKUP TYPES

Markup can be divided into different types based on its function. Fig. 1 describes a taxonomy of markup types. At the highest level, markup is divided into two categories: markup intended for human use and markup intended for computer use. Each of these categories is further divided into subcategories. The principles of the markup types, shown in Fig. 1, are described in the following text.

Markup for Human Use

Markup has been the traditional editing technique used in text publishing. Copy editors have added special marks as instructions *for typesetting* a manuscript to be printed. This kind of markup can be called *presentational* because it is intended to inform the typist about the intended external presentation of the text.

The term "markup" is in some sources used also to cover those notations in documents that are intended *for human reading* to make the text understandable. This type of markup has been divided into *punctuational* and *presentational*.[3] As an example, consider a situation where I want to communicate to my friend Mary Lynn, a proposal to meet her the same day at the statute by Henry Moore in front of the Toronto City Hall, known by Torontonians as The Archer. Text written in haste either by hand on a piece of paper, or by a mobile phone, might first look something like this:

```
April22HiMaryLynnLetusmeettoday4pmatThe
ArcherAiri
```

By punctuational markup I can make this text more readable:

```
April 22 Hi MaryLynn! Let us meet today
4 pm at The Archer. Airi
```

Punctuational markup includes spaces, commas, and other punctuation marks facilitating the separation of words and other syntactic units in text. In addition to the punctuational markup, I might want to use presentational markup to make the text still clearer to read:

```
April 22

Hi MaryLynn!
  Let us meet today 4 pm at The Archer.
Airi
```

Here the presentational markup includes an empty line, beginning of text from a new line, and indentation. In a longer text presentational markup might include page and list numberings, underlinings, and so on.

Markup for Computer Use

The markup intended for computers has to be formal and systematic. The term "markup language" refers to a language with formal syntactic rules for markup. The markup can be regarded as metadata adding some information to some primary data, often intended for human perception. The early markup languages were developed for text processing systems to instruct software the way the content should be formatted. For example, in a UNIX operating system environment the message to Mary Lynn might have been written in the following way:

```
April 22
.sp 1
Hi Mary Lynn!
.in 5
Let us meet today 4 pm at The Archer.
  Airi
```

Here the markup consists of the formatting commands informing the *nroff* text editor how to print the text. The

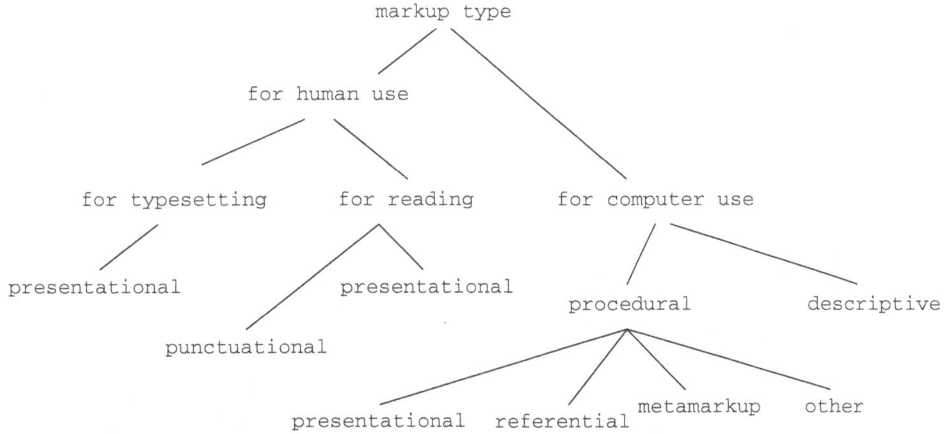

Fig. 1 Taxonomy of markup types.

first nroff command on the second line instructs the text processor to leave one line of blank space and the second command on the fourth line instructs the processor to indent the following text by five white spaces. Also the space in the beginning of the last line represents markup, because in nroff, a line beginning with spaces is an instruction to begin the text on a new line. This kind of markup for a computer software is called *procedural.* Procedural markup is tied to a particular function in software processing, like in the earlier example where `.sp 1` is tied to the line skipping function.

Procedural markup can be used for different types of processing instructions, and accordingly divided into subtypes. The procedural markup intended for formatting is *presentational.* Other subtypes of the procedural markup are referential and metamarkup.[3] *Referential* markup is used to inform the processor to replace a reference by some value. For example, in some Scandinavian text the strings ä and ö might be intended to be replaced by the text processor by the letters ä and ö, respectively. *Metamarkup* includes notations for defining markup rules for a particular application area. The definitions in XML represent metamarkup and some of them will be considered later in the entry.

The formatting instructions given by means of procedural markup as earlier are embedded into the content of the document; changing the formatting requires changing the document. For two kinds of formatting, two documents with the same primary content have to be written. An alternative to the procedural markup is *descriptive* markup describing the structural components of the document without specifying the processing to be performed on them. Different software applications can then process the structure in their own ways. For the purposes of printing or displaying, the format can be attached as a separate *stylesheet* document.

Fig. 2 shows the previous message written by means of descriptive markup. The markup consists of tags of the form <...> and </...>. The tags indicate the beginning and end of the structural components in the message and give also names to the components. A structural component starts by a tag of the form <...> and ends with </...>. The markup does not refer to the external presentation of the message.

Even though procedural and descriptive markup can be seen as alternative types of markup, it is, however, not rare that a particular markup serves both purposes at the same time. The HTML mentioned in the beginning of the article and familiar to many readers is an example of a language where descriptive markup is used to describe the structure of the external presentation of a document. In such a case, descriptive markup is also presentational.

The principle of descriptive markup has been an important facilitator in the evolution of the current information networks where people, organizations, and computers are connected to each other globally. The widespread adoption of the principle was initiated with the open standard called SGML.[1]

```
<message>
<begin>
<date>April 22</date>
<salute>Hi Mary Lynn!</salute>
</begin>
<main_content>
Let us meet today 4 pm at The Archer.
</main_content>
<end>
<salute>Cheers,</salute>
<sender>Airi</sender>
</end>
</message>
```

Fig. 2 An example of descriptive markup.

BRIEF HISTORY OF SGML

The problems related to the automated text processing of documents with embedded formatting instructions were identified in the 1960s. As early as 1967 in a meeting of the Canadian Government Printing Office, William Tunnicliffe pointed out the importance of the separation of information content of documents from their format and called for "generic coding" of documents instead of "specific coding".[4] The idea of generic document coding was an important feature in the language Charles Goldfarb, Ed Mosher, and Ray Lorie invented in 1969 at IBM. The ideas of the language were published in the 33rd annual meeting of the American Society for Information Science in 1970.[5] The language was first called Text Description Language. In his article in the ACM SIGPLAN/SIGOA conference in 1981, Goldfarb adopted the term *Generalized Markup Language* (*GML*, nicely referring also to Goldfarb-Mosher-Lorie) for the language developed at IBM and the term "descriptive markup" to the document coding style in GML.[6] In the same article, Goldfarb emphasized the importance of rigorous markup: the markup should be rigorous facilitating systematic, automated processing of sets of documents of certain types.

The principle of descriptive markup evolved at the time when programming language community started pointing out the difference between procedural and non-procedural programming. In the non-procedural programming, the idea was to give a prescription for solving a problem without showing *how* it is solved.[7] Similarly, descriptive markup is intended to describe the structure of a document without indicating *how* the parts of the structure should be processed. Different processing functions can be attached to the structure, either in the software or in separate specifications. The principle of descriptive markup was implemented in the SCRIBE system even before the implementation of GML.[8] The first implementations served well as a proof-of-concept, but for broader adoption of the principle it was important to find an agreement of standardized rules for descriptive markup. The work toward such rules started in a committee of the International Organization of Standardization (ISO). The first chair person of the committee was Charles Tunnicliffe and the concrete development work was done primarily by Charles Goldfarb. The work resulted in *Standard Generalized Markup Language* (SGML), accepted as an ISO standard 8879 in 1986.[1] The markup in Fig. 2 is an example of SGML markup. To support rigorous markup SGML included the capability to define markup languages by means of *Document Type Definitions* (DTDs). Thus SGML could be used as a *metalanguage* to define special markup languages for special needs as *SGML applications*.

SGML APPLICATIONS

In the 1980s, the definition capabilities of SGML were used, in particular, to define special markup languages for publishing industry, technical documentation, and electronic humanistic texts. Table 1 shows some important SGML applications.

DocBook was developed by private companies especially for authoring and publishing books and articles.[9] Currently, the DocBook schema is maintained by OASIS (Organization for the Advancement of Structured Information Standards, http://www.oasis-open.org/). The development of markup languages for technical documentation was activated strongly by the US Department of Defense under the Continuous Acquisition and Life-Cycle Support (CALS) initiative.[10] The purpose was to support the weapon system acquisition and life-cycle management. The markup needs of electronic humanistic texts differed from the needs of book publishing and technical documentation. A consortium called Text Encoding Initiative (TEI) was established in 1987 to develop and maintain methods for encoding humanistic texts in electronic form. SGML-based TEI guidelines were published in 1994, including, for example, markup vocabulary for prose, verse, drama, and dictionaries.[11]

The most popular SGML-based markup language was born in 1991, when Tim Berners-Lee and Robert Cailliau designed the World Wide Web (WWW) at European Organization for Nuclear Research (CERN).[12] The language was called HyperText Markup Language (HTML),[13] and it was used in the new innovative application to present hypertext documents interlinked to each other on the Internet. In HTML, the SGML-based declarative markup also serves as procedural markup to instruct the web browser in the document presentation and in opening new web pages.

The adoption of WWW expanded rapidly in the beginning of the 1990s. New kinds of businesses evolved, based on the connectivity of people all over the world and connectivity of software applications. A great deal of new business ideas were tested on the web, only a few of them were, however, commercially successful. Drawbacks in the business did not prevent the expansive growth of the Internet. At the end of the century, the number of computers connected to the Internet exceeded a hundred millions.

FROM SGML TO XML

The amount of information resources on the Internet started quickly expanding after the invention of WWW. A rich variety of people and software applications were connected to each other through WWW and had, at least in principle, access to huge information resources with textual and multimedia content. The communication of the applications was, however, often hindered by the differences in the representation of data. This was a great barrier for effective use of the Internet, particularly for business purposes. It became urgent to find some common rules for representing information and information structures within Internet and for exchanging information between applications over the Internet. SGML basically offered such rules, but the rules of SGML were too complicated for the needs of the Internet. One of the problems of SGML was the difficulty of building software supporting SGML in general, not only a particular SGML application like HTML. The development of a restricted form of SGML for the purposes of the Internet

Table 1 Some SGML applications.

SGML application	Main purpose	Developing organization
DocBook[9]	Book and article publishing	First private companies, later OASIS
CALS DTDs[10]	Technical documentation, life-cycle management of weapon systems	US Department of Defense
TEI[11]	Electronic encoding of humanistic texts	TEI Consortium
HTML[13]	Publishing hypertext documents on the WWW	European Organization for Nuclear Research (CERN)

communication started in the mid-1990s by a group of people. A goal was to simplify the language so that the design and implementation of software for it would not be too tedious. The W3C established in 1994 took responsibility for the development work and published the first version of the restricted form of SGML by the name Extensible Markup Language (XML) 1.0 in 1998.[2]

Compared to SGML, the number of rules in XML is clearly smaller, and its character set and resource identification mechanisms are planned for use on the Internet. Text in XML documents is encoded for computers using the Unicode character set. Unicode is intended to serve as a character set for representing textual data for computers written in any natural language of the world, independently, for example, of the writing direction of the language. The markup concepts and the DTD mechanism of XML are inherited from SGML. The descriptive markup in Fig. 2 is an example of XML markup as well as of SGML markup. A great deal of the SGML applications are currently also available as XML applications. For example, the markup recommendations of the TEI are available also for XML encoding. For web publishing, there is the Extensible HyperText Markup Language (XHTML)[14] that facilitates the use of HTML tags by following the rules of XML. For the latest HTML version called HTML5, XMTML syntax has been defined along with the HTML syntax.[15]

MARKUP TECHNIQUES OF XML

The XML is intended to support computerized use, exchange, and processing of information in documents, especially on the Internet. A goal in the XML development has been to keep it as stable as possible. During the years, some needs for changes have, however, evolved and therefore a new version XML 1.1 was published in 2004.[16]

The XML specification of W3C describes the markup rules for XML documents and also partially the behavior of a software module capable to deal with the features common to all XML documents. The module is called an *XML processor*. It is used to read XML documents and check that they follow the rules defined in the specification. In case a DTD is attached to the document instance, the XML processor may also check that the markup follows the constraints in the DTD. XML processor thus performs the parsing of the document. Therefore, an XML processor is often called also an XML *parser* or an XML *validator*.

The XML processor is not an independent piece of software but a module working for a software application. After the parsing the structural components are forwarded to the application. For example, web browsers like Internet Explorer and Mozilla include an XML processor as a component. By opening a file with the filename extention .xml, the XML processor of the browsers checks that the file follows the markup rules of XML and informs about possible errors. Both of the browsers show the file in a pretty-printed form as shown in Fig. 3.

Figs. 2 and 3 showed an example of marking up the logical structure of an XML document. Besides the logical structure, an XML document has a physical structure. The two structures and the corresponding markup are described as follows. At the end of the section, a concise introduction to the DTD capability of XML is provided.

Logical Structure

Even though the markup vocabularies of different XML-based languages differ from each other, there are some common rules all *well-formed* documents have to follow. The logical structure of every XML document is a hierarchy of *elements* indicated by explicit markup. The beginning of an element is shown by a *start-tag* of the form < ... > and the end by an *end-tag* of the form </ ... >. Both tags include the *name* of the element. Element names provide a capability to add semantic information to the structural markup. The text in Fig. 2 is an example of a well-formed XML document. The element names in the markup of the example were chosen such that they tell something about the meaning of the elements to a human reader. The outermost element is called `message` and the element has three *child elements*: `begin`, `main_content`, and `end`. The element called `message` is the *parent element* of the three child elements and also the *root* element of the document. The element

```
- <message>
   - <begin>
        <date>April 22</date>
        <salute>Hi Mary Lynn!</salute>
     </begin>
     <main_content>Let us meet today 4 pm at The Archer. </main_content>
   - <end>
        <salute>Cheers,</salute>
        <signature>Airi</signature>
     </end>
  </message>
```

Fig. 3 The pretty-printed format of the markedup text of Fig. 2 in Mozilla browser.

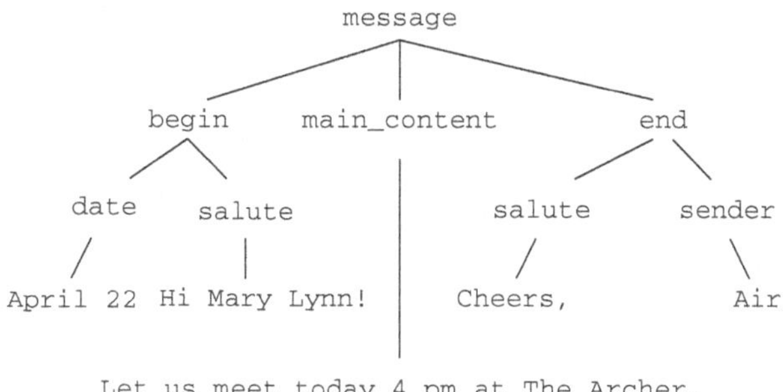

Fig. 4 Graphical representation of the tree structure of the example in Fig. 2.

begin is the parent of two child elements: date and salute. The element end is the parent of two child elements: salute and sender. Graphically, the logical structure of the document is shown in Fig. 4. In the pretty-printed form of web browsers (as shown Fig. 3), the hierarchic structure is utilized by allowing the user to unzoom or zoom branches in the tree structure. The minus character preceding the begin-tag indicates that the element has child elements and the child elements are presented on the screen. By clicking the character –, the child elements will be hidden and the minus character will be replaced by the plus character +.

The text between the start-tag and the end-tag of an element is called the *content* of the element. All elements having the same name in a document belong to the same *element type*.

The markup consisting of tags adds to the text the hierarchic structure and gives names to the structural components. A further means to add information to elements is the use of *attribute specifications*. An attribute specification can be added to the start-tag of an element, after the element name. For example, one might use an attribute to indicate that the content of the element main_content is English:

```
<main_content xml:lang="en">Let us meet
today 4 pm at The Archer.</main_content>
```

Since the capability of presenting content with various natural languages has been found important in XML, a predefined attribute xml:lang has been defined to identify the language in which the content of an element is written. The prefix xml indicates that the name xml:lang is a reserved name from the XML specification. The values of the attribute have to be given by the codes defined by the Internet Engineering Task Force (IETF).[17] In the example, the attribute specification indicates that the content of the element is in English. The example shows that there are two different techniques for providing a piece of data in XML elements: as element contents and as attribute values.

Physical Structure

Each XML document has actually, in addition to the logical structure, also a physical structure. Also the physical structure has to be indicated by markup. The physical structure of an XML document consists of units called *entities*. Each document has a special text entity called *document entity* or *root entity*. All entities referred to directly or indirectly from the root entity are regarded as parts of the physical structure of the document. The entity mechanism can be utilized to include non-textual data in a document. Thus in its physical structure an XML document may be a multimedia document having along with textual parts other forms of data, for example, audio or video data. For example, we might add to the message of Fig. 2 a reference to the photo of the sender by means of the attribute photo.

```
<sender photo="airi-image">Airi
</sender>
```

The attribute value "airi-image" is the name given to the entity elsewhere in the document.

Another type of an entity is a named piece of text introduced in an *entity declaration*. In other parts of the document, an *entity reference* is then used to refer to the text piece, in the same way as macros are used in many programming languages. For example, by giving the name W3C to the text piece

```
"World Wide Web Consortium"
```

we can refer to the text by the entity reference &W3C;. The symbol & starts the entity reference and the semicolon ends it. In processing the document, the XML processor replaces the reference by its value before transmitting data to the application. All entity references in XML documents represent procedural referential markup, not declarative markup. Entities provide an important means to include non-textual data to documents and to support consistency and reuse of the textual content.

Document Type Definitions

The previous sections described what kind of markup is used to indicate the logical and physical structure of a document. Extensible Markup Language also provides metamarkup capabilities to define markup languages for specific domains by means of DTDs. A DTD defines the grammar for the documents of a type. Fig. 5 shows a DTD for a message. The first line shows that the document type is called message and the last line closes the definition. The DTD describes the element types used in the documents of the type message, their names, and the way the documents are structured from elements. Altogether, eight element types are defined. Each of the lines beginning by the word ELEMENT is a grammar rule defining the structure of an element type. The name of the element type is given after

```
<!DOCTYPE message [
<!ELEMENT        message        (begin, main_content, end)>
<!ELEMENT        begin          (place?, date, salute)>
<!ELEMENT        place          (#PCDATA)>
<!ELEMENT        date           (#PCDATA)>
<!ELEMENT        salute         (#PCDATA)>
<!ELEMENT        main_content   (#PCDATA)>
<!ELEMENT        end            (salute, sender*)>
<!ELEMENT        sender         (#PCDATA)>
]>
```

Fig. 5 A Document Type Definition.

the word ELEMENT and the structure of the elements is given between parenthesis after the element type name.

The first element type definition in Fig. 5 defines the root element message. A message is defined to consist of three elements: begin, main_content, and end. The begin element always contains a date and salute, in the beginning possibly a child element called place. The optionality is indicated by the question mark. The notation #PCDATA is used to indicate that an element consists of character data, without having any child elements. The element called end first has a salute and then possibly sender elements. The repetition of zero or more times is indicated by the symbol *. Fig. 2 showed a message following the constraints defined in the DTD. It is called a *valid document* of the type message because it is well-formed and follows the rules expressed in the DTD.

COMBINING MARKUP LANGUAGES

A significant factor in the success of XML has been the idea that the work done in an environment for developing markup vocabularies and software can be reused in another environment without being forced to reinvent well-understood concepts and structures. Combining markup vocabularies from two different environments has required solving two problems: identification problem and name collision problem.

Identification Problem

If concepts defined in an environment are intended to be reused and shared in other contexts, there is a need for the unique identification of the original definitions.

Name Collision Problem

When earlier defined names are adopted from two different contexts, it is possible that the same name is used with different meanings.

These two problems have been solved by means of the *XML namespace* mechanism.[18] A namespace consists of a set of names having a unique identifier. The names may be defined, for example, in a DTD, but no constraints have been set to the way the names are described and defined. For the unique identifier instead, there are formal syntax rules, the identifier has to be given by using the syntax of the Uniform Resource Identifier (URI).[19] The most common form of a URI reference is the Uniform Resource Locator (URL) used in the WWW to refer to resources available on the Internet. For example, the URL http://www.w3.org/ is the address of the main page of the W3C site. A URI reference can also be a Uniform Resource Name (URN) intended for persistent identification of resources to remain the same even when the resource becomes unavailable. As namespace identifiers, URIs are always considered as identifiers of abstract resources. The definitions of the names may be available on a particular Internet site, but the namespace identifier is not regarded as the address of the site even though the format would be that of the URL. For example, if people at the University of Jyväskylä agree of a set of names and "http://jyu.fi/names/" as its identifier, the identifier can be used whether there is something on the web address or not.

In case of namespaces intended for widespread use, the developing organizations may provide some information on the address of the namespace identifier. For example, the W3C has published the URI "http://www.w3.org/1999/xhtml" as the identifier for the element and attribute names in the XHTML language and on the page at http://www.w3.org/1999/xhtml some information about the specifications where the XHTML names are defined.

As mentioned earlier, reusing names requires solving parallel with the identification problem also the name collision problem. In XML documents the name collision of element and attribute names is avoided by means of qualified names. A qualified name consists of two parts: a namespace name as a prefix and a local part. The namespace name is identified in the document by a URI reference, but the name used as the prefix can be chosen locally. Fig. 6 shows an example how a message could be markedup using TEI element names. Instead of choosing own element names like in Fig. 2, the TEI standardization work is utilized. The name tei used locally for the TEI namespace is introduced by the namespace declaration:

```
<message xmlns:tei = "http://www.tei-c.org/ns/1.0">
<tei:opener>
<tei:date>April 22</tei:date>
<tei:salute>Hi Mary Lynn!</tei:salute>
</tei:opener>
<main_content>
Let us meet today 4 pm at The Archer.
</main_content>
<tei:closer>
<tei:salute>Cheers,</tei:salute>
<tei:signature>Airi</tei:signature>
</tei:closer>
</message>
```

Fig. 6 A document using names from the TEI namespace.

```
<message xmlns:tei = "http://www.tei-c.
org/ns/1.0">
```

The name is associated with the URI identifying the TEI namespace. The element names `opener`, `date`, `salute`, `closer`, and `signature` are taken from the TEI namespace.

XML FAMILY OF LANGUAGES

The simplicity of XML has encouraged active development work around XML, including both software development and development of XML applications and related languages. Where SGML has been primarily in use as a format for documents intended for human readers, for example, in the form of HTML documents, the use of XML has extended toward data interchange between software applications.[20] Development of XML-based markup languages has been going on in various standards development organizations. For example, the OASIS (http://www.oasis-open.org/) has coordinated the standardization for health care and business needs.

Probably the most important standards developing organization is the W3C (http://www.w3.org/). The organization was founded in 1994 to coordinate and support international, open development of technologies related to the web. W3C publishes technical reports called *W3C Recommendations*, which are considered to define web standards. The Recommendations and their preliminary versions are published at http://www.w3.org/TR/. During the first 16 years of XML, W3C has developed a family of languages and published Recommendations for over 50 XML-related languages. The intent has been to specify syntactic and semantic rules either for some specific kind of XML data or for data to be used together with XML data for a specific purpose. A web portal maintained by the author of the entry since the year 2000 provides a classification of the languages, and it shows for each language its standardization phase, related specifications, and links to the W3C technical specifications.[21] The classification is introduced and some of the languages in each class are briefly described as follows.

Four main categories on the basis of their purpose have been identified in the XML family. The first category consists of the different versions of *XML* itself. The other three categories are called XML accessories, XML transducers, and XML applications:[20,21]

XML accessories are languages that are intended for wide use to extend the capabilities specified in XML. An example of XML accessories is the *XML Schema* language extending the definition capabilities of XML DTDs. XML Schema allows the use of a variety of data types, for example, boolean, float, int, date, and their validation in conforming software. In addition to a number of built-in data types, the schema designers may define user-derived data types. XML Schema definitions can be written using XML syntax, but other presentations are possible, too. When using XML syntax, the schema is an XML document that can be processed by general XML software.

XML transduces are languages that are intended for transducing some input XML data into some output form. Examples of XML transducers are the style sheet languages Cascading Style Sheets (CSS) and Extensible Stylesheet Language (XSL) intended to produce an external presentation from some XML data, XSL Transformations (XSLT) for transforming XML documents into other XML documents, and XML Query Language (XQuery) for querying collections of XML data both locally and on the web, be it physically stored in XML or viewed as XML via middleware. A transducer language is associated with some kind of processing model that defines the way output is derived from input. From the four example languages, CSS does not have XML syntax while the rest of the languages have.

XML applications are languages that define constraints for a class of XML data for some special application area. As mentioned earlier, XML accessories and XML transducers are often XML-based languages and thus also XML applications. The languages in the XML applications category can be further divided into four subcategories according to the application area:

Non-textual forms of data: The character data of markedup XML are usually shown to the human reader as text. Non-textual data like graphics or voice are attached to the document as external entities. There are, however, also markup languages available to present non-textual data by means of markedup text. In the XML family of W3C such languages are, for example, Synchronized Multimedia Integration Language (SMIL) for multimedia documents, Scalable Vector Graphics (SVG) for vector graphics, and Voice Extensible Markup Language (VoiceXML) to enable access to the web using spoken interaction.

Web publishing: The languages in this group are intended to replace the SGML-based HTML gradually by XML-based representation formats. The most important language in this group is *XHTML*, reformulation of HTML in XML. The latest version of HTML, called *HTML5*, has been defined with two syntaxes: one in HTML and the other in XHTML. Extensible Hypertext Markup Language is a content language aimed at many kinds of devices in addition to laptops and workstations, including TV screens of various sizes, hand-held computers, and portable phones. Therefore, there are several variants of the XHTML markup and also a possibility to embed other markup within XHTML to facilitate displaying non-textual markedup data by browsers. Current browsers already support the use of markup beyond XHTML. For example, Google Chrome, Safari, and Firefox browsers allow combining XHTML and SVG markup.

Semantic Web: To facilitate more effective use of resources on the web, W3C has started to develop rules for adding semantic metadata to the web. Important languages developed for the purpose are Resource Description Framework (RDF) to describe resources, RDF Vocabulary Description Language (RDF Schema) to define RDF vocabularies, and Web Ontology Language (OWL) for publishing and sharing ontologies.

Web communication and services: There is a great need to facilitate secure exchange of data and services between software agents of the Internet. W3C has developed a number of markup languages for the purpose. For example, *XML-Signature* defines syntax and processing rules for XML digital signatures. It is intended to provide integrity, message authentication, and signer authentication services for data. Simple Object Access Protocol (SOAP) is a lightweight XML-based protocol for exchange of information in a decentralized, distributed environment. Web Services Description Language (WSDL) can be used to define web service interfaces and functionalities so that services needed for a particular situation can be automatically accessed and chained with other services.

CONCLUSION

The interconnectivity of people, computers, software agents, organizations, and services on the web is enabled by hundreds of different markup languages, either based on SGML or its restricted form XML. The web users do not necessarily have any need to be aware of the markup. Understanding the principles of markup techniques and markup languages is, however, essential to all information specialists. Also for application domain experts involved in the development of markup languages for the particular domain, it is important to be aware of the possibilities and constraints of markup techniques.

Why XML has been so widely adopted? Some kind of markup is always needed in digital documents to enable automated processing of documents. Compared to other kinds of markup techniques XML provides several benefits. Some of the important benefits are summarized here. First, like SGML, XML is a metalanguage enabling definition of special vocabularies and document structures for various application domains. Rigorous markup using specified vocabularies facilitates automated processing of documents of certain types. For example, it is possible to develop information retrieval tools where the queries are expressed using the terminology of the particular domain. Second, SGML and XML are open standards supporting long-term accessibility of information in data assets of organizations. Information in SGML and XML documents is not accessible by a particular software application only, but by diverse software. And if necessary, the markup is readable also to human individuals. Third, compared to SGML, XML is simpler and provides stronger support for programming. Thus, it has encouraged the development of a great number of software for processing XML data. Last, SGML was developed to be used as a document format, for example, for technical documents and publication industry. XML can be used for the same purposes but also, and is probably used more, as a format for data exchange between software applications. This feature supports interoperability of software applications.

The entry first introduced and classified different types of markup emphasizing the importance of the invention of descriptive markup. Three major milestones in the development of the markup languages were described. First, the development and standardization of the rules for descriptive markup in SGML. Second, the birth of the most important SGML application called HTML for the language of the WWW. Last, the development of XML to support more effective communication on the Internet. An overview of the markup techniques and definition capabilities in XML was given. XML-related development work has been a huge collaborative effort in many standards developing organizations. The sectoral standardization has benefited substantially from the development work of the W3C that has resulted in not only XML but also the namespace mechanism to facilitate combining and reuse of markup vocabularies and over 50 other XML-related standards. The XML family of languages was introduced, and some representatives of the languages were briefly described.

REFERENCES

1. Goldfarb, C.F. *The SGML Handbook*; Rubinsky, Y., Ed.; Oxford University Press: Oxford, U.K., 1990.
2. W3C Recommendation. Extensible Markup Language (XML) 1.0, February 10, 1998, http://www.w3.org/TR/1998/REC-xml-19980210 (accessed November 2014).
3. Coombs, J.H.; Renear, A.H.; DeRose, S.J. Markup systems and the future of scholarly text processing. Commun. ACM **1987**, *30* (11), 933–947.
4. Goldfarb, C. Roots of SGML—A personal recollection, 1996, http://www.sgmlsource.com/history/roots.htm (accessed November 2014).
5. Goldfarb, C. SGML: The reason why and the first published hint. J. Am. Soc. Inform. Sci. **1997**, *48* (7), 656–661. The article is a commentary of the article by Goldfarb, C.; Mosher, E.J.; Peterson, T.I. An online system for integrated text processing. Proc. Am. Soc. Inf. Sci. **1970**, *7*, 147–150.
6. Goldfarb, C.F. A generalized approach to document markup. Proceedings of the ACM SIGPLAN SIGOA Symposium on Text Manipulation. ACM SIGOA Newslett. **1981**, *2* (1–2), 68–73.
7. Leavenworth, B.; Sammet, J. An overview of non-procedural languages. SIGPLAN Not. **1974**, *9* (4), 1–12.
8. Reid, B.K. A high-level approach to computer document formatting. In *Proceedings of the 7th ACM SIGPLAN-SIGACT Symposium on Principles of Programming Languages*; ACM Press; New York, 1980; 32–46.
9. The DocBook Project, http://docbook.sourceforge.net/ (accessed November 2014).
10. CALS Standards, http://www.navsea.navy.mil/nswc/carderock/tecinfsys/cal-std/index.html (accessed November 2014).
11. TEI: Text Encoding Initiative, http://www.tei-c.org/index.xml (accessed November 2014).
12. Berners-Lee, T.; Cailliau, R.; Luotonen, A.; Frystyk Nielsen, H.; Secret, A. The World-Wide Web. Commun. ACM **1994**, *37* (8), 76–82.
13. W3C Recommendation. HTML 4.01 Specification, December 24, 1999, http://www.w3.org/TR/REC-html40/ (accessed November 2014).
14. W3C Recommendation. XHTML™ 1.0 The Extensible HyperText Markup Language (Second Edition). A reformulation of HTML 4 in XML 1.0, January 26, 2000, revised August 1, 2002, http://www.w3.org/TR/xhtml1/(accessed November 2014).
15. W3C Recommendation. *HTML5*. A vocabulary and associated APIs for HTML and XHTML, 28 October 2014, http://www.w3.org/TR/html5/ (accessed December 2014).
16. W3C Recommendation. Extensible Markup Language (XML) 1.1 (Second Edition), August 16, 2006, edited in place September 29, 2006, http://www.w3.org/TR/xml11/ (accessed November 2014).
17. Tags for identifying languages, Network Working Group, Request for Comments: 5646, September 2009, http://tools.ietf.org/html/rfc5646, (accessed November 2014).
18. W3C Recommendation. Namespaces in XML 1.0 (Third Edition), December 8, 2009, http://www.w3.org/TR/REC-xml-names/ (accessed November 2014).
19. Berners-Lee, T.; Fielding, R.; Masinter, L. Uniform Resource Identifiers (URI): Generic Syntax, Network Working Group, Request for Comments: 3986, January 2005, http://www.rfc-editor.org/rfc/rfc3986.txt (accessed November 2014).
20. Salminen, A.; Tompa, F. *Communicating with XML*; Springer: New York/Dordrecht, the Netherlands, Heidelberg, Germany/London, U.K., 2011.
21. Salminen, A. XML family of languages, Overview and classification of W3C specifications, December 1, 2014, http://www.cs.jyu.fi/~airi/xmlfamily.html (accessed December 2014).

Mexico: Libraries, Archives, and Museums

Jesús Lau
Library Services Unit USBI Veracruz (USBI VER), University of Veracruz, Veracruz, Mexico

Abstract
This entry offers a general introduction to the different types of Mexican libraries, museums, and archives, with an emphasis on libraries and related subjects such as serials, book production, and library schools. Literature was consulted and direct data was gathered from Web sites and through telephone interviews of knowledgeable library professionals. Data used in this entry is not all recent. Therefore, it is used mainly as an indicator of the general status of Mexican information development.

GENERAL BACKGROUND

Mexico is a large country, whose official name is Mexican United States, a federal constitutional republic. It is politically divided into 31 states and a Federal District (Mexico City). Its government is presidential with a constitutionally strong Congress and a supreme court. The president is elected for a non-renewable 6-year term and appoints the cabinet. The country's legislature is based on a bicameral Congress: 128-member Senate, and a 500-member Chamber of Deputies, elected for a 3-year term.[1] States provide some funding for education and libraries, as well as setting some of the educational requirements, but policy-making is generally centralized by the federal government. For example, the Ministry of Public Education provides funding and direction, in different levels, to all types of libraries, except special ones. Mexico, as a country, has more than 100 million inhabitants; it is certainly the most populated nation in the Spanish-speaking world. Covering a territory a quarter of the size of the United States of America (U.S.), its economy ranks number 14, according to its Gross National Income, and it ranks number 7 in terms of tourism.[2,3] Mexico is the second largest economy in Latin America. It is a country in an intermediate advanced stage of development with a positive economic performance that is closely linked to the American economy. The official concern in dealing with poverty persists and the per capita income has gone up, although poverty and inequality rates continue to be elevated.[2] Libraries are a crucial service to enhance information development of the country, whether at schools or in the workplace. Therefore they are assumed to be a means to bridge the socio-economic gaps in Mexican society. This entry provides a general description of the libraries, providing a historical introduction, a brief account by type of library, and a description of related subjects, such as book and serial publishing, among other library and information subjects. Museums and archives are also included as repositories for the collection and preservation of culture whose roles complement that of the libraries. The general goal is to give the international reader a general picture of the range of library institutions, stressing their contemporary developments.

HISTORY

Locations for the reproduction, transmission, and promotion of information existed in Mexico well before the Spaniards arrived in 1519. The Aztecs had library-like institutions called Amoxcalli, the house of the Amoxtli, the pictographic codices that recorded economic, social, and political life in this central Mexican Kingdom. This was also the case of other indigenous cultures with urban centers, such as the Maya. Some of the existing codices are preserved, mainly in European institutions, since few Amoxtli works escaped the burning and destruction of the Spanish missionaries in their quest to convert locals to the Catholic Church. The most famous existing codex is the Borgia. It originally included five parts[4] that are now scattered in different European libraries and museums. Libraries in the sense of the western world developed in Mexico after the Spanish Conquest. The first Spanish settlers founded some of the earliest libraries in temples and seminaries, where collections had basically religious books. One of the first books brought to the American continent was a breviary *Libros de Horas* by Jerónimo de Aguilar, the interpreter of the leading conqueror Hernán Cortés. Cortés's party was shipwrecked but managed to save the book in 1511.[4] It is estimated that two decades later there were more books in Mexico because by 1534, the cathedral had officially a library and its own printing press. The first printing press was brought to Mexico from Seville by Jacobo Cromberg, along with the printer Juan Pablos, in 1539. It also became the first printing press in all of the Americas. An early newspaper was published

Encyclopedia of Library and Information Sciences, Fourth Edition DOI: 10.1081/E-ELIS4-120043469

that consisted of loose sheets with news of New Spain and was distributed at the beginning of the sixteenth century by Siguenza y Góngora. The first book to be printed, on the other hand, a religious book, was the *Brief and more compendious Christian doctrine*... (Breve y más compendiosa doctrina Cristiana...) by Zumárraga that is now lost but is recorded in the *Acts of Indias* (Actas de Indias) in the General Archive of Indias in Seville, Spain. These two works made Mexico the first country to publish in the Americas.[5]

The key political position of colonial Mexico, as the crown colony of New Spain, offered the opportunity to import recently edited books from Spain by transatlantic Spanish travelers. Mexico, for example, was one, if not the first, to receive a copy of *Don Quixote* by Miguel de Cervantes, the equivalent of Shakespeare in the Spanish-speaking world. Members of religious groups played an important role in creating libraries, such as Eguiara y Eguren, a religious scholar and author of the first national bibliography on the continent (1755). These groups founded libraries primarily in Mexico and also in colonial America. The colonial libraries were basically for Spaniards and not for Indians or *Mestizos* (inter-racial people with one Spanish and one Indian parent), who were deprived of education or any formal school training. This library/educational discrimination began to change after Mexico's independence (1810) movement[5] when public institutions were decreed to be for the entire population. Mexico was in turmoil during the first half of nineteenth century, with constants revolts and conflicts with European countries and the United States, resulting in the United States gaining more than half of Mexico's territory. Other than the creation of the National Library (1867) and the legal deposit (1812), this was a period of minor library development. Later, when the Republic was consolidated during the Porfirio Díaz regime (1876–1910), libraries were officially open to anyone, but illiteracy was high—only 10% of the population could read. This limited access to written culture continued up to the Mexican Revolution, 1910–1919. After this long internal conflict, libraries began to evolve, and had some initial success with the Vasconcelos public library program that started in 1921,[6] discussed in the public libraries' section of this entry. The decades from 1920 to 1960 were a formational period, with some additional basic library institutions being created, such as the first library school and the library association. The significant library development that occurred after 1970 is described in the following sections of the entry (see Appendix 1).

ACADEMIC LIBRARIES

Mexico has, basically, four types of academic libraries: state university libraries, technological institution libraries, teacher's institutions libraries, and private university libraries. The first three groups, as may be expected, are financed by government, either federal or state, and seldom by municipalities (counties). The total number of universities varies according to the consulted source. The National Association of Universities and Higher Education Institutions, or ANUIES (Asociación Nacional de Universidades e Instituciones de Educación Superior) that includes mainly state universities, and some technological institutes and a few private ones, reports 127 public and 263 private higher education institutions.[7] However, the total for all types of institutions, small and large, is 1482 according to statistics from the National Institute of Statistics and Geography, or INEGI (Instituto Nacional de Estadística y Geografía).[8,9]

State University Libraries

This first group includes the best academic libraries. They belong to the 45 state higher education institutions that are normally the largest in every state and in the Federal District, i.e., Mexico City.[7] There is one state university per state, except in seven, where there are two higher education institutions, and Mexico City, which has several.[7] All of them are autonomous: they can take their own academic and organizational decisions, unlike other higher education institutions in the other categories. State universities provide undergraduate education to 2,528,664, i.e., 36.9%[7,8] of the national student population. Libraries in these institutions are affiliated under the National Council for Library Matters of Higher Education Institutions, or CONPAB (Consejo Nacional para Asuntos Bibliotecarios de Instituciones de Educación Superior) that includes, as full members, 41 members and 8 guest academic libraries whose parent organizations cannot be fully defined as universities.[10] The academic libraries of Mexico City, such as the Autonomous National University of Mexico, or UNAM (Universidad Nacional Autónoma de México) and the Metropolitan University, or UAM (Universidad Metropolitana) are not included, apparently because of their overpoweringly large size and overwhelming influence. Most state universities have a library system that includes a main library, and one per faculty or cluster of faculties or research centers with a director general. This is reflected in the large number of CONPAB libraries, with 713 units. Few universities have fully centralized services. Those that do are newer, i.e., founded after the 1970s. Generally, CONPAB libraries have centralized acquisitions, collection development, and technical services. The larger academic libraries usually belong to the older and larger universities, such as UNAM, regarded as a special case because of its enormous size (see Fig. 1). It is the oldest university in Mexico and one of the oldest in continental America with nearly one-third of a million students, 299,723. Slightly more than half are undergraduate, 167,891; one-third is high school, 107,482; and the rest are postgraduate students.[11] The research output is strikingly higher than any

Fig. 1 UNAM Central Library, Mexico City—by Adolfo Rodríguez.

other institution in the country, with 35% of the scientific output, as measured by the number of refereed journal articles. This academic performance makes UNAM number 150 among the 200 best research universities, according to the British newspaper *The Times Higher Education Supplement* assessment of 2008.[12] UNAM's research activities are dependent on a good library and information service. Including special libraries, UNAM has 142 libraries, with over six million volumes and has the largest library budget for serials, monographs, and electronic resources in the nation. This amount is probably the equivalent of 50% of the total national budget of academic libraries in Mexico. After the National University, the two other large universities are the Universidad de Guadalajara with 195,116 students and 162 libraries,[13] and the Universidad Autónoma de Nuevo León, with an enrollment of 126,000 students and 80 libraries,[14] both located in the two other major cities. Their library systems are also well-funded and well-organized. The rest of the state universities have, in general, large library collections, and hold—like the metropolitan universities of the three major cities—important rare, special, and historical collections; they usually have more professional librarians than other type of libraries.

Besides their own institutional budgets, state university libraries are generally financed through the Integral Program for Institutional Support, or PIFI (Programa Integral de Fortalecimiento Institucional), in addition to their own institutional budgets.[15] PIFI is managed by the General Directorate of Higher Education under the Ministry of Public Education, or SEP (Secretaría de Educación Pública), which uses the funds to set university policies and determine priorities for state-financed higher education. It provides funds on competitive bases to different academic functions, but it has a special fund for academic libraries. Since its inception under a different name in 1980, PIFI has played a decisive role in increasing library collections; acquiring electronic resources, computer equipment, and information technology; training personnel; and furnishing libraries. The challenge that libraries have with these funds is that there is an annual competition for their projects and the money may or may not be awarded, making funding erratic. Librarians do not know if they can count on the funds for the following year. Some changes have been planned to make tri-annual allocations, but, so far, these have not been fully implemented. State university libraries that have been able to attract the most funds, either from PIFI, or from their parent organizations, are UNAM (most successful), and those from the universities in the states of Colima, Jalisco, Ciudad Juárez, Veracruz, Quintana Roo and the Yucatán. In addition there are about 20 other State University library systems whose organization, funding and services are very good. The best accredited universities, included in the previous figures, are grouped in the Mexican Consortium of Universities, or CUMex (Consorcio de Universidades Mexicanas), a body created by SEP, that includes 17 institutions. The library systems of CUMex members generally match the academic excellence of the universities in which they are found, and receive some special funding as a reward for their accreditation achievements (see Fig. 2).

Technological Institute Libraries

Technological institutes total 242, the first having been founded in 1949, plus the large National Polytechnic, or IPN (Instituto Politécnico Nacional),[16] located in Mexico City. IPN is to technological institutes as UNAM is to universities; it was the first and is the largest technological higher education organization in Mexico with 142,861 students. It has 72 libraries, including specialized ones that

Fig. 2 Universidad Veracruzana Library, Boca del Rio, Veracruz—by Ulises Buendía.

serve faculties and research centers in its different campuses. IPN library and information services are larger and better than those of any other technological institution in Mexico, but certainly of a smaller library size when compared against those of UNAM, its State University Library counterpart. Technological institutes, on the other hand, as their name implies, cater mainly to science and technology disciplines, basically engineering, and, to a lesser extent, to management subjects. Technological institutes, originally modeled on the IPN structure, but in an independent network, are run by a centralized directorate in Mexico City under the umbrella of the Ministry of Public Education that provides all the funding and generates library policies at the national level. The network includes engineering, marine, forestry, and agricultural institutes. Their libraries, or information centers, as they are called, have similar information services, including the same type of buildings across the country. Their library development is fairly good, but their budgets are low and their information technology lags behind that of the state university libraries.

There are, in addition, two types of technological universities: technological and polytechnic. Both are newcomers on the Mexican education scene. The first technological universities were founded in 1991.[17] Each of them receives joint funding from the state where it is located and from the federal government. Degrees are of the 2-year college level, called "Técnico Superior Universitario." The current number 65 centrally coordinated from their headquarters in Mexico City. Their total enrollment was 66,660 students nation-wide in 2006,[18] and several had fewer than a thousand learners. The academic structure is a hybrid because they aim to provide, at least by name, technological training with university-based education to support the productive and service sectors. In most states, they are located in cities with no traditional universities—only 30% are in state capitals. The polytechnic universities, on the other hand, are an even newer development within the national education system. They were created to compliment the technological universities, so that college students could pursue higher education following 2 years of college. To date, they number 22 and their funding is awarded in similar proportion by federal and state governments. Libraries at these universities are in the process of basic development with small spaces, usually a classroom-type accommodation, limited budgets and few professional staff. However, there are some exceptions, such as the polytechnic university libraries of Santa Catarina in Nuevo León and in Aguascalientes, with excellent facilities.

Teachers' Institution Libraries

There are 457 teacher's Institutions, usually called *Normales*.[19] In addition, pedagogical and education studies are offered at state and private universities, but their library resources are included under the corresponding type of institution. There are four types—the oldest date from the 1800s. The first one was founded in 1823, and a handful more was created in the following decades, but the rest was founded in the twentieth century. They are in most state capital cities and tend to be well-established. The second type or generation of pedagogical *Normales* is from the previous century, when several were founded outside the state capitals, and even in the rural areas. The third type is the higher education *Normales*, whose studies are equivalent to undergraduate degrees. The fourth group is comprised of a fairly new network of 76 state pedagogical universities (Universidades Pedagógicas) with 206 sub-sites in major urban centers. The universities were started in 1978 when the National Pedagogical University, or UPN (Universidad Pedagógica Nacional) the primary leading institution, was created in Mexico City. Library services at the generally older teachers training institutions range from good to fairly good, while second-generation *Normales* and pedagogical university libraries have poorer development, with smaller collections and less organization. The state UPN's libraries are normally housed in classroom-like facilities with basic information services, except the one in Mexico City that has good library premises and good services.[20] The Pedagogical University sub-sites do not have libraries as such, except for some minor book collections. Teacher's Institution Libraries do not, in general, subscribe to electronic information sources, nor have access to information technology, except for computer and Internet access. In addition, there are more pedagogical and education studies at state and private universities, but they are included under their corresponding type of institutions.

Private University Libraries

Private university libraries vary dramatically according to the size of their parent institutions. According to the Ministry of Public Education, there are 667 institutions of this type. There are a handful of large private universities, over 100 medium-sized, private universities; and over 500 small ones.[21] The large private institutions are, in general, excellent. Their libraries are well-funded and provide excellent information services. An example is the Technological Institute of Higher Education Studies in Monterrey, or ITESM (Instituto Tecnológico de Estudios Superiores de Monterrey). ITESM is the largest private university with a national network of 33 campuses, each with a library. The largest are in Monterrey, Mexico City, and Guadalajara. Other large private universities with excellent libraries include Anahuac with 10 campuses, University of Monterrey (Universidad de Monterrey), Ibero-American University (Universidad Iberoamericana) with 5 campuses outside the national capital, plus other universities with outstanding library services, such as University of the Americas (Universidad de las Americas, Puebla), Valle de México, Technological Autonomous Institute of Mexico (Instituto Tecnológico Autónomo de México), and Panamerican, among others. The private institutions in the second tier are mid-sized. They are normally affiliated with the Federation of Private Mexican Institutions of Higher Education, or FIMPES (Federación de Instituciones Mexicanas Particulares de Educación Superior),[22] a national association that includes 114 institutions. That is about 17% of the private universities, according to the FIMPES Web site. The rest of the private institutions range from the common one-school centered program to the more than two-faculty larger programs. These smaller and newer private universities struggle to have and maintain library services. Their collections and services tend to be minimal and the institutions seldom hire a librarian for their libraries. The Ministry of Public Education regulates their creation and their awarding of university degrees but fails to regulate minimum library standards. The focus of the small institutions, as it is also true for the majority of private universities, is teaching. The faculty members at the small institutions seldom do research, so libraries are not a priority.

In total, academic institutions comprise 1482 libraries, out of the more than 2000 estimated learning centers of all types. State university and large private universities provide the largest library budgets, the fastest growing information collections, and offer the most innovative provision of services. They are also the main customers of international vendors, the leaders in acquisition of technological equipment, and the libraries with the best Internet infrastructure among all types of academic libraries.

PUBLIC LIBRARIES

After the Mexican Revolution of 1910–1919, Jose Vasconcelos, the first minister of public education (1921–1924), created a nation-wide public library program. His dream was to take books to every town in Mexico, and his administration created around 2500 libraries with small holdings that included classic works of literature and technical books.[23] Following his service as minister of public education, he became the first director of the central public library, Biblioteca Mexico, in Mexico City. Many of Vasconcelos' public libraries unfortunately disappeared, in part due to the limited education system and the high illiteracy rate in the country. Five decades later, public libraries entered their second golden period, from the late 1970s up to the present. A strong well-financed federal government strategy to organize public libraries began in 1978, under Guadalupe Carrión, as public libraries' director. In addition to a national plan to develop a library system, the first 5 years focused on reorganizing libraries at a national level, including a study conducted to assess public libraries, and developing indicators and parameters for building, equipping, and creating library collections, as well as completion of a national plan to develop a library system. Additionally, a major achievement was the training of about 500 public library staff members, with a well-organized and intensive full-time 3-month library program offered in three regional centers in the country: Durango, Mérida, and Querétaro.

In 1983, based on the seminal planning work of the previous 5 years, the National Program of Public Libraries was officially announced by the current President and the Minister of Public Education in turn, who appointed Ana María Magaloni as director general. Under the auspices of this program, a strong national public network was created in the next 5 years.[24] The department became the General

Fig. 3 Municipal Public Library, Tlaltetela, Veracruz—by Edna Zamora.

Directorate of Public Libraries, or DGB (Dirección General de Bibliotecas), currently managed by the National Council for Culture and the Arts, or CONACULTA (Consejo Nacional para la Cultura y las Artes) of the Ministry of Public Education. The Directorate finances and manages 7211 public libraries with 36.5 million books. The library system is the largest in Latin America, even larger than that of Brazil, whose population is double that of Mexico. The network has a central public catalog for all holdings of public libraries in the country, using the Dewey Decimal System and the Anglo-American Cataloging Rules. The library staff of the public library network includes 10,485 people, whose library training is, unfortunately rather limited. Only 43 have library technical training, 111 have undergraduate degrees, and only two have master's degrees in library science.[5] However, the general directorate has had library professionals on its staff since its inception in 1978. Perhaps, this fact has been crucial to achieving the current success of the public library network.

Public libraries are grouped into three types: state, regional, and municipal libraries. Their size and services are closely related to their network status. There is a public library in every town with more than 5000 inhabitants. Libraries also vary in size and services from those in the urban centers, which are better equipped, to those in rural towns and villages, where Internet access is almost nonexistent (see Figs. [3–5]).

Public libraries are set up by a joint agreement among the three government tiers. The federal government central office, in Mexico City, is in charge of creating library policies, collection development, acquisitions and technical services. State governments pay for the construction or adaptation of buildings, and the municipal/county authorities, in turn, hire staff and pay for staff salaries. The program has been successful, especially in those states where their governments invest more in the library network, such as is the case in Veracruz and Chiapas. All 31 states and the Federal District have a central public library that is generally large and well-equipped, with good information services. In most cases, these libraries are in charge of the state public library networks, house the state directors, and provide centralized technical services.

Providing Internet access in public libraries has been a major task for most governments at all levels. In 2002, the Bill and Melinda Gates Foundation donated 30 million dollars to Mexican public libraries. The funds were to equip 1500 public libraries with 1–10 computers, train personnel, and introduce the Internet. This grant was the second given outside the United States, after Chile, by the Bill and Melinda Gates Foundation. The Mexican federal government matched the gift with 40 million dollars. Additionally, more libraries were equipped with computers and Internet access with more federal and state funds, and now 38% of the libraries have computers. Some states provide extra funds to promote Internet access, such as the State of Veracruz, with the recent launch of an ambitious program to provide computers to public libraries and to build regional central public libraries, whose constructions showcase modern architecture. The Bill and Melinda Gates Foundation gave their annual 2008 Access to Learning Award to Veracruz for its innovative efforts to connect people from rural and remote communities with the services provided by 20 all-terrain buses converted into mobile-classroom units. They provide information services, free access to computers, and satellite Internet. Veracruz also provides free access to

Fig. 4 Municipal Public Library, Tlacotalpan, Veracruz—by Edna Zamora.

some commercial information databases in their public libraries. The state of Chiapas does this as well, and offers the additional benefit of making the databases open to any remote user within its geographical limits.

The federal CONACULTA Directorate of Libraries is housed in the large, beautiful, seventeenth century historic premises of the Ciudadela, along with the Biblioteca Mexico main public library, as it was originally called, later renamed Biblioteca Vasconcelos. It hosts public library network services and a collection of 250,000 volumes and will soon have additional new premises. A new state-of-the-art building will soon re-open (it opened for a few months, then closed for further construction) at the former Buenavista railroad station in Mexico City.[25] The building, more than 475,000 sq. ft, has a striking modern architectural design, with glass, steel, and concrete playing key roles to create a building that will either be adored or despised, depending on people's artistic perception. A special feature is a botanical garden that gives a natural touch to the building. The design was the result of an international contest with over 592 architects' proposals from all over the world.[25] The library has an auditorium, meeting places, a bookstore, cafeteria, and plenty of room for stacks and services. It is certainly the largest public library in Mexico and in Latin America. User demand is expected to be high, because it is conveniently located next to the new suburban train station, designed to serve most citizens living North of Mexico City.

Fig. 5 Municipal Public Library, Monterrey, Nuevo León.

The Universidad de Guadalajara in the western part of the country has also broken ground on a larger public state library. Since 1861, the University has managed the state public library Juan Jose Arreola. It holds a rich collection of 400,000 historical books and documents. The current building in downtown Guadalajara dates from 1959. However, the collections have outgrown the facility and the new library (43,000 m^2/462,848 sq. ft) will have room for more collections and newer services. The library will be the central unit of a large grand cultural complex that will also include convention facilities. It is planned to open in 2010.

SCHOOL LIBRARIES

School library policies are generally managed by the Sub-Ministry of Basic Education (Subsecretaría de Educación Básica)[26] of the Federal Ministry of Public Education, its 31 state counterparts, and the Federal District. Most, if not all pre-elementary, elementary, junior high, and high schools, have some sort of book collections, even those in remote rural schools. The books may be in a bookcase or in wooden or cardboard boxes, or whatever container is available in the less well-equipped institutions.[25] The Ministry of Public Education has created different programs in the past to provide complementary reading materials to schools. Two of the latest are *The books of the corner* (Los Libros del Rincón), a program that provided between 150 and 300 titles of selected literary materials to every school over 4 years beginning in 1986.[27] This program was superseded by another one that started in 2002, as part of a general reading plan called *Towards a country of readers* (Hacia un país de lectores) that included the *Classroom library* (Biblioteca de aula) program. Its aim is to stock every kindergarten and elementary school classroom with books at the beginning of each school term. In the last 5 years, a staggering figure of over 200 million volumes was given to libraries and classroom collections, making almost nine volumes available to each school child, for the 23 million pupils who attend school. The book stocks include about 50% literary works, and the rest of the books provide general information to support school teaching programs. The titles distributed varied from 218 provided to pre-elementary schools (that received a total of 57 million volumes) to 514 titles provided to elementary schools (that received 78 million volumes), and 488 titles given to junior high schools, who, in turn (that got almost 30 million volumes). These figures also include 51 bilingual titles in Spanish and local indigenous languages.

The book stocks were selected with the participation of teacher focus groups from most states. The program also includes a library training program with a manual on how to organize library materials, how to create library activities and promote reading, plus a set of posters, flyers, and television and radio programs. The teaching staff who runs the program number more than 6000, and include some who work in libraries.[28] As a general comment, book budgets are seldom available for libraries or schools themselves. Material acquisition is centralized in SEP headquarters. Public libraries, on the other hand, support schools' information demand with their open role as community information centers, where buildings and services are more broadly and better structured. Public libraries, in general, tailor their information services to better serve students rather than the average citizen, defining themselves as places for those studying in the elementary education system.

Another library-related action is the federal government's free textbooks program for children that gives a set of books to schools, including those in private institutions, since 1958, although, in the beginning, it did not cover every school and the number of book titles was limited.[29] The total number of volumes distributed in 2007 was a staggering 54,279,051 volumes.[30] A subsidized and free textbook program also exists for high schools (Libros de Texto Gratuitos para Secundaria 149.480.757).[29] The aim is to help students have and/or acquire their required readings. These book programs complement library services, although, as some critics say, it limits information literacy, because kids do not have to search for additional information beyond the compulsory textbook readings. However, this challenge is more due to the prevalent teacher-oriented pedagogical approach than to the free textbook programs. Teachers normally lack extensive reading habits themselves, which sometimes limit the potential academic impact of their classroom book collections and school libraries.

The reading programs in schools and libraries must overcome the limited reading habits of children, and, as stated, of teachers themselves, because basic education tends to be based on rote repetition, where the only source of information is usually the teacher. Teachers who fail to promote reading habits at the time when children learn to read and write waste part of the economic resources devoted to the school library sector. As a result, pupils finish school with limited or no information skills, posing a challenge at subsequent educational levels, where teachers or professors ought to be filling the information competencies gap. School information literacy challenges are reflected in the reading habits of society if one takes as a reading indicator the low number of bookstores, that only total around 1452 in the whole country.[30]

SPECIAL LIBRARIES

Most of these libraries can be grouped into four clusters: 1) science and technology libraries, financed by the National Council of Science and Technology, or

CONACYT (Consejo Nacional de Ciencia y Tecnología); 2) research institute libraries, part of university research centers; 3) government libraries, mostly part of the ministries; and 4) special libraries that are part of private sector industries, service corporations, and/or museums, among other organizations. In the national directory of libraries published by CONACYT in 1976 special libraries were well-documented. Unfortunately this directory has not been updated, in part because these libraries lack an association or a central organization that could promote a directory. Current special libraries can be estimated at between 500 and 600, including academic specialized collections attached to universities. According to García,[31] Mexico ranks second in the total number of special libraries, after Brazil in Latin America. According to Carrión,[32] special libraries have had excellent development in recent decades. Their collections, funding, and professional staff are among the best. However, libraries, in the traditional sense of holding large printed collections and having purpose built buildings, have been decreasing in the last decade to give room to special information services that rely heavily on electronic sources and require fewer staff.

CONACYT has played an important role in special libraries expansion. The Council was founded in 1970 to foster, among other roles, the national research system, with the corresponding goal of creating a national information network. With such a mandate, the 1970s were a decade of increased special libraries creation. CONACYT intensively promoted library training, extending the benefit to university libraries. A special program was set up to send graduate students to study library and information science abroad, especially in the United States. The program lasted 5 years, and achieved the goal of training around 60 MLS professionals (1974–1979). Those who accepted positions in libraries pioneered a period of organization of special and academic libraries, especially outside Mexico City, where professional librarians were in great demand. In conjunction with the graduate program, a library technical staff program operated from 1973 to 1979. The training, involving a two-semester full-time study scheme, was excellent because it included all the subjects required to organize and provide library services. Participants from every state were invited, with the aid of a student CONACYT grant, to attend the program, mainly hosted by the National School of Librarianship and Archives, with a summer version offered once in Ciudad Juárez and Puebla. About 200 library staff personnel participated in the program. A contribution of the trained staff was the implementation of the first basis for a library organization outside Mexico City, where there were virtually no professional librarians, becoming the backbone of library development in those areas. The following sections include more information on special libraries by sub-type.

Science and Technology Libraries

This group of special libraries is closely related to the National Council of Science and Technology. The Council funds 26 basic science and science and technology research centers and their libraries, plus two social sciences institutions: El Colegio de México, and the Mexican unit of Latin American Faculty of Social Sciences, or FLACSO (Facultad Latinoamericana de Ciencias Sociales). This nation-wide science and technology library network subscribes jointly to electronic sources, and organizes an annual library meeting. The larger libraries are those of the Center for Scientific Research and Graduate Education of Ensenada, or CICESE (Centro de Información Científica y Educación Superior de Ensenada), the Research Center of Applied Chemistry, or CIQA (Centro de Investigación en Química Aplicada), and El Colegio de México, a social science think tank that has the largest bibliographic collection in Latin America. Some of these research centers have postgraduate programs focused on research training. Similar social science institutions focusing on local studies are replicated in some states. These institutions generally have good libraries not necessarily supported by CONACYT funding.

Research Institute Libraries

Research institute libraries that serve research communities/centers are also outstanding. UNAM, the national university, produces a great proportion of the national research output, an activity that relies on important specialized collections. Its special libraries number 52, of the total of 142 libraries.[33] Their collections are in paper and in electronic format, and their library staff also number among the best. Additionally, most of the state universities also have special libraries, although fewer than UNAM. The better research institute libraries belong to the five larger universities from Guadalajara, Nuevo León, Puebla, Veracruz, and Universidad Metropolitana in Mexico City. As stated, the IPN, as discussed above, is the largest technological institute. It has 12 special libraries that support different areas of research. Another center with an excellent library is the Center of Advanced Studies and Research, or CINVESTAV (Centro de Investigaciones y de Estudios Avanzados), a center that was formerly part of the National Polytechnic Institute. At a national level, it probably has the largest science and technology collection housed under one roof, and includes some branch libraries in the regional research centers. The Postgraduate College of Chapingo (Colegio de Posgraduados de Chapingo), a specialized agricultural institution that networks with related institutions from other states, has the largest library in its field in Mexico. Private universities do not normally have special libraries, except for ITESM in business information, because, as mentioned, they are mainly teaching institutions with no research or minimal research output.

Government Libraries

Government libraries are, as might be expected, part of ministries, larger government official organizations, and part of federal and state departments. Many of the libraries have leading collections in their fields, such as those in the Foreign Relations Ministry (Secretaría de Relaciones Exteriores), and at the Treasury Ministry Library (Secretaría de Hacienda). The Mexican Congress Library, with legal deposit status, also has a good collection. Another is the National Institute of Anthropology and History, housing an outstanding collection, the largest in this field. Some of the government energy companies have research centers, normally with independent legal status, such as the Mexican Petroleum Institute, or IMP (Instituto Mexicano del Petróleo) that holds the major collection in the country on petroleum-related subjects, and the Institute of Electrical Research Institute (Instituto de Investigaciones Eléctricas) also an excellent information center with the best collection, resources and services in electricity, and secondarily in other energy subjects. A third library on atomic energy is the Institute of Nuclear Research (Instituto de Investigaciones Nucleares).[34] Government statistics on population (census), geography, and macro-statistics are provided by the INEGI, originally founded in 1925. It recently received independent legal status from the government to ensure objectivity in its data gathering. It is in charge of the national census and with collecting most types of socio-economic data. INEGI has a network of 46 information centers, plus 560 deposit libraries. Health science libraries are well-developed, thanks to the Mexican Social Security Institute, or IMSS (Instituto Mexicano del Seguro Social). The IMSS has the largest public health network, serving employees and workers from the private sector. It has some of the largest hospitals, clinics and health care facilities, and its 57 libraries are often the only sources of medical information in the smaller cities. The Institute subscribes on a nationwide basis electronic sources, so that each center has similar access to information sources. The Ministry of Public Health has about 15 good libraries that serve the specialized research institutes (mostly based in Mexico City) conducting medical science research in fields such as oncology, genomics, nutrition, and children's health, among other fields. The judiciary system also has special library units in the different states, in the so-called Culture House (Casa de Cultura), along with the Supreme Court library in the national capital.

Private Libraries

The private sector, i.e., industry, service corporations, and businesses, among others, has fewer special libraries. Data about these libraries is difficult to obtain, but it can be said that some, not all, of the large corporate companies have libraries at their headquarters. The Mexican economy is dependent on foreign corporations, mainly from the United States, and secondarily from European nations. Therefore, the branches located on Mexican soil seldom have information centers or libraries because these services are provided from the headquarters located outside Mexico. Additionally, the advent of electronic services has helped companies to reduce the number of private special libraries because it is now easier to transfer information across borders using seamless Internet and World Wide Web services. Those companies with libraries are mainly in the three largest cities, and, to a lesser extent, in the rest of the country. Some of the best examples are the libraries of the capital's newspapers: *Reforma*, *Excélsior*, *El Financiero*, and *La Jornada*; those in consulting firms, such as Mackenzie; in large law firms and major banks, and in companies like Grupo Condumex, which has a rich collection of historic Mexican publications.

NATIONAL LIBRARY INSTITUTIONS

The national duty of preserving the country's intellectual and cultural heritage is divided among several institutions. The main ones include the National Library that was founded in 1867, although the first law that unsuccessfully attempted to create it dates back to 1846. The first legal deposit decree to help the National Library to collect publications is from 1812, with successive updates since then up to the most recent one in 1991.[35] The National Library was a government run institution up to 1929, when responsibility for it was turned over to the National University (UNAM) that manages and houses it in the main campus. The National Library also became part of the Institute of Bibliographic Research, or IIB (Instituto de Investigaciones Bibliográficas) in 1967. The IIB is divided into two departments, one for the National Library itself, devoted mainly to monographs, and the second for the National Serials Collection (Hemeroteca Nacional de México). The Institute has 26 researchers who are in charge of the national bibliography and other research programs. The two collections are housed in separate units within the same building. They were originally in a former Agustin temple in the historical center of Mexico City until 1979, when a new building was constructed to house them. The Library and the serials collection have the richest bibliographic jewels of the nation: incunabula from Mexico and Europe, unique Mexican monograph copies, and archives and manuscripts from Mexico's colonial period, i.e., fifteenth century, to publications of the twentieth century. These rare and special collections are probably the most important in the former New Spain viceroy cities of Latin America. The National Library collection numbers over 2,286,292 books and documents, including music records, videos, plus the reserved collections. The Library has, as it may be expected, closed stacks, but the study rooms are open to researchers and to the general public. It also offers source cataloging to editors and publishes the national bibliography *Mexican Bibliography* (Bibliografía Mexicana), and allows the public to search their online catalog, called Nautilo. The serials library has two collections: the oldest, including titles from 1722 to 1916, and the contemporary titles. In recent years, it has been converting newspapers from several Mexican cities into digital format. The current digital collection has nine million images to date. This will be a major news source for researchers who live outside the national capital. Both institutions, unfortunately, lack the authority and resources that would be needed to guide acquisitions, technical and library service development for the rest of the libraries at the national level, as is the case in similar institutions in other countries. Their role is mainly to safeguard the national printed materials.

Other libraries use the term "National," such as the central library of the National Polytechnic Institute (Instituto Politécnico Nacional) that specializes in science and technology materials, as well as the library of the National Institute of Anthropology (Instituto Nacional de Antropología). However the term does not really complies with their institutional roles, because they, again, lack a national library leadership or coordination role in their subjects of interest. The Library of the Mexican Congress (Biblioteca del Congreso, 1935) is also a legal deposit center. Its collection covers all subjects and includes rare books from 1511 to 1930, plus 66 manuscripts. In addition, Mexico also has similar organizations that preserve and collect movie reels at the Filmoteca (Films House), and government official archives at the General Archives of the Nation, described in the Archives section. Some Mexican states also have similar institutions.

VIRTUAL/DIGITAL LIBRARIES

Most, if not all, of the virtual libraries have been developed at universities. Only a few libraries include all four elements of the virtual library concept: electronic resources, digitization of materials, software infrastructure, and virtual library services. Most state university libraries and private university libraries subscribe to electronic databases but not all have federated search capabilities. Digitization of collections, mainly historical materials or non-copyrighted materials, is conducted at perhaps 25–30 institutions, including universities and research centers. The principal collections are UNAM's nearly 40,000 digitized theses, Universidad de las Americas (Puebla)'s historical collections, Universidad Veracruzana's historical archives and institutional journals, and the rare archives being digitized at the Universidad Autónoma de Ciudad Juárez, among other collections. In addition, the National Library and the National Serials Collection are undertaking, as stated, the digital conversion of microfilmed national newspapers to digital formats. In terms of software, the first institution to acquire a federated search engine in Mexico and Latin America was the Universidad Veracruzana, in 2003. They also purchased virtual reference software (QuestionPoint),[36] again making it the first library in the Latin American region to do so. Currently about 20 institutions have a search engine and fewer than that offer virtual reference services. The UNAM has worked on the development of an in-house meta search engine, called Hermes, that so far, is just for institutional use.

Repository management software, Personal Digital Libraries has been developed by the Tecnológico de Monterrey, but its use seems to be losing ground with the increased adoption of Dspace, the program created by the Massachusetts Institute of Technology. Another repository management software that is also used, but to a lesser degree, is Greenstone, developed by the New Zealand Digital Library Project at the University of Waikato, using UNESCO funding. A related open access journal repository, the Network of Scientific Magazines from Latin America, the Caribbean, Spain, and Portugal, or REDALyC (Red de Revistas Científicas de América Latina, el Caribe, España y Portugal), started in 2003, was created by the Autonomous University of the State of Mexico, UAEM (Universidad Autónoma del Estado de México). The system includes journals from Latin America, the Caribbean Region, Spain, and Portugal. It currently hosts more than 550 titles in all social and scientific areas with electronic holdings of 100,000 peer-reviewed articles in Spanish, Portuguese, and English. According to REDALyC's official statistics, 70,000 articles are downloaded daily, a good indicator of success.

LIBRARY EDUCATION

Mexican library schools have graduated around 4500 librarians: 4300 with undergraduate degrees, 270 with master's degrees and 15 with doctorates. This means that most professionals working in libraries do not hold a library degree. Those with library degrees work mainly at university and special libraries, because, as stated, school and public libraries seldom have professionals on their staff. There are 11 library and information science programs (see Appendix 2). The first school was founded as early as 1924, but it had its difficulties and closed. Later on, in 1945 was founded what is now the oldest running library School in Mexico City: the National School of Librarianship and Archives (Escuela Nacional de Biblioteconomía y Archivonomía) under the sponsorship of the Ministry of Public Education.[37] The second oldest library school is at the National University (UNAM), also located in Mexico City (1956). These two were the only library schools until 1970, when new library schools were created in the succeeding years. Most institutions offer undergraduate programs, only three offer the master's degree, and just one, UNAM, offers a doctoral program (since 1998), the first one in Spanish-speaking Latin America. Among the programs, four offer distance education degrees, three undergraduate, and one offers a master's degree. Library schools and programs are basically located in the three major cities, except for four programs located in the rest of the country (see Appendix 2). Most schools include the name "library science", except for three that include the terms "documentation", "information science" and "knowledge management and information". Dissertations are required at some of the institutions. Several of the library schools lack a full-time faculty or have a minimum number of professors, except for UNAM, ENBA, SLP and Toluca that have more consolidated faculty. There are also library technical programs at the high school and college level in Mexico City. The newest at the college level, Técnico Superior Universitario, started in 2008 and is offered by the Universidad Veracruzana. Students in this program earn a library technical training certificate in 2 years. Continuing education is a common way to train professional staff. Courses are offered by library associations, the University Library Research Center, or CUIB (Centro Universitario de Investigaciones Bibliotecológicas) at UNAM, and some major libraries.

CUIB is the largest library research center in Latin America, founded in 1981, with a publishing output of 127 books, and the leading library journal in Mexico, as well as the best and largest library collection, and 25 full-time researchers, most of them with a doctorate and recognized by the National System of Researchers of the National Council of Science and Technology. Universities offer in-house "diplomados," informal training programs for their staff, which cover basic library subjects and run for some months.

ACCREDITATION—CROSS-BORDER HIRING OF LIBRARIANS

Although there are few librarians in Mexico, there are a number of librarians who cross the border to work in U.S. libraries. Their degrees are unfortunately not recognized by U.S. libraries because they do not come from library schools with American Library Association accreditation. Librarians who come from the United States and Mexicans who have graduated from library schools in America face the same challenge in Mexico. Their degrees are not fully recognized. Mexicans have the option of undergoing a long process to get government certification that includes complicated paper work from the Mexican Foreign Relations and the Public Education Ministry, and the National University's curriculum review. Most professionals avoid the process—even those who work at academic institutions, where the recognition of foreign library degrees is important for tenure. Librarians who immigrate to the United States normally have to complete a master's degree in the library school field if they want to have the appropriate credentials required by the American library profession. This means that there is an international opportunity to create a library school accreditation agreement between Mexico, the United States and Canada. It would certainly benefit Mexican library school graduates, who could work on either side of the border with an accredited degree. Obviously this task is not easy, because library school programs may need to be aligned and recognized as comparable, that is, they may need to be similar, at least in the basic subjects that are the essence of library schools and information science. The North American countries, Canada, the United States, and Mexico, could follow the pattern of the European Bologna process, which is unifying library school education programs across Europe. Another alternative would be to recognize the accreditation process used in each of the countries.

Accreditation in Mexico is fairly new. The official external evaluation body, the Inter-institutional Committees for the Evaluation of Higher Education, or CIEES (Comités Inter-Institucionales de Evaluación de la Educación Superior) was created in 1991, and the Council for the Accreditation of Higher Education, or COPAES (Consejo Nacional de Educación Superior) dates from 2001. COPAES relies on professional associations, i.e., guilds, or what we call "College of Professionals" to conduct the whole process. Institutions whose programs undergo the evaluation can receive more federal funding and other benefits from the Ministry of Public Education. Library schools and the Mexican Library Association have been slow in pushing for a full accreditation program beyond the evaluation review that they currently undergo. The body that could potentially play the role of accrediting agency for library schools is the National Librarians Guild or CNB (Colegio Nacional de Bibliotecarios), the professional librarian guild in the country. Unfortunately, it is a small organization, currently without the means to fully undertake this role, crucial to increasing the quality of library education in Mexico. There is an accredited library school, the UAEM. However, it received its certification from a social sciences organization; therefore it is not a library body. In conjunction with our library associations, the North American Free Trade Agreement (NAFTA) provides the opportunity to create an accreditation system for the three countries, the United States, Mexico, and Canada, or at least to establish some type of recognition for North American cross-border degrees.

THE U.S. PATTERN

Library science and its practice in Mexico are based on U. S. library principles. For example, university libraries in Mexico use the U.S. Library of Congress Classification system, while public libraries use the Dewey Decimal System, and all libraries that have a bibliographic organization use Anglo-American Cataloguing Rules. There are reasons for these facts: the first librarians to get training went to the US to get their degrees in the early 1920s, and into the seventies, when Mexico established an ambitious library program for academic librarians that launched library development. There were, as mentioned earlier (See Special Libraries section), several tens of scholarships being granted to students to go to the United States to obtain a master's degree in library science or information science. The main library schools that received these students were the University of Texas at Austin, and later the universities of Syracuse, Cleveland, and Denver. The last major group, 23 people, to get a library master's degree at a U.S. library school (University of Wisconsin at Milwaukee), was financed by the ITESM. In addition to these programs, the US has also granted scholarships to several students through the Fulbright program. An institution that additionally has played a key role in promoting library principles is the Benjamin Franklin Library, the official information center of the United States Embassy in Mexico City. Inaugurated in 1942, this was the first public library created by the American government outside the Unites States, and of the few full-sized libraries to remain after recent government downsizing. Many professionals, mainly from Mexico City, had their first library experiences at this library, either as reference assistants or student assistants. Some later became professional librarians, by getting scholarships to obtain a degree in the United States. Between the 1960s and the 1970s, the Franklin Library was one of the best public libraries in Mexico City, and thus a model followed by other institutions in the capital of the country.

SERIALS

The text of this section is an extract from a paper devoted to serials by the author.[38] The oldest circulating serials in Mexico date back to the 1800s, such as *Bulletin, Mexican Society of Geography and Statistics* (Boletín, Sociedad Mexicana de Geografía y Estadística) (1839, ISSN 0188-1442), *Medical Newspaper of Mexico* (Gaceta Médica de México) (1864, ISSN 0016-3813), and *Yearbook of the National Astronomic Observatory* (Anuario del Observatorio Astronómico Nacional) (1881). However, the first serials appeared in Mexico in the 1700s, such as *Literary Newspaper of Mexico* (Diario Literario de México) (1766), *Mercury Flyer* (Mercurio Volante, the first medical magazine in America) (1772–1773), and *Varied Issues on Science and Arts* (Asuntos Varios sobre Ciencias y Artes) (1772–1773). These serials were the first in the American continent.[39] The International Standard Serial Number Agency (ISSN) reports 3431 Mexican periodicals,[40] although it is estimated that there are at least twice as many, due to the fact that many periodicals lack ISSN registration.[41] Journals are, in general, published by state universities and by national research centers financed by the government (usually the federal government). Subject coverage of journals is wide, covering most disciplines and subjects. However the strength is in the social sciences and the humanities, where 60% of the production is published.[41] There is also a significant number of cultural periodicals, like those from other countries. Mexican serials are the best sources for updated academic and scientific information because they publish the best output of researchers and writers. Electronic journals are emerging in good numbers; with some now only published in electronic versions. Library serials number about 10 depending on how one classifies them; several titles have appeared only for short time spans (see Appendix 3).

In terms of comics and magazines, Mexico has a significant number of these, with large audiences. Some of the most popular titles can reach nearly a million copies per week.[42] These periodicals play an important role in fostering reading habits among those who have only a few years of schooling, and even among those who did not have the chance to attend school. Comics are also a huge export to the United States, where Hispanic communities also love to read cowboy and soap opera style stories. As it may be assumed, these serials are the business of private companies who publish numerous titles covering a variety of topics.

Newspapers, on the other hand, have a market usually divided into four tiers according to the geographical locations where the papers are published, a fact that correlates with the importance of the newspapers. First are the dailies from Mexico City. They dominate the market, because of their broader coverage and a good nation-wide distribution system, in addition to being the news agencies for smaller papers. Second in importance are the dailies from the two other major cities, Guadalajara and Monterrey. Both locations have succeeded in distributing their papers to the rest of the major cities. Third are the papers from the medium-sized cities, usually state capitals. They tend to have a distribution limited to the state borders and normally have good publishing facilities. Finally, the fourth tier of newspapers consists of the local community dailies. These periodicals are simple and modest, covering political subjects and local topics relevant to their communities. Many of them struggle to survive with limited resources. Some of the local papers are part of national editing companies, relying on their editorials for in-depth articles. Editing of newspapers from the first three tiers has improved over time. Currently, titles from the largest cities are edited electronically and posted on the Web, some publishing full articles and others putting out only summaries of their main news in their Internet versions.

BOOK PUBLISHING

As stated in the first section of the paper, Mexico was the first country in America to have a printing press in the sixteenth century. This means that Mexico probably has the greatest number of American incunabula that is found at the national library and at some university libraries. Nowadays publishing is an important economic activity, and it is one of the most important in the Latin American region. The other countries that also have a good production are Colombia and Argentina that compete in production. The Mexican book trade is mainly based in Mexico City, where most of the big American and European publishing houses have subsidiaries, plus national companies. After the Spanish civil war several editors migrated to Mexico and contributed to strengthen this industry. Mexican book production covers most subjects but the main output is devoted to basic education, where most of the volumes are printed, according to the statistics of the National Chamber of the Mexican Publishing Industry, CANIEM (Cámara Nacional de la Industria Editorial Mexicana). The country produced 18,682 titles in 2006 according to CANIEM. The production is devoted mainly to basic education (22%), literature (14%), science and technology (12%), and the rest to other subjects, including children books that stand out with 10% of the total publishing output. In terms of copies, basic education gets almost half of the total output with 47.3%, and children books get 20% of all the copies printed. The rest of the production is scattered in the several subjects, such as literature, languages, and philosophy, and psychology. Most of the printing production is, on the other hand, represented by reprintings of titles with 58.6%, new titles by 32.4%, and reeditions with 9%. This amounts 109 million copies.[30] The main costumer for publishers is the Mexican government with the free textbook program, and the acquisition of books for school libraries that was described in the section in earlier sections of this paper.

INFORMATION VENDORS

The proximity to the United States has made Mexico an attractive place for some American and other information vendors to set up offices. For some vendors, like EBSCO and OCLC, after Brazil, Mexico is the second largest library and information market. Companies that have established regional offices, in addition to the two corporations just mentioned, are Swets, Aleph, and Cengage. Other major international companies have local offices to cover the national market. The local information industry has steadily evolved in the last two decades. Business information is a thriving sector, growing faster than information services to the academic community. Information aggregators tend to focus on business information. Some were originally Mexican start-up companies that were later acquired by major overseas companies, such as Infolatina, that was bought by an American information aggregator. Some important information companies in the country are Mercamétrica (directories), IBCON (directories), El Financiero (financial information), and Reforma (syndicated news). Information services are also provided by chambers of commerce. Several of these organizations offer information services to companies and the government. Computer-integrated library systems, on the other hand, probably represent the larger segment in Spanish-speaking Latin America. The most popular one continues to be the Automated System for the Integration of Libraries of the University of Colima, or SIABUC (Sistema Integral Automatizado de Bibliotecas de la Universidad de Colima) created by the University of Colima, which has given away 1500 copies of the software in Latin America, according to a report provided by the institution. This software is nearly free; it requires just a minimum fee of fewer than $2000 for the original acquisition. Additionally, there are at least four companies that have created integral library systems for sale and distribution in Mexico and throughout the region, such as Altair and Janium.[43,44]

LIBRARY ASSOCIATIONS

Library associations date back to 1924, when the first one was founded. The first library conferences were organized in 1927 and 1928. This early association experienced difficulties, not becoming a formal association until 1954, then gaining legal recognition 2 years later, when it adopted the official name of the Mexican Association of Librarians, or AMBAC (Asociación Mexicana de Bibliotecarios, Acción Civil). AMBAC is recognized as the national library association and is headquartered in Mexico City. Since 1956, it has run the largest library conference, an event that became annual in 1977. The conference includes a major vendor exhibition, and its proceedings have been an important source of library literature for many years. It also publishes a quarterly newsletter *News from AMBAC* (Noticiero de AMBAC) that is the oldest continuously published library serial in the country (see Appendix 3). The association has subject sections, with current ones in arts, reading, national information policies, public libraries, school libraries, and information literacy. AMBAC formerly had geographical sections in some of the Mexican states, but they became independent associations when a tax reform affected the fiscal management of AMBAC. The states with associations are Baja California, Chihuahua, Jalisco, Michoacán, and Yucatán. In recent years, AMBAC has been trying to create geographical sections again, but Nuevo León is the only one in existence so far, although three more are in the process of formation. AMBAC does provide some support to the local library associations who continue to view it as their parent organization. The split with state associations has meant that AMBAC membership has not grown and still numbers about 500.

The second most important professional association, although small, is the CNB founded in 1979 in Mexico City. This body only includes librarians who have obtained a university degree. The CNB has, by law, the right to advice government and to conduct evaluation and accreditation processes in library schools because guilds are officially bodies that represent their professional discipline. In addition to CNB, there is the National Council of Library Affairs of Higher Education Institutions, or CONPAB-IES (Consejo Nacional para Asuntos Bibliotecarios de Instituciones de Educación Superior), described in the university libraries section. Some other associations have existed previously, like the Association of Libraries and Institutions of Higher Education and Research, or ABIESI (Asociación de Bibliotecas e Instituciones de Educación Superior y de Investigación), created in 1967, and disbanded in the 1990s. This association's main contribution was the publication of the interlibrary loan code and a set of library standards that are still quoted in the literature. Other short-lived associations, in existence for fewer than two decades have been in the fields of agriculture: the National Association of Agricultural Librarians ANBAGRO (Asociación Nacional de Bibliotecarios Agrícolas); government: Association of Librarians of Governmental Institutions of Mexico, or ABIGMAC (Asociación de Bibliotecarios de Instituciones Gubernamentales de México); and in the field of biomedicine: the Association of Librarians in Biomedicine, or BIBAC (Asociación de Bibliotecarios en Biomedicina), among other bodies. The life and activity of state associations is linked to the size of the library profession in the Mexican provinces, where, unlike in Mexico City, professional librarians are just a handful. The arrival of new library schools in some of the states may foster a local library association development. Generally, library associations and some leading library systems host annual library conferences on general and specialized subjects. These programs are probably the second, if not the premiere, conference offerings in Latin America (see Appendix 4).

INTERNATIONAL LIBRARY COOPERATION

With the most visible international activities, academic libraries lead in collaboration. The most extensive cooperation activity is with U.S. organizations, and to a lesser degree with Latin American and European countries. Mexican border universities often have strong collaborative ties with their counterparts on the other side of the border. For example, the Universidad Autónoma de Ciudad Juárez has borrowing agreements with New Mexico State University and with El Paso Community College, and the CICESE in Ensenada, Baja California, has cooperative agreements with the La Jolla Scripps Research Institute in San Diego. In addition to the academic institutions, the Mexican Library Association has strong links with its international counterparts from Latin American, under the International Federation of Library Associations and Institutions, as well as the principal U.S. library associations that include the American Library Association, the Special Libraries Association, and REFORMA (who have opened paths for cooperation), as well as some state organizations. Cooperation takes the form of visiting speakers attending annual conferences, facilitation of workshops, staff exchanges, and materials exchange. Seal produced an excellent paper documenting U.S.–Mexico collaboration.[45] The best communication venue for U.S.–Mexico cooperation is the FORO, Transborder Library Forum, where some Canadians have also participated, the meeting that began as an annual event in 1991 became, after a decade, a bi-annual conference.[46] It alternates between Mexico and the United States. The FORO was originally organized as a reaction to the NAFTA agreement to strengthen the relationships among border libraries. One of the FORO's byproducts is the multilateral interlibrary loan project between U.S. universities and central Mexican institutions, with the Franklin Library playing a key role facilitating the shipment of bibliographic materials by diplomatic pouch.

ARCHIVES

Like libraries, archives began, in the western sense, after the Spanish conquest of Mexico. Archives were formed during the colonial era in monasteries and churches where registration births, deaths, and property transactions took place. Civic life was directed, in many ways, by the Catholic Church until the nineteenth century. The best source of Mexico's colonial history is the Archives of Indies in Seville, Spain, where the most important records of colonial life are stored. The government had split from the Catholic Church in 1855, creating the national birth registry, when Benito Juárez, then president and a great political reformer, opened the registry office in Veracruz, and the first birth certificate was issued to his daughter in 1859. Several archives of churches and religious groups passed to other government organizations or to especially created archival institutions. The main archive is the General Archives of the Nation, or AGN (Archivos Generales de la Nación), located at the former Lecumberri Prison in Mexico City, where cells now hold different sections of the file collection. The AGN is the leading organization in archives policies and filing standards, with its own organization scheme followed by several archives in the country. Most states have an archive system or structure that coordinates those in the municipalities. Among them are the property offices in each city. They make copies of their documentation to be sent to the state capital's general archives. A similar pattern is followed by birth registries. The new law on information transparency is improving, and will continue to improve, archives, because all government ministries, departments, and official bodies, including public universities, have to include organized archives and make them available to the public via the Web. The body in charge of implementing policies and supervising the legal implementations is the Federal Institute of Information Access.

There are several historical archives located in the large urban centers, mainly those with a colonial past. A survey conducted in 2007 by the Association to Support the Development of Archives and Libraries, or ADABI (Asociación de Apoyo al Desarrollo de Archivos y Bibliotecas en México, AC) identified 142 archives, but this number only corresponds to those that have printed inventory catalogs. The survey classified them in the following categories: 75 parochial archives, mainly from the Catholic Church; 53 state and county archives (included historical and administrative archives); and 14 historical archives covering colonial, independence and revolution materials.[47] The 12 most important private archives are in Campeche, Mexico City, Oaxaca, Puebla, Tamaulipas, and Yucatán. One diocesan archive was reported in the State of Guerrero, in the Southwestern part of the country. Presumably, the archives reported in this study are well-managed, if it is assumed that those who answered have organized archives. However, the total number of historical archives throughout the country may be 3 times this figure. Another study attempting to identify how modern archives were in terms of their organization and storage estimated that 67% of them have a budget that is lower than $25,000 and 10% have budgets of fewer than $100,000 annually. Additional findings were that 85% of the archives have internal regulations and security measures, and 29% have temperature and humidity control systems, and 85% have computers. Most of the archives, 85%, are open to the public. The results of the study are, in general, positive.[48] There are three archive associations, included the one mentioned above, ADABI. This association organizes conferences and meetings and is probably the largest. Two other are the Mexican Association of Libraries and Institutions with Old Collections, AMBIFA (Asociación Mexicana de Bibliotecas e Instituciones de Fondos Antiguos), and the Mexican Association of Private Archives and Libraries, AMABPAC (Asociación Mexicana de Archivos y Bibliotecas Privados, AC). All of these associations have Web sites with membership information. Only two academic institutions offer undergraduate archives studies, they are the National School of Librarianship and Archival Science, or ENBA (Escuela Nacional de Biblioteconomía y Archivonomía) and the Universidad de San Luis Potosí. The first is the older one and has 862 graduates, while the second has just started awarding baccalaureate degrees in archives or records management.

MUSEUMS

Like other institutions discussed in this entry, the organization, collections and economic resources of the 1137 Mexican museums are closely related to the size of the city where they are located. Mexico City ranks number one, with the largest number of museums and with most of the best collections, followed by Guadalajara and Monterrey. The rest of the state capitals have an average of four museums, plus those in the rest of each state outside these capitals. Museums have increased substantially since the beginning of the last century (1907) when there were 38, according to the Mexican Association of Museum Professionals, or AMProM (Asociación Mexicana de Profesionales de Museos).[49] It is also estimated that 60% of the museums are devoted to anthropology and history, 25% to fine arts, and 10% to science and technology, plus other subjects, including children's museums, accounting for about 1%. Along with the classical twentieth century concept of museums, there are also zoos, aquariums, and natural reserves that are not discussed in this paper.

Museums are created and managed by different bodies, including the federal, state, and municipal governments, communities, the private sector, and companies or individuals. The National Institute of Anthropology and History, or INAH (Instituto Nacional de Antropología e Historia),[50] is probably the largest organization that manages museums, 244. It groups museums into six main categories:

1. National museums have country-wide collections and are located in Mexico City. The largest and the best INAH museum is the Anthropology museum that holds some of the most valuable collections of Mexican indigenous cultures.
2. Regional museums cover more than one state and are located in different parts of the country. A good example is the Museum of Cultures (Museo de las Culturas) in Oaxaca.
3. Local museums that are in historical buildings or that hold different collections, such as the Customs House of Ciudad Juárez (Ex-Aduana).
4. Community center museums, such as the outstanding Convent of Tepoztlan (Ex-Convento de Tepoztlán).
5. Community museums hold collections, usually of archeological artifacts, valued by communities.
6. In situ museums whose collections are in archeological sites, where artifacts and information are derived from the same grounds. The most outstanding ones are Chichen-Itza, the Teotihuacan Pyramids, and Uxmal.

The states with the largest numbers of museums, outside Mexico City, include Jalisco with 54 (where Guadalajara is the capital), Veracruz with 18, and Chiapas has the largest number of community museums, 35.

The second organization managing museums is the CONACULTA. This federal governmental body manages 132 museums and galleries. The best are in the Palace of Fine Arts (Palacio de Bellas Artes). Another federal organization that takes care of museums and art galleries is the National Institute of Fine Arts, or INBA (Instituto Nacional de Bellas Artes).[51] It has some excellent museums like National Museum of San Carlos; the Museum of Modern Art and the Tamayo Collection. Private museums run by individuals, companies, and foundations are generally small, however, there are some fine examples of good-sized collections and notable buildings, such as the bank BANAMEX and the Franz Mayer Museum.

Some of the best museums in Mexico City for the general tourist, regardless of the body that manages them, are the mentioned National Museum of Anthropology, Modern Art, Tamayo, National Museum of Fine Arts (Museo Nacional de Arte), and the Papalote (a children's interactive science museum). Smaller thriving museums of interest in the capital include the Frida Kahlo, the Dolores Olmedo Museum that houses Riveras' works and the largest collection of Kahlo's paintings, and the private Franz Mayer Museum for the decorative arts. Guadalajara, the second largest city, also offers some good museums of interest to the outside visitor such as the Regional Museum of Guadalajara and the Popular Arts Museum (Museo de Artes Populares). Guadalajara has undertaken a project to build a Guggenheim museum. A group of private investors paid for a two million dollar feasibility study and the state government financed a call for an architectural building design contest. The planned premises are in a beautiful canyon rim in the outskirts of the city. This initiative may have behind it the idea of competing with Monterrey, located in Northern Mexico, where a cultural corridor has been created in the heart of the city flanked by first class museums, making it the second cultural capital in the country. Its most outstanding museums and galleries are the Contemporary Art Museum, or MARCO (Museo de Arte Contemporáneo), the Museum of Mexican History (Museo de Historia Mexicana), and the Glass Museum (Museo del Vidrio), each housing excellent collections. The rest of the state capitals have fewer collections of smaller size and less financial support. Although there are some that are outstanding, such as the described archeological museums of Oaxaca and Veracruz (see Fig. 6).

Additionally, Mexican archeological sites number in the thousands, and they are certainly living museums. If the sites are lumped together with historical places, the number is 110,442. The challenges of cataloging them are great: 60% are cataloged or are in process, and 173 of them are open to the public, with nearly 10 million visitors per year.[50] The top archeological sites are Mayan—Tulum, and Palenque in addition to those listed—plus the Zapotecan Monte Alban and Mitla in Oaxaca, the Totonaca site Tajin in Veracruz, and the Aztecan Templo Mayor in Mexico City, and finally, the Olmec culture, the earliest known Mexican civilization, that dates back to 3000 years ago with the Tres Zapotes site.

A great feature of Mexican art is the muralist plastic movement that took place after the Mexican Revolution (1921), a time when Mexican identity was redefined. It was basically a nationalistic movement that focused on the indigenous people and on criticism of Spanish and foreign influences. The best-known include David Alfaro Siqueiros, Diego Rivera, José Clemente Orozco, and Juan O'Gorman, among others. Locations with murals in Mexico City by these muralists and those of their followers include the National Palace (Palacio Nacional), the Palace of Fine Arts (Palacio de Bellas Artes), the Central Library at UNAM, and the San Ildelfonso Museum (Museo de San Ildelfonso), among others. There are also murals in the rest of the states.

Fig. 6 Museum of Anthropology, Xalapa, Veracruz—by Héctor Nava.

The best, normally the larger museums, have libraries, such as the National Museum of Art, or MUNAL (Museo Nacional de Arte), Interactive Museum of Economy, or MIDE (Museo Interactivo de Economía), the Museum of Light (Museo de la Luz), and the National Museum of Anthropology (Museo Nacional de Antropología) in Mexico City, and the Museum of Mexican History (Museo de Historia Mexicana) in Monterrey. It is estimated that about 50 museums have libraries. The most outstanding is the large National Library of Anthropology and History attached to the museum of the same name, mentioned in the Special Libraries section of this entry.[52]

Professionals working in museums have degrees in other fields, because there are very few options to get a university degree in this specific subject. The only public university that has a related program for museum professionals at Baccalaureate, Master and Doctorate is UNAM. The studies are in history of art. Additionally, one private university offers a program in the same field and two more on cultural promotion. None of these programs are specifically designed for museum management, but do give the basic background in art. Another option for museum staff is training through courses and workshops organized by the museums themselves and universities and are mainly held in Mexico City.

CONCLUSIONS

This overview of libraries, museums, and archives is just a snapshot because it is difficult to portray the country that is large and has great differences between big and small cities, as well as between urban and rural regions. In conclusion, Mexico has some of the best libraries in Latin America; however, their development is uneven. In terms of growth and quality of library services, state university libraries and large private higher education institutions are in the leaders. However, at the bottom are several smaller public and private academic institutions that lag behind. Special libraries are also among the best libraries with good budgets, collections, and professional staff, but several companies fail to provide information services as part of their organizational structure. The public library system is the largest in Latin America and its growth and improvement has been indeed, a major achievement in the last 25 years. Its collection development is centralized in Mexico City but buildings and staff are the responsibility of the states and the municipalities. School libraries on the other hand, are few, considering the large number of primary and secondary education schools in Mexico, but the government has invested heavily in creating classroom collections, distributing more than 200 million volumes in the last 7 years. Because the number of librarians is inadequate, the country would benefit from more library school graduates. The national information institutions, such as the national library, and the national serials collection have good bibliographic treasures of colonial and contemporary Mexico, but their leading role is limited. There are many museums in Mexico, most of them are devoted to anthropology due to the great interest in pre-Columbian history. The largest number of museums is concentrated in Mexico City and the two other major cities

Appendix 1: Library Chronology

Year	Event
1400	Amoxcalli-Aztec codex (Amoxtli) libraries
1511	First book arrives in Mexico from Europe
1539	First printing press
1555	First book printed in Mexico—Alonso de Molina *Vocabulario en lengua castellana y mexicana*
1788	Opening of the first public library—Turriana Library
1790	First copyright law
1790	Foundation of the first Museum of Natural History
1790	Foundation of the National Archives—Archivo General de la Nación (Original name: Archivo General de la Nueva España)
1825	Foundation of the Mexican National Museum
1867	First decree to create the National Library—Biblioteca Nacional
1882	National Institute of Statistics, Geography, and Informatics (Originally as Dirección, Geografía y Estadística, DGE)—Instituto Nacional de Estadística, Geografía e Informática
1910	Opening of the National Museum of Archeology, History, and Ethnography (formerly known as the Mexican National Museum)
1921	First Department of Public Libraries, Ministry of Public Education—Dirección de Bibliotecas Populares
1922	First public library building—Biblioteca Pública Cervantes
1924/1954	Mexican Association of Librarians—Asociación Mexicana de Bibliotecarios, AC
1939	Foundation of the National Institute of Anthropology and History
1940	The National Museum of Archeology, History, and Ethnography changed its name to National Museum of Anthropology
1945	National School of Library and Archive Sciences—Escuela Nacional de Biblioteconomía y Archivonomía
1956	Opening of the UNAM Central Library Building—Biblioteca Central UNAM

(Continued)

Appendix 1: Library Chronology *(Continued)*

Year	Event
1957	First national library conference—Jornadas Mexicanas de Biblioteconomía, organized annually since 1974
1970	Foundation of the National Council of Science and Technology (An early funding body for special and university libraries)—Consejo Nacional de Ciencia y Tecnología
1970	Labor unions take power at academic libraries, and at universities in general
1972	First library science master's degree—UNAM
1975	First academic library building of a technological institute—IT Saltillo
1978	First Mexican integral (mainframe) library system—LIBRUNAM, UNAM
1983	First release of the library software SIABUC (Most popular free library software)—Universidad de Colima
1984	Foundation of the National Council for Academic Libraries—CONPAB-IES, Consejo Nacional de Asuntos Bibliotecarios de Instituciones de Educación Superior
1988	First librarian to get a Ph.D. (From the United States)—Jaime Pontigo
1999	UNAM Ph.D. program started—UNAM
2003	Mexican Information Literacy Standards are approved for higher education

Appendix 2: Library Science Schools

School	Address	Phone/Fax
El Colegio de México, AC Maestría en Bibliotecología	Camino al Ajusco 20, Pedregal de Santa Teresa, Del. Magdalena Contreras, 10740 México, DF http://www.colmex.mx/	(55) 5449-9909 5449-3000 x2113 Fax: 5645-4584
ENBA—Escuela Nacional de Biblioteconomía y Archivonomía	Calz. Ticomán 645, Col Santa María	(55) 5329-7176
	Ticomán, Del. Gustavo A. Madero, 07330 México, DF	5329-7181
Licenciatura en Biblioteconomía	http://www.enba.sep.gob.mx/	
ÍTESM—Instituto Tecnológico de Estudios Superiores de Monterrey	Eugenio Garza Sada 2501, Col. Tecnológico, Edif. CEDES, Semisótano 1	01800 112-2832
Maestría en Ciencias de la Información y Administración del conocimiento	64849 Monterrey, NL	
	http://www.ruv.itesm.mx/portal/promocion/oe/m/mik/	
UACH—Universidad Autónoma de Chihuahua	Av. Universidad S/N, Cd. Universitaria, Apartado Postal 744, 31240 Chihuahua, Chih. http://www.ffyluach.mx Fax: 414-4932	(614) 413-3449
Licenciatura en Ciencias de la Información		
UANL—Universidad Autónoma de Nuevo León	Av. Alfonso Reyes s/n, Ciudad Universitaria,	(81) 8376-0620
		8376-0780
Lic. en Bibliotecología y Ciencias de la Información	66450 San Nicolás de los Garza, NL	Fax: 8352-5690
	http://www.dsi.uanl.mx	
UASLP—Universidad Autónoma de San Luis Potosí	Álvaro Obregón 64, Col. Centro,	(444) 818-2522 818-9025
	78000 San Luís Potosí, SLP	Fax: 818-2521
Licenciatura en Bibliotecología e Información	http://www.uaslp.mx	
UNACH—Universidad Autónoma de Chiapas Licenciatura en Bibliotecología	Calle Canarios y Av. Central S/N, Col. Buenos Aires, Delegación Terán, San Cristóbal de las Casas, Chis. http://www.unach.mx	(961) 615-1101
UNAM—Universidad Nacional Autónoma de México	Circuito Interior,	College degree
	Ciudad Universitaria, Delegación Coyoacán	(55) 5622-1881

(Continued)

Appendix 2: Library Science Schools *(Continued)*

School	Address	Phone/Fax
Licenciatura en Bibliotecología y Estudios de la Información	04510 México, DF	Master degree and Doctorate
	http://www.unam.mx	(55) 5616-6823
Maestría y doctorado en Bibliotecología y Estudios de la Información	http://www.filos.unam.mx/ POSGRADO/biblio1.htm	
UAG—Universidad Autónoma de Guadalajara	Av. Patria 1201, Lomas del Valle, 3ª. Sección, 45110 Zapopan, Jal.	(33) 3648-8767
Lic. en Ciencias de la Información	http://www.uag.mx	
UAEM—Universidad Autónoma del Estado de México	Av. Universidad Esq. Paseo Tollocan s/n, Cerro de Coatepec, Ciudad Universitaria,	(722) 213-1407
		Fax: 213-1533
Licenciatura en Ciencias de la Información Documental	50110 Toluca, Estado de México	
	http://www.uaemex.mx/	

Appendix 3: Library Science Serials

Title	Editor	Frequency	Address
Biblioteca Universitaria: Boletín Informativo de la Dirección General de Bibliotecas ISSN 0187-750X	Dirección General de Bibliotecas—Universidad Nacional Autónoma de México (UNAM)	Semestral	Biblioteca Central Circuito Interior, Ciudad Universitaria, Coyoacán 04510. México, DF informa@panoramx.dgbiblio.unam. mx http://www.dgbiblio.unam.mx/
Bibliotecas y Archivos ISSN 0185-0083	Escuela Nacional de Biblioteconomía y Archivonomía	Every 4 months	Calz. Ticomán 645, Col. Santa María Ticomán, Gustavo A. Madero, 07330. México, DF biblarch@enba.sep.gob.mx http://www.enba.sep.gob.mx/
Boletín Informativo de ASAR	ASAR, A. C.	Every 4 months	Calle 66, No. 3204, 31410. Chihuahua, Chih. Tel. (614) 411-3672
Hemera—Revista de Ciencias Bibliotecológicas y de la Información ISSN 1665-5834	Hemera	Semestral	Apartado Postal 23-098 BO. San Juan 16001. México, DF Tel. (55) 1509-0554/044 55 2695-8002 http://hemera.galeon.com/
Infobila (Database)	Centro Universitario de Investigaciones Bibliotecológicas, UNAM		Torre II de Humanidades, pisos 12 y 13, Ciudad Universitaria, Coyoacán, 04100. México, DF http://www.cuib.unam.mx
Información, Producción, Comunicación y Servicios ISSN 0188-5847	Infoconsultores, S. C.	Quarterly	Michoacán 30, Desp. 6, Col. Hipódromo, Cuauhtémoc, 06100. México, DF infoconsult@spin.com.mx
Investigación Bibliotecológica: archivonomía, bibliotecología e información ISSN 0187-358X	Centro Universitario de Investigaciones Bibliotecológicas, UNAM	Semestral	Torre II de Humanidades, pisos 12 y 13 Ciudad Universitaria, Coyoacán, 04100. México, DF http://www.cuib.unam.mx
LIBER: Revista de Bibliotecología. ISSN 0188-5847	AMBAC, A. C.	Quarterly	Ángel Urraza 817-A, Colonia del Valle, Benito Juárez 03100. México, DF liber@servidor.unam.mx http://www.ambac.org.mx
Memorias-Jornadas Mexicanas de Biblioteconomía	AMBAC, A. C.	Quarterly	Ángel Urraza 817-A, Colonia del Valle, Juárez 03100. México, DF Tel. y fax: 1152 (5) 5575-3396 http://www.ambac.org.mx
Noticiero de la AMBAC ISSN 0001-186X	AMBAC, A. C.	Quarterly	Ángel Urraza 817-A, Colonia del Valle, Benito Juárez, 03100. México, DF Tel. y fax: 1152 (5) 5575-33-96 ambac@solar.sar.net http://www.ambac.org.mx

Appendix 4: Library Science Conferences

Conference name	Place	Date	Organizing institution
Amigos http://www.udla.mx/amigos	Puebla, Pue.	February (Biannual)	Dirección de Bibliotecas, Universidad de las Américas
Coloquio Internacional de Bibliotecarios http://www.fil.com.mx/cultura/prog04/rub_prof.htm	Guadalajara, Jal.	November/December (First and last week)	Coordinación de Bibliotecas, Universidad de Guadalajara
Coloquio sobre Administración y Liderazgo en Información http://www.uv.mx/bvirtual/coloquio/	Veracruz, Ver.	September (Third week)	Unidad de Servicios Bibliotecarios y de Información, Universidad Veracruzana
Conferencia Internacional sobre Bibliotecas Universitarias http://www.dgb.unam.mx/conf2004.html	Mexico, DF	October (First two weeks)	Dirección General de Bibliotecas, UNAM
CUIB Coloquio Internacional de Investigación Bibliotecológica y de Información cuib.unam.mx/eventos.htm	Mexico, DF	September	Centro Universitario de Investigaciones Bibliotecológicas, UNAM
Congreso Nacional Bibliotecas Públicas http://dgb.conaculta.gob.mx	Site varies	August–September	Dirección General de Bibliotecas, CONACULTA
Encuentro sobre Desarrollo de Habilidades Informativas http://www.uacj.mx/bibliotecas/	Juarez, Chih.	October (Second week)	Dirección General de información y Acreditación, Universidad Autónoma de Ciudad Juárez
Enline@2000 enlinea.mty.itesm.mx/	Monterrey, NL	October	Instituto Tecnológico de Monterrey, Campus Eugenio Garza Sada
Foro Transfronterizo de Bibliotecas http://www.uach.mx/foro/es/	U.S.A./Mexico Site varies	March	Organizing institution varies
Interf@ces http://www.ucol.mx/interfaces/	Colima, Col.	November	Universidad de Colima
Jornadas Mexicanas de Biblioteconomía http://www.ambac.org.mx/	Site varies	May	Asociación Mexicana de Bibliotecarios, A. C.
Foro Social de Información, Documentación y Bibliotecas http://www.fsidyb2006.inforosocial.org/	Site varies	September (Biannual)	Círculo de Estudios sobre Bibliotecología Política y Social (México) y el Grupo de Estudios Sociales en Bibliotecología y Documentación (Argentina)
Reunión Anual CONPAB http://www.conpab.uaslp.mx/default1.htm	Site varies	Site varies	Consejo Nacional para Asuntos Bibliotecarios de las Instituciones de Educación Superior
Reunión Biblioteca de Ciencia y Tecnología IPN	Mexico, DF	August	Instituto Politécnico Nacional
Reunión de Bibliotecarios de la Península de Yucatán http://www.uady.mx/	Merida, Yuc.	October	Dirección de Bibliotecas, Universidad Autónoma de Yucatán

of Guadalajara and Monterrey, and there are some good museums in smaller cities. Archives are probably more evenly distributed throughout the country. Their development varies from very well organized and preserved ones, to small not well-preserved or well-organized archives with scarce resources.

ACKNOWLEDGMENT

Data gathering assistance: Sergio Gómez-Vinales and Jacobo Osuna.

REFERENCES

1. Economist.com. Country briefings: Mexico, http://www.economist.com/COUNTRIES/Mexico/profile.cfm?folder=Profile-Political%20Structure (accessed December 17, 2008).
2. World Bank. Mexico Country brief, http://web.worldbank.org/WBSITE/EXTERNAL/COUNTRIES/LACEXT/MEXICOEXTN/0,,menuPK:338407~pagePK:141132~piPK:141107~theSitePK:338397,00.html (accessed December 17, 2008).
3. SECTUR, *Sube México a séptimo lugar mundial en recepción de turistas*, Boletín 054; Secretaria de Turismo: Mexico, DF, July 2006, http://www.sectur.gob.mx/wb/

sectur/sect_Boletin_054_Sube_Mexico_a_septimo_lugar_mundi (accessed September 8, 2008).
4. Pohl, J. *Libros Antiguos: Códices de las tierras montañosas de México. Mesoamérica*; Fundación para el Avance de los Estudios Mesoamericanos Inc.: Crystal River, FL, http://www.famsi.org/spanish/research/pohl/jpcodices/pohlborgia1.html (accessed September 17, 2008).
5. Fernández de Zamora, R.M. In *La historia de la bibliotecas en México, un tema olvidado*, Proceedings of the 60th IFLA General Conference, Havana, Cuba, August, 21–27, 1994, http://www.ifla.org/IV/ifla60/60-ferr.htm (accessed September 3, 2008).
6. Secretaría de Educación Pública (SEP). *Creación de la Secretaría de Educación Pública, Nuestra Institución, Historia de la SEP*; Secretaría de Educación Pública: Mexico, [No Date]; 2–5, http://www.sep.gob.mx/wb/sep1/sep1_Historia_de_la_SEP (accessed September 13, 2008).
7. Asociación Nacional de Universidades e Instituciones de Educación Superior (ANUIES). *Lista de IES y/o unidades desconcentradas por orden alfabético*, Directorio Nacional de Instituciones de Educación Superior; ANUIES: Mexico, 2008, http://www.anuies.mx/la_anuies/diries/ (accessed September 11, 2008).
8. Instituto Nacional de Estadística Geografía e Información (INEGI) Educación. In *Anuario Estadístico de los Estados Unidos Mexicanos 2005*; INEGI: Mexico, DF, 2005; 17–19, http://www.inegi.gob.mx/prod_serv/contenidos/espanol/bvinegi/productos/integracion/pais/aeeum/2007/Aeeum071. pdf (accessed September 15, 2008).
9. Quijano, A. *Personal Interview*; Puebla, Mexico, September 4, 2008.
10. Consejo Nacional para Asuntos Bibliotecarios de Instituciones de Educación Superior (CONPAB) *Miembros*; CONPAB: Mexico, 2008, http://www.conpab.uaslp.mx/conpabies/integrantes.html (accessed September 15, 2008).
11. Universidad Nacional Autónoma de México (UNAM) *UNAM en números 2008*; Subdirección de Sistemas de Información y Estadística. UNAM: Mexico, 2008, September1–3.
12. Times Higher Education Supplement *World University Rankings 2008*; The Times Higher Education: London, U.K., 2008; 4–5, http://www.timeshighereducation.co.uk/hybrid.asp?typeCode=243&pubCode=1 (accessed September 16, 2008).
13. Vicerrectoría Ejecutiva Coordinación General de Planeación y Desarrollo Institucional, Universidad de Guadalajara (UDG). Numeralia septiembre 2, 2008; UDG: Mexico, http://www.udg.mx/content.php?id_categoria=69&portada=1 (accessed October 10, 2008).
14. Universidad Autónoma de Nuevo León (UANL). *Conoce la UANL*; Universidad Autónoma de Nuevo León: Mexico, 2008, http://www.uanl.mx/international/espanol (accessed October 28, 2008).
15. Comités Interinstitucionales para la Evaluación de la Educación Superior (CIEES). *Informe final: Evaluación de consistencia, resultados y de diseño 2007*; Fondo de Modernización para la educación superior, Secretaría de Educación Pública (SEP): Mexico, March 2008; 2–4, http://www.sep.gob.mx/wb/sep1/fondo_de_modernizacion_para_educacion_superior (accessed October 6, 2008).
16. Secretaría Técnica, Dirección de Evaluación. *Estadística Institucional 2007*; Instituto Politécnico Nacional (IPN): Mexico, 2007; 1–13, http://148.204.103.12/documentos/estadistica_2007.pdf (accessed September 13, 2008).
17. Coordinación General de Universidades Técnicas. Capitulo 2: Universidad Tecnológica por año de Creación. *15 Años 1991–2006 Universidades Tecnológicas, impulsando el desarrollo de México*; Secretaría de Educación Pública (SEP): Mexico, 2008, http://cgut.sep.gob.mx/Libro/1991-2006.HTM (accessed October 1, 2008).
18. Coordinación General de Universidades Técnicas *Estadísticas*; Secretaría de Educación Pública (SEP): Mexico, 2008, http://cgut.sep.gob.mx/estadistica/BIENVENIDA.HTM (accessed October 1, 2008).
19. Subsecretaría de Educación Básica y Normal, Dirección General de Normatividad *Red Normalista*; Secretaria de Educación Publica (SEP): Mexico, 2008, http://normalista.ilce.edu.mx/normalista/index.htm (accessed October 8, 2008).
20. Universidad Pedagógica Nacional (UPN). *Unidades*; UPN: Mexico, 2008, http://www.upn.mx/?q=unidades_upn (accessed September 19, 2008).
21. Presidencia de la República. *Directorio de Instituciones de Educación Superior*; Presidencia de la República: Mexico, 2008, http://www.directorio.gob.mx/comunicacionsocial.php?categoria=9 (accessed October 12, 2008).
22. Federación de Instituciones Mexicanas Particulares de Educación Superior A.C. (FIMPES). *Miembros Afiliados Acreditados, 2008*; Federación de Instituciones de Mexicanas de Educación Superior: Mexico, 2008, http://www.fimpes.org.mx/instituciones_maa.html (accessed September 20, 2008).
23. Fernández Zamora, R.M.; Sametz, L. In *La historia de las bibliotecas en México, un tema olvidado*, Proceedings of the 60th IFLA General Conference, Habana, Cuba, August 21–27, 1994, http://www.enba.sep.gob.mx/Propedeutico/Bibliodist/La%20historia%20de%20las%20bibliotecas%20en%20Mexico.doc (accessed September 12, 2008).
24. Manzanera Silva, N.A. Introducción. In *Las Bibliotecas públicas, análisis de las acciones del gobierno Mexicano, 2001–2006*; El Colegio De México, A.C., Ed.; Biblioteca Daniel Cosió Villegas: Mexico, DF, 2007; 3–9, http://eprints.rclis.org/archive/00013443/ (accessed September 25, 2008).
25. Hernández Pacheco, F. In *Proyecto de la nueva biblioteca Vasconcelos*, Proceedings of the Prospectiva de la Biblioteca Vasconcelos, August 15, 2008; Mexico, 2008.
26. Subsecretaría de Educación Básica. *Evaluación externa del PNL 2006 Organización de Estados Iberoamericanos (OEI)*; Secretaría de Educación Pública (SEP): Mexico, 2008, http://basica.sep.gob.mx/recursos/programas/OEI_PNL2006.zip (accessed September 30, 2008).
27. Castro, M.D. Presente y visión futura de las bibliotecas públicas y escolares frente al hábito lector. In *Mesa Redonda: 45 años de Jornadas: historia y prospectiva de las bibliotecas públicas, las escolares y el hábito de la lectura*, Proceedings of the XXXII Jornadas Mexicanas de Biblioteconomía, Xalapa, Veracruz, Mexico, May, 2–4, 2001.

28. Programa Nacional de Lectura para la educación Básica y Normal.¿Y ahora qué hacemos?. *Bibliotecas escolares y de aula, primaria*; Documentos; Secretaría de Educación Pública (SEP): Mexico [No Date], 17–27, http://lectura.dgme.sep.gob.mx/documentos/man_prim.pdf (accessed September 11, 2008).
29. Comisión Nacional de Libros de Texto Gratuito (CONALITEG), *Historia del CONALITEG 1959–2007*; Secretaría de Educación Pública (SEP): Mexico, 2008, http://www.conaliteg.gob.mx/historia.htm (accessed September 30, 2008).
30. Cámara Nacional de la Industria Editorial Mexicana (CANIEM), *Producción 2006*; CANIEM: Mexico, 2006; 14–19.
31. García, I. Para empezar, hay que recordar: formación profesional e investigación del libro antiguo en México. Rev. Interamer. Bibl. **2005**, *28* (2), 163, http://bibliotecologia.udea.edu.co/revinbi/Numeros/2802/index.htm (accessed November 16, 2007).
32. Carrión, G. *Phone Interview*; Boca del Río: Veracruz, Mexico, September 21–23, 2008.
33. Dirección General de Bibliotecas, *Estadísticas del sistema*; Universidad Nacional Autónoma de México: Mexico, 2007, http://dgb.unam.mx/sbusite/ (accessed October 26, 2008).
34. Pontigo, J. *Phone Interview*; Cuernavaca, Morelos, Mexico, September 14, 2008.
35. Secretaría General; Secretaría de Servicios Parlamentarios; Dirección general del centro de documentación, información y análisis. Órdenes y decretos expedidos de 1812 a 1991, Diario Oficial de la Federación; Cámara de Diputados: Mexico, July, 1991, http://www.diputados.gob.mx/bibliotapotec/decretos.htm (accessed September 17, 2008).
36. Lau, J. *Biblioteca virtual UV (BiV-UV) una plataforma tecnológica para procesos de aprendizaje*, Proceedings of the Reunión CUDI Videoconference, Boca del Rio, Veracruz, Mexico, April 13, 2005.
37. Añorve Guillén, M.A. La formación del bibliotecario en México: 1924, una propuesta de formación integral en el marco de la biblioteca moderna. Invest. Bibl. **2004**, *18*(37), http://www.ejournal.unam.mx/iibiblio/vol18–37/IBI03708.pdf (accessed January 25, 2007).
38. Lau, J. Mexican serials: titles, contents and readers of treasures to tap. Serials Libr. **2002**, *42* (1/2), 115–133, http://www.haworthpress.com/store/Toc_views.asp?TOCName=J123v42n01_TOC&desc=Volume%3A%2042%20Issue%3A%201%2F2 (accessed September 17, 2008).
39. Adleson, S.L. *Personal Interview*; Hermosillo Sonora, Mexico, March 16, 2001.
40. International Standar Serial Number (ISSN), *Number of records from countries with an ISSN national center*. d'Enregistrement des Publications en Series, 2007. http://www.issn.org/files/issn/statistiques/REGISTER-CN-Activity-20072.pdf (accessed October 30, 2008).
41. Rovalo, L. *Personal Interview*; Mexico, DF, May 20, 2001.
42. Rovalo, L. *Administración de publicaciones periódicas: formato impreso y electrónico (Course manual)*; Mexico, DF, May 17–19, 2000.
43. Saavedra, O. *Personal Interview*; Ciudad Juarez: Chihuahua, Mexico, October 23, 2008.
44. Sánchez, S. *Personal Interview*; Merida: Yucatan, Mexico, October 10 2008.
45. Seal, R.A.; Mattes, D. El Préstamo interbibliotecario y el Foro Trinacional de Bibliotecas.. In *Construyendo puentes informativos; experiencias de cooperación entre México y EUA*; Lau, J.; Cortés, J., Eds.; Universidad Autónoma de Ciudad Juárez: Ciudad Juarez, Chihuahua, Mexico, 1998; 95–99.
46. Lau, J. Faculty–librarian collaboration: a Mexican experience. Ref. Serv. Rev. **2001**, *29*, 95–105.
47. Apoyo al Desarrollo de Archivos y Bibliotecas de México (ADABI) *Archivos*; ADABI: Mexico, 2007. http://www.adabi-ac.org/estructuras/vinculacion/marco/vinculacion_estruc.html (accessed October 30, 2008).
48. Palos Ramos, J. *Aplicación de las tecnologías de la información en archivos históricos*, Proceedings of the Reunión nacional de archivos 2003, Aguascalientes, México, September, 24–26, 2003. http://www.agn.gob.mx/archivistica/reuniones/2003/RNA/pdf/PoJuJoPa.pdf (accessed August 28, 2008).
49. Asociación Mexicana de Profesionales de Museos A.C. Balance y perspectivas, Noviembre 2006, http://www.amprom.org.mx/documentos/diagnostico2006.doc.
50. Instituto Nacional de Antropología e Historia (INAH) *Museos*; Instituto Nacional de Antropología e Historia: Mexico, 2008, http://www.inah.gob.mx/Museos/index.html (accessed September 23, 2008).
51. Instituto Nacional de Bellas Artes (INBA) *Museos*; INBA: México, http://www.bellasartes.gob.mx/INBA/Template12/index.jsp?secc_cve=1345 (accessed September 26, 2008).
52. Vargas, L.A. *Phone interview*, Mexico, DF, September 15, 2008.

Modeling Documents in Their Context

Airi Salminen
Department of Computer Science and Information Systems, University of Jyväskylä, Jyväskylä, Finland

Abstract
This entry describes notions and methods for analyzing and modeling documents in an organizational context. A model for the analysis process is provided and methods for data gathering, modeling, and user needs analysis described. The methods have been originally developed and tested during document standardization activities carried out in the Finnish Parliament and ministries. Later the methods have been adopted and adapted in other Finnish organizations in their document management development projects. The methods are intended especially for cases where the goal is to develop an Extensible Markup Language (XML)-based solution for document management. This entry emphasizes the importance of analyzing and describing documents in their organizational context.

INTRODUCTION

Documents serve in organizations as an important means for communication, as a vehicle in work processes, and as organizational memory. Often they are also needed as evidence of the activities in the work processes. The creation and utilization of documents is currently strongly technology-dependent. Documents are created as *digital* documents and software applications are needed to find documents and information available in them. Information in digital documents is lost if the documents cannot be found, if they cannot be presented to human perception, or if they cannot be understood. Understanding the meaning of documents requires, not only understanding the content of the documents, but also understanding at least to some extent the structure of the documents as well as the context where the documents have been created. The importance of the contextual information has been often pointed out especially in the work done on records management and archival research (e.g., McKemmish[1]).

Many enterprises have begun major projects to turn their electronic document management (EDM) environments into environments with more standardized information structures and more effective and secure utilization capabilities. Developing systematic management of digital documents in an organization always requires some kind of standardization, that is, agreeing upon rules for the ways information is presented in documents, in particular, how the content of the documents is structured from information items. If the structure is indicated in the documents in a formal way, software applications can be used to process the documents as a collection of information structures. One approach to indicate the structures in documents is to use some markup language. Extensible Markup Language (XML) is the metalanguage currently widely used to define markup languages for particular needs and to present information in documents in the particular markup language.[2,3] XML is a restricted form of the older markup language called Standard Generalized Markup Language (SGML[4]). XML was developed to offer special support for documents to be distributed over the Internet. The huge number of XML-related development activities initiated after the publication of the first version of XML as a recommendation of the World Wide Web Consortium (W3C) in 1998 shows that XML is becoming a kind of *lingua franca* for the data of the Internet.

In EDM reengineering and standardization projects of organizations, a profound analysis of the document management in the environment is needed. In such an analysis, current documents and document management practices are studied and described and new document structures and document management practices are proposed. It should not be restricted to analyzing document structures and describing them by more or less formal models. To be able to gather the important contextual information, analysis and description of the whole environment is needed. The primary concern in the analysis may be in the documents produced within the organization. EDM development can however also be important in cases in which there is little internal document production. For example, libraries interested in improving the quality of their digital library services need rather profound analysis concerning both the primary documents created outside the library and the secondary documents created within the library, which contain meta information about the primary documents. A library can also participate in an EDM development project as an expert on reader needs. For example, in the document standardization activities of the Finnish Parliament and ministries, the Library of Parliament has provided valuable information about readers of documents and reader needs.[5]

Encyclopedia of Library and Information Sciences, Fourth Edition DOI: 10.1081/E-ELIS4-120044399

This entry describes notions and methods for analyzing and modeling documents in an organizational context. The methods have been originally developed and tested during document standardization activities carried out in the Finnish Parliament and ministries. The implemented standards in the environment concern a major portion of the Finnish parliamentary documents. Later the methods have been adopted and adapted in other Finnish organizations in their document management development projects. The methods have been earlier introduced in Tiitinen–Salminen,[5–10] and experiences of use cases have been reported in Salminen–Nurmeksela.[11–16]

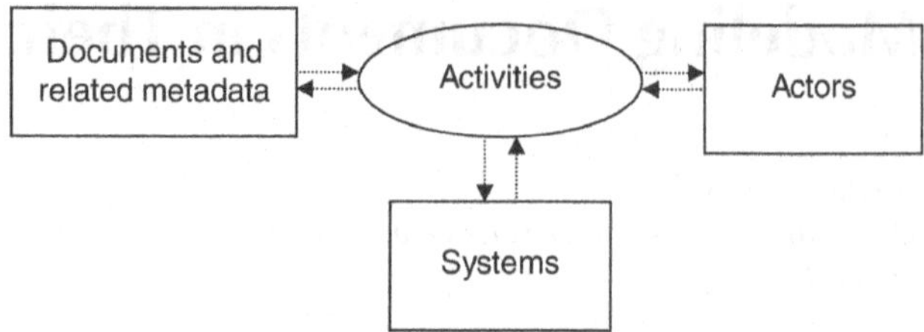

Fig. 1 Components of an EDM environment.
Source: Adapted from Methodology for document analysis, by A. Salminen. In *Encyclopedia of Library and Information Science*, Marcel Dekker, Inc., NewYork, 2000.[9]

EDM CONCEPTS

In EDM development and document standardization, organizations are interested in documents as a means of information management: a means to cluster, organize, store, and transfer information. In particular they are interested in using computers and the digital form effectively. There is therefore a need for associated hardware and software to process the data of documents and to present the content for human perception. When the notion of information is understood according to the sense-making theory of Dervin[17] as "the sense created in a situation, at a specific moment in time and space by a reader" (where Dervin means a human reader), then the information in a document is always subjective. In this entry, the following characteristics are regarded as essential to a *document*:

- It is intended for human perception, to be understood as information pertaining to a topic.
- It has content and one or more external representations.
- The content consists of parts, parts consist of symbols, parts are structured to support human understanding.
- It is stored on media.
- It can be identified and handled as a unit.

Additional characteristics of a *digital document* are

- The content is stored on digital media.
- The document is associated with hardware and software that can identify from the digital content the symbols and the structure of the parts and produce from them external representation to be perceived by humans.

Electronic document management in an enterprise does not concern documents only. Fig. 1 shows the major EDM components. There are basically two types of entities in an EDM environment: activities and resources. An *activity* is a set of actions performed by one or more actors. The *resources* are of three different types: actors, documents and related metadata, and systems. An *actor* is an organization or a person. *Systems* consist of devices, software, and data used to support the performance of activities. Out of all the recorded data in an environment, documents are those possessing the characteristics listed above. The *metadata* describes the content, structure, and context of documents.[18] The contextual metadata includes, for example, information about the actors, activities, and systems in the EDM environment. The broken lines in Fig. 1 show the information flow between activities and resources. Resources are regarded as information repositories in which the information produced in an activity can be stored or from which information can be taken and used in an activity. Information needed and produced during activities is stored in documents and in the related metadata, in the heads and experience of people, in the organizational culture, and in systems. *Information* is thus anything that can be stored in a repository and used in an activity, or that can be produced by an activity and stored in a repository to be later used in an activity (probably in some other environment). In relationship to documents and systems, actors are called *users*. The EDM environments in which a specific organization or person is involved may be quite complex, and the information in an activity making sense to a human actor often comes from many different sources.

XML STANDARDIZATION

Some kind of document analysis is needed in all major document management improvement efforts. Especially SGML/XML standardization has shown to be in some cases a complicated and demanding task. It may take several years, cause tremendous costs, and lead to various effects in the implementing organization as well as in its relationships to other organizations.[11,12,19] On the other hand, also reasonably fast implementation cases have been reported during the last years.[16,20] Experiences in the standardization of the Finnish parliamentary documents have shown the importance of careful analysis of the whole document management environment in the beginning of the standardization.[11,12]

XML as Document Format

SGML and XML offer means for defining and representing information as *structured documents*. Compared to SGML, XML has a smaller set of rules, less optional features, and the referencing mechanism is planned especially for referencing to Internet resources. The logical structure of an XML document is described as a hierarchy of named elements and the elements are indicated by explicit markup. Elements can be associated with attributes to add semantic information. Both SGML and XML are metalanguages, not specifying a specific markup vocabulary or document structure but allowing the definition of specific markup languages for specific purposes.

A characteristic feature to structured document management is that the structure definitions, document instances, and layout specifications can be managed as separate content items. When XML is adopted for structured documents, the structure definitions are called *XML schemas*. Various definition languages have been developed for describing the schemas. Most important of them are the *Document Type Definition* (DTD) mechanism introduced as a part of the XML language[2,3] and the XML Schema language.[21]

Standardization Levels

Development and implementation of specific XML-based languages is part of the multilevel standardization activities going on around the world. Three major interrelated levels of those activities can be identified:

Universal standardization. At this level general rules for wide use for different application areas are developed. The universal standardization activities are coordinated by W3C. Examples of the universal specifications are the XML Linking Language (XLink) intended for describing links between resources[22] and XSLT intended for describing transformations of XML documents.[23] The development work on XML itself is part of the universal standardization activities.

Sectoral standardization. At this level rules for the purposes of a specific sector or application domain are defined. The rules are built on top of the universal rules and they are not necessarily intended to be implemented as such but to be used to tailor further specifications at the local standardization level. The developer is often a consortium of organizations of a specific sector but it may also be a person or a single organization, for example, a software company. W3C and ISO have also published specifications for specific purposes. For example, W3C has developed the XML-based XHTML for Web publishing,[24] and the Text Encoding Initiative (TEI) Consortium participated by several humanistic organizations has published guidelines for encoding electronic texts for scholarly research.[25] The original TEI guidelines were originally based on SGML, later the guidelines have been adapted to XML.

Local standardization. At this level rules for a specific environment are developed. The standardization does not concern documents of the environment only, it concerns also the work of people, technology to be used for working with documents and for using documents, and the ways people of the environment collaborate with each other.

At all levels standardization is a continuing process. The changes in information technology, in organizations, and in business opportunities cause needs to update earlier specifications and to develop new ones. Furthermore, since the specifications are dependent on other specifications, changes in one specification cause needs to change other specifications.

An Example of Local Level Standardization

The SGML/XML standardization of documents produced in the Finnish parliament and ministries is an example of local level standardization. The standardization was initiated by a document analysis carried out in a project called RASKE. The term RASKE comes from the Finnish words "Rakenteisten AsiakirjaStandardien KEhittäminen" meaning the development of standards for structured documents. The methods developed in the project have later been called as RASKE methods. The project was commenced in spring 1994 by the Finnish Parliament and a software company in cooperation with researchers at the University of Jyväskylä.[6] The Ministry of Foreign Affairs, the Ministry of Finance, the prime minister's office, and a publishing house also participated in the project.

Starting the standardization was motivated by document management problems in the Finnish Parliament and government, for example, incompatibilities of systems, disturbing inconsistencies in the document contents, uncertainty concerning the future usability of the information in the archived digital documents, and unsatisfactory retrieval techniques.[6] The document analysis concerned four domains: the inquiry process, national legislative work, Finnish participation in European Union legislative work, and the creation of the state budget. Preliminary DTDs were designed for 21 document types, including, for example, government bill, government decision, government communication, private bill, special committee report, budget proposal, and communication of parliament.

The work of the RASKE project during the period from 1994 to1998 has been followed by several projects in which selected companies have developed and implemented SGML or XML solutions for a specific subset of documents.[11,12,26] The first implemented document repository in SGML form was the archive of laws and statutes, which was published by the Ministry of Justice in 1997. In parliament, the application of SGML started in 1998, and the Ministry of Finance prepared the budget proposal for 1999 in SGML form. The budget proposal is now created in XML format and the transfer from SGML to XML has started also in the parliament. All of the parliamentary documents are available to all citizens on the Internet free of charge.

THE ANALYSIS PROCESS

The analysis as part of EDM development in an organization, often including more or less formal document standardization, has multiple goals:[8]

Understanding the domain and the role of documents on the domain. The document management environment may be a complex network of organizations, people, activities, and documents related more or less to each other. The development work is often at least partly outsourced. Understanding the complex domain may be difficult even to people who have worked in the environment for a long time. The technology experts and consultants may be unfamiliar with the domain, the terminology used there, and the ways people work on the domain. The analysis should offer tools for gaining the understanding.

Communication support. The development process may take several years of cooperation by in-house workers in various units of the organization and consultants. The analysis should help to find a common understanding of the domain.

Understanding the needs of the actors. To succeed in document standardization, the requirements of organizational actors as well as person actors should be carefully analyzed and taken into account in the new solutions.

Support the design of document and metadata schemas. EDM development usually includes schema design for documents or for metadata or for both. The document schema design requires knowledge about current document structures and needs for changes. The metadata schema design again requires wide knowledge about the document management practices in the environment and needs for metadata related to content, structure, and context of documents.

Support the redesign of document production. Major development efforts including document standardization often lead to the redesign of the way documents are produced. For being able to implement effective document processing practices the old practices have to be understood.

Support the specification of requirements for new software systems. The implementation of new solutions often requires new software systems. The document analysis should provide information for specifying the requirements for the software.

Provide documentation for user training. Especially if XML and the structured document approach is adopted, the document authors need understanding of the rules constraining the authoring as well as understanding the needs for the rules. In case of a complex collaborative document production process, each author should also understand his or her role in the whole process. Well written analysis documentation can be used for user training.

A model for the document analysis process is shown in Fig. 2. The circles depict activities, also called *phases*, and the arrows show the control flow specifying the order for starting the activities. The small black circle indicates that all of the following three activities can be started either in parallel or in any order.

The analysis process starts by defining and describing the domain to be analyzed. The domain is an activity whose document management the standardization and improvements will concern. An example of an analysis domain could be creation of the state budget or paper machine manufacturing. Fig. 2 does not explicitly show iteration in the analysis. Once the domain has been defined, any of the subsequent phases may, however, reveal a need to correct or extend previously created models and descriptions. Basically all of the activities may thus proceed to some extent in parallel until the report of the analysis is finished. The domain definition is followed by process modeling, document modeling, and role modeling. Process modeling is used as a means of

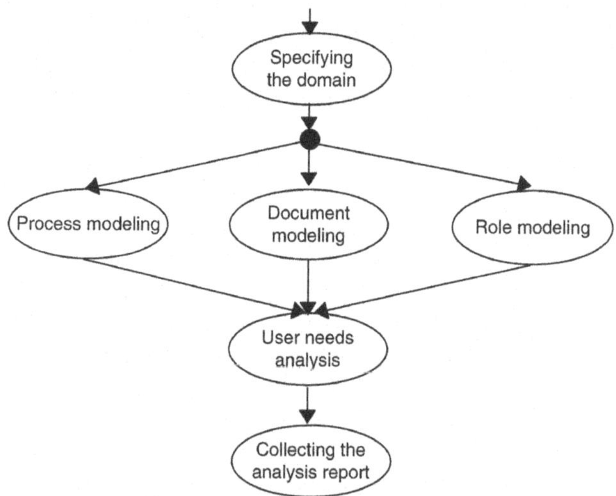

Fig. 2 A model for the document analysis process.

identifying smaller activities on the domain, the organizations responsible for them, and the documents created or used in those activities. Document modeling covers the description of document types, their life cycles, their contents, and relationships to each other. In role modeling the most essential document users are identified and their document management activities are described. The user needs analysis studies the needs concerning future document management. At the end of the analysis process, the analysis report is collected and extended on the basis of the descriptions and models produced in earlier phases. The report includes suggestions for future improvements in document management.

DATA-GATHERING METHODS

An extensive amount of data have to be collected during the document analysis phases. The ways in which the data was gathered in the RASKE project can be divided into three categories: project council meetings, literal sources, and interviews.

Project Council Meetings

A council comprising the analysts and representatives from the document support departments of the organizations involved was set up. At council meetings, the work products of the analysis were evaluated and discussed. These discussions were found to be an effective way of gathering information concerning current document management, requirements for the future, and additional data sources.

Literal Sources

The major literal sources can be divided into the following types:

- Reports of earlier projects and working groups in the EDM area. Considerable activity had taken place during the previous year or two. The reports listed a number of problems and needs.
- Printed documents in the analysis domain. Example documents were copied and carefully analyzed.
- Existing written rules and standards concerning documents. Some of the rules were expressed in statutes, some were instructions given by ministries, and some were more informal instructions. For example, there were written instructions for drafting government bills.
- Systems manuals and instructions. Knowledge about current systems is important in identifying the benefits and problems in them.
- General literature describing the domain. In case of legislation, extensive literature is available.

Interviews

The interviews were divided into the following two types:

- Informal interviews with experts in the domain. Interviews were conducted with people working with documents in the organizations. The interviews were supported by charts and other outcomes of the analysis. The domain experts were mostly chosen by the project council.
- Structured user interviews. People using the documents in the domain either within or outside the subject organizations were interviewed to ascertain their requirements concerning document management. The interviews followed structured questionnaires. The goal of the interviews was to obtain more information about the work and tasks done in the user roles and about the needs associated with those roles. The basis for the design of questionnaires was the sense-making theory.[17] The user needs were connected to situations in the work of the respondents.

MODELING METHODS

The RASKE modeling methods have been chosen from different methodologies and tailored for the purpose of document analysis. XML Schema language and the DTD mechanism have been used as methods for describing detailed document structures. Elm graphs[27] and similar graphical presentations available in XML schema editors have been used for graphical descriptions of document structures. The most important origins of the other modeling methods were in the object-oriented analysis (OOA) methodology,[28] in information control nets (ICNs),[29,30] and in role modeling.[31] One of the most important requirements for the modeling methods was the clarity of notions and models. Except for the formal XML schemas, the models are primarily intended to support communication and understanding of the area by human readers, only secondarily for computers.

Domain Definition and Process Modeling

The domain definition includes the identification of the activity whose document management the improvements will concern and the identification of the major organizational actors of the activity. Process modeling is used as a means to identify smaller activities, organizations responsible for them, and documents created or used in those activities. Variants of ICNs are suitable for describing relationships between activities, actors, and documents.[29,30] Basically, ICN models are process models showing a set of *activity* objects, a set of *resource* objects separated into input resources and output resources, mappings indicating the control flow among the activities, and mappings indicating the information flow. An activity may further be described as an ICN. Figs. 1 and 2 already introduced special variants of ICNs. Fig. 1 showed only one activity circle and but no control flow. Fig. 2 instead showed only the control flow and no resources or information flow. Also, the ICNs used in the domain definition and in the process modeling are special variants of more general ICNs.

Organizational framework

As an ICN, an *organizational framework description* consists of an activity and a set of organizations as input resources. The organizational resources are used in the activity, and their participation can be regarded as an information flow to the activity. Fig. 3 depicts the organizational framework of the domain "creation of the state budget." In the graphical representation, the broken arrows from the organizations to the activity indicate the information flow. They are labeled by identifiers and associated with phrases briefly describing the tasks of the organizations in the activity. Hierarchic relationships of organizations are indicated by nested rectangles.

It is important in modeling EDM to know the relationships subsisting between the major activities, actors, and documents. The document output model and document input model show the business activities of the domain as a process and the organizational actors of those activities. The output model shows the documents produced in the course of the activities, and the input model shows the documents used in the activities.

Document output model

A *document output model* consists of a set of activities which are subactivities of the activity of the whole domain, a set of organizations as resources, and a set of document objects as output resources. In the organizational framework model the participating organizations were indicated as sources of information flowing to the domain activity. In the document output model, explicit information flow is shown only to documents. Organizations can be regarded as input and output resources at the same time. While performing their activities, organizations are not only sources of information; those working in the activities increase their experience and expertise and thus the organizations also increase their information resources. This information flow is not explicitly indicated in the document output model, however. In the graphical representation, organizations performing an activity are listed in the upper part of the activity circle.

Fig. 4 shows a document output model for the creation of the state budget. In Fig. 4 the names of the document types produced in the relevant activities are indicated along the broken arrows. The number in parenthesis following budget proposal refers to different versions of the

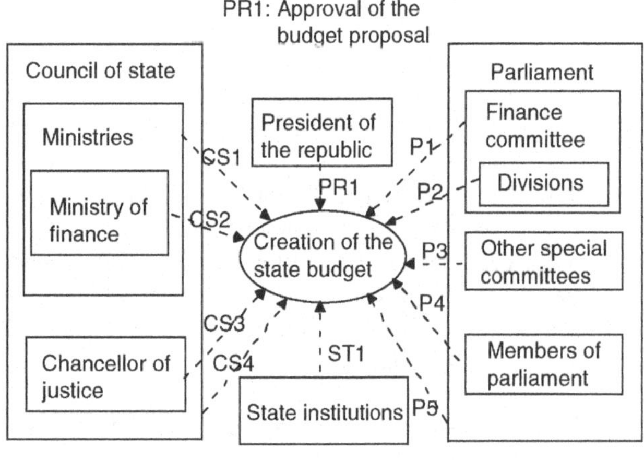

ST1: Preparing proposals

CS1: Preparing ministry proposals
CS2: Collecting the proposals of ministries and preparing the joint budget proposal
CS3: Checking legality
CS4: Presenting the budget proposal

P1: Discussing and reporting its comments concerning the budget proposal
P2: Discussing and working with special areas of the proposal
P3: Preparing statements concerning the area of the special committee
P4: Participating in committee work and voting in the plenary session, preparing budgetary petitions and motions to amend
P5: Presenting the budget after plenary session handling

Fig. 3 Organizational framework for the creation of the state budget.

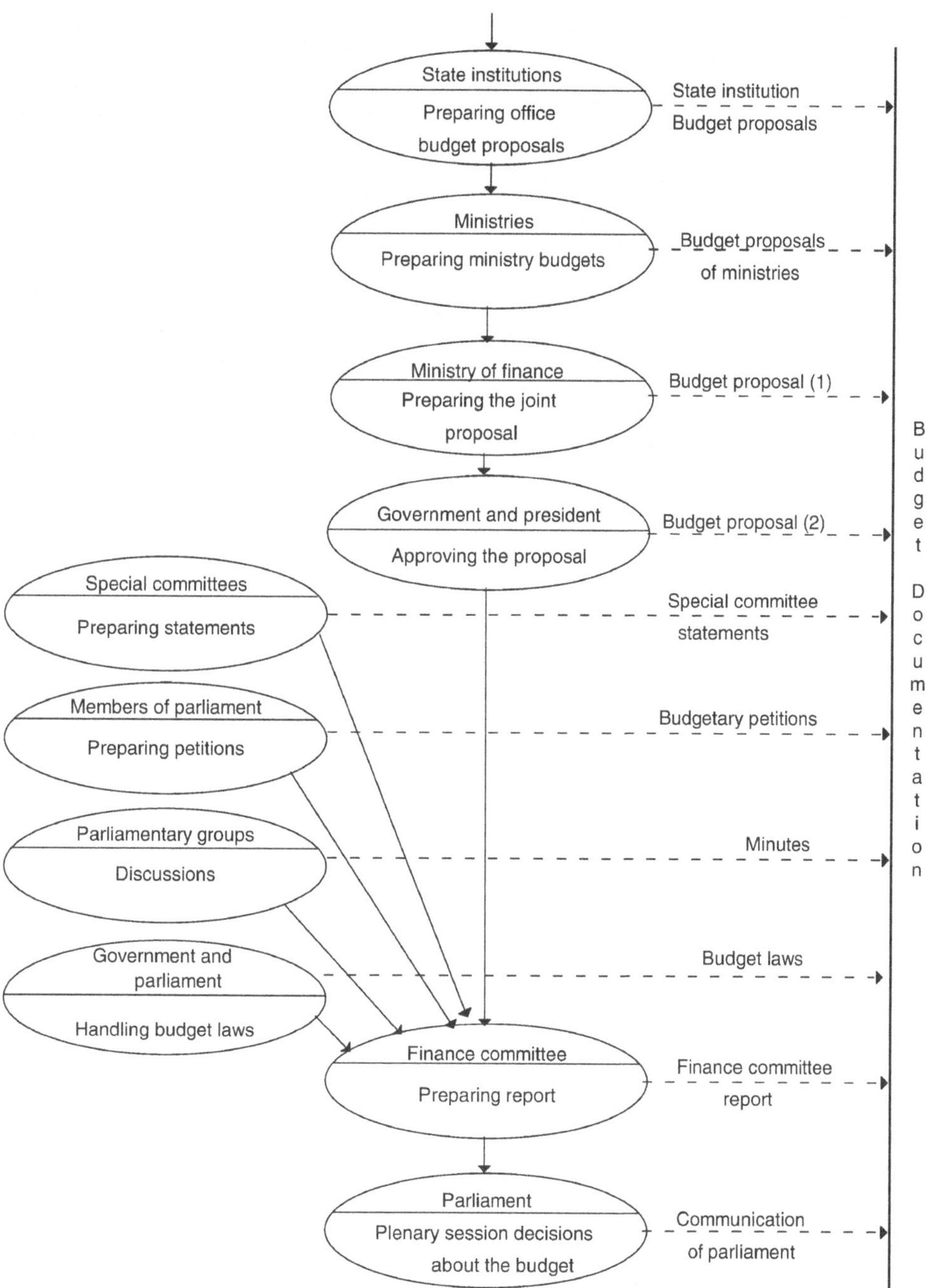

Fig. 4 Document output model for the creation of the state budget.

same document object. The vertical balk line on the right represents the documentation created during an actual work process. Basically the organizations appearing in a document output model are the same as those in the organizational framework figure. For the sake of simplification, some of the organizations may, however, be left out if their tasks are clear. Others may emerge in the course of process description. For example, in the document output model of Fig. 4, the chancellor of justice and divisions occurring in the organizational framework model of Fig. 3 have been omitted whereas the discussions of parliamentary groups have been added. The selection of the correct level of abstraction in the process models is important. The purpose is not to describe all the special cases and details.

In the RASKE project, the document output models were found very useful in the user needs interviews in orienting the respondents to the domain. The models were sent to the interviewees before the interviews, and during the interview the respondents were able to comment on the models and indicate their own place in the model.

Document input model

A *document input model* is otherwise similar to the document output model except that instead of showing the documents produced by the activities, it shows the major documents used in the activities. In the processes analyzed in the RASKE project, the repository of the documents used was much larger than the documentation created during the process. In general, the documentation used in an activity by an organization depends on the information needs of the people working in that activity. Document input models are therefore designed after the user needs interviews.

Document Modeling

The document output model shows the document repository created in the domain. Document modeling is used to give more detailed information about a chosen subset of the document types in the repository. Document modeling may also concern new types not appearing in the current repository. Document modeling is divided into three phases:

- Object modeling
- State modeling
- Content modeling

The origins of object modeling and state modeling are in the object-based modeling methodology OOA of Shlaer and Mellor.[28] Many of the techniques of OOA are also included in the Universal Modeling Language (UML).[32] In object modeling, document objects are identified and described, and their relationships to each other are described in a *document-relationship diagram* (D-R diagram). The dynamic behavior of a document object over time is described in a state model. In content modeling, the structure of documents is analyzed. In case of the XML adoption, content modeling may include the design of preliminary schemas. Much of the modeling of the three phases takes place in parallel and iteratively. Each of the phases is described below.

Object modeling

In object modeling, a *document object* is an abstraction of a set of documents. An important question to be answered is: What are the real-world documents (or the sets of information) to be modeled as a document object? In the document analysis of standardization projects, the goal is to describe the information in units corresponding as closely as possible to those useful for the organization's performance in future document management systems. In current document management practices, however, the partition of information into documents does not necessarily best support information management.

A short textual description is provided in the object model for each document object class. The document objects and their relationships to each other are described graphically in a D-R diagram, corresponding to the information structure diagram of OOA. Fig. 5 shows the D-R diagram for documents created during the creation of the Finnish state budget. In the example, the standardization covers three documents: budget proposal, finance committee report, and communication of parliament. In the diagram, the document objects of the standardization domain are depicted by white rectangles, the external documents by shadowed rectangles. A one-to-one relationship is depicted by a single arrowhead, a one-to-many relationship by a double arrowhead. A conditional relationship is indicated by the letter C.

State modeling

In state modeling, the dynamic behavior of document objects over time is described by the *state transition diagrams* of OOA. State transitions diagrams of UML can also be used.[32] A state transition diagram is a behavioral model showing the behavior of a specific document object over time. The activities shown in the diagram change the values of some attributes of the object. Examples of the diagrams can be found in Salminen,[7] Salminen.[8]

Content modeling

The main purpose of content modeling is to specify the hierarchic structure of the documents in the development domain. The RASKE content modeling methods are intended especially to support XML schema design. In the first stages of the modeling, the major components of documents in a class are described in a *document component description.* The relationships of the components to the components of documents in other classes are described in a *reuse table*.[7] The reuse table is intended for analysis of the current reuse of structural components and for showing new possibilities for reuse. A reuse table is defined for each document object. The collection of reuse tables included in the content model is a way of showing the dependencies of different document types.

Most of the modeling in document analysis usually describes the current situation. In the identification of document objects, however, the analysis should be able to anticipate future needs. Grouping information into document objects may differ from current practices and some of the document types may be totally new. Also, detailed content modeling should take into account the requirements for future EDM. The XML offers a formal language with which to define the detailed structure of document content by a schema. XML authoring tools are available for creating and testing the schemas, and also for showing the schema graphically. Elm graphs[27] were used for graphical descriptions in the RASKE project.

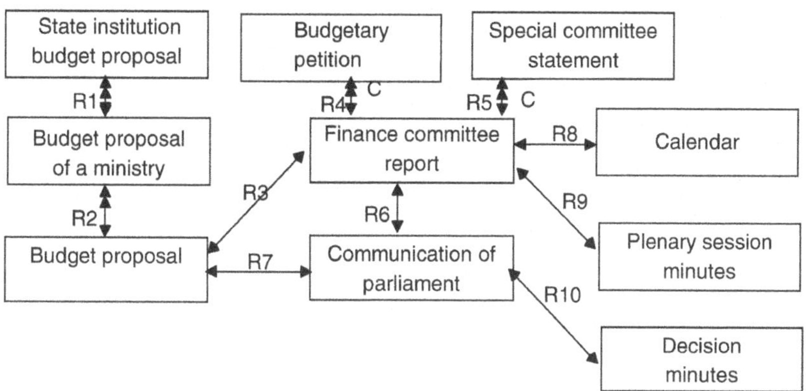

R1: Budget proposal of a ministry is based on state institution budget proposals
R2: Budget proposal is created on the basis of budget proposals of ministries
R3: Finance committee report concerns the budget proposal
R4: Possible budgetary petitions of parliament members are taken into consideration during the preparation of the budget committee report
R5: There may be one or more special committee statements included in the finance committee report
R6: Communication of parliament is created on the basis of the finance committee report
R7: Communication of parliament is a reply to the budget proposal
R8: Finance committee report is mentioned in the parliamentary calendar
R9: Finance committee report is mentioned in the plenary session minutes
R10: The decisions about the budget, included in the communication of parliament, are mentioned in the decision minutes

Fig. 5 A D-R diagram.

Role Modeling

In role modeling the use of documents by actors is modeled by role objects. A *role object* is an abstraction of the document management needs, tasks, and responsibilities of a group of people. Among existing object-oriented modeling methods, the method of Gottlob et al.[31] is flexible enough to describe role hierarchies where a user can play different roles at the same time and where roles can evolve. Fig. 6 shows part of the role hierarchy for the document repository created during the creation of the state budget. Role types are depicted by circles. The role types are connected by arrows to the user class, or to the role types whose objects may take on that role. A person as a user of the repository is considered both as an instance of the root type and as an instance of each role type for which that person qualifies. A user in the *organization* role uses documents in the activities of an organization; for example, as a worker in the organization. The use of documents in a *person* role is not necessarily related to any organization. On the other hand, a user may also be in a person role and organization role at the same time. For example, a user may be at the same time be a client of a public library and a citizen needing information preparatory to moving to another country. The double circle around the organization role indicates that a user may have roles in different organizations at the same time. For example, a person working in the Finnish Parliament as a member of parliament can also be a minister in the Ministry of Finance. During ministerial vacations, a person may take on the role of several ministers at the same time.

With respect to a domain, roles can be divided into internal and external. The users in *internal roles* perform activities in the domain process, whereas the users in *external roles* use documents in some other activities, either in organization roles or as private persons. In the document analysis of companies, all the user roles may be organization roles. Documents created in the public sector are, however, intended for the public and their users may be in a person role not representing an organization in the use situation. Person roles can be classified in different ways; for example, citizen, student, immigrant, senior citizen. The clients of public libraries are typically in person roles while using documents.

Role modeling produces textual descriptions of roles—the way documents are used and the purpose of use. The relationship between document objects and role objects is described in a *document-role relationship table*.[7] In the table the columns are labeled according to document objects and the rows according to role objects. The letters in the table indicate the type of activity performed by a role object in respect to a document object.

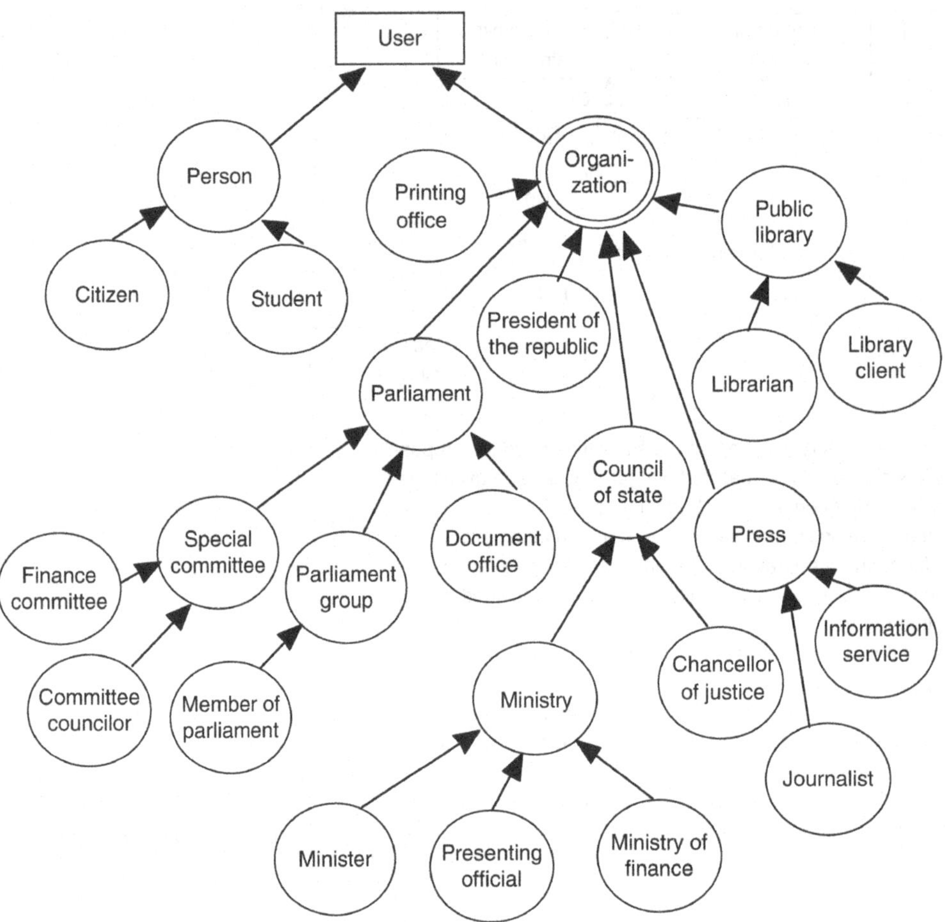

Fig. 6 A part of the role hierarchy for the creation of the state budget.

USER NEEDS ANALYSIS

User needs analysis should cover the document management needs of the individuals and organizations: documents, their use, the systems by which they are used, and the relationships of users. Some of the needs of participating organizations are a starting point for the analysis. More data about the needs of organizations is then collected from literal sources, in the project council meetings, and by the informal domain expert interviews. Needs concerning individuals and groups of persons are part of the needs of the organizations.

Data about the needs of persons are collected by user needs interviews. Structured questionnaires were used in the interviews in the RASKE project. In the questionnaires, data from the following areas were collected:

- Organization and tasks of the organization.
- Personnel tasks in the domain.
- Situations in which documents were used in the domain process and outside the process.
- Documents and information produced and needed in the above situations.
- Systems and databases used in the situations.
- Problems and needs.

The use of documents was associated with specific situations in the work of the respondents on the basis of the sense-making theory.[17]

The user needs interview analysis produces corrections and extensions to the models created in phases started earlier, especially to the outcomes of role modeling. The analysis of the problems and needs is divided according to the document management components—systems, documents, work processes, and interrelationships between actors. The problems and needs of people in different roles are introduced in the final report, which also includes the above-described models and suggestions for improvements in the different document management activities of the organizations.

CONCLUSION

Nowadays documents are mostly authored using information technology. The use of digital data as information in activities of organizations may, however, be impaired by unintegrated and inconsistent solutions. After storing information in nonstandardized ways, probably for three or four decades, the document management environment of an organization may be extremely complicated. To improve the utilization of digital media, careful analysis of the environment is needed. The analysis should cover all the components of document management: documents, their users and use, and the business processes in which the documents are used. The information gathered by the analysis provides valuable information about the context and structure of the documents in the environment. In case of using XML, the structural information can be utilized by XML software, for example, in information retrieval. The contextual information, for example, about the business processes where documents are created, should also be provided as accessible metadata to the users. In Lyytikäinen,[33] we have suggested using the analysis models as contextual metadata and using them as graphical interfaces for information retrieval.

This entry introduced concepts and methods for analyzing documents in their organizational context: A model for the analysis process and methods for data gathering, modeling, and user needs analysis. The methodology was developed and tested in the RASKE project where the goal was to improve the management of Finnish parliamentary documents by standardization. The use of the methods is however not limited to standardization projects. For example, some of the models included in the methodology have been used as a new means to visualize metadata related to European legal documents in Web repositories.[34] The visualization is intended to help the users of European legal information to cope with the complexity of the legal domain in Europe, and to better locate information from correct sources. Similarly, in other application domains and EDM development efforts, the methods introduced in this entry offer means to describe the complex environment and thereby support for improvements.

ACKNOWLEDGMENTS

The results presented in this entry have evolved during the work of the RASKE project. Mika Hirvonen, Kirsi Heiskanen, Kristiina Huhtanen, Matti Järvenpää, Katri Kauppinen, Antti Lehtinen, Merja Lehtovaara, Virpi Lyytikäinen, Pia Norrila, Reija Nurmeksela, Tero Päivärinta, Pasi Tiitinen, and Maiju Virtanen have contributed as RASKE researchers. The cooperation and extensive knowledge of experts in the Finnish Parliament and government as well as in many other organizations has been extremely valuable. Special thanks are owed to Olli Mustajärvi in the Finnish Parliament for his continuous support and cooperation. The financial support of the Finnish Parliament, Ministry of Foreign Affairs, Ministry of Finance, prime minister's office, Technology Development Center of Finland, and Academy of Finland (under Project 48989) is gratefully acknowledged.

REFERENCES

1. McKemmish, S.; Acland, G.; Ward, N.; Reed, B. Describing records in context in the continuum: The Australian Recordkeeping Metadata Schema. Archivaria **1999**, *48* (Fall), 3–43.
2. *In Extensible Markup Language (XML) 1.0;* Bray, T.; Paoli, J.; Sperberg-McQueen, C.M.; Eds.; W3C Recommendation, February 10, 1998. Available at http://www.w3.org/TR/1998/REC-xml-19980210 (accessed September 2007).
3. *Extensible Markup Language (XML) 1.1,* 2nd Edn; Bray, T.; Paoli, J.; Sperberg-McQueen, C.M.; Maler, E.; Yergeau, F.; Cowan, J., Eds.; W3C Recommendation, August 16, 2006. Available at http://www.w3.org/TR/xml11/ (accessed September 2007).
4. Goldfarb, C.F. In *The SGML Handbook*; Rubinsky, Y., Ed.; Oxford University Press: Oxford, U.K., 1990.
5. Tiitinen, P.; Lyytikäinen, V.; Päivärinta, T.; Salminen, A. User needs for electronic document management in public administration: A study of two cases Proceedings of ECIS 2000, European Conference on Information Systems; Hansen, H.R., Bichler, M., Mahrer, H., Eds.; Wirtschaftsuniversität Wien: Wien, 2000; 1144–1151.
6. Salminen, A.; Lehtovaara, M.; Kauppinen, K. Standardization of digital legislative documents, a case study Proceedings of the 29th Hawaii International Conference on System Sciences; Lynn, M.S., Ed.; IEEE Computer Society Press: Los Alamos, CA, 1996; 72–81.
7. Salminen, A.; Kauppinen, K.; Lehtovaara, M. Towards a methodology for document analysis. JASIS **1997**, *48*(7), 644–655.
8. Salminen, A.; Lyytikäinen, V.; Tiitinen, P. Putting documents into their work context in document analysis. Inform. Process. Manag. **2000**, *36*(4), 623–641.
9. Salminen, A. Methodology for document analysis. In *Encyclopedia of Library and Information Science*; Kent, A., Ed.; Marcel Dekker, Inc.: New York, 2000; vol. 67, 299–320.
10. Salminen, A. Document analysis methods. *Encyclopedia of Library and Information Science*, 2nd Ed.; Bernie, C.L., Ed.; Marcel Dekker, Inc.: New York, 2003; 916–927 Revised and Expanded.
11. Salminen, A.; Lyytikäinen, V.; Tiitinen, P.; Mustajärvi, O. Experiences of SGML standardization: The case of the finnish legislative documents Proceedings of the Thirty-Fourth Hawaii International Conference on System Sciences; Sprague, R.H., Jr., Ed.; IEEE Computer Society Press: Los Alamos, CA, 2001; file etegv01.pdf at CD-ROM.
12. Salminen, A.; Lyytikäinen, V.; Tiitinen, P.; Mustajärvi, O. SGML for e-Governance: The case of the finnish parliament Proceedings of the 11th International Workshop on Database and Expert Systems Applications (DEXA 2000); Tjoa, A.M., Wagner, R.R., Al-Zobaidie, A., Eds.; IEEE Computer Society Press: Los Alamitos, CA, 2000; 349–353.
13. Salminen, A.; Lyytikäinen, V.; Tiitinen, P.; Mustajärvi, O. Implementing digital government in the Finnish Parliament. In *Electronic Government Strategies and Implementation*; Huang, W., Siau, K., Wei, K.K., Eds.; IDEA Group Publishing: Hersley, PA, 2004; 242–259.
14. Salminen, A. Towards digital government by XML standardization. *Proceedings of the XML Finland 2003*, XML Finland: Helsinki, 2003; 5–115.

15. Salminen, A. Building digital government by XML Proceedings of the Thirty-Eighth Hawaii International Conference on System Sciences; Sprague, R.H., Jr., Ed.; IEEE Computer Society Press: Los Alamos, CA, 2005; CD-ROM.
16. Nurmeksela, R.; Jauhiainen, E.; Salminen, A.; Honkaranta, A. XML document implementation: Experiences from three cases Proceedings of the Second International Conference on Digital Information Management; Badr, Y., Chbeir, R., Pichappan, P., Eds.; IEEE: Los Alamitos, CA, 2007; 224–229 In.
17. Dervin, B. From the mind's eye of the user: The sense-making qualitative-quantitative methodology. In *Quantitative Research in Information Management*; Glazier, J.D., Powell, R.R., Eds.; Libraries Unlimited: Englewood, CA, 1992; 61–84.
18. Gilliland, A.G. Setting the stage. In *Introduction to metadata. Pathways to digital information*; Gill, T., Gilliland, A.J., Woodley, M.S., Eds.; Online edition, version 2.1; Baca, M., Ed. Available at http://www.getty.edu/research/conducting_research/standards/intrometadata/index.html (accessed September 2007).
19. Fahrenholz-Mann, S. SGML for electronic publishing at a technical society—Expectation meets reality. Markup Lang. Theor. Pract. **1999**, *1* (2), 1–30.
20. Weitzman, L.; Dean, S.; Meliksetian, D.; Gupta, K.; Zhou, N.; Wu, J. *Transforming the Content Management Process at IBM.com*, ACM Press: New York, 2002; 1–15 Case studies of the CHI2002/AIGA Experience Design Forum.
21. Fallside, D.C.; Ed.; XML schema part 0: Primer second edition, W3C Recommendation, October 28, 2004. Available at http://www.w3.org/TR/xmlschema-0/ (accessed September 2007).
22. DeRose, S.; Maler, E.; Orchard, D.; Eds.; *XML linking language (XLink) version 1.0*, W3C Recommendation, June 27, 2001. Available at http://www.w3.org/TR/xlink/ (accessed September 2007).
23. Kay, M.; Ed.; *XSL transformations (XSLT) version 2.0*, W3C Recommendation, January 23, 2007. Available at http://www.w3.org/TR/2007/REC-xslt20–20070123/ (accessed September 2007).
24. A reformulation of HTML 4 in XML 1.0. W3C Recommendation, January 26, 2000, revised August 1, 2002. Available at http://www.w3.org/TR/xhtml1/ XHTML™ 1.0 The Extensible HyperText Markup Language (Second Edition).
25. Text encoding initiative. Available at http://www.tei-c.org/ TEI Home Page.
26. Nurmeksela, R. Facing the challenges in implementing XML: The case of the Finnish parliamentary documents. In *Proceedings of the IASK International Conference E-Activity and Leading Technologies*; Muñoz, M., Freitas, A., Cravo, P., Eds.; IASK International Association for the Scientific Knowledge: Portugal, 2007; 247–255.
27. Maler, E.; El Andaloussi, J. *Developing SGML DTDs. From Text to Model to Markup*, Prentice Hall: Englewood Cliffs, NJ, 1996.
28. Shlaer, S.; Mellor, S.J. *Object Lifecycles Modeling the World in States*, Yourdon Press: Englewood Cliffs, NJ, 1992.
29. Ellis, C.A. Information control nets: A mathematical model of office information flow. ACM SIGMETRICS Perform. Eval. Rev. **1979**, *8*(3), 225–238.
30. Ellis, C.A.; Nutt, G.J. Office information systems and computer science. ACM Comput. Surv. **1980**, *12*(1), 27–60.
31. Gottlob, G.; Schrefl, M.; Röck, B. Extending object-oriented systems with roles. ACM Trans. Inform. Syst. **1996**, *14*(3), 268–296.
32. Booch, G.; Rumbaugh, J.; Jacobson, I. *The Unified Modeling Language User Guide*, Addison-Wesley: Reading, MA, 1999.
33. Lyytikäinen, V.; Tiitinen, P.; Salminen, A. Unifying access to heterogeneous document databases through contextual metadata. In *Effective Databases for Text & Document Management*; Becker, S.A., Ed.; Idea Group Publishing: Hersley, PA, 2003; 93–107.
34. Lyytikäinen, V.; Tiitinen, P.; Salminen, A. Graphical information models as interfaces for Web document repositories Proceedings of the Working Conference on Advanced Visual Interfaces, AVI 2000; Di Gesù, V., Levialdi, S., Tarantino, L., Eds.; ACM Press: New York, 2000; 261–265.

Moldova: Archives, Museums, and Libraries

Hermina G.B. Anghelescu
School of Library and Information Science, Wayne State University, Detroit, Michigan, U.S.A.
Silviu Andrieş-Tabac
Institute of Cultural Heritage, Moldova Academy of Sciences, Chişinău, Republic of Moldova
Elena Ploşniţă
Science Department, National Museum of Archaeology and History of Moldova, Chisinau, Republic of Moldova

Abstract
The present territory of the republic of Moldova was part of the Principality of Moldavia, currently a province of Romania. This territory was annexed by USSR in 1940 and remained under Soviet dominance until 1991, when the country declared its independence from USSR. The establishment of cultural and educational institutions such as libraries, archives, and museums dates back to the early 1800s. The modest beginnings were followed by a period of development during the interwar period. After the country was annexed by USSR in 1940 and until 1991, when it became independent, the Soviet dominance took its toll on all of these institutions. Restricted access to information and rigid censorship became the norm and libraries, archives, and museums were turned by the communist regime into political propaganda tools aimed at supporting the government ideology. Today, these institutions are undergoing a slow process of modernization by opening their collections to the general public, by refocusing their missions, and by redefining their goals. While government financial support remains scarce, new legislation is being adopted in an attempt to align Moldovan libraries, archives, and museums with international standards.

INTRODUCTION

Moldova occupies the area between Romania to the west and Ukraine to the north, east, and south, bordered by the Dniester and Prut rivers (see Fig. 1). With a population of 4 million, two-thirds of Moldovans are of Romanian descent. Other ethnic groups are of Ukrainian, Russian, and Bulgarian origin. The Romanian and Moldovan languages are almost identical and the two countries share a common cultural tradition,[1] which became the subject of a severe Sovietization process in the aftermath of World War II.

HISTORICAL BACKGROUND

The eastern part of the Principality of Moldova was annexed to the Russian Empire under the name of Bessarabia following the Russian-Turkish war of 1806–1812. During the period from 1812 to 1918 the political and legal status of Bessarabia underwent several changes: from a provisional autonomy to a Russian province (gubernie). Upon the dissolution of the Russian Empire the first Parliament of Bessarabia, the Country's Council, voted Bessarabia's union with Romania, on March 27, 1918. The interwar period of development and prosperity for Bessarabia ended on June 28, 1940, when, following the Molotov-Ribbentrop pact, Romania was forced to cede Bessarabia to the USSR. On August 2, 1940, USSR established the Moldavian Soviet Socialist Republic (MSSR), which included a part of the territory of Bessarabia and some districts on the left bank of the Dniester River. During World War II, on July 26, 1941, Romania got Bessarabia back, for a short while. In August 1944, Bessarabia was occupied by the Red Army troops and was again integrated into the USSR.

As a consequence of the perestroika, on August 31, 1989 MSSR's Parliament adopted a law regarding the use of languages in the country's territory. The Romanian language written with the Roman alphabet was declared the official language of the republic. Previously, Russian had been the state language as an attempt of Russification of the majority Romanian population.[2] During the Soviet period the Romanian language was written with the Cyrillic alphabet.[3] After the attempted Moscow Putsch Moldova declared its independence from the USSR on August 27, 1991 and in December of that year joined the post-Commonwealth of Independent States along with most of the former Soviet republics. In September 1990, the Parliament of Transnistria (a strip of land between the Dniester River and the Ukraine) unilaterally declared independence from Moldova. Neither Moldova's

Encyclopedia of Library and Information Sciences, Fourth Edition DOI: 10.1081/E-ELIS4-120044838

Fig. 1 Map of Moldova.
Source: CIA World Factbook.https://www.cia.gov/library/publications/the-world-factbook/geos/md.html).

government nor any other UN-member country has recognized Transnistria's independence. Currently, Moldova aspires to join the European Union. To a great extent, Moldova's recent history has been shaped by its having belonged to the Soviet Union which has left a long-standing legacy in regards to the country's social, political, economic, and cultural life. Today's archives, museums, and libraries in Moldova are a reflection of this legacy.

ARCHIVES

Currently, archives activity in the Republic of Moldova is supervised by the State Archives Department (Serviciul de Stat de Arhivă) of the Republic of Moldova. It is the successor of the Archives Section of MSSR's Board of People's Commissioners (Secţia Arhivelor a Comisariatului Norodnic) of the Ministry of Internal Affairs (1944–1963) and of the Division of Archives (Direcţia Arhivelor) of the Soviet/Council of Ministers of MSSR (1963–1991). Archives activity is governed by the Law Regarding the Archival Collections of the Republic of Moldova (adopted on January 22, 1992 and amended on July 7, 2005), the Regulation of the State Archives Collection (Regulamentul Fondului arhivistic de stat) approved by Government Decision on May 27, 1992, the Regulation of the Public Archives Collection (Regulamentul Fondului arhivistic obştesc), approved by Government Decision on May 30, 1995, and by other legislative and normative acts of more limited coverage.

This legal framework provides for ensuring the conditions of conservation of archival documents and access to them in accordance with international standards. Access to documents is free, once the archives reached repositories at the national level. In general, restrictions on access to documents containing classified information expire after 25 years, restricted access to documents concerning citizens' rights is maintained up to 75 years, and restricted access to marriage records is maintained up to 100 years from the date the document was issued.

Ensuring the physical integrity of documents and access to archival materials in state-controlled archives is difficult due to a series of factors such as: lack of storage space and reading rooms, insufficient equipment, and staff training, under-qualified personnel, inadequate practices that prevent the creation of digital repositories, and most importantly, a lack of managerial strategy and vision at the national level.

The principle of provenance guides all archival activity throughout Moldova. The State Archives Department is responsible for providing centralized record description and inventory. Permanent records are housed by two historic repositories—the National Archives and the Archives of the Social-Political Organizations of the Republic of Moldova—and by specialized central local archives subordinated to national governmental bodies such as the Ministry of Defense, Ministry of Foreign Affairs, Ministry of the Interior, Department of Information and Security, Academy of Sciences, Ministry of Culture, Weather Institute, etc. Intermediary records are preserved in departmental archives or in territorial archives at the municipal and district level. Permanent and intermediary archival institutions oversee the current archives of various institutions, which constitute the source for new records to be transferred to government-level repositories. Guidelines, rules, and regulations ensure the uniform processing of records beginning with their creation. The *Guidelines to Standard Documents and to Retention Periods for the Public Administration, Institutions, Organizations and Businesses in the Republic of Moldova*[4] is such a guide, published both in Romanian and Russian.

The National Archives of the Republic of Moldova—NARM (Arhiva Naţională a Republicii Moldova) constitutes the country's main historical archives and has its origins in the archives of the Governor of the Bessarabia Region, established in 1815 as the first central provincial archives responsible for gathering and preserving the historical archives of the province.[5] However, the foundations for theoretical and practical research of historical documents were laid only at the end of the nineteenth century by the Scientific Commission on Archives of the Bessarabia Province,[6] which was active during the period 1898–1918 and published three volumes of papers. The first historical archives in Chişinău was created within the State Archives only in 1918, after the union of Bessarabia with the Kingdom of Romania. The State Archives in Chişinău were successful in bringing together and organizing collections of historical documents[7,8] it supported the establishment of the journal *Arhivele Basarbiei* (Bessarabia's Archives) (1929–1938)[9,10] as well as the publication of several valuable collections of medieval documents.

In 1945, after World War II, the Archives of the Bessarabia Province (most of them moved to Romania during the war and returned to Moldova in 1954) and part of the central archives of the Soviet Socialist Autonomous Republic of Moldova (republic situated on the left bank of the Dniester River during 1924–1940 as part of the Soviet Socialist Republic of Ukraine), most of which were destroyed during the war,[11,12] were merged and constituted the State Central Historical Archives (Arhiva Istorică Centrală de Stat) of the Socialist Soviet Republic of Moldova and the State Central Archives of the October Revolution and Socialist Construction (Arhiva Centrală de Stat a Revoluţiei din Octombrie şi a Construcţiei Socialiste) of the Socialist Soviet Republic of Moldova. Those two institutions merged in 1958 to create the State Central Archives of MSSR.[13] Today's NARM was created in 1990 by joining the collections of the State Central Archives with those of the State Central Archives for Audio-Visual Documents (Arhiva Centrală de Stat pentru Documente Foto-Fono-Cinematografice), established in 1977.[14,15]

National Archives of the Republic of Moldova preserves all the historical archives (administrative, legal, ecclesiastical, economic, cultural, etc.) of the Bessarabia Province from 1812 to 1944 (except for those transferred to the Odessa Regional Archives,[16] to Cernăuţi in Ukraine, and to some other archives in the USSR, as well as collections still in Romania); all of the archives of MSSR, including the Presidential archives and those of the Parliament and of the Government; civil records up to 1910 (most of which were microfilmed by the Genealogical Society of Utah); and privately donated materials and collections.

The oldest documents date from the end of the fifteenth century. The volume of paper-based documents amounts to almost one million items. In addition, the photo collection numbers about 150,000 negatives, the audio collection consists of over 5000 magnetic tapes, the movie collection consists of over 15,000 movies, and the insurance companies' records represent about 10 linear meters (33 linear feet) of microfilm. The research library contains about 60,000 books and collections of periodical publications, some very rare, dating mostly from the nineteenth and twentieth centuries. All of the materials have inventories and other finding aids, but most of them are in the Russian language which makes research very difficult for non-Russian speaking scholars. It is only after Moldova's independence in 1991 that finding aids in the Romanian language began to be compiled. Some finding aids have been published in Russian or Romanian.[17–21] The NARM is situated in a building specifically constructed in 1964 to serve as an archive and it has 13.5 linear km (44,300 linear feet) of storage space.

National Archives of the Republic of Moldova has a branch in the city of Tiraspol, created in 1976, especially for archived materials focusing on institutions in this particular region situated on the left bank of the Dniester River. In 1988, the collections amounted to 696 archival items. The Transdniester secessionist authorities have turned this branch into the Central State Archives of the Moldovan Republic of Transnistria (Arhiva Centrală de Stat a Republicii Moldoveneşti Nistrene) and it is no longer supervised by the central authorities in Chişinău.[22]

The Archives of the Social and Political Organizations of the Republic of Moldova (Arhiva Organizaţiilor Social Politice ale Republicii Moldova)[23] ensures the preservation of the public archival contents. It was created in 1991, after the nationalization of the Archives of the Communist Party of MSSR and it preserves, in addition to the archives, various other collections of nongovernmental organizations of the Soviet era and the period after Moldova's independence, such as professional associations, trade unions, etc. This is achieved as a result of bilateral agreements between the Archives and these associations and organizations. The Archives has more than half a million items (about 9 linear km/29,528 linear feet), inventories, and other finding aids in Russian and Romanian. The building, which dates from 1978 was purpose-built as an archive and is considered to be the most successful example in Moldova of a building for the preservation of archival materials.

The specialized central archives subordinated to national government offices or agencies are still being organized and they are undergoing gradual implementation of national archival procedures for conservation and access. The most frequently used, both by historians and by the general public, are the Archives of the Civil Registry (Arhiva registrelor de stare civilă) which acts as an agency of the Ministry of Information Development (Ministerul Dezvoltării Informaţionale). It preserves birth, death, and marriage records for the 1911–1944 period, and more recent records for some territorial and administrative regions which no longer exist.[24]

Collections of valuable historical documents are to be found in institutions of national significance all over the country, such as the National Library, the Academy of Sciences of Moldova, and many others. The public broadcasting corporation "TeleRadio-Moldova" and the movie studios "Moldova-film" have significant AV archives of historical importance.

Corporate or organizational archives such as those belonging to universities, academies, religious establishments, and NGOs are generally young or very young and contain documents created during their current activity. Their collections, being recent, are not of historical value at the moment.

Territorial archives, including the municipal archives in Chişinău, Tiraspol, and Bălţi and the archives of regional administrative divisions (*raioane*), host paper-based documents of the local administrations and businesses from the Soviet era and from the post-1991 period. The preservation of materials in these archives is very inadequate, since their budgets depend on the local administrations.

There are no electronic archives or online finding aids in Moldova. Storage, preservation, and access of digitally born documents are addressed by the Law Regarding Electronic Documents and Digital Signatures (Legea cu privire la documentul electronic şi semnătura digitală) adopted on June 15, 2004.

Although, the first article on archival theory in the Romanian language was written by an archivist from Bessarabia,[25] Moldovan archival science has inherited only the theory, methodology, and managerial practices in place in USSR, some fundamental rules, regulations, and practices in use during the Soviet continue to be in force today. At the same time, during the years after Moldova's independence, institutional, and personal contacts with Romanian archivists have resumed and knowledge transfer and exchanges of experience have taken place to the benefit of Moldovan archivists. Representatives of Moldovan archives have attended events organized by the International Council on Archives or by archives within the Commonwealth of Independent States, but implementation of their recommendations is not widespread among Moldovan archivists, who are not very familiar with the content of the recommendations. Most Moldovan archivists are francophone and they have participated in several international training sessions on archival practices organized by the French National Archives.

In 1995, the State University of Moldova established a Department of Archival Studies in the Faculty of History, with a group of 10 students per academic year. Four years later the department was shut down. The curriculum followed the model of library education in the Russian Federation and in Romania based on a textbook published locally in 1997.[26] Many Moldovan archivists received their degrees from the Institute of History and Archival Studies in Moscow or from the School of Archival Studies in Bucharest. This educational system has also been discontinued. Therefore, currently there is no archival education at the graduate level in Moldova. Clerks for secretarial/clerical work in archives are being trained only at the equivalent of an undergraduate level.

There is no professional association for archivists in Moldova. In 1997, the "Paul Gore" Genealogical, Heraldry and Archives Society was established under the patronage of the National Archives of Moldova.[27] The society organizes various scientific activities such as conferences, symposia, and exhibitions. The society gives the "Ioan Halippa" annual award and every other year the "Paul Gore" award recognizes outstanding research and contributions to the field of genealogy, heraldry, archives, and auxiliary sciences. Another professional association is the Society of Historians-Archivists in Transnistria, established in Tiraspol in 1999.[28]

In 1998, the periodical *Pergament—Anuarul Arhivelor Republicii Moldova* (Parchment—Yearbook of the Archives of the Republic of Moldova) started being published by the State Department of Archives, the National Archives and Archives of the Social and Political Organizations. This periodical publishes legislation and regulations in the field, finding aids, archival documents, research studies in archives, and auxiliary sciences as well as book reviews.

In 1994, the Republic of Moldova joined the International Council on Archives. Moldova's archival heritage is under the patronage of the country's UNESCO National Commission and ICOMOS National Committee.

MUSEUMS

Beginning in 1812, in the aftermath of the Russo-Turkish War, Bessarabia's development took place in a new historical context imposed by Czarist Russia that did not favor the national assertion of Bessarabians of Romanian origin. This period of Russian domination in Bessarabia's czarist history offered few opportunities for the development of the national culture but illustrates a great need for training models. It is significant because of the efforts of the society to search for methods of safeguarding and preserving the province's cultural heritage (mainly of archaeological and historical vestiges) and establishing a positive attitude towards the past and its legacy.

The awareness of preserving cultural assets had existed in Bessarabia's society over several centuries and during the early nineteenth century it resulted in the creation of major collections of archeology, history, and antiquities and in the organization of various exhibitions of agricultural, industrial, ethnographic, and art objects. The first public museum was the Zoological, Agricultural, and Crafts Museum, established in 1889 as a result of the Exhibition of Agriculture and Industry which took place the same year in Chişinău. The mission of the museum was twofold: "scientific and practical, to contribute to the development of natural sciences, and to increase the farmers' awareness about the latest developments in the field of agriculture."[29]

Between 1903 and 1905 the museum building was erected in Moorish style, and it was inaugurated on April 30, 1906. Member of all social classes enjoyed the exhibits that highlighted their culture by displaying different kinds of artifacts related to several disciplines such as ethnography, archaeology, history, and numismatics. Donations had a decisive role in developing the museum collections until 1918. The education of the general public was seen as the museum's primary responsibility. The museum was made available to the public under a program that provided access "to local residents from 11A.M. to 2 P.M. on Sundays, and to those visiting from other places and to groups any day at any time."[30] Until 1918, the museum was visited annually by about 25,000 visitors.[31] The second museum in Bessarabia was the Museum of Agricultural and Natural Sciences opened on November 1, 1914 in Tighina (Bender). This first group of museums of natural sciences and ethnography fostered scientific research in these particular fields and boosted the development of a core group of a local scientific elite.

The nineteenth century is known in European museum studies as the century of national museums. Due to the vicissitudes of history, Romanians in Bessarabia could not showcase their history in national museums. However, during the mid-nineteenth century there was a general increase in interest in the country's past and history, which generated interest in collecting and establishing various cultural associations and scientific societies focused on studying the nation and its past through documents and monuments of historical significance. The activity of the members of the Scientific Commission of Bessarabia's Archives (Comisia Ştiinţifică a Arhivelor din Basarabia), of the Historical-Archaeological Religious Society of Bessarabia (Societatea Istorico-Arheologică Bisericească din Basarabia), of the Society for Research of the Dniester Region (Societatea de Cercetare a Ţinutului Nistrean) resulted in the emergence of the concept and design of a museum of archeology.

Despite the fact that these ideas were not implemented, because of the antinationalist policy promoted by the Russian government, they represent an important step in development of attitudes regarding museums. They show an interest in such institutions, as evidence of the awareness of the need to preserve antiquities and to create a national museum of history. Russian czarism could not allow the establishment of national museums in the subordinated provinces. But taking into account the development of museum studies, the development of history as science, and the spiritual needs of the society, czarism imposed a unique concept for history museums highlighting the history of the church (or "church museums").

The establishment of the Church Museum (Muzeul bisericesc) in 1906 in Chişinău is directly connected to the activity of the Historical-Archaeological Religious Society of Bessarabia, founded in 1904. According to its bylaws the mission of the Society was "to collect written documents with religious character, church books, icons, objects of worship; to research archeological and religious materials kept in various state institutions and private collections; in order to create a museum aimed at preserving church antiquities."[32]

This museum remained active until 1940. The creation of the Church Museum meant "a very clear manifestation of the Bessarabians' religious memory. Through this museum the religious thinking and church life continued to preserve their identity in Bessarabia's space within the context of the Russian Empire's imposing uniform religious activities."[33]

The emergence of public museums is one of the most important events in Bessarabia's cultural life during the mid-nineteenth century. Museums were seen as an important factor in the development of national consciousness. They were necessary to preserve traditional values in a society threatened with losing its historical memory. During this period, museums managed to occupy a particular place in social consciousness, the same place as other institutions that preserve human memory such as archives and libraries. Nonetheless, public museums of this period only partially reflected the national culture and society and could not meet the national aspirations of the local population.

Bessarabian museums of the early twentieth century followed the managerial and organization principles of the late nineteenth century Russian museums intermingled with the individual character and structure of their own collections. Until 1918, the development of museums in Bessarabia was mostly of a spontaneous nature, as a reaction against all kinds of factors aimed at cleansing the Romanian population's national identity by the Russian authorities. There was no specific body to coordinate museum activity, the government's role being solely that of recording the existence of such institutions. Museum activity largely relied on private initiative. Prior to World War I there was no specific legislation targeting museum operations.

After the 1918, the unification and the creation of a unitary Romanian state (as a result of which Bessarabia joined Romania), the new Romanian government adopted several pieces of legislation regarding the development of museums in Greater Romania. In April 1932, the Law for the organization of public museums and libraries was adopted, representing the main legislative act that governed the development of these institutions during the interwar period. According to this law, the government became the sole body invested with control over all museums and charged with ensuring the integrity of Romania's museum patrimony. The law defined the scope of the "cultural goods" concept, museums' goals, objectives and their mission and also stipulated the establishment of a Council of Museums, which was to approve the creation and/or closing of museums, to coordinate their activities and operations. Through this law all museums received the status of scientific research institutions. The Zoological, Agricultural and Crafts Museum in Chişinău became the National Museum of Natural History and it was to act as "an institution of scientific research in which all disciplines dealing with natural science were to find their place."[34] In 1926, the first issue of the museum's journal was published: *Buletinul Muzeului Naţional de Istorie Naturală din Chişinău* (Bulletin of the National Museum of Natural History in Chişinău). According to Decree-Law No. 3783 of November 1937 the National Museum of Natural History in Chişinău became Bessarabia's Regional Museum (Muzeul Regional al Basarabiei), with the mission "to gather and study materials documenting Bessarabia from the standpoint of its natural sciences, anthropology, and history. The museum was to become an institute of rigorous scientific research at the regional level and also a central archives and collections repository."[35]

During this period museum scientists engaged in research in the field of natural sciences, conducted archeological digs, and participated in ethnographic explorations which contributed to increasing the museum's holdings. During the interwar period, as during the previous period, Bessarabia's Regional Museum continued to remain the most prominent museum in Bessarabia. During the 1918–1940 period, new museums were established such as: The Antiquities Museum of Cetatea Albă (1919), which published its own journal, *Buletinul Muzeului Cetăţii Albe*; the Fine Arts Museum in Chişinău (1939), two museums of history of religions in Ismail and Bălţi, and the Economic Museum in Bender.

After 1944, when Moldova was incorporated into the USSR, museum history entered a new stage which changed not only the role and significance of museums, and the principles of museum organization and activity but also the concept of museum per se, i.e., the essence of museums as institutions. During the communist period a new approach to museums was implemented: museums were turned into political schools of mass education and indoctrination, they became part of the communist ideological machine. They acquired political-cultural attributes. This process became manifest mostly through the creation of new institutions such as "historical-revolutionary" museums, memorial museums, and antireligious museums.

For many decades, the main method in guiding exhibition activities in museums was the organization of thematic exhibitions while the main criterion for assessing museum activities was the ideological content of the activities they organized. Museums were expected to reflect in their exhibits the achievements of the socialist construction and the superiority of communist lifestyle. In spite of this requirement, museums did not have in their collections items specific to Soviet efforts, which started only in 1917. Therefore, museum objects removed from exhibits were replaced by enlarged texts and slogans, symbols of the communist doctrine.

A new phenomenon in Moldovan museum history was the establishment of antireligious museums, museums of "scientific atheism," in which atheism became a state religion, one of the main components of the communist state ideology. In addition to promoting "scientific atheism," in their instructional and educational activities, museums were required to reflect events of political importance in the nation's life: congresses of the Communist Party, elections of the Supreme Council of the USSR, various V.I. Lenin jubilees, anniversaries of the October Revolution, commemoration of significant events in the history of the USSR, etc. Museums were designed as political stages for socialist events, as powerful weapons of political education, and as a means for illustration and dissemination of the communist doctrine. Despite the museums' efforts to escape the ideological constraints, they remained ideological institutions forced to abide by the communist party's directives, turned into Marxist-Leninist propaganda tools.

Beginning in 1944, when Moldova was incorporated into the Soviet Union, museum activity was coordinated by MSSR's Board of People's Commissioners. In 1946, the institution was called the Council of Ministers of MSSR. In 1953, the Ministry of Culture of MSSR was created, and museums were placed under its jurisdiction. This system of coordination of museum activities remained in place without major changes until 1991. The ideological and propagandistic aspect of museum activities remained the major mission of museums throughout the Soviet regime. According to the communist ideology "museum should occupy a prominent place in promoting the Communist Party policy, thus contributing to building the Marxist-Leninist consciousness and ensuring the quick transition from communism to socialism."[36]

During the Soviet regime the Moldovan museum scene was marked by the emergence of a new category of institutions: "museums of the birthplace region" (muzeul ţinutului natal), featuring collections of local history, natural sciences, ethnography, and art. The name of this kind of museum kept changing during the Soviet period: in 1940 it was called the Republic Museum for the Study of the MSSR Region (Muzeul Republican de Studiere a Ţinutului al RSSM), in 1957 it was called the State

Museum of History and Study of the Birthplace of MSSR (Muzeul de Stat de Istorie Şi Studiere a Ţinutului al RSSM), in 1983 its name changed to the State Museum for the Study of the Birthplace of MSSR (Muzeul de Stat de Studiere a Ţinutului al RSSM). This period was characterized by a significant growth of the number of museums. In 1985, their number amounted to 83.[37]

This period is also significant for the emergence and development of memorial museums, aimed at featuring cultural and political personalities of particular importance in Russia's and the Soviet Union's history and culture while such important personalities at the local level were completely ignored. Leaders of the national cultural, artistic, political movement, or figures that opposed the communist regime were ousted and their contributions to society were completely neglected. A museum network was established nationwide, but there was no variety in their profiles and collections. The Soviet totalitarian system imposed from top down a common vision, a similar museum display regardless of the museum's profile, aimed at highlighting Russia's progressive role in people's life, and at featuring the achievements of the Soviet republics to the well-being of the masses throughout the USSR.

This led to a distortion of national history and culture. During the Soviet regime RSSM, as a simple administrative-territorial subdivision of the USSR, did not have her individual history and therefore there was no museum of national history. During this period, there was a unique history—that of the USSR—that identified itself with the history of Russia. Museums were perceived by public consciousness as agencies of communist propaganda. Particular attention was paid to promote revolutionary ideas. The number of history and revolutionary museums increased through the 1980s and they remained the most important category of museums every Soviet republic had to have. During this period there was no specific museum legislation since everything was coordinated by the omnipotent communist party.

Moldova's independence and sovereignty in 1991 has produced radical changes on the social, economic, and cultural arena. The process of democratization of institutions included museums as well. A characteristic feature of the development of museums after 1991, during the transitional period was to reduce their number. The national revival of Bessarabian Romanians, the democratization of public life, and the new social and political conditions all dictated the closure of political museums and memorial museums devoted to Soviet heroes. At the same time there was a drastic decline in museum visitors. Today there are 70 museums in Moldova, with three national museums: the National Museum of Ethnography and Natural History (originally opened in 1889), the National Art Museum (1939), and the National Museum of Archaeology and History (1983). These are also state museums, as well as local or institutional museums. In December 2002, the Museum Law was approved.

The national association of museographers is called Museion. In 1998, the National Museum of Ethnography and Natural History participated in a European competition—the European Museum Forum—where it received an award. Since 1995, the State University of Moldova, Faculty of History and Psychology, Department of Museum Studies, has prepared specialists for museums. There is a specialized museum journal, and since 1992, two museums have published their own journals: the National Museum of Archaeology and History of Moldova has published *Tyragetia* and the National Museum of Ethnography and Natural History has published the *Buletinul Muzeului*, both journals containing a section for Museum Studies. Since 2005, two museums—the National Museum of Archaeology and History and the National Museum of Ethnography and Natural History have a dual subordination: the Ministry of Culture and Tourism and the Academy of Sciences. Currently, museum activity is focused on researching and establishing a national museum patrimony, on reintegrating in the local circuit the national history and cultural values to reflect the nation's identity and to educate future generations of visitors. Along with the depoliticization of Moldovan museums this will represent radical changes in the development of museums and museum studies in the country.

LIBRARIES

The first public library was established in Chişinău in 1832, as a result of an act issued by the Russian Empire. It began as a very modest private collection of 428 volumes. Bessarabia's civil governor asked neighboring Romania for support to increase the library's holdings, but rigid censorship rules imposed by the czarist regime allowed only 36 volumes to cross the border to be added to the library's collection.[38] For more than a century, the library was moved from one building to another and during the interwar period it occupied several rooms in the City Hall. In 1944, the Central Library of the Moldovan Soviet Socialist Republic was created through the merger of this first public library in Chişinău and the Central Library in Tiraspol.[39,40] In 1961, the library moved into a purpose-built construction where it has continued to operate as the National Library of the Republic of Moldova (NLRM). In 1986, NLRM acquired a second locale in its immediate vicinity, the building of the former Theological Seminary which today hosts the fine arts and the multimedia collection.

In 2007, Moldova reported a total of 2931 libraries:1383 public libraries (including NLRM and the National Library for Children), 1453 school libraries, 21 college libraries,16 academic libraries, 27 medical libraries, 8 agricultural libraries, 20 technical libraries, the Library of the Science Academy, the Parliament Library, the Office for Intellectual Property Library, one trade union library, and one library for the blind. In 2007, a total of 3,148,000 new items were added to these libraries' collections, out of which 1,457,000 (46.28%) were in Romanian, the country's official language. More than 87% of the libraries are in rural areas.

Statistics indicate that in 2007 there was a total of 1,952,080 active library users, of which 853,400 are under 16 years of age.[41] This shows that almost half of the country's population uses libraries despite the dated collections, and even though most of the books are still in Russian and despite the traditional library services often reduced to provision of reading space in old reading rooms. Though the financing of libraries is insufficient and their book stacks are replenished slowly, the number of visits is constantly growing. More than 10 million (10.2 million) people visited libraries in 2005, 3% more than in 2004.[42] Moldova has a very high literacy rate of 96%.

National Library of the Republic of Moldova is the premier library of the country, directly subordinated to the Ministry of Culture and Tourism.[43] National Library of the Republic of Moldova coordinates the project of a shared cataloging system, SIBIMOL, jointly funded by the Ministry of Culture and Tourism and the Soros Foundation for an Open Society, aimed at automating library operations and services by establishing local and interregional networks with shared catalogs, linking them to the NLRM's central catalog, and later making them accessible via the Internet. As of January 2006, NLRM's online catalog contained records for over 140,000 books, 7500 serials, and 21,500 articles from Moldovan periodicals, as well as 1600 AV materials. As of January 1, 2007, NLRM's collections amounted to 2,510,254 items (2,160,941 books and periodicals, 25,624 AV materials, 136,484 graphic documents, 61,142 music scores, 214 manuscripts, and 1885 e-documents). In 2006, NLRM reported 11,654 active users who borrowed 588,720 documents.[44]

Under the Library Law, seven copies of every national publication are to be deposited with the National Library, which then distributes them to other libraries. A "Legal Deposit" department was set up in 1999 to supervise this system and make it work better. In fact, because of the recession, publishers are not honoring their legal obligation, and are depositing 1–4 copies, if any. This makes it impossible to keep a full collection of all the books published in Moldova, and to collect the data needed for the books-in-print catalog. National Library of the Republic of Moldova makes a serious effort to promote its collection and new acquisitions through a series of events: the annual National Book Fair, musical and arts events, literary meetings, lectures, exhibitions, etc. It also does research in a number of fields (history of books, etc.), organizes colloquia and symposia, and produces numerous bibliographies and publications on library science, such as the *National Bibliography* (*Exteriorica*), *Culture in Moldova*, *The National Calendar*, and *The Bibliological Bulletin*. In 1992, NLRM began issuing the quarterly *Magazin Bibliologic* which is distributed to libraries throughout the country to support all librarians' continuing education.

The National Library for Children (NLC) was established in 1944 with an initial collection of 10,000 volumes. Today its collections amount to 260,000 items, including audiovisual materials. Forty-seven percent of its collections are in the Romanian language. The library reports 12,000 users per year.[45] In 1997, NLC became a member of the International Board on Books for Young People.[46] The library has earned a national reputation by organizing the annual Children's International Book Fair.[47]

The Chişinău Municipal Library (CML) is one of the largest and most dynamic in Moldova. It was established in 1877 with a collection of 8073 volumes. By 1932, its collections consisted of 110,000 volumes, 93,800 of them in Russian. In 1941, the library was destroyed by fire. In 1944, it was reestablished by the Soviet authorities under the name of Central City Library. In 1991, it became the Chişinău Municipal Library.[48] Currently, its collections amount to one million volumes. Every year 150,000 patrons use the library's 31 reading rooms. In addition to print materials, CML offers access to electronic books and online databases. One of the branches of CML is a special library, The Public Law Library, situated in a downtown remodeled building equipped with state-of-the-art technology that allows access to legal databases including LexisNexis.[49] Chişinău Municipal Library issues several periodical publications among which is the monthly *Bibliopolis*.

Among special libraries, the Scientific Medical Library (SML) has engaged in a partnership with the North Carolina South East Area Health Education Center. Scientific Medical Library serves as the library of the State Medical and Pharmaceutical University of Moldova. It also acts as the National Medical Library of Moldova. The library collections contain 1,200,000 books, almost all in Russian and very dated. International statistics situate Moldova in the last place in Europe in terms of library expenditures per capita. Unlike Denmark where the governments spends 64.27 Euros per person, in Moldova library expenditures amount to 0.35 Euros (about half a dollar).[50] In 2006, the partnership brought to SML 10,000 medical books and periodicals in English. In addition, the program provided free access to four medical databases.[51] Other special libraries include the Library of the Parliament, established in 1978, with a collection of 11,400 books and 112 periodical titles. The Science and Technology Library was established in 1969 in Chişinău. In 2003, the library reported a collection of 13.5 million volumes.[52] The Library of the Academy of Economic Sciences was established in 1991. It currently holds 330,000 volumes and provides access to online resources. It serves as repository of publications issued by the International Bank for Reconstruction and Development.[53]

The Library of the State University of Moldova, established in 1946, is one of the largest government-sponsored academic libraries, with two million volumes. The Library of the Alecu Russo State University in Bălţi is the only academic library in Moldova that operates in a purpose-built building. The library harbors more than 1 million items and it is the most modern government-funded academic library in Moldova, providing access to electronic databases and e-books. The library also serves as a regional repository for publications issued by the World Bank. Among private universities, the Free International University of Moldova, situated in Chişinău, is the most prominent. Established in 2002 along with the university, the library provides remote access to electronic resources and virtual reference, organizes conferences, publishes conference proceedings and is strongly engaged in the implementation of modern information technologies.

Moldovan library collections are dated and mostly in Russian.[54] Most new books have been donated. Romania has been a major donor. Several public libraries in Romania have developed a sister library program through which they have endowed Moldovan public libraries with Romanian books. Under its Library Support Program and in cooperation with various international organizations, the Soros Foundation has funded a series of programs to support the acquisition of various books and publications: foreign books, subscriptions to international journals, participation in the Pushkin Project. Agencies run by other countries fund the acquisition of foreign publications only. The Alliance Française, for example, contributed books in 1999, under its "100,000 Books for Moldova" program. In the same way, the German Embassy has opened a German-language reading room at CML. The Soros Foundation Moldova supported school libraries with reference materials that helped establish resource enters in elementary and high schools nationwide. In October 1997, librarians in resource centers from the 18 schools attended a 2 day seminar with the motto "Books and Information for Education." The issues covered concerned the role of the school library in school life, the value of reading and its importance for students, use of international standards in library activity, and document classification.[55]

Penetration of the new information technologies into Moldovan libraries is very slow. Because of the country's economic situation, the 1994 Library Law and the Library Support Program, launched in 1998, have done little to improve the financial situation or technical infrastructure of libraries, despite the claim for modernization and vision for the future.[56] Currently, there are 1653 computers for library staff in the entire library system in Moldova (an average of 1.77 computers per library) and only 1126 are connected to the Internet. There are 892 public terminals out of which 737 have Internet connections. Most of these public stations are to be found in academic libraries: 417 computers, 380 with Internet connection.[41] It is also mostly the academic library sector that provides access to foreign databases purchased through a multicountry consortial system, supported by Electronic Information for Libraries (eIFL.net), a nonprofit organization that advocates for the wide availability of electronic resources by library users in transitional and developing countries. The eIFL Direct Moldova consortium comprises 16 major libraries: 10 academic, 3 public, and 3 special libraries.[57]

The National Book Chamber (NBC) was established in 1957 and is responsible for compiling the National Bibliography (books and periodicals, analytical bibliography) and keeping the ISBN and ISSN distribution records. Set up under the Soviets, the Chamber was linked directly to the government through the Publishing Activities Committee, to which it was answerable. Today, it reports to the Ministry of Culture and Tourism. In 2007, NBC celebrated 50 years of existence. An entire issue of *Magazin Bibliologic*[58] was dedicated to this event. A monograph also highlights the institution's achievements during this period.[59]

Librarians of all kinds belong to the Library Association of the Republic of Moldova (LARM), established in 1992 and a member of IFLA (International Federation of Library Associations and Institutions) member since 1994. Occasionally LARM representatives attend international library meetings, book fairs, etc.

Library science education began in 1960 at the State University of Moldova, Department of Library Science, Information Assistance and Archival Studies which offers undergraduate and graduate degrees.[60] Some 25 students graduate every year but after graduation not all of them choose to work in libraries or archives because of the low pay. Librarians also attend professional development courses provided by the Center for Continuing Education in Librarianship, established in 2001 with funding from the Soros Foundation's Training Program. The Center was funded for 3 years and currently is diminishing its activity for lack of financial reasons. The Soros Foundation also covered courses and grants for librarians at specialized institutions abroad and attendance of international conferences. Moldova's Library Law adopted in 1994, with amendments in 2001, 2003, and 2005,[61] specifies the legal status of libraries and includes detailed provisions on library collections within the context of automation of services and digitization of documents. The Library Law also stipulates the role and activity of the National Library Council, that acts as an advisory board on library issues to the Ministry of Culture and Tourism.

Moldova's cultural policy priorities were outlined in the national program "Development and Protection of Culture and the Arts in the Republic of Moldova, 1997–1998," extended to 2000–2005. In November 2005, the *Program on the government's activities for 2005–2009*, named "Modernization of the country — welfare of the people," was initiated, followed by the *Program on the development of the regions, 2005–2015* entitled "Moldovan Village." These programs include a variety of objectives targeting the cultural and educational field such as: the protection of the local cultural heritage; the restoration, and development of the regional houses of culture, libraries, and museums, and "e-culture" that introduce the new forms of promoting culture through electronic media in different sectors of the national culture. In order to implement some provisions of these programs, in 2006 the Ministry of Culture and Tourism elaborated the drafts of several important normative documents and laws: a draft of the Strategy on the Development of a National System of Libraries.[62] It is still to be approved.

In addition to writing long-term programmatic documents, Moldova's policy makers need to substantially support the cultural and educational sector, to contribute to the development of the infrastructure that would facilitate a faster penetration of the new information and communication technologies that would bring progress in every citizen's daily life. The Moldovan information society is still to come.

REFERENCES

1. King, C. *The Moldovans: Romania, Russia, and the Politics of Culture*; Hoover Institution Press: Stanford, CA, 2000.
2. Ciscel, M.H. *The Language of the Moldovans: Romania, Russia, and Identity in an Ex-Soviet Republic*; Lexington Books: Lanham, MD, 2007.
3. Colesnic-Codreanca, L. *Limba Română în Basarabia. Studiu sociolingvistic pe baza materialelor de arhivă (1812–1918) [The Romanian Language in Bessarabia. A Sociolinguistic Study Based on Archival Materials (1812–1918)]*; Editorial Museum: Chişinău, Moldova, 2003.
4. *Indicatorul documentelor-tip şi al termenelor lor de păstrare pentru organele administraţiei publice, pentru instituţiile, organizaţiile şi întreprinderile Republicii Moldova [Guidelines to Standard Documents and to Retention Periods for the Public Administration, Institutions, Organizations and Businesses in the Republic of Moldova]*, Chişinău, 1998.
5. Berzoi, A. Înfiinţarea arhivei Guvernatorului Basarabiei la Chişinău [Establishment of Bessarabia's Governor's Archives in Chişinău]. In *Studii de muzeologie şi muzeografie. Omagiu lui Nicolae Răileanu la 60 de ani, Muzeul Naţional de Istorie a Moldovei*; Tyragetia: Chişinău, Moldova, 2004; Vol. 1, 216–222.
6. Andrieş-Tabac, S. Înfiinţarea Comisiunii Ştiinţifice a Arhivelor din Gubernia Basarabia [Establishment of the Scientific Commission on Archives in the Province of Bessarabia]. In *Pergament. Anuarul arhivelor Republicii Moldova,* 1999; Vol. 2, 23–31.
7. Boga, L.T. Gane, Em. Direcţiunea regională a Arhivelor statului din Chişinău [State Archives in Chişinău, Regional Department]. In: *Inventarul Arhivelor Statului*, Bucureşti, 1939; 341–358.
8. Roman, A. Rolul academicianului Dimitrie Onciul în istoria arhivelor din Basarabia [Academician Dimitrie Onciul's Role in the History of Archives in Bessarabia]. In *Tyragetia. Anuarul Muzeului Naţional de Istorie a Moldovei*, 1995; Vol. 2, 245–254.
9. Corlăteanu-Granciuc, S. Revista "Arhivele Basarabiei" (1929–1938) şi autorii ei [*Arhivele Basarabiei* Journal (1929–1938) and Its Authors]. In *Pergament. Anuarul arhivelor Republicii Moldova*, 1999; Vol. 2, 75–79.
10. Şpac, I. *Revista "Arhivele Basarabiei" (1929–1938). Studiu documentar-informativ* [Arhivele Basarabiei Journal (1929–1938). Research Study]; Bons Offices: Chişinău, Moldova, 2006.
11. Roman, A. Patrimoniul arhivistic al R.A.S.S.M. în perioada interbelică [RASSM's Archival Patrimony during the Interwar Period]. In *Pergament. Anuarul arhivelor Republicii Moldova*, 2000–2001; Vol. 3–4, 136–141.
12. Роман, А.Т.; Руснак, Г.Е. Судьба документального наследия Республики Молдова в годы второй мировой войны [Soarta moştenirii documentare a Republicii Moldova în anii celui de-al doilea război mondial/The Fate of the Republic of Moldova's Documentary Heritage]. In mu uum, 1995; Vol. 4–5, 59–69.
13. Moroz, S. Arhivele, R.S.S.M. în perioada anilor 1920–1960 [MSSR's Archives during 1920–1960]. In *Pergament. Anuarul arhivelor Republicii Moldova*, 2004–2005; Vol. 7–8, 189–196.
14. Kennedy Grimsted, P. *Archives and Manuscript Repositories in the U.S.S.R., Ukraine and Moldavia General Bibliography and Institutional Directory*; Princeton University Press: Princeton, NJ, 1988.
15. Государственные архивы Молдавской ССР [Arhivele de stat ale R.S.S. Moldoveneşti]. *Государственные архивы СССР: справочник [Arhivele de stat ale URSS: călăuză/ USSR State Archives: Guide], Главное Архивное Управление при Совете Министров СССР, Всесоюзный научно-исследовательский институт документоведения и архивного дела, 2 часть, Москва, Изд. «Мысль»*, 1989; 240–248.
16. Андриеш-Табак, Сильвиу. Архивные фонды переданные из Кишинева в Измаил. Учреждения российского периода (1812–1917 гг.) [Fondurile arhivistice transmise de la Chişinău la Ismail. Instituţiile perioadei ruseşti (1812–1917)]. In *Pontes. Review of South East European Studies*, 2004; Vol. 1, 94–114.
17. *Путеводитель по Центральному Государственному Архиву Молдавской ССР [Îndrumător prin Arhiva Centrală de Stat a R.S.S. Moldoveneşti/Guide to the Central Archives of SSR Moldova], Изд,* «Наука» Молдавского филиала Академии Наук СССР: Кишинёв, 1959; 213.
18. *Îndrumător al Arhivei Naţionale a Republicii Moldova* [Guide to the National Archives of the Republic of Moldova]; Chişinău, Moldova, 2004, Part 1, up to 1917, 2nd Ed.
19. *Центральный Государственный Архив Молдавской ССР и его филиал в г. Тирасполе. Краткий справочник [по фондам за 1917–1984 гг.]*, [Arhiva Centrală de Stat a R.S.S. Moldoveneşti şi filiala ei din or. Tiraspol. Scurtă călăuză [prin fondurile din anii 1917–1984/Central Archives of SSR Moldova and Its Branch in Tiraspol. Brief Guide to Fonds 1917–1984] Изд. «Штиинца»: Кишинёв, 1988.

20. *Cancelaria Guvernatorului Basarabiei (1817–1917)* [Bessarabia's Governor's Chancellery]; *Revista fondului*; Chişinău, Moldova, 2003; Vol. 2 .
21. *Jewish Roots in Ukraine and Moldova. Pages from the Past and Archival Inventories*; Miriam Weiner Routes to Roots Foundation: Secaucus, NJ, 1999; by Miriam Weiner in cooperation with the Ukrainian State Archives and the Moldovan National Archives; YIVO Institute for Jewish Research.
22. Тодорашко, З. Г. Обзор архивных фондов Центрального государственного архива Приднестровской Молдавской Республики [Privire generală asupra fondurilor de arhivă din Arhiva centrală de stat a Republicii Moldoveneşti Nistrene]. *Ежеzодный исторический альманах Приднестровья*, [Almanahul istoric anual al Transnistriei/ Annual Historical Almanach of Transnistria], 1997; Vol. 1, 87–89.
23. Cechirlan, A. Arhiva Organizaţiilor Social-Politice a Republicii Moldova: condiţiile preliminare de formare şi locul ei în sistemul arhivelor Republicii [Archives of the Social-Political Organizations in the Republic of Moldova: Preliminary Conditions for Its Establishment and Its Place in Moldova's Archival System]. In *Pergament. Anuarul arhivelor Republicii Moldova*, 2001; Vol. 2, 99–103.
24. Antonovici, D. Registrele de stare civilă—izvor de cunoaştere a strămoşilor noştri [Civil Records: Source for Our Ancestry]. In *Pergament. Anuarul arhivelor Republicii Moldova*, 1999; Vol. 1, 35–40.
25. Gore, P. Arhivele [Archives]. Revista Arhivelor **1924–1926**, *1* (1–3), 8–20.
26. Roman, A. *Arhivistica. Manual*, Chişinău: Universitatea de Stat din Moldova, Chişinău, 1997 [Archival Studies. Manual].
27. Andrieş-Tabac, S. Societatea de Genealogie, Heraldică şi Arhivistică" Paul Gore" la cinci ani de activitate [The "Paul Gore" Genealogy, Heraldry and Archival Science Society at Five Years of Activity]. In *Tyragetia*, 2003; Vol. 2, 353–358.
28. Тодорашко, З. Г. Общество историков-архивистов Приднестровья: становление и первые шаги [Societatea istoricilor-arhivişti din Transnistria: devenirea şi primii paşi/Society of Historians-Archivists in Transnistra: Beginning and Evolution]. *Ежеzодныйисторический альманах Приднестровья*; [Almanahul istoric anual al Transnistriei], 2001; 5, 112–114.
29. Остерман, Албина Безвали, Вера Обьяснительный каталог Музея Бессарабского Земства, Кишинёв, 1912; стр. 1.
30. National Archives of the Republic of Moldova, Fond 65, inventory 2, file 15, 2.
31. Отчёт о работе Земского музея за 1911год, Кишинёв, 1912; стр. 3.
32. Труды Церковно Историко-Археологического Общества, Кишинёв, 1910; том.1, стр. 9.
33. Brihuneţ, E. *Reînfiinţarea Muzeului Antichităţilor Bisericeşti – o necesitate pentru spiritualitatea noastră// Muzeul Bisericesc din Chişinău—geneză, împliniri, pribregii*, [Re-establishment of the Church Antiquities Museum-A Must for Our Spirituality/Chişinău Church Museum-Genesis, Accomplishments, Exile]. Chişinău, Moldova, 2006; 52.
34. Decretul – Lege din 11 noiembrie 1937 [Decree-Law of 11 November 1937]. *Buletinul Muzeului Regional al Basarabiei*; Chişinău, Moldova, 1937; 7.
35. National Archives of the Republic of Moldova, Fond 2011, inventory 1, file 61, 276.
36. Hotărârea CC al PCUS din 12 iunie 1964 Cu privire la ridicarea rolului muzeelor în educaţia comunistă a maselor [Decision of the Central Committee of the Communist Party of the Soviet Union of 12 June 1964 Regarding the Growth of Museums' Role in the Communist Education of the Masses]. *Moldova Socialistă*, 20 iunie 1964; 1.
37. Archives of the Ministry of Culture. Fond Acte, file 23, 14.
38. http://www.bnrm.md/biblioteca/1.2.php Fond iniţial de carte [Initial Collection].
39. Negru, N. *Bibliotecile Basarabiei şi ale Transnistriei şi constiinta de comunitate [Libraries in Bessarabia and Transnistria and Community Consciousness]*; Biblioteca Nationala a Republicii Moldova: Chişinău, Moldova, 2002.
40. Negru, N. Bibliotecile Basarabiei şi conştiinţa de comunitate: 1812–1918 [Libraries in Bessarabia and Community Consciousness: 1812–1918], 9 (1998): 342–344; Bibliotecile Basarabiei şi conştiinţa de comunitate [Libraries in Bessarabia and Community Consciousness]. *Biblioteca*, 1999; 2, 51–53; 6 (1999): 181–183; 7 (1999): 214–216; 8 (1999): 247–248; 9 (1999): 277–280.
41. Data provided by the National Library Council to the National Bureau for Statistics for inclusion in the *2007 Statistical Yearbook*.
42. Number of Libraries in Moldova Diminishes, but Number of Readers Grows Up. Available at http://www.azi.md/news?ID=40562.
43. Anghelescu, H.G.B. The National Library of the Republic of Moldova: old legacies and new identities. Alexandria J. Natl. Int. Libr. Inform. Issues **2004**, *16*/*1*, 3–16.
44. National Library of Moldova. Annual Report 2006. Available at http://www.nlib.ee/cenl/docs/annual_reports/Moldova_annual_report_2006.pdf.
45. Despre Noi—Prezentare Generală [About Us—Overview]. Available at http://www.bncreanga.md/desprenoi.html.
46. IBBY National Sections. Available at http://www.ibby.org/index.php?id=441.
47. Bejan, E. Children's book fair in Moldova. Bookbird **1999**, *37*/*3*, 38–40.
48. Istoric [Historical overview]. Available at http://www.hasdeu.md/ro/index.html?pg=3.
49. Harjevschi, M.; Andritchi, S. *Performing Legal Research: The Moldovan Experience*, 2006; February. Available at http://www.nyulawglobal.org/globalex/Moldova1.htm (accessed August 8, 2008).
50. Osoianu, V. Suntem un neam al cărţii [We are a Nation of book-lovers]. Magazin. Bibliologic. **2008**, *1*/*2*, 59–63.
51. South East Area Health Education Center. NC/Moldovan Library Partnership. Available at http://www.coastalahec.org/library/library-moldova.asp.
52. Biblioteca în Date [Data about the Library]. Available at http://www.iatp.md/brit/biblio2.html.
53. Prezentare generală [Overview]. Available at http://www.lib.ase.md/despre.htm.

54. Anghelescu, H.G.B. Libraries in the Republic of Moldova. In *Encyclopedia of Library and Information Science*; Drake, M.A., Ed.; Marcel Dekker: New York, 2006; online update.
55. Soros Foundation. Soros Foundation Moldova: Activity Report 1997, Chişinău, Moldova, 1998. Available at http://www.soros.md/docs/rep97en.pdf (accessed October 1, 2008).
56. Gologan, L. Viitorul bibliotecilor din Moldova prin prisma societăţii informaţionale: O nouă viziune asupra problemelor cunoscute [Future of Libraries within the context of the Information Society: A new view on old issues]. Magazin Bibliologic **2006**, *1–2*, 43–49.
57. Moldova: Focus on Faculty, Lessons for Libraries. Available at http://www.eifl.net/cps/sections/news/spotlight/2008_01_10_moldova-focus-on-faculty.
58. Magazin Bibliologic, *1*, **2007**.
59. Chiţoroagă, V. *Camera Naţională a Cărţii: 45 De Ani 1957–2002/National Book Chamber the 45th Anniversary 1957–2002/Natsionalnaia Knizhnaia Palata 45 Let 1957–2002*; Camera Naţională a Cărţii: Chişinău, Moldova, 2002.
60. Kulikovski, L. Invăţământul biblioteconomic din Europa în contextul procesului de la Bologna. Ralierea învăţământului biblioteconomic superior din Moldova la acest process [Library Science Education within the Bologna Process. Alignment of Library Science Higher Education to This Process]. *Probleme actuale ale teoriei şi practicii biblioteconomice*; Museum: Chişinău, Moldova, 2005; 37–50.
61. Republic of Moldova. Parliament. Lege cu privire la biblioteci [Law Regarding Libraries], nr. 286/16 November 1994.
62. Moldova: Current Issues in Cultural Policy Development and Debate/Main Cultural Policy Issues and Priorities. Available at http://www.culturalpolicies.net/web/moldova.php?aid=41 (accessed August 8, 2008).

Moving Image Indexing

James M. Turner
School of Library and Information Sciences, University of Montreal, Montreal, Quebec, Canada

Abstract
Several types of moving images are available now, and each has its own indexing needs. In addition, a number of levels of indexing are necessary, depending on the type of image, the type of collection, and the needs of users. In information science, work on providing indexing to the various levels has largely to do with finding ways to recycle text created for other purposes in the processes of production, in order to point to individual shots, sequences, scenes, or chapters. Such text recycling needs to happen automatically, through the application of algorithms developed for this purpose, since indexing at the various levels by humans is prohibitively expensive in most circumstances. Multilingual indexing is an issue in the context of retrieving images in a networked environment. Another issue is access to moving images using indexing approaches other than subject indexing. Tagging of images by users is prevalent in the networked environment, and a discussion of its usefulness is included. Finally, there is some speculation on what the future of moving image indexing might bring.

INTRODUCTION

The term "moving images" is actually a misnomer, since moving images are actually still images that give the illusion of movement when they are displayed in rapid order. For 35 mm film, such as that projected in movie theaters, the rate is 24 images/sec, and for video, the rate is 30 images/sec (the video frame rate actually varies considerably, depending on various technologies and standards). Early attempts at making moving images resulted in a number of intriguing technologies and gadgets such as the thaumatrope, phenakistiscope, zoetrope, praxinoscope, and so on, and today people still enjoy the simple magic of flip books, kaleidoscopes, and animated gifs, along with moving images made using highly sophisticated digital technologies. The first public projection of moving images on film took place in France in 1895. Now, over a 100 years later, many technologies for making moving images are available. Home video cameras are practically a household staple, and even young children learn not only to use them but also to edit their work on computers using software that is easier to use than a word processor.

Large collections of moving images have built up in local, national, and international institutions and in the homes of private collectors. Compared to methods for providing access to books and other text materials, methods for providing access to moving images remain relatively undeveloped. Historically, the landscape of collections of still images, moving images, and sound has been characterized by ad hoc organization. This began with museum collections of paintings, prints, and drawings, and continued through the building of collections of photographs in libraries and archives, and later with moving image and sound collections in studios, libraries, and archives of all types.

Since most formal information was historically consigned to books, all other types of materials came to be considered as special collections, and emphasis was placed on developing cataloging and classification systems for organizing printed materials. Those responsible for the management of audiovisual collections of all types were left to develop their own methods for organization of these collections. For collections of art images, the methods developed by managers of such large and important collections as those at Harvard and Princeton came to be borrowed elsewhere, but essentially, each collection was organized in isolation, its methods based on practical issues and with specific goals in mind, usually to support scholarship in art history.

With some exceptions such as cinematheques, national broadcasters in some countries, the UCLA Film and Television Archive, and the National Audiovisual Institute (Institut national de l'audiovisuel, INA) in France, moving image collections still suffer from levels of organization insufficient to serve useful purposes. In the studios, very little organization occurred until a pressing need developed. The same is true of the television networks, where emphasis has always been placed on the present and the future. With time and the development of technologies not even dreamed of when the production of movies and television programs began, owners of large collections of audiovisual works are coming to realize the importance of archival materials as heritage materials, cultural witnesses, and for their important commercial value.

Encyclopedia of Library and Information Sciences, Fourth Edition DOI: 10.1081/E-ELIS4-120043268

Perhaps the main force driving the progress now rapidly being made in developing methods of organization in recent years has been the arrival of the World Wide Web. The possibilities of networking collections, providing remote access to them, broadening the use of collections, exchanging metadata, and serving a much broader user base are very great. Such possibilities were early recognized in the information science community, and a great deal of work has already been accomplished in addressing the new issues arising from the existence of the Web. Along with this, increased awareness of the immense complexity of developing and coordinating standards of all types, providing for interoperability, access to very large masses of documentation, and preserving digital materials has taught us that a great deal more work needs to be done if we are to achieve the performance levels we so desire from networked systems.

In this entry we focus on issues in indexing moving images so that users with a broad variety of needs can find them. Providing remote access to collections greatly increases the number of potential users. More importantly, it creates new possibilities for using materials. Indexing used to be targeted to specific groups of users. However, in the new environment, the managers of collections cannot even know who will come and use their collections if they provide access to the broad internet community. We discuss the various levels of access, the relationship between text and image, multilingual indexing, indexing other than subject indexing, image tagging, and look briefly at the future of moving image indexing.

LEVELS OF ACCESS

Interestingly, if problematically, there is no consensus on the terminology used for these levels of access in the literature of moving image management. This literature includes the areas of information science, computer science, film studies, literature, popular culture, and cultural studies. The most widely used general term for managing moving image collections is "asset management," a vague, unfortunate term suggesting financial or banking activity and reflecting the preoccupation of the commercial movie studios. However, since it is now deeply implanted, there is no point in trying to control its use. Section, chapter, sequence, scene, and shot are used diversely in various contexts, with meanings sometimes overlapping or outright jumbled. Thus in discussing these issues it is useful, at least until the terminology becomes stable, for authors and others to define clearly what they mean. Various kinds of users need various levels of access to moving images. This needs to be taken into account in building information systems and in providing indexing to their content. Here we discuss levels of access from the point of view of information organization for providing access to users of collections of audiovisual materials.

The notions of *ofness* and *aboutness*, propounded in seminal articles on the subject of picture indexing by Sara Shatford[1,2] and Karen Markey,[3,4] arise from work by the art historian Erwin Panofsky in the area of interpretation of works of art. Panofsky[5] describes three levels of interpetation of images, which he calls pre-iconographic, iconographic, and iconologic. The first level (pre-iconographic) refers to primary or natural subject matter, requiring familiarity with objects and events for interpretation. The second level (iconographic) refers to secondary or conventional subject matter, requiring familiarity with specific themes and concepts for interpretation. The third level (iconologic) refers to tertiary or symbolic subject matter, the meaning of which is derived from complex manipulations impossible to elaborate completely. The levels described by Panofsky have been widely adapted to picture indexing, although the process of interpretation involves a number of inconsistencies. Since the practice applies mainly to art images, we will not discuss it further here. However, it illustrates the notion of levels of access, a concept very much present in indexing moving images.

The levels of access range from whole productions such as movies, through various divisions of such documents, down to individual images or frames from them. A helpful way to contextualize the levels is to define them using the *Rules for Archival Description* (RAD),[6] useful for describing materials down to the item level. For moving images, additional levels need to be added to reflect the granularity required to index moving images in some contexts:

RAD levels: Fonds
- Series
  - Subseries
    - File
      - Item

Additional levels:
- Chapter
  - Scene
    - Sequence
      - Shot
        - Frame

In between the most general level of indexing (in the case of movies, generally the Item level in the RAD hierarchy, although in some cases this could be the series or subseries level) and indexing individual frames, movies can be divided at a number of levels: there are the main divisions such as the "chapters" found on commercial DVDs; each chapter is composed of a number of sequences or scenes, these in turn composed of shots, made up of individual frames. Videos and television programs can have similar divisions, or different divisions, depending on the nature of each work. In the case of television programs, a situation comedy, for example, can be divided by season, episode, and thence as a movie, with sequences, shots, and frames. In contrast, a current events program might have an introduction, a kind of table of contents (roster of what the individual segments will be), the segments themselves, each an individual production, and some concluding material, along with previews of the next week's show.

The level at which a collection needs to be indexed depends on its users and the type of material it holds. For collections that include films along with other types of materials, the most general level is likely what is needed. A research collection will want to offer more detailed information, both in the cataloging and the indexing. A television archive needs tight control over specific information about the production issues. In some cases, individual shots, even individual frames, need to be indexed.

Item-Level Indexing

At the highest, most general level, moving images can be treated as if they were books, for example, in the collection of a public library that offers DVDs of movies to its users. Methods for organizing collections at this level are available through chapters created for this purpose in the *Anglo-American Cataloguing Rules* (AACR2R), presently being replaced by the development of the *Resource Description and Access*[7] rules. Other tools such as Yee's[8] work on moving image cataloging, the *Compendium of cataloging practice for moving image materials*,[9] and the revision of *Archival Moving Image Materials: A Cataloging Manual*[10] offer methods targeted more specifically to moving image collections. These offer rules for providing access points such as author (director), title, the principal players, and so on.

In mixed collections, it is arguably more useful to provide subject access via the same controlled vocabulary that is used for other types of materials such as books. At this level of indexing, this is often perfectly adequate. However, in collections that house only moving images, many in-house controlled and uncontrolled vocabularies can be found. The work of harmonizing these in a networked environment is best accomplished by adopting metadata standards that will foster interoperability. The Association of Moving Image Archivists (AMIA),[11] one of the most important players in the movement to better organize moving image collections jointly with the Library of Congress, is building a union catalog to offer access to moving image collections worldwide. This service is called Moving Image Collections (MIC)[12] and offers portals notably for cataloging and metadata resources and for preservation resources.

Chapter-, Scene-, and Sequence-Level Indexing

At present, these ever-finer levels are mainly found in a production context, notably for finding existing materials to be recycled in new productions. If access at these levels were made more universally available, the systems would of course find new users, because they would permit levels of analysis, comparison, and synthesis of content that are not readily available now. Since the names of chapters are already defined in the context of commercial DVDs, they can be readily included in cataloging records to provide a kind of table of contents for users.

Within each chapter, however, analysis of the scenes, and within these the sequences, are not so readily provided. As we noted, there is not even consensus on the terminology for these divisions. What some call a "scene," for example, is called a "sequence" or even a "shot" by others. Still, a great deal of work is going on in computer science to detect divisions automatically. In general, this works well for shots, although certain types of images confuse the detection algorithm, such as explosions, during which the image content from frame to frame is so different. At the other extreme are cross-fades, in which one scene so slowly becomes another as to fool the algorithm into thinking the scene is continuous. Such problems are relatively minor, however, and with time more sophisticated algorithms will take them into account and a perfect score will be achieved.

Scene and sequence detection are not so simple, however, since they are logical divisions with no easy cues for algorithms that work on the pixels in the image to detect. However, at least with scripted productions, we can imagine algorithms that make use of the script, coding used by editors, and other such documentation, to identify automatically and accurately where there is a scene or sequence change. For the moment, however, human indexers must do this work.

Shot-Level Indexing

Shot-level indexing or shot-by-shot indexing provides a level of access that is very useful in a number of situations. It can be vaguely compared to back-of-the-book indexing, in that users could identify a concept, object, event, or person they wanted to see, look it up in the index, and be led to images of it. If shot-level indexing were available, filmmakers, researchers, film and other historians, students, even the general public would all be able to make good use of it. However, all indexing by humans is expensive and time consuming, so shot-by-shot indexing is carried out at present only if there is a payoff that can justify the cost at the other end, or if it is absolutely necessary in order for users of a collection to be able to do their work. At present there are two principal cases of this, and each has its own needs: stockshot libraries and television newsrooms.

Stockshot libraries are built by recycling material (called outtakes) that was shot for some purpose but never used in the final product. They can be the rejected takes of a shot that did get used, shots the editor simply decided not to use in the final cut, even sometimes material that is shot for stock because a cameraperson on location noticed something nearby that was not part of the shoot, but that he or she felt would be useful material for the stockshot library. Interestingly, in stockshot libraries the shots do not yet have a context. This is provided by the preceding and following shots once they are edited into a production of some kind. Thus the shots need to be indexed as individual entities unrelated to anything else. The only useful way to do this is simply to name the persons, objects, or events seen in the image.

Television newsrooms represent the other case in which shot-by-shot indexing is necessary, this time for the functioning of the newsroom. News events tend to grow, over the period of a day (a gala event), a few days (a factory fire), weeks (an election campaign), months (weather), or years (a war), building on what has already happened. Newsrooms usually have trained searchers on location in the newsroom, who need to be able to hunt down material in a matter of minutes, sometimes even seconds. Because the material usually (but not necessarily) has to do with previous events that are part of the story, there is context. At a primary level, the indexing can be carried out like that of a stockshot library, that is, particular to individual shots. In addition, however, other layers of indexing can be added, for example to relate the shot to its neighbors in the day's shoot, to the events of the previous day, to the story at large, or in a more global context, such as with links to other stories that are related in some way.

In addition, a trend is emerging that will extend in the coming years the pool of moving images cataloged and indexed at the shot level. Large collections gradually being digitized and coming on line will make available many more moving images that can be recycled in other contexts. An interesting example of this is the Institut national de l'audiovisuel (National Audiovisual Institute, INA) in France.[13] Created in 1975 following the breakup of the national broadcaster (Office de radiodiffusion télévision française, ORTF), INA became the official repository for French radio and television when the legal deposit for these was applied starting in 1995. As of 2007, INA had 130 km of shelving space filled with radio and television programs, covering 60 year of radio and 50 year of television. INA's collection is now the largest digitized audiovisual collection in the world. Much of it is already online, and the rest is gradually becoming available.

INA has long practiced shot-level indexing of its collections, but now that the moving image is available online, a mutation is occurring. Instead of simply maintaining their traditional role as audiovisual documents, these take on the additional role of containers from which fragments can be taken for use elsewhere. In this emerging context, today over half of INA's 250 document professionals have taken on editorial duties, packaging these fragments in new ways. Thus the coherence of the original document becomes a single layer of a much more complex process whereby the shots they contain become new resources as they are reconfigured in new uses. Accompanying this process, new metadata is created to document the new context.

We can expect to see this kind of activity become universal practice as other large national collections become available online, offering direct access to the moving image. Use of such collections will probably increase considerably because the shot-level metadata will make useful material easy to find in a number of different contexts. Similarly, the potential user base will be greatly broadened because the networked environment offers the possibility of worldwide sales.

Frame-Level Indexing

At the finest, most specific level individual frames need to be indexed, usually in specialized situations such as for scientific or forensic purposes. For example, indexing describing specific objects and their movement might be used in the case of scientists wishing to study the eruption of a volcano, popcorn popping, cell division, and so on. Forensic uses include the Zapruder film of the assassination of U.S. President John Kennedy, determining the cause of the the space shuttle Challenger exploding, or analysis of the planes crashing into the twin towers of the World Trade Center in New York on September 11, 2001.

This level is also of interest to filmmakers, especially animators, who through their work become intensely aware of the content of each image, how much the image needs to move to ensure that the eye is fooled into seeing natural movement. Norman McLaren famously pointed out that the important part is what happens between the frames.

TEXT AND IMAGE

A great deal of research is going on in computer science, attempting to teach computers to recognize objects and people with a view to generating the indexing automatically. There is some hope that eventually techniques will be developed that will permit this to happen, but progress is slow. Even with still images, the technique of identifying one or more key images, then asking the system to "find me more like this" often yields results that are so off the mark as to be amusing. Only in highly controlled situations are any usable techniques available. However, with so many researchers working on the various problems connected with boundary detection, object recognition, perspective, proportions, spatial relationships, and so on, there is hope that eventually the complexities of these problems will be modeled adequately and that these so-called "low-level" techniques (statistical manipulation of pixels to generate semantics) will make a significant contribution to moving image retrieval. In the best systems, these will work in conjunction with the "high-level" techniques (humans attaching semantic information to images). The discourse in the literature of computer science in this regard most often sees text as a messy problem to be eliminated in favor of fabulous computer techniques that will do the job much better. However, when we consider indexing both still and moving images for storage and retrieval, it quickly becomes clear that text and image are inextricably linked.

We need to use words to retrieve images, and words will remain an important contributor to retrieval strategies. Text is indeed the messy problem computer science researchers identify, but to eliminate it would be to throw the baby out with the bathwater. Text will always be necessary for retrieving images for the simple reason that a great deal of information useful in retrieving images from databases is not available from the images themselves. What is the name of that river in the background? Who is this actor hiding in a pumpkin costume? Is this an actual street scene of the Liberation of Paris or a reenactment? Is that really the campus of Harvard University as it says on the plaque, or is it another campus, or a studio set? What street is that church on? In what city, in what country? Documentary material especially needs text to explain the content of the image. Why is that man crying? How did that child lose its leg? Why is that dog so happy? Where are all those people going? What's going on here?

Using text to get at images is a different problem from that of using text to get at text. In the latter case, direct searches on useful terms can be conducted. The software simply looks for a match. As another layer of search capacity, text queries can be filtered through vocabulary management tools such as a thesaurus or classification to get at other text representations associated with the search string.

With images, however, a cognitive transfer takes place. The indexer looks at the image, and identifies what are the indexable objects. This is akin to assigning meaning to people and objects we encounter in everyday life. We feel a need to identify anything that comes into view, and we use words to do it. Walking along the street, we see a siamese cat approaching and say to ourselves something like, "oh, that's a Siamese cat." If we cannot name the object directly, we are puzzled, and fish through our minds for what it might be if we do not recognize it, and what it is called if we do. We do so in order to satisfy our need to be able to slot everything into some kind of category and thus resolve the discomfort. If we are not able to identify the object or to find some kind of explanation for it, we might erroneously decide it is something else, or ask another person to explain what it is. In extreme cases, fear takes over and we panic.

The phenomenon of dealing with unfamiliar reality is often used as a premise in films about people transported to another century or to another planet. The everyday reality is so different from what they know that the characters need to climb a steep learning curve just to be able to function. When objects or other subject matter are not identifiable, as in fantasy films or with special effects, usually it is because the characters do not yet know what they are either, and in due time an explanation will be given to both the characters and the viewers. A similar situation involves a special culture (say, *Star Trek*) with its own language and conventions, which are known to aficionados but not necessarily to outsiders.

In practice, however, and with ordinary images from everyday life, naming objects is quite easy and direct. Indexers do not need to agonize over finding the best indexing terms, because indexing involves simply naming the persons, objects, or events being portrayed. Things may have more than one name, but if a list is made, the pool of readily available names for an object is quickly exhausted. When all the useful terms are attached to images, the images are retrieved using any of the terms assigned. A number of studies have shown that professional indexers and ordinary users assign the same terms to images of everyday, easily recognizable people, objects, and events. We wouldn't expect an untrained person to be able to index a book adequately, so why are untrained people so good at indexing pictures? The explanation seems to lie in the nature of the material. The objects are common to everyone's reality, and they do not have more than a few names, so that they are easily identified and named. This phenomenon probably explains, at least partly, why Web sites such as Flickr, YouTube, and MySpace work so well. Users find things readily because the useful keywords to assign to them are obvious. Indexing a book, however, involves a lot of synthesis, interpretation, grouping, and so on. In short, it is rigorous intellectual work.

We note in passing that the same indexing approach used for pictures applies to sound. We hear something, and want to know what it is. Once we have attached a name to it, the issue is resolved and we are satisfied. If we cannot name it, we seek help in identifying it. Libraries of stock sounds use the same indexing approach as libraries of stock images, that is, either categorizing the sounds into useful themes or attaching useful keywords to the sounds, or both.

Interestingly, since images are representations of objects and not the objects themselves, we can be easily fooled. Decors in movies, for example, can be shot on location or constructed as sets, or filming can take place in a location that is not the location represented. Thus, in indexing some collections of moving images, provision needs to be made for the real location and the represented location, the real time at which the image was shot and the represented time. Viewers' minds can also be stretched somewhat with representations of the characters. However, the representation of well-known people in movies has to fall within boundaries to which viewers can suspend disbelief. Sounds, of course, can also be faked, and in fact this practice is widespread in movies, to the point where the profession of a Foley artist is to do just that. Again, the database structures of systems that manage this kind of information may need to take this into account, depending on their users and the needs of their users.

Recycling Text

Because of the high costs in both money and time when indexing is created by humans, efforts in information science research are focused on finding ways to reuse text that was created for other purposes in the processes of producing moving images. This involves recycling useful keywords and attaching them to individual shots. An obvious example is the use of closed-captioning subtitles, created for the deaf and for people with hearing loss. These transcribe, more or less faithfully, everything that is said by anyone on or off camera. In some subtitling and closed-captioning systems, additional sound information needed to understand the action is indicated, for example that a telephone is ringing or that there is a knock at the door, not seen in the image. Additional cues advise who exactly is speaking, that someone is not speaking but singing, that sound is coming from a radio, loudspeaker, or other device, what someone is thinking, and so on. When connections are made between closed-captioning text and the corresponding image, a user who remembers a snippet of dialogue can very quickly get to the image during which the dialogue was recited.

Note, however, that the text of closed-captioning has to do with the spoken word. It does not describe the image. Another technology, audio description, adds a special sound track for users of moving image materials who are blind or who have some vision loss. A describer recites text that offers descriptions of what is happening in the image. Users can already decode the story to some degree by following the dialogues and other sound information, but the audio description text uses words to describe aspects of the image that are essential for understanding the action. From the point of view of moving image indexing research, we might say that audio description text complements the closed-captioning text, in that the audio description indexes the image and the closed-captioning indexes the sound.

These two examples give an idea of the potential of recycling text created for other purposes in indexing moving images. There are many, many other kinds of text produced in the process of making moving image documents, and the challenge is to harness these in a way that automates the process of indexing. Other useful texts include the shooting script broken down for the shoot, in which all the decors, props, costumes, accessories, lighting, weather, and so on are described, the editor's logs, created early in the process to help the editor identify individual shots, producer's notes, director's notes, and camera reports.

As is the case with the creation of every other kind of information, moving image production is rapidly moving to a digital environment. Although it is doubtful whether moving image production will ever be entirely digital, it will come very close to that goal. The dream of mining for indexing terms the computer systems used to manage all the textual information needed to make a film is a worthy one. If techniques for parsing and tagging text identified as useful for indexing the image are applied to existing text, and links made from it to the corresponding image, systems that offer access to individual shots can be built.

MULTILINGUAL INDEXING

In the context of globalization, multilingual indexing of moving images is becoming more and more important, even unavoidable. The use of collections that are searchable via the Web can be greatly increased if people all over the world can find them using their own language. The notions that everyday objects are common to everyone's reality, and that they do not have more than a few names at most, can be exploited to automate the indexing of still and moving images in many languages, once they have been indexed in one language, theoretically any language.

We hasten to add that automatic translation of the names of objects is not the same problem as automatic translation of continuous text. In the latter case, the typical messiness and sometimes outright anarchy of natural language offer considerable challenges, and automatic translation of continuous texts has not yet been modeled well enough to give satisfying results, except in highly controlled situations. However, work on these problems continues apace, and progress is steady. In the case of automatically translating the names of objects, the correspondence between languages is much more direct, and there are no grammatical or idiomatic issues to resolve.

Interestingly, it is not even necessary to index each collection in multiple languages for multilingual indexing of moving images to come about. What is needed is online bilingual or multilingual dictionaries, thesauruses, and other vocabulary management tools such as classifications, ontologies, authority lists, semantic maps, and so on. A sample scenario of how searches could work is this: a system could filter through an automatic translator a query made in any language, put the term sought into all other languages available, with each language search the participating databases locally, gather and compile the results, and return the images to the user. One of our studies in this area[14] filtered queries in English and French through eight freely available Web translators, to test how accurate they were in producing a correct term in the other language. The poorest performer of the eight still got the correct answer 72% of the time.

Since objects can have more than one name, a method to measure the success of the correspondence between languages needed to be developed. We used a bilingual dictionary. If the term the automatic translator came up with in response to a query from the source language was one of those listed in the dictionary for the term in the target language, we considered the translation successful. There is good reason to believe this will work well using any languages; however, empirical research that tests across the various families of languages is necessary to prove this conclusively.

What is missing to make automatic multilingual queries possible is infrastructure in the form of online tools and metadata. The online tools involved are the multilingual vocabulary management tools mentioned earlier. A number of these are already available, but not necessarily in multiple languages or with interoperable structures. With time, various interested parties, many of whom are outside the realm of information management, will develop these and put them on line. When that happens, they will be available to exploit.

Exploitation of such tools will be made possible through metadata infrastructure. This involves common or standardized description tools and methods, layers of metadata to make them interoperable, query languages and programming that can exploit the content, and user interfaces that make the behind-the-scenes activity transparent to the user. Available standards and recommendations such as the Dublin Core Metadata Initiative (DCMI), Simple Knowledge Organization System (SKOS), Material Exchange Format (MXF), JPEG2000, and the Resource Description Framework (RDF) are the kinds of tools such a metadata infrastructure needs to include. However, these are not yet mature enough or implanted widely enough to make the dream of universal access to moving images come true.

INDEXING OTHER THAN SUBJECT INDEXING

In information science, the term "indexing" commonly refers to subject indexing. However, more broad definitions of the term include any indicator or other way to point to something, aptly illustrated by the index finger, the finger used to point, apparently the origin for the term. In indexing moving images, a number of access points other than the subject are especially useful in narrowing down long lists of images returned in response to a query. For example, if only a particular type of shot will do, the user might as well specify this in the original query, thus eliminating shots that do not conform and increasing the pertinence of those that do. Such a search strategy supposes that the shots have been indexed using such access points. Following is a discussion of some of these.

Camera angles: How the camera is looking at the object of interest in the image is often important, and sometimes critical. Ready examples of this include aerial views, close-ups of faces, or satellite images. A number of relatively standardized lists of types of shots are available, reflecting terminology in various national and other contexts, and any of these can be used as an authority list. Alternately, codes can be derived from such lists. By attaching these to records of individual shots, access by camera angle becomes available to the user.

Colors: In some kinds of collections, for example specialized collections of any kind of object such as cars, museum objects, clothing, animals, and so on, colors can be critical for the searcher. Dominant colors can be indexed fairly easily using standardized lists, although this can become complicated by the great number of nuances possible. In each situation, a decision on the limits of this needs to be made. Interestingly, in the low-level approaches to indexing, color is one thing searching algorithms can calculate easily, so that in hybrid systems words do not have to be used to provide indexing of colors. For example, the system can calculate the number of pixels within a range of color codes, and return images in which the desired color is dominant.

Time periods: As we noted earlier, there is real time (when the shot was actually taken) and represented time (in scripted productions, when the action takes place). Thus a shot might be taken in 2005 but the action in the film takes place in 1724. If both these dates are indexed, searches on the date become available to the user. Some time periods we might wish to represent are not so precise, so that coding for more vague periods such as the seasons of the year, various moments in a day, or various historical groupings of a number of years is also useful. At the other extreme, sometimes very precise times, including a fraction of a second on a particular date also need to be expressed. A number of coding systems are available for expressing these, for example, the tables available at the end of the Universal Decimal Classification (UDC), which provide for all such cases and more, thus offering a controlled vocabulary that can be used for this purpose.

Geographic spaces: Similarly, there is real location (where the shot was actually taken) and represented location (in scripted productions, where the action takes place). Thus a film might be shot in Argentina but the action in the film takes place in Ireland. Again, separate fields in a database to represent these concepts will allow users to search on either. And again, a number of code lists are available, including a UDC list. Such lists are particularly useful since they permit the expression of political entities (e.g., country names and regions within a country) but also take into account geographical features which cross political borders, such as rivers, mountain ranges, and so on. With the global positioning system (GPS), it is also possible to generate coding to pinpoint precise locations.

Emotion: Indexing human emotions represented in moving images can be helpful to some users, although such indexing is rather hazardous because of the ambiguity involved. It is not always clear to the indexer which emotion is being expressed, especially if there is not enough context. However, in collections where such indexing is desirable, imperfect indexing is still much better than no indexing at all. As with every other kind of indexing, use of some kind of controlled list is desirable, even if it is an in-house list.

Lighting conditions: Whether a shot is taken indoors or outdoors is often significant. Indoors, some description of the degree of luminosity, even broad categories can be helpful, such as very bright studio lighting at one extreme and dim lounge lighting at the other. Outdoors, weather conditions are often useful to describe. Particular times of day can be covered using time period coding, but this does not cover weather and lighting conditions. The sky can be black at high noon because a thunderstorm is about to break. Managers of individual collections will need to decide what level of detail is appropriate. In general, however, a simple, controlled list of lighting conditions is probably enough.

Other indexable special conditions: A number of special conditions are indexable, again for their value in eliminating shots that do not meet such a requirement. These include underwater material, images taken by satellites or shot from space, images shot using infrared cameras or heat-detecting cameras, images reconstituted using computer technology, or anachronistically altered images modified to include a present-day person alongside people long since deceased. Other categories include images using special effects or images shot with special equipment such as fisheye or panoramic lenses.

In addition, we can imagine any number of kinds of special collections of images, for example, images of only mushrooms, stones, cars, types of screws, or furniture. Or collections of microscopic images of diseases affecting cells, forensic photographs, technical aspects of spacecraft or bridges or roofing, and so on. In these cases, the indexing problems will be centered around specialized vocabularies for describing the image content and the level of indexing required.

IMAGE TAGGING

Much has been made of the now rather hackneyed expression "Web 2.0," referring to services available in the context of the evolution of the World Wide Web. Nevertheless, services associated with this concept have been at the heart of the "democratization" of information management, based on the principle that information belongs to everyone and should circulate freely. From the point of view of access to information, this means that technology is loosening the grip of the controllers of information and making it available to everyone. From the point of view of indexing information, this notion challenges the "stranglehold" professionals have on how information is organized and managed. For better or worse, a number of phenomena have sprung up in this context and are now broadly practiced, including communal writing in the form of wikis, building communal classification structures in the form of folksonomies, and journalism in the form of blogs. The phenomenon that concerns us here is user-based indexing, commonly referred to as tagging.

Professional indexers strive for rigor and consistency, and users of the work they produce depend on these qualities in order to do their own work. The practice of indexing both still and moving pictures by untrained persons results in varying quality of indexing. Whether user tagging should even be called indexing or not is open to debate. In discussing the issue, it is important to distinguish among various types of images, because each type has its own indexing needs. For indexing purposes, it is convenient to divide the vast world of images into three categories: art images, documentary images, and "ordinary" images. For our purposes here, the same categories can be used for moving images, although a number of additional useful categorizations are available for these latter.

Art images are interpreted, analyzed, and discussed at length. Thus it is easy to argue that specialized skills are required for indexing them. Indeed, specialized skills are necessary even for looking at them and understanding them. Large bodies of scholarship can build up around even a single painting. Biographical information about artists is often included as part of the discussion. Controversies develop and generate much additional documentation. From an information management point of view, systems for still art images have been constructed mainly to support museums and art history programs in universities, and the way art images have been indexed reflects this perspective. Since the discussion of the levels of interpretation of still art images is outside the scope of this entry, suffice it to say here that historically they have been indexed at an intermediary level of interpretation, avoiding naming individual objects as we find with documentary images and ordinary images. However, now that the relatively recent networked environment has become available, the need to name individual objects in art images is more pressing than ever. In addition, in order to assist scholars, there is a need to gather all the material, whether it be textual, still or moving images, or sound, so that rather complex information systems are needed to manage information about art. Moving images in the form of art films, films about art, films made by artists, and films about artists form part of this corpus and are subject to the needs arising from the same kind of complexity.

However, documentary images are not subject to such needs. The indexing for documentary images involves identifying persons, places, and events by name, and offering explanations that help interpret the image. Although we usually associate documentary images with current events, political, or news items, in the broader sense family photos and videos also fit into this category since they chronicle the same type of information, albeit on a more local, more circumscribed scale. It is easy enough to see the value of indexing such images for those who participated in the event, be it family members or members of a social group, and indeed, these may be the ones best qualified to do the indexing. Similarly, the filmmaker and crew of a documentary may be the ones best equipped to identify and explain the content of the image, since they are so intimately associated with making arrangements for the shoot, are witness to the event, and have made the decisions about exactly how to capture it on film or video.

"Ordinary" images include pictures of animals, flowers, everyday objects, generic scenes, and so on. Examples of the use of ordinary images include illustration, decoration, or as teaching aids in a variety of contexts. Ordinary images can include anything that can be photographed, and the photographer is the "author" or creator of the image. However, in opposition to the situation with art images, the author or creator of an "ordinary" image is not usually important or significant to the user. In general, ordinary images can be indexed by anyone, based on the notion of access to a common reality, since the indexing activity consists of naming the persons, objects, or events in the image. As we mentioned earlier, several studies have shown that untrained users pick the same indexing terms as professional indexers for such images.

For purposes of managing collections of images, it is helpful to note here that the three categories of art, documentary, and "ordinary" images are not necessarily mutually exclusive. For example, an ordinary image can become part of a work of art if an artist decides, for example, to paste a magazine photo of a cup of coffee into a collage. A photographer might think she is merely documenting a person or an event but the resulting photograph is so perfect as to be considered art, or with time become famous for some reason never intended at the outset. In other cases, an image might belong to more than one category simultaneously, for example stock footage of office workers ("ordinary" images) might be sold to makers of corporate videos but for the family and friends of such workers (or actors) the footage also documents their lives (documentary images). We can also imagine the same piece of material ending up in an art film (art images).

Whatever the type of images, the problem remains in using a controlled vocabulary to do the indexing. However, for images other than art images, it is not much of a problem. If we remember that the basic function of indexing is to point to something, then we need also to remember that there can be more than one way of pointing to something. If a number of users add their own tags to images, the possible names for any object are soon covered, and any of the names will retrieve the image. The main function of a controlled vocabulary is to gather synonyms and variants and select a single term for indexing each concept. The reason we bother to do this is largely associated with technology. In the case of controlled vocabularies, the arguments for using them are still sound, but if the technology available skirts the problem they are designed to solve, do we still really need them? As an example, PREserved Context Indexing System (PRECIS) indexing fell by the wayside as computer technology developed because the complexities involved in using the system were no longer necessary. PRECIS made use of software to construct indexing strings and to shunt the strings so that each key term could appear as the entry point in an alphabetical list. However, PRECIS indexing was developed to produce print indexes. Since databases can be searched on any field, it became unnecessary to permute the indexing strings to make available all the entry points to them.

Another discussion in this context is the use of a thesaurus to index ordinary and documentary pictures. The rise of the thesaurus as an indexing tool was largely to do with arranging into semantic networks the vocabulary of specialized areas of endeavor. The notion of using a thesaurus to index a general collection of still or moving images goes against the idea of the thesaurus as a tool for managing the vocabulary of particular areas of endeavor, and supposes the existence of a general thesaurus. Surprisingly, the idea of building a thesaurus for anything that can be photographed is not so farfetched as it seems. A number of moving image collections have built such a tool for indexing their collections. A published thesaurus, the *Thesaurus for Graphic Materials*, was built for indexing documentary and ordinary still images, and is widely used for indexing both still and moving images. A few thousand terms seem to be enough to make such a tool useful, since term creation in this thesaurus and a number of in-house thesauruses seems to level off after a few thousand words.[15]

Another question is how many terms should be attached to each image. As Dizard (2004)[16] puts it, "a picture is worth a thousand words, but which ones?" This is another question related to technology, and the reason for determining limits had to do with the amount of work involved in managing information systems. The point here is that there are no longer technical or managerial reasons for limiting this number. A number of studies have shown that one, two, or three terms are often enough, but this of course depends very much on individual images and on user needs. Today, the answer to the question of how many indexing terms to use is: as many as are useful.

Ultimately, the issue of indexing both still and moving images is economic. The cost of professional indexing is inevitably high, so it seems reasonable to reserve it for art images. For documentary and "ordinary" images, the implicit argument is that indexing by nonprofessionals is better than no indexing at all, also that it is "good enough." In addition, maintaining the tools used for such indexing adds to the costs. Since indexing ordinary and documentary pictures involves attaching names to persons, objects, and events, tagging these with keywords might well be good enough. In the end, it is a moot point, since tagging is free. If costs were involved, it is doubtful whether much tagging would occur at all. Finally, since the term tagging is associated with the practice, purists can easily distinguish between what is "properly" indexed and what is merely tagged.

THE FUTURE OF MOVING IMAGE INDEXING

By using automated techniques and by exploiting text created for other purposes, shot-level access to moving images could become readily available. How this will happen exactly is a matter of conjecture. We note, however, that already computers can easily detect when a new shot is starting because there is a radical change in the image content from one frame to the next when this happens.

Thus a production can automatically be divided into individual shots. We note that distributors of movies in DVD format usually provide chapter divisions with identifying names, allowing users to readily access individual parts of movies. Television programs also have logical divisions, and these are provided in television archives. For example, a current events show will have a number of reports, each cataloged separately and related to the whole. Thus the problem of automatically identifying the useful divisions of moving image productions is already solved. Automatically attaching indexing terms to these divisions is the next problem we need to address.

As we noted in the section on "Shot-Level Indexing," some situations use shot-level indexing by humans. How to attach keywords (synonymous for our purposes with tags and indexing terms) to sections of moving image productions and to individual shots automatically has to do with recycling existing text in a digital environment. As we noted in the section on recycling text, a number of text sources created for other purposes in the processes of production are available. Techniques used in linguistics such as shallow parsing can identify nouns and noun phrases. These are known to be the parts of speech indexers use to represent moving images at the shot level with verbs, adjectives, and adverbs appearing only rarely.

At some point in the not too distant future, production of moving image documents will be nearly entirely digital. It is already largely so. Imagine, then, large modular production databases which house not only the image and the editing information, but also virtually all the text created during the production processes. Imagine further extending the functions of such production databases to include archiving the material. By mining the text modules, parsing the text, and attaching keywords to the corresponding images, all these activities being stages of executing an algorithm, we can imagine indexing individual shots, sequences, scenes, and chapters automatically.

In addition, the work being done in this area by computer science researchers will eventually come to fruition. Because of the immense complexity involved in automatically identifying objects and relationships among them, then attaching semantic information to them, such work is largely experimental and poorly performing at present. However, the day will come when the low-level approaches and the high-level approaches will be usefully combined in hybrid systems that will most likely offer the best performance for retrieval of moving images. We can imagine attaching smart user interfaces to such systems so that they will be able to suggest search strategies using one or the other approach, dynamically, depending on contextual information.

If we add to this equation improved infrastructure that permits the ongoing deposit online of movies and television shows, as well as vast quantities of home video, along with the possibility of downloading all this and viewing it on computer screens, the picture broadens further. We can imagine Web-based systems that search all this material, along with its indexing metadata added automatically via the low-level and high-level approaches, including text in many languages, returning precise results to users of such systems. When that day comes, users will be able to get answers to questions that today cannot even be asked, and a new horizon of possibilities for study and use of the planet's visual heritage will appear.

CONCLUSION

This entry has tried to explain some of the issues surrounding moving images. Although large collections of these have been built since moving images first appeared on film in 1895, methods for organizing such collections remain largely undeveloped, at least when compared to methods for text collections. Apart from their relative recency, moving image collections are not organized so well because they have a number of very different characteristics and thus are not amenable to the same kinds of techniques.

We noted that a number of levels of access need to be provided, depending on the context of the collection and the needs of its users. These range from relatively simple cataloging of DVDs of commercial films to frame-by-frame analysis in scientific and forensic contexts. In some conditions, nonsubject access points are sometimes more useful than subject indexing terms, and a number of these access points are available for moving image documentation. Although a great deal of research in automating the indexing process using low-level approaches is being conducted in the field of computer science, the relationship between text and image is an essential one that will persist. Thus the research in information science focuses on automating the generation of indexing terms from text created for other purposes during the processes of producing moving image documents.

In a global environment, mutilingual indexing is an issue gaining prominence, and work on learning to exploit online vocabularies in many languages contributes to automating the highly desirable provision of access to moving image materials in many languages. The development of Web-based tools of many types, including controlled vocabularies, semantic networks, and bilingual and multilingual dictionaries and thesauruses will foster the acceleration of success in this area.

The need for building systems that can interact with other systems in a networked environment is the strongest force driving the work on information management systems for moving images. Necessarily complex, such systems involve a great deal of thought, planning, discussion, and development. The need to exchange information rapidly and efficiently means that the more interoperable individual systems are with other networked systems, the easier it will be for those involved to accomplish their work. Such goals are eminently worth striving for.

REFERENCES

1. Shatford, S. Describing a picture: A thousand words are seldom cost effective. Catalog. Classif. Quart. **1984**, *4* (4), 13–30.
2. Shatford, S. Analyzing the subject of a picture: A theoretical approach. Catalog. Classif. Quart. **1986**, *6* (3), 39–62.
3. Markey, K. *Subject Access to Visual Resources Collections: A Model for Computer Construction of Thematic Catalogs*; Greenwood Press: New York, 1986.
4. Markey, K. Access to iconographical research collections. Libr. Trends **1988**, *37* (2), 154–74.
5. Panofsky, E. *Meaning in the Visual Arts: Papers in and on Art History*; Doubleday Anchor Books: Garden City, NY, 1955.
6. *Rules for Archival Description*. Planning Committee on Descriptive Standards, Bureau of Canadian Archivists. Rivised version 2008, http://www.cdncouncilarchives.ca/RAD/RADComplete_July2008.pdf (accessed September 2008).
7. JSC RDA. Joint Steering Committee for the development of RDA: Resource Description and Access 2008, http://www.collectionscanada.gc.ca/jsc/rda.html (accessed March 25, 2009).
8. Yee, M.M. *Moving Image Cataloging: How to Create and How to Use a Moving Image Catalog*; Libaries Unlimited: Westport, CT, 2007.
9. *AMIA Compendium of Moving Image Cataloging Practice*, Martin, A.L., Ed.; Association of Moving Image Archivists: Hollywood, CA, 1999.
10. *AMIM2: Archival Moving Image Materials: A Cataloging Manual*, 2nd Ed.; Library of Congress: Washington, DC, 2000.
11. Association of Moving Image Archivists (AMIA), http://www.amianet.org (accessed September 2008).
12. Moving Image Collections (MIC), http://mic.loc.gov (accessed September 2008).
13. National Audiovisual Institute [France], http://www.ina.fr (accessed September 2008).
14. Turner, J.M.; Hudon, M. Multilingual metadata for moving image databases: Preliminary results. In *Advancing Knowledge: Expanding Horizons for Information Science*, Proceedings of the Annual Conference of the Canadian Association for Information Science, Howarth, L.C., Cronin, C., Slawek, A.T., Eds.; University of Toronto Press: Toronto, 2002; 34–45. http://www.cais-acsi.ca/proceedings/2002/Turner_2002.pdf (accessed September 2008).
15. Hudon, M.; Turner, J.M.; Devin, Y. How many terms are enough? Stability and dynamism in vocabulary management for moving image collections. In Proceedings of the 6th International ISKO Congress, Toronto, July, 10–13, 2000, Toronto, Canada, Beghtol, C., Howarth, L.C., Eds.; Williamson, N.J. Ergon: Würzburg, 2000; 333–338.
16. Dizard, W.P. Significa. GCN [Government Computing News], http://www.gcn.com/print/23_29/27391-1.html (accessed September 2008).

BIBLIOGRAPHY

1. *AMIA Compendium of Moving Image Cataloging Practice*, Martin, A.L., Eds.; comp. Johnson, J.D., Tadic, L., Elkins, L., Lee, C., Wood, A. Society of American Archivists, Association of Moving Image Archivists: Hollywood, CA, 2001.
2. Choi, Y.; Rasmussen, E.M. Searching for images: the analysis of users' queries for image retrieval in American history. J. Am. Soc. Inform. Sci. Technol. **2003**, *54* (6), 498–511.
3. Da Sylva, L.; Turner, J.M. Using ancillary text to index web-based multimedia objects. Liter. Linguist. Comput. **2006**, *21* (2), 219–228.
4. Edmondson, R. *Audiovisual Archiving. Philosophy and Principles*; Unesco: Paris, 2004.
5. Egeter van Kuyk, R.H.J. Historical film documentation at the Netherlands information service. UNESCO J. Inform. Sci. Libr. Arch. Admin. **1981**, *3*, 227–34.
6. Lucknow, R.; Turner, J.M. All singing, all talking, all digital; media windows and archiving practice in the motion picture studios. *Archivaria* **2008**, *65* (spring), 165–186.
7. Yee, M.M. *Moving Image Cataloging: How to Create and How to Use a Moving Image Catalog*, Third Millenium Cataloging Series; Libraries Unlimited: Westport, CT, 2007.

RELATED ORGANIZATIONS AND ASSOCIATIONS

1. American Society for Information Science and Technology, Special Interest Group on Visualization, Images, and Sound (SIG VIS).
2. The Association of Moving Image Archivists (AMIA).
3. Audiovisual Roundtable of the American Library Association (ALA).
4. The Coordinating Council of Audiovisual Archives Associations (CCAAA).
5. International Federation of Film Archives (FIAF).
6. International Federation of Library Association and Institutions, Audiovisual and Multimedia Section (IFLA AVMS).
7. International Federation of Television Archives (FIAT).

Multilingual Information Access

Douglas W. Oard
College of Information Studies, University of Maryland, College Park, Maryland, U.S.A.

Abstract
This entry describes the process by which systems can be designed to help users find content in a language that may be different from the language of their query. The discussion of the relatively narrowly construed technical issues that are often referred to as Cross-Language Information Retrieval (CLIR) is situated in the context of important related issues such as information-seeking behavior, interaction design, and machine translation.

INTRODUCTION

The central thesis of Tom Friedman's book *The World is Flat* is that we now live in a world in which technological innovation is creating opportunities for more seamless global interaction than has heretofore been possible.[1] It is important to recognize that "technological innovation" encompasses far more than mere technical innovation—equally important is our ability as a society to learn to productively use the technical capabilities that we can create. This entry examines one such technology: helping users to find information in ways that "flatten" language barriers. In keeping with what is emerging as common usage, we refer to this challenge as Multilingual Information Access (MLIA).

This word "multilingual" can be used in many ways, so let us start by saying what we mean. A multilingual collection is a collection of documents that contains more than just a single language (e.g., English and Chinese). These documents may each contain just one language, or some of the documents might contain words from more than one language. Our interest is in helping a searcher to find the documents that they seek, regardless of the language in which they are expressed. For simplicity, we will assume in this entry that documents are expressed in writing and stored as e-text (i.e., as digital sequences of character codes), but similar approaches have been applied to scanned documents and spoken word collections, and might in the future also be applied to visual languages (e.g., American Sign Language).

Who needs MLIA? We can envision at least two user groups. Perhaps the most obvious is so-called polyglots—people who are able to at least read (and perhaps write) more than one language. For example, more than one billion people who know at least some English are native speakers of some other language. Polyglots can benefit from MLIA in at least three ways: 1) they can find documents in more than one language with a single search; 2) they can formulate queries in the language(s) for which their active vocabulary is largest; and 3) they can move more seamlessly across languages over the course of an information-seeking episode than would be possible if documents written in different languages were available only from different information systems. Monoglots (those who know only a single language) form a second important group. For example, many Americans can read only English, while many citizens of China can read only Chinese. Those populations essentially live in different worlds, worlds that MLIA can help to bridge.

MLIA always involves Cross-Language Information Retrieval (CLIR), in which queries in one language are used to find documents in another. When the user cannot read the document language, some form of translation service will usually be needed. This might be as simple as automatic translation of short snippets, or as complex as on-demand translation by a subject matter expert. There are, however, also cases in which adequate results might be presented without translation. For example, someone who knows only Japanese might search a collection of newspaper photographs that are indexed using only English terms and still easily recognize which of the resulting photographs would best meet their needs.

The remainder of this entry is organized as follows. The next section places MILA in historical perspective and explains (or at least interprets) how and why modern techniques for MLIA evolved in the way that they did. The section "Cross-Language Information Retrieval" then describes the present state of the art for CLIR, the key technical capability in all MLIA applications. The section "The Rest of the Story" builds on that, broadening the coverage to address interaction design and information-seeking processes. Finally, "the entry" concludes with a brief survey of the present state of practice and elucidation of some important open questions.

Encyclopedia of Library and Information Sciences, Fourth Edition DOI: 10.1081/E-ELIS4-120043463

A BRIEF HISTORY OF MULTILINGUAL INFORMATION ACCESS

Gaining access to information in unfamiliar languages has always been an important problem. The intense technological competition that was emblematic of the Cold War in the second half of the twentieth century created a substantial demand on both sides for translation of scientific and technical papers. After some early, and rather disappointing, experiments with automatic translation, the United States National Research Council recommended in 1966 that basic research continue, but that the work of people, rather than machines, provide the principal means for making foreign-language information accessible for the foreseeable future.[2] This recommendation fostered the development of a part of the information industry that focused on translating scientific and technical literature and indexing those translations. Journal articles and so-called gray literature (e.g., technical reports) were translated either prospectively or on demand by a number of organizations, and the World Translations Index (and its predecessors) evolved to provide the needed indexing service for speakers of English.

The economic growth and linguistic diversity of Europe in the second half of the twentieth century provided the impetus for the second major innovation, the development of multilingual thesauri. Oard and Diekema surveyed the genesis of this work, from the first published report (in 1964 from Germany) through publication of the current (1985) version of ISO Standard 5964, which recommends techniques for construction of multilingual thesauri.[3]

Substantial reliance on human translation and thesaurus-based indexing were good choices at the time, but three key events dramatically changed the opportunity space. The most obvious was the end of the Cold War, which resulted in substantial changes in national investment strategies. The International Translations Centre ceased operations in 1997 with the publication of the last volume of the World Translations Index, citing declining demand for their services that resulted from increasing adoption of English as a lingua franca for scientific communication and from declining funding for information science more generally.

The second key event was the rise of the World Wide Web, and in particular the widespread adoption of Web search engines such as Lycos, AltaVista, and Google. Furnas et al. had remarked on what they referred to as the "vocabulary problem" in human–system interaction, observing that "new or intermittent users often use the wrong words and fail to get the actions or information they want."[4] Although the fuzzy-match full-text search capabilities of the 1990s-era Web search engines were far from perfect, experience with that technology began the process of incrementally shifting expectations away from intermediated thesaurus-based search and toward end-user "natural language" search.

The third event, which attracted far less attention at the time, was a remarkable payoff from the investments in basic research that the National Research Council had recommended. Earlier approaches, based on hand-coded rules, had proven to be problematic because the rules could interact in ways that were difficult to anticipate. As a result, at some point adding additional rules in an effort to improve things could actually reduce translation quality. In 1990, a group at IBM Research first published a radical new technique based on one simple idea: machines can learn to translate by using statistical analysis to identify regularities in large collections of translations that were generated by people.[5] Importantly, as more examples are provided, translation quality improves. This "data-driven" approach, which came to be called statistical Machine Translation (MT), is thus well matched to a networked world in which assembling ever-larger collections is increasingly tractable.

These three events, unfolding together in the last decade of the twentieth century, came together to transform both the need for, and the opportunities to provide, automated techniques to support multilingual information access by end users. The spark that ignited the process was a 1996 workshop at an information retrieval conference in Zurich.[6] Early techniques were limited by their reliance on online bilingual dictionaries, but techniques based on statistical machine translation were soon introduced. As described in the next section, this ultimately yielded fuzzy-match full-text search capabilities that accommodate language differences between the queries and the documents remarkably well. End-user search requires more than just accurate ways of finding documents that may be useful, however. Equally important, the user must be able to recognize those useful documents, understand their contents, and (sometimes) draw on that understanding to progressively improve their queries; the section "Conclusion" addresses those issues.

CROSS-LANGUAGE INFORMATION RETRIEVAL

The core capabilities that enable MLIA are indexing and query processing for CLIR. Indexing proceeds in three stages: 1) language and character set identification; 2) language-specific processing; and 3) construction of an "inverted index" that allows rapid identification of documents which contain specific terms. Sometimes the language in which a document is written and the character set used to encode it can be inferred from its source (e.g., *New York Times* articles are almost always written in English, and typically encoded in ASCII) and sometimes the language and character set might be indicated using metadata (e.g., the HTML standard used for Web pages provides a metadata field for specifying the character set). In other cases (or to confirm an initial guess), a very simple form of content analysis can be used to identify those boundaries languages and character sets. The usual approach is to count the frequency of character sequences, and then to guess the language based on similarity to counts computed in the same way for documents written in a known language. For example, the first sentence in this paragraph would yield the following 3-byte sequences: "the", "he ", "e c", " co", "cor", "ore", etc. The technique is easily extended to accommodate multibyte character encodings by counting bytes rather than characters. Language and character set classification using this technique is remarkably accurate (typically well over 95%) for any text that is at least as long as a typical paragraph, so language switching within a single document can sometimes also be detected using this technique.

Once the language and character set are known, the character set can be converted to a standard representation (often Unicode) and two types of language-specific processing are then typically applied: 1) tokenization to identify the terms that could be indexed; and 2) stopword removal to identify terms that need not be indexed (for efficiency reasons). For English, tokenization typically involves splitting on white space and then using rule-based techniques to remove common endings (so-called "stemming"). Identifying "word" boundaries is more complex in "freely compounding" languages such as German, Finnish, and Tamil, and in "unsegmented" languages such as Chinese. Of course, the spoken form of every language exhibits this same tendency to run words together without pauses, so techniques similar to those used in speech recognition for identifying words can be used to identify. The basic idea is to draw on two sources of evidence: we can know most of the words that exist in the language (using a dictionary), and we can guess which word sequences might make sense (e.g., from statistical analysis of word usage). Using these ideas together would tell us that the word "Washington" found in a German document might (from the dictionary) be segmented as "was," "hing," and "ton," but (from usage statistics) that such a segmentation would be unlikely to be correct—in this case we would therefore index the unsegmented word "Washington."

The inverted index used in CLIR is similar in structure to an inverted index used in any information retrieval system, but the information stored in that index may be different. Conceptually, an inverted index includes two parts: 1) a lookup table stored in fast main memory that can be used to rapidly find the "postings" for a specific term (i.e., identifiers for all documents containing that term); and 2) The postings file, which (because of its size) must be stored on the (much slower) hard disk. One of the most important advances in information retrieval system design in the past decade was the widespread introduction of automatic compression techniques for the postings file. Because these techniques are tuned to achieve the greatest compression for the most common terms, stopword removal is no longer essential as an efficiency measure in monolingual applications. In CLIR, however, deficiencies in the translation technique can sometimes yield inappropriate results for translation of very common words. Stopword removal is therefore still common in CLIR applications.

The most obvious distinguishing feature of CLIR is that some form of translation knowledge must be embedded in the system design, either at indexing time or at query time. Essentially, three approaches are possible: 1) translate each term using the context in which that word appears to help select the right translation; 2) count the terms and then translate the aggregate counts without regard to the context of individual occurrences; or 3) compute some more sophisticated aggregate "term weight" for each term, and then translate those weights. Somewhat surprisingly, while the first two of these work about equally well in many cases, term weight translation is typically not competitive.

If the user will ultimately require a machine-generated translation, and if that translation is always into the same language, then a strong case can be made for translating every term in context at indexing time. In its simplest form (which is often adequate), this essentially amounts to simply running a full machine translation system as a preprocessing step prior to building the inverted index. Efficiency arguments against this approach would be hard to make: a translation system fast enough for responsive interactive use at query time would also be fast enough to process every document in all but the very largest collections at indexing time.

When full translation is not needed (e.g., for polyglot users), or when translations into many different languages may be needed to serve a linguistically diverse population, indexing documents using the terms in their original language is typically the preferred system architecture. In this case, considerable efficiency improvements can be obtained by translating term counts rather than term occurrences. The basic approach, first discovered by Pirkola[7] (SIGIR, 1998), is to count every possible query-language translation of each term as having been found in the document. Subsequent refinements resulted in further improvements from using translation probability for individual terms to estimate partial counts[8] and from aggregating translation probabilities for synonymous terms.[9] Regardless of the details, the key idea is to compute "term weights" in the query language rather than in the document language. Many of the commonly used term weighting formulae give more weight to rare terms than to common terms, which comports well with the way professional searchers are trained to enhance the precision of their search using terms that they expect will be highly specific. Since specificity is a feature of the query, it makes sense that computing term weights in the query language would work well.

Among all of the advances in CLIR, none has had anywhere near as large an effect as accurate translation probabilities. The best reported results for systems that lack any notion of translation probability (often called "dictionary-based" techniques) are in the range of 70–80% of what would have been achieved using queries written in the same language as the documents. (These results are normally reported as an average across many topics. The most commonly reported search quality statistics in the CLIR literature is "average precision," which is designed to emphasize the density of relevant documents near the top of a ranked list where most searchers are expected to focus their attention.) The best reported results for systems that use translation probabilities well is closer to 100% of what would have been achieved using same-language queries.[9] It is worth taking a moment to consider what that means—today, we can build systems to search French documents that work (approximately) equally well regardless of whether the query is written in French or in English! Of course, for any specific query the system might do better with French or with English, but on average over repeated use the best systems that can be built today do about equally well in CLIR or monolingual applications.

The key question, therefore, is how to obtain sufficiently accurate translation probabilities. It turns out that this problem was solved for us as one part of statistical MT.[5] The key idea behind statistical MT is that a machine that knows very little about language (e.g., just how to recognize a word) can learn to recognize (and later replicate) patterns of language use by counting what happens in very large collections of examples of language use. Specifically, we give our machine an enormous collection of examples of actual translations (e.g., "man in the moon" and "l'homme dans la lune") and ask it to find the most common alignments of individual terms (e.g., "man" and "l'homme" in this case, but "l'humanite" for "man" in "the evolution of modern man"). If the examples from which the machine learns are representative of the cases to which it will later be applied, the translation probabilities learned by the machine can be quite useful. A full MT system contains additional processing stages, but for CLIR it is often sufficient to simply use the learned translation probabilities directly (with some pruning to suppress the effect of relatively rare random alignments).

THE REST OF THE STORY

There is, however, quite a bit more to the search process than simply automatically creating best-first rankings of documents that the user might wish to examine. Three key questions arise: 1) can people learn to formulate effective queries?; 2) can people recognize useful documents in the result set?; and 3) can people adequately understand the contents of those documents to meet their information needs? Research on these topics is still in its infancy, and moreover we can reasonably expect that as translation technology improves the answers to these questions may change. There will be, therefore, substantial scope for important Library and Information Science research on these questions for some time to come.

The most tractable of these questions at present turns out to be the second one: people seem to be remarkably good at recognizing useful documents using even relatively poor translations. In 2001, the Cross-Language Evaluation Forum (CLEF) started an annual interactive track (iCLEF) to foster research on these questions. In that first year, the focus was on interactive assessment of topical relevance using machine translation. Representative users (in this case, university students) were presented with a written topic statement in a language they knew well (e.g., English) and a set of news stories in some other language that they did not know at all (e.g., Spanish) that had been ranked by a CLIR system and then automatically translated back into the language of the topic statement. Topical relevance judgments made by native speakers of the language in which the news stories were written were used as a gold standard. On average (over several users, each working on several topics), the searchers who did not know the document language agreed with the native speakers about as often as two native speakers would be expected to agree with each other.[10]

Together, those studies indicate that recognizing relevant documents using automatic translation of short summaries or of entire documents is usually not a particularly difficult task. Considerable scope remains, however, for future research on optimally combining the technology for summary generation and translation, for analysis of specific cases in which present technology is not meeting user needs well, and for determining how best to present those results to the user (e.g., as several lists or as a single integrated list).

The third challenge, translating documents well enough that the user can understand their contents, is exactly the goal for which automatic systems for machine translation are optimized. Translation quality can be measured in two ways: 1) an "intrinsic" evaluation in which we ask how similar an automatic translation is to something that a human translator would actually create; or 2) an "extrinsic" evaluation in which we ask how well the reader can accomplish some task using the translation. Intrinsic evaluations provide an important way of assessing incremental progress in the design of machine translation systems, but extrinsic evaluation sheds more light on the ability of present translation technology to meet user needs in multilingual information access applications.

The iCLEF 2004 user studies provided an initial extrinsic evaluation of translation quality, measuring the user's ability to answer factual questions when searching a large collection of news stories in an unfamiliar language. The results of those studies indicated that (on average, across users) only about 70% of the questions could be answered at all, and that (on average, across users and answered questions) only about 70% of those answers were correct. Considering both factors together, those factual questions were answered correctly about half the time.[11]

Jones et al. took this approach further, measuring the utility of an improved machine translation system across four source types (newspaper stories, text-only discussion groups, automatically transcribed news broadcasts, and automatically transcribed talk shows) using a reading comprehension test. They reported about 80% accuracy for answers to factual questions, but only about 50% accuracy for answers to questions that called for some degree of abstract reasoning.[12] From this we can conclude that present machine translation technology can satisfy some user needs, but that further improvements in translation quality will be needed before broadly useful multilingual access applications can be fielded.

The first of the questions posed at the start of this section, whether people can learn to formulate effective queries, is at this point the one we know the least about. The reason for this is simple—to learn very much about this would require long-term studies of real users performing real tasks. But before that can happen we must develop and field real systems capable of supporting those tasks, and those systems don't yet exist. Some insights have begun to accumulate from anecdotal reports of user experiences during structured user studies that have implications for system design. For example, sometimes searchers will recognize a useful term in a translated document and add it to their query, which will only work well if translation of documents and queries are implemented in a consistent manner (which was not the case in early systems). It also seems to be a good idea to inform users when no translation is known for a query term. It is not yet clear how far to take this idea of informing the user—should we show them the translated query? All possible translations for each query term? Alternate translations for some of the terms in a summary or a full document? Perhaps soon we will begin to see studies using Google's new MLIA capability (described below) that will begin to shed light on some of these questions.

CONCLUSION

Adoption of MLIA capabilities in deployed systems seems to have been far slower than the progress on the underlying CLIR technology would support. Deficiencies in current MT systems are undoubtedly a limiting factor in many cases, although applications intended for use by polyglot users would naturally be less affected by those deficiencies. Some cases may reflect a chicken-and-egg paradox: MLIA is needed only for large multilingual collections, but collection development policies in many cases predate the availability of these techniques. Web search would seem to be a natural first mover in MLIA (after all "World-Wide" is the Web's first name!), but there too adoption has been slower than the technology base would support. One commonly cited limiting factor for Web search engines has been the challenge of developing a suitable business model for monetizing MLIA. Regardless of the cause, it seems clear that developing a broader experience base with MLIA techniques will be an important next step.

In May, 2007, Google introduced a rudimentary MLIA capability by coupling query translation (to search Web pages in a different language) with document translation (to translate the result list, and individual results). Such an approach can be easily "bolted on" to any Web search engine since Web search engines typically already include automatic language identification and language-specific processing. (Indeed, Yahoo announced a similar service for German users in 2005, although apparently without much success.) Similar techniques have been used for CLIR research by modifying freely available information retrieval systems that had originally been designed for monolingual applications (e.g., Lucene), and at least one freely available system includes provisions for easily incorporating translation probabilities (Indri's "weighted structured queries"). Some degree of adoption is now also becoming evident among commercial providers of search services. For example, Autonomy now offers cross-language search capabilities (e.g., for enterprise search by multinational corporations).

These emerging capabilities are first steps in the direction of developing a richly multilingual information ecology that could support the next generation of research on information-seeking behavior in such settings. The few studies that have been conducted in recent years have typically focused on single information systems, relatively narrowly scoped collections, and, of necessity, users who have no prior experience with any MLIA application. As more users gain access to a broader range of increasingly capable systems, richer and more nuanced study designs will become possible.

Some open issues remain with regard to the technology base as well. For example, development costs for language-specific processing depend on the number of languages that must be accommodated, but the overall value of processing a specific language varies with the importance to the user of the languages that might be written in that document. With hundreds of written languages in use around the world, a point of diminishing returns may be reached beyond which the development costs for language-specific processing can no longer be justified. In such cases, a simple alternative is to count character sequences (in the same way as for language identification) and then simply index those character sequences. While this works reasonably well for monolingual applications in which the query and the document are written in the same language, how best to integrate translation capabilities into such an architecture is presently less clear.

Another open research question in MLIA is how best to present results from different languages. The challenge in this case arises because present systems for ranking documents in decreasing order of probable utility rely on relative relevance" scores that lack an absolute meaning. The consequence is that we can reasonably hope to determine whether one French document is a better match to the query than another French document, but determining whether an English document is a better match to that query than some French document requires that we create some way of comparing English scores with French scores. Progress on this problem has to date been rather disappointing, with merged result lists often being far less satisfactory than the best single-language result set. Presenting several ranked lists, one per language, is possible, but that approach does not scale well as the number of languages grows.

Result set presentation is a special case of the more general issue of interaction design, for which the research to date has just started to scratch the surface. When first introduced, things that are new are often patterned on things that are already well understood. Newspapers, for example, initially resembled the pamphlets that had preceded them. Later, when newspapers first started providing content on the Web, it resembled a printed newspaper. So it should be no surprise that Google's first try at MLIA looks like, well, Google. New capabilities tend to create their own dynamics, however, with new users bringing new needs, which drives development of new technologies, sometimes ultimately resulting in something that would have been difficult to imagine at the outset. MLIA has progressed far enough at this point for us to begin on that path, but not nearly far enough for us to yet predict where that path will lead us.

ACKNOWLEDGMENTS

The author is grateful to Noriko Kando for initial discussions that led to this entry. This work has been supported in part by DARPA contract HR0011-06-C-0022 (GALE).

REFERENCES

1. Friedman, T.L. *The World is Flat: A Brief History of the Twenty-First Century*; Farrar, Straus and Giroux: New York, 2005.
2. Pierce, J.R. et al. *Languages and Machines—Computers in Translation and Linguistics*; National Research Council: Washington, DC, 1966; ALPAC Report, National Academy of Sciences.
3. Oard, D.W.; Diekema, A.R. Cross-language information retrieval. Ann. Rev. Inform. Sci. Technol. **1998**, *33*, 223–256.
4. Furnas, G.W.; Landauer, T.K.; Gomez, L.M.; Dumais, S.T. The vocabulary problem in human-system communication. Commun. ACM **1987**, *30*(11), 964–971.
5. Brown, P.F. et al. A statistical approach to machine translation. Comput. Linguist. **1990**, *16*(2), 79–85.
6. Grefenstette, G., Ed. *Cross-Language Information Retrieval*; Kluwer Academic: Boston, MA, 1998.
7. Pirkola, A. The effects of query structure and dictionary setups in dictionary-based cross-language information retrieval, 21st Annual ACM SIGIR Conference on Research and Development in Information Retrieval (SIGIR 1998), Melbourne, Australia, August, 24–28, 1998; Croft, W., Ed.; 55–63; ACM, New York, 1998.
8. Xu, J.; Weischedel, R. TREC-9 cross-lingual retrieval, BBN The 9th Text Retrieval Conference (TREC-9), Gaithersburg, MD, November 2000; 13–16, 106–115.
9. Wang, J.; Oard, D.W. Combining bidirectional translation and synonymy for cross-language information retrieval, Proceedings of the 29th Annual International ACM SIGIR Conference on Research and Development in Information Retrieval (SIGIR 2006), Seattle, WA, August 2006, 6–11; Efthimiadis, E.N., Ed.; ACM, New York, 2006; 202–209.
10. Oard, D.W. et al. Interactive cross-language document selection. Info. Retrieval **2004**, *7*(1–2), 205–228.
11. López-Ostenero, F.; Gonzalo, J.; Peinado, V.; Verdejo, F. Cross-language question answering: Searching pasajes vs. searching documents. In *Multilingual Information Access for Text, Speech and Images*; Peters, C., Ed.; Fifth Workshop of the Cross-Language Evaluation Forum (CLEF 2004): Bath, U.K., September 2004; 15–17, 323–333; LNCS, Vol. 3491, Springer-Verlag, Berlin, 2005.
12. Jones, D. et al. ILR-based MT comprehension test with multi-level questions. *Human Language Technologies 2007*, The Conference of the North American Chapter of the Association for Computational Linguistics (HLT-NAACL 2007), Rochester, NY, April 2007; 22–27, 77–80; Companion Volume, Short Papers.

BIBLIOGRAPHY

1. Excellent sources for the latest work on CLIR include the proceedings of the Cross-Language Evaluation Forum (CLEF), (http://www.clef-campaign.org) in Europe, the NACSIS/NII Test Collection Information Retrieval (NTCIR) evaluations (http://research.nii.ac.jp/ntcir) in Japan, and the Forum for Information Retrieval Evaluation (FIRE) (http://www.isical.ac.in/~clia) in India. Contemporaneous reports on earlier CLIR research are also available from the Text Retrieval Conference (TREC) (http://trec.nist.gov) and the Topic Detection and Tracking (TDT) evaluations (http://www.nist.gov/speech/tests/tdt/).
2. For an historical perspective on the developments in MLIA, see the Annual Review of Information Science and Technology, volume 33 (1998). For a broad forward-looking treatment of the subject, see the papers and presentations from the SIGIR 2006 workshop on New Directions in Multilingual Information Access (http://ucdata.berkeley.edu:7101/projects/sigir2006/program.htm).

Museum Accreditation Program

Leah Arroyo
Julie Hart
American Association of Museums, Washington, District of Columbia, U.S.A.

Abstract
For nearly 40 years, the American Association of Museums' Accreditation Program has formally recognized museums' commitment to excellence, public accountability, high professional standards, and continued institutional improvement. Accreditation serves as the museum field's quality assurance and self-regulation.

The Museum Accreditation Program of the American Association of Museums (AAM) formally recognizes museums' commitment to excellence, accountability, high professional standards, and continued institutional improvement. Its purpose is to strengthen individual museums and the entire profession by promoting ethical and professional practices in individual museums and the museum community. Accreditation serves as the field's primary vehicle for quality assurance and self-regulation.

The program assesses how well each museum achieves its stated mission and goals and meets the standards and best practices generally accepted in the museum field. It employs a standardized process of self-study and peer review that incorporates multiple perspectives to ensure balance and fairness. This process draws on the collective wisdom of the field, gathered from participating museums, peer reviewers and the Accreditation Commission, a nine-member, independent and autonomous body that administers the program, and renders all decisions regarding accredited status.

Accreditation offers the following benefits: it certifies that a museum meets the Characteristics of an Accreditable Museum as set forth by the Accreditation Commission, certifies that it has undergone a rigorous process of self-assessment as well as review by its peers, signifies that the museum fulfills its obligations to the public as set forth in its mission and recognizes the institution's commitment to excellence, accountability, high professional standards, and continued improvement.

The accreditation program reflects the diversity of the museum field, accommodating museums' variety in disciplines, from art centers to zoos; budget sizes, from less than $100,000 to $150 million and above; governance types—private, nonprofit, or public—and collecting status, including museums that do not own collections.

After submitting an application, a museum spends a year completing a self-study questionnaire. With Accreditation Commission approval, two peer reviewers conduct a site visit and submit a report, after which the commission votes on accreditation. Peer reviewers are selected from comparable institutions, but with differing areas of expertise targeted for the museum undergoing accreditation. Museums already accredited undergo a subsequent review, or reaccreditation, every 10 years.

In June 1971, 16 museums became the first to be granted accreditation by the AAM. This was a milestone in a process that had begun in 1906, when museum directors came together at the American Museum of Natural History in New York to found AAM and initiate what has become a century-long discussion about developing museum standards and measuring museum performance. Plans for museum accreditation began in earnest in 1967, when President Lyndon B. Johnson asked the U.S. Federal Council on the Arts and Humanities to study the status of American museums and recommend ways to support and strengthen them.

The council enlisted AAM's assistance, and in 1968 the association established a committee to study the idea of an accreditation program for museums. Based on AAM's input, on November 25, 1968, the council issued "America's Museums: The Belmont Report," which stated: "it is urgent that the American Association of Museums and its member institutions develop and agree upon acceptable criteria and methods of accrediting museums." One year later, AAM authorized the Accreditation Committee to define the methods for establishing a program. On June 4, 1970, the committee presented "Museum Accreditation: A Report to the Profession," which outlined the basic principles and framework for AAM's museum accreditation program. Only at that time were the first applications accepted.

Over the years the program has been refined, emphasizing different issues that reflect the issues current to the museum profession: education and program evaluation (1980s), collection management (1990s), and ethics (2000s). Starting in 1986, museums have had to produce collections management policies. In 1996, AAM issued *Characteristics of an Accreditable Museum*, and the

Encyclopedia of Library and Information Sciences, Fourth Edition DOI: 10.1081/E-ELIS4-120044037

following year an institutional code of ethics was required of any museum seeking accreditation. In 2005, AAM revised its standards, self-study questionnaire, and eligibility criteria. See the AAM Web site: http://www.aam-us.org/museumresources/accred/index.cfm.

Accreditation review is voluntary; museums can apply or withdraw at any time. The process is collaborative, involving a dialogue among a museum's staff, governing authority and program staff; the peer reviewers; and the Accreditation Commission. It is also confidential; information provided by museums, and all correspondence and reports, is shared only with program staff, peer reviewers, and the commission.

Museum Architecture and Gallery Design

Volker M. Welter
Department of the History of Art and Architecture, University of California, Santa Barbara, Santa Barbara, California, U.S.A.

Abstract
This entry reviews the history of the architecture of museum buildings in the Western world (Europe and the United States) where the museum as an institution originated. After a brief history of the institution, chronological sections are dedicated to the pre-eighteenth century when the gallery as a room type emerged in France and Italy, the eighteenth century during which basic architectural and spatial requirements of museums were begun to be worked out, the nineteenth century when the museum as a building type was developed, and the twentieth century and beyond when initially modernist museums rejected the nineteenth-century ideal types and at the turn to the current century eclectic and unique architectural designs, so-called signature buildings, became synonymous with museum architecture.

The museum as a distinct building type developed in such European countries as, for example, France, Germany, Italy, Spain, and the United Kingdom, as well, from the eighteenth century onwards, in countries outside Europe. The museum offers spaces for the assembly, display, study, appreciation, and storage of both natural and man-made objects. Typically, the former are taken out of their natural context whereas the latter are removed from their original purpose, either by chance or deliberation, respectively have never been put to any intended use. Again other objects, ranging from works of arts to dioramas, for example, are created specifically for a museum setting.

Historically, the museum derived from institutions of knowledge generation and learning. Architecturally, it stems from the former and also from spaces that housed collections of objects and artifacts. Accordingly, a museum accommodates the functions and activities of collecting, ordering, exhibiting, and commemorating, each determining aspects of its architecture. Over the course of time the form of the museum as an institution changed as its purpose broadened from being a private place of studying and learning to one that displayed objects amassed in the pursuit of wealth or expert scholarship to becoming a public institution visited by both experts and the general public for aesthetic enjoyment and educational purposes.

HISTORY OF THE INSTITUTION

Etymologically, the word museum stems from the Greek word museion which referred both to places of mythological religious worship and institutions of learning. The former were dedicated to the nine muses, goddesses and children of Zeus and Mnemosyne, the goddess of memory.[1] Such places of worship, with or without a shrine, were typically set in nature like, for example, on a hill called museion, opposite of the Acropolis in Athens, on Mount Helicon, on Mount Parnassus, and at Pieria below Mount Olympus, the birth place of the muses. The ancient Greek word also referred to institutions of learning and knowledge such as, for example, the museion in Alexandria that was established in the third century B.C. for scholars of the local academy.[2]

Regardless of this shift in the meaning of the word "from the religious and ethical to the intellectual,"[3] both types encouraged the contemplative withdrawal into the realms of either pastoral nature or a study. Spatially, the former was unconfined, whereas the latter was locatable in two ways. First, as an institution that surveyed and ordered the cultural resources of the city or society of which it was part; second, and more specifically, as the physical space where learning took place.[4] Thus, the museum as "simultaneously an open and a closed concept" (p. 62)[4] determined the development of the institution.

When pondering the universe a medieval scholar may have retreated, for example, into a studio (study). Comparably, Kunstschrank (studiolo or art cabinet), Wunderkammer (curiosity cabinet), and library accommodated for scholarly study collections of typical, rare, and unique objects and artifacts. These spaces became increasingly popular when during the sixteenth century taxonomy and classification emerged as strategies to grasp a world that, from the European point of view, expanded rapidly due to increased overseas trade and political, later also colonial and imperial, relationships with countries on other continents. Often located in domestic buildings, rooms for collections mediated between the world and the home, the public and the private (p. 69).[4]

By the beginning of the seventeenth century the museum had moved from the studio to the galleria, "a space through which one passed, in contrast to the static principle of the spatially closed study" (p. 69).[4] The

Encyclopedia of Library and Information Sciences, Fourth Edition DOI: 10.1081/E-ELIS4-120044114

galleria as a room in which to display a large numbers of objects marked an important beginning of the museum as a distinct building type.

During the eighteenth century foundations of the early modern museum were laid with its twofold emphasis on an educational function and the aesthetic appreciation of the exhibits. The art historian Ernst Gombrich (1909–2001), for example, identified prodesse and delectare, to "profit and delight,"[5] as the two main tasks of the early modern museum. The modern museum emerged when two earlier types of display, the treasure and the shrine, combined to form "the depository and the didactic display" (p. 456).[5] The treasure, for example, royal collections, bolstered the social standing of the owner by overwhelming visitors with a wealth of objects (p. 452),[5] whereas the shrine exhibited selectively objects that were "not simply rare but unique" (p. 453).[5] When such collections were increasingly opened to the public, the treasure was transformed into a depository of "specimens to illustrate the rise of the arts" while the unique objects in the shrine now illustrated the end point of a "road to perfection" (p. 456).[5] In short, the formation of a canon of Western art was decisive for the concept of the modern museum.

From the nineteenth century onwards, the museum became not only more visible within the public realm of the modern city but was increasingly accessible to the public at large, even if it was not always held in public, for example, municipal ownership. The latter was, in the twentieth century, often seen as a direct expression of the social function of the museum. For example, the museologist Alma S. Wittlin (1899–1990) argued in the mid-twentieth century for a shift away from the museum as an expert institution that was also accessible to an educated public towards an educational experience geared primarily at the general public. Wittlin stressed that the modern public museum should value, both primarily and equally, the two tasks of providing enjoyment and education.[3]

Since its inception, the modern museum has oscillated between a didactic exhibition dictated by a canon or any other story and the display of exhibits for pure aesthetic contemplation. In the early twentieth century, many museums began to widen their purpose with public and educational outreach programs, which by the latter part of the century were complemented with entertainment oriented towards consumers and donors alike, and other events in an attempt to alleviate shortfalls in, especially, public funding and to counter charges of elitism. Nevertheless, museums are even today often surrounded by an aura of the extraordinary. This is not only expected by many visitors and donors, but is the tangible result of the "conflicting demands of the civic and hermetic notions" (p. 71)[4] of the museum. The latter two have determined the historic development of this essential institution of Western culture and continue to influence concepts of the contemporary museum as it has been adopted worldwide. Museum architecture likewise operates between potentially conflicting expectations. On the one hand, it should serve the museum as an institution that is dedicated to the exhibition and preservation of the objects in its custody. On the other hand, architects often wish to inscribe into the urban fabric with strong and powerful architectural images the importance of the museum as a civic institution.

HISTORY OF THE BUILDING TYPE

The double roots of the museum in collections of objects and in institutions of learning and knowledge have determined the development of museum architecture. From the former derived the gallery, a typical exhibition room of a museum, whereas the latter influenced the development of the general building type. Museum architecture touches primarily on solutions regarding the display of objects, the organization of exhibitions spaces and the increasingly complex functions of a museum, and the relation of the museum building to the wider built environment. Changing architectural styles were not always of great influence on the development of the building type. Similarly, while the foundation of national and other large museums were crucial for the history of the institution, their architecture was not necessarily of equal importance.

Pre-eighteenth Century

Already European antiquity knew of spaces dedicated to art works like the pinacotheca on the Acropolis in ancient Athens where paintings were displayed in order to honor the gods. Both Vitruvius (fl. later first century B.C) in the Ten Books on Architecture and Pliny the Elder (A.D 23 or A.D 24–79) in his Natural History referred to spaces like, for example, arcaded perambulatories that also accommodated sculptures or mural paintings.[6] Vitruvius explained that because of their at times considerable length such spaces were often decorated with landscape murals and sculptures. Moreover, they were reserved for the domestic architecture of dignitaries with civic obligations, thus the art works were part of a decorative iconographical program focusing on the owner of the house.

During the Renaissance art was begun to be looked at, and accordingly collected, as art. One of the earliest examples of an architectural space created specifically for art exhibits was the Belvedere statue court (Cortile delle Statue) that the architect Donato Bramante (1443 or 1444–1514) designed for the Vatican during the papacy of Julius II (1503–1513).[7] Located to the north of the Belvedere courtyard (Giardino della Pigna), statues were accommodated in niches along the perimeter walls, among them the famous Laocoön group that had been found in Rome in 1506. That the latter was placed in a direct sightline with the adjacent Belvedere Villa may indicate that one goal was to achieve the best possible display of the sculptures (p. 66).[7] While still open to the elements, the court was a marked improvement over the prevailing outdoor displays of ancient sculptures in gardens, loggias, and on terraces.[8,9]

With centrally planned rooms and arcades like perambulatories, Antiquity furnished Renaissance architects with two types of spaces upon which rooms for sculptures and other works of art could be modeled. The top-lit, domed rotunda of the Hadrianic Pantheon (ca. A.D 118–125) in ancient Rome was one model to which museum architects resorted time and again. It probably inspired the circular and top-lit building of the painter Peter Paul Rubens (1577–1640) in Antwerp where his collection of ancient sculptures was displayed (p. 112).[8,9]

Arcaded spaces were evoked in the gallery, a room type of lasting importance for museum architecture. Nowadays, the word refers either to a separate room for a defined group of objects, or to a building dedicated to a class of objects or temporary exhibitions of, for example, contemporary art. Historically, the word gallery referenced a type of room, more long than wide, that in its modern appearance originated in France.[10] Initially functioning as entrance halls and connecting corridors, galleries were used from the mid-fifteenth century onwards to accommodate collections of, for example, antlers, natural objects, or paintings (see appendix: Verzeichnis der im Text besprochenen Galerien).[10] While they derived from ancient arcaded perambulatories as described by Vitruvius, they were enclosed to better suit the northern European climate. Ideally, they were lit by windows on both long sides, but where that was impossible landscape paintings substituted for the view of the surrounding environment.

Galleries developed into a standard element of European palace architecture, but it was in Italy from the sixteenth century onwards that they were also begun to be used for sculptures and paintings, not least due to the excellent provision of light between and opposite the exhibits (p. 3).[3] A prominent example is the nearly 300 ft long gallery in Sabionetta designed ca. 1583–1584 by the Italian architect Vincenzo Scamozzi (1548–1616). It was initially decorated with frescoes of mercenaries, then redecorated with a collection of antlers, celebrating the hunting privilege of the owner, and finally used to exhibit a collection of ancient statues (p. 52).[10] The Antiquarium in Munich was commissioned by Albert (Albrecht) V of Bavaria (1528–1579) for his sculpture collection.[11] The tunnel-vaulted gallery that was rebuilt after its destruction in World War II was designed between 1569 and 1571 by Jacopo Strada (1515–1588), built to a plan amended by Bernhard and Simon Zwitzel, assisted by Wilhelm Egckl (ca. 1520–1588), and from 1586 onwards decorated by Friedrich Sustris (ca. 1540–ca. 1599) (p. 103).[8] It was located on the ground floor of the new building with the library of Albert V on the upper level. Both these examples illustrate that works of art or any other exhibit displayed in these early galleries were typically integrated into a decorative program whose iconography aimed at glorifying the gallery's owner (p. 60).[10]

The conceptual origin of the museum in places of learning and knowledge influenced the beginnings of a distinct building type for the institution. Latest from the sixteenth century onwards contacts of European societies with those on other continents and an increasing awareness of the material heritage of earlier periods of European history resulted in a fascination with collecting unique, rare, and unusual objects and artifacts. Wunderkammern (curiosity cabinets) and Kunstkammern (art cabinets) encapsulated in visible and tangible form the known universe in order to allow scientific inquiry and study.[12] One of the earliest purpose-designed buildings for a collection of this kind was Albert V's new Marstall in Munich which also housed the Kunstkammer. Shortly before he worked on the Antiquarium, discussed above, Egckl had built in 1563–1567 this new edifice (later the Alte Münze) around an open quadrangle with arcaded, open corridors that gave access to the rooms on each level. The art chamber's content was displayed on tables, in cupboards, and hung from the walls in large galleries that stretched around the courtyard on the third level. Rooms for valuable objects were separated in the corners of the quadrangle.[13,14]

Possibly the world's oldest, purpose-designed public museum building was begun in 1679 and opened in 1683 in Oxford, England, for the Ashmolean museum; today it accommodates the Museum of the History of Science. The museum's origin was a universal collection of natural objects and artifacts that Elias Ashmole (1617–1692), an antiquarian, had donated to the University of Oxford after it had originally been amassed by the naturalist John Tradescant, the older (1590–1638), and his son. Installed on the top floor of the new building, the display was supplemented with a lecture room on the ground floor and laboratories in the basement. The building, whose design has been ascribed to either Thomas Wood (1664 or 1665–1695) or Christopher Wren (1632–1723),[15] is of oblong, rectangular shape which ensured gallery proportions for the exhibition space.

Eighteenth Century

At the outset of the eighteenth century one of the earliest architectural plans for a new museum known to us was published in a 1704 essay on an ideal "rarity chamber" for a universal collection of art, curiosities, and natural objects.[16] Art historians have ascribed the pamphlet to the scholar and architect Leonhard Christoph Sturm (1669–1719) (p. 104),[8] (p. 114).[9,17] More recently it has been ascribed to Paul Jacob Marperger (1656–1730).[18] This pamphlet stands in the tradition of writings about curiosity cabinets, art cabinets, and museums that, in the case of the German-speaking countries, for example, stretches back to the 1565 publication *Inscriptiones vel tituli teatri amplissimi* by Samuel van Quiccheberg

(1529–1567); a book written in close connection with the establishment of the Kunstkammer in Munich (p. 336).[17,19] The 1704 essay was illustrated with a plan that showed the ground floor of a three-storey, rectangular building surrounded by a botanical garden, an orangery with foreign plants, and a small zoo of foreign animals. The design of the museum is one of the earliest that assigned separate rooms to different classes of exhibits instead of mixing them in one gallery (p. 114).[9] The relation between exhibition spaces and exhibits was also addressed by recommending a restrained interior decoration that would not conflict with the exhibits. The character of the objects should determine the display which should follow the principles of conservation, good visibility, scientific order, and aesthetic effect (pp. 336–338).[17]

Other ideal museum designs followed. In 1759, Count Francesco Algarotti (1712–1764) described a proposed new museum for Saxony as "a square building with a large courtyard and in each range a Corinthian loggia and one room on either side of it. These eight galleries lead into four corner rooms, each lit by a small dome. A large dome is above the centre of each range lighting the principle room behind the loggia (p. 104)."[8]

The scheme combined galleries along the four sides of a courtyard, each of them divided into two separate units by centrally located rooms. The latter were modeled on the Roman Pantheon and accessible through a columned portico or "Corinthian loggia" as the count had called them (p. 114).[9]

This courtyard plan was for a long time a favorite model for ideal museum designs. A variation inscribed into the larger square a Greek cross with a central room at the crossing of the four arms which, in turn, lead to the circumferential galleries and thus creating four smaller courtyards within the larger quadrangle. This addition increased both gallery space and rooms to accommodate different museums and related institutions like libraries in a single building. For example, the designs with which Jacque-Pierre Gisors (1755–1818) and François-Jacques Delannoy (1755–1835) won in 1778–1779 the Prix de Rome competitions of the French Académie d'Architecture followed this model. Likewise, Étienne-Louis Boullée (1728–1799) designed an ideal museum in 1783 that adopted the basic pattern of a Greek cross inscribed into a square. Envisioned as a multifunctional institution including an art museum, a natural history museum, a print room, a library, and a national monument with statues of French heroes underneath the central dome, the boldness of Boullée's undecorated architecture and its gargantuan seize has proved attractive to many architects ever since. Jean-Nicolas-Louis Durand (1760–1834), another French architect, developed this type of ideal museum into a more practical solution. His *Précis des leçons d'architecture* (1802–1805) included a general design for a museum that was adaptable in size and exact configuration to varying circumstances.[20]

Throughout the eighteenth century important architectural developments also happened on the smaller scale of exhibition spaces and galleries, especially with regard to, first, the relationship between the conceptual order of the displayed objects and the spatial order of the exhibitions rooms, and, second, the architectural settings of exhibits within individual rooms. The first point arose because the integration of objects into decorative schemes may have become overlaid with conceptually ordered displays that emphasized, for example, thematic, formal, and aesthetic principles. The exhibition of sculptures in the gallery spaces of the Villa Albani in Rome, commissioned by Cardinal Alessandro Albani (1692–1779) in the 1740s and completed in the 1760s to a design by architect Carlo Marchionni (1702–1786), was organized along iconographic-thematic principles. These were conceived by art historian Johann Joachim Winckelmann (1717–1768) who grouped together sculptures of the same subject matter (p. 114).[9] Thus the architectural divisions of the exhibition spaces into a sequence of larger and smaller rooms acquired a new importance as the thematic groups of exhibits occupied separate spaces. Beside the art historical logic of such displays, the architecturally interesting issue is the relationship between the spatial sequence of rooms in a gallery or a museum, and the ideal order—formal, aesthetic, thematic and, later, chronological,—in which the exhibits were displayed and, presumably, to be viewed. The plans of the gallery (1767–ca. 1780) at Newby Hall, Yorkshire, England, and of the Museo Pio-Clementino (from 1770 onwards) at the Vatican are exemplary illustrations of this important architectural–museological issue. Both buildings are of vast difference in scale, the English gallery being an annex to a private house whereas the Roman example was an instrument of Papal power with regard to size and ambitions. Nevertheless, architecturally speaking, both buildings center on a circular room in which important exhibits were shown.

Newby Hall's gallery stands in the tradition of small, private art galleries, a distinct British contribution to museum architecture.[21] The architect Robert Adam (1728–1792) extended the main house with a gallery for antique sculptures. The focus was a Pantheon-like rotunda—similar to a circular top-lit sculpture gallery Adam had designed for Kedleston Hall (1758–1763), Derbyshire, England—that was flanked at either side by a square room, a symmetrical arrangement that made the circular room to the center of the plan while the small size of the entire extension kept subtle this hierarchy.

This was different in the case of the Museo Pio-Clementino that was added to the Vatican by the architects Michelangelo Simonetti (1724–1787) and, later, Giuseppe Camporese (1763–1822). To the irregular site the architects responded with a series of spaces, each of a distinct geometric form like, for example, a Greek cross, a rotunda, a hexagon, squares, and rectangles, that wrapped around the east, north, and west side of the Belvedere sculpture court. The new range was originally entered at the north-west corner of the Belvedere courtyard (Giardino della Pigna). From there visitors moved upwards on a grand staircase, built to a design by Simonetti, and towards one of the most impressive rooms of the new museum, the rotunda where sculptures of deities were exhibited. All other art works were arranged thematically in the following galleries. Because the museum was a linear, though irregular sequence of rooms, the conceptual relationship between the latter and the exhibits was both a curatorial and an architectural issue. For example, with the addition of the new galleries, the Belvedere statue court, that had also been remodeled by Simonetti in 1773, was now located at the end of the concourse, accordingly it could be considered either as the highlight of the museum or as its appendix.

The Museo Pio-Clementino was also remarkable for the period design of the interior of the galleries whose neoclassical style alluded to a unity between the ancient exhibits and their contemporary architectural setting. The latter aimed at evoking broadly classical antiquity including original antique Roman mosaics on the floor of, for example, the Rotunda room. A comparable idea of a period setting for exhibits also determined the short-lived Musée des Monuments Français that existed from 1796 until 1816. There the painter Alexandre(-Marie) Lenoir (1762–1839) amassed medieval funeral monuments and other, mainly religious objects that were displayed in a chronological order in a thirteenth-century monastery in Paris.[8] In this case the exhibition spaces were not consciously designed as period rooms but were in a building from the same period as many of the exhibits; thus the latter and the architectural setting interacted particularly closely with each other.

During the eighteenth century some of Europe's best-known museums were founded, some in existing buildings, others in newly erected ones. The Musei Capitolini in Rome was opened to the public in 1735, followed by the Galleria degli Uffizi in Florence in 1743, though the origins of both museums go back much further. The British Museum, the world's first publicly owned museum, was founded in 1753 by an act of Parliament that acquired for the nation the collection of Hans Sloane (1660–1753) that comprised both objects that illustrated natural history and artificialia. The museum opened in Montagu House, a seventeenth-century manor house in Bloomsbury, London, in 1759. In Vienna the Kaiserliche Gemäldegalerie was established in the Upper Belvedere palace (1717–1724) designed by Johann Lukas von Hildebrandt (1668–1745) in 1781. Before that some of the paintings had been displayed in the adapted Stallburg, a stable from before the mid-seventeenth century.[22]

The Louvre in Paris that opened in 1793, occupied a royal palace whose origin stretched back to the twelfth century. Already during the seventeenth century works of arts were shown in the Louvre, for example, the Académie Royale de Peinture et de Sculpture's annual exhibition in the Grande Galerie that had been built between 1595 and 1610 as a connecting corridor. From the mid-eighteenth century onwards these shows were located in the Salon Carré. These two spaces became the germ cells of the Louvre when it was reconceived towards the end of the eighteenth century as the nation's premier museum for works of art. Architecturally, the Louvre is an example of a palace adapted to its new purpose, but regardless, the interior of its galleries influenced many later museums. Already in 1789 top lighting had been installed in the Salon Carré, arguably one of the best light provisions for picture galleries. The painter Hubert Robert (1733–1808) depicted in 1796 also the Grande Galerie with skylights, a proposal that was possibly derived from a ceiling design in a Boullée design for a national library (1784). The gallery, however, had to rely on high sidelighting until 1938 (p. 109).[8] A new grand staircase leading to the galleries and the neoclassical redecoration (1805–1810) of the Grande Galerie by the architects Charles Percier(-Bassant) (1764–1838) and Pierre-François-Léonard Fontaine (1762–1853) were probably inspired by the Museo Pio-Clementino.

New museum buildings were, for example, erected in St. Petersburg, Russia, in Kassel, Landgraviate of Hesse-Kassel, Germany, and in Madrid, Spain. The Kunstkamera (1718–1734) in St. Petersburg housed both Peter the Great's royal collections of natural and artificial objects, and the library of the Academy of Science.[23–25] The Baroque design by the architect Georg Johann Mattarnovy (died 1719) consisted of two oblong, three-storey tall wings to either side of a tower. At the far ends smaller rooms were located followed by galleries in the eastern wing and the library in the western one. The central tower accommodated an anatomical lecture theater and observatories that included a wooden globe (Germany, sixteenth century) with a painted map of the world on the outside and one of the firmaments on the inside. Conceptually, the Kunstkamera stood still in the tradition of curiosity cabinets.

This was also the case in Kassel where the enlightened ruler Landgrave Frederick II (1720–1785) commissioned the Museum Fridericianum (1769–1779), one of the earliest purpose-designed public museum buildings in continental Europe. It combined art galleries with ones exhibiting artifacts, including cork models of famous buildings, and a library.[26] The architect was Simon Louis du Ry (1726–1796). Today, this museum is best known as one of the venues of Documenta, the international exhibition of contemporary art.

In 1785, Juan de Villanueva (1739–1811) began to design a new natural history museum in Madrid which, before its inauguration in 1819, was already rededicated as art museum and later named Museo Nacional del Prado. The neoclassical design is based on an additive architectural design principle whereby suitable geometric forms are selected according to the different functions of various rooms and then brought together in a formal overall composition much like, for example, Durand's schematic museum design. In Madrid, a long, narrow gallery spans between two square end pavilions that is bisected in the center by a perpendicular gallery. The main entrance was in one of the end pavilions from where visitors passed through a skylit circular rotunda. The museums in St. Petersburg, Kassel, and Madrid were physically separated from the palaces of their founders thus making visible their foundation in ideas of the Enlightenment, even though they all were of royal, imperial, or courtly origin.

This was different in the case of museums outside Europe that began to be established in the eighteenth century. Often, they were part of exploratory or colonizing efforts. For example, in North America one the earliest collections of plant specimen and natural objects was founded by the Charleston Library Society, South Carolina in 1773,[27,28] obviously driven by the wish to become familiar with the flora and fauna of the new continent. Other museums were part of the attempts to establish a new society by transplanting elements of the European ones. That museums like, for example, the American Museum in Philadelphia—founded from scratch by Pierre Eugene du Simitière (1737–1784) in 1782 and sold upon his death (p. 7)[28]—were considered to be part of the new society speaks about their popularity. Purpose-designed buildings were apparently erected only in the next century when, for example, the Pennsylvania Academy of the Fine Arts in Philadelphia occupied in 1806 new premises in which a collection of plaster casts was exhibited. The brick cube with a shallow dome, slightly protruding corners, and a door way above which a carved American eagle hovered was designed by John Dorsey (ca. 1759–1821) in a Federal style.[29]

Nineteenth Century

While during the eighteenth century the architectural basics of the museum as a distinct building type were developed, the next century saw their perfection and widespread application.

Architecturally, the century began with three buildings that inspired museum architecture for years to come: the Glyptothek (1816–1830, restored 1972), a sculpture gallery, and the (Alte) Pinakothek (1825–1836, restored 1945), a painting gallery, both in Munich, Bavaria, to designs by Leo von Klenze (1784–1864), and the (Altes) Museum (1823–1830, restored 1960s, sculptures and paintings) in Berlin by Karl Friedrich Schinkel (1781–1841). The Glyptothek was characterized by an exceptionally well-conceived unity between architecture and exhibits, and a chronological display that was mirrored architecturally in a rigidly set route through suites of galleries around a courtyard. Period rooms dominated the settings of sculptures that stood, for example, in rows along walls as to outline the silhouettes while emphasizing the axes of the rooms, were placed as focal points at the end vistas through galleries, or were the center point of individual rooms.

The Altes Museum intertwined skillfully the public realm with the museum space. Schinkel designed a free-standing cube facing the Berlin Stadtschloß (demolished 1950) across the open space of the Lustgarten. A broad stair approaches a screen of double-height columns behind which the entrance is located, a master piece of spatial complexity that, in its original form, led visitors into the building with one flight of steps, took them out again with the next after which the top landing was reached that, from underneath the roof, directed the gaze back towards the city beyond the columns, a view that is now altered by glass panes placed between the columns. Inside, this view was matched by the sublimity of a domed, top-lit, double-height rotunda with a column-supported gallery on which sculptures stood. To either side of this room galleries wrapped around two open courtyards offering strictly sequential routes on each floor.

The Alte Pinakothek revolutionized the spatial organization of galleries. (Fig. 1) The lower floor of the long and narrow building with two slightly protruding end wings was primarily for scholars and offered offices, a library, a print room, and storage space. The publicly accessible upper floor organized circulation spaces and galleries in three parallel bands. A narrow loggia ran from east to west along the southern length of the building. The main band arranged top-lit galleries of slightly different lengths in a rhythm of a-b-a-c-a-b-a that singled out subtly the centermost room. U-shaped cabinets for small paintings opened towards the northern façade in the third band. This arrangement was overlaid with a network of possibly routes that connected axially the galleries with each other in order to mirror in plan the chronological display by schools, while a multitude of north–south links allowed for sudden cross moves, "the spice of museum visits" (p. 138).[9]

Thus early in the century two principle museum plans were available. One, following Durand's ideal museum plan, organized exhibition spaces around one or two courtyards with usually a central, architecturally highlighted space. The other plan was a long, shallow building, typically with projecting pavilions in the center and at both ends. Both types utilized the compositional Beaux-Arts method and were also influential regarding their architectural styles, usually neoclassical or versions of Renaissance styles which, in turn, had revived Greco-Roman architecture. Moreover, they set standards for a civic monumentality of museum buildings. Often, the latter were elevated by broad flights of stairs leading to main entrances in facades that evoked either ancient temples or palatial edifices as exemplified in the forecourt of the new British Museum (1823–1848) by Robert Smirke (1786–1867).

The two basic types differed regarding land use, expendability, and lighting. The courtyard model made

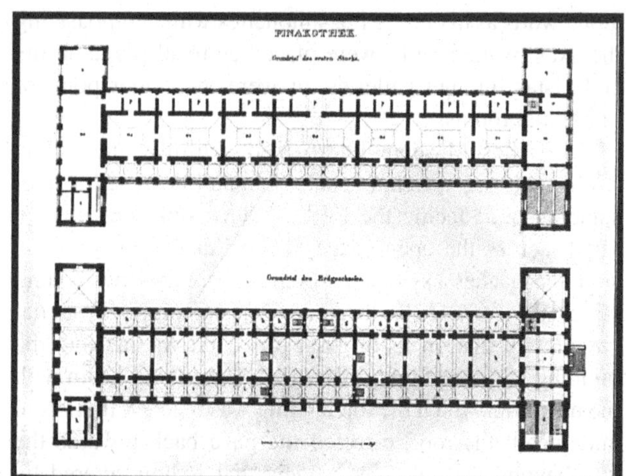

Fig. 1 Leo von Klenze (1784–1864), floor plans of the lower level (bottom) and upper level (top) of the Alte Pinakothek Munich as inaugurated in 1836. The main entrance is at the right end of the lower level. The upper level shows the division into three parallel bands of exhibition rooms and circulation spaces.
Source: Photograph courtesy of Bayerische Staatsgemälde-sammlungen, Alte Pinakothek Munich, Germany.

efficient use of building plots and adding new courts created more galleries. The free-standing, shallow buildings of the other type assured both good light supply on the long sides of, for example, a painting gallery, and excellent light penetration of the interior. The latter became less important with the increased use of iron and glass lanterns from the eighteenth century onwards. That top lighting was beneficial to display works of arts antiquity already knew. The principle had also been employed to light the niches (gabinetti) of the remodeled Belvedere statue court (1773) and in some galleries of the Louvre. The Dulwich Picture Gallery (1811–1814), London, by John Soane (1753–1837), another fine English example of a small art gallery, and the Pinakothek, that proudly displayed lanterns on the roof, were successful modern applications of roof lanterns to exhibition spaces. Until then, galleries had mainly been lit through conventional windows or clerestory windows that provided diagonal light from high above.[30]

At the beginning of the century, only very few European cities like, for example, London, Paris, Rome, and Vienna, were the location of important, even national, museums. By the end of the century, the number of museums had multiplied as the example of the United Kingdom shows. To the 59 museums that existed in 1850, 259 more had been added by 1914 (p. 136).[3] Museums were also established on continents and in countries that were in contact with or colonized by Western powers like, for example, India (Indian Museum, Kolkata, 1814, whose origin goes back to the Asiatic Society of Bengal from 1784), Brazil, (Royal School of Fine Arts, today Escola Nacional de Belas Artes, Rio de Janeiro, 1816, that exhibited a painting collection), and Japan (Museum of the Ministry of Education, today the Tokyo National Museum, 1872).

Architecturally consequential was the adaptation of museum buildings to three developments—growth, specialization, and spatial concentration—that affected museums during the later century. Individual museums grew because with the adoption of didactic displays, chronological or thematic, the need to expand arose as any conceptual order could always be made more comprehensive if allegedly existing gaps in a collection were filled (p. 457).[5] As a response to this growth but also to the increasing separation of individual disciplines in the sciences and the humanities, many museums began to specialize by focusing on select classes of objects. Museums exhibiting together natural objects and man-made artifacts continued to exist, although often older universal collection were dissolved as the dispersal of the Danish Royal Kunstkammer (1650) between ten different museums shows.[31] Regardless, the museum complex, a spatial concentration of different types of museums in the immediate vicinity of each other, gave new spatial form to the idea of a universal collection.

A prime example of these interconnected developments is the Victoria and Albert Museum in London, one of the many museums established from mid-century onwards that were dedicated to the applied arts, their role in modern production, and their relationships with the sciences.[32] A predecessor was the Parisian Hôtel de Cluny that had opened in 1843 with an exhibition of Medieval and Renaissance everyday objects in historicizing settings. Rooted in the contemporary debate about the relationship of the arts and the sciences in an age of capitalism, one goal of these museums was the education of artisans, workers, and citizens in the aesthetics and production of modern commodities. Today's Victoria and Albert Museum was founded as the Museum of Manufactures the year after the 1851 Great Exhibition of the Works of Industry of All Nations in London, opened on its current site as the South Kensington Museum in 1857, and received its current name in 1899. From its inception onwards, the museum was closely allied with a government-initiated school of design.

The museum's early architectural history was intertwined with the rise of iron as a new structural material. Initially, the museum occupied a prefabricated structure, clad with corrugated metal, whose iron and glass roof hovered visibly over the interior spaces. This utilitarian building was elevated to architecture proper in 1862 by two iron and glass exhibition courts that borrowed from church buildings their internal arrangements of central naves flanked by side naves. Another possible source was the iron and glass structure that covered the exhibition court of the new Oxford University Museum (begun 1855), completed 2 years earlier by the architects Thomas (Newenham) Deane (1828–1899) and Benjamin Woodward (1816–1861).[33] In Oxford, the iron structure was integrated into a Victorian Gothic building, in London it was designed in a northern Italian Renaissance style.

This pointed towards a second aspect of the Victoria and Albert museum's architecture viz. that it was a sequence of increasingly formal buildings. The next extension from 1869, another Italianate design by the engineer Francis Fowke (1823–1865), added traditional elements of museum architecture such as, for example, an open courtyard and a temple-like entrance pavilion that included one of the first refreshment rooms ever installed in a museum.

The architecture of this type of museum was integral to its educational mission. In the Oxford University Museum, that hosted science departments, ornaments on structural details were derived from plant forms and shafts of columns were hewn from various British stones. In London, the exterior featured artistically designed terracotta panels, and the interior, for example, mosaics portraying famous artists and murals by Frederic Leighton (1830–1896) depicting the industrial arts at times of war and peace.[34] Instructive decorations had long been a feature of contemporary museum buildings. For example, in the loggia of the Munich Pinakothek murals by Peter (Joseph) von Cornelius (1783–1867) presented the history of painting as a preparation for the true art inside the galleries. In museums of applied art and sciences such details matured from decoration to practical demonstrations of contemporary skills and proclamations of the anticipated merger of arts and sciences. The envisioned renewal of this cooperation was not confined to the small scale of symbolic architectural details, but was also made visible with the museum complex on the larger scale of the modern metropolis.

Specialization did not reject the universal museum as a means to both explore and interpret the world (p. 61).[4] Rather, this idea shifted to a spatial concentration of different museums and educational institutions in the immediate vicinity of each other. In London, the Victoria and Albert Museum was complemented by the Museum of Natural History and the Science Museum. The former was an offspring of the British Museum, housed in a German-Romanesque building (1872–1881) by Alfred Waterhouse (1830–1905). The latter had originally been part of the Victoria and Albert Museum, but was separated in 1909 when the older museum expanded into a new building (1899–1909) by Aston Webb (1849–1930) (p. 131).[9] This cluster in South Kensington comprised also teaching and bibliographical institutions like, for example, the Royal School of Mines, founded in 1851, and the Imperial Institute from 1887, an information brokerage on and for the British Empire. Comparable clusters were formed in other cities. In Vienna, the Naturhistorische Museum (1871–1889) and the Kunsthistorische Museum (1871–1891), both designs by Gottfried Semper (1803–1879) and Carl von Hasenauer (1833–94), faced each other in front of the Hofburg in a symbolic juxtaposition of the arts and nature, respectively, natural sciences. In Berlin, the museum island, a concentration of mainly art museums to the north of the Altes Museum, originated in the idea of Friedrich Wilhelm IV of Prussia (1795–1861) to establish a centre of the arts and the sciences that encompassed the neighboring university founded by Wilhelm von Humboldt (1767–1835) in 1810.

Clusters of museums and educational institutions were also an important element of town planning and planned urban expansion. In 1847, Benjamin Disraeli demanded that vast cities like London needed a forum or Acropolis of cultural institutions that would ennoble "the metropolitan mass."[35] This was echoed, with a different pitch, in the early 1880s by Thomas Coglan Horsfall (1844–1932), director of his own Manchester Art Museum (1877–1953), who proposed to bring with art museums beauty to urban quarters, especially to working class areas.[36] This town planning aspect stretched back in modern times at least to the eighteenth-century Museum Fridericianum that stood proudly on a new public square in Kassel. The grounds for the new Glyptothek and the new Pinakothek in Munich had been outside the city limits, while the South Kensington Museum on the edge of London initiated calls for cheap public transport (pp. 29–30).[32] These contributed to the opening of a station in South Kensington in 1868 by the Metropolitan Railway.

The educational aspect of museums fell on particular fertile ground in the United States where, as already noted, early natural history museums, for example, had a practical role in the settlement efforts. Similarly, the educational and training benefits of art museums were emphasized over collecting art for purely aesthetic enjoyment (p. 37).[32] Accordingly, many museums were initiated by historical societies, libraries, art schools, and colleges, occasionally in collaboration with a private donor. For example, at Yale College, Newhaven, Connecticut, the Trumbull Gallery was named after architect, artist, and diplomat John Trumbull (1756–1843) who had given the art and designed the Greek Revival style building (1831–1832, destroyed 1901) (p. 24).[29] After the South Kensington model of art education and training in combination with a museum had become known widely, for example, through the 1876 Centennial Exposition at Philadelphia (p. 38),[32] comparable museums began to appear in the United States. In Boston, MA, for example, the Museum of Fine Arts that was chartered in 1870 moved into its first building in Copley Square in 1876. The architects, John Hubbard Sturgis (1834–1888) and Charles Brigham (1841–1925) designed a Neo-Gothic brick building (1870–1876, enlarged 1879 and 1890, destroyed) that, while differing in style, took its cues from the London predecessor including, for example, decorative façade panels, instructive interior elements like decorative cast iron stairs, and the installation of entire historic rooms as a backdrop for period exhibits (pp. 29–30).[32]

Within a matter of years the museum had grown out of its premises and, together with changed ideas about museum display that put greater focus on the aesthetic aspect of exhibits and collections; this made necessary a move to another site. Even though the new building, a Beaux-Arts design by Guy Lowell (1870–1927), was only begun in 1906, the plan sums up nineteenth-century thinking about museum buildings. The formal forecourt with projecting wings and the classical style speak of the civic monumentality more pronounced than the old building. The master plan evolved around three design principles: The larger building is composed from smaller units, some with their own entrances, for individual departments and collections, a differentiation between levels according to usage with the public galleries on the upper level and services for scholars on the lower—an idea that von Klenze had already introduced in the Munich Pinakothek—and oblique light through windows as the major light source supplemented by skylights (pp. 41–42).[29]

Twentieth Century and Beyond

The two basic museum types of the nineteenth century never disappeared from the repertoire of possible museum buildings. As late as 1923 the Beaux-Arts inspired plan was considered to be standard.[37] The National Gallery of Art (1936–1941), Washington, D.C., by John Russell Pope (1873–1937), proved that the oblong, shallow building was also transferable to a different period and tasks. Many early twentieth-century museums were mergers and variations of these two types (pp. 38–41),[29] though they were faulted for formalism in plan and elevation. For example, the placement of windows according to style rather than to lighting needs was criticized as was the fact that different functions like moving through a gallery and sojourning in front of an exhibit were not separated spatially. Many museum ideas of especially the first half of the twentieth century aimed to overcome such alleged functional deficiencies with contemporary, modernist designs that would also embody the Zeitgeist.

With "The Museum of Tomorrow" (1929) the architect and planner Clarence Stein (1882–1975) adapted the museum to American metropolitan architecture by designing a skyscraper that would accommodate better both growing collections and the different needs of scholars and the general public.[38] Scholarly collections were placed in galleries along the perimeter of the octagonal building, while public galleries spanned across a central courtyard like spokes of a wheel. Different geographical areas and historical periods were assigned to individual floors that, vertically stacked, made the tower expressive of the conceptual order but created also a rigid spatial sequence. A comparable correspondence determined the ideal museum the architect Le Corbusier (Charles-Edouard Jeanneret, 1887–1965) produced in 1929 for the Mundaneum, a world institute of bibliographical information.[39] A pyramid accommodated a spiral of three parallel naves that wound downwards and symbolized the "chain of knowledge." Both examples drew on the Outlook Tower (1895 onwards), Edinburgh, Scotland, of the biologist and city planner Patrick Geddes (1854–1932), a civic museum that embedded local history into widening geographical areas on each lower floor, an idea Geddes had transferred to a design for an outlook tower in a skyscraper when he visited the United States in 1923.[40]

Stein and Le Corbusier's ideal museums made visible Modernism's comprehensive claim to understanding and designing the totality of modern human life; an assumption that was rooted in a progressive view of history as leading inevitably to Modernism. Modernist museum architecture rejected historical models for the building type, but often adopted the spatially fixed, didactic route through an exhibition. The Museum of Modern Art in New York, that was founded in 1929 and moved in 1939 into a new building to a design by Philip L. Godwin (1885–1958) and Edward Durrell Stone (1902–1978), told the birth of Modernism as a chronological sequence of modern art movements, one following the other, similar to the suite of galleries that mirrored this narrative; a spatial dogmatism that was adhered to as late as 1984 when the architect Ieoh Ming Pei (born 1917) expanded the museum. Similarly the Solomon R. Guggenheim Museum (1943–1959) in New York by Frank Lloyd (Lincoln) Wright (1867–1959) where visitors walk down a ramp that circles around a central atrium. Changing exhibitions are mounted in bays along the perimeter wall. Upward- or downward-directed views across the circular space towards other exhibition cabinets are possible, cross moves are not.

The opposite idea of maximum spatial liberty for both curator and visitor guided the "Museum for a Small City" (1942) by German–American architect Ludwig Mies van der Rohe (1886–1969), a design for a one-storey glass box underneath a flat roof and very few permanent interior installations. The potential difficulties such a museum space poses is demonstrated by Mies van der Rohe's Neue Nationalgalerie (1962–1968) in Berlin where the hall for temporary exhibitions on the upper entrance level suffers from an oversupply of light due to its four all-glass walls. Already at the time of the inaugural exhibition in 1968 floor-to-ceiling curtains were employed to control the flow of light. This reduced the building's transparency which, however, is important for the experience of the space. Consequently, nowadays, the upper-level exhibition hall is mostly used as a grand foyer for the rather cramped permanent exhibition on the lower floor of the building. Regardless, the "museum without walls" (p. 53)[29] developed into an important type of exhibition space for the twentieth century.

Yet it was not the ideal museum envisioned as a modernist glass box but the windowless, artificially lit, so-called white box that liberated the arrangement of a display from almost all architectural restraints. Already the Victoria and Albert Museum had experimented in the 1850s with gas lights to extend the opening hours into the evenings. The collection of the New York Museum of Modern Art was one of the first that was displayed in white boxes, electrically lit, and without direct visual connection to the outside. Not all of these boxes were of purist design. The Yale University Art Gallery (1951–1953), Newhaven, CT, by the architect Louis I(sador). Kahn (1901–74) had a windowless southern façade towards the street that was balanced with a windowed northern façade. Inside, art objects were exhibited under exposed concrete ceilings. Kahn's other two museums, the Kimbell Art Museum (1966–1972), Forth Worth, Texas, and the Yale Center for British Art (1969–1977), Newhaven, broke up progressively the ideal modernist box. The interior of the museum in Texas was covered by narrow vaults, sliced open along the apex in order to let natural light brush down the inner curved surfaces. The second of Kahn's Newhaven projects works with covered atrium spaces that act as light wells and more traditional top lighting.

Flexible, nondetermined exhibition spaces were seen as an opportunity to redefine the relationship between the exhibits, their creator, and the visitor as it was envisioned in exemplary manner by the "open museum" concept of Pontus Hultén (1924–2006), director (1973–1981) of the Musée national d'art moderne, a part of the Centre national d'art et de culture Georges Pompidou in Paris.[41] The architects Renzo Piano (born 1937) and Richard Rogers (born 1933) realized this idea with a building (1971–1977) that sports its structural systems and technical infrastructure on the outside—color-coded as if it were a machine—while the inside offered, at least initially, open plans on the exhibition floors accessible through purely functional entrances on ground level.

Already earlier museums had avoided overly representative entrances, or abandoned them entirely. The brief flight of stairs up the main entrance at the east end of Munich's Pinakothek was inconspicuously located which was perhaps a pointer to the museum's rational provision of various paths through the exhibition. The few steps at the 1909 building of London's Victoria and Albert Museum invited without much intimidation into a space possibly outside of the most visitors' everyday life. The New York Museum of Modern Art could be entered unceremoniously by slipping directly inside from the pavement. The entrances of the Centre Georges Pompidou were equally functional, but regardless of all attempts to popularize museums, the building was criticized as an element of an urban renewal project that also demolished Les Halles, a nineteenth-century wholesale market. This criticism was part of the postmodern questioning of the dominance of modern architecture to which museum architects responded by citing historic museum buildings, proposing to rescue historic buildings by installing museums, and developing alternative architectural models for the institution.

The turn to historic museum buildings is exemplified by the Neue Staatsgalerie (1977–1984) in Stuttgart, Germany, designed by the architects James (Frazer) Stirling (1926–1992) and Michael Wilford (born 1938). The building relied on traditional suites of galleries, referenced historical lighting principles like, for example, the ones used in Soane's Dulwich Picture Gallery, and was organized around a circular, open courtyard modeled on the rotunda of Berlin's Altes Museum. A public path cuts through the rotunda and thus balances any possible monumental or even so-called elitist reading of this space. Historic museum architecture was also cited in the Sainsbury Wing (1987–1991) of the National Gallery, London, by Robert Venturi (born 1925), John Rauch (born 1930), and Denise Scott Brown (born 1930) that replaced a modernist design that had attracted public condemnation by Prince Charles. Now a staircase in the tradition of the Museo Pio-Clementino and the Louvre rises to the upper floor with traditional top-lit galleries.

The use of existing buildings for museums added a new civic dimension to the institution as the older structures may have been monuments or had otherwise an important function for a community. Some of the many museums and galleries designed in Italy by the architect Carlo Scarpa (1906–1978) after the end of World War II in Europe preserved from final destruction ruined monuments of the country's history. In Verona, Scarpa carved the Museo Civico di Castelvecchio (1958–1965) out of on old castle by cutting occasionally even through historic walls in order to achieve a symbiotic relationship between the building and the exhibits. Later in the century, the reuse of buildings became more common that had not originally been intended for museums. Between 1980 and 1990, 13 museums were established along the embankment of the river Main in Frankfurt, Germany, to form a Museumsufer. Some occupied new buildings, some refurbished and enlarged historic private homes like, for example, the villa of the Museum für Angewandte Kunst (1982–1984) that was extended with white cubes by the architect Richard (Alan) Meier (born 1934), and the Deutsches Architekturmuseum (1979–1984) that the architect Oswald Matthias Ungers (1926–2007) designed as a house within a house. The scale was mostly domestic so as to match the art works in the case of art museums and to not disturb the urban design pattern of the embankment. From 1980 to 1986 the Paris train station Gare d'Orsay (1898–1900, architect Victor(-Alexandre-Frédéric) Laloux [1850–1937]), was transformed into the Musée d'Orsay by A.C.T. Architecture (Renaud Bardon (born 1942), Pierre Colboc, and Jean-Paul Philippon). The architect Gaetana Aulenti (born 1927) created the interior design for the exhibition of nineteenth-century art and applied art. While in this case the age of the building and exhibits corresponded, former industrial buildings were also attractive because of the contrasting environment they offered, for example, to contemporary installation artists. One of the earliest examples is the Neue Hallen für Kunst in Schaffhausen, Switzerland, a disused textile factory (1912–1913) that the artist Urs Raussmüller remodeled from 1982 to 1983. Another abandoned industrial building, the monumental Bankside power station (1946–1970, architect Giles Gilbert Scott [1880–1960]) in London was transformed by the architects Jacques Herzog (born 1950) and Pierre De Meuron (born 1950) into the Tate Gallery of Modern Art (1998–2000). While the upper levels offer more conventionally sized gallery spaces, the gigantic former turbine hall challenges artists to conceive site-specific artworks on a scale previously unknown.

Architects also aimed at integrating new museums into cities in ways that made them less monumental. The architect Hans Hollein (born 1934) designed the Städtisches Museum Abteiberg (1972–1982) in Mönchengladbach, Germany, as an urban landscape that avoids most references to traditional museum buildings. Hollein conceived a three-level building that is entered from a platform on top of the highest level. Underneath, two levels of galleries follow a drop in the terrain ending at a museum garden at the lower end of the site. Manifold openings allow for views from the outside into the museum and vice versa, thus connecting directly the building with the urban environment. References to the city's industrial past in the architectural design establish another, more conceptual relationship. While this museum in Germany tried to overcome architecturally expressed civic monumentality, apparently perceived as intimidating, in favor of public accessibility, a later design by Hollein went a step further. In 1990, the architect won a competition for planning a Guggenheim Museum in Salzburg, Austria, whose three floors were to be cut into a mountain within the city limits and lit solely by transparent cones on the latter's top. The design did away with visible architectural links between the museum building and the urban environment and thus seems to question the validity of the historically important conceptual link between the city and the museum as a civic institution. This development, however, did not prevail as the possibly most famous museum of the later twentieth century, the Museo Guggenheim in Bilbao, Spain, is proudly displayed within the city's urban fabric. Like other branches, realized or planned, the Bilbao museum is part of a global expansion of the New York Guggenheim museum. On the local and regional level the museum was essential to a master plan to regenerate economically both the city and the Basque region. The museum's building, an assemblage of titanium sails and waves, was constructed between 1992 to 1997 to plans by the architect Frank O(wen). Gehry (born 1929).

The extraordinary architecture and the economic success of the completed project in Bilbao initiated many new museum buildings at the turn from the twentieth century to the twenty-first. Many institutions commissioned spectacular architectural designs—whose production was helped by ever more sophisticated computer-aided design software—that would function as signature buildings. For example, the Milwaukee Art Museum, Wisconsin, asked architect and engineer Santiago Calatrava (born 1951) to design an extension that would increase the museum's visibility. The Quadracci Pavilion (1994–2001) is an engineering feat with two moveable wings that shade the vaulted glass roof of the 90 ft tall foyer, one of the mainly non-exhibition spaces that were added to the museum. A signature building with generous foyer space was also the goal of the Akron Art Museum, Ohio, that opened in 2007, after the architecture firm Coop Himmelb(l)au of Wolf D. Prix (born 1942) had won a competition in 2001. A three-storey hall is the heart of the extension that makes little gestures towards the old museum in Akron's former post office (1899). Many recent museum buildings feature such central foyer spaces whose size exceeds what is required for circulation purposes. These spaces cater to the needs of the museum as an economic institution as they help to control numerous visitors to blockbuster exhibitions, offer architecturally exciting environments for donor receptions, and generate possible rental income from private and business functions. Thus the signature building has changed the appearance of museum architecture by emphasizing, sometimes dramatically, a space that, however, has been an element of the museum building at least since Durand drew a circle at the center of his ideal museum plan and Schinkel realized the rotunda in the Berlin Museum.

CONCLUSION

Museums are institutions that are deeply rooted in Western civilization. A specific building type began to emerge the moment when the meaning of the museum changed from primarily being a private study to an exhibition space that was publicly accessible. During the eighteenth century architecturally fundamental question about the spatial organization of the museum were worked out, that the nineteenth century perfected in ideal types of museum buildings. The early twentieth century was dominated by a modernist reaction against these ideal museum types, whereas in the later century and the twenty-first century unique signature buildings inscribed visibly into the urban fabric the changed economic condition of museums.

REFERENCES

1. Hesiod, T. In *Works and Days, and Theogonis, Elegies*; Hesiod, T., Ed.; Harmondsworth: Penguin, 1973; 23–26 trans. Dorothea Wender.
2. Watts, E. *City and School in Late Antiquity Athens and Alexandria*; University of California Press: Berkeley, CA, 2006; 146–148.
3. Wittlin, A.S. *The Museum. Its History and its Tasks in Education*; Routledge & Kegan Paul: London, 1949; 1.

4. Findlen, P. The museum: Its classical etymology and renaissance genealogy. J. Hist. Collect **1989**, *1*(1), 59–77 60–62.
5. Gombrich, E.H. The museum: Past, present and future. Crit. Inq. Spring **1977**, *3*(3), 449–470 450.
6. Vitruvius. Ten books on architecture, book 6, chapter 5, paragraph 2. Plinius the Elder, Natural History, book 35, chapter 2.
7. Newhouse, V. *Art and the Power of Placement*; Monacelli Press: New York, 2005; 65–76.
8. Seling, H. The genesis of the museum. Architect. Rev. **1967**, *14*(840), 103–114 February 103.
9. Pevsner, N. Museums. In *A History of Building Types*; Pevsner, N., Ed.; Princeton University Press: Princeton, NJ, 1976; 111–138 111.
10. Prinz, W. *Die Entstehung der Galerie in Frankreich und Italien*; Gebr. Mann: Berlin, 1970; 12.
11. Huth, H. Museum and gallery. In *Beiträge für Georg Swarzenski*; Götz, O., Ed.; Gebr. Mann: Berlin, 1951; 238–245 Henry Regnery: Chicago 244.
12. Impey, O., Macgregor, A., Eds. *The Origins of Museums. The Cabinet of Curiosities in Sixteenth- and Seventeenth-Century Europe*; Clarendon Press: Oxford, 1985.
13. Hartig, O. Die Kunsttätigkeit in München unter Wilhelm IV und Albrecht V, 1520–1579. *Münchener Jahrbuch der bildenden Kunst*, Neue Folge, 1933; Vol. X, 147–252.
14. Seelig, L. The Munich Kunstkammer. In *The Origins of Museums;* Impey, Macgregor, Eds.; Clarendon Press: Oxford, 1985; 76–89.
15. Yanni, C. *Nature's Museums: Victorian Science and the Architecture of Display*; Princeton Architectural Press: New York, 2005; 21.
16. Anonymous. *Die geöffnete Raritäten- und Naturalien-Kammer: Worinnen der galanten Jugend, andern Curieusen und Reisenden gewiesen wird: wie sie Galerien, Kunst- und Raritäten-Kammern mit Nutzen besehen und davon raisoniren sollen ... verfertiget von einem Liebhaber curieuser Sachen*. Benjamin Schillern: Hamburg, 1704. Art historians have ascribed the pamphlet to the scholar and architect Leonhard Christoph Sturm (1669–1719).
17. Berliner, R. Zur älteren Geschichte der Museumslehre in Deutschland. Münchener Jahrbuch der bildenden Kunst **1928**, Vol. V, 327–352 Neue Folge (new series),336–338.
18. Dion, M., Theewen, G., Eds. *Die geöffnete Raritäten-und Naturalien-Kammer ...* ; Salon: Cologne, 2002.
19. Roth, H., Ed. *Der Anfang der Museumslehre in Deutschland. Das Traktat Inscriptiones vel Tituli Theatri Amplissimi von Samuel Quiccheberg Lateinisch-Deutsch*; Akademie-Verlag: Berlin, 2002.
20. Durand, J.-N.-L. *Precis of the Lectures on Architecture: With Graphic Portion of the Lectures on Architecture*, transl. by David Britt Getty Research Institute: Los Angeles, 2000.
21. Jackson-Stops, G. Temples of the arts. *The Treasure Houses of Britain—Five Hundred Years of Private Patronage and Art Collecting*, exh. cat., National Gallery of Art: Washington, D.C., 1985; 14–21.
22. Savoy, B., Ed. Schryen, A. Die k.k. Bilder-Gallerie im Oberen Belvedere in Wien. In *Tempel der Kunst. Die Geburt des öffentlichen Museums in Deutschland 1701–1815*; Philipp von Zabern: Mainz, 2006; 279–303.
23. Markus, T.A. *Buildings & Power. Freedom & Control in the Origin of Modern Building Types*; Routledge: London, 1993; 185–190.
24. Neverov, O. "His Majesty's Cabinet" and Peter I's Kunstkammer. In *The Origins of Museums*; Impey, Macgregor, Eds.; 61.
25. Meijers, D.J. The Kunstkamera of Tsar Peter the Great (St Petersburg 1718-34): King Solomon's house or repository of the four continents?. In *The Architecture of the Museum. Symbolic Structures, Urban Contexts*; Giebelhausen, M., Ed.; Manchester University Press: Manchester, 2003; 17–31.
26. Vercamer, J. Das Museum Fridericianum in Kassel. In *Tempel der Kunst*; Savoy, Ed.; 309–331.
27. Rea, P.M. One hundred and fifty years of museum history. Sci. New Ser **1923**, June 15 *57*(1485), 677–81.
28. Coleman, L.V. *The Museum in America. A Critical Study*; American Association of Museums: Washington, D.C., 1939; 6–7.
29. Searing, H. *New American Art Museums*; University of California Press: Berkeley, 1982; 22–23.
30. von Buttlar, A. Europäische Wurzeln und deutsche Inkunabeln der Museumsarchitektur. In *Tempel der Kunst*; Savoy, Ed.; 35–45, 41–42.
31. Gundestrup, B. From Royal Kunstkammer to the modern museums of Copenhagen. In *The Origins of Museums*; Impey, Macgregor, Eds.; 128–134.
32. Conforti, M. The idealist enterprise and the applied arts. In *A Grand Design. The Art of the Victoria and Albert Museum*; Baker, M., Richardson, B., Eds.; Harry N. Abrams: New York, 1997; 23–47 35–36.
33. O'Dwyer, F. *The Architecture of Deane and Woodward*; Cork University Press: Cork, 1997; 152–283.
34. Dunn, R.; Burton, A. The Victoria and Albert Museum: An illustrated chronology. In *A Grand Design*; Baker, Richardson, Eds.; 49–77 55–56.
35. Disraeli, B. *Tancred or the New Crusade [1847]*, Green and Co.: London 112 Longmans, no year.
36. Horsfall, T.C. *The Study of Beauty and Art in Large Towns*; Macmillan: London, 1883.
37. Gilman, B.I. *Museum Ideals of Purpose and Method*; Harvard University Press: Cambridge, MA, 1923; 143.
38. Stein, C. The art museum of tomorrow. Architect. Rec **1930**, January *67*, 5–12.
39. Le Corbusier, *Le Corbusier 1910–60*, Girsberger: Zurich, 1960; 212–213.
40. Welter, V.M. *Biopolis—Patrick Geddes and the City of Life*; MIT Press: Cambridge, MA, 2002; 130.
41. Serota, N. *Experience or Interpretation. The Dilemma of Museums of Modern Art [1996]*, Thames & Hudson: London, 2000; 14.

BIBLIOGRAPHY

1. Carrier, D. *Museum Skepticism: A History of the Display of Art in Public Galleries;* Duke University Press: Durham, N.C., 2006.
2. Cuno, J., Ed. *Whose Muse? Art Museums and the Public Trust*; Princeton University Press: Princeton, NJ, 2004; Harvard University Press: Cambridge, MA.

3. Gaethgens, T.W. Das Museum um 1800: Bildungsideal und Bauaufgabe. In *Klassizismen und Kosmopolitismus: Program oder Problem? Austausch in Kunst und Kunsttheorie im 18. Jahrhundert*; Griener, P., Ed.; Kolloqium at 6./7. Juni 2001 in Zurich no publisher: Zurich, 2004; 137–162.
4. Giebelhausen, M., Ed. *The Architecture of the Museum. Symbolic Structures, Urban Contexts*; Manchester University Press: Manchester, 2003.
5. Gilman, B.I. *Museum Ideals of Purpose and Method*; Harvard University Press: Cambridge, MA, 1923.
6. Lampugnani, V., Sachs, A., Eds. *Museums for a New Millenium. Concepts, Projects, Buildings*; Prestel: Munich, 1999.
7. McClellan, A. *The Art Museum from Boullée to Bilbao*; University of California Press: Berkeley, 2008.
8. Murray, D. *Museums, their History and their Use*; James MacLehose and Sons: Glasgow, 1904.
9. Newhouse, V. *Art and the Power of Placement*; Monacelli Press: New York, 2005.
10. Newhouse, V. *Towards a New Museum;* Monacelli Press: New York, 1998.
11. Noever, P. *The Discursive Museum*; Hatje Cantz Publishers: Ostfildern-Ruit, 2001.
12. Noordegraaf, J. *Strategies of Display: Museum Presentation in Nineteenth- and Twentieth-Century Visual Culture*; Museum Boijmans Van Beuningen: NAi Publishers: Rotterdam, 2004.
13. Pevsner, N. *A History of Building Types;* Princeton University Press: Princeton, NJ, 1976.
14. Rosenblatt, A. *Building Type Basics for Museums*; John Wiley & Sons: New York, 2001.
15. Savoy, B., Ed. *Tempel der Kunst. Die Geburt des öffentlichen Museums in Deutschland 1701–1815*; Philipp von Zabern: Mainz, 2006.
16. Searing, H. *New American Art Museums*; University of California Press: Berkeley, 1982.
17. Serota, N. *Experience or Interpretation. The Dilemma of Museums of Modern Art [1996]*; Thames & Hudson: London, 2000.
18. Sheehan, J.J. *Museums in the German Art World: From the End of the Old Regime to the Rise of Modernism*; Oxford University Press: Oxford, 2000.
19. Steffensen-Bruce, I.A. *Marble Palaces, Temples of Art: Art Museums, Architecture, and American Culture, 1890–1930*; Bucknell University Press: Lewisburg, PA, 1988.
20. Tilden, S.J., Ed. *Architecture for Art American Art Museums 1938–2008*;; Harry N. Abrams: New York, 2004.
21. Waterfield, G., Ed. *Palaces of Art. Art Galleries in Britain 1790–1990*; Dulwich Picture Gallery: London, 1991.
22. Yanni, C. *Nature's Museums: Victorian Science and the Architecture of Display*; Princeton Architectural Press: New York, 2005.

Museum Collecting and Collections

Robert B. Pickering
Gilcrease Museum and Museum Science and Management Program, University of Tulsa, Tulsa, Oklahoma, U.S.A.

Abstract

Collecting is a central activity to museums. Object-based learning is the underlying principle that museums use to tell their stories to the public through different media such as exhibits, programs, classes, books, and activities. Collecting in museums is usually directed by curators who conduct research, create new knowledge, and present their work through publications, exhibits, and programs. Traditionally, there has always been a tension in museums between saving objects primarily for research versus using objects in educational programs. In recent decades, this tension has become more complicated as a result of other trends relating to changing demographics, new laws, and evolving ethics. In the future, these trends may change how museums build collections.

INTRODUCTION

Museums today come in many sizes, specializations, and perspectives. Most major cities boast of having a number of museums. Art, history, and natural history museums are the most common types. They usually have well-developed audiences and constituents who know what kinds of experiences to expect when they enter the hallowed galleries. In recent decades, many cities, large and small, have developed children's or family museums. To paraphrase Peter Sterling, former director of the Indianapolis Children's Museum, "Children's museums are the only museums defined by audience rather than by subject." Beyond these well-established museums, many different, sometimes quirky, kinds of museums have been opened that focus on the collecting passions of a dedicated and usually wealthy founder or a passionate core group of supporters.

Without doubt, there are more museums and probably more kinds of museums than ever before. Today, over 3,000 of the estimated 17,500 museums in the United States are accredited by the American Association of Museums (AAM), the national organization that sets the standards for professionalism in the field. In addition, there are many other smaller museum organizations that have developed out of regional interests (Colorado Wyoming Association of Museums, CWAM; Mountain-Plains Museum Association, MPMA) or subjects (Museums West Consortium; Association of Science - Technology Centers, ASTC). All of these organizations strive to define practices that assure excellence in collecting practices and collection care, to support a positive working environment for staff, and to provide enjoyable and enriching experiences for visitors.

HISTORY

The idea of museums that provide educational benefits to the public can be traced to the Age of Enlightenment of the seventeenth century. Before that time, royal and noble houses sometimes accumulated objects that reflected the interests and accomplishments of the great names of the time. The collections might have provided personal satisfaction for the owner and have been shared with other royals and nobles, but educating the masses, certainly was not the purpose. Collections and their care were subject to the continuing interest and power of the owners. These collections have sometimes been called "cabinets of curiosities" to denote their rather whimsical and personal origins.[1] Yet, it was precisely this curiosity about the exotic world being discovered by European explorers that started the museum movement which we know today.

Early American museums were part of this "cabinet of curiosities" tradition. Thomas Jefferson, Benjamin Franklin, and Charles Wilson Peale, among many others started personal collections, many of which became the founding collections of the great museums in Boston, Philadelphia, New York, and other early metropolitan areas.

THREE AGES OF MUSEUMS

In thinking about museum collecting in America since the beginning of the Republic, three "great ages" of museum evolution can be described: the age of collection, the age of exhibition, and the age of education. The first great age of this scheme, the "age of collecting," was part of the larger age of exploration that emanated from Europe. The New World, as it was called by the Europeans who came

Encyclopedia of Library and Information Sciences, Fourth Edition DOI: 10.1081/E-ELIS4-120044042

here (understanding that it was not new to those people and cultures that were already here), was the source of great wonder, danger, and opportunity for the Europeans who came and saw a very different world from the one to which they were accustomed. The same wonder, danger, and opportunity must have faced the American cultures that were already here. However, that part of the story is beyond the scope of this entry.

Exploration and collecting go together. Many of the ocean going vessels that left Europe to traverse distant oceans and contact different peoples in search of trade and riches brought back examples of the exotic. Yet the quality of the accumulated collections depends on the training of the collector. Many cultural and natural history objects were picked up by the sailors and passengers on the early voyages to America. The first settlers undoubtedly obtained items from the indigenous people they encountered along the eastern coast. However, it is the rare item that has survived the last three centuries intact and with any information about its origins. During the same period, however, there were individuals who sought to systematically collect and document the new and exotic world in which they were living. These early scientists intended that their work and the objects they collected would be preserved for future generations.

Natural history included the rocks, minerals, fossils, plants, and animals of the new country. The indigenous peoples encountered along the way also were seen as part of nature. Many explorers primarily were interested in the potential wealth that might be obtained from finding gold or silver. Only slightly less important, but often forgotten today, were the riches offered by trees and plants that might have medical, ornamental, or commercial uses. Although economic opportunity may have been the main concern, many of the early expeditions included a scientist who recorded the country through which the expedition passed and the people met along the way. As these ventures expanded across the continent, natural historians were there recording new species with their drawings, descriptions, and preserved specimens. Frequently, artists were part of such expeditions to record the new finds. The works of Mark Catesby and John James Audubon are part of the early naturalist/artist tradition just as the images of Karl Bodmer and Le Page du Pratz recorded the people and customs they encountered. Recently, an excellent new version of Prince Maximilian's travel journals, written while exploring the American West in the early 1830s,[2] has been published. This fine edition also includes excellent illustrations by Karl Bodmer who accompanied the Prince. The Prince and the artist also collected natural history specimens as well as clothing, tools, weapons, and other objects from the American Indian cultures they encountered.

The great age of exploration and collecting continued throughout the eighteenth and nineteenth centuries. In many institutions, systematic collecting continues today. Many great museums, especially in the seafaring countries of Europe, were founded in the age of exploration to care for and to present the odd and curious relics to local audiences. Oxford University's Ashmolean Museum, founded in 1683, was the first institution in Europe to call itself a museum.[3] Within this period, wealthy benefactors, sometimes private individuals and corporate capitalists, as well as government agencies sponsored expeditions of discovery and collecting on the North American continent and beyond. As earlier generations of nobles gained a degree of status and fame from their personal collections, so too did the new rich of the Industrial Revolution and the nascent oil industry, gain from their philanthropy toward collecting and the founding of museums to care for their efforts. The names of Carnegie, Rockefeller, Morgan, Field, and others left lasting legacies for this country by founding some of the great museums that still benefit the public today.

This age of collecting and exploration was a heady time for scientists. The entire world was before them. The extraordinary quantity and variety of natural history specimens being collected around the world, required explanation and some means by which all of the rocks, plants, animals, and other humans could be understood. Many of these objects and the people from distant lands were beyond the experience and the understanding of those whose world view was based on the Bible and local tradition. New ideas based on the observations of geologists such as Sir Charles Lyell and naturalists exemplified by Gregor Mendel and Charles Darwin were converging to revolutionize thinking and the way the world was understood. Naturalists and scientists collected, described, curated, and communicated their finds to other scientists who appreciated their descriptions and systematic organization of the natural world. The revolution of evolution had begun. Decision makers in government and commerce also understood the value to these new discoveries; perhaps not in scientific terms but for their potential economic and political impact. Exhibits of this period often were limited to displays of organisms or objects arranged to illustrate the systematic relationships between the specimens.

The second great age of collecting in museums might be thought of as the age of exhibition and dioramas. Perhaps its roots can be traced to the World Fairs of the late nineteenth and early twentieth centuries. The first World Fair was actually the Great Exhibition of Industry of All Nations held in London in 1851.[3] World Fairs offered an opportunity to bring together the wonders of the industrial world to mass audiences in England and the United States. Major advances in science and technology were presented by the European countries along with the natural history oddities, archaeological exhibits, and exotic races and cultures displayed for the edification and amusement of the public.

In planning America's signature World Fair, the World's Columbian Exposition of 1893 in Chicago, great effort was expended in showcasing past and present cultures from around the world. Frederic Ward Putnam, the director of the anthropology exhibits, and his trusty assistant Franz Boas, sought out, borrowed, and purchased collections of antiquities. George Dorsey, future curator of anthropology at Field Columbian Museum, was sent to South America for collections. Collections representing the Cliff Dwellers of the American Southwest were presented as were W.K. Moorehead's incredible collection of Hopewell artifacts from prehistoric Ohio. Even peoples were on exhibit, not only on the carnival-like Midway, but also next to the anthropology building where Boas encamped a group of Kwakiutl from British Columbia to shock visitors with their savage "cannibal dance." Not to be outdone, the Smithsonian Institution's National Museum mounted its own exhibits featuring the work of Frank Hamilton Cushing among the Zuni Pueblos of New Mexico.

Although the newly appointed University of Chicago anthropologist Frederick Starr supported the educational goal of presenting ancient American cultures through displays, he also had an ulterior motive. He planned and expected that at the end of the Exposition, those massive and valuable collections would come to the Walker Museum of the University of Chicago and thereby be under his control. A good plan from his perspective, but it was not to be. Putnam had lobbied for his vision of a great city museum and influential Chicagoans bought into his plans. Merchant Marshal Field, encouraged by his friend, lumber baron Edward Ayers, gave 1 million dollars to found a museum that became the Field Museum of Natural History. Other Chicago museums, The Museum of Science and Industry (housed in the Fine Arts Building from the World's Fair), the Newberry Library, and the Chicago Academy of Sciences were based on or inspired by the ideals, collections, and architecture of the Columbian Exposition. As varied as these institutions are, as an outgrowth of the Columbian Exposition, their benefit to scientific research, the economic life of Chicago, and the entertainment and education of the public are immeasurable.

Eleven years after the Chicago Fair, St. Louis presented the Louisiana Purchase Exposition. The St. Louis anthropology exhibits topped those in Chicago; it gave new meaning to the concept of "living dioramas."[4] To justify its imperial adventures, the United States brought in dozens of natives from the Philippines to demonstrate the progress the government had made in educating their colonized dependents. A school for Indians of the United States was installed to exemplify the progress made in raising the savage indigenes up the ladder of progress, and an Indian Olympics was held to complement the International Olympic Games. Pygmies were brought from the Congo Free State, and Frederick Starr was sent to the Japanese island of Hokaido to bring back a group of Ainu. Although St. Louis did not gain a great museum, the U.S. National Museum was only too eager to incorporate the magnificent displays into its own collections.

In addition to the many scientists who contributed to these memorable fairs, so too did many artists and technicians apply their skills. Alexander Phimister Proctor, a promising young sculptor, was awarded a commission to create some of the massive animal sculptures in the White City of the Exposition. His background as a western outdoorsman brought an authenticity to his work that served him throughout his long career. Artists such as Carl Akeley and Louis Agazziz Fuertes helped design and create fantastic dioramas for Chicago's new museums. Perhaps for the first time in history, dioramas of entire life scenes, sometimes actual, other times contrived, provided a three-dimensional view into the past that made the viewer feel that they were actually seeing the past. The important point is that the idea of re-creating life behind glass—a permanent record of a particular habitat complete with appropriate plants, animals, insects, and all, or a detailed reconstruction of an activity or scene from an ancient culture—was new and exciting both to the public and to the people who were doing the work. Just as we think of the heady excitement of the early days in Silicon Valley and the computer industry, so were the early days of exhibit development also an exciting and invigorating time. Very talented and dedicated individuals envisioned and created museum environments that have educated and entertained generations of viewers.

While the American Museum of Natural History in New York and Chicago's Field Museum were among the earliest to develop this new approach to museums, they were not the last. From coast to coast, the trend to build larger, more detailed dioramas grew. The Hastings Museum of Natural and Cultural History (Nebraska), the Denver Museum of Nature and Science, and the Los Angeles County Museum of Art are examples.

During the years in which the art of the diorama was being developed, collecting did not stop. However, there was a shift in purpose. Much early scientific collection and exhibition was connected to explorations of evolutionary theory. Scientists looked at rocks and under them to find evidence that either supported or refuted Darwin's new approach to understanding the visible world. In fact, scientific collecting continued to develop in sophistication as did other aspects of science. New techniques of preservation, photography, and eventually, film and audio recording, immensely increased and improved the work of scientists in the field. To the scientist, objects are data. As field work produced more and better data, old theories had to be revised and new theories were developed to explain what the scientists were seeing. First and foremost, science is based on observation. As the number of scientists conducting fieldwork increased dramatically, perhaps exponentially, the need to study, store, and explain their work became more important. The need to systematically organize the increasing collections also became more important. From the earlier focus on specimens in evolutionary research emerged attempts to present the data in its historical context. Thus, the diorama emerged as a way to provide context for specimens.

The age of exhibition, like the age of collecting, has evolved. Advances in computer technology have dramatically improved dioramas but at the same time, signaled their potential demise. In the late 1960s and early 1970s, one of the new terms heard in museums was the "immersion environment." Perhaps Walt Disney should be given credit here. To say that Disney added new life to static dioramas is an understatement. His revolutionary vision created entire environments which engaged multiple senses and provided a wide range of sensory rich, realistic but safe experiences. That he was able to make it work on such a grand scale represents both genius and great organizational skill. His determination to recreate a version of history or the future that entertained and educated, has come to be known as "edutainment." The success of Disney's vision is evidenced by the large paying audiences that have made a trip to the various Disneylands around the world nearly as important as a religious pilgrimage.

While the Disney phenomenon has been viewed by many museum professionals with varying degrees of skepticism, possibly tinged with jealousy,[5,6] there is no doubt that Disney changed the public's standards for the kinds of experiences that they expect. Museums have responded by borrowing some of the ideas and techniques from Disney, and merging them with the museum's mission to present accurate information about nature and culture. In the conflict between entertainment and education, museums usually side with education, but more often today, they attempt to merge the two. The comfortable compromise is the "immersion concept" which strives to put the visitor in the environment with all of its sights, sounds, and, sometimes, smells. Mechanical and computer technology added movement and change to such displays that could not have been provided in earlier decades.

The rain forest exhibit at the Milwaukee Public Museum, a leader in exhibit design for decades, also led in this new direction. The environment was so rich in detail that it is impossible to absorb the entire experience in one trip. This exhibit had two other characteristics that would soon be developed by others. First, there is a reconstruction of a field station within the exhibit so that the visitor can see not only the "natural" environment of the rain forest, but also the "cultural" environment of human activity. In 2002, the Draper Museum of Natural History opened as the fifth museum of the Buffalo Bill Historical Center in Cody, Wyoming, and the first natural history museum built in the United States in the twenty-first century. One of the philosophical underpinnings of that museum is that today, it is no longer possible to separate natural history from human history. They are so intertwined throughout the world that even the concept of nature untouched by human activity is perhaps a relic of the nineteenth century (Fig. 1).

The second imaginative introduction of the Milwaukee Public Museum's rain forest exhibit is that one can enter and explore on at least two levels of the massive gallery: the floor level and the forest canopy level. Today, this may seem a small point, but at the time, providing an immersion experience on one level was a novel experience, letting people experience the environment from a totally different vantage point was simple yet brilliant. Providing a second distinct viewing experience had significant implications and major challenges for the design of the space.

Fig. 1 Beginning in the late nineteenth century, museums used dioramas to interpret and convey information. The Milwaukee Public Museum created many lifelike and dynamic exhibits such as this buffalo hunt.
Source: Photo courtesy of RB Pickering.

Seeing from many directions required much more detail in this artificially produced environment so that, in fact, it did not look artificial.

Innovations in computer technology also may hasten the end of the diorama as we know it and change the role of objects in museums. So too, the increased ease and availability of travel for larger segments of society, has caused the question to be asked, "Why do we need to build a diorama of a distant place on the planet when people can now go there?" Dioramas are both labor and cost intensive. Every tiny element, a leaf, an insect, or a blade of grass, in a diorama is either completely artificial or has been treated so that it will look natural for decades. The expertise to make dioramas is expensive. Moreover, natural history documentaries made for television or massive IMAX screens can provide much more information, empathy, and impact than can a static diorama. These converging trends are causing museums to rethink the concept of what dioramas and the immersion environment might provide. The computer gaming industry has demonstrated that building a virtual environment is both engaging to the audiences and it need not be limited to either a specific location, such as a museum; it does not even have to be limited to reality!

The age of exhibition may not be at an end but it is evolving into the third age—the age of education that includes access to information and experiential learning. Innovative computer technology already can create virtual objects and environments. Will it replace the museum's need for real objects and physical environments? There is no "right" or obvious answer to that question at this time. In fact, there is no single answer. We are currently living through this change and the results will not be known until the public and museums around the world decide, and put their support behind that which they find most engaging. However, there are some trends worth watching. Many museums are rapidly placing collections online for distant learners. They are developing virtual versions and simulations of real exhibitions. Museums recognize that creating an exhibit, especially traveling or temporary exhibits, is very expensive. Even if the exhibit travels over a period of months or years and goes to four to six cities, eventually, the exhibits are dismantled and disappear. Computers now offer the opportunity to simulate the exhibit in perpetuity and also provide a depth of detailed information, sources, and images that could not be included in a real exhibit. Technically, creating a virtual exhibit is already possible and being done. There is no doubt that virtuals provide a lasting record. The more important question is, "Will the public care?" Will virtual exhibits be sought out and seen by the public in the same way that visitors now return to museums to see real objects or works of art that are important to them? Again, we do not know the answer but many within the museum field are concerned about the answer.

Museums have always been populist institutions, although to varying degrees. The idea that the museum exists for the public's benefit, education, and enjoyment has been important for a very long time. For much of the twentieth century, and certainly all of the nineteenth, museums did little to influence or mediate the experience other than to provide objects and labels. The Field Museum, so innovative in its work on dioramas and collections research, also was an innovator in public education. Its education department was established in 1922 to offer classes, lectures, field trips, and a wide range of programs for different audiences. Even more impressive, as early as 1912, Field Museum's Harris Loan Program was established to provide artifacts, specimens, and audiovisual material to Chicago area schools. Access to collections became an important part of the museum experience very quickly.

At least since the 1890s, it has been recognized that access to collections provides excellent learning opportunities for teaching and learning. At the same time, using collections for teaching potentially damages the actual specimens and over time will destroy the specimens. Flowers[7] wrote eloquently about this internal tension. Over 100 years later, this concern still has not been completely resolved, but there are more innovative solutions than in earlier times. Most museums maintain permanent collections for research. Whether the collections are rocks, bird skins, or clothing and textiles, the use of these collections is governed by rules or guidelines. For many museums, the list of people with access is internally restricted to research and collections staff who have the authority and responsibility for those collections. Researchers from outside the institution who have a legitimate reason to work with the collection, have a specific plan of research, and appropriate credentials, usually are granted access. A person from off the street may get access to research collections but not without significant effort.

Over the decades, many education departments have established "education collections" which are available for teaching people of all ages, but primarily for children. Restrictions apply here, too, but access within educational programs does provide children and adults the ability to closely observe and sometimes to touch specimens under the direction of education staff. This kind of access to collections has sometimes been contentious between the curatorial and collections, and education staffs. The reasons for the disagreement are obvious. Curators and collections staffs are responsible for the physical care and long-term preservation of the objects or works. Curators may have actually collected the specimens, and feel proprietary toward them. Understandably, such curators are willing to give access only to those who they trust will treat the objects with the same degree of care and respect.

Educators tend to focus on the audience and the benefit that access provides. That is not to say that educators do not share collections concerns with curators and collections professionals. They do. By working with curators and collections professionals, education departments have been able to obtain specimens that are representative of the subject and can be used in programs. For example, a paleontologist may have hundreds of examples of a common fossil. After evaluation, the curator may decide that some examples are redundant, i.e, they do not provide any different information from other specimens. These may be transferred to the education department for use in programs. For objects that are more delicate than a fossil, such as an example of Lakota bead work or an ancient pottery vessel, educators have also come up with acceptable practices. The object may be secured in an appropriate container so that the audience can handle the container but not the actual piece itself. A high-quality reproduction of the object may also be produced or purchased so that it can be handled instead of the actual specimen. Educators can usually be counted upon to find ingenious ways to provide effective hands-on experiences for audiences without sacrificing important objects.

As valuable as education collections are, they may have inherent problems. Educators sometimes complain that the objects they are given are essentially, "too good to throw away, but not good enough for the permanent collections." Educators do not want to teach with inappropriate or substandard material. They recognize that to do so diminishes the educational experience and essentially disrespects the audience. One innovative solution to this dilemma has been to eliminate completely the education collection and to create a "use code" for all objects in a permanent collection. One method has been to use the colors of the traffic light to signify appropriate use. For example, a "red code" means that the object is rare, delicate, and important for research. Therefore only curators and collections professionals may handle it and the only appropriate uses are research and exhibition. A "yellow code" means that other museum staffers who have had training in handling collections may handle the object. Yellow code objects are used in teaching situations as long as the educator and collections staffs agree on a safe method for handling. A "green code" means that an object can be handled and may eventually have to be discarded because of wear. For this category, education departments may purchase a number of examples of this kind of item and use them over time, replacing damaged ones as they go. The Children's Museum of Indianapolis began this practice in the late 1980s. For example, as many as Ten copies of a particular musical instrument such as an mbira or a drum might be purchased for use in children's programming. One example would be assigned to the permanent collection and be labeled "red" while the others would carry the "green" code and be used in programs. As one instrument was damaged another "green" one would take its place. In this way, all of the objects would be documented and tracked within the same collections management system, permanent collections built and maintained and yet, use of appropriate objects in programs facilitated.

CURRENT TRENDS AFFECTING COLLECTING

Museums, their collections, and their reasons for collecting are a reflection of society as a whole. Many trends that are part of our changing culture also impact museums. Knell[8] provides excellent European perspectives on contemporary and future collecting in museums. By their inherent nature, museums tend to be fairly conservative indicators of change, but change comes, nevertheless. It may not be possible to say how museums will collect or what they will collect in the future but there are some trends worth watching.

A globally significant trend is the rise of the digital age and its amazing ability to provide often instantaneous access to collections around the world. Today, even an armchair hobbyist can have access to images and information that only a few decades ago were available only to top specialists in the field. This is a great advance but not without risks.

Just as the exhibits departments struggle with the competition to their exhibits from computers, television documentaries and other forms of entertainment, and education available today, so too do museum educators struggle with how to compete with the ever-widening number of leisure activities and educational opportunities for the public. No one would dispute that more people now have more access to information around the world than at any time in human history. Therefore, the role of the museum as the presenter of information through objects would seem to be diminishing. Yet, a great deal of the information that is available is unmediated; meaning that the veracity or trustworthiness of the information is not assured. Moreover, the experience of seeing or touching authentic objects cannot be replaced, at this time. Perhaps museums will have an expanding role in providing reliable information about the wide range of subjects presented by museums.

A debate currently within the museum world is to what extent does putting images and data from collections on the Web diminish or increase the role of the museum? Certainly, access to data online reduces the need to visit a particular museum. At the same time, many in the museum world believe that once distant audiences see the virtual image, they will want to come and see the real object or a work of art for themselves. In this sense, putting collections on the Web is a grand advertisement for the real thing. This debate rages (if it can be said that any debate rages in the museum world) as this entry is being written. New audience research will determine how the public is deciding if the virtual is an acceptable substitute for the real.

Although the United States of America is a young nation by world standards, many of our museum collections have now been curated for 100 or more years. Many objects, whether an artist's sketch or a garment made from leather, beads, and hair were not made to last forever; their makers had a shorter term plan in mind. Museums have the responsibility of caring for these collections for our children's children's children—essentially, in perpetuity. If these collections are, in fact, going to survive and be available for research and exhibition for future generations, then conservation of these old collections will become an increasing challenge and cost to museums. The cost of caring for old collections is connected to the cost of making new collections. Many of the great natural history museums have been collecting plant, animal, and geological specimens for a very long time. Today's curators are adding to those collections. Old or newly collected, the collections staff must care for and properly store all of these objects (Fig. 2).

From the perspective of the curator who collects specimens, there are some significant changes that impact collecting today. There are many more laws that restrict the process. The curator, as a representative of the museum, must be knowledgeable about the appropriate laws and make sure that the museum complies with all applicable laws. A museum that does not follow the law loses credibility, and very likely, its audience and its financial support. Individuals and museums that do not follow the laws are liable to legal action.

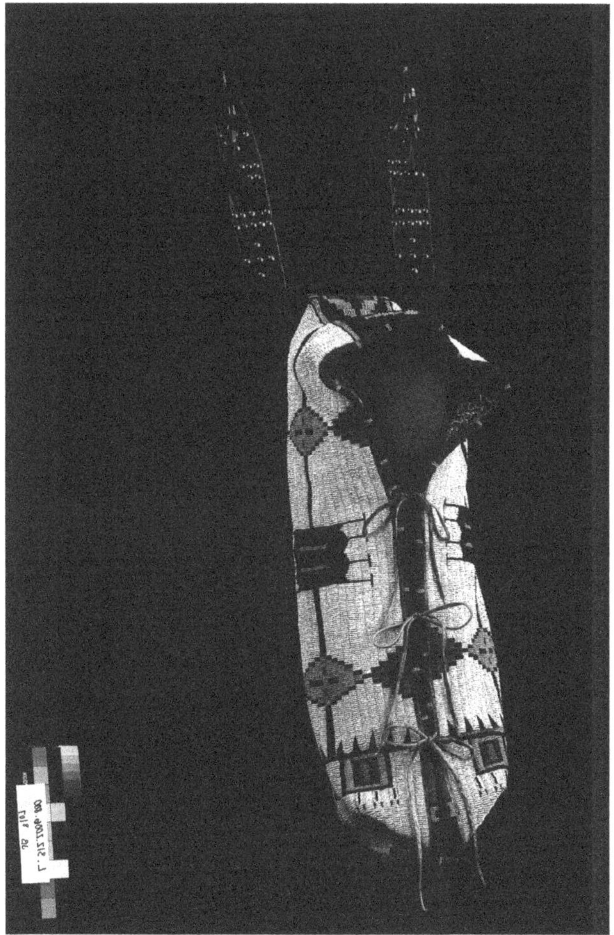

Fig. 2 Older objects, especially those made from perishable materials, will need consistent care to preserve these treasures for future generations. Cheyenne (Tsistsistas) cradle, ca. 1880; wood, tanned hide, glass beads, brass tacks, tin cones, porcupine quills, horsehair.

Source: NA.111.61 Photo courtesy of the Buffalo Bill Historical Center.

As the principal collectors in the museum, curators often determine what will be collected. Research interests have changed over time. In earlier generations, a natural history curator might have focused on the systematic study of a group of plants or animals. Today, a natural history researcher might be delving into DNA rather than looking at bones or feathers. Although those old collections of bones or feathers may yield the DNA needed by contemporary researchers,[9] they can be used to answer new questions. A hundred years ago, an anthropologist might have been out in the field acquiring objects from people in a culture that the anthropologist was sure would be extinct very soon. Perhaps he would have collected some oral histories and stories, too, but museums wanted objects. Today, the anthropologist is more likely to be working with tribal peoples to better understand the objects that were collected. As a result of Native American Graves Protection and Repatriation Act (NAGPRA), the anthropologist may work with federally recognized U.S. tribes to return important sacred and ceremonial objects to the tribe. An art curator today may continue to focus on past periods of artists and art styles and yet, the late nineteenth and the twentieth centuries spawned an explosion of new artists whose contributions and places in history are yet to be determined.

That curators have a central role in collection development is unmistakable, yet the training of curators is another trend that will affect museums in the future. A concern commonly voiced within anthropology and history museums is that for more than a generation, graduate schools have tended to diminish the importance of material culture studies, i.e., working with and researching real objects, (archaeologists sometimes call this "reading" objects) and have emphasized theory and the intellectual aspect of research. While this trend makes considerable sense for creating the next generation of college professors, it means that the skills for handling, studying, and understanding objects are not being transferred to the next generation of curators. Museums and their curators also are interested in the latest theories and the innovations of research, but we also have the collections in our care. If new curators do not have advanced skills in collections-based research and the ability to discriminate between genuine versus modified or fake objects, then the museum and, in fact, the entire public suffers.

While curators direct the building of collections from the inside of the museum, collectors and donors sometimes direct collecting from the outside. Many great collections have been assembled in virtually every collecting field by dedicated and wealthy individuals. Private collecting and collecting for museums can be quite different.[10] However, the history of museums exemplifies how the two merge. Often as they approach the end of their lives or perhaps just the end of their interest in one collecting area, they look for a museum to care for their collections. Many times, this opportunity is a great benefit to the museum. Collectors frequently have more money to spend on acquisitions than do most museums. When the museum and collector work together, the relationship can be very beneficial to all parties including the public who will have access to the once private collection.

The ethics of collecting is evolving rapidly and impacts virtually all areas of collecting and research. The international movement to redress grievances related to art and other possessions stolen by the Nazis is a very visible example but there are others. From stolen religious icons to objects looted from national museums during the Iraq war, museums often find that they are being offered cultural treasures through dealers and donors. Today, the ability to establish clear title and to demonstrate that objects were legally sold and legally obtained by the museum is expected. A museum that does not diligently research such high profile works may find itself in legal difficulty and risk a public relations disaster.

The American NAGRPA law, various United Nations treaties, and laws from individual countries that strive to put control of cultural objects back into the hands from which they were taken are having an increasing impact on museum ethics. These laws pertain to objects, yet their importance is that they redefine the relationship of cultures; usually an indigenous one and a dominant, if not an imperial one. Returning objects does not negate past wrongs but it may well provide a reorientation of respect and responsibility between cultures. Numerous volumes have come out in recent years that explore various aspects of collecting cultural artifacts and relations between museums and indigenous peoples.[11–14]

As positive as these new ethical positions are, they have their extremist proponents too. For example, archaeology explores past cultures and helps this and future generations understand more about how human beings evolved and cultures developed across the world. Archaeology strives to be the scientific and objective way of looking into past cultures. Outside of science, every culture has its own traditions and stories about their origins, their own past, and perhaps their relationships with their neighbors. As previously dominated cultures assert themselves, they also promote their own versions of their histories and sometimes diminish or dismiss the scientific view provided by archaeology. This perspective is understandable, but if taken to an extreme, it refutes archaeology as a legitimate discipline.

While curators direct collecting in many ways, there are cultural trends outside the museum that pertain.[15],[16] For most of the history of this country, the museum-going majority was Euro-American in ethnicity. Laws and practices often eliminated opportunities for racial minorities to take advantage of museums. Cost of admission impacted all poor people regardless of ethnicity. Those restrictions do not apply so much today but there is another aspect of ethnicity that does. The impact of increasing ethnic and cultural diversity is seen in schools, in the workplace, and in churches. Changing demographics also impacts museums. Does every ethnic group have the same museum experience that has evolved in Euro-American museums for more than a century? Do all cultures value the museum experience in the same way, to the same extent? Forward thinking museums will engage their audiences in providing answers to those and other related questions. Together, museums and their audiences will find the answers that work for them. One impact of greater audience diversity is clear; visitors want to see their own histories. For museums of art, history, and anthropology, satisfying an increasingly multicultural audience will require more efforts toward representing cultures that reflect our current society. Alternatively, communities that have felt marginalized or excluded may choose to create their own museums. The Smithsonian's new National Museum of the American Indian and the proposed National Museum of African American History and Culture are prominent examples.

In addition to ethnic differences in perspectives on museums, generational differences also contribute to the changing museum environment. Tom Brokaw's book, *The Greatest Generation*,[17] presented extraordinary acts performed by ordinary people during World War II, both at war and at home. Those who were fortunate to return at all, came home, changed out of their uniforms, and built their lives and this country. A couple of characteristics are worthy of note in the museum context. That generation understood personal sacrifice. Many were committed to making their own lives and the world a better place. They joined organizations, volunteered their time, and gave and raised money for all kinds of public causes. Some members of that generation also were significant collectors of paintings, historical documents, firearms, and many kinds of objects that interest museums.

As that generation passes, many of those collections are being offered to museums. Portions or entire estates are being given to museums as a perpetual memorial to the collector or benefactor. Many museums are also directly benefited from the volunteers who came to museums to learn and to give back to society. As this incredible generation passes, museums, and perhaps our entire society, become poorer for it. There is a critical question as to the philanthropic interests and patterns of giving by subsequent generations. Will the baby boomers and their children be as generous with their time and money? The answer is critical to museums and society in the future.

Beyond demographics, there are psychographics—the interests, needs, and wants that determine the choices people make. Demographics may be thought of as descriptive of an audience while psychographics may be predictive of interests and behaviors. Today's researchers in museums are interested in both. Will the generation now entering kindergarten have the same interests as their grandparents? Will they want to go to a specific place to learn about dinosaurs, ancient cultures, and the art of previous generations? The answers are not readily apparent, but to be successful, museums will have to continually struggle to be relevant and engaging to each new generation.

CONCLUSION

Collecting and preserving objects or works of art and providing access to these collections are the core activities of museums. Over the last three centuries, museums have seen the purposes and techniques of collecting and storing objects change dramatically. Yet, the purpose of collecting—creating new knowledge through research and presenting that knowledge to the public—is still pivotal to the future of museums. New technologies have not only impacted how things are collected, technology now allows the collecting of data that was virtually invisible to former generations. The digital revolution is recasting the opportunities to access the storehouse of knowledge that museum collections represent.

Museums are sometimes thought of as rather quiet, unchanging places where few things happen fast, if at all. There may have been a time when that was true; it is not any longer. To continue to be valued by the public, museums will continue to evolve through internal efforts and external pressures and needs. Museums will continue to reflect what is important to the culture of which they are part. As those cultures evolve, so too will the museum.

REFERENCES

1. Eikelmann, R. *Kunst—und Wunderkammer: Burg Trausnitz*, Zweigmuseum Des Bayerischen Nationalmuseums: München, 2007.
2. Witte, S.S.; Gallagher, M.V., Eds.; *The North American Journals of Prince Maximilian of Wied, Volume I: May 1832–April 1833*; University of Oklahoma Press: Norman, OK, 2008; Translated by William J. Orr, Dieter Karch.
3. Burcaw, G.E. *Introduction to Museum Work*, The American Association of State and Local History: Nashville, TN, 1989.
4. Parezo, N.J.; Fowler, D.D. *Anthropology Goes to the Fair: The 1904 Louisiana Purchase Exposition*, University of Nebraska: Lincoln, NE: Nebraska, 2007.
5. Terrell, J. Disneyland and the future of museum anthropology. Am. Anthropol. **1991**, *93*(1), 149–153.
6. Pridmore, J. Flap at Field Museum. Archaeology **1991**, November/December 60–63.
7. Flowers, W.H. *Essays on Museums and Other Subjects Connected with Natural History*, MacMillan & Co.: London, 1898.
8. In *Museums and the Future of Collecting*; Knell, S.J., Ed.; Ashgate Publishing Company: Burlington, VT, 2004.
9. In *The Research Potential of Anthropological Museum Collections*; Cantwell, A.-M.; Griffin, J.B.; Rothschild, N.A., Eds.; The New York Academy of Sciences: New York, 1981; Annals of the New York Academy of Sciences, vol. 376.
10. Sax, J.L. *Playing Darts with a Rembrandt*, The University of Michigan Press: Ann Arbor, MI, 1999.
11. Ames, M.M. *Cannibal Tours and Glass Boxes: The Anthropology of Museums*, UBC Press: Vancouver, BC, 1992.
12. Cole, D. *Captured Heritage: The Scramble for Northwest Coast Artifacts*, University of Washington Press: Seattle, WA, 1985.
13. Greenfield, J. *The Return of Cultural Treasures*, Cambridge University Press: Cambridge, 1989.
14. In *The Ethics of Collecting Cultural Properties: Whose Culture? Whose Property?*; Messenger, P.M.; Ed.; University of New Mexico Press: Albuquerque, NM, 1989.
15. Belk, R.W. *Collecting in a Consumer Society*, Routledge Press: New York, 1995.
16. Pearce, S.M. *On Collecting*, Routledge Press: New York, 1995.
17. Brokaw, T. *The Greatest Generation: Letters and Reflections*, Random House: New York, 1999.

Museum Computer Network (MCN)

Marla Misunas
Collections Information and Access, San Francisco Museum of Modern Art, San Francisco, California, U.S.A.

Richard Urban
Graduate School of Library and Information Science, University of Illinois, Champaign, Illinois, U.S.A.

Abstract

The museum information professional's association, the Museum Computer Network (MCN), was organized in 1967 during the early years of computerization in museums. Throughout its history MCN has provided conferences, news, and networking opportunities to its members. Through a discussion of key points in the group's development and current activity, the 40 year history of the association is briefly explored.

INTRODUCTION

The Museum Computer Network (MCN), formed in 1967, is a professional association that supports the greater museum community by providing continuing opportunities to explore, implement, and disseminate new technologies and best practices in the field. MCN draws its members from the ranks of museum staff who manage museum Web sites, network infrastructures, visitor services systems, and museum collection management and registration systems.

MCN provides professional development and educational opportunities through its annual conference. A Web site and the MCN-L listserv provide members opportunities to communicate throughout the rest of the year.

This entry offers a brief history of the organization from its inception in the late 1960s through the present.

ORIGINS

In 1965, the New York University (NYU) established the Institute for Computer Research in the Humanities (ICRH) under the leadership of computer scientist Dr. Jack Heller. During its first years of operation, the ICRH developed automation tools for NYU's library and completed the first electronic indexes of the *Répertoire International de Littérature Musicale (RILM)* and the *Revista Filología Española*. Working with the Dag Hammarskjöld Library, Heller created a suite of programs he called the *General Retrieval and Information Processor for Humanities Oriented Studies (GRIPHOS)*.

Heller and the ICRH came to the attention of staff at the Metropolitan Museum of Art in late 1966. Within the next few months, ICRH developed processes for Carl C. Dauterman to analyze porcelain in the Met's collection and had begun exploring a project to create an electronic index of the Met's *Bulletin*. During a visit to the museum, Heller met registrar William D. Wilkerson, who introduced him to the challenges of recording information about the Metropolitan's collections and instigated the series of meetings that was to follow.

In the spring of 1967, directors from 15 New York area museums met to explore ways Heller's work could be used beyond the Met. With funding from the New York Council of the Arts and the Old Dominion Foundation, the consortium formed the MCN to create a prototype system for a shared museum data bank. The administrative committee for the project, chaired by Wilkerson, selected Everett Ellin as its first executive director.

The project recruited curators and registrars to develop a data dictionary that would accommodate the diverse methods used to describe museum collections. The resulting tagged record format allowed for the description of individual objects with separate records for artist biographical information and reference citations. Heller's GRIPHOS system provided the information storage, search, and retrieval infrastructures for the records.

MCN and the Metropolitan Museum of Art, with funding from IBM, organized the first U.S. conference on the topic of museum computing in April 1968. This would be the first of many promotional efforts by Ellin, who was concerned about the growing information crisis in America's museums. In an appendix to the American Association of Museum's (AAM's) influential *Belmont Report*, he described MCN's vision for shared national and international museum data banks that would not only improve museum management practices but also would provide unprecedented access for researchers. Because of the expected costs, MCN

Encyclopedia of Library and Information Sciences, Fourth Edition DOI: 10.1081/E-ELIS4-120044051

advocated for a single network that would handle data for all the museums across the country.

INCORPORATION AND GROWTH

In June 1969, Jack Heller resigned his position at NYU and accepted a position at the State University of New York (SUNY) at Stony Brook. The original grant funding for the MCN pilot project ended in 1970. Of the original 15 partners, only the Metropolitan Museum and the Museum of Modern Art continued to catalog their collections using computerized methods and their own operating funds.

In 1972, the MCN was formally incorporated in the state of New York with David Vance as its first president. An "administrative committee" was comprised of representatives from institutions who had been involved in MCN's formation. Museums could join to receive consultation and advice about computerization projects or as full members with access to MCN software and hardware resources.

In addition to a change in funding structure, this transition marked a change of what kind of "network" MCN represented. Originally conceived as a physical computer network, MCN was to become part of a growing professional network of related cultural heritage computerization projects. Museum Computer Network would be one of the cofounders of a related group known as the Museum Data-Bank Coordinating Committee, which sought to find connections and opportunities for sharing work among a variety of museums including archeology, ethnography, history, natural science, and art museums.

Museum Computer Network was able to attract a number of large institutions as members, allowing it to continue operations and development of the GRIPHOS system. Especially important was the decision by Robert G. Chenhall to select the MCN/GRIPHOS system for the Arkansas Archaeological Survey, which encouraged other statewide surveys to take a similar path.

During this period, MCN began to regularly host annual conferences. Initially the conferences focused on issues relevant for GRIPHOS users, however, over time the conferences attracted representatives from other museums who had not yet implemented a computerized system.

In 1974, David Vance and the MCN office joined Jack Heller at SUNY-Stony Brook.

FROM INSTITUTIONS TO INDIVIDUALS

Toward the end of the 1970s, the operating systems found on IBMs mainframe computers were quickly becoming obsolete, foreshadowing the end for GRIPHOS, which had been tightly tied to those operating systems.

This tight integration had already limited the adoption of GRIPHOS in environments that used non-IBM hardware, a problem for museums which often relied on local university computing centers. Updated packages and user manuals continued to be released, but fewer MCN members were able to support the GRIPHOS software. Vance and Heller worked on migrating GRIPHOS to emerging minicomputers in 1981, but these efforts were soon overshadowed by the microcomputer revolution.

The computer revolution which was changing the business world in the 1980s was reflected in the rapid changes occurring at MCN as well. Cheaper desktop computers along with more accessible software made incorporating computers into their operations more realistic for some museums. This caused the increase in MCN's activity which was evidenced in the composition of *Spectra*. A different audience was looking to MCN for advice on computerization, and for an affinity group of like-minded museum professionals.

While some longtime MCN members continued to advocate for the centralized approach that the organization had been founded upon, museum computerization efforts were increasingly localized with little demand for the large mainframe systems of the 1970s. With dwindling support, the GRIPHOS system was officially retired in 1979.

During MCN's "mainframe" period, only institutions could be members of the organization. Reflecting the change to personal computing, the organization opened up membership to individuals for the first time in 1981. The organization soon attracted a broad spectrum of the museum community using a variety of different approaches to automating their collections.

The MCN Board decided the time had come to make major changes in MCN's structure, some of which were precipitated by funding cutbacks at SUNY-Stony Brook. The State University of New Yorks withdrawal of support meant MCN could no longer afford to pay its longtime staff member and president, David Vance. Vance stepped down as president in early 1986 and was replaced by Ron Kley. The board created a new model of a short-term volunteer president working alongside a grant-funded executive director.

Throughout the 1980s, MCN moved further away from the original vision of a centralized system, choosing instead to emphasize the development of data standards that would allow the exchange of museum information between systems that met local needs. These efforts retained the spirit of the original network, without forcing museums to adopt a single application or hardware platform.

CONSORTIUM FOR THE COMPUTER INTERCHANGE OF MUSEUM INFORMATION

Museum Computer Network continued to envision a structured flow of information between museums and at the end of the 1980s received grants from the National

Endowment for the Humanities and the Pew Trust to create the Computer Interchange of Museum Information (the CIMI project).[1] Headed by David Bearman, the project brought together a group of museum professionals and network industry staff.

Computer Interchange of Museum Information became an independent entity and produced the CIMI Standards Framework in 1993. The Framework recommended the standard fields which could later be used for interchange of information between museums and served as the basis for several test projects. Throughout the 1990s, the CIMI group continued their endeavors; among the members were the Getty Information Institute, the Canadian Heritage Information Network (CHIN), the Eastman Kodak, the Smithsonian, the Museum Documentation Association in the U.K., and of course, MCN.

CONFERENCES AND COLLABORATIONS

Since the first conference in 1968 MCN continued to produce its annual conferences, sharing information on the challenges, and successes of introducing technology into the museum environment. In 1979, MCN held the first conference to which people outside of the group of MCN institutional members were invited. This approach brought in new attitudes and new life into the organization.

Conferences were held in cities all over North America, usually at museums or facilities where members worked. The 1980 conference hosted the first public presentation of the Report of the North American Planning Conference, held at SUNY-Stony Brook that year.

The 1985 meeting was hosted by Dr. Jaime Litvak King of the University of Mexico, and included demonstrations on microcomputers, software, and Apple Mac hardware. The meeting featured preconference workshops for the first time.

Delegates at MCN's annual meeting in Pittsburgh in 1992 welcomed a surprise visitor—presidential hopeful Bill Clinton. Clinton spoke with MCN members who were so impressed that the fall 1992 *Spectra* included a list of delegates who had shaken his hand. Bill Weinstein was the record holder at four handshakes.

San Diego was the setting in 1995 when MCN and the International Conference on Hypermedia and Interactivity in Museums (ICHIM) held a joint conference which kicked off many of the archiving and online efforts of the next several years. Museum Computer Network's president at the time, Leslie Johnston, initiated a relationship with the Smithsonian Institution's archives to store MCN's records, where they are still kept.[2] Museum Computer Network's Web site went online shortly thereafter.

Museum Computer Network continued to forge informal alliances with professional organizations and to produce conferences in conjunction with these groups. Among the collaborators and conference hosts were the CHIN, the Association of Moving Image Archivists (AMIA), the Northeast Documentation Conservation Center (NEDCC), the National Initiative for a Networked Cultural Heritage (NINCH), and numerous others. Museum Computer Network is also an official affiliate organization of the AAMs.

U.S. CONGRESS

The Internet and World Wide Web were expanding rapidly during the early 1990s, and the U.S. Congress was moving to begin regulating and codifying the use of what it termed the "Information Superhighway." The High Performance Computing and Communication Act of 1991 (the Gore bill) led to the introduction of legislation proposed in Congress to support government information and cultural efforts on the Internet.

Early versions of the legislation did not mention museums specifically. Including museums in information superhighway legislation became a priority for Diane Zorich, President of MCN in 1994. Zorich's efforts and the efforts of many others on behalf of the museum community were successful in August of 1994 as stated in a *Spectra* article from the Summer 1994 issue. *Spectra* reproduced AAMs entire announcement, written by Michael Roark from their Government and Public Affairs office. "The Senate Commerce Committee today voted to guarantee the nation's 8000 museums a place in the National Information Infrastructure under the Communications Act of 1994. Museum images, texts, programming, and personnel will soon be accessible to highway travelers." The gist of the bill, according to Roark, was to deregulate sectors of telecommunications industries in exchange for industry support for schools, libraries, hospitals, and museums.

PUBLICATIONS

Information about MCN's activities was first published in the *ICRH Newsletter* along with updates about the progress of the GRIPHOS project which appeared in *Computers in the Humanities* and *Museum News*.

After David Vance relocated to Stony Brook in 1974, he wrote the "MCNews" column that appeared in *Spectra*, the newsletter for the Center for Contemporary Arts and Letters. By 1983, *Spectra* was entirely dedicated to news about MCN activities. The publication schedule was sometimes sporadic but generally followed the quarter system. In 1986, 2600 issues were mailed to 41 countries while *Spectra* was still being distributed at no charge. Issues with literature reviews, featured articles, and conference reports were often done on an extremely low budget, but always with professional editors publishing the sought-after journal. By 1987, organizational focus shifted towards expanding services and working with the AAMs on cooperative ventures. Consequently, the Board decided to expand *Spectra* contents and begin charging for subscriptions. In 1996, the newsletter underwent a complete redesign and by 1999 with the departure of longtime editor Suzanne Quigley, it moved away from MCN news completely. Guest editors organized *Spectra* between 1999 and 2002, when it was self-described as "not a scholarly journal, but rather a community-based current awareness publication focusing on issues and projects of interest to museum information professionals." The new millennium was celebrated with a special small format issue guest edited by Steve Dietz and Scott Sayre featuring thoughts and prophecies from 75 colleagues.

By 2002 rising production costs far out-distanced MCN's subscribers' and sponsors' capacity to pay for them; and the Board reluctantly suspended *Spectra*. The Board's hope was that the journal would eventually be revived on the MCN Web site, but competition for limited resources has not permitted its return.

Spectra's suspension occurred at a dark time for volunteer organizations and membership associations in particular. The "dot com" boom was over, and the tragedies of September 11, 2001 had just occurred. The U.S. economy was experiencing a downturn wherein nonprofit organizations, including museums everywhere, suffered. Nonprofits' budget cuts translated into fewer members for MCN and fewer travel dollars for members.

INTERACTIVE AND ONLINE

The computer ubiquity envisioned for businesses in the 1970s gradually became reality in the 1990s, with the wider availability of personal computers, access to e-mail, and the Internet. Various programs were founded around the country, such as the Electronic Frontier Foundation; the Museum Informatics Project at the University of California, Berkeley; and NINCH. The Getty Art History Information Project launched their Web site and the Networked Access initiative. Museum Computer Network members quickly embraced new technologies which were becoming more and more affordable for smaller institutions not supported by universities or other large entities. The 1990s were a time of growth and expansion for MCN.

The International Conference on Hypermedia and Interactivity in Museums began to hold conferences which focused on the presentation and Web tools in the international museum community. Also in 1996, MCN created their first Internet home page and a discussion list; many museums' Web pages were launched, and thousands of Web pages from all over the world began to come online. In the late 1990s, MCN continued developing its own Web site,[3] which was completely overhauled in 2005.

ANSWERS CHANGE, QUESTIONS REMAIN THE SAME

Over the last 40 years, cycles and recurring themes have occupied the MCN Board. Most of the plans centered around continuing to produce the high-quality conferences and publications for which MCN was well known; and to foster greater member involvement in planning and programs. Board of Directors' strategic planning retreats dealt with these key issues every few years. Each time the focus of the organization shifted slightly, but the premises of supporting the use of technology in museums and supporting museum information professionals did not.

As evidenced in *Spectra* over its 28 year history, desperate straits were always balanced by periods of optimism and growth. Expenses for MCN's ventures increased dramatically over the years and funding was nearly always an issue. Several different management models were tried during MCN's lifetime, including a full-time Executive Director, a part-time Program Director, and various management companies performing administrative duties. Currently, MCN's administrative functions are managed by McPherson Clarke, a Canadian association management company.

MCN TODAY

Governance

Since its incorporation in 1972, MCN has had a volunteer Board of Directors, usually composed of 12 people. Each director is elected for a term of 3 years, and may serve two terms in succession. Directors are expected to contribute to MCN's programs throughout their terms and to participate in several committees, such as Communications, Leadership Development, Membership, Finance, and Marketing. Directors meet monthly by phone and twice a year in person. The Executive Committee handles many of the organization's immediate concerns and is composed of the board officers. The President, Vice President/President-Elect, Treasurer, and Secretary form the Executive Committee. The Treasurer and Secretary are appointed from the Board of Directors, serving a renewable 1 year term. The Vice President serves in that capacity for 1 year and as President for 1 year. The Past President also serves 1 year in an advisory capacity.

Over the years, the bylaws have continued to develop and change. Museum Computer Network bylaws are available in the About Us section of the Web site.[4] The latest strategic plan is also available in the About Us section of the Web site.[5]

SIGs and Chapters

In 1997, MCN created the mechanism to form Special Interest Groups (SIGs) with the establishment of the SIG

Charter.[6] Each SIG provides a forum for MCN members to pursue specific subjects while MCN as a whole focuses on its members' more general concerns. Special Interest Groups may also represent geographic regions, such as the active California SIG.

Contributing to fields within the museum information profession, SIGs provide opportunities for learning new skills, leadership, and growth. Where communication with the MCN Board is indicated, this usually occurs through the Board's SIG Liaison; in some cases, it includes communication with other officers as noted.

Over the years, MCN has formed relationships with various international groups but never formalized these relationships. In 2006, MCN created the mechanism to form separate regional chapters outside North America. In March 2007,

> ...A ceremony marking the establishment of MCN in Taiwan was held at the National Science Council, attended by MCN President Marla Misunas, Academia Sinica Vice President Liu Tsui-jung, and Academia Sinica academician Ovid J. L. Tzeng. Liu also chairs the state-operated National Digital Archives Program (NDAP) which cooperates with the MCN in the organization of the MCN's branch office in Taiwan.[7]

Dr. Der-Tsai Lee, Director of the Institute of Information Science, Distinguished Research Fellow, and Director of Research and Development for the Digital Archive Technologies Program in Taipei, Taiwan, is the chapter's first President.

CONFERENCES LOOK TO THE FUTURE—AND THE PAST

Despite the economic downturn of the 2000s, MCN continued to produce strong conferences. Innovative presentations on current topics drew MCN members both experienced and new to its conferences. The conference theme of 2004, "Great Technology for Collections, Confluence, and Community," focused on the intersection of museums, libraries, and archives, which drew delegates from all three disciplines. This intersection too is a recurring theme, as seen when looking back at *Spectra*, Winter 1989, when a member wrote in for help integrating cataloging information for the three different areas within a museum. The topic of integration remains fluid, as museums couple and decouple their electronic resources.

"Digits Fugit," MCN's 2005 conference, focused on digital preservation and partnered with the Northeast Documentation Association, providing an entire week's worth of educational programs in Boston.

The 34th annual conference in 2006, "Access to Assets: Return on Investment," took an entirely practical approach. The conference showed delegates how the sometimes intangible educational programming for which they are responsible can be shown to be integral to their museum's operation. And whether they bring in funds directly or not, the public expects to have these programs, or will go to other institutions that do.

In 2007, the annual conference celebrated MCN's 40th anniversary, "Building Content, Building Community: 40 Years of Museum Information and Technology." Conference pricing was reduced and conference programming expanded. A full day of plenary sessions focusing on leadership preceded the usual educational sessions and demonstrations, which took place over the remaining 3 days.

COMMUNICATIONS

While publication of *Spectra* ended in 2002, MCN continues to place an emphasis on providing a place for museum technology professionals to communicate. Since 1996, MCN has maintained the MCN-L listserv, which serves as the primary forum for museum professionals to discuss topics from day-to-day operation of a museums technology infrastructure to the impact of emerging technologies on current practice.

FUTURE DIRECTIONS

Museum Computer Network's strategic plan for the years 2007–2010 is comprised of five major sections: Communication, Finance, Leadership Development, Membership, and Programs and Education. Each section of the plan integrates with the other four to establish and maintain initiatives and goals outlined in the plan. Among the goals are those with which MCN boards of directors have long been concerned: increasing membership, improving the association's financial health, continuing to produce quality programs, and keeping members actively involved in program planning. The methods by which the board and committees of the organization work are changing—for example, the board now actively uses its own wiki—but the core aims of the organization remain helping museum staff use technology effectively and helping museum information professionals advance their careers.

REFERENCES

1. http://www.cni.org/pub/CIMI/part1.html#or.
2. http://siarchives.si.edu/findingaids/FARU7432.htm.
3. http://www.mcn.edu.
4. http://www.mcn.edu/about/index.asp?subkey = 4.
5. http://www.mcn.edu/about/index.asp?subkey = 1723.
6. http://www.mcn.edu/groups/index.asp?subkey = 88.
7. http://www.taiwanheadlines.gov.tw/ct.asp?xItem = 67390& CtNode = 39.

BIBLIOGRAPHY

1. American Association of Museums, *America's Museums: The Belmont Report*; American Association of Museums: Washington, DC, 1968.
2. Chenhall, R.G. *Museum Cataloging in the Computer Age*; American Association for State and Local History: Nashville, TN, 1974.
3. Institute for Computer Research in the Humanities, *ICRH Newsletter*; New York University: New York, 1965–1969.
4. Jones-Garmil, K. Laying the foundation: Three decades of computer technology in the museum. In *Wired Museum*; Jones-Garmil, K., Ed.; American Association of Museums: Washington, DC, 1997.
5. Metropolitan Museum of Art, *Computers and Their Potential Application in Museums*; Arno Press: New York, 1968.
6. Museum Computer Network, Spectra. **1974–2002**, *1–29*.

Museum Informatics

Paul F. Marty
College of Communication and Information, Florida State University, Tallahassee, Florida, U.S.A.

Abstract
Museum informatics is the study of the sociotechnical interactions that take place at the intersection of people, information, and technology in museums. This entry presents an overview of museum informatics, covering such topics as information representation, information organization and access, information management, information technology, information interactions, and information professionals in museums. It explores the impact of information science and technology on museums, museum professionals, and museum visitors, and argues that museum researchers must take a sociotechnical approach to studying the use of information resources and technologies in museums.

INTRODUCTION

Museum informatics is the study of the sociotechnical interactions that take place at the intersection of people, information, and technology in museums.[1,2] Over the past few decades, museum researchers and professionals have explored the impact of information science and technology on the people who use museum resources. Museum professionals and museum visitors—including curators, registrars, school children, and scholars—have found their understanding of what museums can and should do dramatically changed by the introduction of new information resources and technologies into museums.[3]

Museums have traditionally served as repositories of objects for the purposes of research, preservation, and education.[4] For thousands of years, museums have acquired, stored, and exhibited objects of art, cultural heritage, natural history, science, and technology. Yet museums are not only repositories of objects; they are repositories of knowledge.[5,6] The modern museum is an information service organization where information about museum collections is just as important as the collections themselves.[7,8] As knowledge repositories, museums store knowledge; as information service organizations, they make this knowledge accessible and usable for their visitors.

Today's visitors to museums—from elementary school children to academic researchers—expect instant access to extensive information about every object in the museum's collections. To meet these expectations, and to serve their clients as effectively as possible, museum professionals have become more skilled in managing information resources in museums.[9] They have honed their expertise in information organization and access, become more sophisticated in the application of information technologies designed or adapted for use in museums, and developed skills in such areas as digitization, information storage and retrieval, collections management systems, and Web-based educational outreach.[10]

The changing needs and expectations of the users of museum information resources have prompted corresponding changes in the capabilities and services provided by museums. This entry will examine those changes, and explore the impact of new information technologies on museums, museum professionals, and museum visitors.

Taking its cue from the scholarly and practitioner literature published on this topic over the past few decades, this entry will examine museum informatics within the context of the museum profession. It is only recently that the field of museum informatics has begun to develop the critical framing and discourse necessary for the advancement of the field as a theoretical area in its own right. While this entry, therefore, focuses primarily on the professional activities of museum informatics, it concludes with a discussion of the importance of moving from practice to theory, and the future of museum informatics as a research area.

INFORMATION RESOURCES IN MUSEUMS

Many types of information resources are important to museums. The most important information resource that any museum possesses is its collection of artifacts. These objects are valuable documents in their own right, providing information about the world's culture, art, history, science, and nature.

Equally important, however, is the extensive information that museum professionals possess about the objects in their care. When a museum acquires a new collection, information about each object is recorded and organized. Museum professionals must know what they have, when they collected it, why it is of significance, where it came from, what condition it is in, etc. They record specific data

Encyclopedia of Library and Information Sciences, Fourth Edition DOI: 10.1081/E-ELIS4-120043944

about each object such as nomenclature classifications; physical dimensions; material analyses; geographical, cultural, and temporal designations; artifact histories; scholarly remarks; condition and conservation records; research notes; and so on. They also maintain related information resources such as donor files, accession records, exhibit histories, research studies, temporary loans records, visitor attendance reports, information requests, etc. (Buck and Gilmore[11] for more information about museum records).

Information Representation

When working with information about their collections, museum professionals rely on principles of information representation to create information surrogates or aggregates that can be manipulated more easily than physical artifacts. Surrogates are created by taking information entities and making them physically or informationally smaller (e.g., catalog card records), while aggregates are single resources that represent groups of information entities based on shared data (e.g., a list of all artifacts accessioned in the same year). Information surrogates and aggregates are usually easier and faster to handle than artifacts themselves, especially when searching, sorting, or manipulating museum resources. In addition, working with object surrogates is safer for artifacts, as museum professionals can research collections, develop exhibits, and work with scholars while artifacts remain safely in storage.

Over the years, museum professionals have used a wide range of tools (such as ledgers, card catalogs, computer databases, and digital collections management systems) to organize and provide access to information representations in museums. While no information representation can duplicate the physical artifact in its entirety, access to a sufficiently detailed information representation can meet the needs of many users, including researchers, scholars, teachers, students, and the general public. For information resources to effectively meet the needs of the museum's users, information must be properly organized and easily accessible.

INFORMATION ORGANIZATION AND ACCESS IN MUSEUMS

Until the 1960s, information resources about museum artifacts were organized into paper records and card files.[12] There were many drawbacks to this paper-based system, especially in terms of information access: only a limited number of individuals could access the files at any one time; and access was restricted to only a few data points, usually accession number, donor name, and occasionally the object's name or classification.

With such a system, answering questions such as "When did we receive this particular artifact?" or "What has this donor given us?" might be simple enough tasks (assuming the card files were kept up-to-date). Searching through and sorting records to answer more sophisticated questions could be laborious and time-consuming. Within the limitations of paper-based systems, certain questions prove virtually impossible to answer, including: "How many oil-based paintings do we have that were painted before 1450?" or "Do we have sufficient numbers and types of shoes to create an exhibit illustrating the history of shoemaking over the past 500 years?" When faced with such questions, even the most knowledgeable and skilled museum employees might be unable to provide satisfactory answers.

This situation improved with the introduction of modern, computerized systems for museum cataloging.[13] Museum professionals were now able to search and sort digital records about their collections using almost any database field. They could store more information about their artifacts, and they could share data more easily with other institutions. Museums had the potential to work together to improve the quality of their information resources and provide better, more useful, and more accurate information to their users; but the realization of this potential did not turn out to be an easy task.

There were few accepted standards for organizing information within museums, and organizational methods were typically institution specific and varied greatly from museum to museum. Given the inherent uniqueness of museum artifacts, it was impossible for one museum to document an object and then share that information with other institutions with the same object. No two institutions would record the same information in their ledgers, or use the same terminology when describing their collections. How, then, could museums develop standards to improve the quality of their records and more easily share data about their collections?

Standards and Metadata

There have been many attempts to create data content, structure, and value standards for documenting and describing museum artifacts.[14] Cultural heritage institutions, for instance, frequently classify collections of man-made objects using a nomenclature system developed in 1978 by Robert G. Chenhall,[15] later revised and expanded by James Blackaby et al.[16] It is difficult to develop a classification system that works equally well across all institutions with widely different kinds of collections. Museum professionals attempting to use Chenhall's nomenclature may encounter many difficult questions, such as: Should an ancient Egyptian document written on a torn piece of papyrus be classified as a material fragment or according to the content of the document? or Should a wine jug from ancient Greece be classified under the generic term "Pitcher, Wine" or the specific term "Red Figure Oinochoe?" Different institutions tend to answer such questions in their own way, thereby making it very difficult to establish standards that can be upheld by all organizations.

Museum professionals at many different institutions are working to solve these problems. The Getty Research Institute has developed detailed vocabularies and thesauri specifically for the use of museums.[17] The products of their research include structured vocabularies such as the Art and Architecture Thesaurus (which provides 131,000 terms for describing cultural materials), the Union List of Artist Names (which contains 293,000 names of artists and architects), and the Thesaurus of Geographic Names (which includes 1.1 million terms for geographical and historical locations). The Getty Research Institute has also developed the Categories for the Description of Works of Art, which establishes a data content standard for describing museum objects and images.

International organizations have developed and evaluated metadata standards to see whether they can be used when describing museum artifacts. The International Committee for Documentation (CIDOC) of the International Council of Museums (ICOM) has led the development of the Conceptual Reference Model (CRM), providing perhaps the most complete model for describing concepts and relationships when documenting cultural heritage objects (http://cidoc.ics.forth.gr/). During the late 1990s, the Consortium for the Computer Interchange of Museum Information (CIMI) evaluated the effectiveness of the Dublin Core Standard for describing museum artifacts, concluding that Dublin Core elements are useful to cultural heritage institutions in the abstract, but potentially problematic when used for institution-specific needs. More recently, academic researchers have been investigating the use of Extensible Markup Language (XML) for describing museum artifacts, and exploring the potential of the Open Archives Initiative for harvesting museum metadata for collections repositories.[18]

Museum associations have also been working to develop standards for best practices when managing museum collections information. The Museum Documentation Association (MDA) in the United Kingdom has developed a standard called SPECTRUM that is a guide to good practice for all museums when documenting their collections.[19] The Visual Resources Association (VRA) has established data content standards for Cataloguing Cultural Objects (CCO), fulfilling much the same purpose as the Anglo-American Cataloguing Rules (AACR2) in library and archives communities.[20]

Data Sharing Initiatives

Efforts to develop international standards acceptable to a range of institutions have resulted in initiatives to build extensive shared collections databases. From local to national levels, collections of digital information resources organize and allow access to a variety of data from museums of all types. The Canadian Heritage Information Network (CHIN) connects hundreds of Canadian museums into one national network, providing a searchable database of millions of museum artifacts and an extensive Virtual Museum of Canada. The Collections Australia Network (CAN) provides a portal for information about Australian museums, including a searchable index of hundreds of thousands of Australian artifacts.

When developing these shared collections, museum professionals often have the opportunity to evaluate different standards and recommend best organizational practices. During the 1990s, the Museum Educational Site Licensing Program explored a variety of issues ranging from data standards to intellectual property rights, when six museums worked with seven universities to share information resources about thousands of digital images.[21] More recently, the Art Museum Image Consortium (AMICO) was able to use the resources of its extensive library of digital images to develop detailed specifications and data dictionaries for institutions scanning and organizing data about images.[22] These projects frequently relied on the resources of their member institutions to test different methods for providing access to distributed sets of artifact data, and for connecting multiple museum databases while accounting for variations in data types, semantics, and query terms.[23]

Museum professionals often form consortia to achieve the common goals of the member organizations collaborating on digital projects. Typically, these consortia are able to undertake projects of greater complexity than any one institution would be able to handle alone. Museum collaborations are usually formed to create a collective digital resource to which all participating organizations will contribute. The Museums and the Online Archive of California, for example, brings together 75,000 object records from 11 cultural institutions in California.[24] The Collaborative (formerly Colorado) Digitization Project brings together cultural heritage materials from institutions across the western United States into one shared resource repository.[25] The Scottish Cultural Resources Access Network has gathered hundreds of thousands of multimedia and text records about Scotland into one central repository.[26] These cooperative endeavors testify to the museum community's commitment to finding new ways of organizing and sharing information resources.

INFORMATION TECHNOLOGY IN MUSEUMS

The first attempts to computerize museum collections occurred in the early 1960s, when several institutions began exploring the potential benefits of automating their collections management with computerized systems.[27,28] These early systems were developed on mainframe systems and used to store descriptive information about museum artifacts. The Smithsonian Institution, for example, developed information systems, such as Smithsonian

Institution Information Retrieval System (SIIRS) and Self Generating Master (SELGEM), which were used at institutions across the country during the 1960s and 1970s. The Museum Computer Network (MCN), founded in 1967, developed and distributed a system called Generalized Retrieval and Information Processing for Humanities Oriented Studies (GRIPHOS) to their member organizations. One of MCN's first projects was to evaluate standards for information organization and access at 12 art museums nationwide, and MCN sponsored the first conference on computers and their potential applications in museums at the Metropolitan Museum of Art in New York in 1967.[29]

Soon, a number of institutions were using mainframe systems to store data about their collections in electronic format. Museum professionals began to meet at a variety of conferences to discuss organizational standards, best practices, and new uses for information technologies in museums. As computers became cheaper, faster, and easier to use, even professionals working for small, poorly funded museums were able to purchase computer systems and database software for collections management. Vendors started developing and distributing collections management systems for many different types of museums. By the 1980s, new technologies had been developed that supported digital imaging, and museums began to experiment with building digital image databases. As the use of digital networks such as the Internet became more widespread, museum professionals found even more ways to share data about their collections. Today, museum professionals face a rapidly evolving information environment, and conferences such as the international conference of Museums and the Web and the annual meetings of the MCN help keep hundreds of museum professionals up-to-date with the latest techniques and methods of bringing museum information resources online.

Museums and Digitization

When museum professionals discuss "digitizing their collections," they refer to a process in which two things can occur: 1) they record in electronic format descriptive data about their artifacts; and 2) they produce some type of digital representation or image of each object. These two activities are often easily confused. When museums first began working with computers, digital imaging was not even a possibility, and when museum professionals referred to "computerizing" their collections, they meant taking descriptive, textual data from their ledgers and card files and converting them into electronic format. Today, with the prevalence of digital cameras and scanners, most museum professionals have expanded their definition of "digitization" to include digital imaging, and it is easy to forget that when a collection is digitized, the museum professionals in charge of the project must do more than produce a digital image of each artifact. They must also record descriptive data about the object (such as its provenance, classification, and composition) in electronic format, and generate new, additional metadata for the electronic object.

Recording data about museum artifacts in digital format offers museum professionals immediate benefits. These benefits include the ability to make a virtually infinite number of perfect copies of digital surrogates, and transmit them over great distances with no loss in quality; to offer new levels of interactivity between objects and users; to take advantage of hypermedia and multimedia to remove objects from the constraints of physical space and present arrangements impossible in physical galleries; to provide remote access to information resources for visitors, scholars, researchers, and students; and to target unique information needs, by broadcasting information resources to wide audiences or narrowcasting information resources to individual users.

The ever present push for digitization has created new problems and exacerbated old ones for museums. These problems include concerns, worries, or fears over such issues as copyright and intellectual property; the potential lessening of the "aura" or authenticity of museum artifacts; the blurring of individual museum identities online; and the potential impact of access to digital surrogates on physical museum visitation. The opportunities and challenges afforded by digitization have prompted new questions and concerns about the rise of the digital museum in the information age.

The Digital Museum

New technologies and online museums mean easier access and wider use of information resources that may previously have been more firmly controlled by the governing institution.[30] Some museum professionals worry that when they digitize their collections and make digital resources available online, they lose control over the museum's intellectual property and other copyrighted materials. Such concerns have prompted some institutions to protect their intellectual property by restricting access to certain types of data or making it difficult to reproduce the content they control. For example, museum professionals may attempt to prohibit the illegal duplication of digital images by embedding visible or invisible watermarks into digital image files.[31] These approaches are only stopgap solutions, however, and a true solution to this problem will only come when the museum community reevaluates its approaches to rights administration and content distribution, developing new economic models for digital cultural heritage.[32]

Another question asked about digital museums concerns whether visitors will stop visiting physical museums as more information about museum collections is available online. This fear has become even more prevalent as the quality of digital artifact representations online has increased; many museums offer extremely high-resolution images of their artifacts online, and some even offer three-dimensional representations that can be manipulated by virtual visitors and examined from all sides. With such features available online, some museum professionals wonder whether museum visitors will still bother to visit the real thing. Fortunately for museum professionals, recent surveys have provided compelling evidence that online museums actually drive physical museum attendance instead of discouraging physical visits; in the majority of studies, planning a museum visit is consistently cited as the primary reason people visit museum Web sites.[33,34] Kravchyna and Hastings[35] found that 57% of museum Web site users visit museum Web sites both before and after they visit physical museums. Similarly, Thomas and Carey[36] found that 70% of museum visitors specifically looked for online information prior to a museum visit, and that 57% said the information they found online increased their desire to visit the museum in person.

Despite the potential challenges, museum professionals remain eager to digitize their collections, prompted no doubt by the growing number of museum visitors who now expect museums to provide access to their collections in digital formats. As the technologies required to build a digital collection become easier to use and cheaper to acquire, more museums have the opportunity to embark upon digitization programs, and more opportunities arise for museum visitors to interact with digital museum collections.

INFORMATION INTERACTIONS IN MUSEUMS

Museum professionals use new information technologies to develop innovative ways of reaching their visitors, online and in-house.[37,38] Inside the museum, interactive kiosks encourage visitors to explore topics in greater depth and at their own pace. Online, virtual museums allow visitors to plan gallery tours, research artifact collections, and learn from interactive educational exhibits. New information technologies have changed how museum professionals achieve their missions, and encouraged museum visitors to embrace the new capabilities of the digital museum.

Museums and the Web

When museums started going online in the 1990s, museum professionals discovered that the Web offered them the potential to provide more than information about their museum's location, hours of operation, and brief descriptions of their collections. They began to explore the capabilities of online exhibits, realizing that increased access to digital collections offered new opportunities for interacting with museum collections and information resources.

Online museums and virtual exhibits have the potential to cover topics in ways not possible in physical museums. For example, Douma and Henchman[39] present an online exhibit that allows visitors to digitally remove layers of a painting (Bellini's Feast of the Gods), examining earlier versions using simulated infrared or x-ray lenses. Gillard[40] explores how the National Museum of American History's HistoryWired project encourages visitors to manipulate a collection of artifacts, uncovering connections between objects along temporal, cultural, and thematic lines. Sayre[41] describes how the Minneapolis Institute of Arts allowed online visitors to follow the restoration of a painting in real time, drawing them into the process and building stronger relationships between the museum and its visitors.

Many museums offer three-dimensional interactive tours online that mimic the experience of visiting the museum in person, while simultaneously opening an array of new possibilities for interaction.[42,43] Online museum visitors, for instance, can compare and contrast artifacts that in real life may not be in the same exhibit or even the same museum. Some institutions have experimented with live online exhibits, using webcasting techniques to interact with global audiences in real time. The Exploratorium in San Francisco, for example, broadcasts live coverage of solar eclipses (online and recently in the virtual world of Second Life) and has developed a related online resource guide (http://www.exploratorium.edu/eclipse/).

New technologies have also offered museum professionals ways to bring information about their collections directly to their audiences. As museums continue to digitize their collections, it has become more common for museum professionals to make their records available online to the general public. These resources are used by a wide variety of online visitors, from recent visitors interested in learning more about artifacts they saw in person, to academic researchers at distant universities searching for particularly unique specimens. As more museums develop online collections databases, museum professionals have explored the potential benefits of linking these databases directly into their online exhibits, providing online visitors with instant access to the latest collections data.[44]

Personalization Technologies

Modern museums can personalize the museum-going experience in ways never before possible. It is now common for museums to offer handheld devices—such as audio guides—to their gallery visitors. In essence, visitors to these museums have their own digital docents that can discuss artifacts of personal interest to them, providing a digital twist on traditional museum guided tours.[45] Using a handheld device, visitors can listen to audio descriptions of works of art, allowing them to explore the gallery's contents in any order and at their own pace.

As handheld computers become less expensive, museum professionals continue to experiment with the capabilities of these devices, offering their visitors detailed text and digital images in addition to audio tracks. Projects that explore the educational potential of mobile computing devices in museums are becoming especially crucial as more museums integrate such systems into their exhibits and learning experiences.[46] Several projects have demonstrated the value of mobile computers for increasing visitor interactions and improving educational experiences in museums.[47,48]

As museum professionals explore new methods of making information on collections available online, revolutionary trends in personalization have occurred in the online museum environment.[49] A growing number of museums, including the Metropolitan Museum of Art, the Virtual Museum of Canada, and the Fine Arts Museums of San Francisco, now allow visitors to create personal digital collections of their favorite artifacts, adding or removing artifacts at will, and returning to view their collections whenever they like. Some museums, such as the Minneapolis Institute of Arts and the Walker Art Center, allow online visitors to group digital artifacts into personal galleries, annotate them with textual descriptions, and share them with other online visitors.

The future of museum personalization can be found in the application of web 2.0 and social computing technologies for online museums; the collaborative social tagging project Steve (http://steve.museum) provides an excellent example of how these technologies can be implemented for museums. It will likely soon be common for museum professionals to encourage their online visitors to draw new connections between artifacts, store those connections on the museum's computers, and share them with other museum visitors. In this way, museum visitors will add value to digital collections, contributing their knowledge to the museum's collections by adding new connections and interpretations across user communities.[50,51]

INFORMATION MANAGEMENT IN MUSEUMS

Information management skills have always been important for museum professionals, who have a lengthy history of working with information resources and technologies.[52] As museum information resources become more technically complex, and the users of those resources become more information literate, the needs and expectations of visitors have become increasingly sophisticated. Users of museum resources are no longer satisfied with limited access to information about museum collections, and many desire 24 hr access to museum data, no matter where the data are located, or how the data are organized. While the ability to manipulate and manage information resources has long been an important skill for museum professionals, meeting these changing expectations can be difficult for museum professionals.

Changing ideas about the museum's position as an information service organization can pose difficult challenges for museum professionals, often requiring them to learn new information management skills and integrate new information technologies into their daily work.[53] Increased access to the digital information resources of libraries, archives, and museums has driven changing expectations from all museum users, including museum visitors and museum professionals, about the information resources museums should provide online and in-house.[54] Users of all types frequently expect digital museums to act more like digital libraries—a situation that puts immense pressure on museum professionals to live up to the changing needs and expectations of their users.

Information Professionals

Museum professionals have become increasingly concerned with the ability of museums to function in the information society, to meet user needs, and to ensure that the right information resources are available at the right time and place, inside or outside the museum. To accomplish these goals, a new role has emerged for information professionals in museums.[55] The success of museums in the information age will depend largely on the work of information professionals trained to deal with the problems of museum informatics and the museum's information needs.

Information and communication technologies in museums change so rapidly that museums need individuals on staff who can guide them through the hazards of planning digitization projects, purchasing collections information systems, or joining online data sharing initiatives. Museum administrators know that if a museum is to participate in the information society, someone at the museum needs to be able to set information policy, manage information resources, administer content management systems, implement metadata standards, evaluate information interfaces, etc. While some technical jobs (including Web design) can be outsourced, museums that do not have in-house skills with museum informatics will find it difficult to meet the constantly evolving demands of their increasingly information-savvy audiences.

MUSEUM INFORMATICS: FROM PRACTICE TO THEORY

The future of museum informatics as a unique research area depends on its ability to bridge multiple disciplines, drawing upon disparate theories and methodologies, and connecting the traditional professional world of museum studies with critical theories from the emerging worlds of new media and digital cultural heritage. Recent publications have been extremely influential in setting an agenda for museum informatics and providing the intellectual framework necessary for the advancement of the field as a research area, a particularly important achievement for an emerging field such as museum informatics.[56,57]

The principal challenge facing the establishment of museum informatics as a unique research area lies in the fact that museum informatics is an extremely interdisciplinary field of study. Researchers interested in the museum's changing role in the information society have drawn upon theories and techniques from dozens of related fields, including digital libraries, human–computer interaction, social network analysis, cognitive science, museum studies, library and information science, etc. While early work in this area focused primarily on how information technologies should be used in museums, researchers are now emphasizing the need for an underlying body of theory and methods for studying museum informatics as well as related fields such as museums and new media or digital cultural heritage.[58]

To explore new theoretical perspectives and to develop new methodologies, researchers and professionals from around the world have joined together to form evolving communities of practice, dedicated to providing guidance to museums and other institutions of cultural heritage as they address important issues in museum informatics.[59] Interest in museum informatics is now widespread, and each year, thousands of people worldwide participate in discussions, projects, and research initiatives related to museum informatics.

Museum professionals and researchers today belong to many different professional organizations and attend a variety of conferences dedicated to exploring museum informatics, including the meetings of such organizations as the MCN, the MDA, the International Council of Museum's International Committee for Documentation, the International Cultural Heritage Informatics Meeting, the International Museums and the Web Conference, and the Institute of Museum and Library Services' WebWise Conference. The published conference proceedings from these meetings, many of which are freely available online, provide important, timely, and often extremely cutting-edge primary resources for individuals interested in studying museum informatics.

The prodigious number of museum informatics-related events (including conferences, training events, symposia, etc.) as well as their regular high attendance are indicative of a continued and widespread professional engagement in this area. In addition, during the last few years, there has been a flourishing of university programs in this area. In the United States and Europe, for example, there are educational programs where students can study exclusively in such areas as museum informatics and digital cultural heritage. These programs are indicative not only of an increase in research activity by academics, but also of the increase in interest and demand by students for resources and publications in the area of museum informatics. To meet this demand, a growing number of scholarly journals now publish papers about museum informatics. The *Journal of the American Society for Information Science and Technology*, the *Journal of Digital Libraries*, and *Curator*, for example, have all published special issues on museum informatics. More recently, the *Journal of Museum Management and Curatorship* has added a permanent section on Digital Heritage to its quarterly issues.

While the increase in publications related to museum informatics (including books, journals, and conference proceedings) is extremely encouraging, the increasing amount of literature has posed challenges for museum informatics researchers. In particular, the natural interdisciplinarity of museum informatics (covering such topics as technology, communication studies, museology, education, information science, etc.) tends to result in a centrifugal approach to publishing, where key pieces of research can appear in very different domains, speaking to very different peer groups. As interest in museum informatics continues to rise, therefore, researchers and practitioners seeking to establish museum informatics as a research area must collaborate to bring together any and all research related to the intersection of people, information, and technology in museums—including both the practical processes and theoretical discourses that relate to the organization, management, and use of museum information resources.

CONCLUSION

The study of museum informatics requires a sociotechnical approach to information resource management in museums. New information technologies have changed the way museum professionals think about the purpose and capabilities of museums. These sweeping changes have affected the way museums manage their information resources, in-house and online, in almost every aspect. The world of museums is being altered constantly by the introduction of new information technologies, as new technologies reshape the job of the museum professional and the overall function of museums in the information society.

To understand these changes, museums must be examined as complex sociotechnical systems that evolve and adapt to meet new challenges. Museum researchers must study museum informatics within complex and interlocking organizational and social contexts affecting the nature of museums in general and the expectations of museum professionals and visitors in particular. In this way, museum professionals and researchers will be able to embrace the growing role of museum informatics in the twenty-first century museum, and continue to explore the sociotechnical implications of people, information, and technology interacting in museums.

REFERENCES

1. Marty, P.F.; Rayward, W.B.; Twidale, M.B. Museum informatics. Ann. Rev. Inform. Sci. Technol. **2003**, *37*, 259–294.
2. In *Museum Informatics: People, Information, and Technology in Museums*; Marty, P.F., Jones, K.B., Eds.; Routledge: New York, 2008.
3. Knell, S.J. The shape of things to come: Museums in the technological landscape. Mus. Soc. **2003**, *1*(3), 132–146.
4. Burkaw, G.E. *Introduction to Museum Work*, 3rd Ed. AltaMira Press: Walnut Creek, CA, 1997.
5. Cannon-Brookes, P. The nature of museum collections. In *Manual of Curatorship*; Thompson, J., Ed.; Butterworths: London, 1992; 500–512.
6. Hooper-Greenhill, E. *Museums and the Shaping of Knowledge*, Routledge: London, 1992.
7. MacDonald, G.; Alsford, S. The museum as information utility. Mus. Manag. Curatorship **1991**, *10*(3), 305–311.
8. Washburn, W.E. Collecting information, not objects. Mus. News **1984**, *62*(3), 5–15.
9. Hamma, K. Becoming digital. Bull. Am. Soc. Inf. Sci. Tech. **2004**, *30*(5), 11–13.
10. Marty, P.F. Museum professionals and the relevance of LIS expertise. Libr. Inform. Sci. Res. **2007**, *29*(2), 252–276.
11. In *The New Museum Registration Methods*; Buck, R.A., Gilmore, J.A., Eds.; American Association of Museums: Washington, DC, 1998.
12. *Museum Registration Methods*, 3rd Ed.; Dudley, D., Wilkenson, I., Eds.; American Association of Museums: Washington, DC, 1979.
13. Chenhall, R.G. *Museum Cataloging in the Computer Age*, American Association for State and Local History: Nashville, TN, 1975.
14. Bearman, D. Strategies for cultural heritage information standards in a networked world. Arch. Mus. Inform. **1994**, *8*(2), 93–106.
15. Chenhall, R.G. *Nomenclature for Museum Cataloging: A System for Classifying Man-made Objects*, American Association for State and Local History: Nashville, TN, 1978.
16. Blackaby, J.; Greeno, P.; Chenhall, R.G. Nomenclature Committee. *The Revised Nomenclature for Museum Cataloging: A Revised and Expanded Version of Robert G. Chenhall's System for Classifying Man-Made Objects*, AASLH Press: Nashville, TN, 1988.
17. Lanzi, E. *Introduction to Vocabularies: Enhancing Access to Cultural Heritage Information*, Getty Trust Publications: Los Angeles, CA, 1998.
18. Perkins, J. A new way of making cultural information resources visible on the web: Museums and the open archive initiative. In *Museums and the Web 2001*; Bearman, D., Trant, J., Eds.; Archives & Museum Informatics: Pittsburgh, PA, 2001; 87–92.
19. McKenna, G.; Patsatzi, E. *SPECTRUM: The UK Museum Documentation Standard*, Museum Documentation Association: Cambridge, England, 2005.
20. Visual Resources Association, *Cataloguing Cultural Objects: A Guide to Describing Cultural Works and Their Images*, American Library Association: Chicago, IL, 2006.
21. In *Delivering Digital Images: Cultural Heritage Resources for Education*; Stephenson, C., McClung, P., Eds.; Getty Research Institute: Los Angeles, CA, 1998.
22. Trant, J.; Bearman, D.; Richmond, K. Collaborative cultural resource creation: The example of the Art Museum Image Consortium. In *Museums and the Web 2000*; Bearman, D., Trant, J., Eds.; Archives & Museum Informatics: Pittsburgh, PA, 2000; 39–52.
23. Moen, W. Accessing distributed cultural heritage information. Commun. ACM **1998**, *41*(4), 45–48.
24. Rinehart, R. MOAC: A report on integrating museum and archive access in the Online Archive of California. D-Lib Mag. **2003**, *9*(1). Available at http://www.dlib.org/dlib/january03/rinehart/01rinehart.html.
25. Allen, N. Collaboration through the Colorado Digitization Project. First Monday **2000**, *5*(6). Available at http://firstmonday.org/issues/issue5_6/allen/.
26. Devine, J.; Gibson, E.; Kane, M. *What Clicks? Electronic Access to Museum Resources in Scotland and E-Learning Opportunities Using Museum Resources*, Hunterian Museum and Art Gallery, University of Glasgow: Glasgow, 2004. Available at http://www.hunterian.gla.ac.uk/what_clicks/index.shtml.
27. Ellin, E. Museums and the computer, an appraisal of new potential. Comput. Humanities **1969**, *4*(1), 25–30.
28. Vance, D. Museum computer network: Progress report. Museologist **1975**, *135*, 3–10.
29. Metropolitan Museum of Art, *Computers and Their Potential Applications in Museums*, Arno Press: New York, 1968.
30. Zorich, D.M. *Introduction to Managing Digital Assets: Options for Cultural and Educational Organizations*, Getty Trust Publications: Los Angeles, CA, 1999.
31. Mintzer, F.; Braudaway, G.; Giordano, F.; Lee, J.; Magerlein, K.; D'Auria, S. Populating the Hermitage Museum's new web site. Commun. ACM **2001**, *44*(8), 52–60.
32. Bearman, D. New economic models for administering cultural intellectual property. In *The Wired Museum: Emerging Technology and Changing Paradigms*; Jones-Garmil, K., Ed.; American Association of Museums: Washington, DC, 1997; 231–266.
33. Haley Goldman, K.; Schaller, D. Exploring motivational factors and visitor satisfaction in on-line museum visits. In *Museums and the Web 2004*; Bearman, D., Trant, J., Eds.; Archives & Museum Informatics: Toronto, CA, 2004. Available at http://www.archimuse.com/mw2004/papers/haleyGoldman/haleyGoldman.html.
34. Marty, P.F. Museum websites and museum visitors: Before and after the museum visit. Mus. Manag. Curatorship **2007**, *22*(4), 337–360.
35. Kravchyna, V.; Hastings, S. Informational value of museum web sites. First Monday **2002**, *7*(2). Available at http://firstmonday.org/issues/issue7_2/kravchyna.
36. Thomas, W.; Carey, S. Actual/virtual visits: What are the links. In *Museums and the Web 2005*; Bearman, D., Trant, J., Eds.; Archives & Museum Informatics: Toronto, CA, 2005. Available at http://www.archimuse.com/mw2005/papers/thomas/thomas.html.
37. In *The Wired Museum: Emerging Technology and Changing Paradigms*; Jones-Garmil, K., Ed.; American Association of Museums: Washington, DC, 1997.

38. In *The Virtual and the Real: Media in the Museum*; Thomas, S., Mintz, A., Eds.; American Association of Museums: Washington, DC, 1998.
39. Douma, M. Henchman, M. Bringing the object to the viewer: Multimedia techniques for the scientific study of art. In *Museums and the Web 2000*; Bearman, D., Trant, J., Eds.; Archives & Museum Informatics: Pittsburgh, PA, 2000; 59–64.
40. Gillard, P. Cruising through History Wired. In *Museums and the Web 2002*; Bearman, D., Trant, J., Eds.; Archives & Museum Informatics: Pittsburgh, PA, 2002. Available at http://www.archimuse.com/mw2002/papers/gillard/gillard.html.
41. Sayre, S. Sharing the experience: The building of a successful online/on-site exhibition. In *Museums and the Web 2000*; Bearman, D., Trant, J., Eds.; Archives & Museum Informatics: Pittsburgh, PA, 2000; 13–20.
42. Galani, A.; Chalmers, M. Can you see me? Exploring co-visiting between physical and virtual visitors. In *Museums and the Web 2002*; Bearman, D., Trant, J., Eds.; Archives & Museum Informatics: Pittsburgh, PA, 2002; 31–40.
43. Paolini, P.; Barbieri, T.; Loiudice, P.; Alonzo, F.; Zanti, M.; Gaia, G. Visiting a museum together? How to share a visit to a virtual world. J. Am. Soc. Inf. Sci. **2000**, *51*(1), 33–38.
44. Besser, H. The transformation of the museum and the way it's perceived. In *The Wired Museum: Emerging Technology and Changing Paradigms*; Jones-Garmil, K., Ed.; American Association of Museums: Washington, DC, 1997; 153–170.
45. Rayward, W.B.; Twidale, M.B. From docent to cyberdocent: Education and guidance in the virtual museum. Arch. Mus. Inform. **2000**, *13*, 23–53.
46. Hsi, S.; Fait, H. RFID enhances visitors' museum experience at the Exploratorium. Commun. ACM **2005**, *48*(9), 60–65.
47. Evans, J.; Sterry, P. Portable computers and interactive multimedia: A new paradigm for interpreting museum collections. Arch. Mus. Inform. **1999**, *13*, 113–126.
48. Woodruff, A.; Aoki, P.M.; Grinter, R.E.; Hurst, A.; Szymanski, M.H.; Thornton, J.D. Eavesdropping on electronic guidebooks: Observing learning resources in shared listening environments. In *Museums and the Web 2002*; Bearman, D., Trant, J., Eds.; Archives & Museum Informatics: Pittsburgh, PA, 2002; 21–30.
49. Bowen, J.P.; Filippini-Fantoni, S. Personalization and the web from a museum perspective. In *Museums and the Web 2004*; Bearman, D., Trant, J., Eds.; Archives & Museum Informatics: Toronto, CA, 2004; 63–78.
50. Bearman, D.; Trant, J.; Chun, S.; Jenkins, M.; Smith, K.; Cherry, R. Social terminology enhancement through vernacular engagement: Exploring collaborative annotation to encourage interaction with museum collections. D-Lib Mag. **2005**, *9*(11). Available at http://www.dlib.org/dlib/september05/bearman/09bearman.html.
51. Lynch, C.A. Digital collections, digital libraries and the digitization of cultural heritage information. First Monday **2002**, *7*(5). Available at http://firstmonday.org/issues/issue7_5/lynch/.
52. Orna, E.; Pettitt, C. *Information Management in Museums*, 2nd Ed. Gower: Aldershot, Hampshire, England, 1998.
53. Marty, P.F. The changing nature of information work in museums. J. Am. Soc. Inf. Sci. Tech. **2007**, *58*(1), 97–107.
54. Rayward, W.B. Electronic information and the functional integration of libraries, museums and archives. In *History and Electronic Artefacts*; Higgs, E., Ed.; Oxford University Press: Oxford, England, 1998; 207–224.
55. Marty, P.F. Meeting user needs in the modern museum: Profiles of the new museum information professional. Libr. Inform. Sci. Res. **2006**, *28*(1), 128–144.
56. Parry, R. *Recoding the Museum: Digital Heritage and the Technologies of Change*, Routledge: London, 2007.
57. In *Theorizing Digital Cultural Heritage: A Critical Discourse*; Cameron, F., Kenderdine, S., Eds.; MIT Press: Cambridge, MA, 2007.
58. Parry, R. Digital heritage and the rise of theory in museum computing. Mus. Manag. Curatorship **2005**, *20*, 333–348.
59. In *The Digital Museum: A Think Guide*; Din, H., Hecht, P., Eds.; American Association of Museums: Washington, DC, 2007.

Museum Management

Gary Edson
Center for Advanced Study in Museum Science and Heritage Management, Museum of Texas Tech University, Lubbock, Texas, U.S.A.

Abstract
Museums must address an increasing array of issues to succeed in the dynamic environment of the twenty-first century. In response to this often-daunting process, the role of institutional management has been assigned greater responsibility and often, greater liability. It must define the museum's mission, justify its legitimacy, and reconcile its relationship with changing constituency expectations. In response to this challenge, museum management is exploring the economic landscape to develop creative and sustainable institutions that serve the interests of the public while negotiating the legal pitfalls, and maintaining the ethics and standards of the international museum community. This entry addresses a number of the issues relating to contemporary museum management. It draws from the precepts of the corporate, as well as the not-for-profit communities, to stimulate understanding of the role and responsibility of inclusive management as a practical response to the complexities of the contemporary museum.

INTRODUCTION

Museums as a part of the rapidly expanding not-for-profit sector must be prepared to adjust to the changing demands. The traditional separation between the not-for-profit and the for-profit worlds is an ever-narrowing gap due to the commonly shared need for money, growth, and prominence. However, unlike the commercial sector, the museum must also conform to the ethics and standards of the professional community and a scrutinizing public. Museum management is often at the epicenter of this shifting landscape of successful achievements and unresolved challenges.

The purpose of museums continues to be service to society, the community, the public and its various constituencies, including those persons that are physically or mentally challenged. The collections are for people, whether those people are the public or researchers. Museums must retain these time-honored values and beliefs while considering escalating expenses, public demands, technology, changing demographics, mergers, outsourcing, governmental regulations, tourism, outcome assessments, and maintaining donor confidence to name but a few issues. The challenges increase exponentially for museums pursuing international interests, such as collections and exhibitions. Nevertheless, the successes are frequent enough to keep dedicated individuals engaged in pursuing the elusive quality customarily called excellence.

The Museum community has endorsed different methods for dealing with management issues in the quest for excellence. Some institutions have turned to the business community for leadership, and others have reinforced core values by relying on museum professionals and more formalized management practices to guide the institution. Both approaches demonstrate the critical concern about museum management in these early years of the twenty-first century.

Often the management of an institution is the least considered aspect of a functional and effective museum. The popular belief is that museums are about unique, often beautiful, and usually significant cultural objects. How those objects are collected, housed, protected, conserved, and exhibited is not and should not be a concern for the average museum visitor. Nevertheless, the "life" of a museum is best represented by the activities that the public never sees, and by the dedication of numerous museum professionals that champion the care and protection of cultural and natural heritage.

This entry will acquaint the reader with a range of museum management issues, processes, and practices. The information will explore the importance of museum management and explain such topics as management structures, personnel management, teamwork and mission, financial management, management planning, and management ethics. Each of the elements is critical to a successful and sustainable museum and its continuing effort to serve the profession and the public.

MUSEUM MANAGEMENT

Museum management is an important but often misunderstood element of the museum profession. Individuals, particularly those entering or preparing to enter the workforce, normally think of museum management as that activity performed by only the director or upper administrators. Many persons associate the idea of management with the "boss." That perspective continues today, although many managers/directors consider themselves leaders instead of individuals who tell others (subordinates) what to do. All

Encyclopedia of Library and Information Sciences, Fourth Edition DOI: 10.1081/E-ELIS4-120053409

museum personnel are involved with management in fact. Every person in a museum, regardless of title, has a position of responsibility that includes accountability, duty, and trust. Everyone should be working to accomplish organizational goals, that is, contributing to the process used to attain what the museum wants to achieve—its defined mission.

The term "management" is likely to be called "administration" in most English-speaking countries. Whereas in the French, Spanish, or Italian tradition of public service it is referred to as "*gestion.*"[1]Although this entry will focus on that aspect of museum management (administration), many of the practices described are applicable throughout the institution. Elements such as budgeting, planning, human resource considerations, communication, teamwork, honesty, and accountability have obvious generalized applications. Museum management is an inclusive concept that involves the judicious use of resources to accomplish an objective. It is both an intellectual and a practical concept.

Museums, as public institutions, exist for the public's benefit, and to be successful, all aspects of their operations should reflect that obligation and commitment. Management is an integral element in maintaining and promoting ethical and legal stability. Collecting, conservation, and research should be executed with a public consciousness, just as the more visible or public-oriented exhibitions and educational programming. These activities are valued elements of museum management. An organization operating in the public interest must manage its affairs properly, but museums as custodians of the cultural, natural, and scientific heritage of a people, region, or nation must function, as nearly as possible, above criticism.

Management and administration are often used to mean the same activity in many locations. The use of "management" in this way applies a collective term describing the "manager" of an organization, for example, a museum. However, management as an act of controlling something successfully can apply throughout the museum, whereas "the administration" is by definition charged with regulating the affairs of the museum. Interestingly, there is no consistent prototype for the general administration (management) of museums. This situation is usually ascribed to the diversity of museum collections and may reflect a lack of understanding of the role of museums in contemporary society. The ambivalence is the result of not knowing whether museums are guardians and interpreters of cultural heritage, repositories for the study of human and natural history, social instruments in community development, or facilities of leisure and recreation.[2]

Museum management is commonly associated with the level of authority within the organizational structure where institutional decisions are made. The museum manager may have different titles, such as director or chief executive officer (CEO), and it is that person who normally makes decisions about the way the museum is organized, the services it provides, and the people it serves. The manager/director is usually hired or appointed by the governing authority, and that person is vested with the authority to make day-to-day operational decisions, including the hiring and disciplining of staff. Managers/directors are expected to provide the leadership, vision, and guidance that are a part of good management.[3]

Organizational management, including the manager/director, represents the essential nature of museum operations. It is that part of the institutional structure that acknowledges and supports the cultural, natural, or scientific experience through carefully prepared and thoughtfully presented exhibitions of collections, quality research, and an insightful plan for preserving objects for future generations.

Effective museum management at any level and in most countries does not occur in a vacuum. All museums operate under some form of governing body—board of directors or trustees, Minister of Culture, or city government. The museum should be established according to the laws of the country or state in which it exists. It should have, as a part of its documentation, a written constitution, statute, or other enabling document that states the museum's legal and financial status. The documentation should confirm that the museum is not organized to make a profit; rather, that it is intended to serve the public need. The concept of not-for-profit maintains the idea that any income generated by the museum is intended for the support of the institution and not for distribution to individual subscribers. This idea seems simple, but the concept is sophisticated, because it includes the principle of philosophical ownership as opposed to physical ownership as found in for-profit organizations. The stakeholders of the not-for-profit organizations are the public, and the governing authority (board) of the museum that represents them. That authoritative body has fiduciary (i.e., evoking public trust) responsibility for the museum. They can make decisions and determine programs, exhibitions, and collections, but may not receive benefits as individuals beyond knowing they have acted as good stewards and responsible trustees.

(NOTE: The terms nonprofit and not-for-profit continue to cause confusion in the international museum community. Nonprofit is interpreted to mean that the museum cannot make money. Whereas, not-for-profit means that the museum is not a commercial enterprise. It is generally accepted that the latter definition is the more acceptable.)

The concepts of public service and philosophical ownership of museums are closely related. The idea of individual (personal) or board (group) ownership of museums as not-for-profit organizations should not exist. There is no physical ownership in the traditional sense because museums are intended to serve a public purpose. This notion of ownership is a very important aspect of the not-for-profit sector. The governing authority (board) governs on behalf of individuals who are not seated at the board table. That group (board) may change and the staff may change, but the "public," although an ill-defined entity, continues to "own" the museum as a holding place for cultural, natural, and scientific heritage.

One of the most important aspects of the organizational documentation is that it reflects the values and beliefs that initiated the need for the museum and that will sustain its continued growth. The museum may be the result of a personal or governmental vision, but that vision must be of appropriate significance to mobilize others into action as supporters and visitors. The beliefs of a museum constitute its value system that differentiates the work of a particular museum from others, or defines critical differences in approach or methods among similar efforts. The management must work to sustain belief in the museum, promote its mission, and advocate its permanence.

The defining institutional attitude that directly connects to management is the museum's mission and policies and provides the organization, its leadership, and staff with a stable foundation upon which to build. The authority of the manager/director generally depends on the laws and regulations under which the museum is established, as well as the internal documents. The regulatory rules may differ from location to location; nevertheless, a primary role of museum management is assisting the museum in achieving consistent results so the institutional mission can be articulated and fulfilled.

The operation of all types of museums is based on teamwork, and this has important implications for the management structure. Managerial (administrative) duties are commonly assigned to the manager/director, and it is normal for that individual to guide the institution toward the desired goal through planning, organizing, directing, and controlling. These four functions of management are applicable throughout an organization. There may be one manager/director for the museum, but there are other managers at different levels. Diversified museum management is exemplified by the processes associated with accessioning and deaccessioning, inventory of collections, educational programming, exhibitions preparation and installation, preventive conservation, integrated pest management, and a continuing list of other practices common to all professionally oriented institutions. The four functions are included at each level of management, though the emphasis on each function may change. The management role fulfilled by the upper administration of the museum is a relatively small, albeit important, aspect of the overall activities of the institution.

Because museums are labor intensive and require a wide range of skills, the management duties may be assigned on different levels, depending on the size and structure of the particular institution. Larger museums may have a structural layer identified as "upper management." This element of the museum includes the manager/director and a number of assistants (senior specialists) identified by different titles. The second layer may be called "middle management" to identify the division heads. These managers have a specialized understanding of certain tasks such as collection management or program development. They are usually responsible for implementing decisions made by upper management as well as supervising employees. Some museums also identify a level of "lower management" that ensures the decisions and plans are executed. These managers have responsibility for tasks of limited duration and include a limited number of support staff.

It is important for all persons with management responsibilities to understand the administrative, legal, and ethical issues applying to their circumstances and the conditions relating to their work. Although these factors also vary from country to country, issues relating to import, export, or transfer of cultural property, endangered species, sacred materials, and human remains have universal implications that must be considered. These issues may significantly influence both museum management and professional practices.[3]

Building and stabilizing an organizational climate is the crux of the concept of public trust as placed in museums. Although a museum's management responsibilities and therefore its structure may differ, there are, nevertheless, certain elements that are common to most. These include the following:

Purpose—a clear understanding of the purpose of the museum in the public interest
Program—maintaining a program consistent with the museum's stated purpose and its available personnel and financial resources
Expenses—supervising programs, management, and related expenses
Promotion—ensuring ethical publicity and promotion, excluding exaggerated or misleading claims
Fund raising—soliciting contributions without payment of commissions or undue pressure
Accountability—producing an annual report that describes program activities and supporting services in relation to expenses and that contains financial statements
Budget—developing and implementing an annual budget approved by the governing body in a form consistent with an annual financial statement

Because museum personnel other than the manager/director may be engaged in completing these tasks, management is often thought of as simply having the ability to get something done by other persons. The manager/director should ensure the museum is a professional, systematic, enjoyable, and socially conscious institution regardless of who performs a particular task. The management must understand and apply principles drawn from research and "best practices" in business and public service, as well as the museum field, to meet these various challenges.

Consideration should be given to a wide range of academic disciplines, including economics, law, psychology, sociology, and information technology.[1] Attention must also be given to management functionality, as the action of measuring a quantity on a regular basis and of adjusting initial plans as actions are taken to reach the intended goal.

The management has a responsibility that embraces all the resources and activities of the museum in fulfilling its various duties. Effective management is the means of ensuring that a museum, regardless of its size or complexity, achieves consistent results so the institutional mission can be fulfilled. It is a necessary element in the development and advancement of a museum. Without proper management, a museum can neither provide appropriate care and use of collections, nor can it maintain and support an effectual exhibition and education program. Public interest and trust can be lost without qualified management, and the museum, as an institution in the service of society,[4] can be jeopardized.

It may be important to gain greater insight into the way museums operate to better understand the museum management process. Who or what authorizes the museum and to whom does it (the museum) report are questions to consider. There are at least four different types of museums based on their authorizing agencies:

Governmental—those museums that are authorized and supported by local, regional, or national governmental agencies.

Private—museums funded and operated by individuals or private organizations. Church museums are included in this group.

University—museums that are attached to colleges or universities and maintained for educational, that is study, collections.

Combination—museums that were initiated by governmental agencies or private organizations and transferred to the other for operational purposes. (This type of museum may be the result of governmental change or the reduction of funding. A nongovernmental organization may be formed to provide funding for the museum to continue the museum's operation.)

The authorizing agency is generally responsible for defining the governing authority for the museum. That authority is often referred to as a Board of Trustees because they are entrusted with oversight responsibility for the museum. That board has fiduciary responsibility of the institution. The governing board (trustees) has the duty and responsibility to manage the affairs of the museum, so its property will not be diverted from the public purposes for which it was entrusted. They hire, evaluate, and when necessary fire the manager/director. They approve the budget and promulgate policies, but should leave the management of the organization to the manager/director.

It is the responsibility of the board to

Clarify the organization's mission

Interpret the mission statement to the public and enhance the organization's public image

Approve goals and objectives and set long-range plans

Establish policies and other guidelines for agency operations

Be legally responsible for all aspects of the organization's operations

Ensure the organization's financial stability and solvency

Hire and support the manager/director and assess his or her performance

There are also boards that give counsel but do not govern. These are advisory boards. They may provide advice to the governing board, the director, or any element of the organization. Advisory boards can be positioned anywhere in the museum structure as long as they are attached to some element. They have only the authority assigned by the governing body. The assigned authority may be extensive or limited, but it must be retractable, that is, someone or some board must have the power to remove the authority granted to the advisory board.

Some museums have a workgroup board. This generally refers to a governing board with minimal or no staff support. Therefore, the board must govern and do the work. Small organizations may have boards with these duel responsibilities. This is not a true board type because it has no assigned location within the organizational structure. It is at the top and everywhere else. Workgroup boards have two different roles and those roles are best served when kept separated.

Governance and management are used to describe the functions or activities by which a board carries out its responsibilities. When a not-for-profit organization has a professional staff, the partnership between the board and staff occurs in fulfilling the management function rather than governance and administration. Boards provide governance and staff does the management and administration functions in theory; however, in practice, the three activities are often intermixed. When this happens, it may be a source of frustration for both the staff and the board. It compounds the issues of "who does what." This complexity is most noticeable when an organization grows and the organizational demands increase. The expansion results in unclear lines of communication, authority, and decision-making, thus causing confusion and organizational dysfunction.

MANAGEMENT STRUCTURE

It may be of value to differentiate between leadership and management before discussing the management structure of museums. These terms are important to the organizational structure of a museum. They acknowledge different characteristics, but are often used interchangeably.

There are good leaders who are good managers just as there are good managers with excellent leadership qualities. However, the opposite is as likely to be true. A good leader is not necessarily a good manager. Managers, by simple definition, are considered experts of efficient organization planning, direction, and control of the operations of a museum. Leaders, on the other hand, are to provide a more visionary reference point for institution attitudes, beliefs, and responsibilities. Leaders set the standard of achievement anticipated by institution personnel such as trust, honesty, personal integrity, efficiency, competency, equity, and dignity. The successful contemporary museum leader is a composite of experiences, skills, and attitudes.

The abilities of the manager/director often influence the organizational structure of a museum. It is also true that a structure appropriate for a smaller museum may not be satisfactory or acceptable for a larger institution. Museums operated as part of a governmental construct may be required to function and be structured according to the management system of the governing body. There is, however, a need to maintain a proper system of operations according to accepted museological practices. A crucial matter for management is therefore to define the structure under which the museum is authorized, governed, supported, and operated. This basic procedure is valuable for existing as well as newly formed museums. Often the management structure is assumed and based on previous practices but lacks clear documentation. A simple diagram or organizational chart can be used to demonstrate lines of authority and information exchange.

The organizational structure may be viewed in different ways. The exact relationship between members of the staff often depends on the perspective of the participants and the practice of the museum. Nevertheless, an organizational diagram (also called a flow chart) is very beneficial in defining structural relationships.

The governing authority is at the top with the director/manager immediately following in the most common organizational structure. The rest of the staff is arranged below according to their relationship with the primary divisions (or functions) of the museum. This arrangement is known as a *hierarchic structure* (Fig. 2) and is an authoritative or top-down approach to institutional management. A second arrangement, often called a *horizontal (or flat) structure* (Fig. 3), spreads the line of contact with the director/manager to give all staff equal access. A third organizational configuration that can function very successfully is the *matrix structure* (Fig. 4). All elements ultimately converge on the director who is the link between the governing authority and the staff regardless of the structural arrangement. The structure may vary, but it should be clearly defined, and care should be taken to involve staff in a range of decision-making roles. One way to promote this exchange is to have a management advisory committee (team). This arrangement allows members of the staff to meet regularly with the director/manager and to discuss issues related to operational activities.

Although certain organizational structures are common across the museum community, each institution by its unique nature has a structure that has evolved over time to meet the particular needs of that institution. The structure of many museums gradually flattens to allow greater access to the director/manager. The more centralized the decision-making authority, the more likely the institutional structure will gravitate in that direction.

A variation of the matrix structure is becoming more common as the museum staff becomes more diverse. Fundraising, marketing, and community engagement personnel often require a coordinated focus group (or committee) that must follow a specific agenda. Fund raising, for example, must establish a systematic process for identifying, developing, and soliciting donors. This process is time consuming and requires intensive communication between members of the team. The team may expand or contract depending on the leader's assessment of a particular project and the approval of the manager/director. Other activities within the museum may be equally well served by using a matrix structure. Communication is a primary factor in organizational structures, but with the matrix structure, that importance increases. The seeming autonomy of the team should not result in unilateral decision-making and unauthorized actions.

Most museums have a management structure that includes at least three components—administration, curation, and operations—regardless of the visual representation that structure may take. All elements of the museum may be the responsibility of one person, or they may accommodate many people. The tri-parted structure allows distribution of various tasks. The division of curation and operation activities is generally based on the concept of collecting and noncollecting areas. This relatively simple structure can be expanded to facilitate increased activities while maintaining clear lines of communication and an easily comprehendible reporting procedure.

The structure may be as simple as the diagram in Fig. 1, or it may be complex with a range of primary, secondary, and tertiary positions, as shown in Fig. 2. Education and exhibitions are often under operations as noncollecting elements of the museum. Budget oversight, fund raising, public relations, and marketing are often a part of institutional management reporting directly to the manager/director. The important issue is to have a clearly defined structure. All museum personnel should know where they fit into the organization and their relationship to other staff members. The organizational chart is a map that defines the system and describes the flow of museum work. It demonstrates the organizational attitude of the institution.

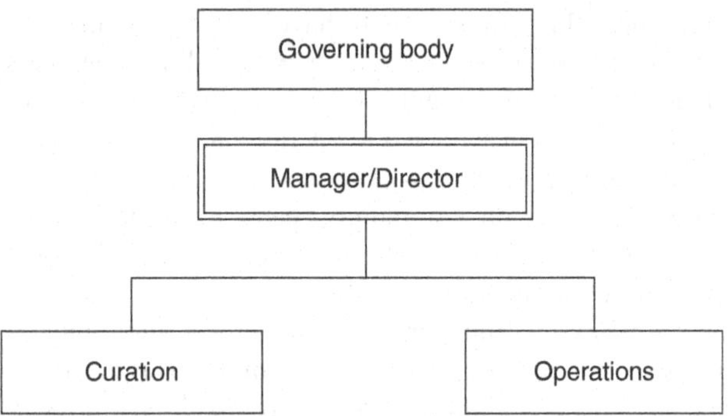

Fig. 1 This diagram shows a simplified *hierarchic* management structure that divides the museum activities between three basic functions. The division is between collecting and noncollecting areas of the museum.

The museum management methods and structures tend to reflect the prevailing practices of national organizations, concepts of business, and levels of development. The management structure of the museum should promote teamwork, communication, and an endorsed sense of purpose regardless of these influences. It is important, in any structure, to have personnel who have adequate experience and training to fulfill the needs of the museum or heritage organization and its stated mission.

The horizontal or flat structure (Fig. 3) is most common in museums where there is a small staff (team) and a shared workload. It has a number of advantages and disadvantages. The staff has greater access to the manager/director, and consequently, this arrangement is popular with the museum personnel. Direct communication with the manager/director has distinct advantages for individuals; however, institutional communication can suffer. Care should always be taken to ensure that there is the circulation of critical information to all parts of the museum.

The third organizational structure found in museums is the *matrix* (Fig. 4). This configuration utilizes many of the same principles as those used in project management. The matrix structure assigns duties to unit leaders and a team of staff members qualified to address a particular task. The team may be responsible for developing an exhibition, designing a gallery, or formulating a fund raising plan. Membership in the team may extend for the entire project or for a specific part, such as the developmental stage. The matrix organizational structure may have overlapping elements that add to the exchange of information and the utilization of personnel.

LEADERSHIP

Museum management must include the issues of identity and leadership development. Consistent with the process of leadership development, museum personnel in many locations are seeking institutional identity based on preservation and dissemination of the cultural patrimony that characterizes the character of the host community. The process of patrimonial protection is ongoing and constantly evolving in a layering process of institutional awareness. Heritage preservation challenges museum identity because it is a form of social consciousness dedicated to communication and eventual understanding in the sense that it is the foundation for redefining the common wealth of humanity.

The issues of museum identity and leadership are of great immediate concern. There are few challenges that a museum must deal with as critical or as immediate as identity. Visitorship, funding, collections, social and cultural affiliations, conservation, and education are but a few of the most obvious issues to be considered within leadership and identity equation. The question of identity as a management issue is fundamental, and includes concerns about the guiding principles for museums as they address decreased funding and increased social and political expectations.

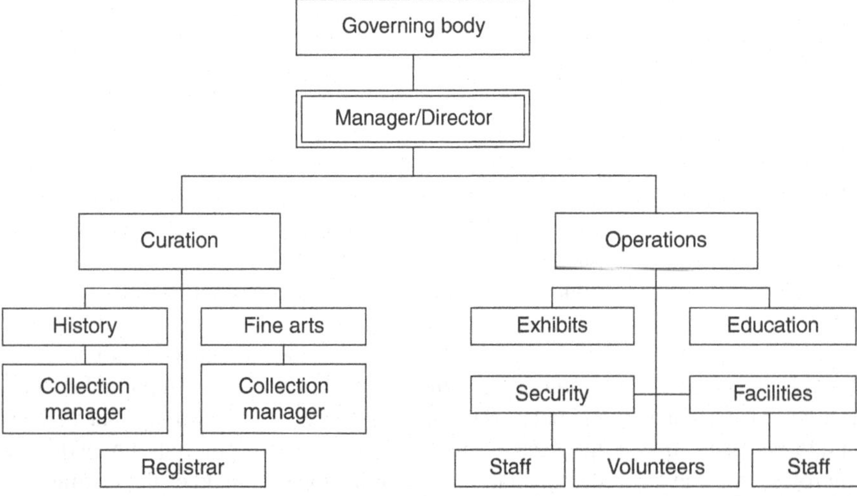

Fig. 2 This is an example of a more complex *hierarchic* structure that includes a second and third layer of museum personnel. The structure can be expanded to include any number of positions.

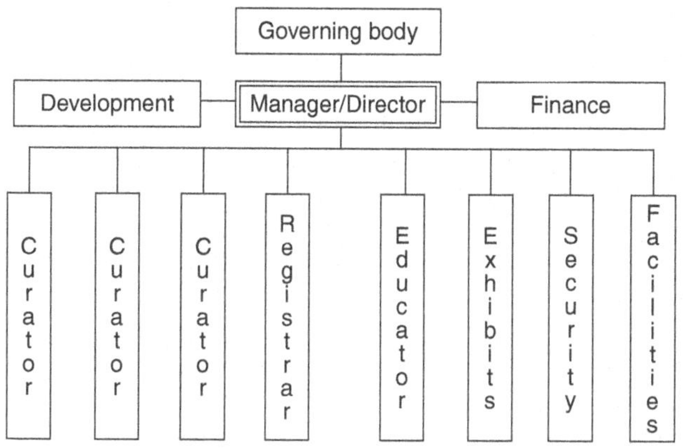

Fig. 3 Example of a horizontal (flat) organizational structure. In this arrangement, all members of the museum staff report directly to the manager/director.

Museum management is directly influenced by the manager/director/leader that often comes from within the ranks of the museum. However, theories about leadership maintain that traditional dependence on paternalistic rule (or materialistic as the case may be) based on status, birth, property, charisma, and power (the so-called "great man" or "great woman" theory of leadership) has been replaced by the less arbitrary measure of knowledge and ability. Although this approach was first advocated many years ago, it appears to remain true during the first years of the twenty-first century. However, this so-called leadership model has evolved at different rates in different part of the world. Privileged leadership continues to be accentuated and implemented by the issues of status and power as epitomized by political appointment. This practice is resident in many locations and is often detrimental to the museum community.

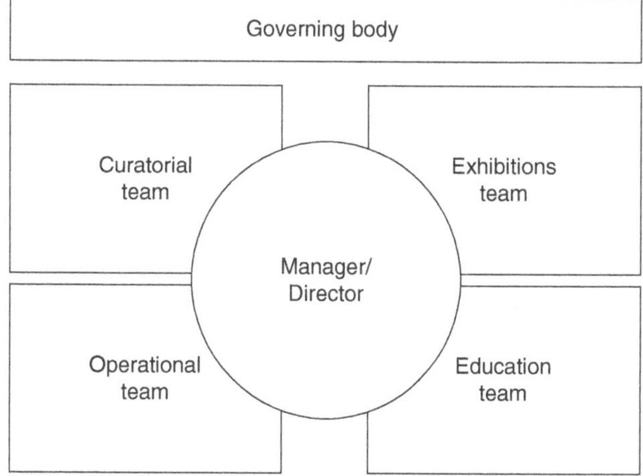

Fig. 4 Matrix organizational structure. Each part of the matrix structure has a level of autonomy, that is, it has a project or activity to accomplish. The team leader or project manager oversees and coordinates planning and resources. The team leader is a facilitator that encourages communication, sees that information and resources are available, calls meetings, and assigns tasks. The team leader reports to the manager/director. The number of teams deployed depends on the needs of the museum and the availability of qualified personnel.

Wise leaders established management teams that balanced the ideas, attitudes, and aspirations of its members to accomplish the stated institutional mission. Early in the knowledge-based leadership process, it was assumed that expertise was the critical factor in effective leadership. However, it was quickly determined that intellect alone was not sufficient to make someone an effective leader. Instead, a participative leadership style that allowed team input in decision-making proved more effective.

PERSONNEL MANAGEMENT

Established values and beliefs drive the museum, good management makes it operate efficiently and effectively, and strong collections give it identity and creditability. Nonetheless, it is the personnel, paid or unpaid, who makes the museum a meaningful and functional place. People generate the activities that other people attend (Fig. 5).

Probably the single most defining characteristic of a nonprofit organization is the people who work within it. The role of the staff is to implement board policy, supervise museum activities, maintain the facilities, manage and recruit volunteers, and handle public relations.[6] However, national laws and the regulations of the country in which the museum is located usually determine the rules and policies regarding employment and work conditions. The employing ministry or other governing authority may also control employment practices, and these regulations may vary greatly from country to country.[7]

Though there is no standard approach for successful personnel management, most criteria are based on cultural assumptions about what such practices should entail and how they are to be achieved and implemented. Regardless of the museum's location, good personnel management requires 1) selecting the right person for the job, 2) determining the work to be done, 3) deciding the way the work is to be accomplished, and 4) managing the relationship between the person doing the work and the other elements

Fig. 5 The inflow and outflow of people involved with the museum.
Source: From Edson.[5]

of the museum. These activities may be accomplished either directly or indirectly, depending on the size and scope of the museum. They are, however, fundamental to the management process.

A primary concern when dealing with personnel issues must be attitude. Attitude is defined as a "way of thinking" that exists in an individual and the workplace. Attitude is a major factor for museums. This attribute is reflected in intangibles such as research and education, as well as the study, care, use, and maintenance of the collections and, perhaps most specifically, in public trust. Personnel that cannot be trusted to invest in the ethics and values of the museum should be trained or redirected. Museums must be value driven. This calls for an attitude of dedication, honesty, and openness. It is a very simple concept. Institutional core values are those qualities that cause people to share their treasures and cause them to support the museum with their participation. Trusted measures are identified with values, and values are identified with trusted museums. Every museum employee and volunteer is a part of that value system.

VOLUNTEERS

Personnel management often includes volunteers used to fill the vacancies in the museum's workforce. Certain services make effective use of volunteers in areas such as classes for children, sales in the museum shop, or housing of collections. Volunteers may also be lawyers, accountants, contractors, teachers, scholars, entertainers, and a range of other persons with specialized skills who contribute their time and effort to support the museum. Volunteer services are so important for some museums that without them, the museum would have to limit its activities.[8] The people working in the museum, whether paid or volunteer, are one of the institution's most valued assets.

The volunteer cadre may also include docents used to guide groups through the museum's exhibitions and teach visiting school classes. These docents should be thoroughly prepared for their duties by the museum staff or a volunteer coordinator. The docent should receive training in all subject matter in which he or she will have to be informed, as well as the teaching of children within the museum context. Such training requires a commitment on the part of the volunteer, as well as a decision on the part of the museum that docents are an important and valued addition to the staff. A rule to remember in using volunteers is that their training and supervision should not take more professional staff time than will the work that the volunteers perform.[8]

TEAMWORK, MISSION, AND POLICY

Of all the factors that contribute to sustained success in museums, one of the most important is creating a cohesive and effective team. Sustaining such a team requires leadership, vision, and a commitment to the value of team effort. The most powerful function of an effective manager/director is that of inspiring others to be part of the team. The transfer of power from one or a few to many involves the delegation of tasks and the sharing of responsibility. The museum with its teams that have "equal value" is a shift in the traditional museum context where authority was vested in a few highly placed individuals.[9]

In addition to selecting qualified personnel, good museum management builds teamwork, develops the institutional vision, and creates an environment where others can work effectively and efficiently to meet institutional goals. Team building extends beyond the museum's administration (manager/director/CEO) office. The manager/director keeps all persons involved and feeling appreciated, so they contribute their best efforts for the good of the museum. Every member of the staff should have a meaningful role in making the museum a successful contributor to the constituency it serves.

Beyond being good practice, teamwork encourages open communication and reduces misunderstandings. As a result, individuals work toward and accept new ideas. The potential for change is heightened and institutional renewal is stimulated. An environment of openness and mutual respect is a hallmark of good management. Management fails when the manager/director loses sight of the mission of the museum, and instead becomes obsessed with issues related to the organization as an entity separate from its purpose. The possibility of this myopia is reduced when team attitudes guide institutional thinking.

A basic element of management and team building is trust, and it is more than a notion of legal or ethical action. Trust is the foundation of positive relationships, both inside and outside the museum. It facilitates a sense of intellectual and emotional security based on mutual respect, honesty, and loyalty. Trust promotes open exchange, constructive assessment, and creative achievement. These elements influence the ability of a museum to accomplish its goals. A shared commitment to respecting individual qualities, maintaining open communication, and promoting the institutional mission is essential for a functional, forward thinking, and professionally oriented museum.

MISSION

Every museum needs a mission regardless of its financial and service orientation, that is, a direction to which all its functions are dedicated. The mission is the heart of the museum's existence. It must be a proactive indication of the organizational intent, and as a ubiquitous statement of mission, it must be endorsed and advocated by the management and staff.

A good mission statement is one that is sufficiently broad to encompass the many possible activities in which the organization may wish to engage and is adequately focused to give proper guidance. This type of broad end statement is philosophical. It results, at least in part, from what the board, staff, and volunteers believe, the world should be, and how the museum complements that perspective. This statement derives from the "idea" of "mission" as a strategy and a commitment. It verifies what the museum is about and what human needs it addresses.

A mission may be a short statement about how a museum wants to be (what it is) and how it wants to be viewed by its audience. Or, it may be the broadest expression that accurately defines the most global ends statement for the organization. It can be brief or broad but accurate and true to ends (outcome) attributes. It should not be a statement of how the organization wants to be or to be seen, but a statement of how the world will be different due to its existence.

It is normally more difficult to identify and articulate the mission of a not-for-profit organization and consequently to develop criteria by which success can be measured.[10] A mission statement is only valuable if it gives some specific guidance on the direction the organization should take in regard to programs, services, and activities. It should be an announcement of the results to be achieved, and a constant reminder of the museum's purpose.

A mission statement is a basic document for all museums as a declaration of purpose, and policies provide the means for achieving the goals of the institution. The governing authority guided by management and staff normally formulate policies, and persons inside and outside the museum should have easy access to these documents. Policies that address specific museum issues should be written to accomplish two primary goals. They are 1) to plan a course of action to influence and determine institutional decisions, actions, and other matters, and 2) to define a course of action for the museum that is considered expedient, prudent, or advantageous.

POLICIES

The governing entity (board) must state what is expected of themselves, the manager/director, and the staff in the policy form of management. When the policies are well formulated, the manager/director knows their limits and the staff is free to pursue institutional objectives within the established parameters. The management should formulate three types of policies:

Philosophical
Resource development
Working

The philosophical policies address ethical issues, resource development policies define allocation of major resources, and working policies are concerned with operational matters. In many organizations, the management generates the first and second types of policies, and the third is staff produced. However, in forward-thinking museums, staff input into the policies regarding ethics is essential, and fund allocation without staff support is often nonproductive. If policies are designed to meet specific needs, then the persons most qualified to identify those needs are the individuals with a detailed knowledge of the organization—the staff. Nonetheless, policy recommendations may emanate from any level of the organization.

Policies are essential to good management. They will undoubtedly differ depending on the institutional mission. However, it is important to establish consistent policy documents that reflect the values and beliefs of the museum and the expectations of staff, as well as define collections' care and use, fiscal matters, physical plant use, and other issues that directly impact upon the ability of the museum to fulfill its mission. Well-defined policies outline the framework in which management and staff can operate and help them make proper decisions. Policies also reassure the public that an institution has given careful consideration to its actions.

FINANCIAL MANAGEMENT

A significant element of all management systems is fiscal accountability. Most museums are subject to a governing authority that determines the financial practices of the institution. The authority may differ and the level of financial oversight may vary, but few museums have complete and unrestricted control over all aspects of their finances. Regardless of the level of flexibility or the source of funding, museums have an obligation to be accountable for the money allocated (given) to them. The process of budget development, fund accountability, and financial planning is generally described as financial management, and while the governing authority may carefully structure the guidelines, the implementation rests with the museum manager/director and subsequently with the staff.

Museums generally use the cash accounting method (instead of the accrual method) for maintaining financial records. Using the cash method income is not counted until the money is received, and expenses are not counted against the budget until they are actually paid. This process differs from accrual accounting in which a transaction is counted (entered into the financial record) when a pledge or commitment is made regardless of when the money or service is received. Likewise, the museum will not record an expense, in cash accounting, until all parts of a project are received, completed, and billed.

Financial management is viewed by many as one of the most difficult aspects of museum management. In reality, the difficulty usually resides in the usability of the budget document. A budget in the simplest terms is a management tool stated in numbers. It is a planning document. Budgeting is more than balancing expected revenues with expenditures. It indicates the money available, the money needed (by projection), and the difference between the two. It also allows management to determine the most appropriate alternatives for resource allocation. A budget, in most instances, is a statement of intent that is used to guide an institution's activities. It empowers museum management to decide how to use financial resources most effectively.

The relationship between the mission-oriented goals and financial resources is critical, and budget formulation is an integral part of the planning and management process. Actual spending and receipts can be tracked against planned targets as an instrument of managerial control. Variances between expenditures and the projected budget may signal the need to slow spending or increase income, or to shift resources from one category or financial commitment to another. Differences in spending or in revenues that are more than incidental departures from the planned amounts require the management's attention.

FUNDING SOURCES

Most museums receive income from different sources. Primary support in many locations comes from the governing authority, but even in those cases, additional income may come from admission charges, the museum shop, donations, or food service. Museums have several financing opportunities:

Admission charge
Museum shop
Food service
Marketing
Tourism
Gifts
Voluntary contributions (donations)
Corporate sponsorships
Publishing
Travel tours
Membership
Grants

The financial prospects are often dependent on the imagination, commitment, and work of the management in coordination with the governing authority. An analysis of the museum's mission, location, collections, programming, and other assets will give an idea of the funding potential of the particular institution. Not every museum has every financial opportunity, but most museums have several possibilities. Care should be taken to determine possible restrictions or prohibitions by regional or national rules before initiating nontraditional financial schemes.

The ultimate gauge of good financial management is the quality of the service provided and the relevance of that service to the museum's mission. The budget must therefore relate to the mission and the money should be used to further that mission. In formulating a budget, museum management should consider two distinct principles: 1) use established policy as a guide to planning and projections, and 2) make efficient use of funds by carefully considering how much things cost and how the money is obtained.

It should be acknowledged that budgeting is an ongoing process. It is not something done once a year and ignored the rest of the time. A budget is a working document that should be reviewed monthly by the manager/director, the appropriate staff members, and members of the museum's governing authority. This scrutiny is important because neither income nor expense can be predicted with total accuracy. Regular review is the only way museum management can know its financial standing.

MANAGEMENT PLANNING

Planning is critical to successful museum management. It is vital for all museums as a basis for supervision by the governing authority, sound management by the manager/director and staff, effective fund acquisition and utilization, and meaningful program evaluation in fulfilling the museum's mission. Every museum can be improved, and effective planning is an integral aspect of the improvement process.[11]

Museum planning should be an inclusive activity that considers the museum's history, mission, collections, staff, facilities, funding, community support, audience, political status, local and regional problems, and other environmental and social potentialities for making decisions that will guide the museum into the future. This planning process allows the museum (management and staff) to assess, redefine, and implement its mission, programming, exhibitions, and the audience served. There is a close connection between the planning process and marketing because the planning must precede the marketing, and the marketing analysis of a museum is a part of the planning process.

Planning may include any or all of the following:

Finance/revenue: These are issues related to the current and future funding needs of the museum and its ability to secure sufficient resources to support activities for the execution of its stated mission.

Community needs and involvement: These issues refer to changing community needs and the museum's ability to develop effective responses appropriate to its mission and priorities.

Human resources: These issues concern the recruitment, training, and retaining of sufficient qualified personnel with adequately diverse backgrounds to fulfill staff and volunteer service needs.

Organizational/structural: These issues evaluate the museum structure to determine the best configuration to meet current and future museum and community needs through the provision of quality, cost-effective services.

Communications/visibility: These issues ask how the museum can make itself more visible and inform the public about its mission and services and consider what resources will be needed to execute the processes of gaining greater visibility.

National agenda: Assuming the museum is part of a national group, the institutional agenda should support increased awareness and advocacy of national issues such as funding, accountability, and standards.

Service effectiveness: These issues relate to evaluation of services, programs, and exhibits and the results to measure museum effectiveness in meeting the needs of targeted populations, and ensuring that marginal services will be enhanced or discontinued.

A museum should undertake planning to reaffirm or to modify its mission—why it exists, what its purpose is, and what it does—and to agree on its vision—what it wants to be and do in the coming years. The ultimate product of the planning process is a guide to govern the activities of the museum. It is not the purpose of the plan to decide what should be done in the future, but to decide what should be done now to make desired things happen in the future.

For museums, planning is essential to success; however, flexibility, adaptability, and creativity are elements of the planning process that must be carefully considered. This does not mean changing the museum's mission in response to social or financial opportunities. The traditional practice of relying on a five-year plan, however, is no longer practical because the cultural, financial, political, and social environment changes rapidly. The successful adaptation to change requires establishing a stable means for the museum to accomplish its mission, despite challenging external or internal conditions.

Elements of the museum that should be considered in the planning process are the following:

Mission
Organization
Decision-making
Fund raising
Resource allocation
Performance evaluation
Organizational effectiveness

Financial planning is an integral part of the planning process of museums. The allocation of resources is a significant element in setting organizational goals and fulfilling them. Depending on the needs of the museum, budget planning will assume varying degrees of importance. However, in all cases, considering the financial realities of the organization will play an important part in the development of a strategic plan.

The development of a financial plan may extend far into the future, and in all cases, it is an ongoing activity. Financial planning as a process implies intentional preparation for the future and must promote growth in a rational and achievable way. Budget and financial stability must be a part of all planning. A careful look must be taken at the feasibility of proposed services, programs, and exhibitions, not to mention staff and facility expansion. One of the most difficult elements of financial planning is projecting future income. This is an area where good information and experience cannot be underestimated.

Without planning, the organization's effort will be haphazard, the outcome unpredictable, and the management indecisive. Planning should focus on achieving the most appropriate connection between a museum and the environment in which it operates. The environment means those conditions that exist both inside and outside of the museum that have a say over its operations. Effective planning deals with the issues that develop along the margin between the inner workings of the museum and outer influences. Planning should delineate a strategy for success.

It is the governing authority's responsibility to see that planning takes place. The staff can encourage planning through the director, but ultimately the board (trustees) must start the process because, it is responsible for the welfare and effectiveness of the museum. The board, therefore must not only assure planning takes place and oversee the process, it must actively participate in the process.

SELF-ASSESSMENT

Information is an important part of the management of any organization, and to be of value, the information must be based on evaluation and assessment. Proper decision-making requires dependable information gathered in systematic ways. An assessment can be conducted on the entire institution, as with the accreditation self-study, or it can be used to assess one aspect of the museum such as financial development, public relations, and marketing, or volunteer involvement.

Self-assessment is a part of planning and one way to determine the effectiveness of the museum and the method for deciding the value or purpose of the institutional mission. Planning is a process through which a museum may

Identify needs in society
Define its relation to the mission of the museum

Evaluate its capabilities as a museum
Assess its external environment
Set objectives for the museum
Select strategies for the museum
Design programs for the museum
Determine a budget for the museum
Evaluate performance of the museum

A part of the assessment process is called environmental scanning. Environmental scanning is a means for the museum to systematically examine and compile data on the factors that are significant to the organization today and in the future. Centralizing this information will help the museum to understand the realities that are a part of developing the strategic plan. This process looks at the activities around the museum to determine influencing factors that may alter the future of the organization in a positive or negative way. Most of the time, these influences are monitored in an informal way. It can be very beneficial to the museum to look carefully at factors that have an impact upon the following areas:

Economics
Legal or regulatory
Politics
Technology
Society
Demographics
Competition

PLANNING METHODS

Planning is a necessary element of every museum. The collecting plan defines the objectives of institution collecting. A collection management plan (or policy) addresses a range of issues related to collection care and use, including accessioning, deaccessioning, loaning, cataloging, exhibiting, conserving, and storing objects and specimens. There are also exhibitions, financial, marketing, long-range, human resources, and strategic planning that must be considered.

In preparing any institutional plan, it is essential to be clear about who are the intended recipients of this documentation. It is often the expectations of this audience that will determine the type and structure of plan that is appropriate. For example, the requirement by government, or local authorities (city or nation/state) for museum strategic plans may differ from the information gathered for the internal document. (It is often the case that what government bodies require is something more akin to a business plan.)

A strategic plan, regardless of the format, is the result of careful and extensive research and strategic thinking by the museum. It is a disciplined effort to produce fundamental decisions and actions that will shape and guide what a museum is, what it does, and why it does what it does.[12] Strategic planning is important to museums as a basis for strong governance by the board, sound management by the executive and staff, effective fund raising by both the board and the staff, and constructive program evaluation by all participants in fulfilling the museum's mission.

There are various ways to develop a strategic plan. The two most common planning processes are the "goals approach" and the "vision of success approach." Each of these methods has a different anticipated outcome, but either may serve as a starting design for the museum.

The goals approach is a commonly used method for planning. That process requires the museum to establish goals and objectives for itself and to develop strategies to achieve the anticipated outcomes. This approach can be effective if there is general agreement on the established goals and objectives, and if those goals and objectives are adequately detailed to guide the development of strategies. This process is most effective when there is a hierarchical management structure with leadership that can establish goals for the museum.

The vision of success approach is another recognized form of planning. In this approach, the museum develops an "ideal" picture of itself in the future as it successfully fulfills its mission. This approach is most usable when it is difficult to identify strategic issues directly or if no specifically agreed upon goals and objectives exist. The vision approach is also effective when drastic changes are necessary, and the development of future achievement can provide the concepts that enable organizational members to identify necessary changes.

A commonly used method for analyzing the institutional assets is called SWOT.[13] This technique calls for an examination of the institution's strengths, weaknesses, opportunities, and threats. It is a process and not an end unto itself. It is, however, an effective method for gathering information to be used in the planning process.

In initiating the planning process, it is not necessary to have a consensus. Different ideas, approaches, and unique viewpoints are good as a starting point for museum analysis. This kind of self-assessment should be an ongoing part of the planning and management activities of the museum.

MANAGEMENT ETHICS

No profession can survive without a body of ethics as the dynamic principles developed to reflect a changing environment. Comprised of ideals and values that guide individual and group conduct, ethics can be defined in terms of these two groups. Individual ethics are "value statements," such as rules, positions, and inferences, which incorporate ideas such as good and bad, and right and wrong.[14] Group ethics include customs and codes that monitor an individual's behavior for the benefit of a group. Ethical

Fig. 6 Ethics is a body of correct actions that reinforces the concept of the museum as a trusted resource and the means for recognizing the highest common good. The worth of an activity is not derived from the purposes it seeks to achieve, but from its being in accordance with a policy that respects a code of ethics. **Source:** From Edson.[16]

theory involves how people see reality, why they associate "value" within it, and how they respond to it.[15]

Ethics seeks to establish principles of right behavior that may serve as action guides for individuals and groups (see Fig. 6). The activities an individual, manager/director, or staff member, performs consciously and willingly and for which that person is responsible (accountable) are within the domain of ethics. Therefore, ethical concerns ought to be common to all areas of the museum. It is naïve to assume that ethics is the responsibility of the management (administration or board of trustees) and not that of the general workforce. Ethical reasoning is a part of every decision, and is fundamental to interaction with other members of the museum profession and the public. Every act or action associated with the museum profession has a related ethical matrix (Fig. 7).

Ethical responsibility is evidenced by interaction inside and outside the organization and the way a museum conducts its activities. An ethical museum is one in which all participants acknowledge professional standards and

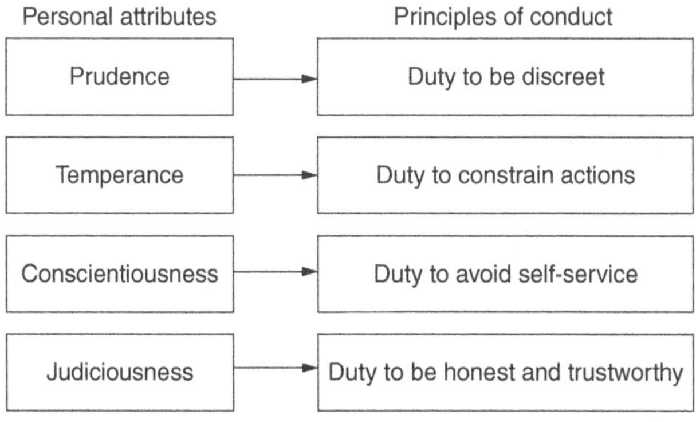

Fig. 7 The relationship of attributes to conduct. **Source:** From Edson.[17]

where those principles are exemplified by the museum's activities. The public perception of a museum's ethical correctness (trust) revolves around its collections' stewardship, as well as its dealings with fiscal and institutional accountability. The numbers of ethical issues related to museum management are increasing, and they go well beyond the traditional concerns for use of collections and money. There are also national and international laws that influence an increasing array of museum activities regardless of the museum size or location. Museums should have policies that delineate organizational rules and responsibilities, as well as to guide the manager/director in management duties.

Ethics is more than following the rules. It is a holistic endorsement of doing the right thing. A code of ethics is a part of the process of creating and maintaining an ethical institution and ensuring proper management. However, it is only a part of the equation. An ethical museum is one in which all participants acknowledge the core values such as loyalty, honesty, integrity, respect for others, and pursuit of excellence, and where those values are promulgated in the context of the museum's mission.

CONCLUDING COMMENTS

Museums, as institutions in the service of society, are a reflection of the high level of social development enjoyed in many areas of the world. They require personnel (management and staff) with varied educational and decision-making backgrounds. The balancing of these efforts result in a properly functioning museum. The modern museum must be an informative, professional, systematic (in its collection care and planning), enjoyable, and socially active institution. To meet this challenge, management must include the application of practices developed by research, economics, law, education, and physical plant management combined with the latest technology. The exact arrangement of these elements in an effective model may change, but the concern for the management process enjoys equivalent importance in most locations.

Working in a museum involves public trust and entails great responsibility, including steadfast personal integrity. Ironically, the role of the manager/director with all its responsibilities and obligations is among the least well-defined positions in the contemporary museum. This impreciseness reflects the wide range of managerial duties that include the technological, political, and social capabilities required to manage and lead a museum in uncertain and demanding times. The manager/director must be a public representative, service advocate, and museum professional capable of securing essential resources for the museum while maintaining the integrity of the institution. The manager/director must have the scholarly and administrative skills to promote the mission of the museum, as well as the ability to explain critical issues that may not be understood by the public. No job description can completely describe all the variables that might be encountered in museum management.

Because management is accountable for the way the museum conducts itself, it should be inspired by a high standard of public service and ethical conduct. If those ideals are overlooked or ignored, the museum will cease to warrant public trust and support. Conversely, a museum guided by proper management will establish the identity of the institution with reference to the social and cultural environment, and position it for future growth and influence. It is certain that a museum cannot survive without a sense of growth, identity, leadership, and vision. Management is therefore about the future of the museum and the people associated with that institution.

The contemporary museum evokes a feeling of prestige and a sense of pride that inspires and reassures visitors. It grants a measure of certainty in uncertain times. The value of a museum is in direct proportion to the services it gives to the emotional and intellectual life of the people. Proper management by an individual dedicated to serving the interests of the public, protecting cultural and natural heritage, and promoting goodwill and understanding will ensure that trust is not denied.

REFERENCES

1. Edson, G. Museum management. In *Running a Museum: A Practical Handbook*; Boylan, P., Ed.; International Council of Museums: Paris, France, 2004; 134.
2. The Museum Organization. Encyclopaedia Britannica Library, from Encyclopaedia Britannica 2005 Deluxe Edition CD-ROM Encyclopaedia Britannica, Inc., Chicago, IL, May 19 2007. Copyright (c) 1994–2003 (accessed May 4, 2008).
3. Edson, G. Museum management. In *Running a Museum: A Practical Handbook*; Boylan, P., Ed.; International Council of Museums: Paris, France, 2004; 133.
4. ICOM *Code of Ethics for Museums*; International Council of Museums: Paris, France, 2006; 14.
5. Edson, G. *Museum Ethics*; Routledge: London, U.K. and New York, 1997; 91.
6. Genoways, H.; Ireland, L. *Museum Administration: An Introduction*; Altamira Press, A Division of Rowman & Littlefield Publishers, Inc.: Walnut Creek, New York, and Oxford, 2003; 83.
7. Boylan, P. Managing people. In *Running a Museum: A Practical Handbook*; International Council of Museums: Paris, France, 2004; 147.
8. Burcaw, G.E. *Introduction to Museum Work*, 2nd Ed.; AASLH Press: Nashville, TN, 1983; 40–41.
9. Suchy, S. *Leading with Passion: Change Management in the 21st Century Museum*; AASLH Press: Nashville, TN, 2004; 78.
10. Wolf, T. *Managing a Nonprofit Organization*; Fireside Books: New York and London, U.K., 1990; 7.
11. Edson, G.; Boylan, P. Museum management. In *Running a Museum: A Practical Handbook*; International Council of Museums: Paris, France, 2004; 144.
12. Byron, J. *Strategic Planning for Public and Nonprofit Organizations: A Guide to Achieving and Sustaining Organizational Achievements*; Jossey-Bass: San Francisco, CA, 2004.
13. Genoways, H.; Ireland, L. *Museum Administration: An Introduction*; Altamira Press, A Division of Rowman & Littlefield Publishers, Inc.: Walnut Creek, New York, and Oxford, 2003; 82.
14. Winter, J.C. The way to somewhere: Ethics in American archaeology. In *Ethics and Values in Archaeology*; Green, E.L., Ed.; The Free Press: New York, 1984; 36–47.
15. Brody, C. *Museum Science Program*; Texas Tech University: Lubbock, TX, 2002; 36, Unpublished thesis.
16. Edson, G. *Museum Ethics*; Routledge: London, U.K. and New York, 1997; 31.
17. Edson, G. *Museum Ethics*; Routledge: London, U.K. and New York, 1997; 7.

Museum Registration and Documentation

Dixie Neilson
University of Florida, Gainesville, Florida, U.S.A.

Abstract

Keeping documentation on museum objects is vital to good museum management. Important polices such as the Collection Management Policy that enumerates what and how the museum will collect objects, and the museum's code of ethics that defines acceptable behavior of staff, boards of directors, and volunteers provide the framework for long-term museum management. Records of accession and deaccession procedures contain specific information on the objects, their donors, and the reasons for their inclusion in, or removal from, the museum collection. Documentary files contain sections on appraisals, condition reports, correspondence, deed of gift or purchase information, notes, and shipping records. Records of loans to and from the museum are important historical documents and contain details of condition reports, photography, loan agreements, shipping details, and correspondence between parties. All files should be kept in perpetuity and preserved through the safeguards of backup documentation, protection from hazards, and deterioration and destruction.

INTRODUCTION

Museum collections are comprised of more than objects or specimens, also included are the documents and data pertaining to the objects. Documentation consists of official and legal transactions such as accessions records, loan contracts, field notes, scientific analysis, and deaccession records. Museums must establish recordkeeping procedures as a matter of responsible collections care; without supporting documents museum objects would be worthless. Keeping information relating to the collection (including any objects that may be loaned to the museum or be housed there for any reason) is one of the primary duties of the registrar. Records concerning permanent collection objects are deemed to be a part of the museum's collection and equal in stature to the objects to which they pertain; their importance cannot be overstated.

The goal of this entry is to introduce the topic of museum registration, particularly as it pertains to recordkeeping and to fully describe the collections documents and how to house them in a responsible manner. A brief background of the history of registration assists the reader in understanding the transition from early museums where the function was merely to display objects and was purely curatorial in focus, to the museum of today as educational institutions with vast resources that detail not only the object, but its place in our cultural history.

Important policies and documents under the control of the registrar are discussed such as Collections Management Policies, Codes of Ethics, and creating the documentary files for Accession and Deaccession and Loans. Philosophical and legal reasoning is offered to explain and inform each topic.

HISTORY OF REGISTRATION

The Museum at Alexandria, founded by Ptolemy in the third century B.C. may have been the first institution to use the term museum, meaning "seat of the Muses," but with a group of scholars and a library, it was more of a philosophical, educational organization. The Museum was the name given to a collection of objects owned by Lorenzo de'Medici in fifteenth-century Florence. Even then the term referred to a concept of comprehensiveness more than a building. By the seventeenth century Europeans were using the term to describe collections of curiosities. The Ashmolean Museum, built in 1683, housed the collection of Elias Ashmole and is considered the prototype of museums as we know them today.

Museum personnel in the earliest times were trained in a specific discipline and knew little of the larger concept of the museum as a whole, or its place in society. The apprenticeship nature of early training of museum staff gave little opportunity for the introduction of new ideas or methods, and the growth of museology, or museum studies as we know them.

When the Tammany Society of New York City opened its American Museum in 1791, it promised that all donations would be accepted, and the generous donors' names would be inscribed in a large register, a book kept just for that purpose. The duties of the "Keeper" of the museum included recording presents given to the museum and insuring that no visitor remove or injure any of the articles belonging to the museum. Thus the concept of a staff member dedicated to the care and control of objects was confirmed.

In 1880 Steven C. Brown was named Registrar for the United States National Museum that would become the

Encyclopedia of Library and Information Sciences, Fourth Edition DOI: 10.1081/E-ELIS4-120043237

Smithsonian Institute. His duties included shipping, storage, accessions, recording of objects, and the distribution of objects and specimens.

Henry Watson Kent addressed the 5-year-old American Association of Museums (AAM) in 1911, and presented a complete procedure for accessioning articles. By 1925 John Cotton Dana had described various staff descriptions as he schooled apprentices at the Newark Museum. The registrar would be responsible for receiving and recording accessions, labeling, creating storage lists, filing and maintaining documents, care of photographs and negatives, inventories of book collections and in particular, the care of objects on exhibition.[1] Thus began a transition from the arenas of display with vague practices and few rules, to professionalized institutions honoring and preserving the country's cultural heritage. Emphasis on training led to industry-wide standards of care and responsibility. Some formalized instruction through public education furthered professional development. By the second half of the twentieth century, post-World War II Americans looked to museums as a popular leisure activity. In response, widespread training programs for a variety of museum staff positions began in earnest.

In 1977 the Registrars Committee was recognized as an official Standing Professional Committee of AAM.

> The mission of the Registrars' Committee (RC-AAM) is to give assistance to the AAM and its regional associations in their objectives of sound professional preparation and promotion of high standards and, specifically, shall endeavor to increase professionalism among museum registrars through educational programs and publications, establish standards of professional practice, and create an atmosphere of understanding and respect, of communication and cooperation among registrars, between registrars and other museum professionals, and between registrars and individuals in related service fields.[2]

Registration Today

Today the duties of the registrar still resemble the earliest models, but with many additional responsibilities. At the same time they also have new tools to assist them. In particular the computer has enhanced collection management care. It facilitates many tasks such as generation of reports and compilations of collections formerly done by hand. Software programs exist to assist museums of any size and budget and have truly changed the way museums conduct much of their business.

A registrar oversees the operations that affect collections and manages risk, space, information, and people. It is generally recognized that museum collections are comprised of more than objects or specimens, but also of documents and data. Documentation consists of official and legal transactions such as accessioning, the process that makes the object property of the museum, deaccession records documenting the removal of objects from the collection, loan contracts, donor and artist information, field notes, scientific analyses, business archives, and factual information about the objects. The term "Collections Manager" is often used interchangeably with "Registrar" to describe registration duties, literally the person who manages the collections held by the museum. Our focus, however, is on museum documentation therefore the term registrar, one who records and preserves collection information as a part of collections care, will be used in this entry.

MUSEUM DOCUMENTATION

Several types of documents are common to most museums no matter their size. While each museum may design and create their own documentation specific to the needs of their discipline, much of the content is common to all museums. Museums record their standards and practices in their incorporating documents. Writing policies, some relating to collecting and exhibiting museum objects, and others which inform the ethical behavior of the director, staff, board of directors, and volunteers, are now common practice and required for accreditation by the AAM. Files related to legal ownership of every object in the collection, and exhibition files spanning the history of the museum are important parts of a museum's documentation.

Policies

The best policies are created by a team made up of appropriate staff members so that each department's needs and individual concerns may be discussed prior to policy being set. Ethical considerations as well as the physical mechanism for carrying out these policies should be discussed and understood by the staff. New hires should be given copies of relevant policies so all staff stay current with procedures within the museum. While there are many policies that may govern a museum or a department within a museum, two in particular are considered key by AAM for every collecting institution, the Collection Policy and the museum's Code of Ethics Policy.

Collections management policy

Vital to good museum management is a written Collections Management Policy. A Collections Management Policy defines the direction of collecting that will be undertaken by the museum, spells out the criteria for selecting acceptable objects for its permanent collection and designates authority in selecting additions to the collection. It should also outline the procedures by which the policy is carried out. This policy is the capstone of the museum's documentation, and may be consulted in cases where museum collection procedures are in question. In legal cases concerning museum objects the Collections Management Policy will serve as proof of a museum's standard practices.

Not all objects that enter a museum are destined to become part of the permanent collection. Unlike the early directive of the Tammany Museum, museums today do not, and should not, accept all objects that they are offered. Storage space and staff time are often limited and it is considered irresponsible to the rest of the collection to accept an object that will never be utilized. Objects that seem far outside the collecting scope of the museum may be rejected as legal donations by the Internal Revenue Service (IRS). For example, the donation of a violin to a museum that collects modern art may be called into question. The museum could be asked to show proof that a violin is an acceptable gift by submitting its Collections Management Policy to the courts. Therefore, careful consideration must be given in formulating the policy. It should be based upon the museum's mission, goals, and past history. It should not be so restrictive that normal collecting is hampered, yet it should not be so broad as to be meaningless. Its purpose is to identify the collecting priorities of the museum and to serve as a guide in the identification of potential purchases and appropriate gifts. The policy should incorporate existing areas of interest, as demonstrated by past collecting efforts, as well as desirable areas of expansion. It must take into consideration the organizational structure of the museum and all laws, guidelines, ethical standards, and appropriate practices. Common Collections Management Policy criteria include quality, relatedness, utility, control, and ethical considerations.

Quality is to be considered relative to the museum's existing collections. While it is ideal to acquire objects of impeccable excellence, the minimum standard for acquiring an object is that it be as good as or better than a similar object already in the collection. After reasonable determination of authenticity—verification of scholars, provenance, testing, etc.—the object will be graded according to esthetic merit and condition. Objects in poor condition should not be accepted unless the museum is reasonably sure funds exist for restoration or repair.

Relatedness is graded according to existing collections; it should fill a need or gap among existing holdings and enhance the overall collections. If it duplicates another object, will the collection be strengthened by having two or more similar objects?

Utility is defined by how well the object enhances the museum's goals and resources, and takes the following into consideration: exhibition potential, does the museum foresee exhibiting the object and with what frequency? Is the object's medium a limitation to its usefulness?

Control must be taken into consideration if there are any encumbrances accompanying an object that will have a negative impact on the museum's ability to manage the collection or are contradictory to ethical standards embraced by the museum. Donors should be discouraged from placing any restrictions on their gift. Donor stipulations regarding retention and/or exhibition schedule may inhibit the museum's exhibition programming. No promises should be made about how often or how long an object will be exhibited. Often donors do not consider the negative impact of a lengthy exhibition time on their gift. They may not be familiar with environmental concerns such as over exposure from light and heat. Donor restrictions should not prevent the removal of the object through sale or trade from the collection. Any restriction that prevents the museum from its normal activities of exhibition and care should be avoided.

A statement should be included in a letter of acceptance from the director of the museum confirming that all objects must conform to the museum's ethical standards. These include ethical standards regarding collecting as established by the AAM, the Association of Art Museum Directors (AAMD) and United Nations Educational Scientific and Cultural Organizations (UNESCO). Museums will generally not accept human remains, objects that are suspected of being war loot or stolen during international conflicts, endangered species, or objects imported or obtained illegally.

Code of ethics policy

Museums in the United States are grounded in the tradition of preservation of cultural heritage. Nonprofit museums are organized as public trusts, holding their collections and information as a benefit for those they were established to serve. Members of their governing authority, employees, and volunteers are committed to the interests of these beneficiaries. The law provides the basic framework for museum operations. As nonprofit institutions, these museums comply with applicable local, state, and federal laws and international conventions, as well as with the specific legal standards governing trust responsibilities. Legal standards are a minimum. Museums and those responsible for them must do more than avoid legal liability; they must take affirmative steps to maintain their integrity so as to warrant public confidence. They must act not only legally but also ethically.[3]

Codes of ethics exist for many staff positions within a museum, including Boards of Director, directors, curators, registrars, museum store managers, educators, and volunteers. Since 1999 the AAM has required every museum applying for accreditation to have their own specific Institutional Code of Ethics tailored to their collection and mission statement. They require that it be approved by the museum's governing authority. While not all museums apply for accreditation, most follow the AAM blueprint for the creation of an institutional ethical code, demonstrating to the public how seriously the museum takes its role as steward of the collections it holds in the public trust. Museums must be committed to public accountability and be transparent as far as their day-to-day operations. Further, having a Code of Ethics cements responsibility to the collection in the minds of all staff. Guidelines and instructions for writing codes can be found on the AAM Web site, as well as in many reference materials. Topics include governance, responsibility to the collection, acquisition procedures, deaccession and disposal methods, public accountability and professional conduct, responsibility to the public, and conflict of interest for staff, volunteers, and members of the governing authority. Among these duties, one of the highest is to maintain truthful, complete, and accurate records of each object within the collection. This duty most often resides with the registrar and the information contained in the registration files.

Registration Files

Two types of files under the control of the registrar are: Documentary Files, those which contain accession and deaccession information about the individual objects in the museum's permanent collection, and Exhibition Files that relate to all exhibitions of the museum's collection as well as loaned objects from other institutions and/or individuals. Files containing research on individual objects, such as their historical or cultural significance, are generally gathered and maintained in the curatorial department, and are not included in the discussions here.

Accession numbers

Once the museum has confirmed that a new acquisition (addition to the collection whether by donation or purchase) is to take place the registrar should assign an accession, or inventory, number to the gift and its objects.

While each museum may choose its method of creating accession numbers, one traditional system uses a tripartite number that begins with the year of the gift, followed by a number designating its place among gifts given that calendar year by all donors, followed by a number designating each individual object's place within that gift. For example, if Mr. Smith donated three paintings, all given on a particular day in 2009, and it is the fifth gift the museum has received from all its donors that year, the number for the gift would be 2009.5. Numbers are assigned within that gift, to each individual object. Painting one will be designated as 2009.5.1, painting two will be 2009.5.2 and painting three will be 2009.5.3. In cases where the object may have several components, such as a tea set or a pair of shoes, a suffix may be added indicating that the objects are part of a larger set. In the example of a tea set, the gift may be 2009.7 while the tea pot is 2009.7a, a saucer may be 2009.7b, and a cup 2009.7c. Generally this system is used when all objects together form one exhibitable object. One saucer without the cup is not likely to be exhibited, nor one shoe without the other.

Documentary files

Every object belonging to the museum should have, at the least, some reference in a registration documentary file. Registration files document both the acquisition process and the care information for the objects in the museum's collection. They are distinct from curatorial files, often maintained outside the registration department. While curatorial matters are not the subject of this commentary, for the sake of clarity the difference is important to understand. Curatorial files contain research information on the individual objects as well as bibliographic references, exhibition histories, and other information of a curatorial nature that is pertinent to the display and use of the objects. Each file pertains to one object in the collection, and those may be arranged alphabetically by object name or type. Curators build these files as research is conducted and the objects are exhibited. Conceivably, not all objects will have a file if no information has been gathered or the object has not yet been displayed. Curatorial files may also exist on objects not in the collection of the museum, but which are similar in nature to those which the museum collects, for reference purposes.

Registration files, often called documentary or accession files, however, are created immediately upon the acquisition of new objects, perhaps even prior to the object's receipt by the museum. They record the acquisition event, whether by donation, purchase, transfer, bequests or other means, as well as subsequent care information. These files include incoming and outgoing receipts, deeds of gift, gift agreements or purchase information, loan agreements, condition reports, copyright licenses, letters of correspondence, packing and shipping documentation, object photographs, appraisals, and insurance records. Registration files in natural history museums may also include collection maps detailing the location of archeological digs, permits, licenses, and import/export documentation.

It is not necessary, or even desirable due to space limitations, to have an individual documentary file for each separate object because much of the content would be duplicated in each. Each file represents one gift, no matter how many objects are in that gift. If one donor, for example, gave the museum ten paintings at one time all of the documentation for the gift would be in one documentary file. The delivery information, the correspondence, the gift agreement and so on relates to one event. It would be redundant to have ten copies of each piece of documentation contained in ten separate files. Purchases, as opposed to gifts, are considered individual events, therefore each purchase is represented by one documentary file.

Creating the accessions file

Although retention schedules for many businesses recommend that files be purged after a certain number of years, museum records should be retained forever. Provenance (ownership histories) field records, conservation treatments, and the like, cannot be traced without the retention of all records no matter how long ago they were created.

File with manila folders (or other similar types of folders) inside contain and separate the documents by subject. For long-term preservation of the original legal documents, such as the deeds of gift, they should be created using acid-free paper and stored separately in an acid-free folder. A fire-resistant filing cabinet kept in a secure location is an excellent repository for these documents. It is important to understand that any archival or acid-free file that contains documents on non-archival paper will, over time, lose its archival quality. The acids will migrate and contaminate any archival documents. Copies of these documents should be made for inclusion in the documentary file, while the archival master should be handled as little as possible.

Tabs on the exterior of the file folder contain the accession number of the gift, the name of the donor, and a brief description of the gift, for example, 2009.2.1-15, John Smith, 15 Masks. Files should be maintained in accession number order, which will also be a chronological order in which the accessions were made. File cabinets storing this or any other important documentation should not sit directly on the floor, but be raised at least three inches to protect against any water that may accumulate on the floor during a fire or flood emergency. Manila folders within the file will hold a variety of information depending on the museum's discipline. Common folder contents are: APPRAISAL, CONDITION REPORTS, CORRESPONDENCE, DEED OF GIFT, PURCHASE INFORMATION, INCOMING/OUTGOING RECEIPTS, LOANS, PHOTOGRAPHY, PUBLICATIONS, and NOTES. When marking the content of the manila file it is advisable to write directly on the folder's tab rather than applying a gummed label which will fall off the folder as it ages and dries out.

Each section of the file, described below, contains information regarding the legal status, the care and condition, and all other pertinent documentation relating to the objects in the collections. Proper maintenance of these files is one of the highest priorities of the registrar's job.

Appraisals

Donors preparing to make a gift to the museum often do so with the intent that they will take a charitable contribution tax exemption. In cases where the value of the contribution exceeds a certain dollar amount, the Internal Revenue Service requires that a certified appraisal be done on the object no longer than sixty days before the gift is made. Museum ethics prevent the staff from supplying a donor with an appraisal for a donation they expect to receive. Indeed, staff should remain at arm's length concerning any appraisal done for a potential donor. Should a donor ask for a recommendation or help in finding a qualified appraiser, the museum should supply the donor with a list of area appraisers, preferably three or more names, none with significant ties to the museum. This is done to prevent even a suspicion that the donation hinges on a favorable appraisal in which the value of the object may be overstated. Similarly the museum should not pay for the appraisal nor any services provided by the appraiser including travel, meal, or hotel reimbursement. The IRS now requires that appraisals be done by certified appraisers who are recognized as such by a professional appraisal organization and to follow generally accepted appraisal standards. The law further calls for severe penalties for appraisers who intentionally under/over value property.[4]

A museum may accommodate an appraiser's visit to the museum to view the object, should it be housed there prior to the donation. The museum staff may also assist the appraiser by providing photographs or other supporting documents, as long as the choice of the appraiser and the funds to pay him/her comes directly from the donor.

Because the appraisal is solicited and paid for by the donor, the museum should not assume that the documentation produced will be shared with the museum at the time of the donation. It is not unreasonable to ask the donor if the museum may have a copy of the appraisal in order to make sure that the insurance value placed on the object by the museum is accurate. Often donors will volunteer a copy of the appraisal, especially when they understand that it insures proper valuation for their gift. Copies of the appraisal are kept confidential, and should be kept in the object's documentary file.

At times the museum may choose to have one or more of its own objects examined and appraised for a variety of reasons usually related to insuring the collection or loan documentations. In cases where the museum already holds title to these objects, there is no conflict of interest and therefore no problems associated with the museum paying for the services of the appraiser. Care should be taken to only hire those appraisers who have been certified by a professional appraiser's organization. Valuations placed on objects by those without these credentials may be questioned or disallowed in the future.

Note that insurance values, often placed on loan agreements, are distinct from appraisals and may be assigned to museum objects by curators or others knowledgeable about the type of object. Insurance values may be higher than appraised values because they reflect not only the object's value, but also compensation for staff time in handling repair or replacement issues, should something be damaged.

Condition reports

Many publications offer detailed descriptions on how to write a condition report, and sample pages are provided for recording damage to many types of medium. Therefore this section will only deal with general practices regarding condition reporting. Many different condition report formats exist, each one particular to the type of medium of the object. A museum is free to design its own condition report form but care should be taken to use terms common in standard museum practice and those appropriate for the object's medium.

A condition report is an account of an object's physical state at any given time. When an object first enters the museum, whether as a new acquisition or a loan, an examination should be conducted and the report written. Condition reports done at the time of acquisition establish a baseline of the object's physical status. Follow up examinations, done as part of an inventory or in preparation for an exhibition of the object, can be compared to the original report. If discrepancies are noted they may signal a problem with storage conditions that should be remedied. For example, buckling or wavy paper can indicate high humidity levels in storage areas; dry and cracked wooden items may signal that environmental conditions are too dry; these should be adjusted for proper object maintenance.

Condition reports done on objects coming to the museum on loan are done to confirm that both the borrower and lender are in agreement about the condition of the object and that no damage has occurred in transit. Loaned items should be examined immediately upon their unpacking at the borrowing institution. If there is a discrepancy between a condition report written by the lender and the report done by the borrowing registrar, the lender should be notified immediately. Objects with damage should not be displayed and may need to be returned to the lender for restoration or repair. Reports are completed again just prior to the object's return to its museum to insure it is being returned in the same condition as when it arrived. By careful examinations both before and after the exhibition, a museum may avoid accusations of responsibility for damage that did not occur on its premises.

Condition examinations are ideally conducted in a well-lit and clean environment. Common tools that assist with this process are: soft pencils, forms, rulers and or calipers, clean white gloves, flashlight, ultraviolet light, magnifying glass and/or jeweler's loupe, a rolling cart to transport objects and a metal measuring tape (a cloth or plastic tape will stretch over time and become inaccurate and should therefore not be used however care should be taken that a metal tape does not scratch the object).

Several methods exist to describe the location of damage on an object. Because condition reports are often consulted by someone other than the reporter it is vital that the location and the damage are described clearly and definitively. A zone method divides a canvas or other two-dimensional object into top, middle, and bottom sections as well as right, left, and center sections. Damage is noted, for example, in the top left corner of the object, or bottom center, accurately conveying the location of concern. A second method of determining location is the axis method, in which damage may be described as located, for example, five inches to the left, and three inches up from the bottom. It is also acceptable to describe the location using the subject of the object. "There is a crack just above the man's eyebrow," can be just as clear as either of the previous methods described. The method used is not important as long as the information can be understood by any reader.

Damage is described in terms of length, width, color, shape, or another appropriate physical property. It is not necessary to determine the cause of the damage however, if known, that is helpful information. The extent of damage is referred to as negligible, slight, moderate, marked, and extreme.

Condition reports are to be stored in the object's documentary file and reviewed periodically. New information from subsequent examinations should be written on the original form and dated to indicate that it is not an original comment. Having all information on one sheet insures a much better historical report on the overall condition and is more efficient than locating and consulting several pages of old documentation.

Correspondence

Written correspondence between the museum and the donor can be important in determining the donor's intent to gift an object to the museum. In some cases heirs have disputed the validity of a gift made by a family member when that donor is no longer present to confirm their wishes. Correspondence between the museum and the donor often reveals clear intent to give the object to the museum. Courts will rule according to the donor's intent, often found within correspondence, despite the lack of a deed of gift or other receipt. This circumstance underscores the need for all file documentation, especially correspondence, to be permanently retained in the object's file.

Deeds of gift

Once the object offered for donation has been accepted by the museum the registrar will generate a deed of gift or similar conveyance spelling out the terms of acceptance. The deed should contain the name, address, and telephone number of both the donor and the museum, and a description of the object including as appropriate, title, artist, country of origin, medium, and dimensions. The donor states on the agreement that he has full ownership and authorization to make the gift, that he gives up all rights of ownership (with the possible exception of copyright) that the gift is unrestricted, and was not acquired by illegal means, and that the donor is not receiving any goods or services in exchange for the gift. The museum should stipulate in writing that it accepts the gift. A letter of thanks from the museum usually suffices for written acceptance.

Two identical deeds are created on acid-free paper. The donor signs and returns both copies to the museum for signature by an authorized member of the staff. It is important, but not a legal requirement, for the museum representative to be the last signatory on the deed in order to prevent the donor from making unexpected additions to the agreement. Once the deeds have both been signed by the museum representative one fully-executed agreement is returned to the donor and the other is filed in an acid-free folder in a fire-resistant file cabinet dedicated only to archival materials. (Note: some file cabinets are referred to as "fireproof" a misnomer; at high temperatures of lengthy duration, metal cabinets can be destroyed by fire.) The deeds of gifts should be handled as little as possible in an effort to conserve them as long as possible. Copies of the deed are placed within the object's documentary file.

While a deed of gift is a succinct document containing much of the information related to the donation, it is not a necessary component of the legal transfer from the donor to the museum. The law stipulates that for a valid transfer to take place there must be: 1) an offer; 2) an acceptance of the offer; and 3) physical transference of the object to the museum out of the control of the donor. Transfer may occur for example, when a donor writes a letter to the museum offering an object, the museum responds favorably to the offer and the donor delivers the object to the museum. A full and legal gift has not been made if any of these three components has not occurred. Therefore when a donor wishes to take a tax deduction in a particular year it is incumbent on the registrar to insure that the museum has actual physical control of the object by year's end. Physical control means "under the museum's care" and includes storage at a facility where the museum has contracted to store the object. As of yet, the IRS does not consider the gift complete if it is removed from the donor but still enroute to the museum.

Bequests

In some cases donors will request, through their wills, that some of their property be donated to a museum upon their death. These are considered gifts but there are special considerations involved. In essence, a bequest is an offer to a museum. The museum may or may not be aware of the plans of the donor; ideally the donor will have discussed their interest in making a gift after their passing, and the museum will have a chance to accept or decline the offer. In many cases the bequest comes as a surprise to the museum. Museums are under no obligation to accept post mortem offers, just as they are under no obligation to accept any other offer. In cases where the museum declines the offer the executor of the will makes other arrangements for the object. If the bequest is accepted, the executor may sign the deed of gift and handles the transfer in place of the donor. Bequest documentation should be included in the documentary file, however it is not necessary for a copy of the will to be submitted to the museum as it may contain other, sensitive material. It may be permissible to photocopy just the pertinent section of the will for inclusion.

Purchase information

Not all acquisitions are made through donations. Museums often purchase objects for their collections, either from reputable dealers, auction houses, or private sales. In those cases there will be no deed of gift and a sales receipt will suffice as the conveyance of title. Details of the sales are still important and should be retained. If the purchase was done through an auction the catalog may be filed in the documentary file, along with any known provenance or dealer information that may be historically relevant.

Incoming and outgoing receipts

Receipts should be issued for any potential collection object coming into the museum or leaving it, even temporarily. Office furniture and equipment and personal objects are not treated in the same manner as collection objects and are excepted from this discussion. Objects may enter the museum to be reviewed as potential acquisitions at the request of the director or curator; as objects of scholarly study, loans, or, least desirably, as unsolicited objects left as a museum donations. A receipt should be issued that clearly states the owner's name, address, telephone number, e-mail address, or other contact information. The receipt should state the purpose for which the object is left, and the expected date, if any, that the object will be returned to its owner. The object should be described fully enough to assist in identifying it, should that be necessary. Materials and dimensions are helpful, as is a short narrative recognizable by a lay person. Therefore a description of "a painting" will not suffice should the object become separated from its identifying information. More helpful would be "a framed painting, 16 × 20 in., oil on canvas, subject is a dog wearing a party hat."

All receipts should bear the name and signature of the person receiving the object, as well as the person depositing the object. Terms under which the object will be held, such as responsibility for insuring the object, should be noted on the receipt. The addition of language describing the duty of the owner to keep the museum apprised of their contact information helps reduce the chance that loaned objects will be forgotten by the lender and become abandoned property in the museum. Although many states now have abandoned property laws specifically to aid museums in the acquisition or disposal of abandoned objects, the process is cumbersome and time consuming, particularly if the object is not wanted by the museum. Registration staff should strive to return deposited objects promptly for the same reason. No object should remain in the museum without proper documentation.

A receipt should not substitute for a loan agreement; if the object is expected to remain in the custody of the museum for a significant length of time, or the museum has plans to use or exhibit the object, a loan agreement should be written that will spell out the responsibilities of both the lender and borrower, including insuring the object. See Loan Documentation below for further information.

Outgoing receipts are to be issued for any collection object leaving the museum, no matter how short the duration. The receipt should contain the same information as on the incoming receipt. If permanent collection objects leave the museum for conservation, photography, or similar purposes, a copy of the outgoing receipt should be given to the security staff who notes that the object is out of the building. The security staff should likewise be informed when the object returns to the museum. If an object is given back to its owner the receipt should state that the object is not expected to return. Under no circumstances should any object leave the building without a record of its removal. All receipts should be filed in the object's Shipping folder; they may be useful as records of the object's movement.

Loan records

Upon the return of an object that has been lent to another institution, a copy of the loan agreement should be placed in the object's documentary file with the original remaining in the loan file. Records of loans to other institutions are retained as part of the object's provenance. While this information may also be recorded on the museum's collection database, it is important to have the original loan agreement that contains all the information pertaining to the loan. Having the agreement at hand may assist with future grant applications that request the museum's loan history.

Standards of care include the responsibility to limit the number of hours sensitive objects are exposed to light. Light exposure records for individual objects should include times when the object has been on loan, just as they would for objects on exhibition in their home museum. Having a copy of the loan agreement can assist in the calculation of these hours. Incoming and outgoing loans are discussed in a later section. Further information concerning loans is discussed in a later section.

Photography

Documentary photography is an important part of any object's file. When an object first enters the collection a photograph, even one of low quality, is immediately taken, marked with the object's accession number, and stored in the Photography section of the file. Documentary photographs are to be used only for object identification; their quality is not adequate for publication.

In ideal circumstances all objects would have a series of publication-quality photographs taken as soon as they enter the collection as a part of the accession procedure. Unfortunately staff availability and financial resources often preclude this from occurring right away. If and when a publication-quality photograph does become available it can be stored in this file. If it is stored in another location, such as in a curator's or publicity manager's office, its existence should be noted in the documentary file. Additionally, surrogates of the image should be linked to the object's record in the collection database and in the museum's digital asset management system as appropriate. Publication-quality photography may also be held by the donor, gallery, or auction house from which the object came. These sources are often willing to provide the photos to the museum.

Copyright considerations should be observed when planning to publish any photograph of museum objects. While "fair use" or "educational use" may be defenses, it should not be assumed that any museum use of photographs is allowed. In addition to artist rights, the photographer often holds copyright protection. It is a wise decision to note any copyright information in the object's database.

Registration staff often assume the task of photographing one or more objects in the permanent collection for documentation purposes. For efficiency, a time is set aside when photography of a number of objects can occur at once. Objects to be photographed are grouped according to size to avoid frequent camera adjustments. Very small objects may benefit from having a ruler, a coin, or other measuring device placed in the photo in order to help the viewer determine the object's size accurately.

A neutral background is selected so that visual distractions do not interfere with the photograph. Depending on the size of the object a neutral background can be created by placing a piece of foam board or cloth behind the object. Wide rolls of photography paper (purchased from local photography stores) may be hung on the wall behind larger objects.

Photo flood lights are placed on both sides of the object at approximately the same height as the camera and about six to eight feet from the object. Cool burning lights specifically for studio photography are used. Nonetheless, use of any light is judicious as all light exposure can damage most objects by varying degrees. Lights are not placed in close proximity to objects, nor are they left burning when the object is not actively being shot.

Each object is photographed by itself to avoid any confusion or background interference. Lighting must be adequate and care is taken that shadows do not fall across the object. Should there be important markings on the object, more than one photograph may be necessary. Markings on the bottom or reverse of the object are also included. The object's accession number may be legibly written on an index card or similar paper tag, and displayed prominently in the photograph without interfering with the subject. This aids in identification of the object absent any writing on the photograph.

The viewfinder area is filled with the object and the focus is as sharp as possible. While some photographic errors can be reduced or corrected with digital manipulation it is better to take a good quality shot the first time.

When possible framed works are unframed prior to being photographed otherwise glare can hamper the quality of the final product. If unframing is not possible the use of polarizing screens and/or filters helps to reduce any reflection. If glare persists lighting should be moved until the glare is reduced or eliminated. When photographing a flat object from above, the camera must be secured by a tripod or strap around the neck of the photographer so that it does not fall onto the object. Use a secure tripod or keep the camera's strap around your neck at all times.

Publications

From time to time the objects in a museum's collection may appear in publications. Whether they are scholarly texts, museum catalogs, newspaper articles, museum receptions, or another form of printed media, copies of the publication are retained, and stored in the object's documentary file. If the publication is a book or other cumbersome format, a reference to the publication and note about where the book is stored in the museum should be placed in the file. Similarly, if the reference is an Internet site a note in the file listing the URL and the date it was first posted is acceptable. Because of the transient nature of the Internet, it is best to print a hard copy of the Web page showing the object and its reference. This does not apply to aggregate Web sites where large groups of objects are published, such as ArtStor or the California Digital Library, for example.

Notes

The notes section of the documentary file is meant to hold all notes, memos, and internal correspondence concerning the object. Memos written to alert staff that an object is entering or leaving the building, requests for preparation work or installation schedules should all be retained and filed in chronological order. Leaving these types of notes intact and available in the file will assist future staff who research an object's movements.

Other sections

Depending on the museum's discipline and governance there may be other types of information that is gathered and preserved in the documentary file. Natural history museums may have sections for field notes, maps, excavations, among other things; zoos and aquariums may have information on their "living collections' fish and animals" historic homes may have files relating to furniture restoration, and so on. No matter the discipline an accurate history of the museum, its collections, and the objects themselves can only be assured if the information is clearly documented and carefully preserved. The staff must keep in mind that electronic storage devices such as computers and their software programs will become outdated and the information held by them may not be accessible if it has not been kept up-to-date.

Deaccessions

Museums generally accept objects into their collections through the process of accessioning, an act of recording and processing the object and its documentation. Acceptance of any object into a museum's collection is a thoughtful process taking into consideration the benefit the museum and its visitors will enjoy, the ability of the museum to care for the object, its suitability for exhibition, its appropriateness for the collecting mission of the museum, its quality, its freedom from excessive donor restrictions, as well as all laws, guidelines, and ethical considerations. The decision often involves the staff, collection committees, boards of directors, as well as the donors. Laws regulating museums and their collections are promulgated by state and federal laws including those involving the Internal Revenue Service. Every attempt is made to accession wisely. Objects in museums validate our culture and the heritage of peoples around the world. Museum personnel take this fiduciary responsibility very seriously, realizing that public trust is sacred. Donors give objects to the museum with the expectation that the objects will be kept, cared for, and preserved for future generations to come. Museums are loathe to act in a manner that would imply that this trust is misplaced. Making a decision to permanently remove an object from the collection for any reason is therefore done in a thoughtful and well-considered manner. Museums exist to serve its public and to do so they must have the confidence of their community. Deaccessioning is related to the museum's purposes, policies, resources (staff, physical facilities, acquisition, and conservation funds), and long-term goals and is not intended to be a reflection of the particular tastes of the period or individuals involved. A decision to deaccession objects in the permanent collection should be considered not only in light of the law, but with regard to the museum's public trust.

From time to time it may be necessary to remove objects from the collection in the interest of constantly improving the collections and maintaining a high standard of esthetic quality and historical importance. Museums must retain the right to deaccession any item, however acquired, which does not meet standards which demonstrably enhance existing collections, esthetically fulfill an identifiable instructional purpose, or contribute in significant ways to an academic or research program. Deaccessioning and disposal of museum objects must be conducted in accordance with museum policy and any applicable state and federal laws. Criteria applied to deaccessioning and disposal are as stringent as those applied to the museum's acquisition process, and reflect professional standards of ethics as established by the Association of Art Museum Directors and the American Association of museums.

Regulations cover the circumstances under which an object may be deaccessioned, as well as what may be done with any funds or other proceeds realized by this process. These regulations apply to a wide variety of museum disciplines whose objects may break, wear out, or degrade to such a state as to render them useless for the museum's purposes. Living history museums often use their objects in educational demonstrations which contribute to their deterioration. Zoological collections include living mammals and fish whose remains must be removed from the museum collection at death.

Authority to deaccession

The authority to determine the disposal method lies with the museum director and the board of directors. Criteria, authority, and procedures for deaccessioning should be contained in the museum's Collections Management Policy. Legal consultation will help insure that all existing laws and regulations are satisfied by the procedures adopted by the museum and incorporated in its policy. Depending on the size and discipline of the museum, and the value of the object in question that authority may shift. In a natural history museum, where scientific specimens that have little or no market or scientific value are added and removed from the collection as a matter of course, the decision may rest with the curator or others working with the collection. In a publicly funded art museum where the object is of significant value, or a majority of the museum's collection is being considered for deaccession, the state's attorney general may be consulted to ensure that the terms of the sale are fair and reasonable and that the purpose of the organization is promoted by these actions. The greater the object's value the higher the decision-making authority must be.[5] A general guideline is that the level of authority to remove an object should be equal to or higher than the level of accessioning it.

Criteria for deaccessioning

Objects meeting certain criteria are deemed acceptable to deaccession. Such criteria include the following: the museum's inability to preserve or care properly for the object; the extent to which an object may, in the context of the collections, be redundant or a duplicate of equal or inferior quality; an infestation or other condition of an object which cannot be ameliorated that makes it dangerous to other objects in the collections; the object's lack of relationship to the museum's collections; objects below museum quality standards, either intrinsically or relatively, in comparison with objects of the same type in the collections; the existence of an object in the collections in violation of UNESCO Convention on the Means of Prohibiting and Preventing the Illicit Import, Export and Transfer of Ownership of Cultural Property; objects determined to have been missing over five years; specimens that are deceased, or the discovery that an object has been misattributed, falsely documented, and/or is considered to be a forgery (in which case the museum's records must be changed to reflect the object's rightful attribution). In some cases objects may still be useful for study purposes and can be retained; deaccessioning does not demand that an object be removed from the museum.

Verification of records

The museum must confirm clear and unrestricted title to any object being considered for deaccession. The records of donation, if any, must be consulted to ascertain that no contractual contingencies in a gift prevent a deaccession. Legal counsel may need to review the validity of any restrictions that have been placed on collection objects that may interfere with the deaccession process. No collection object that has been acquired by gift or bequest with a restriction as to its retention should be deaccessioned while said restriction remains in effect, unless the retention of the object presents a clear, physical danger to other objects in the collections or unless it is proven that the object is held in violation of the UNESCO Convention on the Means of Prohibiting and Preventing the Illicit Import, Export and Transfer of Ownership of Cultural Property.

Precatory (nonbinding) stipulations which do not impose any accompanying legal obligation are respected to the extent possible, unless modified by the donor, or if the donor is not living, the donor's heirs or legal representatives. If the object is unrestricted the museum may proceed with the deaccession. Unless stipulated in the accession documents, donor notification of deaccession procedures is not necessary. An object given to a museum without restriction becomes the museum's property to be administered as the museum sees fit. Some museums adopt a good-will policy under which the donor or surviving family may be notified of a deaccession but this is done only as a volunteer practice.

The deaccession procedure

All deaccession action must be approved by the governing authority. In areas where, in the opinion of the director or board of directors, museum staff expertise is not adequate to determine suitability for deaccessioning on the basis of authenticity or quality, outside professional advice is secured. Expert opinions may be sought from outside consultants who are acknowledged specialists in the field.

Once it has been determined that no detriment to the deaccession exists, the museum generates a written justification for the deaccession of the object in accordance with the criteria for deaccession described above. This justification generally includes an estimate of the object's current value, a recommendation for the method of disposal, and the date acquired; value at time of acquisition (if known); the source of acquisition, and stipulations, if any, detailing terms of the gift or bequest, and, if appropriate, an estimate of the amount of money that can be expected from this act. This justification and any report of the proceedings is included in the object's documentary file.

Disposal of deaccessioned objects

Deaccessioned objects may be transferred or donated to other museums or agencies as appropriate, they may be sold, donated, exchanged, or if necessary, may be destroyed.

Any sales should be conducted openly, preferably at auction. An object may be offered for donation or exchange to another museum or suitable institution for the express purpose of keeping that object available to the public. As mentioned above, in some circumstances the museum may elect to retain the object but reduce its status and subsequent level of care, to be used for educational purposes. Of course this would not be a factor where it was determined that the object had been stolen or otherwise illegally obtained, and in the case where the object was a living specimen, if it had died.

Ethical considerations in art museums demand that no employee, representative, or agent of the museum may receive any benefit, including the right to purchase any work of art removed from the collection. A conflict of interest may arise if employees may both suggest that a work of art be removed from the collection and purchase or otherwise receive that work of art once it has been removed.

As stipulated by the AAM and endorsed by the American Association of Art Museum Directors, all proceeds from the sale of works of art may be used only to acquire other works of art for the collection or to fund conservation of its collection. Ideally the museum will use the funds to purchase a similar yet superior work of art to that being removed. This considers the wishes of the donors who gave the original object to the museum. By selecting a similar work of art the intentions of the donor are presumed to attach to the newly purchased work of art. Works acquired with the proceeds of sales of donated items should, if feasible, be credited as an original gift from the donor of the work that was sold.

A recent debate in the nonprofit museum community has arisen that surrounds proceeds from the sales of collections objects that fund building projects, facilities maintenance, or other institutional operations. The 1992 code of ethics for the American Association of State and Local History offers the following guidance concerning proceeds: Collections shall not be deaccessioned or disposed off in order to provide financial support for institutional operations, facilities maintenance, or any reason other than the preservation or acquisition of collections.[6] In 1994 the AAM promulgated a revised code of ethics which contained a similar statement:

> Disposal of collections through sale, trade or research activities is solely for the advancement of the museum's mission. Proceeds from the sale of nonliving collections are to be used consistent with the established standards of the museum's discipline, but in no event shall they be used for anything other than acquisition or direct care of the collections.[7]

The definition of direct care has been left to the individual museum.

While the law has been more receptive to a broad interpretation of use of deaccession procedures, common ethical practices support the more strict understanding. A museum's mission invariably centers on the maintenance and use of its collections. When the collections are treated as assets they cannot serve the public trust. Museums facing serious financial difficulties argue that without this source of income they will shut down completely and will not be available to serve the public at all. This debate underscores the reality that laws can be enforced whereas ethical codes uphold the integrity of the profession and may be more demanding than the law.

Records of deaccession procedures

Complete and accurate records, including photographs and documentation of the circumstances of its disposal, are maintained on each object removed from the collections. At a minimum the records should include copies of the original accession documents, the museum's written justification for deaccession, any records of expert opinion, the record of disposal method and use of proceeds, and a photograph of the object. These records are kept in perpetuity but not stored with the documentary files of the current collections. The registrar adjusts the records to reflect the deaccession action.

Loan Documentation

Duty to loan

In July of 2000 the AAM wrote guidelines on exhibiting borrowed objects. An excerpt from the guidelines says this:

> Over time human societies have increasingly turned to their museum to provide a special place, a *sacred precinct*, for the display of significant objects and ideas created by human civilization. Since no museum contains or could contain, all objects worthy of admiration and understanding, museums have traditionally exhibited not only objects from their own collections but also objects from other museums and private individuals and organizations. Borrowing objects allows museums to provide more comprehensive exhibits and to make objects accessible that would otherwise be seen only by a few.[8]

Most museums have within their Collections Management Policy criteria and procedures to both make and receive loans. As educational institutions museums welcome the opportunity to exhibit objects from other areas, and to use those objects to enhance and highlight their own collections. Loan agreement forms are usually generated by the registration department and the documentation that ensues is permanently housed in that department. Like other museum documents, these records are kept in perpetuity.

The registrar's role in loan discussions centers on the objects that will be loaned. The registrar, as manager of the collection, keeps the schedule of the objects that have been selected for its own upcoming exhibitions, as well as those that are scheduled to travel to other institutions. The registrar also oversees conservation schedules and maintains environmental exposure records that indicate the maximum amount of time an object can be responsibly displayed. Decisions to loan or accept a loan are usually made by the director and curator, keeping in mind those important considerations. A registrar's records must be kept up-to-date and accurate in order to contribute to a wise decision.

Loan requests

When an object is requested for loan by another museum the registrar may request that the borrowing museum complete a Facilities Report, a standard but lengthy report that details the building construction, the environmental controls, exhibition and storage areas, the expertise of the staff and the handling, and collection practices followed by the borrower. Careful review of this document may reveal concerns surrounding the loan. Any issue the lender has with the borrowing museum or staff should be addressed and cleared up before the loan process proceeds.

In addition to the institutional practices of the borrowing museum, the lender should be concerned with the reason for the loan request and the circumstances for the exhibit. It is standard practice not to lend objects to individuals. Museums collections are maintained for the benefit of the public and it is hard to justify their exclusive use for any one individual. When museum objects are on loan they should be afforded the same standard of care and protection as when they are in their own museum environment. Private homes or offices cannot replicate the security nor the controlled atmosphere that a museum can. Additionally, tax regulations require donors to relinquish complete control over the items for which they have received a charitable contribution exemption. If donated property was lent back to the donor, even temporarily, the deduction could be called into question. Staff members of the museum, including the board and volunteers, have a duty not to receive any personal benefit from their positions. Lending museum objects to a staff member is a direct and serious violation of this ethical consideration.

Some institutions have a policy of only lending to a certain type or size of museum. Some may lend only to educational museums, some to museums within their state, some only to institutions their size or larger. Many larger museums will not consider loaning an object to another institution that has not been accredited.

Loan agreements

Once a loan has been accepted by the lending museum the registrar crafts a loan agreement with responsibilities of both lender and borrower clearly designated. Loan agreements may be written by either the borrower or lender. In some cases both institutions write an agreement to insure their particular concerns are met. In this case the registrar should carefully review each document to make sure they do not conflict with each other, nor with state regulations.

Components of the agreement include: a description of the object being lent, dates both of the arrival and return of the object and dates of the public exhibition, name of exhibition, instructions on what to do if an object is damaged, caution against cleaning or altering any work in any way, including reframing; the expected standard of care for the object, the necessity of condition reporting, who may pack and transport the object, who may handle the object at the borrowing museum, cost assignments for transportation, conservation, framing, and insurance, information on how to unpack and repack, and who insures the work in transit and on site. The lender may ask for a diagram of the gallery and layout of the show in order to check the anticipated traffic patterns. A covered vitrine, a raised pedestal, or stanchions may be requested to protect fragile objects in high density areas. Other issues that may be contained in the agreement concern who may get invited to the opening reception, courier or travel costs to be reimbursed, and any sales costs for museum catalogs or other exhibitions support materials.

Once the registrar has completed a written agreement with all the supporting information, two originals are sent and signed, each museum keeping one of the originals. Copies of the agreement may go to the director, the curator, and the business office. The original loan agreement should be kept on file in perpetuity and copies made from which to work.

Creating the loan file

The loan file is the repository of every scrap of information pertaining to the loan, from the first loan request to the object's return. A loan number may be assigned in a similar manner as are accession numbers. A commonly used system uses an alpha-numeric designation such as Outgoing Loan (OL) or Incoming Loan (IL) followed by the year in which the loan will begin plus the number of loans that have been created for that year. For example, the third outgoing loan in 2009 would bear the number OL2009.3. Depending on the database, if any, different configurations of the prefixes may be used to help sort the loan information.

Tabs attached on the exterior of the file folder contain the loan number, the exhibition dates, and the institutional name of the lender/borrower. Files are maintained in a chronological order. File cabinets should not sit directly on the floor, but be raised at least three inches to protect against any water that may accumulate on the floor during a fire or flood emergency.

Manila folders within the file will hold a variety of information depending on the museum's discipline. Common incoming loan folder contents are CONDITION REPORTS/PHOTOGRAPHY, CORRESPONDENCE, INSURANCE, LOAN AGREEMENT, NOTES, PUBLICATIONS, and SHIPPING. Outgoing loan folders may contain the same designations with the addition of FACILITY REPORT. When marking the content of the manila file it is advisable to write on the folder's tab rather than applying a gummed label which may fall off the folder as it ages and dries out.

An additional folder within in the exhibition files should be designated LOANS DENIED. Historical information on loans which have been requested from the museum but for whatever reason did not occur. Correspondence between the borrower and lender concerning the denied loan are kept here.

Condition reports: Incoming

Condition reports insure that both the borrower and lender are in full agreement on the condition of the loaned objects. While a condition report done as a matter of standard operations for collection objects aids in long-term tracking of condition, a condition report done in a loan situation protects each institution from unfounded claims of damage. Incoming loan objects should arrive at the borrowing museum with an individual condition report for each object. If there are no reports the receiving registrar should prepare them and immediately send copies to the lending museum. While it is an imposition of time and effort, the protection afforded the borrowing museum is priceless. Numerous manuals exist to aid in completing condition reports on a wide variety of materials. Consulting an appropriate form will aid the speed with which one can complete this process.

Condition reporting is best managed by a two-person team. One person reads the existing report (or writes one, if no report exists) while the other examines the object to confirm the report. Should damage to the object be discovered that is not on the report, the lending registrar should be notified. Judgment should be used to determine if the damage is slight and was just overlooked, in which case the registrar may add the observations to the report, sign and date them, or is new damage that has occurred in packing or transit. If damage to an incoming crate or container is obvious the damage should immediately be reported to the shipper, as well as to the lending registrar, preferably while the drivers are still on premises. The packing material in a damaged container should not be discarded; it may hold shards or other material necessary for the repair of the object. It can also indicate how the damaged happened, which may impact the person financially responsible for the damage.

The loan agreement contains instructions on what to do when damage is found. Under no circumstances should the borrowing museum staff attempt to unframe, clean, repair, or alter the object in any way without written permission of the lender. A telephone conversation to the lender should be followed by a fax or e-mail detailing the damage in writing along with photographs of the damage. The lender should reply, in writing, giving instructions on how to proceed. If the lender is not familiar with museum procedure (in the case of a private lender, for example) the options can be outlined to the lender so they may grant written permission, in writing, to have the repair made.

If after the object has been examined and its condition is as stated in the report, the examiner should so indicate by writing "No Change" on the report, sign and date it. It is not necessary to reiterate any damage that is already listed on the report.

When the loan period comes to an end, a second round of condition reports is completed for each object. On the original report it may again be noted "No Change" if the object is in the same condition as when the first review was done, along with the examiner's signature and date. If damage has occurred while on the borrower's premises it should be reported immediately to the lender following any instructions in the loan agreement and noting the damage on the condition report. It is helpful to include any photographs of the damaged area with the report.

Condition report: Outgoing

When sending an object to another museum, the object is carefully examined for condition. Numerous manuals exist to aid in completing condition reports on a wide variety of materials. Consulting an appropriate form will aid the speed with which the process can be completed. A photograph or rough sketch on which indicators pointing to each area of damage has been drawn, makes the report easier to understand. Any observations should be clearly written so that anyone reading the report will understand what is being conveyed. As with all condition reporting, it is easiest to accomplish using a two-person team. One person will examine the object and report verbally, while the other makes accurate notes on the report.

Should the loan be to multiple venues, and/or there are many objects in the loan, a condition report notebook should be compiled in a three-ring binder and sent along with the objects. In addition to condition reports and accompanying photographs the notebook may include any special packing or exhibiting instructions, a crate list indicating which objects are contained in each crate, and contact information for the registrar, curator, and publicity person. Packing instructions may be on paper and in an electronic format. A video of packing or assembling complicated objects can be invaluable.

Correspondence

Prior to a loan being realized there will be correspondence, generally between the borrowing and lending curators, that will contain information such as details of the exhibition, the reason for the exhibition, why certain objects are being requested, other lenders to the exhibition, and stipulations concerning the loan. All of this information is important and may answer future questions or assist in settling any disputes. These notes should be retained in the correspondence folder.

Insurance

Proof of insurance for either party should be retained in this file. Often the borrowing institution will issue a Certificate of Insurance that confirms that the borrowed objects are covered by the borrowing museum's policy. Either the borrower or the lender may choose to insure the objects. This information should be contained within the loan agreement.

Loan agreement

The original signed loan agreement should be preserved in this folder. Because it is a legal document it should remain as pristine as possible. Copies may be made and circulated to those staff members directly involved with the loan (including the development officer), however the original should remain in the file.

Notes

This section of the loan file should store any internal notes between staff referring to any meetings, schedules, requests for labor, or any similar material.

Publications

Any catalog created for an exhibition which contains references to the museum's objects should be kept as a record of the exhibition. Any exhibition opening invitations, copies of newspaper or magazine articles should also be retained. Pertinent online articles should be printed out and filed with the URL and the date accessed noted.

Shipping

Any shipping invoices, correspondence to shipping companies, bills of lading, or any documentation concerning the movement of objects pertaining to the exhibition should be stored here.

PROTECTION OF RECORDS

In addition to maintaining the information the registrar assumes responsibility for the physical safety of the files. Long-term retention is the goal; ideally the information will be readily available for the life of the museum, no matter how long that may be. Acid-free materials and folders should be used for all legal documents and records that are deemed archival. Acid-free pages should not be stored with acidic pages nor stored in acidic file folders as the acid will migrate and contaminate the acid-free materials. All pages should be free of paper clips, staples, and creases, factors that degrade paper. File labels should be written directly on the folder, not attached by a sticker that will fall off once the glue ages. The file cabinets should be stored in an environment conducive to long-term preservation. High heat and humidity conditions should be avoided. Because much of the material contained within the files may be sensitive, the files should not be accessible to the public, nor to any staff not directly involved with collections care. Storage in a locked cabinet is preferred. Staff should be reminded that the information contained in the files is confidential and should not be shared with others.

The material in the documentary files may be duplicated in part in a museum's computerized data management system. Backup procedures should be done on a regularly scheduled basis to insure that the material is up-to-date, accurate, and safely maintained. Backup records should not be stored in the same building as the computer.

A secure offsite location, known by more than one person is recommended for all backed up computer records. Unless they are on a network server that automatically stores and backs up documentation. Because data management systems constantly evolve, they are not part of the further discussion of records management.

All records must remain secure from hazards such as fire, theft, and water damage. Slower acting agents of destruction also present a hazard to the collection such as light exposure, pests, acid reactions to paper, and mishandling. Safeguards should include restricting food, drink, and smoking from record areas, nearby fire extinguishers (and the training to use them), and a system for locking and monitoring access. Managing collections is a rigorous task. Even museums with few resources can design systems to safeguard both the collections and its pertinent records.

CONCLUSION

A museum's documentary records on its objects are unique and irreplaceable assets of the organization and should be systematically collected and preserved. These records allow personnel to properly care for and access the museum's collections. Records prove ownership, describe the material in the collection, and document loans. They insure that museum collections are physically and intellectually available for collections management, interpretation, exhibition, and research. They demonstrate accountability for the collections. Today, as the public demands more accountability from those who steward objects of cultural heritage, it is more important than ever to preserve this important documentation. Governing authorities such as the AAM regulate what information a responsible museum should preserve.

Documentary records can be considered secure as long as information is entered in a timely manner, access is restricted to those working directly with the records, errors are corrected as soon as they are discovered, and the museum's standards of practice address the importance of these files and their contents.

REFERENCES

1. Buck, R. *Registrars and Registration Go Back to the Future*; American Association of Museums: Boston, MA, April 27–May 26, 2006.
2. RCAAM Operating Rules and Procedures, 1978.
3. http://www.aam-us.org/museumresources/ethics/coe.cfm.
4. Pension Protection Act of 2006, H.R. 4, section 6695A.
5. Malero, M.C. *A Legal Primer on Managing Museum Collections*; Smithsonian Books: Washington, DC, 1998.
6. American Association for State and Local History. *Statement of Professional Ethics*; 1992. Available at http://www.aaslh.org.
7. American Association of Museums. *Code of Ethics for Museums*; 1994. Available at http://www.aam-us.org/aboutaam/coe.cfm.
8. American Association of Museums. *Guidelines on Exhibiting Borrowed Objects*; 1990. Available at http://www.aam-us.org/museumresources/ethics/borrowb.cfm.

Museum Studies

Marjorie Schwarzer
Museum Studies Department, John F. Kennedy University, Berkeley, California, U.S.A.

Abstract

Defined at its most basic level, "museum studies" sometimes referred to as "museology" or "museum science" is the study of museums. Since its origins in the early 1900s, its development has been tied to ongoing discussions within associations like the American Association of Museums (AAM) and the International Council on Museums (ICOM) about how best to train those who work in professional roles in museums. Beyond its emphasis on practical training, museum studies scholarship also explores museums' cultural, political, and historical roles within society. Universities and other research institutions, like the Smithsonian and the Getty, offer a range of museum studies courses, graduate degrees, workshops, research, and publications. There is debate about how to approach the study of museums. The entry below offers discussion on these issues from a historical perspective. It largely focuses on the United States, although it should be noted that museum studies programs and scholarship exist around the world. Given the complexity of the museum field and museum studies and the number of individuals who have made contributions to its advancement, the discussion below is by no means exhaustive or complete.

INTRODUCTION

Defined at its most basic level, "museum studies" sometimes referred to as "museology" or "museum science" is the study of museums. This study, according to the Smithsonian Institution Center for Education and Museum Studies, encompasses "the ideas and issues involved in the museum profession—from the practical, day-to-day skills needed to operate a museum to theories on the societal role of museums."[1] Museum studies is interdisciplinary and is thus undertaken by individuals from a variety of backgrounds and disciplines, including, but not limited to: 1) university professors and other scholars who incorporate museums as part of their research or apply their academic discipline (e.g., Anthropology) to an understanding of various aspects of museums, 2) university faculty who teach courses to students who are pursuing academic degrees in museum studies, 3) adjunct instructors who are employed by museums or are retired professionals and teach one or two university courses on topics like museum collections management or museum ethics, 4) practitioners in museums or in independent research institutions who research and publish studies about different trends in museum practice (e.g., visitor studies), and 5) individuals who hold academic degrees and/or certificates in museum studies.

Museum studies departments are housed at a select number of universities throughout the United States and around the world, either as sections of traditional academic departments, such as a Department of Anthropology or Art History, or as stand-alone departments in Schools of Education, Liberal Arts, Library Sciences, or Continuing Education. Other museum studies departments are run by educational and research divisions of large institutions, such as the Smithsonian Institution. Typically museum studies departments offer services like workshops, conferences, publications, and reports related to museum work, research and credit courses that lead to a certificate or master's degree in museum studies. These courses cover topics such as museum history and theory; administration; marketing; collections management; education; technology; exhibition design, ethics and law; and community outreach.

A variety of organizations, ranging from professional museum associations to academic presses, publish journals and books that disseminate museum studies research. Some publications are theoretical in nature and address different philosophies on the role and meaning of the museum in society. Others take on more practical aspects of museum work such as how to design exhibitions and public programs, preserve a specific kind of fragile artifact, understand museum audiences, or measure economic viability. Still others meld theory and practice. In addition to academic journals and books, museum studies research is disseminated through trade publications and professional committee newsletters.

Despite the growing number of museum studies publications, researchers, college-level courses, and universities that offer a master's degree or certificate in museum studies, there is little agreement or cohesiveness within the field. Since the institution of the museum encompasses a staggering array of organizations, collections, disciplines, organizational structures, public services, economic models and professional practices, it follows that the field of

Encyclopedia of Library and Information Sciences, Fourth Edition DOI: 10.1081/E-ELIS4-120044038

museum studies is equally disparate. Many professionals who work in museums are not acquainted with or knowledgeable of the field of museum studies. Likewise, many museum studies scholars, researchers, and professors have limited direct work experience in museums.

Given the varied perspectives, there are lively debates about the nature, stature, and future of museum studies. These debates address issues such as: 1) standardization of curriculum and accreditation of university and other museum studies training programs; 2) the knowledge, skills, and learning outcomes that museum studies curriculum should strive for; 3) appropriate subfields of study, such as visitor studies, curatorial studies, ethics, legal issues and educational learning theory; and, of course, 4) the ever-changing nature of museums themselves. Museum studies scholars have been instrumental in framing key intellectual issues in the field including the repatriation of looted objects, the role of indigenous peoples in creating museum displays of their culture, how the design of galleries shapes the visitor's experience, and the tensions between creating entertaining blockbuster shows and more scholarly interpretations of collections.

EARLY HISTORY OF MUSEUM STUDIES

The history of museum studies is tied to the development of museums as professional workplaces, and the ongoing need for trained employees. It should be noted that although most museum practitioners and academicians agree that a museum is a professional workplace, some do not believe that museum work is a distinct profession, another contention in the debates about museum studies.[2]

Stemming from their beginnings as royal and priestly cabinets of curiosities and then private collections in Europe during the fifteenth and sixteenth centuries, early museums were eclectic, described by museum historian Edward Alexander as "individualistic and unorthodox," and subject to decisions by wealthy collectors and benefactors that were "uncertain, haphazard, and wasteful."[3] Even as museums became more accessible and thus more accountable to the public during the seventeenth and eighteenth centuries in France and England, and likewise in the nineteenth century in the United States, no attention was given to developing a coherent set of practices, or focused study of, the growing phenomenon of gathering art and natural science collections, studying, and classifying them, arranging them in publicly accessible displays, and managing their care and upkeep.

As museums grew in number, especially in major cities in the United States after the Civil War, great attention was paid to amassing collections and developing an architecture to house them that communicated grandeur. But no internal system existed for training employees to manage or care for them. Most museums were run by their founders, their founders' relatives, or other volunteers who had personal financial cushions and could forgo a salary. A high number listed their occupation as "amateur archaeologist" or "volunteer." Some doubled as benefactors, donating their own collections and inheritances to keep their museum afloat. In short, museums remained the purview of wealthy hobbyists.

In 1891, G. Browne Goode, a curator at the Smithsonian Institution, wrote the first American book to lay out ideas for the professional management and organization of museums. In *The Museums of the Future*, he opined that not just anyone could run a museum. Museums needed employees who possessed a "museum sense" meaning that they understood the unique qualities of collections, exhibitions, and public display.[4]

A collective "museum sense" was slow in coming. Professionals working in other types of scholarly and public organizations had begun to develop a collective sense of profession in the nineteenth century. Several autonomous professional associations—for example, the American Bar Association (1878), the American Historical Association (1880), and the American Library Association (1881)—were born at that time. In 1889, the first association of museum workers—the Great Britain Museums Association—was founded in York, England. It held meetings where various ideas and practices were discussed. In 1902, British museum workers published the field's first professional journal: *Museum Journal*. Those working on the other side of the Atlantic Ocean were intrigued. The Salt Lake City Museum of Utah was the first foreign museum to join the Great Britain Museums Association, and Americans began to sail to England to participate in meetings.

In 1905 at the Smithsonian Institution a group of museum workers who had been attending the meetings in England set forth a charter for an independent American museum association. The next year, in New York City, at the American Museum of Natural History, 71 individuals working in art, natural science, and history museums held the foundational conference of the American Association of Museums (AAM). Within a year, they had recruited 160 founding members (mostly curators). Their idea was straightforward. Museums, whether devoted to art, science, history, or a combination of all three, had common interests and goals. Therefore, people working within them would benefit from a formal network through which to share practices. As the Smithsonian reported: "the importance of this movement so auspiciously inaugurated cannot be overestimated, since the opportunity for interchange of views will surely stimulate the activities of museums everywhere. . ."[5]

American Association of Museums became a forum for workers (they called themselves "workers" through the 1940s, then used the term "museum people," and finally, around the late 1950s, the then-disputed term "professional") to develop their own voice, while remaining obedient to their places of work, and their patrons.[6] Scarcely anyone knew how to organize exhibits, deal with artifacts, or run museums. Scarcely any literature existed that described what a museum was and what it should do. In 1907, Frederic A. Lucas, curator of the Museums of the Brooklyn Institute of Arts and Sciences, wrote about the shortage of information and workers in an expanding field. Where could he find trained taxidermists, landscape artists, and preparators to help create exhibitions?[7] That same year, *The Nation* ran an editorial noting that despite the shortage of workers, wealthy philanthropists continued to found new museums. What was needed, the editorial suggested, was a specialized curriculum devoted to training a cadre of curators to advance the work of museums. This curriculum should include a thorough understanding of classical antiquities, as well as an understanding of how European museums operate. Around the same time, A. R. Crook, curator of the Illinois State Museum of Natural History, surveyed AAM members and synthesized their ideal qualifications needed to run a museum. His recommendations were: "a knowledge of museum history and philosophy; a grasp of exhibit techniques; skill in soliciting materials and money; good health; and the ability to handle a canoe."[8] Thus, two courses covering the fundamentals of museum work (minus the canoe) were created, one in Iowa and the other in Pennsylvania. In 1907 in Iowa City, Homer Dill, an anthropologist and taxidermist, set up a "Taxidermy and Plastic Art" teaching lab and course at the University of Iowa Museum of Natural History. His students went on to direct natural science museums in Denver, Ann Arbor, and Minneapolis. A year later in Philadelphia, Sara Yorke Stevenson, curator at the University of Pennsylvania Museum of Archeology and Anthropology and an expert on ancient Egypt, taught a course in museum work at the Pennsylvania Museum and School of Industrial Arts, now The University of the Arts.[9] Her course emphasized Greek, Roman, and Egyptian antiquities and their classification, as well as techniques for educating the public about these artifacts.

Demand for the fledgling museum training courses was high. "We cannot furnish enough graduates to supply the demand for curators and other workers," Dill reported to the AAM.[10] Yet, collectors and other prominent citizens who continued to found museums had little interest in training a workforce. Dill, Stevenson's, and others' efforts were discontinued. Throughout the next decades, seasoned museum workers remained in such scarce supply that, in its first code of ethics, AAM warned museums not to steal employees from another institution without the prior consent of the director. "A museum may not properly offer a position to an employee of another museum with which it has regular and intimate relations without having first notified the director of its intentions to do so."[11]

In the 1920s, two charitable foundations—the Carnegie Corporation and Rockefeller Family Foundations—advanced the cause of training museum workers. In face of accusations of their undue political influence on educational institutions like libraries and museums, these foundations realized the value of an autonomous organization of museum workers. In 1923, the Laura Spelman Rockefeller Memorial Foundation gave AAM its first grant which was soon followed by support from the Carnegie Corporation. This support launched five activities that helped to establish a collective "museum sense" of professional practice, laying the groundwork for many of the practices embraced today by museum studies departments. They were: 1) a code of ethics; 2) a monthly journal called *The Museum News*; 3) a partnership with the National Park Service (NPS) to establish trailside museums (nature centers) to teach visitors about flora, fauna, and geology; 4) training programs; and 5) data gathering.

American Association of Museums' 1925 code of ethics—the field's first such guidelines—emphasized the public function of museums, noting that "the life of the museum worker, whether he be a humble laborer or a responsible trustee, is essentially one of service." The code also promoted the virtues of loyalty, sincerity, tactfulness, and courtesy in the workplace, warning that "jealous acts, gossip, inquisitiveness, sarcasm, practical jokes, while often thoughtless, are always uncharitable."[12] Despite the ethical code, early issues of *The Museum News*, edited by Harold Madison, director of the Park Museum in Providence, Rhode Island, often printed gossip items. These included betrothals, summer vacations, and other life events of AAM members. However, the journal also provided short articles on new acquisitions and new kinds of educational programs offered at member museums and announcements of the availability of equipment, such as cases, shelves, collecting jars and the like. *The Museum News* offered tips for providing better public service, including the advice to let visitors touch objects when possible, perhaps the first iteration of the interactive education movement that decades later would become a serious subject of study in many museum studies departments.

The NPS trailside museum initiative was an important development because it represented the first coordinated effort between museum workers to develop a cohesive group of museums with similar styles of architecture, display, and educational interpretation. Lessons learned from establishing the first trailside museums inspired the first museum exhibition design manual, written in the late 1930s, by Ned Burns, head of the NPS Museum Division.[13]

The Carnegie Corporation, headed by Frederick Keppel, a former dean at Columbia University, directly helped to advance efforts to train museum workers. Keppel was a proponent of adult education, in vogue because of the rush of non-English speaking immigrants into American cities. Possibly influenced by the work of John Dewey who was on Columbia's faculty while Keppel was a dean there, Keppel believed that museums were ideal places to expose America's adult population to higher cultural values. Keppel began by training a museum workforce, sponsoring museum workers to travel to Europe to study the museums there. He then steered support to the first sustained museum training course in the country established in 1921 at Harvard University by Paul Joseph Sachs, son of Samuel Sachs, financier and founder of the banking firm Goldman/Sachs.

The Harvard curriculum emphasized materials, chemistry, application techniques, and new restoration technologies like x-ray equipment. Sachs' famous course "Museum Work and Museum Problems" covered not only art restoration, but museum history, philosophy, and management. He stressed that his students needed "educated eyes" in order to observe artwork closely and recognize the telltale flourishes of important artists. Sachs forged alliances between his students, the AAM (he served on its board) and the inner circles of the art world. Sachs "insisted that the museum must remain 'firmly in the control of a trained elite, [which would] maintain standards of quality independent of the contingent values of daily life.' "[14] His illustrious disciples went on to lead America's best-known art museums, including the Museum of Modern Art, the St. Louis Art Museum, and the Toledo Museum of Art.[15]

While the Harvard museum course focused on applying the values of connoisseurship to the nation's elite art museums, three contemporaneous training courses in the United States emphasized other areas of the museum field. In 1923, at the Newark Museum, Louise Connolly initiated a program that trained primarily young female apprentices in library work and museum education. Two members of the first graduating class of the Newark program—Dorothy H. Dudley, registrar at the Metropolitan Museum of Art, and Irma Bezold Wilkinson, registrar at the Museum of Modern Art—went on to write the first manual of standard techniques in collections documentation.[16] From 1926 to 1929, Laura Bragg, director of the Charleston Museum (the nation's oldest museum) worked closely with AAM to pioneer a summer course at Columbia University in New York that included an apprenticeship in Charleston. Its goal was to emphasize the community educational role of museums and, in Bragg's words, "to make clear the ideals of the modern museum and the potential scope of its activities and influence."[17] Starting in 1929, with funds from the Rockefellers, the Buffalo Museum of Science trained museum workers in the design and construction of natural science dioramas and exhibitions, including those at NPS trailside museums. This program was run by longtime AAM board member Chauncey Hamlin as well as Carlos Cummings who went on to write a classic museum text that compared world's fair displays to museum exhibitions.[18] Museum training courses were also founded in Europe and South America during this era.

As trained men and women found employment in museums, the field gathered and analyzed data to guide their work. Until the 1920s, the majority of written materials available to museum workers consisted of reams of technical information on taxidermy techniques. A perusal through AAM's 1928 *Bibliography of Museums and Museum Work* reveals only one article (by John Cotton Dana, director of the Newark Museum) discussing the value of public service. The majority of articles are on the details of taxidermy. Carnegie now began to fund research projects to cover other subjects, including the first studies of museum fatigue. From 1924 to 1928, Yale University psychology professors, Edward Stevens Robinson and Arthur Melton studied how visitors used exhibits, with an eye to creating environments and buildings that would be less tiring and more invigorating.[19] Their work influenced directors to advocate for less cluttered displays and more comfortable viewing galleries. In 1928, Carnegie underwrote the first intensive cross-comparative study of museums. Paul Marshall Rea, a former director of the Charleston Museum, studied 104 museums and compared attendance and population data for their locales. He produced a dense study with 150 pages of elaborate logarithmic calculations and suggested such innovations as branch museums (urban institutions opening branches in outlying areas) and other cost efficiencies.[20] Museum training and research programs were largely discontinued during World War II, when museums, like the rest of the nation, focused on the war effort. Yet these foundational efforts framed the importance of professional conferences and networks, publication of data and information, and training courses to advance and improve museums.

MUSEUM STUDIES IN THE SECOND HALF OF THE TWENTIETH CENTURY

After World War II, interest in training museum workers grew significantly. Through the Commission for the Protection and Salvage of Artistic and Historic Monuments (known as the "Roberts Commission" and housed at the National Gallery of Art), American museum specialists traveled to postwar Europe to assess the damage war had levied on the continent's monuments, masterworks, and archives. These specialists included Paul Sachs and many of his former students at Harvard. The Commission was named for Owen Roberts, Justice of the U.S. Supreme Court. With fresh memories of the damage World War II had wreaked on Europe's cultural landscape, museum directors from throughout the world founded international organizations like UNESCO and ICOM (International Council of Museums), dedicated to the protection and advanced public understanding of the world's cultural and education heritage. The need for training museum personnel at all levels was a significant topic of discussion, "enshrined in the basic charter setting out ICOM's role, with particular reference to the objectives of UNESCO."[21] "If we must have museums at all in the postwar world" declared Metropolitan Museum of Art director Francis Henry Taylor in 1945, then they "desperately ... need to be overhauled and reorganized. But this overhauling ... must be intellectual as well as physical."[22]

One urgent necessity was the training of personnel to manage and care for museum collections, a process that was becoming increasingly specialized. Until World War II, recordkeeping had primarily been the responsibility of curators, often referred to as "keepers," a title still used in Great Britain. As the postwar examinations made abundantly clear, museums around the world had "kept" collections, but had largely neglected to care for them.[23] Collections documentation systems had existed since the 1910s. But the first coordinated collections management and care training efforts did not begin until the second half of the twentieth century. In 1955, at the New York State Historical Association in Cooperstown, Paul Sachs' former students, Sheldon Keck and Carolyn Kohn Keck taught the first course in painting conservation. In 1959, Sheldon opened the first training program for art conservators at New York University. Other training labs were founded at the University of Delaware (1951) under the tutelage of historian Charles Montgomery and Oberlin College (1952) by conservator Richard D. Buck. Much of the impetus for delegating this work to a specialist came from the rising value of art and the increased number of traveling exhibitions.

Americans were also traveling in greater numbers, due to the postwar economic boom and greater focus on leisure time activities. Outdoor museums like Colonial Williamsburg and those run by NPS began to develop educational programs for families and produce manuals for workers in how to create these programs.

Freeman Tilden's classic guide to educational interpretation at historical sites, *Interpreting our Heritage*, was released in 1957 and is still a benchmark in the field.[24] Other museum trends, especially in exhibition design, were analyzed in the field's first independent journal, *Curator*, founded in 1958 and published by the American Museum of Natural History. In 1959, Edward Alexander, one of the twentieth century's most prolific writers on museum history, founded the Seminar for Historical Administration at Colonial Williamsburg. Like museum training programs before it, the purpose of the summer-long seminar was to address the "critical shortage of adequately trained personnel ... to staff [museums]." Alexander's curriculum included courses in museum history, educational interpretation techniques, administration, and how to conduct research.[25]

Increasing university resources and new government agencies led to a boom in new museums on campuses and in cities during the 1960s, and an expanded interest in developing resources for those wishing to work within a growing sector. The Smithsonian Center for Museum Studies was founded in 1965, along with university-based training programs including the University of Wisconsin in Milwaukee (1963), Cooperstown Graduate Program (New York, 1964), and the Museology program at the University of Leicester (United Kingdom, 1966). In 1969, ICOM's newly formed International Committee for the Training of Personnel (ICTOP) held a major symposium on the professional training needs of museum workers at the University of Leicester. Among the issues explored were the lack of recognition within universities of museology as a valid academic discipline and the need for an internationally recognized basic syllabus and training standards.[26] Under the guidance of Smithsonian specialist Nancy Fuller, the initial ICOM Basic Syllabus for graduate-level Professional Museum Training was published in 1971. The components and emphasis of this syllabus has been revised several times in the ensuing decades to assure that it reflects changes in the museum field.

During the 1970s, despite the international calls for a standardized curriculum, in the U.S. universities founded museum studies training programs to meet local and regional needs. Like the early individualistic museums, discussed above, these programs were eclectic and reflected the expertise and strengths of their founders as well as their trends in their locales. John F. Kennedy University (JFKU)'s Department of Museum Studies, founded in the San Francisco Bay Area in 1974 by Deborah Kirschman, drew on the then-unique community focus of the Oakland Museum as well as the experimental educational work of the Exploratorium, Berkeley Art Museum, and San Francisco Museum of Modern Art. The George Washington University (GWU)'s program, founded in Washington, D.C. in 1976 by a committee of professors in the Art History, Anthropology, and American Studies departments, distinguished itself in museum education, curriculum development and law, drawing on its proximity to the Smithsonian Institution. Both JFKU and GWU created professional journals to disseminate current museum research to others in the field. John F. Kennedy University's Museum Studies Journal was discontinued in 1988. Another early program was founded at New York University in 1977 by Flora Kaplan. New York University's program emphasized art history, conservation, and exposure to the diverse landscape of museums throughout New York City. University of Delaware's program (1972) emphasized history and the decorative arts; Bank Street College's program (1978) was known for embracing progressive educational techniques.

These programs, as well as others forged during the 1970s, benefited from the large increase in philosophical and practical guides to museum work. Texts published during this era addressed a range of subjects, from the expanding role of museums' education departments, to calls for accountability that were emerging from the growth in government funding, to modern architecture, to the future of museums in uncertain times (a recurring theme in the field of museum studies). They included such seminal publications as Ellis Burcaw's *Introduction to Museum Work* (1975); Barbara Newsom and Adele Silver's *The Art Museum as Educator* (1978), and Edward Alexander's history text *Museums in Motion* (1979). The growing numbers of disparate museum studies programs led to the founding of AAM's Museum Studies Curriculum Committee in 1973 (now known as the Committee on Museum Professional Training [COMPT]). Like ICTOP, COMPT members have continually argued for standards and rigor within curriculum and scholarship. As Patrick Boylan, chairman of ICTOP, noted in 1987: "There is [still] no unanimous view about the form, content or extent of training for museum staff."[26]

Museum studies changed radically during the 1990s. The popularity of cultural and postcolonial studies in universities, coupled with high-profile controversies at several museums over the content of exhibitions, led to intensive analysis of the politics, ideology, and values inherent in museums by scholars (for example, Tony Bennett, James Clifford, and Donna Haraway). With museums reeling from the Robert Mapplethorpe and *Enola Gay* scandals on one hand, and the passage of the Native American Graves Protection and Repatriation Act on the other, art historians and anthropologists posed difficult questions. What was the relationship between cultural displays and the cultural assumptions of the people who created those displays? How had the museum acquired their collections and who really owned those collections? Who was the museum really for?

Concurrently, the growth of children's museums and interactive science centers led to intensive attention to the educational theories like multiple intelligences (Howard Gardner), and constructivist learning (George Hein). With interactive displays seemingly blurring the lines between education and entertainment, academicians accused museums of "dumbing down" while educators defended their attempts create to more accessible programs. More debate ensued as government cutbacks and financial retrenchment led to increased calls for accountability, ethical decision-making, and greater attention to the museum-going public. Key texts by scholars like legal expert Stephen E. Weil and educational researchers John Falk and Lynne D. Dierking advanced the thinking in these areas. In his edited book, *The New Museology*, Peter Vergo, an art historian and theorist at England's University of Essex, published a collection of essays that aimed to open the door toward a "radical reexamination of the role of museums within society."[27] These growing and sometimes bitter debates contributed to new research and ways of thinking about the core issue that concerns museums: the improvement of museums. All of these debates were undertaken in museum studies curriculum and literature. Dissertations on museums grew in number, as did conferences, symposia, and workshops.

Toward the end of the 1990s, the spread of digital technology radically impacted museum studies. In the late 1990s, museum studies departments at JFKU, GWU, and Harvard University offered the first courses in museum studies and technology, taught respectively by Richard Rinehart, Kym Rice, and Katherine Burton Jones. This area of study has grown substantially in the last decade, with attention paid to researching how to create more accessible online databases, caring for digital assets, communicating through online social networks, developing technology in exhibitions, and so on. Another result of online technology has been the spread of distance-learning and online courses in museum studies.

Despite or perhaps because of the growth of museum studies as an area of scholarship and professional training, the debates continue. Is museum studies a subset of larger academic disciplines or is it a field in its own right, meriting a separate Ph.D.? Does museum studies curriculum really train future professionals to successfully lead museums in all of their complexity? Are there too many museum studies programs and initiatives for a relatively small sector of the nonprofit economy, or are there not enough for a creative industry that continues to found new institutions and create new initiatives?[28] Would museum studies programs benefit from industry accreditation standards, or would these standards confine a curriculum and area of study that thrives on adapting to rapid changes in the marketplace? All of these questions and others point to a robust future for the field of museum studies.

ONLINE MUSEUM STUDIES RESOURCES

American Association of Museums (AAM)—http://www.aam-us.org/

American Association for State and Local History (AASLH)—http://www.aaslh.org/

Canadian Heritage Information Network—http://www.chin.gc.ca/English/index.html

Committee on Museum Professional Training—http://www.compt-aam.org

Getty Trust—http://www.getty.edu/

International Committee for the Training of Personnel (ICTOP)—http://icom.museum/international/ictop.html

International Council of Museums (ICOM)—http://icom.museum/

National Association for Interpretation—http://www.interpnet.com/

National Park Service Museum Management Program—http://www.nps.gov/history/museum/

Smithsonian Institution Center for Education and Museum Studies—http://museumstudies.si.edu/

Visitor Studies Association—http://www.visitorstudies.org/

ACKNOWLEDGMENT

In addition to her role as chair of the Museum Studies department at John F. Kennedy University in Berkeley, California, the author has served on the board of AAM's Committee on Museum Professional Training and participated in professional colloquia about the nature and future of museum studies sponsored by organizations like the American Association of Museums, the Getty Institute, Smithsonian, and Florida State University. She acknowledges the many points of view, resources, and individuals whose perspectives she was not able to include in this entry.

A version of this text first appeared in *Riches, Rivals and Radicals: 100 Years of Museums in America* by Marjorie Schwarzer, American Association of Museums (Washington, D.C., 2006).

REFERENCES

1. http://www.museumstudies.si.edu/
2. August, R.S. So you want to start your own profession! Fable, Fulfillment or Fallacy? Museum Stud. J. Fall **1983**, *1* (2), 16–25.
3. Alexander, E. *Museums in Motion: An Introduction to the History and Function of Museums*; American Association of State and Local Histories: Nashville, TN, 1979; 239.
4. Browne Goode, G. *The Museums of the Future*; Smithsonian: Washington, DC, 1891; 445.
5. Smithsonian Institution archives, carton 007450-011, Box 34.
6. Edson, G.; Dean, D. *Handbook for Museums*; Routledge: London, U.K., 1996; 205.
7. Lucas, F.A. quoted in Museum News January **1965**, 13.
8. Cushman, K. Museum studies: The beginnings, 1900–1926. Museum Stud. J. Spring **1984**, *1* (3), 9–11.
9. Lesko, B. Sarah Yorke Stevenson, http://www.brown.edu/Research/Breaking_Ground/bios/Stevenson_Sara%20Yorke.pdf.
10. Schrimper, G.D. The University of Iowa Museum of Natural History: An historical perspective. J. Iowa Acad. Sci. **1992**, *99*, 92.
11. AAM *1925 Code of Ethics for Museum Workers*; AAM: Washington, DC, 1925; 4.
12. American Association of Museums, *Code of Ethics for Museum Workers*; AAM, Washington, DC, 1925.
13. Burns, N.J. *Field Manual for Museums*; National Park Service: Washington, DC, 1941, 63.
14. Tassel, J. Reverance for the object: Art museums in a changed world. Harvard Mag. September–October **2002**, 50.
15. Tassel, J. Reverence for the object. Harvard Mag. September/October **2002**, 48–58. 98.
16. Dudley, D.H.; Bezold, I. *Museum Registration Methods*; The American Association of Museums: Washington, DC, 1958.
17. Allen, L.A. *A Bluestocking in Charleston: The Life and Career of Laura Bragg*; University of South Carolina Press: Charleston, SC, 2001; 140–148.
18. Cummings, C.E. *East is East and West is West*; Buffalo Museum of Science: Buffalo, NY, 1940.
19. Robinson, E.S. *The Behavior of the Museum Visitor*; American Association of Museums: Washington, DC, 1928.
20. Rea, P.M. *The Museum and The Community: A Study of Social Laws and Consequences*; The Science Press: Lancaster, PA, 1932.
21. Boylan, P.J. The training of museum personnel: A major concern of ICOM and of UNESCO for forty years. Museum no. 159, **1987**, *39* (4), 225–231.
22. Taylor, F.H. *Babel's Tower: The Dilemma of the Modern Museum*; Columbia University Press: New York, 1945; *7*.
23. De Borhegyi, S. Curatorial neglect of collections. Museum News January **1965**, 35.
24. Tilden, F. *Interpreting our Heritage*; University of North Carolina Press: North Carolina, 1957.
25. Tramposch, W.J. A companion to change: The seminar for historical administration, 1959–1984. Museum Stud. J. Fall **1984**, *1* (4), 8–19.
26. Patrick J. Boylan, The training of museum personnel: a major concern of ICOM and of UNESCO for forty years. Museum, No. 159 **1987**, *39* (4), 225–231.
27. Vergo, P., Ed. *The New Museology*; Reaktion Books: London, U.K., 1989.
28. Spiess, P.D. II Museum studies: Are they doing their job? Museum News November/December **1996**, 32–40.

BIBLIOGRAPHY

1. Alexander, E.P. *Museum Masters: Their Museums and Their Influence*; American Association of State and Local History: Nashville, TN, 1983.
2. Alexander, M.; Alexander, E.P. *Museums in Motion: An Introduction to the History and Functions of Museums, 2nd Ed.; AltaMira Press: Lanham, MD, 2007.*
3. Anderson, G., Ed. *Reinventing the Museum: Historical and Contemporary Perspectives on the Paradigm Shift*; AltaMira: Walnut Creek, CA, 2004.
4. Bennett, T. *The Birth of the Museum: History, Theory, Politics*; Routledge: New York, 1995.
5. Carbonell, B.M., Ed. *Museum Studies: An Anthology of Contexts*; Blackwell Publishing: Oxford, U.K., 2004.
6. Conn, S. *Museums and American Intellectual Life, 1876–1926*; University of Chicago Press: Chicago, IL, 1998.
7. Cushman, K. Museum studies: The beginnings, 1900–1926. Museum Stud. J. Spring **1984**, *1* (3), 8–17.
8. Daedalus: Journal of the American Academy of Arts and Sciences. America's Museums, Summer **1999**.
9. Duncan, C. *Inside Public Art Museums*; Routledge: New York, 1995.
10. Genoways, H., Ed. *Museum Philosophy for the Twenty-First Century*; Alta Mira Press: Walnut Creek, CA, 2006.
11. Glaser, J.R. Museum studies in the United States: Coming a long war for a long time. Museum no. 159, **1987**, *39* (4), 268–274.
12. Karp, I.; Lavine, S.D., Eds. *Exhibiting Cultures: The Poetics and Politics of Museum Display*; Smithsonian Institution Press: Washington, DC, 1991.

13. McClellan, A., Eds. *Art and Its Publics: Museum Studies at the Millennium*; Blackwell: Malden, MA, 2003.
14. Schwarzer, M. *Riches, Rivals and Radicals: One Hundred Years of Museums in America*; American Association of Museums: Washington, DC, 2006.
15. Sherman, D.J.; Rogott, I., Eds. *Museum Culture: Histories, Discourses, Spectacles*; University of Minnesota Press: Minneapolis, MN, 1994.
16. Vergo, P., Ed. *The New Museology*; Reaktion Press: London, U.K., 1989.
17. Weil, S.E. *Making Museums Matter*; Smithsonian Institution Press: Washington DC, 2002.
18. Weisz, J.; Roxana, A. Series Ed. In *Codes of Ethics and Practice of Interest to Museums*; American Association of Museums: Washington, DC, 2000.

Museum Web Sites and Digital Collections

David Bearman
Jennifer Trant
Archives & Museum Informatics, Toronto, Ontario, Canada

Abstract

Museums adopted the Web early, building on their experience with videodisc and CD-ROM publications in the 1980s and early 1990s. From the first, they introduced experimental features including visitor feedback, three-dimensional (3D) walk-throughs, and deep coverage targeted at niche audiences. Only with the maturation of the genre did they routinely have basic hours and location information for visitors as part of their sites. Consistently, museum use of the Web has been programmatically driven, emphasizing exhibitions and events, rather than collections databases and privileging browsing over site-searching (though supporting search engines). Over the next years, museums will increase the amount of location-based content delivery and aim content at cell phones, pdas, and similar devices being carried by their potential audiences.

INTRODUCTION

The World Wide Web (the Web) has provided an easy way for museums to reach their many audiences, publishing a range of materials about their institutions and collections, and creating spaces for their varied constituents to engage with each other, and with the content of collections. Following its release in 1993[1] the Web was rapidly adopted by museums (a development traced in the proceedings of the Museums and the Web conferences (1997–). Today, 15 years after its release, having a Web site is considered a necessity by museums. This rapid adoption of the Web by museums reflects the fit between museum needs for widespread dissemination of multimedia content and the ease with which the functionality embodied in the Web supports programmatic needs.

Museums care for information as much as they care for collections. The Web enabled relatively easy publication of complex documents, richly illustrated in color (something that the economics of print publication was making more and more difficult). The broad reach of the Web enables contact with both local constituencies, and international networks of potential tourist visitors and subject-specialist scholars. Broadcast of basic information about the institution (such as location, hours, and exhibition program) and narrow-cast of in-depth information for particular audiences (such as teacher-packets and interpretive programs for schoolchildren) are enabled by the same technology.

Museums were well positioned to take advantage of the Web through early experiments in multimedia. They remain leaders in the use of social computing technologies, because of the true fit between these tools and the desire to engage communities—based in part on the new museology.[2]

HISTORY OF MUSEUMS ON THE WEB

Background

Museum adoption of the Web in the mid-1990s built on a decade of museum experiences with hypertext, networking, and multimedia. By 1993, museums were widely exploiting stand-alone interactive image and text on kiosks within the museum, often using videodisc or CD storage.[3] While these technologies enabled distribution outside the museum on fixed digital media, the reach of these publications was extremely limited when compared to the near ubiquity that the network now provides. Authoring tools were proprietary and often difficult to use, and run-time environments were closely prescribed and often hardware-based.

Museum networking on private, proprietary connections had been available in the 1970s, and national networks (such as the Canadian Heritage Information Network) and regional ones (such as the Museum Computer Network GRIPHOS application), had been built. But prior to the Web, networking databases was expensive, limited to text only, and for institutional rather than public needs; early French experiments with public access to Minitel reached out more broadly. Immediately prior to the advent of the Web, in the late 1980s and early 1990s, open protocols developed for access to (predominantly text) files over the Internet—such as archie [for ftp] and gopher for files—were experimentally employed by some museums. The most radical aspect of the Web was that it enabled true multimedia. While initially only text and image, for a community that had struggled with side-by-side monitors for text and image videodisc display, and hardware-dependent CD-Rom authoring, this was a major breakthrough.

Encyclopedia of Library and Information Sciences, Fourth Edition DOI: 10.1081/E-ELIS4-120043512

Early Cultural Web Experiments

Most museum technology professionals were probably introduced to the possibility of networked access to cultural heritage information by the Library of Congress' exhibit of *Treasures from the Vatican* which was delivered over the Internet[4] from January to April 1993, even before European Organization for Nuclear Research (CERN) board decided to make the World Wide Web publicly available, using the alpha release of the first popular Web browser, Mosaic.[5] A few might even have seen the exhibit of Soviet materials released in the previous year, before any inkling of the Web had spread beyond CERN. Outside of academia, uptake was only slightly slower. The French Ministry of Culture site on the Lascaux caves, which first appeared late in 1994 played an important role in alerting generalists to the benefits of publishing cultural content on the Web.[6]

Some museums in the academic sphere were introduced to the Web before commercial browsers made their debut in late 1994. Teaching and research collections took the lead by implementing Web access to their existing databases. As early as August 1993, the University of Illinois's Krannert Art Museum launched a hypermedia exhibit on the Web; the University of California at Berkeley, Museum of Paleontology had a site underway by September which by year-end included a walk-through of the Dinosaur halls and an interactive guest book. The University of Virginia Rosetti Archive had launched an experimental Web site with digital collections, exhibits, and educational materials by the spring of 1994. The Perseus Project, a digital library that was under development since the spring of 1987, was quick to try out Web-based access methods.[7] These early scholarly initiatives pointed out a new audience for museum collections content. In January 1994, the Exploratorium became the first nonacademic museum site on the World Wide Web.

However, the Web was not seen as the only viable solution to networked access to linked image and text for a few years. In late 1994, when the Getty Museum Educational Site Licensing Project launched its competition for University participation in a museum image sharing project, one element in evaluation was whether the participants had the capacity to develop applications to deliver networked multimedia. Several contenders had existing, non-Web, applications that were in experimental use, and were selected in part based on that. However, by the time the first MESL applications appeared a year later, all but one of the Universities employed Web protocols rather than the special solutions each had been expected to have to create to deliver multimedia over the Internet.[8]

Early Museum Web sites

It is tempting to paint a path from simple to complex museum Web site–from brochure, to exhibit, to shop, to online collection, to social network, to semantic Web—but the history of museum use of the Web is not linear. Many museums first saw the Web as an experimental space in which they could develop hypermedia and test very demanding digital delivery scenarios. It was only with the broad public popularity of the Web that museums came to realize that their sites ought to include basic "brochure" information.

It is still surprising to many that the first sites built by museums often lacked such fundamental elements as museum hours (and especially location information), and that some of the earliest museum Web sites included collections, exhibitions, educational interactives, and even what we would now think of as social networking features.

The citation given by GNN (The Global Network Navigator) in 1994 to the Paleontology Server at The University of California Museum of Paleontology[9] read:

> The server is an interactive natural history museum available over the Internet. This museum without walls is well organized and makes interesting use of large graphics. You can learn about phylogeny, the "Tree of Life," or examine photographs of Great White Sharks off the California coast, which proves that paleontologists study living things as well as fossils.

Other early adopters included the Museum of Natural History, London[10]; the Science Museum, London; and the Canadian Museum of Civilization.

MUSEUM PROGRAMS ONLINE

Web pages of museums have evolved to reflect the range of museum programming. An informational core, which presented the museums' physical reality in cyberspace, soon formed the required "brochure."[11] The basic elements of a museum Web site included information about the museum, location, maps and admissions, details of exhibits and current events such as tours, a profile of the collections, possibly with some highlights, perhaps some detail about the institution's history, a welcome from the director, information about museum membership and giving to the museum, facilities rental, and the museum store. Extended features often centered around special exhibitions, and then were "archived." Education materials, for teachers could be exhibition related, or related to the permanent collection. If this sounds like a reiteration of the physical museum, in many ways it was. Each department found its place on the Web, and early museum sites often reflected the concerns of their internal leads.[12]

Online Museum Exhibitions

As with the physical site, most museums' preferred way to display their collections online has proven to be as part of an online exhibition. The fundamental advantage of the Web is that it offers opportunities for additional content and broader audiences. From the first, exhibitions were about more than simply showing museum objects with juxtaposed text; the object was to create an experience in multiple sensory dimensions, not unlike that of entering a real-world exhibit. In early 1994, when "fast" Web access meant someone was using a 14.4 mbps modem, the Smithsonian's "The White House Collection of American Crafts," (which opened on the Web on April 25, 1994), included extensive video and audio clips of the curator talking about selected pieces and handling them in ways that would not be possible during the exhibition.[13] In addition, each artist was asked to answer a series of questions about their work, which was not part of the exhibition itself. An important element of the exhibit, novel at the time, was what we would now think of as a "social networking" feature that allowed visitors to add comments to a comment book.[14]

In 1995, the Museum of Modern Art, New York (MOMA) was developing online exhibitions to accompany many of its physical shows. Like many museums, it still lacked an infrastructure to support its online activity so sites for "Annette Messager," "Video Spaces: Eight Installations," and "Mutant Materials in Contemporary Design" were hosted for MOMA by the School of Visual Arts.[15]

Within a short time, museums developed a range of interpretive materials to augment online exhibits. These were often aimed at specific niche audiences, such as games for children, pre- and post-visit guides for families, learning packages for teachers, and extensive scholarly research pathways, and have become a standard way both to market the in-house show and to extend its useful lifetime. Most museums today will have an online surrogate or augmentation of current exhibitions on their sites. In addition, many will provide access to past exhibits, which of course are no longer accessible in the physical world, even if they are not truly serving a guaranteed, permanent archival function.

Substantial research has been undertaken on storytelling and narrative presentation online in support of museum exhibitions. But museums are aware that their efforts are often subverted by the fact that their visitors do not "enter by the front door" and read the linear script as written by curators, but rather reach the museum by search engines taking them deep into the interpretive narration.[16]

Online Events

Museums have found the low cost of entry to broadcasting over the Internet highly attractive, in part because of their interactive capability (though the facility for narrow-casting provided by Web-based programs is equally important). Using the network to bridge geography is a common strategy, whether this is the virtual reuniting of a dispersed work, or the creation of a real-time multipoint event. As an example of the latter integrated into a museum's educational program, from February 11–21, 1997, the Exploratorium site provided live interactions with astronauts servicing the Hubble Space Mission. In two shows daily, they combined live feeds from the orbiting shuttle, science demonstrations, videoconferencing with researchers across the country, and questions from the audience.[17] Since then, at the Exploratorium and many other science museums worldwide, regular interactions between scientists and school children via Webcasting, have become standard features of museum programming. At the Natural History Museum (London) these Web-based features now occur daily.[18]

Social Experiences

Museums envision themselves as gathering places designed to encourage thinking, generate dialogue, and occasionally create controversy. So the social potential of the Web was seen as crucial to its museum implementations long before the mainstream invented the rubrics Web 2.0 and social computing. Partnerships with schools were the first territory explored by museums, and this rapidly led to the teachers, and then the students, contributing content back to the museum.[19] Applications that enabled visitors to provide their views followed swiftly.[20]

By 1997, museums were inventing mechanisms for user feedback missing from the Web at large. Web designers for the Smithsonian Institution's *Revealing Things* exhibit envisaged users as both "designers of their personal exhibits" and "contributing objects and stories to the presentation... chang(ing) the experience for themselves and others."[21]

Early observers recognized that user-generated (or user-contributed) content and the interaction of the Web would challenge the authority of museums. Some celebrated that,[22,23] while others were concerned. The resulting dialogue clarified the differences between authority and authenticity and helped museums position themselves vis-à-vis their varied publics.[24]

Some museums, led by the National Museum of the American Indian in Washington and Te Papa in New Zealand—two national institutions that were first opened during the "Web-Age," began to construct architectures that enabled them systematically to obtain and use the insights of indigenous informants to bring a perspective from within the societies that originally created artifacts to bear on museum documentation.[25] The Encyclopedia of New Zealand encourages and incorporates user-contributed content.[26]

Because one of the problems museums face is that of describing the objects in their collections, and providing access to them in ways that visitors find useful, engaging volunteer catalogers over the Internet was explored in the 1990s. In the MESL project, the Fowler Museum's experience of obtaining remote assistance in describing part of its African collection from Columbia University was held up as a justification for the effort involve in putting collections online.[27] The Fine Arts Museum of San Francisco had early success with volunteer keywording of its Thinker database.[28,29] But action came with the success of social tagging at del.icio.us and flickr in 2004. Organized investigation of the potential for folksonomy in the steve. museum project[30,31] coincided with implementations of nonresearch taggers, the most extensive of which is at the Powerhouse Museum in Sydney.[32] Early findings are that many people find it rewarding to tag, and will generously give their time to museums if asked. The resulting tags are mostly relevant and not terms that the museums have in their own documentation.[33,34]

Museums have also been attracted by the engaging power of serious games, especially as a means of attracting and keeping the attention of younger audiences and people who might be alienated by more traditional methods of teaching. An excellent example, Launchball at the Science Museum of London, winner of several "best of the Web" awards in 2008, including one at the South by Southwest Interactive Festival.[35] Similarly, the power of providing visitors with sophisticated tools with which to construct their own meanings and publish them to the Web, has been successfully used by museums to engage visitors, as with the film editing widget at the American image exhibit of the Maxwell Museum of Anthropology.[36]

Museums are also finding that they can meet potential audiences in engaging social spaces created by others, including commercial services. Social computing spaces such as FaceBook, Flickr, and YouTube are attracting museum attention and programming.[37–39]

Virtual Experiences

Museum exhibitions are three-dimensional (3D) installations designed to offer context to objects so that they may be better understood. It is not surprising, then, that efforts to create 3D environments on the Web attracted museum interest from the first. In 1993, the University of California Berkeley Museum of Paleontology demonstrated the potential of exhibition walk-throughs. By 1997, museums were regularly providing remote visitors with 3D experiences over the Web—both walk-throughs of spaces, and 3D models of artifacts.[40,41] Quickly, though, the community realized that we didn't need elevators in Web museums; the logical models of museum information-space were more effective when they didn't mirror the architecture—and historic organic growth—of physical museum spaces.

Early reports featured natural history educators using 3D modeling to teach morphology, registrars providing information to potential researchers prior to shipping a fragile item, and school teachers exciting students into careful observation. Reconstructions also tested historical hypotheses.[42] The Science Museum in Milan provided remote 3D access to "working" models of Leonardo Da Vinci's inventions, including those never built in the real world, in 1999, and allowed avatars representing individuals logged in from remote locations to "join" each other in an experience[43,44] similar to that museums are now exploring virtual worlds such as Second Life.[45]

Museums have also successfully used the Web to offer a window onto otherwise "back-room" museum processes. Projects like those that chronicled the lengthy conservation of works of art at the Minneapolis Institute of Arts[46] helped museums demystify some of their professional processes.

Some museums (along with universities, governments, and many other institutions) have taken up a virtual presence in these virtual worlds today. Often, they have done so, like the Exploratorium, explicitly in order to provide experiences that are not possible in the physical world, such as experiencing Brownian motion by riding on a dust particle.[47] Others are content to see virtual worlds as useful because avatars provide an emotional extension of humans into the virtual world and thereby enhance interpersonal communication that might otherwise occur through online chatting or bulletin boards alone.

Evaluators are still trying to determine when these kinds of experiences were necessary, and when they might be simply entertaining, or even distracting. Investigation about how to bridge the physical space of the museum and the virtual space of the Web is ongoing.[48] Findings have often seemed counterintuitive; for example, after years of experimentation, museums have discovered that bookmarking, per se, is not something that visitors do at museums, though museum professional repeatedly hypothesized that it would be a highly rewarding application.[49]

Searchable Collections

Although "virtual collections" and "digital museums" are concepts that are often associated with museum use of the Web, they have their roots, and their primary appeal, outside of the museum culture, in broader society and in academia. Many early "virtual museums" such as the Virtual Louvre or the Artchive, were creations of individual enthusiasts rather than institutions.

Online catalogs have not been the primary goal of museums on the Web, in direct contrast to libraries, who have seen the OPAC as the first point of contact with their online public. Some institutions with close academic ties, particularly if their collections were assembled for research or teaching, made their collections catalog searchable on the Web early. For example, the American Museum of Natural History had its Library catalog online in 1996.[50] The Fine Arts Museums of San Francisco (FAMSF)—an early adopter of digital imaging technology—had over 65,000 works online for viewing at its "Thinker" site in 1996,[51] and encouraged its Web visitors to "be the curator!"

The FAMSF site included teachers' guides and online tours of temporary exhibitions as well.

Museum collections catalogs are difficult for the nonspecialist to interpret and are often better suited for expert use. These text databases often only include rudimentary data often without any images, or with only one relatively low-resolution image. Because the primary audiences museums wish to reach through the Web are not only "researchers" but potential visitors, additional contextual and interpretive materials have priority.[52] One approach to making the museum catalog more accessible has been to link it to familiar interfaces. Integrating museum databases with other sources of information, especially to enable graphical displays that are intuitive to end users, was a desire of museums before the Web and suggested as an early objective of Web implementations;[53] with the advent of Ajax and techniques for Web mashups, integrating museum data with data and tools from other sites, there have been successful implementations in museums. By dragging multiple images from the public sources on the Web, researchers have been able to recreate 3D renderings of historical sites as if they were flying through them.[54] Many "museum-like" applications, such as the mashup (combination) of ornithology data with map coordinates, have emanated from university laboratories.[55]

Still in its infancy, but growing quickly, geo-encoding of museum collections enlists the potential of location-aware information delivery based on open APIs (Application Programming Interfaces) to put museum objects where the audience is physically, rather than expecting the audience to come to the museum. By geo-encoding the locations of important events in the life of an object into its digital record, museums use the same Web-based infrastructure that is evolving to tell people in passing cars about local restaurants and other commercial offerings, to inform them about the cultural artifacts that are native to the area in which they find themselves, even if these are in museum collections thousands of miles away. This has potentially revolutionary consequences for how people relate to the spaces in which they live, and for museums it has the capacity to "turn the museum inside out" and show its collections in the contexts in which they were made, used, or collected.[56]

Collecting and Preserving

Museums, particularly art museums that have contemporary culture as part of their collecting mission, or those that are dedicated to understanding contemporary events, such as science centers, face a special challenge since they not only need to use digital methods to provide the public with access to their collections, but also are challenged to collect and exhibit digital works.

Art museums, self-consciously collecting *avant garde* digital art, were the first to encounter the challenges of exhibiting and preserving born-digital collections.[14,57,58] Some early examples, such as "Gallery 9" as of December 1998, can still be seen at the Internet Archive.[59]

Increasingly science museums and even history museums are being challenged to collect digital artifacts as these artifacts have an impact on everyday life. A community museum, might, for example, have to collect digital artifacts in order to document community involvement in a planning process conducted using environmental impact mapping in a collaborative Web space.[60] This process, conducted over many months, relied on visualization tools, models, and data that were specific to the community, and logged hundreds of citizens participating in the discussion and illustrating their points by digitally generating representations of different possible futures. Science museums which are experimenting with making science news feeds a part of their on-site exhibition, such as the Minnesota "Science Buzz" project, or which are creating opportunities for visitor feedback by cell phone as at the Liberty Science center, will need to consider just what place an archival record of these interactions has in documenting the museum programs.

Ongoing digitization programs are retrospectively creating digital versions of photographic surrogates kept by museums for identification and documentation purposes. But while in libraries retrospective digitization is sometimes cast in terms of preservation (for the digital copy holds the same informational content as the original), in museums digital surrogates will never take the place of original museum artifacts. Although digitization projects in museums are primarily about access they have spin-off preservation benefits by reducing the impact of repeated handling for reference purposes, and have, unfortunately, also sometimes left us with the only copies of works once in museums but lost through war or natural disaster.

IMPACT ON MUSEUMS

In its brief 15-year history, the World Wide Web has already had significant impact on museums as institutions.

Sectoral Identity: The Museum Domain

At MW97, Cary Karp proposed that museums ought to have a place in the Internet domain name system.[61] By 2000, he had led ICOM and the J. Paul Getty Trust in an effort to obtain a high level domain for museums in the belief that high level domains would proliferate and that a distinctive one for museums would serve their needs to be recognizable in Web space.[62,63] Although widely publicized in the museum community, the new top level domains have not had the impact socially that was expected in 2000. Museums, which generally maintained their identities in "dot org" or "dot edu" space, have not made the switch to "dot museum" in appreciable numbers. At present it seems unlikely that they will because newer top level domains, introduced after the national domains and the three original ones for commerce, civil organizations, and education, have not captured the popular imagination in other sectors either.

Outreach

Though the distinction of museums as high level domains did not enhance their sectoral visibility, Web technologies are being deployed successfully to raise the profile of individual institutions and their programs. Many museums are using RSS (really simple syndication) to narrowcast the contents of their sites to those with specific interests in their topic. By tagging their content with a variety of highly specific descriptors, and using RSS to distribute a feed of news items, they enable aggregation and representation of museum content in diverse contexts. The 24 hr museum, now culture 24, aggregates news about U. K. museum activities, and presents it as an integrated museum-related RSS feed.[64] RSS has also been used to create content streams that are used to animate museum exhibition environments.[65,66]

Some museums are encouraging viral marketing[67] in order to build mini-communities of interest around particular parts of their content. Museums are actively engaged in blogging, podcasting, and even in posting videos to YouTube. And the "fans" of museums on social sites such as Facebook, are being used to promote its activities to their friends.

Like other institutions influenced by academia and libraries, museums were caught off-guard by the overwhelming success of search engines. By 1997, reports already revealed that while museums were expending much energy in authoring visually and intellectually enticing sites, their content was organized narratively and linearly while most of their users were finding specific content in searches and then linking directly into the museum site at the level of that content. Museums have responded to their users "entering by the window rather than the front door" in several different ways. Some museums have taken great care to be fully available to search engines—hiring Search Engine Optimization (SEO) consultants, inviting crawlers, making metadata for the search engines to use, identifying resources with URIs and other digital identifiers, and attending to the requirement for persistent addressing. Others have become engaged with libraries and universities promoting the use of the Open Archive Initiative (OAI) protocols for harvesting museum collections data. The Consortium for Computer Interchange of Museum Information (CIMI) led a well-publicized effort to adopt OAI for museums, but the limitations of the Dublin Core metadata framework essentially defeated this effort, despite funded attempts to overcome them.[68]

Some museums are watching carefully to see how the Semantic Web evolves and what kinds of discovery can be provided by geo-aware methods. When museums were first introduced to the semantic Web in 2002, the excitement level was high[69,70] however as these technologies evolved and it became clearer that semantic Web accessibility of collections depended not just on metadata but on quite sophisticated metadata expressed in Resource Description Framework (RDF) with a defined ontology, the enthusiasm gave way, outside academic circles, to watching and waiting.[71] In 2008, with the launch of some more sophisticated toolsets demonstrating the potential of semantic Web approaches, some cautious renewed interest is being expressed, but as always the barriers to museum making their collections available in this way are that they lack the resources and often the knowledge of their collections, to create the necessary metadata. Meanwhile, geo-aware devices in phones and automobiles, and an array of services that might be built upon these, are attracting significant attention in museums whose collections were gathered from locations around the globe and can often be best interpreted in those contexts, if they could be discovered there by tourists or locals.

Staffing and Resource Allocation

The Web has created new opportunities for museums to reach their audiences and conduct their missions, but it did so at a cost. In effect, each museum has now opened another branch. While early museum Web sites were often projects of one or two dedicated people (or even unauthorized "skunkworks"), increasingly museums have learned that their Web presence requires all the manpower and programming attention of a second venue.[72]

Maintaining a quality Web site makes both technical and program content demands on the museum. Staff throughout the institution become responsible for updating the public face of their departments and programs as represented on the Web. Data that was created for internal purposes needs to be revisited and repurposed for public access. As information is created digitally for use in-house, on the museum Web site, in virtual exhibits and in syndicated content for "cultural events" sites and ticketing agents, the need to manage digital objects that can be reused for a variety of purposes increases. The technical sophistication demanded by such reuses has led museums to implement Digital Asset Management and Digital Rights Management systems in addition to traditional Collections Management Systems that keep track of the physical collection of the museum.

User expectations based on the evolution of nonmuseum Web experiences impinge on acceptance of the museum product and force the museum to continuously upgrade its capabilities and offerings. And requirements imposed by governments, for example to provide accessibility to those with physical handicaps, now extend to online visitors.

Museums face the challenge of retaining skilled staff. In a project-driven culture, where much work is often outsourced developing institutional capacity is an issue. Many museums don't have programming staff on site and so are stretched to take full advantage of the potential of the Web.

Even maintenance becomes a great challenge, since the Web imposes a constantly changing technical requirement on the museum. Information technologies within the institution and servers providing access to the outside world must be maintained. Specialist staff must learn about online education, online fundraising, online publication, and other online programming skills. Technical standards that were optional for institutions without interconnections become mandatory. And in-service education becomes necessary. Ongoing venues for professional development include annual conferences such as Museums and the Web, the meetings and listservs of organizations such as the Museum Computer Group (United Kingdom) and the Museum Computer Network (USA), the Association of Science and Technology Centers, The Visitor Studies Association, and to some extent the work of the International Council of Museums' Committees on Documentation (ICOM/CIDOC) and Visual Information (ICOM/AVICOM). Emerging online communities of professionals include ExhibitFiles.org and conference.archimuse.com.

Business Models

In the early days of the Web, museums and other social institutions, wondered if it had income potential, and if so whether they wanted to exploit that source. Quite a few museums were caught up in the early widespread notion that the Web might be a source of significant new income. Museums lived through the dot.com boom and bust; while only a few (notably the Museum of Fine Arts Boston, museum shop[73]) succeeded in making money from it, none went out of business as a consequence. However, some museums joined high-profile consortia with universities to provide online education, and these did collapse in the bust of 2001. Since then few museums have made online commerce a priority. However, most museum Web sites have e-commerce functionality (often delivered by an outside provider) to support basic store purchases, membership sales, and occasionally online ticketing. Although advertising emerged as a means of making income from the Web in the early twenty-first century, other than a few high-profile sponsorship relationships (such as British Telecom and Tate) museums have not introduced advertising on their sites. For the present, anyway, museums are treating the Web as a service to be provided for free and without commercial advertising, even when they charge for access to the physical museum and actively solicit sponsorship for on-site exhibitions.

Outside the museum community, museums are perceived to be making money from the sale of rights and reproductions; however, far from being a major source of new income, online licensing has become a cost-center for most museums.[74,75]As well as requiring costly research in order to discover the rights inherent in collections, museums often pay fees to use materials online themselves. Efforts to make the works available under Creative Commons licenses or free to scholars have not proved very attractive to museum administrators, who, unlike their counterparts in libraries, have historically incurred high costs in making images available and recovered some of that cost through fees. Experiments with access for noncommercial uses at the Victoria & Albert Museum and The Metropolitan Museum of Art are, however, ongoing. The Creative Commons was not flexible in offering museums a license that worked for them, until the CC+ license of 2008, which some museums may now be ready to consider.

In 1997 more than 30 high-profile art museums joined to form the Art Museum Image Consortium (AMICO). The purpose of AMICO was not to earn income for the museums, though it developed a successful licensing scheme that ultimately recovered its costs of rights clearance (which are quite high for art of the past century), but to find a way to serve university and school students high-quality digital reproductions by reducing transaction costs.[75,76] Its success attracted the Mellon Foundation which launched ArtStor, a program with similar objectives which subsequently absorbed AMICO and now licenses a collection of art reproductions (much not sourced from museums) to higher education.

Despite these experiments, museums have generally not followed either the commercialization route or the licensing route. The trend is toward more open access, with mission-related goals of accessibility and education guiding museums to make content available on the Web without restrictions, but within the context of museum programming rather than as discrete objects in searchable databases.

Issues Facing Museums Online

From the first, museums have been concerned that their move of programming to the Web increase opportunities for participation. Early implementations were highly sensitive to average slow access speeds and low resolution monitors, and present implementations avoid proprietary tools. The Digital Divide continues to echo in museum discussions. As public institutions museums don't want their choice of delivery channel to exclude users.

Using the Web in a socially responsible way has led museums to open themselves up to challenges to their ownership of objects in their collections (creating, for example, avenues that can be used by those claiming they benefited from Nazi war loot), their interpretation of objects in their collections (enabling alternative accounts from aboriginal communities for instance) and ensuring accessibility.

Finally, museums are beginning to alter their measures of success. Instead of counting "visitors" to the museum itself, or to its Web sites, some museums are beginning to find ways to measure their audiences or impact even when the content of the museum is seen or used somewhere other than the museum site.[77] It is likely that syndication of content on other nonmuseum sites, as the Library of Congress and Powerhouse Museum are now experimentally doing with photographs from its collections in the Flickr Commons,[78] will become a growing trend. Museums are slowly ceding control of their content in order to reach audiences through as many channels as possible.

CONCLUSIONS

Museums have long used new media technologies, be they murals, dioramas, films, or interactive Web pages, to help explain the complexities of their collections to many diverse audiences. They publish a wide range of materials, from printed ephemera (in-gallery hand-outs) to scholarly tomes (exhibition catalogs), in a wide range of formats. From its outset, the Web has proven a suitable platform for delivering many types of information to many different users, and museums have adopted its many potentials. As the Web interpenetrates real space, with portable, geo-aware devices like the iPhone™, museums will find that it continues to serve their goals: engaging communities with collections and encouraging active learning and participation.

REFERENCES

1. Connolly, D. A little history of the World Wide Web. 2000. http://www.w3.org/History.html (accessed April 29, 2008).
2. Vergo, P., Ed. *The New Museology*; Reaktion Books: London, U.K., 1989.
3. Bearman, D. Museum interactives. Arch. Museum Info. **1993**, *7* (2), 6.
4. Library of Congress. Rome reborn: The Vatican library & renaissance culture. 1993 [2002] http://www.loc.gov/exhibits/vatican/.
5. Bearman, D. Exhibits on the Internet. Arch. Museum Info. **1993**, *7* (1), 8.
6. [editor]. Out of the caves. In The Washington Post; January 28, **1995**; A 14.
7. Crane, G. The Perseus project and beyond: How building a digital library challenges the humanities and technology. D-Lib Magazine January **1998**. http://www.dlib.org/dlib/january98/01crane.html (accessed April 28, 2008).
8. Trant, J. The museum educational site licensing project. Spectra, J. Museum Comput. Network **1995**, *22*, (Winter 1994–1995), 19–21. http://www.archimuse.com/papers/jt.mesl.spectra9502.
9. University of California Museum of Paleontology. Awards and reviews of the University of California Museum of Paleontology Website. 2001, July 30, 2001 http://www.ucmp.berkeley.edu/museum/reviews.html (accessed June 17, 2008).
10. T1 Rex: Street Cred. Wired **1999**, *7*(3). http://www.wired.com/wired/archive/7.03/streetcred_pr.html.
11. Garzotto, F.; Discenza, A. Design patterns for museum Web Sites. In *Museums and the Web 1999: Proceedings*, Bearman, D., Trant, J., Eds.; New Orleans, LA, 1999. http://www.archimuse.com/mw99/papers/discenza/discenza.html (accessed June 15, 2008).
12. Bearman, D.; Trant, J. Survey of museum Web implementations, 2005. Arch. Museum Info. **2006**. http://www.archimuse.com/research/mwbenchmarks/report/mwbenchmarks 2005.html (accessed January 31, 2008).
13. National Museum of American Art. In *"The White House Collection of American Crafts" and Exhibit*; 1994. http://web.archive.org/web/19980130054030/http://nmaa-ryder.si.edu/whc/invirtutourmainpage.html (accessed October 14, 2008).
14. Dietz, S. Curating on the Web: The museum in an interface culture. In *Museums and the Web 1998: Proceedings*; Bearman, D.; Trant, J., Eds.; Toronto, ON, Canada, 1998. http://www.archimuse.com/mw98/papers/dietz/dietz_curatingtheweb.html (accessed June 15, 2008).
15. Museum of Modern Art, N. Y. 1996, November 11, 1996, http://web.archive.org/web/19961111103911/www.moma.org/webprojects.html.
16. Nordbotten, J. Entering through the side door—a usage analysis of Web presentations. In *Museums and the Web 2000: Proceedings*; Bearman, D.; Trant, J., Eds.; Archives & Museum Informatics: Minneapolis, MN, 2000.
17. Exploratorium, T. Hubble Servicing Mission: Looking Beyond Boundaries; 1997. August 17, 2000 [archive date].
18. Natural History Museum, L. Nature live online: Live Webcast. 2008. http://www.nhm.ac.uk/nature-online/nature-live/live-webcast/live-webcast.html (accessed April 30, 2008).
19. McKenzie, J. Building a virtual museum community. In *Museums and the Web 1997: Proceedings*; Bearman, D., Trant, J., Eds.; Los Angeles, CA, 1997. http://fromnowon.org/museum/museweb.html (accessed June 15, 2008).
20. Glasser, S. New ideas/new audiences. In *Museums and the Web 1997: Proceedings*; Bearman, D., Trant, J., Eds.; Los Angeles, CA, 1997. http://www.archimuse.com/mw97/speak/glasser.htm (accessed June 15, 2008).
21. Gradwohl, J. Revealing things: An experiment in museum Web Sites. In *Museums and the Web 1997: Proceedings*; Bearman, D., Trant, J., Eds.; Los Angeles, CA, 1997.
22. Walsh, P. The Web and the unassailable voice. In *Museums and the Web 1997: Proceedings*; Bearman, D., Trant, J., Eds.; Los Angeles, CA, 1997. http://www.archimuse.com/mw97/speak/walsh.htm (accessed June 15, 2008).
23. Smith, A. The museum as a forum for the nation. In *Museums and the Web 1998: Proceedings*; Bearman, D., Trant, J., Eds.; Toronto, Ontario, Canada, 1998. http://

www.archimuse.com/mw98/papers/smith_a/smith_a_paper.html (accessed June 15, 2008).

24. Bearman, D.; Trant, J. Authenticity of digital resources: Towards a statement of requirements in the research process. D-Lib Magazine June **1998**. http://www.dlib/org/dlib/june98/06/bearman.html (accessed April 28, 2008).
25. Witcomb, A. The end of the Mausoleum: Museums in the age of electronic communication. In *Museums and the Web 1997: Proceedings*; Bearman, D., Trant, J., Eds.; Los Angeles, CA, 1997. http://www.archimuse.com/mw97/speak/witcomb.htm (accessed June 15, 2008).
26. Williams, S. Te Ara—The encyclopedia of New Zealand: An encyclopedia created for the Web. In *Museums and the Web 2007. Proceedings*; Toronto, Ontario, Canada, 2007. http://www.archimuse.com/mw2007/papers/williams/williams.html (accessed June 15, 2008).
27. Trant, J. Enabling educational use of museum digital materials: The Museum Educational Site Licensing (MESL) Project. In *The Electronic Imaging and Visual Arts Conference (EVA)*, Florence, Italy; 1996. http://www.archimuse.com/papers/jt.eva.florence.9602.html (accessed January 31, 2008).
28. Futernick, B. On access points in The Thinker. 2003. http://www.thinker.org.
29. Futernick, B. Keyword indexing the thinker. To J. Trant: e-mail message. August 15, 2005.
30. Bearman, D.; Trant, J. Social terminology enhancement through vernacular engagement: Exploring collaborative annotation to encourage interaction with museum collections. D-Lib Magazine **2005**, *11*(9). http://www.dlib.org/dlib/september05/bearman/09bearman.html (accessed September 11, 2006).
31. Chun, S.; Cherry, R.; Hiwiller, D.; Trant, J.; Wyman, B. Steve.museum: An Ongoing experiment in social tagging, folksonomy, and museums. In *Museums and the Web 2006: Selected papers from an international conference*, Albuquerque, NM, Trant, J., Bearman, D., Eds.; 2006, http://www.archimuse.com/mw2006/papers/wyman/wyman.html (accessed September 11, 2006).
32. Chan, S. Tagging and searching—serendipity and museum collection databases. In *Museums and the Web 2007. Proceedings*; Trant, J.; Bearman, D., Eds.; Toronto, Ontario, Canada, 2007. http://www.archimuse.com/mw2007/papers/chan/chan.html (accessed October 15, 2006).
33. Trant, J. Exploring the potential for social tagging and folksonomy in art museums: Proof of concept. New Rev. Hypermedia Multimedia **2006**, *12* (1), 83–105http://www.archimuse.com/papers/steve-nrhm-0605preprint.pdf (accessed June 15, 2008).
34. Trant, J.; Wyman, B. Investigating social tagging and folksonomy in art museums with steve.museum. World Wide Web 2006 (WWW2006): Collaborative Web Tagging Workshop: Edinburgh, Scotland, 2006. http://www.archimuse.com/research/www2006-tagging-steve.pdf (accessed January 31, 2008).
35. Science Museum. Science Museum's Launchball game wins international media award, 2008. http://www.sciencemuseum.org.uk/about_us/press_and_media/press_releases/2008/03/launchball_game.aspx (accessed June 15, 2008).
36. Maxwell Museum of Anthropology, U. o. N. M. The American image: The photographs of John Collier Jr.: Propaganda filmmaker. 2007. http://americanimage.unm.edu/propagandafilmmaker.html (accessed July 15, 2008).
37. Bernstein, S. Where do we go from here?: Continuing with Web 2.0. In *Museums and the Web 2008. Proceedings*; Trant, J., Bearman, D., Eds.; Montreal, Quebec, Canada, 2008. http://www.archimuse.com/mw2008/papers/bernstein/bernstein.html (accessed March 31, 2008).
38. Burnette, A.; Alexander, C.; Dark, D.; Hart, D.; Rossi, J.; Minor, N. Beyond launch: Museum videos on YouTube. In *Museums and the Web 2008. Proceedings*; Trant, J., Bearman, D., Eds.; Montreal, Quebec, Canada, 2008. http://www.archimuse.com/mw2008/papers/hart/hart.html (accessed March 31, 2008).
39. Dawson, B.; Trépanier, G.; McDonald, F. Social presence: New value for networked museum audiences. In *Museums and the Web 2008. Proceedings*; Trant, J., Bearman, D., Eds.; Montreal, Quebec, Canada, 2008. http://www.archimuse.com/mw2008/papers/dawson/dawson.html (accessed March 31, 2008).
40. Calvo, C.M.; Hansen, C.C.; Rosenberger, A. The digital Darwins project. In *Museums and the Web 1997: Proceedings*; Bearman, D., Trant, J., Eds.; Los Angeles, CA, 1997. http://www.archimuse.com/mw97/speak/calvo.htm (accessed June 15, 2008).
41. Quackenbush, A.; Toomey, R.; Schroeder, E. QuickTime virtual reality and museums on the Internet. In *Museums and the Web 1997: Proceedings*; Bearman, D., Trant, J., Eds.; Los Angeles, CA, 1997.
42. Devine, J. Reconstructing Rosie: A digital experiment in facial reconstruction. In *Museums and the Web 2001: Proceedings*; Trant, J., Bearman, D., Eds.; Seattle, WA, 2001.
43. Paolini, P.; Barbieri, T. Cooperative visits for museum WWW sites a year later: Evaluating the effect. In *Museums and the Web 2000: Proceedings*; Bearman, D., Trant, J., Eds.; Minneapolis, MN, 2000. http://www.archimuse.com/mw2000/papers/barbieri/barbieri.html (accessed June 15, 2008).
44. Paolini, P.; Gaia, G.; Barbieri, T.; Alonzo, F. Cooperative visits for museum WWW sites. In *Museums and the Web 1999: Proceedings*; Bearman, D., Trant, J., Eds.; New Orleans, LA, 1999. http://www.archimuse.com/mw2000/papers/barbieri/barbieri.html (accessed June 15, 2008).
45. Marty, P.; Twidale, M.; Urban, R. A second life for your museum: 3D multi-user virtual environments and museums. In *Museums and the Web 2007. Proceedings*; Toronto, Ontario, Canada, 2007. http://www.archimuse.com/mw2007/papers/urban/urban.html (accessed June 15, 2008).
46. Sayre, S. Sharing the experience: The building of a successful online/on-site exhibition. In *Museums and the Web 2000: Proceedings*; Trant, J., Bearman, D., Eds.; Minneapolis, MN, 2000. http://www.archimuse.com/mw2000/papers/sayre/sayre.html (accessed June 15, 2008).
47. Rothfarb, R.; Doherty, P. Creating museum content and community in second life. In *Museums and the Web 2007: Proceedings*; Trant, J., Bearman, D., Eds.; Archives & Museum Informatics: Toronto, Ontario, Canada, 2007. http://www.archimuse.com/mw2007/papers/rothfarb/rothfarb.html.

48. Barry, A. Creating a virtuous circle between a museum's on-line and physical spaces. In *Museums and the Web 2006: Proceedings*; Bearman, D., Trant, J., Eds.; Albuquerque, NM, 2006. http://www.archimuse.com/mw2006/papers/barry/barry.html (accessed June 15, 2008).
49. Bowen, J.; Filippini-Fantoni, S. Bookmarking in museums: Extending the museum experience beyond the visit? In *Museums and the Web 2007. Proceedings*; Toronto, Ontario, Canada, 2007. http://www.archimuse.com/mw2007/papers/filippini-fantoni/filippini-fantoni.html (accessed June 15, 2008).
50. American Museum of Natural History. December 18, 1996 [archive date]. American museum of natural history research Web. http://web.archive.org/web/19961218225054/http://amnh.org/ (accessed April 30, 2008).
51. Fine Arts Museums of San Francisco. The Thinker Imagebase: 60,000 works of art, 1996, December 19, 1996 [archive date].
52. Sumption, K. Beyond museum walls—A critical analysis of emerging approaches to museum Web-based education. In *Museums and the Web 2001: Proceedings*; Trant, J., Bearman, D., Eds.; Seattle, WA, 2001. http://www.archimuse.com/mw2001/papers/sumption/sumption.html.
53. Bearman, D. Museum strategies for success on the Internet. Museum Collections and the Information Superhighway Conference, Science Museum, London, U.K., 1995. http://web.archive.org/web/20010211004518/http://www.nmsi.ac.uk/infosh/bearman.htm (accessed April 30, 2008).
54. Microsoft Live Labs. In *Photosynth at TED Conference. Photosynth Team Blog*, 2007. http://labs.live.com/photosynth/blogs/CommentView,guid,721172f9-f94f-4cee-93ec-88e7274cca53.aspx (accessed April 30, 2008).
55. Cornell Ornithology Lab. eBird 2008. http://ebird.org/ (accessed April 30, 2008).
56. Liberge, L.; Gerlings, J. Cultural heritage on the map. In *Museums and the Web 2008. Proceedings*; Trant, J., Bearman, D., Eds.; Montreal, Quebec, Canada, 2008. http://www.archimuse.com/mw2008/papers/liberge/liberge.html (accessed March 31, 2008).
57. Cook, S. Researching and presenting a history of new media: Ten years of the Banff New Media Institute. In *Museums and the Web 2005: Proceedings*; Vancouver, British Columbia, Canada, 2005. http://www.archimuse.com/mw2005/papers/cook/cook.html.
58. Cook, S.; Graham, B. A curatorial resource for upstart media bliss. In *Museums and the Web 2001: Proceedings*; Trant, J., Bearman, D., Eds.; Seattle, WA, 2001. http://www.archimuse.com/mw2001/papers/graham/graham.html (accessed June 15, 2008).
59. Walker Art Center. Gallery 9. 1998, December 2, 1998. http://web.archive.org/web/19981202203145/www.walkerart.org/gallery9/ (accessed April 30, 2008).
60. Suen, I.-S.; Borich, T.O. 3D visualization in community-based planning. J. Extension **2004**, *42*(6), http://www.joe.org/joe/2004december/tt2.shtml.
61. Karp, C. The international museum community's position in the Internet domain name system. In *Museums and the Web 1997: Proceedings*; Bearman, D., Trant, J., Eds.; Los Angeles, CA, 1997.
62. Karp, C. The further adventures of the museum top-level Internet domain. Cultivate Interactive 2003. http://www.cultivate-int.org/issue9/musenic/.
63. Karp, C.; Hamma, K. A top level domain for museums. In *Museums and the Web 2001: Proceedings*; Trant, J., Bearman, D., Eds.; Seattle, WA, 2001. http://www.archimuse.com/mw2001/papers/hamma/hamma.html (accessed June 15, 2008).
64. Pratty, J. The 24 hour museum tunable RSS news feed. In *Museums and the Web 2005: Proceedings*; Bearman, D., Trant, J., Eds.; Vancouver: British Columbia, Canada, 2005. http://www.archimuse.com/mw2005/papers/pratty/pratty.html (accessed June 15, 2008).
65. LaBar, W. Exhibit commons: Using the Internet for a new exhibit paradigm. In *Museums and the Web 2006: Proceedings*; Bearman, D., Trant, J., Eds.; Albuquerque, NM, 2006. http://www.archimuse.com/mw2006/papers/labar/labar.html (accessed June 15, 2008).
66. LaBar, W.; Balsamo, A.; MacDonald, D.; Minneman, S.; Winet, J. Science mobilized: Bringing up-to-the-minute headlines into the museum and back out again: The times square of science and techn. In *Museums and the Web 2007. Proceedings*; Toronto, Ontario, Canada, 2007. http://www.archimuse.com/mw2007/papers/macdonald/macdonald.html (accessed June 15, 2008).
67. de Vet, M. Buzz and viral marketing as a PR tool for museums: A Dutch case study. In *Museums and the Web 2006: Proceedings*; Bearman, D., Trant, J., Eds.; Albuquerque, NM, 2006. http://www.archimuse.com/mw2006/papers/devet/devet.html (accessed June 15, 2008).
68. Marty, P.F.; Cole, T.; Sandore, B.; Kaczmarek, J.; Prom, C.; Shreeves, S. Now that we've found the 'Hidden Web' what can we do with it? The Illinois open archives initiative metadata harvesting experience. In *Museums and the Web 2002: Proceedings*; Trant, J., Bearman, D., Eds.; Boston, MA, 2002. http://www.archimuse.com/mw2002/papers/cole/cole.html (accessed June 15, 2008).
69. Dingley, A.; Shabajee, P. Today's authoring tools for tomorrow's semantic Web. In *Museums and the Web 2002: Proceedings*; Trant, J., Bearman, D., Eds.; Boston, MA, 2002. http://www.archimuse.com/mw2002/papers/dingley/dingley.html (accessed June 15, 2008).
70. Miller, E. Weaving meaning: The W3C's semantic Web initiatives. In *Museums and the Web 2002: Proceedings*; Trant, J., Bearman, D., Eds.; Boston, MA, 2002. http://www.w3.org/Talks/2002/04/20-sw/ (accessed June 15, 2008).
71. Hyvönen, E.; Junnila, M.; Kettula, S.; Saarela, S.; Salminen, M.; Syreeni, A.; et al. Finnish museums on the semantic Web: The user's perspective on Museum Finland. In *Museums and the Web 2004: Proceedings*; Bearman, D., Trant, J., Eds.; Washington DC/Arlington, VA, 2004. http://www.archimuse.com/mw2004/papers/hyvonen/hyvonen.html (accessed June 15, 2008).
72. Getchell, P.; LaKind, D. Zero to a million in one year flat. In *Museums and the Web 2000: Proceedings*; Trant, J., Bearman, D., Eds.; Minneapolis, MN, 2000. http://www.archimuse.com/mw2000/papers/getchell/getchell.html (accessed June 15, 2008).
73. Tanner, S. Reproduction charging models & rights policy for digital images in American art museums; August 2004. http://www.kcl.ac.uk/kdcs/pubs/USMuseum_SimonTanner.pdf (accessed December 13, 2008).

74. Tanner, S.; Deegan, M. Exploring charging models for digital cultural heritage: Digital image resource cost efficiency and income generation compared with analog resources. June 2002. http://heds.herts.ac.uk/mellon/title.html (accessed December 13, 2008).
75. Bearman, D. The economics of publishing cultural heritage content online: The AMICO experience. *International Cultural Heritage Informatics Meeting: Proceedings from ichim03*, École du Louvre, Paris, France, Perrot, X., Ed.; 2003.
76. Bearman, D.; Trant, J. Economic, social and technical models for digital libraries of primary resources. New Rev. Info. Network. **1998b**, *4*, 71–91. http://www.archimuse.com/papers/amico/index.html (accessed June 15, 2008).
77. Chan, S. Towards new metrics of success for online museum projects. In *Museums and the Web 2008. Proceedings*; Trant, J.; Bearman, D., Eds.; Montreal, QC, Canada, 2008. http://www.archimuse.com/mw2008/papers/chan-metrics/chan-metrics.html (accessed March 31, 2008).
78. Oates, G. The commons on Flickr: A primer. In *Museums and the Web 2008. Proceedings*; Trant, J.; Bearman, D., Eds.; Montreal, Quebec, Canada, 2008. http://www.archimuse.com/mw2008/papers/oates/oates.html (accessed March 31, 2008).

BIBLIOGRAPHY

1. General introductions to the issues of museum and technology can be found in the following:
2. Din, H.; Hecht, P., Eds. *The Digital Museum: A Think Guide*; American Association of Museums: Washington, DC, 2007.
3. Marty, P.; Jones, K., Eds.; *Museum Informatics: People, Information, and Technology in Museums*;, Eds. Routledge: New York, London, 2008.
4. The annual Museums and the Web conference publish peer-reviewed papers surveying the broad range of activity on the Web. Other conferences have been mentioned above.

Museums

Leslie Madsen-Brooks
Boise State University, Boise, Idaho, U.S.A.

Abstract

Museums are diverse institutions—and grow more so. Few museums have remained untouched by shifting paradigms of research, education, and leisure activities. During the late twentieth century, museums increased their emphasis on their public educational missions. As part of these efforts, museums and related institutions, such as planetaria, botanical gardens, and zoos, are embracing new ways of engaging with audiences, for example through new technologies or during special events that emphasize civic discourse. Despite the opportunities offered by these new approaches, museums continue to wrestle with issues of funding and larger cultural politics.

INTRODUCTION

Museums are slippery institutions in that many of them are reevaluating their missions and redistributing their resources to meet the challenges of an increasingly urbanized culture, digital communications, and national and global environmental and cultural crises. This entry provides an overview of the state of museums in the early twenty-first century.

This entry begins with a definition of museums and a brief bit of museum history, then moves into more detailed descriptions of the contemporary functions of a museum: collections and research, exhibition and education, civic outreach, and leisure destination. There follows a list, with brief descriptions, of a dozen different types of museums. This entry then looks at current opportunities and challenges within the museum field—technology, civic discourse, funding, and politics—before concluding with an overview of professionalization processes. This entry is appended by a list of resources—professional organizations, books, journals, and websites—that allow for further learning about museums and the museum field.

WHAT IS A MUSEUM?

Definition

Museums are sites where objects, ideas, and cultural beliefs are represented and contested. More so today than in the past, they embody the intersection of expert knowledge with more local ways of knowing.

The International Council of Museums defines a museum as a nonprofit organization that conserves, studies, and exhibits "the tangible and intangible heritage of humanity and its environment" for the "education, study, and enjoyment" of the public.[1] The U.S. federal government, through the Museum and Library Services Act, defines museums similarly, requiring in addition a professional staff and regular public exhibitions.[2] The American Alliance of Museums (AAM) Code of Ethics for Museums notes that their common denominator is making a "unique contribution to the public by collecting, preserving, and interpreting the things of this world." The Code recognizes various types of museums, many of them places that those outside the museum profession might not consider to be museums, for example, botanical gardens, aquaria, zoos, and historic sites.[3] The Institute of Museum and Library Services tracks 35,000 U.S. museums and related institutions—such as botanical gardens and aquaria—which the AAM estimates employ 400,000 Americans and generate 850 million visits per year.[4]

HISTORY

The earliest "museums" were religious sites dedicated to the muses (mouseion) of ancient Greece. By 340 B.C.E., Greek philosophers such as Aristotle were founding lyceums to further scholarly study and discourse, and some of these sites were home to collections of plants and other biological specimens. Between about 200 and 60 B.C.E., the Romans became enamored of Greek statuary and art, and many public spaces as well as private homes in Rome featured Greek art. As time passed, Roman homes as well came to contain frescoes and moveable paintings.

By the time of the Renaissance, traders and explorers provided Europeans with biological specimens and cultural artifacts from around the world. The wealthy class began to collect these objects in cabinets, drawers, and even entire rooms dedicated to flora, fauna, and cultural curiosities. These Wunderkammer, or cabinets of curiosity, are often cited as the first "real" museums because

Encyclopedia of Library and Information Sciences, Fourth Edition DOI: 10.1081/E-ELIS4-120053390

they attempted to organize knowledge, as represented by biological specimens and material culture, within architectural space. In 1682, Elias Ashmole donated his collection to Oxford University to found the Ashmolean Museum; in 1686, he codified the museum's structures in a memo on the museum's income, governance, and operations. This museum was one of the first to be open to the public.[5]

While European museums came out of a tradition of aristocracy and the practices of elite travelers, collectors, and patrons, American museums arose out of different impulses. From their earliest days, American museums have been more entrepreneurial in that they tend to articulate their usefulness to society in terms of value to individuals and to communities.[6] Throughout the nineteenth century, American museums were concerned with uplifting the masses and, in particular, assimilating new immigrants through the twin processes of education and enculturation. Free lectures and increased access to works of art, scientific specimens, and displays of new technology were meant to showcase American ingenuity and improve Americans' cultural and scientific literacy.

As the nineteenth century progressed, museums collected not only the best artistic production and most interesting scientific specimens of their own region, but from their nation's colonial territories as well. In the twentieth century, foreign governments and indigenous peoples raised questions about the ethics and legality of the acquisition of this cultural patrimony. In response, museums in the developed world continue to rethink how they represent "others" within their galleries and halls, while many museums in the developing, formerly colonized, world attempt to divorce themselves from the colonial heritage at the core of their museums' missions and collections.

In the twentieth century, many museums increased their focus on public education, particularly on the education of children. Museums targeting young visitors emphasized hands-on activities, role-playing, and kinesthetic exercises that engage the whole body. Families thus became a core constituency of the museum-going public, and museums extended their outreach to families and neighborhood groups, thereby building the institutions' sensitivity to the interests and needs of local and regional inhabitants.

FUNCTIONS

In the edition of the *Encyclopedia of Library and Information Science* published in 1968, James L. Swauger named three basic functions of museums: collection, study, and communication.[7] Twenty-first century museums have embraced a much broader, and at the same time very granular, spectrum of functions. Collecting remains at the core of many museums' missions, and the study of these collections—whether they may be centuries-old textiles, natural history museum specimens, or oil paintings—by scholars is still an important function of museums that own art and artifacts. Today, however, museums function just as much as institutions of public education, civic outreach, and leisure or "edutainment."

Collections and Research

Historical museums, art museums, and natural history museums have at their core a collection of objects—artifacts, fine arts or crafts, or scientific specimens. Museums place these objects on permanent or temporary exhibit, but in museums with larger collections, an object may never go on display. For example, the Smithsonian Institution in Washington, D.C., has more than 138 million objects in its possession; even within its 19 museums, 194 affiliate museums, and 9 research centers, it would be impossible to exhibit all of those objects in any human lifetime.[8]

Museums acquire objects in numerous ways. Scientists and anthropologists collect specimens and artifacts in the field, in the best cases adhering to local and international ethical guidelines regarding the acquisition of objects. Individual collectors give objects to museums during their lifetimes or bequeath them to the institution upon their death. Museums also purchase art, artifacts, and other objects, or trade with other museums to secure these objects for their collections. Zoos, aquaria, and gardens additionally have breeding and cultivation programs that increase their collections.

Museum collections can be contentious. Stakeholders and members of the public have called into question museums' ownership of sacred tribal objects, human remains, and ancient art. In the United States, this critique resulted in the 1990 North American Graves Protection and Repatriation Act (NAGPRA), which requires any institution receiving federal funding to return to the original tribes sacred objects, human remains, funerary artifacts, and related objects.[9] Internationally, agreements among countries and museums have made institutions more responsible for determining the provenance of objects in the hopes of reducing the traffic, for example, of archaeological artifacts and early art from their countries of origin. Most notable among these agreements may be the 1970 United Nations Educational, Scientific and Cultural Organization (UNESCO) Convention, which regulated the traffic of cultural artifacts, and particularly antiquities, from one country to another.[10]

Most museums allow researchers access to objects not currently on display. Many collections are open to the public by appointment, but some institutions restrict access to fragile or otherwise sensitive collections to scholars who provide relevant credentials. Curators and archivists at these museums frequently provide finding aids online, as well as guidelines on how to handle and photograph (or not) specimens, artifacts, and ephemera in the collections.

Increasingly, museums with collections are digitizing their texts and placing photos of their artifacts online as well. Many art museums let website visitors create "collections" of their favorite pieces of art. One museum that has made its digital collections particularly accessible is the Powerhouse Museum in Sydney, Australia, which has harnessed visitors' interest in its collections to expand the museum's understanding of both its objects and its visitors. The Powerhouse collections' online interface allows visitors to "tag" objects with vernacular words and phrases, adding to its curatorial taxonomy of the museum's objects a vernacular "folksonomy."[11]

Exhibits and Education

Museums are best known for their exhibitions. Exhibitions largely take two forms. The first type displays artifacts from a museum's—or several museums'—collections, with the goal of giving visitors a comprehensive overview of, for example, an artist's work, military aircraft, or animals of the Pleistocene. The second type of exhibit—which has come to dominate larger museums' exhibition design—is less focused around objects, but is fabricated to provide a particular learning experience. For example, an exhibit on climate change may not lend itself to the exhibition of artifacts; in this case, an exhibition designer would create interactive exhibits that are less dependent on artifacts and more focused on informational panels, multimedia presentations, and hands-on activities designed to facilitate learning about the phenomenon.

As increasing numbers of cultural organizations compete for the same pool of funding, many of the larger museums have turned to "blockbuster" exhibitions. Examples of this type of exhibition include King Tut and the Golden Age of the Pharaohs by National Geographic and the Supreme Council of Antiquities of Egypt, The Vatican Collections—The Papacy and Art and Van Gogh in Arles.[12] These exhibitions are so popular that visitors must reserve tickets in advance and enter the museum at a specific time. These exhibitions have been criticized for needlessly endangering works of art by shipping them around the world, for shifting the focus of museums from curatorial scholarship to marketing and visitor numbers, and for driving traffic from smaller museums toward those that can afford to mount these expensive exhibitions.[13] Supporters of blockbuster exhibitions claim they bring new audiences and revenues to museums, as well as make world-famous art and artifacts more accessible to the public.

Not all exhibitions are curated by experts. Community curation, or the selection and interpretation of objects by museum outsiders, takes many forms. In 1991, the Walsall Museum in the United Kingdom invited townspeople to nominate their own collections for display at the museum. This "People's Show" became so popular that it was repeated in later years at Walsall and elsewhere.[14] In 2007, the Tech Museum of Innovation in San Jose, CA, invited inhabitants of the virtual world Second Life to prototype exhibits in the virtual world; several of these prototypes were fabricated and exhibited in the real-world Tech Museum.[15]

Some curators are skeptical of crowdsourcing, but others see an opportunity for museums to curate the endless digital stream of user-generated content. In the analog world, museums have long filled this role of identifying information and items relevant to their communities and organizing content for visitors.[16] Thanks to interactive digital displays—multitouch tables are but one example of this technology—museums' curation of this content need not be limited to their websites; curators and educators can literally place the information at users' fingertips on the exhibition floor. Some of these exhibitions sit at the nexus of libraries and museums. For example, the Emerging Issues Commons is a physical gallery in the Hunt Library of North Carolina State University's Centennial Campus in Raleigh. Using multitouch tables and walls, visitors can interact with dynamic, data-driven graphics, watch historical and contemporary videos showcasing how the public has addressed the state's problems, view relevant social media streams, learn how state government policies come into being, and recommend solutions to current and emerging challenges. The gallery has a companion website where visitors may continue their engagement at home.[17]

Museums use their websites to expand their audience beyond visitors to their physical sites. News of events, exhibition previews, and even searchable collections all have proven to be of interest to web visitors. Individuals and organizations that lack the resources or interest to host visitors in a physical space are increasingly creating online "museums." The best resource to date on these online museums is the Museum of Online Museums (MoOM), which includes links not only to revered institutions such as the National Portrait Gallery and the United States Holocaust Memorial Museum, both of which are in Washington, D.C., but also to such virtual exhibits as a locomotive horn sound file collection, the Museum of Soviet Uniform Caps, and the Gallery of Firework Label Art.[18]

Leisure Destination

Individuals and families turn to museums not just for learning experiences, but as leisure destinations. Over the past several decades, museums have struggled to balance their appeal as leisure destinations with their educational missions, and family groups are at the center of this tension. Although families may come to museums to help their children learn, the visit is as much about forging family and individual identity as it is about the exhibition's content. In fact, recent visitor studies have analyzed not only what individual visitors perceive in exhibits, but also what they say to one another in family groups.

This research also takes into account the fact that any given museum is but one island in an archipelago of a family's learning resources.[19] Families are looking for time and space to spend together in an era where family time is less plentiful and childhood is compressed.[20]

Museums and similar sites are not stand-alone institutions, but part of a leisure landscape. For example, Carole Blair and Neil Michel have demonstrated that the Astronauts Memorial at the Kennedy Space Center Visitor Center in Orlando, FL, is part of the same cultural landscape as Disneyworld.[21] Similarly, the Smithsonian Institution museums are part of a larger touristic experience in Washington, D.C. Accordingly, a museum's education and marketing teams need to think beyond the walls of their institution when planning for visitors.

Civic Outreach

Traditionally, a museum's functions have been dictated by the type of museum it is (e.g., art museum, children's museum), but in recent years more museums have been crossing over into other areas of inquiry and expanding their public service missions. Museums are motivated to make this shift as they reevaluate their missions in light of changing patterns of public life and civic participation online and offline. Part of this effort has been providing free or inexpensive space for people to interact informally in public.[22]

These museum programs are diverse and frequently focus on children and youth—but without the feel of a more traditional museum education program. For example, the Boston Children's Museum in Massachusetts has entered into numerous collaborations with other institutions in the city, developing community open spaces within several office complexes near the museum.[23] The de Young fine arts museum in San Francisco engages high school students as "museum ambassadors" who lead interactive activities at classrooms and community centers and offer tours at the museum.[24] The National Museum of American Jewish History in Philadelphia, PA, formed a neighborhood action bureau that trained high school students to interview longtime residents about race relations and other neighborhood issues, particularly relations between Jewish Americans and African Americans.[25]

In Africa, where many museums have sought to divorce themselves from their colonialist roots, museums are focusing on community service, particularly in urban areas that have been stressed by immigration from rural regions. The Musée des Civilisations in Abidjan, Côte d'Ivoire, participated in the project "African Ingenuity: Creative Recovery and Recycling." The museum produced an exhibit of recycled and repurposed objects and drew attention to living conditions and caste systems within major African cities.[26] Other museums in Africa, including the National Museum of Nigeria, are moving from a mission of merely collection, preservation, and exhibition to a more proactive role in fostering healthy urban development, for example by opening up, via exhibitions, conversations about traffic jams, the relative safety of the suburbs over the cities, or mosquito eradication efforts.[27]

Museums and related institutions around the world have recently invested considerable resources in explaining climate change and encouraging visitors to consider ways to address this global crisis. Sometimes the engagement is very subtle, for example in the British Museum's gigapixel exhibit *Stories in the Rock*, which uses exceptionally large-format photographs of petroglyphs in part to tell an older climate-change story of the desertification of the Arabian Peninsula.[28] In other cases, institutions tackle climate change head-on. In 2015, The Long Beach Aquarium of the Pacific in Southern California, for example, convened a climate change summit that brought together policymakers; scientists from the government, university, and nonprofit sectors; industry representatives; and members of the public to identify critical areas of research that might provide solutions to Southern California's vulnerability to rising temperatures, drought, and coastal flooding.[29] Some scholars and museum professionals have recently called for using the accelerating climate change crisis as an opportunity to shift museums' approaches to preservation. Rather than addressing heritage—and particularly historic sites and other significant places in a community—as something that can be preserved perpetually, cultural institutions should, they argue, help visitors and the wider community adapt to new realities and to heritage loss.[30]

TYPES OF MUSEUMS

Museums come in many forms, including those listed as discussed the following list. Due to budget constraints, new technologies, patron or community interests, and changes in staff, museums are always innovating and partnering with other organizations, forging new kinds of institutions. This list, therefore, is by no means exhaustive.

Art museums: Art museums collect, exhibit, and conserve arts and fine crafts. Unlike natural history museums and science centers, which have wide appeal, especially among families, art museums have long battled with a public perception that they are elitist institutions. Indeed, the spare white, hushed galleries dotted with security guards, coupled with abstract artworks that may feel emotionally or intellectually inaccessible to laypeople—these may decrease enthusiasm for an institution significantly. However, like most other museums, art museums have been undergoing a transformation to make themselves more appealing to families and laypeople. For example, the Louvre in Paris has programs specifically targeting families, as well as workshops for children age 4 and older.[31] The Museum of Modern Art in New York City offers "Tours for Fours" and "Tours for Tweens" to satisfy young visitors, as well as family art workshops and films.[32]

Natural history museums: Traditionally, natural history museums' exhibitions housed hundreds, if not thousands, of preserved specimens of plants and animals (e.g., taxidermied mounts or skeletons). In the late nineteenth and early twentieth centuries, glass cases of specimens gave way to habitat group dioramas that placed animals in context but in many cases were loaded with cultural messages about nuclear families and patriarchy.[33] These aging dioramas, which were expensive to install and are not simple to renovate, are gradually being replaced by more interactive, multimedia exhibits and, in some cases, even older approaches to natural history display. For example, the renovated mammal hall that opened in 2003 at the Smithsonian's National Museum of Natural History features single, magnificent taxidermied mammals—a more "big game" approach to display—in lieu of habitat groups. Through video screens on walls and floor, shifting lights, and targeted sounds, visitors to the exhibition experience changing weather patterns on the veldt and in the forest. Natural history museums are also increasingly targeted at laypeople; instead of having rows of dioramas or specimens labeled with species' common and scientific names and a bit of explanatory text, exhibits are themed and narrative. The Smithsonian mammal hall, for example, welcomes visitors to a "Mammal Family Reunion."[34]

Science centers: Science centers (sometimes called science and technology centers) take a decidedly less object-oriented approach to museum exhibition in that most science centers do not have collections in the sense that other museums do. Science centers are intensively hands-on, informal learning environments that encourage observation, curiosity, role-playing, cooperation, and a sense of discovery.[35] Like children's museums, science centers are audience-focused rather than exhibits-centered (and by extension, curator-centered). The Exploratorium, which was founded in San Francisco in 1969 by noted physicist Frank Oppenheimer, is often credited with being the first science center.[36]

Children's museums: Children's museums seek to provide an enriching experience for young visitors, particularly those in their communities. The first children's museum, the Brooklyn Children's Museum in New York, was founded in 1899; today there are 300 children's museums worldwide. Like science centers, children's museums emphasize hands-on learning, discovery, and play. Also like science centers, they tend not to have large collections, although the Brooklyn Children's Museum has 29,000 natural history specimens and cultural artifacts.[37]

Museums of history or anthropology: History museums collect artifacts and ephemera related to the specific region or era reflected in the museum's mission. Very large museums, such as the National Museum of American History in Washington, D.C., have the space and staff resources to collect a wide range of artifacts from all eras of American history. Other museums, such as the Computer History Museum in Mountain View, California, focus their collections and exhibitions around more specific objects. These museums' exhibitions might be celebratory, informative, or commemorative. One particularly interesting approach to history is embodied by the Jim Crow Museum of Racist Memorabilia at Michigan's Ferris State University, which collects and exhibits objects—contemporary and historical—that draw on racist stereotypes of African Americans. The museum not only documents a history of hate but also serves as a resource for civil rights organizations.[38]

Living history museums: At these sites, historical reenactors wear the clothes and perform the tasks of people living in an earlier era. At some sites, these reenactors may serve as docents, who explain what they are doing and its significance to visitors, and even give visitors an opportunity to try a task or chore. The Living History Farms in Iowa are an example of such a site. At other living history museums, the reenactors are historian actors who never break from character. Some sites blend these two approaches. For example, at Plimoth Plantation in Massachusetts, Native American staff at the Wampanoag Homesite dress in Native historical garb but serve as interpreters rather than actors in order to better inform visitors about Native American culture today and in the past. Yet in the English Village portion of Plimoth Plantation, interpreters portray the daily life and special events experienced by specific settlers in 1627.[39]

Historic house museums: Historic house museums concern themselves with the conservation, maintenance, and interpretation of homes—and often their accompanying landscapes—of historic significance. The exhibition and education programs of these museums usually focus on the everyday lives of the former inhabitants of the house.[40] The notable exceptions to this practice are U.S. plantation house museums, 80% of which, according to one survey, either do not mention the contributions of slaves or trivialize their presence at the site.[41]

Community-based museums: Community-based museums take many forms, but all insist on representing and serving the people in their communities. "Community" can be defined narrowly, to include a museum's immediate community, or more broadly, to encompass a regional or ethnic mission. For example, the Smithsonian's Anacostia Community Museum sits in a largely African-American community in Washington, D.C., but focuses on African- American history and culture as well as its community's history.[42] In its exhibitions on art, history, the environment, and people, the Oakland Museum of California aims to be responsive to its immediate community.[43] Community museums are among those most likely to partner with other cultural organizations and institutions; take, for example, the Heart of Brooklyn cultural partnership among the Brooklyn Museum, Brooklyn Public Library, Brooklyn Botanic Garden, Prospect Park, Prospect Park Zoo, and the Brooklyn Children's Museum to promote learning and access to collections.[44]

Indigenous museums: In the United States and elsewhere, European immigrants and others long have been fascinated with the culture of the land's indigenous peoples. Individual and institutional collectors amassed—through means ethical and unethical—vast collections of native art and material culture. Museums used these artifacts—some of them sacred objects that native peoples felt should not be put on display—to represent indigenous cultures in ways that were not always accurate and in many cases were racist. With the rise of native self-determination movements in the 1960s and 1970s, indigenous peoples increasingly sought to represent themselves in museums.[45] The result has been the establishment of museums that either were established by native peoples or in partnership with them. The largest example of this in the United States is the National Museum of the American Indian in Washington, D.C. In Australia, the Aboriginal Heritage Unit works with native communities to establish cultural centers to represent their cultural heritage and "keeping places" to safely and securely house artifacts.[46]

Planetaria: A planetarium is a large theater designed for educational and entertaining presentations about objects in the solar system, Milky Way galaxy, and the larger universe. Usually these theaters have a dome-shaped ceiling and walls, as well as seats that recline backward so that audiences can comfortably look upward to see stars projected onto the dome. Planetarium shows may mimic space flight, instilling in viewers a sense of the universe's scale and the relative size and distance of night sky objects. The original planetarium shows used optical "star ball" projectors that simulated the movements of planets and stars relative to Earth. Contemporary planetarium shows tend to use digital projectors that allow for virtual travel into the night sky.[47]

Botanical gardens and arboreta: Botanical gardens and arboreta showcase plants and trees. These gardens not only serve as respites from urban or suburban landscapes but also conserve local, native, or endangered plants. Increasingly, these gardens target multiple users: runners, teachers and students, families with small children, the elderly, artists, and research scientists. For example, the Huntington Botanical Gardens in San Marino, CA, features a children's garden with hardy plants, low tunnels overgrown with vines, and fountains at toddler height.[48]

Aquaria and zoos: Aquaria and zoos display and conserve animals that live in freshwater and saltwater and on land. Although long criticized by animal activists and others for keeping animals in restricted spaces and barren environments, many zoos and aquaria have sought to replicate animals' habitats in order to foster breeding and conservation. Of particular current interest is amphibian conservation because large numbers of frogs and other amphibians are threatened with extinction due to habitat loss and a highly infectious disease. Other high-priority conservation projects include ocean habitats and elephants.[49]

OPPORTUNITIES

Technology

Museums are increasingly embracing the opportunities of the digital, networked age. Many museums have gone beyond websites that provide information, choosing instead to offer online visitors an interactive virtual experience—and in some cases, let visitors contribute to the site's content. Visitors comment on museums' blogs and Facebook pages, contribute videos of their museum experiences, enter videos they made into museum-sponsored contests, tag items in museum collections in crowdsourced projects, and share photos on Instagram and Flickr.

Many museums have smartphone apps that allow visitors to engage more deeply with exhibition content. In late 2015, the Brooklyn Museum released ASK Brooklyn Museum, an app that lets visitors ask real-time questions of art historians and educators who use Bluetooth-aware sensors to determine next to which works visitors are standing at the moment they use the app.[50] Monticello, Thomas Jefferson's former estate, developed an app in 2014 that shares haunting details about the slaves who lived and died there.[51] A coalition of museums in the United Arab Emirates share an app, MuseumsUAE, that provides visitors with information about each museum, including which museums are closest to them. In addition, as visitors check in at each museum, the app awards virtual badges that reveal additional information about each museum.[52]

A slightly older yet still compelling use of digital technology is the United States Holocaust Memorial Museum's Mapping Initiative, which uses Google Earth to map and interpret sites of historical and 21st-century genocide. Google Earth users can explore burned-out villages in Darfur and view accompanying texts and photographs documenting the destruction and loss of human life. The museum has similarly mapped the Holocaust, providing photographs, texts, and animated maps that demonstrate the scope of Nazi crimes against humanity.[53]

Civic Discourse

As explained earlier in this entry (see section "Civic Outreach"), museums are already reaching out to their communities in various ways. In an age of reduced funding for public education, large-scale human suffering, and local and global environmental crises, many museums and similar cultural and scientific institutions are redoubling their outreach efforts. These new activities go beyond bringing objects and lessons to school classrooms or setting up temporary exhibits in public venues. Increasingly, museums see themselves not merely as institutions that perform civic outreach, but as institutions that facilitate civic discourse.[54]

As part of this effort, some museums have teamed with universities and scientific organizations to promote efforts, such as Café Scientifique, where scientists and laypeople gather informally to discuss current issues in science. Cafés Scientifiques meet in locations around the world, including— to name just a few—Uganda, Iran, Israel, Bulgaria, Finland, Mexico, Chile, and the Philippines.[55] These and other efforts at promoting civic discourse—symposia, forums, and more—challenge traditional notions of the museum as a single site where people walk quietly through large halls, gazing at or interacting with objects. Some museum professionals find this shift disconcerting and not entirely within the missions of their museums, but others feel museums must be more proactive in leading and facilitating discussions and conversations lest museums become irrelevant in the larger everyday culture.

CHALLENGES

Politics

Museums the world over feel pressure to modify their exhibition content as a result of broader cultural and political landscapes. One particularly stunning—and oft-cited—example of this pressure resulted in the Smithsonian's National Air and Space Museum cutting back significantly on a 1995 exhibit commemorating the dropping of the atomic bombs on Hiroshima and Nagasaki. Complaints from veterans and conservative political groups convinced the museum to change the exhibition from one that looked at the decision to drop the bomb, the bombing itself, and its aftermath to a much smaller one centered around the restored fuselage of the *Enola Gay*, the plane that dropped the bomb.[56]

Criticism of this exhibition and others has led the public, politicians, and museum professionals to ask what exactly is the purpose of a museum, and particularly of a history museum. When it comes to interpreting events such as the bombing of Japan, what is the proper role of a museum, especially if it receives state or federal funding? Should the museum commemorate the bombing with displays of artifacts accompanied by simple, factual labels (even though these facts will likely be contentious); celebrate the contributions of the innovators and soldiers who brought about the end of the war in the Pacific; or look more critically at the bombing based on what we have learned, for example, about radiation during the past half century? Should museums be places where people's beliefs are challenged, where people are asked to think critically about commonly held notions about science and culture? Or should museums be a place where a culture's beliefs and knowledge are showcased uncritically? These are questions that are far from settled within communities and cultures around the globe, but professionals in museum fields tend to see museums as institutions of education that on occasion challenge visitors' understanding of the world and their places in it.

Contemporary transnational politics and events also affect museums in the short- and long-term. In the second decade of the twenty-first century, the rise of the self-styled "Islamic State" (ISIS) operating in Syria and Iraq not only touched off a human rights and refugee crisis of tremendous proportions; it also threatened the ancient cultural patrimony of the region. Jihadist fighters blew up signature historic sites in Palmyra, Syria, and the Islamic State funds its terror in part by selling antiquities on the black market.[57] Prior to the rise of ISIS, the Taliban and Al Qaeda looted museums, destroyed antiquities, and obliterated historic sites, including the famous 150 ft tall Bamiyan Buddhas carved into a cliff in central Afghanistan.[58] As a result, in some parts of the world, the physical security of museums and historic sites has taken on new urgency and importance.

Funding

Securing adequate money to maintain their collections and exhibits, as well as fund their education and outreach efforts, has been a perennial problem for many, if not most, museums. Museums typically rely on financial support from a combination of government agencies, foundations, and private fundraising. In the United States, funding for educational institutions shifts depending on which political party is in power in Washington, D.C., and even when funds are available, often those projects that favor the dominant political party's ideology receive funding over those that present alternative views.

To keep their doors open, most museums charge admission fees. It can be difficult to strike a balance between the amount of money a museum needs to collect and what the average visitor—and particularly the average family—is willing to pay. The result is typically a modest admission fee, although some museums charge no admission. For example, the Smithsonian Institution offers free admission to all its museums, and the United Kingdom features more than 50 free national museums.[59] In January 2009, French President Nicolas Sarkozy announced that French citizens aged 18–26 would gain free admission to public museums and monuments, including the Louvre—which set off its own controversy because non-French residents of France saw this policy as discriminatory.[60] Other museums raised their admission fees considerably in the 2000s. In 2004 the Museum of Modern Art in New York

City reopened with a new building and a $20 fee for adult visitors, representing a 60% increase in ticket prices, and in 2008 the California Academy of Sciences in San Francisco also opened a new facility with a $24.95 admission fee for adults, a significant increase over its previous ticket price of $10.[61] By late 2015, the Academy's price had risen to $34.95 for adults and $29.95 for youth.[62]

Coupled with stiff competition for private grants and government funding, museums' modest revenue means museum professionals, like many who work in the nonprofit sector, tend to receive salaries far below those of professionals in the corporate sector. While many people enjoy long careers in the museum field, lower paid positions experience a good deal of turnover as younger employees realize they might not be able to balance their personal budgets on such incomes. Those who remain in the field alternately describe it as enriching and frustrating; they have big ideas and ideals, but they may lack funding and public support for their projects.

PROFESSIONALIZATION AND TRAINING

The museum field boasts countless areas of specialization, but among them are curating, education, exhibit development, conservation, historic preservation, organizational management, development (fundraising), evaluation, and marketing and public relations. Depending on the size and status of the museum, some of these career tracks begin with entry-level jobs that require little prior experience or training. Others, such as curation or conservation, typically require advanced degrees in relevant disciplines. Museum professionals have advanced degrees in fields as diverse as museum studies, art history, library science, education, integrated pest management, conservation, and nonprofit management.

Undergraduate programs in museum studies are relatively rare; graduate degree and certificate programs are far more common. The best museum studies programs provide their students with a historical perspective on museums, a solid theoretical grounding in areas of interest to the student (e.g., education, curation, marketing), and access to internships at the best regional and national institutions. The Smithsonian Institution keeps an updated list of museum studies programs internationally.[63]

CONCLUSION

Museums are dynamic institutions. While conservative curators, researchers, and some patrons might see collections and their exhibition as museums' raison d'être, the museum-going public, museum educators, and others continue to make museums more responsive to community needs and thus more relevant to people's everyday lives. "Collaboration," "public outreach," and "civic discourse" are key terms in this new paradigm—one that undoubtedly will persist in this highly networked, digital age.

ASSOCIATIONS

1. International Council of Museums http://icom.museum/.
2. American Alliance of Museums http://www.aam-us.org.
3. Institute of Museum and Library Services, http://www.imls.gov.
4. Association of Science and Technology Centers, http://astc.org/.
5. The Association for Living History, Farm and Agricultural Museums, http://www.alhfam.org/.
6. Association of Zoos and Aquariums, http://aza.org/.
7. American Public Gardens Association, http://www.publicgardens.org/.
8. American Association for State and Local History, http://www.aaslh.org/.
9. Visitor Studies Association, http://www.visitorstudies.org/.
10. More museum-related organizations listed at http://museumstudies.si.edu/websites.htm.

Resources for Further Learning

Books

1. Anderson, G. *Reinventing the Museum: Historical and Contemporary Perspectives on the Paradigm Shift*, 2nd; AltaMira Press: Lanham, MD, 2012.
2. Carbonell, B.M. *Museum Studies: An Anthology of Contexts*; Blackwell Publishing: Malden, MA, 2004.
3. Falk, J.H.; Lynn, D.D.; Susan, F. *Principle, in Practice: Museums as Learning Institutions*; Altamira Press: Lanham, MD, 2007.
4. Falk, J.H.; Beverly, S. *Thriving in the Knowledge Age: New Business Models for Museums and Other Cultural Institutions*; Altamira Press: Lanham, MD, 2006.
5. Genoways, H. Ed. *Museum Philosophy for the Twenty-First Century*; Altamira Press: Lanham, MD, 2006.
6. Gurian, E.H. *Civilizing the Museum*; Routledge: London, U.K., 2006.
7. Harvey, D.; Perry, J. Eds., *The Future of Heritage as Climates Change: Loss, Adaptation and Creativity*; Routledge, New York, 2015.
8. Hooper-Greenhill, E. *Museums and the Shaping of Knowledge*; Routledge: London, U.K., 1992.
9. Karp, I.; Christine, M.K.; Steven, D.L. Eds., *Museums and Communities: The Politics of Public Culture*; Smithsonian Institution Press: Washington, DC, 1992.
10. Karp, I.; Kratz, C.A.; Szwaja, L.; Ybarra-Frausto, T. *Museum Frictions: Public Cultures/Global Transformations*; Duke University Press: Durham, NC, 2006.
11. Karp, I.; Steven, D.L. Eds., *Exhibiting Cultures: The Politics and Poetics of Display*; Smithsonian Institution Press: Washington, DC, 1991.
12. Lord, B.; Gail, D.L. *The Manual of Museum Planning*; AltaMira Press: Walnut Creek, CA, 2002.
13. Macdonald, S. Ed., *A Companion to Museum Studies*; Blackwell Publishing: Malden, MA, 2006.

14. Marstine, J. Ed., *New Museum Theory and Practice: An Introduction*; Blackwell Publishing: Malden, MA, 2006.
15. McClellan, A. *The Art Museum From Boullée to Bilbao*; University of California Press: Berkeley, CA, 2008.
16. Pearce, S.M. *Museums, Objects and Collections: A Cultural Study*; Leicester University Press: Leicester, U.K., 1992.
17. Roberts, L. *From Knowledge to Narrative: Educators and the Changing Museum*; Smithsonian Institution Press: Washington, DC, 1997.
18. Schwarzer, M. *Riches, Rivals, and Radicals: 100 Years of Museums in America*; American Association of Museums: Washington, DC, 2006.
19. Silverman, L. *The Social Work of Museums*; Routledge: London, U.K., 2010.
20. Weil, S.E. *Making Museums Matter*; Smithsonian Institution Press: Washington, DC, 2002.

Magazines and Journals

1. ASTC Dimensions (Association of. Science and Technology Centers). http://www.astc.org/pubs/dimensions.htm.
2. Curator: The Museum Journal. John Wiley & Sons, Inc., New York. http://www.curatorjournal.org/.
3. Journal of Museum Education. Museum Education Roundtable. Washington, DC. http://museumeducation.info/jme.
4. Muse. Canadian Museums Association. Ottawa, Ontario. http://www.museums.ca/site/muse_current.
5. Museum Magazine. American Alliance of Museums. Arlington, Virginia. http://www.aam-us.org/resources/publications/museum-magazine.
6. Museums and Social Issues. Taylor & Francis. Abingdon, Oxfordshire. http://www.maneyonline.com/loi/msi.
7. Museum History Journal. Taylor & Francis. Abingdon, Oxfordshire. http://www.maneyonline.com/loi/mhj.
8. Museum Management and Curatorship. Taylor & Francis. Abingdon, Oxfordshire. http://www.tandfonline.com/loi/rmmc20.

Websites

1. Global Museum http://www.globalmuseum.org/.
2. HEREIN System (European heritage policies)http://www.herein-system.eu/.
3. Museum 2.0 http://museumtwo.blogspot.com/.
4. Museum Stuff http://www.museumstuff.com.
5. Museums and the Web: Archived conference papers and presentations http://www.archimuse.com/conferences/mw.html.
6. Smithsonian Center for Education and Museum Studies http://museumstudies.si.edu/.

References

1. "Museum Definition." http://icom.museum/the-vision/museum-definition/ (accessed December 2015).
2. http://name-aam.org/uploads/downloadables/EXH.spg_11/5%20EXH_spg11_What,%20if%20Anything,%20Is%20a%20Museum__Dillenburg.pdf (accessed December 2015).
3. http://aam-us.org/resources/ethics-standards-and-best-practices/code-of-ethics (accessed December 2015).
4. http://aam-us.org/about-museums; http://aam-us.org/about-museums/museum-facts (accessed December 2015).
5. Abt, J. The origins of the public museum. In *A Companion to Museum Studies*; Macdonald, S., Ed.; Blackwell Publishing: Malden, MA, 2006; 115–134.
6. Schwarzer, M. *Riches, Rivals and Radicals: 100 Years of Museums in America*; American Association of Museums: Washington, DC, 2006; 7pp.
7. Swauger, J. Museums and museology. In *Encyclopedia of Library and Information Science,* Kent A. et. al., eds. Marcel Dekker, Inc.: New York, 1968; 301–327.
8. http://newsdesk.si.edu/factsheets/facts-about-smithsonian-institution-short (accessed December 2015).
9. National Park Service, U.S. Department of the Interior. Laws, Regulations, and Guidance: National NAGPRA, 1990. http://www.nps.gov/nagpra/MANDATES/INDEX.HTM Accessed December 2015.
10. UNESCO. *Convention on the Means of Prohibiting and Preventing the Illicit Import, Export and Transfer of Ownership of Cultural Property*, 1970. http://portal.unesco.org/en/ev.php-URL_ID=13039&URL_DO=DO_TOPIC&URL_SECTION=201.html (accessed December 2015).
11. http://www.powerhousemuseum.com/collection/database/browsekeywords.php (accessed December 2015).
12. Art history and the "blockbuster" exhibition. Art Bull. **1986**, *68* (3), 358–359.
13. Penny, N. Preface. In *The Ephemeral Museum: Old Master Paintings and the Rise of the Art Exhibition*; Haskell, F., Ed.; Yale University Press: New Haven, CT, 2000; viii–xiv.
14. Mullen, C. The people's show. In *Interpreting Objects and Collections*; Pearce, S.M., Ed.; Routledge: London, U.K., 1994; 287–290.
15. Simon, N. Event Announcement: The Tech Virtual's First Exhibition opens June 4. Museum 2.0; June 2, 2008, http://museumtwo.blogspot.com/2008/06/event-announcement-tech-virtuals-first.html (accessed December 2015).
16. Byrd Phillips, L. The temple and the bazaar: Wikipedia as a platform for open authority in Museums. Curator: Mus. J. **2013**, *56* (2), 226.
17. https://iei.ncsu.edu/resources/emerging-issues-commons/ (accessed December 2015).
18. http://www.coudal.com/moom/ and http://www.coudal.com/archive.php?cat=cat_moom (accessed December 2015).
19. Ellenbogen, K.M.; Luke, J.J.; Dierking, L.D. Family learning in museums: Perspectives on a decade of research. In *Principle, in Practice: Museums as Learning Institutions*; Falk, J.H., Dierking, L.D., Foutz, S., Eds.; Altamira Press: Lanham, MD, 2007; 17–30.
20. Patchen, J.H. Defining our museum audience: An extraordinary opportunity. In *Museum Philosophy for the Twenty-First Century*; Genoways, H., Ed.; Altamira Press: Lanham, MD, 2006; 247–254.
21. Blair, C.; Michel, N. Commemorating in the theme park zone: Reading the astronauts memorial. In *At the Intersection: Cultural Studies and Rhetorical Studies*; Rosteck, T., Ed.; Guilford Press: New York, 1998; 29–82.
22. Falk, J.H.; Sheppard, B.K. *Thriving in the Knowledge Age*; Altamira Press: Lanham, MD, 2006; 67pp.
23. Falk, J.H.; Sheppard, B.K. *Thriving in the Knowledge Age*; Altamira Press: Lanham, MD, 2006; 138pp.

24. https://deyoung.famsf.org/education/k-12-students/museum-ambassadors (accessed December 2015).
25. Hamilton-Sperr, P. *Museums in the Life of a City: Strategies for Community Partnerships*; American Association of Museums: Washington, DC, 1995; 19pp.
26. Savane, Y. African ingenuity: Recovery and recycling artisans. In *Museums and Urban Culture in West Africa*; Adande, A.B.A., Arinze, E., Eds.; West African Museums Programme: Oxford, U.K., 2002; 139–142.
27. Ikwueme, P.I. Nigeria: Urbanisation and heritage. In *Museums and Urban Culture in West Africa*; Adande, A.B.A., Arinze, E., Eds.; West African Museums Programme: Oxford, U.K., 2002; 151–158.
28. Louw, M.; Crowley, K. New ways of looking and learning in natural history Museums: The use of gigapixel imaging to bring science and publics together. Curator: Mus. J. **2013**, *56* (1), 96.
29. Aquarium gathers experts to help make long beach a climate resilient city. *Pacific Currents Fall*, 2015; 5. http://www.aquariumofpacific.org/downloads/CURRENTS_FALL_15.pdf (accessed December 2015).
30. Sutter, G.C. book review, The future of heritage as climates change: loss, adaptation and creativity. Mus. Manag. Curatorship; Harvey, D.C., Perry, J., Eds.; **2015**, *30* (4), 359–361.
31. http://www.louvre.fr/familles/activites#tabs and http://petite galerie.louvre.fr/article/individuel-ou-famille (accessed December 2015).
32. http://www.moma.org/learn/kids_families/gallery_talks (accessed December 2015).
33. Haraway, D. Teddy bear patriarchy: Taxidermy in the Garden of Eden, New York City, 1908–1936. Social Text **1984–1985**, *11*, 20–64.
34. http://www.mnh.si.edu/mammals/ (accessed December 2015).
35. Bitgood, S.; Serrell, B.; Thompson, D. The impact of in- formal education on visitors to museums. In *Informal Science Learning: What the Research Says about Television, Science Museums, and Community-Based Projects*; Crane, V., Nicholson, H., Chen, M., Bitgood, S., Eds.; Research Communications Ltd: Dedham, MA, 1994; 61–106.
36. http://www.exploratorium.edu/about/history (accessed December 2015).
37. http://www.brooklynkids.org/exhibits (accessed December 2015).
38. http://www.ferris.edu/jimcrow/ (accessed December 2015).
39. http://www.plimoth.org/what-see-do/wampanoag-homesite; http://www.plimoth.org/what-see-do/17th-century-english-village (accessed December 2015).
40. Foy Donnelly, J.; Foy McNicholl, G. *Interpreting Historic House Museums*; Altamira Press: Walnut Creek, CA, 2002; 18pp.
41. Eichstedt, J. Museums and (in)justice. In *Museum Philosophy for the Twenty-First Century*; Genoways, H., Ed.; Altamira Press: Lanham, MD, 2006; 127–137.
42. http://anacostia.si.edu/ (accessed December 2015).
43. http://museumca.org/ (accessed December 2015).
44. http://www.heartofbrooklyn.org/ (accessed December 2015).
45. Simpson, M.G. *Making Representations: Museums in the Post-Colonial Era*; Routledge: London, U.K., 1996; 135pp.
46. James, B. 'Keeping places' in the Timor Sea Region. Mus. Int. **2003**, *55* (3–4), 30–37. 35pp.
47. http://www.technewsworld.com/story/71409.html (accessed December 2015).
48. http://www.huntington.org/WebAssets/Templates/general.aspx?id=16566 (accessed December 2015).
49. https://www.aza.org/conservation-commitments-and-impacts/ (accessed December 2015).
50. https://itunes.apple.com/us/app/ask-brooklyn-museum/id949540325?mt=8 (accessed December 2015).
51. http://www.npr.org/sections/alltechconsidered/2015/08/02/428126511/an-app-tells-painful-stories-of-slaves-at-monticellos-mulberry-row (accessed December 2015).
52. https://www.invasivecode.com/uae-museum.html (accessed December 2015).
53. http://www.ushmm.org/learn/mapping-initiatives (accessed December 2015).
54. Koke, J.; Schwarzer, M. Eds., Civic discourse: Let's talk. Mus. Soc. Issues **2007**, *2*(2).
55. http://www.cafescientifique.org/ (accessed December 2015).
56. Kohn, R.H. History and the culture wars: The case of the Smithsonian Institution's Enola Gay exhibition. J. Am. Hist. **1995**, *82* (3), 1036–1063.
57. http://www.npr.org/sections/parallels/2015/09/05/437616132/as-isis-destroys-artifacts-could-some-antiquities-have-been-saved (accessed December 2015).
58. http://www.al-monitor.com/pulse/originals/2014/01/arab-world-heritage-museums-destruction.html (accessed December 2015).
59. http://www.nationalmuseums.org.uk/what-we-do/encouraging_investment/free-admission/ (accessed December 2015).
60. http://www.theguardian.com/artanddesign/2009/may/27/louvre-free-entry-policy-complaint (accessed December 2015).
61. http://archives.sfexaminer.com/sanfrancisco/california-academy-of-sciences-will-be-twice-the-price/Content?oid=2145189 (accessed December 2015).
62. http://www.calacademy.org/admission (accessed December 2015).
63. http://museumstudies.si.edu/training.html (accessed December 2015).

Museums and Community

Tamara Biggs
Chicago History Museum, Chicago, Illinois, U.S.A.

Abstract

In spite of Charles Willson Peale's ideal of a democratic museum, most in the early nineteenth century were either eclectic and intimidating, or filled with sham amusements. In the late nineteenth and early twentieth centuries, museums began to consider their educational mission on an equal par with collecting and research. A lack of representation in mainstream museums led to the foundation of many American and international ethnic museums, beginning with African American museums in the 1960s, giving voice to cultures often excluded from the historical narrative. Larger institutions responded to societal demand for inclusion by engaging community advisory boards and first voice perspective through oral history. The most recent museum community to develop has been online, and crosses traditional barriers of race, class, and gender. Innovative museums looking to the future have invited visitors to participate in the narrative process.

INTRODUCTION

The ever-changing relationship between museums and their communities is a topic which reflects the fluid landscapes of culture and technology. The industry which began as a smattering of avid scholars amassing personal collections has grown through the efforts of individuals and organizations to become a global network of public resources. Presentation and accessibility have improved to attract a wider demographic, and in the past 50 years a staggering array of cultures and viewpoints has come into the public eye through the establishment of ethnic and neighborhood museums. The relationship between community and museum has been personalized through the collection of firsthand accounts and the involvement of community advisory groups, while information is becoming ever more accessible through the reaches of the Internet. The predominant trend in the history of the relationship between museums and their communities is a steady increase in the appeal and availability of information to all facets of the population.

BODY OF TEXT

Early American Museums

The founder of the first American museum, Charles Willson Peale, struggled with some of the same issues as museums of the twenty-first century. Namely, how does one endeavor to attract, educate, and entertain the broadest possible audience while maintaining a commitment to research and scholarship? Peale believed that government financial support would make both of these ideals possible. In an address to the state legislature of Pennsylvania, printed in *Poulson's American Daily Advertiser*, December 18, 1810, Peale said

> In Europe, all men of information prize a well regulated museum, as a necessary appendage to government, but in several parts of that quarter of the earth, the means of visiting those repositories, are within the reach of particular classes of society only, or open on such terms or at such portions of time, as effectually to debar the mass of society, from participating in the improvement, and the pleasure resulting from a careful visitation.[1]

Peale solicited the new American government to provide public monies so that he could operate a museum that would offer "rational amusement" to a wider swath of society; he articulated a more democratic intent than the models in Europe. Believing that natural history could "promote National and Individual happiness,"[2] he experimented with presentation techniques, using his fine artistic skills to paint backdrops for mounted specimens. At the end of the gallery, he even included a three-dimensional natural setting, with trees, shrubs, and a pond, for a collection of mammals, reptiles, amphibians, and birds. But he could neither gain public funding nor attract enough visitors to pay the 25¢ admission fee to keep the doors open. The Philadelphia Peale Museum closed in 1827 shortly after his death, and the collection was largely sold off to P. T. Barnum and Moses Kimball.

Two of Peale's sons, Rembrandt and Rubens, also tried their hands at museums, opening one in Baltimore, and later one in New York. Rubens had an especial flare for marketing: he installed gas lighting to attract visitors at night, and he hosted (for the substantial fee of $650) the blockbuster of the day—the first Egyptian mummy brought to America. The effectiveness of such entertainment events is recorded in his detailed accounts. For

Encyclopedia of Library and Information Sciences, Fourth Edition DOI: 10.1081/E-ELIS4-120044072

example, visitorship spiked during the Mummy's six weeks of display, and generated $1842 of income.[3]

Like the Peale family's, many early American museums actively appealed to public interests in an effort to increase visitation. In their endeavors to remain solvent, they struggled with the tension between entertainment and education, often including such elements as wax figures and vaudeville-like performances. P. T. Barnum had no qualms about promoting amusement and hokum before science in his New York Museum, to the extent that when the museum burned in 1870, he abandoned the museum business and devoted his attention to the circus.

On the other hand, early private collectors, more concerned with their own education than that of the public, joined to form societies and share information.

> The naturalists who studied and collected natural history objects typically shared a commitment to self-improvement, group collaboration and national advancement. They created local societies to link the layers of individual activity—private conversations, semi-private correspondence, exchange of specimens, and presentation of ideas—into a collaborative project to identify and map all species in the American landscape.[4]

While the public may have been allowed into the sanctums of these societies, they found no aids to help them understand what they saw. There were few docents or legible labels, and the species were organized for efficient storage, not pleasurable viewing. Indeed, the societies became just one more way to establish the elite standing of well-heeled Americans. Museum theorist Stephen E. Weil put it this way: "Museums were created and maintained by the high for the low, by the couth for the uncouth, by the washed for the unwashed, by those who knew for those who didn't but needed to know and who would come to learn."[5] Neither the P. T. Barnum types nor the natural history societies democratized the natural sciences as Peale had yearned to do.

Birth of Museum Education

Beginning in the 1870s, Alpheus Hyatt at the Boston Society of Natural History, aided by teacher Lucretia Crocker, worked to attract a more general public. They hired guides, "introduced special evening and Saturday classes, produced guidebooks, and added more descriptive charts and posters to displays. . . ."[6] After the Civil War, systematic displays (with rows of species organized by their biological relationship to one another) became the norm for "serious museums." But teachers and the general public exerted their influence to produce more attractive and understandable displays. George Brown Goode, the Smithsonian Institution's Associate Director, said in the SI's first circular, that the museum had three roles: museum of record, museum of research and museum of education. In other words, the Smithsonian established public education on equal footing with collecting and research.

Into this milieu came John Cotton Dana. Primarily a librarian, he first revolutionized that field in Denver, where he headed the Denver Public Library from 1889 to 1898. He believed that libraries', and later museums', prime mission is relevance and usefulness. He was instrumental in changing the library from "a closed temple of 'wisdom undisturbed' to an open workshop of delight and learning"[7] by introducing open stacks, a special business library, a children's library, community rooms, branch libraries, and foreign language collections to serve immigrant populations. When he relocated to Newark, New Jersey to become head of the Free Public Library in 1902, he also took on the task of developing a museum using the same principles of usefulness to the public. Noting that the citizens of Newark had access to landmark temples of art and natural history across the river in New York City, he concluded that what was needed was a museum of, by and for Newark—a museum that was "supported by, and. . .duty bound, to try to be of direct value and service to a city of industries. . .for the pleasure and advantage of our chiefest patron—the people of Newark. . . ."[8] Among the innovations there during his lifetime were hiring an educational advisor, making 300 trips to museums to learn what worked or didn't for others, holding public forums to gain insight into public desires, mounting a wide range of exhibitions (such as clay products of New Jersey with "the daily presence of a skilled potter," or immigrant textiles collected through schoolchildren), lending collections to classrooms, establishing one room as a children's museum, and forming a junior museum club.

Dana spread his revolutionary ideas through letters to *The New York Times*, a series of small volumes under the general title "The New Museum," papers at the annual meeting of the American Association of Museums (founded in 1906), and finally by the founding one of the nation's first museum studies programs at the Newark Museum in 1925.[9] The New Museum continues his legacy through innovations such as the High School Art Program (HSAP), one of the first museum education programs in the country to engage at-risk teenagers in contemporary art, launched in 1980.

Ethnic Museums

The next sea change for museums and community came with the Civil Rights movement. While scholarship on the history of blacks was well developed by the early twentieth century, the dearth of African Americans in museum positions that could influence the interpretive course meant that mainstream museums continued to teach and display a distorted and biased version of America's past.

Consequently, in the 1960s and 1970s, blacks formed their own community-based museums to show that they indeed held an integral place in history: The DuSable Museum of African American History in Chicago, Illinois (1961); The Charles H. Wright Museum of African American History in Detroit, Michigan (1965); the African American Museum and Library at Oakland, California (1965); and the National Afro-American Museum and Cultural Center in Wilberforce, Ohio (1972). Most recently, Congress chartered the newest Smithsonian museum, the National Museum of African American History, in 2003. The NMAAH will allow African American scholars and educators a federally supported institution to preserve, study, and share their unique place in American history.

The establishment of Latino art and culture museums followed on the heels of the movement for African American Museums: El Museo del Barrio in New York City (1969); The Mexican Museum in San Francisco (1975); Chicago's Mexican Fine Arts Center Museum (now the National Museum of Mexican Art, 1982); the Mexic-Arte Museum in Austin, Texas (1983); and many others since then. Their shared first-voice identity "utilizes Latino self-expression as a lens for examining parallel experiences shared by many cultural communities...."[10] Carlos Tortolero of Chicago's NMMA reiterates that the museum is an expression of the Mexican American community, but that it is a place for everyone. "We want both the local community and the mainstream world to visit...so that we can break down some of the barriers....If only our own people come here, we will have failed our mission."[10]

Because The Native American Graves Protection and Repatriation Act (NAGPRA) of 1990 coincided with the licensing of many Indian casinos, American Indians had the legal means to reclaim many of their ancestors' remains and sacred artifacts from American museums at the same time that they were gaining the financial ability to house them properly. This convergence of circumstances has contributed to a renaissance on many reservations, and the establishment of approximately 300 tribal museums and cultural centers. The noteworthy Mashantucket Pequot Museum in Connecticut (1998) is a 308,000 square foot complex that cost $193 million.

Dozens upon dozens of ethnic museums now operate in the United States, some of them arising early in the twentieth century, such as the Jewish Museum in New York in 1904, and Chicago's Polish Museum of America in 1935. The numbers, however, have burgeoned since the 1970s. These new ethnic museums range in size from small storefront operations run by volunteers to large initiatives such as the Japanese American National Museum in Los Angeles, California (1992); the Arab American National Museum in Detroit, Michigan (2005); and the newly expanded Wing Luke Asian Museum in Seattle, Washington (2008). The Chicago Cultural Alliance, formed in 2006, boasts a membership of 25 Chicago-area ethnic museums, historical societies, and cultural centers that represent Cambodian, Swedish, Scottish, Irish, East African, African American, Mexican, Puerto Rican, Lithuanian, Latvian, Polish, Arab, Korean, Filipino, Japanese, Asian Indian, American Indian, Chinese, and Brazilian communities. Detroit's Cultural Exchange Network is a similar consortium of ethnic arts groups, and other cities have equally rich arrays of cultural assets. Immigrant populations may be Americanized, but they are not—indeed, they resist—becoming homogenized. Dr. Rosa Cabrera, senior urban anthropologist at the Field Museum in Chicago, asserts that these communities and their museums have a reciprocal benefit—that the very process of establishing a museum shapes community identity.[11]

International Examples

The United States is not alone in the outgrowth of small neighborhood or ethnic museums. El Museo Shan-Dany was founded in 1986, through the cooperation of Mexico's Instituto Nacional de Antropologia e Historia (INAH) and the community leaders of Santa Ana del Valle, Oaxaca. The project was inspired by the discovery of several archeological burial sites during plaza and road construction. INAH did not judge the artifacts to be of a high enough caliber for display in the national museum, but they were extremely important to the identity and patrimony of the people of Santa Ana. El Museo Shan-Dany became a model for the formation of 16 other museums in neighboring villages. Together they comprise The Union of Community Museums of Oaxaca, and like the Chicago Cultural Alliance, they do joint planning, fundraising, programming, and marketing.[12]

The Lower East Side Tenement Museum, opened in 1988, does not focus on a particular ethnicity. Instead, its community is defined by the former residents of 97 Orchard Street, an estimated 7,000 people from more than 20 nations between 1863 and 1935, when landlords chose to evict rather than invest in meeting new building codes. The museum connects its historic stories to the plight of current immigrant communities, many of them toiling in sweatshops just as the residents of Orchard Street 100 years before them. According to founder Ruth Abram, "Behind every door is a family with a different religion, a different language, each special and unique. But in the hallways, stoops, and streets, all those people are together pursuing the American Dream...."[13] Because its mission is to promote tolerance through the historical perspective, the museum's programs ask what policies and attitudes persist as obstacles to immigrant families today.

Like the Tenement Museum, the District Six Museum was formed to preserve a neighborhood consciousness. But District Six did not have a "time capsule" building to resuscitate. In fact, there was no neighborhood at all after the Apartheid government of South Africa declared in 1966 that it would be "white" and the homes and businesses of the multiethnic residents razed. Some 60,000 people were relocated, but they never stopped fighting to regain the right to return. In 1989, the Methodist Church, one of the few structures left standing, became the center for an outpouring of collective memory, inscribed by former residents on a huge floor map. The Museum served as a tool to preserve memory and fight to reclaim the neighborhood for the dispossessed, a battle won in 1998. The Museum continues to work with community memory in the renovated Methodist Church.[14,15]

Te Papa Tongarewa, the National Museum of New Zealand opened in 1998, does not give voice to its native minority through a special museum. Rather, the government adopted the concept of unified collections and narratives developed via a bicultural partnership. Tangata Whenua (the Maori, those who belong to the land by right of first discovery) and Tangata Tiriti (the Europeans, those who belong to the land by right of the Treaty of Waitangi) worked together to interpret the cultural heritage and environment of New Zealand, drawing equally on Maori and western knowledge systems. Te Papa's marae, or Maori meeting house, symbolizes this collaborative and consensual effort. A marae is a sacred place inhabited by ancestors; indeed the house IS the ancestor. Rigid protocols protect both the marae's power and the well-being of those who enter. The museum created a marae that gives all people the right to enter because of their shared history.[16,17]

In 1999, the Tenement Museum, together with the District Six Museum (South Africa); the Gulag Museum (Russia); the Liberation War Museum (Bangladesh); Maison des Esclaves (Senegal); National Park Service (U.S.A.); Memoria Abierta (Argentina); Terezin Memorial (Czech Republic); and the Workhouse (United Kingdom) founded the International Coalition of Historic Site Museums of Conscience (now known as the International Coalition of Sites of Conscience) to unite institutions whose mission is to preserve difficult histories in order to enable an educated citizenry to build civil societies. The Coalition Web site states, "By initiating new conversations about contemporary issues through a historical lens, places of memory can become new centers for democracy in action. But the power of historic sites is not inherent; it must be harnessed as a self-conscious tactic in the service of human rights and civic engagement." Since its founding with the above 9 institutions, the Coalition had grown to 17 accredited sites in 2008. Regional Networks led by accredited members in Russia, Asia, Africa, and South America bring together an additional 20–30 organizations for joint projects, workshops, one-on-one consultations, and other activities to build the capacity of emerging initiatives and strengthen the collective memory. An Immigration Network of 1 European and 13 American members formed in 2008 to foster an international dialogue on current immigration issues. An additional 100 affiliate members around the world support the mission.[18]

ICOM

The International Council of Museums (ICOM) is an older and larger organization founded in Paris in 1946 at the initiative of American Chauncey J. Hamlin, previously president of AAM and then president of the board of the Buffalo Society of Natural Science. The organization immediately established a cooperation agreement with United Nations Educational, Scientific and Cultural Organization (UNESCO), and within the first few years, 53 countries were active members. It has grown to currently boast 26,000 members from 151 countries. ICOM's mission includes professional cooperation and exchange, advancement of professional standards and ethics, and interpretation and preservation of the world's natural and cultural heritage, both tangible and intangible. Since its inception, ICOM has been a valuable ally for local museums to protect and repatriate cultural assets, through such initiatives as standardizing the ethics of acquisition, "One Hundred Missing Objects" publications that fight illicit traffic of cultural property, and the International Committee of the Blue Shield that provides preservation aid in emergency situations. This concrete aid to keeping tangible culture in the hands of the community that created it is accompanied by theoretical assistance in democratizing museums. Conferences, workshops, and publications on such topics as "Local Museums and Cultural Development Outside Large Centres" (1954), "The Most Effective Means of Rendering Museums Accessible to Everyone" (1958), and "Museum as a Cultural Centre in the Development of the Community" (1960) were early innovations. The theme of the 1995 ICOM conference in Stavanger, Norway, was "Museums and Community." ICOM also invests in capacity building for community museums, most notably training staff at the Nubia Museum (1993–2001), and facilitating training in new technologies in museums in Caribbean countries (2001). Recently ICOM has turned its attention to sustainable cultural tourism, recommending that museums promote "participatory democracy by bringing together heritage resources and their neighbouring communities, stimulating community based development through heritage tourism that contributes to poverty alleviation without compromising the integrity of heritage resources."[19]

AAM's Museums and Communities Initiative

Mainstream museums have become increasingly attuned to diversifying the communities they serve, reaching out through innovative program partnerships, target audience marketing, special exhibitions highlighting local ethnic communities, multilingual labels, accessible design, and other new methods of inclusive interpretation. These cultural accessibility issues were important enough that the American Association of Museums conceived the Museums and Communities Initiative in 1998. AAM convened a national task force, held six community dialogues around the country through 2001, and passed a Museums and Community Resolution in 2002,[20] urging all museums to be active and collaborative in their communities. In 2002, AAM published two volumes to assist museums in becoming more community minded: *Mastering Civic Engagement: A Challenge to Museums*, and *A Museums and Community Toolkit*. AAM also hosted seminars on building community connections in Los Angeles and Philadelphia in 2003, and Chicago and New Orleans in 2004. While the grant-funded initiative ended in 2007, AAM continues to encourage the work between museums and community. AAM members can access current information on its Web information center.[21]

In 2007, AAM took its community focus abroad, converting its International Partnership Among Museums (IPAM) program into the Museums and Community Collaboration Abroad (MCCA). From its inception in 1980 through the end of the program in 2007, the IPAM program made possible over 245 museum exchanges that focused on administration, collections care, education, research, marketing, and design. MCCA programs emphasize exchange projects that go beyond the museums and into the communities. The first granting cycle included a project that partnered the tiny Black Pine Animal Park in Indiana, with only three paid staff, with the struggling Dushanbe Zoo in Tajikistan. The Black Pine Animal Park prospers because of its ability to mobilize volunteers and in-kind donations, and through AAM's MCCA they have embarked on a training program for Dushanbe to adapt the Black Pine model to the Tajik community.[22]

The National Park Service

In 2001, the Advisory Board of the National Park System, chaired by renowned historian John Hope Franklin, issued a report entitled "Rethinking the National Parks for the 21st Century," in which they called on the agency to use the Parks not just for recreation, but as springboards for intellectual and cultural enrichment. They admonished that the Parks "must ensure that the American story is told faithfully, completely, and accurately. . . .Our nation's history is our civic glue." Said Franklin, "The places that commemorate sad history are not places in which we wallow,. . . but instead places in which we may be moved to a new resolve, to be better citizens. Explaining history from a variety of angles makes it not only more interesting, but also more true."[23] Northeast Regional Director Marie Rust responded by holding a workshop focused on civic engagement and agency in New York in December 2001. The Civic Engagement Initiative

> is the National Park Service's challenge to itself, to find new ways to revitalize its mission of preserving and interpreting our nation's natural and cultural heritage. Forming meaningful partnerships with the very people most invested in the parks will instill in them a sense of ownership, and ensure the relevance of NPS resources and programs.[24]

Oral History

Oral history is one way for mainstream museums to record the experiences and inner lives of those ". . . absent from the historical record—workers, dissenters, recent immigrants, ethnic minorities, and farmers. . . ."[25] This valuable tool had its beginnings even before the early days of recording devices, when such projects as documenting the narratives of 2,300 former Slaves was conducted by Works Progress Administration journalists. Its use exploded in the 1960s and 1970s, and some believe it has yet to reach its full potential. Richard Rabinowitz, president of the American History Workshop, notes that oral history videos in exhibitions allow the visitor to experience a conversation with the subject, not a lecture from "a masked authority figure with a very remote kind of knowledge."[26] A milestone for the Smithsonian Institution's National Museum of American History was the 1987 exhibition A More Perfect Union: Japanese Americans and the U.S. Constitution. As a lesson on the constitution, the NMAH decided to tell a story of its violation: the saga of 110,000 U.S. citizens of Japanese descent who were held in internment camps during World War II. Selma Thomas, the filmmaker on the project, reflects,

> We wanted to create a document that was incontestable. . .but the oral history also gives it a humanity that is often lacking in other kinds of documents. . . .You're asking a person to relive a painful moment and make it part of the public record. It's very invasive. But unless they do it, some part of the historical record is missing from the public forum.[27]

Oral history projects have proven even more integral to community museums than to mainstream museums. The Alutiiq Museum in Kodiak, Alaska, makes its collection come alive by showing artifacts to elders and recording their explanations of use and meaning. Recordings are also a means to preserve the Alutiiq language, in danger of dying with so few living native speakers. While the Alutiiq Museum is focusing on oral history as a tool to preserve its culture, the Japanese American National Museum has reached out to multiple cultures to preserve the history of a neighborhood. In its 2002 exhibition, "Boyle Heights: The Power of Place," oral histories of Jewish, Japanese, Mexican, Italian, Armenian, Russian Molokan, and African American families, conducted by a team of scholars, volunteers, and university and high school students, revealed the evolution of the neighborhood, and how these ethnicities interrelated. According to

Associate Curator Sojin Kim, the teenagers actually collected some of the most interesting stories, because the older interviewees were more open to sharing their stories with the young people than with scholars.[27] The Boyle Heights project achieved a more diverse visitorship for the museum, and fostered a sense of pride in the participants.

Community Advisory Groups

Mainstream museums often invite community advisors to shape their exhibition, collection, and educational programs. The Denver Museum of Nature and Science has enjoyed the benefit of a Native American Resource Group since the mid-1970s. From 2003 to 2005, the Chicago History Museum employed a 15-member Teen Council to develop a Web site, a program series, and an exhibition, and also to create content by collecting 100 oral histories of growing up in the city. The Royal British Columbia Museum in Victoria, B. C., Canada, not only worked with Nuu-cha-nulth tribal members on a 1999 exhibition about their artworks, but the Nuu-cha-nulth also served as paid "hosts" in the galleries. Nuu-cha-nulth youth came to a deeper knowledge of their own culture by explaining it to non-native visitors. In the 1980s, the Field Museum in Chicago established the Center for Cultural Understanding and Change to help the museum connect with and understand its contemporary urban community. It convened a forum entitled "Conversations on Pluralism and Identity in America" and in 1998 launched Cultural Connections, an annual series of six programs, each jointly presented by two Chicago area ethnic museums. One pitfall for museums that convene community advisory groups for special projects is that they often disband them when the project is complete. Relationships must be based on more than just the museum's agenda. Says Claudine K. Brown of the Nathan Cummings Foundation, "Each partner should be in a better position for having participated in the process."[20]

Communities on the Net

New trends in museum communities include those growing through the Internet. As early as 1996, The Fine Arts Museum in San Francisco launched "The Thinker ImageBase" (http://www.thinker.org) with 80,000 images from its collection, stating "The collections belong to the people of the City and County of San Francisco" and that the museum's mission was to be more a resource than a repository. By 2003, it was noted that many museums had more virtual visitors than real visitors.[28] Online communities can convene people for activities, discussions, games, exhibitions, stories, research, collaboration, and much more. The Carnegie Science Center in Pittsburgh, Pennsylvania created the social networking site, Braincake, in 2006, as part of the Girls, Math and Science Partnership. Girls aged 11–17 years join this upbeat virtual community, whose tag line is "Smart. Sweet," to participate in programs, get homework help, find out about scholarship and career opportunities, and blog about science.[29] In 2008, Tate Modern in London, England, opened the Great Tate Mod Blog, inviting Web visitors to help shape the development of their new wing by posting photographs and ideas of their favorite spaces on a "mood board."[30] Museums are also taking advantage of existing social networking and other Web 2.0 sites. For example, the Chicago History Museum joined the MySpace community in 2008, and its profile reads "female; 101 years old; mood: cultured; interests: hearing and telling stories." At the time of this writing, most of her friends were other museums.[31] In 2006, San Francisco, California's Exploratorium mixed real and virtual world experiences by inviting avatars (a virtual representation of oneself) to gather in the museum's Second Life amphitheater to view a live Webcast of the total solar eclipse in Turkey. Second Life is an enormous, multiuser, three-dimensional online virtual world that people visit through their avatars, and explore virtual environments built by other people's avatars. The museum also hosts events and tests prototypes on "Exploratorium Island," their corner of the Second Life world. A staff avatar can make a presentation and take questions from an international avatar audience.[32]

The information superhighway may connect a museum with visitors from around the world or down the block, but access is not universal. Poverty keeps away both the real and the virtual visitor in what has come to be known as the "digital divide." Even though the United States is among the most networked nations in the world, the 2000 U.S. Census reported that among children 3–17, 77% of white households and 72% of Asian households had computers with Internet access, while only 43% of African American children and 27% of Latino children had Internet at home.[33] While the gap is certainly narrowing, pockets of isolation exist in both urban and, perhaps even more so, rural regions of the United States.

Visitor-Generated Content

The Tech Museum of Innovation in San Jose, California, brought the real and virtual worlds even closer when it launched The Tech Virtual Experiment. In early 2008, the museum posted an open call on Second Life for avatars, individually or in virtual collaborations, to develop and design museum exhibits. Of the 50 virtual exhibitions created by hundreds of avatars, seven were converted to the real world and installed in the Virtual Test Zone gallery in June 2008.[34] This kind of visitor-generated content may be an increasing trend embraced by museum innovators, but many museums still fear dilution of their authority. In 2005, Marymount Manhattan College Art Professor, David Gilbert, turned the museum world on its ear with a guerilla audio tour project called Art Mobs. His students produced unauthorized audio guides to works in

New York's Museum of Modern Art (MoMA), that they offered to the general public via the Internet, at a time when museums were only beginning to ponder the possibilities of downloadable media content. Says Gilbert, "we are democratizing the experience of touring an art museum; we are offering a way for anyone to 'curate' their own little corner of MoMA."[35] Since then, many museums have begun to realize that they can ride the crest of this wave, and many welcome a far flung audience to the table to participate in the creation of history, culture, and meaning. The Minnesota History Center invited Minnesotans to suggest topics for their October 2008 exhibition celebrating the sesquicentennial of the state. They received over 2,700 entries. Each of the 150 subjects chosen for display includes a photo and testimonial of the person who nominated it. Minnesota Historical Society director Nina Archabal asks, "Who better to tell us about Minnesota than the people who live here?"[36] In March, 2008, the Brooklyn Museum in New York made an open call to artists to submit a work of photography that represented the theme "The Changing Faces of Brooklyn," along with a 100-word statement. Next they invited the general public to evaluate the submissions using an online evaluation tool. 3,344 evaluators cast 410,089 evaluations for the 389 entries. The photographs were curated by the crowd, and the top 20% were installed in the exhibition gallery at the Museum from June 27 to August 10, 2008.[37,38] These online initiatives redefine the very nature of community—online visitors choose to join the virtual community based on personal interest, completely independent of their class, gender, ethnic profile, or national origin.

CONCLUSION

While there remain many bastions of curated culture that do not embrace the notion of accessibility and community involvement, the evolutionary arc of museums over the last 200 years tends toward greater inclusion. The introduction of first voice into a mainstream museum can offer new authentic and personal perspectives on a shared past. But just like the difference between memoir and biography, first voice narratives and mainstream historical analysis both hold value. In combination, they produce a synergy of meaning that provides empowerment and self expression at the same time as a sense of context in the overall course of human society. Mainstream museums can offer a stitching together of the patchwork of many first voice stories, but where the lines are drawn can be contentious territory. Museums and communities often struggle over who owns the narrative. These tensions are not limited to mainstream museums, as the politics of inclusion and exclusion play out in ethnic museums as well. Those in the dominant culture often consider minority groups to be homogenous, but a little interaction is enough to reveal the remarkable diversity within each group.

In spite of the challenges of community collaboration, it is one of the key strategies for museums to become and/or remain relevant. In an October 2008, keynote speech, Jonathon Katz posited that society is trending from empathy to agency. He cited the fact that the gaming industry, which operates on agency, has overtaken the gross sales of the film industry, which banks on empathy. He advised museums to embrace this trend toward agency, and to provide means for visitor influence on the content and experience in programs, galleries, and online.[39] Nina Simon agrees; on her museum 2.0 blog, she says "In a world where visitors want to create, remix, and interpret content messages on their own, museums can assume a new role of authority as 'platforms' for those creations and recombinations."[40] The museum of the future will prosper if it invites its visitors to enter the narrative process.

ACKNOWLEDGMENTS

I would like to thank Rosemary Adams, director of publications at the Chicago History Museum, for her editorial eye; Nina Simon for turning me on to the remarkable online museum community; my daughter Katie Biggs-Wrona for writing the insightful introduction; and David Kavesh for his relentless support.

REFERENCES

1. Brigham, D.R. Social class and participation in Peale's Philadelphia Museum. In *Mermaids, Mummies, and Mastodons: The Emergence of the American Museum*; Alderson, W.T., Ed.; American Association of Museums: Washington, D.C., 1992; 79.
2. Kholstedt, S.G. Entrepreneurs and intellectuals: Natural history in early American museums. In *Mermaids, Mummies, and Mastodons: The Emergence of the American Museum*; Alderson, W.T., Ed.; American Association of Museums: Washington, D.C., 1992; 23.
3. Durel, J.W. In pursuit of a profit. In *Mermaids, Mummies, and Mastodons: The Emergence of the American Museum*; Alderson, W.T., Ed.; American Association of Museums: Washington, D.C., 1992; 60.
4. Kholstedt, S.G. Entrepreneurs and intellectuals: Natural history in early American museums. In *Mermaids, Mummies, and Mastodons: The Emergence of the American Museum*; Alderson, W.T., Ed.; American Association of Museums: Washington, D.C., 1992; 28.
5. Weil, S.E. The museum and the public. Museum Manage. Curatorship **1997**, *16*(3), 257–271.
6. Kholstedt, S.G. Entrepreneurs and intellectuals: Natural history in early American museums. In *Mermaids, Mummies, and Mastodons: The Emergence of the American Museum*; Alderson, W.T., Ed.; American Association of Museums: Washington, D.C., 1992; 37.
7. Dana, J.C. In *The New Museum: Selected Writings by John Cotton Dana*; Peniston, W.A., Ed.; The Newark Museum

and The American Association of Museums: Washington, D.C., 1999; 164.
8. Dana, J.C. In *The New Museum: Selected Writings by John Cotton Dana*; Peniston, W.A., Ed.; The Newark Museum and The American Association of Museums: Washington, D.C., 1999; 117.
9. Booth, E.T. *Apprenticeship in the Museum*; The Museum: Newark, NJ, 1928.
10. Zamora, H. Identity & community: a look at four Latino museums. Museum News **2002**, *81*(3), 39.
11. Cabrera, R. *Beyond Dust, Memories and Preservation: Roles of Ethnic Museums in Shaping Community Ethnic Identity*, Unpublished doctoral dissertation; University of Illinois at Chicago: Chicago, IL, 2008.
12. Cohen, J.H. The Shan-Dany Museum: community, economics and cultural traditions in a rural Mexican village. Human Org **2001**, Fall *60*(3), 272–280.
13. Seitz, S.; Miller, S. *A Tenement Story: The History of 97 Orchard Street and the Lower East Side Tenement Museum*, The Lower East Side Tenement Museum: New York, 1999; 10.
14. http://www.sitesofconscience.org/sites/district-six/what-happened-here/en/.
15. http://www.sitesofconscience.org/sites/district-six/how-is-it-remembered/en/.
16. http://www.tepapa.govt.nz/TePapa/English/AboutTePapa/AboutUs/WhatWeDo/The+Concept.htm.
17. http://www.tepapa.govt.nz/TePapa/English/AboutTePapa/AboutUs/WhatWeDo/Corporate+Principles.htm.
18. http://www.sitesofconscience.org/about-us/en/.
19. http://icom.museum/.
20. Conwill, K.H.; Roosa, A.M. Cultivating community connections. Museum News **2003**, *82*(3), 69.
21. http://www.aam-us.org/museumresources/ic/mip/engage.cfm.
22. http://www.aam-us.org/mcca/About.cfm.
23. http://www.nps.gov/civic/about/how.pdf.
24. http://www.nps.gov/civic/.
25. Chew, R. Collected stories: The rise of oral history in museum exhibitions. Museum News **2002**, *81*(6), 31.
26. Chew, R. Collected stories: The rise of oral history in museum exhibitions. Museum News **2002**, *81*(6), 32.
27. Chew, R. Collected stories: The rise of oral history in museum exhibitions. Museum News **2002**, *81*(6), 33.
28. Muller, K. The culture of globalization. Museum News **2003**, *82*(3), 62.
29. http://www.braincake.org/whoweare.aspx.
30. http://modblog.tate.org.uk/.
31. http://myspace.com/chicagohistorymuseum.
32. http://www.exploratorium.edu/worlds/secondlife/index.html.
33. http://www.census.gov/prod/2001pubs/p23-207.pdf.
34. http://museumtwo.blogspot.com/2008/06/community-exhibit-development-lessons.html.
35. http://mod.blogs.com/art_mobs/.
36. http://discovery.mnhs.org/MN150/index.php?title=Main_Page.
37. http://www.brooklynmuseum.org/exhibitions/click/stats.php.
38. http://www.brooklynmuseum.org/exhibitions/click/quick_facts.php.
39. Katz, J. Joint Meeting of the Association of Midwest Museums and the Mountain Plains Museum Association, Kansas City, MO, October 21–25, 2008.
40. http://museumtwo.blogspot.com/2008/10/future-of-authority-platform-power.html.

BIBLIOGRAPHY

1. Alexander, E.P.; Brennan, N.; Brigham, D.R.; Durel, J.W.; Helm, R.; Kohlstedt, S.G.; Kulik, G. In *Mermaids, Mummies, and Mastodons: The Emergence of the American Museum*; Alderson, W.T., Ed.; American Association of Museums: Washington, DC, 1992.
2. Ames, K.L., Franco, B.; Frye, L.T., Eds. *Ideas and Images: Developing Interpretive History Exhibits*; American Association for State and Local History Book Series; Clark, S. Sageser, Ed.; AltaMira Press: Walnut Creek, CA, 1997.
3. Bunch, L.G. Flies in the buttermilk: museums, diversity, and the will to change. Museum News **2000**, *79*(4), 32–35.
4. Cabrera, R. Beyond museum walls. Museum News **2006**, *85*(4), 35–38.
5. Din, H., Hecht, P., Eds. *The Digital Museum: A Think Guide*; American Association of Museums: Washington, D.C., 2007.
6. Isaac, B.; Harjo, S.S.; Lomawalma, H.; McKeon, C.T.; West, R.W. NAGPRA at 10: Examining a decade of the Native American Graves Protection and Repatriation Act. Museum News **2000**, *79*(5), 42–75.
7. Karp, I.; Kratz, C.A. *Museum Frictions: Public Cultures/Global Transformations*, 1st Ed.; Szwaja, L., Ed.; Duke University Press: Durham, NC, 2007; January.
8. Rosenzweig, R.; Thelen, D. *The Presence of the Past: Popular Uses of History in American Life*, Columbia University Press: New York, 1998; November 12.
9. Schwarzer, M. *Riches, Rivals and Radicals: 100 Years of Museums in America*, American Association of Museums: Washington, DC, 2006.
10. Steinbach, L. Civic engagement in a digital age: an even greater challenge to museums. Museum News **2003**, *82*(3), 27–57.
11. Weil, S.E. *Making Museums Matter*; Smithsonian: Washington, DC, 2002.

Museums and Their Visitors: Historic Relationship

Samuel J. Redman
Department of History, University of California, Berkeley, Berkeley, California, U.S.A.

Abstract

The makeup of the museum visitor is perhaps one of the most challenging aspects of museum history for historians to uncover. Historians of museums have often noted that before the field of Visitor Studies grew to prominence, museums often envisioned their audiences as nameless, faceless masses. Historians have either painted this public as composed of members of the privileged elite or as those receptive to being shaped by the elite cultural institutions. This entry examines how the museum visitor has been discussed by both museum professionals and historians of museums in the nineteenth and twentieth century United States.

The Victorian museum visitor leaves but ghostly images in photographs and paintings of historic exhibition halls. Natural history museums greet the Victorian audience with objects grouped comparatively by type or geographic location, which form seemingly endless, straight lines within cold, glass cases. Art museums greet the same visitors with top to bottom walls of paintings or paintings along single lines intend to represent the development of art from its "primitive" forms to its highest (read) European incarnations. The Victorian museum visitor would hardly recognize most contemporary museums in either the United States or Europe, save for the seemingly timeless Greco-Roman architectural façade that masks the past century of change protected within the museum's walls. Museum audiences and visitors, unlike exhibition spaces, collections acquisitions, architectural developments, and institutional changes, leave little documentation of their change over time. Historic visitors to museums have traditionally been treated by scholars in either one of two contradictory terms; they either represented the bourgeoisie elite of a given region or time period, or they have represented the faceless masses subjected to the social control of the elites governing the museums themselves. For more on this contradictory viewpoint related to museum audiences, see Conn.[1] Other scholars have argued that American museums have, since their origins, been geared more towards educating broader audiences than European museums.[2] Museums today, unlike their earlier manifestations, make deliberate efforts to empirically understand who their audiences are, how they learn, and what most interests them. This also helped allow modern museums make conscientious efforts to educate wide-ranging audiences, including children and the disadvantaged. Museums also increasingly work to include their visitors in their presentation of knowledge. Computer-based guest books, blogs, touch screen monitors, and other new technology allow visitors to "talk back" to exhibitions and participate in their development. While most recognize these developments as being, on the whole, overwhelmingly positive, others criticize that museums have gone too far to embrace a brand of "edutainment" and long for a return of a museum "golden age" that, in truth, never really existed. In fact, the use of quantitative analysis by museums in efforts to better understand their audiences and how they learn has made museums both more effective and more enjoyable. This entry will attempt to trace the history of museum audiences and their representation in the historical literature. This entry focuses mainly on the history of museums in the United States from the late nineteenth century to the present. This entry does not focus on the growing body of literature focusing on professionalized Visitor Studies, but rather, it examines the nature of the more casual, yet concerted dialogue about museum audiences in which museum professionals engaged throughout the late nineteenth century to the present.

In his study of the intellectual history of American museums, the historian Steven Conn notes that, "Museum audiences are elusive quarry for the historian," as "They left little trace of themselves and did not register with and specificity in the official records of most museums."[3] Before the 1920s, many museums understood their visitors in terms of one or two basic categories often limited a dichotomy of either adults or school groups. Many museums associated with universities differentiated between school groups and students from the university, sometimes even noting which courses required students to visit the campus museum. Beyond that, however, historians are left with only the museum professionals' speculation on their patrons. Museums did not typically record the educational background of adults visiting the museum and their understanding of how to cater to their audiences continued to be limited. Generally, most museum archives are devoted primarily to the maintenance of a record articulating the development of collections, general institutional policy, and exhibition spaces. Archives are perceived as generally silent on the subject of audiences; however, historians can gain clues to their nature upon close readings of the available sources. The contrast in the available documentation related to collections and exhibitions vis-à-vis the available documentation for museum audiences is perhaps telling. It might be argued that museums considered their collections and exhibitions as a greater priority to the health of the institution, leading directly to the ratio of available archival materials.

By the turn of the last century, museums and museum professionals were seriously contemplating the experience of the visitor to their institutions. Franz Boas, the illustrious cultural anthropologist working at the American Museum of Natural History (AMNH) engaged in just the sort of intellectual debate that characterized the discourse surrounding the experiences of the museum visitor during this time period in a 1907 exchange in the journal *Science*. In responding to a review penned by a curator at his former institution, the Field Museum of Natural History (FMNH) in Chicago, Boas chose to broaden the discourse and entitled his response "Some Principles of Museum Administration." Boas, in comparing two institutions that were well known as significant research institutions vis-à-vis the sleepy American universities at the time, explains, "Museums may serve three objects. They may be institutions designed to furnish healthy entertainment, they may be intended for instruction and they may be intended for the promotion of research." Boas was perhaps one of the most significant researchers working in the United States at this time and yet he explains in the article that the "value of the museum as a resort for popular entertainment must not be underrated."[4] Boas, despite much of what is said in this article, was never fully understood by historians to be a great popularizer. He also adds that, "every attraction that counteracts the influence of the saloon and the racetrack is of great social importance." Museums, therefore, should be both entertaining and intellectually stimulating. George Dorsey, the curator from FMNH who initially offered his critique of the exhibits at the AMNH, longed for the good old days of museum exhibitions. Dorsey comments, "Such exhibits as those above [at the AMNH] characterized might with some degree of propriety be found in the lower grades of the public school, but they certainly do not seem worthy of an institution with claims to be foremost of American museums." Dorsey argues that if the AMNH's leadership truly desires for objects to serve the purpose of educating the general public, they should simply pack them up and send them off to the public schools around the region. He concludes condescendingly, "thus the ideal of this scheme might be more easily and cheaply realized."[5]

For many curators at the early part of the past century, however, museum exhibits were intended to be forums for the presentation of the most recent available research. While the tension between creating cutting-edge research and the desire to popularize major ideas existed throughout the course of the twentieth century, several factors forced museums to begin changing. While a significant number of important exceptions exist, many of the top researchers in fields such as anthropology, biology, and geology began taking academic job posts in universities as opposed to curatorial positions in natural history museums. In fields such as ethnology and archaeology, the rise of new cultural patrimony laws governing the international transport of objects of cultural patrimony resulted in the decrease of certain types of collections arriving in museums. This claim is not without its problems. Certain institutions maintained, on the surface, a steady flow of objects into their collections, though, in the case of anthropological collections in museums, it is important to differentiate between archaeological and ethnographic material. The Hearst Museum of Anthropology at the University of California, Berkeley offers an example of this phenomenon. During the Great Depression and Second World War, when international travel and the purchase of objects from indigenous peoples became increasingly difficult, an increased number of archaeological expeditions allowed the museum to continue to grow at a steady pace in terms of the number of objects accessioned per year.

While the visitor experience was becoming more commonly discussed in various forums utilized by museum professionals, summations of the health of individual museums, or museums as a whole, began not with attendance figures but rather notable collections acquisitions and the development of research programs. Visitors were not left out of documents produced by museums entirely, however, and the visitors experience is hinted at on certain occasions. In a 1908 article summarizing the annual reports of several major institutions, F.A. Lucas notes that the Carnegie Museum's annual report expressed dissatisfaction with the fact that the museum had been opened to the public before the exhibits were ready to host them.[6] Lucas further notes the troubles of the Brooklyn Museum, which complained of having too many tasks without the necessary resources to address them. Two items that the Brooklyn Museum's annual report disparages are a lack of labels for objects and disarranged exhibit cases. It does not take a vast leap of the imagination to begin to understand how a visitor might experience the self-described disarranged and unlabeled, exhibits of the Brooklyn Museum during this time period. Attendance figures, though not included in Lucas' opening remarks on the health of American museums, are included in his commentary later on, presented alongside the attendance figures for several major institutions. Lucas notes that attendance figures, in his estimation, are commonly misunderstood:

> We are accustomed to regard the number of visitors to a museum as a measure of its importance and public

usefulness, but it may more properly be looked upon as an indication of its interest for the public and to some extent the state of the weather. If it is of interest to the public, there is small doubt but what it will prove to be useful.[7]

Lucas also gives an indication of how museums were beginning to understand their audiences. He notes that visitors to the U.S. National Museum (now the Smithsonian Institution) are largely out-of-town tourists, while many of the other major metropolitan museums, such as the FMNH and AMNH, host primarily local and regional residents. Lucas is also quick to point directly to the construction of a new, elevated train station in New York near the AMNH as the direct cause for a spike in attendance. Lucas writes, "Museum attendance, as shown by the report of the U.S. National Museum, is subject to great fluctuation and, like sun-spots, has its maximum and minimum periods." Lucas utilizes similar experiences from museums in London to conclude his analysis on the topic. Clearly then, museums were coming to a better understanding of their audiences by 1908, and this was starting to coalesce in the national and international discourse.

Art museums in the first half of the twentieth century understood themselves as serving multiple audiences. One of these audiences was the student of art. In 1915, Edith R. Abbot examined the experience of the art student as museum visitor in *The Metropolitan Museum of Art Bulletin*. Abbot notes that, "A sculptor comes to visit the classical collection. For him the antique marbles are all lessons in transcription; it is not enough to connect them with the past, their relation to the types of today is quite as pertinent." While these audiences were certainly welcomed to the museum, Abbot argues that the art student is best served by the museum by taking a guided tour, "with some one whose eye is . . . keen." Abbot also notes, however, "The instructor who is familiar with the resources of the Museum is in requisition in all of these instances as guide rather than as teacher. It is only when individuals or groups of persons arrange in advance for a series of appointments that museum instruction can be called organized in any sense."[8] While articles like Abbot's lack the quantitative evidence utilized in later forms of visitor studies, it is demonstrative of attempts to examine anecdotal experiences to improve various types of visitor experiences.

By the late 1920s certain museums were attempting to better understand their audiences through quantitative rather than qualitative methods of observation. Instead of providing anecdotal evidence of the background of the audiences, or reporting casual curatorial strolls through exhibitions spaces in attempts to gauge how much audiences were learning, articles from this period, along with museum annual reports begin to demonstrate attempts at quantitative analysis. In the December 1929 issue of the *Pennsylvania Museum Bulletin* (now the Philadelphia Museum of Art), the museum reported the results of a survey during the first year of its occupation of a new facility. The simple survey was given to one thousand of the first million visitors to the museum. The survey consisted of six basic questions related to the visitor's occupation, place of residency, mode of transportation to the museum, what prompted the visitor to come to the museum, what the visitor liked about the museum, and suggestions for improvement. The occupations of those visiting the museum represent rather basic categories separated into men and women, then subdivided into basic categories such as businessmen, salesmen, lawyers, doctors, and factory workers. Unsurprisingly, students represented the largest number of visitors in the male category. Tellingly, however, male individuals working in manufacturing were well represented in the survey; in short, the museum's audience was more complex than the anonymous hoards of art students assumed to have been visiting museums by previous estimates. The Philadelphia Museum of Art, unlike many of its counterparts including the Metropolitan Museum of Art in New York, was becoming well known as an institution that not only eschewed discouraging the working classes from visiting the museum, in fact, the museum worked to reach out to them. The Philadelphia Museum of Art also ran the School of Industrial Arts. Additionally, the museums advertisements on streetcar lines are indicative of this commitment to the working classes. For more on the development of the Philadelphia Museum, see Conn.[9] To provide further evidence of this, lawyers, making up an estimated 6000 visitors, barely outpaced farmers, who represented 5000 of the 1,000,000 total. A majority of the art students visiting the museum were women (23,000), yet they were outpaced many times over by housewives (264,000). Housewives, in fact, represented over a quarter of the total number of museum visitors represented in the survey.[10]

A vast majority of the visitors represented in the survey were from the metropolitan Philadelphia region, though a roughly equal number of visitors arrived from the suburbs of Philadelphia as did those from other regions of Pennsylvania (nearly 11%). A majority of visitors arrived to the museum by private car, though various types of public transportation, when combined, greatly outpaced this number. Over half of the visitors learned about the museum through word of mouth, though over 40% were prompted to go to the museum due to some form of advertisement, many of which were placed on streetcars. Housewives and farmers mostly enjoyed the period rooms, students and artists appreciated the paintings—as did the factory workers—and architects and engineers appreciated the museum building itself as much as they enjoyed the exhibits. The most common suggestion for improvement was a desire for a greater number of lectures, a desire for a café, and better modes of transportation to and from the institution. The museum report concludes that the institution does not simply represent a small portion of the public, but rather a large cross-section of the population. That said, the museum attracted, "a proportionally large number of people from those groups whose vocations make them most dependent upon a knowledge and study of works of art."[10]

In reading the 1929 report on the Pennsylvania Museum's survey, one is struck by not only the broad cross-section of the population visiting the museum, but also the wide range of reactions to the institution, most of which were positive. The report concludes that it was initiated in an attempt to better the museum's service to the public. This report complicates the notion that museums in the United States were simply gathering points for the bourgeois elite of a given community. The vast number of farmers and factory workers visiting the museum indicate that it was not simply a form of entertainment for the upper class. Additionally, the roughly proportionate female visitors (54.8%) to male visitors (45.2%) indicate that museums were neither sites of male or female domination.[10]

Though quantitative forms of analysis were becoming increasingly available, broad assumptions related to museum audiences and visitors remained the currency of academics and museum professionals that attempted to be the authority on the subject. In a 1940 article appearing in *Science*, Marcus S. Goldstein posited a number of questions on museum visitors but then noted, "I am not acquainted with the literature on museum administration, and research based on the above queries may already be available." Rather than familiarizing himself with this literature, Goldstein believed his assumptions, and the assumptions of those around him, to be interesting enough for publication, "In any case, my own observations (and the response of a number of other individuals with whom the subject has been discussed support these views), point to the following conditions...." While many of Goldstein's arguments prove to be interesting and valid, (e.g., museum exhibitions should have movement to attract a broader audience) a complete lack of evidence beyond his assumptions prevent the argument from being wholly effective.[11]

The experience of visiting museums in both the United States and Europe changed swiftly after the close of the Second World War. Museums in the United States began hiring educators who worked directly with visitors, curatorial staff, and perhaps most importantly, the docents who guided tours through museum exhibits. Docents were trained to guide tours aimed toward educating specific types of audiences, rather than repeating the same tour for every group. Art museums, specifically, had taken the lead role in working with young children in the field of museum education following the Second World War.[12] More specifically, art museums in cities like Indianapolis, rather than the major metropolitan museums of Chicago or New York, assumed the lead role in developing children's art classes or workshops in museums. In addition to developing new exhibition spaces specifically aimed at childhood education, museums were changing the nature of how school groups visited museums. Whereas previously museums would encourage school groups to tour the entire museum in a single day, museums such as the Denver Natural History Museum (now the Denver Museum of Nature and Science) began encouraging teachers to tie visits closely with classroom materials. By the late 1950s, museums were discouraging schools from bringing in groups for general visits, and strongly encouraging these types of classroom-related visits. An example of this type of guideline can be found in its annual report.[13] Attendance in museums in both the United States and in many places in Europe boomed following the Second World War. Long lines awaited newly reopened museums on the coasts or in vulnerable areas including the British Museum in London and the Metropolitan Museum of Art in New York, both of which had been closed or redacted during the course of the war. The Denver Natural History Museum, Art Institute of Chicago, and numerous other American museums broke attendance records as the Second World War came to a close. Americans, as the war waned on, possessed a far greater amount of disposable income than during the latter years of the Great Depression, and one manner in which they spent their new income was at museum turnstiles. Theodora Kroeber, wife of the famed American anthropologist, Alfred Kroeber, describes in her biography of her husband their waiting in line with throngs of Londoners to visit the reopened British Museum of Natural History.[14] Museum visitors again availed themselves to many of the most prized works of arts possessed by these institutions that were placed in storage or sent inland, to other museums for safekeeping.

By the 1950s, in addition to changing methodologies related to collections, loans and exchanges, the goals of various types of museum exhibitions, were continuing to evolve. In 1957, the *Los Angeles Times* described the development as the museum shifting its gaze from the exhibition cases themselves to those that were supposed to be looking at the cases. The *L.A. Times* reporter argued that when museums did in fact begin to attempt to understand the museum visitor, it noted that they were generally uninterested in many of the ideas presented to them. "Perhaps," the *L.A. Times* reported, "it was because the presentation was uninspired."[15] Generally, museum curators by this time were taking fewer risks in their exhibitions. By 1954, a pair of museum commentators and curators, Donald Collier and Harry Tschopik, Jr. commented in *American Anthropologist*, "Most importantly, the newer exhibits have not, to date, reflected any systematic or integrated plan, and treatment of many problems of current theoretical interest..." Unlike museums of the first half of the twentieth century, exhibits did not address matters of "current theoretical interest."[16] Instead, museums presented basic educational materials and served as introductions to broader topics. Museums had become more analogous to introductory textbooks than scholarly journals. Interestingly, the notion of educating the public via exhibitions and the production of top-notch research continued to be somewhat at odds. This was especially true in university-based museums. In 1953, in discussing the continued desire for a new anthropology building, the anthropology department at the University of California, Berkeley circulated a memorandum that noted museum research and the use of collections for exhibition spaces were somewhat at odds, "The use of the collections for undergraduate teaching exhibits frequently conflicts with their use for research, when materials in an exhibition case are needed for a research project, and the reverse situation also arises."[17]

Popular notions surrounding museums, however, were anything but fully changed by the 1960s. In 1963, another *L.A. Times* reporter argued that if the word, "museum" came up in a word association game, his response would be "stuffed Indian." This word association response, the reporter then argues, would have been inaccurate, "Because museums are moving magically these days."[18] The postwar period of American history also meant the development of new museum facilities in many parts of the country. This development, in turn, lead to greater pressure for museums to draw larger crowds. Museums began responding to these pressures by hosting a greater number of major, "blockbuster" exhibitions on topics of popular interest, thus changing the visitor experience.

While most museums were essentially developing educational programming without quantitative analysis informing the decision-making process, museum professionals during the 1960s and 1970s worked to better understand their audiences and develop programming specifically attuned to the need of the public. In 1975, an article in the journal *Studies in Art Education*, estimated that 93% of the art museums in the United States sponsored educational programs. Of those programs, no serious, systematic documentation of the programs' effectiveness or scope had been attempted. In other words, while museums were attempting to educate their audiences utilizing more refined processes, they possessed little understanding of how well they were working.[19]

By the late 1980s and early 1990s, museums were arriving at a more complex understanding of their audiences. In 1989, a study of several American art museums that corroborated with another study in England demonstrated that those visiting art museums were typically "in the upper educational, occupational and income groups, younger than the population in general (average age is 34) and active in community and leisure-time organizations."[20] While natural history and science museums were understood as catering to audiences differently than art museum, the common notion that museums were synonymous with the upper class of western society continued to stick, and arguably with some supporting evidence. One of the authors of the 1989 study, would, 1 year later, argue that the one of the most important factors in turning a nonart museum visitor into a regular patron was not parental encouragement or the entrance into a new tax bracket, but rather, having art lessons as a child. The most important factor however, between visitors and non-visitors, was simply being offered the opportunity to visit the museum in the first place.[21]

In 1999, the Smithsonian's National Museum of American History featured an exhibit on the history of sweatshops in the United States. The exhibit, which covered a subject that was challenging for many visitors to the museum, provided a guest book for visitor comments. Mary Alexander, an educator employed by the Smithsonian, published many of her observations related to the visitors' reactions and comments to the exhibit, which was entitled, "Between a Rock and Hard Place: A History of American Sweatshops, 1820–Present." The following year, the results of Alexander's study were published in the academic journal, *The Public Historian*. The exhibit is representative of attempts by museums to better understand—and subsequently cater to—their visitors. The process of documenting the audience's reactions to an exhibition, studying these reactions, and then disseminating the results of the study in an academic journal would have been unheard of throughout most of the twentieth century. As Alexander's study demonstrated, museum audiences were, by-and-large, understanding many of the complex and challenging themes presented in the displays. Alexander reported the comments of the visitors to museums in a fashion that might surprise some, arguing that their comments were "intelligent, articulate, sophisticated, and sometimes vehement."

Several years before the Smithsonian exhibition on sweatshops in American history, the American Association of Museums developed a report entitled, "Excellence and Equity: Education and the Public Dimension of Museums." The report examines museums and spaces of public education and offers 10 guidelines for improving and maintaining the role for museums well into the future. For the American Association of Museums, the changes occurring related to the professionalization of museum education represented progress. Analysis of this document can be found in Crew.[2] The changes occurring in museums during the closing decades of the twentieth century did not go undisputed. In 1991, John Terrell, a Curator of Anthropology at the FMNH compared the contemporary museums to Disneyland, calling for a return of, "The Good Old Days," when academic departments were responsible for the development of exhibition spaces. The problem with Terrell's commentary, however, is that "The Good Old Days," as he envisions them, never really existed. Terrell notes that while museum curators were responsible for exhibitions from the founding of the museum through the 1960s, the museum displayed some of its most popular exhibitions. What Terrell carefully ignores, however, is that some curators were not simply just "mediocre in their exhibit talents"; some curators deliberately misled the public and the press in order to push for greater attendance, including a notable example of Henry Field at Terrell's own Field Museum in the display of a set of European human remains from the

Magdalenian Period. (Henry Field, upon the occasion of the display of the Field Museum's Magdalenian Girl.) Field called the display of the specimen a "chance to fire the imagination of Chicago."[22] In connection with the skeleton, Field purchased an ivory harpoon point he claimed to have been found near the remains. Field began referring to the projectile point as the possible cause of death for the woman, and labeled it in the exhibition space as such. No archaeological evidence exists to make this claim, and it is unclear as to whether or not the projectile point even came from the same site at all. Despite the tenuous nature of the evidence, however, Henry Field, the museum, and the popular media, eagerly ran with the story. The museum and the press further speculated on the story of Magdalenian Girl's murder as coming at the hands of a jealous lover. By the time the remains arrived in Chicago, the press had latched firmly onto the story, splashing it on the front pages and further speculating on the circumstances of the prehistoric woman's death, and the public became fascinated. The first Saturday of her display, 22,000 visitors, a record crowd, came to view the skeleton firsthand.[23] Despite the fact that over a decade had gone by since her first appearance in Chicago, lectures on the subject of Magdalenian Girl were still selling out following the Second World War, as long as they included dramatizations of the circumstances of her demise.[24] In other words, possessing a doctorate in an academic discipline (like Henry Field) does not prevent an individual from being disingenuous or an effective communicator. On the other hand, educators with specialized knowledge of communicating ideas on a broad level have, on the whole crafted exhibits in museums which are arguably more interesting and entertaining than those developed by previous generations of scholars. My point here, of course, is not that educators are above the human temptation to exaggerate claims or make mistakes, but rather, than academic credentials does not prevent these types of errors. Like Dorsey before him, Terrell misjudged the modes of crafting the visitor experience in his own day-and-age. In the interest of full disclosure, the author is a former employee of the Field Museum.

Terrell and those still pining for a return to an age before the professionalization of education departments within museums would be wise to heed the words of A.E. Parr, the director of the American Museum of Natural History, who wrote upon the conclusion of the Second World War,

> "... to see as the goal of reconversion only a reversal to an earlier state of happier memory, and to seek mainly the reestablishment of previous contacts with fellow sufferers rather than attempt to reenter the turbulent main stream which left them on its shores for a while. This is the deepest pitfall across the path of the natural history museums today."[25]

Museums today understand their visitors and audiences much more effectively than throughout the course of most of their history. Anecdotal assumptions about what makes a museum effective have been replaced in a successful manner with quantitative analysis. While visitor surveys and the hiring museum professionals with backgrounds in education have proven to be a positive development for these institutions, they cannot fully replace the casual observation of exhibition halls on a day-to-day basis. Curators would be well served to spend more time in their own exhibitions, working directly with visitors and observing docent tours rather than assuming they understand their constitution. Additionally, curators should avoid the assumption that their galleries were either more effective or possessed some a greater form of academic rigor in the "Good Old Days." While museums at the turn of the last century did, in fact, present a more complex exhibition of their subject matter, the over-verbalization and emphasis on theory made many exhibits more pedantic than effective. While the Victorian museum visitor would hardly recognize most of their own cultural institutions, museums, and their audiences, have largely profited from these developments.

REFERENCES

1. Conn, S. *Museums and American Intellectual Life, 1876–1926*; University of Chicago Press: Chicago, IL, 1998; 19–20.
2. Crew, S. Who owns history?: History in the museum. Hist. Teach. November **1996**, *30* (1), 83.
3. Conn, S. *Museum and American Intellectual Life, 1876–1926*; University of Chicago Press: Chicago, IL, 1998; 19.
4. Boas, F. Some principles of museum administration. Sci. New Ser. June 14, **1907**, *25*, 921–933.
5. Dorsey, G. The anthropological exhibits at the American Museum of Natural History. Sci. New Ser. April 12, **1907**, *25* (641), 584–489.
6. Lucas, F.A. The work of our larger museums as shown by their annual reports. Sci. New Ser. January 3, **1908**, *27* (679), 33–36.
7. Lucas, F.A. The work of our larger museums as shown by their annual reports. Sci. New Ser. January 3, **1908**, *27* (679), 35.
8. Abbot, E. Problems of museum instruction. Metropol. Mus. Art B. September **1915**, *10* (9), 193–194.
9. Conn, S. *Metropolitan Philadelphia: Living with the Presence of the Past*; University of Pennsylvania Press: Philadelphia, PA, 2006; 211.
10. Report of a survey of visitors to the museum in its first year. Bull. Penn. Mus. December **1929**, *25* (130), 2–11.
11. Goldstein, M. The museum as a potential force for social enlightenment. Sci. New Ser. August 30 **1940**, *92* (2383), 197–198.
12. Brown, J. The museum as educator. Art Educ. November **1953**, *6* (7), 5–6.
13. Denver Natural History Museum, Annual report, 1958.
14. Kroeber, T. *Alfred Kroeber: A Personal Configuration*; University of California Press: Berkeley, CA, 1970; 198.

15. Thrapp, D. Museum's dioramas enthrall; Los Angeles Times, February 3, **1957**.
16. Collier, D.; Tschopik, H. Wenner-Gren foundation supper conference: The role of museums in American anthropology. Am. Anthropol. New Ser. Oct. **1954**, *56* (5), 768–779.
17. Unknown Author. *The Importance of the Anthropology Collections in Teaching and Research*; Dated December 16, 1953. Bancroft Library, CU-5 Series 2, University of California, President, 1931, 83–100A, Anthropology.
18. Seidenbaum, A. Once-stuffy museum now magic teacher; Los Angeles Times, April 28, **1963**, L2.
19. Newsome, B. An examination of visual arts education in museums. Stud. Art Educ. **1975**, *16* (2), Arts in the Community, 54–56.
20. Hendon, W.; Costa, F.; Rosenberg, R. The general public and the art museum: Case studies of visitors to several institutions identify characteristics of their publics. Am. J. Econ. Sociol. April **1989**, *48* (2), 231–243.
21. Hendon, W. The general public's participation in art museums: Visitors differ from non-visitors, but not as markedly as case studies have indicated. Am. J. Econ. Sociol. October **1990**, *49* (4), 439–457.
22. Yastrow, E.; Nash, S. Henry Field, collections, and exhibit development, 1926–1941. In *Curators, Collections, and Contexts: Anthropology at the Field Museum, 1893–2002, Anthropology, New Series, No. 36*; Field Museum of Natural History: Chicago, IL, 2003; 137.
23. Yastrow, E.; Nash, S. Henry Field, collections, and exhibit development, 1926–1941. In *Curators, Collections, and Contexts: Anthropology at the Field Museum, 1893–2002, Anthropology, New Series, No. 36*; Field Museum of Natural History: Chicago, IL, 2003; 136–138.
24. Bull. Chicago Nat. Hist. Mus. **1946**, *19* (1–2), 8.
25. Parr, A.E. *In Transition*; American Museum of Natural History; New York, Annual report, 1945; 9.

BIBLIOGRAPHY

1. Anderson, G., Ed. *Reinventing the Museum, Historical and Contemporary Perspectives on the Paradigm Shift*; Alta Mira Press: Walnut Creek, CA, 2004.
2. Conn, S. *Museum and American Intellectual Life, 1876–1926*; University of Chicago Press: Chicago, IL, 1998.
3. Nash, S.; Feinman, G., Eds. *Curators, Collections, and Contexts: Anthropology at the Field Museum, 1893–2002, Anthropology, New Series, No. 36*; Field Museum of Natural History: Chicago, IL, 2003.

Museums as Place

Peter Davis
Han-Yin Huang
International Centre for Cultural and Heritage Studies, Newcastle University, Newcastle upon Tyne, U.K.

Abstract
Theoretical approaches to place have been the domain of geographers, sociologists, psychologists, and, to some extent, museologists and academics with an interest in culture and heritage. This entry positions museums within these theories, in particular exploring how contemporary museum practices deal with place representation. Particularly relevant here are the changing nature of places caused by globalization and migration. Alternative approaches to exploring places enshrined in the philosophical approaches of ecomuseology are also discussed.

INTRODUCTION

Place is a complex concept, and few places are as potentially emotive as the museum environment. Place is inevitably linked to concepts of identity and community; museums attempt to construct the identities and histories of places and their communities, making them institutions with challenging responsibilities. This entry reviews the theoretical approaches to places that have been explored by geographers, sociologists, and psychologists and attempts to position museums within them. Globalization and the changing nature of places are of increasing relevance to museums and are discussed briefly before exploring views about place representation enshrined in the philosophical approaches of ecomuseology. Here geographically defined places and the complexities of their landscape, natural resources, archaeology, history, and contemporary culture offer an alternative museum model for the celebration of the tangible and intangible characteristics of place.

THEORIES OF PLACE AND THEIR RELEVANCE TO MUSEUMS

> .... Les Salants is dead throughout the summer, panting and parching in the wind and heat. But to me, it's still home. Not the most beautiful place in the world, or even the most welcoming. But it's my place
>
> —Joanne Harris, *Coastliners*

The image that Joanne Harris paints of her fictional village of Les Salants, located on a small island off the coast of Brittany, France, is that of an imperfect place; isolated, desolate, and inward-looking, it is a place rich in family rivalry and feud where the community scrapes a living from the sea. Nevertheless, despite its frailties and uncertain future, for the central character it remains "my place," a place—according to the islanders—to which "everything returns."

All people have their own place, or perhaps several places, where they feel they "belong." Terms such as "belonging," "sense of place," "identity," and "community" are all related to—or confused with—ideas about place. Perhaps it is unsurprising then that place, and the more elusive "sense of place" have been a research focus in several disciplines, including geography, anthropology, ecology, psychology, sociology, and cultural and heritage studies. A variety of terms seeking to capture the relationship between people and place, including "sense of experience,"[1] topophilia,[2] place identity,[3] place attachment,[4] and insidedness, local sentiment, or community sentiment[5,6] have been coined. Discussion has sought and found inspiration from cross-disciplinary evaluation.[7–9] So, for example, although the physical geographer may examine place as a defined geographical entity, "the sentiments of attachment and detachment that human beings experience, express and contest in relation to specific places"[8] have been increasingly examined by human geographers as a result of psychoanalytical, social, and environmental approaches. Place lies at the heart of human geography[9] with Yi-Fu Tuan, Edward Relph, and Anne Buttimer being regarded as pioneers in reflecting on place and "sense of place" from experiential perspectives.[10,11] These three authors' understanding of place puts people at the heart of the concept. Tuan[12] reminds us that a sense of place goes beyond aesthetic appreciation, while Relph[13] demands that we examine the idea in terms of "authenticity"; Buttimer[14] argues that place is something that must be experienced rather than described. All emphasize that place provides "a world of meaning."[11]

Encyclopedia of Library and Information Sciences, Fourth Edition DOI: 10.1081/E-ELIS4-120044341

Tuan[15] sees space and place as mutually defined terms: "what begins as undifferentiated space becomes place as we get to know it better and endow it with value." Similarly Casey agrees that the place must be experienced: "there is no knowing or sensing a place except by being in that place, and to be in a place is to be in a position to perceive it."[16] This has resonance with Escobar's[17] view that place is not simply "a constructed reality"—a physical space—but it is also "a category of thought," a conceptualization of identity. This is an important issue for museums, because they also seek to conceptualize place. Museums also add an additional layer of complexity because they frequently attempt to portray a place not only as it can be experienced today, but also seek to create a vision of a place at an earlier point in history. Museums may attempt to take us back to the mediaeval past when discussing social histories, or deep into the Mesolithic to explain archaeological finds, or into the Mesozoic to explore dinosaur diversity. Dioramas of environments, re-created streets, house interiors, immersion habitats, and digitally created worlds are all utilized by curators and designers to create illusions of places past and present, attempting to provide a "real" and truthful experience.

There is an interesting contrast then between the illusion of places and events that museums create within their walls, and the experience the visitor has at a heritage site. These *in-situ* encounters with place and the past become part of our lived experience and may—arguably—be more meaningful as a result. Smith[18] regards this "affect" of place as being of particular significance in order to understand the meaning of heritage and heritage sites. She writes:

> Heritage as place, or heritage places, may not only be conceived as representational of past human experiences but also of creating an affect on current experiences and perceptions of the world. Thus, a heritage place may represent or stand in for a sense of identity and belonging for particular individuals or groups.

If the word "museum" is substituted into this paragraph for the term "heritage" it makes equally sound reasoning. The idea of place is vital to our understanding of the significance of museums to society, helping us to comprehend—and question—the role museums have in constructing identity.

Place theories make us ask what meanings and values are museum buildings—as place entities themselves—endowed with? With their imposing architecture and sense of power, permanence, and purpose museums are an essential feature of our mental maps of familiar places. They are a reference point in our physical landscape and help us to navigate spaces. So, for example, the museums that grace the waterfront of Stockholm (Sweden) are signifiers and guides to the physical and cultural landscapes for local people and tourists alike. For the local person with a strong attachment to place and memories of childhood (and later), visits to a local museum building are also significant in placing museums within our cognitive geography. It is accepted that memory and place are strongly connected and Casey suggests that "we might even say that memory is naturally place-oriented or at least place-supported."[19] Hummon[5] also addresses the social dimensions of place and the emotional investment and meanings attached to it. Of especial interest to museums are his views on the personal and social meanings of place, how a "symbolic locale"—such as a museum building—serves as an extension of self and community identity. For many people then, museum buildings are a part of the tangible landscape and consequently important in their own right through providing a beacon for a sense of belonging and a symbol of permanence.

The notion that "place provides a world of meaning"[11] demands that we question how museums construct and convey meanings and values about a place—its history, its natural environment, its cultural landscape, and its people—and how they represent a range of identities and memories. How do museums help their visitors to position themselves within a community, to find a "place" in the social, cultural, and physical world, to affect them? Museums are a cultural tool that societies, communities, and even nations have used to construct and express a sense of identity and belonging, but what elements of place feature in the collections held by museums, and are there restrictions on what can be exhibited to represent place? How are objects selected from this store of artifacts to construct "truth," a narrative about a place, peoples, histories, or events that took place there?

Before exploring these ideas further, it is essential to discuss the nature of museums themselves. All museums are not the same, indeed, their diversity is extraordinary. They can be managed and financed centrally by the state, by local authorities, by charitable trusts, and by private individuals. They may exhibit specialist collections or hold a diverse range of artifacts and specimens. They may have high levels of funding and professional staffing or be small volunteer-run institutions. They may identify their audience as being international or national tourists, or only local people; they may appeal to elite audiences or they may regard themselves as being family oriented. They can be located in large cities or in remote rural areas. All these variations influence how individual museums determine their role in society, and consequently how they might wish to interpret their place. What image of "their place" might they attempt to portray in their exhibitions, and who makes those decisions? It is evident that the complexity and diversity of museums make it dangerous to generalize about the relationships between museums and place.

The situation is complicated further by the types of collections that museums have amassed over time.

Collections may be of international scientific and historic interest or be of purely local significance. Collections can have immediate or explicit links to local places (a locally collected herbarium, a collection of local landscape paintings, or ceramics from a local pottery) or may gain an association with a place over time, an inferred link. Thus a stuffed polar bear or a collection of French impressionist paintings held by a museum in an industrial northern city in the United Kingdom might not have explicit links with the immediate locality. Nevertheless, generations of local visitors have "appropriated" them; for local people these items constitute elements in the memories and knowledge of "their" museum in their city, they have become a part of their place.

Where does this leave National Museums and their "universal" collections? Large national museums, such as the Smithsonian, the British Museum, or the Louvre, portray a global view of place. The British Museum, for example, does, of course, hold collections which enable it to interpret aspects of British history but most of its galleries present a global perspective, using artifacts to celebrate ancient civilizations and the diverse cultures of the world. These exhibitions also represent Britain and the British as traders, explorers, and especially, as colonists. Objects exhibited here are not only a testament to humankind's ingenuity and craftsmanship, but also a record of the acquisition of places and their natural resources, and of the subjugation of people. Perhaps it is unsurprising that the objects themselves, rather than people or place, are the principal focus of interpretation in the British Museum. For this reason much of the following discussion ignores national museums, as they say little about the more familiar places within which we locate ourselves.

Museum Management–Music Information

What then are the key theoretical components of place that museums have to consider in relation to their audiences and their exhibitions? Relph[13] places particular emphasis on time, suggesting that the length of time in a locality appears to play an important part in how it is perceived by the individual; other studies[20] support the view that the longer a person stays in a place, the more strongly he or she is attached to it, and especially so if they were born there. Attachment may therefore differ between long-term residents and more recent immigrants.[5,6] However, recent research[21] in Lancashire (United Kingdom) has revealed that incomers have an ability to place themselves "in an imaginary landscape which is central to people's sense of belonging." The authors refer to this phenomenon of contemporary attachment to place as "elective belonging," where "Belonging is not that of an individual to a fixed community rooted in place, but rather, one in which the place becomes valuable to the individual."[22] It appears that incomers grasp the opportunities places make available to them, and that they frequently become involved as active players in local social networks. Tuan[12] suggests that an individual's perception of place also varies according to the stage of life he or she has reached, but other variables—for example, gender, education, religion, class, occupation—must also surely come into play. The nature of the person–time–place interaction demands that museums be aware of its complexity and of the range of knowledge about and attitudes to place that occur among its visitors. Long-term residents may have a very different place identity to that of more recent arrivals, but the latter may be more receptive to innovation by, and participation in the museum.

Museums can be confident that even though every individual has their own unique concept of place, strong elements of place are frequently shared with others.[23] So, for example, in the redesigned (2007) galleries of Sheffield's Weston Park Museum, two of the elements chosen to represent Sheffield (United Kingdom) as a distinctive place are its past and current involvement in the steel and cutlery industries, and the contemporary natural history of the wooded river valleys that are so characteristic of the city. The link is made between the valleys and their industrial archaeology as it was here that water powered early industrial activity. These attributes have been interpreted by the museum's professional staff using a range of local objects and specimens from the collections, but also using local voices and experiences—in text and oral/visual presentations—to provide meaning.

The dynamic interaction between people and place—the creation of the cultural landscape—is particularly significant for museums. Lippard[24] suggests that every individual interacts with place differently, whereas Agnew[25] proposes that "Common experiences and interests create an emotional attachment and self-definition peculiar to the specific place in which the locales of enduring social relationships are concentrated. This is local identity or sense of place." It would seem that this author regards a shared local identity as being the same concept as sense of place. However there are dangers for museums in these imagined, shared identities, the ways that communities "remember" the past. Watson[26] illustrated how the subject matter for the new (2004) Great Yarmouth (United Kingdom) museum became focused on the herring fishing industry, the theme chosen by local people during an extensive consultation process as the most significant historical narrative for the town. Fishing surpassed all other suggested topics despite the fact that it was (short) seasonable work that even in its heyday (1913) employed only a small percentage (5.6%) of Yarmouth people. By 1968, only five boats were active and the demise of herring fishing in 1971 was not publicly mourned. Historical research indicated that other industries—especially tourism, and silk and crepe manufacture—had been far more important in establishing the town's prosperity. However, in popular imagination, fishing had a deep historical legacy; it was a picturesque tradition where people lived in harmony with the sea and the coastal landscape, something that Great Yarmouth people could identify with and be proud of. As a consequence, the new museum has proved to be popular and has been significant in restoring local pride. Due to the widespread public consultation, and the strength of collective memory about the fishing industry that this demonstrated, the museum had little choice but to embrace a myth about place and reinforce it.

So can museums ever construct and celebrate an "authentic" or "truthful" sense of place? By carefully selecting artifacts and stories that trigger an emotional response they may have the ability to do so, reminding visitors of significant moments in local history, or—as in Sheffield Museum—introducing the past through engaging media such as oral histories and by introducing the visitor to key elements of the tangible and intangible cultural landscape. However, Watson's[26] research reminds us that museums must recognize the complexities of place and history and Lippard[24] hints that place must be interpreted from multiple perspectives. This is important for museums if seeking to reach a wide audience, and especially so when dealing with "difficult" histories. For example, Crooke's[27] discussion of the presentation by museums of the contested histories of conflict in South Africa and Northern Ireland clearly demonstrates the value of presenting multiple, contested viewpoints about places and their histories.

Identity, including place identity, is not only socially constructed but also constantly shifting. Thus although the distinctive characteristics of places can to an extent be quantified at a point in time by identifying key tangible and intangible elements, for example using the "Parish Maps" and "Illuminated Alphabets" promoted by Common Ground,[28–30] the dynamic nature of "local identity" and "sense of place" is much more elusive, it is a chameleon concept. Shifting identities pose a real challenge for museums and demands that they collect contemporary evidence to represent changes in place. Some disciplines in museums, for example, art or archaeology, find this more challenging than others. However, other museum specialists—social historians, anthropologists, and natural scientists—are continually documenting change not only by collecting objects and specimens but also using digital recording media. So while not all museums will dedicate efforts to this goal contemporary practices in collecting have been reviewed by many individual museums. At Te Papa (New Zealand):

> Since the early 1990s, collection development has increasingly aimed to represent the visual culture and history of Pacific peoples in New Zealand. The scope is broad and ranges from contemporary high art and fashion through to new forms of weaving, tīvaevae, and tapa that migrants have brought with them to New Zealand. Complicating this changing curatorial focus is the fact that many island-based communities have become more transnational in nature as a result of developments in telecommunications, air travel, email, and print media.[31]

Such strategic approaches to documenting a changing material culture that reflects place are now a feature of most museums' collecting policies. Museums—as Te Papa does—must also acknowledge that new communication media enable people to be more aware of their place by making comparisons with the homelands of other communities.

The dynamic and emotional dimensions of place enable Cresswell[9] and Lippard[24] to propose that place is somewhere to be lived, experienced, and explored from inside. In contrast, an outsider, or visitor, can only observe "landscape" as they lack the longer term, intimate experience of a place. Similarly, Cross,[6] proposes that sense of place is comprised of two aspects: relationship to place and community attachment. Anyone can build a relationship to place, even temporarily as a visitor, but she emphasizes that communities—insiders—relate and attach themselves to a place in many ways, and that those processes and feelings about place are dynamic. Hummon[32] also sees sense of place as having two separate features, namely an interpretive perspective on the environment and an emotional reaction to it. While these theorists fail to address how the transition from outsider to insider, or from not belonging to belonging occurs, these views suggest that museums can never really provide a true experience of place for insiders, those communities that belong. Museums can interpret place but cannot convey the emotional dimension that locals have, simply because emotional attachment to place lies in the locality, not inside the museum. This is something of a paradox as most local or regional museums regard local people as their key target audience. So in order to best interpret place in museums, we firstly need to be aware that continual revision of ideas and concepts in exhibitions is necessary to successfully capture its dynamic local nature and secondly, to try to provide an emotional, affective experience. Ultimately museums have to make choices not only about the vision of place and the histories of place that they wish to portray, but also *how* places are interpreted. To really affect visitors they need to employ a full range of media and innovative design techniques, but in truth full representation of place will always be out of reach, an illusion.

If place theory tends to suggest that most museums will deliver an interpretation of place for consumption by "outsiders," this may help to explain patterns of museum visiting by holiday-makers or tourists to local museums, where people are making an investment of time in order to better understand a place. However, these theoretical approaches fail to totally explain why some museums (such as Glasgow Museums, Scotland, or the Watercolour Museum, Tjörn, Sweden) appear to develop an emotional relationship with their local communities, encouraging ownership and involvement, while many other museums fail to do so. O'Neill[33] links the success of Glasgow's museums in terms of community relationships to the organization's drive to create a more positive identity of the city and its people, so that it is a place its inhabitants are proud to belong to.

Proshansky et al.[34] use the term "place identity" to approach this issue of how individuals react to "their place," linking their ideas to notions of the self, or self-identity. They define place identity as "... cognitions [that] represent memories, ideas, feelings, attitudes, values, preferences, meanings, and conceptions of behavior and experience which relate to the variety and complexity of physical settings that define the day-to-day existence of every human being."[35] The authors attribute five functions to place identity, namely recognition; meaning; expressive-requirement; mediating change; and anxiety and defense. Of particular relevance to museums is the recognition function, which affirms a sense of continuity and environmental stability by allowing an individual to recognize their physical world; museum exhibitions can reinforce feelings of historical attachment and permanence of place. The "meaning function" that serves as the source of an individual's perception of place and their behaviour is also interesting in terms of how visitors react to museum environments or "museum places"; quiet and reflective gallery spaces may play a role in allaying anxiety. The notion of mediating change is interesting for museums, and may help us to understand how Glasgow's museums (mentioned above) have created an emotional bond with their local communities. The transition from once industrial city to a city of learning and culture has certainly been aided and supported by the museum's vision of Glasgow as place; here we observe the museum as both mediator of change and advocate for place.

For Proshansky et al., place identity is predominantly cognitive. By contrast, Dixon and Durheim[36] propose a discursive approach to place identity, relocating its construction from "the vault of the mind" to "the flux of human dialogue." They suggest that actions such as "blaming, justifying, derogating, excusing, excluding and all of the other things people do with words" construct place. Museums can be identified as an element in this "flux of human dialogue"; they have the potential to act as an inclusive venue for discussion about place identity with their communities. The need to consult with all communities is especially important for museums, where the concept of multiple voices and multiple interpretations of places and their histories is gradually being accepted. Previously "hidden histories" and untold stories have begun to emerge as part of wide-reaching postmodernist changes in practice in museums.[37,38]

PLACE, COMMUNITIES, AND IDENTITIES IN A GLOBAL WORLD

In the early 1990s, globalization theorists revitalized concerns about the demise of local identities, the loss of place. They argued that due to the movement of peoples, objects, capital, and information across large distances, life for most people is not restricted to one place, to a defined locality with fixed boundaries. New media of communication played a crucial role here, enabling rapid contact over long distances, leading to the instability and fragmentation of face-to-face community exchanges, which for some writers[39] was the essence of social life. Other developments—shopping malls, corporate logos, fast food—pointed to the dilution of the unique nature of places and the emergence of "placelessness."[13]

However, by the mid-1990s, a different view of globalization began to appear[40–42] that explored how globalization could encourage the reworking of social relationships and generate new approaches to localization. Central to these arguments are that place, or the local, are not subsumed by the national or international, rather that nation or the region are composed of innumerable places; in Lefevbre's words "the worldwide does not abolish the local."[43] Robertson popularized this view as "glocalisation" where "globalisation has involved the reconstruction of 'home,' 'community,' and 'locality.' "[44]

So how do we think about our place—the local—within a globalized world? Massey's[41,45] views on "progressive sense of place" are especially helpful as they demonstrate how individuals move into and out of places; this can happen irregularly or with a regular pattern. Massey regards "coming and going" as crucial to understanding how people develop or perceive their relationship to place. The implication here is that knowing another place, or other places, is essential to understanding your own. Appadurai[46] takes this argument a stage further by suggesting that localities are socially produced through processes of boundary definition; delineating the boundary of place is achieved by making comparisons—aided by global flow—with adjacent places. Individuals and communities create a shared identity that provides boundaries that lie beyond physical features such as fences, walls, rivers, or mountains. The line drawn between communities, between places, is socially constructed, invisible, and dynamic, and often difficult to define.[9,39,47] Consequently globalization makes us question firstly the nature of the communities museums are attempting to serve, and secondly how local places should be represented by museums in terms of the different reconstructions of "locality" and "place" influenced by globalization.

One major feature of globalization is the movement of peoples. Hall[48] refers to the concepts of the "contact zone" and transculturation to explore how culture and identity is constantly changing through these interactions and mutual influences. He argues that intense encounters with different cultures, where one identity negotiates with the "copresence" of another identity or identities and where elements of cultures fuse together, lead to identities with multiple frames. Diaspora discourse has been significant in terms of understanding place; indeed, these views about shifting cultures are also true for place identities. Consequently museums must try to acknowledge and reflect such dynamism. No single identity is pure and is "always already 'the product,' in part, of a long history, of connections with the beyond, with other places."[49] A place can also be "hybridized" under multiple influences through the passage of time, and museums need to respond to and document such change. One relevant example here is Sheffield Museum's (2008) temporary exhibition on Sudanese immigrants to the Yorkshire city, which explored the reasons for their migration, the ways in which they have adapted to new lives and developed new communities, and how they feel now about their homeland. Similarly Tyne and Wear Museum's temporary exhibition (2008) "Destination Tyne and Wear" uncovered and described the history of the region's migrant communities and demonstrated how they helped to shape its culture from the nineteenth century onward. Immigrant voices are used to give powerful and emotive recollections of movement and settlement, demonstrating how the import of new ideals, new cultures, has enriched the region, creating a new, vibrant, and changed culture. The exhibition reflects on the ways that the region has become a different place, but one that all its inhabitants can share pride in.

Some observers feel that immigrant individuals and families cannot immediately identify with places (and hence their museums) because they are strangers; this feeling of "not belonging" can be even stronger for refugees and exiles "who did not leave their homes voluntarily."[50] However, this conclusion is refuted by researchers who, in relation to their study group in Lancashire, state that

> ... we agree with proponents of globalization theory. Although in our four locations there continue to be people who live in the vicinity of where they were brought up, these are not necessarily the people who feel they belong there. It is the perceptions and values of incoming migrant groups, which more powerfully establish dominant place identities and attachments ... people's sense of being at home is related to reflexive processes in which they can satisfactorily account to themselves how they come to live where they do.[51]

This research is significant for museums, reminding them that incomers rapidly adapt to new places and adopt a sense of belonging to that place. Strategic approaches for museums require inclusive recognition of its multiple communities.

Interestingly, Halls' "back-to-basics" model of cultural change, invites a different response to globalization, one that turns inward to more "closed" definitions of culture and place with "the revival of an attachment to more 'local,' or fixed, or placed aspects of culture."[52] This model is reflected in the continuing growth of small museums dedicated to celebrating place at a local scale. The *hembygdmuseum* movement in Sweden, for example, a network of some 1400 small social history museums, seeks to capture and even fossilize place and time by conserving vernacular houses, landscapes, and their associated material culture.

Similarly, concerns for the general "loss of place" has led to movements which emphasize local culture and heritage and attempt to defend local distinctiveness. However, Harvey[39] notes that place is always subjected to influences beyond its immediate boundaries and consequently by the need to adapt. Places compete against each other for capital investment, production, and consumption, yet decry the loss of distinctiveness and authenticity. Similarly, Massey[47] argues that places cannot be understood without the "consciousness of its links with the rest of the world" and asks that the possibility of developing a progressive, "global" sense of place be considered. This global responsibility is echoed by several new museums, including the Museum of World Culture in Gothenburg, Sweden, which promotes the world as place, and creates exhibitions on subjects such as *Aids* and *Human Trafficking* that reflect connections across the world rather than divisions and difference.

PLACE AS MUSEUM

Interestingly, Tuan regarded museums as poor channels to communicate place because "[t]he museum, after all, consists wholly of displaced objects"[53] and "[t]he effort to evoke a sense of place and of the past is often deliberate and conscious."[54] Tuan rejects the creation of a sense of place using artifacts and artificial situations. Other researchers[55] have similarly suggested that:

> It might be argued that the complexity of place and what it represents to individuals and communities [means] that the traditional museum can never capture its elusive qualities. It is impossible for the curator to acquire place, carefully label it and store it in an acid-free container. Museums can acquire fragments of place, and exhibit them together to re-create their version of place, but that is all. The essence of place lies beyond the museum, in the environment itself, and is defined by the individuals and the communities that live there.

So is a different museum model required to try to capture and celebrate places? Place theory indicates that individuals and communities attach deep significance to their place and particular sites within it. Various mechanisms exist to conserve the sites or objects that possess special significance, at every level from the World Heritage Site to the Tree Preservation Order. So, for example, in England the preservation and interpretation activities of English Heritage, Natural England, and the National Trust have helped to proclaim the significance of heritage sites, adding labels, signposts, or other markers in a process that has witnessed the "musealisation" of place. "Experts" who attach their own meanings to sites or objects have largely carried out these processes, not the local people or visitors who experience them. There is a paradox here, in that these organizations declare what is important on a national scale, but until recently have only rarely taken local needs or interests into consideration. This can mean that the features of the immediate environment that local people value most may not be protected, and even where they are that the associated histories or stories told are too "academic," irrelevant or take no heed of local knowledge.

A new museological approach demands two important changes in attitude. The first of these, the realization that the museum has a role in documenting places (sites) beyond the walls of the museum as well as constructing place in its exhibitions, has been largely accepted. The second demand—community empowerment—is beginning to be met in developed, and some developing, countries. One new philosophical approach that recognizes these needs is ecomuseology, which has the potential to provide local people with a process for rescuing fragments of heritage, a building, redundant factory, a habitat, intangible heritage, or a way of life from loss or destruction, and also helps them to express a deep conviction to preserve and deepen their sense of place.

Empowerment became a key feature of ecomuseum philosophy and practice as it emerged in the late 1960s and early 1970s.[56] Its two main proponents, Hugues de Varine and Georges Henri Rivière (1897–1985) were central to the development of new ideas about place, communities, and heritage. The first experiments with ecomuseology occurred in French Regional Natural Parks and other rural areas in the late 1960s. Later developments focused on postindustrial urban areas, most famously at Le Creusot-Montceau in Burgundy (1974).[57] The latter established not only political, social, and regeneration ideals but cemented the concept of the "fragmented museum," which encouraged the visitor to explore the local area by visiting several local heritage sites. This split-site approach has since become the most common feature of ecomuseums worldwide. By this time the ecomuseum had taken the notion of place, expressed as "territoire" (territory), as a cornerstone of its philosophy and industrial heritage had been identified as of particular significance, a situation that was in tune with the growing "industrial museum" movement of the 1970s.

The word "ecomusée" was devised in September 1971 by De Varine to express new museological approaches to community–heritage–place interactions. Rivière's[58] definition of the term ecomuseum includes many of the key concepts—local identity, territory, landscape, a sense of history, and continuity—that appear to be important in creating a sense of belonging. Perhaps the most significant features of Rivière's definition are the repetition of the word "population" (the emphasis on communities) and the idea of the ecomuseum having "limitless diversity," a suggestion that the ecomuseum can be anything local people and museum professionals want it to be, and that it is a malleable concept.

One of the most interesting features of Rivière's definition[58] is the comment that "it is an interpretation of space—of special places in which to stop and stroll." Here is the link to place—the ecomuseum is not limited to a building or even a museum site, but it encompasses everything within the region it refers to as its "territoire." Here, key sites have special meaning and are integrated into the museum. Heritage is not defined, but the assumption is that it is more than just sites and material culture, encompassing memories, folklore, music, and song. At the extreme, the ecomuseum includes everything within its territory. Intangible local skills, behaviour patterns, social structure, and traditions are as much a part of the ecomuseum as the tangible evidence of landscapes, geology, wildlife, buildings and objects, and people and their domestic animals. As Van Mensch[59] observed "it has become increasingly difficult to discern where the 'museum' stops and the 'real world' begins."

There have been many attempts to state succinctly what an ecomuseum is. Rivard[60] compared the traditional museum (= building + collections + experts + public) to the ecomuseum (= territory + heritage + memory + population). Varine suggested that the label "ecomuseum" was nothing more than an opportunity to run with new ideas, to be imaginative, and to initiate new ways of working.[61] Despite the problems of definition, the flexibility of the ecomuseum model has meant that some 400 are now found worldwide, on every continent, with the recent growth in Asian countries being especially marked. Here, the processes of creating ecomuseums have been frequently linked to meeting demands for sustainable tourism, encouraging conservation, and interpretive practices of places that will ultimately benefit local people. It is this trend that led Davis[62] to define the ecomuseum as "a community-driven museum or heritage project that aids sustainable development." It is this link to economic development through low-level tourism that has encouraged the rapid adoption of ecomuseum practices worldwide. Now fully established in Europe, and especially France, Spain, Portugal, Italy, and Sweden, the concept is now emerging strongly in South America and especially Asia, with significant numbers created in Japan and China.

The one characteristic that appears to be common to all ecomuseums is their pride in the place that they represent. This is true whatever the nature of the ecomuseum, whether it be a rural farming community in mainland China, a scattered group of heritage sites on a Japanese peninsula, an old farm settlement in Brittany, or abandoned terraces in northern Italy. This pride is expressed in a variety of ways. It can be seen in the careful design of an exhibition, in the sheer pleasure people take in performing local music and dance, the pride in demonstrating weaving skills, or delivering bold and imaginative interpretation. Ecomuseums encourage dialogue with local people as well as inviting visitors to explore their territory, which can only promote a better understanding of sense of place and local identity.

CONCLUSION

Museums have an affinity with places and their peoples. The origins of public museums in the nineteenth century are often associated with "local" or "civic" pride, the museum being perceived as a venue to reflect on the natural and cultural characteristics of a place and the achievements of its people. However, in the twenty-first century the rapidly changing nature of places—in terms, for example, of their spatial characteristics, ethnicities, and cultures—require museums to adapt to new needs and find different techniques—and new models—to engage with and represent changing local communities, and to construct images of place that meet local demands.

REFERENCES

1. Lovell, N. *Locality and Belonging*, Routledge: London, U.K., 1998.
2. Tuan, Y.F. *Topophilia: A Study of Environmental Perception, Attitudes, and Values*, Prentice-Hall Inc: Englewood Cliffs, NJ, 1974.
3. Proshansky, H.M.; Fabian, A.K.; Kaminoff, R. Place identity: Physical world socialization of the self. J. Environ. Psychol. **1983**, *3*, 57–83.
4. In *Place Attachment*; Altman, I., Low, S.M., Eds.; Plenum Press: New York and London, 1992.
5. Hummon, D. Community attachment: Local sentiment and sense of place. In *Place Attachment*; Altman, I., Low, S.M., Eds.; Plenum Press: New York and London, 1992.
6. Cross, J.E. What is Sense of Place? 12th Headwaters Conference Western State College November, 2–4, 2001. Available at http://www.western.edu/headwaters/archives/headwaters12_papers/cross_paper.html (accessed January 30, 2008).
7. In *Key Thinkers on Space and Place*; Hubbard, P., Kitchin, R., Valentine, G., Eds.; Sage: London, U.K., 2004.
8. *The Dictionary of Human Geography*, 4th Ed.; Johnston, R.J., Gregory, D., Pratt, G., Watts, M., Eds.; Blackwell Publishing: Malden, MA, 2000.
9. Cresswell, T. *Place: A Short Introduction*, Blackwell: London, U.K., 2004.
10. Cresswell, T. *Place: A Short Introduction*, Blackwell: London, U.K., 2004; 19.
11. In *Key Thinkers on Space and Place*; Hubbard, P., Kitchin, R., Valentine, G., Eds.; Sage: London, U.K., 2004; 5.
12. Tuan, Y.F. *Space and Place: The Perspective of Experience*, Edward Arnold Ltd: London, U.K., 1977.
13. Relph, E. *Place and Placelessness*, Pion Limited: London, U.K., 1976.
14. Buttimer, A. Home, reach and the sense of place. In *The Human Experience of Space and Place*; Buttimer, A., Seamon, D., Eds.; St Martins Press: New York, 1980.
15. Tuan, Y.F. *Space and Place: The Perspective of Experience*, Edward Arnold Ltd: London, U.K., 1977; 6.
16. Casey, E. How to get from space to place and back again in a fairly short stretch of time: Phenomenological prolegomena. In *Sense of Place*; Field, S., Basso, K., Eds.; School of American Research Press: Santa Fe, CA., 1996; 18.
17. Escobar, A. Culture sits in places: Reflections on globalisation and subaltern strategies in localisation. Polit. Geogr. **2001**, *20*, 139–174.
18. Smith, L. *Uses of Heritage*, Routledge: London and New York, 2006.
19. Cresswell, T. *Place: A Short Introduction*, Blackwell: London, U.K., 2004; 86.
20. Hay, R. Sense of place in a developmental context. J. Environ. Psychol. **1998**, *18*, 5–20.
21. Savage, M.; Bagnall, G.; Longhurst, B. *Globalization and Belonging*, Sage Publications: London, U.K., 2005.
22. Savage, M.; Bagnall, G.; Longhurst, B. *Globalization and Belonging*, Sage Publications: London, U.K., 2005; 80.
23. Rodman, M.C. Empowering place: Multilocality and multivocality. In *The Anthology of Space and Place: Locating Culture*; Low, S.M., Lawrence-Zúñiga, D., Eds.; Blackwell: Malden, MA., 2003.
24. Lippard, L. *The Lure of the Local:Place in a Multicentered Society*, New Press: New York, 1997.
25. Agnew, J. Place and politics in post-war Italy: A cultural geography of local identity in the provinces of Lucca and Pistoia. In *Inventing Places: Studies in Cultural Geography*; Anderson, K., Gale, F., Eds.; Longman Cheshire: Melbourne, 1992; 52–71.
26. Watson, S. History museums, community identities and a sense of place: rewriting histories. In *Museum Revolutions: How Museums Change and Are Changed*; Knell, S., Macleod, S., Watson, S., Eds.; Routledge: London and New York, 2007; 160–172.
27. Crooke, E. Dealing with the past: Museums and heritage in Northern Ireland and Cape Town, South Africa. Int. J. Museum Stud. **2005**, *11*(2), 131–142.
28. Clifford, S.; King, A. Losing your place. In *Local Distinctiveness: Place, Particularity and Identity*; Clifford, S., King, A., Eds.; Common Ground: London, U.K., 1993; 7–29.
29. Clifford, S.; King, A. *From Place to PLACE: Maps and Parish maps*, Common Ground: London, U.K., 1996.
30. Common Ground. *Promotional Leaflet: Common Ground*, Common Ground: London, U.K., 1996.
31. http://www.tepapa.govt.nz/TePapa/English/CollectionsAndResearch/Collections/PacificCultures/Contemporary/ Te Papa (2008) Contemporary collecting.
32. Hummon, D. Community attachment: Local sentiment and sense of place. In *Place Attachment*; Altman, I., Low, S.M., Eds.; Plenum Press: New York and London, 1992; 262.
33. O'Neill, M. Museums and identity in Glasgow. Int. J. Heritage Stud. **2005**, *12*(1), 29–48.
34. Proshansky, H.M.; Fabian, A.K.; Kaminoff, R. Place identity: Physical world socialization of the self. J. Environ. Psychol. **1983**, *3*, 57.
35. Proshansky, H.M.; Fabian, A.K.; Kaminoff, R. Place identity: Physical world socialization of the self. J. Environ. Psychol **1983**, *3*, 59.

36. Dixon, J.; Durheim, K. Displacing place identity: A discursive approach to locating self and others. Brit. J. Social Psychol. **2000**, *39*, 27–44.
37. Mason, R. Cultural theory and museum studies. In *A Companion to Museum Studies*; Macdonald, S., Ed.; Blackwell Publishing: Oxford, U.K., 2006; 17–32.
38. Witcomb, A. *Re-imagining the Museum*, Routledge: London and New York, 2003.
39. Harvey, D. From space to place and back again. In *Mapping the Futures: Local Cultures, Global Change*; Bird, J., Curtis, B., Putnam, T., Robertson, G., Tickner, L., Eds.; Routledge: London, U.K., 1993.
40. Lash, S.; Urry, J. *Economies of Signs and Spaces*, Sage: London, 1994.
41. Massey, D. *Space, Class and Gender*, Polity: Cambridge, MA, 1994.
42. Robertson, R. Glocalisation: Time-space and homogeneity-heterogeneity'. In *Global Modernities*; Featherstone, M., Lash, S., Robertson, R., Eds.; Sage: London, U.K., 1995.
43. Brenner, N. The urban question as a scale question: reflections on Henri Lefevbre, urban theory and the politics of scale. Int. J. Urban Reg. Res. **2000**, *24*, 361–378.
44. Robertson, R. Glocalisation: Time-space and homogeneity-heterogeneity'. In *Global Modernities*; Featherstone, M., Lash, S., Robertson, R., Eds.; Sage: London, U.K., 1995; 30.
45. Massey, D. Power geometry and a progressive sense of place. In *Mapping the Futures: Local Cultures, Global Change*; Bird, J., Curtis, B., Putnam, T., Robertson, G., Tickner, L., Eds.; Routledge: London, U.K., 1993.
46. Appadurai, A. *Modernity at Large*, University of Minnesota Press: Minneapolis and London, 1996.
47. Massey, D. The conceptualization of place. In *A Place in the World?: Places, Cultures and Globalization*; Massey, D., Jess, P., Eds.; The Open University & Oxford University Press: Milton Keynes, 1995; 45–85.
48. Hall, S. New cultures for old. In *A Place in the World?: Places, Culture and Globalization*; Massey, D., Jess, P., Eds.; Oxford University Press: Oxford, U.K., 1995.
49. Massey, D. The conceptualization of place. In *A Place in the World?: Places, Cultures and Globalization*; Massey, D., Jess, P., Eds.; The Open University & Oxford University Press: Milton Keynes, 1995; 67.
50. Rose, G. Place and identity: A sense of place. In *A Place in the world? Places, Cultures and Globalization*; Massey, D., Jess, P., Eds.; Oxford University Press: Oxford, U.K., 1996; 87–132.
51. Savage, M.; Bagnall, G.; Longhurst, B. *Globalization and Belonging*, Sage Publications: London, U.K., 2005; 29.
52. Hall, S. New cultures for old. In *A Place in the World?: Places, Culture and Globalization*; Massey, D., Jess, P., Eds.; Oxford University Press: Oxford, U.K., 1995; 200–201.
53. Tuan, Y.F. *Space and Place: The Perspective of Experience*, Edward Arnold Ltd: London, U.K., 1977; 114.
54. Tuan, Y.F. *Space and Place: The Perspective of Experience*, Edward Arnold Ltd: London, U.K., 1977; 198.
55. Corsane, G.; Davis, P.; Murtas, D. Place, local distinctiveness and local identity: ecomuseum approaches in Europe and Asia. In *Heritage and Identity: Engagement and Demission in the Contemporary World*; Anico, M., Perelta, E., Eds.; Routledge: London and New York, 2009; 47–62.
56. Davis, P. *Ecomuseums: A Sense of Place*, Leicester University Press/Continuum: London and New York, 1999.
57. Davis, P. *Ecomuseums: A Sense of Place*, Leicester University Press/Continuum: London and New York, 1999; 66–67.
58. Rivière, G.H. The Ecomuseum: An evolutive definition. Museum **1985**, *37* (4), 182–183.
59. Van Mensch, P. Museology and the management of the natural and cultural heritage. In *Museums and the Environment*; De Jong, R., Ed.; Southern Africa Museums Association: Pretoria, 1993; 57–62.
60. Rivard, R. Museums and ecomuseums—questions and answers. In *Okomuseumsboka – identitet, okologi, deltakelse*; Gjestrum, J.A., Maure, M., Eds.; ICOM: Tromso, Norway, 1988; 123–128.
61. Varine, H.; L'Écomusée. In *Vagues – une anthologie de la nouvelle muséologie*; Desvallées, A., Ed.; Editions W. Macon: Paris, 1992; [Originally published in *La Gazette* {Association des musées canadiens} 1978, 11, 28–40].
62. Davis, P. Ecomuseums and sustainability in Italy, Japan and China: Concept adaptation through implementation. In *Museum Revolutions: How Museums Change and are Changed*; Knell, S.J., MacLeod, S., Watson, S., Eds.; Routledge: London and New York, 2007; 198–214.

Music Information Retrieval

Kjell Lemström
Department of Computer Science, University of Helsinki, Helsinki, Finland

George Tzanetakis
Department of Computer Science, University of Victoria, Victoria, British Columbia, Canada

Abstract

This entry gives an overview of the area of music information retrieval. More specifically, it focuses on what has been done for retrieving polyphonic musical documents both in symbolic and audio forms. It also describes research efforts to combine symbolic-based and audio-based approaches.

INTRODUCTION

The spread of the Internet and the creation of the World Wide Web have offered exciting real-world problems for existing and novel theories and methods. Among the large amount of digital documents publicly available, there is a large number of musical documents, in various formats, that should be retrievable in musically pertinent and user-friendly ways.

This entry focuses on content-based techniques, as opposed to the text-based methods, developed for retrieving music from large databases of polyphonic music. In a typical setting the query pattern to be searched for is a short musical excerpt that can be given, e.g., by humming or playing an instrument, or by recording a snippet from a sound recording. In this entry, we divide the techniques in two categories depending on whether they are based on symbolic or audio representation. In general, the symbolic methods are appropriate for a *query-by-humming* application, where an occurrence of a query forms only some portion of the whole polyphonic structure of the matching part in the database. The audio methods are used for *query-by-example* applications, where the query constitutes a possibly distorted snippet taken from the underlying database.

The symbolic techniques developed for content-based music retrieval are based either on string or on geometric representation. The "Symbolic Techniques" section gives an overview on techniques and results that are obtained by using these frameworks. In the section "Audio Techniques," we provide a survey of different content-based problems using audio representations that have been proposed. The survey is structured based on the type of query used, the information extracted and the specificity of the desired results. Finally in the section "Bridging Symbolic and Audio Content-Based Music Retrieval," we conclude the entry by some ideas on how to bridge the gap between the symbolic and audio techniques.

SYMBOLIC TECHNIQUES

Symbolic music representations, such as the Western Common Music Notation (CMN) or Music Instrument Digital Interface (MIDI), are most often used for storage purposes: they include detailed information for artists or, in the case of MIDI for musical instruments, how to perform the stored music. Although performances differ from each other, the listener still perceives them as the same musical works. This justifies the use of symbolic representations for content-based music retrieval purposes. The advantage of performing retrieval in the syntax level (i.e., using a symbolic representation as opposed to audio) is the possibility to search for occurrences that are embedded in the music structure, such as a melody line in a polyphonic orchestration—the occurrence may even be distributed among several instruments of the orchestration.

Choosing the representation. There are several important, intrinsic features of music and the application that need to be taken into account to have effective retrieval results, the most important being:

1. the inherent polyphony of real-world music,
2. location invariance to allow occurrences to reside anywhere in the database, not just in incipits (the "opening line" of the music; usually the first four bars of the melody),
3. transposition invariance to allow matching music in different keys,
4. time scaling invariance to allow matching music in different tempi, and
5. tolerance to "noise" caused by various sources (the database may contain unexpected musical embellishments, a conversion process may have caused errors, the hummed/played query pattern contains inaccuracies).

Together these five features form a complex problem field and they all have to be considered already when choosing a suitable representation.

Encyclopedia of Library and Information Sciences, Fourth Edition DOI: 10.1081/E-ELIS4-120043656

Previously, the symbolic representations used for content-based music retrieval have been based either on string[1–4] or geometric representations.[5–10] Of the five aforementioned properties, the first one has the strongest impact on choosing an appropriate representation. As opposed to monophonic music, which is relatively naturally representable by using string representation, casting polyphonic music to linear strings[11–14] is often not effective.[15] However, string matching has been adopted to some restricted cases, as discussed below. When using the string matching framework, the properties (3) and (4) are dealt with at the representational level, the remaining ones by the methods solving the specific problems.

The geometric representations, on the other hand, accommodate equally and naturally to both monophonic and polyphonic music. This discrimination has led most of the recent studies on symbolic content-based music retrieval to focus on the geometric representations. With the geometric framework the properties (2–5) are typically dealt with the methods solving the problems.

Using String Matching Framework

Problem definition

When using the string matching framework, the polyphonic content-based music retrieval problem is casted to a slightly modified string matching problem. In this case the usual setting is such that the pattern to be searched for is monophonic while the database to be searched is polyphonic. To this end, let us represent both the musical pattern $P = P_1, \ldots, P_m$ and the database $T = T_1, \ldots, T_n$ as strings of sets of integers. Thus, in a string S (corresponding either to P or T) each S_i models a chord and is formally a subset of an integer alphabet Σ. Let us denote by q the size of the largest chord in S, i.e., $q = \max \{|S_i| \mid 1 \leq i \leq m, n\}$. The polyphonic structure may consist of K parallel monophonic *voices*. In such a case each S_i consists of pairs $\langle k, h\rangle_i \in K \times \Sigma$ in order to be able to track the voicing information. Naturally, if $q = 1$, S is monophonic; otherwise it is polyphonic. Each S_i thus corresponds to a chord of notes, and is comprised of notes having their onsets simultaneously. This representation is also known as *onset-based representation*.[15]

The content-based music information retrieval (MIR) problem is as follows. Given a long database $T = T_1, \ldots, T_n$ and a relatively short music query pattern $P = P_1, \ldots, P_m$, the task is to find all locations in T where P occurs. Here an occurrence might mean an exact, transposed, or approximate occurrence.

We define that there is an *exact occurrence* of P at position j, if $P_i \in T_{j+i-1}$ holds for $i = 1, \ldots, m$. Furthermore, there is a *transposition invariant occurrence* of P at position j, if there is an integer d such that each $(P_i + d) \in T_{j+i-1}$.

When both P and T are monophonic, an exact and a transposition invariant occurrence means that $P_i = T_{j+i-1}$ and $(P_i + d) = T_{j+i-1}$ for each i, respectively. A k approximate occurrence of P is found if there is a subsequence P' of T, such that P' can be obtained from P by using k or fewer editing operations. An *approximate transposition invariant occurrence* is defined accordingly.

Results

When dealing with the polyphonic content-based music retrieval problem, in some limited cases it may suffice to heuristically reduce the polyphonic music structure in a monophonic one and then apply classical string matching algorithms. See, for instance Blackburn and DeRoure[16] and Uitdenbogerd and Zobel[17] for such reduction heuristics. The power of the onset-based representation becomes evident when searching for *distributed occurrences* of the pattern. In such a case the pattern appears in consecutive positions within the database but may jump across the voices (or the voicing information is simply absent).

If transposition invariance is not needed the edit distance framework can be used in a straitforward manner.[11,12,18] The combinatorial explosion in the transposition invariant case can be avoided by chopping the possibilities in n-grams (strings of length n).[19] When the degree of polyphony is high, however, this may prove not to be an efficient solution because of the large number of generated n-grams. Another possibility is to split the pattern to bare intervals that are searched individually.[13] This requires a two-pronged search: the candidates found in the first phase have to be examined in another phase to discard discontinuous patterns (the subsequent interval does not begin in the note where the former ends). When the voicing information is available, one can also look for a transposition invariant occurrence that minimizes the number of jumps across the voices.[14]

Using Geometric Framework

Problem definition

Let us now introduce the geometric framework and consider the content-based music retrieval problems as point pattern matching ones. The points are real values in a d-dimensional real space $\mathbb{R}^d$; at times the space needs to be discretized to the integer space $\mathbb{Z}^d$ for efficiency purposes.[5,7] In a typical case, music is represented by using two dimensions: one (horizontal) dimension represents the note *onset time* (i.e., when the associated note is to be invoked), the other (vertical) gives the *pitch* (i.e., the perceived height of the note) information. To consider the note durations, several extensions to this basic point setting have been suggested[6,9,20] (see below).

In this way, the symbolic content-based music retrieval problems can be seen as special cases of point pattern matching (an excellent tutorial to point pattern matching can be found in Mäkinen and Ukkonen).[21] Let us consider this more formally. Given two point sets P and T, where typically $|P| \ll |T|$, both being finite subsets of $\mathbb{R}^d$ ($\mathbb{Z}^d$), the general task is to search for pairs (f, τ) where f is a transformation ($f \in F$) and $\tau \subset T$, such that $f(P)$ matches τ. To take care of the properties (2) and (3) (cf. above), the set of allowed transformations includes *translations*, denoted by F_t, where a constant vector is added to each point in P. Time scaling invariance (property (4)) is obtained by including *scales*, denoted by F_s, in which case distances to a common origin are multiplied by a constant. Depending on the application, a *match* may be exact or approximate; in the latter case an appropriate similarity measure needs to be selected. Please note that by definition, as opposite to the string matching case, an exact match allows "extra intervening" elements in T.

The most typical problems are exact point pattern matching and largest common pointset matching under translations. In *exact point pattern matching under translations* the quest is to find $f \in F_t$ such that $f(P) \subset T$. The straightforward way to include approximation in this is to allow a minimum number of unmatched points of P. To that end, the *largest common pointset matching under translations* looks for the largest $\tau \in T$ where $\tau \subset f(P)$ for some $f \in F_t$. The respective problems including scalings are defined analogously.

Results

In the following we assume that P and T are lexicographically ordered. (Let $(a,b),(a',b') \in \mathbb{R}^2$. In a *lexicographic order* vector $(a,b) \leq (a',b')$ if and only if $a < a$ or ($a = a'$ and $b \leq b'$).) If that is not the case, they can be ordered in $O(|P| \log |P|)$ time and $O(|T| \log |T|)$ time, respectively. Moreover, recall that typically $|P| \ll |T|$.

Matching under translations. The exact point pattern matching problem under translations is solvable in $O(|P||T|)$ time and $O(|P|)$ working space.[6] However, the solution has an expected running time of $O(|T|)$. For deterministic point pattern matching algorithms quadratic running times seem to be the lower bound.

THEOREM 1. [8] *THE LARGEST COMMON POINTSET PROBLEM UNDER TRANSLATIONS IS 3SUM-HARD.*

If we assume that $|T| = n$ and $|P| = \Theta(|T|)$, according to Theorem 1 an $o(|P||T|)$ time algorithm for largest common pointset would mean that there is an $o(n^2)$ algorithm for the 3SUM problem, which would be an unexpected theoretic breakthrough. (Given n numbers, the 3SUM problem is to find whether there are three numbers a, b, and c among them for which $a + b + c = 0$ holds.)

A straightforward algorithm solving the largest point pattern matching under translations runs in $O(|P||T|\log(|P||T|))$ time.[22] The algorithm calculates translation vectors from each point in the pattern P to each point in T. The translations are subsequently sorted in order to find the translation giving the maximal occurrence. With a better sorting routine the running time can be improved to $O(|P||T|\log|P|)$.[6]

To date, no deterministic algorithm is known to solve the problem in a quadratic time. It may be that the largest point pattern matching under translations is also `SORTING X + Y`-hard, in which case Ukkonen et al.'s algorithm may already be an optimal solution. (Given two sets X and Y of n numbers, the `SORTING X + Y` problem is to sort the set $X + Y = \{x + y \mid x \in X, y \in Y\}$.)

By accepting that some of the true occurrences may not be found, faster solutions are obtainable. To this end one can either use subquadratic time approximation algorithms,[8,9] or a solution based on discretized values and an indexing schema similar to inverted files used for natural language information retrieval.[5]

Indexing. Exact solutions based on indexing face two major problems; let us assume an index T for T that is built in time $f(n)$. First, Theorem 1 implies that it is 3SUM-hard to create largest common pointset queries using T, working in $g(m)$ time and holding $f(n) + g(m) = o(n^2)$. Second, the number of the possible translation vectors is exponential in the length of T and, therefore, a total index would also require exponential space.

In addition to the inverted file approach, recently two more indexing schemes have been proposed. The first uses a *metric index* working under earth moving distance.[20] However, it seems difficult with this approach to support translations or partial matching with polyphony. Another method is to use a sparse index and a statistical filtering approach to search for promising areas in T. This approach relies heavily on the power of filtration but seems to be several orders of magnitude faster than the online (nonindexing) algorithms, both in the exact point pattern matching and in the largest common pointset problem.[10]

Note durations. There are several suggestions on how to equip symbolic representations with note durations. A natural idea is to replace the points (representing the note onsets) with horizontal line segments, where the length of the segment represents the duration of the corresponding note.[6] Then the task becomes to search for a translation so that the segment patterns, representing P and T, intersect as much as possible. Interestingly enough, this modified problem is solvable in $O(|P||T| \log (|P||T|))$ time, and if reduced to integer space, in $O(|P||T| \log |P|)$ time.[6] The space reduction also enables the use of a more general distance function considering consonance/dissonance aspects of the music in hand.[7] Other possibilities include the use of earth moving distance when the durations are represented as the weight of the points[20] or the use of a third dimension to represent the durational information.[9]

Matching under translations and scaling. For the moment, it has not been widely studied how to have both translation and scaling invariance at the same time. The problem in combining these two invariances is due to that the former is an additive, while the latter is a multiplicative property. Recall that the translation invariance actually captures two features: transposition and location invariances. The obvious way to achieve scaling invariance would be the use of a logarithmic encoding of the time axis. That way, however, only occurrences starting at the origin chosen for the logarithmic scale would be found thus losing the location invariance.

A naïve solution for solving largest common pointset problem under translations and scaling works in time $O(|P|^3\ |T|^3)$. First, the translation vectors are calculated, in a lexicographical order, from each point in the pattern to each point in the database. This gives $|P|$ increasing sequences of vectors (pairs of real values) each of length $|T|$. Then, each possible time scaling value is selected by choosing two vectors from two distinct sequences; there are $O(|P|^2\ |T|^2)$ possibilities in this choice. For each time scaling value, the maximum co-occurrence between pattern and database needs to be determined. This can be done by checking whether each of the remaining $|P| - 2$ sequences (each containing $|T|$ vectors) includes a vector that accords with the chosen scaling factor. This is feasible in $O(|P||T|)$ time. These found candidates are to be verified by checking that the associated pitch intervals also match.

In order to avoid the high polynomials in the running time, it has been suggested to consider only those scalings that appear within a window whose width is chosen independently of the size of P and T.[9]

AUDIO TECHNIQUES

A wide variety of different retrieval scenarios have been explored using audio-based techniques. In many cases they can be formulated as "query-by-example" applications in which the user provides a possibly distorted snippet and looks for similar music pieces in a large collection. Even for the cases where the "query-by-example" view is not a perfect fit it is a reasonable approximation. For example, genre or style classification can be formulated as a retrieval problem where given a piece of music or a genre label the system returns other pieces in the same genre or style. In addition even in the cases of systems with no notion of a query such as audio-based music browsing systems based on exploration many of the underlying techniques and algorithms are the same.

A rough taxonomy of audio-based MIR systems can be created along the following major "dimensions": query type, extracted information, and specificity. Although for presentation purposes we describe these various stages and types of information separately, successful MIR systems typically utilize multiple of these stages and representations. The citations provided are mainly representative of existing research and its diversity rather than being an exhaustive list.

Query Type

Probably the most common type of query is a piece of music in audio format (query-by-example). The goal of the MIR system is to retrieve other pieces of music from a large collections that sound "similar" to the example query. This problem is typically formulated as a nearest neighbor problem between audio content representations which are described in more detail below. Other query possibilities are based on metadata such as genre,[23] style,[24] mood,[25] or artist name.[26] These problems are typically formulated as classification problems and solved using a supervised learning approach. In such an approach the MIR system is "trained" to classify music pieces it has not encountered before by analyzing music pieces that have been labeled by a human. This is done in order to create statistical models that can predict the correct label with high accuracy for data that has not been encountered before. A variety of such "classifiers" have been proposed including Gaussian mixture models, decision trees, artificial neural networks (ANNs), and support vector machines (SVMs). More details can be found in textbook such as Theodoridis and Koutroumbas.[27]

Although not as explored as the previous two approaches to queries another interesting possibility is for the user to "perform" some aspect of the desired returned results. Examples of such "performed" queries include beat-boxing,[28] humming,[29,30] singing,[30] tempo by tapping, or even matching the retrieved music to the speed of jogging and more generally specific exercise goals.[31]

Representations and Extracted Information

A variety of different sources of information can be used as the basis for creating audio music retrieval systems. To some extent the traditional musical aspects of melody, harmony, rhythm, and instrumentation have inspired similar types of audio analysis. The most direct modeling is through sequences of feature vectors that statistically represent the time varying timbral characteristics of a music piece. Frequently features proposed for speech recognition such as the Mel-Frequency Cepstral Coefficients (MFCCs)[32] are utilized. MFCCs summarize spectral information (the energy distribution of different frequencies) by taking into account the characteristics of the human auditory system. Such features depend on the instrumentation of a piece, how the timbral "texture" changes over time as well as how humans perceive this information.

In other cases, for example in cover song identification or automatic chord detection, it is desired to have a representation that is related to the pitch content of the music rather than the specifics of the instruments and voices that are playing. Although a full music score generated by an automatic transcriptive system could be used, unfortunately current transcription technology is not robust enough to be used reliably. Instead the most common pitch content representation is the Pitch and Pitch Class Profile (other alternative names used in literature are pitch histograms and chroma vectors). The pitch profile measures the occurrence of specific discrete musical pitches in a music segment and the pitch class profile considers all octaves equivalent essentially folding the pitch profile into 12 pitch classes. The pitch profile and pitch class profile are strongly related to the underlying harmony of the music piece. For example, a music segment in C major is expected to have many occurrences of the discrete pitch classes C, E, and G that form the C major chord.

Automatically extracting information related to rhythm is also an important component of audio MIR systems and has been an active area of research for over 20 years. A number of different subproblems within this area have been identified and explored. The most basic approach is finding the average tempo of the entire recording which can be defined as the frequency with which a human would tap their foot while listening to the same piece of music. The more difficult task of beat tracking consists of estimating time-varying tempo (frequency) as well as the locations in time of each beat (phase). Rhythmic information is hierarchical in nature and tempo is only one level of the hierarchy. Other levels frequently used and estimated by audio MIR systems are tatum (defined as the shortest commonly occurring time interval), beat or tactus (the preferred human tapping tempo), and bar or measure. For some MIR applications such as automatic classification it is possible to use a representation that provides a "salience" value for every possible tempo—e.g., the beat histograms described in Lu, Liu, and Zhang.[23]

Beat analysis approaches can be characterized in different ways. The first and most important distinction is by the type of input: most of the earlier beat tracking algorithms used a symbolic representation while audio signals have been used more recently. Symbolic algorithms can still be utilized with audio signals provided an intermediate transcription step is performed—typically audio onset detection. Another major distinction between the algorithms is the broad approach used which includes rule-based, autocorrelative, oscillating filters, histogramming, multiple agent, and probabilistic. A good overview of these approaches can be found in Chapter 4 of Klapuri and Davy.[33]

In many modern pop and rock recordings each instrument is recorded separately and the final mix is created by a recording producer/engineer(s) who among other transformations add effects such as reverb or filtering and spatialize individual tracks using stereo panning cues. Information about this production process can be reverse-engineered from the recording and although not strictly musical in the traditional sense can be used to build more effective MIR systems. For example, the amount of stereo panning and placement of sources remains constant in older recordings that tried to reproduce live performances compared to more recent recordings that would be almost impossible to realize in a live setting. Stereo panning features have recently been used for audio classification.[34]

Specificity

Given a particular query as well as a representation that captures relevant musical content information the user expects to retrieve a set of results that are "similar" in some way to the original query. A variety of different "similarities" have been explored with varying degrees of specificity. The most specific type of retrieval is audio fingerprinting where the goal is to return other instances of the exact same recording possibly subject to noise, minor edits (such as hand clapping removal), and audio compression.[35] Audio fingerprinting can be used for discovering copyright violations as well as associating metadata with music pieces. Remixes also correspond to the same underlying recorded performance, however, with the addition of extra musical materials such as drum loops and beats. In cover song identification the goal is to find other recordings of the same song that are performed by different musicians and instrumentation.[36] Content-based features for cover song identification must capture higher level musical constructs such as chord progressions and not be sensitive to instrumentation changes. Pitch and pitch class profiles are frequently used for this purpose. Artist,[24] album and genre similarity[23] although to some extent artificial tasks have the advantage that it is relatively straightforward to obtain ground-truth using existing metadata associated with files and therefore provide qualitative comparisons between different feature sets for describing audio content.

Specificity also relates to the amount of relevant results returned by the system which has implications about the methods used for matching. High-specificity results typically only return few relevant objects and therefore typically require calculating some kind of similarity or matching function between the query and all items in the collection. For low-specificity queries such as, e.g., based on a genre label the number of retrieved objects is typically much larger and therefore amendable to a different type of approach. When there is sufficient label data supervised machine learning techniques can be used to "train" statistical models of the data that can directly "classify" a music piece with a discrete category. Retrieval can then be more efficiently performed by randomly selecting pieces and returning as relevant only the ones that have the correctly assigned label avoiding full comparisons of the query with the entire collection.

Evaluation

Music information retrieval is a new growing research area and one of the major challenges that researchers have to face is evaluation. A lot of the early work in MIR and still a large part of existing work is performed with in-house datasets which makes systematic comparison of different approaches and algorithms impossible. Since 2005 MIREX (the MIR Evaluation eXchange) http://www.music-ir.org/mirex2007/index.php/Main_Page has been an effort to address this problem and provide comparisons and evaluations on common datasets. It is a community-based formal evaluation framework coordinated and managed by the International Music Information Retrieval Systems Evaluation Laboratory (IMIRSEL) at the University of Illinois at Urbana-Champaign (UIUC). Every year based on interest by the community a set of different tasks are proposed and research groups around the world submit their algorithms for comparative evaluation. One of the challenges with MIREX is that the datasets used are not provided to the participants and therefore all submitted algorithms must be executed at UIUC. This to some extent also prevents "overfitting" of submitted systems to the particular data collection. Browsing the results for each task is a great way to see what the current state of the art is and which groups are active in each task. There are multiple metrics that can be used to evaluate different systems even for the same task. In order to provide a rough picture of the current state of the art we provide representative results of the "best" performing systems for some of the MIREX audio-based tasks: genre classification 68.29% (7000 30-sec clips, 10 genres, MIREX2007), audio mood classification 61.50% (600 30-sec clips, 5 moods, MIREX2007), and audio artist identification 48.14% (30-sec clips, x artists, MIREX2007). All these results show percentage of clips correctly classified using a threefold cross-validation scheme where one-third of the data is used for testing and two-thirds for training and the process is repeated three times. Other results include audio music similarity 0.568 (100 random queries from 7000 songs, evaluated by human graders with a fine score between 0 and 10, score is the normalized sum of fine-grained human similarity decisions, MIREX 2007) and audio tempo extraction 94.29% (percentage of at least one tempo correct, MIREX 2006).

User Interfaces

Ultimately any MIR system needs to be used by humans. Music listening is a personal, subjective, enjoyable experience which automation should enhance and support. Therefore, the interaction with the user is a critical and essential component of MIR research that has been gaining importance as the field matures. One of the interesting directions in this area is content- and context-aware user interfaces that rely on automatic audio analysis techniques to inform the visual presentation of music collections. Such interfaces typically employ content-based audio feature extraction as described previously followed by dimensionality/visualization techniques that map the extracted features into visual attributes or positions of objects. Self-organized maps (SOM) are used in the Islands of Music system to map audio feature vectors to positions in a two-dimensional grid which is colored using a map metaphor.[37] Musicream utilizes principal component analysis (PCA) to assign colors to disks that represent individual music pieces and to adjust the playlist composition by using a water tap metaphor.[38]

BRIDGING SYMBOLIC AND AUDIO CONTENT-BASED MUSIC RETRIEVAL

The obvious possibility for bridging symbolic and audio content-based music retrieval is to use an automatic polyphonic music transcription method for extracting a symbolic representation from an audio signal, and then to apply some of the methods described in the section "Symbolic Techniques." Nevertheless, automatic polyphonic transcription is a hard technical problem for which there is no current general-purpose and reliable solution, although there has been remarkable progress in this direction.[33]

In some cases it is possible to combine symbolic and audio content-based music retrieval approaches without requiring a full music transcription system. For example, it is possible to use the monophonic reduction (recall from the section "Using String Matching Framework") in order to use symbolic queries for audio databases[39] or to retrieve a symbolic score from a score collection by using a polyphonic audio query.[40] More generally, the polyphonic audio-score alignment can be used to discover the respective parts of an audio signal and a score.[41,42] An *off-line* application for such an alignment is in the back-end of a query-by-humming system: the back-end is needed in order to playback the part of an audio file that corresponds to the found occurrence, in a symbolic music file, of a hummed query. *Online* audio-score alignment is needed in computer accompaniment.[43]

ACKNOWLEDGMENTS

Kjell Lemström was supported by the Academy of Finland (Grant #108547).

REFERENCES

1. Mongeau, M.; Sankoff, D. Comparison of musical sequences. Comput. Humanities **1990**, *24*, 161–175.
2. Ghias, A.; Logan, J.; Chamberlin, D.; Smith, B.C. Query by humming—Musical information retrieval in an audio

database. *ACM Multimedia 95 Proceedings*, San Francisco, CA, 1995; 231–236.

3. McNab, R.J.; Smith, L.A.; Bainbridge, D.; Witten, I.H. The New Zealand digital library MELody inDEX. D-Lib Mag. **1997**. Available at http://www.dlib.org/dlib/may97/meldex/05witten.html.
4. Lemström, K. *String matching techniques for music retrieval*; University of Helsinki, Department of Computer Science, 2000; Ph.D. thesis, Report A-2000-4.
5. Clausen, M.; Engelbrecht, R.; Meyer, D.; Schmitz, J. Proms: A web-based tool for searching in polyphonic music. *Proceedings of the International Symposium on Music Information Retrieval (ISMIR'00)*, Plymouth, MA, October 2000.
6. Ukkonen, E.; Lemström, K.; Mäkinen, V. Sweepline the music!. *Computer Science in Perspective—Essays Dedicated to Thomas Ottmann*; Springer-Verlag: New York, 2003; vol. 2598, 330–342 of *Lecture Notes in Computer Science*.
7. Lubiw, A.; Tanur, L. Pattern matching in polyphonic music as a weighted geometric translation problem. *Proceedings of the 5th International Conference on Music Information Retrieval*, Barcelona, October 2004; 289–296.
8. Clifford, R.; Christodoulakis, M.; Crawford, T.; Meredith, D.; Wiggins, G. A fast, randomised, maximal subset matching algorithm for document-level music retrieval. *Proceedings of the 7th International Conference on Music Information Retrieval*, Victoria, BC, October 2006; 150–155.
9. Romming, C.A.; Selfridge-Field, E. Algorithms for polyphonic music retrieval: The Hausdorff metric and geometric hashing. *Proceedings of the 8th International Conference on Music Information Retrieval (ISMIR'07)*, Vienna, October 2007; 457–462.
10. Lemström, K.; Mikkilä, N.; Mäkinen, V. Fast index based filters for music retrieval. *Proceedings of the Ninth International Conference on Music Information Retrieval (ISMIR'08)*, Philadelphia, PA, September 2008; 677–682.
11. Bloch, J.J.; Dannenberg, R.B. Real-time accompaniment of polyphonic keyboard performance. *Proceedings of the 1985 International Computer Music Conference*, Vancouver, BC, 1985; 279–290.
12. Holub, J.; Iliopoulos, C.S.; Mouchard, L. Distributed string matching using finite automata. J. Automata Lang. Comb. **2001**, *6*(2), 191–204.
13. Lemström, K.; Tarhio, J. Transposition invariant pattern matching for multi-track strings. Nord. J. Comput. **2003**, *10*(3), 185–205.
14. Lemström, K.; Mäkinen, V. On minimizing pattern splitting in multi-track string matching. J. Discr. Algorithm. **2005**, *3*(2–4), 248–266.
15. Lemström, K.; Pienimäki, A. On comparing edit distance and geometric frameworks in content-based retrieval of symbolically encoded polyphonic music. Musicae Scientiae **2007**, *4a*, 135–152.
16. Blackburn, S.; DeRoure, D. A tool for content based navigation of music. *ACM Multimedia 98 Proceedings*, Bristol, 1998; 361–368.
17. Uitdenbogerd, A.L.; Zobel, J. Manipulation of music for melody matching. *ACM Multimedia 98 Proceedings*, Bristol, 1998; 235–240.
18. Dovey, M.J. A technique for "regular expression" style searching in polyphonic music. *The 2nd Annual International Symposium on Music Information Retrieval (ISMIR'01)*, Bloomington, IN, October 2001; 179–185.
19. Doraisamy, S.; Rüger, S.M. An approach towards a polyphonic music retrieval system. *The 2nd Annual International Symposium on Music Information Retrieval (ISMIR'01)*, Bloomington, IN, October 2001; 187–193.
20. Typke, R. *Music Retrieval Based on Melodic Similarity*; Utrecht University: the Netherlands, 2007; Ph.D. thesis.
21. Mäkinen, V.; Ukkonen, E. Point pattern matching. In *Encyclopedia of Algorithms*; Kao, M., Ed.; Springer-Verlag: New York, 2008; 657–660.
22. Wiggins, G.A.; Lemström, K.; Meredith, D. SIA(M)ESE: An algorithm for transposition invariant, polyphonic content-based music retrieval. *Proceedings of the International Conference on Music Information Retrieval (ISMIR '02)*, Paris, October 2002; 283–284.
23. Tzanetakis, G.; Cook, P. Musical genre classification of audio signals. IEEE Trans. Acoust. Speech Signal Process. **2002**, *10*(5), 293–302.
24. Li, T.; Ogihara, M. Music artist style identification by semi-supervised learning from both lyrics and content. *ACM International Conference on Multimedia*, New York, 2004; 364–367.
25. Lu, L.; Liu, D.; Zhang, H.J. Automatic mood detection and tracking of music audio signals. IEEE Trans. Acoust. Speech Signal Process. **2006**, *14*(1), 5–18.
26. Ellis, D.P.W.; Whitman, B.; Berenzweig, A.; Lawrence, S. The quest for ground truth in music artist similarity. *International Conference on Music Information Retrieval (ISMIR)*, Paris, 2002.
27. Theodoridis, S.; Koutroumbas, K. *Pattern Recognition*, 3rd Ed.; Academic Press: London, 2006.
28. Kapur, A.; Benning, M.; Tzanetakis, G. Query by beatboxing: music retrieval for the DJ. *Proceedings of the International Conference on Music Information Retrieval (ISMIR)*, Barcelona, 2004.
29. Ghias, A.; Logan, J.; Chamberlin, D.; Smith, B. Query by humming: Musical information retrieval in an audio database. ACM Multimedia **1995**, 213–236.
30. Dannenberg, R.B.; Birmingham, W.P.; Tzanetakis, G.; Meek, C.; Hu, N.; Pardo, B. The MUSART testbed for query-by-humming evaluation. Comput. Music J. **2004**, *28*(2), 34–48.
31. Oliver, N. Kreger-Stickles, L. Papa: Physiology and purpose-aware automatic playlist generation. *Proceedings of the International Conference on Music Information Retrieval (ISMIR)*, Victoria, BC, 2007.
32. Davis, S.; Mermelstein, P. Experiments in syllable-based recognition of continuous speech. IEEE Trans. Acoust. Speech Signal Process **1980**, *28* 357–366.
33. Klapuri, A.; Davy, M., Eds. *Signal Processing Methods for Music Transcription*; Springer: New York, 2006.
34. Tzanetakis, G.; Jones, R.; McNally, K. Stereo panning features for classifying recording production style. *Proceedings of the International Conference on Music Information Retrieval (ISMIR)*, Vienna, 2007.
35. Cano, P.; Battle, E.; Kalker, T.; Haitsma, J. A review of algorithms for audio fingerprinting. *Proceedings of the*

International Workshop on Multimedia Signal Processing (MMSP), Virgin Islands, 2002.
36. Ellis, D.; Poliner, G. Identifying cover songs with chroma features and dynamic programming beat tracking. *Proceedings of the International Conference on Audio, Speech and Signal Processing (ICASSP)*, Hawaii, 2007.
37. Pampalk, E.; Dixon, S.; Widmer, G. Exploring music collections by browsing different views. Comput. Music J. **2004**, *28*(2), 46–62.
38. Goto, M.; Goto, T. Musicream: New music playback interface for streaming, sticking, sorting and recalling musical pieces. *Proceedings of the International Conference on Music Information Retrieval (ISMIR)*, London, 2005.
39. Suyoto, I.S.H.; Uitdenbogerd, A.L.; Scholer, F. Searching musical audio using symbolic queries. IEEE Trans. Audio Speech Lang. Process. **2008**, *16*(2), 372–381.
40. Pickens, J. et al. Polyphonic score retrieval using polyphonic audio queries: A harmonic modeling approach. *Proceedings of the International Conference on Music Information Retrieval (ISMIR)*, Paris, 2002.
41. Hu, N.; Dannenberg, R.B.; Tzanetakis, G. Polyphonic audio matching and alignment for music retrieval. *Proceedings of the IEEE Workshop on Applications of Signal Processing to Audio and Acoustics (WASPAA)*, Mohonk, NY, 2003.
42. Fremerey, C.; Müller, M.; Kurth, F.; Clausen, M. Automatic mapping of scanned sheet music to audio recordings. *Proceedings of the Ninth International Conference on Music Information Retrieval (ISMIR'08)*, Philadelphia, PA, September 2008; 413–418.
43. Dannenberg, R.; Raphael, C. Music score alignment and computer accompaniment. Commun. ACM **2006**, *49*(8), 38–43.

Music Librarianship

Holly Gardinier
Honnold/Mudd Library, Libraries of The Claremont Colleges, Claremont, California, U.S.A.

Sarah R. Canino
Dickinson Music Library, Vassar College, Poughkeepsie, New York, U.S.A.

Carl Rahkonen
Harold S. Orendorff Music Library, Indiana University of Pennsylvania, Indiana, Pennsylvania, U.S.A.

Abstract

This entry explores the major aspects of music librarianship beginning with a review of the core literature, types of music libraries, professional organizations, and music librarianship as a career. The general areas of acquisition, cataloging, classification, reference, and preservation are examined as they relate to the unique needs of music. Future challenges to the profession are summarized.

DEFINITION

Music librarianship is a specialization of librarianship that involves the acquisition, cataloging, and preservation of music materials in audio, visual, print, and digital formats and the provision of instructional and reference services to the users of these materials.

LITERATURE

In 1893, James Duff Brown[1] wrote the first manual describing the organization of a music library. Books and collections of essays about music librarianship offering an historical perspective include McColvin,[2] Bryant,[3] McColvin and Reeves,[4] Redfern,[5,6] Jones,[7] and Turbet[8] written from the British point of view and Wallace,[9] Hill,[10] Bradley,[11] Mann,[12] Ochs,[13] and Cassaro[14] viewed from the American perspective. Additionally, Bradley[15] compiled a collection of seminal articles published about music librarianship up until 1973. Timely essays summarizing the state of the profession appeared in *Notes*, the official journal of the Music Library Association, by Watanabe (1981),[16] by Davidson (1993),[17] and by contributors in the field in a special millennial issue.[18] In *American Music Librarianship: a Biographical and Historical Survey*,[19] Bradley acknowledged the pioneers who built collections, devised classifications, and developed cataloging codes. She later documented the literature of the field in her exhaustive bibliography *American Music Librarianship: a Research and Information Guide*.[20]

TYPES OF MUSIC LIBRARIES

Academic Libraries

Academic music libraries primarily serve students, faculty, and visiting scholars. Collections are driven by the evolving curriculum of the institution and are important resources supporting its educational mission. Such collections tend to be interdisciplinary in scope and are augmented by musical archives of importance to the institution and the locale. Critical editions, study scores, sound and visual recordings, and monographs and periodicals on music-related topics form the basis of these scholarly collections. Depending on the curriculum, performing editions with parts are often well-represented in the collection.

Academic music libraries employ music librarians, frequently with advanced degrees in music, to administer the collection, develop and catalog it, provide instruction, and answer reference questions. The work of the music librarians is usually supported by library and/or student assistants.

Academic music collections may be incorporated within a general academic library or exist as a separate branch library. Often music collections were initiated in music departments and later incorporated into the administrative structure of the institution's academic library.

Research Libraries

Research libraries are administered by an organization, founder, or foundation. As a result, these collections may be more narrowly focused in accordance with the mission of the supporting body than their counterparts in

Encyclopedia of Library and Information Sciences, Fourth Edition DOI: 10.1081/E-ELIS4-120043861

academia. Examples of research library collections may be found worldwide in societies, foundations, museums, and church, monastery, or other spiritual organizations, for example, the Moravian Music Foundation (the United States), the International Library of African Music (South Africa), Internationale Stiftung Mozarteum Biblioteca Mozartiana (Austria), English Folk Dance and Song Society, Vaughan Williams Memorial Library (the United Kingdom), and Biblioteca Apostolica Vaticana (Italy). Staffing of these collections ranges widely. Research music libraries may employ music librarians with advanced degrees or expertise in specific areas of music. However, small collections may be administered by knowledgeable volunteers.

Conservatory Libraries

Conservatory libraries, at institutions such as the Curtis Institute of Music (the United States), Royal College of Music (the United Kingdom), and Sibelius Academy (Finland), serve students, faculty, and visiting artists. Similar to the academic library, their collections are driven by curricula; however, the emphasis is generally on performance and pedagogy. Performing editions with parts, orchestral excerpts, sound and visual recordings, and monographs on performance issues are augmented with the basic resources found in academic libraries. Conservatory libraries may also perform an archival role relating to the institution or to artists of local interest. Conservatory music libraries hire music librarians to administer the collection, develop and catalog it, provide access and bibliographic instruction, and answer reference questions.

Public Libraries

Public library music collections are shaped by the size and resources of the community they serve as well as the significance of local historical music events. They are funded by local government and most contain some music-related monographs and small popular music audio/visual collections. However, large public library collections such as those found in major cities are similar to research collections. While public libraries may maintain archival collections of local music history, the primary aim of the library is to circulate materials and provide access to members of the community. Public libraries with large music collections employ several music librarians. In smaller public libraries, the tasks of collection development, cataloging, and reference may fall to those librarians who have an interest in the subject.

Music Information Centres

Music Information Centres are national organizations that collect, document, and promote the music of the supporting country. Services are provided to anyone worldwide with an interest in the music of the country. Collections include scores, recordings, and biographical and research materials. In addition to administration, collection development, cataloging, and reference, Music Information Centres are charged with promoting the music of their country through various activities. Since 1939, the American Music Center has served this purpose for the United States.

National Libraries

National libraries are generally responsible for "acquiring, cataloguing, and maintaining copies of the national bibliographic output and preparing the national bibliography."[21] These library collections combine characteristics of public and research libraries and Music Information Centres. Like public libraries, national libraries are funded by a government and provide services to its citizens. However, national music libraries are broader in their collection scope than most public libraries and may include scores, sound and visual recordings, and monographs and periodicals on music-related topics. Similar to Music Information Centres, they collect and promote the music of their country. Often they are required by legislation to serve as a repository for copyrighting newly published music and many also set cataloging and other policies for libraries in their country. Music collections in national libraries are staffed by music librarians. Some of the many important national libraries with substantial music collections include: the British Library (the United Kingdom), Bibliothèque Nationale de France (France), Bayerische Staatsbibliothek (Germany), Oestererreichische Nationalbibliothek (Austria), Biblioteka Narodowa (Poland), Rossiyskaya Gosudarstvennaya Biblioteka (Russia), and the National Diet Library (Japan). Though often considered a national library, the Library of Congress (the United States) was created to serve the members of Congress.

Performance Libraries

The purpose of a performance library is to meet the specialized needs of performers and performing organizations. These library collections include few of the music reference and sound and visual recordings found in other types of music libraries. In these libraries, the music librarian is responsible for obtaining the music needed for performance each season through purchase or rental, organizing and maintaining parts acquired by the organization, and marking parts with directions for performance as required by the conductor of the work. Librarians from many of these organizations are served by a professional society, the Major Orchestral Librarians Association (MOLA).

Because of its global lending policy and extensive holdings, the Edwin A. Fleisher Collection of Orchestral

Music, at the Free Library of Philadelphia, is the world's largest lending library of orchestral performance material.

Media and Broadcast Libraries

Significant changes have taken place in the collections of radio and broadcasting station libraries. In the United States, until recently, radio stations maintained large collections of physical recordings. With the rise of Internet radio stations, digitized collections are being amassed for streaming. Many traditional stations are digitizing recordings to offer content via both Internet and terrestrial radio.

In Europe, radio broadcast libraries, such as the British Broadcasting Corporation Music Library, traditionally provided scores for broadcast performances. Over time, some collections changed their focus as has Radio France, Documentation Musicale which originally provided performance scores for its orchestra, Orchestre National. It now acts as a national documentation center promoting contemporary music. In the past, Sveriges Radio Förvaltning, Musikbiblioteket commissioned works for radio and television performance, thus it contains autograph manuscripts of Swedish composers in addition to other performance scores.

PROFESSIONAL ORGANIZATIONS

IAML: International Association of Music Libraries, Archives, and Documentation Centres (http://www.iaml.info)

Established in 1951, IAML provides an international forum for music libraries, archives, and documentation centers with an interest in the collection, preservation, access, and dissemination of musical sources. Open to individuals and institutions interested in the goals of the association, this trilingual organization utilizes professional and national branches, subject commissions, committees, and working groups to accomplish its aims. Institutional and individual members number approximately 2200. National branches support IAML at the local (country) level. Communication is facilitated by the IAML-L listserv and the journal of the organization, *Fontes Artis Musicae*, published in English, French, and German. IAML holds a major annual conference, hosted in a different country, to encourage member participation.

IAMIC: International Association of Music Information Centres (http://www.iamic.net)

Since 1986, IAMIC has served as an international organization for the 41 Music Information Centres that make up its membership. IAMIC fosters the sharing of resources and collaborative projects to further the aims of the association. Recent projects include the *2009 IAMIC Annual List*: a "reference for performers seeking to expand their new music repertoire."[22] Communication is provided via *IAMIC News* on the IAMIC website. Like IAML, IAMIC's annual conferences are held in different countries to allow equitable opportunities for attendance.

MLA: Music Library Association (http://www.musiclibraryassoc.org)

Founded in 1931, MLA is a professional organization "devoted to music librarianship and all aspects of music materials in libraries."[23] MLA's over 2000 members are primarily music librarians from the United States and Canada; however, membership is open to all institutions and individuals, regardless of professional status, who support the work of the association. MLA is composed of committees, roundtables, and interest groups which work to further the goals of the association. Regional chapters support MLA on the local level. Communication is promoted through the listserv MLA-L, an online newsletter, and the organization's quarterly journal, *Notes*. MLA publications facilitate the work of music researchers and librarians and articulate the responsibilities and training of the music librarian. MLA holds a major annual conference, hosted in a different area of North America, for information-sharing among members.

MOLA: Major Orchestral Librarians' Association (http://www.mola-inc.org)

Organized in 1983, MOLA is an international association which supports the work of librarians in professional performance organizations by sharing resources and information related to the performance library arena. As of January 2009, MOLA comprised 249 member organizations, representing over 400 individual librarians, and 18 individual honorary members. Members exchange information through the association's online discussion forum and a quarterly newsletter, *Marcato*. MOLA publications facilitate the work of the members and articulate the responsibilities and training of the orchestral librarian. Annual meetings are hosted by MOLA members.

MOUG: Music OCLC Users Group (http://www.musicoclcusers.org)

In 1977, MOUG was formed as a task force of the Online Computer Library Center, Inc. (OCLC) to examine issues regarding OCLC's implementation of the MARC (Machine-Readable Cataloging) music format for scores and sound recordings. From its early concentration on cataloging issues, the group expanded its scope to encompass the use of OCLC products in activities such as music acquisition and reference. Communication is facilitated by the *Music OCLC Users Group Newsletter*. Membership is open to individuals and institutions that are interested in the goals of MOUG and, as of January 2009, totaled 207 personal and 229 institutional members. Because there is much overlap in membership between MLA and MOUG, annual meetings are held together.

ARSC: Association for Recorded Sound Collections (http://www.arsc-audio.org/index.html)

ARSC, founded in 1966, is of particular interest to music librarians since music libraries tend to have large collections of sound recordings. ARSC's mission is to share knowledge and education about recording preservation, cataloging, history, and copyright law. The Association comprises 1072 individual and institutional members. It publishes the *ARSC Journal* and a newsletter. Annual conferences are held throughout the United States.

IASA: International Association of Sound and Audio Archives (http://www.iasa-web.org)

Established in 1969, IASA promotes international cooperation between libraries, archives, museums, and private collectors that preserve recorded sound and audiovisual materials. As of January 2009, interest in the work of the IASA is reflected in its 215 institutional and 180 individual memberships. Members share expertise in digitization and preserving sound in electronic formats.

The association publishes the *IASA Journal* semi-annually, and also issues an electronic bulletin, and various technical reports. Annual conferences are held in locations around the world.

CONSIDERING A CAREER IN MUSIC LIBRARIANSHIP

The ability to read musical notation coupled with a background in singing or playing a musical instrument and/or participating in a musical ensemble is essential for carrying out the responsibilities of a music librarian. For example, music catalogers must be able to read musical notation to determine the form of a piece and other identifying elements, such as key, used in descriptive cataloging; those who purchase music and provide reference service must possess knowledge of musical notation to be able to select items for a collection and to answer questions that require score identification; and those who are in charge of binding music must understand how scores and parts are used to make appropriate binding choices.

Besides a library master's degree, music librarians need a broad background in music including substantial undergraduate coursework. Often a second master's degree in music is required for those preparing to assist academic scholars. A reading knowledge of foreign languages, especially German, is invaluable in working both with the music and the secondary literature. Knowledge of current digital resources and applications is expected, and practical experience in the profession is valued. An excellent way to gain experience for entry into the profession is through an internship in a music library as part of a library degree-related graduate program.

The Music Library Association supports mentorship activities and its website[24] offers information about job requirements, a directory of library school offerings in music librarianship, and up-to-date details about career prospects. In April 2002, the MLA's Library School Liaison Committee drafted a report[25] outlining the core competencies of music librarians. Published in 2004, *Careers in Music Librarianship II*[26] offers a realistic picture of the profession through essays by professionals in the field that describe their experiences as music librarians and their assessments of career path options.

While small collections may employ only one music librarian, larger collections are better served with at least one music subject specialist and a specialized music cataloger. Thus, career advancement may only be achieved through moving on to a larger institution or taking on more varied responsibilities in the current job. Some music librarians find that managing a music library provides excellent experience for advancement to library supervisory and administrative positions. On the other hand, large academic and public libraries that employ a number of music librarians may offer opportunities for advancement within their library organizations.

DEVELOPING COLLECTIONS

Typically, music libraries contain books on music, audio and visual recordings, music scores, and specialized reference tools, indexes, and periodicals. The large collections of printed music and sound recordings make music libraries unique. Many music library collections originally focused on Western classical music and have expanded their scope to include popular genres and world music.

Acquiring music materials is challenging because they are published in multiple manifestations and recorded in different versions. In addition, the same work may be published under different titles in different languages, further complicating the issue. Traditional book vendors rarely handle music scores so acquiring these materials requires working with specialized music vendors and publishers. Book vendors may handle recordings; however, obtaining foreign and specialized labels can be challenging and require the services of knowledgeable recording vendors. Fling's *Library Acquisition of Music*[27] presents a detailed examination of the music acquisition process and its inherent complexities. *A Basic Music Library*,[28] now in its third edition, was written to identify what constitutes a music library core collection of scores and recordings.

Scores

Music librarians acquire scores in different manifestations for different purposes. As Krummel observed, "Musical documents are physically distinctive for reasons which are essentially musical" (p. 327).[29] Scores are published in different formats to meet users' needs. For example, in the nineteenth century a market developed for scores to be used by concertgoers, who wanted scores to follow while listening. To be portable full scores were published in a reduced size that could easily slip into a pocket. Today, these scores are referred to as miniature, pocket, or study scores and are often used by students in analyzing music.

Likewise, the demand of musicians for scores to study and perform resulted in the publication of piano-vocal scores, also called vocal scores. Piano-vocal scores feature the orchestral music reduced or arranged for piano while maintaining the original vocal parts. These types of scores can be used by vocalists to rehearse their parts without requiring the full instrumental accompaniment.

Those interested in performance practice seek historical/critical editions of scores prepared from an in-depth examination of all known primary sources. These scores present the most authoritative versions of a musical work as scholars in the field have determined. A critical report, detailing the editorial practices, identifying the autograph and/or copyist's manuscripts consulted, and outlining research issues, often accompanies each volume. Music librarians may spend a good portion of their acquisition budget on standing orders to obtain these scholarly critical editions of music.

Scholars want to consult a composer's manuscripts, sketches, and the earliest printed editions of music to determine a composer's intentions. When original materials are unavailable facsimiles are sought. Researchers also seek access to modern scholarly editions that reflect current scholarship.

Performers who use a music library may range in skill from beginners to professionals. For the less-skilled amateurs simplified editions, in which the composition has been reduced to the basic thematic line and an easy accompaniment, are requested. Skilled musicians look for scores reproduced with sensitivity to the intentions of the composer that do not dictate performance practice through editorial accretions. Modern publishers use the term *Urtext*, "original text," for performing editions that attempt to distinguish editorial markings from those of the composer. Editorial practices used in producing *Urtext* editions vary by publisher. Performing editions may include indications of fingering, bowing, phrasing, tempo, and articulation markings not found in the composer's manuscript.

Some libraries collect octavo and sheet music. The term "octavo" originates from the size of the paper folded into eights and is the size commonly used in publishing choral music. Sheet music is printed on large unbound sheets of paper and is the format commonly used for popular music. The late nineteenth and early twentieth centuries witnessed the heyday of sheet music publishing. Sheet music is of historical interest for its song texts and illustrative covers that document events and offer insights into the popular culture of the period.

Unique sheet music collections in the public domain, such as the *19th-Century California Sheet Music Project*,[30] have been digitized to make the collections available for online viewing. Duke University,[31] the University of California at Los Angeles,[32] Johns Hopkins University,[33] and Indiana University[34] maintain their own sheet music websites and also make their collections accessible through the catalog of the Sheet Music Consortium. The Consortium, hosted by the UCLA Digital Library Program, works to build an open collection of digitized sheet music using the Open Archives Initiative standards.[35] Their website facilitates searching sheet music collections from many institutions, including the Library of Congress, through a common interface.

Like digital sheet music collections, access to electronic music scores is a recent development. Begun as the Variations Project, Variations2[36] for scores brought Indiana University to the forefront of digitizing music. The Sibley Music Library at Eastman[37] and the Eda Kuhn Loeb Music Library at Harvard[38] are examples of other libraries that have digitized scores in the public domain and offer access through their library websites. Collaborative websites of content-related library holdings, such as *CFEO: Chopin's First Editions Online*,[39] are also new developments. In 2007, the Internationale Stiftung Mozarteum, Salzburg, in cooperation with the Packard Humanities Institute, Los Altos, California, completed a groundbreaking project to digitize the *Neue Mozart Ausgabe* (W. A. Mozart's complete works).[40]

In the commercial arena, Alexander Street Press has been a pioneer in licensing access to copyrighted music (Boosey & Hawkes Study Scores) through their electronic database *Classical Scores Library*. *CD Sheet Music*, also available through ebrary, sells access to digitized older editions of scores in the public domain. Individual scores can be purchased and downloaded through a variety of vendors such as *Digital E-Print Delivery* from J. W. Pepper.

Audio and Visual Recordings

When Thomas Edison patented his phonograph in 1877, the way we listen to music changed forever. Before that time we could only hear music in live performance, but after the invention of sound recording, music could be captured and listened to at any time and in almost any place. This invention made recordings of music a commodity that could be collected. Sound recordings eventually became just as important as scores to music libraries. In practice, music librarians strive to coordinate the audio and score titles collected to facilitate study and performance. Variant performances of the same work, sometimes in different instrumentation, are collected to allow users the opportunity to hear different interpretations.

Edison's phonograph recorded on fragile wax cylinders. The machine was purely mechanical, not needing electricity, and it was quite portable. This made it ideal for use in ethnographic fieldwork. The earliest cylinders of music recorded in this fashion were made by Jesse Walter Fewkes and date from the 1880s. Cylinders had several disadvantages. First, the maximum recording time on each cylinder was around three minutes; therefore, to record even a movement of a work could take multiple cylinders. They were better suited to recording popular songs and ethnographic examples rather than classical music. Second, cylinders were a fragile medium. They were made of wax or similar materials and were prone to breaking, sensitive to high temperatures, and wore down as they were being played. For these reasons, early music libraries generally did not establish large cylinder collections. Today most of these collections are found in ethnographic sound archives, like the American Folklife Center at the Library of Congress, the Archives of Traditional Music at Indiana University, Bloomington, and the Phonogramm-Archiv in Berlin.

In 1887, Emil Berliner invented and patented the gramophone that recorded on discs. These were less bulky and easier to store than cylinders, making sound recording collection more practical for libraries. Although early commercial 78 rpm discs played for about three minutes, the same as a cylinder recording, record players were developed where one could stack discs and play them one after another in sequence. This facilitated listening to lengthy classical works. For these reasons discs triumphed over cylinders in the war of competing formats.

Many technological advances were applied to disc recordings. These included making discs from new materials that were less heavy, bulky and fragile, using electrical microphones for recording and amplifiers for playback (adapted from radio), and an electric lathing process. Eventually discs featured microgrooves. Slowing the speed to 33 1/3 rpm increased the recording time to more than twenty minutes per side. They were called LPs (Long Playing recordings) and they soon featured significantly improved sound quality with high fidelity and stereo. The LP disc became the most widely collected sound recording medium by libraries.

In the 1930s, magnetic sound recording was developed in Germany. Two competing formats emerged: wire and magnetic tape. Early magnetic tape was backed with paper and was a fragile medium which could tear or lose its magnetic surface. After World War II, magnetic tape continued to be developed in the United States, especially by the 3M Corporation, the makers of Scotch Tape. Their magnetic tape was made of newly invented plastics and offered a more permanent medium. Magnetic tape won over wire in the competing magnetic recording formats. In the early 1960s, the Phillips Corporation of the Netherlands developed the cassette tape which eventually became the most widely used recording medium in the world.[41,42]

Magnetic tape also made possible the recording of video. Video recorders and players featured a rotating steel head that produced a recording of much higher quality, equivalent to a much faster tape speed. The home recording video market also had two competing formats, Betamax from Sony and VHS from JVC. VHS eventually became the standard format for home video recording, even though it was bulkier and not as technically advanced as Betamax, partially because VHS tapes could record up to six hours of video, compared to only one hour for Betamax. This longer time made possible the recording of feature-length films on a single VHS cassette.

Music libraries did not fully embrace collecting magnetic recordings, except for VHS tapes, and continued to collect LPs, since they offered higher quality audio and a permanent medium that could not be recorded over. Reel-to-reel tapes, which were more cumbersome to use than LPs, were found in professional applications such as studio recording, concert, or ethnographic field recording, and by audiophiles. Cassette tapes, and to a lesser extent 8-track tapes, were collected primarily by public libraries for their circulating audio collections.

In the late 1970s, a century after Edison's first patent, digital recording was commercially developed. The compact disc (CD) was invented jointly by Phillips and Sony. They avoided the major mistake made with the cassette tape in that CDs would be a permanent recorded medium, like LPs. During the final two decades of the twentieth century, the CD replaced the LP as the default prerecorded music medium. The video equivalent of the CD is the digital video disc (DVD). Like the CD, the DVD was initially a playback only medium, but personal computers eventually made both the CD and DVD into recordable mediums. The February 19, 2008 announcement by Toshiba that it would no longer develop, market, or manufacture high definition DVD players and recorders, marked the triumph of Blu-ray over High Definition DVD in the fierce competition of formats for the next generation of video recordings.

Like audio recordings, commercial vendors are beginning to license access to streaming video content. Alexander Street Press markets the *Opera in Video* and *Dance in Video* databases that feature performances and video clips of interviews with artists.

No one could have anticipated the coming of the Internet revolution. This began with the development of the Personal Computer (PC) in the 1970s, and as millions of these computers became networked, with ever increasing transmission and computing speeds, the Internet came into its own in the 1990s. The Internet made possible the easy recording and sharing of digital audio files. The Napster website gained notoriety for sharing audio files. Individuals could find literally millions of sound recordings, both legal and illegal under copyright laws, and download them onto their own personal computers. The Recording Industry Association of America (RIAA) sued Napster and won. Now Napster works with the recording industry and charges a modest fee for each digital file.

Recorded sound is progressing to the digital file. One can listen to music on computers and on portable devices, such as the iPod. Libraries have adapted to this revolution by subscribing to digital listening services, such as Napster, Rhapsody, *Classical Music Library* and *Smithsonian Global Sound* from Alexander Street Press, *DRAM* from the Anthology of Recorded Music, Inc., and *Naxos Music Library* from the Naxos Digital Services Ltd. These listening services feature hundreds of thousands of digital tracks of music, far beyond the ability of most music libraries to provide by purchasing physical recordings. Libraries subscribe annually for a fee which allows their patrons access, but not the downloading of files. Most libraries are engaged in determining the appropriate balance between ownership and access for their users and continue to purchase CDs based on the needs of their institution.

Reference Tools

The basic print bibliographies of music reference sources are Duckles,[43] Marco,[44] Brockman,[45] and Foreman.[46] Beginning in 2001, with *Grove Music Online* (now part of *Oxford Music Online*), publishers started to offer electronic access to some core music reference titles such as the *Harvard Dictionary of Music* and *Baker's Biographical Dictionary of Musicians*.

Thematic catalogs offer unique access to library collections. They authenticate a musical work by identifying it through its opening and/or major musical themes given in musical notation, referred to as *incipits*. Thematic catalogs also distinguish works by key, opus, and thematic catalog number and provide information about the composition's publication history, variant editions, and relevant bibliographic literature.

Other unique music reference tools include repertoire guides and graded lists, discographies, and song indexes. Musicians consult repertoire guides and graded lists in search of new works to perform. These sources include information about the musical characteristics of a composition and its performance difficulties, instrumentation, publisher, and performance timing. Discographies are bibliographies of sound recordings that offer information about a particular musician's recordings or document the recorded evolution of musical forms and genres. Song indexes provide access to large songbook collections through song title, composer, subject, and the words of the song text.

Important to music research are indexes to the critical editions of composers' complete works and to the historical monuments of music. For many years Charles[47] Heyer[48] served as the definitive sources for this information. Subsequently, Hill and Stephens[49] compiled an updated bibliography of the historical sets and series, collected editions, and monuments of music whose specific content is being entered into an electronic database version and hosted by a number of aggregators.

Music scholars use the *Répertoire International des Sources Musicale*, *The International Inventory of Musical Sources (RISM)*, to locate music manuscripts and early printed music, works on music theory, and libretti held in libraries, archives, monasteries, schools, and private collections. Only portions of *RISM* are available via electronic access, these being *Series A/II: Music Manuscripts After 1600* and the *U. S. Libretto Database*.[50]

The Internet has become a major resource for music reference information.[51] Large collections of music-related materials have been digitized and organized by individuals, organizations, and institutions, such as the music collections of the Library of Congress' *Performing Arts Reading Room*.[52] Websites enable musicians, scholars, organizations, and libraries to promote their works and offer contact information and/or access to their collections.

Indexes and Abstracts

The basic indexes/abstracts to music periodical literature are: *The Music Index Online*, *The International Index to Music Periodicals* (*IIMP*), and *Répertoire International de Littérature Musicale* (*RILM*). *RILM*, "the first automated abstract journal in the humanities,"[53] features abstracts in English and, most recently, in the language of publication for articles, *festschriften* (collections of celebratory essays), dissertations, and reviews in 140 languages. Although varying in coverage, journal databases such as *Journal Storage: the Scholarly Journal Archive (JSTOR)* and *Project Muse* provide a form of indexing through searchable full-text access to runs of music journals.

The *Retrospective Index to Music Periodicals, 1800–1950* (*RIPM*), indexes runs of music periodicals published before 1950 from around the world. Index coverage is intended to dovetail with *RILM*.[54] This index is available in print, CD-ROM, and electronic formats. The *RIPM Online Archive of Music Periodicals* provides full-text access to the journals indexed in *RIPM*.

CATALOGING

Music catalogers follow the same rules *Anglo-American Cataloging Rules* (AACR 2 rev.) and use the same tools, for example Machine Readable Cataloging (MARC)

Records and Library of Congress Subject Headings (LCSH) as other catalogers; however, music has specialized provisions for bibliographic description and access. These specialized provisions and music cataloging guidelines are detailed in books written by Smiraglia[55] and Weitz.[56–58] In 2006, Smiraglia published a bibliography of literature relating to music cataloging.[59]

Music cataloging practices are geared towards collections of Western classical music. This music exists in written form, either printed or in manuscript. It could be a score, showing all the parts of an ensemble displayed vertically, or a part showing the music performed by one member of an ensemble. Music libraries traditionally collect scores and parts up to nine parts. If a work has ten or more parts, such as a band, orchestral, or wind ensemble piece, it is usually housed in a separate performance ensemble library. Girsberger's *Manual for the Performance Library*[60] provides guidance in how to organize ensemble libraries.

The composer has served as the primary point of access in music cataloging. This assumption dates from the mid-nineteenth century when cataloging rules were first being developed.[61] Establishing the title of a piece of music has always been problematic because of the various languages used by publishers and composers, and because there are many generic forms in Western classical music, such as sonatas, concertos, and symphonies, with many pieces identified only by these generic titles. Thus, uniform titles become essential in music cataloging as a way to standardize variant titles and titles of generic forms. Also subject headings and in part, music classification systems largely rest on these standard musical forms. With the advent of musical sound recordings, the same cataloging conventions were applied.

Sheet music is "musical notation printed on sheets of paper that remain unattached and unbound at the time of sale" (p. 1).[62] For years, music catalogers did not catalog sheet music because of its popular and ephemeral nature, and because there were no cataloging guidelines for sheet music. But as large sheet music collections began to be preserved and made available, cataloging became necessary. A working group of the Music Library Association developed cataloging guidelines for sheet music.[62]

Music Uniform Titles

Uniform titles are more widely used in music cataloging than in any other cataloging context. Uniform titles make it possible to find a composition listed in one place, no matter its language, form, or physical arrangement. Music is published in various languages, so there frequently needs to be a single uniform title that draws together (collocates) the same musical work from various publishers. Also, music is frequently composed in a generic form. Uniform titles are needed to distinguish a particular generic piece from others of the same form by the same composer. Finally, since the very earliest time of music publication, music has been commonly published in collections and anthologies. These anthologies need generic uniform titles to identify and group together collections, usually under a composer's name. Thus, music cataloging recognizes three types of uniform titles: Distinctive titles, Form titles, and Collective titles. Distinctive titles are unique titles, given by the composer, in the original language, for example Debussy's *Prelude to the Afternoon of a Faun* = [Prélude à l'après-midi d'un faune]. Form titles are used for "generic" works such as sonatas, symphonies, and songs. They follow a specific structure: [Form, instrumentation, number, key], for example Beethoven's *Pastoral Symphony* = [Symphonies, no. 6, op. 68, F major]. Collective titles are used for collections and anthologies of music, for example Bach, Johann Sebastian. *Neue Ausgabe sämtlicher Werke* = [Works].

Library catalogs that display uniform titles alphabetically under the composer's name allow users to see all manifestations of a work listed together. Electronic catalogs that allow linking to an item with the same uniform title are valuable tools to collocate, identify, and locate a specific piece of music. Music library users benefit by being aware of the way uniform titles are used to organize music. For detailed information about music uniform titles consult Koth.[64]

Music Subject Headings

Library of Congress Subject Headings (LCSH) for music are unique because they fulfill two functions: to retrieve books about music and to retrieve the actual music itself. The headings used to find books about music are true subject headings. Those used to retrieve music could more properly be called form headings. Terms describing musical forms, such as sonatas, concertos, and symphonies, may be used in both types of music headings, those for finding information about a form, as well finding compositions in that form. Generally, if the term is in the plural, it retrieves the music itself. If it is in the singular, it retrieves books about that subject as a musical form. For example, the subject heading "Concertos" will retrieve scores and recordings of concertos, while "Concerto" will retrieve books about the concerto. This works for most musical forms; however, one exception is "Songs." There is no singular subject heading "Song" for books about this musical form. The heading "Songs–History and criticism" is used.

All the music subject headings from the LCSH (to 1997) have been gathered in a single volume. For further study, this work includes an excellent seventy-five page introduction by Young about the workings of music subject headings.[65]

The Future of Music Cataloging

Cataloging is at the very beginning of a new age. As international committees attempted to update the AACR2, they found that the traditional way of cataloging was less functional in the Internet environment. They began creating a new standard for cataloging called the RDA (Resource Description and Access), marking a fundamental change in cataloging practices.

The MARC record has been at the center of cataloging for more than 30 years and may be approaching the end of its life. As cataloging migrates to web-based standards such as Dublin Core and MODS (Metadata Object Description Schema), cataloging elements will retain their semantic value, the meaning of their controlled vocabulary, but they may lose their syntactic value, which comes from the precise order in which these terms are arranged. The many thousands of MARC records created in the twentieth century will still form the core of data for cataloging records into the future, regardless their format. Knowledge of music cataloging practices will continue to help library users find the music they seek.

CLASSIFICATIONS

Today most academic libraries in the United States use the Library of Congress Classification (LCC). The "M Schedule" for music,[66] was devised by Oscar Sonneck in 1902 to meet the needs of an existing collection, the Library of Congress. Since its inception, LCC has been amended to accommodate popular music, world music, and other new areas of music research. Smiraglia's *Shelflisting Music*[67] provides guidance in how to construct LCC call numbers.

Conceived as a way to organize all knowledge, the Dewey Decimal Classification (DDC) was drafted by Melvil Dewey in 1876. Adopted by public, research, and some academic libraries the DDC is the most used classification globally.[68] Inherent problems in DDC were its inability to adapt to new musical forms and genres and its lack of a provision to separate music scores from music literature. Some libraries addressed this problem by adding a prefix "M" for music scores before the Dewey class number while others elected to reclassify their collections to LCC. The revision of "780 Music" of Dewey (DDC20) attempted to resolve these problems by creating a faceted system allowing scores to be segregated from music literature. It also added classification numbers for folk and popular music and modeled the classification of musical instruments on the wider encompassing Sachs–Hornbostel system which distinguishes instruments by how sound is produced.[69]

Over the years, a number of music classification systems were formulated as examined by Krummel,[70] Elliker,[71] McKnight,[72] and Bradley.[73] For example, a classification specifically for music scores was devised by George Sherman Dickinson, Professor of Music, and the first music librarian at Vassar College, Poughkeepsie, NY (USA). In his classification system, *The Classification of Musical Compositions: A Decimal-Symbol System*,[74] published in 1938, Dickinson recognized that not one system could serve each library type equally. The result is a system that can be modified to conform to different types of music libraries and the needs of their users. The Dickinson classification system was used by a number of music libraries in the northeastern United States. However, because the Dickinson classification utilizes special music symbols, many libraries have adopted classification that are more compatible with integrated library systems.

For audio collections, libraries may choose not to classify recordings but to organize them in accession order. This arrangement offers the most economical use of space because room is not left to interfile new items. Some music libraries elect to use the record label and label number as a way to organize recordings. Both arrangements have the benefit of avoiding the decision of where to classify a disc when it includes works of different genres by different composers.

If recordings are classified libraries often adapt LCC or DDC. Some music libraries use the *Alpha-Numeric System for Classification of Sound Recordings* (ANSCR)[75,76] intended to facilitate browsing in public libraries. ANSCR arranges recordings in a hierarchy of subject, composer or subcategory, title, and performer's name.

PRESERVATION

Music libraries will continue to have LP and CD collections, as well as collections of recorded magnetic tape in various formats. The challenge in keeping these collections valid and useful is twofold: preservation and access. An LP is a great medium for preservation; even discs 60 years old or older will play well if not worn, warped, or scratched. However, challenges remain of maintaining working playback equipment and obtaining replacement parts. Magnetic tape formats are becoming obsolete and finding working playback machines is becoming difficult. For these reasons, many libraries are digitizing their analog collections for purposes of preservation and access.

Preservation needs to be considered even for digital formats. The oldest CDs are now nearly 30 years old. They can be subject to oxidation and damage from wear and tear. Digital media require migration to newer digital formats to keep them useful. Sound recording archivists held a conference at the Library of Congress in 2001, which took into consideration problems of access, preservation, and intellectual property for folk heritage sound recording collections.[77] Most recently, Indiana University and Harvard University published audio preservation standards[78] based on their tests of new technology.

For print collections, attention must be taken to process materials for long-term use. Since music is used in performance, it must be bound to lay flat on a music stand. Special binding provisions are needed for parts, comb bindings, and nonstandard sized items. Carli's *Binding & Care of Printed Music*[79] presents a detailed examination of the issues of paper conservation and binding and offers how-to information for in-house conservation steps.

ETHNIC AND WORLD MUSIC

Music libraries have traditionally collected materials in Western classical music, but ethnic and world music have become common in collections over the past three decades. In 1994, MLA published a technical report examining world music in libraries.[80] The term "world music" is a popular current alternative for such terms as primitive, non-Western, ethnic, and folk music. Its broadest definition is simply all types of music from around the world. In this context the definition expands beyond the purely popular idiom to include all styles of music with ethnic or foreign elements.[81]

With the growth of worldwide systems of communication and commerce, librarians will feel increasing demands for materials characterized as world music. Reference questions pertaining to world music have become more numerous in recent years, as college and public school curricula have emphasized cultural diversity and interest in globalization. Music education majors now look for examples of ethnic music to teach in the classroom. Public librarians face ever greater numbers of patrons seeking music of their ethnic heritage.

The techniques used to handle Western classical music do not always easily apply to world music. Certain basic assumptions are made about Western classical music: that it exists in a written form and can be identified in an historical context from written sources; that the composer serves as the primary point of access; that uniform titles can be created according to what is found in written sources; and that subject access and classification rest on standard forms. World music is less likely to exist in a written form, since it may be passed on by aural tradition. The composer may be unknown, thus the performer, informant, or even the collector may have to serve as primary points of access. Music in aural traditions may vary with each performer and even with each performance. The title of a work may exist in variant forms and may not be found in any written source. Finally, world music frequently exists in forms and genres that cannot be identified in written sources, thus subject access and classification may require special provisions.

Many music reference tools also address world music; however, there are also specialized sources. One of the best is the 10-volume *Garland Encyclopedia of World Music*[82] which is also available in electronic format. Each volume covers an area of the world. This work is not an encyclopedia in the traditional sense, where one could look up a specific term. Rather, it should be thought of as a collection of well laid-out and illustrated scholarly articles written by experts. To find specific information, readers need to use the detailed indexes. Other specialized reference works are cited in annotated bibliographies by Schuursma[83] and Post.[84]

Subject access to world music presents special problems. LCSH are designed for use primarily with Western classical music. A basic tenet of these headings is that they tend to use genre or form of a composition as the initial entry point. This becomes a problem with world music, because it tends to scatter headings of music from a specific geographic region throughout the catalog. Examples of LCSH forJapanese music include: "Ballads, Japanese," "Buddhist hymns, Japanese," "Folk Songs, Japanese," "Hymns, Japanese," and "Songs, Japanese."

Another tenet of LCSH is that they use only the most specific heading that fits and typically do not add more general headings. For example, Japanese koto music would receive the subject heading "Koto music" and not "Music–Japan." If this music is in a specific form, such as a sonata, it would be cataloged under "Sonatas (Koto)." Patrons need to know details about the music in order to find the specific subject heading.

Libraries with large collections of world music have tended to use the Murdock's *Outline of World Cultures*[85] to augment subject access to their collections. Additional information about subject access to world music materials may be found in Kaufman[86] and in Pierce.[87]

FUTURE CHALLENGES

Music, as a humanities discipline, has been slow to enter the digital environment. While journals were the earliest format to be digitized in other fields, music journals are relatively recent inclusions in *JSTOR* and *Project Muse*; however, other music formats are much further behind. Projects for digitizing musical scores are uneven in coverage and not fully developed. The physical practicalities of using digital scores for performance have yet to be successfully addressed. Currently, some databases of copyrighted music permit access to scores by allowing users to pay per item download. Others allow users to view scores for study purposes but not to perform from the digitized versions. Digital audio content from commercial databases is broadening, but is still representative of only particular recording labels or specialized subject areas. Alarmingly, lacking are provisions for perpetual access to the content of these digital audio and music resources. In addition to physical hurdles to overcome, in general, non-book materials are plagued with much more complex limitations imposed by copyright law than are books.

Because music materials are not in step with other disciplines, music libraries have been slower to feel the problems and challenges which face general libraries in the first decade of the new millennium, and music librarians are only beginning to realize these changes in their daily work. In the area of collection development questions of access vs. ownership are further complicated because not as many music-related items are yet available electronically. Music publishers tend to be small businesses and are often reluctant to fund the development of new electronic resources.

Aside from digitization, music-related materials themselves are changing. For example, the field of music study has expanded in new directions. It is increasingly interdisciplinary, focusing on cultural, ethnic, racial, and gender issues, and requiring new reference tools and resources.

The future of sound recording looks very much like the past. The issue of retention of older formats and their playback equipment while acquiring new formats continues to be a challenge. The history of sound recording has been characterized by competing formats, and we still have competing formats today. Digital files can be in a variety of formats such as WMV, RealAudio, MP3 and AAC. There is absolutely no guarantee that today's audio file will play on a computer even 5 years from now, let alone into the foreseeable future. All digital file sound recordings, just like other computer media, will have to be migrated to newer formats as they are developed and become the standard for that time.

In the digital age, academic music institutions are expected to provide course reserve listening assignments in digitized form. This new service requires acquisition and training in the use of software and hardware, beyond the simple scanners needed by their counterparts in other disciplines.

The Indiana University Digital Library Program proposes to create Variations3, a digital music library system, modeled after Indiana's highly successfully electronic Variations music library, which can be deployed at other academic libraries. In support of instruction and learning, the system will enable institutions to digitize and provide online access to recordings and scanned scores for use with annotation and analysis tools.[88]

Historically, music libraries have been somewhat autonomous from general collections because of their many nontraditional needs. Integrated library systems provide a benefit for increased collaboration with colleagues in other disciplines but also a downside. With integrated library systems the special needs of music materials often take a backseat to the general needs of book materials. Music libraries are finding themselves pressured to standardize procedures and to abandon specialized classifications.

However, new technology can offer new opportunities. It is hoped that new digital resources will offer a wider range of access points tailored to musicians' needs such as song text, date of composition, exact instrumentation, edition, and type of score. Especially useful would be sources that display for recordings liner notes and for scores the first page of music, if not the entire composition, to allow users to view editorial practices, typography, and page layout.[89]

While the idea of librarians as teachers is gaining acceptance in all disciplines, students especially benefit from help in evaluating music resources and effectively finding music materials in the largely book-oriented library online catalogs. The expanding interdisciplinary scope of music research brings new patrons who need to familiarize themselves with the different procedures, equipment, and classifications found in music libraries. Blotner observed greater need for instruction to address the growing number of databases.[90] Users seek help in selecting the appropriate database to consult, in formulating search strategies, and in evaluating search results. Recognizing this need, in 2004 MLA published *Music Library Instruction*.[91] Physical barriers that are inevitable with separate music library facilities or collections are reduced through electronic access to portions of the collection or to a music librarian by email, chat, blogs, and social networking tools.

Space issues are increasingly a problem for many older libraries and music libraries are no exception. As patrons look to accessing audio music and course reserves from their computers, academic libraries are using space formerly devoted to on-site listening areas to meet other needs. Computer work areas, group study spaces, and classrooms are taking their place.

Digitization of reference tools and primary resources offer an opportunity to improve reference service and foster communication with a broader range of users. The future of music librarianship requires that music librarians, who best know the field of music and its users, advocate for and participate in the design of music reference tools, library systems, and digital resources that advance music scholarship and satisfy the needs of those who study, perform, and enjoy music.

REFERENCES

1. Brown, J.D. *A Guide to the Formation of a Music Library*; Library Association Series, No. 4; Simpkin, Marshall, Hamilton, Kent & Co.: London, U.K., 1893.
2. McColvin, L.R. *Music Libraries: Their Organisation and Contents, with a Bibliography of Music and Musical Literature*; Grafton: London, U.K., 1937–38; 2 Vols.
3. Bryant, E.T. *Music Librarianship: A Practical Guide*, 2nd Ed.; with the assistance of Guy Marco; Scarecrow: Metuchen, NJ, 1985.
4. McColvin, L.R.; Reeves, H. *Music Libraries, Including a Comprehensive Bibliography of Music Literature and a Select Bibliography of Music Scores Published Since 1957*; Completely rewritten, revised, and extended by Jack Dove; A. Deutsch: London, U.K., 1965; 2 Vols.
5. Redfern, B.L. *Organizing Music in Libraries: Selected Papers of the Music Library Association, Presented at Its 1942 Meeting*; Philosophical Library: New York, 1966.

6. Redfern, B.L. *Organising Music in Libraries*, 2nd Ed.; C. Bingley: London, U.K., 1978–1979; 2 Vols.
7. Jones, M. *Music Librarianship*; Clive Bingley: London, U.K., 1979.
8. Turbet, R., Ed. *Music Librarianship in the United Kingdom: Fifty Years of the United Kingdom Branch of the International Association of Music Libraries, Archives, and Documentation Centres*; Ashgate: Aldershot, U.K., 2003.
9. Wallace, R., Ed. *The Care and Treatment of Music in a Library*; American Library Association Committee on Cataloging, Contribution, No. 1; American Music Library Association: Chicago, IL, 1927.
10. Hill, R.S., Ed. *Music and Libraries: Selected Papers of the Music Library Association, Presented at Its 1942 Meeting*; Music Library Association: Washington, DC, 1943.
11. Bradley, C.J. Comp. *Manual of Music Librarianship*; Music Library Association: Ann Arbor, MI, 1966.
12. Mann, A., Ed. *Modern Music Librarianship: Essays in Honor of Ruth Watanabe*; Pendragon: Stuyvesant, 1989.
13. Ochs, M., Ed. *Music Librarianship in America*; Eda Kuhn Loeb Music Library: Cambridge, MA, 1991.
14. Cassaro, J.P., Ed. *Music, Libraries, and the Academy: Essays in Honor of Lenore Coral*; A-R Editions: Middleton, 2007.
15. Bradley, C.J., Ed. *Reader in Music Librarianship*; Microcard Editions: Washington, DC, 1973.
16. Watanabe, R. American music libraries and music librarianship: An overview in the eighties. Notes **1981**, *38* (2), 239–256.
17. Davidson, M.W. American music libraries and librarianship: Challenges for the nineties. Notes **1993**, *50* (1), 13–22.
18. Griscom, R., Ed. Music librarianship at the turn of the century. Notes **2000**, *56* (3), 563–664.
19. Bradley, C.J. *American Music Librarianship: A Biographical and Historical Survey*; Greenwood: New York, 1990.
20. Bradley, C.J. *American Music Librarianship: A Research and Information Guide*; Routledge: New York, 2005.
21. Benton, R. Libraries, types of music libraries, national libraries. In *Grove Music Online*; *Oxford Music Online* (accessed January 31, 2009).
22. http://www.iamic.net/projects (accessed June 14, 2009).
23. http://www.musiclibraryassoc.org (accessed June 14, 2009).
24. http://www.musiclibraryassoc.org/employmentanded/index.shtml (accessed June 14, 2009).
25. http://www.musiclibraryassoc.org/pdf/Core_Competencies.pdf (accessed June 14, 2009).
26. Elliot, P.; Blair, L., Eds. *Careers in Music Librarianship II: Transitions and Traditions*; Music Library Association Technical Reports, No. 29; Scarecrow: Lanham, MD, 2004.
27. Fling, R.M. *Library Acquisition of Music*, Music Library Association Basic Manual Series, No. 4; Scarecrow: Lanham, MD, 2004.
28. Music Library Association. *A Basic Music Library: Essential Scores and Sound Recordings*, 3rd Ed.; American Library Association: Chicago, IL, 1997.
29. Krummel, D.W. Musical functions and bibliographical forms. The Library December **1976**, *31*, 327–350.
30. http://people.ischool.berkeley.edu/~mkduggan/neh.html (accessed June 14, 2009).
31. http://library.duke.edu/music/sheetmusic/collections.html.
32. http://digital.library.ucla.edu/apam (accessed June 14, 2009).
33. http://levysheetmusic.mse.jhu.edu (accessed June 14, 2009).
34. http://webappl.dlib.indiana.edu/inharmony/welcome.do (accessed June 14, 2009).
35. http://digital.library.ucla.edu/sheetmusic (accessed June 14, 2009).
36. http://www.dlib.indiana.edu/variations/scores (accessed June 14, 2009).
37. http://urresearch.rochester.edu/handle/1802/292 (accessed June 14, 2009).
38. http://hcl.harvard.edu/libraries/loebmusic/collections/digital.html (accessed June 14, 2009).
39. http://www.cfeo.org.uk/dyn/index.html (accessed June 14, 2009).
40. http://dme.mozarteum.at/DME/nma/nmapub_srch.php?l=2 (accessed June 14, 2009).
41. Wallis, R.; Malm, K. *Big Sounds for Small Peoples: The Music Industry in Small Countries*; Pendragon: New York, 1984.
42. Manuel, P. *Cassette Culture*; University of Chicago Press: Chicago, IL, 1993.
43. Duckles, V.H.; Reed, I.; Keller, M.A. *Music Reference and Research Materials: An Annotated Bibliography*, 5th Ed.; Schirmer Books: New York, 1997.
44. Marco, G.A. *Information on Music: A Handbook of Reference Sources in European Languages*; Libraries Unlimited: Littleton, CO, 1975–1984; 3 Vols.
45. Brockman, W.S. *Music: A Guide to the Reference Literature*; Libraries Unlimited: Littleton, CO, 1987.
46. Foreman, L. *Information Sources in Music*; Saur: München, 2003.
47. Charles, S.R. *A Handbook of Music and Music Literature in Sets and Series*; Free Press: New York, 1972.
48. Heyer, A.H. *Historical Sets, Collected Editions, and Monuments of Music: A Guide to Their Contents*, 3rd Ed.; American Library Association: Chicago, IL, 1980; 2 Vols.
49. Hill, G.R.; Stephens, N.L. *Collected Editions, Historical Series & Sets & Monuments of Music: A Bibliography*; Fallen Leaf: Berkeley, CA, 1997.
50. http://hcl.harvard.edu/libraries/loebmusic/isham/rism.html (accessed June 14, 2009).
51. http://library.music.indiana.edu/music_resources (accessed June 14, 2009).
52. http://www.loc.gov/rr/perform/new.collections.html (accessed June 14, 2009).
53. Brook, B.S. The road to RILM. In *Modern Music Librarianship: Essays in Honor of Ruth Watanabe*; Mann, A., Ed.; Pendragon: Stuyvesant, NY, 1989; 85–94.
54. http://www.ripm.org/about_ripm.php (accessed June 14, 2009).
55. Smiraglia, R.P. *Describing Music Materials: A Manual for Descriptive Cataloging of Printed and Recorded Music, Music Videos, and Archival Music Material for Use with AACR2 and APPM*, 3rd Ed.; revised and enlarged with the assistance of Taras Pavlovsky; Soldier Creek Music Series, No. 5; Soldier Creek Press: Lake Crystal, MN, 1997.
56. Weitz, J. *Music Coding and Tagging: MARC 21 Content Designation for Scores and Sound Recordings*, 2nd Ed.; Soldier Creek Press: Belle Plaine, MN, 2001.

57. Weitz, J. *Cataloger's Judgment: Music Cataloging Questions and Answers from the Music OCLC Users Group Newsletter*; Libraries Unlimited: Westport, CT, 2004.
58. Weitz, J. *Music Cataloging and Instructional Text and Workbook*; Greenwood Press: Westport, CT, 2007.
59. Smiraglia, R.P. *Bibliographic Control of Music, 1897–2000*; compiled and edited with the assistance of J. Bradford Young. Music Library Association Index and Bibliography Series, No. 32; Scarecrow Press: Lanham, MD, 2006.
60. Girsberger, R. *A Manual for the Performance Library*, Music Library Association Basic Manual Series, No. 6; Scarecrow Press: Lanham, MD, 2006.
61. King, A.H. *Printed Music in the British Museum: An Account of the Collections, the Catalogues, and Their Formation, up to 1920*; Clive Bingley: London, U.K., 1979.
62. Schultz, L.; Shaw, S., Eds. *Cataloging Sheet Music: Guidelines for Use with AACR2 and the MARC Format*; Music Library Association Technical Reports, No. 28; Soldier Creek Press: Lanham, MD, 2003.
63. http://library.music.indiana.edu/collections/uniform/uniform.html (accessed June 14, 2009).
64. Koth, M.S. *Uniform Titles for Music*, Music Library Association Technical Reports, No. 31; Soldier Creek Press: Lanham, MD, 2008.
65. Young, J.B. Introduction to the structure and use of Library of Congress subject headings for music and material about music. In *Music Subject Headings: Compiled from the Library of Congress Subject Headings*, 2nd Ed.; Hemmasi, H., Ed.; Soldier Creek Press: Lake Crystal, MN, 1998; 1–28.
66. Library of Congress, *Library of Congress Classification M: Music*; Library of Congress, Library Cataloguing Distribution Service: Washington, DC, 2007.
67. Smiraglia, R. *Shelflisting Music: Guidelines for Use with the Library of Congress Classification*, 2nd Ed.; Music Library Association Technical Reports, No. 30; Scarecrow Press: Lanham, MD, 2008.
68. http://www.oclc.org/dewey (accessed June 14, 2009).
69. Hornbostel, E.M. von; Sachs, C. Classification of Musical Instruments. Galpin Soc. J. **1961**, *14*, 3–29.
70. Krummel, D.W. The origins of modern music classification. In *Festschrift Albi Rosenthal*; Elvers, R., Ed.; Hans Schneider: Tutzing, Germany, 1984; 181–198.
71. Elliker, C. Classification schemes for scores. Notes **1994**, *50* (4), 1269–1320.
72. McKnight, M. *Music Classification Systems*; Music Library Association Basic Manual Series, No. 1; Scarecrow Press: Lanham, MD, 2002.
73. Bradley, C.J. Classifying and cataloguing music in American libraries: A historical overview. Catalog. Classif. Quart. **2003**, *35* (3/4), 467–481.
74. Dickinson, G.S. *The Classification of Musical Compositions: A Decimal-Symbol System*; Vassar College: Poughkeepsie, NY, 1938.
75. Saheb-Ettaba, C.; McFarland, R.B. *ANSCR: The Alpha-Numeric System for Classification of Recordings*; Bro-Dart: Williamsport, PA, 1969.
76. Hansen, L.L.; Saheb-Ettaba, C. *ANSCR: Supplement, 1988*; Professional Media Service: Gardena, CA, 1988.
77. *Folk Heritage Collections in Crisis*; Council on Library and Information Resources: Washington, DC, 2001.
78. http://www.dlib.indiana.edu/projects/sounddirections (accessed June 14, 2009).
79. Carli, A. *Binding and Care of Printed Music*; Music Library Association Basic Manual Series, No. 2; Scarecrow Press: Lanham, MD, 2003.
80. Rahkonen, C., Ed. *World Music in Music Libraries*; MLA Technical Reports, No. 24; Music Library Association: Canton, OH, 1994.
81. Rahkonen, C. World music in the music library. Coll. Music Soc. Newsl. October **1999**, *6*.
82. *Garland Encyclopedia of World Music*; Garland: New York, 1998–2002; 10 Vols.
83. Schuursma, A.B. *Ethnomusicology Research: A Select Annotated Bibliography*; Garland: New York, 1992.
84. Post, J.C. *Ethnomusicology: A Guide to Research*; Routledge: New York, 2004.
85. Murdock, G.P. *Outline of World Cultures*, 6th rev. Ed.; Human Relations Area Files: New Haven, CT, 1983.
86. Kaufman, J. *Recordings of Non-Western Music, Subject and Added Entry Access*; Music Library Association Technical Reports, No. 5; Music Library Association: Ann Arbor, MI, 1977.
87. Pierce, D.I. What do you do when hotchiku music arrives in the library? Providing access to world music materials. In *World Music in Music Libraries*; Rahkonen, C., Ed. MLA Technical Reports, No. 24; Music Library Association: Canton, OH, 1994; 41–59.
88. http://www.dlib.indiana.edu/projects/variations3 (accessed June 14, 2009).
89. Gardinier, H. *Access Points Perceived as Useful in Searching for Music Scores and Recordings*; PhD dissertation. University of California: Los Angeles, CA, 2004.
90. Blotner, L.S. Music libraries of tomorrow: Virtual or concrete, harmony or discord?. In *Music, Libraries, and the Academy: Essays in Honor of Lenore Coral*; Cassaro, J.C., Ed.; A-R Editions: Middleton, WI, 2007; 67–79.
91. Campana, D., Ed. *Music Library Instruction*; Music Library Association Basic Manual Series, No. 3; Scarecrow Press: Lanham, MD, 2004.

Name Authority Control

Janifer Gatenby
Online Computer Library Center (OCLC), Leiden, The Netherlands
Karen Smith-Yoshimura
Online Computer Library Center (OCLC), San Mateo, California, U.S.A.

Abstract
The purpose of name authority control is to facilitate searching and browsing by 1) ensuring retrieval of all the works of a person, personal identity such as a pseudonym, family name, or organization where they may be published under different name versions over time and in different places; 2) enabling other works by the same identity to be retrieved from any one work; 3) by eliminating works of other identities with the same name; and 4) by concise name indexes that ensure efficient browsing. Authority records may include name variants, and these are distinguished from related names of other identities of the same person. Records also contain differentiating information and, most importantly, identifiers that are the key elements facilitating linking. Differentiating information differs for personal and organization names. The creation of authority records is a labor-intensive process, and the trend is toward creating locally and sharing internationally. Consolidated sources are important for facilitating reuse and as key resources in linked data. Input data are accepted from a variety of sources, including biographical sources, encyclopedias, institution records, and crowdsourced systems. Different models and encoding systems are detailed.

INTRODUCTION

There are multiple purposes of name authority control. Firstly, name authority control facilitates searching and browsing by ensuring retrieval of all the works of, or about, a person, personal identity such as a pseudonym, family name, or organization where they may be published under different name versions over time and in different places, and ensuring that they are retrieved with the same form of name that the specific community will understand (e.g., "Confucius" in Anglo-American communities, and "孔 子" in CJK [Chinese, Japanese, and Korean] communities). Name versions differ in different languages; in particular, transliteration practices differ by language. There are also differences in name forms among regions sharing the same language such as Belgian Flemish and Dutch name forms. Geographic names are prime examples: Firenze (Italian), Florenz (German), and Florence (French and English). Name authority records also enable other works by the same identity to be retrieved from any one work, at the same time eliminating works of other identities with the same name. Name indexes can be created from authority records instead of bibliographic records so that the indexes are more concise, ensuring faster and more efficient browsing.

In librarianship, name authority control is traditionally the process of collecting together different versions of a name and recording them together in a name authority record along with differentiating information. Names in bibliographic records' access points are linked to name authority records either via a name form or by an identifier. In traditional library practice, the authority record indicates a preferred name form that is used in bibliographic records. The most common form of name used in the official language of the community is generally selected as the "preferred form," and the preferred form can vary from one community and language to another. Where there are different persons or organizations sharing the same name, the usual practice is to extend the preferred form of name in an authority record with additional differentiating information such as dates or profession in the case of persons, and location in the case of organizations. However, identifiers are now replacing the concept of preferred name.

NAME CONTROL OR IDENTITY CONTROL?

As stated earlier, name authority control allows the differentiation of different persons and organizations with the same name. The International Standard Name Identifier (ISNI)[1] makes a clear distinction between a name, an identity, and a person or an organization. A person may have one or more names, such as a maiden name, married name, change of sex name, and name in a different script, but only one identity. A person may also have one or more identities that he or she uses to present creative works publically. Where a person has multiple name forms, within a MARC (Machine Readable Cataloging) authority record one is marked as preferred and others as name variants. The Virtual International Authority File (VIAF)[2] and ISNI, being crafted from multiple sources, have moved away from the traditional library concept of a

Encyclopedia of Library and Information Sciences, Fourth Edition DOI: 10.1081/E-ELIS4-120050533

preferred form of name, allowing preferred names to differ according to source. Preferred name is challenged by some professional communities that do not designate "one preferred form" but identify which forms are used in particular contexts, both geographic and temporal.[3] For scholars, VIAF and ISNI have not gone far enough, but the notion of a preferred form of name is endemic even outside the library community, for example, in the knowledge organization systems (KOS) such as thesauri, classification schemes, subject heading systems, and taxonomies, and that is reflected in the W3C SKOS standard.[4]

NAMES AND NAME VARIANTS

Meryl Streep has only one public identity that she uses for her creative works. VIAF includes Streep, Meryl (Mary Louise), as the name form on her birth certificate is Streep, Mary Louise. Her married name Gummer, Mary Louise, is mentioned in Wikipedia and could also be considered as a name variant (Fig. 1). Changes in the preferred forenames and change of name due to marriage are not considered as constituting a change of identity as there is not necessarily a wish by the person to separate his or her creative output corresponding with a name change. Researchers, for example, will mention the ensemble of their publications in their curriculum vitae where they have been published over a lifetime involving name changes.

Alternative name forms that do not usually indicate a change in identity can take variant forms including names in different scripts or transliterated with different schemes, changes due to change of sex, marriage, or legal declaration.

PSEUDONYMS AND MULTIPLE IDENTITIES

Kingsley Amis in Fig. 2 is an example of an author writing under three different identities: writing as himself and writing under two different pseudonyms. His works attributed to each of the three different identities are clearly separated. In this case, the association of pseudonyms with the real person is public but that is not always the case. For example, J.K. Rowling chose to create a pseudonym Robert Galbraith[5] so that she could write in a different genre and have her works in the new genre judged without any influence of the successful Harry Potter series. When the relationship between a pseudonym and a real person is or becomes public, the works tend to become associated with the real person as well as the pseudonym; for example, they may be republished or released in collected works. One example is John Wyndham, the main pen name of John Wyndham Parkes Lucas Beynon Harris (July 10, 1903, to March 11, 1969). Under an earlier pen name, John Beynon, he wrote *Secret People,* but this is now published under John Wyndham. As a general rule, separate authority records should be made for each identity used as a public identity. This allows the history of works to be accurately traced, enabling catalogs to respond to questions such as "under which identity was the work conceived and first published?" The authority records related to each of the public identities should be linked where the relationship is public. Encyclopedias such as Wikipedia tend to have only one entry for a person, grouping all public identities. This entails the need for one-to-many relationships in linking especially

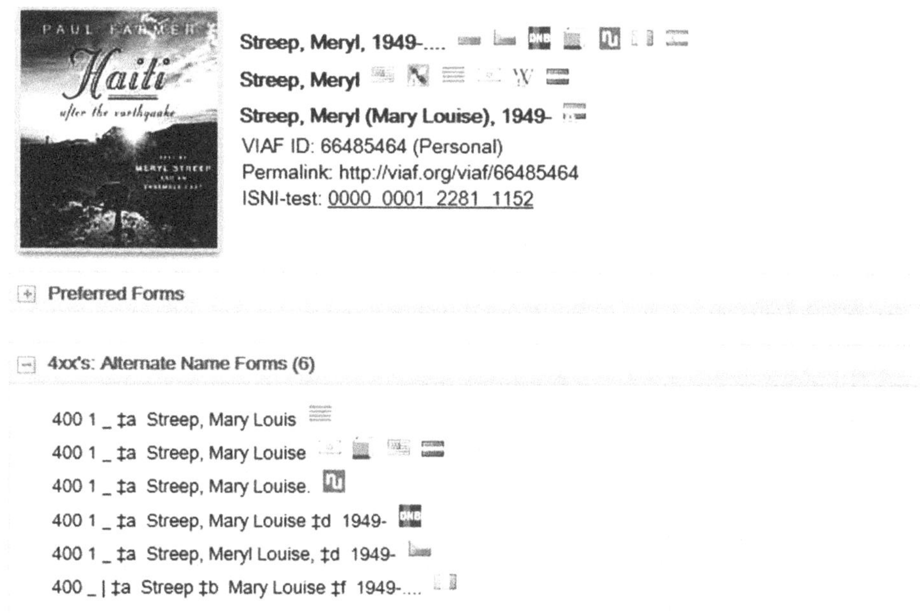

Fig. 1 Image of VIAF authority cluster for Meryl Streep.

Fig. 2 Kingsley Amis and his two pseudonyms.

from library authority records to encyclopedias. For example, VIAF links its clusters to Wikipedia and ISNI includes MusicBrainz links in its records (including links to library authority records).

Figs. 3–5 from VIAF indicate that VIAF and ISNI have three separate records for the three separate public identities of Kingsley Amis. All but one VIAF source considers Robert Markham to be a separate identity, whereas two sources (National Libraries of Poland and Catalonia) have declared the name as a variant name.

When is there a change of identity? Authority records include name variants and related identities. Practices differ among libraries. The same name can be declared to be

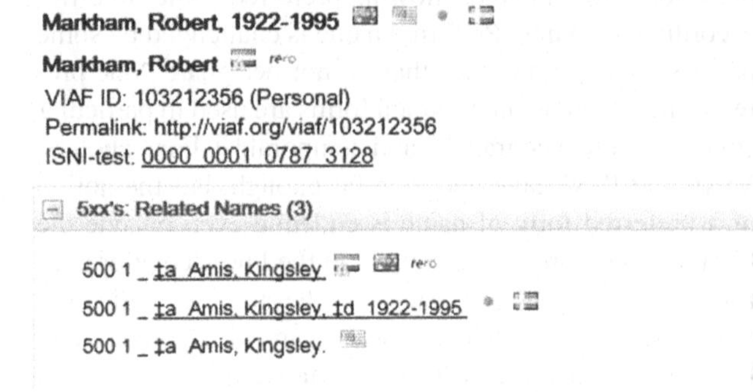

Markham, Robert, 1922-1995
Markham, Robert
VIAF ID: 103212356 (Personal)
Permalink: http://viaf.org/viaf/103212356
ISNI-test: 0000 0001 0787 3128

5xx's: Related Names (3)

500 1 _ ‡a Amis, Kingsley
500 1 _ ‡a Amis, Kingsley, ‡d 1922-1995
500 1 _ ‡a Amis, Kingsley.

Fig. 4 Image of VIAF cluster for Robert Markham.

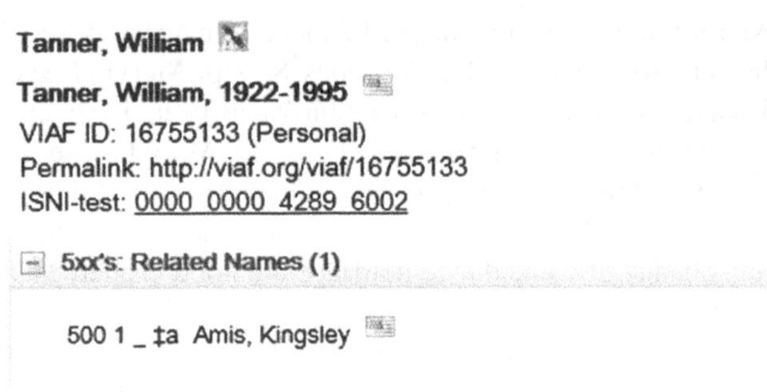

Tanner, William
Tanner, William, 1922-1995
VIAF ID: 16755133 (Personal)
Permalink: http://viaf.org/viaf/16755133
ISNI-test: 0000 0000 4289 6002

5xx's: Related Names (1)

500 1 _ ‡a Amis, Kingsley

Fig. 5 Image of VIAF cluster for William Tanner.

a name variant by one library and the name of a related identity by another. The VIAF includes many examples of these among its clusters, as in the case of Robert Markham. As the concept of public identity is core to ISNI, and giving separate ISNIs to each separate identity is critical,

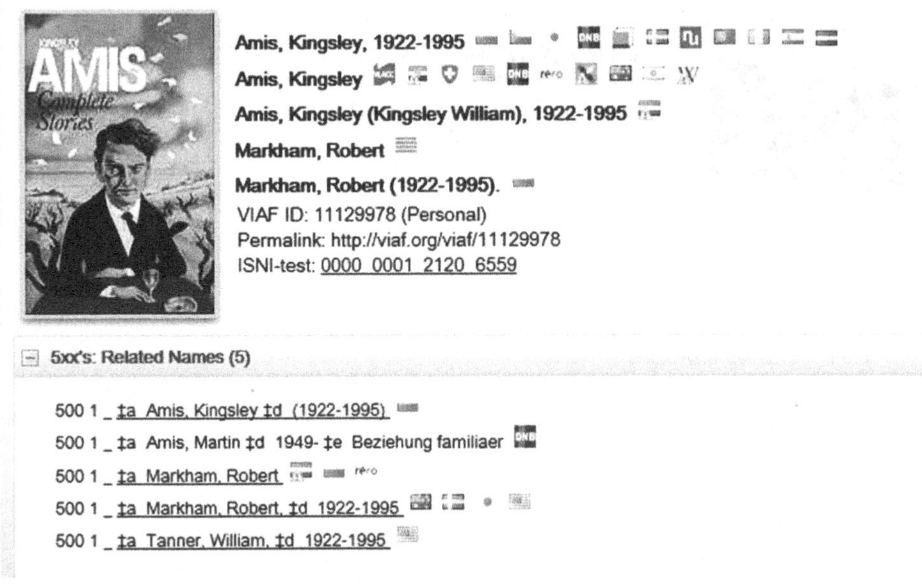

Amis, Kingsley, 1922-1995
Amis, Kingsley
Amis, Kingsley (Kingsley William), 1922-1995
Markham, Robert
Markham, Robert (1922-1995).
VIAF ID: 11129978 (Personal)
Permalink: http://viaf.org/viaf/11129978
ISNI-test: 0000 0001 2120 6559

5xx's: Related Names (5)

500 1 _ ‡a Amis, Kingsley ‡d (1922-1995)
500 1 _ ‡a Amis, Martin ‡d 1949- ‡e Beziehung familiaer
500 1 _ ‡a Markham, Robert
500 1 _ ‡a Markham, Robert, ‡d 1922-1995
500 1 _ ‡a Tanner, William, ‡d 1922-1995

Fig. 3 Image of VIAF cluster for Kingsley Amis.

the ISNI Quality Team has produced a policy document[6] defining when a name form should be regarded merely as a name variant or as belonging to another identity (both identities being linked in the ISNI database by a "Other identity same Person" link) and is working closely with VIAF to encourage adoption of consistent treatment.

UNDIFFERENTIATED NAMES

Many library systems include a feature that will generate name authority records from the name forms in the name fields in bibliographic records. Links are then made between the generated authority records and the name fields from which they were derived. One such system is Centraal Bibliothek Systeem (CBS), used by the Deutsche Nationalbibliothek (DNB).[7,8] The DNB makes a distinction between the records that are generated by program and those that are made by catalogers using biographical information from multiple sources including that published within a work, encyclopedias, and contacts with creators directly or through their publishers. However, it should be noted that not all undifferentiated names are machine-generated. For example, in Library of Congress/ Name Authority Cooperative Program (LC/NACO),[9,10] undifferentiated authority name records have been created by catalogers for the purpose of making catalog access points where there was insufficient information available at the time to create separate authority records. Undifferentiated authority records control a name string and may bring together works by different identities sharing the same name string. They serve a purpose to facilitate search and browse within the file in which they were generated. However, their utility beyond the one file is limited. Undifferentiated data cannot be used confidently in a broad networking environment and become a serious problem when exposed in Linked (Open) Data. For this reason, the Program for Cooperative Cataloging has a new policy as of November 13, 2013, stating that no new undifferentiated authority name records will be created.[11]

ORGANIZATION NAMES AND HIERARCHIES

Organizations, including institutions, corporate bodies, and less formal groups of individuals, pose their own problems for name authority control. Like individuals, names may change over time without a change of identity, for example, a university library may be given the name of an emeritus person. Organization names are often abbreviated and the sequence of words within a name string may be altered, for example, the University of Sydney and Sydney University. These are examples of name variants for organizations. More often, a change of name reflects a change in scope, purpose, or ownership, constituting a change of identity. For example, a name with the same words in a different sequence can sometimes be the same organization and sometimes a different organization and many abbreviations and acronyms can be shared among identities.

Organizations raise other issues from their structural perspective. The same name may represent separate identities for the same organization—a legal, a commercial, a branding, and a contracting identity. Some of the organizations, depending on the nature of their activity, insist on the need for separating these identities. Organizations also have hierarchies. Depending on the needs for information processing, representing these hierarchies can be very important.[12] Within authority records, hierarchies can be represented using related name fields plus relationship type.

DATA ELEMENTS: DIFFERENTIATING CRITERIA AND INFORMATIONAL METADATA

In order to separate different identities with the same name, library authority records include differentiating elements, in particular date of birth and/or death that may be included in the preferred name form. In the preferred name form, distinguishing data may also be included such as occupation, fuller forms of forename, and name qualifiers such as Jr. (Junior). More data can be included in supporting fields such as the new MARC fields introduced for compatibility with the new rules Resource Description and Access (RDA)[13] that allow for more granularity in data encoding and, therefore, provide new possibilities for exploiting the information. These are special coded dates, associated place, address, field of activity, affiliation, occupation, gender, family information, and associated language.

Other data included in authority records that also play an important differentiating role include titles of works, identifiers of works, associated languages, and occupation. VIAF considers coauthors and performers as well when merging or differentiating, and ISNI has extended the differentiating criteria to include instrument and voice for musicians and performers.[14]

The important elements for differentiating organizations with the same or similar name strings are geographic location, organization type (e.g., university or hospital), and name use (e.g., legal or brand).[15] Dates are important for organizations as well. However, they are less frequently included in the authority records than those for persons as they are not widely known. Therefore, the use of dates as a criterion of disambiguation for organizations in automated processing is less reliable. Similarly, works published by organizations tend to have generic titles such as "Annual report" and so are less useful for disambiguation of organizations. Relationships between individuals and organizations are important complementary elements. A person record can include institutional affiliations and links to other persons. Organization records can include links to related persons and to other organizations. Recording the precise type of relationship is now replacing the more generic "see also" that is implied from the existence of the related field within an authority record.

The International Federation of Library Associations (IFLA)'s mandatory elements for internationally shared resource authority records (MLAR) report recommends mandatory elements required for records to be suitable for international sharing.[16]

In other domains, the emphasis on differentiating criteria can vary. Encyclopedias such as Wikipedia[17] and MusicBrainz[18] tend to use similar criteria to libraries, whereas Rights Management Societies may use passports and other official documents, together with dates, all of which is regarded as confidential data. ORCID[19] relies on e-mail address as the main differentiating element, and this is usually marked as confidential.

Archival authority records, though built on the library authority control tradition, are in general much richer than library authority records. The identity part of information, that is, the management of names, is much in line with the library practices. The difference is in the descriptive information about the entity. While libraries tend to create detailed records for bibliographic resources and smaller authority records with just enough information to differentiate identities, archival authority records include extensive, supportive, descriptive information such as biographical and genealogical data, called "contextual information." The detail in archival authority records can be richer than that in the records of associated resources.

> Archival authority records, however, need to support a much wider set of requirements than is the case with library authority records. These additional requirements are associated with the importance of documenting information about records creators and the context of records creation in archival description systems. As such, archival authority records go much further and usually will contain much more information than library authority records.[20]

RELATING BIBLIOGRAPHIC AND AUTHORITY RECORDS

Many libraries exemplified by the contributors to the LC/NACO file link from bibliographic records to authority records principally by name string. The name string of the preferred name form is included in the bibliographic records with optionally a reference to the authority record identifier. The fact that preferred name forms may contain dates and qualifiers that are nonname elements reflects this usage. While it allows the use of authority records without imposing actual links, it has limitations:

- The preferred name form in the authority record needs to be stable, so dates are not consistently added to headings where known and they are not updated when a person dies, though they can be recorded in other fields in the authority record.
- Differentiating metadata is in both the preferred heading and in supporting fields within the authority record.
- It necessitates the choice of a single preferred name form, whereas many name variants merit equal weight, for example, in a bilingual or multilingual country such as Canada or Switzerland. Name forms in multiple scripts provide another example where multiple preferred forms should be possible.
- It makes global changes of bibliographic records a lengthy practice where each corresponding bibliographic record needs to be updated when the preferred name in an authority record changes, for example, in the case of a typographical correction or a change of name.
- In the case that it is necessary to split an authority record into two or more separate identities, the global change procedure is even more complicated and inadvertent omissions are common.

Many library systems store only an identifier in the bibliographic record, making global change a far less onerous task but as not all do, these problems remain, particularly when records are split and one identifier is retained.

To begin to overcome these problems, it is necessary to systematically use identifiers when linking from bibliographic to authority records. This is a new recommendation of the Program for Cooperative Cataloging.[21]

IDENTIFIERS

Where multiple preferred forms are allowed within an authority record, identifiers become the essential element and are used for reliable linking. The number of data elements necessary to establish identity and distinguish from other identities with the same name varies depending on the commonness of the name. For example, two persons could have the same name and be born in the same place on the same date. In this case, the name of their parents or other data elements such as profession would differentiate them. Because the number of elements is not finite, identifiers serve to act as shorthand for the ensemble of metadata elements within an authority record. Identifiers are concise, easily sharable elements, and are the key elements in linked data. In 2008, an IFLA Working Group on Functional Requirements and Numbering of Authority Records[22] concluded that development of a system of international scope to issue and maintain authority identifiers was unlikely to happen. Nevertheless, they recommended the use of the VIAF cluster number as an alternative with a close watch on the development of the ISO working group on the ISNI. Three years later in

November 2011, the ISNI-IA announced the ISNI database with 1 million assigned identifiers. In 2 years of operation, the number of assigned identifiers has grown to 7.5 million with 30 contributors.[23]

The key identifiers for international use are ISNI, VIAF, and ORCID. ORCID started in 2012 with the aim of providing identifiers for researchers to use in submission of articles for publication and in grant applications. Thus, an ORCID can be assigned and an authority record can be born before the researcher has actually published. Another identifier that is used internationally is the Interested Party Identifier (IPI) of the International Society of Authors and Composers (CISAC).[24] This identifier is used in the music industry in particular, but access to it is restricted because it links to confidential information. Thus, CISAC became one of the early drivers of ISNI to act as an independent neutral identifier for cross-database and cross-domain linking.

RECORD CREATION AND REUSE

Creating high-quality authority records takes time and research. The training for LC/NACO certification is 5 days.[25] The British Library, for example, often contacts authors through their publishers to determine whether they have previous publications. Apart from a work in hand that may contain biographical information, there are many sources on the web that can be consulted including encyclopedias such as Wikipedia and MusicBrainz, personal web pages, institutional web pages, biographical dictionaries, and trade information such as Scholar Universe,[26] Scopus,[27] Web of Knowledge,[28] and Amazon.[29]

Considering the high cost of creating authority records, libraries seek to reuse existing authority records wherever possible. Records made by national libraries are made available to other libraries for reuse.

In the mid-1970s, the Program for Cooperative Cataloging established the LC/NACO program and database that currently includes over 7 million records. As well as the Library of Congress, participants include the British Library, National Library of Medicine, National Agricultural Library, and national libraries of Mexico, New Zealand, Scotland, South Africa, and Wales, and over 200 other participant libraries.[30] The records are freely available via web search and as linked data. The LC/NACO file contributes to VIAF that started in 2003. In January 2014, VIAF included 33 sources, of which LC/NACO is just one. National libraries and library networks worldwide have contributed to VIAF as well as the Getty Museum and Perseus Digital Library hosted by Tufts University. Wikipedia data are harvested and appear as a source within VIAF, and ISNI started contribution to VIAF in 2013. VIAF clusters data from its sources and makes it available for consultation via a web interface and by an SRU API (Application Program Interface). The data are also available for harvesting by bulk downloads and for diffusion as linked data. VIAF contains 34 million authority records, of which more than 26.4 million are personal name and 5.1 million are corporate name records. Name/title (1.8 million) and geographic name (400,000) authority records make up the total. It has become a significant international resource for libraries and linked data. This is evidenced by its traffic with close to a million personal visits a year.[31]

VIAF is a major source within the ISNI database. ISNI is an international database maintained by a not-for-profit consortium, the ISNI-IA. The database scope is different from VIAF; though it includes VIAF, it does not include its name/title records, meeting, or geographic name records and excludes undifferentiated and sparse records. On the other hand, ISNI's scope is larger than VIAF with 28 other contributors from multiple domains: rights management, trade, and education and professional societies. In particular, it includes more researchers, musicians, and publishers. Like VIAF, ISNI's data are clustered, but the records are flagged for confidence and there are strict rules for assignment. ISNI also defines extensive vocabularies, for example, creation roles, relationship types, organization types, name use, and matching types. There is a freely available web interface and SRU enquiry API and RDF (Resource Description Framework) serialization.[32,33]

Name disambiguation is a common requirement for databases in multiple domains. Rights management societies collect money for reuse of resources and need to track down rights holders. Online stores such as Amazon and iTunes need disambiguated identities in order to provide, for example, "more by this author or performer" searches and biographical information. Search engines are also beginning to provide such information. Examples are Amazon's Author Central program[34] and Google's knowledge graphs.[35]

Just as libraries use external sources for creating authority records, their records are being reused in other domains. The major Internet search engines harvest data from VIAF and ISNI such that, for example, the VIAF search API accounts for 98% of external access and averages about 5 million searches a week.[31] The lack of authority control in institution repositories has been recognized as a major problem for retrievability.[36] The University of North Texas Libraries[37] has estimated that less than 35% of researchers can be found in VIAF and LC/NACO sources. Consequently, it has built a name authority system that allows access to VIAF, LC/NACO, Wikipedia, and ORCID and builds links at the same time.

The level of reuse and sharing is necessary to enable libraries, archives, and all organizations involved in the creative domains to concentrate on local identities, especially as the scope of authority control must be broadened to include many more types of publication, both physical and digital. Name authority control of the authors of journal articles was long avoided by libraries but is now being embraced in cooperating systems such as ISNI and

ORCID and in the OCLC Research activity on registering researchers in library authority files.[38]

CROWDSOURCING

Crowdsourcing is increasingly important for enriching and correcting data. A large number of databases are based on crowdsourcing such as Wikipedia and MusicBrainz, social networking sites, and professional networking sites such as Mendeley,[39] RePec,[40] AuthorClaim,[41] ResearchGate,[42] and PublicationsList.[43] ORCID too is based on researchers self-registering.

The major drawbacks of sourcing data from the public at large are risks of incompleteness and inconsistency in detail and quality. Moreover, in the current information environment, quality is more needed than ever. The question is how to benefit from crowdsourcing as a powerful means of enhancing quality and enriching data in authoritative systems and at the same time making sure of the quality of the input. Such a model requires careful monitoring and a solid policy for resolving conflicts. ISNI has setup a monitored crowdsourcing system. The general public is encouraged to enrich and correct data, but the data that are collected trigger an e-mail alert to the Quality Team at the British Library and the Bibliothèque nationale de France. In this way, ISNI strives to achieve a balance between curated data from the library world and other domains and individual knowledge. ORCID too is striving to find a balance between data input by researchers and that input on their behalf by their institutions.

MATCHING AND CLUSTERING

VIAF and ISNI collect data from multiple sources. Both use similar matching algorithms; VIAF then creates clusters and ISNI creates composite records. Where names, dates, and title of a work match from different sources, a match is made. In the absence of a direct match, other metadata elements are considered such as subjects, classification, active time period, nationality, coauthors, institutional affiliations, publishers, instruments, and uncommon title words. In addition, ISNI assigns two confidence scores; one in the data itself and another in the matching. Some records are flagged as possible matches needing manual review or retry against new data or with revised matching algorithms. ISNI also seeks to find sources that are rich in elements that can help cluster sources with different differentiating elements. For example, MusicBrainz encyclopedia was harvested so that it could help match data from the performers' rights management data that contains identity dates and instruments with other sources containing names and works only.

LINKED DATA

In the words of Corine Deliot of the British Library "Linking is not a new concept in librarianship. Within databases, bibliographic records contain links to authority records. Even WorldCat, to which thousands of libraries worldwide contribute, links to only one name authority file, to LC/NACO. The newly coined linked data extend links beyond databases to multiple Internet sources. The Internet was a method of linking computers (useful, but difficult, and not interesting to most people); the Web is a way of linking content (pages) held on computers (interesting and useful to people); linked data are a way of linking information (interesting to people and very useful to machines). This opens up new possibilities for machine to machine processing and new services that depend fundamentally on accurate identification of entities." Linked data add context to links and provide to bibliographic databases the capability of links to a myriad of authority files and resources.

Cross-domain linking is a trend. Wikidata, the pool available to all language versions of Wikipedia, has been populated with VIAF and ISNI identifiers via the "VIAFBot," and so far the German and English versions of Wikipedia include these identifiers.[44–46] In the Netherlands, the universities' Current Research Information System called National Academic Research and Collaborations Information System uses the national union catalog's authority file to register researchers receiving government funding.[47]

Links too can be complicated, not necessarily a simple one-to-one relationship as is seen in the case of Wikipedia that generally has just one page per person, grouping all known pseudonyms. One-to-many and many-to-one links are necessary.

Error correction is a major challenge with linked data. The more links there are, the more difficult it is to stamp out an error in the same way that it can be difficult for a person to suppress a former address. ISNI (which has 18 million links) has a notification system that pushes error corrections to all known sources. Acceptance of such notifications is a condition of ISNI membership and data contribution.

ENCODING AND MODELS

Data models, data rules, and encoding are closely related. Rules determine the semantics of data elements and how to construct them, for example, how to abbreviate and how to sequence elements. Examples of rules for library cataloging include *Anglo-American Cataloging Rules*, 2nd ed. (AACR2),[48] *Personennamendatei* (PND),[49] and the French rules AFNOR NF-Z44-061.[50] RDA[13] has been introduced first to replace AACR2 but is likely to become an international cataloging code replacing all the national and regional rules. In the archival world, there is ISAAR (CPF).[51] The early library rules have a common model of a bibliographic record for a publication linked to one or more authority records (names, subjects, places, etc.) where names of authors, editors, illustrators, translators, etc., are linked to authority records. RDA are new rules brought into being for two main purposes; to be international rules that could replace the myriad of national cataloging codes and to reflect a new model, Functional Requirements for Bibliographic Records (FRBR)[52] and its associated Functional Requirements for Authority Data (FRAD).[53] In the new model, the production of bibliographic data is not viewed as simply creating bibliographic records but as a process of creating descriptive information about the four FRBR Group 1 entities; the work (original creation), expression (content level), manifestation (publication level), and item (physical level), as well as information for the Group 2 entities (agents) defined by the FRAD model. RDA also articulates the roles of authority records that can be linked to any of the three theoretical FRBR levels. For example, authority records for authors and composers are linked at the work level, whereas translators, illustrators, and performers are generally linked at the expression level and publishers may be linked at the manifestation level.

There are many standards in practice for encoding authority records. Schemas determine the name of record elements and how they are structured. They include MARC in its many variations, in particular, MARC21[54] and UNIMARC[55] and MADS,[56] with various encoding options, including ISO 2709, XML, RDF, Turtle, and JSON. The experimental Bibliographic Framework Transitions Initiative (BIBFRAME)[57] is being developed as a replacement for MARC21 and a general model for expressing and relating bibliographic data, including name authorities. In addition, the emerging BIBFRAME authority schema[58] may serve as an enriched alternative to the schema.org[59] schema that is used by major search engines to harvest metadata from web pages. In the archival world, there is EAC-CPF,[60] natively expressed in XML with alternative serializations in RDF.

TRENDS

Libraries have traditionally shared their data, and that sharing is increasingly international and cross-domain with the emergence of freely available, consolidated sources such as VIAF and ISNI as databases, enquiry targets, and linked data. The data are being harvested and used in library systems as well as institutional systems and Wikidata and Wikipedia. Maintenance of authority data is federated with an emphasis on local creation and international sharing. With increased sharing, there is a greater need for standard and consistent labeling of such things as pseudonyms and for usage of common vocabularies such as relationship terms and organization types. It is important to maintain data locally and also within consolidations to ensure correct clustering, data consistency, and quality linked data. Multiple web sources and linked data are facilitating information gathering as library and archive data are coming together with data from multiple domains and crowdsourced resources. Authority data are being extended to link from all types of creative works, physical and digital.

ACKNOWLEDGMENT

The author wishes to acknowledge the very valuable input from Anila Angjeli, Pauline Chougnet, Alan Danskin, Corine Deliot, Michael Docherty, Andrew MacEwan, Richard Moore, Karen Smith-Yoshimura, and Alison Woods.

REFERENCES

1. ISO 27729-2010: Information and Documentation: International Standard Name Identifier (ISNI). International Organisation for Standardization: Geneva, Switzerland, 2010.
2. Virtual International Authority File (VIAF). Web site http://viaf.org(accessed February 12, 2014).
3. Smith-Yoshimura, K.; Michelson, D. Irreconcilable differences? Name authority control & humanities scholarship, http://hangingtogether.org/?p=2621 (accessed February 12, 2014).
4. Simple Knowledge Organization System. Web site. (SKOS). http://www.w3.org/2004/02/skos/ (accessed February 12, 2014.
5. Robert Galbraith. Web site http://robert-galbraith.com/ (accessed February 12, 2014).
6. ISNI Quality Team. *Pseudonyms, Married and Maiden Names*; An ISNI policy document, 2013.
7. Deutsche Nationalbibliothek. Web site http://www.dnb.de (accessed January 19, 2014).
8. CBS TM Metadata management solution. http://www.oclc.org/cbs.en.html (accessed February 12, 2014).
9. Program for Cooperative Cataloging: Name Authority Cooperative Program. Web site http://www.loc.gov/aba/pcc/naco/ (accessed February 12, 2014).
10. Byrun, J.D. NACO: a cooperative model for building and maintaining a shared name authority database, January 2003, http://www.sba.unifi.it/ac/relazioni/byrum_eng.pdf.
11. Program for Cooperative Cataloguing. RDA guidelines. Web site. http://www.loc.gov/aba/pcc/rda/PCC%20RDA%20guidelines/Z01%20008%2032%202014rfeb.pdf (accessed February 12, 2014).
12. Bide, M. ISNI and the identification of publishers and other media businesses. Unpublished discussion paper, August 2012.
13. Library of Congress. Resource description and access (RDA) Information and Resources in Preparation for

RDA. Web site. http://www.loc.gov/aba/rda/ (accessed February 12, 2014).
14. MacEwan, A.; Angjeli, A.; Gatenby, J. The International Standard Name Identifier (ISNI): The evolving future of name authority control. Cat. Classif. Q. **2013**, *51* (1–3), 55–71.
15. Gatenby, J. ISNI and I2: expanding the use of an identifier to serve multiple needs. In *The Information Exchange Environment, The Critical Component: Standards*, ALCTS Papers on Library Technical Services and Collections series revised citation ALCTS Publishing, 2015, http://www.ala.org/alcts/resources/monographs/critical-component (accessed May 9, 2016).
16. IFLA UBCIM Working Group on Minimal Level Authority Records and ISADN. Mandatory data elements for internationally shared resource authority records, 1998 (known as "MLAR"), http://www.ifla.org/VI/3/p1996-2/mlar.htm(accessed February 12, 2014).
17. Wikipedia. Web site http://www.wikipedia.org (accessed February 12, 2014).
18. MusicBrainz. Web site http://musicbrainz.org (accessed February 12, 2014).
19. ORCID. Web site http://orcid.org (accessed February 12, 2014).
20. ISAAR (CPF): Norme Internationale sur les notices d'autorité utilisées pour les Archives relatives aux collectivités, aux personnes ou aux familles, 2ème édition 2011, http://www.ica.org/10230/normes/isaar-cpf-norme-internationale-sur-les-notices-dautorit-utilises-pour-les-archives-relatives-aux-collectivits-aux-personnes-ou-aux-familles-2me-dition.html (accessed February 12, 2014).
21. PCC Task Group on the Creation and Function of Name Authorities in a Non MARC Environment. Report, http://www.loc.gov/aba/pcc/rda/RDA%20Task%20groups%20and %20charges/ReportPCCTGonNameAuthInA_NonMARC_Environ_FinalReport.pdf (accessed February 12, 2014).
22. Tillett, B.; Patton, G.E. *A review of the feasibility of an International Standard Authority Data Number (ISADN)*. Prepared for the IFLA Working Group on Functional Requirements and Numbering of Authority Records, July 1, 2008, http://archive.ifla.org/VII/d4/franar-numbering-paper.pdf (accessed February 12, 2014).
23. International Standard Name Identifier (ISNI). Web site http://www.isni.org (accessed February 12, 2014).
24. IPI (Interested Parties Information). Web site http://www.ipisystem.org/SUISASITES/IPI/ipipublic.nsf/pages/index1 (accessed February 12, 2014).
25. LC/NACO training schedule, http://www.loc.gov/aba/pcc/naco/outline.html (accessed February 12, 2014).
26. Scholar Universe. Web site, http://www.scholaruniverse.com/ (accessed February 12, 2014).
27. Scopus. Web site, http://www.elsevier.com/online-tools/scopus (accessed February 12, 2014).
28. Web of Knowledge. Web site. http://wokinfo.com/ (accessed February 12, 2014).
29. Amazon. Web site. http://www.amazon.com (accessed February 12, 2014).
30. LC/NACO contributors. http://www.loc.gov/aba/pcc/stats/PCCvsLCNACOContributions.pdf (accessed February 12, 2014).
31. Hickey, T. NISO/DCMI Webinar: Cooperative authority control: the Virtual International Authority File (VIAF), December 4, 2013, http://www.slideshare.net/BaltimoreNISO/nisodcmi-webinar-cooperative-authority-control-the-virtual-international-authority-file-viaf?ref=http://www.niso.org/news/events/2013/dcmi/authority/ (accessed February 12, 2014).
32. Gatenby, J.; MacEwan, A. ISNI: a new system for name identification. NISO, ISQ (Inform. Stand. Q.), **Fall 2011**, *23*(3), http://www.niso.org/apps/group_public/document.php?document_id=7255 (accessed February 12, 2014).
33. ISNI. Data element values, http://www.isni.org/filedepot_download/130/356 (accessed February 12, 2014).
34. Amazon. Author Central. Web site https://authorcentral.amazon.com/ (accessed February 12, 2014).
35. Google. Knowledge Graph. Web site https://www.google.com/intl/es419/insidesearch/features/search/knowledge.html (accessed May 9, 2016).
36. Salo, D. Name authority control in institutional repositories. Cat. Classif. Q. **April 2009**, *47* (3/4), http://minds.wisconsin.edu/handle/1793/31735 (accessed February 12, 2014).
37. Tarver, H.; Waugh, L.; Phillips, M. Implementing name authority control into institutional repositories: a staged approach, http://or2013.net/sites/or2013.net/files/UNT-proposal.pdf (accessed February 12, 2014).
38. OCLC Research. Registering researchers in authority files, 2014, http://www.oclc.org/research/activities/registering-researchers/progress.html (accessed February 12, 2014).
39. Mendeley. Web site http://www.mendeley.com/ (accessed February 12, 2014).
40. RePEc (Research Papers in Economics). Web site http://repec.org/ (accessed February 12, 2014).
41. Author Claim. Web site http://authorclaim.org/ (accessed February 12, 2014).
42. ResearchGate. Web site. https://www.researchgate.net/home.Home.html (accessed February 12, 2014).
43. Publications List. Web site. http://publicationslist.org/ (accessed February 12, 2014).
44. Klein, M.; Kyrios, A. VIAFbot and the integration of library data on Wikipedia. Code4lib journal issue 22, October 14, 2013, http://journal.code4lib.org/articles/8964.
45. Klein, M. The ropebridges: authority control in Wikidata, Hanging Together, May 9 2013, http://hangingtogether.org/?p=2878.
46. Klein, M. "Allow me to reintroduce myself," say those in Wikidata and VIAF, Hanging Together, September 25, 2013 http://hangingtogether.org/?p=3331 (accessed February 12, 2014).
47. Digital author identifier (DAI). Web site. http://www.surf.nl/en/themes/research/research-information/digital-author-identifier-dai/digital-author-identifier-dai.html (accessed February 12, 2014).
48. Anglo-American Cataloging Rules, American Library Association, Canadian Library Association and Chartered Institute of Library and Information Professionals. Anglo American Cataloging Rules http://www.aacr2.org/ (accessed February 12, 2014).
49. Die Gemeinsame Normdatei (GND). http://www.dnb.de/DE/Standardisierung/GND/gnd_node.html (accessed February 12, 2014).

50. AFNOR NF Z 44-061, 1er juin 1986 Catalogage: forme et structure de vedettes noms de personne, des vedettes titres, des rubriques de classement et des titres forges, http://www.boutique.afnor.org/norme/nf-z44-061/documentation-catalogage-forme-et-structure-des-vedettes-noms-de-personnes-des-vedettes-titres-des-rubriques-de-classement/article/746004/faq (accessed February 12, 2014).
51. International Council on Archives. International Standard Authority Record ISAAR. Web site http://www.icacds.org.uk/eng/ISAAR%28CPF%292ed.pdf (accessed February 12, 2014).
52. IFLA. *Functional Requirements for Bibliographic Records*; IFLA: The Hague, the Netherlands, 2009, http://www.ifla.org/publications/functional-requirements-for-bibliographic-records (accessed February 12, 2014).
53. IFLA Working Group on Functional Requirements and Numbering of Authority Records (FRANAR) *Functional Requirements for Authority Data: A Conceptual Model*; IFLA: The Hague, the Netherlands, 2008, http://www.ifla.org/files/assets/cataloguing/frad/frad_2013.pdf (accessed February 12, 2014).
54. Library of Congress. MARC21 Format for Authority Records. Web site http://www.loc.gov/marc/authority/ecadhome.html (accessed February 12, 2014).
55. Willer, Myrna. UNIMARC Manual. Authorities Format 3rd edition. München: K.B. Saur, 2009 (IFLA series on bibliographic control, 38) http://www.ifla.org/publications/ifla-series-on-bibliographic-control-38 (accessed May 9, 2016).
56. Library of Congress. MADS Metadata Authority Description Schema. http://www.loc.gov/standards/mads/ (accessed February 12, 2014).
57. Library of Congress. BIBFRAME model and vocabulary. http://www.loc.gov/bibframe/docs/index.html (accessed May 9, 2016).
58. BIBFRAME. Authority Schema. Web site http://bibframe.org/documentation/bibframe-authority/ (accessed February 12, 2014).
59. Schema.org. Web site http://schema.org/ (accessed February 12, 2014).
60. Society of American Archivists. Encoded Archival Context. Corporate Bodies, Persons, and Families (EAC-CPF). Web site. http://eac.staatsbibliothek-berlin.de/ (accessed February 12, 2014).

National Archives

Helen Forde
Department of Information Studies, University College London, London, U.K.

Abstract

The scope of this entry covers the development of national archives from antiquity to the present day, charting the changes in the understanding of what constitutes a national archive and the differences between countries throughout the world. It looks at the different positions of national archives within governments, at their varying responsibilities, the scope of their holdings, and the activities which they undertake.

INTRODUCTION

National archives are the repositories of the selected records of government, in whatever medium, normally preserved in a government building and made accessible to the public. As in other archives they gain their authenticity from retention in official custody which in this case maintains their value as evidence of decisions and subsequent implementation by government. The reasons for maintaining a national archive are also much the same as for any other archive but often on a larger scale; the official record plays a role in society by ensuring that the rights of the individual and of government are documented and retained over time. Thus a national archive may contain diverse material ranging from treaties or boundary agreements on a national scale to the personal details of births, marriages, and deaths or the financial rights of individuals. The word *archive* covers both the historic records and the organization which looks after them but the context makes it clear which definition is referred to.

The concept of a national archive appears relatively simple at first sight, but on further investigation proves to be a highly diverse subject with many variations. This discussion is necessarily limited, due to the global scope of the subject and the availability of information, but the recent comparative work undertaken by the European Union (EU) demonstrates the value of deeper investigation. It is also clear that the concept changes and develops over time depending on the regime which it documents; these changes will continue, not least as greater global importance is placed on the right of all citizens to official information.

The footnotes indicate the main sources used and it must be emphasized that where examples are given the information is provided by the country cited and it has not been possible to verify it independently. It should also be noted that they are intended to be exemplars only and citing one does not mean that other countries do not follow the same practices. The regions of the world cited are those adopted by UNESCO.[1]

HISTORICAL CONTEXT

The concept of ensuring the survival of key government documents dates back to antiquity although the recording format has changed over the centuries. The need for administrations to make their promulgations and laws public initially led to inscriptions being made on stone and clay tablets, foreshadowing the more sophisticated use of papyrus, parchment, paper, and ultimately electronic documents in the hands of those in power.

The survival of records in antiquity and their secure buildings is patchy—in some countries, such as Egypt, actual records survive but not the buildings; "Rarely indeed has there been a bureaucracy as record conscious as that of ancient Egypt. It not only used records as tools of management but also contributed toward making record—consciousness integral and important in the life of people"[2] Elsewhere in the ancient world buildings, such as the Metroon in Athens or the Tabularium in Rome, which used to house the records of administrations, are known to have existed but their contents have not survived. The concept, however, was well developed and understood; for example, the tradition of keeping the royal archives with registers of the documents in Babylon was maintained by Alexander, the Great when he conquered the Persians in 333 B.C. The Greeks also influenced later Ptolemaic and Roman Egypt, bringing enhanced administrative skills which included quite sophisticated record keeping. In the Roman Empire, the Tabularium became the seat of the imperial archives after Caesar before the system was reformed by Diocletian (284 A.D.) and the previously centralized government became a migratory body, taking its documents with it. Many of such archives disappeared between the fifth and seventh centuries during the barbarian invasions in central and western Europe but the tradition of national—or at least regime—record keeping was to some extent maintained by the Arabs. Evidence for this is found in the Fatimid administration of Sicily from the tenth

Encyclopedia of Library and Information Sciences, Fourth Edition DOI: 10.1081/E-ELIS4-120044542

century where advanced techniques of making, arranging, and preserving the records of the administration were introduced.

Northern Europe lagged behind these traditions, though by the time of Charlemagne (769–814 A.D.) codification of the law and some concept of the importance of keeping central administrative records must have been quite widespread. Evidence such as Domesday Book (1086), compiled for William the Conqueror in England, suggests that at least some of the information gathered for the survey was already available in written form by that time. The Normans instituted considerable administrative changes throughout their territories in Europe, including registers of grants and taxes as well as writs of instruction, most of which, in England were kept by the king in the Curia Regis and subsequently in the Chancery or government secretariat.

Elsewhere in Europe similar developments occurred, though frequently the archives related to powerful independent areas such as the city states in Italy, or the duchies in France. The archives of the kingdom of Aragon (modern Spain) date from 1346 and the first formal amalgamation of archives to form a type of national archive there occurred in 1542 with the foundation of the Archivo de Simancas. Two centuries later, the Hungarian historic archive was founded (1756) and most European administrations already held archival material essential for managing each country or region and its citizens by the end of the eighteenth century. However, the French Revolution is widely regarded as the moment at which the birth of national archives took place. The Archives Nationales, as an organization, was created in 1790 and legally established by law in 1794, centralizing the archives of France, making them available to the public and establishing an archival network throughout the country. The impetus came from the need to legitimize and preserve the archives of the new government, to rearrange those of the Ancient Regime and to take charge of confiscated documents regarded as part of the national heritage.

Similar changes occurred in the Netherlands, Italy, Germany, and Spain following the Napoleonic Wars of the early nineteenth century as the abolition of existing regimes necessitated control by new administrations. This confirmed the concept of a division between an historic national archive—relating to previous regimes—and current national records which in time would be selected for transfer to a place of permanent security.

Elsewhere in the world many of the governments and dynasties which relied on written communications had long established archives. The preeminent example is that of China where the magnificent chests in which the Ming emperors (1368–1644) kept their archives are still maintained in the Forbidden City in Beijing. Slightly later in Russia, Peter the Great initiated reforms when he issued an instruction to regulate transfers to the Russian Imperial Archive in 1720, an interesting development demonstrating the importance he attached to the official record. Other countries or rulers also maintained their archives privately, for reasons of legitimacy, reference or self aggrandizement in a more or less complete state and transferred them to official national repositories when these were created. For some, this moment came with the expansion of government in the nineteenth century. In South America the Argentinean national archives was founded in 1821, the Mexican in 1823, the Bolivian in 1825, the Venezuelan in 1836, the Brazilian in 1838, and that of Peru in 1861. In Iceland the first national archive was housed in the attic of the Cathedral of Reykjavik in 1882; shortly afterwards, and on the other side of the world a national archive was created in India when the Imperial Record Department was established in Calcutta in 1891. As in some other countries a formal national archives was not established in the United States until the early part of the twentieth century since all government departments held their own records.[3]

The catastrophic events of the two World Wars in the twentieth century precipitated further changes in the history of the national archives.[4] Radical alterations to the constitutions and legal systems of Germany, Italy, and the Russian central and eastern European countries changed previous concepts and in 1992 Michel Duchein[5] categorised three distinct groups as

- Centrally controlled systems in countries such as Bulgaria, Czechoslovakia, Poland, Romania, and the USSR where all archives, except for personal documents, were regarded as part of the state archive fonds following Lenin's decree of June 1, 1918 outlining their status.
- Dispersed control systems in countries such as Switzerland where each canton is separate archivally, with no national archive laws or standards.
- Intermediate systems in countries such as
  - Germany where the federal (Lände) archives are separate but a compliance system is enforced
  - Italy where provincial archives are part of the State Archive and municipal archives are controlled by regional Superintendents appointed by the Director General
  - Spain where the state archives have their own network of repositories but the regional authorities are given most of the archival power by the state
  - England where the national and local archives are not connected other than where public records, subject to the authority of the Lord Chancellor, are deposited locally
  - France where the national and local archives are governed by the same laws but the Archives Nationales is under the Director General of the French Archives and the local archives are under the supervision of the General Inspectors.

Since then the emergence of independent countries formerly part of the USSR, and changes in the Balkan areas of southern Europe have resulted in further developments of national archives. Theses have included Estonia which established a National Archive in 1998, Lithuania which did the same in 2004, and the Slovak Republic which created the National Archives Service in 2002.

Elsewhere in the world, the second half of the twentieth century saw a proliferation of national archive legislation and a burgeoning of national archive buildings and organizations. Information on these can be accessed from the relevant national archive Web site.

In the Pacific area these included

- The Australian National Archive which was created as a result of the Archives Act of 1983
- The Japanese National Archive which started as a government department in 1971 though it is now an independent agency following an amendment to the Archive Law in 2001
- The Malaysian National Archive created in 1963 although it was actually founded 6 years earlier as the Public Record Office and
- Archives New Zealand which was established in 2005 following new legislation although the archive had existed from much earlier.

In Africa many ex-colonial countries scrambled to establish archives as symbols of independence and legitimacy; these included

- Kenya which established a National Archives and Documentation Service in 1965.
- Mozambique which divided the library and archive to form a national archive in 1976.
- Ethiopia which opened its National Archives in 1979.
- South Africa where the State Archives Service became the National Archives in 1996.

Amongst the Arab countries

- The Lebanon passed legislation establishing the National Archives in 1977.
- Tunisia finally renamed the archive (which had served in various state capacities since 1874) as the National Archive in 1988.

In the Caribbean, national archives were established

- In the Bahamas in 1971.
- In Puerto Rica in 1972.
- in Jamaica in 1982.

The above are all examples, many other countries have established national archives and will continue to do so as administrations change and boundaries alter. However the progression of national archives through the centuries demonstrates the importance attached to the secure maintenance of official papers and the legitimacy which the possession of such documents confers on a regime.

ISSUES

Reviewing the development of the national archives as described above it is abundantly clear that no two are exactly alike. The European Commission came to the conclusion that "It is impossible to say that there is a 'typical' 'National Archives service, exemplifying a general pattern, which applies to a greater or lesser extent throughout the European Union.'"[6] If that is so for Europe, how much more true is it for the rest of the world, given the variety of histories, legal, and administrative differences?

Position of National Archives in Government

National archives are established by law in the country to which they relate. The provisions of each piece of legislation will dictate the activities undertaken by the directors and the staff of the archive, but all statutes embrace the three basic principles of selection, preservation, and access.

Different interpretations abound about the scope of these responsibilities, dependant on the financial and professional skill resources available. Selection of material is, in many ways, the most controversial since it is open to accusations of partisanship and bias, political, social, and economic. Even unwittingly archivists can shape the future historical perspective depending on which records are selected for permanent preservation and for national archives this may be a bigger issue than for a smaller, more local organization. This perception, of the official record whether it be national or local, has played a part in the proliferation of community archives, often established in localities or amongst the ex-employees of a business no longer operating, to add an additional, unofficial dimension to history.

The impact of freedom of information legislation has also accelerated the ways in which all public archival organizations have widened access to their holdings. Improved service delivery is a growing trend, with some of the national archives leading the way, not least since for the developed countries it has been possible to employ additional specialists who have skills in audience development, digitization, and education. The growth in interest in genealogy has been behind many of these developments and it has been possible to widen access to the relevant records as well as others following the development of digitization techniques. In consequence, a world wide audience is now a target for many access programs.

The different attitudes between administrations to the correct place for national archives within government are clearly demonstrated by scrutinizing their location; the report on European archives in 2005 shows that the majority of the 25 national archives surveyed were the responsibility of the relevant Ministry of Culture (14); three others were situated within the Ministry of Education, two within the Ministry of the Interior, two within the Ministry of Justice, three within the Office of the Prime Minister, and one within that of Science policy.[7] These statistics suggest that although it is widely acknowledged that archives are part of modern public administration, they, and in particular those which are sometimes referred to as historic archives, are more comfortably placed under the aegis of culture. In other parts of the world the same is broadly true, judging by those national archives which offer information of this sort on their Web sites. The Arab world has a tendency to give the oversight of the archives to the presidential or prime ministerial office as do a few Latin American countries but elsewhere the trend is toward culture and heritage. Many of these ministries have additional responsibilities ranging from the Status of Women (Canada) to Heritage and Sport in some African countries and in Australia, contributing to the impression that the organizations within their aegis are something of a ragbag. In just a few places, such as New Zealand, Japan, and the United States the national archive is a department or agency in its own right in government.

The variance in the position of national archives throughout the world is indicative of the problem of explaining their dual role in not only promoting access to the past but also in ensuring good current record keeping in government.

Responsibilities of National Archives

Strictly speaking, the scope of an archive of a government or regime would be limited to managing the records of the transactions of that body and its predecessors. In practice, the work undertaken in different countries is surprisingly variable. The titles have also changed over the years ranging from the very Victorian, and confusing, title of Public Record Office used in England and Malaysia (by now changed in both) to State Archives in Austria, Italy, Poland, and quite a number of other countries. "National" is the preferred term for most but transfer between the two has been quite common, the progression usually being from "state" to "national." South Africa switched from the title State Archives Service to National Archives and Record Services in 1996 with a mission to foster a national identity and the protection of rights. Swaziland is also very clear that these issues are central to the mission of the Swazi National Archives—which "is to empower Swazi citizens to fully participate in their country's social, political, and economic life through the equitable development, preservation, and protection of the Swazi cultural heritage."[8]

These, and other similar statements elsewhere reflect the difference between the two terms, *state* denoting "a nation or territory considered as an organized political community under one government" and *nation* "a sovereign state of which most of the citizens or subjects are united also by factors which define a nation, such as language or common descent.[9]" Others however have adopted the term state with rather different meanings—in Denmark the State Archives is the collective name for the Danish National Business Archives, the Danish Data Archives, the Danish National Archives, and the four regional archives. In Georgia, the historic archive and the modern record archive are both referred to as state organizations although in practice they both contain much more than just the records of government.[10] In Latvia, the State Archive consists of the Latvia State Historical Archive, the State Archive of Latvia, Latvia State Archive of Audiovisual Documents, State Archive of Personnel Files and 11 Regional State Archives, as well as the Archival Inspection, the Conservation Laboratory, and the Archival Training Centre with Library.[11] The scope of the term therefore appears to vary according to the historical development of each archive and although some use the term national for specific reasons it seems likely that others are less concerned about the precise definition but more concerned to ensure that the various elements within the sphere of the archive are well looked after.

The governments of ex-colonial countries in many parts of the world have struggled with the concept of their former rulers that the records of the earlier administration are the property of the colonial power. In many cases, the provision of copies of the records concerned have been provided to ensure that the information about the ex-colony is available in the place of origin, but for some this is inadequate and disputes remain. Many of the arguments hang on the concept of *respect des fonds* and the integrity of the complete archive. Demands for restitution are often argued on the same basis as the return of museum objects to their place of origin. In the Philippine Islands, however, a conscious effort was made to re-create a national identity by handing over the Spanish archives of various agencies to the Americans at the Treaty of Paris in 1898, despite the fact that the records are in archaic Spanish and now rarely understood. "The National Archives, both as an institution of colonial creation and as a collection of records of colonial control, reinforces the *imagined* [my italics] idea of nationhood."[12]

A few national archives are combined with libraries, either as a result of historic connections or as a rationalization of existing services. In Bolivia, the national library and archive have existed together since an economy measure in 1935; in Eritrea, the Research and Documentation Centre which is in the process of establishing the national archives encompasses the national library as well as other printed documentation and exists to collect all types of materials relating to the country. Much the same argument was behind the formation of the national Library and Archives Canada where the two were merged as partners in 2004; the vision is that of being the "stewards of a collection that is the keystone of Canada's national documentary heritage, a collection of national scope and importance."[13] In the United Kingdom, the National Archives is moving in somewhat the same direction but more as the centre for government information than as the provider of all official documentary material both manuscript and printed.

Scope of National Archive Holdings

The scope of national archive holdings might seem self-evident but in practice many have gaps in the records which they hold and many also hold material which might appear to be not strictly within a brief definition of their remit. Even the meaning of the phrase "national archive holdings" is not static since increasingly many countries include material amongst their holdings which is not necessarily the result of government activity but that of others in a government related role. This recognizes the value of nongovernmental organizations (NGOs), in particular, those that have been divorced from central government policy departments and operate in a more independent way. In effect, national archive policy must stem from and reflect current government's means of working and ensure that as complete a picture as possible is maintained for future reference. Government is not limited to strict boundaries in an information rich society.

The narrow definition might also lead to the assumption that a national archive would have the responsibility for the selected material from *all* government departments. A quick look at the available evidence makes it clear that this is far from true. Disregarding secret or classified records the EU report on archives in the enlarged EU[14] identified some clear trends; 12 of those surveyed took in neither the records of Parliament nor the Department of Defense, eight did not have Foreign Ministry records, four did not have the records of the President or Prime Minister's Office, two had neither the records of the Department of Finance nor those of the Interior and one did not have material emanating from the Department of Justice. The omission of the records of Parliament are understandable since national archives are usually established for the executive arm of government and special arguments on security grounds may be adduced for the some of the Defense records, but many of the others seem to negate the principles of openness which democratic countries are at pains to proclaim. Only eight out of the 25 EU national archives held the records of all the major departments of government and three were denied custody of as many as five or six departments, seriously limiting their ability to ensure the survival of a full record of activity.

Information about the gaps in the holdings of other countries is hard to find as it is not included on Web sites and no global survey has been undertaken; however, it seems likely that all over the world some governments still restrict the scope of the holdings in their national archives while maintaining a cloak of democratic access.

Issues to do with access to sensitive material have dominated the history of national archives, in particular with changing regimes. Attitudes vary according to stance; those who are successful in overthrowing a government which they regard as illegal are often keen to demonstrate this by reference to archival material. For the same reason, the previous regime may have left much activity undocumented or destroyed material which could prove compromising. The Japanese government, as just one example, destroyed almost all the records of their wartime administration both at home and in occupied territories, but it has happened in many places at different times. Distrust of official custody has also made it difficult to resolve the eventual custody of reports and documentary material held as a result of national legal proceedings such as international criminal tribunals or truth and reconciliation commissions. In South America, Africa, and parts of Europe where the latter have been held, the issues have been very carefully considered to ensure that previous victims are comfortable with the designated repository for the archive. In the case of the reunification of Germany in 1991, the level of concern over free access to the Stasi files of the German Democratic Republic (which held immense amounts of personal detail) were so high that a separate archive was established to manage the records. Many German archivists felt that special arrangements were unnecessary and that this compromised the existing system, but a pragmatic solution had to be found. Other countries have had to resort to similar ways of dealing with highly sensitive material.

The impact of data protection and freedom of information legislation on national archives has been no less dramatic than for other archives—in many ways it has been greater. The resources allocated to ensuring that the right information is available to the right people at the right time have had to be huge; quite apart from the records management issues surrounding the custody of personal information in electronic formats the requirement to provide information freely has necessitated new procedures, additional departments, and dedicated staff. In many countries, the lead has been taken by the national archives but has sparked controversy about the responsibilities which then ensue.

An added change to the role of twenty-first century national archives is that they may now no longer be the obvious place of custody for material which crosses international borders. Globalization and improved communications has led to world wide organizations such as the United Nations and its various branches as well as commercial businesses which know no boundaries. Thus while international diplomatic activity may be on record in the national archives the decisions to which they relate may well not be part of the official record, bringing a further dimension to the search for archival sources.

Turning to the question of material which is held in many national archives, but which might not be expected, is also interesting. The issue of the custody of private archival material in national archives is one which has generated considerable debate. The theory that national archives exist for purely administrative material is fine on paper and is often adhered to more strictly by national archives which have been established relatively recently such as Cyprus or Sweden. In practice, it is often less easy to distinguish between the official material and that which is frequently generated by individuals in the course of their duty. Additionally, for many countries the national or state archive may be, or have been in the past the only available repository for private papers. In Scotland the National Archives holds a considerable number of family, legal, and estate papers; and records of businesses, societies, and institutions. In Cuba the holdings cover all those papers that relate to a civil society including papers of those who contributed to cultural and political life. In Canada the remit of the Library and Archives is so wide that they solicit every type of material from Canadians on their Web site—"Anyone who feels that they have valuable materials, whether published or unpublished, and regardless of media, is encouraged to offer them to Library and Archives Canada (LAC)."[15] This sort of statement is powerful in creating a national vision and the new title chosen by the Canadians—"Library and Archives Canada"—indicates the inclusiveness of their collecting policy; *Directions for Change* states that the combined organization "will play a significant role in the government of Canada and within the library, archival, cultural heritage, and learning communities in Canada."[16] In India too it is recognized that the rich collection of private papers, acquired through donation or gift, and held in the National Archives complements the public records. Elsewhere some limitations are imposed such as in Australia where the private paper holdings are limited to those of prominent people such as governors-general, prime ministers, ministers, secretaries, and High Court judges. Indeed, to clarify the scope of their holdings the Web site of the National Archives of Australia specifies what it does not hold, and presumably will not accept. This includes information on convicts, on colonial migration, on nineteenth century Australian history including exploration or colonial administration, land title or settlements and records of births, deaths, and marriages. In England, although the National Archives has some private papers deposited in earlier periods, the policy is to encourage potential depositors to select another, more appropriate archive.

Legal papers are frequently part of the holdings of national archives although not specifically administrative documents relating to government. In Portugal, the National Archives has oversight of the district archive services to which the records of civil registration, the courts, and the notaries public must be transmitted. In the Caribbean, legal holdings are part of the material held in the Bahamas and in Latin America, judicial material from the sixteenth century is kept in Ecuador, and the records of tribunals from about a century later in Argentina. In Europe, the National Archives of the Czech Republic holds judicial records as does the National Archives in Hungary which emphasizes the importance of many of the judicial papers of the second half of the twentieth century as an essential part of the history of a turbulent era.[17] In Scotland, the National Archive holdings include legal records such as registers of deeds and land holdings (seisins), Chancery records, and adoption records leading to considerable use of their legal search room by lawyers. In England, the judicial exhibits produced as evidence in law courts and now held in the National Archive constitute a wonderful rag bag of items, hardly archival but adding much substance to similar legal reports. In Iceland, the records of the Supreme Court are regarded as public records and are transferred accordingly to the National Archives.

Ecclesiastical documents are another category of archive frequently found in national repositories though not within the strict definition of such organizations. In many cases this is due to historical accident, since the national archive may have or have had a wide remit as the only obvious place of safe deposit. This is often the case where the church in earlier periods acted as part of the civil administration, registering baptisms, marriages, and burials and providing the mechanism for proving wills. The necessity for court proceedings associated with the latter resulted in a need to ensure that documents were kept and often copied for safety; in England, the records of the Prerogative Court of Canterbury (testamentary court of the Archbishop of Canterbury) are available at The National Archives and form a valuable source for family historians. In Luxembourg, the archives of the Hospice of St John with genealogical information as well as evidence of the activities of the church from the thirteenth century are maintained in the National Archives. In Portugal, an extensive archive of ecclesiastical material is held in the National Archive of Torre do Tombo including diocesan and monastic papers.

Private papers, legal reports, and ecclesiastical documents all form part of many national archives but the twentieth century brought the advent of material in other formats—photographs, tapes, film, and electronic formats. In some countries these are accepted as any other deposit of selected archival material; the National Archive and Record Administration (NARA) in the United States multimedia collections include nearly 300,000 reels of motion picture film and more than 200,000 sound and video recordings. In Australia, as in some other countries, the audiovisual holdings comprise not only those produced by government (200,000 film and video items), but also audiovisual material from Australian Broadcasting Corporation (ABC), Film Australia, Australian Film, Television and Radio School (AFTRS), Special Broadcasting Service (SBS), Defense, and many other government agencies. In other national archives such as Malta, Kenya, Costa Rica, and Yemen such collections, though smaller, are an essential part of the history of each country since audiovisual material, especially television footage, may be the only archival material which survives for some twentieth century events. Not all national archives contain audiovisual archives, however, partly due to the specialized nature of the material; in England the British Film Institute acts as an agent for The National Archives and the BBC maintains its own archive. Practical considerations make this a more convenient arrangement, obviating the need to maintain the facilities for viewing such material in the National Archives and ensuring that the collections are looked after by specialists. Elsewhere the broadcasting organizations also often maintain their own archival material, particularly commercial firms. In Thailand, by contrast, the government is planning to establish the Royal Private Film Archive as the place to preserve the King's moving and still pictures. The Coordinating Council of Audio-visual Archive Associations (CCAAA) which was established by UNESCO in 2001, has recommended that "Deposit conditions should apply to publicly funded archives with recognised national responsibilities and should apply to both commercial and noncommercial productions,"[18] but it is not specified which organization this should be and it will undoubtedly vary according to circumstances.

Scope of National Archive Activity

If the scope of the holdings of national archives is diverse then the scope of the activities undertaken worldwide under this aegis is even more so. The description which each organization gives itself is revealing: some call themselves national archives and leave the interpretation to a vision statement, often backed up by a mission statement—for example the National Archives of Scotland or of Brazil; others include records management in the title to indicate a greater than just historic role, such as the National Archives and Records Administration of the United States of America; others use the term National Archive Services such as the Botswana National Archives and Records Services, or National Archival Services in countries such as Norway where the term encompasses a wider range of archive institutions than simply the designated national institution. The word "services" is used increasingly, documenting a global perception that while the historic archive must be maintained in its own right as a record of events, it is also imperative that every archive, whether national or other, serves the citizens of the country in which it is situated in a number of spheres.

A survey of Web sites on which national archives identify their raisons d'être makes it clear how diverse these activities can be. In India, their vision is to help in spreading a feeling of national pride in the documentary cultural heritage and ensuring its preservation for posterity. The National Archives is concerned to develop the best means of conserving the records, to foster good relations between archives both at home and abroad, to increase access, and develop greater professionalism amongst creators, custodians and users. In the United States, the aspiration goes further with a vision that "all Americans will understand the vital role records play in a democracy, and their own personal stake in the National Archives."[19] Although the title of the organization proclaims that they form the records administration arm of government, in the mission statement it is not explicitly stated, support for democracy, and the promotion of civic education being more prominent. In Kenya, the National Archive is clear that it has a vision to excel as an archives service in the view of all Kenyans and to serve as the Memory of the Nation; the Web site cites the overall activities of the service, which are common to many countries in the world, as continuing to

- Advise public offices on proper records management.
- Select valuable records for permanent preservation as archives.
- Store and preserve archives in the repositories.
- Publicize availability of information resources in our custody through computerization of indexes, digitization, World Wide Web; and through use of other communications and information technologies.
- Promote access to public records and archives for reference and research purposes, or just for leisure and enjoyment.[20]

The Australians manage to encompass some philosophy about their approach to record keeping in their mission statement, referring to best practice in management from the point of creation and their concern to develop, manage, and promote a visible, known, and accessible national collection. This argues a confidence which is also visible in the statements issued by the Malaysian National Archive with a vision of molding a knowledgeable nation that values its national heritage, and a rather simpler mission which repeats the overall purpose of all national archives namely acquisition, conservation, and preservation but also includes popularizing the archives and national heritage and making the National Archives a resource and research centre. This introduces an academic element which is shared among some other national archives, such as Greenland, suggesting links to higher education. Finally, in the Netherlands another issue is explicitly raised, that of wishing to play a leading role in archive policy and to advise the State Secretary effectively, a point followed in the mission statement of The

National Archives in the United Kingdom where that is developed into information management—"The National Archives is at the heart of information policy—setting standards and supporting innovation in information and records management across the United Kingdom, and providing a practical framework of best practice for opening up and encouraging the reuse of public sector information."[21]

It is clear that national archives fulfill a number of roles many of which are very similar and have been so for some time. Other roles are being developed not least on account of the dual role of preserving the past for the future but also ensuring that current records, increasingly in electronic format, are properly managed. Some, such as the State Archives of China, divide their activities, and their premises and staff, so a clear distinction is made between the two roles; others run a multifaceted operation connecting the past and the present with a view to ensuring the survival of it all for the future. Much depends on the scale of the organization and available funding; in a few countries large sums of private money supplement government support, but for defined purposes. The obvious example is that of the presidential libraries in the United States which are administered by the National Archives and Records Administration but with private endowments. Elsewhere the more modest official sums available require archives to bid for exterior funding to support digitization programs or even basic improvements to buildings and storage areas. In areas of the world where the workforce constitutes the major part of the annual expenditure all effort will be put into reducing that to a bare minimum; elsewhere the limiting factor may not be the size of the workforce but the untrained element.

CONCLUSION

National archives are a defined but diverse group, carrying out both basic and more advanced archival work on behalf of governments. The scope of what they do is limited by resources and by the type of national archive system, as well as the national perception of the role of archives in modern society. The diversity is important as it reflects the differing characteristics of each country, historic, legal, and cultural factors, and, as recognized by the EU, "it would be inappropriate even to contemplate a 'model' of a National Archives service."[22] If that is true for the EU, it is equally applicable to other areas of the world, let alone impossible to impose. Much of the value of national archives is contained in what each can offer to its very varied citizens.

REFERENCES

1. http://www.unesco.org/cgi-bin/webworld/portal_archives.
2. Posner, E. *Archives in the Ancient World*; Society of American Archivists: Chicago, IL, 2003; 73.
3. Details of many of these archives can be found on the UNESCO portal. http://www.unesco.org/cgi-bin/webworld/portal_archives.
4. Links to the national archives of the individual countries in the European Union can be found on http://vlib.iue.it/hist-eur-integration/Archives.html.
5. Duchein, M. The history of European archives and the development of the archival profession in Europe. Am Archiv **1992**, *55* (winter), 14–24.
6. European Commission. *Report on Archives in the Enlarged European Union*, 2005; 37.
7. European Commission, *Report on Archives in the Enlarged European Union*, 2005; 38.
8. http://www.gov.sz.
9. Oxford English Dictionary.
10. See web page. http://archive.gol.ge.
11. http://www.arhivi.lv.
12. Punzalan, R.L. Archives of the new possession; Spanish colonial records and the American creation of a "national" archives for the Philippines. Archiv Sci **2006**, *6* (3–4), 381–392.
13. http://www.collectionscanada.gc.ca.
14. European Commission, *Report on Archives in the Enlarged European Union*, 2005; 39.
15. http://www.collectionscanada.gc.ca/collection/003-340-e.html.
16. http://www.collectionscanada.gc.ca.
17. http://www.mol.gov.hu.
18. http://www.ccaaa.org/ccaaa_heritage.pdf.
19. http://www.archives.gov.
20. http://www.kenyarchives.go.ke.
21. http://www.nationalarchives.gov.uk.
22. European Commission, *Report on Archives in the Enlarged European Union*, 2005; 37.

National Biological Information Infrastructure (NBII)

P. Bryan Heidorn
Graduate School of Library and Information Science, University of Illinois at Urbana-Champaign, Champaign, Illinois, U.S.A.

Annette Olson
Biological Resources Division, U.S. Geological Survey, Reston, Virginia, U.S.A.

Abstract

The United States National Biological Information Infrastructure (NBII) is a collaborative program with the mission of improving online access to the country's information about its biological resources. Coordinated by the Biological Informatics Program Office of the U.S. Geological Survey (USGS), the NBII provides a distributed infrastructure for scientific information provided by national, state and local governments, universities, museums, private organizations, and international collaborations. Concentrating on the fields of biodiversity and ecology, the NBII's main audience is considered U.S. land managers, scientists, and policy makers, but specific programs also support educators as well as private citizens. The NBII catalogs and links to data and information resources, provides searches of Web sites, develops tools for the integration and display of data, and synthesizes the latest information on select subjects; it also supports the development and use of standards and technological tools. The NBII is the only organization within the United States with the mandate and experience to organize and deliver the depth and breadth of biological information to the people.

INTRODUCTION

The U.S. NBII (http://www.nbii.gov) is a broad, collaborative program to make accessible online the nation's biological data and information, especially in the fields of biodiversity and ecology. The NBII includes over 250 agencies and organizations, with coordination and program management provided by the Biological Informatics Program of the U.S. Geological Survey (USGS). Because biological information comes from numerous public and private partners, and is found in multiple formats (e.g., datasets, maps, documents, and images), pooling these resources is a significant management and organization challenge. Many individuals and organizations, however, have recognized the value in discovering otherwise hidden information, in having rapid access to new data, and in data integration; this recognition has driven the formation and operation of the NBII over the past 15 years.

Calls began in 1993 for a national, digital system "to collect, house, assess, and provide access to the scientific information needed to understand the status of the nation's biological resources, the trends in the changes of that status, and the causes of those changes."[1] Digital system initiatives already were underway for genomic, medical, and molecular information, and various government agencies, universities, and other organizations felt that an infrastructure was needed for biodiversity and ecological information. These calls led to the creation of the original NBII within the U.S. Department of the Interior (DOI) in 1994. The NBII initially focused on developing standards and infrastructure to support the linking of specific data and information. Further calls for the expansion of the program, to a "next generation" NBII (p. 30),[2] yielded a viable, distributed infrastructure for linking and providing a wider breadth of information online.

The current NBII seeks to meet information needs defined by the U.S. government, by NBII partners, and by outside users, which include researchers, resource managers, policy makers, educators, students, and others. Its efforts emphasize credible, scientific information from the government agencies (federal, state, and local), museums, university collections, gene banks, nongovernmental organizations, botanical and zoological gardens, libraries, bibliographic services, as well as other sources. The NBII has four approaches to gather and disseminate information from these disparate sources: 1) improving standards and technology; 2) working with various regions to meet local information needs; 3) supporting data sharing on national or global issues (e.g., invasive species); and 4) creating the network for integrating local to global knowledge. The resulting infrastructure has both centralized and distributed components: the NBII National Program Office at USGS maintains the standards and protocols, a data repository, a search engine, and Web sites; and distributed offices feed in data from various sources and support specific information portals. Both the Program Office and the distributed projects also help develop tools to synthesize, integrate, and apply biological information.

Overall, while the NBII's general mission has remained relatively constant since its inception in 1994, it has grown

Encyclopedia of Library and Information Sciences, Fourth Edition DOI: 10.1081/E-ELIS4-120043271

with the opportunities afforded by new technology and with new partnerships from local to global levels. The next section addresses the history of the NBII, as well as its mission, goals and strategy, and its organizational structure. The NBII's extensive and complex relationship to other organizations is discussed in sections for Regional Foci, Thematic Foci, National Standards and Technology, and Knowledge Integration.

HISTORY

Throughout American history, many leaders and agencies have recognized the value of information on its biological resources. Shortly after the United States was formed, Thomas Jefferson charged Meriwether Lewis with gathering knowledge about the landscape, soil, plants, and animals of the West during the Lewis and Clark Corps of Discovery trip to the Pacific Ocean.

> Your observations are to be taken with great pains & accuracy, to be entered distinctly, & intelligibly for others as well as yourself, to comprehend all the elements necessary. . .[3]

Lewis collected extensive field notes and specimens during the 1804–1807 trip. In the two centuries that have followed, hundreds of local, state, and federal agencies and projects, universities, museums, and private citizens have amassed huge amounts of diverse data and information. Unfortunately, there has been no overarching plan to organize and make these disparate collections accessible. The NBII was created to help find and serve information about our nation's biological resources.

The origins of the NBII can be traced, if not to Jefferson, then at least back to a 1993 report by the National Research Council (NRC), titled "A Biological Survey for the Nation."[1] In this report, the NRC recognized the value of interoperability and of linking disparate information types from distributed sources via the Internet, thus providing better and quicker access to scientifically reliable information on biological resources. The NRC recommended that the DOI create a "National Biotic Resource Information System" (NBRI) that would develop new methods to collect and distribute data and information about data, as well as promote standards to ensure compatibility among information sources. The NBRI would especially support database development and coordination at local, regional, and national levels. To help address the multiple issues identified in the NRC report, including that of information management, the U.S. Secretary of the Interior Bruce Babbitt created the National Biological Survey (NBS) within the DOI in 1994; the NBS included the NBRI as one of its major components. The NBS was later renamed as the National Biological Service.

The following year, President Clinton signed Executive Order 12906[4] and created the National Spatial Data Infrastructure (http://fgdc.gov/nsdi/) to coordinate acquisition and access to geographic data. In recognition of the parallel objectives of the NSDI and the NBRI, Secretary Babbitt renamed the NBRI to the "NBII." The NBII began work early on standard vocabularies in order to interlink data and information. An initial focus of the NBII was to assist the NSDI by writing the Biological Data Profile of the Federal Geographic Data Committee (FGDC) Metadata Content Standard. Metadata is information that describes data and datasets, (both geospatial and non-geospatial); this standard carries both metadata and actual data content, such as specimen descriptions. The NBII also joined the partnership for the Integrated Taxonomic Information System (ITIS; http://www.itis.gov), an authority for organism names and taxonomy, and supported development of the National Vegetation Classification Standard, part of a collaborative program between the USGS and the National Park Service.

In 1996, the entire NBS was folded into the USGS and was renamed the Biological Resources Division (BRD); the Office of Biological Informatics and Outreach (OBIO, which later would become the Biological Informatics Program) of the BRD then became the official coordinator of the NBII. Work continued on standards, on building partnerships, and on building Web sites to disseminate information. This work resulted in a number of awards, including the 1997 APEX Award, the 1999 Government Technology Leadership Award, Best Feds on the Web (1999); and the 1998 and 1998 Renew America National Awards for Environmental Sustainability.

Over the next few years, more entities and organizations expressed the need to expand the NBII to meet the initial mission as proposed by the NRC. In 1998, the Biodiversity and Ecosystems Panel of the President's Committee of Advisors on Science and Technology (PCAST) provided strong support. The PCAST reiterated the role of the NBII in society in a report to President Clinton titled "Teaming with Life: Investing in Science to Understand and Use America's Living Capital."[2] The cover letter by John A. Young's states "The PCAST report provides a roadmap to bringing the vast advances in information technology to the field of biodiversity in order to develop a 'next generation' national biological information infrastructure. Such capacities will allow researchers and resource managers worldwide to make full use of information generated on ecosystems and biodiversity." The PCAST proposed the most suitable configuration for this "next generation NBII" as being a distributed system of data sources, complemented with multiple entry points, or "nodes."

The PCAST report was the decisive factor, and in 2000, the U.S. Congress appropriated funds for the development of a NBII node-based infrastructure. In 2001, the NBII initiated two thematic and six regional nodes, including the

Fisheries and Aquatic Resources Node (http://far.nbii.gov), and the Pacific Northwest Node (http://pnwin.nbii.gov). These nodes identify, compile, and disseminate information by working with partners associated with a specific region, issue, or research data need. Today, there are eight regional nodes and four thematic nodes, along with similar, smaller projects, as discussed in more detail below.

The new node structure brought additional local and national partners into the NBII. The thematic work, however, as well as the NBII's continued work with standards, meant that the NBII also needed to develop strong ties with international entities. In 2001, the NBII began a formal collaboration with the Global Biodiversity Information Facility (GBIF; http://www.gbif.org), an international effort to meet the framework of the Rio Convention on Biodiversity, which proposed a worldwide information and data exchange, as well as training in informatics for developing countries. One objective of GBIF, with which the NBII has close coordination, is to provide a global, online infrastructure for primary biodiversity data, especially museum specimen information. The NBII helped support the standards and protocols needed for this broad effort, and became the U.S. representative and the U.S. node of GBIF. Beginning in 2002, the NBII also began helping the NATO Information Management Committee of the NATO Research and Technology Agency with the design of the NATO Science, Research, and Technology Network (STARNET), and the International Council for Science (ICSU) recognized the NBII as the U.S. World Data Center for Biodiversity and Terrestrial Ecology. In 2003, the NBII helped launch the Global Invasive Species Information Network (GISIN; http://www.gisinetwork.org). That same year the NBII also became a leading member of the Inter-American Biodiversity Information Network (IABIN; http://www.iabin.net), which helps coordinate and network biodiversity information from the Western Hemisphere, and it helped launch the IABIN Invasives Information Network (I3N) search system (http://i3n.iabin.net/search/mercury_search.html). The NBII has continued to join in other international information partnerships, such as the Conservation Commons.[5]

Today, the NBII partnership includes more than 250 agencies and organizations contributing their expertise, data, equipment, facilities, and labors directly to create and support standards, to strengthen the NBII infrastructure, and to increase the pool of accessible information.

MISSION, GOALS, AND STRATEGIES

The current NBII mission is similar to its original mandate and is defined as *providing the nation with a mechanism for accessing the vast amount of existing biological and natural resources data, information products, and analytical tools that support and enhance science-based decision-making.*[6]

The NBII mission encompasses all biological and natural resource data and applications for the nation, a very complicated task requiring wide coverage from molecular work and genetics, to species interactions, to biomes, to related resource information such as water and geology. Thus, the NBII Steering Team formulated its Strategic Plan[6] from the plans of both the DOI and the USGS Biological Informatics Program in which the NBII is housed, and from input from multiple parties, including NBII partners, other stakeholder groups, and Congress. These groups specifically requested ecological information to support a "better understanding of current environmental conditions, develop predictions about the future, and provide options for adopting a course of action or response to these conditions (p. 1)."[6] The NBII thus focuses on three knowledge domains: 1) species information, including biosystematics and nomenclature, habitat requirements, and population dynamics; 2) landscape level information, including land, vegetation, and water classifications and status; and 3) the environmental drivers behind trends in invasive species, wildlife diseases, climate change, and human impact.

The NBII's methods of information management fall within the science and practice of "biological informatics," or "bioinformatics," which creates and utilizes techniques for compiling, linking, organizing, storing, integrating, synthesizing, and delivering biological data and information, as well as tools to help analyze and apply this information. The terms bioinformatics and biological informatics often have been used more narrowly to denote biomolecular information only, but both terms actually address all scales of biological data from the molecular to ecosystem levels.

For each of these knowledge domains, the NBII has four main goals (p. 8):[6]

- Develop the framework to support knowledge discovery and creation for the nations' biological and ecological resources.
- Create an integrated library by systematically discovering, acquiring, organizing, storing, updating, and making available scientific data and information from diverse sources. Ensure that this library responds to the information needs of land and resource managers and other stakeholders and users.
- Lead the development, selection, and distribution of tools and standards necessary to facilitate system-wide interoperability and allow meaningful interactions with scientific data and information.
- Empower NBII users by creating an awareness of the NBII and its capabilities and providing support to enable users to directly apply NBII products and services within their own areas of concern.

To meet these goals, the NBII coordinates with the many other organizations that have developed similar regional or thematic interests and resources. Consequently, a web of projects and funding has emerged. Recently, funding for NBII operations has been flat or declining (p 132),[7] and much increasing in-kind work through partnerships is critical for the NBII to meet its goals. For example, according to a 2005 DOI Investment Overview,[8] partners provided the equivalent of $3 for every one the NBII spent in 2002. This funding and leveraging environment influences the projects on which the NBII can focus. Many pressing national concerns, however, are not fully met under the current funding regime. For example, most natural history collections are not digitized and remain inaccessible over the Internet.

Organization

The NBII is managed by the Biological Informatics Program of the USGS, based in Reston, VA, and is led by the NBII Steering Team, consisting of USGS employees (Fig. 1).

The figure shows how multiple groups provide input on information needs, goals, and objectives. One such group is the Biodiversity and Ecosystems Informatics Working Group (BioEco; http://www.bioeco.gov), established under the White House's Office of Science and Technology Policy in 1997 to improve the coordination of federal biodiversity and ecosystem informatics activities. The NBII also receives input directly from the scientific communities through staff who attend scientific meetings and participate in discussions with outside scientific committees and associations. Finally, the hundreds of partners in the NBII federation provide input either directly to the Steering Team or via project managers.

In building the national infrastructure, the NBII has four organizational approaches: national themes, regional foci, network standards and technology, and knowledge integration. Staff within the thematic and regional foci concentrate on discovering, incorporating, and integrating data specific to a region or theme, as well as in creating application tools. The Network Standards and Technology and the Knowledge Integration groups assist in this process, but also provide overarching standards, tools and applications, and technical support for all NBII Web sites and repositories. Many project managers and staff are based at a USGS or partner science centers that specialize in their subject, such as the USGS Center for Biological Informatics (CBI) in Denver, CO, while additional Program staff are based in Reston; project managers within each approach, however, commonly work closely with managers in others, in person or remotely. The main projects within each approach are detailed below.

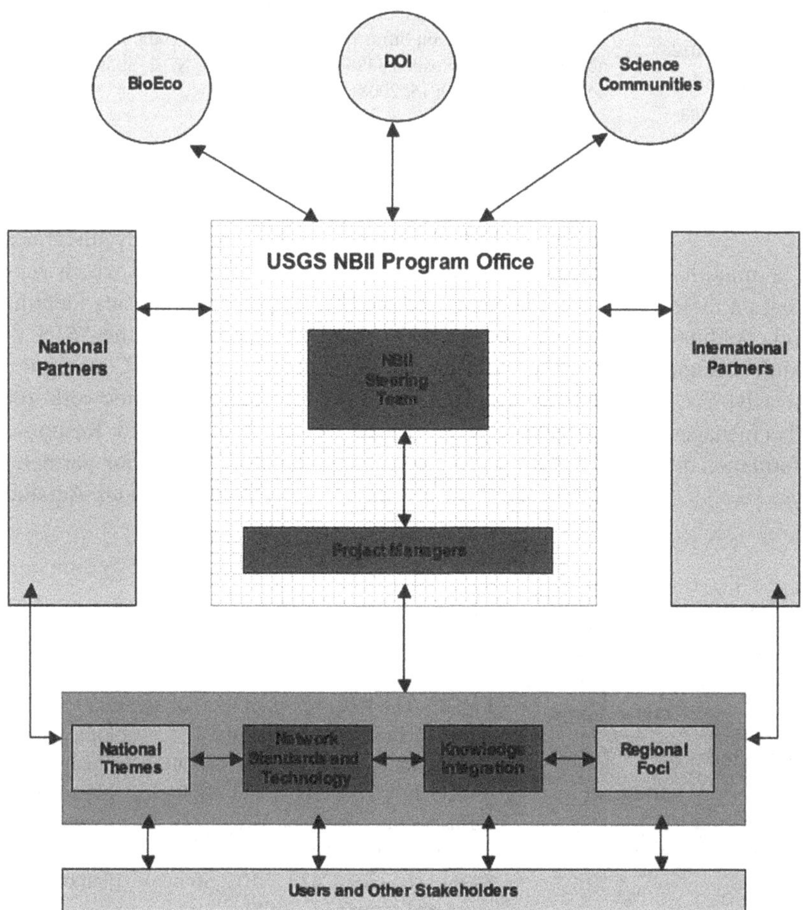

Fig. 1 Organization of the NBII's activities. **Source:** Modified from Ruggerio, M.; Marcia McNiff, M.; Olson, A.; Wheeler, B. Strategic Plan for the U.S. Geological Survey Biological Informatics Program: 2005–2009; U.S. Geological Survey, Biological Resources Discipline, 2005; 1–22, http://www.nbii.gov/images/uploaded/8496_1178901646922_BIO5yrPlan.pdf (accessed March 15, 2008).[9]

Regional Foci

Data issues and collections often have a geographical basis and orientation, thus information users often seek a regional approach to sharing data. A NBII regional focus, or "node," includes local and regional partners who work with a NBII regional manager to help determine the data priorities for that region, and then to develop, acquire, and manage that content. The resulting Web site within the NBII system provides an entry point to that regional data and information, which also becomes accessible to the general NBII user community through the main NBII Web site and overarching tools. Eight regions currently have projects underway, and the strategic plan calls for the implementation of 12 nodes to effectively blanket the country (Fig. 2; Table 1).

Different regional nodes can have different subject and resource foci, depending on their partners' needs. The Pacific Northwest Information Node (PNWIN; http://pnwin.nbii.gov) makes available information about forests, as well as other subjects. The Southern Appalachian Information Node (SAIN; http://sain.nbii.gov) was one of the first nodes to form, and it combines information and resources to improve productivity, resource management, and sustainable development within its region. An example SAIN project includes assisting the Appalachian State University in developing a Southeast Herbaria Network to support the digitization of and improved access to botanical collections. A more recent formation, the Mid-Atlantic Information Node (MAIN; http://main.nbii.gov) provides online access to biodiversity information about the Chesapeake Bay area, as well as expanding into other subjects.

National Themes

Many environmental issues are relevant in a majority of regions. To help research and decision-making on these issues, the NBII provides a layer of national-level coordination by constructing several major thematic information nodes: Bird Conservation, Wildlife Diseases, Invasive Species, and Fisheries and Aquatic Resources. It also manages smaller thematic projects, such as collecting information on Amphibians, Botany, and Pollinators.

Table 1 Regional nodes of the NBII.

Regional node	States
Active nodes	
California	California
Central Southwest/ Gulf Coast	Arkansas, Louisiana, Oklahoma, and Texas
Mid-Atlantic	Delaware, District of Columbia, Maryland, Pennsylvania, Virginia, and West Virginia
Mountain Prairie	Kansas, Montana, Nebraska, North Dakota, South Dakota, and Wyoming
Northeast	Connecticut, Maine, Massachusetts, New Hampshire, New Jersey, New York, Rhode Island, and Vermont
Pacific Basin	Hawaii, Guam, and the island nations of the Pacific
Pacific Northwest	Idaho, Oregon, and Washington
Southern Appalachian	Alabama, Kentucky, Mississippi, and Tennessee
Future nodes	
Alaska	Alaska
Great Lakes	Illinois, Indiana, Iowa, Michigan, Minnesota, Missouri, Ohio, and Wisconsin
Southeast	Florida, Georgia, North Carolina, and South Carolina
Southwest	Arizona, Colorado, Nevada, New Mexico, and Utah

Source: Strategic Plan for the U.S. Geological Survey National Biological Information Infrastructure (NBII) July 2005; National Biological Information Infrastructure: Reston, VA, 2005, http://www.nbii.gov/images/uploaded/8496_1165236262413_NBII_Strategic_Plan.pdf (accessed March 15, 2008).[6]

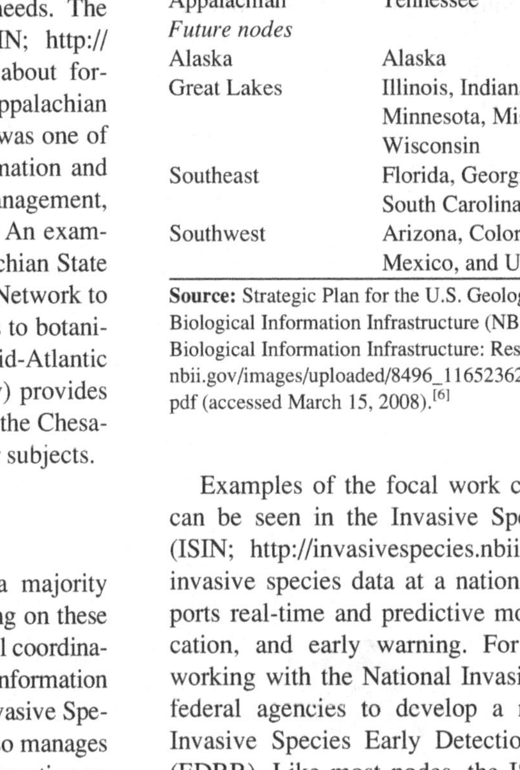

Examples of the focal work conducted within a node can be seen in the Invasive Species Information Node (ISIN; http://invasivespecies.nbii.gov), which integrates invasive species data at a national level and which supports real-time and predictive modeling, species identification, and early warning. For example, the ISIN is working with the National Invasive Species Council and federal agencies to develop a national framework for Invasive Species Early Detection and Rapid Response (EDRR). Like most nodes, the ISIN has major partners; among them in this case are the Nonindigenous Aquatic

Fig. 2 The NBII regional foci, or "nodes."
Source: Strategic Plan for the U.S. Geological Survey National Biological Information Infrastructure (NBII) July 2005; National Biological Information Infrastructure: Reston, VA, 2005, http://www.nbii.gov/images/uploaded/8496_1165236262413_NBII_Strategic_Plan.pdf (accessed March 15, 2008).[6]

Species Project of the USGS Florida Integrated Science Center, and the National Institute of Invasive Species Science at the USGS Fort Collins Science Center. Another example of the NBII's thematic work is the Wildlife Disease Information Node (http://wildlifedisease.nbii.gov), which helps operate the Chronic Wasting Disease Data Clearinghouse and is helping build the National Highly Pathogenic Avian Influenza Early Detection Data System.

National Standards and Technology

The remaining two NBII organizational approaches, Network Standards and Technology, and Knowledge Integration, help provide the means to link to and serve all the information from various partners.

Interlinking data and information depends in part on a common vocabulary, or standard. Scientists use different techniques for research and thus original data differs in the types and scales of measurements. Supplying metadata provides an opportunity to document the resource (e.g., dataset, information product, tool, etc.) with a common vocabulary. This way, researchers know what they are comparing, and thus can implement conversions if necessary. Metadata also adds value by supplying keywords and information about provenance, quality, timeliness, and authority.

As previously mentioned, one of the first projects of the NBII was to create the FGDC Biological Data Profile (http://www.fgdc.gov/standards/projects/FGDC-standards-projects/metadata/biometadata/). Work also continues in support of ITIS and the Vegetation Mapping Classification. Other work in standards includes

- *The Biocomplexity Thesaurus* (http://thesaurus.nbii.gov/)—an online thesaurus of scientifically reviewed biological terms and preferences for use. Begun in 2002, the NBII develops and maintains the thesaurus in partnership with CSA (previously known as Cambridge Scientific Abstracts). It includes over 15,000 terms on subjects such as aquatic sciences and fisheries, life sciences, pollution, social sciences, ecotourism, and, now incoming, fire ecology, and management.
- *The Darwin Core* (http://wiki.tdwg.org/twiki/bin/view/DarwinCore/WebHome)—a derivative of the Dublin Core standard, the Darwin Core deals specifically with natural history museum specimens and other primary species data. In partnership and with support from the NBII, the Biodiversity Information Standards (until recently known as the Taxonomic Databases Working Group; TDWG; http://www.tdwg.org) develops Darwin Core and similar standards.
- *The Geospatial Interoperability Framework* (http://www.nbii.gov/portal/community/Communities/Toolkit/Geospatial_Framework/)—a data strategy to reduce development time for geospatial applications, based on the International Standards Organization (ISO) standards and the Open Geospatial Consortium (OGC) specifications. It is integrated with other core NBII Framework standards and protocols, such as the Universal Description, Discovery and Integration (UDDI) protocol.

The NBII continues to create or adopt, and then implement new standards, such as for ecological datasets, multimedia resources, and observational records. The NBII also is investing in the development of semantic Web technology for biological data through Spire (http://spire.umbc.edu/) and others entities, allowing the linking of common terms and scientific concepts.

In addition to standards, many activities within the NBII require technological support. The CBI, which is also managed by the USGS Biological Informatics Program, provides a significant portion of this technical support. It houses the majority of the servers, supplies the security, provides Web services, researches new bioinformatic techniques, and helps create protocols, tools, and applications. Further, the NBII provides technological support to partner systems, for instance, it houses a mirror of the GBIF's data.

Knowledge Integration

The NBII accesses data and information from a variety of organizations. Its mandate is to compile and, where possible, to facilitate the integration of this data and information in order to support the discovery, comparison, and use by a wide variety of users. The NBII provides information directly to individual users through its Web sites, search engine, and other tools; it also shares information with research institutions and other agencies, with organizations that help compile, integrate, and synthesize information, and with other distributed networks that help feed data from multiple organizations (Table 2; see http://www.nbii.gov/portal/community/Communities/Toolkit/NBII_Partners/ for a complete list). The level of integration depends on the format of the data, customer needs, and the technology on hand.

The objective of NBII knowledge integration activities is to bring together scientifically credible data and information in a manner that not only maintains attribution, provider ownership, and the integrity of the data, but also adds value by applying standards and by providing further, similar data resources. This objective is a challenge in light of the great variability in information and in source organizations. Many suppliers do provide information available in preset, standardized formats, easily served by the NBII through a catalog or other appropriate means. More often, however, information suppliers with different base infrastructures serve the NBII with collections of varying sizes and in different formats, including record-level databases, datasets, maps, images, documents, and

Table 2 Sample NBII data and information partners.

U.S. federal government	U.S. local and state governments	Nonprofits	Universities	Multisector and international
U.S. Fish and Wildlife Service	California Department of Fish and Game	Conservation International	University of California	International Ocean Biographic Information System
U.S. Bureau of Land Management	Colorado Division of Wildlife	Ecological Society of America	City University of New York	FishBase
U.S. Department of Agriculture	Illinois Department of Natural Resources	Natural Science Collections Alliance	Colorado State University	Global Biodiversity Information Facility
USGS Gap Analysis Program	New York City, Borough of Queens	Association of Fish and Wildlife Agencies	Appalachian State University	CBD Clearing-House Mechanism
Smithsonian Institution	Chattanooga-Hamilton County Regional Planning Agency	Bernice Pauahi Bishop Museum	Columbia University, Earth Institute	Eastern Brook Trout Joint Venture
Greater Yellowstone Coordinating Committee	Galveston Bay Estuary Program	Appalachian Trail Conservancy	Boise State University, Raptor Research Center	BirdLife International
U.S. Department of Energy	Wyoming Game and Fish Department	NatureServe	Cornell University	Global Invasive Species Programme

species lists. Thus, the NBII must find and apply multiple, flexible integration methods. Furthermore, the act of integration may reveal gaps in the information, and the NBII may then support initiatives to gather the missing data. Finally, in many cases, the methods to gather or integrate biological information may be difficult to use or nonexistent; thus, the NBII also develops new protocols, data processing programs, and other tools to assist in data integration.

The NBII has multiple knowledge integration activities: the key activities are the cataloging of information sources, data harvesting from multiple servers and indexing them in one location, the hosting of collections, the coordination of experts, and the provision of platforms through which the information can be accessed.

Catalogs and Collections: The identification, prioritization, description, and linking of important data and information sources is the first step in integrating information, and has been a NBII focus for the past several years. The NBII's regional and thematic operations describe and document data resources using the NBII Resource Catalog standard, which aids in searching these resources from any NBII Web site. Other multiagency partnerships contribute to specialized catalogs or data collections that are also served through the NBII's search portal, including

- *The NBII Metadata Clearinghouse* (http://mercury.ornl.gov/nbii)—a program of the NBII and the U.S. Department of Energy's Oak Ridge National Laboratory in Tennessee. The Clearinghouse provides detailed descriptions of thousands of biological data sets.
- *The Natural Resource Monitoring Partnership* (NRMP; http://nrmp.nbii.gov)—provides Web-based tools developed by the NBII for the NRMP. These tools are for sharing natural resource monitoring project locations, and a library of monitoring protocols.
- *The NBII LIFE* (http://life.nbii.gov/; recently known as the NBII Digital Image Library; http://images.nbii.gov)—a growing, searchable collection of images related to nature and the environment. A variety of NBII partners contribute the images and detailed metadata about those images. This library is also setting up harvesting mechanisms with other image libraries that have similar metadata.

Harvesting Partner Sites: The NBII's partners help provide biological data and information such as abstracts, databases, species pages and lists, and maps. The NBII constructs software programs to "crawl" the partner sites, and the partner provides services that help open hidden or blocked information, or to make the process easier. Examples of the information exchanged include species pages from NatureServe, datasets from the Long-Term Ecological Research (LTER) Program, and reports from the UNESCO Man and the Biosphere programme (MAB). The NBII also links to national and international collections networks such as the Mammal Networked Information System, MaNIS (http://manisnet.org/) and HerpNET (http://www.herpnet.org/), a global network of herpetological collections data. Finally, the NBII is partnering with other major informatics initiatives, for example, within the fields of hydrology and geology, to share information.

Web Crawling: The NBII also uses software to crawl public Web sites. A NBII staff member first researches a site, such as the U.S. Fish and Wildlife Service (http://www.fws.gov), and constructs a software program to crawl the site, called a "spider." The spider starts at a designated page, copies it, and then crawls the hyperlinks from that page to the next set of pages, and so on to a depth set by NBII staff. Exception lists are generated for each site to exclude irrelevant information. As the crawler returns Web pages, available metadata is attached, and the pages then are served through the NBII. Crawling has some drawbacks, but the NBII is dedicating staff to refining the process.

Hosting: The NBII provides infrastructure to the data networks of selected partners such as ITIS, the Fire Research and Management Exchange System (http://frames.nbii.gov), and the Terrestrial and Aquatic Gap Analysis Program (GAP; http://gapanalysis.nbii.gov), a national program that integrates data on land cover, species distributions, and land stewardship to determine gaps in the protection of species. The NBII also hosts Web sites or provides other technological support for partners: it helped develop and maintains the U.S. Web site for IABIN, along with the I3N (http://i3n.iabin.net), and the I3N cataloging tool.

Expert Coordination: Within the NBII's regional and thematic activities, as well as within overarching projects, much effort is put into finding and enlisting the experts in a field, one of the best data resources available. The NBII brings together experts in workshops on critical topics and helps maintain expert directories, such as the Taxonomic Resources and Expertise Directory (TRED; http://tred.nbii.gov). The NBII also provides gateways to outside expert databases.

Collaborative Platforms: The NBII provides a password-protected virtual collaboration space, (http://my.nbii.gov), where one can join communities, find project-related documents have discussions, and share information in a dynamic, secure environment. Specific communities have been set up for projects such as the Appalachian Trail Environmental Monitoring Program and the Multistate Aquatic Resources Information Systems.

EXAMPLE OF THE FOUR APPROACHES

A good example of how the NBII applies the four different approaches to making biological information accessible is with the use of species occurrence data, especially museum collection information and observational records. Species occurrence data can be used by land managers, scientists, and policy makers to predict current, past, and future distribution of species; to identify biodiversity hot spots; to predict the impact of road construction; or to help model the impact of climate change. Museums and research institutions have long held historical records of occurrences, but this data has not been readily available over the Internet. Global Biodiversity Information Facility is now providing an online platform for serving such information. Through its regional and thematic projects, the NBII finds collections and catalogs them; it also helps recruit museums to join GBIF and make their museum records available. As one necessary component, GBIF and the NBII assisted and helped support financially the development of the standards needed for data integration, including the Darwin Core, the FGDC Biological Data Profile, and species names from ITIS. Once the records at each of the thousands of museums are in a standard format, GBIF uses transport protocols to query and transfer the information over the Internet. The NBII and GBIF helped support development of these transfer protocols, including the Distributed Generic Information Retrieval (DiGIR) protocol currently in use, and now a protocol combining DiGIR and others, called TAPIR (http://www.tdwg.org/standards). The NBII sponsors two to three workshops a year on the implementation of DiGIR protocols. Finally, the NBII also assists with the development of geospatial applications, such as the Geospatial Interoperability Framework, in order to help provide a common platform for serving the collected information from thousands of providers.

All of these activities extend past the U.S. borders. Through the NBII–GBIF partnership and other partnerships, the NBII provides global access to U.S data and collections, representing them to the international community, but it also brings critical data directly back to the United States that is useful for investigating the impact of invasive species, climate change, and other environmental issues.

CONCLUSION

Knowledge about the biological world is critical to our health and prosperity, and best practices to ensure that information is organized and accessible are vital. Prior best practices concerned providing and storing handwritten copies, as Jefferson instructed Lewis:

> Your observations are to be taken with great pains & accuracy, to be entered distinctly & intelligibly for others, as well as yourself, to comprehend all the elements necessary, with the aid of the usual tables, to fix the latitude and longitude of the places at which they were taken, and are to be rendered to the war office for the purpose of having the calculations made concurrently by proper persons within the US. s[sic]everal copies of these as well as of your other notes should be made at leisure times, & put into the care of the most trust-worthy of your attendants, to guard by multiplying them against the accidental losses to which they will be exposed. A further guard would be that one of these copies be on the paper of the birch, as less liable to injury from damp than common paper.[3]

Today, information can be also stored digitally and made available over the Internet to a broad range of users, thus helping society make informed decisions about the use of our biological resources. The NBII attempts to discover, organize, and add value to information from the molecular level to the ecosystem level, and then disseminate it. To accomplish this task it has developed partnerships with local, state, and federal agencies and well as intergovernmental bodies and private organizations. Because of the interconnectedness of the world's biological resources and the people within it, the NBII mission has come to include the coordination of information at a global scale. In so doing, the NBII has shepherded in a new global information network that has been recognized by distinguished scholarly and public panels as both incredibly successful and valuable.[10–13]

The same government and private study groups, committees, and task forces have also recognized the huge challenges in providing access to our natural resource knowledge base, as well as acknowledging gaps in the knowledge we do have. The information that we now have through the NBII's efforts does not begin to approach the volume and diversity that we need to make informed decisions. The NBII will continue to face daunting challenges in the political, social, and technological spheres. Our demands for food, water, shelter, medicines, and energy require that we develop a much greater understanding of the biological world. Greater understanding can only be built on data and information that have been gathered over the centuries and are still being gathered. We can hope that society has the will and foresight to support the NBII to the degree necessary to accomplish this massive undertaking, since there is no other organization in the United States with the mandate and experience to address the breadth of the issue.

ACKNOWLEDGMENTS

Sincere thanks to Kate Kase, NBII Program Manager, Anne Frondorf, former NBII Program Manager, and Ron Sepic, NBII Information Liaison, for providing information upon request, and to Vicky Cooper, NBII Graphic Designer, for updating the graphics.

REFERENCES

1. National Research Council (NRC), *A Biological Survey for the Nation*, National Academy Press: Washington, DC, 1993; ISBN: 0309049849. Available at http://www.nap.edu/html/bio/ (accessed March 3, 2008).
2. President's Committee of Advisors, Science and Technology (PCAST), *Panel on Biodiversity and Ecosystems. Teaming with Life: Investing in Science to Understand and Use America's Living Capital*; Office of Science and Technology Policy: Washington, DC, 1998.
3. Jefferson, T. Thomas Jefferson's instructions to Meriwether Lewis June 20, 1803. In *Thomas Jefferson and Early Western Explorers*; Transcribed and Edited by Gerard W. Gawalt, Manuscript Division, Library of Congress. (Available Library of Congress, American Memory Collection).
4. Office of the President, Executive Order 12906, Coordinating geographic data acquisition and access: The national spatial data infrastructure. Fed. Reg. **1994**, *59*(71), 17671–17674. Washington, DC, 4. Available at http://www.archives.gov/federal-register/executive-orders/pdf/12906.pdf (accessed March 15, 2008).
5. NBII Formally Joins the Conservation Commons, NBII access: Newsletter of the national biological information infrastructure. Summer **2007**, *10*(3).
6. *Strategic Plan for the U.S. Geological Survey National Biological Information Infrastructure (NBII) July 2005*; National Biological Information Infrastructure: Reston, VA, 2005. Available at http://www.nbii.gov/images/uploaded/8496_1165236262413_NBII_Strategic_Plan.pdf (accessed March 15, 2008).
7. United States Government Accountability Office. *Environmental information: Status of federal data programs that support ecological indicators* (*GAI-05-376*), Report to Congressional Requesters. September 2005. Available at http://www.gao.gov/new.items/d05376.pdf.
8. Department of the Interior. *DOI budget year 2005 IT investment overview*, USGS-5–USGS-10. Available at http://www.doi.gov/foia/DOI%202005%20IT/Capital%20Asset%20Plan%20Summaries/DOI%20BUDGET%20YEAR%202005%20IT.2.pdf.
9. Ruggerio, M.; Marcia McNiff, M.; Olson, A.; Wheeler, B. *Strategic Plan for the U.S. Geological Survey Biological Informatics Program: 2005–2009*; U.S. Geological Survey, Biological Resources Discipline, 2005; 1–22. Available at http://www.nbii.gov/images/uploaded/8496_1178901646922_BIO5yrPlan.pdf (accessed March 15, 2008).
10. My.NBII.Gov Wins Government Solutions Award, NBII access: Newsletter of the National Biological Information Infrastructure. Summer **2002**, *5*(3).
11. ITIS and TRED Win Links2Go Taxonomy Awards, NBII access: Newsletter of the National Biological Information Infrastructure. Fall **2000**, *3*(4).
12. SAIN Wins ESRI Award, NBII access: Newsletter of the National Biological Information Infrastructure. Fall **2002**, *5*(4).
13. Three USGS Biologists Honored by State Department, NBII access: Newsletter of the National Biological Information Infrastructure. Fall **2004**, *7*(4).

BIBLIOGRAPHY

1. NBII publications page, http://publications.nbii.gov.

National Historical Publications and Records Commission (NHPRC)

Keith Donohue
National Historical Publications and Records Commission, Washington, District of Columbia, U.S.A.

Abstract
The National Historical Publications and Records Commission (NHPRC) is the grantmaking arm of the National Archives and Records Administration, supplying financial support for projects that preserve and provide access to historical records of national significance housed in collections across the country. Each year, the NHPRC awards grants, based on its annual appropriations, to state and local government archives, nongovernmental archives, historical documentary editing projects, and other nonprofit organizations. It currently runs 10 grant or subvention programs and one fellow program. Since 1964, the NHPRC has awarded nearly $175 million to some 4400 projects in all 50 states, the District of Columbia, and other special jurisdictions. As part of the National Archives, the Commission is chaired by the Archivist of the United States and governed by a 15-person advisory board, unique among Federal agencies since it includes appointees and representatives of all three branches of government—the Executive, Legislative, and Judiciary.

DOCUMENTING DEMOCRACY: THE NATIONAL HISTORICAL PUBLICATIONS AND RECORDS COMMISSION

The National Historical Publications and Records Commission (NHPRC) is the grantmaking arm of the National Archives and Records Administration, supplying financial support for projects that preserve and provide access to historical records of national significance housed in collections across the country. Each year, the NHPRC awards grants, based on its annual appropriations, to state and local government archives, nongovernmental archives, historical documentary editing projects, and other nonprofit organizations.

The National Archives serves American democracy by safeguarding and preserving the records of our Federal Government, ensuring that the people can discover, use, and learn from this documentary heritage. Continuing access to the essential documentation of the rights of American citizens and the actions of their government helps support democracy, promote civic education, and facilitate historical understanding of our national experience.

As part of the National Archives, the Commission is chaired by the Archivist of the United States. A 15-person advisory board serves as Commissioners, and they are charged with reviewing all of the applications and recommending projects to the Archivist which projects to fund. Unique among Federal agencies, the Commission is represented by all three branches—the Executive, Legislative, and Judiciary, as its members include two Presidential appointees and representatives from the Department of State and the Department of Defense; a member from each house of Congress and a representative from the Library of Congress; and a representative appointed by the U.S. Supreme Court. Rounding out the advisory body are representatives from the professional societies of archivists, historians, documentary editors, and records administrators. An Executive Director, appointed by the Archivist, reports to the advisory board and manages a small administrative staff at the NHPRC offices in the National Archives headquarters in Washington, D.C.

Since 1964, the NHPRC has awarded nearly $175 million to some 4400 projects in all 50 states, the District of Columbia, and other special jurisdictions. From the papers of America's Founding Era to contemporary electronic records, the NHPRC documents democracy, linking the records of the Federal Government with historical materials across the country. It awards grants through the following funding categories:

- *State and National Archival Partnership Grants* to build a national archival network by strengthening archives and historical records programs in each of the states. *Only state government agencies, or their designated fiscal agents, are eligible to apply.*
- *Digitizing Historical Records* to digitize nationally significant historical records collections and make the digital versions freely available on the Internet.
- *Electronic Records Projects* to support efforts that will lead to sustainable electronic records archives that preserve digital records with enduring historical value.

Encyclopedia of Library and Information Sciences, Fourth Edition DOI: 10.1081/E-ELIS4-120044827

- *Professional Development Grants for Archives and Historical Publishing* to improve the training and education of professionals in the archival and historical publishing communities.
- *Strategies and Tools for Archives and Historical Publishing Projects* to develop new strategies and tools that can improve the preservation, public discovery, or use of historical records.
- *Archives—Basic Projects* to reveal "hidden collections" in archives by processing materials in backlogs.
- *Archives—Detailed Processing Projects* to conduct detailed processing and preservation of collections of national significance.
- *Publishing Historical Records* to publish historical records of national significance.
- *Publishing Historical Records-Founding Era* to publish the records of the Founding Era of the United States. *Open only to the previously funded projects dedicated to publishing the papers of John Adams, Benjamin Franklin, Thomas Jefferson, James Madison, George Washington, and records that document the Ratification of the Constitution and the First Federal Congress.*
- *Publication Subventions* to enable nonprofit presses to publish volumes of historical documentary editions. *Open only to assist publication of NHPRC-sponsored or -endorsed editions.*
- *Historical Editing Fellowships* to allow publications projects to host Historical Documentary Editing Fellowships. *Open only to NHPRC-sponsored or -endorsed publishing projects.*

A Brief History

Imagine a national archive double the size and scope of the National Archives. According to the 2004 National Archives and Records Administration Plan, traditional archival holdings total 2.9 million feet. Extrapolating data from earlier surveys, we estimate that state archives alone hold about 2.7 million feet. The mental jump is easy if you count state archives and records repositories which house the documentary heritage of governments from Alaska to Florida. This American archives increases exponentially when the hundreds of city and local government archives are added to the mass. Imagine the American archives connected to a Web of the many other private institutions, nongovernmental organizations, and community associations, home to billions of documents, images, recordings, and other clusters of information. *Where History Begins*, a 1998 report by the Council of State Archivists, estimated nongovernmental repositories held 4 million cubic feet. This *archives of archives* runs like a great river through our national consciousness: official government records at all levels providing the essential evidence for documenting our political democracy, and billions of other records and papers complementing our understanding of our diverse history and culture.

En masse, the archives defeat every hope of completion. Archivists cannot save it fast enough; researchers cannot ever reach the bottom. Order is provisional, always. Selecting what to save, what to discard, and how to organize and make public the records embedded in the great American archives is the central challenge to all those engaged in documenting democracy.

The NHPRC is a mechanism within the National Archives and Records Administration for reaching out to and connecting thousands of archives, and records repositories across the country dedicated to preserving and publishing the primary sources of the American story in its many forms. For the past 45 years, the Commission has awarded grants to help strengthen the network of state government and local archives and to make public documentary materials in possession of the Government and those in private hands.

"National archives have a natural history of their own." So wrote J. Franklin Jameson and the Assistant Committee on the Documentary Historical Publications of the United States Government to the Committee on Department Methods in its 1908 report. Their report laid out the case for a Federal program in conjunction with a National Archives, which would publish the documentary materials, whether issued by the Federal Government or not, that would "meet more fully the needs of the Government, of historians, of the public, and be a source of credit to the nation." Commonly known as the Keep Commission, after its chairman, Charles H. Keep, the Committee on Department Methods was a panel appointed by President Theodore Roosevelt to review the efficiency of operations of the Federal Government. The Assistant Committee was chaired by historian Worthington C. Ford, and had as its members: Charles Francis Adams, Charles M. Andrews, William A. Dunning, Albert Bushnell Hart, Andrew C. McLaughlin, Alfred T. Mahan, Frederick J. Turner, and its Secretary, J. Franklin Jameson. The Assistant Committee's full report can be found in *John Franklin Jameson and the Development of Humanistic Scholarship in America*, Vol. 3, The University of Georgia Press: Athens, Georgia (2001), pp. 56–71.

Jameson and his fellow historians had been gently twisting the government's arm for some time. One of the first tasks undertaken by the American Historical Association after its founding in 1884 focused on the need for a national archival system, and as early as 1891, calls went out for a commission empowered to publish the national record. The natural history of the archives and a national publishing program evolved slowly. Fifty years after the call, the answer finally came with the establishment of the National Archives and the National Historical Publications Commission.

As envisioned by Jameson, the national program would support publishing of two classes of documentary materials:

> The one class consists of lists, inventories, indexes, and calendars in the exact or restricted sense of that term, which are intended to serve the officials and the public as finding-lists or guides to the materials kept in the official repository. . . . The other is that of publications which consist of documents printed at full length, such as the Journal of the Continental Congress, the Official Records of the War of the Rebellion, the old American State Papers, or almost any other of the historical publications of the American government. It is submitted that the main question with respect to such a plan is, What collections of material hitherto unprinted are most needed in order that the history of this country may be elucidated to its citizens?
>
> —MEMORANDUM respecting the organization and administration of the proposed National Archives, by J.F. Jameson, Director of the Department of Historical Research in the Carnegie Institute of Washington, November 30, 1927. The full memorandum can be found in *John Franklin Jameson and the Development of Humanistic Scholarship in America*, pp. 257–270.

The old-fashioned elegance of Jameson's question notwithstanding, the sentiment lies beneath the mission of the NHPRC's ongoing work as the grantmaking affiliate of the National Archives and Records Administration.

The National Archives and the National Historical Publications Commission (NHPC) were born on the same day in 1934 after about 50 years of gestation. The idea, put simply, was for the Archives to be the steward of the national record and the Commission to select, publish, and tell the story of eminent and important figures from that national record and, importantly, from the archives and records not under the control of the Federal Government, including local and state government, colleges and universities, other nongovernmental organizations, and individuals. Implicit in the idea of the Commission is that the papers of Thomas Jefferson, to take one example, are part of America's documentary heritage, belonging to all of the people, no matter who owned the particular original documents.

The Commission itself met sporadically during the Great Depression, through the war years, and afterward. In 1950, however, a chance encounter took place in The White House that proved catalytic. Impressed by Volume 1 of *The Papers of Thomas Jefferson* presented to him by Julian Boyd and the Princeton University Press, President Harry Truman proposed a comprehensive program for the publication of the public and private writings of persons who have contributed greatly to the development of the United States. A spirited debate over the proposal ensued among historians, and the Commission worked through 1952 to expand and refine its scope.

Early in 1954, a final report to President Eisenhower, *A National Program for the Publication of Historical Documents*, recommended 361 individuals as worthy of consideration for a national publications program, and it singled out 112 persons, including the five Founding Fathers, for immediate attention. Together with the Jefferson papers, these series became the core of the NHPC's editions program. The report also recommended selective editions for 107 individuals, and three series called for the Federal Government, rather than a private publisher, to produce the documentary editions on the Constitution and the First Federal Congress.

An additional report to President Kennedy (*Report to the President containing a proposal by the National Historical Publications Commission to meet existing and anticipated needs over the next ten years under a National Program for the collection, preservation, and publication, or dissemination by other means of the documentary sources of American History*, Washington, D.C.: Government Printing Office, 1963) laid the groundwork for approaching Congress for appropriations, and in 1964, the Commission was funded for a national grants program: the Public Law 88–383, signed by President Lyndon Johnson on July 29, 1964. By November of that year, the NHPC awarded its first grants—a total of $350,000—for historical documentary editions.

Another decade slipped by, and the National Archives changed into the National Archives and Records Service (as part of the U.S. General Services Administration. NARS became the National Archives and Records Administration when the agency gained independent status in April, 1985) and NHPC became the NHPRC, acknowledging its responsibility for preservation of original records as well as publishing through grants and other assistance. With the increased responsibility for "records," NHPRC's budget shot up to $2.5 million in Fiscal Year 1975, and the Commission recognized that to effectively carry out its preservation mission, it had to involve the states. The Commission mandated and began working with State Historical Records Advisory Boards for planning and grant review, then for implementation of those plans, actual archival strategies, and operations, and finally for regrants to local archives and records centers within the states. The 1998 reauthorization of the NHPRC made explicit the *raison* for the NHPRC, amending the language of the enabling legislation to include the Commission's training and education programs, and its partnership with the states:

> Section 4, Duties and Functions (a) The Commission shall make plans, estimates, and recommendations for historical works and collections of sources it considers appropriate for preserving, publishing or otherwise recording at the public expense. The Chairman of the Commission shall transmit to the President and the Congress from time to time, and at last biennially, the plans, estimates, and recommendations developed and approved by the Commission. (b) The Commission shall cooperate with, assist

and encourage appropriate Federal, State, and local agencies and nongovernmental institutions, societies, and individuals in collecting and preserving and, when it considers desirable, in editing and publishing papers of outstanding citizens of the United States, and other documents as may be important for an understanding and appreciation of the history of the United States. (c) The Commission may conduct institutes, training and educational programs, and recommend candidates for fellowships related to the activities of the Commission and may disseminate information about documentary sources through guides, directories, and other technical publications. (d) The Commission may recommend the expenditure of appropriated or donated funds for the collecting, describing, preserving, compiling and publishing (including microfilming and other forms of reproduction) of documentary sources significant to the history of the United States and for the activities described in subsection (c). (e) The Archivist of the United States may, within the limits of available appropriated and donated funds, make grants to State and local agencies and to nonprofit organizations, institutions, and individuals for those activities in subsection (d) after considering the advice and recommendations of the Commission.

The Impact of NHPRC Grants

NHPRC awards have helped identify, preserve, and make public the original papers and documents of the Founding Fathers—George Washington, John Adams and Family, Thomas Jefferson, Alexander Hamilton, James Madison, and Benjamin Franklin. Other multivolume editions trace the history of the first Congress, the first Supreme Court, and Ratification of the Constitution. And two hundred or so other Americans—rebels and mavericks, explorers and fighters for justice and equal rights, Presidents and pioneers—have had their legacy preserved and published through printed volumes that number in the hundreds, reels of microfilm that stretch into thousands of feet, and new Web sites on the Internet. Among the noteworthy figures are Martin Luther King, Jr., the expeditions of Lewis and Clark, Abraham Lincoln, Thomas Edison, and many more. These papers projects provide easy access to our documentary heritage—but these are not endings in and of themselves.

Rather, the publishing function of NHPRC is only the beginning, and the effect of its grants ripple out to new interpretative works—dozens of biographies, histories, textbooks, and reconsiderations. Drawing on the works of the 27-volume edition of *The Papers of Alexander Hamilton*, historian Ron Chernow recently published a new monumental biography that may restore Hamilton's reputation and place in American history. Virtually every new American history or historical biography has tapped into the rich vein of source materials uncovered through NHPRC-supported projects.

Plays based upon the words of slaves and the newly emancipated have emerged from the primary sources uncovered through NHPRC support, along with documentary films and television programs—from *The Civil War* to *Emma Goldman*. New curricula have been created at history classes in high schools, colleges, and universities, and new editions of textbooks reflect what educators have learned through close examination of these published primary sources. On the Internet, users can read the original documents of Eleanor Roosevelt, listen to Kennedy White House tapes from the Cuban Missile Crisis, or read a "mini-edition" of the *Papers of Frederick Douglass*. And these new stories have the ripple effect of deepening and broadening people's understanding of their own history and the individual's place in the American story.

To grasp the impact of the program, take the example of the Freedom History Project, a highly selective edition of documents pertaining to black American life in the years between the beginning of the Civil War and the advent of Reconstruction. The Freedom History Project has kept a cumulative tabulation of how people are using its publications. For example, the papers have been cited in 23 reference works, 15 documentary editions, 130 monographs, 212 scholarly articles and essays, and 68 college-level textbooks and anthologies. At least 152 college courses have made use of the work, as well as 41 teacher workshops, 8 publications for elementary and middle school teachers, 3 CD-ROMs, 9 books for young readers, 24 books for popular audiences, 9 exhibits, 6 films, 11 television programs—including Ken Burns's Civil War series, 16 radio programs, 80 stage productions, and 176 Web sites. One of the editors of the project, Steven Hahn, also wrote *A Nation Under Our Feet: Black Political Struggles in the Rural South from Slavery to the Great Migration* (The Belknap Press of Harvard University Press) which received the 2004 Pulitzer Prize for History. Virtually every scholar of American history has benefited, at one time or another, from works preserved and published through the NHPRC. And even all of these related "products" produced out of the primary sources are still means to an end: to give citizens a better understanding of our nation.

Understanding of our democracy, history, and culture, however, is not limited to the study of great men and women, nor is the American story complete without broad access to the documentary heritage of our states and territories, our great cities and towns, and the records held in smaller repositories across the nation. The NHPRC began to fund the underlying archival work of identification and preservation of documents and records in 1974 through grants to local archival institutions. Coupled with the direct grants to state archives and historical repositories for records preservation and access, the accumulative impact has been to strengthen and develop a national archival system.

Grants through this program have helped preserve and make accessible documents and records throughout the country—from the records of the Rhode Island towns' meetings to ratify the U.S. Constitution to the oral histories of the Crow tribe in Montana. NHPRC helped the Boston Schools Desegregation-Era Records Project find and preserve records in danger of being lost in a flooded basement, and the Cook County (IL) Local Records Commission discover Chicago's original record of the city council's vote for incorporation from September 1833, long thought destroyed by the Great Chicago Fire of 1871. Through finding aids and database construction, individual users are now able to go online and search through photographs of Colorado's railroads at photoswest.org, daguerreotypes from Harvard University, the whaling industry at the Nantucket Historical Society, and the University of Pittsburgh's Archives of Industrial Society. Genealogists are able to drill down into the records of pioneers and early settlers to Utah. Environmentalists can dig through the archives of the Sierra Club at the University of California's Bancroft Library. Researchers and historians can visit scores of historical societies, libraries, universities, archives, and state and local governments, and their chances of finding the evidence they seek have been greatly improved through NHPRC grants. A complete list of grants from 1976 onward can be found on the NARA Web site at http://www.archives.gov/grants/funded_endorsed_projects/states_and_territories/.

Just as the documentary editions and records program grants produce results beyond their own intrinsic worth, the NHPRC also has invested in other ways to strengthen the archival infrastructure. Since 1967, the Commission has awarded fellowships in documentary editing, and for the past 38 years has sponsored a two-week summer seminar for editors known informally as "Camp Edit," most recently at the University of Wisconsin. In 2008, the Commission also established its Archives Leadership Institute, also at the University of Wisconsin, to provide leadership training to the next generation of archivists and records managers.

Through grants to national professional associations, such as the Society of American Archivists, the National Association of Government Archives and Records Administrators, the Association for Documentary Editing, and others new archival tools and techniques have developed—from basic handbooks for archivists to greater dissemination of sophisticated electronic descriptive tools and standards, such as MARC and Encoded Archival Description. In the wake of the devastating hurricanes Katrina and Rita, the NHPRC entered into a groundbreaking partnership with the Council of State Archivists (CoSA) to provide disaster preparedness training for archives and records centers, and through grant support it helped in the recovery efforts in Alabama, Texas, and Louisiana. Out of this partnership and the longstanding partnership with CoSA, new efforts are underway to establish a Partnership for America's Historical Records that would provide bloc grants to the states, and in 2008, the NHPRC began a new program to allow the states—through their historical records advisory boards—to undertake new programmatic initiatives and to plan for a true national archival network.

The NHPRC was the first Federal agency to fund research and development efforts to preserve electronic records—records either "born" digital or digitized—beginning in the late 1980s and continuing through this day at projects such as the San Diego Supercomputer Center's Distributed Custodial Preservation (DCP) Center for electronic records. The DCP Center will develop a cost model for providing preservation services for electronic records by developing the iRODS (integrate Rule-Oriented Data System, http://www.irods.org) to meet the needs of state archives and other repositories. More recent efforts in digitization are helping archives digitize entire collections, helping preserve records ranging from the work of natural conservation pioneer Aldo Leopold to an exploratory effort to bring online the works of the Founding Fathers.

Results of all this Federal funding can be measured by finding aids or cubic feet of records been saved, research requests of visitors through the doors or Web sites of thousands of repositories. In the greater sophistication the archival field brings to its task of preserving and publishing. In the sheer number of hidden collections now exposed and neglected records uncovered in a courtroom basement or warehouse attic. But the data say what data everywhere says. These measures are not the end. The real measure is in the connection made between the National Archives and Records Administration, the national archival system, and the millions of American citizens who use and benefit from the record of our democratic experiment.

The NHPRC is a bridge to and from the National Archives and the thousands of repositories where the essential evidence is channeled and stored. NHPRC provides funding and leadership. It is a signal commitment from the Federal Government to the local historian in Peralta, New Mexico, to the graduate student in Knoxville, Tennessee, to the genealogist in Juneau, Alaska, to readers, searchers, and explorers of our democracy, history, and culture wherever they may be.

National Libraries

Ian McGowan
Former Librarian, National Library of Scotland, Edinburgh, U.K.

Abstract
The entry describes the various attempts that have been made to define the role and functions of national libraries. The historical background is reviewed, beginning with the royal libraries of Europe, and examining the growth in the number of national libraries in nineteenth-century Latin America and in the postcolonial world of the twentieth century, leading to the most recent wave of national library creation following the dissolution of the Soviet Union. The main collaborative organizations of national libraries are described and the prospects for national libraries in the changing circumstances of the digital age are considered.

INTRODUCTION

Any consideration of national libraries should begin with the definition of what a national library is and what it does. Since every national library is distinctive, if not unique, in its historical origins, development, functions and position within a country's library system, it is not surprising that in the past a simple definition has proved elusive. The evolution of these attempts at a definition is traced, from the earliest, mainly under the auspices of UNESCO, to the more recent approaches that tend to focus on roles rather than functions.

A brief historical overview of national libraries and their services is provided, grouping them into the successive waves by which they appeared, from the early royal libraries of Europe to the new national libraries of the post-Soviet world. This is followed by a more detailed look at the complex and varied evolution of a few notable examples. Since the 1960s there has been significant growth in the main cooperative organizations that national libraries have created in order to pursue collaborative projects and these organizations are described, together with the activities that they have made possible.

Finally, the prospects for national libraries in the digital age are considered, including the threats that are posed by the alternative providers of the information previously only accessible in the large collections of national and research libraries, and the opportunities that exist for extending national libraries' reach, for example through Web-based services.

WHAT IS A NATIONAL LIBRARY?

The question of definition is one that has exercised many writers on national libraries. Because these libraries can differ dramatically in size and function, their nature is not subject to a straightforward, and short, definition. In the well-known comparison suggested by one of the most prolific and respected of thinkers about national libraries, Maurice Line, "national libraries are in fact rather like dogs: dogs also exhibit an enormous variety, but we somehow recognize them all as dogs [. . .] Anything that is said about national libraries (or dogs) is almost certain not to apply to one or another specimen. Just about the only thing they (dogs and national libraries) have in common is that they all have very hearty appetites."[1]

With the notable exception of the work of Esdaile,[2] the literature on national libraries before the mid-twentieth century is sparse, authors perhaps assuming that their nature was self-evident. However, stimulated by a series of seminars sponsored by UNESCO in the 1950s and 1960s, the discussion about national libraries, what functions they should have and what role they should play in a country's overall provision of library services, became more intense and systematic. In 1966, K. W. Humphreys summarized the various activities of national libraries and divided them into three categories—essential, desirable, and inessential.[3] The essential functions included the holding of an outstanding collection of the nation's literature, the receipt of publications by legal deposit, wide coverage of the scholarly literature of other countries, the publication of the national bibliography, operating as the national bibliographical information center, the publication of catalogs, and the creation of exhibitions. The desirable functions were seen as the organization of interlibrary lending, coordination of the nation's manuscript and archive activities, and research on library techniques. Other activities, described as "functions of the national library service which are not necessary functions of the national library" were the international exchange service, the distribution of duplicates, the provision of books for the blind, professional training, and advice and assistance to other libraries on library techniques.

Encyclopedia of Library and Information Sciences, Fourth Edition DOI: 10.1081/E-ELIS4-120044742

Another approach to the classification of national libraries is exemplified by Burston's analysis by type.[4] This identifies institutions such as "cultural national libraries"—those libraries providing services to major administrative regions, sometimes formerly independent, of federal states. "Dual-purpose libraries" include "national-academic libraries" and "national-public libraries," which combine their national responsibilities with services aimed at specific groups, as well as "national-parliamentary libraries," such as the Library of Congress in the United States and the National Diet Library of Japan, which not only serve the country's legislature but also operate as de facto national libraries. The growth of national subject libraries was seen as a recognition of the fact that no one library could hope to achieve complete coverage of global publishing output, but this might still be feasible in a particular subject area, especially in scientific and technical fields, for example those covered by the National Library of Medicine and the National Agricultural Library in the United States.

Sylvestre's *Guidelines for National Libraries*,[5] prepared and published under the auspices of UNESCO's General Information Programme, advanced the definition of a national library by describing the functions "on which there exists a very large measure of agreement." According to these *Guidelines*, the fundamental task of the national library is to acquire, preserve, and make accessible the publications of the country, and legal deposit legislation is seen as the most effective means to make this collection of the nation's literature as comprehensive as possible. The national library should also acquire foreign literature, although Sylvestre recognizes the practical and financial limitations to this aspect of collection building, and suggests that in some instances the national library might be best suited to promoting and monitoring a national acquisitions plan, aimed at the avoidance of duplication of effort by other collecting institutions, rather than seeking to acquire foreign material widely itself. The collection of manuscripts of national significance, other than public records, should also be given high priority. The national library should normally contain a country's national bibliographic agency, responsible for compiling the current and retrospective national bibliographies. The national library's public services should aim to complement, rather than duplicate, those offered by the nation's other libraries, and should be supported by adequate reading rooms, reprographic facilities, current catalogs, professional advice, and permanent and special exhibitions. Sylvestre places more weight than earlier writers about national library functions on the need for programs to ensure the preservation of library collections, including then novel techniques such as digitization, and recognizes the conflict inherent in satisfying the needs of present researchers while safeguarding collections for future generations. The *Guidelines* suggest that national libraries need to seek public support through consultation with their users, and engage in research related to the improvement of services. They should encourage the development of nationwide library networks, using the best technology currently available, but making sure that their services are accessible to libraries at various levels of technological development. The national library should act as the clearing house for the international exchange of publications and participate in international library programs, regional and worldwide. Sylvestre suggests that national libraries should preferably be separate organizations with a clear mandate to provide nationwide services, but when they are attached to another institution, such as a university, the services to that parent institution should not have a detrimental effect on national services. Whether responsibility for national library services lies with a single institution or is distributed between two or more institutions, the national library should be the lead body for promoting cooperation among the country's libraries.

Line's *National Library and Information Needs*[6] is described by the author as complementary to Sylvestre's *Guidelines*, in that it considers national libraries from the point of view of national information needs, rather than from national libraries' existing practice. In this analysis, Line identifies the paradox that developed countries are most likely to be able to afford and already have a national library, but their need for a national library is less than that of the developing countries, who may find it more difficult to justify in economic terms. The sequence of documents on national libraries published by UNESCO was continued by Cornish,[7] who discusses the various functions that a national library might reasonably be expected to exercise and the impact of new information technology on the way a national library should carry out those functions. He acknowledges the difficulty of defining a national library, and concludes that there are only three characteristics that most have in common: they are funded mainly from the public purse, they are open to the public, and they act as the major archive of printed material produced within the country concerned. *Guidelines for Legislation for National Library Services*,[8] designed to be of particular use to developing countries without a satisfactory legislative basis for the national library, proposes an updated definition that encompasses both the "heritage" and "infrastructure" responsibilities that a modern national library should embrace:

> National library: an institution, primarily funded (directly or indirectly) by the state, which is responsible for collecting, bibliographically recording, preserving and making available the documentary heritage (primarily published materials of all types) emanating from or relating to its country; and which furthers the effective and efficient functioning of the country's libraries through the management of nationally significant collections, the provision of infrastructure, the coordination of activities in the country's library and information system, international

liaison, and the exercise of leadership. These responsibilities are formally recognised, usually in law.

Reexamining the position of national libraries in the digital environment of the twenty-first century, Brindley suggests a definition based on roles rather than functions: support for research, preserving the cultural heritage and providing a locus for national cultural identity, support for the knowledge economy, support for education and lifelong learning, support for community development, support for citizens, and leadership for the library system.[9]

It can be seen from these evolving definitions that many activities can reasonably, but not necessarily, form part of what the national library does. In addition to the commonly encountered tasks of collection building and management, the national library may offer services to a specific target audience, such as the scientific, business, and industrial communities, or develop cultural programs for the wider public—a "Centre for the Book," musical performance, lectures, exhibitions. It may maintain the agencies assigning International Standard Book Numbers (ISBNs) and International Standard Serial Numbers (ISSNs), promote research and development in areas relevant to library and information services, and manage information and document supply networks.

The legislative position of national libraries exhibits as much variety as the work they perform. Typically they are answerable to a ministry with responsibility either for education or for culture and the arts, although there are many variations to this pattern. A number of national libraries have a direct link to the office of the head of the government, and this arrangement can be of particular benefit to the institution. It is not uncommon for a national library to have a representative, nonexecutive board providing advice and guidance, and in some cases direct managerial control.

HISTORY AND DEVELOPMENT OF NATIONAL LIBRARIES

Europe

The earliest form of national library, that of a library founded on the collections of royal and aristocratic personages, expanding through the acquisition of collections from a variety of sources, taking on the responsibilities of legal deposit and a range of services to a wider public, can be seen in many of the national libraries of Europe. The Austrian National Library, for example, which was established in 1920, can be seen as heir to the library of the Holy Roman Empire and the Hapsburg Imperial Court Library (Fig. 1). Some libraries retain their royal identity, for example Sweden's Kungliga biblioteket, the Bibliothèque royale de Belgique, Denmark's Kongelige Bibliotek, and the Koninklijke Bibliotheek of the Netherlands. Others have made their "national" role explicit, for example Spain's Biblioteca Real, which assumed the title Biblioteca Nacional as early as 1836.

Not all European national libraries have their origin in royal libraries. Learned and patriotic societies are another historical starting point: The National Library of Ireland was founded in 1877 on the basis of the collections of the Royal Dublin Society; The Slovak National Library grew from the national cultural organization Matica slovenská. Hungary's National Széchényi Library honors in its name the donor of its first collection, Count Ferenc Széchényi (1754–1820), who saw the establishment of a national library as the natural accompaniment to a national academy of sciences, and until 1949 the Library operated within the framework of the National Museum. Other national libraries had affiliations with private organizations and individuals: the National Library of Scotland

Fig. 1 The Austrian National Library, Heldenplatz.
Source: Photograph: Austrian National Library.

was founded, with a substantial private endowment for running costs, on the basis of a gift to the nation of its collections by the Faculty of Advocates, a private legal association. The National Library of Portugal illustrates the link that sometimes existed between early forms of legal deposit and the control and censorship of publications. The Library can date its origin to the creation of the Mesa Censória in 1768, which examined works submitted for publication and received a copy of each work that was approved for publication and printed. Italy has libraries called Biblioteca Nazionale Centrale in both Florence and Rome. The newer institution in Rome, founded in 1876, reflected the desire to furnish the new capital of a united Italy with a symbol of the national culture. National responsibilities continue to be divided between the two libraries, although both collect material of national interest. Florence, for example, houses the national bibliographic agency, while Rome maintains the National Centre for Manuscripts.

In some instances the functions of a university library have been combined with national responsibilities: in the case of the National Library of Finland and the National Library of Norway, for example, it is only in recent years that they have separated organizationally from the universities of Helsinki and Oslo. The National Library of the Czech Republic, housed in the famous complex of buildings known as the Klementinum, was born out of the University Library of Prague, which received a donation of books from the Emperor Charles IV in 1366. In 1769 the library was open to the public and later in the century was named "Public and University Library." In 1935, in the period of the Czechoslovak Republic, it became the National and University Library, and has been known as the National Library since 1990.

In all these cases, however varied, the concept of nationhood is obviously a vital factor in the libraries' creation. The National Library of Bulgaria, for example, is the oldest cultural institution in the country, dating from 1878, shortly after the country gained its independence from the Ottoman Empire. In 1747 the public library which was to be the forerunner of the National Library of Poland was founded in Warsaw by the brothers Józef Załuski, Bishop of Kiev, and Andrzej Załuski, Bishop of Cracow. By the 1780s the library was placed under the control of the Commission for National Education and had received the right of legal deposit. After the partition of Poland in 1795, the library's collections were moved to St. Petersburg. It proved possible to recover some of this material after the Russian Revolution and the end of hostilities between Russia and the independent Polish Republic, but much had been lost and therefore could not be returned to the new National Library of Poland, established in 1928. After the Nazi assault on Poland, many of the National Library's collections were destroyed, either at the time of the invasion or after the Warsaw Uprising of 1944, as part of the attempt to obliterate all manifestations of Polish culture. Unfortunately such attacks on national cultural identity are not just a matter of history, as the destruction of the National Library in Sarajevo in 1992 sadly demonstrated.

Latin America

The rise of the national library as an explicit statement of national identity is linked, in particular, to the emergence of newly independent states in Latin America at the beginning of the nineteenth century. These new nations naturally wanted to ensure that their history and literature was recorded and retained and also to demonstrate their independent status through the symbols of statehood. In some instances, the new national libraries were created on the basis of existing institutions. The National Library of Colombia, for example, had its origins in the Real Biblioteca Pública del Nuevo Reino de Granada, which opened to the public as early as 1773; the National Library of Ecuador similarly originated in the Biblioteca Pública founded in 1792. The National Library of the Republic of Argentina traces its roots to the creation of the Biblioteca Pública de Buenos Aires after the Revolution of 1810. Others, such as the National Library of Peru, owed their existence to the country's proclamation of its independence—its governor, José de San Martín, issuing the ordinance establishing the national library only a matter of weeks after proclaiming Peru independent in 1821, and also donating his own collection of books to the library. The foundation of the National Library of Chile in 1813 made it one of the first state institutions created after Chile's declaration of independence in 1810, although its core collection was the existing colonial library of the Jesuits. The National Library of Brazil, inaugurated in 1810, the same year as the Biblioteca Pública de Buenos Aires, is unusual in that it owes its foundation collections to events many miles away in Europe. One of the casualties of the Lisbon earthquake of 1755 was the royal library, and following its destruction a new royal library was assembled which included the collections of the bibliographer Diogo Barbosa Machado and books from the Portuguese Jesuit colleges. When the forces of Napoleon entered Portugal, the royal family and the royal library departed for the then colony of Brazil. When João VI returned to Portugal in 1821, the royal library remained, becoming public property after the proclamation of Brazil's independence in 1822. It was not uncommon for the national libraries of Latin America to be associated closely with a university. The National Library of Chile was linked to the Universidad de Chile until 1852; the National Library of Colombia was attached to the National University after 1867. In North America, the National Library of Mexico also has long-standing associations with the National Autonomous University of Mexico. Although the first attempts to establish a national library of Mexico date to the 1830s, it was not until 1856 that a decree of the President proposed the establishment of the National Library, which came into existence the following year after the suppression of the University of Mexico and the assigning of its building and books to the National Library. The National Library was not immune from the political upheavals experienced by Mexico in the nineteenth and early twentieth centuries, but with the granting of autonomy to the University of Mexico in 1929, control of the National Library passed from a department of government to the University itself, and is now under the administration of the Institute of Bibliographic Investigation. The National Library still forms part of the cultural complex on the university campus, Ciudad Universitaria.

National Libraries in the Postcolonial World

The former British Dominions (self-governing territories of the British Commonwealth) tended to have developed library systems at a relatively early stage in their political and economic development. The National Library of New Zealand (in Māori Te Puna Mātauranga o Aotearoa) was formed by the merger of three institutions: the General Assembly Library created in 1858 to serve Members of Parliament; the Alexander Turnbull Library, a research collection bequeathed to the nation and opened to the public in 1918; and the National Library Service, which brought the Country Library Service and the School Library Service together in 1945. The updated legislation of the National Library of New Zealand Act 2003 placed more emphasis on the responsibilities of the Library toward Māori heritage and knowledge, and extended legal deposit to electronic publications.

Library and Archives Canada/Bibliothèque et Archives Canada (LAC) was created in 2004 with the merger of the National Library of Canada (dating from 1953) and the National Archives of Canada (dating from 1872), thereby establishing one of the few organizations in the world to bring together an existing national library and national archives. The intention was not simply to bring two sets of functions under a single administration, but to create a fully integrated knowledge-based institution. The legislation establishing Library and Archive Canada introduced the term "documentary heritage" to encompass all recorded information about the country, including electronic media, which are now subject to legal deposit. Library and Archives Canada also harvests a representative sample of Canadian Internet sites for preservation purposes.

Before the creation of the National Library of Canada, national library functions fell to the Library of Parliament. Similarly, Australia's Commonwealth Parliamentary Library, inaugurated in 1902 after the model of the Library of Congress, enjoyed the legal deposit privilege from 1912 and formed the basis of the National Library of Australia. The National Library Act 1960 separated the National Library from the Parliamentary Library and a new building for the Library was opened in Canberra in 1968. The Library has been at the forefront in exploring the preservation of digital information, and is committed to the exploitation of its collections through digital technologies.

In the twentieth century a further wave of national libraries accompanied the emergence of new nations in the postcolonial period. This was seen clearly in Africa, although the term "bibliothèque nationale" was used more frequently in francophone Africa than "national library" in Anglophone countries, where a national library service was often introduced. In Ghana, for example, which gained its independence from Britain in 1957, the Ghana Library Board was established to set up and manage public libraries. However, it is also responsible for the George Padmore Research Library, which acts as a National Library in the absence of a statutory body. The Kenya National Library Service was established by an Act of Parliament in 1965 in order to develop public library services, but it too carries out a range of services within the remit of a national library, such as acquiring comprehensively material published in Kenya and abroad about the country, providing bibliographic and reference services, and publishing the national bibliography. A similar picture is seen in Botswana, where a Division of the Botswana National Library Services administers the acquisition of books by legal deposit and produces the *National Bibliography of Botswana*. Zambia also lacks specific legislation for a national library service, but the Zambia Library Services, a unit in the Ministry of Education, undertakes a range of national functions. The National Library of Nigeria was established by the National Library Act 1964, which was unusual among national library legislation in that it called for the creation of a branch of the National Library in each of the country's States. As a result of the political situation in the country, as well as the familiar financial pressures, the Library still has some way to go in achieving the goal, although branches now exist in some 14 States. Uganda has taken the step of repealing its Public Libraries Act 1964, which established a Public Libraries Board responsible for managing libraries nationally in Uganda, and replacing it with the National Library Act 2003. Responsibility for libraries had already been decentralized in 1997 by new local government legislation, and the 2003 Act established the National Library of Uganda as an advisory body for national library policy and the executive body for managing legal deposit, maintaining the national collection, and publishing the national bibliography. The national libraries of Africa face the most challenging conditions of any national libraries. The economic and political environment in which they operate, and the competing needs of other pressing social and economic concerns, can make the role of the national library seem marginal. Nevertheless, in many countries the impact they make in support of national library services and the importance they have as national symbols are clearly significant.

The most developed national library of sub-Saharan Africa is undoubtedly the National Library of South Africa. Until its creation in 1999, South Africa had two libraries performing national library functions, the South African Library in Cape Town, founded in 1818, and the State Library in Pretoria, founded in 1887. For historical reasons both libraries received South African publications by legal deposit legislation which dated back to the middle of the nineteenth century. The South African Library, formerly the South African Public Library, developed as a national reference library, whereas the State Library operated as both a public and a national library, being a center for national functions such as exchange agreements, bibliographical information, and interlibrary lending. The new National Library, created from the reconstitution of these two libraries as a single entity on two sites, was seen as reflecting the goals of democratic, postapartheid South Africa.

The national libraries of North Africa are distinguished by rich historical collections, particularly of manuscripts, their national status tending to center on the preeminence of their collections rather than their role in a system of national information provision. The National Library and Archives of Egypt, founded in 1870, and the National Library of Tunisia, founded in 1885, for example, both contain collections predating the creation of these libraries by many centuries. Both are now embracing the possibilities provided by new technology to digitize and make available their collections internationally. In Morocco, the Bibliothèque Générale et Archives, established in 1926, undertakes the functions of a national library through the legal deposit privilege and the publication of current and retrospective bibliographies, as well as the collection of manuscripts and the production of catalogs of manuscripts. The National Library of Algeria traces its history to 1835 but considers its new library building, fully opened in 1998, essential for its mission of providing access to information for a wide public, including children and young people, who are seldom catered for specifically by national libraries.

The distinction between a national library and a national library service, which is a recurring theme in any account of national libraries, is illustrated by the different development paths taken in Jamaica and in Trinidad and Tobago. The National Library and Information System of Trinidad and Tobago (NALIS) was created by legislation in 1998. This legislation formalized the integration of three public library systems, the Trinidad Public Library, founded as a subscription library in 1851; the Carnegie Library, opened in 1919; and the Central Library of Trinidad and Tobago, established in 1941. The result was a structure that provided traditional public library functions through its administration of a network of branch and mobile libraries, as well as school and special libraries, while meeting the heritage obligations of a national library, including the maintenance of a legal deposit collection and the creation of the national bibliography. On the other hand, the National Library of Jamaica began its operations in 1979 against a backdrop of an existing public library system and its role in coordinating the national information system depends on its ability to manage various cooperative relationships among autonomous bodies.

The national libraries of Asia generally were founded relatively recently, although they may have much earlier historic roots. The National Library of Thailand, for example, like many European national libraries, was founded on the basis of a number of royal libraries, brought together in 1905. As well as the buildings within the National Library complex in Bangkok, there are now 17 provincial branches of the National Library throughout Thailand. The Library not only has the oldest and largest collection of manuscripts and printed books in the country, but also provides a range of services, such as training courses and document delivery, to other libraries. It is the National Bibliographic Agency of the country, assigning ISBNs and ISSNs and publishing the national bibliography. The forerunner of the National Library of China, the Metropolitan Library, was also created at the beginning of the twentieth century (1909) at a time of expanding Western influence and operated as a legal deposit library from 1916. From 1928 the Library was known as the National Peiping Library, and after the founding of the People's Republic of China as the Beijing Library. Its de facto national status was recognized when it was renamed the National Library of China in 1998. It contains the largest collection of Chinese books in the world and the largest collection of foreign books in China. It serves the country's library system by acting as a center for library research and development, as the national bibliographical center, and the center for national information networks. These national functions extend to the responsibilities the Library has for three important national cultural projects: the National Cultural Information Resources Sharing Project, the Chinese Rare Book Facsimile Project, and the Rural Area Book Distribution Project. The implementation of the National Digital Library of China Project and the National Library of China Phase II approved in 2001 illustrates the way that the rapid growth of China as an economic power is permitting substantial investment in the country's information infrastructure.

The emergence of many of the national libraries of the region can be seen as part of the process of national building in the postcolonial period. The National Library of Malaysia began as a unit in the National Archives of Malaysia in 1966, before becoming a separate federal department under the National Library Act 1972. A high priority for the Library is the collection of materials published in and about Malaysia and the Library's Centre for Malay Manuscripts contains the world's largest single institutional collection of Malay manuscripts. The Library's building is itself an unusual physical expression of national identity, since its design was inspired by the traditional Malay headdress, reflected in the shape of the building's roof and symbolizing Malaysia's achievement and culture. The National Library of Indonesia was established in 1980 as the result of the amalgamation of four existing libraries. In 1989, a further merger with the Centre for Library Development extended the Library's responsibilities. As well as undertaking the common national library functions such as building the national collection and providing bibliographical and reference services, the Library develops national policies in the library sphere. Through the Provincial National Library, a division of the National Library of Indonesia, it maintains a presence throughout the country. In Sri Lanka, the National Library developed to encompass documentation services when in 1990 it became the National Library and Documentation Centre with a clear mandate to provide information resources to the whole population. Its central role has been demonstrated in recent years through the leadership it has brought to the reconstruction of libraries following the devastation caused by the tsunami of December 2004. The National Library of Singapore was established in 1958, although its origins can be traced to the Singapore Institution founded in the 1820s. Since 1995 it has been under the administration of the National Library Board and integrated into a national system including regional, community, and children's libraries, with all publicly funded libraries in the country linked to the totality of the country's information resources. In Singapore the role of libraries has been recognized as crucial for the successful development of a knowledge-based economy, and the *Library 2010 Report* defines its current objective as "to bring the world's knowledge to Singapore to create a positive social and economic impact."

The origins of the National Library of India date to 1836 and the creation of the Calcutta Public Library, a subscription library that from its earliest days made provision for limited use free of charge by indigent scholars and others who were unable to afford the subscription. At the end of the nineteenth century an Imperial Library was formed to serve the needs of the Government, and with an amalgamation of this library with the Calcutta Public Library in 1903, a new Imperial Library, functioning as a general reference and public library, was born. It was intended that it should contain all works written about India in all languages as well as standard reference works. After gaining its independence, the Government of India changed the name of the Library to the National Library of India.

Of the national libraries with a role to serve the legislature, the National Diet Library, Japan, resembles most closely the Library of Congress in its responsibilities. This is not coincidental, as there was significant input to the discussion about the shape of national library services in Japan after the Second World War on the part of an advisory mission of representatives from the Library of Congress and the American Library Association. New legislation governing the National Diet Library came into effect in 1948. The National Diet Library merged with the old Imperial Library (founded in 1872 and renamed the "National Library" in 1947) to form a single national library providing services to the Diet of Japan and to the general public.

The Post-Soviet World

Following the collapse of the Soviet Union and the subsequent political changes in Central and Eastern Europe, many of the national libraries of the region received a new lease of life. The national libraries of the Soviet Republics began to operate as the cultural representatives of independent states. The redrawing of national borders, in the former Yugoslavia, for example, created sovereign states from previous federations and the national library took its place as a national symbol among other cultural institutions, such as national museums and galleries.

In the case of the Baltic States, their national libraries had been founded after the end of the First World War as the result of an earlier reordering of European nations. The Estonian State Library was founded in 1918, at first primarily for the use of the members of Parliament. It developed as a public library during the Soviet period, but was renamed the National Library of Estonia in 1988. As well as assuming responsibility for building the national collection of works published in and about Estonia, it once more became the library of the national Parliament. The National Libraries of Lithuania and Latvia were established in 1919, both with the title of State Library, emerging from the turbulence of the twentieth century as National Libraries on the restoration of their countries' independence in 1990 and 1991, respectively. The Vernadsky National Library of Ukraine and the National Parliamentary Library of Georgia combine national responsibilities and services to the general public with support for Parliament and government bodies. Some aspects of Soviet library organization survive, as in Armenia, for example, where the National Library of Armenia coexists with the National Book Chamber of Armenia, which remains the center of national bibliographical activity.

In the Russian Federation, the Russian State Library in Moscow (Fig. 2), formerly the Lenin State Library of the USSR, and the National Library of Russia in St. Petersburg, formerly the State Public Saltykov-Shchedrin Library, are the two libraries that both exhibit in one form or another the characteristics of a national library, including the privilege of legal deposit. The Russian State Library has its origins in the collections of printed books and manuscripts bequeathed by Count Nikolai Petrovich Rumiantsev to the nation on his death in 1826. In 1861 the collections were transferred from St. Petersburg to Moscow and, supplemented by other private collections and

Fig. 2 The Russian State Library, Moscow.
Source: Photograph: Russian State Library.

selected art works from the Hermitage, opened to the public as the Moscow Public and Rumiantsev Museum in 1862, in effect the city's first publicly accessible library. After the Revolution of 1917 there was a period of substantial growth as numerous private and institutional collections entered the Museum. In 1925 the museum objects were dispersed to other institutions, including Moscow's Museum of Fine Arts (now known as the Pushkin Museum), and the library collections were retained in what was renamed the Lenin State Library. In the Soviet period the Library grew to be the largest in the country, extending into a new complex of buildings constructed in the 1950s, and it remains one of the largest in the world. After the breakup of the Soviet Union, the remit of the Library was adjusted accordingly, no longer being responsible for coordinating the work of the libraries of what had been the Union Republics, and it received the designation of Russian State Library in 1992. The closer coordination of its activities with those of the National Library of Russia dates from this time.

The National Library of Russia was founded as the Imperial Public Library in St. Petersburg by Catherine the Great in 1795 on the basis of the Załuski collection, removed from Warsaw. It was intended to supplement this collection with others already in government hands, including the libraries of Voltaire and Diderot, although in practice it was many decades before these collections were transferred to the Library. The Library's main purpose would be to maintain a complete collection of books in Russian, wherever published, and books about Russia in all languages. The planned opening of the Library's building on Nevsky Prospect in the center of St. Petersburg was delayed by Napoleon's invasion of Russia in 1812 when the most valuable collections were removed from the city for safekeeping, and the Library was finally opened to the public in 1814. Through the efforts of a series of energetic directors, including Modest Andreevich Korf, whose influence has been likened to that of Panizzi at the British Museum, the Library grew through the nineteenth century to become one of the most notable in Europe. After the Revolution, the Library was known as the Public Library of Russia and, like its counterpart in Moscow, absorbed many library collections from individuals, public bodies, and religious foundations. In 1932 it was renamed in honor of the famous Russian satirist Mikhail Evgrafovich Saltykov-Shchedrin (1826–1889). In 1941 the Library's most precious items were again evacuated when the invading Nazis threatened the city. With great difficulty the Library remained open during the Siege of Leningrad (1941–1944) when the remaining collections were distributed on the lower floors and in underground shelters. The Library's pressing problems of accommodation, felt throughout the twentieth century, were finally addressed with the construction of a new building in the 1990s. Its designation as the National Library of Russia in 1992 confirmed the national functions that it had undertaken to a greater or lesser extent throughout its history, but allowed it a greater independence of action in carrying them out than it had experienced before.

Some Notable National Libraries

While it is impossible in the space available to consider the historical development and individual characteristics of each of the national libraries of the world, a closer consideration of a small number of notable examples can give an indication of their range and complexity.

Bibliothèque nationale de France

The Bibliothèque nationale de France (Fig. 3) is generally regarded as having the strongest claim to being the first

Fig. 3 Bibliothèque nationale de France.

national library. Tracing its foundation to 1368 as the royal library of Charles V, it was the first to receive the country's publications through a system of legal deposit, introduced in France by the Ordonnance de Montpellier of Francis I in 1537. This decreed that a copy of every book printed in France should be deposited in the royal library at Blois and that every book printed abroad and sold in France should be offered to the library for purchase. The library was also the first to be styled "national" when the title of the royal library was changed in 1789 at the time of the French Revolution. By the first quarter of the eighteenth century, as a result of its continual growth, the library reached the point when it needed to be reorganized in some systematic way in order to be managed efficiently and so five separate departments, including Printed Books, Manuscripts, and Prints, were established. From the 1720s, under the king's long-serving librarian, Abbé Jérome Bignon, the library also became more accessible to the generality of scholars. After the Revolution the library was greatly enhanced by collections confiscated from suppressed monasteries and French émigrés who had not been successful in removing them from the country. The private libraries of Louis XVI and Marie-Antoinette were among the many that entered the national collections at this time, as the library rapidly doubled in size, helped by the spoils of Napoleon's armies. At this time the library occupied part of a complex of buildings adapted from other uses on and around the rue de Richelieu in Paris. In 1856 more of the complex was given over to the library and the government architect Henri Labrouste combined a restoration of existing buildings with newly built book stacks and the famous *salle de travail* which opened in 1868. In the twentieth century, responding to the pressure, familiar to all national libraries, for more space for continually expanding collections, the library had to find various ingenious solutions for extending accommodation on the rue de Richelieu site, which allowed no horizontal development and was subject to strict controls over any change in its appearance. This increased storage capacity in central Paris was supplemented by three annexes at Versailles built between 1934 and 1971. A radical new phase in the history of the library was heralded by the announcement by the President of the Republic on July 14, 1988 of the construction of a new library which would provide not only conventional storage (albeit in a controversial series of book-shaped glass towers) but would also exploit the most up-to-date technological solutions for the management of information. The new building opened to the public in December 1996.

The British Library

The history of the British Library illustrates some of the complexities that accompany the development of national libraries and the way in which they often reflect the constitutional arrangements of the states they serve. The British Library is the national library of the United Kingdom, but since the United Kingdom is a federal state of four countries, two of which (Scotland and Wales) have their own national libraries, the British Library has a particular responsibility also to act as the national library of England. The British Library is a relatively new institution, established by The British Library Act of 1972, but brought together individual institutions with a much longer history: the British Museum Library, the National Reference Library of Science and Invention (the Patent Office Library), the National Central Library, and the National Lending Library for Science and Technology (Boston Spa). Further additions were the British National Bibliography and the Office for Scientific and Technical Information in 1974, the India Office Library in 1982 and the British Institute of Recorded Sound in 1983. The library departments of the British Museum date to the foundation of the Museum itself in 1753. The wealthy physician and collector Sir Hans Sloane directed in his will that his collections of printed books and manuscripts, as well as his collections of botanical, zoological, and mineralogical specimens, should be offered to the nation for £20,000. Thanks to a lottery, this sum was raised, together with sufficient funds to acquire the Harleian Manuscripts collected by Robert and Edward Harley, Earls of Oxford, as well as to provide a home for the collections and an endowment for their upkeep. These collections, which formed the basis of the Museum, were enhanced by the acquisition of others, such as the Old Royal Library, presented by George II in 1757, and by the legal deposit privilege. In 1823, shortly after the death of George III, the Museum was presented with the remarkable "King's Library," with the proviso that it should be retained as a separate entity. The King's Library doubled the size of the Museum's collections of printed books at a stroke, and a special gallery was created for it in the new Museum building designed in the Greek style by Sir Robert Smirke. When the British Library's new St. Pancras building was opened in 1998, the King's Library was housed in a striking six-story glass tower, visible to those entering the building and a vivid reminder of the continuity of collecting from the eighteenth century to the present day.

Before the construction of the St. Pancras building, for many users the British Library meant the round Reading Room, built within the quadrangle of Smirke's Museum building in the 1850s to a concept by Antonio Panizzi, the Museum's inspirational and energetic Principal Librarian. However, the institutions brought together by the British Library Act provided a wealth of other services, not only to individual researchers, but also to the scientific community, commerce, and industry as well as to other libraries worldwide. Many users of the Library's services would be unaware that their information requirements, presented to their local library service, would be satisfied with the help of the British Library. The National Central Library and National Lending Library for Science and Technology merged in 1973 to form the British Library Lending Division, later the Document Supply Centre, coordinating and providing loans and supplying documents internationally. The British National Bibliography, unlike the other constituent parts of the British Library, had operated as a commercial company, publishing weekly listings of all British publications, and in its new home in the British Library became a leader in the production of machine-readable catalog records and their exploitation in computerized library management systems.

Die Deutsche Nationalbibliothek

The history of the German national library reflects the political turmoil of the twentieth century. As a relatively new unified European state, Germany inherited a rich legacy of State libraries, such as the Preussische Staatsbibliothek in Berlin, and the Bayerische Staatsbibliothek in Munich, but no national library as such. The national library was established as the Deutsche Bibliothek after the reunification of Germany in 1990 through a merger of the Deutsche Bücherei Leipzig and the Deutsche Bibliothek Frankfurt. The Deutsche Bücherei was established in 1912 on the initiative of the book trade, the city of Leipzig, center of publishing in the German Reich, and the Kingdom of Saxony. Its remit was to collect, catalog, and make available free of charge German and foreign-language literature published in Germany and German-language literature published abroad. At the end of the Second World War and the division of Germany into four zones by the occupying Allies, a second depository library, the Deutsche Bibliothek, was set up in Frankfurt am Main in the American zone. With the later emergence of two German states, these two libraries became the national libraries of the German Democratic Republic (Leipzig) and the Federal Republic of Germany (Frankfurt). As the two states became one, the two libraries integrated their activities as the Deutsche Bibliothek, which changed its name in 2006 to the Deutsche Nationalbibliothek.

The Library of Congress

The foremost representative of those national libraries whose primary purpose is to serve the legislature of the country, the Library of Congress was established in 1800 by the Congress of the United States when Congress itself transferred from Philadelphia to Washington, D.C., the new capital city. By moving, Congress lost its access to the existing libraries of New York and Philadelphia and $5000 was appropriated to establish a reference library for Congress, consisting mainly of immediately relevant works, for example on public law and legislative procedures. By 1814 the library had grown to some 3000 volumes when it was completely destroyed by British troops who set fire to the Capitol Building during the War of 1812? Former President Thomas Jefferson immediately offered his personal library, to be purchased on Congress's own terms, as a replacement. The offer aroused some controversy as the library contained literary, scientific, and philosophical works as well as legal and political material, but the purchase was authorized and the collection of over 6000 works was duly bought in January 1815 for $23,950. The present Library of Congress still maintains the comprehensive collecting policies that have their origin in Jefferson's belief that all subjects are potentially important to a nation's legislators. In 1816 restrictions on the use of the library were eased, so that in practice access was allowed to scholars in general, but it remained in scale and nature a library for Congress, "national in no sense but ownership."[10] The tenure of Librarian Ainsworth Rand Spofford, which extended from 1864 to 1897, saw the library strengthened by improved copyright legislation that required deposit at the Library of Congress as a condition for copyright protection for a wide range of printed material, including music, maps, and photographs. To accommodate the growing collections, in 1886 Congress authorized a new library building, now known as the Jefferson Building, completed in 1897, which made a statement about the wealth, prestige, and values of the nation as well as housing the collections in the then most technologically advanced library building in the world. The collections were seen as a resource for the nation and during Spofford's term as Librarian, the library's opening hours were extended to every weekday and eventually to evenings as well.

Even longer serving than Spofford, Herbert Putnam oversaw in his 40 years in the office of Librarian (1899–1939) a tenfold increase in the size of the collections, staff, and funding. A notable achievement was the creation of a centralized cataloging service, supplying printed catalog cards to the country's libraries, supported by other central services such as the national union catalog and interlibrary loans. Putnam also looked overseas to collect material from other countries, for example the Yudin library of Russian literature and important collections of oriental books, and no fewer than three copies of the Gutenberg Bible were acquired with the Vollbehr collection in 1930. The expansion of collections, staff, accommodation, and services continued through the twentieth century, making the library a world resource for scholarship and research, as well as continuing its role of information provision for Congress. Although the library rejected the suggestion that its name should be changed to National Library, and was careful not to claim any directing role over the rest of the nation's libraries, its leadership in many areas of library and information services could not be doubted. Its policy of large-scale acquisition of foreign publication meant that it was the most successful of the national libraries of the world in maintaining the concept of a comprehensive collection. Its pioneering developments in library automation and the digitization of collections to make them accessible remotely have been emulated by many other national libraries wishing to adapt their traditional role of collecting institutions to the changing circumstances of digital technology and the world of the Internet.

NATIONAL LIBRARY ORGANIZATIONS

The Conference of Directors of National Libraries (CDNL) is described as "an independent association of chief executives of national libraries, established to facilitate discussion and promote understanding and cooperation on matters of common interest to national libraries worldwide."[11] The Conference was established in 1974 and meets annually, providing an important framework for international collaboration. Being open to all the national libraries of the world (the list of national libraries on the Web site of the International Federation of Library Associations now contains over 160 entries[12]), there are practical difficulties in members attending each meeting and partly for this reason a number of regional organizations has been established focusing on national libraries: La Asociación de Bibliotecas Nacionales de Iberoamérica (ABINIA), the Conference of Directors of National Libraries of Asia and Oceania (CDNLAO), the Standing Conference of National and University Libraries of Eastern, Central and Southern Africa (SCANUL-ECS), and the Conference of European National Librarians (CENL).

La Asociación de Bibliotecas Nacionales de Iberoamérica's aims are to encourage the exchange of knowledge and experience among the national libraries of Latin America, for example through collaborative training and the promotion of new information technologies and conservation techniques. Joint initiatives include digitization projects, of the nineteenth-century Latin American press for example, and the creation of a union catalog of Ibero-American musical records.[13] La Asociación de Bibliotecas Nacionales de Iberoamérica has a special concern to promote the adoption of appropriate and adequate legislation for national libraries.

The 26 members of CDNLAO similarly promote cooperation and the exchange of information.[14] The CDNLAO Newsletter[15] records the activities of the Conference and publishes reports and research from the national libraries of the region. The Libraries of Asia and the Pacific Directory,[16] an initiative of CDNLAO, supported by the National Library of Australia, aims to provide a single access point for retrieval of information about the functions, services, and collections of libraries in Asia and the Pacific region.

The SCANUL-ECS was founded in 1994 with the following aims: to support and develop national and university library services in the areas covered by Eastern, Central, and Southern Africa; to promote interchange, contact, and cooperation among national and university libraries in the region; to collect, coordinate, and disseminate information on library activities; to encourage increased contact among members and the international library community; to organize and encourage conferences, seminars, workshops, and subject meetings; to initiate and implement regional projects and resource sharing; and to promote the participation of the information sector in the major socioeconomic activities in the region.[17] In support of these aims SCANUL-ECS organizes meetings, supports case studies, and publishes a newsletter.

The CENL, founded in 1987, states its aim to be "increasing and reinforcing the role of national libraries in Europe, in particular in respect of their responsibilities for maintaining the national cultural heritage and ensuring the accessibility of knowledge in that field," and explicitly elaborates the rationale for a collaborative approach: "National libraries need to secure their own position in order to establish the conditions necessary for free and unhindered access to information and documentation. This information must be, as far as possible, complete, clearly organised, prompt, and reliable. More than ever before, it is therefore necessary to develop new models of cooperation, to divide work tasks and share resources. National libraries can act as a focus within a cooperative network."[18] Conference of European National Librarians draws its membership from the national librarians of the member states of the Council of Europe and acts through annual meetings as well as through specific projects and initiatives. Its mission[19] is to support the European national libraries in their role to

- Give everybody fast, comprehensive, multilingual, and long-term access to their collections and information, and wherever appropriate without cost.
- Build the European Digital Library.
- Safeguard European national cultural heritage and knowledge.
- Do research and development to improve user services of national libraries.
- Promote cultural diversity and multiliguality as basic values of the European culture.
- Cooperate with other cultural heritage institutions, universities, publishers, and information providers on a European as well as on a global level.

The Conference expanded from the original 11 national librarians from Western Europe with the growth of links to the national libraries of Eastern Europe through the 1990s. The Conference's priority areas for activity have remained as defined at the first meeting: harmonization and innovation of national policy concerning libraries; implementation of new information technology in the libraries; standardization of data structure and communication interfaces within a European network; and preservation and conservation of important collections in Europe. The Conference working groups illustrate the concerns that are at the forefront of thinking on national libraries in Europe. For example, the challenge to the concept of legal deposit posed by electronic publishing prompted the creation of a "Statement on the development and establishment of voluntary deposit schemes for electronic publications,"[20] which reflects the level of cooperation currently enjoyed by national libraries and publishers and draws on the need to share the experience of those countries which already have legislation for electronic deposit or developed voluntary deposit schemes.

The European Library (TEL), the Web service of CENL,[21] gives access to the resources of 48 national libraries in Europe in 20 languages. These resources are both bibliographic, such as catalogs and collection descriptions, and digital (including some 300 photographs of Europe's national libraries). The European Library states that it exists to open up the universe of knowledge, information, and cultures of all Europe's national libraries, and aims to provide equal access to promote worldwide understanding of the richness and diversity of European learning and culture. Starting in 2006, the European Digital Library project, funded by the European Union and managed by CENL, built on TEL with the aim of integrating the digital content of the main European national libraries into a single multilingual service, Europeana,[22] launched in prototype at the end of 2008. Europeana encompasses not only libraries, but also museums, archives, and audiovisual collections, and is managed by a team based at the national library of the Netherlands, Koninklijke Bibliotheek. The management team is tasked with recommending a business model that will ensure Europeana's long-term sustainability as a cross-domain portal that will bring together existing digital content and provide support for further digitization of Europe's cultural and scientific heritage.

Conference of Directors of National Libraries coordinates its activity with the other main forum for the national libraries of the world, IFLA's National Libraries Section.[23] The Section's *Strategic Plan 2007–2009*[24] lists its goals as

- To promote the universal availability of information by such activities as encouraging the creation and building of national libraries, the development of national legislation for national libraries—especially legal deposit dispositions and preservation activities—and to promote the convergence of information and heritage institutions.
- To serve as a forum to share and learn from the experience of the practical problems of national libraries, in order to promote benchmarking, best practices, and quality models, and to improve management skills.
- To promote research in fields of interest to national libraries, always considering the opportunities to share experiences with other groups within IFLA and in close cooperation with CDNL, and to promote the development and implementation of standards.

As well as producing its regular *Newsletter*,[25] the Section organizes sessions and workshops at the annual World Library and Information Congress, collaborates with other Sections of IFLA on the Congress program, and contributes to specific projects in support of its strategic plan.

FUTURE TRENDS: NATIONAL LIBRARIES IN THE INTERNET AGE

In 1998, Line posed the question "What do national libraries do in the age of the Internet?"[26] One new activity is to attempt to manage the information that the Internet has given birth to. While most national libraries still strive to acquire the nation's printed output (and some also cover

Fig. 4 Kongelige Bibliotek, Copenhagen.

various types of nonprint media), usually by a form of legal deposit, the scope and nature of electronic and Web-based publishing presents particular challenges. As legislation changes to bring electronic publications within the scope of legal deposit, for example in Denmark,[27] Norway, and the United Kingdom,[28] national libraries are faced with a series of new responsibilities. The global nature of the Internet can obscure or confuse the national origin of a digital publication. Once the material is identified, systematic methods of harvesting, sometimes volatile and ephemeral, information must be implemented. Information may be subject to legal or voluntary deposit, but contains embedded links that refer to material that is beyond the scope of these arrangements. Other digital publications may contain technological systems to limit or prevent access or copying and rely on changing hardware and software platforms. National libraries now have to devise structures to manage digital information and build digital repositories that address these issues of acquisition, access, and preservation. With the dramatic increase in the resources available via Internet search engines and as a result of commercially funded mass digitization projects, national libraries are looking beyond their former roles and services to find new ways to exploit their collections, whether they be in digital or traditional forms. As well as developing their own individual Web-based services, they are forging new partnerships and working collaboratively, nationally and internationally, to create gateways such as Libraries Australia[29] and TEL, or supranational digital libraries such as the projected European Digital Library and the prototype World Digital Library.[30]

Such initiatives might suggest that the day of the national library as a physical expression of national identity and prestige is now gone. However, with major new national library buildings recently completed or planned in countries as dissimilar and widespread as Denmark (Fig. 4), Belarus, Peru, Latvia, the United Kingdom, the Czech Republic, France, and Korea (where a major new building is to house the National Digital Library), the evidence is that many nations continue to value the symbolic presence of the national library as the visible expression of their history and culture.

REFERENCES

1. Line, M.B. Changing perspectives on national libraries: a personal view. Alexandria **2001**, *13*(1), 44.
2. Esdaile, A. *National Libraries of the World: Their History, Administration and Public Services*, 2nd Ed.; Hill, F.J., Ed.; Library Association: London, U.K., 1957.
3. Humphreys, K.W. National library functions. Unesco Bull. Libr. **1966**, *20*(4), 158–169.
4. Burston, G. National libraries: An analysis. In *National libraries*; Line, M.B., Line, J., Eds.; Aslib: London, U.K., 1979; 87–98.
5. Sylvestre, G. *Guidelines for National Libraries*; UNESCO: Paris, 1987.
6. Line, M.B. *National Library and Information Needs: Alternative Means of Fulfilment, with Special Reference to the Role of National Libraries*; UNESCO: Paris, 1989.
7. Cornish, G.P. *The Role of National Libraries in the New Information Environment*; UNESCO: Paris, 1991.
8. Lor, P.J. *Guidelines for Legislation for National Library Services*; UNESCO: Paris, 1997.
9. Brindley, L.J. The role of national libraries in the twenty-first century. Bodleian Libr. Rec. **2002**, *17*(6), 464–481.
10. Esdaile, A. *National Libraries of the World: Their History, Administration and Public Services*, 2nd Ed.; Hill, F.J., Ed.; Library Association: London, 1957; 291.
11. http://consorcio.bn.br/cdnl/index.htm.
12. http://www.ifla.org/VI/2/p2/national-libraries.htm.
13. http://www.abinia.org.
14. http://www.nla.gov/lap/aboutcd.html.

15. http://www.ndl.go.jp/en/publication/cdnlao.
16. http://www.nla.gov/lap/aboutlap.html.
17. http://www.scanul-ecs.org/constitution.asp.
18. http://nlib.ee/cenl/about.php.
19. http://nlib.ee/cenl/statement.php.
20. http://nlib.ee/cenl/docs/05-11CENLFEP_Draft_Statement 050822_02.pdf.
21. http://theeuropeanlibrary.org.
22. http://www.europeana.eu.
23. http://www.ifla.org/VII/s1/index.htm.
24. http://www.ifla.org/VII/s1/annual/sp01–2009.htm.
25. http://www.ifla.org/VII/s1/index.htm#Newsletter.
26. Line, M.B. What do National Libraries do in the age of the Internet?. Ariadne **1998**, (13), 6–7.
27. Larsen, S. Preserving the digital heritage: new legal deposit act in Denmark. Alexandria **2005**, *17*(2), 81–87.
28. Field, C. Securing digital legal deposit in the U.K.: The legal deposit libraries act 2003. Alexandria **2004**, *16*(2), 87–111.
29. http://librariesaustralia.nla.gov.au/apps/kss.
30. http://www.worlddigitallibrary.org.

BIBLIOGRAPHY

1. Cole, J.Y.; Aikin, J. Eds.. *Encyclopaedia of the Library of Congress: for Congress, The Nation & the World*; The Library of Congress in association with Bernan Press: Washington, DC, 2004.
2. *Historia de las bibliotecas nacionales de Iberoamérica*, 2nd Ed. Universidad Nacional Autónoma de México: Mexico City, 1995.
3. Line, M.B.; Line, J., Eds. *National Libraries 2: 1977–1985*; Aslib: London, U.K., 1987.
4. Line, M.B.; Line, J., Eds. *National Libraries 3: 1986–1994*; Aslib: London, U.K., 1995.
5. Sturges, P.; Neill, R. *The Quiet Struggle: Information and Libraries for the People of Africa*, 2nd Ed.; Mansell: London, U.K., 1998.
6. Periodic surveys of the literature on national libraries can be found in *Alexandria: The journal of national and international library and information issues* and in the chapters on national libraries in the volumes of *Librarianship and Information Work Worldwide*.

National Library of Medicine

Kathel Dunn
National Library of Medicine, Bethesda, Maryland, U.S.A.

Abstract
The National Library of Medicine (NLM) is one of 27 Institutes and Centers of the National Institutes of Health (NIH), located just outside Washington, DC in Bethesda, Maryland, United States. The NLM is responsible to the Department of Health and Human Services (HHS) and to the Congress, which annually reviews its programs and appropriates funds for its operation. The institution was and continues to be a leader in applying computer technology to the handling of large databanks of medical information. This entry provides an introduction to the National Library of Medicine by first discussing some of the library's history and then shifting focus to organizational structure, administration, extramural programs as well as various other aspects of the library.

INTRODUCTION

The National Library of Medicine (NLM) is one of 27 Institutes and Centers of the National Institutes of Health (NIH), located just outside Washington, DC in Bethesda, Maryland, United States. The NLM is responsible to the Department of Health and Human Services (HHS) and to the Congress, which annually reviews its programs and appropriates funds for its operation. The institution was and continues to be a leader in applying computer technology to the handling of large databanks of medical information. Today, it is the largest library of the health sciences in the world. Extensive information about the programs described here is on the NLM's website at www.nlm.nih.gov.

The National Library of Medicine is independent of the other national libraries but works closely with the Library of Congress and the National Agricultural Library in a number of areas to ensure, for example, that acquisitions policies are complementary and cataloging practices are consistent.

Most of the library's programs are housed in three buildings at the southeast corner of the National Institutes of Health campus. Two library divisions, Extramural Programs and Specialized Information Services, as well as some of the staff from Library Operations and the Office of Computer and Communication Systems (OCCS) are housed in leased facilities a couple of miles away. The NLM building, occupied in 1962, contains the collections, technical processing, public services, and administrative offices on five floors (three below ground). The remaining programs are housed in the adjacent Lister Hill National Center for Biomedical Communications Building, a 10-story structure dedicated in 1980, and in the Natcher Conference Center, across the street and north of the other NLM buildings. The permanent full-time staffing level of the library in 2012 was about 800. The appropriation for the year ending September 30, 2012 was $337 million.

HISTORY OF THE LIBRARY

The National Library of Medicine had its origin with a collection of books in the office of the U.S. Army Surgeon General, established in 1818. The first request for funds for the library—$50 for medical books—appeared in the 1836 estimate of expenses for the Surgeon General's Office, and, in 1840, the office issued its first "catalogue of books in the library." The year 1865, when John Shaw Billings assumed charge of the collection, marked a turning point in the development of the library. By 1880 the collection contained 50,000 books and 60,000 pamphlets. Within that decade, books and journals were regularly going out on loan to physicians, and thousands of reference inquiries were being answered annually.

Just as important as the increase in the collection was the publication of reference and bibliographical works inaugurated by Billings. In 1879, there appeared the first issue of *Index-Medicus, a Monthly Classified Record of the Current Medical Literature of the World*. The following year, volume 1 of the *Index-Catalogue of the Library of the Surgeon General's Office* was published. This project was a combined author and subject listing of monographs and periodical literature in the library. Fifteen years later, in 1895, volume 16 appeared, thus concluding the first series of the *Index-Catalogue*. The work contained a total of 176,364 author and 168,557 subject entries for books and pamphlets, as well as subject entries for 511,112 journal articles. William Welch, professor of pathology at the Johns Hopkins Medical School, claimed that the Index-Catalogue was America's greatest contributions to nineteenth-century medicine.[1] The holdings of

Encyclopedia of Library and Information Sciences, Fourth Edition DOI: 10.1081/E-ELIS4-120049545

the library in 1895—the year Billings retired—included 116,847 books and 191,598 pamphlets.

When Billings assumed charge of the library in 1865, it was housed in the Riggs Bank Building in Washington. In 1866, the collection was transferred to Ford's Theatre. These facilities, however, were also woefully inadequate, and, in 1887, the library and the Army Medical Museum moved into a newly constructed, three-story, red brick building that Billings and architect Adolph Cluss had designed on the Washington Mall. The library remained there until 1962, when it moved to new quarters in Bethesda.

The official name of the library, the Library of the Surgeon General's Office, remained in effect until 1922. In that year, it was changed to the Army Medical Library. Thirty years later, in 1952, the secretary of defense redesignated the library as the Armed Forces Medical Library, thus making it a joint agency of the three military departments. The last change came in 1956, when the institution officially became the National Library of Medicine and was transferred to what is now the Department of Health and Human Services. A source of detailed information about the development of the NLM is *A History of the National Library of Medicine*.[2]

LEGISLATION

Senators Lister Hill (Alabama) and John F. Kennedy (Massachusetts) introduced the legislation that established the National Library of Medicine and authorized construction of necessary facilities. After wrangling about the location of the library, Congress finally passed the bill, and it was signed into law by President Eisenhower on August 3, 1956. The act established the library, created a board of regents to advise it, and left the question of where the library should be located up to the board. The legislation mandated that the library

- Acquire and preserve books, periodicals, prints, films, recordings, and other library materials pertinent to medicine
- Organize the materials...by appropriate cataloging, indexing, and bibliographical listing
- Publish...catalogs, indexes, and bibliographies
- Make available, through loans, photographic, or other copying procedures...materials in the library
- Provide reference and research assistance
- Engage in such other activities in furtherance of the purposes of this part as (the surgeon general) deems appropriate and the library's resources permit

The NLM Board of Regents advises the HHS secretary on matters of policy affecting the library. Ten regents, drawn from academia, the health sciences, librarianship, public life, and industry, are appointed by the secretary for 4-year terms. In addition to the appointed members, there are nine ex officio members who are high-ranking federal officials in related fields, including the surgeons general of the Army, Navy, Air Force, and Public Health Service. Pioneering heart surgeon Michael E. DeBakey, whose persuasiveness in the halls of the Congress was instrumental in the passage of the NLM Act, was a member (and chair) of the first NLM Board of Regents. Reacting with dispatch to the act's provision for a new building, that original board, at their second meeting, recommended that a 10-acre tract on the campus of the National Institutes of Health in Bethesda, Maryland, be designated as the site of a new building for the National Library of Medicine. Five years later, in 1962, the library moved from the Washington Mall to its new $7 million building in Bethesda.

The wording of the original legislation has been amended several times. The six functions listed above have been expanded with a seventh: "publicize the availability from the Library of the above products and services..."; and an eighth: "promote the use of computers and telecommunications..." Other congressional actions have had a profound effect on the library: the Medical Library Assistance Act (MLAA) of 1965, also championed by Dr. DeBakey, which created a program of grants and called for the establishment of a system of regional libraries, the joint resolution establishing the Lister Hill National Center for Biomedical Communications (1968), and the legislation creating the National Center for Biotechnology Information (1988), and the National Information Center on Health Services Research and Health Care Technology (1993).

Administration

The recommendations in a 1944 American Library Association report called *The National Medical Library: Report of a Survey of the Army Medical Library* would lay the foundation for the modern era of library practices. In the succeeding decades the Library would hire a Library Director, Brad Rogers, (1948) and ensure that he received training in library science; implement a collection development policy, with accompanying manual (1951), the first edition of the Army Medical Library Classification, a scheme for arrangement of books on medicine and preclinical sciences, designed for use in conjunction with the Library of Congress Classification, also as recommended by the *Report of a Survey* (1944). Rogers, though a physician selected from the Army Medical Corps, was sent to Columbia University to obtain a librarian's degree. In his role as Director of the Army Medical Library, Rogers was asked to modernize the library, provide it with more professional management and better organization and make it relevant to Congress.[3] He oversaw the transition of the library from the military to the civilian sphere, the construction of a new building, and the tremendous job of moving the collection from Washington to Bethesda. It was Rogers who laid much of the groundwork for the present-day National Library of Medicine, including the planning and early development of MEDLARS® (Medical Literature Analysis and Retrieval System) and the creation of the Medical Subject Headings (MeSH®) vocabulary, both of which figure prominently in the library's reputation as a leader in scientific communication.

Succeeding Rogers was Martin M. Cummings, a scientist, educator, and administrator, appointed in 1963. In the two decades under his guidance, the library assumed new responsibilities in a number of areas: a grants program, audiovisual facilities, research and development, specialized toxicology information services, and the introduction of a national online information retrieval services (MEDLINE® 1971). Cummings retired in late 1983, and in May 1984, Donald A.B. Lindberg, was named by the secretary of Health and Human Services to succeed him. Dr. Lindberg continues in that post today.

Lindberg, who at the time of his appointment was director of the Information Science Group and professor of pathology at the University of Missouri School of Medicine in Columbia, is an expert in the field of medical informatics—the use of computers and communications technology in medicine. Lindberg's tenure has been marked by a number of major initiatives: an extensive long-range planning process and publication of a detailed long-range plan for the library,[4] a practical means of end-user searching of the NLM databases, the establishment at NLM of the National Center for Biotechnology Information and the National Information Center on Health Services Research and Health Care Technology, and the transition to the Internet and the Web as the primary distribution method for NLM information and data, the development of health information resources for the general public, and tremendous expansion in the amount of biomedical literature, scientific data, and health information that is freely available on the Web.

Organizational Structure

The NLM's organizational structure consists of an office of the director and six major operating components. The office of the director includes all the centralized management functions: planning, personnel, budget, contracting, purchasing, public communications, and equal employment opportunity. The director is assisted by a deputy director, a deputy director for research and education, an associate director for health information programs development, an assistant director for policy and development, and an associate director for administrative management. There are two assistant directors in the specialized areas of health services research information and high performance computing and communications (HPCC).

The major NLM components include the following:

- *Library Operations* (acquisition, cataloging, indexing, reference services, preservation, interlibrary loan, online database management, health services research information, the National Network of Libraries of Medicine, and history of medicine)
- *Extramural Programs* (grant administration)
- *Specialized Information Services* (toxicology and environmental health information)
- *Lister Hill National Center for Biomedical Communications* (research and development)
- *National Center for Biotechnology Information* (programs in molecular biology information and sequence databases)
- *Office of Computer and Communications Systems*

Mission and Long Range Plans

The laws that shape and animate the National Library of Medicine are further informed by the Library's mission, and Long Range Plans, which add form and function to Library products and services. In the words of its Director, Donald A. B. Lindberg: "The purpose of the National Library of Medicine, flat out, is to acquire, organize and disseminate the biomedical knowledge of the world for the benefit of the public health. I mean, that's clear, and most people here understand that very well. It's one of the reasons we function efficiently."[5] NLM had no long term plan when Lindberg arrived. "My predecessors were good, made wise decisions and needed no plan, but I needed one."[6] Though a 1993 law would later require all agencies within the Department of Health and Human Services to have a strategic plan that defined its mission, goals, and the means by which it will measure its progress in addressing specific national problems, needs, or challenges related to its mission over the course of at least 5 years,[7] NLM's first strategic plan was in place a full 6 years before that law, in 1987, and has followed with successive plans, to include the current Long Range Plan, *Charting the Course for the 21st Century: NLM's Long Range Plan 2006-2016* (http://www.nlm.nih.gov/pubs/plan/) . NLM's current Long Range Plan has as its core four goals:

- Seamless, uninterrupted access to expanding collections of biomedical data, medical knowledge, and health information
- Trusted information services that promote health literacy, improve health outcomes, and reduce health disparities worldwide
- Integrated biomedical, clinical, and public health information systems that promote scientific discovery and speed the translation of research into practice
- A strong and diverse workforce for biomedical informatics research, systems development, and innovative service delivery

The library's commitment to meeting its legislative mandate, its mission, and its goals is visible in its print and digital collections, along with a commitment to public access to scholarly publications; its databases, where bibliographic data, full-text, scientific data, and consumer health information are organized and made accessible to scientists, health professionals, and the public; vocabularies that underpin NLM's databases, and are also widely used in external product development; intramural research and development in computational biology, information retrieval, knowledge representation, natural language processing, imaging, and communications; grant funding of external informatics research and training; and through outreach, exhibits and training, where the library connects its products and services with the communities that need them.

COLLECTIONS

Print

In 2013, NLM's print collection held 20,869,244 items, comprising in part 863,182 monographs, 1871–present; 1,451,840 serials; and 17,372,682 manuscripts. The library broadly collects materials in the areas of biomedicine and the related areas of the life sciences, items that document the practice and teaching of medicine broadly defined, demonstrate how health services are organized, delivered, and financed, chronicle the development and implementation of policy that affects research and the delivery of health services, and illustrate the public perception of medical practice and public health. Since the mid-1990s, there have been added emphases and expansions in collecting in the subject areas of fundamental life sciences research; chemistry, physics, engineering; public health issues to include disaster management and bioterrorism; and complementary and alternative medicine.[3,8] These areas correspond to relatively recent extensions of the Library's responsibilities in health services research, with the Congressionally directed founding of the National Center for Biotechnology Information in 1988, the National Information Center for Health Services Research and Technology in 1993, and the Disaster Information Management Research Center (DIMRC) in 2008. This broadening of scope reflects a goal set for NLM in the Board of Regents' Long Range Plan for 2006–2016. The print collection contains material in virtually every written language and from every country. The Library is guided in its selection process through its current Collection Development Manual (CDM), available online at: https://www.nlm.nih.gov/tsd/acquisitions/cdm/index.html, has antecedents in previous manuals dating back to 1951.

Historical

The judicious collecting of important medical works by nineteenth-century library director John Shaw Billings resulted in the nucleus of the library's rare book and medical history collection. The ongoing accrual of rare books and manuscripts, as well as the acquisition of current monographs and periodicals for over a century, has made the library's holdings in the history of medicine one of the finest research collections in the world. The earliest medical work in the library is an Arabic manuscript of 1094. The earliest dated printed work is Rabanus Maurus, "*De sermonum proprietate*," published in Strasbourg in 1467. Altogether, the library owns over 580 incunabula. There are over 5000 volumes in the library printed in the sixteenth century; and nearly 65,000, including serials and theses, printed in the seventeenth and eighteenth centuries. The library holds not only most of the great landmark works of medicine, but also many less well-known works necessary for historical research, often in several successive editions and translations. Some of the volumes in the collection are the only known copies that survive.

Among the library's historical research collections are the modern manuscript items, dating from 1700. Many of these items were acquired over the past century as part of the general collecting of historical materials. However, to help preserve a record of the present and provide sources for future research in the history of medicine, the library has a "current manuscripts" acquisitions program as well. These new collections are, at times, supplemented by selected oral history interviews. The NLM also has a collection of some 60,000 pictures relating to the history of the health sciences and a significant collection of historical audiovisuals and motion pictures. The library's acquisition of significant manuscript materials, its collecting of rare books and monographs, and its publication of historical bibliographies help to give the scholar access to the history of medicine, just as other NLM functions supply bibliographical assistance for current research and information.

Preservation

The library has a committed focus on preservation of the collection in keeping with its national role as the library of last resort for other libraries, as well as its legislative mandate to preserve the books and other works it has acquired. One of the first steps in that process is collecting and maintaining the print collection. From 1986 to 2007, the Library microfilmed approximately 105,000 volumes of serial and monograph volumes printed on deteriorating paper.[9] NLM stopped microfilming opting instead to provide digital access to selected collection holdings.

In 2011, the Library instituted a nationwide, cooperative, voluntary program with National Network of Libraries of Medicine (NN/LM) guaranteeing retention of clinically significant titles in print. The program, called MedPrint, identified approximately 250 journals as the primary set of materials to preserve in print. At the end of 2012, NLM had received 15 signed agreements from institutions representing all eight NN/LM regions. Of the 250 titles identified in the MedPrint program, libraries across the country had made commitments to all but 10 titles. The goal of the program is to get commitments for 12 copies of each MedPrint title, with NLM's copy being the 13th. Thirty-nine of the 250 titles now have 12 or more commitments.[10]

Collection Access

The library ensures the discoverability to its print collection through its online catalogs, LocatorPlus, and the NLM Catalog. In March 2013, NLM began using RDA: Resource Description and Access for all original cataloging of modern material, replacing the Anglo-American Cataloging Rules, second edition.

The print collection is available to the public onsite through the Library's History of Medicine and Main Reading Rooms. The print collection circulates beyond the Library's doors through the Library's interlibrary loan program, a service begun in 1870, when loan service was first established to make volumes from the Library's collections available to distant libraries and physicians.[11] Onsite use of the print collection, though, is declining with in-person visits to the Main Reading Room decreasing throughout the late 1990s and 2000s.

In 2013, 1.4 million document requests were filled throughout the network using DOCLINE, the Library's own system for interlibrary loan requests and management. The number of interlibrary loan requests filled via DOCLINE peaked in 2002 at 3,038,934.[12] In 2013, NLM instituted scan on demand, offering library users throughout the world the option of having a monograph, if copyright-free, fully scanned and a PDF copy sent to the requestor. A scanned copy of the monograph is then placed in NLM's digital repository.[13] The results of a 2012 national survey of librarians who participate in DOCLINE largely attributed the decline in interlibrary loans to the availability of materials online and though not stated, presumably available online without charge; and the greater availability of online journals through package deals that even smaller libraries could afford, or participate in through consortia. Changes in how users interact with the collection are seen most readily in the inception and growth of the Library's digital collections.[12]

Public Access to Journal Literature

Launched in February 2000, PubMed Central® (PMC), a free archive of biomedical and life sciences journal literature, was developed and is managed by NLM's National Center for Biotechnology Information (NCBI). In keeping with NLM's legislative mandate to collect and preserve the biomedical literature, PMC serves as a digital counterpart to NLM's extensive print journal collection. In 2012, PubMed Central held 2,540,2952 articles and 1,149 journal titles.[14] The NIH Public Access Policy ensures that the public has access to the published results of NIH funded research. It requires scientists to submit final peer-reviewed journal manuscripts that arise from NIH funds to the digital archive PubMed Central immediately upon acceptance for publication. To help advance science and improve human health, the Policy requires that these papers are accessible to the public on PubMed Central no later than 12 months after publication.

Digital Collections

NLM also maintains "Digital Collections," a free online archive of nonjournal biomedical resources. All the content in Digital Collections is in the public domain and freely available worldwide. Digital Collections provides preservation of and unique access to NLM's rich, historical resources. In 2012, the Digital Collections Repository held 6979 texts and 70 audiovisuals. The Digital Collections encompass subject areas of Medicine in the Americas, 1620–1920; Cholera Online, 1817–1900; NLM Publications and Productions; Tropical Disease Motion Pictures; The Public Health Film Goes to War; and the NIH Annual Reports.[15]

In 1998, NLM introduced the web site "Profiles in Science," a web site that makes the archival collections of prominent biomedical scientists available to the public through modern digital technology.[16] The collections have been donated to the NLM and contain published and unpublished materials, including books, journal volumes, pamphlets, diaries, letters, manuscripts, photographs, and audio tapes and other audiovisual materials. The collection includes famous American scientists and public health figures such as Oswald Avery and C. Everett Koop, plus Nobel laureates Christian Anfinsen, Julius Axelrod, Joshua Lederberg, and Martin Rodbell.[16]

Born Digital

Started as a pilot in 2009, "Health and Medicine Blogs," is a unique repository of archived health blogs, developed by NLM in collaboration with the Internet Archive. Collected blogs feature the perspectives of physicians, nurses, hospital administrators, and other health professionals. The Library has also collected blogs of patients chronicling their experiences with conditions such as cancer, diabetes, and multiple sclerosis. These blogs illustrate the public perception of medical practice, provide insight into the health care environment, and document medical innovations and medical education in the twenty-first century.[17]

DATABASES

Ever since the Library's earliest days, it had dual roles, one in which it built and maintained a print collection, and one in which it indexed the medical literature, making it accessible at the article level for not just on-site users, but to users throughout the world, through the publication of the indexes, the *Index-Catalogue* and the *Index Medicus*. From *Index Medicus* to MEDLINE/PubMed®, NLM has continued its role in aiding users worldwide in the discovery of information contained in the biomedical literature, while expanding its services to include other kinds of information and data. During the first 25 years of its online services, NLM charged modest fees to recover the cost of online access via commercial telecommunications networks. When Internet access became prevalent in the mid-1990s, NLM was able to make its databases freely available.

MEDLINE/PubMed®

Currently, MEDLINE/PubMed is the premier biomedical database in the world, providing free access to MEDLINE, NLM's database of citations and abstracts in the fields of medicine, nursing, dentistry, veterinary medicine, health care systems, and preclinical sciences. PubMed links to full-text articles found in PubMed Central or at publisher web sites, and other related resources.[18] In 2013, PubMed held 23 million records, 5,669 journals currently indexed for MEDLINE, 61% of the citations linking to full-text, 18% linked to free full-text; and in a typical day 3.5 million Web searches are recorded (730,000 users), 5.5 million record views (1.7 million users), and 75,000 mobile searches (18,000 users).[19] The Entrez system that delivers PubMed is developed and maintained by the National Center for Biotechnology Information (NCBI). NCBI improves users' search experience following a Discovery Initiative model, using automated methods to draw users' attention to related data that do not necessarily appear as part of the original search. Various "ads" on results pages provide links to related articles and citations, queries, gene names, gene symbols, free full text, protein and nucleotide records, and accession numbers.[20] In 2013, NCBI debuted PubMed Commons (http://test.ncbi.nlm.nih.gov/pubmedcommons), a new system that enables researchers who are PubMed authors to share their opinions about scientific publications indexed in the PubMed database.[21]

Today NLM has over 295 databases, resources, and application programming interfaces (APIs), on biomedicine, toxicology, hazardous substances, lactation medicine, household products, genes, and consumer health. MedlinePlus Connect, a system for linking electronic health records (EHR) systems to NLM consumer health content, and ClinicalTrials.gov, with detailed information on human subject studies, are two resources that have significant impact on information for patients, and patient care. A list of NLM databases, resources, and APIs can be found on this page: http://wwwcf2.nlm.nih.gov/nlm_eresources/eresources/search_database.cfm

MedlinePlus Connect

MedlinePlus Connect, launched in 2010, is a system to link patient portals, electronic health record (EHR) systems, and health IT systems to consumer health information from MedlinePlus.gov. MedlinePlus Connect meets the meaningful use requirement of the HITECH Act (Health Information Technology for Economic and Clinical Health), part of the American Recovery and Reinvestment Act (ARRA) of 2009, which seeks to improve American health care delivery and patient care through an unprecedented investment in Health IT (HIT). The provisions of the HITECH Act are specifically designed to work together to provide the necessary assistance and technical support to providers, enable coordination and alignment within and among states, establish connectivity to the public health community in case of emergencies, and assure the workforce is properly trained and equipped to be meaningful users of certified Electronic Health Records (EHRs). Meaningful use is a Center for Medicare and Medicaid Services (CMS) payment incentive program for the use of certified EHRs by hospitals and providers in a way that meets specific requirements.[22]

MedlinePlus

MedlinePlus Connect uses the MedlinePlus web site, a popular portal to consumer health information. The site offers authoritative, up-to-date health information, without advertisements, and is available anytime, anywhere for free.[23] A Spanish-language version, MedlinePlus en español (http://medlineplus.gov/spanish) is also available. MedlinePlus pages contain carefully selected links to Web resources with health information on over 900 topics. MedlinePlus follows a list of guidelines for the inclusion of web sites. The MedlinePlus health topic pages include links to current news on the topic and related information. The public can also find preformulated searches of the MEDLINE/PubMed database, which allow them to find references to latest health professional articles on a topic. The A.D.A.M. medical encyclopedia brings health consumers an extensive library of medical images and videos, as well as over 4000 articles about diseases, tests, symptoms, injuries, and surgeries. Drug and supplement information is available from the American Society of Health-System Pharmacists (ASHP) via AHFS® Consumer Medication Information, and Natural Medicines Comprehensive Database Consumer Version.[24]

ClinicalTrials.gov

ClinicalTrials.gov, launched in February 2000 to implement provisions of the Food and Drug Administration Modernization Act (Public Law 105-115), that required creation of a centralized, consumer-friendly online listing of clinical trials of drugs for serious and life-threatening conditions. In an effort spearheaded by NLM, the National Institutes of Health (NIH) developed this site in collaboration with all NIH Institutes and the U.S. Food and Drug Administration (FDA). The database now has more than 160,000 clinical trials and observational studies, with studies in locations in all 50 states and 185 countries and includes summary results tables for more than 11,000 trials. It is the only public source of results data for many trials. In 2007, the FDA Amendments Act mandated deposit of registration data for an expanded set of trials of FDA regulated drugs, biologics, and devices and deposit of summary results for trials of approved products. The ClinicalTrials.gov results database was launched in September 2008 to implement the clinical trials provisions of this law. Submission of adverse event information was optional when the results database was released and became mandatory in September 2009. In 2013, ClinicalTrials.gov saw 95 million page views per month, 60,000 visitors per day.

MEDICAL TERMINOLOGIES

NLM is home to a number of medical terminologies that it creates and curates for use in its own products, and for use by others in commercial and free products. A standardized medical terminology is often used within a database in such a way that it enables users to interact with the database using their own words and have their words connect with other words like theirs (synonyms, or ones with the same meaning) using the controlled vocabulary. NLM also licenses SNOMED CT®, a clinical terminology, designated as a U.S. standard for electronic health information exchange in Interoperability Specifications produced by the Healthcare Information Technology Standards Panel.[25]

Medical Subject Headings (MeSH)

MeSH is the National Library of Medicine's controlled vocabulary thesaurus. It consists of sets of terms naming descriptors in a hierarchical structure that permits searching at various levels of specificity. The MeSH thesaurus is used by NLM for indexing articles for the MEDLINE/PubMED database and for the NLM-produced database that includes cataloging of books, documents, and audiovisuals acquired by the Library. MeSH, in machine-readable form, is provided at no charge via electronic means. MeSH descriptors are arranged in both an alphabetic and a hierarchical structure.

The MeSH thesaurus is used by NLM for indexing articles from 5600 of the world's leading biomedical journals for the MEDLINE®/PubMED database. It is also used for the NLM-produced database that includes cataloging of books, documents, and audiovisuals acquired by the Library. Each bibliographic reference is associated with a set of MeSH terms that describe the content of the item. Similarly, search queries use MeSH vocabulary to find items on a desired topic.[26,27]

Unified Medical Language System (UMLS)

The National Library of Medicine (NLM) produces the Unified Medical Language System® (UMLS®) to facilitate the development of computer systems that behave as if they "understand" the meaning of the language of biomedicine and health. As part of the UMLS, NLM produces and distributes the UMLS Knowledge Sources (databases) and associated software tools (programs) for use by system developers in building or enhancing electronic information systems that create, process, retrieve, integrate, and/or aggregate biomedical and health data and information, as well as in informatics research.

By design, the UMLS Knowledge Sources are not limited to particular applications; they are multipurpose. Developers will find that they can be applied in systems that perform a range of functions involving one or more types of information, e.g., patient records, scientific literature, guidelines, public health data. The associated UMLS software tools assist developers in customizing or using the UMLS Knowledge Sources for particular purposes. The Unified Medical Language System (UMLS) integrates and distributes key terminology, classification and coding standards, and associated resources to promote creation of more effective and interoperable biomedical information systems and services, including electronic health records. All UMLS Knowledge Sources and associated software tools are free of charge to U.S. and international users. There are three UMLS Knowledge Sources: the Metathesaurus®, the Semantic Network, and the SPECIALIST Lexicon. The Metathesaurus contains over 150 source vocabularies, such as MeSH®, RxNorm, SNOMED CT®, ICD-9-CM, ICD-10-CM, CPT®, and LOINC®. Many of the vocabularies are designated as U.S. health standards for electronic health records.[25]

RxNorm

RxNorm is two things: a normalized naming system for generic and branded drugs; and a tool for supporting semantic interoperation between drug terminologies and pharmacy knowledge base systems. RxNorm is a controlled vocabulary for drugs, providing normalized names and codes for clinical drugs and links its names to many of the drug vocabularies commonly used in pharmacy management and drug interaction software, including those of First Databank, Micromedex, MediSpan, Gold Standard Alchemy, and Multum. By providing links between these vocabularies, RxNorm can mediate messages between systems not using the same software and vocabulary. RxNorm is the U.S. medication standard for health data exchange.[25,28]

SNOMED CT

SNOMED Clinical Terms (SNOMED CT) is an extensive clinical terminology that was formed by the merger, expansion, and restructuring of SNOMED RT® (Reference Terminology) and the United Kingdom National Health Service (NHS) Clinical Terms (also known as the Read Codes). It is the most comprehensive clinical vocabulary available in English (or any language). SNOMED CT is concept-oriented and has an advanced structure that meets most accepted criteria for a well-formed, machine-readable terminology. It has been designated as a U.S. standard for electronic health information exchange in Interoperability Specifications produced by the Healthcare Information Technology Standards Panel and has also been adopted for use by the U.S. Federal Government, through the Consolidated Health Informatics (CHI) Initiative, for several clinical domains.[29]

Coordination of Clinical Terminologies

NLM is the central coordinating body for clinical terminology standards within the Department of Health and Human Services (HHS). NLM works closely with the Office of the National Coordinator for Health Information Technology (ONC) to ensure NLM's efforts are aligned with the goal of the President and HHS Secretary for the nationwide implementation of an interoperable health information technology infrastructure to improve the quality and efficiency of health care. NLM supports, licenses, or develops key Clinical Vocabularies identified for Meaningful Use and HIPAA transactions: SNOMED CT®, LOINC®, and RxNorm. NLM represents the United States on matters related to the structure and content of SNOMED CT, as member of the International Health Terminology Standards Development Organisation (IHTSDO®). NLM provides uniform distribution for more than 150 clinical vocabulary standards and HIPAA administrative code sets through the UMLS Metathesaurus.[30]

Value Set Authority Center

In 2012, in cooperation with the Office of the National Coordinator for Health Information Technology, and the Center for Medicare and Medicaid Services (CMS), NLM launched the Value Set Authority Center (VSAC).[31] VSAC currently serves as the authority and central repository for the official versions of value sets that support Meaningful Use 2014 Clinical Quality Measures (CQMs). The VSAC provides search, retrieval, and download capabilities through a Web interface and APIs. The VSAC will maintain and update the value sets consistent with the overall process for maintaining and updating the 2014 CQMs themselves. Through the VSAC, NLM draws upon the UMLS Metathesaurus and its responsibility as the central coordinating body for clinical terminology standards within the Department of Health and Human Services (HHS) to assure the on-going validity and accuracy of the value sets. In the future, the VSAC will provide authoring tools for users to create value sets.[20]

RESEARCH AND DEVELOPMENT

There are two divisions within NLM that conduct research: the Lister Hill National Center for Biomedical Communication (LHNCBC) and the National Center for Biomedical Information (NCBI). Lister Hill Center conducts and supports research and development in high quality imagery, medical language processing, high-speed access to biomedical information, intelligent database systems development, multimedia visualization, knowledge management, data mining, machine-assisted indexing, and electronic health records to facilitate patient-centric care. NCBI conducts research in basic and applied research in computational, mathematical, and theoretical problems in molecular biology and genetics; and data representation and analysis, including the development of computer-based systems for the storage, management, and retrieval of knowledge relating to molecular biology, genetics, and biochemistry. Both Lister Hill Center and NCBI have Boards of Scientific Counselors (BOSC) who review the work of their intramural researchers; and both offer training opportunities for post-doctoral fellows. NLM's Board of Regents delineated specific research directions for NLM overall and Lister Hill Center and NCBI in particular, in the 2006–2016 Long Range Plan, in Goal 3: Integrated biomedical, clinical, and public health information systems that promote scientific discovery and speed the translation of research into practice.

NCBI

Within the Long Range Plan, NCBI was specifically charged with developing linked databases for discovering relationships between clinical data, genetic information, and environmental factors and that NCBI should

- Lead the development of repositories of information on human variation that will be essential tools for discovering the associations between genes and disease
- Continue to be the computational and database focal point in a trans-NIH program to connect clinical and genotypic data from large, long-term studies
- Assume a leadership role in this effort (make data available, protect privacy, and inform public) and thus contribute to the transformation of clinical, genomic, and environmental information into better evidence-based medicine and improved patient care

NCBI's molecular biology information resources are based on sequence repositories upon which curated and annotated sets of data resources are built. Information ranges from genetic sequence data to entire genomes, protein sequences and structures to chemical structures and assays, as well as clinical data paired with genotypes. The primary source for NCBI sequence data is GenBank, the NIH genetic sequence database. GenBank is an annotated collection of all publicly available DNA sequences.[3] GenBank is part of the International Nucleotide Sequence Database Collaboration, which comprises the DNA DataBank of Japan (DDBJ), the European Molecular Biology Laboratory (EMBL), and GenBank at NCBI. These three organizations exchange data on a daily basis.[20] Eleven taxonomy divisions within GenBank contain sequences for over 380,000 species.[20]

LHNCBC

Within the Long Range Plan, the Lister Hill Center was specifically charged with promoting the development of next-generation electronic health records to facilitate patient-centric care, clinical research and public health. Additionally, the Plan encouraged NLM and Lister Hill to

- Enhance these efforts in response to specific U.S. government priorities and feedback from those attempting to implement standards in current electronic health records and personal health records, regional health information exchanges, clinical research systems, and public health applications
- Build on its long development and policy studies related to electronic health records by promoting work to define and develop the next generation of electronic health records (EHR)
- Promote development and use of advanced electronic representations of biomedical knowledge in conjunction with electronic health records
- Continue to promote research and development on robust and scaleable approaches to synthesizing, representing, updating, and deploying electronic knowledge and decision algorithms for use in conjunction with electronic health records

In 2008, Lister Hill debuted an NLM Personal Health Record (PHR), with an early version aiming to help individuals who are caring for their elderly parent(s) and/or young children. The goal of the NLM Personal Health Record is to help individuals manage health care for themselves and their relatives. The PHR is intended to serve as a test-bed for patient-specific and reminder-based consumer education information, validating and improving NLM clinical vocabularies, studying consumers' use of PHR systems, studying the potential of PHR-based educational reminder systems to improve prevention, and as a potential vehicle for gathering information during clinical trials. The PHR supports the entry and tracking of key measurements, test results, prescriptions, problems, immunizations, and future health appointments.[33]

Also in 2008, LHNCBC researchers initiated an effort to develop an open source text de-identification tool. The tool, called Clinical Text De-identification (CTD) system, is software that complies with the privacy rule of the Health Insurance Portability and Accountability Act (HIPAA). The rule requires the removal of 18 individually identifiable health information elements that could be used to identify the individual, the individual's relatives, employers, or household members. In 2011, LHNCBC researchers conducted a study of the CTD tool against four state-of-the-art systems and found that the CTD was superior in the detection of personal names in clinical reports than the methods of the other four systems.[33]

Extramural Programs

The Extramural Programs Division (EP) administers extramural grant programs for NLM as authorized by the Medical Library Assistance Act (MLAA) and Public Health Service Act. EP's first grant awards were issued in 1965. Funds are expended as grants-in-aid to the extramural community in support of the Library's mission. Review and award procedures conform to NIH policies. EP awards several categories of grants, all of which pertain to biomedical informatics and the management and dissemination of biomedical knowledge. Biomedical informatics research applies computer and information sciences to improve the access, storage, retrieval, management, dissemination, and use of biomedical information. Applications are received through "parent" NIH funding announcements or through special funding opportunity announcements issued by EP. Each year, NLM makes new and/or continuing awards in these five grant categories: Research Projects, Resources, Career Development, Research Career Training, and Small Business Research & Development. NLM's EP FY2012 base budget for grant awards was $44,281,000, the same amount as in FY2011. One hundred thirty-seven new and continuing awards were made with NLM's appropriated funds. An additional $3.3 million in co-funding was received for 11 awards from other NIH and Department of Health and Human Services (DHHS) sources. FY2012 funds were awarded to 35 organizations in 32 states.[33]

OUTREACH, EXHIBITIONS, AND TRAINING

NLM conducts its outreach primarily through the National Network of Libraries of Medicine (NN/LM), its network of over 6000 organizations throughout the country. These include academic medical libraries, hospital, pharmaceutical and other special health sciences libraries, information centers, public libraries, and community-based organizations with an interest in promoting access to health information. The NN/LM was created through the Medical Library Assistance Act of 1965 (Public Law 89-291), which both authorized NLM's extramural programs of grant assistance to improve the nation's medical library and health communication resources as well as establishing the Regional Medical Library Network (now called the National Network of Libraries of Medicine). The introduction of an extension of the National Library of Medicine to the rest of the country through the NN/LM caused some contention at first among health sciences libraries, but in time the creation of the Network only served to strengthen the ties to health sciences libraries and extend NLM's influence.[34] Other offices and divisions that conduct outreach are the Office of Health Information Program Development, which sponsors specialized programs in outreach to elementary through high school students in choosing careers in health; a program called VIVA!, peer tutoring for the Latino population in Texas and elsewhere; and Native American outreach through NLM representation at American Indian Pow-Wows through the Mid-Atlantic area. The division of Specialized Information Services (SIS) also conducts outreach, focusing on reaching special populations of minority populations through its United Negro College Funds Special Programs (UNCFSP) HBCU Access Project; debuting an outreach effort in 2012 to Black Greek Letter Organizations to combat health disparities; training in the use of NLM resources through partnerships with minority health professional organizations; and through the development of special population web sites focusing on health information including the American Indian Health Web Portal, Women's Health Resources, Arctic Health Web Site, and the Refugee Health Information Network (RHIN).[33]

National Network of Libraries of Medicine (NN/LM)

Today, the NN/LM is comprised of eight regions throughout the country, each led by a Regional Medical Library (RML), through a contract awarded every 5 years from the National Library of Medicine. The current Regional Medical Libraries are based at the University of Massachusetts, University of Pittsburgh, University of Maryland, Baltimore, Houston Academy of Medicine/Texas Medical Center, University of Utah, University of California, Los Angeles, University of Illinois at Chicago, and the University of Washington. These Regional Medical Libraries employ staff that vary in size from five to eleven, and extend the National Library of Medicine's reach and assistance to medical libraries through education and training and outreach, and the reduction of health disparities.

With the assistance of other NN/LM members, the RMLs do most of the exhibits and demonstrations of NLM products and services at health professional, consumer health, and general library association meetings around the country. In FY2012, NLM and NN/LM services were exhibited at 29 national and 281 regional, state, and local conferences across the United States.

RMLs and other network members conduct many special projects to reach underserved health professionals and to improve the public's access to high quality health information. Virtually all of these projects involve partnerships between health sciences libraries and other organizations, including public libraries, public health departments, professional associations, schools, churches, and other community-based groups. In FY2012, the NN/LM initiated 232 outreach projects which target rural and inner city communities and special populations in 37 states, the District of Columbia, U.S. Virgin Islands, Puerto Rico, and Guam.[33]

DIMRC

A relatively recent addition to NLM's outreach efforts was the creation of a Disaster Information Management Research Center. Recognizing the untapped potential of libraries, librarians, and information services to aid in the nation's disaster management efforts, the Long Range Plan (2006–2016) recommended the creation of a Disaster Information Management Research Center to help with national emergency preparedness, response, and recovery efforts. As part of NLM's SIS division, DIMRC is tasked with the collection, organization and dissemination of health information resources and informatics research related to disasters of natural, accidental, or deliberate origin. NLM has a long history of providing health information to prepare for and respond to all types of disasters, and has developed a number of tools and advanced information services designed for disaster and emergency. NLM provided information for the Bhopal, India gas leak in 1984 and helped create local disaster information centers following Hurricane Mitch in Central America. NLM's Hazardous Substances Data Bank (HSDB®), a comprehensive toxicology database, provides the framework for the Wireless Information System for Emergency Responders (WISER®), a resource used by emergency responders to assist with the management of chemical, radiological, and biological emergencies. WISER was used in Louisiana after Hurricane Katrina, and in Iraq to help identify potentially toxic substances. More recently, NLM assisted public health officials responding to H1N1 influenza, earthquakes in Haiti and Chile, the Gulf of Mexico oil spill, and the Japanese radiation event, by providing timely, evidence-based information.[35]

Exhibitions

NLM hosts major exhibitions in its rotunda. Designed to appeal to the interested public as well as the specialist, these exhibitions highlight the Library's resources and are an important part of NLM's outreach program. The most recent exhibition is *Native Voices: Native Peoples' Concepts of Health and Illness*, exploring the interconnectedness of wellness, illness, and cultural life for Native Americans, Alaska Natives, and Native Hawaiians. Through the extensive use of interviews and media, visitors discover how Native concepts of health and illness are closely tied to the concepts of community, spirit, and the land. NLM sent out 25 copies of 12 exhibition titles, to 156 host venues, most in libraries, in 43 states, and five international locations during 2012. Host venues and their audiences had positive and favorable responses to the traveling exhibition program. All exhibitions also feature an online counterpart as well.[33]

Training

The fourth goal of the Long Range Plan 2006–2016 is a strong and diverse workforce for biomedical informatics research, systems development, and innovative service delivery. NLM meets this goal in part through its training programs, from its early career fellowship program for recent library science graduates, to mid-career training opportunities in biomedical informatics, funded support for academic training in biomedical informatics, fellowships in medical informatics and senior level career support for health sciences librarians preparing for director-level positions in academic health sciences libraries.[36] Many health sciences library directors, distinguished informatics researchers, and leaders in health information technology are graduates of these programs.

CONCLUSIONS

As the National Library of Medicine moves more fully into the twenty-first century, it can see the fulfillment of many initiatives begun in the last century: the greater availability of the scholarly literature through online repositories, and through its own web sites of digital collections and the integration of and use of its databases and terminologies into others' work through the creation of apps, and repurposing of terminologies used in other settings. The National Library of Medicine also continues to chart its future, through its research and development branches, the awarding of extramural grants, and through its investment in the future in training a biomedical workforce. The underlying commitment of the National Library of Medicine remains the same: the acquisition, organization, and preservation of the biomedical literature for the public.

REFERENCES

1. *Memorial Meeting in Honor* of the Late Dr. John Shaw Billings; Medical Library Association, April 25, 1913; p. 10.
2. Miles, W.D. *A History of the National Library of Medicine*; The Library: Bethesda, MD, 1982.
3. U.S. Department of Health and Human Services, National Institutes of Health, National Library of Medicine. *Collection Development Manual of the National Library of Medicine*, 4th Ed.; 2004 (accessed December 19, 2013).
4. National Library of Medicine (US) Board of Regents. *Long Range Plan*; The Library: Bethesda, MD, January 1987.
5. National Library of Medicine. *NLM Welcome Video*; National Library of Medicine: Bethesda, MD, 2002.
6. Jeff, E. Innovation at NIH: Donald Lindberg, senior statesman for medicine and computers, Breakinggov.com, http://breakinggov.com/2012/05/16/innovation-at-nih-donald-lindberg-senior-statesman-for-medicin/ (May 16, 2012).
7. *Government Performance and Results Act of 1993*, Public Law 103-62, 103rd Congress, January 5, 1993.
8. Womack, K.; Eannarino, J. Collection Development Manual: CDM, Presentation to the NLM Associate Fellows, Bethesda, MD, September 16, 2013.
9. National Library of Medicine. Fact sheet: Preservation and collection management program, http://www.nlm.nih.gov/pubs/factsheets/preservation.html (accessed December 19, 2013).
10. National Library of Medicine. Medprint—Medical serials preservation program, http://www.nlm.nih.gov/psd/print_retention_about.html (accessed December 19, 2013).
11. National Library of Medicine. 175 years: A fantastic voyage, http://apps.nlm.nih.gov/175/index.cfm (accessed December 19, 2013).
12. Collins, M.E. DOCLINE Users Group Meeting, Presentation at the Medical Library Association, Boston, MA, May 2013.
13. Frant, L., National Library of Medicine. NLM digital programs, Presentation at the Medical Library Association, Boston, MA, May 6, 2013.
14. National Library of Medicine. PMC overview, http://www.ncbi.nlm.nih.gov/pmc/about/intro/ (accessed December 19, 2013).
15. National Library of Medicine. About digital collections, http://collections.nlm.nih.gov/about (accessed December 19, 2013).
16. National Library of Medicine. About profiles in science, http://profiles.nlm.nih.gov/ps/display/About (accessed December 19, 2013).
17. National Library of Medicine. NLM web collecting FAQs, http://www.nlm.nih.gov/webcollecting/ (accessed December 19, 2013).
18. National Library of Medicine. Fact sheet: PubMed: MEDLINE Retrieval on the World Wide Web, http://www.nlm.nih.gov/pubs/factsheets/pubmed.html (accessed December 19, 2013).
19. Canese, K. PubMed update, Presentation at the *Medical Library Association Meeting*, Boston, MA, May 2013.
20. U.S. Department of Health and Human Services, National Institutes of Health, National Library of Medicine.

Programs and Services. Fiscal Year 2011. (accessed January 6, 2014).
21. PubMed commons: A new forum for scientific discourse, *NCBI Insights* (blog), October 22, 2013, http://ncbiinsights.ncbi.nlm.nih.gov/2013/10/22/pubmed-commons-a-new-forum-for-scientific-discourse/.
22. National Library of Medicine. MedlinePlus connect, http://www.nlm.nih.gov/medlineplus/connect/overview.html (accessed December 19, 2013).
23. National Library of Medicine. About MedlinePlus, http://www.nlm.nih.gov/medlineplus/aboutmedlineplus.html (accessed December 19, 2013).
24. National Library of Medicine. ClinicalTrials.gov background, http://clinicaltrials.gov/ct2/about-site/background (accessed December 19, 2013).
25. National Library of Medicine. Medical terminologies at NLM, https://www.nlm.nih.gov/medical-terms.html (accessed December 19, 2013).
26. National Library of Medicine. Fact sheet: Medical subject headings MeSH, http://www.nlm.nih.gov/pubs/factsheets/mesh.html (accessed December 19, 2013).
27. National Library of Medicine. Fact sheet: Unified medical language system, http://www.nlm.nih.gov/pubs/factsheets/umls.html (accessed December 19, 2013).
28. National Library of Medicine. RxNorm overview, http://www.nlm.nih.gov/research/umls/rxnorm/overview.html (last modified January 6, 2014).
29. National Library of Medicine. Supporting Interoperability—Terminology, subsets, and other resources from NLM, http://www.nlm.nih.gov/hit_interoperability.html (accessed December 19, 2013).
30. National Library of Medicine. NLM launches value set authority center, http://www.nlm.nih.gov/news/value_set_authority_center.html (accessed December 19, 2013).
31. National Library of Medicine. Value set authority center, https://vsac.nlm.nih.gov/ (accessed December 19, 2013).
32. National Library of Medicine. GenBank overview, http://www.ncbi.nlm.nih.gov/genbank/ (accessed December 19, 2013).
33. U.S. Department of Health and Human Services, National Institutes of Health, National Library of Medicine. Programs and Services. Fiscal Year 2012.
34. Humphreys, B.L. Adjusting to progress: interactions between the National Library of Medicine and health sciences librarians, 1961–2001. J. Med. Libr. Assoc. **2002**, *90* (1), 4–20.
35. National Library of Medicine. Fact sheet: Disaster information management research center, http://www.nlm.nih.gov/pubs/factsheets/dimrcfs.html (accessed December 19, 2013).
36. National Library of Medicine. Training and outreach, https://www.nlm.nih.gov/training.html (accessed December 19, 2013).

Natural Language Processing for Information Retrieval

Elizabeth D. Liddy
School of Information Studies, Syracuse University, Syracuse, New York, U.S.A.

Abstract

Natural language processing (NLP) is the computerized approach to analyzing text that is based on both a set of theories and a set of technologies. Although NLP is a relatively recent area of research and application, compared with other information technology approaches, there have been sufficient successes to date that suggest that NLP-based information access technologies will continue to be a major area of research and development in information systems now and into the future.

INTRODUCTION

Natural language processing (NLP) is the computerized approach to analyzing text that is based on both a set of theories and a set of technologies. And, being a very active area of research and development, there is not a single agreed-upon definition that would satisfy everyone, but there are some aspects, which would be part of any knowledgeable person's definition. I offer the following definition: Natural language processing is a theoretically motivated range of computational techniques for analyzing and representing naturally occurring texts at one or more levels of linguistic analysis for the purpose of achieving human-like language processing for a range of tasks or applications.

Several elements of this definition can be further detailed. First, the imprecise notion of "range of computational techniques" is necessary because there are multiple methods or techniques from which to choose to accomplish a particular type of language analysis.

"Naturally occurring texts" can be of any language, mode, genre, etc. The texts can be oral or written. The only requirement is that they be in a language used by humans to communicate to one another. In addition, the text being analyzed should not be specifically constructed for the purpose of the analysis, but rather that the text be gathered from actual usage.

The notion of "levels of linguistic analysis" (to be further explained in the section titled "Levels of Natural Language Processing") refers to the fact that there are multiple types of language processing known to be at work when humans produce or comprehend language. It is thought that humans normally use all of these levels because each level conveys different types of meaning. But various NLP systems use different levels or combinations of levels of linguistic analysis, and this is seen in the differences among various NLP applications. This also leads to much confusion on the part of nonspecialists as to what NLP really is, because a system that uses any subset of these levels of analysis can be said to be an NLP-based system. The difference between them, therefore, may actually be whether the system uses "weak" NLP or "strong" NLP.

"Human-like language processing" reveals that NLP is considered a discipline within artificial intelligence (AI). And although the full lineage of NLP does depend on a number of other disciplines, because NLP strives for human-like performance, it is appropriate to consider it an AI discipline.

"For a range of tasks or applications" points out that NLP is not usually considered a goal in and of itself, except perhaps for AI researchers. For others, NLP is the means for accomplishing a particular task. Therefore, you have Information Retrieval (IR) systems that use NLP, as well as machine translation (MT), question-answering, etc.

Goal

The goal of NLP as stated above is "to accomplish human-like language processing." The choice of the word "processing" is very deliberate and should not be replaced with "understanding." For although the field of NLP was originally referred to as natural language understanding (NLU) in the early days of AI, it is well agreed today that although the goal of NLP is true NLU, that goal has not yet been accomplished. A full NLU system would be able to:

1. Paraphrase an input text.
2. Translate the text into another language.
3. Answer questions about the contents of the text.
4. Draw inferences from the text.

Although NLP has made serious inroads into accomplishing goals 1–3, the fact that NLP systems cannot, of themselves, draw inferences from text, NLU still remains the goal of NLP.

Encyclopedia of Library and Information Sciences, Fourth Edition DOI: 10.1081/E-ELIS4-120008664

There are more practical goals for NLP, many related to the particular application for which it is being used. For example, an NLP-based IR system has the goal of providing more precise, complete information in response to a user's real information need. The goal of the NLP system here is to represent the true meaning and intent of the user's query, which can be expressed as naturally in everyday language as if they were speaking to a reference librarian. In addition, the contents of the documents that are being searched will be represented at all their levels of meaning so that a true match between need and response can be found, no matter how either are expressed in their surface form.

Origins

As most modern disciplines, the lineage of NLP is indeed mixed and still today has strong emphases by different groups whose backgrounds are more influenced by one or another of the disciplines. Key among the contributors to the discipline and practice of NLP are the following: Linguistics focuses on formal, structural models of language and the discovery of language universals—in fact, the field of NLP was originally referred to as computational linguistics; computer science is concerned with developing internal representations of data and efficient processing of these structures; and cognitive psychology looks at language usage as a window into human cognitive processes and has the goal of modeling the use of language in a psychologically plausible way.

Divisions

Although the entire field is referred to as natural language processing, there are in fact two distinct focuses: language processing and language generation. The first of these refers to the analysis of language for the purpose of producing a meaningful representation, whereas the latter refers to the production of language from a representation. The task of NLP is equivalent to the role of reader/listener, whereas the task of natural language generation is that of the writer/speaker. Although much of the theory and technology are shared by these two divisions, natural language generation also requires a planning capability. That is, the generation system requires a plan or model of the goal of the interaction to decide what the system should generate at each point in an interaction. We focus on the task of natural language analysis, because this is most relevant to library and information science studies.

Another distinction is traditionally made between language understanding and speech understanding. Speech understanding starts with, and speech generation ends with, oral language and, therefore, rely on the additional fields of acoustics and phonology. Speech understanding focuses on how the "sounds" of language as picked up by the system in the form of acoustical waves are transcribed into recognizable morphemes and words. Once in this form, the same levels of processing, which are used on written text are used. All of these levels, including the phonology level, are covered in "Levels of Natural Language Processing"; however, the emphasis throughout is on language in the written form.

BRIEF HISTORY OF NATURAL LANGUAGE PROCESSING

Research in natural language processing has been going on for several decades dating back to the late 1940s. Machine translation (MT) was the first computer-based application related to natural language. Although Weaver and Booth[1,2] started one of the earliest MT projects in 1946 on computer translation based on expertise in breaking enemy codes during World War II, it was generally agreed that it was Weaver's memorandum of 1949 that brought the idea of MT to general notice and inspired many projects.[3] He suggested using ideas from cryptography and information theory for language translation. Research began at various research institutions in the United States within a few years.

Early work in MT took the simplistic view that the only differences between languages resided in their vocabularies and the permitted word orders. Systems developed from this perspective simply used dictionary lookup for appropriate words for translation and reordered the words after translation to fit the word-order rules of the target language, without taking into account the lexical ambiguity inherent in natural language. This produced poor results. The apparent failure made researchers realize that the task was a lot harder than anticipated, and they needed a more adequate theory of language. However, it was not until 1957 when Chomsky[4] published *Syntactic Structures* introducing the idea of generative grammar, did the field gain better insight into whether or how mainstream linguistics could help MT.

During this period, other NLP application areas began to emerge, such as speech recognition. The language-processing community and the speech community then were split into two camps with the language-processing community dominated by the theoretical perspective of generative grammar and hostile to statistical methods, and the speech community dominated by statistical information theory[5] and hostile to theoretical linguistics.[6]

Because of the developments of the syntactic theory of language and parsing algorithms, there was such enthusiasm in the 1950s that people believed that fully automatic high-quality translation systems[2] would be able to produce results indistinguishable from those of human translators, and such systems should be in operation within a few years. It was not only unrealistic, given the then-available linguistic knowledge and computer systems, but also impossible in principle.[3]

The inadequacies of then-existing systems, and perhaps accompanied by the overenthusiasm, led to the ALPAC (Automatic Language Processing Advisory Committee of the National Academy of Science–National Research Council) report of 1966.[7] The report concluded that MT was not immediately achievable and recommended it not be funded. This had the effect of halting MT and most work in other applications of NLP at least within the United States.

Although there was a substantial decrease in NLP work during the years after the ALPAC report, there were some significant developments, both in theoretical issues and in construction of prototype systems. Theoretical work in the late 1960s and early 1970s focused on the issue of how to represent meaning and developing computationally tractable solutions that the then-existing theories of grammar were not able to produce. In 1965, Chomsky[8] introduced the transformational model of linguistic competence. However, the transformational generative grammars were too syntactically oriented to allow for semantic concerns. They also did not lend themselves easily to computational implementation. As a reaction to Chomsky's theories and the work of other transformational generativists, case grammar of Fillmore,[9] semantic networks of Quillian,[10] and conceptual dependency theory of Schank[11] were developed to explain syntactic anomalies and provide semantic representations. Augmented transition networks of Woods[12] extended the power of phrase-structure grammar by incorporating mechanisms from programming languages such as LISP. Other representation formalisms included Wilks' preference semantics[13] and Kay's functional grammar.[14]

Alongside theoretical development, many prototype systems were developed to demonstrate the effectiveness of particular principles. Weizenbaum's ELIZA[15] was built to replicate the conversation between a psychologist and a patient, simply by permuting or echoing the user input. Winograd's SHRDLU[16] simulated a robot that manipulated blocks on a tabletop. Despite its limitations, it showed that natural language understanding was indeed possible for the computer.[17] PARRY[18] attempted to embody a theory of paranoia in a system. Instead of single keywords, it used groups of keywords and used synonyms if keywords were not found. LUNAR was developed by Woods[19] as an interface system to a database that consisted of information about lunar rock samples using augmented transition network and procedural semantics.[20]

In the late 1970s, attention shifted to semantic issues, discourse phenomena, and communicative goals and plans.[21] Grosz[22] analyzed task-oriented dialogues and proposed a theory to partition the discourse into units based on her findings about the relation between the structure of a task and the structure of the task-oriented dialogue. Mann and Thompson[23] developed Rhetorical Structure Theory, attributing hierarchical structure to discourse. Other researchers have also made significant contributions, including Hobbs and Rosenschein,[24] Polanyi and Scha,[25] and Reichman.[26]

This period also saw considerable work on natural language generation. McKeown's discourse planner TEXT[27] and McDonald's response generator MUMMBLE[28] used rhetorical predicates to produce declarative descriptions in the form of short texts, usually paragraphs. TEXT's ability to generate coherent responses on-line was considered a major achievement.

In the early 1980s, motivated by the availability of critical computational resources, the growing awareness within each community of the limitations of isolated solutions to NLP problems,[21] and a general push toward applications that worked with language in a broad, real-world context,[6] researchers started reexamining nonsymbolic approaches that had lost popularity in early days. By the end of the 1980s, symbolic approaches had been used to address many significant problems in NLP, and statistical approaches were shown to be complementary in many respects to symbolic approaches.[21]

In the last 10 years of the millennium, the field was growing rapidly. This can be attributed to the following: 1) increased availability of large amounts of electronic text; 2) availability of computers with increased speed and memory; and 3) the advent of the Internet. Statistical approaches succeeded in dealing with many generic problems in computational linguistics such as part-of-speech identification, word sense disambiguation, etc. and have become standard throughout NLP.[29] Researchers of NLP are now developing next-generation NLP systems that deal reasonably well with general text and account for a good portion of the variability and ambiguity of language.

LEVELS OF NATURAL LANGUAGE PROCESSING

The most explanatory method for presenting what actually happens within a natural language processing system is by means of the "levels of language" approach. This is also referred to as the synchronic model of language and is distinguished from the earlier sequential model, which hypothesizes that the levels of human language processing follow one another in a strictly sequential manner. Psycholinguistic research suggests that language processing is much more dynamic, because the levels can interact in a variety of orders. Introspection reveals that we frequently use information we gain from what is typically thought of as a higher level of processing to assist in a lower level of analysis. For example, the pragmatic knowledge that the document you are reading is about biology will be used when a particular word that has several possible senses (or meanings) is encountered, and the word will be interpreted as having the biology sense.

Of necessity, the following description of levels is presented sequentially. The key point here is that meaning is conveyed by each and every level of language and that because humans have been shown to use all levels of language to gain understanding, the more capable an NLP system is, the more levels of language it will use (Fig. 1).

Phonology

This level deals with the interpretation of speech sounds within and across words. There are, in fact, three types of rules used in phonological analysis: 1) phonetic rules for sounds within words; 2) phonemic rules for variations of pronunciation when words are spoken together; and 3) prosodic rules for fluctuation in stress and intonation across a sentence. In an NLP system that accepts spoken input, the sound waves are analyzed and encoded into a digitized signal for interpretation by various rules or by comparison to the particular language model being used.

Morphology

This level deals with the componential nature of words, which are composed of morphemes (the smallest units of meaning). For example, the word *preregistration* can be morphologically analyzed into three separate morphemes: the prefix *pre*, the root *registra*, and the suffix *tion*. Because the meaning of each morpheme remains the same across words, humans can break down an unknown word into its constituent morphemes to understand its meaning. Similarly, an NLP system can recognize the meaning conveyed by each morpheme to gain and represent meaning. For example, adding the suffix *-ed* to a verb, conveys that the action of the verb took place in the past. This is a key piece of meaning, and in fact, is frequently only evidenced in a text by the use of the *-ed* morpheme.

Lexical

At this level, humans, as well as NLP systems, interpret the meaning of individual words. Several types of processing contribute to word-level understanding (the first of these being assignment of a single part of speech tag to each word). In this processing, words that can function as more than one part of speech are assigned the most probable part of speech tag based on the context in which they occur.

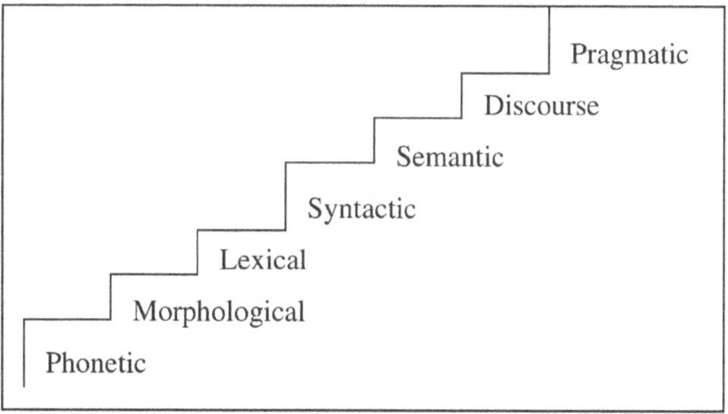

Fig. 1 Model of synchronized language processing.

In addition, at the lexical level, those words that have only one possible sense or meaning can be replaced by a semantic representation of that meaning. The nature of the representation varies according to the semantic theory used in the NLP system. The following representation of the meaning of the word *launch* is in the form of logical predicates. As can be observed, a single lexical unit is decomposed into its more basic properties. Given that there is a set of semantic primitives used across all words, these simplified lexical representations make it possible to unify meaning across words and to produce complex interpretations, much the same as humans do.

launch(a large boat used for carrying people on rivers,
lakes harbors,etc.)((CLASS BOAT PROPERTIES
(LARGE)(PURPOSE(PREDICATION
(CLASS CARRY(OBJECT PEOPLE))))

The lexical level may require a lexicon, and the particular approach taken by an NLP system will determine whether a lexicon will be used, as well as the nature and extent of information that is encoded in the lexicon. Lexicons may be quite simple, with only the words and their part(s) of speech, or may be increasingly complex and contain information on the semantic class of the word, what arguments it takes, and the semantic limitations on these arguments, definitions of the sense(s) in the semantic representation used in the particular system, and even the semantic field in which each sense of a polysemous word is used.

Syntactic

This level focuses on analyzing the words in a sentence to uncover the grammatical structure of the sentence. This requires both a grammar and a parser. The output of this level of processing is a (possibly delinearized) representation of the sentence that reveals the structural dependency relationships between the words. There are various grammars that can be used and that will, in turn, impact the choice of a parser. Not all NLP applications require a full parse of sentences; therefore, the remaining challenges in parsing of prepositional phrase attachment and conjunction scoping no longer stymie those applications for which phrasal and clausal dependencies are sufficient. Syntax conveys meaning in most languages because order and dependency contribute to meaning. For example, the two sentences "The dog chased the cat." and "The cat chased the dog." differ only in terms of syntax, yet they convey quite different meanings.

Semantic

This is the level at which most people think meaning is determined; however, as we can see in the above defining of the levels, it is all the levels that contribute to meaning. Semantic processing determines the possible meanings of a sentence by focusing on the interactions among word-level meanings in the sentence. This level of processing can include the semantic disambiguation of words with multiple senses; in an analogous way to how syntactic disambiguation of words that can function as multiple parts of speech is accomplished at the syntactic level. Semantic disambiguation permits one and only one sense of polysemous words to be selected and included in the semantic representation of the sentence. For example, among other meanings, "file" as a noun can mean either a folder for storing papers, or a tool to shape one's fingernails, or a line of individuals in a queue. If information from the rest of the sentence were required for the disambiguation, the semantic, not the lexical level, would do the disambiguation. A wide range of methods can be implemented to accomplish the disambiguation, some which require information as to the frequency with which each sense occurs in a particular corpus of interest, or in general usage, some which require consideration of the local context, and others which use pragmatic knowledge of the domain of the document.

Discourse

Although syntax and semantics work with sentence-length units, the discourse level of NLP works with units of text longer than a sentence. That is, it does not interpret multisentence texts as just concatenated sentences, each of which can be interpreted singly. Rather, discourse focuses on the properties of the text as a whole that convey meaning by making connections between component sentences. Several types of discourse processing can occur at this level; two of the most common are anaphora resolution and discourse/text structure recognition. Anaphora resolution is the replacing of words such as pronouns, which are semantically vacant, with the appropriate entity to which they refer.[30] Discourse/text structure recognition determines the functions of sentences in the text, which, in turn, adds to the meaningful representation of the text. For example, newspaper articles can be deconstructed into discourse components such as lead, main story, previous events, evaluation, attributed quotes, and expectation.[31]

Pragmatic

This level is concerned with the purposeful use of language in situations and uses context over and above the contents of the text for understanding The goal is to explain how extra meaning is read into texts without actually being encoded in them. This requires much world knowledge, including the understanding of intentions, plans, and goals. Some NLP applications may use knowledge bases and inferencing modules. For example, the following two sentences require resolution of the anaphoric term "they," but this resolution requires pragmatic or world knowledge.

> The city councilors refused the demonstrators a permit because they feared violence.
>
> The city councilors refused the demonstrators a permit because they advocated revolution.

Summary of Levels

Current NLP systems tend to implement modules to accomplish mainly the lower levels of processing. This is for several reasons. First, the application may not require interpretation at the higher levels. Second, the lower levels have been more thoroughly researched and implemented. Third, the lower levels deal with smaller units of analysis (e.g., morphemes, words, and sentences), which are rule governed versus the higher levels of language processing, which deal with texts and world knowledge, and which are only regularity governed. As is seen in the following section on approaches, the statistical approaches have, to date, been validated on the lower levels of analysis, whereas the symbolic approaches have dealt with all levels, although there are still few working systems that incorporate the higher levels.

APPROACHES TO NATURAL LANGUAGE PROCESSING

Natural language processing approaches fall roughly into four categories: symbolic, statistical, connectionist, and hybrid. Symbolic and statistical approaches have coexisted since the early days of this field. Connectionist NLP work first appeared in the 1960s. For a long time, symbolic approaches dominated the field. In the 1980s, statistical approaches regained popularity as a result of the availability of critical computational resources and the need to deal with broad, real-world contexts. Connectionist approaches also recovered from earlier criticism by demonstrating the utility of neural networks in NLP. This section examines each of these approaches in their foundations, typical techniques, differences in processing and system aspects, and their robustness, flexibility, and suitability for various tasks.

Symbolic Approach

Symbolic approaches perform deep analysis of linguistic phenomena and are based on explicit representation of facts about language through well-understood knowledge representation schemes and associated algorithms.[21] In fact, the description of the levels of language analysis in the preceding section is given from a symbolic perspective. The primary source of evidence in symbolic systems comes from rules and lexicons developed by humans.

A good example of symbolic approaches is seen in logic- or rule-based systems. In logic-based systems, the symbolic structure is usually in the form of logic propositions. Manipulations of such structures are defined by inference procedures that are generally truth preserving. Rule-based systems usually consist of a set of rules, an inference engine, and a work space or working memory. Knowledge is represented as facts or rules in the rule base. The inference engine repeatedly selects a rule whose condition is satisfied and executes the rule.

Another example of symbolic approaches is semantic networks. First proposed by Quillian[10] to model associative memory in psychology, semantic networks represent knowledge through a set of nodes that represent objects or concepts and the labeled links that represent relations between nodes. The pattern of connectivity reflects semantic organization (i.e., highly associated concepts are directly linked, whereas moderately or weakly related concepts are linked through intervening concepts). Semantic networks are widely used to represent structured knowledge and have the most connectionist flavor of the symbolic models.[32]

Symbolic approaches have been used for a few decades in a variety of research areas and applications such as information extraction, text categorization, ambiguity resolution, and lexical acquisition. Typical techniques include explanation-based learning, rule-based learning, inductive logic programming, decision trees, conceptual clustering, and K nearest neighbor algorithms.[6,33]

Statistical Approach

Statistical approaches use various mathematical techniques and often use large text corpora to develop approximate generalized models of linguistic phenomena based on actual examples of these phenomena provided by the text corpora without adding significant linguistic or world knowledge. In contrast to symbolic approaches, statistical approaches use observable data as the primary source of evidence.

A frequently used statistical model is the Hidden Markov Model (HMM) inherited from the speech community. The HMM is a finite state automaton that has a set of states with probabilities attached to transitions between states.[34] Although outputs are visible, states themselves are not directly observable, thus "hidden" from external observations. Each state produces one of the observable outputs with a certain probability.

Statistical approaches have typically been used in tasks such as speech recognition, lexical acquisition, parsing, part of speech tagging, collocations, statistical machine translation, statistical grammar learning, etc.

Connectionist Approach

Similar to the statistical approaches, connectionist approaches also develop generalized models from examples of linguistic phenomena. What separates connectionism from other statistical methods is that connectionist models combine statistical learning with various theories of representation; thus, the connectionist representations allow transformation, inference, and manipulation of logic formulas.[33] In addition, in connectionist systems, linguistic models are harder to observe because connectionist architectures are less constrained than statistical ones.[21,35]

Generally speaking, a connectionist model is a network of interconnected simple processing units with knowledge stored in the weights of the connections between units.[32] Local interactions among units can result in dynamic global behavior, which, in turn, leads to computation.

Some connectionist models are called localist models, assuming that each unit represents a particular concept. For example, one unit might represent the concept "mammal," whereas another unit might represent the concept "whale." Relations between concepts are encoded by the weights of connections between those concepts. Knowledge in such models is spread across the network, and the connectivity between units reflects their structural relationship. Localist models are quite similar to semantic networks, but the links between units are not usually labeled because they are in semantic nets. They perform well at tasks such as word-sense disambiguation, language generation, and limited inference.[36]

Other connectionist models are called distributed models. Unlike that in localist models, a concept in distributed models is represented as a function of simultaneous activation of multiple units. An individual unit only participates in a concept representation. These models are well suited for natural language processing tasks such as syntactic parsing, limited domain translation tasks, and associative retrieval.

Comparison Among Approaches

From the above section, we have seen that similarities and differences exist between approaches in their assumptions, philosophical foundations, and source of evidence. In addition to that, the similarities and differences can also be reflected in the processes each approach follows, as well as in system aspects, robustness, flexibility, and suitable tasks.

Process

Research using these different approaches follows a general set of steps, namely, data collection, data analysis/

model building, rule/data construction, and application of rules/data in system. The data collection stage is critical to all three approaches although statistical and connectionist approaches typically require much more data than symbolic approaches. In the data analysis/model building stage, symbolic approaches rely on human analysis of the data to form a theory, whereas statistical approaches manually define a statistical model that is an approximate generalization of the collected data. Connectionist approaches build a connectionist model from the data. In the rule/data construction stage, manual efforts are typical for symbolic approaches, and the theory formed in the previous step may evolve when new cases are encountered. In contrast, statistical and connectionist approaches use the statistical or connectionist model as guidance and build rules or data items automatically, usually in relatively large quantity. After building rules or data items, all approaches then automatically apply them to specific tasks in the system. For instance, connectionist approaches may apply the rules to train the weights of links between units.

System Aspects

By system aspects, we mean source of data, theory, or model formed from data analysis, rules, and basis for evaluation.

Data. As mentioned earlier, symbolic approaches use human introspective data, which are usually not directly observable. Statistical and connectionist approaches are built on the basis of machine-observable facets of data, usually from text corpora.

Theory or Model Based on Data Analysis. As the outcome of data analysis, a theory is formed for symbolic approaches whereas a parametric model is formed for statistical approaches, and a connectionist model is formed for connectionist approaches.

Rules. For symbolic approaches, the rule construction stage usually results in rules with detailed criteria of rule application. For statistical approaches, the criteria of rule application are usually at the surface level or underspecified. For connectionist approaches, individual rules typically cannot be recognized.

Basis for Evaluation. Evaluation of symbolic systems is typically based on intuitive judgments of unaffiliated subjects and may use system-internal measures of growth such as the number of new rules. In contrast, the basis for evaluation of statistical and connectionist systems are usually in the form of scores computed from some evaluation function. However, if all approaches are used for the same task, then the results of the task can be evaluated both quantitatively and qualitatively and compared.

Robustness

Symbolic systems may be fragile when presented with unusual or noisy input. To deal with anomalies, they can anticipate them by making the grammar more general to accommodate them. Compared to symbolic systems, statistical systems may be more robust in the face of unexpected input provided that training data is sufficient, which may be difficult to be assured of. Connectionist systems may also be robust and fault tolerant because knowledge in such systems is stored across the network. When presented with noisy input, they degrade gradually.

Flexibility

Because symbolic models are built by human analysis of well-formulated examples, symbolic systems may lack the flexibility to adapt dynamically to experience. In contrast, statistical systems allow broad coverage and may be better able to deal with unrestricted text[21] for more effective handling of the task at hand. Connectionist systems exhibit flexibility by dynamically acquiring appropriate behavior based on the given input. For example, the weights of a connectionist network can be adapted in real time to improve performance. However, such systems may have difficulty with the representation of structures needed to handle complex conceptual relationships, thus limiting their abilities to handle high-level NLP.[36]

Suitable Tasks

Symbolic approaches seem to be suited for phenomena that exhibit identifiable linguistic behavior. They can be used to model phenomena at all the various linguistic levels described in earlier sections. Statistical approaches have proven to be effective in modeling language phenomena based on frequent use of language as reflected in text corpora. Linguistic phenomena that are not well understood or do not exhibit clear regularity are candidates for statistical approaches. Similar to statistical approaches, connectionist approaches can also deal with linguistic phenomena that are not well understood. They are useful for low-level NLP tasks that are usually subtasks in a larger problem.

To summarize, symbolic, statistical, and connectionist approaches have exhibited different characteristics; thus, some problems may be better tackled with one approach and other problems by another. In some cases, for some specific tasks, one approach may prove adequate, whereas in other cases, the tasks can get so complex that it might not be possible to choose a single best approach. In addition, as Klavans and Resnik[6] pointed out, there is no such thing as a "purely statistical" method. Every use of statistics is based on a symbolic model and statistics alone is not adequate for NLP. Toward this end, statistical approaches are not at odds with symbolic approaches. In fact, they are rather complementary. As a result, researchers have begun developing hybrid techniques that use the strengths of each approach in an attempt to address NLP problems more effectively and in a more flexible manner.

NATURAL LANGUAGE PROCESSING APPLICATIONS

Natural language processing provides both theory and implementations for a range of applications. In fact, any application that uses text is a candidate for NLP. The most frequent applications using NLP include the following:

- Information retrieval. Given the significant presence of text in this application, it is surprising that so few implementations use NLP. Recently, statistical approaches for accomplishing NLP have seen more use, but few systems other than those by Liddy[37] and Strzalkowski[38] have developed significant systems based on NLP.
- Information extraction (IE). A more recent application area, IE focuses on the recognition, tagging, and extraction into a structured representation, certain key elements of information (e.g., persons, companies, locations, and organizations) from large collections of text. These extractions can then be used for a range of applications including question-answering, visualization, and data mining.
- Question-answering. In contrast to Information Retrieval, which provides a list of potentially relevant documents in response to a user's query, question-answering provides the user with either just the text of the answer itself or answer-providing passages.
- Summarization. The higher levels of NLP, particularly the discourse level, can empower an implementation that reduces a larger text into a shorter, yet richly constituted abbreviated narrative representation of the original document.
- Machine translation. Perhaps the oldest of all NLP applications, various levels of NLP have been used in MT systems, ranging from the word-based approach to applications that include higher levels of analysis.
- Dialogue systems. Perhaps the omnipresent application of the future, in the systems envisioned by large providers of end-user applications. Dialogue systems, which usually focus on a narrowly defined application (e.g. your refrigerator or home sound system), currently use the phonetic and lexical levels of language. It is believed that use of all the levels of language processing explained above offer the potential for truly habitable dialogue systems.

CONCLUSION

Although NLP is a relatively recent area of research and application, compared with other information technology approaches, there have been sufficient successes to date that suggest that NLP-based information access technologies will continue to be a major area of research and development in information systems now and far into the future.

ACKNOWLEDGMENT

Grateful appreciation to Xiaoyong Liu who contributed to this entry while she was a Ph.D. student and a Research Assistant in the Center for Natural Language Processing in the School of Information Studies at Syracuse University.

REFERENCES

1. Booth, A.D., Locke, W.N., Eds.; Historical Introduction. In *Machine Translation of Languages*; The Technology Press of MIT and Wiley: New York, 1955; 1–14.
2. Bar-Hillel, Y. The present status of automatic translation of languages. Adv. Comput. **1960**, *1*, 91–163.
3. Hutchins, W.J. Machine translation: A brief history. In *Concise History of the Language Sciences: From the Sumerians to the Cognitivists*; Koerner, F.F.K.; Asher, R.E., Eds.; Pergamon Press: Oxford, U.K., 1995; 431–445.
4. Chomsky, N. *Syntactic Structures*; Mouton: The Hague, the Netherlands, 1957.
5. Shannon, C. The mathematical theory of communication. Bell Syst. Tech. J. **1948**, *27*, 398–403.
6. Klavans, J.L.; Resnik, P. *The Balancing Act: Combining Symbolic and Statistical Approaches to Language*; MIT Press: Cambridge, MA, 1996.
7. National Academy of Science Language and machines: Computers in translation and linguistics. In *A Report by the Automatic Language Processing Advisory Committee (ALPAC)*; National Academy of Sciences: Washington, DC, 1966.
8. Chomsky, N. *Aspects of the Theory of Syntax*; The MIT Press: Cambridge, MA, 1965.
9. Fillmore, C.J. The case for case. In *Universals in Linguistic Theory*; Bach, E., Harms, R., Eds.; Holt, Rinehart and Winston: NewYork, 1968; 1–88.
10. Quillian, M. Semantic memory. In *Semantic Information Processing*; Minsky, M., Ed.; MIT Press: Cambridge, MA, 1968.
11. Schank, R. Conceptual dependency: A theory of natural language understanding. Cogn. Psychol. **1972**, *3* (4), 552–631.
12. Woods, W.A. Transition network grammars for natural language analysis. Commun. ACM **1970**, *13* (10), 591–596.
13. Wilks, Y. An intelligent analyzer and understander of English. Commun. ACM **1975**, *18* (5), 264–274.
14. Kay, M. Functional grammar. In Proceedings of the Fifth Annual Meeting of the Berkeley Linguistics Society; Chiarello, C., Ed.; Berkeley Linguistics Society, 1979; 143–158.

15. Weizenbaum, J. ELIZA—A computer program for the study of natural language communication between man and machine. Commun. ACM **1966**, *9* (7), 36–43.
16. Winograd, T. *Understanding Natural Language*; Academic Press: New York, 1972.
17. Gazdar, G.; Mellish, C. *Natural Language Processing in Prolog*; Addison-Wesley: Wokingham, England, 1989.
18. Colby, K.M.; Weber, S.; Hilf, F.D. Artificial paranoia. Artif. Intell. **1971**, *2* (1), 1–25.
19. Woods, W.A. Progress in natural language understanding: An application to lunar geology. In AFIPS Conference Proceedings; AFIPS, 1973; 441–450.
20. Woods, W.A. Procedural semantics for a question-answering machine. In Proceedings of AFIPS Pall Joint Computer Conference; AFIPS, 1968; Vol. 33, 457–471.
21. Manaris, B. Natural language processing: A human– computer interaction perspective. In *Advances in Computers*; Zelkowitz, M., Ed.; Academic Press, Inc.: San Diego, CA, 1998; Vol. 47, 1–66.
22. Grosz, B.J. The representation and use of focus in a system for understanding dialogs. In Proceedings of Fifth International Joint Conference on Artificial Intelligence, IJCAI '77, Cambridge, MA; IJCAI, 1977; 67–76.
23. Mann, W.C.; Thompson, S.A. Rhetorical structure theory: A theory of text organization. In *Discourse Structure*; Polanyi, C., Ed.; Ablex: Norwood, NJ, 1987.
24. Hobbs, J.; Rosenschein, S. Making computational sense of Montague's intensional logic. Artif. Intell. **1977**, *9* (3), 287–306.
25. Polanyi, L.; Scha, R. On the recursive structure of discourse. In *Connectedness in Sentence, Discourse and Text*; Ehlich, K., van Riemsdijk, H., Eds.; Tilburg University: Tilborg, 1983; 141–178.
26. Reichman, R. *Getting Computers to Talk Like You and Me*; MIT Press: Cambridge, MA, 1985.
27. McKeown, K.R. *Text Generation*; Cambridge University Press: Cambridge, 1985.
28. McDonald, D.D. Natural language generation as a computational problem: An introduction. In *Computational Models of Discourse*; Brady, M., Berwick, B., Eds.; MIT Press: Cambridge, MA, 1987.
29. Jurafsky, D.; Martin, J. Speech and language processing: An introduction to natural language processing. In *Computational Linguistics, and Speech Recognition*; Prentice-Hall: Upper Saddle River, NJ, 2000.
30. Liddy, E.D. Anaphora in natural language processing and information retrieval. Inf. Process. Manag. **1990**, *26* (1), 39–52.
31. Liddy, E.D.; Paik, W.; McKenna, M. Development and implementation of a discourse model for newspaper texts. In Proceedings of the AAAI Symposium on Empirical Methods in Discourse Interpretation and Generation; 1995.
32. Dinsmore, J. Thunder in the gap. In *The Symbolic and Connectionist Paradigms: Closing the Gap*; Lawrence Erlbaum Associates: Hillsdale, NJ, 1992; 1–23.
33. Wermter, S.; Riloff, E.; Scheler, G. Learning approaches for natural language processing. In *Connectionist, Statistical, and Symbolic Approaches to Learning for Natural Language Processing*; Wermter, S., Riloff, E., Scheler, G., Eds.; Springer-Verlag: Berlin, Germany, 1996; 1–16.
34. Manning, C.D.; Schütze, H. *Foundations of Statistical Natural Language Processing*; MIT Press: Cambridge, MA, 1999.
35. Kay, M.; Gawron, J.M.; Norvig, P. *Verbmobil: A Translation System for Face-to-Face Dialog*; Center for the Study of Language and Information: Stanford, CA, 1994.
36. Lange, T.E. Hybrid connectionist models: Temporary bridges over the gap between the symbolic and the subsymbolic. In *The Symbolic and Connectionist Paradigms: Closing the Gap*; Dinsmore, J., Ed.; Lawrence Erlbaum Associates: Hillsdale, NJ, 1992; 237–289.
37. Liddy, E.D.; Myaeng, S.H. DR-LINK's linguistic-conceptual approach to document detection. In Proceedings of First Text Retrieval Conference TREC-1; NIST: Gaithersburg, MD, 1993.
38. Strzalkowski, T. *Natural Language Information Retrieval*; Kluwer Academic: Boston, MA, 1999.

BIBLIOGRAPHY

General Texts

1. Allen, J.F. *Natural Language Unsderstanding*, 2nd Ed.; Benjamin/Cummings: Redwood City, CA, 1995.
2. Berwick, R.C. *Computational Linguistics*; MIT Press: Cambridge, MA, 1989.
3. Charniak, E. *Statistical Language Learning*; MIT Press: Cambridge, MA, 1993.
4. Brady, M.; Berwick, R.C., Eds. *Computational Models of Discourse*; MIT Press: Cambridge, MA, 1983.
5. Charniak, E.; Wilks, Y.A., Eds. *Computational Semantics*; North-Holland Press: Amsterdam, the Netherlands, 1976.
6. Schank, R.C.; Colby, K.M., Eds. *Computer Models of Thought and Language*; W.H. Freeman: San Francisco, CA, 1973.
7. Cohen, P.; Morgan, J.; Pollack, M. *Intentions in Communication*; MIT Press: Cambridge, MA, 1990.
8. *Frame Conceptions and Text Understanding*, Metzing, D., Ed.; Frame Conceptions and Text Understanding,? De Gruyter: Berlin, Germany, 1980.
9. Gazdar, G.; Mellish, C. *Natural Language Processing in Prolog: An Introduction to Computational Linguistics*; Addison-Wesley Press: Reading, MA, 1989.
10. Grishman, R. *Computational Linguistics: An Introduction*; Cambridge University Press: New York, 1986.
11. Harris, M.D. *Introduction to Natural Language Processing*; Reston Publishing Co.: Reston, VA, 1985.
12. Jurafsky, D.; Martin, J. *Speech and Language Processing*; Prentice-Hall: Upper Saddle River, NJ, 2000.
13. Klavans, J.; Resnik, P. *The Balancing Act: Combining Symbolic and Statistical Approaches to Language*; MIT Press: Cambridge, MA, 1997.
14. Manning, C.; Schuetze, H. *Foundations of Statistical Natural Language Processing*; MIT Press: Cambridge, MA, 1990.
15. Strzalkowski, T., Ed. *Natural Language Information Retrieval*; Kluwer Academic Press: Dordrecht, the Netherlands, 1999.
16. Rustin, R., Ed. *Natural Language Processing*; Algorithmics Press: New York, 1973.

17. King, M., Ed. *Parsing Natural Language*; Academic Press: London, U.K., 1983.
18. Grosz, B.J.; Sparck-Jones, K.; Webber, B.L., Eds. *Readings in Natural Language Processing*; Morgan Kaufmann: San Mateo, CA, 1986.
19. Schank, R.C.; Abelson, R. *Scripts, Plans, Goals, and Understanding*; Lawrence Erlbaum Associates: Hillsdale, NJ, 1977.
20. Lehnert, W.; Ringle, M.H., Eds. *Strategies for Natural Language Processing*; Lawrence Erlbaum Associates: Hillsdale, NJ, 1982.
21. Tennant, H.R. *Natural Language Processing*; Petrocelli Books: New York, 1981.
22. Wilks, Y.A.; Slator, B.M.; Guthrie, L.M. *Electric Words: Dictionaries, Computer, and Meanings*; MIT Press: Cambridge, MA, 1996.
23. Winograd, T. *Understanding Natural Language*; Academic Press: New York, 1972.
24. Winograd, T. *Language as a Cognitive Process*; Addison-Wesley: Reading, MA, 1983.
25. Young, S.; Bloothooft, G. *Corpus-Based Methods in Language and Speech Processing*; Kluwer Academic Publishers: Dordrecht, the Netherlands, 1997.

Relevant Journals

1. Artif. Intell.
2. Cogn. Sci.
3. Comm. ACM.
4. Comput. Humanit.
5. Comput. Intell.
6. Comput. Linguist.
7. Comput. Speech Lang.
8. IEEE Trans. Intell. Syst.
9. Inf. Process. Manag.
10. J. Am. Soc. Inf. Sci.
11. J. Artif. Intell. Res.
12. J. Doc.
13. J. Logic, Lang. Inf.
14. J. Nat. Lang. Eng.
15. Lit. Linguist. Comput.
16. Mach. Transl.
17. Mind Lang.
18. Nat. Lang. Linguist. Theory.

Conferences

1. American Association for Artificial Intelligence (AAAI).
2. Applied Natural Language Processing (ANLP).
3. Association for Computational Linguistics (ACL).
4. Empirical Methods in Natural Language Processing (EMNLP).
5. European Association for Computation Linguistics (EACL).
6. Human Language Technology Workshop (HLT).
7. International Conference on Computational Linguistics (COLING).
8. International Joint Conference on Artificial Intelligence (IJCAI).
9. North American Chapter of the Association for Computational Linguistics (NAACL).
10. Special Interest Group in Information Retrieval (SIGIR).
11. Text Retrieval Conference (TREC).

Electronic Resources

1. AI on the Web: http://www.cs.berkeley.edu/~russell/ai.html. The site provides pointers to other sites on the Web with information on Artificial Intelligence. It has a section on natural language processing, and it lists homepages of people who are active in the field, companies, research groups, journals, software, etc.
2. Natural Language Processing and Computational Linguistics Links: http://www-a2k.is.tokushima-u.ac.jp/member/kita/NLP/nlp.html. Another NLP site that provides links to pagers, technical reports, on-line proceedings, organizations, NLP people, and so on.
3. Statistical Natural Language Processing and Corpus-Based Computational Linguistics: An Annotated List of Resources: http://www-nlp.stanford.edu/links/statnlp.html. This web site is maintained by Christopher Manning. It provides links to many useful tools and toolkits such as part-of-speech taggers, language modeling toolkits, etc. It also has pointers to various corpora, lexical/morphological resources, educational resources, and mailing lists.
4. The ACL NLP/CL Universe: http://www.aclweb.org/u/db/acl/. The largest index of computational linguistics and natural language processing resources on the Web. It features a search engine that should allow you to find specific NLP-related Web pages.
5. The Association for Computational Linguistics site: http://www.aclweb.org. The Association for Computational Linguistics is the major international organization in the field.
6. The Computation and Language E-Print Archive: http://xxx.lanl.gov/archive/cs/. The Computation and Language E-Print Archive is a fully automated electronic archive and distribution server for papers on computational linguistics, natural language processing, speech processing, and related fields.
7. The Language Technology Helpdesk: http://www.ltg.ed.ac.uk/helpdesk/faq/index.html. Frequently asked questions of the Human Communication Research Center at the University of Edinburgh.
8. The Linguistic Data Consortium: http://www.ldc.upenn.edu/. An open consortium of universities, companies, and government research laboratories. It creates, collects and distributes speech and text databases, lexicons, and other resources for research and development purposes. The University of Pennsylvania is the LDC's host institution.

Network Management

Robert J. Sandusky
University Library, University of Illinois at Chicago, Chicago, Illinois, U.S.A.

Abstract

Network management includes activities related to the design, construction, and operation of communications networks, which are performed by a network management organization. Network management is inherently a distributed activity because a network includes equipment distributed across multiple locations. Network management work is described in terms of the five dimensions of network management as defined by the International Standards Organization: fault, configuration, performance, accounting, and security management. Network management work is further described as a melding of design and real-time supervisory control work, depending upon effective information management and coordination of activities within the network management organization and with external organizations, including customers, peer organizations, and equipment and service providers.

INTRODUCTION

Network management includes activities related to the design, construction, and operation of communications networks, which are one type of distributed infrastructure. Network management activities are performed by a network management organization (NMO). An NMO is one of many types of information technology service organizations and, as discussed here, is responsible for the design, monitoring, and evolution of distributed infrastructure (an assemblage of hardware, software, and services) in its particular organizational context. The network itself is the primary object of the NMO's work and the NMO generally has little influence over how the network is used by other members and affiliates of the organization. An NMO may be a single organization but will typically interact with multiple organizations including customers, peer organizations collaborating to provide network services, and vendors. Network management, in all but the simplest cases such as a home or small single-site local area network (LAN), is inherently a distributed activity: a network usually includes equipment distributed in multiple locations. At the smaller end of the scale, equipment may be located in multiple rooms or on multiple floors of a building (referred to as a LAN). In more complex cases, the equipment may be located in multiple buildings (on a campus or across a metropolitan area, often referred to as a MAN, or metropolitan area network), in multiple cities, or even multiple countries (a WAN, or wide area network). This entry will assume, for purposes of illustration and discussion, a MAN or WAN unless otherwise noted.

This entry begins with a brief description of the types of components that make up a MAN or WAN and are the network components that require management. The five major dimensions of network management, as defined by the International Standards Organization (ISO) as part of the Open Systems Interconnection model, are used to introduce the range of activities associated with management of complex networks. Next, how design work is approached in NMOs is discussed in terms of the classic "waterfall" software development life cycle. The dynamic and collaborative nature of work within an NMO is described in terms of two interrelated modes of working: design work and real-time supervisory control work. Finally, the critical role of information management is described in the context of a disaster recovery/business continuity test.

WHAT IS MANAGED IN A NETWORK?

Networks, including the Internet, closed or private networks built by organizations, and smaller-scale LANs, are composed of several classes of components. Applications (e.g., Web sites, enterprise databases, digital libraries, e-mail systems) made accessible to remote users, messages carried by the network (i.e., frames, packets), end-user computers (i.e., client computers), server computers (e.g., Web servers, file servers, proxy servers), routers, switches, hubs, equipment racks, link signaling devices (i.e., link encryptors, digital signaling units/digital "modems"), access lines (e.g., the Ethernet cabling from client computers to a local switch, router, or hub), wireless access points, and long-distance telecommunications circuits (e.g., the higher-capacity, leased digital line between network locations usually connecting routers to each other).[1] All of these network components, except the cables, contain software and configurable parameters and all must be managed in order to provide effective network services that evolve to meet demand and keep pace with technical

Encyclopedia of Library and Information Sciences, Fourth Edition DOI: 10.1081/E-ELIS4-120044293

innovations. Vendor-provided software for configurable components must be tested and implemented to fix bugs, patch security holes, and to add functionality. The NMO also monitors the network in real-time for failures, errors, traffic bottlenecks, etc., and corrects problems by issuing commands to change component state and by swapping failed components with replacements. The NMO also monitors actual usage patterns and takes requests for new services into account as part of its network design and provisioning work.

The NMO must have the means to organize information about all the elements of the network in order to manage these components. The NMO must also have a set of operating parameters that, in combination with the network components, can enable the NMO to create appropriate standard operating procedures (SOPs) and ancillary support systems such as trouble ticket, configuration management, test scheduling, and reporting systems.

DIMENSIONS OF NETWORK MANAGEMENT

A conceptual framework associated with the ISO's Open Systems Interconnection model for communications systems is used to organize the full range of network management activities.[2] While originally focused on network management, this framework may be used to characterize the management of distributed computing systems more generally. The OSI framework is broken down into five functional areas: fault management, configuration management, performance management, accounting management, and security management.

Fault management is the detection, diagnosis, and correction of problems, or faults, in a network. Network components asynchronously generate fault data as messages, referred to as alarms, which are categorized as major, minor, and informational depending upon their significance or impact. Major alarms are generated when a network component fails due to hardware failure, software failure, or because the component can no longer be contacted by the network management systems (i.e., it has become isolated from the rest of the network). Minor alarms are generated when less critical events are detected, such as a performance threshold being exceeded, a burst of transmission errors is detected, or a failure of a subcomponent (e.g., a single interface card failure on a large router). Informational messages are generated for a variety of reasons, do not require direct attention by the real-time supervisory control (RTSC) staff, but are logged and available if needed (e.g., an anomalous but automatically recoverable condition, such as a communications protocol error). As alarms are generated, they are propagated to the NMO via both a real-time and an archival path. Alarms are sent to network management workstations that are continuously monitored by RTSC staff and to databases for long-term alarm storage. Propagation of alarms to the network management workstations supports the real-time work of isolating and correcting faults requiring direct intervention by NMO staff. Examples of faults requiring real-time intervention include failures that do not automatically recover or large-scale failures that trigger the performance of a SOP. Propagation of alarms to databases provides comprehensive historical data for postevent, trend, or long-term fault analysis. Faults are logged in a database using a record format that includes date, time, location, fault codes, and other information of potential use in diagnosis, correction, or to support subsequent, long-term analysis. To support fault diagnosis, NMO staff use diagnostic test tools and component status query commands to retrieve real-time component status, and various component activation/deactivation commands to alter component status or component operating parameters. NMO staff are trained in troubleshooting procedures, and have access to SOPs for monitoring the network, documenting fault conditions in trouble tickets, and problem escalation (i.e., when to contact next-level expertise and/or management if a fault cannot be corrected in a timely manner). Trouble tickets are created for all faults requiring intervention. The trouble ticket is a locus for a textual narrative of the situation as it unfolds, providing capabilities to combine descriptions of evidence, activity, causal hypotheses, as well as a record of interpersonal, intra-, and inter-organizational communications. To correct faults that have been diagnosed, the NMO staff use commands to alter physical configurations (e.g., to replace a failed component with a backup component), manually activate a deactivated component, or to modify the operating parameters of affected components.

Configuration management is the set of capabilities that allow the NMO to set up and modify the network's physical and logical configurations. Following initial implementation the network's physical and logical configurations will change "to alleviate congestion, isolate faults or meet changing user needs."[2] Configuration changes may be unplanned, caused by network faults, or as a result of NMO staff action in response to a fault or changing, real-time network conditions, or as part of a preplanned configuration change. Faults often cause spontaneous network reconfigurations, such as removal of a long-distance telecommunications link from the network topology. Networks must be fault-tolerant: their internal complexity (the large number of varied and interconnected components) and reliance on long-distance telecommunications links result in frequent (e.g., several per day) single component failures. Therefore, networks must be designed to tolerate all single-component failures in order to be considered minimally reliable. In order to provide availability on the order of 99.9% or higher, the design must tolerate the simultaneous failure of any two components. In some situations, networks are designed to tolerate all dual-component failures as well as a subset of three-component failures. Network components are designed to attempt automatic recovery following failures, and many failures are corrected automatically. In a significant percentage of cases, NMO diagnosis and correction are required to either effect component recovery (e.g., manually reactivating a component) or to temporarily reconfigure the network so connections and traffic flow around the failure (e.g., moving a LAN's connection from its failed default router to an available connection on an alternate router). Planned network reconfigurations take two forms: predesigned modifications that are intended to be permanent, such as changes made to address new requirements, and predesigned modifications that are intended to be temporary, such as those that are part of disaster recovery/business continuity plans. Adding, modifying, or removing routers, interface cards to a router, or telecommunications circuits between routers are examples of common planned permanent configuration management activities. Network planning and design work is required prior to implementation of either a new network or a significant revision to an existing network. One of the implications of designing a fault-tolerant system is the need to preplan the organization's responses to a range of anticipated fault events including normal, single-component failures (e.g., loss of a long-distance telecommunications link) or high-impact failures (e.g., complete loss of connectivity for a network site, whether it is caused by natural disaster, massive telecommunications link failure, fire, simultaneous failure of both primary and backup routers, etc.). Preplanning work is complex, and results in the creation of SOPs that guides NMO reconfigurations in response to classes of failures (see discussion below in the section on "Perspectives on Network Management Work").

Performance management refers both to the capabilities in the network that support measurement of network use and the expertise within the NMO to analyze data, justify recommendations for change, and plan the configuration changes needed to support emerging or anticipated network uses. NMOs are interested in understanding and documenting past usage patterns, comparing current usage patterns to historical patterns, and using both historical and current data to support the capacity planning process. While performance monitoring occurs in real-time as the RTSC staff continuously monitor utilization of network components like routers and long-distance telecommunications links, the bulk of performance management activities are performed "off-line" by design staff. Network components periodically—every few minutes—log levels of usage by writing data to network management servers for later analysis. Network components may also generate fault messages or alarms when utilization levels exceed certain thresholds to enable real-time supervisory staff to respond with network configuration changes. Networks and their protocols are designed to be tolerant of fluctuations in network traffic or topology, so real-time intervention is not usually required. Performance management is part of the longer-term network design process and involves analysis of the logged performance data in order to detect changes in usage patterns that lead to modifications in the network's configuration. For example, increasing network traffic between two locations may lead to installation of higher capacity routers, telecommunications links, reconfiguration of the network topology, or a combination of the three.

Accounting management is the set of capabilities that allows the NMO to collect and manage usage and configuration data, track costs, and charge network users according to the tariffs, service level agreements, or contracts that are in place. Several network components may be capable of generating and transmitting usage data that may be fed into an off-line accounting or billing system (e. g., routers and servers running shared applications may generate data that are fed into a billing system). Costs of other components, such as cables, routers, or equipment racks, may have their costs allocated on some other basis (such as employee head count or a count of connections), or may be factored into usage-sensitive charges. NMOs evaluate the costs, benefits, and complexity of collecting and correlating large amounts of data and negotiating customer agreements in order to produce detailed bills against other approaches that don't require detailed usage-based calculations (e.g., simpler, flat-rate or percentage-allocated cost-recovery arrangements). The simpler approaches are particularly useful for networks built to support the internal operations of an organization. NMOs providing services to the public, such as land-line and mobile telecommunications organizations, are more likely to develop usage-sensitive procedures.

Security management is concerned with control of physical access to network components, end-point authentication, user authentication, key management for encryption, end-to-end data encryption, security log management, monitoring emerging security threat vectors and developing organizational responses, and firewall management. Security management has two objects in the network management context: first, the network itself must be secured (e.g., control the access to router management ports which are used to issue reconfiguration commands to the router; ensure that physical access to network equipment at all locations is controlled; manage NMO staff authentication and access); second, the network must support the security requirements of the users and applications transmitting data across the network (e.g., providing encryption of telecommunications circuits; end-to-end encryption of data streams; management of encryption keys). In environments with high security needs, including financial institutions, health care organizations, and commercial organizations in highly competitive markets, security management responsibilities are concentrated in an independent part of the organization, with a management chain distinct from the RTSC and technical staffs. A separate management chain encourages, enforces, and makes a high degree of transparency possible through establishment of arms-length relationships between different parts of the NMO. NMOs with these types of stringent needs will also employ a comprehensive internal auditing process, augmented by recurring external audits. Security logs, like fault logs, identify date, time, location, and diagnostic information. Security logs should be reviewed regularly in order to identify unusual usage patterns or to correlate successful and unsuccessful access attempts by users and intruders alike. Several of the activities included in security management, including encryption key management and developing responses to emerging security threats, are complex management challenges in a distributed environment (see the entry "Authentication and Authorization," p. 413).

PERSPECTIVES ON NETWORK MANAGEMENT WORK

Network management depends upon the blending of actions performed by people with a range of skills and expertise, and these actions depend upon information management practices. Design and RTSC work patterns are defined, and the central role of information management in network management is described. These two work patterns are discussed in the context of the five dimensions of network management. The section concludes with a description of a complex yet typical activity, a disaster recovery test (DRT), which illustrates the relationship between information and activity in distributed infrastructure management.

Patterns of Work

Network management combines patterns of both design and RTSC work. Research has shown that design work and RTSC work have different rhythms and patterns that, in network management, are coordinated to perform fault, configuration, performance, accounting, and security management. RTSC work is event driven, dynamic, and involves the interaction of multiple workers with complex systems.[3] Malfunctions in the operation of these systems can result in serious consequences such as the loss of human life or financial loss. Signs of malfunction must often be recognized and responses formulated within minutes or seconds in order to prevent adverse consequences. By contrast, design work has different patterns and rhythms than RTSC work and is characterized as being self-paced (as opposed to being event-driven), reflective (as opposed to being time-constrained), and creative.[3–5] The object of design work is usually to iteratively create, study, or revise some artifact like a document, a set of specifications, a product, or a system, such as a data communications network. In network management, there are frequently occasions when workers who usually do design work join the RTSC staff to perform event-driven and time-constrained work, particularly with regard to fault and configuration management. This section will first describe how an NMO for a WAN is organized. How new network implementations are managed is described next, followed by a description of the role of information management in network management work. Finally, the five dimensions of network management (above) are discussed in terms of design work and RTSC work.

The NMO for a large network, such as a national-scale WAN, includes a staff of technical specialists who provide depth of knowledge in particular technologies, the RTSC staff, budget, accounting, and administrative support staff, and executive management. Categories of technical specialists include network hardware engineers, network software engineers, data security specialists, and circuit/topology experts. Network hardware engineers are specialists in network equipment, signaling equipment, electrical requirements, lower-level network protocols, and troubleshooting. The most skilled network hardware engineers will have degrees in computer or electrical engineering. Network software engineers are more likely to be trained in computer science, and will have expertise in higher level network protocols, software debugging, software development, and software engineering processes (e.g., the waterfall systems development life cycle discussed below). Circuit/topology experts manage the leased long-distance telecommunications circuits and the relationships with the vendor or vendors from whom they are leased, and are responsible for managing the network topology. Security specialists may have backgrounds in either engineering or computer science, but will focus on authentication, authorization, dedicated security hardware (e.g., link encryptors and firewalls) and encryption key management processes. In large NMOs, the security experts will be in a separate group and report to a different manager than do the hardware and software engineers in order to maintain arms-length relationships and help ensure that security procedures and standards are not compromised by expediency (e.g., cost or schedule pressures). In total, these technical experts are referred to here as "members of the technical staff."

The RTSC staff is organized into three shifts, with shift supervisors who report to the supervisory control manager. The RTSC staff are the people who work most directly and most often with the network itself, monitoring the network's health and configuration (fault and configuration management). The RTSC staff also act as the human interface between the network and the NMO's internal and external customers. The RTSC staff work in one or more centralized network control rooms. RTSC staff backgrounds are likely to vary from some who have university degrees in a variety of technical and nontechnical fields, to those who have experience in real-time operations but little or no postsecondary education.

The budget and accounting staff rely upon information generated by and about the network to manage billing, budgeting, and financial planning. The executive managers often have backgrounds that include a degree in a technical field and experience as a member of the technical staff. As managers, they will have a well-developed model of the technology and the ability to perform cross-community coordination with the various NMO groups (members of the technical staff, RTSC staff, accountants), internal and external customers, and vendors.

Network design and software engineering processes have many parallels, and can be described by well-known life cycle models such as the "waterfall" model of software development (Fig. 1). In both situations, the goal is to create a new object: the network or piece of software. The life cycle begins with the identification and documentation of *requirements*. Given a set of relatively stable requirements, one or more *design* alternatives can be produced to satisfy the requirements. Given agreement on a design, *implementation* of the object can begin. As the object is created, each discrete piece undergoes *testing*, and the object is ultimately tested as a whole. After successful testing, the object is released and goes into *maintenance* (software) or goes into *production operation* (network). The life cycle is repeated as new requirements emerge. Each of these subsequent iterations can be managed using the same life cycle model: new requirements are documented, a network design revision is created, and the changes are implemented, tested, and made operational. The NMO is responsible for managing the entire implementation/revision life cycle for its network, and the cycle can be reiterated many times throughout the useful life of the network. Typical types of new requirements for a network include expanding the network into new locations, increasing capacity, or adding support for new data transmission protocols.

In order to design a new network (or modify an existing network), requirements must be gathered to inform the network design (network locations, traffic patterns and types, security and reliability requirements, service level requirements, cost parameters, etc.). During the network design process, engineers use a combination of formal, algorithmic, and professional heuristic processes. For example, given a certain expected traffic load, algorithmic tools can be used to define the number, arrangement, and sizes of routers and the circuits connecting them. The arrangement of routers and circuits is referred to as the network topology. WANs are never designed as a completely interconnected mesh (i.e., each site linked directly to each other site, Fig. 2), so the topology must be carefully designed to provide adequate support for the traffic patterns and service-level expectations while minimizing operating costs: long-distance circuits between cities are often leased from a telecommunications provider and have recurring monthly costs (Fig. 3). The set of equipment and services needed can then be acquired, installed, and tested. Any moderately complex network is, when built, an ecosystem comprised of a wide variety of equipment and services, including cables, equipment racks, signaling devices (e.g., encryptors and digital "modems"), routers, and network management servers and workstations. Each type of equipment (e.g., routers) can be thought of as a species within the ecosystem. Engineers plan and manage installation and testing of hardware and services at each site (the routers, link signaling

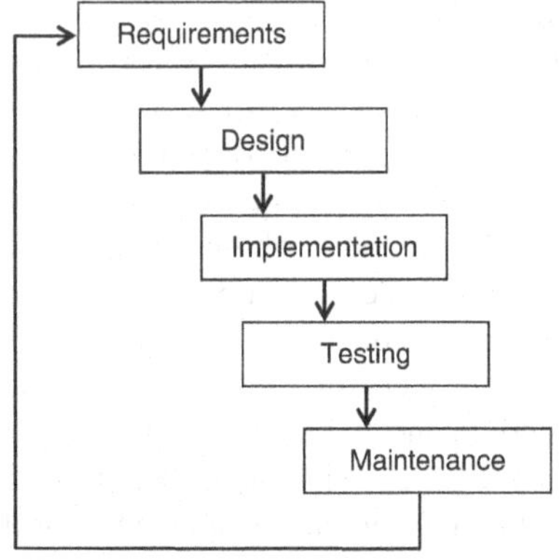

Fig. 1 The "waterfall" systems development life cycle.

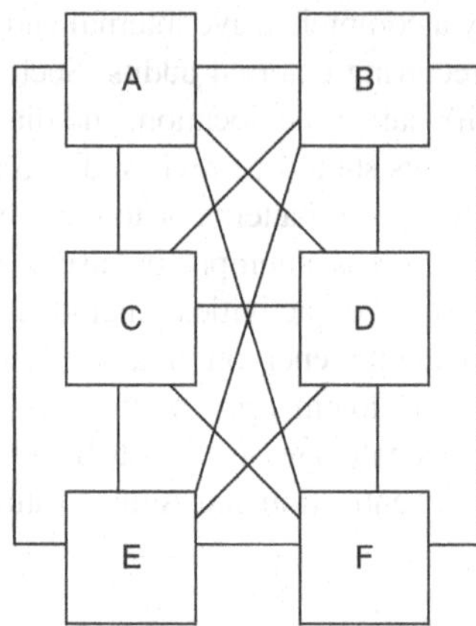

Fig. 2 Full mesh topology, where A, B, C, D, E, and F are network sites.

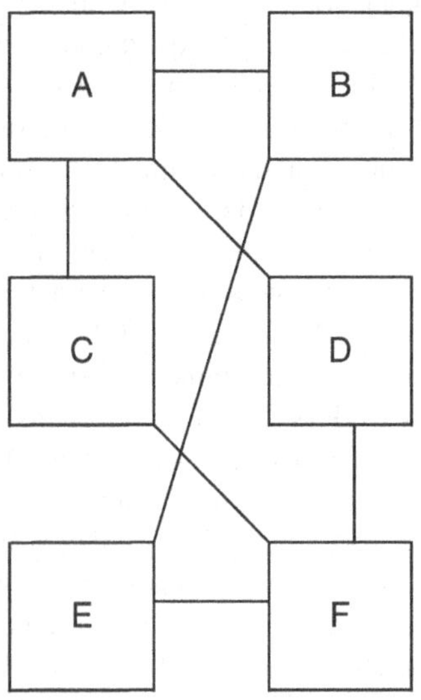

Fig. 3 Optimized network topology, where A, B, C, D, E, and F are network sites.

devices, switches, hubs, racks, long-distance telecommunications circuits, wired and wireless access points, and cables). Software engineers define and test connection parameters and system options within routers, link signaling devices, and any other software-configurable network components. RTSC staff monitor and control the systems as they are installed and tested, perform routine tasks (on both a daily and per-shift basis) and respond to faults. Documentation, policies, and SOPs are developed and refined throughout the planning, implementation, and testing phases. Customer endpoints (LANs, hosts, servers, and applications) are connected to the network, tested, and the new network is in production operation and maintenance mode. Following initial implementation of a network, configuration change tends to be gradual, to replace failed equipment, replace a species (e.g., routers) with an upgraded version, or to make modifications in response to changing user or organization needs. Whether initial installation or incremental upgrade, network reconfigurations include both physical changes (replacing a hardware component), software changes (modifying software parameters related to the component, also known as provisioning), and changes to the documentation.[6]

Management of distributed infrastructure, including network management, is information-intensive work. Each kind of equipment included in the network is managed by its own workstation-based suite of applications tailored to manage that layer of technology. Each of these systems contains a database (the Management Information Base, or MIB) that provides a representation of the configuration of that layer of the network, providing an accurate, one-to-one correspondence to the physical network configuration. Information in each MIB is, however, isolated and few tools exist to provide effectively merged views of data from all layers of the network. SOPs are created, using an iterative process of proposal, negotiation, and testing, in order to define preplanned and vetted operational sequences for use in routine and nonroutine but anticipated situations. SOPs are organization and context specific, reflecting organizational values and priorities as well as the combinations of technology that make each WAN unique (e.g., kinds of equipment and locations). Some (SOPs) are so commonly used that the RTSC staff has them memorized and the paper documents are only used by newcomers or as referents during discussion. Other procedures, like disaster recovery procedures, are hopefully never actually used. Versions of these types of procedures are often modified into test scripts, which are used once and then discarded.

The NMO staff creates formal databases and other information management tools to serve the specific needs of the NMO, such as trouble ticket, configuration management, and test scheduling systems. Other formal information systems include the vendor provided MIBs and the NMO's own SOPs. Other more situated and less formal information systems included are handwritten notes and collections of information assembled by individuals, created spontaneously by the NMO staff in order to allow them to do their work more effectively. The informal systems often combine information drawn from one or more formal information sources. The combination of information from multiple sources results in new information compounds[7] that highlight, through processes of extraction, juxtaposition, and integration of domain semantics, what is salient in a domain rich with information.[8] People from all parts of the organization spend a great deal of time seeking and gathering bits of formal data, adding the organization-specific stuff of meaning and context, and producing useful, but often difficult to find and manage collections of information. These informal information compounds are often expressed in tabular format in order to represent relationships between physical and logical objects. The relationships of logical objects (like the symbolic or mnemonic name of a network device) to physical objects (like a port on a router or a cable) are enormously important during troubleshooting or in planning for network changes. These information compounds are a means by which the members of the NMO can introduce the organization-specific data about customers, purpose, and meaning into both the real-time supervisory control and design environments. However, maintaining the integrity of these informal representations over time is difficult due to the high rate at which changes are made to the network configuration.

Schematic drawings of relationships between network devices are another common information compound useful in highlighting important relationships between discrete elements in the network. These, too, are prone to problems caused by change and poor document maintenance.

Patterns of Work and Dimensions of Network Management

The degree to which members of the technical staff, who are primarily responsible for network design work, and the RTSC staff, who are responsible for monitoring and controlling the network in real-time, share and coordinate the work associated with the five dimensions of network management varies by dimension, and is influenced by the values, priorities, and other characteristics of the NMO. The work patterns described below are based upon network management work as practiced in a large financial institution,[9] but are typical of any NMO operating a WAN in a context where high security, reliability, and availability are expected.

In terms of fault management, members of the technical staff will be engaged in the requirements definition and implementation of equipment and software related to fault management. Software engineers may develop or customize systems for managing alarm data in either real-time or for fault diagnosis or post hoc fault analysis. Members of the technical staff do not participate routinely in fault monitoring activities: this is the responsibility of the RTSC staff. However, under certain conditions, such as during real-time troubleshooting, members of the technical staff merge with the RTSC staff—usually joining together in the network control room—to isolate and resolve a difficult problem as quickly as possible.

Faults requiring intervention occur frequently in large networks, often because of the complex hardware and software configurations located at each network site or because of problems with the telecommunications circuits that connect network locations to each other. An NMO creates procedures (SOPs) that define the canonical responses to typical fault situations. RTSC staff use the SOP as a reference when responding to typical faults, which should result in rapid service recovery performed in a standardized manner. If the standard response does not work, the RTSC staff moves into troubleshooting mode in order to restore service to affected users (by perhaps reconfiguring the network so that redundant or alternate components can be used by the affected users), isolate and characterize the outage, document the outage in a database (by creating a trouble ticket that serves as a collection point for alarms, actions taken, actors involved; a trouble ticket created in response to nonroutine events becomes a narrative of the NMOs collective actions), and escalate the situation (i.e., notify management and next-level technical support, including hardware and software engineers who are responsible for network design and are typically expert in relatively narrow areas such as circuits, routers, or security; or possibly equipment or service providers).

Configuration management is primarily performed by members of the technical staff using a reflective, self-paced, and creative design process, although the RTSC staff are involved for the implementation, testing, and ongoing maintenance. A standard implementation process, such as the waterfall process described above, is typically used to manage preplanned, permanent configuration changes. The RTSC staff may make temporary configuration changes in response to network faults, or as part of the execution of a SOP (e.g., see the description of a DRT, below).

Performance management is almost entirely done by members of the technical staff in a reflective process where data collected by the network is compiled and analyzed. In rare cases, real-time network congestion may bring RTSC and design staff together in the control room for real-time analysis and intervention. These rare real-time situations are likely to cause a network capacity review by members of the technical staff.

Accounting management is also almost entirely a post hoc, off-line activity. RTSC have little to do other than ensure that the accounting data is being collected continuously. Accounting data is usually important to the NMO even in cases where detailed usage tracking is not done; usage information is still likely to be used to demonstrate NMO and network relevance as well as to help apportion network costs to customer organizations.

Security management involves members of the technical staff most directly and includes managing access control, user accounts and passwords, and encryption key management procedures. The RTSC staff does get involved, particularly in diagnosing suspected link encryption or data encryption problems. In a 24 hour, high-security environment, additional control procedures are required to manage access to "superuser" passwords that may need to be accessed from a secure location, such as a safe, when required for fault resolution.

Information and Activity in Network Management

An example of how an NMO plans and conducts a disaster recovery, or business continuity, test (DRT) is indicative of the ways the design and RTSC staffs interact and of the reliance of the NMO on effective information management. The DRTs in a WAN are complex. The DRT scenario assumes that the entire network site, its servers, and LANs at that the site have all been disabled (e.g., due to a fire, flood, etc.). A private network with high standards for availability would set as a network design requirement the ability to survive the complete loss of any network site by providing connectivity at an alternate, backup site. This requirement directs many other decisions and activities. For example, the need to redirect huge flows of data from a failed site to a backup site has an impact on the initial design of the network and its topology, as well as the way recovery mechanisms within the network are customized. The NMO also commits significant human resources from the technical and RTSC staff to create SOPs that will support this sort of recovery within the target times, which require complete network and server recovery within a few hours of the outage. The SOP likely contains scores of steps that are to be performed in a preplanned sequence, often by multiple organizations working in coordination. Such a complex document must be created and reviewed by both RTSC and technical staffs: the members of the technical staff are subject matter experts with deep knowledge of a narrow technical specialty, while the RTSC staff have broad working knowledge of the range of network technologies, but with less technical depth. The RTSC staff's "big picture" view of the network and the organizational environment allows them to contribute information about how activities should be sequenced and coordinated, both within and across the participating sites. People from multiple organizations and sites must be familiar with the procedures and rehearse them regularly. Backup data must be transmitted regularly, often on a continuous transaction-by-transaction basis, or by using daily data transfers. In either case, these data transfers become part of the RTSC staff's ongoing responsibilities.

The planning for a DRT begins a couple of months before the test date. A DRT director, usually a manager, is assigned responsibility for planning and running the test. Draft test scripts are distributed, which are modified versions of the SOP. The modifications reflect the goals and exceptions for the current test. (It is, as a practical matter, nearly impossible to take a major site out of the network for the 18–24 hours it takes to run a disaster simulation and test all of the recovery and fallback procedures. The tests are invariably limited to some degree to accommodate other competing requirements.) Conference calls are held where the site being tested, the NMO, and any other sites involved in recovery of servers "walk through" the script, looking for errors, sequencing problems, negotiating modifications, and inserting proper articulation and control points (e.g., periodic management conferences to review progress and status when the test is executed). Members of the technical staff and RTSC staff are present at all of the planning meetings and participate in the discussions and negotiations. The SOP is designed to serve as a canonical text in that it embodies the actions to be taken in the event that an "ideal" disaster occurs: a complete, total disaster at the site that would render it unusable. As such, the SOP embodies a "best practice" approach to dealing with a disaster, providing guidance on the most reliable way to effect the recovery of each piece of the failed environment at the backup sites. At the start of the test, the disaster itself is simulated, and how the simulation is to be performed is part of the test script. Specific dates and times are included in the test script to provide a rough sense of what it means to be on or behind or ahead of schedule during the test, values which are not included in the canonical SOP.

As the test date nears, it is discussed during the normal change and scheduling meetings to ensure the readiness of the NMO and other direct participants, to allow new information to be integrated into the schedule and plan, and to ensure awareness by a wider range of people and organizations who may be conducting other activities that overlap with the DRT. The day before the test begins, a final meeting is held, attended by representatives from all locations with responsibility for conducting the DRT. This meeting is the last opportunity for cancellations, late modifications to the test script, discussion of resource conflicts, times, etc.

The DRT begins a couple of hours before dawn, and RTSC staff from the NMO are responsible for many of the first steps to reconfigure the network to support movement of servers and other systems from the site under test to various recovery sites at other locations across the network. The third shift NMO staff cannot participate in daytime planning meetings that have occurred during the past week, and so they rely upon the written test schedules and scripts, plus any information passed verbally to them by the previous shift staff. They are also likely to have other network reconfigurations to perform during the same time period, near the end of their shift. If this part of the day goes well, the NMO will be in good shape for the entire weekend. If not, the political fallout could last for weeks. The site disaster will be simulated by disabling all of the network connections from other network sites to the site under test, in effect isolating that site from the rest of the network. The NMO RTSC staff issue status commands to ensure that the circuits are inactive. Alarms printers and displays record the disables as well as hundreds of other, cascading events. Network elements, represented by icons, change from green to red on many of the workstations. The NMO RTSC staff contact the test director to report that their current task is completed.

Contingencies are bound to arise in any event this complex. One site may get a late start; there may be problems reading a tape when trying to restore a software image at the backup site. The NMO is also likely to be dealing with normal problems, such as circuit problems that are causing high error rates and affecting network performance. In real time, processes move forward at the many participating sites. Some parts of the process get stuck and require intervention; some succeed; others simply fail, and the test script is modified on the fly in a continuous series of phone calls and negotiations. When the reality of the test day proves problematic, people can refer to the plan and make on-the-spot decisions about how to work around the difficulty: steps may be done in the "wrong" order, certain steps skipped, or certain steps repeated. These variations must be noted at the NMO as they occur, both to keep track of the test status in real time and as information to be used to modify the underlying SOP and subsequent similar test scripts.

The duration the DRT and other tests may span shift boundaries, making it necessary for accurate status to be passed from shift to shift. Managers from the NMO need status and may be on site or at home. The technical staff members supporting this and other simultaneous tests need to be aware of the status of the major test and adjust their weekend activities accordingly. The NMO must coordinate its activities through the DRT manager. As the test runs, problems may occur which must be resolved. Some parts of the test may be omitted in response to unexpected problems to avoid compromising the entire test.

The final event associated with a DRT is the postmortem held the following week. The participants in the postmortem are the same as those who participated in the many pretest meetings. The DRT director in effect grades the performance of the participants. The NMO and other organizations are held responsible for problems arising during the test. Responsibility for resolving each problem is publicly assigned. Resolution of problems assigned to the NMO may involve modifying the SOP or making configuration changes to the network. Even though problems occur during the DRTs, they are, due to the careful preplanning and test-day coordination, almost always considered successful.

CONCLUSION

Network management is not exclusively a technical issue of routers, telecommunications links, servers, applications, and the interconnections of LANs via metropolitan or WANs. Effective network management depends upon the blending of design and RTSC work to support all dimensions of network management: fault, configuration, performance, accounting, and security management. Effective organization and control of complex, dynamic information is also important to the NMO, as it enables the recording and communication of large amounts of information in forms that incorporate the values of the NMO and the larger organization within which it is embedded. While the five dimensions of network management form a common basis for organizing network management across a wide variety of organizations, the details of network management practice are situated and influenced by security requirements, available technical expertise, and budget. The concerns of network management apply as well to other situations in which distributed infrastructure must be managed.

Standards published by the Internet Engineering Task Force (IETF) have come to dominate network management practice. The most important of these are the Simple Network Management Protocol Version 3 (SNMPv3), defined in Requests for Comment 2571–2575.[10–14] Further information about the technical aspects and best practices of network and infrastructure management, including how SNMPv3 is used in practice, can be found in a number of works, including Limoncelli–Muller.[15–18]

REFERENCES

1. Panko, R.R. *Business Data Networks and Telecommunications*, 6th Ed.; Pearson Prentice Hall: Upper Saddle River, NJ, 2007.
2. Klerer, S.M. The OSI management architecture: An overview. Network **1988**, *2* (2), 20–29.
3. Jones, P.M. Cooperative work in mission operations: Analysis and implications for computer support. Comput. Support. Coop. Work Int. J. **1995**, *3* (2), 103–145.
4. Bucciarelli, L.L. An ethnographic perspective on engineering design. Des. Stud. **1988**, *9* (3), 159–168.
5. Schön, D.; Bennett, J. Reflective conversation with materials. In *Bringing Design to Software*; Winograd, T., Ed.; ACM Press: New York, 1996; 171–184.
6. Wang, H.H. *Telecommunications Network Management*; McGraw-Hill: New York, 1999.
7. Paepcke, A. Information needs in technical work settings and their implications for the design of computer tools. Comput. Support. Coop. Work J. Collab. Comp. **1996**, *5* (1), 63–92.
8. Goodwin, C. Professional vision. Am. Anthropol. **1994**, *96* (3), 606–633.
9. Sandusky, R.J. Infrastructure management as cooperative work: Implications for systems design. Comput. Support. Coop. Work J. Collab. Comput. **2003**, *12* (1), 97–122.
10. Harrington, D.; Presuhn, R.; Wijnen, B. *An Architecture for Describing SNMP Management Frameworks*, RFC 2571; Internet Engineering Task Force, 1999, http://www.ietf.org/rfc/rfc2571.txt (accessed August 7, 2008).
11. Case, J.; Harrington, D.; Presuhn, R.; Wijnen, B. *Message Processing and Dispatching for the Simple Network Management Protocol*, RFC 2572; Internet Engineering Task Force, 1999, http://www.ietf.org/rfc/rfc2572.txt (accessed August 7, 2008).
12. Levi, D.; Meyer, P.; Stewart, B. *SNMP Applications*, RFC 2573; Internet Engineering Task Force, 1999, http://www.ietf.org/rfc/rfc2573.txt (accessed August 7, 2008).
13. Blumenthal, U.; Wijnen, B. *User-based Security Model (USM) for Version 3 of the Simple Network Management Protocol (SNMPv3)*, RFC 2574; Internet Engineering Task Force, 1999, http://www.ietf.org/rfc/rfc2574.txt (accessed August 7, 2008).
14. Wijnen, B.; Presuhn, R.; McCloghrie, K. *View-based Access Control Model (VACM) for the Simple Network Management Protocol (SNMP), RFC 2575*; Internet Engineering Task Force, 1999, http://www.ietf.org/rfc/rfc2575.txt (accessed August 7, 2008).
15. Limoncelli, T.A.; Hogan, C.J.; Chalup, S.R. *The Practice of System and Network Administration*, 2nd Ed.; Addison-Wesley: Upper Saddle River, NJ, 2007.
16. Burke, J.R. *Network Management: Concepts and Practice, A Hands-on Approach*; Pearson Education: Upper Saddle River, NJ, 2004.
17. Morris, S.B. *Network Management, MIBs and MPLS*; Prentice Hall: Upper Saddle River, NJ, 2003.
18. Muller, N.J. *LANs to WANs: The Complete Management Guide*; Artech House: Boston, MA, 2003.

Network of European Museum Organisations (NEMO)

Frank Birkebæk
Roskilde Museum, Roskilde, Denmark

Abstract

European professional museum organizations joined together in 1992 in order to establish a political network of museums that would be able to act on a supranational level within the EU.

The Network of European Museum Organisations (NEMO) was founded in 1992, based on a Danish initiative. The intention was to establish a cooperation between the museum organisations within the then EC. Besides Denmark, Great Britain and Holland were the other driving forces in furthering this work.

The Maastricht Treaty made the need for NEMO even more evident and gave the network a clearer political dimension. After Maastricht, museums had to be able to act on a supranational level.

NEMO is an initiative for professional museums organizations, but professionally staffed state institutions and committees are invited to join from other countries, where no nationwide organisations exist. NEMO is set up with minimum bureaucracy. It is informally structured and has led to a flexible and workable organisation.

NEMO's members meet for 2–3 days every year. The meetings are held in rotation in the member countries, and are led by the chairman and the executive committee, who together monitor the work in NEMO and prepare for the annual meeting. The secretariat follows the chairman.

NEMO tries to get the expenses for running the secretariat and network financed by EU programs. The executive committee meets 2–3 times a year. One of these meetings is held at Brussels, and includes meetings with other cultural networks, with the cultural committee of the Parliament, and with the relevant offices of the Commission.

NEMO has made the presence of museums felt in the EU, and it is the duty of NEMO to bring museums into the current political debate. NEMO does so, by means of its meetings and contacts at Brussels, by taking part in conferences, by cooperating with other networks, by the distribution of information on the work and necessity of museums, by written submissions, and, especially, by contributing to different EU programs. The latest example is the compilation of a standard loan agreement for museums, which will make it easier to procure mobility of collections within Europe.

NEMO has brought about a close cooperation between museum organisations within the EU, and gaining knowledge and understanding each other has been one of the most important results of NEMO's activities. NEMO has also been part of the inspiration behind a new attempt to create a global collaboration among professional museum associations.

NEMO's Web site is a meeting point for museums that are looking for partners for projects. NEMO' Web site is also the forum for dissemination of information from EU that is relevant for museums.

Today, NEMO is considering its role in the future. Will it be obliged to be formal in order to meet the demands of formality from EU authorities? Or can it stay informal and keep the flexibility of an independent network?

Encyclopedia of Library and Information Sciences, Fourth Edition DOI: 10.1081/E-ELIS4-120044829

Networked Knowledge Organization Systems/Services (NKOS)

Marianne Lykke
Information Interaction and Architecture, Royal School of Library and Information Science, Aalborg, Denmark

Abstract
The NKOS Community is described in this entry. NKOS (http://nkos.slis.kent.edu/) is an informal network of academics and practitioners who are interested in the use of knowledge organization systems (KOS) in networked information environments. The general aim of the community is to enable KOS to act as networked information services (both machine-to-machine and human–computer), and support the description and retrieval of information resources on the Internet. The community is a forum for presentation and discussion of KOS applications, and interchange of ideas, from technical issues to intellectual, semantic, and terminological problems related to the use of KOS. The participants come from a variety of disciplines, and from academia as well as practice, and interact and communicate by a diverse set of means: annual workshops in the United States and Europe, a Web site, a mailing list, and publication of special journal issues and working papers about contemporary issues. The NKOS community represents topical diversity, informality, and multiple perspectives on networked KOS applications. There is an implicit danger that this variety diverts the focus and discussion. However, it appears from the analysis that the constancy in the organization of the activities and the well-established peer review process is adequate to attract participants, maintain satisfactory quality, and keep focus in multiplicity.

INTRODUCTION

Networked Knowledge Organization Systems/Services (NKOS) is an informal network of academics and practitioners from a variety of disciplines who are interested in the use of knowledge organization systems (KOS) in networked information environments. The notion of KOS covers a wide range of systems from authority files, classification systems, thesauri, gazetteers, and ontologies.

The NKOS network interacts and communicates by a diverse set of means. Since 1997, there has been an NKOS workshop each year, at either the Joint Conference on Digital Libraries (JCDL) or the European Conference on Digital Libraries (ECDL). In addition, NKOS Special Sessions have been held occasionally at other conferences or seminars. NKOS-related special issues have appeared in the online Journal of Digital Information (JoDI) in 2001 and 2004 and in the printed journal *New Review of Hypermedia and Multimedia* (NRHM) in 2006. A variety of KOS-related documents have been proposed and emerged from the NKOS community.

The community operates a mailing list, http://listserv.oclc.org/archives/nkos-l.html, today hosted at the Online Computer Library Center (OCLC). Diane Vizine-Goetz, OCLC oversees the list. From June 2001 to May 2007 the archive of the NKOS mailing list was hosted by the National Science Foundation (NSF) DLI2.[1] There is access to information about activities and means of communication at the NKOS Web site (http://nkos.slis.kent.edu/), hosted and administered by Marcia Zeng, Kent State University.

This entry is a description of the NKOS community, its interests, and activities. The remainder of the entry is organized as follows. Section "Aims, Participants, and Topical Focus" provides an overview and discussion of the aims, participants, topical focus, and themes that NKOS covers. Section "The NKOS Workshops and Special Sessions" presents the NKOS workshops and other NKOS meetings. Section "Special Journals Issues" discusses the special journal issues and other related documents proposed and developed within the NKOS community. Section "Conclusion" sums up and concludes about the contribution of NKOS.

AIMS, PARTICIPANTS, AND TOPICAL FOCUS

NKOS is devoted to the discussion of the functional and data model for enabling KOS as networked interactive information services to support the description and retrieval of diverse information resources through the Internet.[1]

From the start the NKOS community and its primary means of communication, the NKOS workshops were planned to be an *informal* meeting place for researchers and developers, a forum for discussions and interchange of ideas and experiences. In calls participants are encouraged strongly to present problems or lessons learned that will benefit from workshop discussion. Substantial, extensive discussions, with "crosscutting discussion points," is a crucial goal for the NKOS workshops.[2] At every the

Encyclopedia of Library and Information Sciences, Fourth Edition DOI: 10.1081/E-ELIS4-120044732

workshop a portion of the meeting time is reserved for informing about research and development projects, current as well as planned, deliberately with the idea of exchanging ideas and identifying collaborative development opportunities.

The workshops invite participants internationally from the industry as well as academia, and looking at the workshop programs participants also embrace a wide range of disciplines and professionals: thesaurus, taxonomy and ontology developers, digital library and information infrastructure developers, library, museum and archive professionals, standard developers, user interface designers, and knowledge managers. The workshops bring together developers of traditional KOS tools such as classification schemes and thesauri and developers of newer semantic tools such as ontologies and topic maps, and as such provide a meeting room where recent KOS development can take advantage of the vast body of knowledge from more traditional systems and where the practices for traditional KOS structures can benefit from the technological advances being developed to improve semantic access to Web content.

The main, overall workshop topics are themes related to KOS applications and networked implementation of KOS, ranging from technical challenges, terminology and standards development, identification of user needs, and understanding of the advantages and the general scenario for searching and navigating networked knowledge organization systems. Over the years the NKOS members have discussed the four essential discussion points that was developed already at the second NKOS workshop in 1998:[2]

1. The data model: what kind of data model is needed to support the interactive use of thesauri and other terminologies in online information services such as digital libraries? What data elements and/or relations are needed to convey the content of these resources?
2. The functional model: how do users want to use thesauri and other authority files in searching and resource description? What kind of access is important in exploring or "navigating" through the thesaurus?
3. Thesaurus-level metadata and thesaurus registries: what thesaurus-level metadata is needed to represent the scope, structure, size, ownership, access constraints, etc. of a thesaurus so that potential users will know what is available and how to access and use it?
4. The business/intellectual property model: what types of collaborative agreements and partnerships are necessary between thesaurus owners? What kinds of relationships are possible between owners of vocabularies published over a public network and users?

These topics have appeared at almost all workshops, and may be considered the main topical focus. Beyond these basic topics most of the workshops have had a special theme in the call for proposals, with the purpose to cover proactively up-coming issues and problems relevant to networked KOS. During time the community has picked up emerging issues such as cross walks and vocabulary mapping, interoperability, user-centered approaches to design and development. Consequently, the NKOS community has covered KOS related issues from multiple perspectives. Table 1 provides an overview of all the workshops NKOS in the United States and Europe from 1997 to 2008, with indication of their special issues and themes.

THE NKOS WORKSHOPS AND SPECIAL SESSIONS

The main activity for the NKOS community is the NKOS workshops, with NKOS workshops in the United States since 1997 (US NKOS workshops) and in Europe since 2000 (EU NKOS workshops).

The very first NKOS workshop was held in the United States in June 1997 at the 2nd ACM International conference on Digital Libraries. Also the following workshops in 1998, 1999, 2000, and 2001were hosted by ACM Digital Libraries Conferences. From 2001 the host was ACM and IEEE Joint Conferences on Digital Libraries (JCDL), continuing until 2005. After a break in 2006 and 2007, the 2008 US NKOS workshop was held as a Joint NKOS/ CENDI workshop. CENDI: the Commerce, Energy, NASA, Defense Information Managers Group.

Joseph Busch, Taxonomy Strategies organized the first NKOS workshop. Later workshops were organized by a large group of people, with Linda Hill, University of California, Gail Hodge, Information International Associates, Marcia Lei Zeng, Kent State University, and Diane Vizine-Goetz, OCLC as the regular and primary organizers over the years.

From the start the workshops were international with participants from the United States as well as European countries. As a result, workshops were also held in Europe from 2000, still with broad international participation.[3–6] The European Conference on Digital Libraries (ECDL) hosts the European workshops. Traugott Koch, Max Planck Digital Library, Douglas Tudhope, University of Glamorgan, and Marianne Lykke Nielsen, Royal School of Library and Information Science have been the principal organizers.

The NKOS workshops are peer-reviewed, with a formal call for proposals and a program committee. The organization group and the program committee are dynamic, and consist typically of a set of earlier organizers and new people, in order to keep simultaneously the primary scope and add new perspective. The program committee is multidisciplinary and international, and represents a wide range of professionals, disciplines, and interests.

Table 1 NKOS workshops, 1997–2008.

Workshop	Location	Workshop theme
US NKOS 1997	ACM Digital Libraries Conferences, United States	Metadata and thesauri
US NKOS 1998	ACM Digital Libraries Conferences, United States	Standards for networked terminology/thesauri/ classification/authority systems
US NKOS 1999	ACM Digital Libraries Conferences, United States	Thesauri registry and data models
US NKOS 2000	ACM Digital Libraries Conferences, United States	Networked knowledge organisation systems, with special focus on ontologies and gazetteers
EU NKOS 2000	European Conference on Digital Libraries, Portugal	European initiatives and projects/options for global cooperation
US NKOS 2001	ACM Digital Libraries Conferences, United States	Classification crosswalks and vocabulary mapping
US NKOS 2002	Joint Conferences on Digital Libraries, United States	Digital gazetteers
US NKOS 2003	Joint Conferences on Digital Libraries, United States	Transformation of traditional KOS to new semantic tools
EU NKOS 2003	European Conference on Digital Libraries, Norway	Standards in networked KOS
EU NKOS 2004	European Conference on Digital Libraries, United Kingdom	User-centered approaches
US NKOS 2005	Joint Conferences on Digital Libraries, United States	Interoperability and integration of KOS
EU NKOS 2005	European Conference on Digital Libraries, Austria	User-centered strategies
EU NKOS 2006	European Conference on Digital Libraries, Spain	Semantic Web applications of KOS in Digital Libraries
EU NKOS 2007	European Conference on Digital Libraries, Hungary	KOS in next-generation digital libraries
US NKOS 2008	JOINT NKOS/CENDI, United States	New dimensions, e.g., mapping, collaborative KOS development
EU NKOS 2008	European Conference on Digital Libraries, Denmark	User centered systems and Terminology Registries

Source: http://nkos.slis.kent.edu/ (accessed January 2009).[1]

In 2004 the EU NKOS workshop was held in collaboration with Sebastian Ryszard Kruk, National University of Ireland, who comes from the semantic web community. The purpose was to have a special session, highlighting semantic web applications of KOS in Digital Libraries. The session was chaired by Thomas Baker, Goettingen State and University Library and Bernhard Haslhofer, ARC Seibersdorf research, Studio Digital Memory Engineering.

In 2003, 2005, and 2008 NKOS events were held three times yearly: workshops at JCDL in the United States and at ECDL in Europe, and NKOS Special Sessions at the DCxxxx International Conference on Dublin Core and Metadata Applications (DCxxxx). The first special session was held at DC2003 in Seattle. The session explored the relationship between metadata structures and values, and discussed the traditions and innovations in controlled vocabulary use in the networked environment. The second special session was held at DC2005 in Madrid, and focused on the practical applications of networked KOS. The last DC special session was held in Berlin in 2008. The presentations covered topics such as the combined use of KOS and social tagging, controlled vocabulary in metadata for semantic web usages, and metadata and terminology registries.

In 2008, the conference of the American Society of Information Science and Technology (ASIST) hosted a NKOS meeting, which was a new invention and meeting platform. The meeting was held as a panel discussion that addressed important issues around standards and applications. A registry for controlled vocabularies at the Library of Congress was presented, the architecture of the OCLC Terminology Services, and a MeSH indexing tool for Health Science Repository System. The panel was a continuing effort of the ASIST Standards Committee in order to promote awareness of standards.

SPECIAL JOURNAL ISSUES

The workshops do not publish workshop proceedings, but publish the Power Point presentations at the workshop Web site.[1] However, NKOS-related special issues have appeared in the online Journal of Digital Information (JoDI) in 2001 and 2004 and in New Review of Hypermedia and Multimedia (NRHM) in 2006. These special issues have their origin and evolve from the NKOS workshops where the participants are encouraged to submit papers based on their NKOS presentations. However, the calls for papers are open calls within the topical scope of networked KOS.

The first special issue of the JoDI evolved from the EU NKOS 2000 workshop, held in Lisbon.[7] The focus was European initiatives and projects, and the issue presented five papers on the general workshop themes, on both conceptual aspects and technical implementations of knowledge organization systems. The papers covered the development of a four-language multilingual social thesaurus, exploration of the potential of thesaurus facet structure in query formulation, problems of semantic mapping between thesauri, approaches to the mapping and understanding of equivalence and hierarchical relationships between terms from different subdomains, and the use of the Unified Modeling Language (ULM) for representing ontologies and mapping from Extensible Markup Language (XML) encodings and UML.

The second special issue was published in JoDI in 2004 with its origin in the two NKOS workshops, held in 2003 in the United States and Europe, respectively.[8] Three of the five accepted papers represent classical NKOS topics. The first paper reported a reengineering project of a traditional thesaurus structure to an ontology structure for conceptual reasoning and automatic use. The second paper discussed automatic mapping and creation of intervocabulary associations, and the third paper concerned development of protocols for distributed access to thesauri. The fourth paper was a theoretical paper discussing the role of knowledge organization systems and arguing that the effective teaching of scientific concepts may be facilitated by digital library systems, which provide integrated knowledge organization structures. In the paper a system was presented, based on a strongly structured model of scientific concepts that integrates a domain-specific KOS with associated metadata and specialized learning models. The fifth paper reviewed the topical notion of the semantic web, and argued that the semantic web is based on a restricted and static sense of meaning. The last paper was long for a conventional journal paper, but as JoDI is an electronic journal, it was possible to publish the extended historical treatment of the semantic web. This is precisely in the spirit of the NKOS community that focuses on facilitating informal communication of new perspectives and viewpoints.

The third special issue was published in the *New Review of Hypermedia and Multimedia* in 2006. The issue had its origins in the EU NKOS workshops, held in 2004 and 2005, although the majority of contributions resulted from an open call for papers.[9] The themes were typical for NKOS. One paper reported research evaluating automated subject classification of textual Web pages with categorization rules based on a controlled vocabulary. The second paper continued the automatic indexing theme by reporting on a variety of natural language processing techniques that have been used in combination to improve information retrieval, including query expansion. Semantic interoperability was the topical focus of the third paper that reported results from a major project by the Food and Agriculture Organization (FAO) in mapping two large agricultural thesauri. The fourth paper described a freely faceted classification method that allows the free combination of concepts in complex subject descriptors. A Web demonstrator illustrated its application to a small set of bibliographic records. The last paper reported on initial results from proof of concept projects conducted by the Metropolitan Museum of Art and the steve.museum collaboration.

The NKOS community has proposed and initiated the development of several working papers. Linda Hill and Interconnect Technologies drafted in 1996 document defining and describing a set of thesaurus attributes.[10] A reference documents for data elements was developed in 1998, and later updated in 2001 and 2008.[11] Gail Hodge drafted a taxonomy of knowledge organization systems in 2000.[12] A document describing a vocabulary mark-up language was published in 2000.[1]

As a whole, the special issues and working papers represent well the objectives and topical focus of the NKOS community. All three journal issues are a mix of the classical NKOS topics related to the use and development of KOS and up-coming topics such as user-oriented approaches to design and development, social tagging, and KOS as a teaching facility. Similarly, the NKOS-related documents cover classical NKOS topics.

CONCLUSION

The analysis of NKOS community and its activities shows that the NKOS community is an active network which enables presentation and discussion of the use and development of KOS. The community is international and multidisciplinary with participants from a variety of fields such as information science, library science, computer science, semantic web community, and language engineering. Correspondingly, the participants come from academia as well as practice. The network facilitates informal interchange of ideas, viewpoints, and approaches by a diverse set of means, a Web site, mailing list, workshops, journal papers, and working papers.

The overall focus is KOS, but this topic is approached from many different angles, from technical issues to intellectual, semantic, and terminological problems, standardization and registries, from design, development, and use of KOS applications. NKOS is a topical broad forum, and provides room for completed and on-going research, early and mature development projects, and demos of prototypes as well as full applications. The review of the NKOS activities shows clearly that the community covers multiple KOS-related issues from a large set of disciplinary perspectives.

This topical diversity, multiple perspectives, and informality in communication should be considered an advantage in its richness and complexity, but the multiplicity might also be a disadvantage and "Achilles' Heel," with an implicit danger of lack of focus and mixed quality. However, it seems from the analysis of the activities and the fact that the community has existed more than 10 years that the more or less constant organizing committees in the United States and Europe, and the well established peer review process is adequate and sufficient to maintain satisfactory quality, attract participants, and keep focus in multiplicity.

REFERENCES

1. http://nkos.slis.kent.edu/.
2. http://nkos.slis.kent.edu/dl98_workshop_preliminary.html.

3. Tudhope, D. ECDL 2003 workshop report: Networked knowledge organisation systems/services workshop: Evolving standards. D-Lib Mag. **2003**, *9*(9).
4. Nielsen, M.L. ECDL 2004 workshop report: Networked knowledge organisation systems/services (NKOS). D-Lib Mag. **2004**, *10*(10).
5. Tudhope, D. Report on the 4th European networked knowledge organisation systems/services workshop. Mapping knowledge organization systems. D-Lib Mag. **2005**, *11*(11).
6. Koch, T. Report on the 5th European networked knowledge organisation systems/services (NKOS) workshop. D-Lib Mag. **2006**, *12*(10).
7. Hill, L.; Koch, T. Networked knowledge organisation systems: Introduction to a special issue. J. Dig. Inform. **2001**, *1*(8).
8. Tudhope, D.; Koch, T. New applications of knowledge organization systems: Introduction to a special issue. J. Dig. Inform. **2004**, *4*(4), Article no. 286.
9. Tudhope, D.; Nielsen, M.L. Introduction to knowledge organization systems and services (special issue). New Rev. Hypermed. Multimed. **2006**, *12*(1), 3–9.
10. http://nkos.slis.kent.edu/Thesaurus_Registry.html.
11. http://nkos.slis.kent.edu/registry3.htm.
12. http://nkos.slis.kent.edu/KOS_taxonomy.htm.

New Zealand Aotearoa: Libraries

Heather M. Lamond
Massey University Library, Palmerston North, New Zealand

Abstract

This entry provides an overview of libraries and library services in New Zealand Aotearoa. Taking as a starting point British colonization in 1840, the entry follows the development through until the present day. In addition to outlining the four major library sectors of public, academic, school, and special libraries, it also includes detail of the National Library of New Zealand. Education for librarianship in New Zealand is described along with descriptions of professional associations. Finally, some issues and challenges in New Zealand libraries are identified.

INTRODUCTION

Situated at the bottom of the Southern Hemisphere in the Pacific Ocean, New Zealand consists of two major islands (North and South), and smaller surrounding islands. It was originally settled prior to A.D. 1300 by Polynesian people from the eastern Pacific islands. It is believed that they made landfall along the eastern coast of New Zealand[1] (p. 35). For the ensuing almost 350 years, the indigenous people of Aotearoa lived without European contact or influence and a community with a strong oral history and tradition developed. The tāngata whenua (people of the land) Māori lived in independent subtribe groups.

The first European discovery in 1642 was by Dutch explorer Abel Jansen Tasman, who mapped portions of the west coast of both islands. Subsequently, some 120 years later, New Zealand was effectively rediscovered by British Captain James Cook in 1769.

The beginnings of European settlement were in the late 1700s and early 1800s, primarily by whalers and sealers, with the first traders and missionaries following shortly after. New Zealand became annexed to the British Crown in 1840 with the signing of the Treaty of Waitangi, and by this time there were only a few hundred Europeans living in the country.[2] The Treaty is now considered the founding document of New Zealand Aotearoa as a nation. The British understood that the Treaty granted sovereignty to the British Crown, whereas the Māori chiefs that signed the document understood they were granting governance to the Crown but not sovereignty. The differences between the two versions (one in English and one in Māori) have been a point of tension and debate since 1840.

The wave of settlers that followed the declaration of British sovereignty were predominantly those looking for a better life than they were leaving behind, with an image of a society that was both egalitarian and equal. Literacy levels were relatively high among the settlers and those who had low levels of reading ability were determined to better both themselves and their society.[3]

New Zealand today has a population of over 4.8 million people. While it is truly multicultural, with recent high immigration rates from the Pacific, Asia, and the Middle East, the Treaty of Waitangi establishes a formal bicultural framework for Māori and Pakeha (non-Māori) to work within. To this end, New Zealand has three official languages—English, Te Reo Māori, and, since 2006, sign language.

The impacts of British colonization can be clearly seen in the government and the legislative structure. While there was a brief period of provincial government in the nineteenth century, this was short-lived, so unlike Australia and the United States, New Zealand does not have state or provincial government. This has led to more cooperative developments on a national scale.

New Zealand has a state schooling system that is free for all 5–19-year olds and compulsory for all 6–16-year olds.[4] While achievement rates for New Zealand students in the OECD PISA reports are higher than average (ranked seventh in 2009),[5] on closer inspection, the education system is not serving all students equally well. There are higher numbers, in particular, of Māori children leaving school before eighteen, and one in four New Zealanders over the age of fifteen does not hold any educational qualifications. Low literacy levels among Māori are an ongoing concern, and various Māori education initiatives have been developed over the years to address these gaps.

The New Zealand economy was traditionally based on primary industries, with a focus on agriculture, forestry, and fishing exports to drive the economy. In recent times, there has been a shift in focus for development with subsequent government investing in manufacturing innovation, the knowledge economy, and tourism. While the primary industries continue to make the most significant contributions to the economy, the newer areas of emphasis

Encyclopedia of Library and Information Sciences, Fourth Edition DOI: 10.1081/E-ELIS4-120044984

are having an impact and are an attempt to spread the risk in times of recession and slow growth.[6] New Zealand does suffer in terms of the global economy being geographically isolated from many of its major markets. The increasing financial cost of freight and concern about the environmental footprint of long-distance exporting places the country at a disadvantage when seeking new markets, as well as the barrier of trade protection measures in potential markets. Free trade negotiations are a priority for New Zealand governments, and it is a party to the Trans-Pacific Partnership Agreement negotiations.

While New Zealand is a well-developed first-world nation, in recent times, there has been increasing concern about levels of child poverty and a widening divide between the socioeconomic classes.[7,8] Improving technology infrastructure is one method that is being proposed to address these gaps. Ultrafast broadband is to be rolled out nationwide by 2020.[9]

LIBRARY ORIGINS AND LEGISLATION

The first library in New Zealand is thought to have been a Mechanics' Institute and Library that opened in Auckland in 1842,[10] and in 1854, the first Provincial Council libraries were founded.[10] The 1874 Census states that there were 161 public libraries and other literary institutes in New Zealand at that time. However, these were not public libraries as we know them now, but private members' collections. In 1879, the Auckland Free Public Library was formed from the previous Mechanics' Institute and was the first of its kind in the country with other centers following suit thereafter. By 1926, there were 435 public libraries listed.[10] However, the majority of these libraries were still subscription based. In 1934, only the Timaru Public Library was lauded by Munn and Barr (a commissioned report on libraries in New Zealand) as being completely free for its constituents to use.

The General Assembly Library (established to meet the needs of central government representatives) was first established in Auckland in 1856, and subsequently moved to Wellington when the more southern city was established as the capital city in 1864.[3] The National Library Service was initially formed in 1945 as an amalgamation of a collection of national services, and in 1965 was merged with the General Assembly Library and the Alexander Turnbull Library (a private collection gifted to the country) to become the National Library of New Zealand.

The first academic/tertiary library was established in Dunedin in 1869 at the then University College of Otago, with other centers such as Christchurch (1873), Auckland (1883), and Wellington (1899) following shortly after.[11]

Much of the development of New Zealand libraries following the pioneer period was as a result of a report commissioned from the Carnegie Corporation by the New Zealand Library Association (NZLA)—commonly known as the Munn-Barr report and published in 1934. A similar report was researched and written for Australia's libraries and published in 1935 (known as the Munn-Pitt Report). In addition to the recommendations of the Munn-Barr report, which governed the strategic development of libraries for the next 50 years,[12] New Zealand was the beneficiary of several Carnegie grants to both build libraries and fund development of collections and librarians.

LEGISLATION

The primary piece of legislation governing public libraries in New Zealand has its origins in the original Public Libraries Act of 1869. It provided, in principle, for local authorities to be authorized to charge a rate for library funding, that management of libraries would sit with the local authority, and that admission to libraries should be free. The current legislation covering public libraries is the Local Government Act 2002, and in essence it lists a library as a core service for consideration (although does not obligate any local authority to provide a library), and states that where a library is provided, constituents must be able to join free of charge. While public libraries are in general free to join, there has been a history of some libraries charging for borrowing some items. This could stem from the original intent of the 1869 Act, when it was not envisaged that public libraries would be lending libraries.[10] Recent lobbying attempts by the Library and Information Association of New Zealand Aotearoa (LIANZA) to ensure core library services are provided free of charge in all local authorities were not successful.

The National Library Act 1965 was enacted when the National Library Service amalgamated with the Alexander Turnbull Library and the General Assembly Library. This Act was repealed in 2003, and replaced with The National Library of New Zealand (Te Puna Mātauranga o Aotearoa) Act 2003.

Other legislations that impact on New Zealand libraries are the Copyright Act 1994 and associated regulations, privacy laws, classification laws, and laws and regulations concerning digital access. The New Zealand Bill of Rights Act 1990 is designed to protect citizens from discrimination and, although not an Act, the Treaty of Waitangi as a founding constitutional document plays a large part in guiding libraries' moves toward biculturalism.

NATIONAL LIBRARY

The National Library of New Zealand officially came into being in 1965, although its seeds were planted much earlier in a variety of national library services. Key among these was the Country Library Service (started in 1938), which sent bulk loans of books to small rural libraries. The other key national service was the School Library Service that began in 1942. These two services were amalgamated in 1945 to form the National Library Service. Then in 1965, the Alexander Turnbull Library and the Parliamentary library were added and the National Library became an official entity.

The National Library of New Zealand has, as its purpose in The National Library of New Zealand (Te Puna Mātauranga o Aotearoa) Act 2003, to collect and preserve documentary heritage and taonga (treasures), to supplement and further the work of other New Zealand libraries, and to work collaboratively with other institutions having a similar role. The current work of the National Library is focused on providing easy access for all New Zealanders to the information and resources they need to turn knowledge into value.[13]

In 2011, the National Library along with Archives New Zealand was integrated into the Department of Internal Affairs. In late 2012, the National Library reopened to the public after a three-year refurbishment of the building and service. During the closure, mass digitization projects were undertaken that now provide over 250,000 online images and two million pages of historical newspapers. More than 2000 at-risk audio recordings were also digitized during this period.

In its role of working collaboratively and furthering all New Zealand libraries, the National Library has been the driving force behind several major innovative projects. Highlights include the following:

- Te Puna Services—a partnership with New Zealand libraries that facilitates shared cataloging, interlibrary loan, and the maintenance and searching of the National Union Catalogue (http://natlib.govt.nz/librarians/te-puna).
- EPIC (Electronic Purchasing in Collaboration), which provides access to a range of online databases to libraries in a collaborative purchasing model (http://www.epic.org.nz/).
- DigitalNZ is a collaboration between more than 120 partners to make access and discovery of digital content relevant to New Zealand easier (http://www.digitalnz.org/).
- Aotearoa People's Network Kaharoa (APNK) provides free access to broadband internet services via public libraries and marae around New Zealand (http://www.aotearoapeoplesnetwork.org/).
- Kōtui is a shared library management system and discovery service that public libraries can join by subscription, thereby reducing cost to individual libraries and increasing shared capability and knowledge (http://www.kotui.org.nz/).

The Library is also working with New Zealand publishers and other stakeholders on epublishing and elending models in order to establish a workable solution to the issue of ebooks in libraries. Through Services to Schools (http://natlib.govt.nz/schools), the National Library provides critical literacy and resourcing support to teachers and students throughout the country.

The collections of the National Library are both heritage and general. Under the legal deposit clause in the National Library Act 2003, two copies of all material published in physical format are to be sent to the National Library for the collection. The general collections are primarily held and developed to support the Library's reference services and the Services to Schools collection. Heritage collections include the Alexander Turnbull Library (see below) and other collections of material significant to the history of New Zealand.

The Alexander Turnbull Library

A "library within a library," the Alexander Turnbull Library began life as the private collection of Alexander Horsburgh Turnbull, born in Wellington in 1868. By the time of his death in 1918, the collection held 55,000 items including books and other print items that he bequeathed to the Crown to "form the nucleus of a New Zealand National collection"[14] (p. 1). The collection has been added to continually over the years with a strong but not sole focus on information relating to New Zealand and the Pacific. It also includes an outstanding collection regarding John Milton—a particular interest of Turnbull's. Most of the material in this collection is for use in specialized Reading Rooms within the National Library building and it is predominately a closed access collection as befitting its value and worth.

PUBLIC LIBRARIES

New Zealand's public libraries are administered and funded solely from local government. There are 290 local public libraries across 78 local authorities and the range in size, scale, and capability is vast. Auckland Libraries (formed by a local government amalgamation in 2010) is the largest public library system in Australasia with 55 library branches across the system. As outlined in the legislation section, there is no legislative requirement for a local authority to provide a library service, but in reality, most people have access to a public library within their region. Libraries are funded usually from a levy made on property owners, which is gathered by the local authority. This local government funding usually contributes around 80% of the library's annual income. Further income is generated from overdue loan penalties and value-added services such as business research services and digital collections.

With the cessation of the Country Library Service in the late 1980s and mass local government amalgamations in 1989, it became unviable for many small rural libraries to continue as a local government function. In an echo of the subscription libraries of the pioneer days, some of these libraries have continued to function as community membership libraries.[15]

LIANZA published Public Library Standards regularly, with the most recent edition in 2004. With the establishment of an independent Association of Public Library Managers (APLM) in 2007, the updating of the Standards has become a priority for this group to undertake, and at the time of writing, these are yet to be published. In 2012, APLM released the refreshed Strategic Framework for Public Libraries 2012–2017, which outlines a bold direction for the sector in coming years. The eight key priorities from the framework for the coming five years are to

- Work with New Zealand authors, publishers, and booksellers to develop a whole-of-country approach to deliver an ebook solution that meets the needs of all parties
- Develop an evidence-based model of measurement that can be used to demonstrate public libraries' value and contribution to outcomes and for benchmarking purposes
- Identify or develop business models that make it easy for collaboration on a regional, national, and cross-sector basis in association with the local government New Zealand
- Explore a nationwide partnership with schools to deliver content and reading support in schools and across the Network for Learning, in association with the Ministry of Education and the National Library of New Zealand
- Collaborate with the National Library of New Zealand to deliver a National Year of Reading program to celebrate the joy of reading and improve literacy levels in New Zealand
- Develop a national approach to workforce planning, skills development and recruitment, and, in association with LIANZA, foster leadership for the new generation of libraries
- Investigate the opportunities for the development of whole-of-country digital solutions to ensure public library content and services are delivered in the mobile environment
- Dramatically increase the range of New Zealand's unique and legacy content available in digital format, in association with the National Library of New Zealand, universities, and other appropriate national and international partners[16]

Services provided in New Zealand public libraries include lending and reference collections in many formats (e.g., DVDs, CDs, MP3, ebooks, online databases, and research tools). Many provide mobile libraries in order to serve communities that are further away from their physical branch as well as outreach services to community members with special needs. Through the APNK free internet access is provided at 149 sites around the country, with libraries that are not part of the network also providing internet access, although non-APNK libraries sometimes charge a small fee for access. Children's and young people's services are offered nationwide, and many public libraries work closely with their local schools to provide tailored programs and services at appropriate levels. Provision of ebooks through public libraries is increasing in New Zealand, primarily through a consortial approach to purchasing and local solutions.[17]

The reinventing of public libraries as community spaces or hubs has been a recent and strong development in New Zealand, with many libraries being either refurbished or moving in to completely new buildings in the last decade or so. The library as place has led to new models of community service being provided from library buildings, such as community meeting rooms, flexible furniture, cafeterias, and multimedia computing suites, and of course the expert help that goes along with them. There have also been some significant developments bringing libraries, museums, and galleries into one space (e.g., Puke Ariki in New Plymouth) as well as some libraries providing services that have traditionally been provided by local authorities (e.g., rates payments, dog registration, cemetery records, etc).

SCHOOL LIBRARIES

While there are more than 2550 school libraries across all age levels of the compulsory sector, it is not a legislative obligation of schooling in New Zealand to provide a library service. As schools have considerable freedom in how they manage their own environments and budgets, the quality of any school library can vary greatly from school to school. School libraries in the main suffer from being both underfunded and undervalued in many schools in the country, with the importance of professional, qualified staff not uniformly recognized or understood.[11] Of course, there are exceptions of well-funded and supported school libraries, but these are not common, and in the LIANZA Remuneration Survey, school librarians are the lowest paid of all sectors across all roles.[18]

Both the School Library Association of New Zealand (SLANZA) and the National Library are active proponents in this sector. SLANZA provides advocacy and professional development for those working in school libraries through a range of resources and events. The National Library, through the Services to Schools section, provides a range of support services to schools, librarians, teachers, and learners. These include a curriculum service where resources are sent to schools around the country to assist teachers and school librarians in teaching the curriculum. They also provide advisory services to teachers and school librarians as well as offering an online chat reference service to students called "Any Questions."[19]

The New Zealand curriculum identifies five key competencies: thinking; using language, symbols, and text; managing self; relating to others; and participating and contributing.[20] While these concepts are very broad, it is possible to place developing information literacy skills and using library resources effectively within them. School librarians face an ongoing advocacy challenge to build strong working relationships with both school management and teachers to embed information and research skills in to day-to-day teaching.

In 2012, the New Zealand Government requested that the Education and Science Select Committee carry out an "Inquiry into 21st century learning environments and digital literacy."[21] Following submissions to the Select Committee by SLANZA, LIANZA, and various individual libraries, it is encouraging to note that the important role of both school and public libraries in the twenty-first century learning has been highlighted as an area for further investigation by the government.

ACADEMIC LIBRARIES

New Zealand's tertiary education system is made up of eight universities that are public institutions; eighteen government-funded Institutes of Technology or Polytechnics (ITPs) that offer tertiary education with a focus on technical, vocational, or professional education, but also encourage research particularly in applied or technological areas; and three Wānanga (Māori teaching and research institutions) with sites throughout the country. While all tertiary institutions receive government funding, most (especially the universities) seek additional revenue through research and development and other commercial initiatives. Government funding is currently allocated according to four broad education performance indicators: qualification completion rate, course completion rate, retention, and progression. In addition, a stand-alone government fund, the Performance Based Research Fund (PBRF), is allocated according to the standard of research output from an institution.

While the Munn-Barr report of 1934 stated that "[t]he college libraries of New Zealand do not even approach accepted overseas standards"[10] (p. 35), the same cannot really be said today. Development in the university libraries took a turn for the better in the 1960s, with increasing budgets for building collections that were relevant and necessary for the teaching and research activities of their institutions. This was a result primarily of the Parry Report[22] that urged an immediate injection of funds to libraries. It was not, however, until the advent of electronic access to scholarly databases and later full-text online academic journals that vast improvements were seen. University libraries are still subject to the constant vagaries of budget allocations from the university and ever-increasing subscription costs. In recent times, the open access movement has offered alternatives for both scholarly publishing and scholarly collections of university libraries.

All the university libraries contribute to the New Zealand interlibrary loan scheme, and there are also reciprocal borrowing arrangements in place between most of them. Consortial purchasing of electronic packages increases the buying power for what is still a small market by working with universities in Australia through the Council of Australian University Librarians Electronic Information Resources Consortium (CEIRC), of which all the New Zealand university libraries are members.

The ITP libraries have also had mixed fortune since their establishment in the 1960s as technical institutes. Woefully underfunded during this stage, the institutes were widely criticized for the state of their libraries. The 1990s saw a loosening of control by the central government over the qualifications and courses that the ITPs could offer, and this era saw them begin to offer undergraduate degree courses. In order to be accepted as meeting New Zealand Qualifications Authority (NZQA) standards significant, investment in their libraries was required, and many ITP libraries experienced phenomenal growth as a result.

As with the university libraries, the ITP libraries continue to struggle against variable funding and increasing vendor costs. As subsequent governments continue to review and alter tertiary education policies, these all have a flow-on effect to the library budget.

Wānanga were established in the early 1980s but were not officially recognized under the Education Act 1989 until the early 1990s. Wānanga were established to provide a tertiary education option for Māori, which was a distinct experience from the mainstream universities and ITPs. The rationale for wānanga can best be stated as "... characterized by teaching and research that maintains, advances, and disseminates knowledge and develops intellectual independence, and assists the application of knowledge regarding ahuatanga Māori (Māori tradition) according to tikanga Māori (Māori custom)."[23]

As tertiary academic institutions, all three types of libraries offer similar services to their patrons, including lending, reference services, information literacy teaching, collection development and management, and ensuring access to large collections of print and electronic resources. Increasingly, the academic library is taking on other roles such as computing and learning services and providing flexible spaces for group research and projects. Several institutions have had major refurbishment to match the new vision of what an academic library is. Discovery services are a relatively new development in terms of providing access to resources for patrons as libraries continue to strive toward a solution that delivers quality results to users in the most painless way possible and are still a work in progress in many institutions. Other recent developments are focusing on embedding library and research skill development into the online learning environment using teaching and learning pedagogy and tools, developing digital institutional repositories, and starting to work with researchers in the eresearch field.

SPECIAL LIBRARIES

Special libraries exist to meet the information needs and requirements of their parent bodies. Included in this group are libraries serving government departments, medical libraries, corporate and law libraries, as well as those from the not-for-profit sector. They can be described as having a narrow scope in both collection and online resources, but greater depth to that collection than is possible in a more general library.

There are approximately 300 libraries in this sector in New Zealand, the earliest of which can be traced back to the establishment of the nation with various court libraries and scientific collections, including those of the Royal Society of New Zealand.[10]

Special libraries are in general funded directly by their parent body, and some have needed at times to be very inventive to raise additional funding with initiatives like accepting overseas interns for a fee and even teaching English in overseas centers. In an increasingly tight economic climate, special libraries need to work very hard to demonstrate their value to their funders, particularly when there is a common misconception that everything is available on the internet. By developing subject-specific expertise in the required narrow fields of knowledge, special librarians help to preserve their role, but they also need to be vigilant in marketing their specialist skills and services to their clientele. There has also been a broadening of role as evidenced by the increasing variation in position titles from librarian to information manager or knowledge manager. While some corporate libraries have been lost over the last decade, it appears there has been an increase in special library workers in the noncommercial sector.[24]

Of particular significance in this Sector are the Crown Research Institute (CRI) libraries. There are eight different institutes, each with a specialist research library service to meet the needs of scientists and technicians working in their fields to further research in areas such as environmental, agricultural, and food research.[25]

The Parliamentary Library that began as the General Assembly Library in 1856 was part of the National Library from 1965 until 1985. It was felt then that separating the Library out again would help to clarify its purpose as the library for parliamentarians,[3] and in 1986, its name was changed from the General Assembly Library to the Parliamentary Library. While the Library had in the past fulfilled many of the roles of a National Library, since the separation, it has been able to focus much more on providing an efficient and effective information service to members of parliament, parliamentary staff, and research units from its vast collections of both print and digital material as a special library.

EDUCATION AND THE PROFESSION

Education for Librarianship

As a result of New Zealand's geographical isolation, the education of librarians was a concern as early as 1910, when the first NZLA Conference set one of their aims to be to improve the "status and qualifications"[26] of New Zealand librarians. Given that there were no library training opportunities within New Zealand, this invariably meant travel to either the United Kingdom or the United States.

By 1942, the NZLA was ready to offer a general certificate course by correspondence, and there were forty-six students in the first intake. It was a requirement for enrolment that students must be currently employed in a library for at least fifteen hours a week and the nature of the course was both practical and theoretical. In 1946, the first postgraduate diploma was offered and was taught from within the National Library Service from the then newly formed New Zealand Library School. The Diploma was considered a professional qualification and would take one academic year of full-time study in Wellington.

This model of library education and training was to remain in place for almost a further 40 years. After several years of discussion and planning, the Certificate course moved to the Wellington Teacher's College and the Diploma to Victoria University of Wellington in 1980.[27] Since 1980, most qualifications have been renamed as information management courses, the Diploma has been upgraded to a Master's degree, and a Doctor of Philosophy degree has been introduced. In 1996 the undergraduate education was moved to the Open Polytechnic of New Zealand.

The Victoria University of Wellington is the only educational provider offering postgraduate qualifications. Current options are postgraduate certificates and diplomas, in addition to the master of information management degree with a library science endorsement. Victoria also offers the option of PhD study in the School of Information Management, although there have been very few enrolments focusing on topics in librarianship to date. Victoria courses are offered both by distance education and on campus in Wellington.

The Open Polytechnic of New Zealand offers subdegree programs in LIS as well as undergraduate bachelor of arts or applied science degrees in library and information science. The Open Polytechnic is a distance education provider.

Te Wānanga o Raukawa offers a one-year diploma or a three-year undergraduate bachelor degree in information management, with a specific aim to develop bilingual and bicultural managers of Māori information resources in Māori and non-Māori organizations.

Professional Registration

After several years of debate, planning, and consultation around the need to improve the standing of librarianship as a profession, in 2007, LIANZA introduced its Professional Registration scheme. The scheme is an open, voluntary scheme that provides a framework for continuing professional development and accreditation with like organizations outside New Zealand. It is designed to firmly position library and information management as a graduate profession, as registrants must hold a recognized degree in library studies. Similar in structure to CILIP's Chartership scheme, the Professional Registration scheme required registered librarians to revalidate every three years by submitting a reflective journal of development and learning. While still relatively new, the scheme aims to benefit librarians, employers, and the public as a whole by providing both the motivation and means to continually upskill. LIANZA's scheme has reciprocal recognition with CILIP, allowing registered New Zealand librarians to be recognized as equivalent to chartered librarians in the United Kingdom.

The LIANZA Professional Registration scheme has a body of knowledge adapted from the IFLA guidelines, with the significant addition at the time of an eleventh element regarding indigenous knowledge frameworks. Both LIANZA and Te Rōpū Whakahau (an association for Māori library workers) have worked diligently to have this eleventh element internationally accepted as part of the LIS Body of Knowledge with the support of the IFLA SIG on Indigenous Matters, and they are to be congratulated that this amendment to the IFLA guidelines has been made in 2013.

Professional Associations

The NZLA, trading as LIANZA, came into existence in 1910 in Dunedin, following the first conference of library leaders. It was incorporated under its own statute, NZLA Act 1939, and celebrated its centenary with the publication of the Association's history in 2010.[26] LIANZA is a membership organization with both individual and institutional members and has as its vision to "... be the vibrant, vital professional voice for those engaged in Librarianship and Information management."[28] LIANZA operates the Professional Registration scheme for librarians and information professionals as well as providing an annual conference, continuing professional development program, regular publications, and high-level advocacy on behalf of members with central and local government.

Te Rōpū Whakahau was formed in 1992 as a SIG of LIANZA and in 1996 was incorporated as an independent organization. It was formed as a specialist support network for Māori staff working in libraries and to build understanding and capacity for all when working with Māori patrons or Māori information. There is a formal partnership between LIANZA and Te Rōpū Whakahau that assures the two associations' work together in the pursuit of bicultural development of librarianship in New Zealand. Notable achievements for Te Rōpū Whakahau have been the development and delivery of CPD courses nationwide to increase bicultural awareness in LIS workers, working with The National Library of New Zealand to develop Māori subject headings for use in library catalogs, and working with Te Wānanga o Raukawa to deliver library education in a Māori environment.

Over the decades, other professional associations have come into being to serve specific needs and sectors. Notable examples are the SLANZA, APLM, and the New Zealand Law Libraries Association (NZLLA). Sector specific groups are also in existence within LIANZA's structure in the form of Special Interest Groups (SIGs) and these include HealthSIG, SLIS (Special Libraries), and the Digital Libraries SIG, to name a few.

Issues and Challenges

Biculturalism

As described earlier, New Zealand is in the unique position of having a founding document in the Treaty of Waitangi that essentially requires two distinct cultures to live as equals in one nation. The reality of colonization is of course quite different to this ideal, and true biculturalism remains a challenge for the country as a whole.

Since a resurgence of Māori culture and language in the late 1980s, there has been considerable movement along the bicultural continuum in libraries and information services. Two key research reports have contributed to these developments "Te Ara Tika: Maori and Libraries" and "Te Ara Tika: Guiding Voices."[29,30] The project that led to their publication during the 1990s was jointly commissioned by LIANZA and Te Rōpū Whakahau.

Evidence of the development of bicultural library services includes such practical things as bilingual signage, bilingual staff, special and separate collections of Māori material, Māori artwork, and adhering to the Treaty of Waitangi appearing in libraries' strategic plans and goals. With the twenty-first century has come a deeper commitment to understanding of a Māori worldview in many leading institutions. For example, the National Library's "Bicultural Implementation Plan" shows great potential.[31] Te Rōpū Whakahau continues to work toward helping non-Māori library staff achieve authentic bicultural understanding and knowledge, but maintaining this momentum will be a challenge for some time to come.

The Waitangi Tribunal is a central government body established to settle claims brought against the Crown by Māori under the Treaty of Waitangi. A recent report (WAI-262) on a claim relating to ownership of intellectual property and cultural treasures or taonga makes it clear that in order to truly meet the needs of Māori, libraries need to consider not just the services offered to Māori clients but also how Māori information and knowledge is cared for and preserved.[32] Having a deep understanding of the indigenous knowledge frameworks at play is critical to achieving this.

The Digital Revolution

As we enter the twenty-first century, all libraries face the challenge of remaining relevant in the digital world. As the general purpose of libraries has not changed, the challenge in particular is demonstrating relevance and value to stakeholders and decision-makers that fund libraries. These challenges are felt just as strongly in New Zealand as in the rest of the world. A particular vulnerability for New Zealand public libraries is the lack of any legislative obligation for local authorities either to provide public library services or to ensure that those services are provided free of additional charge. As costs continue to increase and local authorities must spread levy income further, libraries can seem an easy way to cut spending, especially when there is a common misunderstanding of the continued importance and relevance of libraries in the digital age. This misconception is common across all library sectors.

The digital divide in New Zealand (due both to the physical lack of high-speed broadband in remote areas, and the comparatively high cost of data traffic) is both an opportunity and challenge for New Zealand libraries. Libraries are well placed to help address the divide (if they are funded to do so), but, at the same time, they will inevitably move to providing more services that are only available online, thereby underserving some parts of the population and further exacerbating the issue. Of course, at the same time libraries support developing their customers' information and digital literacy skills as part of their everyday work, and this will go a long way to bridging the digital divide.

As more and more information is created online and shared on the internet, there will be an increasing need to address the preservation of digital New Zealand knowledge and information for future use and research. With the National Library undertaking a biannual all-of-domain web harvest and maintaining the National Digital Heritage Archive (NDHA), steps are being taken that are both sustainable and forward-looking. Many institutions also maintain digital repositories of local research and theses, as well as a community "kete" or repository movement gaining momentum to capture local stories, images, and media. Of course, in relation to the discussion on biculturalism, automatic harvesting of digital content can be a fraught process where different ownership or intellectual property paradigms are in place, and this will need to be handled carefully to fall within the WAI-262 settlement guidelines.

CONCLUSIONS

Since the earliest days of pioneer settlement, New Zealand's libraries have struggled in an environment of both geographic and intellectual isolation. The Munn-Barr report of 1934 was very disparaging of the situation then but provided a clear path to improvement that was followed for a further five decades. The National Library of New Zealand, LIANZA, and leading libraries have since also provided insightful, innovative, and at times, groundbreaking leadership in the profession.

New Zealand has at times led the world, for example, in nationally acknowledging the importance of indigenous knowledge frameworks, developing an all-of-country digital preservation strategy, and establishing collaborative library purchase and collection agreements. Indeed at times, the nature of being an isolated, small country has been of benefit, allowing more agile, creative solutions to be formulated and implemented relatively quickly.

New Zealand libraries and librarians face the same challenges of underfunding and misconception that all libraries face in the twenty-first century, and they will need to meet these challenges with strength of purpose and commitment for many years to come, while continuing to innovate and think creatively to remain as Munn and Barr put it in 1934, the "community storehouses of knowledge and culture, not in the sense of compulsory educational institutions but as places where people may obtain help, self instruction, or recreation whenever they require it."[10]

REFERENCES

1. Royal, T.A.C. Māori. In Te Ara—The Encyclopedia of New Zealand. 2011, http://www.TeAra.govt.nz/en/maori (accessed January 2013).
2. Wilson, J. History. In Te Ara—The Encyclopedia of New Zealand. 2011, http://www.TeAra.govt.nz/en/history (accessed January 2013).
3. Martin, J.E. In *Parliament's Library 150 years*; Steele Roberts: Wellington, New Zealand, 2008.
4. Wilson, J. Society. In Te Ara—The Encyclopedia of New Zealand. 2009, http://www.TeAra.govt.nz/en/society (accessed January 2013).
5. Organisation for Economic Co-operation and Development. PISA 2009 results: Executive summary. 2010,

http://dx.doi.org/10.1787/888932343342 (accessed January 2013).
6. Country Report: New Zealand. 2012, http://ezproxy.massey.ac.nz/login?url=http://search.ebscohost.com/login.aspx?direct=true&db=anh&AN=78302166&site=eds-live (accessed January 2013).
7. OECD, *Doing Better for Children*, OECD Publishing. Paris, France, 2009, http://dx.doi.org/10.1787/9789264059344-en.
8. Office of the Children's Commissioner. Child poverty in New Zealand. 2010, http://www.occ.org.nz/home/childpoverty/about_child_poverty (accessed December 2012).
9. Ministry of Business Innovation and Employment. Ultrafast broadband initiative. 2012, http://www.med.govt.nz/sectors-industries/technology-communication/communications/broadband-policy/ultra-fast-broadband-initiative (accessed January 2013).
10. Munn, R.; Barr, J. In *New Zealand Libraries: A survey of conditions and suggestions for their improvement*; Libraries Association of New Zealand: Christchurch, New Zealand, 1934.
11. Fields, A.; Young, R. In *Informing New Zealand: Libraries, Archives and Records*, 5th ed.; Open Polytechnic of New Zealand: Lower Hutt, New Zealand, 2007.
12. Exon, F.C.A.; Exon, M.J.; Calvert, P.J. *Review of Library and Information Services in Australia and New Zealand*; British Library Board: Boston Spa, England, 1995.
13. National Library of New Zealand. About the Library. 2012, http://natlib.govt.nz/about-us (accessed December 2012).
14. Barrowman, R. *The Turnbull: A Library and Its World*; Auckland University Press: Auckland, New Zealand, 1995.
15. Jenner, M. In *Small Libraries of New Zealand*; Bay of Plenty Polytechnic: Tauranga, New Zealand, 2005.
16. Association of Public Library Managers. *Public Libraries of New Zealand: A Strategic Framework 2012–2017*; Association of Public Library Managers & Local Government New Zealand: Wellington, New Zealand, 2012.
17. Association of Public Library Managers. Ebooks and digital media service. 2011, http://www.publiclibrariesofnewzealand.org.nz/article/new-ebooks-and-digital-media-service-regional-consortia (accessed December 2012).
18. Library and Information Association of New Zealand. LIANZA Remuneration Survey - November 2010. 2010, http://lianza.org.nz/sites/lianza.org.nz/files/lianza_remuneration_survey_report_2010.pdf (accessed January 2013).
19. National Library of New Zealand. Services to schools. 2012, http://schools.natlib.govt.nz/about (accessed December 2012).
20. Ministry of Education. New Zealand Curriculum online. 2012, http://nzcurriculum.tki.org.nz/ (accessed January 2013).
21. Education and Science Select Committee (New Zealand House of Representatives). Inquiry into 21st century learning environments and digital literacy 2012, http://www.parliament.nz/NR/rdonlyres/FD34151C-744B-4B49-86F2-6FE5850123AE/256992/DBSCH_SCR_5695_Inquiryinto21stcenturylearningenvir.pdf (accessed December 2012).
22. McLintock, A.H. 'The Parry Report', from An Encyclopaedia of New Zealand, originally published in 1966. Te Ara—The Encyclopedia of New Zealand 2009, http://www.TeAra.govt.nz/en/1966/education-university-university-of-new-zealand/14 (accessed January 2013).
23. New Zealand Qualifications Authority. Wānanga, http://www.nzqa.govt.nz/audience-pages/wananga/ (accessed January 2013).
24. Henczel, S.; Ralph, G.; Sibthorpe, J. Special libraries. In *Global Library and Information Science: A Textbook for Students and Educators*; Abdullahi, I., Ed.; de Gruyter: Berlin, Germany, 2009; 253–269.
25. Anderson, B.; Bowden, M.; Cahalane, R.; Clements, C.; Dyer, M.; Matero, R.; Speakman, A.; Wickers, D. *Crown Research Institute Libraries*. LIANZA, 2012, http://www.lianza.org.nz/crown-research-institute-libraries (accessed November 2013).
26. Millen, J. *Te rau herenga—A Century of Library Life in Aotearoa: The New Zealand Library Association and LIANZA 1910–2010*; LIANZA: Wellington, New Zealand, 2010.
27. Ronnie, M. *Education for Librarianship in New Zealand and the Pacific Islands*; Mansell: London, U.K., 1996.
28. Library and Information Association of New Zealand. LIANZA. 2012, http://lianza.org.nz/ (accessed January 2013).
29. MacDonald, T. *New Zealand Library and Information Association. Te Ara Tika : Māori and Libraries : A Research Report*; New Zealand Library & Information Association: Wellington, New Zealand, 1993.
30. Szekely, C. *Te ara tika = Guiding Voices : Māori Opinion on Libraries and Information Needs; New Zealand Library and Information Association and Te Rōpū Whakahau*; Maori Library and Information Workers' Association: Wellington, New Zealand, 1997.
31. National Library of New Zealand. *Bicultural Implementation Plan, 2010–2012: Living Draft : Summary, March 2010*; National Library of New Zealand: Wellington, New Zealand, 2010.
32. New Zealand Waitangi Tribunal. Ko Aotearoa tēnei : a report into claims concerning New Zealand law and policy affecting Maori culture and identity. 2011, http://www.waitangi-tribunal.govt.nz/news/media/wai262.asp (accessed January 2013).

Non-governmental Organizations and Information

Lynne M. Rudasill
Steve W. Witt
University of Illinois at Urbana-Champaign, Champaign, Illinois, U.S.A.

Abstract

The advent of global civil society has highlighted the importance of the nongovernmental organization as a factor in the development of the information society. Understanding this phenomenon is essential for those interested in the dissemination of information surrounding various actors in civil society. Here we define the nongovernmental organization, discuss the different types of nongovernmental organizations and the areas in which they are active. The development of these organizations is discussed as well as future scenarios. Most importantly, the place of these organizations in information society, and interaction of the organizations with libraries, archives, and others in the pursuit of free and equitable access is explored.

INTRODUCTION

Nongovernmental organizations or NGOs are sometimes thought to be prominent examples of the effects of globalization. These organizations are ubiquitous in the world of interconnected, interdependent social movements. The mention of any major natural disaster brings to mind the work of the International Federation of the Red Cross and the Red Crescent Societies. Humanitarian relief efforts frequently include the work of Oxfam or Doctors without Borders. Environmental threats often find Greenpeace at the forefront of the fight to publicize and remedy the results. In 1997, the International Campaign to Ban Land Mines received the Nobel Peace Prize as had three other organizations before it. All of these organizations are examples of international NGOs.

What is an NGO? When and why did they develop into major players on the world scene? Why are they important to libraries and information science? How do they interact with individuals, states, and other international organizations? What do they do?

DEFINING THE NONGOVERNMENTAL ORGANIZATION

The problem with defining a term like "nongovernmental organization" is very similar to that of defining other self-referential terms. Although it seems simple at first, the mere definition of the term does not express the wide ranging implications of the concept. Literally, a nongovernmental organization might be assumed to be any group that is not part of a state organization and does not receive direct funding from a state government. This simple definition would include a wide range of organizations from humanitarian relief agencies to criminal syndicates, from religious organizations to multinational corporations. Further exploration of the term provides us with a little more specificity. Generally, these organizations are privately funded, either directly through philanthropic organizations or individual members. Occasionally, however, government may play a role in their funding, or use the NGO as a funnel for distribution of assistance. In many countries, the state plays a role in the development and certification of NGOs. The missions of NGOs tend to focus on the remediation of some societal problem, or publicize some perceived injustice. They have alternatively been referred to as "the conscience of the world" or the "warning voice."[1] Several themes are repeated when attempting a more granular meaning for the NGO. They are not entirely governmentally supported or founded, although government policies might have been a major reason for their genesis. They usually have defined goals and objectives relating to the creation of a civil society. They frequently work at the grassroots level to provide aid, education, and, most importantly for the librarian, information both to the audience they are trying to provide services to, and to a wider audience of policy-makers, state organizations, funding agencies, and actors on the international stage. The most useful advocacy tool of any NGO is information. Whether it is in the form of pamphlets distributed to a target population, a report to a funding agency, a public relations campaign, or a policy planning interaction with other organizations, the dissemination of information is key to the work of any NGO.

There are also many variants to the basic concept of the NGO. Related non-state actors include a variety of organizations such as the donor-organized nongovernmental organizations (DONGO), the governmentally organized nongovernmental organization (GONGO), the quasi nongovernmental organization (QUANGO), the grass-roots organization (GRO), and the intergovernmental organization (IGO). They can be international in nature, or very local. After the antiglobalization riots during the

Encyclopedia of Library and Information Sciences, Fourth Edition DOI: 10.1081/E-ELIS4-120043551

WTO economic summit in Seattle in 1999 the term "wild NGOs" came into use to denote NGOs that sought change through less-than-peaceful means of protest. Table 1 lists many of the terms and formats of these organizations including those terms used in several different countries.

The areas in which NGOs are active include a list of societal issues such as human rights, economic, and agricultural development, education, humanitarian relief, environmental degradation, health, international security, and economic development. Several of these areas are explored in depth later in this essay. NGOs might be social movement organizations, grassroots groups, religious organizations, or even the philanthropic organizations that fund other NGOs.

HISTORY OF NGO DEVELOPMENT

It should be noted that at one time, the theory of state sovereignty provided no recognition for organizations outside of other sovereign states as power-holders. The state and its leaders interacted with other states in the development and application of policies both within and outside of its borders. This is sometimes referred to as the Westphalian model of sovereignty. In the late nineteenth century, non-state actors began to influence policy-making and intergovernmental relations. These organizations evolved into today's nongovernmental organizations. One of the ultimate purposes for the NGO is to earn a place at the table when local, national, and international policy-making is taking place. This has truly changed the dynamic of the relationship between the NGO and the state.

Table 1 Typology of organizations.

BINGO——Business NGO
CBO—Community-based Organization
Citizens' Organizations—Local NGOs (commonly used in Japan)
Civic Advocacy Organization—Frequently used to refer to community-based organizations in the United States
CONGO—Conference of NGOs in Consultative Relationship with the United Nation
CSO—Civil Society Organization
DONGO—Donor-organized nongovernmental organization (can be governmentally organized, United Nations organized, or private)
GONGO—Government organized nongovernmental organization
GRINGO—NGO with a symbiotic relationship with a government
GRO—Grassroots Organization
IGO—International governmental organization (e.g., the United Nations, World Trade Organization, OECD, OAS)
INGO—International nongovernmental organization (e.g., Red Cross/Red Crescent, OxFam, Amnesty International)
NGDO—Nongovernmental Development Organization
NGO—Nongovernmental Organization
NPO—Non-Profit Organization (used in United States frequently for philanthropic organizations)
PANGO—Party-affiliated Organization (mostly Latin American)
PDO—Private development organization
PSO—Public Service Organization
QUANGO—Any organization that relies on government funding, but is administratively distinct from the state
SMO—Social Movement Organization
VO—Voluntary Organization
"Wild" NGO—Newly developed NGOs interested in the negative effects of globalization

The development of NGOs before and after World War I was quite rapid. Whether in spite of, or because of, the devastating "War to End All Wars" and the Great Depression in the United States, the growth in the number of NGOs was quite steady in the first three decades of the twentieth century. The 1940s saw the advent of the NGO as a recognized societal actor. But the true political power of these organizations was yet to be realized. Exponential growth in the number of NGOs occurred at the end of the twentieth century. The Yearbook of International Organizations first listed nongovernmental organizations, in 1949. The three categories of nongovernmental organizations listed there totaled 73 organizations in all.[2,3] In the 2008–2009 edition of the work, 11,859 organizations were noted as Cluster 1 NGOs.[4] It is interesting, but not surprising, that the rapid multiplication in the number of NGOs coincided with the expansion of the Internet as a tool for the dissemination of information.

Few publications concerning NGOs existed before the 1950s. The Online Computer Library Center's (OCLC) WorldCat lists 49 books and 114 serials published for the time period between 1900 and 1950 if one searches for "nongovernmental organizations" as a keyword search. The decade between 1990 and 1999 shows 7553 book records and 209 serial records in the database. A search for the first half of the current decade reveals almost 5437 books and 96 serials records.[5] Clearly, in recent years, publications by or about these agents of civil society and change have increased almost as exponentially as the organizations themselves.

This growth can also be seen in the relationship between NGOs and the United Nations. When the United Nations was chartered (itself an international governmental organization), 44 NGOs were legitimized through the authority found in Article 71 of the UN Charter. This entry states:

> The Economic and Social Council may make suitable arrangements for consultation with non-governmental organizations, which are concerned with matters within its competence. Such arrangements may be made with international organizations and, where appropriate, with national organizations after consultation with the Member of the United Nations concerned.[6]

In addition to this mention, Resolution 288 B(X) provided consultative status to recognized NGOs in 1950. In 1968, ECOSOC Resolution (XLIV) further defined this relationship and Resolution 1996/31 established three categories of consultative status—general consultative status; special consultative status; and inclusion on the roster. Most recently, the Millennium Declaration provided a new mandate to enhance the partnership of the NGOs and the United Nations.[7,8]

At the state level, different nations have different reactions to the development of organizations within their boundaries that seek to share power. In more democratized areas, these reactions range from encouragement to benign neglect. In other cases, the development of organizations that give voice to the intrinsic problems of an area is frowned upon and varying controls are in place to prevent any thought of power sharing or governmental influence by these organizations. In still other states, the development of NGOs is fostered and sometimes the goals and influence of the organization are coopted for political ends.

THE PROS AND CONS OF THE NGO

Traditionally NGOs have been held in high regard by many governments and intergovernmental organizations, as well as individuals. There are three empowering aspects of NGOs. First, they are seen as having a good deal of expertise in the area to which they relate. The data produced by NGOs in exploring their target population or issue provides them with a great deal of information concerning the problems, issues, and policies that might be necessary to obviate a perceived need. Second, and related to this expertise, is the credibility they have in the promotion their agendas. They have been seen as free from the pressures that might arise from government funding or close ties to a business or industry. Even when the NGO is employed as a way of pushing government aid out to a population, the organization itself is considered an independent and frequently more efficient avenue for distribution than the state. Examples of this are particularly apparent in the delivery of humanitarian aid after natural and man-made disasters. Finally, many NGOs are perceived as having broad and effective networks to deal with problem issues. Although there are some exceptions, primarily due to cultural conditioning, NGOs are very good at reaching out to other organizations for both moral and financial support. The relationship between mass media and the NGO is usually a strong bond due to the importance of public relations for the organization and the issues it addresses.

In recent years, especially since the events surrounding the WTO-associated riots in various countries, the image of the NGO as an independent, peaceful change agent has been somewhat tarnished. The "wild NGOs" active in these events frequently represented more radical even anarchist movements. In addition to behavioral problems, some questions have arisen regarding the accountability of many of these organizations. Less-democratic governments have used this as an excuse to shut down or at least severely limit the work of many NGOs. The existence of funding outside of the sphere of the state can be perceived as a threat and many instances exist of government policy interfering with the work of the NGO that receives its funds from an agency beyond its borders. Regulations for reporting are becoming more common in the state–NGO relationship.

NGOS AND INFORMATION

Information Dissemination

Other than increasing the amount of material written about NGOs, what impact do these organizations have on the library, the archive, or the larger information society? These organizations are both producers and consumers of large amounts of sometimes difficult-to-capture information. Ostensibly, grassroots organizations seek to send a flow of information downward to the clients and interested parties affected by the group. Information on weather patterns, water resources, health, and human rights are pushed out to the target populations. In this way, the NGO creates and disseminates information for its client base. This client base is also frequently the source of information the NGO needs to engender awareness of the issues and problems in its area of expertise. Using the client-generated information, NGOs must also push information upward to funding agencies, government agencies, and the international community for the purposes of financial support and influence. Information flows between the funding body and the organization in the form of reports, grant requests, and information bulletins. If the NGO has an affiliated relationship with a larger body such as a coordinating council or other international governmental organization an exchange of ideas, plans, statistics, or other information types is shared. Additionally, information may flow to a larger audience through publications and media outlets. Frequently, the information generated by the local agency will be passed up an information avenue to a coordinating council and ultimately to a supranational agency such as the United Nations for consideration in policy planning. A variety of information flows can be seen in Fig. 1.

Information Types

The production of information comes in many forms and formats. Information outflow from the organizations to funding and state agencies can include physical and financial progress reports, narrative reports, annual reports,

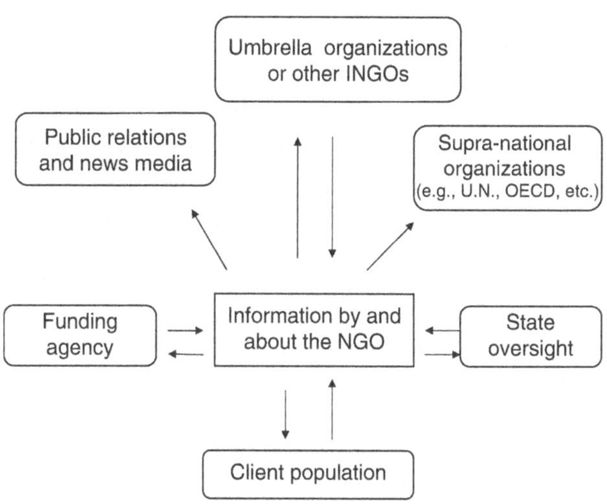

Fig. 1 Information dissemination.

annual budgets and work plans, published studies, internal studies, baseline and impact data, participatory appraisals, process documentation research, internal evaluation exercises, records, diaries, "significant changes," field notes, dialogue with community members and field observations, and meeting minutes. The funding agencies for the NGOs studies provide project and program proposals, documents describing program strategies and interests, annual budgets and "summary justifications," news clippings, trends, and networks, workshops and fairs, publicity documents, meeting minutes, field visit reports, evaluations and reviews, consultant reports/expertise, and monitoring missions.[9]

Some of these documents may be a matter of public record, but most are not. Most of these documents are typical examples of grey literature. They are not widely distributed, and do not easily find their way into the traditional publication cycle. Those that are actually created electronically are rarely archived, and often difficult to find due to the lack of technological know-how on behalf of their creators. A researcher may come across a report during a field interview, and then be unable to obtain a copy when returning home. The temporary nature of these documents is of concern for the scholar and researcher as well as the librarian or archivist.

More easily accessible materials are frequently those that the organization uses to provide public relations and outreach for its clientele or cause. Well-established and financially supported organizations can often afford to maintain some kind of Web presence. In some cases this presence consists of basic information about the program, how to contact staff, and a mission statement. More robust sites include publications such as reports and newsletters, press releases, mailing lists, donor information, and a variety of policy statements. Although the information on these sites is more accessible, it is not always as stable as the print materials an organization might produce, and is subject to becoming inaccessible over time.

Following is a description of information flows of some of the types of NGOs whose information is widely sought or interact regularly with information professionals and librarians.

Human Rights Information

Perhaps the most publicly known NGOs are those that focus on human rights and social justice issues. Some of the most prominent of these include Human Rights Watch, Amnesty International, and the Child Rights Information Network, which operate on an international basis. Human rights NGOs, particularly those that advocated for the abolition of slavery in the nineteenth century, are among the first documented NGOs after the advent of the current nation-state system. Currently, human rights NGOs focus on topics that range from state-initiated abuses of power to the cultural and economic aspects of human rights outlined in the UN Universal Declaration of Human Rights.

Unlike NGOs that focus on development or education, these groups often operate counter to official government policy and action. This complicates the ability of these organizations to collect and disseminate information, secure funding, and receive technical support. Often support to disseminate reports and research comes from international organizations and transnational communities. This unstable relationship between human rights NGOs and their host countries was quite visible in Uzbekistan in recent years when almost all NGOs with international support, including educational and developmental groups, were closed down.

The dangers faced by these NGOs and their workers affects researchers and librarians since the dissemination of documentation emanating from human rights NGOs can be difficult to verify and attribute. Additionally, primary source materials from these NGOs that become widely available have the potential to imperil those who work under repressive regimes and seek to work and cooperate with NGOs anonymously.

Following the flows of human rights information through NGOs provides a view of a vast and interconnected group of organizations that operate on local, national, regional, and international levels with the explicit goal of documenting and disseminating information related to human rights and related issues. In a sense, information flows from these organizations in an inverted pyramid as seen in Fig. 2, with local NGOs, researchers, and advocates pushing information upward in the system toward the larger organizations that in turn publicize, reuse, and consolidate information towards a worldwide audience that ranges from nations and intergovernmental bodies to the general public and researchers of social phenomena.

The data these NGOs rely upon in this stream consists of published and unpublished information. Many NGOs routinely collect published information from traditional

Fig. 2 Information flow—human rights.

print and electronic media, other NGOs, IGOs, and governmental sources to incorporate into reports, press releases, and handbills. Depending on the scope and scale of the NGO, these "collections" maintained by NGOs are on one extreme, collected, cataloged, and distributed electronically to staff throughout the world, such as the system employed by Amnesty International. At the other extreme, collections simply pileup in office corners without systematic processing or organization.

Unpublished information from these NGOs consists of the actual data or primary source material gathered from within a community or region by the NGO's staff and researchers. This "data" can consist of anything from interviews with prisoners and witnesses of abuses to an accounting of local demographic information. This data is also integrated into research reports and other publications of the NGO. Like published collections within an NGO, this unique data is collected and archived based upon the scope and capacity of the organization. Unlike the published collection, these vast unique repositories of local and regional knowledge are largely inaccessible to outside researchers and organizations, and represent one of the least stable and inaccessible forms of grey literature.

Much of the current information pattern is heavily reliant on the growth of the Internet and availability of cellular- and satellite-based communications technologies. Information can be disseminated quickly and often synchronously to a large audience as violations occur, impacting greatly the potential to inform the public and promote remedial action. In addition, organizations once isolated are now networked to enable direct communications and collaboration. The 1984 Vallerti Agreement formed one of the first of these networks, linking aid and social justice organizations to worker organizations, activists, and effectively facilitating community-based research through the Interdoc network. This in turn led in 1990 to the Association for Progressive Communications' online network and ultimately to Interdoc.[10] The advent of the World Wide Web and open source technologies that allow organizations to create online communities and groups has further provided organizations with access to the Internet, with the capacity to disseminate information and share expertise among social justice and human rights NGOs.

Internet technologies also provide the various publics of an NGO with a venue through which to access information. For example, the organization HURIDOCS maintains a search engine that provides access to documentation and materials from over 3000 Human Rights NGOs, effectively linking these groups and their potential impact to researchers and members of civil society around the world.

Human Rights NGOs also work to educate people about the concept of human rights as formally defined by the United Nations and legally defined within countries. Human Rights Education was catapulted into the mainstream when the UN made 1994–2004 the "Decade for Human Rights Education." The UN's focus on Human Rights Education, which continues today, provided NGOs with funding from organizations ranging from governments, UN bodies, and foundations such as Soros to educate and broadly disseminate human rights information to the general public, the legal community, and even military groups. Through these initiatives, many resources ranging from curricular materials to research on outcomes were developed throughout the world. Some of this is available through the Office of the United Nations High Commissioner for Human Rights though most is dispersed throughout the world's NGO community.

It is evident that the Internet quickly became a tool for protecting and promoting human rights, but has also impacted upon traditional modes of information management within organizations, requiring organizations to allocate more resources towards technology and focus on information organization, metadata, and a notion of an audience broader than a local population or government. In most instances, NGOs have opted to emphasize technical infrastructure and Web-based resource development. Most NGOs, especially those that operate locally or regionally, do not employ information professionals or maintain and archive digital and print materials that are produced. Additionally, a formal library to collect and organize research materials, publications, and archival records is the exception rather than the norm among NGOs.[11–13] This fact heightens the need for larger international NGOs to actively collect, organize, and archive materials from the local organizations. University libraries, research consortia, and associations can also potentially address these needs through collaborative digitization and archival programs.

Development and International Assistance NGOs

Development and international assistance NGOs work toward economic development within a country. In this context economic development includes activities aimed at building a society's capacity to provide for the welfare of its people. Activities range from institution building, developing markets, educating farmers, and providing technical assistance and material resources among others.

Unlike many Human Rights NGOs, NGOs that work in development often partner directly and openly with their own and other governments plus international organizations such as the World Bank and the UN's Food and Agricultural Organization (FAO). This often presents to the public and general researcher a confusing network of governmental, nongovernmental, and quasigovernmental organizations that works with similar communities and often in partnership on the same program. For example, the U.S. Agency for International Development and FAO might simultaneously fund an NGO whose aim is to alleviate famine in Liberia.

The number of organizations that may work in a region to address a problem potentially causes much confusion and can inhibit the provision of aid. For example, the lack of information coordination was acutely visible in the aftermath of the South Asian Tsunami when multiple governments and aid organization sent resources and personnel to assist in recovery and redevelopment efforts.

The shape of information flow within the development community is more pyramid shaped, with knowledge and technical expertise moving from larger organizations such as governments, universities, IGOs, and large NGOs. This knowledge moves through a variety of conduits. Often knowledge transfer occurs through direct exchange and training. For example, an NGO that works in the area of water quality and access might receive support from a larger organization that funds university experts to consult with and train a local community in the development and maintenance of an efficient and sustainable water purification system. These experts from the academic community may also receive funding from various government research grants for their field work.

Technology and mobility have also contributed to providing access to knowledge and information. For example, Book Aid, a U.K.-based NGO, works directly with communities to select and disseminate books and other reading materials to set up lending libraries. On the technical side, JSTOR, initially an NGO funded by the Mellon Foundation and whose mission is to archive and provide wide access to prominent scholarly journals, initiated a program through which universities and nonprofit organizations in African countries are eligible for free access to the entire electronic collection.

As in the case of Human Rights NGOs, the Internet and similar technologies have allowed the structure of information flows to begin changing from one in which knowledge flowed mainly one direction to a growing structure through which NGOs increasingly have the capacity to share knowledge and expertise, creating a flow that may resemble more of a churning motion than linear trajectory.

Educational NGOs

Educational NGOs focus on a myriad of topics, ranging from human rights, as noted above, to health education, literacy, and ICT proficiency. These organizations constitute a subgroup in the development category, yet for the information society, many educational NGOs overlap heavily with services offered by libraries and information professionals.

ICT Education

Greater access to technology and the realization of the potential for knowledge and information to empower people and enhance capacity-building programs fuels the need for and expansion of ICT education programs within the NGO community. These programs include skill and technology development for NGOs and community-based projects to provide education on the use of ICTs to support everything from small business and entrepreneurs to virtual student exchanges.

For example, the International Institute for Communication and Development, a Dutch NGO, maintains multiple programs throughout Africa, Latin America, and the Caribbean to promote capacity building in ICT expertise and sharing knowledge among organizations across regions through networked-based technologies. In addition to capacity building, this NGO works closely with iEARN, an NGO that facilitates student exchanges and international friendships with a vast network of affiliated offices in nearly 120 countries. iEARN in turn collaborates and works with NGOs, IGOs, and governments around the globe, constituting another vast and churning network of information exchange and communication maintained by NGOs and facilitated by ICTs.

Literacy Education

Literacy education, including basic, computer, cultural, and economics is a major activity among NGOs in the developed and developing world. Many literacy programs, especially those that promote adult literacy and reading to children partner directly with public and school libraries and work in consultation with librarians and their associations. For example, Baby Talk, a U.S.-based NGO, operates its early reading intervention program within local public libraries and community centers. On an international level, the UN has denoted 2003–2012 as the Literacy Decade. Similar to the impact on human rights education, UN denotation has increased the level of funding for organizations involved in literacy education through both the UN and foundations from Carnegie to Starbucks.

Information Literacy is also an educational component within NGO literacy education. As noted by Jackman and Jones, information literacy is an essential piece in capacity building as individuals and organizations gain greater access to information through open markets and greater access to technology.[14] Libraries and information professionals are poised to provide information literacy training to NGOs at a time when these organizations are adopting ICTs and developing new systems to organize and disseminate knowledge. In addition, library-focused associations such as IFLA and the U.S.-based ACRL are dedicating increasing energy to information literacy education and dissemination of materials to assist librarians and other information professionals improve their education programs.

Library Professional Development

Library professional development programs are also widely funded and delivered by NGOs. The MacArthur, Mellon, and Carnegie foundations all fund programs to educate and train library leaders in both developing and more developed countries. The Mortenson Center for International Library Programs, which is housed at the University of Illinois at Urbana-Champaign, offers exchanges and training programs within the United States, Russia, and Africa through a combination of support from these foundations. Beyond foundations, some of the other major funders of library-related NGO programs include UNESCO, and numerous government-sponsored grant and development programs that focus on both national and international capacity building.

ACCESS TO KNOWLEDGE (A2K) MOVEMENT

The global A2K movement focuses simultaneously on human rights, ICTs, and education in an effort to advocate for access to knowledge. The movement is based on the premise that access to knowledge is central to the well-being of societies, communities, and individuals.[15] A2K organizations work as both policy advocates and providers of direct assistance. NGOs in the A2K community directly support, and in many ways parallel, the work and missions of libraries through their advocacy, access, and educational missions.

A2K policy advocates focus on national and international policy such as copyright, accessibility standards, and technical protocols. One of the major campaigns of the movement is to reform the World Intellectual Property Organization (WIPO) to limit new treaties and standards that impede access to information while shifting WIPO's focus away from intellectual property protection toward an agenda that would promote knowledge creation and developmental assistance. The International Federation of Library Associations (IFLA) works closely with IGOs and NGOs in the A2K community, notably through their work with the UN's World Summit on the Information Society (WSIS).

As noted above, many NGOs provide developmental assistance in the form of access to information and training. These programs parallel and complement the A2K movement by virtue of work they promote and perform. Electronic Information for Libraries (eIFL.net) works within this A2K community to support and advocate access to electronic resources by working with libraries in developing countries to negotiate affordable subscriptions and build capacity to develop, disseminate, and preserve locally produced knowledge.

Through policy work and development assistance, the A2K NGOs encompass the numerous legal, economic, and technical issues that library professionals in all nations face. These issues include digital copyright, privacy, data security, and advocacy for the profession and its global community of users.

NGO ARCHIVES AND COLLECTIONS

A variety of archives exist for nongovernmental organizations. These include true archives of all organizational papers and more loosely collected works by and about organizations. Some NGOs such as Oxfam recognize the importance of an information archive and have the resources to maintain their own archival materials. Others, with fewer resources or a briefer history, rely upon others to collect and preserve their materials.

For example, the University of Colorado at Boulder maintains archival materials from the American Friends Service and various other pacifist movements. On a more global basis, the Database of Archives of Non-Governmental Organizations (DANGO) is attempting to maintain an information archive of the activities of a large number of organizations in Great Britain that have been in existence since 1945. On the other side of the globe, the Center for the Study of Cooperative Human Relations at Saitama University in Japan houses a large collection of what is referred to as "Citizens Records" going back to the 1970s. This includes the publications of a large number of NGOs and grassroots organizations published both in Japan and elsewhere.[16–18]

In addition to formal archives, some educational institutions support the dissemination of information to answer the questions that NGOs might have in various areas. A good example of this is the Women's Human Rights Resources Programme at the University of Toronto. The program has developed a database of resources to assist those working in the area of the legal rights of women in Canada and elsewhere that can be queried. This is ultimately what many NGOs strive to do—provide easily accessible information to a client base and beyond.[19,20]

CONCLUSION—THE FUTURE OF GLOBAL CIVIL SOCIETY

The concept of global civil society as exemplified by the existence of NGOs will continue in importance in the future. The exponential growth of these organizations that was witnessed in the last part of the twentieth century and the beginning of the twenty-first century will no doubt slow in the future. However, the organizations will always spring up where there is need for joint action, information dissemination, and a seat at the table of policy-makers. These are ultimately the purposes for which these organizations exist. If the organizations are true to their goals, they should hope they will fade from view as the problems and issues they highlight are addressed. In the meantime, it is likely that less-democratic countries will continue to challenge their work, especially those working in the area of human rights. More stable democratic regimes will no doubt attempt to make these organizations more accountable for both their actions and their finances. The library community needs to start now to capture the information production of these groups and assist organizations create and disseminate the information at the heart of all NGOs.

REFERENCES

1. Willetts, P., Ed. *The Conscience of the World: The Influence of Non-governmental Organisations in the U.N. System*; The Brookings Institution: Washington, DC, 1996.
2. Suter, K. *Global Order and Global Disorder: Globalization and the Nation-State*; Praeger: Westport, CT, 2003.
3. Union of International Organizations. *Yearbook of International Organizations*, 2nd Ed.; Editions de l'Annuaire des Organisations Internationales S.A.: Geneve, Suisse, 1949; 170–173.
4. Union of International Organizations. *Yearbook of International Organizations*, 43rd Ed.; Union of International Organizations: Brussels, Belgium, 2008; 3.
5. Online Computer Library Center (OCLC) WorldCat. Available at http://www.worldcat.org/advancedsearch.
6. Charter of the United Nations. Available at http://www.un.org/aboutun/charter/.
7. United Nations, Committee on Non-Governmental Organizations. Available at http://www.un.org/esa/coordination/ngo/committee.htm.
8. Millennium Declaration. Available at http://www.un.org/millennium/declaration/ares552e.htm.
9. Ebrahim, A. *NGOs and Organizational Change: Discourse, Reporting, and Learning*; Cambridge University Press: Cambridge, U.K., 2005.
10. Murphy, B.M. Interdoc: The first international non-governmental computer network. First Monday **2005**, *10*(5), 1–14. Available at http://www.firstmonday.org/issues/issue10_5/murphy/index.html (accessed May 2007).
11. Brophy, P.; Halpin, E. Through the net to freedom: Information, the Internet and human rights. J. Inform. Sci. **1999**, *25*(5), 351–464.
12. Halpin, E. An evaluation of the child rights information network: Examining information management in a global NGO—Part one. Can. J. Inform. Libr. Sci. **2002/2003**, *27*(3), 25–44.
13. Halpin, E. An evaluation of the child rights information network: Examining information management in a global NGO—Part two. Can. J. Inform. Libr. **2002/2003**, *27*(4), 31–54.
14. Jackman, L.; Jones, L. Information Literacy, Information Communication Technologies (ICTs), and the Non-governmental Organization (NGO)/Nonprofit World: A Practitioner's Perspective, White Paper prepared for UNESCO, the U.S. National Commission on Libraries and Information Science, and the National Forum on Information Literacy, for use at the Information Literacy Meeting of Experts, Prague, The Czech Republic. Available at http://www.nclis.gov/libinter/infolitconf&meet/papers/jackman-fullpaper.pdf.
15. Shaver, L.B. Defining and measuring access to knowledge: Towards an A2K index. J. Law Policy Inform. Soc. **2008**, *4*(2), SSRN: Available at http://ssrn.com/abstract=1021065.
16. Peace and Justice Collection, University of Colorado at Boulder. Available at http://ucblibraries.colorado.edu/archives/collections/peace.htm.
17. Database of Archives of Non-Governmental Organisations (DANGO). Available at http://www.dango.bham.ac.uk.
18. Center for the Study of Cooperative Human Relations. Available at http://www.kyousei.iron.saitama-u.ac.jp/modules/xfsection/article.php?articleid=5.
19. Women's Human Rights Resources Database. Available at http://www.law-lib.utoronto.ca/diana/whrr/index.cfm?sister=utl&CFID=165034&CFTOKEN=85616084.
20. Human Rights Information and Documentation System, International (HURIDOCS). Available at http://www.huridocs.org.

BIBLIOGRAPHY

1. Brecher, J.; Costello, T.; Smith, B. *Globalization from Below: The Power of Solidarity*; South End Press: Cambridge, MA, 2000.
2. Iriye, A. *Global Community: The Role of International Organization in the Making of the Contemporary World*; University of California Press: Berkeley, CA, 2002.
3. Korten, D.C. *Getting to the 21st Century: Voluntary Action and the Global Agenda*; Kumarian Press: West Hartford, CT, 1990.
4. Martens, K. *NGOs and the United Nations: Institutionalization, Professionalization, and Adaptation*; Palgrave Macmillan: New York, 2005.
5. Witt, S.W., Ed. *Changing Roles of NGOs in the Creation, Storage, and Dissemination of Information in Developing Countries*; K.G. Saur: Munich, Germany, 2006.

North American Serials Interest Group

Jill Emery
Portland State University Library, Portland, Oregon, U.S.A.

Abstract

The North American Serials Interest Group (NASIG) was founded in 1985 and hosted their first conference at Bryn Mawr College in 1986. NASIG is an independent organization that promotes dialogue and professional growth among all members of the serials information community. NASIG is a membership-driven organization that holds an annual conference to represent the diverse interests of the serials community.

INTRODUCTION

The North American Serials Interest Group (NASIG) was founded in 1985 after 16 American librarians attended the United Kingdom Serials Group (UKSG) Meeting in 1984 and began to discuss what it would take to create a similar organization in North America. Becky Lenzini, who was a librarian working for the Faxon Company, and John Riddick, a librarian working at Central Michigan University, started a study group to investigate the feasibility of a North American Serials Group. An ad hoc executive council was formed that included John Riddick and Becky Lenzini as cochairs, Tina Feick (Boley) as vice-chair, Susan Davis (SUNY-Buffalo) as treasurer, Marilyn Gonseiwsky(Cal Poly-San Luis Obispo) as secretary, and Lenire Wilkas as the first newsletter editor. Dues were initially set at U.S. $15. Membership solicitation began and the first conference site, Bryn Mawr College, was selected. In addition, a site selection committee made up of John Riddick, George Lupone (Cleveland State University), and Tina Feick did site visits in Ohio to find the location for the second conference.

The first *NASIG Newsletter* appeared in January 1986. In the meantime, Leigh Chatterton from Boston College and Mary Beth Clack from Harvard were appointed to serve as the first conference program chairs. Denison University in Granville, Ohio, was selected as the site for the second conference. By May 1986, membership had grown to 324 members and draft bylaws for the organization had been distributed. In June 1986, the first conference took place and remains the highest ranking conference in the history of NASIG. The first elections took place in November of 1986 where the bylaws were approved by the membership and NASIG was well on its way.

NASIG's 10th anniversary conference was held at Duke University in 1995 and was a wonderful celebration of the organization's decade of history. Members recollected that while the organization has continued to grow, they maintained an enthusiasm and dedication to the organization that has been unparalleled. NASIG's 20th anniversary was held in Minneapolis, Minnesota, in 2005. This celebration noted that NASIG continued to work on refining its function as an organization and the ongoing development of their governance. In 2010, NASIG celebrated its 25th anniversary in Palm Springs, California. Financial planning, membership development, and technological planning have become the main issues of the organization during its maturity.

Permanent archives for the organization were established in 2003 at the University of Illinois, and an archivist position was created to archive. Today, NASIG is a financially stable organization that holds a world-recognized annual conference in North America and continues to provide a forum that promotes the communication, understanding, and sharing of ideas among all members of the serials and electronic resource information community.

MEMBERSHIP

NASIG has continued to grow and prosper. Having reached a membership high of close to 1500 members in the early part of the millennium, NASIG now holds a steady membership of around 725 members. The membership dues have grown to keep up with the economic climate and currently are at U.S. $75 for regular members and U.S. $25 for retired and student members. In 2010, an organizational membership category was created and instituted. The rate for this membership category is U.S. $1500. The organizational member rate allows for a dedicated table at the annual conference vendor exposition, recognition of the organization's membership on the NASIG website, and the ability to designate three individuals in the organization as NASIG members.

Personal membership benefits include access to the online membership directory, presenter's handouts from

Encyclopedia of Library and Information Sciences, Fourth Edition DOI: 10.1081/E-ELIS4-120049516

the annual conference, and access to the *NASIG Proceedings* archive. In addition, members also receive the NISO (National Information Standards Organization) member rate for NISO webinars, reduced rates for the annual conference and webinars, and a discount subscription rate to *The Serials Librarian*. Lastly, members also get biweekly e-mails of *Serials E-News* from UKSG.

NASIG ORGANIZATIONAL STRUCTURE

NASIG has an executive board made up of the following positions: President, Vice-President/President-Elect, Past President, Secretary, Treasurer, six Members-at-Large, and ex officio member in the form of the *NASIG Newsletter* Editor-in-Chief. Each member of the executive committee serves as a direct liaison to NASIG's committees and task forces. The current committees are Awards and Recognition, Bylaws, Conference Planning, Continuing Education, Database and Directory, Electronic Communications, Evaluation and Assessment, Financial Development, Membership Development, Mentoring, Nominations and Elections, Program Planning, Publications and Public Relations, Site Selection, and Student Outreach. There is currently one task force, Core Competencies. In addition, there are individuals appointed to the positions of Archivist, Conference Coordinator, Conference Proceedings Editors, Newsletter Editor-in-Chief, and Registrar.

Each committee has a formal written charge from the Board, which is reviewed and modified as needed by the executive board. Any current NASIG member is eligible to serve on a committee and can indicate their preference for committee appointments by submitting a volunteer form. The vice-present/president-elect is responsible for all committee, task force, and board liaison appointments. In general, committee members are not allowed to serve more than two consecutive terms on any given committee.

AWARDS AND SCHOLARSHIPS

The greatest benefits that NASIG provides to the information community are the numerous awards the organization provides. Currently, there are eight awards sponsored by NASIG each year. The John F. Riddick student grant award is the oldest award offered by NASIG. The grant provides conference expenses and a one-year membership to current library and information science students. The grant was named after one of the cofounders and first elected presidents of NASIG, John F. Riddick. It was his idea to begin to offer student grant awards in 1988, and they have been successfully granted since the inception of the award. Many members of the NASIG student grant awards have gone on to become leaders in the library and information science field in addition to serving in leadership roles in NASIG as committee chairs and on the executive board. To date, 162 student grants have been awarded and NASIG is recognized as a leading organization in the profession in fostering and mentoring new professionals.

The next oldest award is the Horizon Award, which was created to advance the profession by providing promising new information professionals with the opportunity to accelerate their knowledge and understanding of serials by networking and interacting with all members of the serials information environment from vendors to other librarians. This award is granted to professionals who have three or less years' experience in their serials-related position and have not previously attended the NASIG annual conference. To date, there have been 27 Horizon Award winners and many of those winners have gone on to serve as NASIG committee chairs and executive board members.

In 1998, NASIG awarded the first Fritz Schwartz Serials Education Scholarship. The scholarship is named in honor of Fritz Schwartz, who was a well-known and highly respected authority on Electronic Data Interchange (EDI), the Internet, and library standards. He was a frequent and well-received speaker at NASIG conferences. This award is open to qualified graduate-level students in any NASIG member country (Canada, Greenland, Mexico, or the United States) who demonstrate serials-related work experience and a desire to pursue a professional serials career after earning their degree. To date, 16 Fritz Schwartz Serials Education Scholarships have been granted. The winner is awarded a U.S. $3000 scholarship as well as a student grant award to attend the NASIG conference for the year in which the scholarship is granted and a one-year free membership to the organization.

In 1999, the Marcia Tuttle International Grant Award was created to provide funding for an individual working in any area of the serials information chain to foster international communication and education through activities involving some aspect of serials. The award provides a U.S. $3000 grant and a one-year free membership. This award is only given as qualifying applications are received, so there are years where this award is not granted. To date, eight awards have been made for research projects based in or working with China, Europe, Eastern Europe, and the Middle East.

Another premier award developed and offered solely by NASIG is the Mexican Student Grant Award. This award grants assistance to a Mexican student of library/information science to attend the annual conference and to receive a one-year free membership in the organization. This award was first created in 2001 and has been awarded almost every year since then with 11 recipients of the award to date. The Mexican students enjoy the recognition as well as the opportunity to participate in the national library conference event in the United States.

The Champion Award was created in 2005 in conjunction with the 20th anniversary of NASIG. The Champion Award is selectively given to members of NASIG who have a long history of dedicated service to the organization to honor their contributions both to NASIG and to the profession at large. To date, only two Champion Awards have been made, the first to Tina Feick, a founding member of NASIG and active member in the serials information chain. The second recipient, Susan Davis, is also a founding member of NASIG and has also been extremely active in the serials profession throughout her career. Both award winners served as President of NASIG at one point in their careers.

In 2006, NASIG created the Serials Specialist Award in order to provide conference travel funding for a promising paraprofessional working with serials to advance their knowledge and understanding of serials work. Along with the travel stipend, the award winner also gains a year's free membership to NASIG. There have been eight recipients of the serials specialist award to date.

The Rose Robischon Scholarship Award was created in 2009 to honor NASIG member Rose Robischon who had two decades of service to NASIG. She served as a chair on numerous committees and was the NASIG Treasurer from 2005 to 2007. The scholarship provides the recipient with funding to attend the annual conference in the year that it is awarded. The award is open to any NASIG member who currently holds a position where their primary responsibilities cover some form of serials management or enterprise and for whom travel to the conference cannot be covered by their employing institution or organization. Preference is given to applicants who have not been able to previously attend NASIG and who can show a benefit in their application for attending the conference. To date, there have been four award winners for this scholarship.

The most recent award is one that was developed in conjunction with UKSG. The award is named in honor of John Merriman in recognition of the role he played both in UKSG and with the development of NASIG. John was the conference organizer of UKSG and was the person who extended an invitation to 16 American serial librarians in 1984, which led to the creation of NASIG. The John Merriman Joint NASIG/UKSG Award pays for one UKSG member to travel to the NASIG conference each year and for one NASIG member to travel to the UKSG conference. The award is open to any member of each organization and consists of travel expenses up to U.S. $3000 for the attendance at the other conference but does not cover the expense of attending the local conference. Current board members of either organization are not eligible for the award. The committee vetting the award is made up of members from both organizations. To date, six members of NASIG/UKSG have been able to experience each other's conference and learn how serials are managed in different areas of the world.

CONTINUING EDUCATION

NASIG sees the need for finding ways to better support the ongoing educational needs of its members and the serials community. In addition to the annual conference, NASIG has sponsored local and regional continuing education activities such as the North Carolina Serials Conference and the Ohio Valley Group of Technical Services Librarians annual meeting as well as numerous CONSER and Serials Cataloging Cooperative Training Programs offered by the Library of Congress. In 2012, NASIG began offering a quarterly webinar series including sessions on open-source integrated library systems, library use of publisher metadata, and effective negotiation. NASIG has also partnered with the NISO allowing NASIG members to register for NISO continuing education events at a discounted rate. This has been a well-utilized partnership for NASIG and NISO.

PARTNERSHIPS & OTHER OUTREACH

In addition to UKSG, the Library of Congress, and NISO, NASIG has sought to forge partnerships with other relevant organizations. Most specifically, in 2009, NASIG entered into an information sharing agreement with the Association for Subscription Agents and Intermediaries to help promote events of both organizations. As part of its student outreach efforts, NASIG established the Student Ambassador's Program, which links NASIG members with North American library and information science programs. The presentations that NASIG ambassadors give to LIS students are often the first time that a student has heard of the organization or become aware of that specialization in the profession.

NASIG PUBLICATIONS

NASIG has two primary publications that it produces on a regular basis. The first is the *NASIG Newsletter*, which is produced quarterly each year and covers the business and membership news and information. The newsletter is expanded upon with the use of the *NASIG Blog*, which is updated four to six times a month. Begun in 1986, the newsletter with the inception of the organization has been produced regularly since then. In the early 2000s, the *NASIG Newsletter* moved online and is now produced entirely electronically. Certain segments such as the President's Corner, conference reports, and member updates have been an integral part of the newsletter since its inception. All issues of the *NASIG Newsletter* are freely available here: http://www.nasig.org/publications_newsletter.cfm.

In addition to the *NASIG Newsletter*, the *NASIG Conference Proceedings* have also been produced since the inception of the organization. The conference proceedings fully encapsulate the scholarship and presentations given each year at the annual conference. The *NASIG Conference Proceedings* appear each year in *The Serials Librarian*, and NASIG and the publishers of *The Serials Librarian* have enjoyed a joint partnership in bringing this area of knowledge and expertise for 27 years. An electronic version of all of the conference proceedings are made available on the NASIG website to NASIG members. The *NASIG Conference Proceedings* are highly cited works, and it is to the organization's credit that this level of scholarship is brought to publication each year.

NASIG has recently developed a statement of *Core Competencies for Electronic Resource Librarians*. As an emerging area of the profession, this document has become a useful publication for students, early career professionals, and employers who wish to describe these specialized positions and the criteria upon which to evaluate the performance of those who hold them.

ANNUAL CONFERENCE

The annual NASIG conference is considered the go-to event for technical services librarians and collection management librarians involved in the selection and management of ongoing subscription services and more recently the management of electronic resources. The conference brings together a mix of librarians, publishers, intermediaries, and service providers in one event for concentrated programs on serials and electronic resource management. Initially, the conference was held on universities with the attendees staying in campus dorm rooms during the intercession periods for the university/college. This dictated the annual conference occurring during May and/or June each year between spring and summer terms. Over the years, as colleges campuses began to charge more and the meeting became more popular, it was found that hotel conference centers were often competitive in both amenities and location. For this reason, NASIG's membership voted in 2013 to move the conference from the university setting to the hotel environment. The conference has remained in the May/June time frame since long-term members and attendees have come to expect the conference being held in this time frame.

The location of the annual conference varies each year to allow for attendance by local members and others within the library and information science community who may otherwise not get to travel to conferences.

The conference typically runs for four days and usually occurs over a weekend. The first day of the conference includes preconferences that are additional cost to the main registration and provide in-depth exploration of various topics. In the evening of the first day is the opening reception and welcome to the location from the conference planners and local members of the community. The second and third days are full conference days with plenary sessions kicking off the conference each day followed by breakout sessions that attendees can choose from to attend. In addition, there are usually lunch breaks provided that allows plenty of time for networking and joining up with colleagues. There are usually evening opportunities presented as well for attendees, and NASIG has a long tradition of trying to pick locations with either minor or major league baseball games occurring for blocks of members/attendees to attend as well. The last day of the conference is usually a half day to allow for travel arrangements. In addition to programmed events, there are committee meetings, a members' business meeting/town hall event, as well as various networking opportunities that focus on the use of specific management tools or products.

In 2010, NASIG instituted a vendor showcase for vendors and publishers to have an opportunity for a dedicated "sales" time period. This is usually held prior to the opening session on the first day, and attendees/members have an opportunity to interact with their friends and colleagues on a business level prior to the conference beginning. This event was seen as controversial for some NASIG members since the intent of the annual conference was meant as meeting of the minds from all areas of the serials and continuing resources community and not a sales event. However, the past few years have shown that having this minor business opportunity upfront has benefitted both the corporate institutions involved with NASIG as well as providing the librarians to explore products and content they might not otherwise know.

CONCLUSION

NASIG has been and continues to be a vital organization in the library and information profession. It provides opportunities for new librarians and information specialists to become professionally active and participate in an environment that is nurturing and engaged in many activities from publishing, to attendance at the annual conference, to committee work. NASIG offers multiple opportunities for engagement and for forging a sense of community who may otherwise become lost in larger professional organizations such as the American Library Association and its myriad of divisions and committees. NASIG was founded with the ideology that would remain an independent organization that promotes dialogue and professional growth among all members of the serials information community. NASIG has not only succeeded in this vision but continues to prosper upholding the principles its founders developed 27 years ago.

OCLC: A Worldwide Library Cooperative

Jay Jordan
OCLC Online Computer Library Center, Inc., Dublin, Ohio, U.S.A.

Abstract
This entry describes the history, governance, and current activities and plans of OCLC Online Computer Library Center, a nonprofit, membership, computer library service, and research organization dedicated to the public purposes of furthering access to the world's information and reducing library costs. OCLC and its member libraries cooperatively produce and maintain WorldCat—the OCLC Online Union Catalog.

INTRODUCTION

OCLC, Online Computer Library Center is a nonprofit, membership, computer library service, and research organization. Since its founding in 1967 by university presidents in Ohio, OCLC's mission has been to further access to the world's information and reduce library costs. At this writing, more than 69,000 libraries participate in a worldwide cooperative that extends to 112 countries. Libraries use OCLC services to help manage their collections and provide reference services to end-users.

OCLC has approximately 1200 employees, with some 860 on its main campus in Dublin, Ohio. In the United States, OCLC has offices in California, Colorado, Kansas, New Jersey, Pennsylvania, Washington state, and Washington, DC. There are also 16 offices in these countries: Australia, Canada, China, France, Germany, Mexico, the Netherlands, Switzerland, and the United Kingdom (Fig. 1).

HISTORY

Founded in 1967 by librarian Frederick G. Kilgour and the Ohio College Association (a group comprising the presidents of Ohio's private and public colleges and universities), OCLC was originally called the Ohio College Library Center. In 1971, OCLC pioneered the digital revolution in libraries with the introduction of its first service, the Online Union Catalog (today called WorldCat) and Shared Cataloging System. Since then, enormous changes in computer technology and telecommunications have occurred. The original terminals, computers, and telecommunications network have given way to several succeeding generations of technology, each of which has been faster, better, cheaper, and smaller than its predecessor.

The advent of the Internet in the mid-1990s, and then the World Wide Web, caused a sea change for libraries and librarianship. The sheer volume of electronic information, coupled with the emergence of search engines that appeared to offer viable alternatives to library services, presented libraries with new challenges.

OCLC enters the twenty-first century and its fourth decade with services and strategies that are intended to help libraries not only cope, but thrive, in an environment of continuous change. To that end, OCLC at this writing was pursuing two strategic objectives: 1) to weave libraries into the World Wide Web and the Web into libraries and 2) to extend the cooperative to provide more value to more libraries around the world.

GOVERNANCE

OCLC's governance has always been closely intertwined with the use of OCLC services and the growth of WorldCat, the OCLC Online Union Catalog. Membership is based on the use of OCLC services and contribution to the OCLC cooperative.

From 1967 to 1977, membership in OCLC was limited to institutions in Ohio and governance of OCLC resided in a nine-member board of trustees elected by Ohio member institutions of the Ohio College Library Center. In 1977, the Ohio membership relinquished control of OCLC and established a governance structure that extended membership to libraries and other institutions outside Ohio. The governance structure that was implemented in 1978 consisted of three parts: Members, Users Council, and Board of Trustees. This structure provides libraries with an institutionalized role in governing the cooperative whereby members elected Members Council delegates, who in turn elected six members of the 15-member OCLC Board of Trustees.

In 2002, the governance structure was modified to complement new services, increased international activity, and new forms of contribution. The name of Users Council was changed to Members Council. The Board and Members Council broadened the definition of "contribution," which since 1978 had included current cataloging and holdings information. Contribution was defined as

Encyclopedia of Library and Information Sciences, Fourth Edition DOI: 10.1081/E-ELIS4-120043963

OCLC's Chartered Objectives

As set forth in OCLC's Articles of Incorporation, the objectives of OCLC are to "establish, maintain and operate a computerized library network and to promote the evolution of library use, of libraries themselves, and of librarianship, and to provide processes and products for the benefit of library users and libraries, including such objectives as increasing availability of library resources to individual library patrons and reducing rate-of-rise of library per-unit costs, all for the fundamental public purpose of furthering ease of access to and use of the ever-expanding body of worldwide scientific, library and educational knowledge and information."

Fig. 1 OCLC charter.

"intellectual resources provided and shared by libraries and other institutions through the products and services of OCLC and its affiliates for the benefit of other members of the cooperative."

There were three levels of membership participation: Governing Members, Members and Participants. Governing members were institutions that contractually agree to contribute metadata to WorldCat, including all current cataloging and holdings as described in the "OCLC WorldCat Principles of Cooperation," and to make the information available for the benefit of all participants in the OCLC cooperative. Governing members received credits from OCLC for their contributions to WorldCat and received a discount on OCLC services. Governing members elected delegates to the OCLC Members Council, which in turn elects six members of the Board of Trustees.

Members, like governing members, embraced the OCLC values of commitment to collaboration by contributing intellectual content and by sharing resources. While they were not contractually bound to contribute all of their current cataloging to WorldCat, they did contract to contribute to cooperative products or services provided by OCLC and its affiliates. They also received a discount on OCLC services. Representatives from member institutions were eligible for election to Members Council and the Board of Trustees.

Participants contracted to use OCLC products and services without any obligation to return any intellectual content to the cooperative. While participants did not have a direct vote in the affairs of the cooperative, they are encouraged to provide input to their networks, service centers, and Members Council delegates.

The second part of the governance structure was the Members Council, which provided a formal institutional means for the governing members to participate in election of trustees and policy decisions. The OCLC Members Council consisted of 66 delegates who met three times a year. Elections were conducted by OCLC-affiliated networks and regional service centers in the United States and around the world.

Members Council delegates had three main responsibilities: 1) to elect six delegate librarians to the OCLC Board of Trustees; 2) to ratify amendments to the OCLC Articles of Incorporation and Code of Regulations; and 3) to provide advice and counsel to OCLC. The number of delegates each network or service center may elect is based on a formula that takes into account service revenues in cataloging and resource sharing.

A typical Members Council meeting took 2.5 days. The meeting was organized along an annual theme adopted by the delegates. In 2006–2007, the theme was "OCLC Organizational Dissonance: The New Harmony." On February 5–7, 2007, delegates for the first time met outside the United States in Quebec City, Quebec, Canada.

Much of the work (the providing of advice and counsel to OCLC) of the Council was done in small groups that are asked to address specific questions and issues. These groups were organized along service areas, such as cataloging and metadata, digital libraries and research, global librarianship, cooperative reference and preservation/electronic collections, and resource sharing. Additional groups were organized by library type: systems and state libraries; government and special libraries; research libraries; public libraries; private academic libraries; and state academic libraries. These groups produced minutes, which were forwarded to the Members Council Executive Committee. This activity resulted in a written report of significant issues that is sent to OCLC management for comment and possible action and feedback to the Council. This communication, both formal and informal, helped the OCLC cooperative stay in close touch with its member libraries and constituents.

The third part of the governance structure was the Board of Trustees, which was composed of six trustees elected by the Members Council, five trustees elected by the Board itself from fields outside librarianship such as law, finance, government and business, and three board-elected trustees from the general library community. The President of OCLC is an ex-officio trustee. The Board sets strategic goals and policy, approves plans and programs for achieving those goals, hires and evaluates the chief executive officer, approves annual budgets, oversees audits and other reports pertaining to the financial condition of OCLC.

Membership and participation in OCLC continues to become more global. Revenues from international operations in fiscal 2008 were $56.2 million, which was about 23% of total revenues of $246.4 million. That compares with 9.3% of revenues in fiscal 2000. In the past 10 years, the number of libraries participating in OCLC outside the United States has increased from 6000 to almost 14,627 and the number of countries from 75 to 112. In 2007–2008, there were 17 Members Council delegates elected from outside the United States.

In 2007, the OCLC Board of Trustees recognized that as OCLC was becoming an increasingly global cooperative, its governance must be adjusted to ensure representation and participation by members around the world and conducted another periodic review of OCLC's governance. In 2008, the membership adopted a new governance structure for the OCLC cooperative. The new structure is designed to extend participation in the OCLC cooperative to an increasing number of libraries and cultural heritage institutions around the world. It includes regional councils that send delegates to a Global Council, which in turn elects six members of a 15-member Board of Trustees. The transition to the new structure was under way in 2009 and was coordinated by representatives of the 2008/2009 Members Council and the Board of Trustees. In 2009, regional councils were established in the Americas region, the Asia Pacific region, and Europe, the Middle East and Africa, with the first Global Council meeting set for 2010.

FINANCES

Throughout OCLC's history, the organization has funded its operations and paid for research and development with revenues generated by services provided to member libraries. OCLC does not rely on government appropriations, foundation funding, or membership assessments. OCLC's financial philosophy can best be summed up by the introduction to the financial section of the fiscal 2008 annual report reads:

> OCLC is a nonprofit, membership, computer library service, and research organization whose public purposes of furthering access to the world's information and reducing library costs dominate its plans and activities. In support of these purposes, OCLC strives to maintain a strong financial base by operating in a business-like manner in order to accommodate growth, upgrade technological platforms, conduct research and development and still subsidize worthwhile projects for the benefit of libraries and their users. OCLC follows a conservative, nonaggressive accounting and operating philosophy in maintaining its financial reporting and internal control systems."[1] (OCLC 2007/2008 Annual Report, p. 50)

OCLC WORLDCAT

At the heart of the OCLC cooperative is the WorldCat bibliographic database, which member libraries and OCLC cooperatively produce and maintain. WorldCat is the world's largest Online Union Catalog, and among the most consulted databases in higher education. Each WorldCat record contains a bibliographic description of a single item and a list of institutions that hold the item. Institutions share these records, using them to create local catalogs, arrange interlibrary loans, and conduct reference work. Institutions contribute records for items not found in WorldCat using the OCLC shared cataloging system.

Since 1971, more than 130 million records have been added to WorldCat. These records describe materials that span five millennia of recorded knowledge, from approximately 3400 B.C. to the present. Records are in eight formats: books, continuing resources (serials), sound recordings, musical scores, maps, visual materials, mixed materials, and computer files. A member institution adds a new record to WorldCat every 10 sec.

WorldCat has become a unique library resource that is consulted by librarians and library users around the world. It is the result of the concept of shared cooperative cataloging, advanced by OCLC's founder and first president, Frederick G. Kilgour. Shared cataloging not only increased the productivity of library staffs, it also increased the availability of information for library users.

Using the OCLC cataloging system, a cataloger searched the database for a bibliographic record for the item being cataloged. If a record was found, the cataloger used it for the library's catalog. If no record was found, the cataloger created a new record and input it into WorldCat. Thus, shared cataloging made it possible for only one library to create an original catalog record for an item and then provide a means for other libraries to use that same record for their catalogs.

Today, libraries find records they can use for current cataloging 94.6% of the time. Thus, for every 100 books cataloged, only about six required original cataloging. It is possible to catalog up to 14 titles an hour when records are resident in WorldCat, compared with two to three an hour when an original cataloging record must be created.

The ability to edit records and add information in real time meant that contributors could see cataloging results immediately, and any member library connected to the system could use the new information right away. Economies of scale increased as the number of records in the database and number of users grew.

Through WorldCat, OCLC has provided libraries with over $1 billion in services based on cooperative cataloging and resource sharing. These services have not only been at low cost, but have saved libraries billions of dollars in potential duplicate costs. Today, libraries use WorldCat to help them select, order, catalog and get materials ready for shelves, and arrange interlibrary loans. WorldCat is now available to people everywhere on the Internet through WorldCat.org (see below). WorldCat is also available to library users as a reference database

OCLC Worldcat statistics by format
June 30, 2007

Type of material	Number of records	Percentage of total	Locations on LC records	Locations on participating	Locations on member-input	Location of items cataloged
Books	72,166,205	83.90%	594,439,084	373,798,972	70,291,465	1,038,529,521
Continuing resources format [*Serials*]	3,490,048	4.06%	19,380,291	15,3 69,184	608,641	35,358,116
Visual	2,804,530	3.26%	488,015	22,532,443	19,190	23,039,648
Maps	1,168,069	1.36%	1,635,135	3,410,395	84,561	5,130,091
Mixed materials	787,880	0.92%	17,478	543,194	1,052	561,724
Sound recordings	3,215,057	3.74%	3,497,696	22,518 ,124	1,858,612	27,874,432
Scores	1,927,684	2.24%	1,624,017	7,514,673	2,117,208	11,255,898
Computer files	451,050	0.52%	69,452	1,428,652	2,415	1,500,519
Totals	86,010,523	100.00%	621,151,168	447,115,637	74,983,144	1,143,249,949

Compiled from cataloging file statistics: Analysis of online bibliographic records

Fig. 2 OCLC WorldCat statistics by format.
Source: OCLC annual report 2006/2007.

through the OCLC FirstSearch service. The continuing evolution of WorldCat is discussed later in this entry (Fig. 2).

WORLDCAT ENRICHMENT AND QUALITY CONTROL

OCLC member libraries and OCLC maintain a proactive and rigorous quality control program that includes cooperative efforts at the national and international levels. To ensure the quality of WorldCat, all participating libraries are required to comply with specified cataloging standards. The quality control program includes both manual correction of records or elimination of duplicates by OCLC staff and selected participating libraries and automated software that corrects headings and other items automatically.

In the Enhance Program, specially authorized users may lock and replace most full-level member-input bibliographic records in WorldCat, including national-level records. Through the Cataloging in Publication (CIP) Upgrade Program, OCLC works with materials vendors to accelerate the upgrading of CIP records in WorldCat and provide libraries with full cataloging records as soon as possible after publication. A number of OCLC member libraries and OCLC participate in the Program for Cooperative Cataloging (PCC), an international cooperative effort coordinated by the Library of Congress and aimed at expanding access to library collections by providing useful, timely and cost-effective cataloging. As part of the PCC, WorldCat is the host database for the CONSER (Cooperative Online Serials) program in which libraries and publishers build and maintain a comprehensive database of authoritative bibliographic information for serials. OCLC also employs automated techniques in maintaining the quality of WorldCat records.

OCLC member libraries have been able to upgrade minimal-level records and add information, such as call numbers and subject headings, to many of the records in WorldCat. However, major changes to many records have been restricted to participants in the Enhance Program. In response to requests from the cataloging community, in 2009, OCLC started the Expert Community Experiment, in which OCLC libraries with full-level cataloging authorizations were able to improve and upgrade many more WorldCat master bibliographic records. The experiment was expected to result in more corrections and additions to master bibliographic records and more timely actions to correct record problems. The experiment was inspired by long-standing requests from members to be able to do more—and more immediate—upgrading of WorldCat records. The experiment also allowed OCLC to test a "social cataloging" model involving the existing community of cataloging experts who have built WorldCat record-by-record over the past four decades. Interest in such an experiment had grown with the launch of WorldCat Local and with the popularity of other socially cooperative ventures, such as Wikipedia.

In 2008, OCLC began the Next Generation Cataloging and Metadata service pilot, which explored the viability of capturing ONIX metadata upstream from publishers and vendors and enhancing that metadata in WorldCat. A variety of academic and public libraries, publishers, and vendors are participating in the pilot. In 2009, OCLC was preparing to publish case studies and findings from the pilot and to routinely ingest, create, and enhance metadata in WorldCat and output enhanced data in MARC and

ONIX. The start of the pilot last year coincided with the recent release of a "Report on the Future of Bibliographic Control" by the Working Group on the Future of Bibliographic Control, which was formed by the Library of Congress to address changes in how libraries must do their work in the digital information era.

WORLDCAT AND INFORMATION STANDARDS

WorldCat is based on MARC ("Machine-Readable Cataloging"—a format for communication of bibliographic information in machine-readable form developed at the Library of Congress in 1967) and *Anglo American Cataloging Rules* 2nd Edition. MARC21, the current format, represents a harmonization of U.S. and Canadian MARC. There are other MARC formats, such as U.K. MARC and UNIMARC, which is intended to be a global MARC standard.

In the 1990s, the Internet and then the World Wide Web changed the nature of publishing and information seeking. Cataloging information evolved into metadata, and the library community (AACR2/MARC) was not the only group creating and distributing metadata about electronic resources. In 1991, the OCLC Office of Research began studying Internet resources and their potential impact on library operations. In 1995, the National Center for Supercomputing Applications (NSCA) and OCLC held a workshop in Dublin, Ohio to discuss metadata semantics. The result was the Dublin Core, a 15-element metadata set intended to be interoperable and also allowing for author-generated description. In 2001, the American National Standards Institute approved the Dublin Core as NISO Z39.85-2001, and in 2003 it became an ISO standard (ISO 15836). In 1999, WorldCat began supporting Dublin Core as well as MARC21/AACR2.

OCLC was the host for the Dublin Core from its founding in 1995–2005, when it became a public, not-for-profit Company based in Singapore. The founding members of the new legal entity were the National Library Board Singapore and the National Library of Finland.

EVOLUTION OF WORLDCAT

Since 1971, OCLC had built and maintained WorldCat on its own proprietary system that it had developed in-house and continuously modified and updated. From 2001 to 2005, OCLC was engaged in a major project to move WorldCat to a new platform based on hardware and licensed software with widespread industry adoption. This was an important step in OCLC's strategy to evolve WorldCat beyond bibliography into a globally networked, Web-based information resource that would also provide links to digital objects in other knowledge repositories. The switch from a monolithic legacy system to hardware and licensed software with widespread industry adoption enabled OCLC to develop new component applications based on open architectural models that provide improved interoperability within OCLC services and also with external services.

The new WorldCat platform supports additional standards such as Dublin Core and IFLA (International Federation of Library Associations and Institutions) standards for bibliographic records and Unicode, a character coding system designed to support the worldwide interchange, processing, and display of written texts of the diverse languages of the world. In 2007, WorldCat supported the following scripts for cataloging: Arabic, Bengali, Chinese, Cyrillic, Devanagari, Greek, Hebrew, Japanese, Korean, Latin, Tamil, and Thai. OCLC has also moved beyond bibliography to enrich WorldCat with new types of metadata and content such as book cover images, summaries, authors' notes and reviews.

GROWTH OF WORLDCAT

WorldCat has grown continuously since it began operation on August 26, 1971. In 2002, the number of records in WorldCat reached the 50 million after 31 years of shared cataloging. Libraries added the next 50 million records in just 6 years, with the 100 millionth record attained in 2008. The number of holding symbols in WorldCat reached 1 billion in 2005, and by 2009 had climbed to 1.4 billion. This growth is attributable to improvements in automated, batchloading processes and to the new technological platform with its Unicode capabilities that support 12 language scripts noted above, which makes it practicable for an increasing number of international organizations to merge their national union catalogs or other large files with WorldCat.

OCLC was also working to make it easier for national libraries and others to keep their union catalogs in synch with WorldCat. In 2008, the Dutch Union Catalogue started updating WorldCat in real time using SRU technology. In 2009, WorldCat's second SRU record update implementation began operation with Libraries Australia. Records appearing in the Australian National Bibliographic Utility now show up 5 second later in WorldCat. This machine-to-machine process is definitely introducing system-wide efficiencies that benefit the entire cooperative.

It is interesting to note that the language composition of WorldCat has changed over the past decade, with the percentage of records in languages other than English going from 38% in 1998 to slightly over 50% in 2008 (Fig. 3).

CATALOGING

In 2002, OCLC launched the Connexion cataloging service on a new technological platform. It combined functionality from existing OCLC services such as CORC,

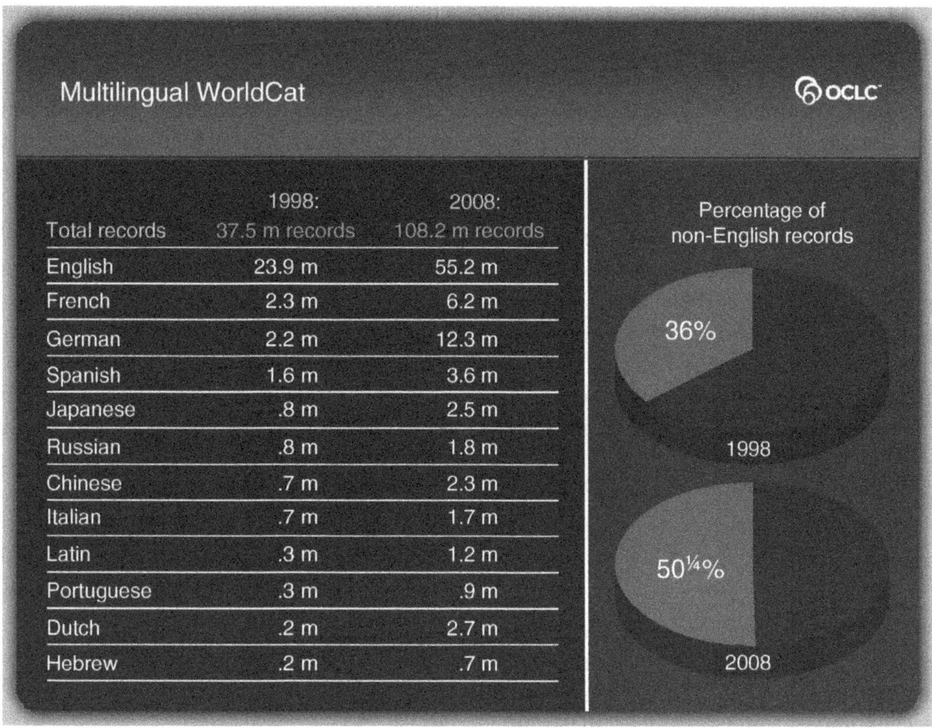

Total records	1998: 37.5 m records	2008: 108.2 m records
English	23.9 m	55.2 m
French	2.3 m	6.2 m
German	2.2 m	12.3 m
Spanish	1.6 m	3.6 m
Japanese	.8 m	2.5 m
Russian	.8 m	1.8 m
Chinese	.7 m	2.3 m
Italian	.7 m	1.7 m
Latin	.3 m	1.2 m
Portuguese	.3 m	.9 m
Dutch	.2 m	2.7 m
Hebrew	.2 m	.7 m

Fig. 3 Languages in WorldCat.
Source: OCLC.

CatExpress, the Cataloging Micro Enhancer, Passport, and WebDewey. Connexion supports cataloging of all materials and formats from a single interface that the library can customize. It provides access to WorldCat, linked authority control, automatic classification, and the ability to build subject guides.

OCLC metadata and cataloging services are designed to help libraries manage their collections and increase the speed at which materials are made available for patron use. In addition to the online shared cataloging service described above, OCLC provides batch processing and Web-based cataloging systems that libraries use to catalog materials and maintain information on their physical and electronic collections.

These services include: automatic delivery of cataloging information with new books received from book vendors; automatic upgrading of cataloging records; workstation software that can be used on the cataloging system to automate certain cataloging tasks; cataloging system for Chinese, Japanese, and Korean ("CJK™") library materials; cataloging software for Arabic library materials; a Web-based copy cataloging system for small libraries with low volumes of cataloging (CatExpress); an authority control service; online, batch and microcomputer-based retrospective conversion services to convert older library cataloging records, usually cards, to machine-readable form; contract cataloging and processing service that acquires, catalogs and adds necessary labels to library materials, including videos, DVDs, and CDs as well as books; and a terminologies service.

The oldest OCLC metadata service is the Dewey Decimal Classification (DDC) system, created by Melvil Dewey and first published in 1876. He established Forest Press in 1911 to edit, publish, and distribute the classification. In 1988, OCLC was asked to assume control of Forest Press. Subsequently, OCLC has published 20th, 21st, and 22nd editions of the DDC, 12th, 13th, and 14th abridged editions, and three electronic versions. The DDC has been translated into 30 languages and is used by over 200,000 libraries in 135 countries. Editing of the DDC is done at the Library of Congress. The DDC is available in both print and electronic versions.

In 2007, OCLC introduced a terminologies service, which provides access to multiple controlled vocabularies to enable creation of consistent metadata for library, museum, or archive collections. The vocabularies include: the Dublin Core; the Art & Architecture Thesaurus of the Getty Vocabulary Program, which describes objects of art as well as the processes and materials from which the objects are made; Newspaper Genre List from the University of Washington, Māori Subject Headings/Ngā Ūpoko Tukutuku from the National Library of New Zealand; and Thesauri for Graphic Materials I and II from the Library of Congress. One goal of the terminologies service is to make it easier for museums and archives to participate in the OCLC cooperative.

WORLDCAT COLLECTION ANALYSIS

Launched in 2005, WorldCat Collection Analysis provides data mining and manipulation capabilities that enable libraries to determine subject coverage in their collections and compare their collections with peer libraries to identify titles held in common and gaps in their collections. The service now includes: peer library comparisons, analysis of library collection and comparison to all holdings in WorldCat, and interlibrary loan analysis, which enables OCLC Resource Sharing users to determine how their collections are being used by others, as well as how they are supplementing their collections via interlibrary loan. Future developments include analysis of circulation usage statistics.

WORLDCAT SELECTION

In December 2006, OCLC introduced the WorldCat Selection service, which is based on ITSO CUL (Integrated Tool for Selection and Ordering at Cornell University Library). The service allows selectors of library materials to view new title data from multiple vendors in a single system. Acquisitions staff export selected records to load into the ILS to complete the ordering process. Staff can share selection decisions with others in their institution. The system streamlines selection, saves time and costs, and requires no software to load. The service now has these library materials vendors as partners—Aux Amateurs de Livres, Blackwell, Casalini libri, China National Publishing Industry Trading Corporation, Coutts, Erasmus, Howard Karno Books, Harrassowitz, Leila Books, Lindsay & Croft, Touzot. and YBP Library Services.

eSERIALS HOLDINGS SERVICE

In 2006, OCLC launched the eSerials Holdings Service, which helps libraries manage their eSerials collections. It automatically sets and updates WorldCat holdings for ISSN-based electronic serials each month. OCLC currently partners with EBSCO, OCLC Openly 1Cate, Serials Solutions, and TDNet on this service. About 1.8 million holdings have been set automatically in the past year. This service helps lower costs and increase the visibility of a library's eSerials collection to searchers and ILL librarians via FirstSearch, Resource Sharing, and Open WorldCat.

REFERENCE AND RESOURCE SHARING

OCLC's reference and resource sharing services build on and strengthen the tradition of interlibrary cooperation. OCLC introduced its online interlibrary loan service in 1979, and its online end-user reference service, FirstSearch, in 1991. Since then, the two services have become closely connected, based on the notion that searching, retrieval and delivery of information should be merged into a single, integrated service that would provide information to the user when and where needed.

The interlibrary loan service enables libraries to select holdings information electronically from WorldCat and to send requests for materials to other libraries in the OCLC network. For the year ended June 30, 2008, libraries conducted 10 million interlibrary loans online through OCLC.

The direction of resource sharing could be seen in OCLC ILLiad software that integrated borrowing automation, lending automation and electronic document delivery into one Web-based customer interface. Library users could easily send and track requests electronically through the Web while the system automatically processed filled requests and contacted users when requests were completed.

In 2009, OCLC further refined its consortial borrowing service with the introduction of WorldCat Navigator. The service manages returnable and nonreturnable items, and integrates with circulation systems to create a discovery-to-delivery tool.

QUESTIONPOINT

In 2002, with the Library of Congress, OCLC introduced QuestionPoint, a virtual reference desk collaborative service that includes e-mail, phone, walk-up, and fax capabilities. In 2004, OCLC acquired the assets of the 24/7 cooperative reference service project of the Metropolitan Cooperative Library System, Los Angeles, California, which enables library users to ask questions and get answers from qualified reference staff in real time on the Internet. In 2009, more than 1900 libraries were using QuestionPoint in 23 countries, and more than 1500 libraries were participating in the 24/7 reference cooperative, including 13 statewide services, the nationwide enquire service in the United Kingdom, and an additional 15 major regional services. The service handled questions in 26 languages. In 2008, the three-millionth reference question was logged on the service.

QuestionPoint uses the expertise of librarians to provide answers to questions, research guidance, and help navigating the Internet. Libraries may brand their own customized versions of QuestionPoint. For example, the Netherlands Public Library Association has customized QuestionPoint into Al@adin, a Web-based network of librarians in 50 libraries that delivers reference assistance to any library user in the country. Al@din answers questions locally and nationally and can seamlessly refer them to other QuestionPoint users around the world. QuestionPoint subscribers maintain a Global Knowledge Base, which contains 18,000 records in 10 languages. In

2008, a chat widget was introduced that give libraries the ability to embed a snippet of HTML code throughout their Web pages and in a variety of environments, thereby providing access to the QuestionPoint service.

eCONTENT

Initially, OCLC services were designed for use by librarians to help manage their collections. When the FirstSearch service was launched in 1991, it was the first end-user reference system in the library community. Indeed, FirstSearch was in some respects as revolutionary in its early days, before the advent of the Web and search engines, as online shared cataloging had been 25 years earlier. Before FirstSearch and its user-friendly, menu-driven interface, online database searching was the exclusive preserve of reference librarians who alone knew how to devise search strategies to navigate complex and expensive databases. The library community rapidly adopted FirstSearch.

In use in more than 22,000 libraries, FirstSearch provides library end-users with desktop access to bibliographic, abstract, and full-text information from approximately 84 databases. It also provides document delivery of print and electronic materials and permits library users to request interlibrary loans. In the year ended June 30, 2008, there were 79.7 million searches conducted on FirstSearch.

OCLC FirstSearch Electronic Collections Online (ECO) provides cross-journal searching and access to electronic versions of 5600 journals and over 2.2 million full-text articles from 70 publishers. Accessible as a database on FirstSearch, ECO enables libraries to assemble, circulate, manage, and archive large collections of academic and professional journals on the World Wide Web. ECO provides links to other databases, WorldCat holdings information, and access to the OCLC interlibrary loan service. Libraries could also obtain bibliographic records that matched their journal subscriptions in order to facilitate access to the collection from the library's online public access catalog (OPAC).

In addition to WorldCat, OCLC produces eight databases that are available on FirstSearch:

- OCLC Union Lists of Periodicals includes more than 7 million location listings of local information linked to over 750,000 bibliographic records for periodicals WorldCat.
- OCLC ArticleFirst (15 million records) includes bibliographic citations from over 12,600 serials, covering science, technology, medicine, social science, business, the humanities, and popular culture.
- Electronic books include 675,000 records for online electronic books cataloged by OCLC member libraries.
- OCLC ECO provides cross-journal searching and access to electronic versions of 5600 journals and over 4.2 million full-text articles.
- OCLC PapersFirst (6.9 million records) gives access to individual papers presented at every congress, symposium, exposition, workshop, and meeting added to The British Library Document Supply Centre since October 1993.
- OCLC ProceedingsFirst (192,000 records) provides tables of contents of presented papers from conferences worldwide.
- OCLC WorldCat Dissertations and Theses (8 million records) provides access to the dissertations and theses available in OCLC member libraries.
- CAMIO (Catalog of Art Museum Images Online) provides more than 95,000 high-quality art images from prominent museums around the world.
- ArchiveGrid provides access to nearly 1 million descriptions of archival collections held by thousands of libraries, museums, historical societies, and archives worldwide.
- OAIster provides access to 19 million records pointing to open archive collections, contributed by over 1000 organizations worldwide.

In July 2009, OCLC planned to make available all of its eContent resources through a single discovery platform—WorldCat.org. (see below). It will provide libraries with a single and familiar access point to their content and collections available anytime, anywhere. It also adds functionality that has been in high demand from users—social software, citation management, and tagging.

ELECTRONIC BOOKS

In the mid-1980s, the OCLC Office of Research had experimented with electronic books with EIDOS, the Electronic Information Delivery Online System. With the envisioned system, a user could search for a document and browse tables of contents and index pages and, if desired, request the actual text. Staff developed a prototype system, but it did not go into production. In the early 1990s, OCLC, with the American Association for the Advancement of Science, launched the world's first peer-reviewed medical journal, the Online Journal of Current Clinical Trials. OCLC also experimented with different technological approaches to electronic journals until settling on the current ECO model in 1997. Thus, OCLC was no stranger to electronic books and journals when the technology of the World Wide Web made such electronic publications practicable.

In 2002, OCLC acquired the assets of NetLibrary, a provider of electronic books and textbooks. The NetLibrary division provides electronic book content and tools to libraries. NetLibrary's collection contains more than 171,000 titles from 400 publishers, with 90% of new, incoming content published within the last 3 years. The collection includes 7000 eAudiobooks. OCLC MARC records are included with all NetLibrary eBook and eAudiobook purchases, and holdings are automatically set in WorldCat for member libraries. The multilingual interface is available in Chinese, Dutch, English, French, German, Japanese, Korean, Spanish, and Thai.

DIGITAL COLLECTION SERVICES

In 2003, OCLC began making available CONTENTdm, a software package that facilitates WorldCat access to photos, graphics, and other objects in digitized special collections of libraries and other cultural heritage institutions. In 2006, OCLC acquired DiMeMa (Digital Media Management), the organization that developed and supports CONTENTdm software, which was distributed by OCLC and used by more than 450 institutions to manage their digital collections. In 2008, OCLC added Unicode support to CONTENTdm, thereby extending the software's application in the United States and throughout the world to organizations with primary source materials in many languages. OCLC is now building the OCLC Digital Repository, which will integrate CONTENTdm collections with WorldCat. The metadata for some 100,000 items has already been harvested from 105 organizations and is already in WorldCat.

The DLF/OCLC Registry of Digital Preservation Masters, introduced in 2004, helps libraries build a central, shared registry of digital formats that all participating institutions may one day contribute to and use. By accessing the registry, a library can identify items already digitized and make informed decisions about what items they need to digitize, thereby reducing duplication of effort.

The OCLC Digital Archive provides long-term access and preservation for digital collections. Libraries can share their collections with the world or limit access for their own administrative purposes. Objects can be added one-at-a-time or in batches in a variety of formats. The Digital Archive follows the Reference Model for an Open Archival Information System, which has been adopted as an ISO standard. Dissemination Information Packages from the Digital Archive conform to the Metadata Encoding and Transmission Standard.

Web Harvester, introduced in 2008, allows users of Connexion and CONTENTdm to captured Web-based documents and Web sites from the live Web and manage the collected content as part of their overall digital collection management program.

OCLC also provides high-quality preservation microfilming and digital scanning services for libraries, operates preservation microfilming and digital scanning services for libraries, archives, historical societies, and museums. OCLC has digitized the microfilmed papers of George Washington, Thomas Jefferson, and Abraham Lincoln for the American Memory Project of the Library of Congress. OCLC operates preservation centers in the United States in Bethlehem, Pennsylvania; Lacey, Washington; and Richmond, Virginia; and in Winnipeg, Manitoba, Canada.

INTEGRATED LIBRARY SYSTEMS

With the merger with Pica BV in the Netherlands in 1999 and the formation of OCLC EMEA, OCLC reentered the local systems business. Pica was a well-established local systems provider, primarily in Europe with its LBS and CBS systems. LBS is an integrated local library management system that supports acquisitions, cataloging, and circulation. The CBS (Central Library System) provides the infrastructure for the creation and management of union catalogs and tools for regional interlibrary loan. There are CBS installations at the Royal Library of the Netherlands, the German National Library, and the National Library of Australia, and at ABES (Agence bibliographique de l'enseignement supérieur) in France, to name a few.

OCLC EMEA also develops and maintains three other library management systems acquired through acquisitions. The OLIB (originally developed by Fretwell Downing Informatics) library management system is installed in about 250 organizations worldwide. In 2008, OCLC EMEA completed a 5-year project to create new public catalog site for the U.S. National Archives and Records Administration based on OLIB. The SunRise library system (originally developed by Sisis) is installed in more than 150 libraries, primarily in Germany, Switzerland, and the Netherlands; the Bavarian State Library is a SunRise user. The Amlib system has some 500 installations in Australia, Africa, and the United States.

OCLC's long-term strategy for the ILS is to create an infrastructure to deliver a large-scale, network-based workflow solution to manage library business processes. The design of the future library management environment will comprise a number of important aspects. It will be an evolutionary process, with new service implemented in a building block process that will eventually become a unified solution. The new services can also be integrated into a library's existing infrastructure and current library management system. The notion is to preserve the functionality of the ILS, but at the same time enhance it by placing it in a network environment, and extending it to manage print, licensed, and digitized material with one solution.

OCLC PROGRAMS AND RESEARCH

On July 1, 2006, OCLC combined operations with RLG, a nonprofit organization of over 150 research libraries, archives, museums, and other cultural memory institutions. By the end of 2007, RLG's services in online cataloging, resource sharing, and digitization/imaging had been integrated with OCLC's. RLG's program initiatives are being continued as RLG-Programs, a new division of OCLC Research. This unit, based in San Mateo, California, combines RLG's successful tradition of identifying issues and building consensus among research institutions with OCLC's research capacities and robust prototyping capabilities. The combined memberships represent a critical mass of libraries, museums, archives, and other cultural heritage institutions.

OCLC Research staff have developed the following work agenda:

- Supporting new modes of research, teaching, and learning.
- Managing the collective collection of the cooperative.
- Renovating descriptive and organizing practices.
- Modeling new service infrastructures.
- Participating in architecture and standards activities.
- Measuring and assessing end-user behaviors.

The Office of Research, established by OCLC Founder Frederick G. Kilgour in 1978, is one of the world's leading centers devoted exclusively to the challenges facing libraries in a rapidly changing environment. The mission of OCLC Research is to expand knowledge that advances OCLC's public purposes of furthering access to the world's information and reducing library costs. This mission is achieved through the integration of computer, library, and information sciences into research activities including experimentation, prototyping, standardization advancements, studies, and research collaborations. Main areas of research include content management, interoperability, knowledge organization, system and service architecture, and collection and user analysis.

OCLC Research also provides programs that benefit the larger library community. The OCLC/ALISE Library and Information Science Research Grant Program funds research projects by full-time academic faculty in schools of library and information science. The Visiting Scholar program brings experienced professionals to OCLC to work with staff, facilities, and data resources. The Distinguished Seminar Series brings distinguished information professionals to OCLC to discuss their research activities.

OCLC Research develops and provides source code free of charge to the library community for use and further development. OAICat and OAIHarvester are OCLC open-source software programs that implement OAI protocols for data storage and harvesting in support of institutional repositories. DSpace, the open-source repository software created by MIT, uses OAICat to support its OAI (Open Archives Initiative) capability. OCLC Research has also released an algorithm that provides instructions for implementing Functional Requirements for Bibliographic Records on bibliographic databases.

In 2008, OCLC Research staff engaged in variety of projects, including studying the information behaviors of college students. They were also closely involved in launching the WorldCat API and Developers Network, creating a WorldCat widget for use in Facebook and other social Web sites and developing a service that makes different metadata standards interoperable. They also contributed to the enhancement of OCLC's terminology-based services, the release of a production version of WorldCat Identities, the testing of the Registry of Copyright Evidence and an examination of circulation data from libraries that are members of the OhioLINK consortium. Also in 2008, OCLC Research opened an office at the University of St. Andrews in Scotland to better serve the needs of research libraries and other cultural heritage institutions in Europe.

ADVOCATE FOR LIBRARIES

Libraries have been increasingly urging OCLC to become more active as an advocate for libraries. OCLC pursues this role in a variety of ways. OCLC researchers serve as advocates for libraries in the development of standards. For example, OCLC researchers are active in the Dublin Core Metadata Initiative (see above). OCLC officers and senior managers are involved in national and international professional activities in the library and information community in such groups as the OAI Steering Committee, the Digital Library Federation Steering Committee, the JISC/FAIR (Focus on Access to Institutional Resources—United Kingdom), ALA's Library Business Alliance, NISO's Board of Trustees and Standards Development Committee, and the IFLA Standing Committee on Cataloging.

Another advocacy effort is the Jay Jordan IFLA/OCLC Early Career Development Program, which provides early career development and continuing education for library and information science professionals from countries with developing economies On an annual basis, up to six individuals, including a theological librarian, are selected for participation in this intensive 5-week Fellowship program. Four weeks are based at OCLC's headquarters in Dublin, Ohio, United States; 1 week is based at OCLC in Leiden, Netherlands. The program gives Fellows opportunities to meet with leading information practitioners, visit libraries, and explore topics including information technologies, library operations and management, and global cooperative librarianship. The Fellows visit selected North American and European libraries, cultural heritage institutions, and library organizations. The Fellows also observe OCLC's governance structure in action, gaining insight into issues affecting the global library cooperative. Fellows give presentations about their home countries and libraries, meet leading information professionals, and discuss real-world solutions to the challenges facing libraries today. The Fellows translate their learning and experiences into specific professional development plans that guide their continued growth as well as their personal contributions to their home institutions and country of origin. Since the program began in 2001, there have been fellows from Brazil, China, Colombia, Georgia, Ghana, India, Indonesia, Jamaica, Kenya, South Korea, Malawi, Malaysia, Mauritius, Moldova, Morocco, Nepal, Pakistan, Philippines, Rwanda, Serbia, South Africa, Sri Lanka, Trinidad and Tobago, Turkey, Uganda, and Vietnam.

In 2009, OCLC launched the OCLC Minority Librarian Fellowship program designed to provide a unique opportunity for aspiring library professionals from historically under-represented groups. The Fellowship program offers an opportunity to be part of the world's leading library cooperative. The 12-month program offers the selected Fellow two, three-month assignments within specific divisions of OCLC, and one six-month assignment with a specific operating unit within the OCLC organization.

OCLC also develops studies and other information sources that OCLC members can use in their planning and, indeed, in their own advocacy activities. Here is a sample of recent reports.

- "Five-Year Information Format Trends" outlines trends in popular and scholarly materials, digitization projects, and Web resources.
- "Libraries: How They Stack Up" compares library economics and activities to other sectors, professions, and destinations in the worldwide economy.
- "OCLC Library Training and Education Market Needs Assessment Study" produced in conjunction with the Members Council Task Force on OCLC's role in staff development.
- "Libraries and the Enhancement of E-learning" is a white paper issued in 2003 by the OCLC E-Learning Task Force to help frame discussions as to what roles libraries and the OCLC cooperative might play in e-learning.
- "Perceptions of Libraries and Information Resources: A Report to the OCLC Membership" (2005).
- "Sharing, Privacy, and Trust in Our Networked World" (2007).

In 2004, OCLC issued "The 2003 OCLC Environmental Scan: Pattern Recognition." This report to the OCLC membership identified trends that are affecting libraries, museums, and archives in five landscapes: social, economic, technology, research and learning, and library. The *Scan* was based on interviews with 100 information professionals and a review of 300 relevant articles and papers. The report has been well received by OCLC members, some of whom were using it for their own strategic planning efforts. In 2004, the Association of Library Collections and Technical Services, a division of the American Library Association, awarded the authors of the *Scan* a Presidential Citation.

In 2008, OCLC published *From Awareness to Funding: A Study of Library Support in America*. Using a $1.2 million grant from the Bill & Melinda Gates Foundation, OCLC partnered with the Leo Burnett marketing agency to conduct research about library funding, and to evaluate the potential of a large-scale library marketing and advocacy campaign to increase awareness of the library's role in the community.

WEBJUNCTION

Started in 2003 with a $9.2 million grant from the Bill and Melinda Gates Foundation, WebJunction has become a thriving online community of library staff that supports peer-to-peer sharing through online discussions and distributed content publishing. There are over 40,000 registered members and 90,000 unique monthly visitors. There are 15 community partners, most of them state libraries that operate customized versions of WebJunction. The site also hosts 700 online courses for continuing education and 17 custom learning communities for library staff that are sponsored by library service organizations. In 2009, WebJunction launched learning communities for the Research Learning Group, ILLiad (resource sharing) and for library staff outside the United States.

WEAVING LIBRARIES INTO THE WEB: OPEN WORLDCAT

In 2003, OCLC launched the Open WorldCat pilot program to determine the feasibility of providing new services that would integrate the collections of OCLC member libraries into heavily used Web sites. The notion was to make it easy for a person who is looking for information via a search engine to end up finding it in a nearby library. To do this, OCLC would make WorldCat records directly available to the general public for the first time via the Web. Heretofore, WorldCat had been available only through participating libraries.

OCLC began the pilot after extensive consultations with the Board of Trustees, Members Council, regional service providers, and member libraries. The consensus was that it was something the cooperative had to try since numerous studies had indicated that people were turning increasingly to the Web first for their information needs, often ignoring libraries when doing research. The pilot offered the possibility of raising the visibility of libraries on the Web.

In the first phase, users could access links to Open WorldCat through selected Web sites, including Alibris, Abebooks, Antiquarian Booksellers Association of America, BookPage, and HCI Bibliography. In the second phase, 2 million records from WorldCat were made available on search engines, such as Google and Yahoo! Search, with links to the Web-based catalogs of 12,000 academic, public and school libraries participating in OCLC.

In 2005, Open WorldCat became an ongoing program, making bibliographic records of library-owned materials in WorldCat visible and accessible to Web users through popular search engines such as Google, Yahoo! and Ask. com. OCLC has also made it easier to get to member libraries' catalogs by adding always-there access to Open WorldCat from toolbars on FireFox, Google, and Yahoo! Another feature enables users in the United States to buy books online that they find in Open WorldCat; they can then donate a portion of the sale proceeds to the Open WorldCat library of their choice.

WORLDCAT.ORG

On August 8, 2006, OCLC introduced the WorldCat.org Web site. It offers a search box that people can download and use to search all the records and location listings in WorldCat. For the first time, collections in OCLC member libraries became visible on the Internet to people everywhere. This was one of the signal achievements in the history of the OCLC cooperative, testifying not only to the vision of OCLC's founder Frederick G. Kilgour, but to the perseverance and hard work of catalogers and librarians who have built WorldCat record by record since 1971.

By reaching into the working and learning patterns of today's information consumers, Open WorldCat raises the visibility of libraries and other cultural heritage institutions on the Web. It enables information seekers to guide themselves to quality information contained in libraries in an increasingly seamless fashion. It gives users knowledge management tools that enhance their use of the library, both for traditional collections and, increasingly, for digitized special collections.

WORLDCAT LOCAL

In 2008, OCLC introduced WorldCat Local, a compelling user environment that provides a single interface to the collections of a library. It interoperates with locally maintained services such as circulation, resource sharing and resolution to full text to create an integrated experience for library users. WorldCat Local searches the entire WorldCat.org database and presents local and group library holdings at the top of the results list, as well as ownership details for WorldCat libraries outside the local library and consortium.

With the implementation of WorldCat Local, OCLC began providing a local connection to cloud computing. It is a service provided to the library across the Internet that eliminates costs to the library for hosting, operating, and maintaining software. WorldCat Local is "activatable," which means that library staff configure the service from their library using their library's policies. This configuration is done using an online questionnaire that ideally requires the involvement of staff from both public services and technical services.

WEB SERVICES

Web services enable applications to interconnect over the Web through machine-to-machine interfaces. They cover a wide range of activities that let people tap into computing power on the Web.

In addition to WorldCat.org, WorldCat Local and the WorldCat Identities mentioned above, OCLC has also introduced other Web services in the past 5 years. The xISBN service, developed by OCLC Research, supplies International Standard Book Numbers (ISBNs) associated with an individual intellectual work, based on information in the WorldCat database. It finds all related editions of a book, including paperback, hardback, audiobook, foreign and out-of-print. Easily incorporated into library catalogs, the service is available free to OCLC cataloging members and for a fee to others.

The WorldCat Registry is a Web service, which enables a library to manage its institutional identity more efficiently. On a secure Web platform, a library can create and maintain a single profile that includes information of use to the library's consortium members, technology vendors, eContent providers, funding agencies, and other partners. This access enables the library to automate routine tasks such as activation of a new subscription service or renewal of an existing one. In 2008, the Registry included more than 120,000 institution records for OCLC and non-OCLC members.

In 2008, OCLC established the WorldCat Developer's Network by inviting a small group of developers from OCLC cataloging institutions in North America and Europe to use the WorldCat API (Applications Programming Interface) to build applications that would guide people from the Web to library services. These developers could then link WorldCat information to Internet applications as well as presentations, blogs, and e-mails. This shared development will enhance the creativity and usage of WorldCat.

GOOGLE AND OCLC

In 2008, OCLC and Google agreed to exchange data to will facilitate the discovery of library collections through Google search services. OCLC member libraries participating in the Google Book Search™ program, which makes the full text of more than 1 million books searchable, may share their WorldCat-derived MARC records with Google to better facilitate discovery of library collections through Google. Google will link from Google Book Search to WorldCat. org, which will drive traffic to library OPACs and other library services. Google will share data and links to digitized books with OCLC, which will make it possible for OCLC to represent the digitized

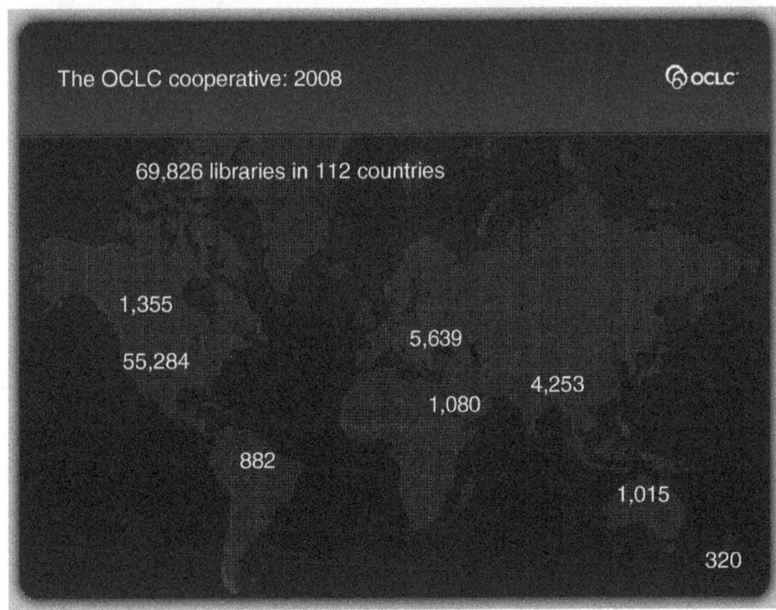

Fig. 4 The OCLC cooperative: 2008.
Source: OCLC.

collections of OCLC member libraries in WorldCat. OCLC began online operations in 1971 with 54 academic libraries in Ohio. In 2008, more than 69,000 libraries in 112 countries had a unique holding symbol in the WorldCat database and were participating in some way in the OCLC global cooperative (Fig. 4).

U.S. ACTIVITY

For the year ended June 30, 2008, revenues from U.S. operations were $190.2 million, or 77.2% of total revenues of $246.4 million. Here are a few highlights of U.S. activities in fiscal 2008.

- University of Washington Libraries enters 100 millionth bibliographic record in WorldCat on April 1, 2008.
- State Library of Ohio begins using WorldCat Local production version.
- Mellon Foundation awards OCLC $145,000 grant to conduct data exchange study with seven RLG Programs art museum partners.
- Orbis Cascade Alliance and OCLC are working together to migrate the Alliance's Summit union catalog of 38 libraries to a consortial borrowing solution.

ACTIVITY OUTSIDE THE UNITED STATES

Revenues from operations outside the United States in fiscal 2008 were $56.2 million, or 22.8% of total revenues. Here are some highlights of OCLC activities outside the United States for fiscal 2008 (year ended June 30, 2008).

OCLC ASIA PACIFIC

- OCLC Beijing Representative Office established on July 25, 2007.
- National Library of China to load Chinese records into WorldCat.
- National Central Library, Taiwan to load Chinese records into WorldCat.
- Completed loading of the National Union Catalog of Australia into WorldCat.
- Completed loading of the National Union Catalog of New Zealand into WorldCat.

OCLC CANADA

- University of Manitoba to use OCLC Canada LTS for outsourced cataloging.
- Edmonton Public Library to use OCLC Canada LTS for outsourced cataloging of Chinese language materials.
- Twelve new governing members to catalog on OCLC.
- Six new Canadian publishers to contribute eBooks to the NetLibrary collection.
- Presented the first OCLC Symposium in Canada during Canadian Library Association annual conference on Social Networking and Web 2.0.

OCLC LATIN AMERICAN AND THE CARIBBEAN

- More than 48,000 records from RedALyc (scientific journals from Latin America, Spain, and Portugal) were loaded into WorldCat with access to article level full text.

- The National Library and Information System Authority of Trinidad and Tobago became the first national library in the Americas offering the QuestionPoint service to provide virtual reference services.
- The Pedro Henriquez Ureña National Library in the Dominican Republic joined OCLC as a cataloging member.
- More than 470,000 records of scientific material related to agriculture and animal research from Embrapa (Brazil) were loaded into WorldCat.
- State of Jalisco Public Library system (Mexico) began using NetLibrary eBooks.

OCLC EUROPE, THE MIDDLE EAST AND AFRICA

- Signed an agreement with the UKB (Association of Dutch University Libraries, the Royal Library, and the Library of the Royal Academy of Sciences) in the Netherlands to continue managing the Dutch national information infrastructure.
- Loaded into WorldCat bibliographic files from the National Library of Sweden, Swiss National Library, Hebis, and Bavarian State Library.
- Migrated LinkUK data to UnityUK creating a single national union catalog in the United Kingdom.
- Introduced the Netlibrary platform for distribution of Dutch eBooks to Dutch public libraries.

FUTURE DIRECTIONS

Since 1971, OCLC has provided libraries with $3.7 billion in products and services. WorldCat is in the workflows of most parts of the library, including acquisitions, cataloging, reference, resource sharing, and circulation. OCLC products and services have not only been at low cost, but have saved libraries millions of dollars. Clearly, the OCLC cooperative has worked well for 37 years. Going forward, OCLC will provide local, group, and global nodes that work together seamlessly and symbiotically as it continues to pursue its mission of furthering access to the world's information and reducing the rate of rise of library costs.

REFERENCE

1. OCLC Annual Report 2000/2001; OCLC Online Computer Library Center, Inc.: Dublin, OH, 2000/2001; 61.

Older Adults' Information: Needs and Behavior

Kirsty Williamson
Caulfield School of IT, Monash University, Caulfield, Victoria, Australia and School of Information Studies, Charles Sturt University, Wagga Wagga, NSW, Australia

Terry Asla
Senior Lifestyles Researcher, Seattle, U.S.A.

Abstract

The proportion of older adults, usually defined as aged 60 or 65 and over, is expanding rapidly in the populations of many countries of the world, leading to the expectation that they should have growing importance from a research perspective. It is therefore surprising that there have been few substantial studies of the information needs and behaviors of this group, apart from research of which the principal focus is library services. This entry discusses the major studies that have been undertaken on the topic, mentioning library studies only where relevant. Library services are not part of the purview and are dealt with only briefly. The introduction discusses definitions of "older adults," why there is an imperative for studying this large, diverse group and the role played by research with a library focus. The entry then examines what is known about human information behavior (HIB) in the context of everyday life information focusing particularly on information needs, the sources used to meet those needs and the role of residential context (for the very old and frail) where this is relevant. Where possible, the findings are discussed in terms of the three age groups into which older adults are sometimes divided: the young aged (60–74), the old–old (75–84), and the very old (85+). Recently, the concept of the Fourth Age has been introduced into the HIB field. The Fourth Age describes people who have multiple disabilities and are usually in the last stage of their lives. The physical, cognitive, and social losses of the Fourth Age have significant impact on HIB. Since computers and the Internet have now become such important tools in the information-seeking process, the next section of the entry focuses on these topics. The conclusion is that further research is needed, that people in the wide age span from 60 to 65 plus should not be treated as homogeneous in their needs, and that the Internet be included in future research but that it should be examined in the context of other sources of everyday life information.

INTRODUCTION

The goal of this entry is to explore what we know about the information needs and behaviors of older adults. To do this, we need to begin by defining the group at the center of the discussion, involving as it does a very large age span that needs to be further subdivided for meaningful conclusions to be reached.

Defining "Old"

The simplest, most comparable, and widely used definition of "old" is chronological age (p. 9),[1] also referred to as calendar age. In the United States, because the Social Security Act of 1935 was viewed as "old-age security legislation" intended for people aged 65 and older (p. 184, 200),[2] this age became, officially and in common parlance, the time when old age was said to begin (p. 258).[3] The age of 60 plus is the definition of "old age" accepted by most developed countries, though there is no UN standard numerical criterion.[4] It should be noted that the age at which citizens are eligible for the old-age pension is set to rise over the next few years to 67 in countries such as United States, the United Kingdom, and Australia, the adjustment considered necessary because of the increased life span now occurring.[5–7]

Because of the disparate physical and cognitive differences noted among adults aged 60 and older, gerontologists early on divided the aged into three groups commonly designated as the young aged (60–74 years), the old–old (75–84), and the very old or "oldest old" (85 +). In the field of library and information science, most researchers have continued to treat older people as one group, aged over 60 or 65. There have been exceptions, which include Turock[9] and Wooliscroft,[10] who, in their work about older people and libraries, have found the three subgroups useful. Today, the "very old" group is often referred to as the "oldest old"[11] the designation that Asla et al.[12] used in their 2006 article in *Library and Information Research*.

Even the division of the aged into three groups did not solve problems for researchers who found a wide disparity in abilities among members of each of the specific groups. Consequently, gerontologists developed Fourth Ages

Encyclopedia of Library and Information Sciences, Fourth Edition DOI: 10.1081/E-EISA-120053437

theory, with the Fourth Age referring to that time in life described as "the disability zone" (p. 31).[8] Members of the Fourth Age are identified by specific, measurable physical, cognitive, and social losses, which have significant impact on their lives and also on HIB: vision, hearing, cognition, chronic illnesses, and mobility. Thus researchers who employ the Fourth Age definition "are assured of studying a homogeneous group of individuals approaching the end of life."[13] Recently, the concept of the Fourth Age, describing people in the "disability zone" and usually in the last stage of their lives, was introduced into the HIB field by Asla,[13,14] whose study was undertaken in two retirement communities in the United States.

In this entry, we review literature where "older adults" are regarded as aged at least 60 years, but we also describe what is known about how baby boomers might bring changes in HIB as they reach the age of 60 plus as the oldest ones have already done. Where possible, the sub-age groups, mentioned earlier, will be discussed in relation to key topics of discussion.

The Imperative for Studying Older Age Groups

Of crucial importance in any consideration of the information needs and behavior of older people is the effect of the very large generation labeled as "baby boomers" (persons born between 1946 and 1964). While the youngest baby boomers have yet to turn 60, there is growing interest in the future impact on the public library of the library and HIB needs of this cohort.[15] A key argument for focusing research attention on older age groups stems from the fact that the proportion of older people is increasing and becoming quite significant. The phenomenon of the burgeoning older population is well known in the developed world. In the United States, the number of people aged 65 and over at the time of the 2010 Census was more than 40 million or 13% of the total population. Between 2000 and 2010, the population 65 years and over increased at a faster rate (15.1%) than the total US population (9.7%).[16] Between 2010 and 2050, the US population aged 65 and over is projected to grow to 88.5 million, with the baby boomers, who began turning 65 in 2011, being largely responsible for this increase. By 2030, when all of the baby boomers will have turned 65, the percentage of the US population aged 65 and over will be 19% (compared to 13% in 2010) and will rise slightly again by 2050.[17] In 2030, when the last baby boomer turns 65, the demographic landscape will have changed significantly. One of every five US citizens—about 72 million people—will be an older adult.[18] The number of people in the oldest age group (85+) is also projected to rise dramatically from 5.8 million in 2010 to 8.7 million in 2030 and 19 million in 2050 (4.3% of the US population, up from 2.3% in 2030), again because of the effect of the baby boomers.[17]

In Australia, where the lead author of this entry lives and where a major study of the information-seeking behavior of the older population was undertaken, there are comparable statistics. At the time of the 2011 Census, 3.1 million people were aged 65 or over, accounting for about one in seven Australians.[19] Between 1971 and 2011, the proportion of Australia's older people increased from 8.3% to 14%. The projected increases are to 22% in 2061 and to 25% in 2101. For those aged 85 years and over (the age group most apt to be in or entering the Fourth Age), numbers had more than tripled, to 420,300 between 1971 and 2011, with proportions increasing from 0.5% to 2% of the population over that period. This group is projected to grow rapidly, to 5% by 2061 and to 6% by 2101.[20]

Like Australia and the United States, all of the world's developed nations face the same problem of rapidly aging populations. Given such large increases in numbers and population percentages, it is imperative that there be an increase in research in all fields, including in the "information" arena.

Library-Based Research

Starting with the 1975 White House Conference on Aging, there were a large number of studies and discussions focusing on the provision of library services to older people, some emanating from the American Library Association (ALA). In recent years, the number of such studies has declined dramatically despite the increased aging of the population, as noted by Perry.[21] The White House Conferences on Aging, held every 10 years, involve events sponsored by the ALA, the latest in 2005 titled "Libraries, Lifelong Learning, Information and Older Adults."[22] The ALA has also provided guidelines for library services to older adults.[23] An important resource, the database AgeLine, produced by the American Association of Retired Persons and available on EBSCO Host, is a very useful resource provided in some public libraries. Decker provides a worthwhile discussion of baby boomers in relation to the US public library system, focusing on facilities, services, technology, and library staff.[24] Her article draws on several papers presented at a conference in NSW (Australia) in 2009: "Next chapters: public libraries for older adults in Australia and New Zealand" and published in the journal, *Australasian Public Libraries and Information Services*. The papers cover a range of needs, services, and age cohorts, including baby boomers.[25] Earlier library-based research focused primarily on audits of services, programs, and the allocation of library resources for older patrons, for example, Turock and Ip.[9,26] A recent study using this approach was undertaken by Perry.[21] Unfortunately, most of these studies treated older users as a homogeneous group aged about 65 years and older. Since library services are not central to this entry, studies where libraries are the focus are not discussed further unless they shed significant light on needs and behaviors associated with everyday life information.

Everyday Life Information Seeking

What do we know about the needs of older adults for information for everyday life and how these needs are met? There are few projects that have explored this topic in any depth. We know that "health" is an important topic for older people and that there have been a number of studies of older people in relation to health information.[27–29] Other studies have focused on online access for older people and people with disabilities, with "information" being an obvious concomitant.[30] Other examples are provided later.

Two of the major studies of information seeking, published during the 1990s, took different approaches to the topic. Chatman[31,32] studied the information world of 55 women, who lived alone in a retirement community in a southern US city and whose average age was 82 years (age range 68–100). Using what she termed "social network theory" and an ethnographic approach during the 2-year study, she explored the women's information and recreational needs, as well as the sources routinely used in response to those needs. For her, the term "social network" referred to the interpersonal communications that assist people in meeting problems and her focus was on the role of personal networks, for example, family, friends, neighbors, or professionals, in meeting the needs of older women. Williamson[33,34] used an ecological framework, taking into account the physical and social environments of her participants, to explore the information-seeking behavior of her 202 older adults, aged 60 and over. The sample included 146 persons who were aged 60–74 (the young-aged), 44 persons aged 75–84 (the old–old), and 12 individuals aged 85 and older (the very old). The data were collected by interview (three with each participant) in both city and rural areas.

A further major multidisciplinary study employing the Fourth Age rather than chronological age was recently completed by Asla.[13,14] Significant findings about the HIB of this specific group emerged from this study, which was undertaken in two retirement communities in the Midwestern US.

Information Needs

Chatman identified six broad areas where older people needed help: 1) *dealing with loss*, including loss of material possessions, friends and family, familiar and known surroundings, health, and control over one's life events; 2) *death and dying*, pertaining not only to one's own death but to the death of loved ones; 3) *the aging process*, the first dimension concerned with maintaining a high level of involvement in social and personal interests, known to be important in successful aging; the second concerned with sexism due to the unequal standards applied to men and women with regard to physical attractiveness as they age; 4) *uncertainty about the future*, focusing on worries such as "being a burden, going to a nursing home, dying, poor health, or financial concerns"; 5) *fear of crime*, particularly affecting women; and 6) *loneliness*, again particularly acute for women who are four times as likely to be widowed as men. Chatman confirmed these broad areas in her own research but also found that the women had significant needs in such areas "as health, financial problems, and general news about activities in which one could become involved" (p. 78).[32]

Williamson's approach[33,34] was to build on earlier projects about information-seeking behavior of the broader community, as well as studies of older people from other fields, for example, Tinker et al.[35] from gerontology and Nussbaum et al.[36] from communication. This enabled comparison with these studies. As with other studies of the information needs of older people, health was the number one topic for the sample as a whole. The second topic of concern was income and finance, and recreation was the third. These topics have all emerged as important in other studies. Other topics, in descending order of importance, included government, consumer, housing and accommodation, retirement benefits, crime and safety, environment, pharmaceuticals, holidays, legal, transportation, family and personal, education, employment, services (e.g., meals on wheels), and volunteer opportunities. Voluntary work was found to be an important topic in phase 2 of Wicks' North American study, the phase involving the younger of his two cohorts who were not living in residential communities.[37] This topic is likely to be a significant interest of baby boomers who are now beginning to be part of the "young aged" group.

Asla's study[13,14] findings, regarding the daily living information needs of his Fourth Age cohort, were similar to those of Williamson. The first of the two exceptions was "adaptive devices" for which about 80% of participants expressed a need for information, mostly for vision and hearing losses. The second was "safe mental challenges," noncompetitive activities such as matching wits with television game shows like *Wheel of Fortune* (these were encompassed, in a more minor way, in Williamson's "recreation" category).

Research focusing on the likely library needs of baby boomers as they retire from their full-time occupations suggests that some of their information needs, right through the stages of their older age, are likely to be different from the past[10,38–40] especially given the better health they will experience and their increased life expectancies. The literature indicates that additional important information needs will be connected to issues of successful retirement and the challenges of aging well, estate planning, travel, genealogy, and employment planning that will be different from the past in that baby boomers may wish to continue working, although in a more flexible capacity than in the past, or may have to work to sustain the lifestyles they want. The latter scenario is more likely in the case of the younger boomers who are likely to face more financial hardship than the older cohort.[41] Projected worker shortages mean that governments are now encouraging people to work longer.

What do we know about the differences in information needs of the three groups within the broad older cohort? The Williamson study found that the younger aged had a need for more information topics and that the range of information needs diminished as people became part of the "old–old" or the "very old" cohorts. The exceptions were the topics health, income, recreation, and pharmaceuticals, where the needs remained strong as people age. Asla, too, found that information needs declined, although this decline could sometimes be slowed by outside intervention, such as providing people in the Fourth Age with opportunities designed to help them maintain their role identities. For example, in one of the retirement communities, residents were given roles such as "librarian" or "artist."

Information Sources

Given that social networks underpinned Chatman's study, she undertook a deep exploration of the interpersonal relationships and support provided to study participants. The residential setting was crucial here as it meant that there were many "neighbors."

Although Chatman found some use of professionals (e.g., doctors, lawyers) as sources of information, she did not find as strong dependence on professionals as Williamson did among the old–old and very old (but not the young aged). Chatman[31] found the mass media to be important in mediating access to the larger world for those who were now isolated from it. The most frequently used medium was television, followed by books, newspapers, radio, and magazines. Wicks[37] and Williamson[33,34] also found that the media were very important, with newspapers, television, printed information, and radio all being in the top six most used sources in the Williamson study. A recent study has focused on media use by older adults.[38] Both Chatman and Williamson found that there was considerable use of libraries that, in Chatman's case, occurred through the outreach service offered to the retirement community.

In the Williamson study, the list of six sources that were very frequently used in information seeking or acquisition, regardless of topic, included (along with the media sources) family members at number 1, and friends at number 3. Nevertheless, there was a difference in source use according to age, which to some extent mirrored the "information needs" picture in that the young aged used more sources, particularly media sources, than the "old–old" or the "very old" cohorts. The two oldest groups set particular store by medical professionals and paraprofessionals for meeting key information needs and also were more reliant on family members and, to a lesser extent, on friends. As Chatman found, "friends" from earlier life stages were not a key information source for some of the very old since members of this group were becoming increasingly isolated due to failing health and the loss of friends through death or other circumstances. Also, they sometimes appeared to be unable to sustain the effort needed to maintain friendships. Asla,[13,14] whose study like Chatman's was undertaken in the small world of retirement communities, found that key information sources were caregivers, usually one specific family member or an individual who was "like family" (including retirement community staff members). Other key informatants were intimate social networks, including other family members and close friends. Other sources included wider social networks; mass media; small world sources such as resident meetings and information grounds; and outside professional and institutional sources. Asla also found proxy information seekers (i.e., people who sought information on behalf of those needing the information) became increasingly important, as also demonstrated by Pálsdóttir's Icelandic study of frail elderly still living in their own homes.[43]

Information Literacy of the Very Old (the Fourth Age)

This is a topic that has been discussed in the literature, to a limited extent. Williamson and Asla[44] discussed issues of whether commonly discussed definitions of information literacy are appropriate for people in the Fourth Age and thus whether general definitions of information may be found wanting for this group. The multiple disabilities experienced by people in the Fourth Age are likely to have a major impact on information literacy, which is usually strongly linked to textual information. Williamson and Asla postulated that the first and foremost element needed for sustaining information literacy in this last stage of life is maintaining a healthy relational system, thus facilitating communication. Another component is attempting the "compression of information illiteracy" where the focus is to help people maintain the information literacy skills, which they have developed earlier in their lives. Asla explores these issues in his thesis.[14]

Residential Communities

The effect of retirement communities on information-seeking behavior was important to the Chatman study,[31,32] the first phase of the Wicks' study[45] and to Asla's study of the Fourth Age.[13,14] The sample for Wicks study consisted of 15 people residing in one of two residences for seniors, the majority of whom were in the "oldest-old" age group (mean age was 83.6). Wicks found that participants relied largely on meetings to find out what was happening in their residential setting. Wicks concluded that "information flow within seniors' accommodation is crucial and becomes even more important as age and functional abilities decline" (p. 23). He discussed the role of staff in this and called for research on information dissemination in residential communities. Asla confirmed these findings about the importance of information provision within the small world. He also found that the opportunity for his participants to do internal voluntary work related to their personal role identities was important. Especially in one of Asla's two retirement communities, management consciously tailored volunteer opportunities to residents' interests. This challenges the conclusion of Wicks who found that lifelong role identity played no significant part in the information behavior of his retirement community participants.

Computers and the Internet

The Internet is making a major difference to the information-seeking behavior of the "young aged" as is made clear in the study of baby boomers by Williamson et al.[15,25,46] The study was undertaken with baby boomers in 2005–2007, meaning that some of the participants would now be part of the "young aged." There was mainly a continuity of information needs as revealed in the earlier major studies, with health information needs being particularly important. While participants, as before, wanted access to a wide variety of information in as many formats as possible, they were making considerable use of the Internet for a range of information needs. As one technologically savvy participant commented, "apparently there's quite a growing trend towards self-diagnosis [on the Internet]." Another spoke of relying a lot "on electronic media...I access electronic databases like Medline to find out about medical issues."

Although the percentage of older people who go online has risen as the technological revolution has proceeded, there are still big differences between younger and older age groups. While, for the first time ever, more than half of Americans aged 65 or older went online in 2012 (59%), they still lagged behind younger Americans in technology adoption (p. 1).[46] Moreover, Internet use and broadband adoption in this age group each fell off notably starting at approximately age 75. Some 68% of Americans in their early 70s went online in 2012, and 55% had broadband at home. By contrast, Internet adoption fell to 47% and broadband adoption fell to 34% among 75–79 year olds (p. 2). Physical, cognitive, and sensory losses are major impediments for the very old or people in the Fourth Age.[47] In Australia, 83% of the population went online in 2012–2013, but age group percentages fluctuated from 97% of people aged 15 to 17, to 46% of those who were 65 or over.[48]

Dickinson and Gregor[49] found that "technology is frequently presented as a panacea for the support needs of the ageing population" but that research did not support that conclusion. Research shortcomings included "failure to distinguish between the effects of training/support and computer use; misattributing causality; [and] inappropriately generalizing results from a different population" (p. 744). With technology use declining as people become increasingly old, electronic information delivery is unlikely to meet their needs. While half of Asla's Fourth Age participants used, or had recently used computers and/or the Internet, by the end of the 2-year study, not one participant had been able to independently master, let alone successfully maintain a new computer or Internet skill. As their physical and cognitive health failed, they needed more and more technical support and services, and had to rely more and more heavily on proxy information seekers.[13,14] Wales[50] saw the Internet for frail and vulnerable older people (including those in daycare centers and residential homes) as "a person issue before a technology issue." While some may be able, with assistance, to learn Internet skills for themselves, a personal approach is needed because of the physical limitations of the people involved and the unfamiliarity of the technology and its benefits to many older people (p. 41). Even the younger aged may not be satisfied by electronic information delivery alone. A key finding of Wicks' study of nonresidential older people[37] was that they strongly preferred obtaining information through interpersonal contact and print sources rather than through electronic delivery despite the increasing preference of governments to delivery of information via the Web (p. 20).

There is a large body of literature about computer use in relation to disabilities, much more likely to affect the very old/oldest old and, to a lesser extent, the old–old. The use of assistive technology, such as large print keyboards and enlarged text on screens, can be greatly beneficial and help to prolong Internet use.[51,52] There is also no shortage of advice in the literature on interface design issues.[53,54]

There has been some useful research undertaken regarding e-health literacy and collaborative learning.[55–57] Xie conducted a series of experiments focused on computer-based training, to encourage participants to play a greater role in their health management. The experiments showed improvements in skills and attitudes. Participants reported that their learning had affected their participation in their own health care and provided positive feedback on the intervention.[57]

Conclusion

To date, there have been few substantial studies of the information needs and behaviors of older adults that have not been limited to a library context. Given the fact that the proportion of older people is increasing and becoming quite significant, at least in the developed world, there is scope for more research to take place. It is important that future research take account of the very wide age span from aged 60 or 65 upward, and that this group is no longer treated as homogeneous in its needs, behaviors, and environmental contexts. It will also be important to include the use of the Internet for information seeking by the older age groups as this area is under-researched at present, but it is particularly important that it should be examined in the context of other sources of everyday life information. Studies that span all sources of everyday life information are likely to be most fruitful, given the finding of the extensive Williamson study (pre-Internet), confirmed in other literature, that "no one source is able to provide all the information needed by a very diverse older group" (p. 267).[58] Williamson, the first author of this entry, added that "it is also imperative to consider the likelihood . . . that older people will be slower than other groups to accept computer-based sources of community information." This prediction of almost 20 years ago is, at this stage, turning out to be correct. With regard to tomorrow's Fourth Agers—those who have employed computers and the Internet in the workplace—the second author's research[14] suggests that the physical, social, and cognitive losses associated with the Fourth Age will make it increasingly difficult to maintain those skills, let alone master new ones. Research into viable outside intervention and support to offset or delay this HIB challenge is badly needed.

REFERENCES

1. Rowland, D. *Aging in Australia*; Longman Cheshire: Melbourne, Vic, Australia, 1991.
2. Graebner, W. *A History of Retirement in America: The Meaning and Function of an American Institution 1885–1978*; Yale University Press: New Haven, CT, 1980.
3. Thane, P. The twentieth century. In *A History of Old Age*; Thane, P., Ed.; Thames Hudson, Ltd: London, U.K., 2005; 263–300.
4. World Health Organization. *Definition of an older or elderly person*; 2009, http://www.who.int/healthinfo/survey/ageingdefnolder/en/print.html.
5. Social Security Administration. *Retirement planner: Full retirement age*; 2014, http://www.ssa.gov/retire2/retirechart.htm/.
6. The Government UK. *State pension age timetables*; 2014, https://www.gov.uk/government/uploads/system/uploads/attachment_data/file/310231/spa-timetable.pdf.
7. Australian Government Department of Human Services. *Age pension eligibility basics*; 2014, http://www.humanservices.gov.au/customer/services/centrelink/age-pension.
8. Lamdin, L.; Fugate, M. *Elder Learning: New Frontier in an Aging Society*; The Oryx Press: Phoenix, AZ, 1997.
9. Turock, B.J. *Serving the Older Adult: A Guide to Library Programs and Information Sources*; Bowker: New York, 1982.
10. Wooliscroft, M. Library services to elderly people. In *Libraries after 1984: Proceedings of the LAA/NZLA Conference: Brisbane*; Library Association of Australia: Sydney, New South Wales, Australia, 1985; 418–427.
11. National Institute on Aging. *The future of aging*; 2003, http://www.niapublications.org/pubs/microscope/chapter5.pdf.
12. Asla, T.; Williamson, K.; Mills, J. The role of information in successful aging: the case for a research focus on the oldest old. Libr. Inf. Sci. Res. **2006**, *28* (1), 49–63.
13. Asla, T.; Williamson, K. Unexplored territory: information behaviour in the Fourth Age. Inf. Res. Int. Electron. J. **March 2014**, *20* (1), http://www.informationr.net/ir/20-1/isic2/isic32.html#.VVvK7GOc6M0.
14. Asla, T. *The Fourth Age: human information behavior and successful aging*; Unpublished doctoral dissertation, Charles Sturt, Bathurst, New South Wales, Australia, 2014, http://www.openthesis.org/documents/Fourth-Age-Human-Information-Behavior-601676.html.
15. Williamson, K.; Bannister, M.; Makin, L.; Johanson, G.; Schauder, D.; Sullivan, J. Wanting it now: baby boomers and the public library of the future. Aust. Libr. J. **2006**, *55* (1), 54–72.
16. US Census Bureau. *The older population: 2010* (2011 census briefs), http://www.census.gov/prod/cen2010/briefs/c2010br-09.pdf.
17. US Census Bureau. *The next four decades. The older population in the United States: 2010 to 2050* (Population estimates and projections), 2010, http://www.census.gov/prod/2010pubs/p25-1138.pdf.
18. U.S. Center for Disease Control. *The state of aging health in America 2013*, http://www.cdc.gov/aging/pdf/state-aging-health-in-america-2013.pdf.
19. Australian Bureau of Statistics. *Where and how do Australia's older people live? Reflecting stories from the 2011 census*; 2013, http://www.abs.gov.au/ausstats/abs@.nsf/Lookup/2071.0main+features602012-2013.
20. Australian Bureau Statistics. *3222.0—Population projections, Australia, 2012 (base) to 2101*, http://www.abs.gov.au/ausstats/abs@.nsf/Lookup/3222.0main+features32012% 20(base)%20to%202101.
21. Perry, C.A. Information services to older adults: initial findings from a survey of suburban libraries. Libr. Q. Inf. Community Policy **2014**, *84* (3), 348–386, http://www.jstor.org/discover/10.1086/676491?uid=3739808&uid=2&uid=4&uid=3739256&sid=21104560579551.
22. American Library Association. Final report to white house conference on aging. Ref. User Serv. Q. **2005**, *45* (2), 130–132.
23. *American Library Association*. Guidelines for library and information services to older adults *(Library Services to an Aging Population Committee, Reference Services Section, Reference and User Services Association of the American Library Association)*; 2008, http://www.ala.org/rusa/resources/guidelines/libraryservices.
24. Decker, E.N. Baby Boomers and the United States public library system. Libr. Hi Technol. **2010**, *28* (4), 605–616.
25. Williamson, K. Creating the new village green: the impact of the retirement of the baby boomers on the public library. APLIS **2009**, *22* (2), 83–88.
26. Ip, L. Public library services to older Pennsylvanians: a decade review. Public Libr. Q. **1992**, *12* (1), 41–61.
27. Gollop, C.J. Health information-seeking behavior and older African American women. Bull. Med. Libr. Assoc. **1997**, *85* (2), 141–146.
28. Yates, C.; Stoodley, I.; Partridge, H.; Bruce, C.; Cooper, H.; Day, G.; Edwards, S. Exploring health information use

by older Australians within everyday life. Libr. Trends **2012**, *60* (3), 460–478.

29. Eriksson-Backa, K.; Ek, S.; Niemelä, R.; Huotari, M. Health information literacy in everyday life: a study of Finns aged 65–79 years. Health Informatics J. **2012**, *18*, 83–94, http://jhi.sagepub.com/content/18/2/83.short/.
30. Williamson, K.; Wright, S.; Schauder, D.; Stillman, L.; Jenkins, L. Levelling the playing field: The role of libraries in providing online services for people with disabilities. Paper presented at *ALIA 2000, Capitalising on Knowledge*, held at the National Convention Centre Canberra, Australia, 23–27 October 2000, http://conferences.alia.org.au/alia2000/proceedings/kirsty.williamson.html.
31. Chatman, E. Channels to a larger social world: older women staying in contact with the greater society. Libr. Inf. Sci. Res. **1991**, *13*, 281–300.
32. Chatman, E. *The Information World of Retired Women*; Greenwood Press: Westport, CT, 1992.
33. Williamson, K. The information needs and information-seeking behaviour of older adults: an Australian study. In *Information Seeking in Context, Proceedings of an International Conference on Research in Information Needs, Seeking and Use in Different Contexts*; Vakkari, P., Savolainen, R., Dervin, B., Eds.; Taylor Graham, London, U.K./Los Angeles, CA, 1997; 337–350. Tampere, Finland.
34. Williamson, K. Discovered by chance: the role of incidental learning acquisition in an ecological model of information use. Libr. Inf. Sci. Res. **1998**, *20* (1), 23–40.
35. Tinker, A.; McCreadie, C.; Salvage, A. *The Information Needs of Elderly People—An Exploratory Study*; Age Concern Institute of Gerontology: London, U.K., 1993.
36. Nussbaum, J.F.; Thompson, T.; Robinson, J.D. *Communication and Aging*; Harper and Row: New York, 1989.
37. Wicks, D.A. Older adults and their information seeking. Behav. Social Sci. Libr. **2004**, *22* (2), 1–26.
38. Niemelä, R.; Huotari, M.L.; Kortelainen, T. Enactment and use of information and the media among older adults. Libr. Inf. Sci. Res. **2012**, *34* (3), 212–219.
39. Kleiman, A. Global greying: successful strategies for bridging information gaps with the elderly population. In *63rd IFLA General Conference Program and Proceedings*, IFLA, 1997; http://www.ifla.org/IV/ifla63/63klea.htm.
40. Nevill, D. Directions and connections for boomers and seniors. Public Libr. **2004**, *43* (5), 256–259.
41. Kahlert, M. The impact of the baby boomers on public libraries: myth and reality. APLIS **2000**, *13* (1).
42. Hamilton, M.; Hamilton, C. *Baby Boomers and Retirement: Dreams, Fears and Anxiety*; Australia Institute: Sydney, New South Wales, Australia, 2006; Discussion Paper 89, http://www.tai.org.au/documents/dp_fulltext/DP89.pdf.
43. Pálsdóttir, Á. Relatives as supporters of elderly peoples' information behaviour. Inf. Res. **2012**, *17* (4) paper 546, http://InformationR.net/ir/17-4/paper546.html.
44. Williamson, K.; Asla, T. Information behaviour of people in the fourth age: implications for the conceptualization of information literacy. Libr. Inf. Sci. Res. **2009**, *31* (2), 76–83.
45. Wicks, D. Micro-roles and the information-seeking behaviour of seniors. In *Proceedings of the 27th Annual Conference of the Canadian Association for Information Science*, Université de Sherbrooke, Quebec, Canada, June 9–11, 1999, http://www.cais-acsi.ca/proceedings/1999/Wicks_1999.pdf.
46. Williamson, K.; Bannister, M.; Sullivan, J. The crossover generation: baby boomers and the role of the public library. J. Librariansh. Inf. Sci. *42* (3), 179–190.
47. Pew Research Center. Older adults and technology use, 2014, http://www.pewinternet.org/files/2014/04/PIP_Seniors-and-Tech-Use_040314.pdf.
48. Stark-Wroblewski, K.; Edelbaum, J.K.; Ryan, J.J. Senior citizens who use e-mail. Educ. Gerontol. **2007**, *33* (4), 293–307.
49. Australian Bureau of Statistics. *8146.0—Household use of information technology 2012–2013*, http://www.abs.gov.au/Ausstats/abs%40.nsf/mf/8146.0.
50. Dickinson, A.; Gregor, P. Computer use has no demonstrated impact on the well-being of older adults.. Int. J. Hum.-Comput. Stud. **2006**, *64* (8), 744–753.
51. Wales, R.J. A person issue before a technology issue. In *HCI and the Older Population, A Workshop held as part of HCI 2004, Leeds, U.K.*; Goodman, J., Brewster, S., Eds.; 2004, 41–42, http://www.dcs.gla.ac.uk/utopia/workshop/lahteenmaki.pdf.
52. Williamson, K.; Stillman, L.; Bow, A. Online information and communication services for people with disabilities. Internet Res.: Electron. Netw. Appl. Policy **1999**, *9* (2), 161–171.
53. Williamson, K.; Wright, S.; Schauder, D.; Bow, A. The Internet for the blind and visually impaired. J. Comput.-Mediat. Commun. **2001**, *7* (1), http://jcmc.indiana.edu/vol7/issue1/williamson.html.
54. Lahteenmaki, M.; Kaikkonen, A. Designing for aged people communication needs. In *HCI and the Older Population, A Workshop held as part of HCI 2004 at Leeds, UK*; Goodman, J., Brewster, S., Eds.; 2004, http://www.dcs.gla.ac.uk/utopia/workshop/lahteenmaki.pdf.
55. Xie, B. Older adults, e-health literacy, and collaborative learning: an experimental study. J. Am. Soc. Inf. Sci. Technol. **2011**, *62* (5), 933–946.
56. Xie, B. Experimenting on the impact of learning methods and information presentation channels on older adults' e-health literacy. J. Am. Soc. Inf. Sci. Technol. **2011**, *62* (9), 1797–1807.
57. Xie, B. Improving older adults' e-health literacy through computer training using NIH online resources. Libr. Inf. Sci. Res. **2012**, *34* (1), 63–71.
58. Williamson, K. *Older adults: information, communication and telecommunications*; Unpublished doctoral dissertation: RMIT, Melbourne, Victoria, Australia, 1995.

One-Person Libraries

Judith A. Siess
Information Bridges International, Inc., Champaign, Illinois, U.S.A.

Abstract

A one-person librarian (OPL) is a person who works in a one-person library. What does that mean? An OPL is the only librarian (or only professional librarian) in a library or information center. The OPL does everything from acquisitions, cataloging, circulation, and reference, even dusting the shelves and vacuuming the carpet, if necessary. It is a situation in which there are no professional peers with whom to share problems and ideas, or to commiserate with when things get tough. The OPL often does not have to go through layers of administration to get approval for purchases or new programs. OPLs know exactly what is going on their libraries: what is being checked out, what questions are being asked, who is using the library, etc. The OPL is often perceived as the "information guru" in the organization—the one to whom everyone comes for answers. Finally, any and all successes (and, of course, failures) of the library are also those of the OPL. They can make of it whatever is in their vision and power.

Other names for an OPL are solo, sole-charge librarian, or one-man band. The movement, and even the term OPL, can be attributed to Guy St. Clair, the original founder of *The One-Person Library: A Newsletter for Librarians and Management.*

INTRODUCTION

A one-person librarian (OPL) is a person who works in a one-person library. What does that mean? An OPL is the only librarian (or only professional librarian) in a library or information center. The OPL does everything from acquisitions, cataloging, circulation, and reference, even dusting the shelves and vacuuming the carpet, if necessary. It is a situation in which there are no professional peers with whom to share problems and ideas, or to commiserate with when things get tough. The OPL often does not have to go through layers of administration to get approval for purchases or new programs. OPLs know exactly what is going on their libraries: what is being checked out, what questions are being asked, who is using the library, etc. The OPL is often perceived as the "information guru" in the organization—the one to whom everyone comes for answers. Finally, any and all successes (and, of course, failures) of the library are also those of the OPL. They can make of it whatever is in their vision and power.

Other names for an OPL are solo, sole-charge librarian, or one-man band. "Until about twenty-five years ago, one-person librarianship as a recognized branch of specialized librarianship and information services did not exist."[1] The movement, and even the term OPL, can be attributed to Guy St. Clair, original publisher of *The One-Person Library: A Newsletter for Librarians and Management.*

Although there are OPLs all over the world, this entry focuses on their history and activities in English-speaking countries, mainly the United States, Canada, the United Kingdom, and Australasia.

BRIEF HISTORY OF THE OPL MOVEMENT

1972: Guy St. Clair was invited to lead a discussion at the 1972 Special Libraries Association (SLA) annual conference in Boston, Massachusetts, on "The One-Man Library." He said he would do so only if the title was changed to "The One-Person Library." This is the first instance of the term OPL being used. Hundred of OPLs attended the session, overflowing the room.

1976: St. Clair's first article on the OPL was published, followed by several workshops and seminars.

1984: St. Clair founded *The One-Person Library* newsletter with Andrew Berner.

Early 1980s: The One-Man Bands group of Association of Special Libraries and Information Bureaux (ASLIB) was formed in the United Kingdom. The group is no longer active.

1986: The first book on OPLs, *Managing the One-Person Library*, was published by St. Clair and Joan Williamson.

1986: The One-Person Library Support Group was established as part of the Toronto, Canada, chapter of the SLA. First chair was Penny Lipman, Rio Algom, Ltd. This is the first OPL group we know of anywhere in the world. It is still very active.

1987: The first 2-day continuing education course on one-person librarianship was taught at the SLA annual conference in Anaheim by Guy St. Clair, who taught similar courses until 1998.

1988: At the SLA annual conference in Denver, Martha Rose (Marty) Rhine led two roundtables on one-person libraries. She circulated a list to obtain participants' names

Encyclopedia of Library and Information Sciences, Fourth Edition DOI: 10.1081/E-ELIS4-120044565

and addresses so they could keep in touch. Ninety-nine people signed the list.

1988: Using the list as a base, Marty formed the Solo Librarians Caucus of the SLA, with an initial membership of about 100.

1991: The Solo Librarians Caucus became a full-fledged division of the SLA. Judith Siess was the first chair.

1991: Guy St. Clair was inaugurated as president of the SLA.

1991: *The Best of OPL* was published, consisting of selections from the first 5 years of the newsletter.

1995: One-Person Australian Librarians (OPAL) was formed as a special interest group of the Australian Library and Information Association after the Health, Law and Specials Conference in Sydney. Georgina Dale, Toni Silson (now Kennedy), and Therese Bendeich were its first leaders.

1996: The first German OPL Roundtable was held, organized by Evelin Morgenstern of the Deutsches Bibliotheksinstitut/German Library Institute (DBI), Berlin, Germany.

1997: AspB (the German Special Libraries Working Group), devoted its biennial conference to small special (OPL) libraries.

1997: VdDB (Verein der Diplom-Bibliothekare), an association of professional librarians in Germany, established the OPL Kommission, with Regina Peeters as chair. This special working group offers continuing professional education programs for OPLs at least twice per year.

1997: *Das Robinsoon-Crusoe Syndrom und was man dagegen tun kann* (The Robinson Crusoe Syndrome and What You Can Do About It) was published, with reports from 24 German OPLs describing their work.

1997: The Solo Librarian's Sourcebook by Judith Siess was published.

1997: The first meeting of Special Librarians (many of them OPLs) in the Midlands (SLIM) was held in Birmingham, England. Chris Crabtree and Margaret Brittin were the founders.

1998: A Most Delicate Monster: The One-Professional Special Library by Jean Dartnall was published in Australia.

1998: Information Bridges International purchased *The One-Person Library* newsletter. Judith Siess was the new editor/publisher.

1999: Special Librarians in London (SLIL) was founded by Bert Washington of Sports Marketing Surveys. This function is now fulfilled by the Industrial and Commercial Libraries Group of CILIP.

1999: The Workplace Libraries discussion list was launched April 1999, by the Library Association (now CILIP, Chartered Institute of Library and Information Professionals; United Kingdom). (Now discontinued.)

1999: An electronic discussion list just for OPLs was established by the Library Association. (Also discontinued.)

1999: The Workplace '99 Initiative was started by the LA to increase awareness of commerce, industry, government, and voluntary institution libraries. Lyndsay Rees-Jones and Mark Field are the LA Professional Advisors for Special Libraries. (Discontinued, but Rees-Jones is still actively assisting solos.)

1999: A Solo Professional network was set up by Steve Witowski of the East Midlands Branch of the LA. (No longer active.)

2000: The first meeting of Special Librarians in Cambridge (SLIC) was held in England. Lis Riley was the founder. (Still active.)

2000: OPAL published its first book, *Evaluating Websites.*

2000: Initiative Fortbildung für wissenschaftliche Spezialbibliotheken und verwandte Einrichtungen (Initiative for Special Libraries and Similar Institutions) was formed in German as DBI was being dissolved.

2004. The OPL Archives were established by Judith Siess at the University of Illinois at Urbana-Champaign (where both she and Guy St. Clair received their library degrees). Material in the archives includes copies of all issues of *The One-Person Library* newsletter; books on OPLs from the United States, the United Kingdom, and Australia; copies of many articles by and about solos and OPLs.

2005. *The Essential OPL, 1998–2004: The Best of Seven Years of The One-Person Library: A Newsletter for Librarians and Management*, was published by Judith Siess, with Jonathan Lori.

2006. *The New OPL Sourcebook* was published by Judith Siess.

How many OPLs are there? Because of their size, there is no accurate count of OPLs, but the following figures are available. The SLA estimates that close to 60% of their more than 11,000 members are OPLs. That is nearly 7000 OPLs in special libraries alone! (The Solo Librarians Division of SLA grew to nearly 1000 members before a decline that paralleled that of SLA as a whole. In 2007 there were nearly 700 members, the fifth largest division in the organization.) A large percentage of U.S. public libraries have no more than one professional librarian. Most school libraries have only one professional (if that many), as do most hospital libraries. Small law firms are unlikely to have more than one professional, and prison and church or synagogue libraries are lucky if they have any degreed staff. There seems to be a consensus that about one-third of the world's libraries are one-person or one-professional operations.

WHERE DO OPLs WORK?

Most OPLs work in special libraries. A special library is one serving a specialized or limited clientele, with specialized or limited materials and services. The emphasis is often on providing information, rather than on books. The collection is usually small. The OPL nearly always reports to a nonlibrarian, and the library is part of, but not considered critical to, the parent organization's main mission. Most OPLs (about 80%) are solo by chance, with only 20% by choice. However, a lot of OPLs that started by chance now like it so much that they would not go back to a large library.

According to St. Clair and Williamson,[2] a library with an OPL may be the organization's first library, newly established and unsure of how many staff it needs, destined to grow to include a larger staff. It can also be a downsized library, formerly having several librarians, but due to less demand, less money, or less awareness of need, now be reduced to one professional. Or, it can also be a right-size library, one that needs only one well-trained and efficient professional to serve the organization's information needs. This is probably the most common situation.

Although many OPLs work for corporations, there are other opportunities. Following are just a few of them.

Law Libraries

Librarians serving private practice or small law or bar associations are often OPLs, as are law librarians in government institutions such as courts or agencies, and some public law libraries, but these make up only about 15% of law librarians. Most law librarians in academia and law schools, where a library is required for accreditation, are not OPLs. Only 29% of law librarians have law degrees, but nearly all (80%) have library degrees. Most employers look to their law librarians to save billable hours of the lawyers, to save attorneys' time and billable hours looking for information, and to add to revenues by having the librarian perform billable information searches for clients. Sometimes they are also looking for other capabilities, such as archives, records management, managing dockets, conflicts checking, and supervising paralegals. The future will probably see an expansion of the law librarian into other areas, including skill-based resource management, client current awareness services, research for client and practice development, supporting speaking opportunities (speeches and seminars), research or reference and/or technology training for clients, internal and client newsletters, web page design, content, management, coordinating continuing legal education programs, managing paralegals, and formal legal research training for new staff. (Note: If librarians are asked to perform research for clients, they should be sure it is included in the firm's profitability analysis.) The issues facing legal OPLs are the need for rapid delivery of information, often with price insensitivity; the currency and accuracy of the information; the high degree of confidentiality expected; deciding the fine line between legal research and interpretation; and dealing with summer interns or law clerks. Also, academic law librarians are becoming increasingly responsible for teaching legal research techniques to students. Other issues not unique to law librarianship are timeliness, currency, accuracy, thoroughness, detail, rising costs, and burnout, and an emphasis on the practical uses of information. Academic law librarians get more involved in research, history, and comparative law. In a summary of several studies of how lawyers find information, researchers found that 50–60% of them do not go to librarians for help, even if they have trouble finding the information themselves. They do not use the librarian to learn how to search, only to provide the documents they identify from their own search.

Prison or Jail Libraries

Most states require the provision of access to legal materials to inmates (although some have decided to close all their prison libraries). Most prison libraries remain one-person positions, despite staffing-level recommendations. Most prison librarians are professionals. Prison librarians have problems motivating their inmate assistants due to turnover and lack of a strong work ethic. They are also concerned with confidentiality, and the dividing line between legal reference and legal advice. Another hot current issue is the computerization of prison libraries. Prisons are reluctant to replace books with computers because of the potential for online crime. Jail libraries are usually smaller and less likely to hire a professional. The emphasis is on access to legal materials and recreational reading as a form of behavior control or self-improvement. Lack of funds, censorship, and low status are major issues. Personality traits needed by prison or jail librarians include an understanding of the political climate of the institution, survival skills, patience, a sense of humor, ability to follow the rules, and a professional demeanor.

Hospital Libraries

Hospitals used to be required to employ professional librarians for accreditation; however, they are now only required to provide access to appropriate materials. However, most hospitals still have libraries and librarians. Except in the large medical schools and hospitals, the librarian is often an OPL. The needs of physicians are similar to those of lawyers—rapid delivery of current and accurate information, price irrelevant, and with a practical application. Many hospital librarians are also involved in patient service, archives, consumer health information, and administration of physician continuing education. Some librarians are even part of the treatment team—this practice is increasing with the advent of higher training levels for librarians and the computerization of medical information. Hospital libraries frequently have a staff of volunteers of varying degrees of training and commitment with which to work. This may or may not help the OPL's workload. The Medical Libraries Association offers a certification program in medical librarianship. Although certification is not required for all medical librarian positions, it is strongly encouraged.

Museum or Zoo Libraries

Museums, zoos, and libraries acquire, describe, and make accessible to us the records of human experience, covering life sciences, education, business, philosophy, and art. Not all museums or zoos have libraries. The American Zoo Association/Librarian Special Interest Group (AZA/LSIG) consists of zoo and aquarium librarians, as well as individuals in zoos and aquariums that are responsible for their institution's library and operations. Formed in 1978, AZA/LSIG now has more than 90 members from zoos and aquariums spread across three continents. Some zoos use volunteers to staff their libraries, whereas many others combine the job of librarian with another position. These libraries have historically been underfunded, understaffed, and underused. Facilities range from just a collection of books and magazines for staff use to a fully organized and professional-directed information collection. The library is likely to have a relatively large number of volunteers. Nearly all the libraries provide reference service to staff, members, and the general public. Few circulate items beyond the staff, provide online searching, perform document delivery, or have access to the Internet.

Church or Synagogue Libraries

Many churches and synagogues have libraries. Some are staffed by volunteers (often a retired librarian or schoolteacher), but some of the larger ones hire professional librarians. Nearly all these are one-person positions. The church library functions as a centralized place for materials for church programs (a sort of learning and resource center), with the specific aim of promoting the spiritual development of its users. There are no specific educational requirements for the church librarian, but dedication, friendliness, ability to work with details, neatness, patience, and a sense of humor are suggested—the same criteria as for an OPL. Funding is usually minimal, as is pay, but it is a rewarding field for the dedicated.

Public Libraries

Surprisingly, a large number of OPLs work in public libraries. Nearly 80% of public libraries serve populations of fewer than 25,000 and are staffed by no more than one professional.[3] The library director is the heart of the library, representing the library to the community, the board, and the staff. Public librarians face similar issues as corporate or other types of librarians: a sense of intimacy with their patrons, overwork, doing it all, dealing with nonlibrarians as supervisors (the library board). The librarian and the board are often at odds about the role each should play. OPLs in public libraries also face some unique issues: building maintenance, bond issue, etc. Another issue unique to public libraries is the relationship to the school system. Some communities may not understand the necessity to support two separate library systems. Pay for directors of small public libraries is often abysmal; there are personnel issues and long hours, but, as with all OPLs, you run the show.

Public or Private School Libraries

School librarians and media specialists are often OPLs. Many of them serve two or more school libraries, with volunteers (often students) staffing the library when the librarian is not there. All professional school librarians must also have a teaching certification. They are seen as an extension of the classroom and often assist teachers with special projects, as well as running the library and teaching library skills to the students. Some even have such varied duties as story hours, teaching reading or English, computer instruction, advisor to student groups, running the bookstore, and lunchroom supervision.

Information Brokers

The work of information brokers falls into two main categories: information retrieval and delivery, and information organization. The latter is often called information consulting. He or she may design and produce databases, perform primary and secondary research, obtain documents, perform abstracting and indexing, evaluate libraries, manage libraries, perform outreach and public relations, perform translations, act as a records manager, train librarians, write or edit books, articles, or newsletters—or almost anything else you can imagine. What does it take to be a successful information broker? Patience, speaking and writing and telephone skills, organizational skills, a sense of humor, ability to integrate disparate concepts, problem-solving ability, perseverance, broad base of knowledge, dedication and hard work, enjoying working alone, ability making decisions, ability to prioritize, energy, intelligence, creativity, computer skills, confidence, optimism, and the ability to sell yourself and your services—in other words, the same skills as a good OPL.

Market Researchers

An increasing number of librarians work in the competitive intelligence (CI) field, usually as OPLs. CI is the gathering of information that will assist a company in maintaining its competitive edge. (It is not, as some think, only gathering information about one's competitors. It also includes information about a company's customers, keeping up with technology and anything else that makes the company better able to compete.) Librarians are exceptionally well qualified to do CI, being trained to search for, analyze, organize, and disseminate information. They are experienced in working in an interdisciplinary environment. They already have their own networks. Other traditional library competencies that transfer well to CI include online searching, the reference interview, current awareness, knowledge of bibliographic tools, computer skills, written presentation skills, and time management.

Other Opportunities

The nontraditional sector is probably the fastest-growing area of librarianship. A librarian's skills can be applied in many fields. One can be a representative for a library supplier, a writer or publisher, a consultant, work for a market research firm, a not-for-profit organization, a government agency, a document delivery service, an association library, in website development, or for a library consortium or network. Job opportunities are limited only by your imagination, creativity, interest, and persistence.

WHAT DOES AN OPL DO?

The tasks of an OPL fall into the following categories:

Managerial

- Manage any clerical employees or volunteers available, including hiring, discipline, and firing.
- Manage one's own time, including learning to deal with interruptions.
- Create and distribute publicity for the library. This may include a weekly newsletter, articles in the organization's publications, and open houses.
- Organize library files and, because there is no one else to do it, file.
- Write monthly and annual reports to management.
- Prepare, distribute, and evaluate user surveys to determine user desires, attitudes, and satisfaction.
- Keep and analyze a wide variety of statistics.

Technical

- Locate, evaluate, and order books and magazines, often for the entire organization, not just the library.
- Follow up on orders.
- Check books and magazines in and out, and keep statistics on what is and is not being used.
- Answer questions from people within the organization, whether they come in by telephone, mail, e-mail, fax, or in person. These requests for information may use resources in the library or involve ordering articles from another library. Often these are "rush" requests with a deadline that can be as short as within the hour. Other questions involve extensive research and a written summary.
- Teach users how to find information, in the library and on the Internet.
- OPLs are often in charge of the organization's audiovisual equipment (slide projectors, etc.).
- Evaluate new electronic services and sources; arrange a demonstration or trial period, if possible; and recommend or make the final purchase decision. This may include computer, systems, and software, too.
- Troubleshoot or repair equipment such as computers, photocopiers, printers, and even entire networks.
- OPLs are often asked to create web pages for an organization's Intranet or Extranet, and sometimes serve as the organization's webmaster.
- In addition to the above, OPLs are often in charge of an organization's archives or records. OPLs in hospitals are often given responsibility for tracking physician continuing medical education and/or patient or consumer education materials.

Professional

- Participate in local, regional, national, or even international library organizations and networks. OPLs often serve in leadership positions.
- Keep up with the library and information worlds by reading professional literature and following electronic discussions.
- Arrange for one's own continuing education—attending seminars, professional conferences, and courses.

Financial

- Pay bills.
- Purchase office supplies, catalog cards, copy paper, computer media, etc.
- Prepare the library budget.
- Track library expenses.

Why would anyone want to be an OPL? The three most common reasons are independence, variety, and an enhanced feeling of self-worth. OPLs enjoy the ability to run their show, plan their own schedule, and set their own priorities, with a minimum of supervision (and interference). The life of an OPL also has its drawbacks. The most commonly mentioned problems are professional isolation, lack of clerical support, the need for reporting to a nonlibrarian, and low pay.

Because many OPLs are OPLs by choice, obviously the pros must outweigh (or at least equal) the cons. Perhaps the key is in fitting the right person to the job. Most people agree that an OPL should be flexible and creative, biased toward service, able to share and build coalitions, idealistic, resourceful, curious, self-confident, and patient. In addition, the OPL should be able to work alone; manage time, think analytically, and see the big picture; have a sense of humor, good organizational skills, good recall, excellent oral and writing skills, and a high tolerance for frustration. Can these skills be taught? They probably cannot, but the specific tools and techniques to make the most of them can be learned, either in library school, on the job, or through continuing education. An OPL must also have confidence in making good decisions, an entrepreneurial attitude, comfort with networking, proficiency in gathering supporters, a lot of flexibility, good time management and balancing of priorities, a love for the profession, ability to cope with lots of bosses and patrons who think they are the only client, a readiness to take risks and learn something new every day, a passion and enthusiasm, and a willingness to dive in to do anything.

HOW DOES AN OPL HELP THEIR ORGANIZATION ACHIEVE ITS GOALS?

All employees must be involved in their organization's goals, but this is especially important for OPLs. They must ensure that the library is seen as a critical part of the organization and that it is involved in mission-critical issues. The library's mission statement must closely mirror the mission of the organization. The library must also be relevant to the lives of its users. The OPL knows more about the organization and its business, the users and their needs, and how to collect, organize, and disseminate information than anyone else in the organization because of its strategic position as the information hub.

Power makes organizations run. An OPL must know the organization's corporate culture—its shared beliefs, values, and assumptions. The OPL also learns how the organization is formally structured and how it actually works, who is in power and who is not; what information the organization needs, who needs it, how it flows within the organization, team dynamics, and communication.

The OPL's customers are management, other professionals, secretaries and other clerical staff, manufacturing workers, the mailroom, and perhaps even the cleaning staff. All these are potential customers of the library. Ideally, all should be treated equally, but it would be foolish not to recognize that one will be much faster to respond to an inquiry from the president or managing director of the organization than from a worker on the assembly line. However, it is the importance of the answer to the continued existence of the organization, not the position of the customer on the organizational chart that matters. Users do not want information, they want answers. They want their problems solved. This answer could be an article, a book, a list of references or websites, or even a summary report with the answer to the question. This is how the library can best add value. Clients also expect the library to help lower their cost of doing business—by saving them time and, therefore, money. Another way the OPL helps the organization is by making information convenient for them. This can mean anything from taking requests over the Internet to putting databases and research services on their desktops.

OPLs must be proactive and anticipate what customers will need and be sure they can meet the demand. This involves planning, thinking, anticipating, and taking the initiative. The keys are communication with and to customers, and taking responsibility for information (evaluating it for content and quality). OPLs find out what customers need by observing, listening, and reading both the library and industry literature.

The OPL should also be involved in "knowledge management." Knowledge management is the art of making creative, effective and efficient use of all the knowledge and information available to an organization all for the benefit of clients. Its implementation requires a review of the organization's values, culture, infrastructure, and management of intellectual assets. Knowledge management is a new focus on information and knowledge, creating a knowledge-valuing environment, where information is shared, managed, and used. Librarians in general, and OPLs in particular, are perfectly situated to be the knowledge management leaders in an organization. They already understand the organization and its information flows. Their people skills and customer service orientation allow them to work well with all levels of the organization, from the factory floor to the highest levels of management. They can find information, evaluate it, and produce analytical reports of its significance.

THE FUTURE OF ONE-PERSON LIBRARIANSHIP

Librarianship will increasingly depend on technology. However, the computer or the Internet will not be able to answer every question, will not replace the human touch, and cannot greet the user with a smile. Technology must be seen and designed as just another tool to solve problems, not an end in itself, leading us only to find new ways to use new technology. The costs, benefits, and impact on users of any proposed innovation must be weighed before its adoption.

Many people expect that the information user of the future will not have to come to the library at all, relying on Internet, phone, or e-mail access. Libraries may indeed go virtual, but there will always be a need for a physical repository somewhere and someone to decide what to put in it, devise an order for it, and arrange access to it.

More and more librarians, especially OPLs, will be working outside libraries in an organization or on their own. The location of a librarian in a physical library may be unnecessary and, in some cases, undesirable. In the corporate sector, librarians are moving out of the library into the business units, working alongside other professionals to provide the information needed for informed decisions right at the point of the decision. Partnering or team-building skills will become even more vital in the future in the corporate world. This is also important outside the for-profit arena, as librarians are increasingly required to work as part of research or project teams in organizations, participate in clinical rounds in hospital rounds, and support teams of attorneys working on large, involved cases. In the electronic future, the librarian's world will become wider.

Medical librarians are already moving out of the library and into the future. One example is clinical librarianship, where the medical librarian receives special, accelerated medical training and then becomes a part of the patient team. The librarian accompanies the physicians on rounds. Equipped with a laptop computer, a wireless modem, an Internet connection, and access to medical databases, the librarian can often provide instant answers to clinical questions. When the answer cannot be found immediately, the librarian returns to the library (or their desk or cubicle) and engages in a lengthier search, delivering the answer (not raw data or articles) to the physician within hours.

Instead of OPLs being downsized out of existence as many fear, it is likely more will be created. Some of these will be, unfortunately, from the downsizing of larger libraries, but many more will come from the realization that information is absolutely necessary for an organization's success and that a trained information professional, that is to say a librarian and not a computer person, is the best one to handle this responsibility. To quote St. Clair:

> [managers] will find that they get more value for their money by employing one highly skilled and effective librarian/information specialist instead of a team - however small - of generalists who are not as skilled. There is also recognition in the profession that one-person librarianship just might become a standard for library staffing in the future. [Often] one excellent, efficient, and enthusiastic librarian or information specialist is preferable to two or more who do not provide the same level of service for users.[4]

Although there have been drastic changes in the information climate since he wrote these words, the desire for good library service or good information delivery has not changed. Because of the following, the OPL more than ever is able to serve an organization's information needs with little or no assistance:

- Advances in technology, including networking, electronic information available online or on the Web at little or no cost (in money or time)
- Concentration of librarian resources on mission-critical functions and outsourcing or elimination of nonessential services
- Increasing capability of users to find answers to noncomplex questions, or for law librarians or attorneys using electronic resources to perform their own legal research, thus allowing librarians to focus on business, medical, or international issues
- Better training and education for librarians in general and OPLs in particular; a heightened sense of professionalism by OPLs, accompanied by more attendance at continuing education events; and increased interpersonal networking and establishing of professional cooperative relationships

There will, of course, continue to be challenges. The idea that "everything is on the Internet and is free" is a serious problem. OPLs must show their clientele that they have only found the tip of the information iceberg and the rest can best be found with the assistance of a librarian. A second major challenge is downsizing. All librarians, but OPLs in particular, need to demonstrate their value to management on a daily basis. They have a responsibility not only to keep the information professional in the organization, but also to demonstrate to future generations of librarians how great it is to be an OPL.

Fundamentally, OPLs around the world are the same; yet, there are some critical differences. The concept of one-person librarianship has not been well known outside the United States, Canada, the United Kingdom, Australasia, and Germany. Although there undoubtedly are many OPLs around the world—in fact, they may predominate—there is no good way of reaching them. They are most likely working in "less-developed" nations in small libraries in small communities or charitable institutions, and are unlikely to be degreed librarians (or to have even had any library training at all). Managers and even library directors are not library professionals. Library work is not valued. Job responsibilities for trained librarians may be limited to technical processing (choosing books, cataloging them, checking them in and out), with no time for helping people with their information needs.

The full potential of technology is unrealized in much of the world. Even e-mail and electronic lists cannot be used because some of the smaller libraries do not have access to a network, but need to dial up to use their e-mail and they only get the chance to do this once or twice per day. Some libraries do not even have a computer. In many countries, library resources and organizations are less plentiful. Problems with currency fluctuations and the resultant high cost of online services and journals can cause major problems for many OPLs. Educational systems outside the United States are structured quite differently. There is not always an emphasis on customer service.

It is almost certain that there will be more OPLs in corporate and other institutional settings, and probably even in public and academic settings. Although some may see this as a bad thing, it can be an opportunity for those who enjoy working alone. Networking is now and will continue to be imperative for survival. Fortunately, this is getting easier every day. There are multitudes of electronic discussion lists. Organizations serving OPLs are growing and beginning to cooperate. For those in developing countries, networking is even more important. Therefore, it is incumbent on experienced OPLs to establish and maintain mentoring relationships with OPLs elsewhere so that they will no longer feel alone.

REFERENCES

1. St. Clair, G. *Dealing with downsizing: A guide for the information services practitioner*; SMR International: New York, 1996; Vol. 6 SMR special report.
2. St. Clair, G.; Williamson, J.W. *Managing the New One-Person Library*, 2nd Ed. Bowker Saur: New York, 1992.
3. St. Clair, G. The one-person library: an essay on essentials. Spec. Libr. **1976**, *67*(3), 233–238.
4. St. Clair, G. The one-person library: an essay on essentials re-visited. Spec. Libr. **1987**, *78*(4), 267.

BIBLIOGRAPHY

Articles

1. Buchanan, L. The smartest little company in the world. Inc. **1999**, *21*(1), 42–54.
2. DiMattia, S. Going solo: wise is a force of one. Libr. J. **2000**, *125*(12), 40–41—Cover article, profile of Olga Wise, Compaq, Austin, TX.
3. Siess, J.A. The MLS is not enough: one SOLO librarian's view. One-Pers. Libr. **1995**, *12*(5), 4–7.
4. Siess, J.A. The future of SOLO librarianship. AALL Spectr. **1997**, *2*(2), 10–12 —Cover article in journal of the American Association of Law Libraries.
5. Siess, J.A. Flying solo: librarian, manage thyself. Am. Libr. **1999**, *30*(2), 32–34.
6. St. Clair, G. The one-person library: an essay on essentials. Spec. Libr. **1976**, *67*(3), 233–238.
7. St. Clair, G. The one-person library: an essay on essentials re-visited. Spec. Libr. **1987**, *78*(4), 263–270.

Books

1. Berner, A. St. Clair, G.L. *The Best of OPL: Five Years of the One-Person Library*, Special Libraries Association: Washington, DC, 1990; —Especially great for new OPLs, a history of the profession in very readable form (general considerations, management strategies, advocacy, marketing, profiles, helpful tips, bibliography).
2. Berner, A. St.; Clair, G.L. *The Best of OPL, II: Selected Readings from The One-Person Library: a Newsletter for Librarians and Management, 1990–1994*, Special Libraries Association: Washington, DC, 1996.
3. Kennedy, S.E., Ed. *Reference Sources for Small and Medium-Size Libraries*, 6th Ed.; American Library Association: Chicago, IL, 1999.
4. Moorman, J. *Running a Small Library: A How-To-Do-It Manual*; Neal-Schuman: New York, 2006.
5. Peeters, R. The Robinson Crusoe Syndrome and What You Can Do About It—24 detailed descriptions of OPLs in Germany with a strong emphasis on pragmatic approaches to problem solving (in German). 1987.
6. St. Clair, G.; Williamson, J. *Managing the One-Person Library*; Butterworth-Heineman: Stoneham, MA, 1986.
7. St. Clair, G.; Williamson, J. *Managing the New One-Person Library*, 2nd Ed.; Bowker Saur: New York, 1992.
8. Siess, J.A. *The SOLO Librarian's Sourcebook*; Information Today, Inc.: Medford, NJ, 1997; (out of print).
9. Siess, J.A. *The OPL Sourcebook*; Information Today, Inc: Medford, NJ, 2001; (out of print).
10. Siess, J.A. *The New OPL Sourcebook: A Guide for Solo and Small Libraries*; Information Today, Inc.: Medford, NJ, 2006.
11. Siess, J.A.; Lorig, J. *The Essential OPL, 1998–2004: The Best of Seven Years of The One-Person Library: A Newsletter for Librarians and Management*; Scarecrow Press: Metuchen, NJ, 2005.
12. White, H.S. *Librarians and the Awakening from Innocence: A Collection of Papers*; G.K. Hall: New York, 1989; —The first collection of Herb's writings, this should be read, memorized, and followed by all librarians.

Journals

1. *Flying Solo*, Special Libraries Association: Washington, DC Solo Librarians Division —Quarterly, free with membership.
2. *National Network*, Medical Libraries Association: Chicago, IL Hospital Libraries Section —Quarterly, included with membership.
3. *Rural Libraries*, Clarion University: Clarion, PA Center for the Study of Rural Librarianship—Semi-annual.

Associations

1. Association of Independent Information Professionals (AIIP), http://www.aiip.org, 7044 So. 13th St., Oak Creek WI 53154-1429 U.S.A., voice: 1-414-766-0421, fax: 1-414-768-8001, email: aiipinfo@aiip.org; the premiere organization for independent librarians outside of traditional libraries, members must own or rent their own facilities (not for library fee-based services within libraries).
2. Kommission-fur One-Person Librarians, part of the Verein der Diplombibloiothekare (VdDB) and Berufsberband Infor mation und Bibliothek (BIB), website: http://homepages.uni-tuebingen.de/juergen.plieninger/vddb-opl/, c/o Regina Peeter s, Europaisches Ubersetzer-Kollegium, Kuhstrasse 15–19, 47638 Straelen, Germany, voice: 02834-7158, fax: 02834-7544, email: euk.straelen@t-online.de, discussion list: send email to majordomo@izn.niedersachsen.de, "subscribe opl".
3. One Person Australian Libraries (OPAL) of the Australian Library and Information Association (ALIA), website: http://www.alia.org.au/sigs/opals, membership in ALIA required to join OPAL; Australian Library and Information Association (ALIA), PO Box E441, Kingston ACT 2604, Australia, voice: 61-02-6285-1877, fax: 61-02-6282-2249, email: enquiry@alia.org.au; discussion list: ALIAOPAL, listserv@alia.org.au.
4. OPL Section, Private Law Libraries Special Interest Group, American Association of Law Libraries, focuses on

OPLs in private law firms, discussion list: PLL-OPLL-L, listproc@aall.wuacc.edu.

5. Solo Librarians Division, Special Libraries Association, website: http://www.sla.org/divisions/dsol membership in SLA required to join the Solo Division. (Special Libraries Association, 1700 18th St., NW, Washington DC, 2009, voice: 1-202-234-4700); discussion list: SLA-DSOL, to subscribe, send an email to sla-dsol@lists.sla.org with message subscribe sla-dsol yourfirstname, your lastname; discussions of OPL issues and quick answers to your questions, if you're only going to join one list, it should be this one, membership in the Division or SLA not required.

Others

1. OPL Archives, University of Illinois at Urbana-Champaign, Library, http://web.library.uiuc.edu/ahx/ala/archon/controlcard.php?id=8287&q=85%2F9%2F10.
2. Paul, M.; Crabtree, S. *Strategies for Special Libraries*; Freeland Library and Information Services: Camberwell, Victoria, Australia, 1995.
3. SMR International: New York SMR International Special Reports (out of print, but may be available from some libraries).
4. St. Clair, G. *Finances and value: How the one-person library is paid for; SMR special report*; SMR International: New York, 1995a.
5. St. Clair, G. *One-Person Librarianship: The Authority of the Customer*; SMR International: New York, 1995b.
6. St. Clair, G. *The One-Person Library in the Organization*; SMR International: New York, 1995c.
7. St. Clair, G. *What the One-Person Library Does*; SMR International: New York, 1995d.
8. St. Clair, G. *Dealing with downsizing: A guide for the information services practitioner; SMR special report 6*, SMR International: New York, 1996a.
9. St. Clair, G.L. *One-Person Libraries: Checkliste als Orienteirungshilfe fur den Betreib von OPLs*, Deutsches Bibliotheksinstitut: Berlin—in German, 1996b.
10. St. Clair, G.L. *One-Person Libraries: Aufgaben und Management. Handlungshilfe fur den Betrieb von OPLs*, Deutsches Bibliotheksinstitut: Berlin—in German, 1998; Arbeitshilfen fur Spezialbbliotheken, Band 8.

Online Catalog Subject Searching

Danny C.C. Poo
School of Computing, Department of Information Systems, National University of Singapore, Singapore

Christopher S.G. Khoo
School of Communication and Information, Nanyang Technological University, Singapore

Abstract

The Online Public Access Catalog (OPAC) is an information retrieval system characterized by short bibliographic records, mainly of books, journals, and audiovisual materials available in a particular library. This, coupled with a Boolean search interface and a heterogeneous user population with diverse needs, presents special problems for subject searching by end users. To perform effective subject searching in the OPAC system requires a wide range of knowledge and skills. Various approaches to improving the OPAC design for subject searching have been proposed and are reviewed in this entry. The trend toward Web-based OPAC interfaces and the developments in Internet and digital library technologies present fresh opportunities for enhancing the effectiveness of the OPAC system for subject searching.

OVERVIEW

An OPAC database records are usually derived from the MARC (MAchine Readable Cataloging) format. The records are brief bibliographic descriptions enriched with a small number of controlled subject descriptors (often taken from the Library of Congress Subject Headings) and a classification number (usually a Library of Congress or a Dewey decimal class number). The database records, thus, contain minimal information for searching—little more than the author, title, publication year, subject description, and a class number.

The subject descriptors are selected to reflect the subject content of the item as a whole rather than to provide in-depth indexing of the information contained in the item.[1] For example, if a book contains many articles, subject descriptors are not assigned for each article but only to the overall topic of the book.

For periodical publications, only the periodical as a whole is described. Individual journal articles are usually not recorded in the database. This is in contrast to indexing and abstracting databases that provide keyword searching in the abstract and even the full text of articles, and provide exhaustive indexing of the content of journal articles. However, the distinction between OPACs and other kinds of information retrieval systems is blurring. Increasingly, OPACs are also providing links to full-text document, electronic books, and Internet resources.

Most of the online catalogs in use today are what Hildreth[2] termed second-generation OPACs. Most OPACs are Boolean retrieval systems that perform exact matching and require the search query to be specified as a Boolean expression. Typical search features include the choice of keyword searching (i.e., searching for individual words in the title and subject fields) or field searching with automatic truncation (e.g., searching for a whole title or author name), the use of Boolean operators to combine two or more terms, the use of a truncation symbol, and limiting a search to specific fields. *The onus is on the user to translate the user's information need into the subject headings and indexing terms used in the OPAC database and to refine the search based on the initial search result.*

Because most OPAC systems now offer Web access, OPAC interfaces are increasingly Web interfaces in the form of web pages containing HTML forms. Such interfaces are mainly form-filling interfaces. The user selects the type of search and the fields for searching either by entering the query in the appropriate input box or by toggling the appropriate checkbox or radio button. For keyword searching, the search expression can include Boolean operators as well as indications of which field(s) to search.

OPAC users are heterogenous, varying widely in background, age, subject interests, and computer and information literacy. So the OPAC has to be designed to cater to a wide range of users, ranging from users who have little knowledge of what a catalog contains and have little experience with computer terminals to librarians who are experienced in online database searching and who require the system to have powerful search capabilities.

Encyclopedia of Library and Information Sciences, Fourth Edition DOI: 10.1081/E-ELIS4-120008863

SUBJECT SEARCHING

OPAC searching is of two types:

- Specific-item searching (or known-item searching), where the user is trying to locate a particular item that the user knows of and has some information about (e.g., the author or fragments of the title)
- Subject searching, where the user wants to retrieve any item(s) on a particular topic.

The distinction between these two types of searching is fuzzy. A search often involves both types of searching. What begins as a specific item search often ends up as a subject search, especially if the specific item search fails to locate the desired item. Both types of searching have their particular problems. This entry focuses on the problems with subject searching.

Slone[3] distinguished between two types of subject searching: unknown item searching and area searching. In an area search, the OPAC is used to identify the area in the library where materials on a particular topic are located. Online searching is kept to a minimum, and the user relies on shelf browsing to identify specific relevant items. In contrast, unknown item searchers rely on the OPAC to identify the specific relevant items.

Subject searching is an important activity that constitutes a major proportion of OPAC searches. However, estimates of the proportion of subject searches vary, partly because the proportion varies with the type of library and user group, and partly because of the practical difficulty of distinguishing subject searches from other kinds of searches.

In a nationwide survey of U.S. libraries in the early 1980s, Matthews et al.[4] found that about 59% of online catalog use involved subject searches. Recent studies of OPAC transaction logs obtained percentages of subject searching ranging from 35 to 60%.[5–10] It is possible that the actual proportion of subject searching is even greater than reported because some of the keyword title searches actually represent subject searching.

A number of studies found subject searching to be the most common type of OPAC searching,[6,9,11] although other studies found a decline in subject searches and an increase in title searches.[10,12,13] Two studies of university OPAC use found that undergraduate students tend to do subject searching, whereas graduate students and faculty tend to search by author or title and do subject searching only when working outside their own fields.[13,14]

KNOWLEDGE NEEDED FOR SUBJECT SEARCHING

To perform effective subject searches requires the following kinds of knowledge:

1. Knowledge of the fields in the bibliographic records that can be used for subject searching and their characteristics.
2. Knowledge of the thesaurus system or subject headings list from which subject descriptors are selected and assigned to each bibliographic record.
3. Knowledge of search strategies and when and how to apply them.
4. Knowledge of the search capabilities provided by the OPAC system and how to use them.
5. Knowledge of the subject area.
6. Knowledge of how to translate an information need into a searchable query.

Borgman[15] divided the knowledge needed into three types:

1. Conceptual knowledge of the information retrieval process—how to translate an information need into a searchable query.
2. Semantic knowledge of how to implement a query in a given system—how and when to use system features.
3. Technical skills in executing the query—basic computing skills and the skill of formulating search statements in the syntax required.

The main fields in the bibliographic record that contain subject information are the title fields, subject fields, and class number fields. Each subject field contains a subject descriptor or subject heading selected from the Library of Congress Subject Headings (LCSH) or from some thesaurus [e.g., the U.S. National Library of Medicine's MEdical Subject Headings (MESH)]. A subject descriptor comprises a main descriptor and optionally a number of modifiers called subheadings or subdivisions. To know what descriptor and modifiers to use when searching the subject field, the user has to consult the Library of Congress Subject Headings or thesaurus, which may be searchable online or available only in printed form.

Knowledge of the thesaurus structure, how the descriptors are selected to represent the subject content of a work, and how the descriptor–modifier combinations are constructed is important for searching the subject field effectively. Knowledge of the thesaurus structure includes knowing the kinds of relations (broader term, narrower term, related term, etc.) used in the thesaurus and how to make use of these relations.

In selecting terms to search in the subject field, users should be aware of the following two principles used by indexers when selecting descriptors from the thesaurus:

1. Descriptors are selected that summarize the content of the whole item rather than index all the concepts contained in the work. This suggests that when searching the subject field, the user should use a term

or descriptor that is broader than the concept of interest.
2. When selecting a descriptor to represent a concept in a work, the most specific descriptor that matches the concept is used (the rule of specific entry), and usually only one descriptor is used to represent a concept. An item that is assigned the descriptor "Fishes" will usually not be assigned descriptors for specific types of fish (e.g., "Sharks" or "Goldfish"). So, to locate books on all kinds of fishes, the descriptor Fishes and all narrower terms should be used for searching.

An alternative way of doing subject searching is to search for keywords in the title and subject fields. Keyword searching in the title field is particularly appropriate when there is no descriptor that matches exactly the concept that the user is interested in. The disadvantage is that a concept may be expressed by several synonymous words, each having several variant forms, and that all the synonyms and variant forms have to be used in the search to retrieve all the relevant records. In addition, keyword searches may retrieve many nonrelevant records if the keyword has more than one possible meaning.

One field that is often overlooked in subject searching is the class number field. To search this field effectively requires knowledge of the classification system and notation used. The user also needs to consult the appropriate classification schedule to identify the correct class numbers to use. The major advantage of class number searching is that it allows the user to browse neighboring numbers and find related works. This is similar to browsing at the shelves. One problem with the class number search is that only one class number is assigned to an item, even if the item covers more than one topic.

Author fields can also be used for subject searching, inasmuch as publications by the same author tend to be on the same or related topics.

Although most online catalogs have subject, title, class number, and author fields, the catalogs vary in the search capabilities provided, in the search language used for searching these fields, and in the design of the search interfaces. To perform effective subject searches, the user needs to know the search features available and how to use them.

Also needed is the more general skill of translating an information need into a searchable query. This may involve visualizing what information is needed to satisfy the need, the kind of book that is likely to contain the desired information, the content or topic of the book, and the terms than can be used to represent the topic. Some knowledge of the subject area is needed to think up broader terms, narrower terms, and related terms for searching and for looking up appropriate descriptors in the thesaurus.

Slone,[3] in a study of OPAC use in a public library, found generating search terms was crucial to a successful unknown item search. When term generation was difficult, unknown item searches failed. She found that users who performed very narrow searches tended not to find what they needed. Users who performed broad searches and then narrowed the search, by selecting terms from the search results to use in a new search, were more successful. However, many users had so little knowledge of what they sought that they were not able to generate related terms to initiate a search.

An appropriate search strategy is thus needed to apply all the above knowledge creatively to perform an effective subject search. Search strategies can be divided into initial strategies and reformulation strategies. Initial search strategies are used in formulating the initial search request. Reformulation strategies are used for formulating subsequent search requests to improve the search result after reviewing the initial search result. Reformulation strategies include broadening strategies for increasing the number of relevant records retrieved and narrowing strategies for decreasing the number of unwanted records retrieved.

PROBLEMS USERS HAVE WITH SUBJECT SEARCHING

Numerous studies using a variety of research methods have found that users have difficulty performing subject searches in online catalogs. Problems experienced by users include the following:[8,16–18]

- Users have difficulty matching their search terms with those used in the online catalog.
- They have difficulty identifying terms that are broader or narrower than their topic of interest.
- They lack understanding of the thesaurus structure and the Library of Congress Subject Headings.
- They don't know how to broaden the search and increase the search result when too little or nothing is retrieved.
- They don't know how to narrow the search and reduce the search result when too much is retrieved.
- They don't know how to use Boolean operators and truncation and how to limit keyword searches to specific fields. They are generally not aware of the more sophisticated capabilities of the OPAC system.
- They don't know how to translate their information need into a Boolean search statement.
- They have difficulties with spelling.
- They have difficulty formulating a search command using the search language of the system.

Slone[3] found that 60% of unknown item searchers in a public library OPAC were frustrated and 40% were disappointed. Only 20% were relaxed or content.

To obtain optimal results in subject searches often requires using more than one search strategy. The typical online catalog user does not know the range of strategies that can be used or the limitations of each strategy. Users lack much of the knowledge described in the section "Knowledge Needed for Subject Searching" above.

A high proportion of OPAC subject searches result in null sets or zero postings.[6–8,19] Spelling and typographical errors are among the most common errors.[7,8,10,19] More help is clearly needed to help users recover from spelling and typographical errors and guide them to related terms that may retrieve items with useful information.

Studies of OPAC transaction logs have found that few users make use of Boolean operators in their searches (e.g., Connaway).[10] Users are also confused about the difference between keyword searching and searching by subject headings. Connaway et al.[14] found that many users searched the subject field when a keyword search might have been more appropriate. Hildreth[20] found that most users do not understand how the OPAC system processes their keyword searches.

IMPROVING THE DESIGN OF OPAC SYSTEMS

Numerous writers have suggested how the on-line catalog can he designed to help users perform more effective subject searches. The suggested improvements can be divided into the following categories:

1. Develop more helpful and user-oriented interfaces.
2. Develop graphical and direct manipulation interfaces.
3. Develop interfaces for browsing.
4. Enhance catalog records with more subject and table of contents information.
5. Provide query expansion and query formulation support.
6. Provide non-Boolean best-match search capability.
7. Provide relevance feedback and query refinement capability.
8. Incorporate search heuristics.
9. Incorporate search trees and knowledge-based techniques.

These solutions are briefly reviewed below.

Design More Helpful and User-Oriented Interfaces

Simple changes to the OPAC screen design can help users improve their searching significantly. Such improvements to the OPAC screen can be identified by analyzing the OPAC transaction log. Blecic et al.[21] analyzed the transaction log of a university OPAC system, identified the main errors made by users, and then made simple changes to the OPAC screen, such as simplifying and clarifying the wording in the introductory screens, using the same book for all search examples, placing the keyword search option as the first option, and making certain help messages more prominent. An analysis of the transaction log 6 months later found a statistically significant reduction in errors and more effective searches. Ballard[22] had also found that the amount of keyword searching increased when keyword search was listed as the first option on the OPAC screen. In a follow-up study, Blecic et al.[23] found that some of the initial improvements did not hold over time, indicating that the same OPAC screen design can affect different user groups differently, especially in a changing computing environment.

Hildreth[20] found that users seldom read help screens. Nevertheless, they expressed a strong interest in context-sensitive search assistance from the system while conducting their searches. Context-sensitive help messages displayed on the same screen as the search result can guide the user on how to improve the search. When no record or few records are retrieved, the system can suggest shortening the search phrase, substituting synonyms or more general terms, or retrying the search using a different search method. When too many records are retrieved, the system can ask the user to enter additional search words or enter limiting criteria to narrow the search. The messages could tell the user what to do, how to do it, and why it may improve the result.[24] However, online prompts can provide only a limited amount of help. Some search strategies require an understanding of the bibliographic record, controlled vocabulary, cataloging rules and online searching, and too much information about "what to do, how to do it, and why" will overwhelm the user.

Some researchers have called for OPAC systems to incorporate models of the user and the user's task and situation. Such an OPAC can provide different search screens, use different search strategies, and guide the user in different ways according to:

- Whether the user is a new OPAC user or an experienced user.
- Whether the user is knowledgeable about the subject area.
- Which stage of a project the user is at.[25–27]
- Whether the search is a continuation of an earlier search.[28]
- What the goal of the user is in performing the search.[27,29,30]

While clearly desirable, it is not yet known how user models can be incorporated into OPAC systems effectively.

Graphical and Direct Manipulation Interfaces

With new developments in interface technology as well as advancements in Internet and Web-related technologies, such as Dynamic HTML, new types of graphical OPAC interfaces are likely to be developed, which incorporate 2-D and 3-D images, animation, virtual reality, and direct manipulation capabilities that allow users to manipulate objects on the screen. Such techniques can be used to help users visualize relationships between search terms as well as documents and help users to browse the OPAC database. They can also be used to help users understand search strategies and make the manipulation of search results and OPAC records more intuitive. Some ideas for the use of icons, animation, manipulation, and metaphor have been explored in prototype OPACs.

Lee[31] described an animated, object-based OPAC interface that featured 2-D and 3-D interactive objects such as card catalog drawers, bookshelves, and cassette tapes that could be manipulated. Bovey[32] described an online catalog for a collection of cartoons. The set of cartoons retrieved in a search was displayed on a time line showing the number of cartoons published on each month and year. The user could use the mouse to point to a place on the time line to select a cartoon published at a certain time. Chung[33] explored how virtual reality can be incorporated in an OPAC interface.

Pejtersen[34] described a prototype online catalog of fiction materials called the Book House, which used the metaphor of a house as a search environment, with different rooms in the house representing different user groups (e.g., children and adults) and different kinds of searching. Each room in the house had objects that could be manipulated to represent different aspects of a search. Animations were used to suggest the type of search, and icons were used to represent different dimensions of the classification system e.g., a globe to represent the geographical setting, a clock to represent the time dimension, and theater masks to represent the emotional experience provided by the books. Records retrieved were represented as a bookcase of books, and individual records were displayed as text in an image of an open book.

Develop Interfaces for Browsing

Most OPAC systems require the user to think up appropriate terms for searching. This is difficult if the user is not knowledgeable in the subject area. Moreover, few users know how to identify the appropriate Library of Congress subject heading to use. A browse interface reduces the user's cognitive load by requiring only that the user recognizes relevant concepts. Three main approaches have been proposed for an OPAC browse interface: browsing the classification system or the class numbers assigned to library items, browsing Library of Congress Subject Headings, and browsing a semantic network of associated terms.

Class number browsing makes use of the principle that books on similar topics are assigned the same or neighboring class numbers. Users take advantage of this when they browse the library shelves. Class number browsing on the OPAC provides an online equivalent of shelf browsing—especially if the books' table of contents are available online for scanning. OPAC records can be displayed in class number order to facilitate such browsing. Beheshti[35] proposed using object-oriented graphical interfaces with images of books representing bibliographic records on the OPAC screen. Book titles can be superimposed on the spines of the book images, and these can be arranged by class number on the image of a bookshelf. If the classification system uses a hierarchical notation (e.g., the Dewey decimal classification system), the user will be able to broaden or narrow a search by using a shorter or longer class number and to zoom in on the detailed class number for a specific subject. For the Library of Congress classification system, which uses an enumerative notation, Huestis[36] has formulated an automatic method of identifying ranges of class numbers.

Some writers have proposed making the Library of Congress Subject Headings thesaurus available online for users to browse. Subject headings have broader terms and narrower terms, as well as several levels of subdivisions that can be browsed hierarchically. However, the list of subject headings and subdivisions for some subject areas may be too extensive to browse easily. Allen[37] and Massicottee[38] have proposed ways of reducing the length of subject heading displays by replacing many headings with broad conceptual categories and summarizing all headings beginning with the same initial word or phrase with one line containing just that word or phrase followed by an asterisk to indicate that the line can be expanded.

The Library of Congress Subject Headings can be further enhanced with a network of associated terms to form a rich semantic network. Associations between terms can be based on the co-occurrence of two terms in the same bibliographic record. Associations suggested by Bates[39] include title keywords with the assigned subject headings, two subject headings assigned to the same book, subject headings and the class number label (taken from the classification system), as well as two words in the same title. Such an enhanced thesaurus or semantic net increases the chances of the user's initial terms matching one or more terms in the system and allows the user to explore a rich network of links and associations.[39]

Lin[40] reviewed various ways of displaying a semantic network on a browse screen: hierarchical displays, network displays with links and nodes, scatter displays (graphical dotted images produced by mapping high-dimensional data to a 2-D visual space), and map displays which apply the geographical map metaphor to information space.

Web interfaces provide a natural way of navigating and browsing a semantic network using hypertext links (hyperlinks). For example, in most Web OPAC interfaces, bibliographic fields that are displayed in the search result screen can be clicked on by using a mouse device. Clicking on a subject heading displayed in a bibliographic record automatically sends a search request to the OPAC system to search for other records containing the specific subject heading.

Enhance Catalog Records with More Subject and Table of Contents Information

Catalog records can be enhanced with more subject information in a number of ways:[41–44]

- Include the book's table of contents in the record.
- Include selected terms from the back-of-book index.
- Include in the record terms from the Library of Congress Subject Headings that are related to the assigned subject headings and terms in the classification schedule that correspond to the assigned class number.

Enhancing the catalog records in the above ways will increase the probability of retrieving relevant records and reduce the number of searches that retrieve no records. It will also allow the user to use more specific terms in a search rather than the possibly broader subject descriptors used in the subject fields.

The disadvantage of enhancing catalog records in these ways is that more nonrelevant records will be retrieved and it is much more likely for a search to retrieve too many records for the user to scan.[45,46] This will place a heavier burden on the user to know how to narrow a search when too many records are retrieved.

Traditionally, fiction books are not assigned subject descriptors in online catalogs. However, fiction books constitute the major proportion of loans in public libraries, and effort is now being made to assign subject headings also to fiction materials.[47]

Provide Query Expansion and Query Formulation Support

OPAC users need more help with query expansion to identify broader, narrower, and related terms to use in a search, and with query formulation to formulate a Boolean query in the search language of the system. A number of prototype OPAC systems have explored the use of an online Library of Congress Subject Headings or some other thesaurus or semantic network to help users identify alternative search terms and controlled subject descriptors to use.[48] This has been shown to be useful and effective.

Drabenstott et al.[49–54] developed a prototype OPAC system that matched the user's query terms with entries in the Library of Congress Subject Headings and displayed the exact and partial matches for the user to select. If the user's terms matched a "see" reference, this was automatically replaced with the authorized subject heading. The user could then browse the thesaurus structure to view broader, narrower, and related subject headings as well as the subdivisions.

Poo and Khoo et al.[55] in a prototype expert intermediary interface called the E-referencer used a knowledge base of associations between title keywords and subject headings. The keyword-subject heading associations were derived by analyzing several years of catalog records. For each title keyword, all the subject headings associated with it (i.e., assigned to titles containing the keyword) were identified and assigned a score equal to the number of times the heading was assigned. The raw scores were then normalized by dividing by the highest score (the score obtained by the most frequent subject heading). The normalized scores were used to represent the strength of the association between the title keywords and subject headings. This knowledge base was then used to identify the subject headings that were most highly associated with the users' query terms.

Larson[56,57] and Micco and Pop[58] have proposed an indirect way of query expansion by clustering records in the library database by the class numbers assigned to the records. The title keywords and subject headings of all the records in each cluster are then used as index terms to the cluster. A keyword search would retrieve not just the records containing the keyword but all other records belonging to the same cluster as the retrieved records. A list of retrieved clusters, with their class number and some descriptive phrase, can be displayed for the user to select.

The OPAC interface can also incorporate some degree of natural language processing to allow users to express their information need in natural language and have it converted it automatically to a Boolean query. ALEX-DOC[59] was one natural language retrieval front end that performed linguistic analysis to match the user query with terms in the thesaurus and constructed a Boolean search statement using a set of transformation rules. Researchers have developed other automatic methods for constructing Boolean queries from natural language statements (e.g., Salton).[60]

Provide Non-Boolean Best-Match Search Capability

Information retrieval researchers have advocated a "best-match" retrieval approach with relevancy ranking for the OPAC system. In such a system, records containing some or all of the user's terms are retrieved, and relevancy ranking is performed to display the records in decreasing order of probable relevance—with the records that most closely match the user's query being shown first. A major advantage of best-match systems is that natural language queries can be processed by the system and users need not formulate Boolean queries.

Best-match retrieval approaches include the vector-space model and the probabilistic model[61] and are commonly used in Web search engines and full-text retrieval systems. The Okapi system[62–64] is a well-developed experimental OPAC system that used a probabilistic best-match approach. Relevancy ranking is available in the Library of Congress OPAC system (URL http://catalog.loc.gov/) but is still generally uncommon in OPAC systems. Extended Boolean retrieval models that combine the strengths of Boolean retrieval with best-match relevancy ranking have also been proposed.[65–67]

Best-match retrieval requires different indexing structures and search mechanisms in the back end of the OPAC system than those used for Boolean retrieval. An alternative to using best-match search engines in the OPAC system is to incorporate some relevancy ranking capabilities in the OPAC front end residing on the user's desktop computer or in a middleware or metasearch engine that sits between the OPAC server and the user's computer. This can then behave as an intelligent agent to retrieve a large number of records from multiple OPAC servers and perform relevancy ranking on the records retrieved.[55,60,66,68–70]

Incorporate Search Heuristics and Relevance Feedback Capability

Hildreth[24] pointed out that "to optimize retrieval results in subject searching, more than one search approach may have to be employed in the overall search strategy.... Conventional information retrieval systems place the burden on the user to reformulate and re-enter searches until satisfactory results are obtained." Cherry[5] analyzed zero-hit subject field searches and found that converting the queries to other search forms such as keyword subject, keyword title or title searches would have obtained useful hits in 71% of the cases. An OPAC system can use automated search algorithms to reformulate the user's search query and refine the search criteria to improve the search results.

Cheng[71] described a front end to the OPAC system at the University of Illinois, Urbana–Champaign, which executed a sequence of strategies to help the user improve the search results. When an initial search did not find a subject heading, the front end performed a sequence of modifications on the search string, including adding a truncation sign, displaying alphabetically similar headings, separating the words and searching by using the Boolean AND, and finally searching for the words in the title. If the title search retrieved a relevant record, the system extracts the first subject heading from the record and continued the subject search with that heading.

Automated search heuristics can also be used to simulate relevancy ranking. The E-Referencer system[55,68] first formulated a narrow search to retrieve and display the most relevant records. Broadening strategies were applied gradually to retrieve additional records, which were appended to the end of the display. Because the records retrieved by the broadening strategies were less likely to be relevant than those retrieved by the initial search, the result is a list of records roughly in order of probable relevance.

Search algorithms can also be used to perform relevance feedback: the user can indicate which of the retrieved records are relevant, and an automatic procedure can attempt to retrieve other relevant records by analyzing the records already retrieved to extract appropriate terms to include in a new search.[24,72]

The CITE system[73] performed a frequency analysis of the subject headings that occurred in the records that the user indicated to be relevant. It then displayed a ranked list of the subject headings for the user's selection. Classification numbers from the relevant records were then used together with the selected headings in a best match search.

In the Okapi system,[63,74] the automatic query expansion facility took the subject headings and classification numbers from records chosen by the user and assigned each a weight based on the number of chosen records in which they appeared. Later versions of Okapi made use of interactive query reformulation where users can select the subject headings to use in a new search. The researchers found that fewer users took up query reformulation than expected and concluded that a better balance between automatic and interactive query reformulation had to be designed.[75,76]

Incorporate Search Trees and Knowledge-Based Techniques

Although using a fixed sequence of search heuristics and query reformulation procedures have been shown to improve the search effectiveness, more flexible and sophisticated methods for selecting appropriate search strategies in response to different situations might work better than a fixed sequence of heuristics. Expert systems or knowledge-based systems have been proposed for online searching. An expert system that embodies within it the knowledge and skills of a librarian or "search intermediary" for carrying out online bibliographic searches is called an expert intermediary system.

Several researchers have attempted to apply knowledge-based techniques to information retrieval. Gauch[77] and Ford[78] surveyed some of the more well-known systems. Most of these have focused on abstracts and full-text databases, rather than library OPACs. They have also focused on the selection of query terms from a thesaurus or semantic net representing the knowledge base. Chen[79] and Khoo[80] present designs of expert intermediary systems that focus on search strategies and rules for selecting them.

Chen's system[81,82] was the most ambitious expert intermediary system developed for OPAC subject searching, with many search strategies and knowledge bases. However, the prototype was applied to a very small database and narrow domain, and it is not clear whether it can be scaled up easily to a real library database.

Drabenstott et al.[50–53] has developed a prototype OPAC system that uses search trees or decision trees that represent how experienced librarians might select a search strategy and formulate a search statement. The decision tree was represented as a flowchart and was developed on the basis of an analysis of user queries captured in OPAC transaction logs.

The E-Referencer[55,68–70] was a prototype expert intermediary system for searching OPACs on the Web. It was implemented as a proxy server that mediated the interaction between the user and Boolean OPAC servers. It processed the user's natural language query, mapped the query words to Library of Congress subject headings, selected a suitable search strategy, and formulated an appropriate search statement to send to the library system. Based on the user's relevance feedback on the search results, it further selected a strategy for refining the search. The knowledge incorporated in the E-Referencer comprised:

- A conceptual knowledge base that mapped free-text keywords to subject headings.
- Search strategies coded in the system.
- Initial search strategies for converting the user's natural language query to a Boolean query.
- Reformulation strategies for refining a search, including broadening strategies, narrowing strategies, and relevance feedback strategies.
- Rules for selecting an appropriate search strategy in the form of a decision tree.

MULTIPLE LIBRARY OPACs SEARCH

With the advent of Internet and the high-speed delivery of information via efficient networking infrastructure, multilibrary OPAC and electronic databases, search has now become a reality and is becoming a necessity in the offering of library services. In Poo,[83] Poo and Khoo discuss the problems with Information Overload, a phenomenon brought about through the globalization of information via the Internet and demonstrate how various state-of-the-art technologies can be applied to enhance user's experience in multicatalog and electronic database search.

CONCLUSION

Users have many kinds of problems performing subject searches in OPAC systems. Typical users do not have the range of knowledge and skills needed for effective subject searching. This entry has surveyed possible improvements that can be made to OPAC system design.

With developments in Internet and Web browser technologies, many of the proposed improvements can be instituted without major changes to the OPAC back end system. Changes can easily be made in the design of the web pages used as an interface to the OPAC. Dynamic HTML, Javascript, and Java applets can be used in Web OPAC interfaces to provide users with more assistance and to implement more interactive direct manipulation features. Improvements that require access to a knowledge base or more processing power can be implemented in a middleware program (metasearch engine or intelligent agent) that sits between the user's computer and the OPAC server. The middleware can be implemented as Java servlets that use the Z39.50 Information Retrieval protocol or the internet HTTP protocol to communicate with the OPAC server. Solutions using Java applets and Java servlets have been implemented in a number of systems.[55,69,83,84]

OPAC interfaces are playing increasingly expanded roles. They now provide access not just to records of books and journals held by a library but also to multiple library systems, to full-text documents and journal articles, and to databases and other resources on the Internet. OPAC interfaces are increasingly becoming digital library interfaces and even Web portals, providing a window to the world of information. This presents new challenges for developing OPAC interfaces for subject searching.

REFERENCES

1. Chan, L.M. *Library of Congress Subject Headings: Principles and Applications*; Libraries Unlimited: Littleton, CO, 1978; 159.
2. Hildreth, C.R. Pursuing the ideal: generations of online catalogs. In *Online Catalogs, Online Reference: Converging Trends*; Aveney, B., Butler, B., Eds.; American Library Association: Chicago, IL, 1984; 31–57.
3. Slone, D.J. Encounters with the OPAC: on-line searching in public libraries. J. Am. Soc. Inf. Sci. **2000**, *51*(8), 757–773.
4. Matthews, J.R.; Lawrence, G.S.; Ferguson, D.K. *Using Online Catalogs: A Nationwide Survey*; Neal-Schuman: New York, 1983; 144.
5. Cherry, J.M. Improving subject access in OPACs: an exploratory study of conversion of users' queries. J. Acad. Librariansh. **1992**, *18*(2), 95–99.
6. Hunter, R.N. Successes and failures of patrons searching the online catalog at a large academic library: a transaction log analysis. RQ **1991**, *30*(3), 395–402.
7. Peters, T.A. When smart people fail: an analysis of the transaction log of an online public access catalog. J. Acad. Librariansh. **1989**, *15*(5), 267–273.
8. Wallace, P.M. How do patrons search the online catalog when no one's looking? Transaction log analysis and implications for bibliographic instruction and system design. RQ **1993**, *33*(2), 239–252.
9. Zink, S.D. Monitoring user search success through transaction log analysis: the WolfPAC example. Ref. Serv. Rev. **1991**, *19*(1), 49–56.
10. Connaway, L.S.; Budd, J.M.; Kochtanek, T.R. An investigation of the use of an on-line catalog: user characteristics and transaction log analysis. Libr. Resour. Tech. Serv. **1995**, *39*(2), 142–152.
11. Nelson, J.L. An analysis of transaction logs to evaluate the educational needs of end users. Med. Ref. Serv. Q. **1992**, *11*(4), 11–21.

12. Larson, R.R. The decline of subject searching: long-term trends and patterns of index use in an on-line catalog. J. Am. Soc. Inf. Sci. **1991**, *42*(3), 197–215.
13. Millsap, L.; Ferl, T.E. Search patterns of remote users: an analysis of OPAC transaction logs. Inf. Technol. Libr. **1993**, *12*(3), 321–343.
14. Connaway, L.S.; Johnson, D.W.; Searing, S.E. Online catalogs from the users' perspective: the use of focus group interviews. Coll. Res. Libr. **1997**, *58*(5), 403–420.
15. Borgman, C.L. Why are on-line catalogs still hard to use? J. Am. Soc. Inf. Sci. **1996**, *47*(7), 493–503.
16. Markey, K. *Subject Searching in Library Catalogs: Before and After the Introduction of Online Catalogs.* OCLC Library, Information and Computer Science Series; OCLC Online Computer Library Center: Dublin, OH, 1984; Vol. 4, 77.
17. Ensor, P. User practices in keyword and Boolean searching on an online public access catalog. Inf. Technol. Libr. **1992**, *11*(3), 210–219.
18. Kaske, N.K.; Sanders, N.P. *A Comprehensive Study of Online Public Access Catalog: An Overview and Application of Findings*, OCLC: Dublin, OH, 1983; OCLC/OPR/RR-83/4.
19. Ferl, T.E.; Millsap, L. The knuckle-cracker's dilemma: a transaction log study of OPAC subject searching. Inf. Technol. Libr. **1996**, *15*(2), 81–98.
20. Hildreth, C.R. The use and understanding of keyword searching in a university on-line catalog. Inf. Technol. Libr. **1997**, *16*(2), 52–62.
21. Blecic, D.D.; Bangalore, N.S.; Dorsch, J.L.; Henderson, C. L.; Koenig, M.H.; Weller, A.C. Using transaction log analysis to improve OPAC retrieval results. Coll. Res. Libr. **1998**, *59*(1), 39–50.
22. Ballard, T. Comparative searching styles of patrons and staff. Libr. Resour. Tech. Serv. **1994**, *38*, 293–305.
23. Blecic, D.D.; Dorsch, J.L.; Koenig, M.H.; Bangalore, N.S. A longitudinal study of the effects of OPAC screen changes on searching behavior and searcher success. Coll. Res. Libr. **1999**, *60*(6), 515–530.
24. Hildreth, C. Beyond Boolean: designing the next generation of online catalogs. Libr. Trends **1987**, *35*(4), 647–667.
25. Kuhlthau, C.C. Inside the search process: information seeking from the user's perspective. J. Am. Soc. Inf. Sci. **1991**, *42*(5), 361–371.
26. Kuhlthau, C.C. *Seeking Meaning: A Process Approach to Library and Information Services*; Ablex Publishing: Norwood, NJ, 1993.
27. Hert, C.A. User goals on an online public access catalog. J. Am. Soc. Inf. Sci. **1996**, *47*(7), 504–518.
28. Spink, A. Multiple search sessions model of end-user behavior: an exploratory study. J. Am. Soc. Inf. Sci. **1996**, *47*(8), 603–609.
29. Belkin, N.J.; Chang, S.J.; Downs, T.; Saracevic, T.; Zhao, S. *Taking Account of User Tasks, Goals and Behavior for the Design of Online Public Access Catalogs, ASIS '90*, Proceedings of the 53rd ASIS Annual Meeting, Toronto, November 4–8, 1990; Learned Information: Medford, NJ, 1990; Vol. 27, 69–79.
30. Belkin, N.J.; Marchetti, P.G.; Cool, C. Braque: design of an interface to support user interaction in information retrieval. Inf. Process. Manag. **1993**, *29*(3), 325–344.
31. Lee, N.S. Multimedia visualizer: an animated, object-based OPAC. Inf. Technol. Libr. **1991**, *10*(4), 297–310.
32. Bovey, J.D. A graphical retrieval system. J. Inf. Sci. **1993**, *19*(3), 179–188.
33. Chung, S.H. *A VRML-Based 3D OPAC*, M.Sc. thesis; Nanyang Technological University, School of Applied Science, 1998.
34. Pejtersen, A.M. New model for multimedia interfaces to online public access catalogues. Electron. Libr. Int. J. Minicomput. Microcomput. Softw. Appl. Libr. **1992**, *10*(6), 359–366.
35. Beheshti, J. Browsing through public access catalogs. Inf. Technol. Libr. **1992**, *11*(3), 220–228.
36. Huestis, J.C. LC classification numbers in an online catalog for improved browsability. Inf. Technol. Libr. **1988**, *7*(4), 381–393.
37. Allen, B. Improved browsable displays: an experimental test. Inf. Technol. Libr. **1993**, *12*(2), 203–208.
38. Massicottee, M. Improved browsable displays for online subject access. Inf. Technol. Libr. **1988**, *7*, 373–380.
39. Bates, M.J. Subject access in online catalogs: a design model. J. Am. Soc. Inf. Sci. **1986**, *37*(6), 357–376.
40. Lin, X. Map displays for information retrieval. J. Am. Soc. Inf. Sci. **1997**, *48*(1), 40–54.
41. Atherton, P. *Books Are for Use: Final Report of the Subject Access Project to the Council of Library Resources*; Syracuse University Printing Services: Syracuse, NY, 1978; 172 ED 156 131.
42. DeHart, F.E.; Reitsma, R. Subject searching and tables of contents in single-work titles. Tech. Serv. Q. **1989**, *7*(1), 33–51.
43. Markey, K. Searching and browsing the Dewey decimal classification in an online catalog. Cat. Classif. Q. **1987**, *7*(3), 37–68.
44. Michalak, T.J. An experiment in enhancing catalog records at Carnegie Mellon University. Libr. Hi Tech **1990**, *8*(3), 33–41.
45. Byrne, A.; Micco, A. Improving OPAC subject access: the ADFA experiment. Coll. Res. Libr. **1988**, *49*(5), 432–441.
46. Lancaster, F.W.; Connell, T.H.; Bishop, N.; McCowan, S. Identifying barriers to effective subject access in library catalogs. Libr. Resour. Tech. Serv. **1991**, *35*(4), 377–391.
47. MacEwan, A. Electronic access to fiction. Vine **1997**, *105*, 41–44.
48. Paice, C. Expert systems for information retrieval? Aslib Proc. **1986**, *3*(10), 343–353.
49. Drabenstott, K.M.; Vizine-Goetz, D. *Using Subject Headings for Online Retrieval: Theory Practice, and Potential*, Academic Press: San Diego, CA, 1994.
50. Drabenstott, K.M.; Vizine-Goetz, D. Search trees for subject searching in online catalogs. Libr. Hi Tech **1990**, *8*(3), 7–20.
51. Drabenstott, K.M.; Weller, M.S. Testing a new design for subject searching in online catalogs. Libr. Hi Tech **1994**, *12*(1), 67–76.
52. Drabenstott, K.M. Enhancing a new design for subject access to online catalogs. Libr. Hi Tech **1996**, *14*(1), 87–109.
53. Drabenstott, K.M.; Weller, M.S. Failure analysis of subject searches in a test of a new design for subject access to online catalogs. J. Am. Soc. Inf. Sci. **1996**, *47*(7), 519–537.

54. Drabenstott, K.M.; Weller, M.S. The exact-display approach for on-line catalog subject searching. Inf. Process. Manag. **1996**, *32*(6), 719–745.
55. Khoo, C.; Poo, D.; Toh, T.-K.; Hong, G. E-Referencer: transforming Boolean OPACs to web search engines. In *International Federation of Library Associations*, 65th IFLA Council and General Conference, Bangkok, August 20–28, 1999; The Hague, Netherlands, 1999; Vol. 6, 56–63.
56. Larson, R.R. Classification clustering, probabilistic information retrieval, and the online catalog. Libr. Q. **1991**, *61*(2), 133–173.
57. Larson, R.R. Evaluation of advanced retrieval techniques in an experimental online catalog. J. Am. Soc. Inf. Sci. **1992**, *43*(1), 34–53.
58. Micco, M.; Popp, R. Improving library subject access (ILSA): a theory of clustering based in classification. Libr. Hi Tech **1994**, *12*(1), 55–66.
59. Hildreth, C.R. *Intelligent Interfaces and Retrieval Methods for Subject Searching in Bibliographic Retrieval Systems*; Cataloging Distribution Service, Library of Congress: Washington, DC, 1989; 80.
60. Salton, G. A simple blueprint for automatic Boolean query processing. Inf. Process. Manag. **1988**, *24*(3), 269–280.
61. Harman, D. Ranking algorithms. In *Information Retrieval: Data Structures & Algorithms*; Frakes, W. B., Baeza-Yates, R., Eds.; Prentice-Hall: Englewood Cliffs, NJ, 1992; 363–392.
62. Walker, S. Improving subject access painlessly: recent work on the OKAPI online catalog projects. Program **1988**, *22*(I), 21–31.
63. Walker, S.; Vere, R. *Improving Subject Retrieval in Online Catalogues: 2. Relevance Feedback and Query Expansion*, British Library Research Paper; British Library: London, U.K., 1990; Vol. 72.
64. Robertson, S.E. Overview of the Okapi projects. J. Doc. **1997**, *53*(1), 3–7.
65. Fox, E.; Betrabet, S.; Koushik, M.; Lee, W. Extended Boolean models. In *Information Retrieval: Data Structures & Algorithms*; Frakes, W.B., Baeza-Yates, R., Eds.; Prentice-Hall: Englewood Cliffs, NJ, 1992; 393–418.
66. Lee, J.H.; Kim, M.H.; Lee, Y.J. Ranking documents in thesaurus-based Boolean retrieval systems. Inf. Process. Manag. **1994**, *30*(1), 79–91.
67. Radecki, T. Trends in research on information retrieval—the potential for improvements in conventional Boolean retrieval systems. Inf. Process. Manag. **1988**, *24*(3), 219–227.
68. Khoo, C.; Poo, D.; Toh, T.-K.; Liew, S.-K.; Goh, A. *E-Referencer: A Prototype Expert System Web Interface to Online Catalogs, ECDL'98*, Research and Advanced Technology for Digital Libraries 2nd European Conference 1998; Nikolaou, C., Stephanidis, C., Eds.; Springer-Verlag: Berlin, Germany, 1998; 315–333.
69. Poo, D.; Toh, T.K.; Khoo, C. Design and implementation of the E-Referencer. Data Knowl. Eng. **2000**, *32*, 199–218.
70. Poo, D.; Toh, T.K.; Khoo, C. *Search Interface for Z39.50 Compliant Online Catalogs over the Internet, HICSS-32*, Proceedings of the 32nd Annual Hawaii International Conference on System Sciences, Software Technology Track, Multi Media Database and Internet Mini Track (USA), Hawaii, January 5–8, 1999; IEEE: New York, 1999; 50–57.
71. Cheng, C.-C. Microcomputer-based user interface. Inf. Technol. Libr. **1985**, *4*(4), 346–351.
72. Lynch, C.A. *The Use of Heuristics in User Interfaces for Online Information Retrieval Systems, ASIS '87*, Proceedings of the 50th ASIS Annual Meeting; Ching-Chih, C., Ed.; Learned Information: Medford, NJ, 1987; Vol. 241, 148–152.
73. Doszkocs, T.E. CITE NLM: natural-language searching in an online catalog. Inf. Technol. Libr. **1983**, *2*(4), 364–380.
74. Hancock-Beaulieu, M.; Walker, S. An evaluation of automatic query expansion in an online library catalogue. J. Doc. **1992**, *48*(4), 406–421.
75. Hancock-Beaulieu, M.; Fieldhouse, M.; Do, T. An evaluation of interactive query expansion in an online library catalogue with a graphical user interface. J. Doc. **1995**, *51*(3), 225–243.
76. Beaulieu, M. Experiments on interfaces to support query expansion. J. Doc. **1997**, *53*(3), 8–19.
77. Gauch, S. Intelligent information retrieval: an introduction. J. Am. Soc. Inf. Sci. **1992**, *43*(2), 175–182.
78. Ford, N. Knowledge-based information retrieval. J. Am. Soc. Inf. Sci. **1991**, *42*(1), 72–74.
79. Chen, H.; Dhar, V. Cognitive process as a basis for intelligent retrieval systems design. Inf. Process. Manag. **1991**, *27*(3), 405–432.
80. Khoo, C.S.G.; Poo, D.C.C. An expert system approach to online catalog subject searching. Inf. Process. Manag. J. **1994**, *30*(2), 223–238.
81. Chen, H. *An Artificial Intelligence Approach to the Design of Online Information Retrieval Systems*, Ph.D. dissertation; New York University: New York, 1989.
82. Chen, H. Knowledge-based document retrieval: framework and design. J. Inf. Sci. **1992**, *18*(3), 293–314.
83. Poo, D.; Khoo, C. *Multi-library Catalog and Electronic Database Search for Lay-Users*, Pre-World Library Summit Seminar, April 22–23, 2002.
84. Ayres, F.H.; Nielsen, L.P.S.; Ridley, M.J. BOPAC2: a new concept in OPAC design and bibliographic control. Cat. Classif. Q. **1999**, *28*(2), 17–44.

Online Library Instruction

Beth Evans
Library, Brooklyn College, City University of New York, Brooklyn, New York, U.S.A.

Abstract
Online library instruction, or instruction in information skills delivered over the Internet, varies in its content, levels of technical complexity and intended audiences. Public libraries and special libraries, academic libraries and school libraries, graduate schools of library and information studies, library organizations, commercial vendors, and individuals all provide library instruction in an electronic environment. Delivering library instruction through the Internet is a new approach for educating learners and researchers using technology. It comes at a time of an increasing desire for librarians to educate themselves and their users and follows a history of librarians applying technology in education.

INTRODUCTION

A child studying in the Denver Public Library learns how to navigate through the online public access catalog using a specially designed interface for children.[1–3] A lawyer at the Miami office of a national firm is referred to information about electronic resources on the library website by the law librarian at the firm.[4] A library school student takes an online distance education class in "Managing Change in Information Environments" through the University of Pittsburgh FastTrack MLIS program using a computer at a cybercafe in Clarksburg, West Virginia.[5] Library paraprofessionals at Northwestern University Libraries, once trained on the job with a video on handling library materials, now acquire new skills on their own with a self-paced, Web-based tutorial.[6]

Online library instruction, or instruction in information skills delivered over the Internet, varies in its content, levels of technical complexity and intended audiences. Public libraries and special libraries, academic libraries and school libraries, graduate schools of library and information studies, library organizations, commercial vendors, and individuals all provide library instruction in an electronic environment. Delivering library instruction through the Internet is a new approach for educating learners and researchers using technology. It comes at a time of an increasing desire for librarians to educate themselves and their users and follows a history of librarians applying technology in education.

HISTORY

The Need for the Teaching Librarian

Three major American library associations have recently crafted mission statements identifying ongoing education and professional development as critical for practicing professional librarians.[7–11] Embedded in each of these statements is the understanding that librarians who upgrade their skills are better equipped to further the information education of their constituents. Increasingly, librarians are expected to be both learners and teachers. They are expected to understand different learning theories and adapt them to the different learning styles of students.[12,13] The purpose, according to theorists, is to position librarians to make lifelong learners of information seekers.[14] Fig. 1 shows an exercise from a Web-training tutorial.

The Emergence of Distance Education

Distance education allows learners to become educated in many disciplines where barriers of time and place may have once prevented them from accessing instruction.[16,17] Early distance education was often delivered through correspondence courses mailed to students and extension courses taught by faculty who traveled to remote sites.[18–20] Technology has expanded the options in delivering distance education. Although higher education may have been slow to adapt to the new methodologies,[21] according to the National Center for Education Statistics, one third of colleges and universities in the United States offered distance learning courses in 1998, and 20% of the schools not offering distance education courses at the time had plans to do so within the following three years.[22] Furthermore, if Gary Smith is correct that degrees offered for online study are recognized to be of equal value to degrees offered for a traditional course of study,[23] a major social, political, and economic barrier to students choosing online learning will be removed.

Though the Open University in the United Kingdom is often cited as the model institution offering an entire curriculum remotely since 1970,[24] colleges in the United

Encyclopedia of Library and Information Sciences, Fourth Edition DOI: 10.1081/E-ELIS4-120008804

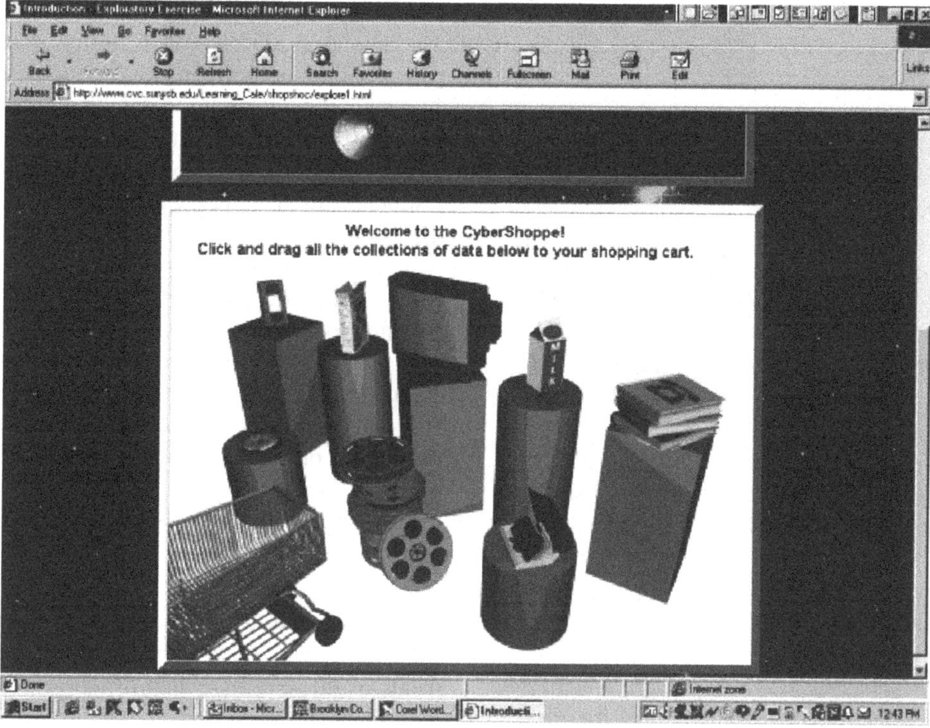

Fig. 1 An exercise from the Learning Café, an online information literacy tutorial. Tutorial exercises that allow for interactivity on a Web site are believed to increase student learning.(From Scarlatos.)[15]

States have offered technologically facilitated courses since the beginning of the twentieth century. Technologies that have enabled distance learning around the world have included standard radio and television transmission; microwave; cable; open circuit; closed circuit, and satellite transmission; teletext; telephone; audio conferencing; faxsimilie; videodisc; slow scan video; sideband FM transmission; and Instructional Television Fixed Services. Distance education programs have partnered universities with each other and with broadcasting networks, foundations, and corporations.[25–28]

Online Education as Distance Education

Linda Harasim makes the point that

> [o]nline education is not the same as distance education, although it shares some of the same attributes. Both are any place, any time, and largely text-based. However, the critical differentiating factor is that online education is fundamentally a group communication phenomenon. In this respect, it is far closer to face-to-face seminar-type courses.[29]

Whether the current examples of online library instruction conform to Harasim's model is a reflection of the evolving thinking about the purpose and method of library instruction, the varied audiences targeted, the content delivered, and the methods of delivery employed.

SETTING THE STAGE FOR ONLINE LIBRARY INSTRUCTION

Predictors and Predecessors

Looking to the future of libraries and librarians in the last two decades of the twentieth century, a number of writers foretell of the lessening of the importance of the physical library collection, the increasing availability of electronic resources, and the subsequent decreasing need for librarians to work in a dedicated, physical location. F. Wilfrid Lancaster describes libraries as becoming "disembodied," necessitating that in order "[t]o survive, the librarians must get out of the library."[30] Carolyn Dusenbury and Barbara G. Pease consider the lessening importance of having a physically present librarian in a physical library with particular respect to library instruction:

> Can we continue to expect users to come to our place at our pre-set time in order to learn what they need to learn? Can we expect all users to be equally motivated or equally ready to learn at the same time? These questions combined with staff and budget shortages are causing careful re-examination of how resources are deployed and how effective current programs are.[31]

The Library and the Early Days of Distance Education

Librarians have long been sensitive to the desire of students to learn research skills at their own convenience. Reference desks were established in libraries to provide point-of-need research assistance.[32–34] Similarly, an essential concept in distance learning is timing delivery to connect with the learner at the moment of need. The early efforts of libraries to use technology to reach and assist researchers studying on their own predate the widespread use of the Internet. In the 1980s and early 1990s, libraries saw video and satellite television as ways to instruct without an instructor being present.[35] Programs such as Elginet in Illinois,[36] the Library Video Network in Maryland and, nationally,[37] the Global Library Project at the Library of Congress[38–41] and the Library and Information Science Distance Education Consortium[42] developed and delivered staff and pre-professional training videos and information programming to the public. Fig. 2 shows the Library and Information Science Education Consortium website.

Computer Assisted Instruction (CAI) in Libraries Prior to the Internet

The computer-assisted demonstration

Librarians began to use the computer to assist with instruction as personal computers became more ubiquitous in libraries and on college campuses during the 1980s. At the same time as the growth in the availability of computers in the library, there was an increase in library reliance on online searching of remote subscription databases. Electronic classrooms with multiple computers available for all students were yet to come, but in the 1980s librarian instructors used computers with projection systems for live demonstrations of online resources to catch the attention of students and to give them a realistic sense of an online searching environment.[43] Moreover, librarians continue to teach with computer-assisted demonstrations using laptops and portable projection systems when the computer classroom in their library may not be available and they work with students in noncomputer equipped classrooms outside the library.[44]

Live assistance and hand-on, computer-based learning

The computer, as a tool to assist with learning information skills, moved out of the hands of the instructor and into the hands of the students when libraries gained access to or built computer classrooms. Librarians teaching in person instructed students in practical skills, particularly in online searching.[45] Linda Friend describes the new role academic librarians were able to play as consultants for their patrons who were paying for personal accounts on online systems. These remote users were working without detailed manuals and were likely to need help choosing

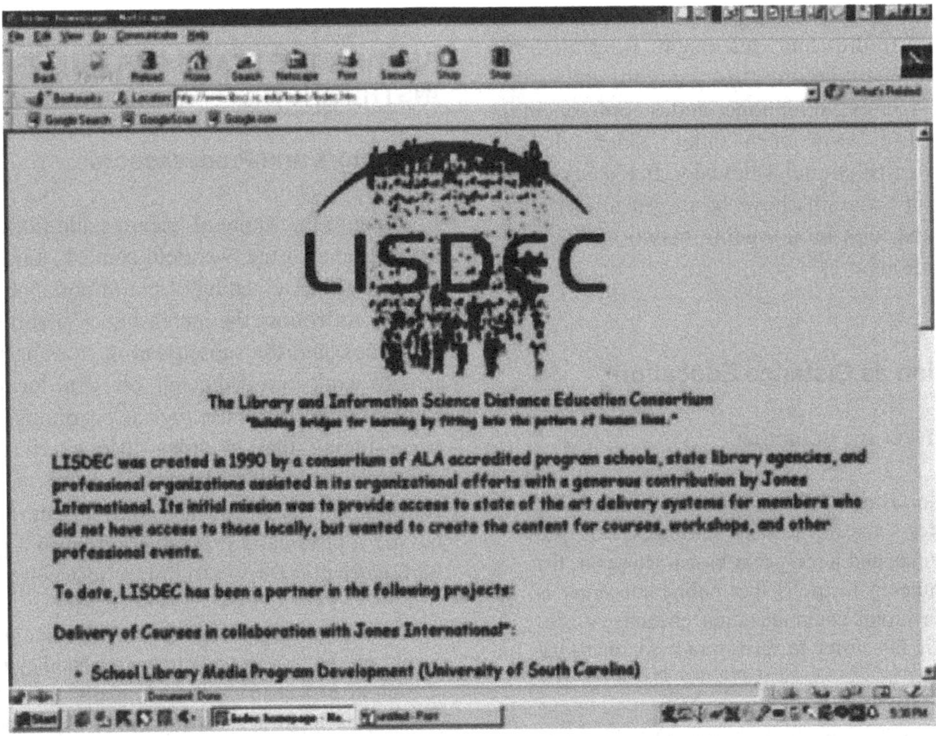

Fig. 2 Web site for the Library and Information Science Distance Education Consortium. Before wide-spread use of the Web, consortia fostered distance learning in librarianship through televised workshops.(From Barron.)[42]

search terms and constructing a search. Librarians provided initial patron training sessions in person and were then on call to do follow-up troubleshooting for students working at remote locations.[46] In addition to librarians giving live, hands-on instruction in searching vendor-provided databases, librarians also used the electronic library classrooms to instruct in how to use the online library catalog, or online public access catalogs (OPAC).[47] The OPAC has typically been a library-created database and not a subscription product available from a vendor. Requiring no per-search or connection-time fees, the OPAC was often the first publically available, end-user electronic resource in a library and an important candidate for classroom exploration.

Tutorials for independent learning

With the increasing presence of the personal computer in academic libraries, librarians began to develop computer-assisted instruction software to meet their local training needs. Instruction continued to focus on online searching as one content area. Nancy Fjällbrant observes the affinity between method and content in discussing CAI tutorials developed to teach online searching: "[o]nline information retrieval is an interaction dialogue between the user and the host computer. It is, therefore, hardly surprising that computer-based learning packages have been developed for online training purposes."[48] Tutorials for online searching instruction primarily targeted graduate students and faculty. Nonetheless, in addition to developing CAI for these advanced researchers, academic librarians created CAI applications to provide basic library instruction for large numbers of undergraduate students.

Librarians designing tutorials for stand-alone computers often used Hypercard and Macromedia's Authorware and Director. Instruction librarians who did not see themselves as technologically sophisticated praised these tools for their simplicity to learn and use.[49] Modules were developed and saved on CD-ROMs that could be mounted on individual library or campus lab computers,[50,51] set up in information kiosks,[52] or offered to students to use at remote sites. Andrew Cox, writing in 1997 with a historical perspective on pre-Internet CAI delivery, points out an advantage of students learning from the nonnetworked CAI modules. When students are working in the Web-environment, they can easily click their way out of their focused task. Students using tutorials in the stand-alone environment, however, are not as easily sidetracked.[53] Nonetheless, despite the possible drawbacks of delivering instruction through the Internet, as libraries began to go online, Web-delivered instruction began to replace CAI delivered on stand-alone workstations and on local area networks (LANs) restricted to the library or campus.

THE INTERNET, LIBRARIES AND ONLINE LEARNING

The Case for CAI

Arguments in favor of creating computer-based instruction have withstood the migration of delivery from stand-alone computers and LANs to delivery over the Internet. Supporters of CAI reason that student use of the computer-based instruction frees up staff time and offers a consistent set of material.[50,51] Additionally, when learning with live instruction, students are limited to learning from one individual. A CAI tool usually reflects the talent and ideas of a number of creators, and students gain from the expertise of all. Furthermore, when a librarian is not available to assist them, students may use a computer-learning module at their own convenience and work at their own pace. Working with a computer application provides students with a nonjudgmental environment where they may be more comfortable venturing with answers to questions posed or reviewing material taught early on in the tutorial. In addition, because CAI can be used outside of class, instructors do not need to give up any of their teaching time to allow for library instruction. Lastly, computer-based instruction can also reach upper-level transfer students who may have missed the standard library instruction offered in conjunction with a freshman class.[54–58] The many benefits of CAI and the increasing availability of Internet access have encouraged librarians to develop instructional tools to work in a number of teaching situations online.

Instructional Opportunities for Online Library Instruction

The advent of World Wide Web browsers has offered libraries new ways to instruct their remote users and the ability to reach more users than they can with stand-alone, CD-ROM tutorials. Online library instruction may be designed to orient users to a physical library or a library website through a virtual tour. The online instruction may focus on a single library tool such as an online public access catalog or on a vendor-provided database. It may provide general information literacy skills, focus on computer skills, teach research skills in the context of a given course, or deliver a full curriculum in library and information studies. The intended audience for online library instruction may be the public served by a single library or library system, K–12 students at a school, undergraduate and graduate students, faculty and staff at a college or university, library school students, working professionals in any field, librarians and library staff, individuals interested in upgrading their technology skills, and Internet surfers who may chance upon the website of a library providing instruction.

The virtual tour

Web-based information delivery has allowed many library services to be offered remotely. Consequently, researchers often may feel no need to visit the physical library. Librarians working with these remote patrons have often been eager to put a face on their virtual presence, or they have wanted to prepare visitors for what to expect before they visit an actual library, or they have created virtual libraries that have no physical equivalent as an access point to electronic information. Library virtual tours have been developed that make use of a range of Web technologies and give the distant user a sense of being in a physical place. The Stephens-Burnett Library at Carson-Newman College in Tennessee includes a virtual library tour module as part of a four-part instruction package. The virtual tour includes still images of each floor of the library and text descriptions.[54,55] The Texas Agricultural and Mechanical University Evans Library Educational Media Services Department used Spin Panorama to update its original virtual library tour of still photographs and give a more realistic view of the six floors of their library annex.[59–61] Using Macromedia Flash, librarians at the Baruch College of the City University of New York have created a virtual tour of the Newman Library with music and text available in nine languages.[62,63] Jeff Bobicki's Libtech, a virtual library in the Active World Librarea, connects to Bobicki's writings on library technology topics and biographic information about authors through links embedded in book and face images.[64–67] Each method of providing an online library tour orients information seekers so that they are better equipped to find what they need when they visit the physical library or continue to explore the virtual library website.

Focus on a single resource: the popular database and the OPAC

Librarians ponder if one day all library instruction will be built into every database they acquire for researchers. Successful, intuitive systems, it has been suggested, could eliminate the need for teaching librarians and serve as sufficient guides for doing research.[68,69] Recognizing the limitations of database software design as it currently exists for the end users, both remote and in the library, librarians in many environments have developed online tutorials focused on heavily used, individual electronic resources. Institutions with large numbers of potential users, such as public universities or urban library systems, cannot give extensive live instruction in their online catalog or heavily used aggregated database to thousands of users, but they can reach any one of these patrons with an OPAC or a database tutorial.[70–72] Database providers often provide help screens and tutorials to accompany the systems they design.[73,74] But, as Anne Tubbs Prestamo observes, users of electronic resources often do not use the built-in help links that come with most databases. Librarians who know the learning styles of their own clientele best may be the most appropriate instructors to design online help for these resources.[72]

Teaching information literacy skills

Arguments against librarians investing time in developing CAI for individual resources include concerns that the interface and search options may change or the library may cancel its subscription to the product. Frequent changes in the appearance and functionality of information resources remain part of the impetus to design an information literacy approach to library education. Furthermore, advocates for teaching information literacy skills suggest that librarians move away from tool-based instruction and adopt a concept-based approach to library instruction instead.[14] In designing CAI that teaches students how to use the online catalog and individual databases, librarians intended to package tool-based instruction and consequently free more of their time for concept-based instruction in the live classroom. Nonetheless, librarians have also developed online tutorials to deliver basic information literacy, or critical thinking skills. Nancy H. Dewald found, in 1999, that a majority of the online library tutorials noted by the ALA Library Instruction Round Table fell into this category of teaching general, information literacy skills.[75]

Colleges and universities that traditionally offered in-person classes have begun to supplement their curricula with distance education courses to provide an extensive range of information literacy tutorials. Commercial online education providers, however, such as the e-global library of Jones International, have also offered tutorials in library research skills for those studying through an institution partnered with Jones and for individuals willing to pay for the service.[76,77] Regardless of the provider, online information literacy skills tutorials are often modular with each module being made available as it is developed.[78] Though not tied to the academic courses of study that students will choose for their majors, basic online library instruction at academic institutions is often embedded in freshman courses designed to ease the transition from high school to college. Basic library tutorials are included as part of English composition courses generally required of all college students.[54,58,79,80]

Alternatively, librarians may develop basic library instruction modules without a guaranteed group of users in mind and seek out a small pilot group in one academic department when the online modules are ready to deliver.[81] Additionally, developers may find that online information literacy modules are adopted and required by faculty in a range of courses soon after the library makes them broadly available. Although the tutorial designers may create instruction modules with a look and feel designed for freshmen and sophomores, upper classmen are likely to use the tutorials and need to be considered as a potential audience in the design process.[78] A library may also consider offering its basic library instruction tutorial with multiple interfaces to appeal to its various targeted audiences.[82] Furthermore, a library may need to develop information literacy modules with varied content reflecting the developmental stages of student learning or a progression of skills.[83,84]

Discipline-specific online library instruction

An information literacy, or basic library skills, approach to research education, though it seeks to serve the needs of many, may be found to fall short in helping learners with specific, deep, and complex research assignments. Consequently, library instruction, live and online, in the university, is thought to be most effective when tied to the research work required of students registered in discipline-specific classes. Course-related library tutorials have been developed for courses in business,[85] criminal justice,[82] engineering,[86,87] chemistry,[88] biology,[89,90] modern languages,[91] and Latin American studies[92] as well as other disciplines.

Creating and successfully implementing course-related, Web-based instruction depends on cooperation between the library and college departments. A department may invite the campus library to develop a tool to assist with teaching research specific to a discipline.[85,92] An advantage of course-related library instruction is that departments are likely to pool resources with the library and jointly seek funding to cover the cost of technologically enhanced learning tools.[91] When developing course-related tutorials, the librarian typically will discuss their development and use with the classroom instructors who will be teaching the course prior to their delivery. When the classroom instructors are not familiar with the tools the library has created, the students, who are required to use the tools for problem solving in their classes, quickly become frustrated and see both their instructors and the library as falling short of adequately preparing them for their tasks.[89]

Library instruction tied to courses presents opportunities for collaboration and sharing among students, faculty, and librarians. In the Learning Links Project, jointly run by the Spanish and Portuguese Department and the Scholarly Communications Center of the library at Rutgers University in New Jersey, graduate students in Spanish language and culture courses developed websites and prepared multimedia material that the undergraduates used in their own study.[91] Students in a library media course at Georgia State University had an opportunity to do collaborative Web development online with a sister library in Toulouse, France.[93] Additionally, librarians who develop course-related, online resources have something substantive to share with their colleagues in the library. A librarian with responsibility for collection development in a particular subject area may rework, to suit his or her own instructional needs, a course-related tutorial developed by a colleague working in another discipline.[82]

Online library instruction as a credit course

Many institutions have designed online library instruction to teach broadly applied information literacy skills or to support specifically focused college courses. Though these modules and tutorials may be connected with individual courses, the library content is adjunct to the course content. Learning the library content may contribute to the students' earning a grade but achieving these skills is not an end in itself. Colleges and universities do offer a number of examples of library instruction comprising the complete content of online, credit-bearing courses. Moreover, the examples of information-skills courses offered for credit at academic institutions often have in common interinstitutional ties or multidisciplinary content. In some situations, in order to make the creation of the tutorial worth the time and resources required, extensive application of the finished tool is required.

The Utah Academic Library Consortium currently supports a credit-bearing, information literacy tutorial Internet Navigator offered in 10 public and private colleges and universities throughout Utah.[94] Fig. 3 shows the opening screen. Each participating school has independently selected the department that offers the course, has determined the amount of technical support needed, and has set tuition according to its own guidelines.[95] Mercy College in New York State and Hasharon Distance College in Israel partnered to deliver an eight week, eight module course on research using the Internet. Students at Hasharon take the required course in their first semester, are encouraged to connect their research to what is needed for their other classes, and use the subscription online resources offered by the hosting college in the United States. The instructor of the course notes the special cultural challenges of teaching across national boundaries.[96]

Interdisciplinary fields such as women's studies and area studies, or topics students develop that cross over discipline boundaries are challenging for both the classroom instructor and the librarian to teach and for students to research successfully. A brief, single session in the library is not adequate to introduce the major research tools from all the included disciplines. Nor is one individual instructor expert in the range of fields that may comprise an interdisciplinary topic. Consequently, interdisciplinary studies are good candidates for any method of library instruction that is not bounded by the constraint of a single session with a single instruction librarian in the library. Patricia J. Herron and Lily G. Griner have had an opportunity to teach a live, one credit research course in Latin American Studies and integrated a Web component, a noninteractive research guide, into

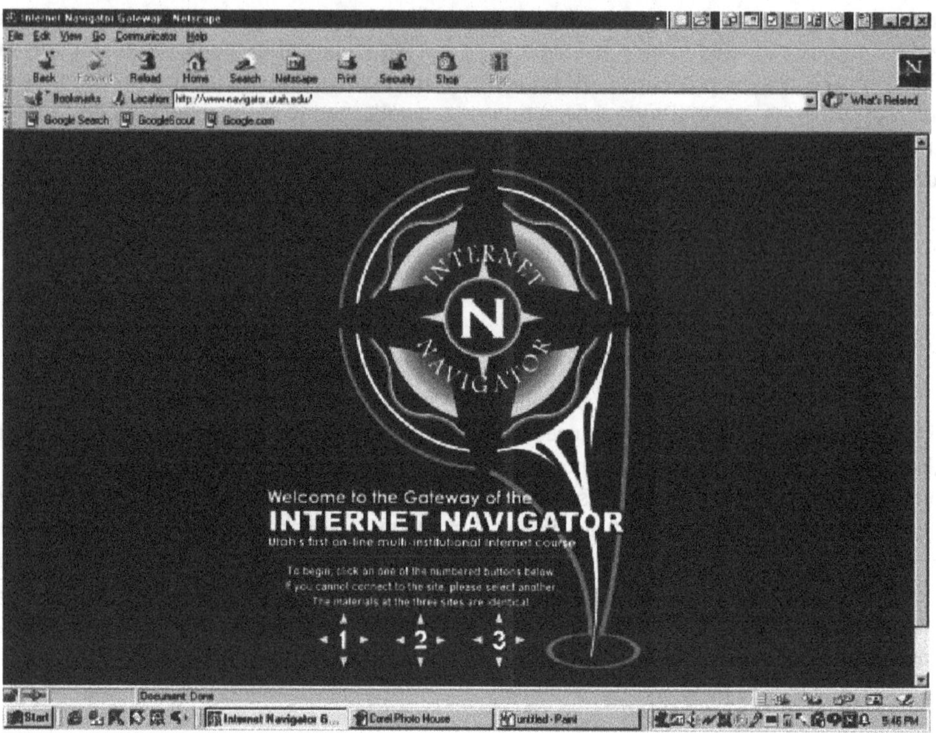

Fig. 3 The opening screen of the Utah Academic Library Consortium's Internet Navigator Tutorial. Library tutorials have been developed for use as credit-bearing courses implemented across a number of institutions.(From Hansen.)[95]

the course they teach. The guide is extensive, reflecting the many fields upon which an interdisciplinary course draws. It was designed for students to print out and use in support of their other Latin American Studies courses.[92]

Online library instruction in schools of library and information studies

Graduate programs in library education are increasingly providing opportunities for instructors to develop credit-bearing online courses in information skills. Thirty-six colleges and universities in 25 states in the United States and in Canada offer graduate students in library and information studies distance education opportunities.[97] In 2001 the United States Institute of Museum and Library Services awarded two of seven grants to universities and colleges with projects designed to recruit and educate students in library and information science through distance education.[98] Distance education programs in developing nations such as India and Thailand recognized the limited availability of computers and reached out to future librarians and information professionals with numerous study centers to provide online learning.[99–101] The Open University in the United Kingdom, educating a more affluent population, has encouraged personal computer ownership since the late 1980s and facilitated online learning in all disciplines including library and information studies.[102] The British Open University Library, once faulted for not opening its doors to part-time students,[103] began extending access to electronic resources to all students in the late 1990s.[104,105] This access is invaluable to distance learners in information studies. Fig. 4 shows the website of the University of Pittsburgh online MLIS program.

Online instruction for librarian professional development

Practicing librarians and library support staff continue to need instruction in understanding, using, and instructing in standard library operations, new resources, and technology systems. Commercial providers may concentrate on marketing one or two library-specific training tools,[106] offer a diverse listings of online tutorials in Internet research skills,[107] or provide a full catalog of online training options for both library and specialized technology skills with broad applications within and outside a library setting.[108,109] Library consortia and organizations also have offered practicing librarians online training.[110–112] In the fall of 2001, the Illinois State Library launched LibraryU, a clearinghouse of free tutorials aimed primarily at library staff and administrators, but they are also of use to library users.[113,114] The advantages of libraries turning to outside providers to provide on line training to upgrade the skills of their own professionals and staff are that training can be offered in an extensive range of topics and carefully targeted to the needs of selected individuals. For smaller libraries with limited staff and local talent, turning outside of their own institution is the only option for professional

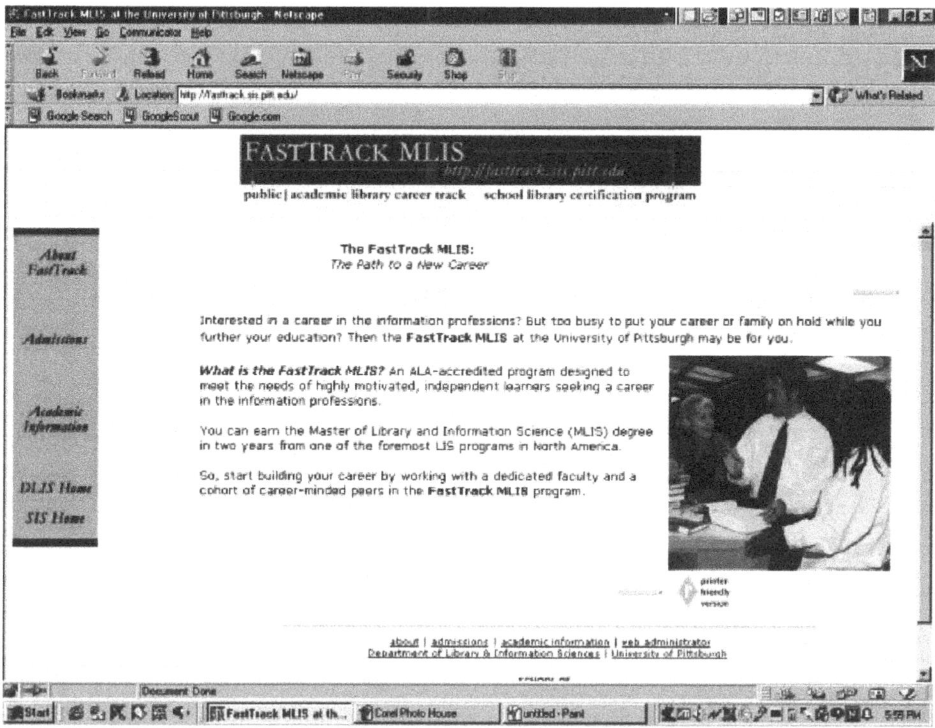

Fig. 4 The Web site for the FastTrack MLIS at the University of Pittsburgh School of Information Science. Graduate programs in library and information science are increasingly enabling future librarians to obtain a degree through distance learning.(Source: University of Pittsburgh.[5]

development. Fig. 5 shows a Webpage from an online workshop for professional librarians.

Options in Technology for Online Library Instruction

In addition to taking advantage of the many opportunities to offer online library instruction to a wide-ranging audience, libraries have experimented with an array of technologies to deliver online library instruction. Often libraries will mix different forms of technology in order to meet the different levels of students' needs and to work more effectively within the technological limitations of the library. Central Queensland University in Australia, for example, offers tutorial modules through the Web, but gives each participating chemistry graduate student an introductory video on the broad topic of information access and two CD-ROMs on searching the OPAC and on general database search strategies.[88]

The examples of online library instruction suggest that for online courses to be developed, librarians need to be skilled in their disciplines, adept in pedagogy, and in some situations able to negotiate the politics of passing a curriculum through a campus evaluation process. Furthermore, in order to design and deliver online library instruction in the Internet environment, librarians must be skilled in using a range of sophisticated and rapidly changing Internet-based technologies. Librarians have delivered online library instruction that has succeeded on different levels of functionality. Static Web pages have evolved into interactive, multifunctional sites. Some faculty have used courseware software to deliver their course content, while others have embellished their sites with streaming video and audio. Students have come to interact online with the course website, their professor, and their classmates. With each technology they choose, librarians have looked to appeal to their learners and to be effective teachers.

Moving beyond the static web page to web site interaction

The earliest and simplest uses of Web technology for teaching have involved construction of websites of information embedded with hyperlinks to related information. Librarians have designed sites as guides to major disciplines or tied directly to individual courses. The sites may reflect a particular instructor's syllabus and library assignments and can double as handouts students may download and study for their courses. Librarians may also offer questions and quizzes on the websites and require students to print out and answer the questions in a traditional manner.[92,115–117] As technological developments have given librarians the opportunity to reach a virtual community in a number of ways, advocates of using the Internet for instruction have urged librarians to think differently about how they can teach using a website. Bridget Loven and

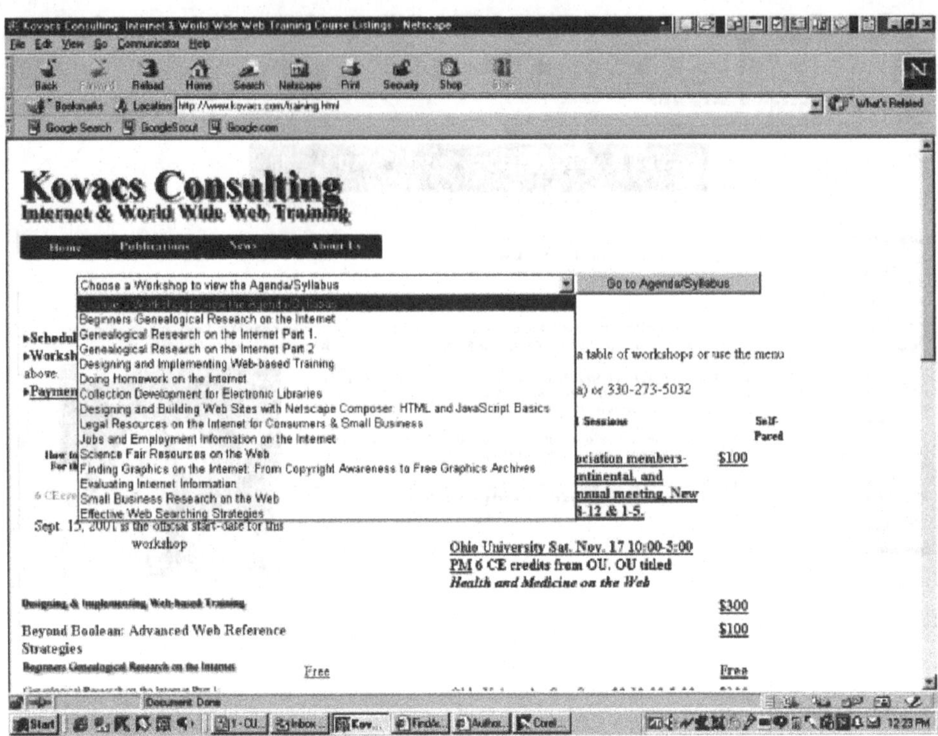

Fig. 5 The Web site for Kovacs Consulting. Independent trainers offering Web-based workshops provide continuing education opportunities for practicing librarians.Source: Kovacs Consulting.[107]

others stress that librarians "go beyond merely 'digitizing' handouts that already exist."[118] Websites designed for teaching should take advantage of technology that creates an environment as similar to a live situation as possible.

Although eager to create complex, technologically enhanced library instruction websites, libraries with a limited, in-house knowledge base may find themselves restricted to choosing only development tools that do not require extensive programming knowledge.[71] Nonetheless, library administrators may also consider the need to create online instruction tools as an opportunity to expand on the skills of the librarians working in their institution,[119] an occasion to hire nonlibrarians to do the development,[50] or a chance to find partners with the necessary skills outside of the library. Such varied strategies have enabled libraries to be at the forefront of online instruction with cutting-edge technologies and also to use low-end technologies in new and ingenious ways. The library at the University of Tennessee at Knoxville found that by positioning itself to be the pilot project for streaming video on campus, the Telecommunications and Network Services unit of the college provided network and digitizing support for them to build a virtual library tour.[120,121] Librarians at Bowling Green State University in Bowling Green, Ohio, conversely, used the simple ability to edit HTML source code from their Web-based catalog results screens, ready-made graphics, text written to appeal to students, and hyperlinks to create a Web-based tutorial for basic library instruction.[70,122] Because of Internet design restrictions on the Bowling Green campus, the authors looked for ways to achieve interactivity without the benefit of server-side scripts. Fig. 6 shows the opening screen of a virtual tour of the University of Tennessee Libraries. Fig. 7 shows the Bowling Green State University interactive tutorial FALCON.

Librarians have also used javascript programming and Macromedia Shockwave to enable their Web tutorials for interactive learning. Quizzes, such as those included in the tutorial for the library at the University of Nevada, Las Vegas,[123] depend on javascript to allow students to answer multiple choice questions online. The information literacy tutorial (TILT) at the University of Texas at Austin[124,125] and the Data Game at Colorado State University Libraries[126] instruct in basic library skills with appealing and often humorous Shockwave presentations that move as the viewer clicks and makes choices. Including exercises that require the learner to be more than a passive reader is frequently recommended for good library tutorial design.[75,127,128] Hyperlinking, scripting, and Shockwave have all given libraries different ways to integrate exercises into tutorial lessons and to include quizzes that require student input.

Reaching out to the online learner through electronic mail

Clicking on radio buttons and making selections from pull-down menus that are included as part of the exercises

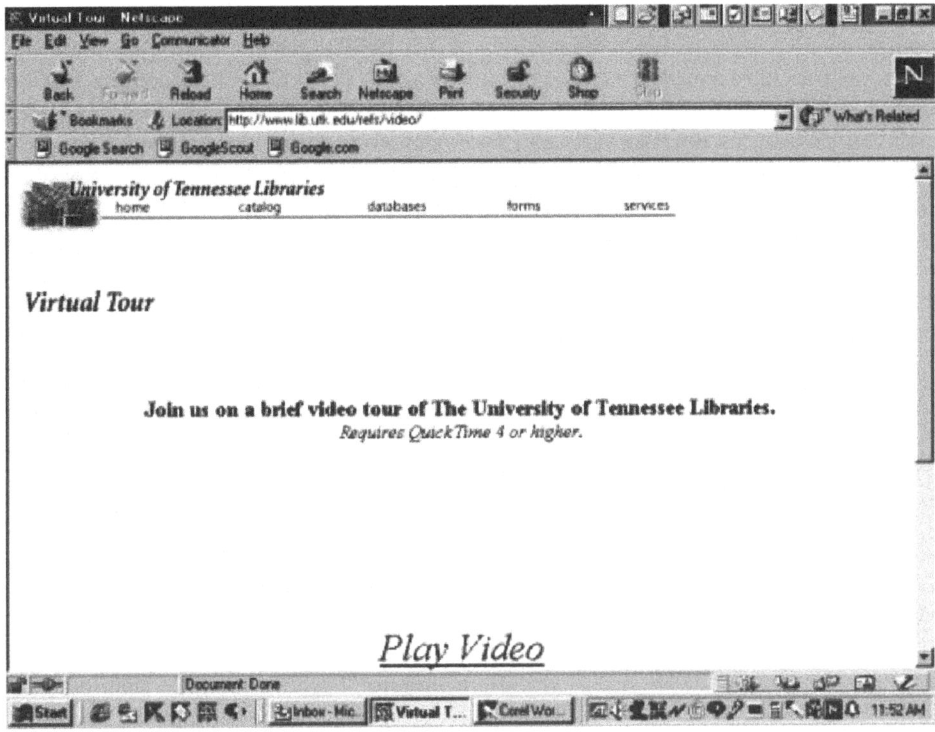

Fig. 6 Virtual Tour of the Hodges Library at the University of Tennessee at Knoxville. A QuickTime movie played on a Web site can substitute for an orientation tour of the library.Source: University of Tennessee Libraries.[121]

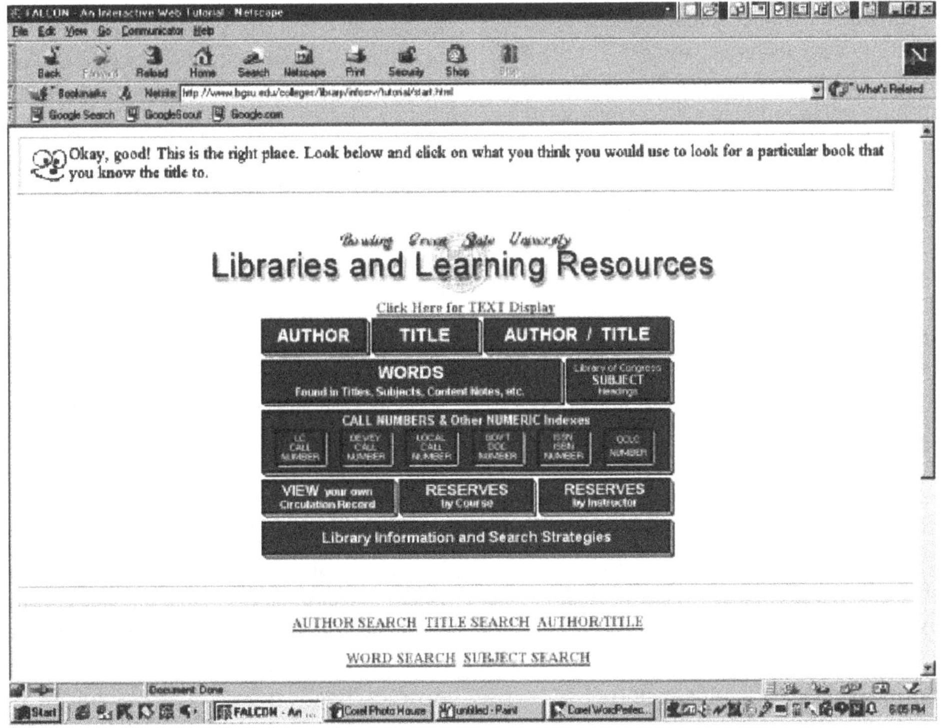

Fig. 7 FALCON, the interactive tutorial created for the libraries at Bowling Green State University in Bowling Green, Ohio. ©2001 Stefanie Hunker (used by permission of the author). Often a library tutorial may focus on a single resource and allow for interactivity without server or client-side scripting. Source: From Hunker.[122]

or quizzes on an instructional website may give users of library tutorials a sense of active participation in the learning process. However, libraries have aimed to increase the interactive experience of online learning so that the student's interaction can be with the librarian instructor, or with other students, whenever possible, rather than only with a computer program or a website. Prior to the widespread use of graphical Web browsers, librarians reached out directly to potential users by delivering lessons in segments through e-mail. The librarians have instructed faculty, students, and staff, both affiliated and unaffiliated with their institutions. The e-mail instruction opened an opportunity for a direct, online conversation with an individual librarian.[129–131] Even when libraries are able to offer instruction through the Web, as Sigrid Kelsey points out,

> [t]he e-mail messages constitute a form of pro-active outreach; in contrast the web pages [are] a passive method of instruction largely dependent upon the participants' initiative to educate themselves.[132]

Sending out instruction modules through e-mail may be seen as proactive, but once students have an invitation to e-mail an instruction librarian, the amount of student feedback may vary greatly. One librarian, who had established a mailing list of 109 interested readers for her seven-week sequence of lessons, received three e-mail queries from her students.[132] Another librarian, however, running an online course with three graduate students in a school media program, sent out over 650 course-related e-mail messages, most dealing with technical issues.[93] Academicians will often cite the large amount of e-mail that may be associated with running an online course to counter the belief that online education provides an opportunity to teach larger classes with no increase in instructor workload. Instructors have documented that running an online course and reading and answering student e-mail is more time consuming than running a traditional class.[133] Teaching librarians in all capacities, who make themselves available to their students through e-mail, are as vulnerable to an unknown quantity of contact as instructors in other disciplines. Despite the potential for an overwhelming student response to an e-mail invitation offering support, however, librarians who offer their contact information to students and who also collect student e-mail addresses when they have the opportunity may find they have facilitated communication with individuals who might otherwise have held back from their instructor and remained reluctant to ask questions.

Expanding the connection with conferencing software, courseware, chat, and co-browsing

Telecommunications facilities allow the remote learner to communicate and to learn as part of a social process, what Søren Nipper calls "the key element in the conceptual development of third generation models of distance learning."[134] E-mail opened the first door of communication in the virtual classroom. Conferencing software and courseware have added features that enable the online classroom to mirror the physical classroom more fully. Conferencing or threaded discussion software allows for asynchronous discussion among students and instructors. An instructor posts text for consideration or poses a question and students respond. Each student's response is posted on a growing stream of responses to the initial posting. New topics engender new streams of responses.

Students may not be any more responsive as a group when their class includes a threaded discussion than they are when they sit in a live classroom. Consequently, instructors have a responsibility to keep students involved in an online threaded discussion.[96] Faculty may have to cajole reluctant students to participate and require them to refer to the discussion content in their written assignments.[24] As with physical classrooms, some students are more willing to participate than others. Conversely, students who may be reluctant to talk in a traditional classroom may be more comfortable and willingly express themselves in a written discussion setting.

Multifunction courseware packages such as TopClass,[135] eCourse,[136] WebCT,[137] and Blackboard[138] have expanded instruction possibilities for librarians offering course-integrated and credit-bearing instruction. The packages do not require the instructor to know hypertext mark-up language (HTML). They allow teachers to incorporate text documents and multimedia on their course sites, manage multiple courses, give online examinations, and monitor their students' achievement and grades. The software may provide an area for student biographies and images so that student working together virtually can attach faces to names of classmates. One application originally designed for business conferencing, Microsoft's Netmeeting, integrates a camera and audiobridge to allow online library instruction to include audio and visual connections in real time.[18]

A number of courseware packages allow for chat or synchronous discussion in addition to threaded discussion forums.[80,91] Chat, or software that allows typed conversation in realtime, is becoming increasingly popular with libraries of all types. Businesses and dot-com information services such as Webhelp[139] use chat to provide real-time customer service and to answer a range of queries.[140–142] Chat allows libraries to extend their reference services with point-of-need assistance and may be used to answer reference questions as well as to instruct.[143–145] Chat can be useful for librarians running online classes. It enables them to set up online office hours and have real-time conversations with their remote learners. Fig. 8 shows a website[145] where online chat can be used for communication.

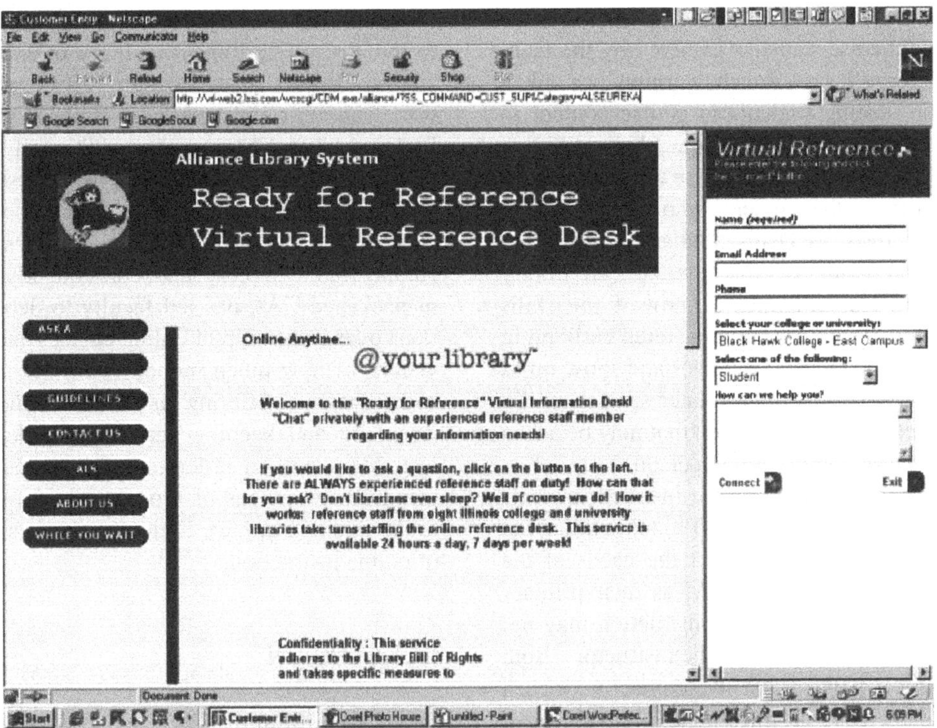

Fig. 8 The Virtual Reference Desk (Library Systems and Services) of the Illinois-based Alliance Library System. Chat software allows librarians to provide round-the-clock reference assistance and help with research. Source: Alliance Library System.[145]

Chat as a tool for classroom interaction is limited by the typing abilities of those communicating and the tendency of chat conversations to become disjointed. Furthermore, most libraries currently offering chat service do not have the capability to engage more than one user synchronously with a librarian and each other. An emerging Web technology that is likely to replace chat and eliminate the tendency of conversations to become fragmentary is Voice over Internet Protocol (VoIP). Using VoIP, teaching librarians and remote learners can speak to each other using their computers and avoid the typing required in chat.[146–148] A drawback of VoIP is that it requires users on both ends to upgrade their computers with expensive peripheral hardware. It was not until chat software that did not require the client computer user to download any plug-ins became available that librarians began to set up chat services. Until the cost of having access to VoIP drops and the procedures for installing it are simplified, librarians are not likely to see it as practical for providing remote assistance and instruction.

Some software libraries have used, other than courseware, incorporates a chat function and may also allow for collaborative Web browsing. Collaborative Web browsing is useful for online library instruction when a librarian is working in real time with an individual student doing Internet research. The screen exchange allows the remote student to show the librarian unsuccessful strategies and results and the instructor to show effective alternative search techniques.[149–151]

Assessment of Online Library Instruction

Usability, learning outcomes, and learner/instructor preferences

Recent studies of alternative teaching methods in libraries have found that students learn equally well with live instruction and with online tutorials.[90,152,153] Such evidence may encourage libraries with shrinking resources to embark on a program of online instruction. Nonetheless, libraries and all institutions of learning that have a distance learning program in place need to evaluate individually if the way in which they are teaching is effective and should be continued.[154,155] Teachers and administrators have to consider student feedback on the usefulness and appropriateness of the online instruction methodology in addition to examining evidence of student learning.[85]

The Emerging Technologies in Instruction Committee of the Instruction Section of the Association of College Libraries provides a number of criteria libraries may use to evaluate their instructional tutorials.[156] Early on in the process of designing a tutorial, libraries can evaluate how usable their online instruction is by organizing focus groups of testers who mirror their potential users.[78] Measuring the usability of an online instructional tool, nonetheless, differs from measuring the effectiveness of the instruction carried within the tool. Whereas computer and telecommunications technology makes tracking the use of instructional material possible in ways that could not have been done before so much information became available electronically,[157] the use statistics gathered by the technology do not measure how much learning has taken place. In addition, testing students in course content in online learning situations presents unique challenges that would not exist in a live classroom where the student seen attending a course is the student who arrives for a test.[96,158,159] Moreover, as Denis Madland and Marian A. Smith point out, with specific reference to library instruction, educators would like to know if the skills learned through a library tutorial administered early on in the college career of a student carry over and show up as ability in a student doing research in later semesters.[160] The question, nonetheless, is a question that may be asked of all library instruction, online and in person.

Libraries may find that using online instruction meets their needs to reassign professional staff to other tasks, but online instruction may not meet all of the needs of the students who are asked to use the CAI as their primary tool of learning. Furthermore, online instruction may not meet all the needs or desired goals of the instructors. Both students and instructors may favor live contact with each other and doubt that electronic correspondence is the most efficient or effective way to communicate with each other. Students encountering all library tools virtually through a CAI module may look for opportunities to use the physical library collection,[161] value anything they can take away in print from a session with an online tutorial,[58,90] and give highest ratings to the time spent with a librarian in person when their lessons couple traditional and online learning.[80] Moreover, in some situations, computer-based instruction may be contraindicated. Students in a freshman program at California State University at San Marcos were not confident in their computer skills. This weakness, coupled with difficult subject matter, inhibited learning.[79] Additionally, according to one study, students tracked into online library instruction modules as an alternative to live instruction show a high rate of failure to complete the instruction as offered.[153] In addition, student ownership of a personal computer has been found to impact on the ability of participants in a sequence of online library instruction to do well in the course.[86] Colleges and universities requiring that students learn through CAI need to consider this imbalance in outcomes as they plan a campus computer infrastructure and, alternatively, debate requiring all incoming students to own or lease a personal computer.

Economic viability

In addition to determining if online instruction is an effective teaching tool, researchers and administrators are interested in assessing the economic value of developing online learning.[162,163] Librarians may assert that online instruction saves money without giving specific evidence of the facts.[56,153] V. Lonnie Lawson, however, did a cost analysis of developing CAI for library tours in comparison to the cost of staffing live library orientation visits. The analysis showed that the high cost of investing in hardware can outweigh the cost-savings in staff time.[164] Polley Ann McClure argues, additionally, that the use of technology in education is still in the research and development stage where the costs of development are a long way from being recovered.[165] The desire of academic administrators to reuse, and, consequently, prorate the cost of packaged CAI, has led faculty to debate their institutions over ownership of online courses and has challenged visions of how much money could be made by colleges and universities offering instruction online.[166] Moreover, designing and keeping current multiple versions of an instruction tool in order to reach learners who may be using older versions of browsers, have slow connections to the Internet, or have limited vision is an added expense of online instruction.[78,84,120]

CONCLUSION

Individual institutions of education, including libraries, will find themselves reviewing programs of online education at other institutions as well as in their own settings to decide if such programs should be implemented, need to be redesigned, or are doing well to serve their purpose. Beyond the programmatic level, nonetheless, these same institutions and academicians everywhere are considering the place of online education in the greater philosophical framework of what is the fairest and best way for an individual to learn.[167] Concurrent with the discussion about the overall value of online education, moreover, librarians have been engaged in an ongoing dialog to define themselves clearly as educators, rather than guardians or deliverers of information. Electronic resources and telecommunications connectivity have removed the content of libraries from the physical structures of these institutions. Traditional library users have gone into cyberspace seeking out information and taking it where they find it. Librarians who see that their users are turning to this new online setting, look for ways to continue to play a role in the information-seeking experience for these online adventurers, even as they continue to serve a physical public.[168] Just as providing the information alone may never have been enough of a role to play to satisfy librarians who recognize that knowledge is more than information, developing ways to make information more understandable remains an important goal for librarians in an online environment. Whether they play this role in the design of the systems that deliver information, or stand aside from the information systems as partner-explorers with the information seekers, librarians continue to recognize the importance of researchers having successful experiences in their search for and assimilation of information. Remembering that the information seeker is the reason that information is gathered has encouraged librarians to migrate with their users into the online environment. Providing online library instruction has enabled librarians to meet their users where they are working and make the connection from one physical space to another across the digital information sphere.

REFERENCES

1. Denver Public Library. In *Kid's Catalog Web*; http://kcweb.coalliance.org/kcweb/kcHome (accessed July 10, 2001).
2. Cedrone, M. *Children and their Use of Online Public Access Catalogs*; http://www.pages.drexel.edu/~mec24/index.html (accessed July 10, 2001).
3. Sandlian, P. *The Kid's Catalog Project: Customizing Networked Information*. Emerging Communities: Integrating Networked Information into Library Services, 30th Annual Clinic on Library Applications of Data Processing University of Illinois at Urbana/Champaign, April, 4–6, 1993; The Board of Trustees of The University of Illinois, 1993. http://www.cni.org/docs/illinois.dpc/sandlian.html (accessed July 10, 2001).
4. Kaskey, S. The law librarian as trainer. Legal Ref. Serv. Q. **1999**, *17* (3), 37–38.
5. University of Pittsburgh, School of Information Science, *FastTrack MLIS*; http://fasttrack.sis.pitt.edu/ (accessed August 21, 2001).
6. Bond, E. Creating an interactive multimedia training program. In *Promoting Preservation Awareness in Libraries: A Sourcebook for Academic, Public, School, and Special Collections*; Drewes, J.M.; Page, J.A., Eds.; Greenwood: Westport, CT, 1997; 256–259.
7. American Library Association ALA*Action* 2005; http://www.ala.org/work/alaction2005.html (accessed August 24, 2001).
8. American Library Association. In *Education and Continuous Learning*; http://www.ala.org/work/educationbrochure.html (accessed August 24, 2001).
9. McClure, L.W. Education for health sciences librarians. In *Encyclopedia of Library and Information Science*; Kent, A., Ed.; Marcel Dekker, Inc.: New York, 1997; Vol. 60, 64–83. Supp. 23.
10. Medical Library Association. In *Platform for Change: The Educational Policy Statement for the Medical Library Association*; http://www.mlanet.org/education/platform/index.html (accessed August 21, 2001).
11. Special Library Association. In *Mission Statement, Vision and Strategic Plan*; http://www.sla.org/content/SLA/strategic/slanplan/index.cfm (accessed July 12, 2001).
12. Kilcullen, M. Teaching librarians. In *Encyclopedia of Library and Information Science*; Kent, A., Ed.; Marcel Dekker, Inc.: New York, 2001; Vol. 69, 365–380. Supp. 32.
13. Kilcullen, M. Teaching librarians to teach. Ref. Serv. Rev. Summer **1998**, *26* (2), 7–8.
14. Oberman, C. Introduction. In *Read this First: An Owner's Guide to the New Model Statement of Objectives for Academic Bibliographic Instruction*; Dusenbury, C.; Fusich, M.; Kenny, K.; Woodard, B., Eds.; ACRL: Chicago, IL, 1991; 1–4.
15. Scarlatos, T.; Evans, B. *Welcome to the Cybershoppe!* http://www.cvc.sunysb.edu/Learning_Cafe/shopshoc/explore1.html (accessed September 19, 2001).
16. Maggio, T.G.; Blazek, R. On-campus and off-campus programs of accredited library schools: A comparison of graduates. J. Educ. Libr. Inf. Sci. **1990**, *30* (4), 315–329.
17. Beitz, N.C. Academic advisement for distance education students. J. Educ. Libr. Inf. Sci. **1987**, *27* (4), 280–287.
18. Pival, P.R.; Tuñón, J. Netmeeting: A new and inexpensive alternative for delivering library instruction to distance students. Coll. Res. Libr. News **1998**, *59* (10), 758–760.
19. Barron, D.D. Distance education in United States library and information science education. In *Encyclopedia of Library and Information Science*; Kent, A., Ed.; Marcel Dekker, Inc.: New York, 1993; Vol. 52, 72–85. Supp. 15.
20. Olsgaard, J.N. The impact of a distance education program on enrollment patterns. J. Educ. Libr. Inf. Sci. **1987**, *27* (4), 272–279.
21. Barron, D.D. Alternative delivery of library and information science education: Introduction. J. Educ. Libr. Inf. Sci. **1987**, *27* (4), 219–222.
22. National Center for Educational Statistics. In *Distance Education at Postsecondary Education Institutions: 1997–98*; http://nces.ed.gov/pubsearch/pubsinfo.asp?pubid = 2000 013 (accessed July 22, 2001).
23. Smith, G. In *Distance Learning: Perspectives from a Library Technologist and Student*, National Online Meeting 19th: 1998, National Online Meeting Proceedings, New York, May, 12–14, 1998; Information Today: New York, 1998; 365–374.
24. Mason, R. From distance education to online education. Internet High. Educ. **2000**, *3* (1/2), 63–74.
25. Barron, D.D. Faculty and student perceptions of distance education using television. J. Educ. Libr. Inf. Sci. **1987**, *27* (4), 257–271.
26. Barron, P.P. Production of a telecourse in library and information science: Jump over the moon: Sharing literature with young children. J. Educ. Libr. Inf. Sci. **1987**, *27* (4), 247–256.
27. Faibisoff, S.G.; Willis, D.J. Distance education: Definition and overview. J. Educ. Libr. Inf. Sci. **1987**, *27* (4), 223–231.
28. Wilson, S. The sky's the limit: A technology primer. J. Educ. Libr. Inf. Sci. Spring **1987**, *27* (4), 233–239.
29. Harasim, L. Shift happens: Online education as a new paradigm in learning. Internet High. Educ. **2000**, *3* (1–2), 41–61.
30. Lancaster, F.W. Future of librarians lies outside the library. Cathol. Libr. World **1980**, *51*, 388–391.
31. Dusenbury, C.; Pease, B.G. The future of instruction. J. Libr. Adm. **1995**, *20* (3/4), 97–117.
32. Ensor, P. Virtual library instruction: Training tomorrow's user today: Remembering our in-library clients. In *Recreating the Academic Library*; La Guardia, C., Ed.; Neal-Schuman: New York, 1998; 221–230.
33. Eadie, T. Beyond immodesty: Questioning the benefits of BI. Res. Strategies **1992**, *10* (3), 105–110.
34. Brundin, R.E. Education for instructional librarians: Development and overview. J. Educ. Libr. Inf. Sci. **1987**, *27* (4), 177–189.

35. Hammond, N. New technologies to the aid of the user education programme. In *User Education in Academic Libraries*; Fleming, H., Ed.; The Library Association: London, 1990; 121–139.
36. Vision Research Consortium. In *Investigation of Partnership Models Between Libraries and Cable-Based Telecommunications Providers: A Study Commissioned by the Library and Information Commission and the Cable Communications Association: Final Report, Elginet Case Study*; http://www.librariesandcable.co.uk/54.htm (accessed July 24, 2001).
37. Baltimore County Library. *What is Library Video Network?*; http://www.bcpl.net/~inlib/what.html (accessed July 24, 2001).
38. Library of Congress Fiveson named director of global library project. Libr. Congr. Inf. Bull. February 6, **1995**, *54*(3), gopher://marvel.loc.gov:70/00/loc/pubs/lcib/1995/vol54.no3/10 (accessed July 24, 2001).
39. Library of Congress. In *PR94-143: Film/TV Producer to Head Global Library Project*; http://www.loc.gov/today/pr/1994/94-143 (accessed July 24, 2001).
40. Library of Congress. In *PR95-37: Northern Telecom to Award $1 Million to LC*; http://www.loc.gov/today/pr/1995/95-037 (accessed July 24, 2001).
41. Library of Congress. *Madison Council Highlights*; http://lcweb.loc.gov/development/council.html (accessed July 24, 2001).
42. Barron, D. *LISDEC: Library and Information Science Distance Education Consortium*; http://www.libsci.sc.edu/lisdec/lisdec.htm (accessed July 24, 2001).
43. Bell, S.J. Using the live demo in online instruction. Online **1990**, *14*, 38–42.
44. MacDonald, B.S. Class act: Designing a portable approach to multimedia library instruction for the remote classroom. Res. Strategies **1998**, *16* (2), 127–133.
45. Bruce, C.S. Educating users of remote online systems. In *Encyclopedia of Library and Information Science*; Kent, A., Ed.; Marcel Dekker, Inc.: New York, 1994; Vol. 54, 155–182. Supp. 17.
46. Friend, L. Independence at the terminal: Training student end users to do online literature searching. J. Acad. Librariansh. **1985**, *11* (2), 136–141.
47. Wiggins, M.E. *Hands-On Instruction in an Electronic Classroom. A Final Report to the U. S. Department of Education of a Research and Development Grant Awarded to Establish a Fully-Equipped Electronic Training Room and Test the Effectiveness of Hands-On Instruction in Learning the NOTIS OPAC and Silver-Platter ERIC*; ERIC, 1994. ED369391.
48. Fjallbrant, N. Recent trends in online user education. IATUL Q. **1988**, *2*, 228–236.
49. Niemeyer, C. Authorware for computer-assisted instruction. Libr. Hi Tech **1997**, *15* (1–2), 133–144.
50. Forys, M. Library explorer: A voyage toward self-directed learning. Internet High. Educ. **1999**, *2* (1), 5–9.
51. Dixon, L.; Garrett, M.; Smith, R.; Wallace, A. Building library skills: Computer-assisted instruction for undergraduates. Res. Strategies **1995**, *13* (4), 196–208.
52. Pasicznyuk, R. Application development for user instruction: Constructing an interactive kiosk. Colo. Libr. Summer **1995**, *21*, 44–45.
53. Cox, A. Using the World Wide Web for library user education: A review article. J. Librariansh. Inf. Sci. **1997**, *29* (1), 39–43.
54. Kocour, B.G. Using web-based tutorials to enhance library instruction. Coll. Undergrad. Libr. **2000**, *7* (1), 45–54.
55. Kocour, B.G. *Virtual Tour*; http://news.cn.edu/kocour/virtual.htm (accessed August 7, 2001).
56. Edwards, R.G. Web tutorials for education students: A practical alternative to traditional library instruction-basic issues and concerns. Behav. Soc. Sci. Librar. **2000**, *18* (2), 17–25.
57. Ardis, S. Creating internet-based tutorials. Inf. Outlook **1998**, *2* (10), 17–20.
58. Vander-Meer, P.F.; Rike, G.E. Multimedia: Meeting the demand for user education with a self-instructional tutorial. Res. Strategies **1996**, *14* (3), 145–158.
59. Xiao, D.Y. Experiencing the library in a panorama virtual reality environment. Libr. Hi Tech **2000**, *18* (2), 177–184.
60. Xiao, D. *PanoramaVR Tour Sterling C. Evans Library Annex*; http://library.tamu.edu/edms/tour/anxtour.htm (accessed July 30, 2001).
61. Mosley, P.A.; Xiao, D. Touring the campus library from the World Wide Web. Ref. Serv. Rev. **1996**, *24*(4)7–14, 30.
62. Downing, A.; Klein, L.R. A multilingual virtual tour for international students: The web-based library at Baruch College opens doors. Coll. Res. Libr. News **2001**, *62* (5), 500–502.
63. Klein, L.R. *William and Anita Newman Library Virtual Tour*; http://newman.baruch.cuny.edu/about/v_tour/ (accessed July 30, 2001).
64. Bobicki, J. *Overview of Librarea*; http://www.swrlss.org/aw1.html (accessed July 30, 2001).
65. Bobicki, J. *Welcome to Librarea*; http://www.jefftech.net/jack1.html (accessed July 30, 2001).
66. Active Worlds; http://www.activeworlds.com (accessed July 30, 2001).
67. California Virtual Campus, Statewide/Rural Regional Center. In *Professional Resources*; http://www.cvc4.org/web_pages/library_resources/professional_resources.htm (accessed July 30, 2001).
68. Rapple, B.A. In *The Electronic Library and the Future Function and Training of Librarians*. National Online Meeting 19th: 1998, National Online Meeting Proceedings, New York, May, 12–14, 1998; Information Today: New York, 1998; 307–331.
69. Grassian, E. Librarian-teachers and the virtual library. In *Recreating the Academic Library*; LaGuardia, C., Ed.; Neal-Schuman: New York, 1998; 203–219.
70. Dennis, S.; Broughton, K.M. FALCON: An interactive library instruction tutorial. Ref. Serv. Rev. **2000**, *28* (1), 31–38.
71. Johnson, A.; Sager, P. Too many students, too little time: Creating and implementing a self-paced, interactive computer tutorial for the libraries' online catalog. Res. Strategies **1998**, *16* (4), 271–284.
72. Prestamo, A.M.T. In *Development of Web-Based Tutorials for Online Databases*. National Online Meeting 19th: 1998 National Online Meeting Proceedings, New York, May, 12–14, 1998; Information Today: New York, 1998; 275–287.
73. EBSCOhost. In *EBSCOhost Help*; http://ehostvgw20.epnet.com/help/EBSCOhost.htm (accessed August 26, 2001).

74. Proquest. In *Proquest Guided Tour*; http://www.proquest.com/hp/Features/PQDTour/ (accessed August 26, 2001).
75. Dewald, N.H. Transporting good library instruction practices into the web environment: An analysis of online tutorials. J. Acad. Librariansh. **1999**, *25* (1), 26–31.
76. Heilig, J.M. E-Global library: The academic campus library meets the Internet. Searcher **2001**, *9* (6), 34–43.
77. *Jones E-Global Library*; http://www.egloballibrary.com/index.html?page = /home.html (accessed August 22, 2001).
78. Bender, L.J.; Rosen, J.M. Working toward scalable instruction: Creating the RIO tutorial at the University of Arizona Library. Res. Strategies **1998**, *16* (4), 315–325.
79. Sonntag, G. Using technology in a first year experience course. Coll. Undergrad. Libr. **1999**, *6* (1), 1–16.
80. Getty, N.; Burd, B.; Burns, S.K.; Piele, L. Using courseware to deliver library instruction via the Web: Four examples. Ref. Serv. Rev. **2000**, *28* (4), 349–359.
81. Scholz, A.M.; Kerr, R.C.; Brown, S.K. PLUTO: Interactive instruction on the Web. Coll. Res. Libr. News **1996**, *6* (6), 346–349.
82. Jayne, E.A.; Arnold, J.; Vander-Meer, P.F. In *Casting a Broad Net: The Use of Web-Based Tutorials for Library Instruction*, Off-Campus Library Services Conference 8th. The Eighth Off Campus Library Services Conference Proceedings, Providence, RI, Central Michigan University: Mount Pleasant, MI, 1998; 197–205.
83. Samson, S. What and when do they know? Web-based assessment. Ref. Serv. Rev. **2000**, *28* (4), 335–342.
84. Fowler, C.S.; Dupuis, E.A. What have we done? TILT's impact on our instruction program. Ref. Serv. Rev. **2000**, *28* (4), 343–348.
85. Donaldson, K.A. Library research success: Designing an online tutorial to teach information literacy skills to first-year students. Internet High. Educ. **1999**, *2* (4), 237–251.
86. Curl, S.R.; Reynolds, L.J.; Mai, B.; Macklin, A.E.S. Reality check: Asynchronous instruction works. Coll. Res. Libr. News **2000**, *61* (7), 586–588.
87. Byers, D.F.; Wilson, L. *The Web as A Teaching Tool.*, National Online Meeting 17th: 1996 National Online Meeting Proceedings, New York, May, 14–16, 1996. Information Today: New York, 1996; 31–36.
88. Orr, D.; Duncum, C.; Wallin, M. CHEMPAGE: A model for exploring the Internet for professional development. Aust. Libr. J. **1998**, *47* (2), 183–189.
89. Orians, C.; Sabol, L. Using the Web to teach library research skills in introductory biology: A collaboration between faculty and librarians. Issues Sci. Technol. Librariansh. Summer **1999**, *23*. http://www.library.ucsb.edu/istl/99-summer/article2.html (accessed August 22, 2001).
90. Kaplowitz, J.R.; Contini, J. Computer-assisted instruction: Is it an option for bibliographic instruction in large undergraduate survey classes? Coll. Res. Libr. January **1998**, *59* (1), 19–27.
91. Kessleman, M.; Khanna, D.; Vazquez, L. Web authorware and course-integrated library instruction: The Learning Links project at Rutgers University. Coll. Res. Libr. News **2000**, *61* (5), 387–390. 402. http://www.ala.org/acrl/webauthor.html (accessed August 22 , 2001).
92. Herron, P.J.; Griner, L.G. Research strategies and information sources in Latin American studies: A one-credit, Web-based course. Res. Strategies **1999**, *17* (1), 11–21.
93. Hindes, M.A. Can Web-based instruction foster information literacy? School Libr. Worldw. **2000**, *6* (2), 88–101.
94. Utah Academic Library Consortium. In *Internet Navigator*; http://www-navigator.utah.edu/ (accessed August 3, 2001).
95. Hansen, C.; Lombardo, N.T. Toward the virtual university: Collaborative development of a web-based course. Res. Strategies **1997**, *15* (2), 68–79.
96. Rao, S.; Ickowitz, C. In *Developing a Distance Learning Course on Using the Internet for Research*, National Online Meeting 22nd: 2001. National Online Meeting Proceedings, New York, May, 15–17, 2001. Information Today: New York, 2001; 413–421.
97. American Library Association. In *ALA Accredited LIS Programs that Provide Distance Education Opportunities*; http://www.ala.org/alaorg/oa/disted.html (accessed August 22, 2001).
98. Institute of Museum and Library Services. In *IMLS Responds to Nation's Shortage of Librarians Funds Recruitment, Education and Technology Training*; http://www.imls.gov/whatsnew/current/071701-1.htm (accessed August 7, 2001).
99. Kanjilal, U. Education and training of library and information science professionals through distance mode: Challenges for the Infira Gandhi National Open University in the next millennium. FID Rev. **1999**, *1* (2/3), 44–49.
100. Kanjilal, U. Reaching out to distance learners in library and information science at the Indira Gandhi National Open University. Inf. Dev. **1997**, *13* (1), 19–22.
101. Sacchanand, C. The information science programs of the School of Liberal Arts, Sukhothai Thammathirat Open University (STOU), Thailand. J. Educ. Libr. Inf. Sci. **1996**, *37* (2), 191–199.
102. Jones, A. Providing home computing facilities for students learning at a distance. Educ. Inf. **1990**, *8* (4), 313–324.
103. Library Association Library doors shut on Open University. Libr. Rec. **1991**, *93* (10), 676.
104. Whitsed, N. A look at the Open University Library. Electr. Libr. **1997**, *15* (5), 369–371.
105. Carty, J.; Stark, I.; Van der Zwan, R. Towards a strategy for supporting distance-learning students through networked access to information: Issues and challenges in preparing to support the doctorate in education. Educ. Inf. **1996**, *14* (4), 305–316.
106. LibraryTools.com. http://www.librarytools.com (accessed September 7, 2001).
107. Kovacs Consulting. *Internet and World Wide Web Training*; http://www.kovacs.com/training.html (accessed August 22, 2001).
108. Element K. http://www.elementk.com/ (accessed August 24, 2001).
109. Smart Force. http://www.smartforce.com (accessed August 24, 2001).
110. Neale, J. NYLINK Advisory Group Meeting, Albany, NY, April, 25, 2001.
111. Metropolitan New York Library Council Exploring online courses: An interview with Jacqueline Mundell. @Metro **2001**, *6* (3), 1.
112. Special Library Association. In *Learn with SLA*; http://www.sla.org/content/learn/index.cfm (accessed July 12, 2001).

113. Illinois State Library. In *LibraryU*; http://www.libraryu.org (accessed September 7, 2001).
114. Levine, J. *[WEB4LIB] Re: Web-Based Training on Library Skills*; http://sunsite.berkeley.edu/Web4Lib/archive/0105/0124.html (accessed September 7, 2001).
115. Au, K.N.; Tipton, R.L. In *Webpages as Courseware: Bibliographic Instruction on the Internet*, National Online Meeting 18th: 1997. National Online Meeting Proceedings, New York, May, 13–15, 1997. Information Today: New York, 1997; 21–25.
116. Gray, D. Online at your own pace: Web-based tutorials in community college libraries. Va. Libr. **1999**, *45* (1), 9–10.
117. Northern Virginia Community College. In *Library Tutorial*; http://www.nv.cc.va.us/library/tutorial/ (accessed August 22, 2001).
118. Loven, B.; Morgan, K.; Shaw-Kokot, J.; Eades, L. Information skills for distance learning. Med. Ref. Serv. Q. **1998**, *17* (3), 71–75.
119. Evans, B. The authors of academic library home pages: Their identity, training and dissemination of Web construction skills. Internet Res. **1999**, *9* (4), 309–319.
120. Crowther, K.N.T.; Wallace, A.H. Delivering video-streamed library orientation on the Web: Technology for the educational setting. Coll. Res. Libr. News **2001**, *62* (3), 280–285.
121. University of Tennessee Libraries. In *Virtual Tour*; http://www.lib.utk.edu/refs/video/ (accessed August 26, 2001).
122. Hunker, S.D. *Falcon: An Interactive Web Tutorial*; http://www.bgsu.edu/colleges/library/infosrv/tutorial/tutor1.html (accessed August 22, 2001).
123. University of Nevada at Las Vegas. In *U LV Library Tutorials*; http://library.nevada.edu/help/tutorial/index.html (accessed August 26, 2001).
124. The University of Texas System Digital Library. In *TILT: Texas Information Literacy Tutorial*; http://tilt.lib.utsystem.edu/ (accessed August 26, 2001).
125. Dupuis, E.A. *Designing Interactive Instructional Environments*; http://staff.lib.utexas.edu/~beth/Presentations/Interact/ (accessed August 20, 2001).
126. Colorado State University. In *The Datagame Game*; http://lib.colostate.edu/datagame/datagame.html (accessed August 31, 2001).
127. Association of College and Research Libraries, Instruction Section Teaching Methods Committee. In *Tips for Developing Effective Web-Based Library Instruction*; http://www.lib.vt.edu/istm/WebTutorialsTips.html (accessed August 22 , 2001).
128. Dewald, N.H. Web-based library instruction: What is good pedagogy? Inf. Technol. Libr. **1999**, *18* (1), 26–31.
129. Jensen, A.M.; Sih, J. Using E-mail and the Internet to teach users at their desktops. Online September/October **1995**, *19*, 82–86. http://www.onlineinc.com/onlinemag/OL1995/SepOL95/jensen-sih.html (accessed June 15, 2001).
130. Burke, J. Using E-mail to teach: Expanding the reach of BI. Res. Strategies **1996**, *14* (1), 36–43.
131. Butros, A. Using electronic mail to teach MELVYL MEDLINE. Med. Ref. Serv. Q. **1997**, *16* (1), 69–75.
132. Kelsey, S.E. Library user education: Implementing an E-mail bibliographic instruction course at a college library. LLA Bull. **1999**, *61* (4), 222–225.
133. Liu, Y.; Thompson, D. Teaching the same course via distance and traditional education: A case study. ERIC **1999**.
134. Nipper, S. Third Generation Distance Learning and Computer Conferencing. In *Mindweave: Communication, Computers and Distance Education*; Mason, R.; Kaye, A., Eds.; Pergamon Press: Oxford, 1989; 63–73http://www-icdl.open.ac.uk/mindweave/chap5.html (accessed August 22, 2001).
135. WBT Systems. In *TopClass e-Learning Suite*; http://www.wbtsystems.com/products/products.html (accessed August 26, 2001).
136. eCollege. In *eCourse*; http://www.ecollege.com/solutions/Teaching_Course.html (accessed August 26, 2001).
137. WebCT. In *WebCT*; http://www.webct.com (accessed August 26, 2001).
138. Blackboard. In *Welcome to Blackboard*; http://www.blackboard.com (accessed August 26, 2001).
139. Webhelp. In *Webhelp*; http://www.webhelp.com (accessed August 26, 2001).
140. Tomaiuolo, N.G. Aska and you may receive: Commercial reference services on the web. Searcher **2000**, *8* (5), 56–62. http://www.findarticles.com/m0DPC/5_8/61945075/p1/article.jhtml (accessed August 8, 2001).
141. Lipow, A. "In your face" reference service. Libr. J. **1999**, *124* (13), 50–52.
142. Livereference. In *Group on Live Reference Services for Librarians*; http://groups.yahoo.com/group/livereference (accessed August 8, 2001).
143. Francoeur, S. *The Teaching Librarian: Digital Reference*; http://pages.prodigy.net/tabo1/digref.htm (accessed August 8, 2001).
144. In *Facets of Digital Reference, The Virtual Reference Desk.* Conference Proceedings of the 2nd Annual Digital Reference Conference, Seattle, WA, October, 16–17, 2000; Kasowitz, A.S., Stahl, J., Eds. http://www.vrd.org/conferences/VRD2000/proceedings/index.shtml (accessed August 22, 2001).
145. Alliance Library System; In *Ready for Reference: Virtual Reference Desk*; http://vrl-web2.lssi.com/wcscgi/CDM.exe/alliance/?SS_COMMAND = CUST_SUP&Category = ALSEUREKA (accessed September 19, 2001).
146. Schuyler, M. Meet your new friend VOIP. Comput. Libr. **2000**, *20* (6), 56–57.
147. Brinsmead, A.M.; Lang, G.M.; McTavish, L. In *Create Online Learning for Where It's Going To Be, Not Where It's Been: An Online Pedagogy for 2006*, WebNet 99, World Conference on the WWW and Internet Proceedings, Honolulu, HI, October, 24–30, 1999. ED448699.
148. Learn, L.L. Internet telephony: The next killer application? (Or, how I cut my long-distance phone bill to nothing!). Libr. Hi Tech News June **1995**, *123*, 12–19.
149. Anderson, E.; Boyer, J.; Ciccone, K. In *Remote Reference Services at the North Carolina State University Libraries*, Facets of Digital Reference, The Virtual Reference Desk, Conference Proceedings of the 2nd Annual Digital Reference Conference, Seattle, WA, October, 16–17, 2000; http://www.vrd.org/conferences/VRD2000/proceedings/boyer-anderson-ciccone12-14.shtml (accessed August 8, 2001).

150. Lieberman, H.; Van Dyke, N.; Vivacqua, A. *Let's Browse: A Collaborative Web Browsing Agent*; http://lieber.www.media.mit.edu/people/lieber/Lieberary/Lets-Browse/Lets-Browse.html (accessed August 8, 2001).
151. Sidler, G.; Scott, A.; Wolf, H. In *Collaborative Browsing in the World Wide Web*, Proceedings of the 8th Joint European Networking Conference, Edinburgh, Scotland, May, 12–15, 1997; http://www.tik.ee.ethz.ch/~cobrow/papers/jenc8/jenc8.html (accessed August 8, 2001).
152. Foust, J.E.; Tannery, N.H.; Detlefsen, E.G. Implementation of a web-based tutorial. Bull. Med. Libr. Assoc. **1999**, *87* (4), 477–479.
153. Holman, L. A comparison of computer-assisted instruction and classroom bibliographic instruction. Ref. User Serv. Q. **2000**, *40* (1), 53–60.
154. Tobin, T.; Kessleman, M.A. Evaluation of web-based library instruction programs. INSPEL **2000**, *34* (2), 67–75.
155. Vargo, J. Evaluating the Effectiveness of Internet Delivered Courseware. In *AusWeb97 Conference Program and Papers*; http://ausweb.scu.edu.au/proceedings/vargo/index.html (accessed July 31, 2001).
156. Association of College Libraries, Instruction Section, Emerging Technologies in Instruction Committee. In *ACRL/CNI Internet Education Project: Selection Criteria*; http://www.cwru.edu/affil/cni/base/selection.html (accessed August 15, 2001).
157. Newmarch, J. Courseware on the Web: An Analysis of Student Use. In *AusWeb97 Conference Program and Papers*; http://ausweb.scu.edu.au/proceedings/newmarch/index.html (accessed July 31, 2001).
158. Guernsey, L. For those who would click and cheat. N.Y. Times April **26, 2001**, *150,* Circuits. Sec. G, page 8, col. 3.
159. Software Secure. In *Securexam*; http://www.softwaresecure.com/ (accessed August 31, 2001).
160. Madland, D.; Smith, M.A. Computer-assisted instruction for teaching conceptual library skills to remedial students. Res. Strategies **1988**, Spring*6*, 52–54.
161. Wright, C.A. Applications of the model statement to a basic information access skills program at Penn State University. In *Read this First: An Owner's Guide to the New Model Statement of Objectives for Academic Bibliographic Instruction*; Dusenbury, C.; Fusich, M.; Kenny, K.; Woodard, B., Eds.; ACRL: Chicago, 1991; 22–29.
162. Carr, S. Is anyone making money on distance education? Chronic. High. Educ. February 16 **2001**, *47*, 23. http://chronicle.com/free/v47/i23/23a04101.htm (accessed August 30, 2001).
163. Garson, G.D. The political economy of online education. In *Encyclopedia of Library and Information Science*; Kent, A., Ed.; Marcel Dekker, Inc.: New York, 1999; Vol. 65, 192–208. Supp. 28.
164. Lawson, L. A cost comparison between general library tours and computer-assisted instruction programs. Res. Strategies **1990**, *8* (2), 66–73.
165. McClure, P.A. Technology plans and measurable outcomes Educom Rev. **1996**, *31* (3), 29–30.
166. Carnevale, D. New intellectual property policy at Stevens is a model, both sides agree. Chronic. High. Educ. November 22 **2000**. http://chronicle.com/free/2000/11/2000112201u.htm (accessed August 30, 2001).
167. Young, J.R. Author warns students—and colleges—to avoid on-line education. Chronic. High. Educ. November 3, **1999**. http://chronicle.com/free/99/11/99110302t.htm (accessed September 2, 2001).
168. Kent, C.M. Is Anyone at Home?. In *Recreating the Academic Library*; LaGuardia, C., Ed.; Neal-Schuman: New York, 1998; 257–264.

Online Public Access Catalogs (OPACs) *[ELIS Classic]*

Kevin Butterfield
Wolf Law Library, College of William and Mary, Williamsburg, Virginia, U.S.A.

Abstract
In one form or another, from a mental list in the mind of the librarian, to book catalogs, card indexes, and online information retrieval systems, some type of meta access has existed to guide library users through library collections. Over the last 40 years, these constructs of paper and wood evolved into Online Public Access Catalogs (OPACs). When the catalog shifted out of drawers and off of three by five cards to become a networked, universally accessible entity, its role in the library shifted as well. The OPAC competes with the World Wide Web, metadata registries, search engines, and more sophisticated database structures for attention. Amongst this assortment of access mechanisms, the purpose of the OPAC has become muddled. The OPAC has now become one information source among maOnline Public Access Catalogs (OPACs)ny and one of a number of portals for accessing library collections and beyond.

INTRODUCTION

As long as there have been libraries there have been catalogs. In one form or another, from a mental list in the mind of the librarian, to book catalogs, card indexes, and online information retrieval systems, some type of meta access has existed to guide library users through collections. Over the last 40 years, these constructs of paper and wood evolved into Online Public Access Catalogs (OPACs). When the catalog shifted out of drawers and off of three by five cards to become a networked, universally accessible entity, its role in the library shifted as well. The OPAC competes with the World Wide Web, metadata registries, search engines, and more sophisticated database structures for attention. Amongst this assortment of access mechanisms, the purpose of the OPAC has become muddled. The OPAC has now become one information source among many and one of a number of portals for accessing library collections and beyond.

HISTORICAL DEVELOPMENT

The OPAC is understood to be the technological device that replaced the card catalog. The card catalog had in turn replaced the book catalog form that preceded it. The widespread acceptance of the card catalog at the beginning of the twentieth century reflected a trend towards standardization. The format used by these card catalogs lasted well into the 1990s and represented the influence of mass production in libraries. Catalog cards were first written by hand in library script, then typed, and ultimately ordered from vendors or the Library of Congress. Later they were produced via bibliographic utilities such as OCLC using MARC records. Each change in turn marked a move toward a more efficient means of record creation and maintenance.

The widespread acceptance of the online catalog in the early 1980s marked a trend toward experimentation in library catalog design.[1] However, the card catalog still has a strong influence on how current OPACs have been developed. Current systems and usage patterns are historical artifacts of the library card catalog. The OPAC interfaces and usage patterns embody a history of assumptions made during the card era.[2] At the time online catalogs were developed, the library catalog had reached a remarkable degree of standardization and stasis as a device. The standardization arose from the mass production of cards and from the cultural acceptance of the card catalog as an access device. Online catalogs upset that stasis, and it appears that the standardization enjoyed during the era of the card catalog will not return for some time.[2]

Online catalogs did not develop during a crisis situation. There was no pressing need to find an alternative to the card catalog. The technological capability was there, so the attempt was made to apply the new technologies to the existing systems and routines. Thus OPACs were not brought about by a revolution, but by an evolution of need. A large catalyst in this development was the creation and widespread acceptance of MARC. Use of MARC led to lower cataloging production costs and a greater standardization of description. The first attempts at library automation revolved around card production, acquisitions, and serial control. As the data formerly typed by hand or printed onto three by five cards was encapsulated and transmitted via the MARC formats, libraries and bibliographic utilities began to amass archives of bibliographic records. A natural next step for these libraries was to experiment with making access to these archives available to librarians, libraries, and the public by adapting or

Encyclopedia of Library and Information Sciences, Fourth Edition DOI: 10.1081/E-ELIS4-120045435

creating search interfaces and emerging computer and database technologies. Early library automation centered on using these records to computerize circulation functions. This tendency to apply new technology to existing systems and routines is a common response to technological advance. There seemed to be no overwhelming burden under which librarians and users toiled that motivated them to push for the development and implementation of online catalogs. Consequently, the OPAC was not expected to be a great improvement over previous catalog formats. It was simply seen as a better, faster way to realize desirable system and cost efficiencies.[2]

The cost and capabilities of computer and communications technologies shaped the ability of libraries to realize these efficiencies, as well as drove the dominant trends in library automation over the last three decades.[3] In the specific case of OPACs, four factors can be seen as necessary for their development and acceptance:[2]

1. The technology had to be available.
2. It had to be available at a price that was perceived as cost efficient by potential purchasers.
3. The systems had to be acceptable to users with their specific needs.
4. Online catalogs had to mesh with the goals of the libraries that developed or purchased the system.

The requisite technology for the birth of online catalogs (other than the MARC record structure perhaps) developed outside the library profession. This parallels the current trend in digital library development. Digital libraries initially arose out of the engineering and computer science disciplines before catching on in libraries. In the early days of OPAC development, library collections still revolved around monographs and serials, in various physical formats. Automated library access to monographic holdings developed after automated access to journal literature in most fields was well established.[4] Many of the design features of the prototype online catalog systems, however, did not mimic the automated systems for access to journal articles.

The card catalog remains as the most influential parent of online catalogs and reinforces the evolutionary nature of their development. Online databases of journal articles, for example, did not emulate printed abstracts and indexing tools to the extent that early online catalogs emulated the printed card catalogs.[2] This may have been an outgrowth of the fact that the same MARC record used to produce a catalog card was being used to create an on-screen display. Libraries did not switch en masse from card catalogs to OPACs. Large bibliographic utilities such as OCLC were still producing cards for libraries during this transition period. As a result, there was no immediate or revolutionary change in the basic record structure. It still had to play a dual role.

The development of Integrated Library Systems (ILS) and OPACs has been a response to needs for efficient production and maintenance workflows within libraries. Needs for efficient authority control, inventory tracking of serials, circulation, and acquisitions were among the initial reasons for their development. Most systems developed out of MARC-based cataloging systems or commercial online circulation systems. In both of these instances, automation of library staff functions came first. Efficient production and maintenance routines were the chief attraction of online catalogs, not enhanced access. To the extent that access was discussed, an increased number of access points to bibliographic records were stressed, rather than enhanced user access possibilities.[2] Much of this can be traced to the relative lack of search engine and interface design development at the time, but it also demonstrates the continued influence of the card catalog paradigm.

Although several academic libraries offered enhanced keyword searching early in OPAC development, it was not until the advent of the World Wide Web that we see real pressure from users to develop more sophisticated search and display mechanisms for OPACs. As the field of interface design began to thrive and better, faster more efficient search mechanisms became standard on the Internet and within commercial databases, the pressure to develop more effective services to users of OPACs grew. The World Wide Web and the perceived universal access to content it provides have raised expectations for OPAC interface design.

The imagined production efficiencies hoped for from ILS and OPACs were within the library as an institution, not efficiencies to be realized by the users of information systems. Initially, online catalogs were much more attractive to libraries and librarians than they were to users.[2] In terms of automating arduous tasks and maintaining tighter bibliographic control, the systems were a boon to libraries. Unfortunately interface design at the time was not as sophisticated an area as today. This resulted in often-difficult interactions with the catalog as users attempted to grasp the new technology.

Online catalog development initially was supported by underfunded institutions (e.g., libraries) and the systems needed to be designed for a broad, untrained user population. Database and user interface design were not, then, traditionally part of the librarians experience. This was definitely the case during these early days. These two facts may explain why online catalogs were not on the leading edge of bibliographic storage and retrieval development and reflect the evolutionary, rather than a revolutionary, nature of their development.[2] These systems were designed not to replace, but to enhance and continue preexisting practice.

There were three major types of OPAC systems developing during these early years: in-house, consortium, and package or turnkey systems.[5] Of the pioneering in-house systems, the Library Control System (LCS) of the Ohio State University Libraries is perhaps the best known. Developed by IBM for the university in the late 1960s, it developed from a circulation system to an online catalog. The LCS planners did not envision patrons conducting their own searches at public terminals nor did they plan on replacing the card catalog with LCS. Nevertheless, both of these things came to pass.

Notable milestones introduced by LCS in 1978 included the ability to store and display full bibliographic records, the provision of subject access to records, and the ability to browse through subject heading lists.[5] Other pioneering in-house systems were Northwestern University's Northwestern Online Total Integrated System (NOTIS) and the Virginia Tech Library System (VTLS).

Libraries and library consortia that have designed and developed online catalogs locally to provide access to their databases of MARC records represent another type of online catalog development. What sets these online catalogs apart from those such as LCS and NOTIS is their radical departure from the card catalog as the model for online searching. The database structure and search methods of these catalogs were modeled largely after commercial information retrieval systems such as DIALOG and BRS. The challenge for these online catalogs was not merely to apply the models used by these information retrieval systems but to also preserve the traditional functions of the catalog and to produce a retrieval system that could be used by novices without assistance.[5] Dartmouth College Library developed an end-user, self-explanatory, user interface to the BRS retrieval system as their online catalog in the early 1980s by creating a database using Dartmouth's OCLC transaction tapes. These MARC records were converted to BRS's internal record format. The project was innovative in its interface design goals and it uses of a record structure other than MARC.

One of the more significant consortial endeavors was begun in 1977 by the University of California system. Dubbed MELVYL, the purpose of the catalog was to make it possible to use the separate collections of the university's libraries as a single collection or to allow a user at any campus to access the collection at any other campus. Since some of the UC libraries used OCLC and others used RLIN, MELVYL became the first catalog to successfully merge OCLC and RLIN records into a single database. The prototype version went operational in 1981. As a public-access retrieval system, MELVYL was innovative in that it had a file structure that supported keyword access and Boolean queries, a patron interface that included two user-selectable dialog modes (menu-guided and command language) and an extensive "help" facility.[5]

During the 1970s commercial vendors began to replace large university libraries as the principal developers of computer-based library systems.[3] Among the reasons were libraries' lack of funding and research and development staffing. Commercial vendors were able to fund development more consistently; however, they did not always understand the access needs of patrons. These were more inventory control systems with a searchable front end for the public than true information retrieval systems. Early online systems evolved according to the hardware and software systems of the era. Those that ran on proprietary operating systems and hardware fell away replaced by those that ran on operating systems thought of as industry standards.[6] These turnkey systems were implemented in libraries often with mixed results.

The economic and technical realities of the 1980s favored increased autonomy and local library responsibility.[3] A reaction to the economies of scale of the online technologies developed. In the 1980s administrators tried to regain much of the control over their own operations and decision making that they gave up to the networks in the 1970s.[3] Many institutions of higher education were getting out of the systems design, development, and support business.[2] Libraries began either purchasing entire systems from vendors or assembling ILS modules from several different vendors to create systems that fit their needs.

During the 1990s, integrated systems design became the exclusive domain of vendors. However, libraries and universities began exploring a tangential subject, that of digital library development. With the explosion of the World Wide Web in the mid-1990s, many information retrieval systems and search engines were developed to locate, organize, and retrieve information on the Web. The OPACs, as information retrieval systems, were, in many cases, left behind. They are now beginning to find a role in this new information landscape. The interfaces for these early OPACs tended to be less user friendly than their paper-based predecessors. The strongest pressure for the adoption of online catalogs came not from users, but from library management. Again, a need to find better, faster ways to realize production and management efficiencies was a driving force. However, the more online catalogs are expected to perform the functions of inventory control, acquisitions, cataloging, and public access to the collection, the less likely it is that public users will have a system well designed for public use.[7]

WHAT DO OPACs Do?

The OPAC serves as a public face on a library's ILS. The ILS controls the following functions:

- Circulation (keeping track of items checked out and by whom)
- Cataloging (keeping and offering access to materials)
- Acquisitions (acquiring new items and tracking payments for them)
- Serials (tracking periodicals, claiming missing, or nonreceived items and binding)
- The OPAC
- Interlibrary loan (cooperative sharing of library materials)

At the core of the majority of ILS is the MARC record. Although there are innovative systems using BRS/Dataware, SGML/XML, or SQL to reformat data, typically a MARC/AACR2r-based bibliographic record serves as the focal point for all functions. Order, serial check-in, item, and circulation records "hang" off of it. The bibliographic record acts as a surrogate for the item describing its provenance, content, and container. The ancillary records document financial transactions related to acquisition, continued maintenance, and usage by the public. The OPAC interface translates MARC tags within the records to display labels read more easily by the public (i.e., 100 becomes author, 650 becomes subject).

A great deal of effort must be put into translating tags into labels that make sense to nonlibrarians. Also, given the large number of tags in the typical MARC record, the OPAC displays can run quite long. This has given rise to the traditional brief record display in today's OPAC. Typically one MARC tag generates one labeled field unless the system is instructed to collapse fields together. The library can, depending upon the ILS involved, control what gets displayed and in what order.

The OPACs will search MARC records by author, keyword, corporate name, class number, title, series author/title acronym, ISBN/ISSN/LCCN, subject heading keyword, and subject heading browse. In addition, most OPACs offer phrase and keyword searching. Keyword searching within OPACs has become problematic. Web search engines lead users to believe that OPACs provide deeper access to content than they actually do. The OPAC keyword search is dependent upon the keywords being used within the MARC record. A Web search engine keyword query may mine the full text of an item in an effort to locate the terms used. Since an OPAC consists of item surrogates rather than complete text, the results are not the same.

A review of OPAC search logs may reveal that users attempt to use the OPAC as if it were a Web search engine without knowledge of the classification and subject heading structures inherent in it. Content enhancement of the basic OPAC record would allow the user to take full advantage of the abilities of the basic OPAC, let alone the future incarnations. Addition of abstracts, table of contents, back of the book indexes, etc. would greatly enhance the search experience.

Advanced OPACs allow users to sort and save search results for export in specific data formats. Results can be imported into programs for creating bibliographies or databases. Increased access is also available to patrons for reviewing their circulation records or, in the case of academic libraries, print and retrieve reserve materials for classes.

The OPACs began as stand-alone systems unique to each library, much the same as card catalogs. If a user wished to search the online catalogs of multiple institutions, they would need to locate the catalogs for each and run their search repeatedly. As networking and the Internet came to the fore, more and more OPACs became linked via academic, regional, and statewide consortia. Consortia allow for simultaneous searching across member catalogs or group specific types of libraries together in clusters depending upon the subjects they represent (law, theology, etc.) or their status (academic, public, etc.). Consortial catalogs allow users to search the catalogs of multiple institutions at once, collate the results, and request materials needed through cooperative borrowing arrangements. This allows users access to the combined catalogs of many public and academic libraries with enhanced borrowing functions. It facilitates cooperative collection development among the institutions involved, as they will now be able to see where collections overlap. This has become more prevalent as libraries shift from the paradigm of collecting materials "just in case they are needed" to providing access to materials "just in time."

In addition, bibliographic utilities placed public search interfaces on their union catalogs. OCLC's WorldCat and FirstSearch allow users to search across OCLC's database and retrieve records for items throughout the world. The OCLC's Intercat and CORC projects have extended the scope of the catalog beyond traditional media. Increasingly, recent journal holdings are being made available to libraries through aggregator databases. In a number of cases, vendors will hook the holdings of a particular journal title in their databases to the MARC record in the library's OPAC, allowing users to find the print version of the text should the full text not be available in the vendor's database.

These recent enhancements to OPACs have allowed them to serve as gateways or proxy servers to licensed databases. The ILS patron database can be used to verify that an individual has authorization to access the databases and ensure that the library functions within licensing agreements. Also, additional enhancements have allowed title-level access to aggregator databases, and hooks to holdings that allow reverse access as well. Methods have become available that allow users to jump directly from an OPACs bibliographic record to a Web site or electronic file, text, or journal. Use of the 856 MARC field as a linking technology or bridge between the catalog record and the item described has made this commonplace. It alters, significantly, definitions of the catalog. Now the catalog not only describes what the library owns, but also what the library potentially has access to. These developments illustrate a growing convergence of portal development and OPAC design. Through this portal-OPAC, the user gains access to resources and people far beyond what earlier, more traditional definitions of a catalog would allow.

HOW EFFECTIVE ARE OPACS?

Users come to the OPAC with a particular need for information. However, they tend to search the OPAC as if it were a Web search engine. While various metadata schemes exist to provide more structure to Web-based information, they are not in widespread use. As successive generations of users, savvier at searching, come to expect natural language oriented, full text searching and retrieval, the OPACs interface and search capabilities begin to look dated in structure and potential. The surrogate record structure does not lend itself easily to that type of query. Most users are unaware of the catalog's structure and are unable to use it effectively.

OPACs depend on user expertise for reasonably successful operation. Given their increased use of search engines on the Web, it is hard for users to understand that they cannot find everything in the catalog by using their own vocabulary, as they would doing a Web search, but must use a precoordinated subject heading system that does not necessarily match their language usage or topical vocabulary. The OPACs are very bad at subject searching often due to poor authority control and subject heading assignment and the fact that increasingly students and the public attempt to search the OPAC as they would search with an Internet search engine. These two insufficiencies combine to provide poor search results. With international access to OPACs on the Web, automation in multilingual and multiscript environments becomes important. Some vendors support this, but not all.

There appears to be a need to break the public pieces of the ILS away from the administrative functions related to the collection and other licensed databases. One system cannot do all of this effectively while still clinging to the vestiges of a card catalog. Not all of this is the fault of the OPAC. Descriptive cataloging has not yet mastered bibliographic control of electronic or digital items with the same degree of expertise as it has the medium of print. Innovative OCLC-led projects such as Intercat and Cooperative Online Resource Catalog (CORC) experimented with the ability of OPACs and the MARC format to access and describe electronic objects. Much progress has been made, specifically in describing and providing access to e-journals, but, despite great strides forward, library systems still lag behind many of their Web search engine counterparts. More work is needed to create descriptive metadata that focuses on content, not containers, and public displays that distill for users the information they require to find and retrieve items while, at the same time, balancing the needs of libraries for full, robust, standardized record keeping. An OPAC can only display and interpret the information it contains. It cannot make up for inefficiencies in the catalog record.

CONCLUSION

It is becoming more and more clear that in the future library catalogs will no longer retain their exclusive role as the sole portal to the collection. More and more items are being cataloged in separate registries or via links and portal systems. The catalog becomes, then, one of many access tools. What is not clear is what will be the connecting force between all of these registries and the catalog.

MARC was created as a method of communicating bibliographic information. It is not necessarily the best method for organizing information within a database. New, more object-oriented methods have developed since MARC came on the scene. Mark-up languages such as XML as well as developments in descriptive metadata will improve functionality of the OPAC and allow for a more flexible container or packet structure for the data. Leveraging these technologies would make OPAC function more flexible and allow for the integration of other data structures. All of these technologies also play into the OPACs function as a user interface for the catalog. Compared to other search engines prevalent on the Internet, the OPACs interface seems very dated.

Library automation vendors vie with each other to deliver a system that can stand as a true client/server, multitiered, graphical, Web-enabled, Unicode-enhanced, object-oriented integrated library system built on an industry-standard relational database management system.[6] And so the standard is set for the current generation of library automation systems. The OPAC's general characteristics will include a client/server architecture; support for multiple character sets, preferably through Unicode; a windows-based graphical user interface for library staff; a Web interface for library users; use of a standard relational database system; a Z39.50-compliant server; import and export of MARC records; and Electronic Data Interchange (EDI).[6]

REFERENCES

1. Cochrane, P.A.; Markey, K. Catalog use studies—Since the introduction of online interactive catalogs: Impact on design for subject access. Libr. Inf. Sci. Res. **1983**, *5* (4), 338.
2. Peters, T.A. *The Online Catalog: A Critical Examination of Public Use*; McFarland & Company: Jefferson, NC, 1991; 10–14.
3. De Gennaro, R. Library automation and networking: Perspectives on three decades. Libr. J. **1983**, *108* (7), 243–274.
4. Lynch, C.A.; Berger, M.G. The UC MELVYL medline system: A pilot project for access to journal literature through an online catalog. Inf. Technol. Libr. **1989**, *8* (4), 372.
5. Hildreth, C.R. Online public access catalogs. Annu. Rev. Inf. Sci. Technol. **1985**, *20*, 246–254.
6. Breeding, M. A new look at large-scale library automation systems. Comput. Libr. **1999**, *19* (8), 36–37.
7. Estabrook, L. The human dimension of the catalog: Concepts and constraints in information seeking. Libr. Res. Tech. Serv. **1983**, *27* (1), 71.

Ontologies and Their Definition

Jos de Bruijn
Digital Enterprise Research Institute, University of Innsbruck, Innsbruck, Austria
Dieter Fensel
Institute of Computer Science, University of Innsbruck, Innsbruck, Austria, and National University of Ireland, Galway, Galway, Ireland

Abstract
This entry introduces ontologies as a potential "silver bullet" for knowledge management, enterprise application integration, and e-commerce. Ontologies enable knowledge sharing and knowledge reuse. The degree to which an ontology is machine-understandable, its formality, is determined by the language used for the specification of the ontology. There exists a trade-off between the expressiveness of an ontology language and the modeling support it provides for the ontology developer. This entry also describes how different knowledge representation formalisms, together with the Web languages XML and RDF, have influenced the development of the Web ontology language OWL.

INTRODUCTION

The current Web and current enterprise application integration (EAI) systems lack standards and formal descriptions that impede information sharing and reuse, and cooperation between individuals and organizations. This problem is illustrated in the Web while performing a search. A search query typically returns many unrelated results, and information from such search results needs to be manually extracted from the source and manually combined with different sources. Inside organizations this problem is illustrated by the overlap in the data maintained by many applications. This overlap is often hard to detect. Even when such an overlap is identified, it is hard to deal with because the relation between data in different applications is often difficult to precisely characterize.

Ontologies can potentially solve these problems by facilitating knowledge sharing and reuse through formal and real-world semantics.[1] Ontologies, through formal semantics, are machine understandable. A computer can process data annotated with references to ontologies and through the knowledge encapsulated in the ontology deduce facts from the original data. Ontologies make knowledge explicit, thus making it easier to see what kind of data are maintained by an application and to understand the meaning of the data. Therefore, ontologies facilitate the discovery of overlaps, and thus enable interoperability between heterogenous systems. Furthermore, ontologies are intended to be shared models of a certain domain facilitating cooperation between different applications and even between different partners within that domain.

ONTOLOGIES AND THE SEMANTIC WEB

The term "ontology" originally comes from philosophy, where it stands for the universal theory of existence. The term ontology has been adopted by several Artificial Intelligence (AI) research communities; these were originally the knowledge engineering, natural-language processing, and knowledge representation communities. In the late 1990s, the notion of ontologies also became widespread in fields such as intelligent information integration, information retrieval on the Internet, and knowledge management.[2]

In AI, the term ontology refers to a description of a part of the world in a program. Ontologies were developed to facilitate knowledge sharing and reuse. A common definition of the term ontology, used by many researchers in the field of ontologies, is given in Gruber:[3] "An ontology is a formal explicit specification of a shared conceptualization." A conceptualization is an abstract simplified view of the world that we wish to represent for some purpose. The ontology is a specification because it presents the conceptualization in a concrete form. It is explicit because all relevant concepts and constraints of the domain are explicitly defined. It is formal, which means that the ontology should be machine processable. It is shared—the ontology captures consensual knowledge.[2]

According to Fensel,[1] ontologies, through formal, real-world semantics, and consensual terminologies, interweave human and machine understanding. The real-world semantics are not captured by Gruber's definition, but we feel that this is a very important property of ontologies. It is the real-world semantics that allow sharing and reuse of ontologies by both humans and machines.

Encyclopedia of Library and Information Sciences, Fourth Edition DOI: 10.1081/E-ELIS4-120039479

A reason for the increasing interest in ontologies nowadays comes from the development of the Semantic Web.[4] The Semantic Web can be understood as knowledge management on a global scale. Tim Berners-Lee, inventor of the current World Wide Web and director of the World Wide Web Consortium (W3C), envisions the Semantic Web as the next generation of the current web, where the information will be machine readable and the services will be automated. According to Fensel[1] "The explicit representation of the semantics underlying data, programs, pages, and other web resources will enable a knowledge-based web that provides a qualitatively new level of service." Ontologies provide such an explicit representation of semantics. The combination of ontologies with the web enables overcoming of many of the problems in knowledge sharing and reuse and information integration.

Ontologies interweave human and computer understanding of symbols. These symbols, also called terms (We mean here by "term" the word which is used to specify a certain concept.) and relations, can be interpreted by both humans and machines.

The meaning for the human is presented by the term itself, which is usually a word in natural language, and by relationships between terms that are understandable to humans. An example of such a human-understandable relationship is the superconcept–subconcept relationship (often denoted by the term is-a). This relationship denotes the fact that one concept (the superconcept) is more general than another (the subconcept). An example would be the superconcept person, which is more general than the subconcept student. Fig. 1 shows an example concept hierarchy (taxonomy), where the more general concepts are located above the more specialized concepts.

Concepts describe a set of objects in the real world. For example, the concept PhD-Student aims to capture all existing Ph.D. students. One such Ph.D student is Peter, modeled in Fig. 1 as a box. Peter has an instance-of relationship to the concept PhD-Student. This instance-of relationship means that the actual object is captured by the concept PhD-Student. Because of the formal relationships between the concepts PhD-Student, Student, Researcher, and Person, Peter must also be an instance of the concepts Student, Researcher, and Person.

These relationships are fairly easy to understand for the human reader. As the meaning of the relationships is formally defined a machine is able to reason with them and draw the same conclusions as the human reader. That which is implicitly known to humans (a human knows that every student is a person), is formally and explicitly encoded into these relationships, so that they can then be understood by a machine. In a sense, rather than the machine gaining real "understanding," it is able to process "understandings of humans" and draw conclusions through logical reasoning.

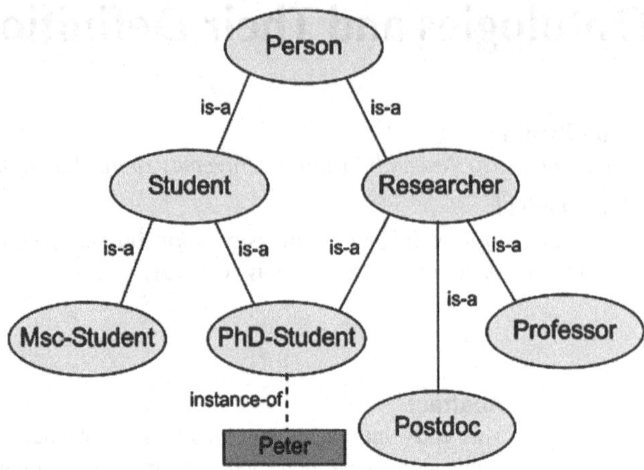

Fig. 1 Example is-a hierarchy (taxonomy).

Types of Ontologies

There exist many different ontologies built for many different types of applications, which vary in the detail they express and the generality of their uses.

WordNet, for example, aims to cover all of the English language by providing a natural-language description for each English term and then specifying simple relationships, such as synonym (equivalent terms) and hyper-/hyponym (more/less general terms), between terms.[5] The scope of WordNet is very broad (all of the English language), the level of detail is relatively low, and the relationships are quite simple. The term descriptions are limited to natural language and are thereby not machine understandable.

Cyc is another example of an ontology with a very broad scope attempting to capture all commonsense knowledge (e.g., space and time), but with a high level of detail.[6] There are many very strict formal relationships between different terms. These formal relationships are machine-understandable.

We will refer to the scope of the ontology as the generality of the ontology; the level of detail is the expressiveness of the ontology. We provide a more detailed description of the generality and expressiveness of ontologies below and use these as dimensions to classify existing ontologies.

Generality of Ontologies

Because ontology is a specification of a shared conceptualization within a particular community, domain experts, users, and designers need to agree on the concepts and relations that are specified in the ontology. Such an agreement can be difficult to achieve. By layering the necessary knowledge in different ontologies based on generality, all parties need not agree to all ontologies. Agreement on the concepts and relations in the ontology is only required for the utilized top-level ontologies and for the specific domain and application ontologies.[7]

In the literature, we generally find three common layers of knowledge, corresponding to three different types of ontologies, based on their levels of generality, namely:[1,2,8,9]

- *Generic (or top-level) ontologies*: Capture general, domain-independent knowledge (e.g., space, time, etc). Examples are WordNet and Cyc. Generic ontologies are shared by a large number of people across different domains.[5,6]
- *Domain ontologies*: Capture the knowledge in a specific domain. An example is UNSPSC, which is a product classification scheme for vendors.[10] Domain ontologies are shared by the stakeholder in a domain.
- *Application ontologies*: Capture the knowledge necessary for a specific application. An example could be an ontology representing the structure of a particular web site.

The separation between these three levels of generality is not always strict. For example, WordNet contains some domain-specific relations and Cyc contains domain-specific microtheories (modules of the ontology).

Although sometimes other types of ontologies (such as representational ontologies or task ontologies) are distinguished, the above three types of ontologies are commonly referred to in the literature and serve as the most useful separation of ontology types according to generality.

Expressiveness in Ontologies

Orthogonal to the generality of ontologies is their expressiveness. The expressiveness of ontology is typically, but not necessarily, determined by the ontology language; the expressiveness of the ontology language is the upper bound for the expressiveness of the ontologies that are specified using this language. We distinguish several levels of expressiveness partly based on the ontology spectrum introduced in McGuinness[11] (see also Fig. 2). These are:

Controlled vocabulary: A list of terms. An example is Dublin Core.[12]

Thesaurus: Relations between terms, such as synonyms, are additionally provided. An example is WordNet.[5]

Informal taxonomy: There is an explicit hierarchy (generalization and specialization are supported), but there is no strict inheritance; an instance of a subclass is not necessarily also an instance of the superclass. An example is the Yahoo! Dictionary.[13]

Formal taxonomy: There is strict inheritance; each instance of a subclass is also an instance of a superclass. An example is UNSPSC.[10]

Frames: A frame (or class) contains a number of properties and these properties are inherited by subclasses and instances. Ontologies expressed in resource description framework schema [RDF(S)] fall in this category.[14]

Value restrictions: Values of properties are restricted (e.g., by a data type). Ontologies expressed in OWL Lite (see the section on "Ontology Language" below) fall in this category.

General logic constraints: Values may be constraint by logical or mathematical formulas using values from other properties. Ontologies expressed in OWL DL (see the section on "Ontology Language" below) fall in this category.

General logic constraints: Very expressive ontology languages, such as those seen in Ontolingua or CycL, allow first-order or even higher-order logic constraints between terms and more detailed relationships, such as disjoint classes, disjoint coverings, inverse relationships, part–whole relationships, etc.[6,15] Note that some of these detailed relationships, such as disjointedness of classes,

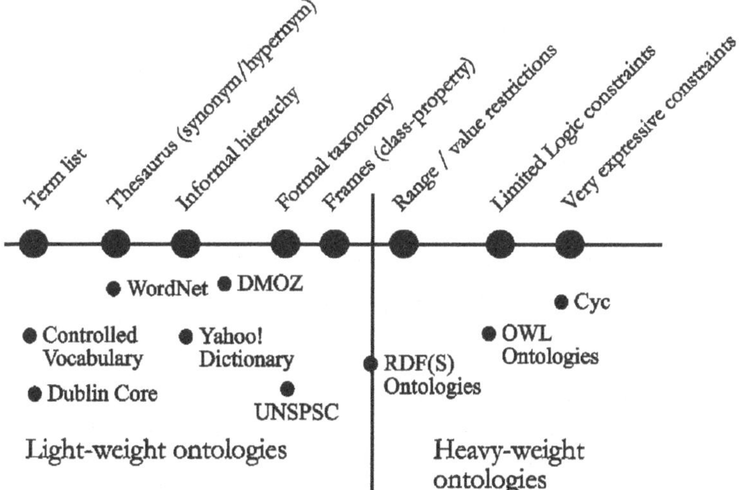

Fig. 2 An ontology expressiveness spectrum.

are also supported by OWL DL (and even OWL Lite), which indicates that the borders between the levels of expressiveness remain fuzzy.

Besides the distinction between different levels of expressiveness, Fig. 2 also shows the distinction between lightweight and heavyweight ontologies, as introduced in Corcho,[16] as well as several examples of ontologies according to their location in the ontology expressiveness spectrum. Lightweight ontologies include concepts, properties that describe concepts, relationships between concepts, and concept taxonomies. Heavyweight ontologies also (perhaps instead of "also" you could write "extend lightweight ontologies to") include axioms and constraints, such as value and cardinality restrictions.

ONTOLOGY LANGUAGES

In the areas of knowledge engineering and knowledge representation, interest in ontologies really started taking off in the 1980s with Knowledge Representation systems, such as KL-ONE and CLASSIC.[17,18]

An important system for the development, management, and exchange of ontologies in the beginning of the 1990s was Ontolingua, which uses an internal KIF (Knowledge Interchange Format) representation, but is able to interoperate with many other Knowledge Representation (ontology) languages, such as KL-ONE, LOOM, and CLASSIC.[15,19]

The languages used for ontologies were determined by the tool used to create the ontologies. Systems like KL-ONE, CLASSIC, and LOOM each used their own ontology language. The Ontolingua system was capable of translating ontologies between different languages using the KIF language as an interchange language. The languages and tools can be understood as interdependent, but also somewhat orthogonal, where we have the language on one axis and the tool on the other. For example, KL-ONE, CLASSIC, and LOOM all have their basis in Description Logics, while KIF has its basis in first-order logic.[20]

In the early 1990s, KIF could be seen as a standard for ontology modeling. The language was used in prominent tools, such as Ontolingua, and in important ontology engineering projects, such as TOVE (Toronto Virtual Enterprise) and The Enterprise Ontology.[21,22]

Later on in the 1990s, ontologies began to be applied to the World Wide Web. SHOE, for example, used ontologies to annotate web pages using formal ontologies embedded in HTML documents.[9] Ontobroker and its successor On2broker, developed in the late 1990s, uses ontologies not only to annotate web pages, but also to formulate queries and derive answers.[23] Ontobroker (and On2broker) provides an annotation language, which is used to annotate HTML documents with references to ontologies. The ontology (the terminology used by the annotation language) is specified using the representation language based on F-Logic.[24] Finally, OntoBroker uses a query language for the retrieval of documents based on their annotations. This query language is a subset of the representation language.

These ontology languages have all influenced the ontology languages for the Semantic Web. Below, we describe the different languages on the Semantic Web. We describe the history and development of the ontology languages in the context of the Semantic Web, starting with RDF(S) and moving to OWL.

Toward an Ontology Language for the Semantic Web

In this section, we describe the languages that are used to enable the Semantic Web and provide a basis for the development of ontology languages for the Semantic Web. The goal of such development is to establish one Web ontology language, developed by the W3C, as well as other web-enabled ontology languages, which will collectively form a basis for the W3C OWL language.

In the late 1990s the idea of a Semantic Web boosted the interest in the development of ontologies even further.[4] The general conviction, held by the W3C, is that for the Semantic Web an ontology language needs to be developed that is both compatible with current Web standards and layered on top of them. The language needs to be expressed in XML and preferably layered on top of RDF(S) (see the subsections below for an overview of these languages). We will present the Web ontology language OWL, which has been developed as an ontology language for the Semantic Web.

An (perhaps too) often used depiction of the vision of Semantic Web languages, originally presented at XML2000 (http://www.w3.org/2000/Talks/1206-xml2k-tbl/slide10-0.html) by Tim Berners-Lee, is shown in Fig. 3. This so-called Semantic Web language Layer Cake depicts the different kinds of languages envisioned to be used on the Semantic Web. The layering of languages on the Semantic Web is both a syntactic and a semantic layering of languages.

The two bottom layers in the Layer Cake, Unicode-URI and XML (Schema), consist of existing standards and provide a syntactical basis for the Semantic Web languages. Unicode provides an elementary character-encoding scheme, which is used by XML. The Uniform Resource Identifier (URI) standard provides a means to uniquely identify and address documents and, more generally, resources, on, but also outside, the Web. All concepts used in the languages located higher in the Layer Cake can be specified using Unicode and are uniquely identified by URIs.

We will describe the XML, RDF(S), and ontology layers below. We will not cover the Logic, Proof, and Trust layers here. The Logic layer on top of the ontology language layer in the Semantic Web tower seems a little strange because current ontology languages have a good

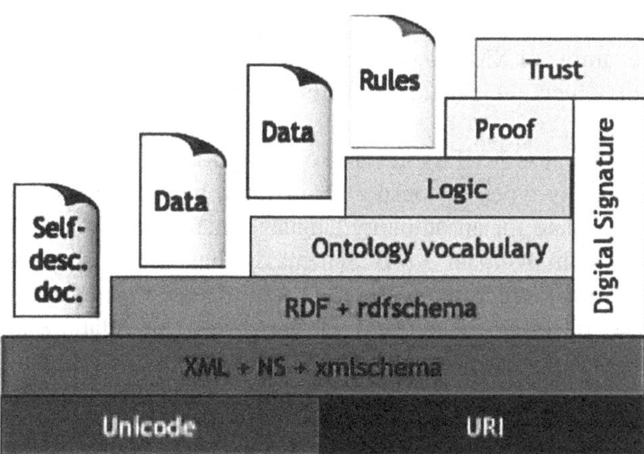

Fig. 3 The Semantic Web Language Layer Cake.
Source: http://www.w3.org/2000/Talks/1206-xml2k-tbl/slide10-0.html.

grounding in logic. There is some debate on this logic language layer; some say a more expressive logic language should be layered on top of the ontology language.[25] It could also be argued that this is not an appropriate layering; that the ontology language should be the top language and that applications should use it directly. However, there is a general conjecture that a more expressive rule language is required. There is currently a proposal for a Semantic Web Rule language, which is layered on top of OWL.[26] The Proof and Trust layers are not well understood, but most likely refer to the application and not to some specific language (the application could prove some statement by using deductive reasoning and a statement could be trusted if it is proven and digitally signed by some trusted third party). The user would very likely play an important role in the Trust layer because it is the user that should decide whether or not some information source should be trusted.

Extensible Markup Language

Extensible Markup Language (XML) is a language for describing data in a structured or semistructured manner.[27] Data are described using a number of tags with arbitrary names that can contain other tags or arbitrary data. A tag may contain attribute-value pairs. Furthermore, tags can be nested yielding a tree-based data structure. The names of the tags can be chosen arbitrarily by the creator of the XML document. This means that an XML document can be understood by a human reader if the name of the tags and the structure are chosen with care by the author and the reader understands the language used by the author. But even then problems can arise, because different people have different associations with terms. For example, some people would argue that the concept "Animal" includes humans, whereas others might feel uncomfortable being classified as an animal, and thus do not consider the term to include humans.

Because an XML document is formally structured using tags, it is possible to process the document using a machine if there is an agreement about the structure of the document [using a document type definition (DTD) or XML Schema, discussed below]. However, a machine cannot understand the meaning of an XML document, as the tags are arbitrarily chosen by the author. The data in an XML document can only be processed in a prescribed way by organizing tags in a specific syntactical structure. The major benefit of using XML as the foundational layer of other languages is the fact that it presents a standardized way of representing data structures. Structures in higher-level languages can be mapped to structures in XML. Furthermore, XML makes use of the URI concept and provides namespace support. Also, XML enables the use of Unicode for character encoding and provides a standardized way of identifying the character encoding of a document.

An example XML document is shown in Fig. 4. The root element is "student," denoted by the <student> start and the </student> end tags. All data are enclosed in elements nested within this root element.

If the XML document from Fig. 4 is sent from one machine to the other, the other machine can only process the document if it knows the schema of the document (i.e., the exact syntactical structure) and if it knows how to process the data enclosed in the document.

We illustrate this requirement of being aware of the exact schema and the way of processing each element with the XML document in Fig. 5. One can see that both XML documents aim at representing exactly the same information. The data in both documents have the same meaning (i.e., the same semantics), but the way it is represented (the syntax or structure) is different. For example, where the document in Fig. 5 uses the element PhD-Student to denote a Master's student, the document in Fig. 4 uses the Student element, together with a Type element containing the data PhD, to denote a Ph.D. student. A human looking at the documents can see that they both represent the same student. A machine processing the document, however, does not see the similarity between the two documents because it has no means of relating different names and different structures.

```
<student>
   <name>Jos de Bruijn</name>
   <type>PhD</type>
   <birthdate>1979-06-23</birthdate>
   <email>jos.debruijn@deri.org</email>
</student>
```

Fig. 4 XML document "Student.".

```
<phdstudent>
   <name>Jos de Bruijn</name>
   <dateofbirth>23-6-1979</dateofbirth>
   <contact>jos.debruijn@deri.org</contact>
</phdstudent>
```

Fig. 5 Sample XML document "PhD-Student."

XML can be used as a format for data exchange between machines, in which case all parties taking part in the exchange need to agree on a common structure for the XML document, a common DTD or XML Schema. Furthermore, all parties need to agree on how to process these structures, i.e., they need to agree on the semantics of the XML tags, even though XML does not provide support for this. Another possible use of XML, as it is done in the Semantic Web, is to use it as the serialization language for other languages. This has the additional advantage of the possibility of reuse of many XML parsers, validators, and other XML-related tools.

Document type definitions

The structure of an XML document can be described using a DTD. A specific DTD describes the constraints on the structure of an XML document for it to be valid with respect to that DTD. A DTD describes the structure of a class of XML documents. Agreement on a DTD between different parties allows exchange of XML documents that conform to the DTD. However, note that only agreeing on a specific DTD is not enough for understanding all valid XML documents, as only the structure (the allowed tags) is described and not the meaning of these tags. A simple DTD describing the class of XML documents to which the document of Fig. 4 belongs is shown in Fig. 6.

XML Schema

Just like DTD, XML Schema is used as a language to describe classes of XML documents. As with DTD, the structure of XML documents is prescribed by the schema.[28] A major difference between DTD and XML Schema is the fact that the latter has a broad range of (simple) data types (e.g., string and integer) and the possibility to form (arbitrarily) complex data types. An example of XML Schema for the class of XML documents to which the document in Fig. 4 belongs is shown in Fig. 7.

```
<!ELEMENT student (name, type, birthdate, email)>
<!ELEMENT name (#PCDATA)>
<!ELEMENT type (#PCDATA)>
<!ELEMENT birthdate (#PCDATA)>
<!ELEMENT email (#PCDATA)>
```

Fig. 6 Document type definition for "student" example.

Because XML Schema also allows for the specification of many types of constraints, it would be a more suitable candidate for an ontology language than DTD. The main problem with an XML Schema is that it describes the physical structure (syntax) of an XML document but not the meaning (semantics) of the data. The relationship between ontology and XML Schema can be seen as analogous to the relationship between a conceptual database schema (e.g., an EER diagram) and a physical database schema (e.g., a relation database schema).[29]

Klein et al. examined the relation between a specific ontology language, namely, OIL, which is a predecessor of OWL (see below), and XML Schema.[29,30] One of the results of the comparison was that OIL has more expressive power when it comes to expressing knowledge and XML Schema has more expressive power when it comes to the structure of the data (e.g., there is no such thing as ordering in OIL) and data types (there are no data types other than string in OIL and to completely axiomatize different data types would be complex; OWL adopts XML Schema data types). Here again, it is stressed that ontology provides a domain theory and not the structure of a data container (like an XML Schema does), which explains most of the differences between the two.

Resource Description Framework Schema

The RDF is the first language developed especially for the Semantic Web. It was developed as a language for adding machine-readable metadata to the existing data on the web. It uses XML for its serialization to realize the layering as depicted in the Semantic Web Language Layer Cake (Fig. 3). Resource description framework schema extends RDF with some basic (frame based) ontological modeling primitives.[14] There are such primitives as classes, properties, and instances. Also, the instance-of, subclass-of, and

```
<xs:schema xmlns:xs="http://www.w3.org/2001/XMLSchema">
  <xs:element name="student">
    <xs:complexType>
      <xs:sequence>
        <xs:element name="name" type="xs:string"/>
        <xs:element name="type" type="xs:string"/>
        <xs:element name="birthdate" type="xs:date"/>
        <xs:element name="email" type="xs:string"/>
      </xs:sequence>
    </xs:complexType>
  </xs:element>
</xs:schema>
```

Fig. 7 XML Schema for "student" example.

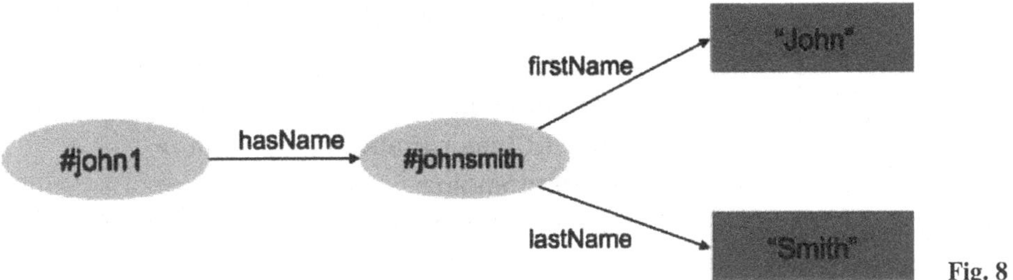

Fig. 8 Sample RDF graph.

subproperty-of relationships have been introduced enabling creation of class and property hierarchies.

The RDF(S) (referring to the combination of RDF and RDF Schema) is not very expressive compared to many other ontology languages, as it just allows the representation of concepts, concept taxonomies, and binary relations. In the ontology expressiveness spectrum of Fig. 2, RDF(S) has the expressiveness of formal taxonomies combined with frame-based representation.

Resource description framework has the subject–predicate–object triple, commonly written as P(S,O), as the basic data model. An object of a triple can in turn function as the subject of another triple, yielding a directed labeled graph, where resources (subjects and objects) correspond to nodes and predicates correspond to edges. Furthermore, RDF allows a form of reification (a statement about a statement), which means that any RDF statement can be used as a subject in a triple; however, reification is not reflected in the formal semantics of RDF, and thus no additional conclusions can be drawn from the use of reification. A sample RDF graph is shown in Fig. 8. The corresponding triples notation is shown in Fig. 9; the RDF/XML serialization is shown in Fig. 10.

An XML Schema prescribes the order and combinations of the tags (the structure) in an XML document. In contrast, RDF Schema only provides information about the interpretation of the statements given in an RDF data model, but does not say anything about the syntactical appearance of the RDF description. Resource description frameworks can, in fact, be seen as an extension to RDF. Resource description frameworks provide for a means to define classes, class hierarchies, properties (binary relations), and property hierarchies. The classes and properties of RDF(S) can be instantiated in RDF (Fig. 11).

We have described the foundational Semantic Web languages XML and RDF(S). These languages are used as the lower layers in the Semantic Web Language Layer Cake, on top of which more expressive languages can be layered.

```
(hasName, #john1, #johnsmith)
(firstName, #johnsmith, "John")
(lastName, #johnsmith, "Smith")
```

Fig. 9 RDF triples.

OWL

Using the DAML + OIL language[32] as the basis, the W3C Web Ontology working group has created a new ontology language for the Semantic Web; one that implements true layering on top of RDF(S) and incorporates the wishes of many stakeholders, both academic and industrial. The Web Ontology Language OWL consists of a set of three strictly layered dialects, namely OWL Lite, OWL DL, and OWL Full.[33] This means that OWL Lite is a subset of OWL DL and OWL DL is a subset of OWL Full.

OWL is an extension of RDF(S). There are, however, some problems when layering OWL on top of RDF(S).

In Fig. 12 we see a very simple example of OWL, corresponding to the "student" example introduced earlier (see Fig. 4). Because of the very verbose RDF/XML syntax, this example is very hard to read. Fig. 13 presents the abstract syntax form of this simple OWL ontology. Note that the abstract syntax can only be used for the OWL Lite and OWL DL sublanguages. Note also that even the abstract syntax is quite complex for such a simple definition (just one class with four properties). This complexity originates from the Description Logic origins of OWL. The properties are defined separately from the classes instead of as a part of the classes.

It is possible to define the local property restrictions in OWL, thereby regaining some of the frame-based modeling possibilities originally introduced in OIL.[32]

```
<rdf:RDF
  xmlns:rdf="http://www.w3.org/1999/02/22-rdf-syntax-ns#"
  xmlns:s="http://description.org/schema/">
  <rdf:Description about="john1">
    <s:hasName>
      <rdf:Description about="#johnsmith">
            <s:firstName>John</s:firstName>
            <s:lastName>Smith</s:lastName>
      </rdf:Description>
    </s:hasName>
  </rdf:Description>
</rdf:RDF>
```

Fig. 10 RDF/XML serialization.

```
<rdf:RDF>
  <rdfs:Class rdf:about="#student">
  </rdfs:Class>
  <rdf:Property rdf:about="#birthdate">
    <rdfs:domain rdf:resource="#student"/>
  </rdf:Property>
  <rdf:Property rdf:about="#email">
    <rdfs:domain rdf:resource="#student"/>
  </rdf:Property>
  <rdf:Property rdf:about="#name">
    <rdfs:domain rdf:resource="#student"/>
  </rdf:Property>
  <rdf:Property rdf:about="#type">
    <rdfs:domain rdf:resource="#student"/>
  </rdf:Property>
</rdf:RDF>
```

Fig. 11 Example of RDF(S) ontology.

Problems with OWL and Language Layering on the Semantic Web

In the language layering on the Semantic Web, we can distinguish syntactic layering (RDF uses a subset of XML, so every RDF document is valid XML) and semantic layering (every valid RDF statement must be a valid OWL Full statement). There is syntactic layering between Unicode, XML, and RDF and semantic layering between RDF and RDF schema [i.e., the RDF(S) meaning of constructs incorporates the RDF meaning of constructs] and now also between RDF(S) and OWL Full.[25]

The following are the problems we have found with the current OWL language and the layering on top of RDF(S):[1,25,34]

- It is not possible to fully layer a Description Logic-style language on top of RDF(S). The first problem is the fact that in RDF(S) keywords in the language are allowed to occur in RDFS ontologies. For example, one can create subclasses of rdf: type. Using the language constructs in the language itself is not possible in a first-order framework, because first-order logic does not allow for redefinition of the language. The second problem is the mixing of identifiers for classes, properties, and individuals. In RDF(S), the same individual can be a class and an individual at the same time. This cannot be captured in a first-order framework, because predicates are not allowed to occur in the place of terms.
- OWL Lite is the least expressive of the species of OWL. However, it still requires a fully fledged Description Logics reasoner and is therefore not as "Lite" as it seems. It turns out that features such as disjunction and negation can be expressed in OWL Lite, even though these constructs are not explicitly represented in the syntax. Horrocks[35] shows how several features of OWL DL can be expressed using the constructs of OWL Lite. In fact, the only features in OWL DL that cannot be expressed in OWL Lite are

```
<rdf:RDF>
  <owl:DatatypeProperty rdf:about="#birthdate">
    <rdfs:domain>
      <owl:Class rdf:about="#student"/>
    </rdfs:domain>
    <rdfs:range rdf:resource="&xsd;date"/>
  </owl:DatatypeProperty>
  <owl:DatatypeProperty rdf:about="#name">
    <rdfs:domain>
      <owl:Class rdf:about="#student"/>
    </rdfs:domain>
    <rdfs:range rdf:resource="&xsd;string"/>
  </owl:DatatypeProperty>
  <owl:DatatypeProperty rdf:about="#type">
    <rdfs:domain>
      <owl:Class rdf:about="#student"/>
    </rdfs:domain>
    <rdfs:range rdf:resource="&xsd;string"/>
  </owl:DatatypeProperty>
  <owl:DatatypeProperty rdf:about="#email">
    <rdfs:domain>
      <owl:Class rdf:about="#student"/>
    </rdfs:domain>
    <rdfs:range rdf:resource="&xsd;string"/>
  </owl:DatatypeProperty>
</rdf:RDF>
```

Fig. 12 Example of OWL ontology.

```
Class(a:student)

 DataProperty(a:birthdate
  domain(a:student)
  range(xsd:date))
 DataProperty(a:email
  domain(a:student)
  range(xsd:string))
 DataProperty(a:name
  domain(a:student)
  range(xsd:string))
 DataProperty(a:type
  domain(a:student)
  range(xsd:string))
)
```

Fig. 13 OWL example using abstract syntax.

arbitrary number restrictions and nominals (individuals in class descriptions).

- OWL DL is a language created by a standards committee, and is thus necessarily a compromise between the wishes of different stakeholders. The most important design goal was to create a sublanguage for which the satisfiability problem is decidable. OWL DL is equivalent to the SHOIN(**D**) Description Logic.[36] It is known that this language is decidable, but there are currently no reasoners for this language, nor is there a known algorithm for deciding satisfiability of OWL DL ontologies. The major problem is dealing with nominals (individuals in class definitions). Arguably, it would have been better to restrict the language to SHIQ(**D**), which underlies the OIL language, a predecessor of OWL. Several optimized algorithms and implementations have been developed for reasoning with SHIQ, such as Racer and FaCT++.
- OWL Full is completely semantically layered on top of RDF(S). In this respect, it accommodates all wishes for a Web ontology language. However, the semantics for OWL Full are very hard to understand and entailment in OWL Full is not computationally decidable.[37] Furthermore, ontologies provide a vocabulary for more expressive language in the Language Layer Cake (see Fig. 3), such as rule languages, and as a result this undecidability is propagated to the higher layers.
- Current proposals are for rule languages on top of the OWL layer on top of the OWL DL species, because of the nonstandard semantics of OWL Full and the nondecidability of the language. The most prominent proposal for a Semantic Web rule language is SWRL, which layers on top of OWL DL.[26] Because SWRL combines the full expressive power of an expressive Description Logic with the full expressive power of (function free) Horn Logic, the language is in general undecidable.[26]

We think OWL Full will probably not be used very much on the Semantic Web because the semantics is very hard to understand and it is very hard to deal with in an automated way. Even now, most research involving OWL focuses on OWL DL. Most practical applications will most likely use a subset of OWL DL, which is efficiently computable. However, wide-scale application of OWL on the Semantic Web will have to show what requirements arise when the language is actually put to use. It can, however, be argued that entailment (proving that one ontology is the logical consequence of the other; this is the problem that is undecidable in OWL Full) will not be the most common reasoning task, in which case OWL Full can be very useful.

For a more elaborate critique of the different species of OWL and language layering on the Semantic Web, we refer the reader to de Bruijn.[38]

CONCLUSIONS

We have introduced ontologies as a potential "silver-bullet" (cf. Fensel[1]) for knowledge management, EAI, and E-commerce (which is in fact EAI on an interorganizational level) for the following practical reasons:

- Ontologies are shared by a group of stakeholders in the domain.
- Ontologies interweave formal semantics with real-world meaning.
- Ontologies relate a human-understandable domain description with a machine-understandable description.

Because of these attractive properties, ontologies enable knowledge sharing and knowledge reuse. However, it turns out that we are not done with the introduction of the concept of ontologies. The degree to which an ontology is machine-understandable, its formality, is determined by the language used for the specification of the ontology. This also applies to the expressiveness of the ontologies (i.e., the degree of detail to which the domain can be described in the ontology), which is limited by the expressivity of the ontology language.

Actually, what an ontology looks like and what can be expressed by an ontology are entirely determined by the ontology language used. We have also seen that there exists a trade-off between the expressiveness of an ontology language and the modeling support it provides for the ontology developer. The use of Description Logics[20] in current ontology languages, such as OWL,[33] limits the understanding of developed ontologies, because of the decoupling of classes and properties. Fully fledged inferencing is necessary to determine the properties for certain classes.

We have described how different knowledge representation formalisms, such as first-order logic, frames, and Description Logics, together with the Web languages XML and RDF, have influenced the development of the current Web ontology language OWL.

The existence of version 1.0 of OWL does not mean the development of ontology languages will stop. Horrocks et al. identify several possible future extensions and improvements of OWL, which include support for modularization, closed world reasoning, and the unique names assumption.[35] Furthermore, there is a current proposal for a Semantic Web rule language, which has been submitted to the W3C.[26]

Online Public–Organizational

REFERENCES

1. Fensel, D. *Ontologies: A Silver Bullet for Knowledge Management and Electronic Commerce*, 2nd Ed.; Springer-Verlag: Berlin, Germany, 2003.

2. Studer, R.; Benjamins, V.R.; Fensel, D. Knowledge engineering: principles and methods. Data Knowl. Eng. **1998**, *25*(1–2), 161–197.
3. Gruber, T.R. A translation approach to portable ontology specification. Knowl. Acquisition **1993**, *5*(2), 199–220.
4. Berners-Lee, T.; Hendler, J.; Lassila, O. The semantic web. Sci. Am. **2001**, *284*(5), 34–43. Available at http://www.sciam.com/article.cfm?articleID=00048144-43-10D2-1C70-84A9809EC588EF21&ref=sciam.
5. Fellbaum, C. *WordNet: An Electronic Lexical Database*; MIT Press: Cambridge, MA, 1999.
6. Lenat, D.B. CYC: a large-scale investment in knowledge infrastructure. Commun. ACM **1995**, *38*(11), 33–38.
7. Meersman, R. Semantic ontology tools in IS design. Proceedings of the ISMIS'99 Conference, Warsaw, Poland, June 1999.
8. Guarino, N. Formal ontology and information systems. In *Formal Ontology in Information Systems*, Proceedings of FOIS'98 Trento, Italy, June 6–8, 1998; Guarino, N., Ed.; IOS Press: Amsterdam, the Netherlands, 1998; 3–15.
9. Heflin, J.; Hendler, J. Dynamic ontologies on the web. Proceedings of the 17th National Conference on Artificial Intelligence (AAAI-2000); AAAI/MIT Press: Menlo Park, CA, 2000; 443–449.
10. The United Nations Standard Products and Services Code (UNSPSC). Available at http://www.unspsc.org/.
11. McGuinness, D.L. Ontologies come of age. In *Spinning the Semantic Web: Bringing the World Wide Web to Its Full Potential*; Fensel, D., Hendler, J., Lie-berman, H., Wahlster, W., Eds.; MIT Press: Cambridge, MA, 2003.
12. Weibel, S.; Kunze, J.; Lagoze, C.; Wolf, M. RFC 2413—Dublin Core Metadata for Resource Discovery; September 1998.
13. http://www.yahoo.com/.
14. Brickley, D.; Guha, R.V. RDF Vocabulary Description Language 1.0: RDF Schema. W3C Recommendation. Available at http://www.w3.org/TR/2004/REC-rdf-schema-20040210/.
15. Farquhar, A.; Fikes, R.; Rice, J. The ontolingua server: a tool for collaborative ontology construction. Int. J. Hum. Comput. Stud. **1997**, *46*(6), 707–728.
16. Corcho, O.; Fernández-López, M.; Gómez-Pérez, A. Methodologies, tools, and languages for building ontologies, where is their meeting point? Data Knowl. Eng. **2003**, *46*(1), 41–64.
17. Borgida, A.; Brachman, R.J.; McGuinness, D.L.; Resnick, L.A. CLASSIC: a structural data model for objects. Proceedings of the 1989 ACM SIGMOD International Conference on Management of Data, 1989; 59–67.
18. Brachman, R.J.; Schmolze, J. An overview of the KL-ONE knowledge representation system. Cogn. Sci. **1985**, *9*(2), 171–216.
19. Genesereth, M. Knowledge interchange format. Proceedings of the 2nd International Conference on the Principles of Knowledge Representation and Reasoning (KR-91) Morgan Kaufman, 1991; 238–249. See also http://logic.stanford.edu/kif/kif.html.
20. Baader, F.; Calvanese, D.; McGuinness, D.L.; Nardi, D.; Patel-Schneider, P.F. *The Description Logic Handbook*; Cambridge University Press: Cambridge, U.K., 2003.
21. Grüninger, M.; Fox, M.S. Methodology for the design and evaluation of ontologies. Proceedings of IJCAI'95, Workshop on Basic Ontological Issues in Knowledge Sharing, Montreal, QC, 1995.
22. Uschold, M.; King, M.; Morale, S.; Zorgios, Y. The enterprise ontology. The Knowl. Eng. Rev. **1998**, *13*(1), 31–89.
23. Fensel, D.; Decker, S.; Erdmann, M.; Schnurr, H.P.; Studer, R.; Witt, A. Lessons learned from applying AI to the web. Int. J. Coop. Inf. Syst. **2000**, *9*(4), 361–382.
24. Kifer, M.; Lausen, G.; Wu, J. Logical foundations of object-oriented and frame-based languages. J. ACM **1995**, *42*(4), 741–843.
25. Patel-Schneider, P.F.; Fensel, D. Layering the semantic web: problems and directions. Proceedings of the 2002 International Semantic Web Conference, Sardinia, Italy, 2002.
26. Horrocks, I; Patel-Schneider, P.F.; Boley, H.; Tabet, S.; Grosof, B.; Dean, M. SWRL: a semantic web rule language combining OWL and RuleML. W3C Member Submission. Available at http://www.w3.org/Submission/2004/SUBM-SWRL-20040521/ .
27. The eXtensible Markup Language. Available at http://www.w3.org/XML/ XML.
28. XSD. XML Schema Definition. Available at http://www.w3.org/XML/Schema.
29. Klein, M.; Fensel, D.; Van Harmelen, F.; Horrocks, I. The relation between ontologies and XML schemas. In *Electronic Transactions on Artificial Intelligence*, Special Issue on the 1st International Workshop "Semantic Web: Models, Architectures, and Management," 2001.
30. Fensel, D.; Van Harmelen, F.; Horrocks, I.; McGuinness, D.L.; Patel-Schneider, P.F. OIL: an ontology infrastructure for the semantic web. IEEE Intell. Syst. **2001**, *16*(2).
31. Beckett, D. RDF/XML Syntax Specification (Revised). W3C Recommendation. Available at http://www.w3.org/TR/2004/REC-rdf-syntax-grammar-20040210/.
32. Fensel, D.; Van Harmelen, F.; Horrocks, I. OIL & DAML+OIL: ontology languages for the Semantic Web. In *Towards the Semantic Web: Ontology-Driven Knowledge Management*; Davies, J., Fensel, D., van Harmelen, F., Eds.; John Wiley: Chichester, England; Hoboken, NJ 2003.
33. Dean, M.; Schreiber, G. OWL Web Ontology Language Reference. W3C Recommendation. Available at http://www.w3.org/TR/2004/REC-owl-ref-20040210/.
34. Horrocks, I.; Patel-Schneider, P.F. Three theses of representation in the semantic web. Proceedings of the 12th International Conference on World Wide Web (WWW2003), Budapest, Hungary, 2003; 29–47.
35. Horrocks, I.; Patel-Schneider, P.F.; Van Harmelen, F. From SHIQ and RDF to OWL: the making of a web ontology language. J. Web Semant. **2003**, *1*(1), 7–26.
36. Horrocks, I.; Patel-Schneider, P.F. Reducing OWL entailment to description logic satisfiability. Proceedings of the 2003 International Semantic Web Conference (ISWC 2003), Sanibel Island, FL, 2003.
37. Patel-Schneider, P.F.; Hayes, P.; Horrocks, I. OWL Web Ontology Language Semantics and Abstract Syntax. W3C Recommendation. Available at http://www.w3.org/TR/2004/REC-owl-semantics-20040210/.
38. de Bruijn, J.; Polleres, A.; Lara, R.; Fensel, D. OWL DL vs. OWL Flight: conceptual modeling and reasoning for the Semantic Web. Proceedings of the 14th International World Wide Web Conference (WWW2005), Chiba, Japan, 2005.

Open Access Scholarship and Publishing

Malcolm Getz
Department of Economics, Vanderbilt University, Nashville, Tennessee, U.S.A.

Abstract

Open access publishing helps scholars to be more productive and to reach larger audiences. The challenge for entrepreneurs and universities is to design systems for publishing that take advantage of the digital technologies, offer substantial intellectual value, and are cost effective. Authors, publishers, libraries, and readers are changing their roles as the methods of financing publication shifts in part from readers to authors.

INTRODUCTION

At the beginning of the twenty-first century, the growth of the Internet changed the economics of scholarly publishing. The dramatic and sustained increases in prices of paper-based materials had narrowed access to scholarship.[1] In contrast, the publication of digital materials on the Internet expanded and accelerated access and lowered costs. Indeed, substantial quantities of high-quality material became available to readers worldwide without charge. Such open access scholarship changed the relationship between authors and readers with fundamental shifts in the roles of publishers and libraries. Open access publication supports collaboration, a wider range of publishing opportunities, and access to wider audiences. There is a concern, however, that its openness may foster disorder that may make it less valuable than it could be.

FROM CONVENTIONAL TO DIGITAL PUBLISHING

The conventional print books and periodicals of the twentieth century involved both the up-front cost of editing and typesetting along with the substantial variable cost of paper, printing, and mail for each copy shipped. Publishers earned revenue from selling subscriptions to their readers and libraries sufficient to cover both the up-front and variable costs. The publishers typically charged higher rates to libraries than to individuals, particularly for journals. For many scholarly books and journals, revenues to publishers from libraries were predominant, effectively paying for most of the publisher's up-front costs and more. For many journals, prices to libraries grew beyond plausible association with production and distribution costs.[2] Moreover, the libraries incurred significant additional costs in managing their purchases, registering each item in a database to sustain control and access, and providing space to store the materials.[3] Under such pressure, library budgets did not expand enough to sustain their collecting programs. The number of publications and growth in the number of pages expanded faster than the purchasing power of library collection budgets and the libraries bought a smaller share of all that was available. In addition, print had considerable delays from the time an author submitted her work until it was in the hands of readers.[4]

The digital revolution changed many of these costs while accelerating the process. Digital materials are often stored once on the Internet, or a few times for security, rather than on each campus. Materials offered by subscription may be licensed as whole databases rather than by individual title, reducing each library's processing costs. Open access materials particularly, but often all digital materials, are fully searchable by individual words with freely available search services that not only point to items by content but reveal the importance of the item in wider streams of scholarly work. The digital documents whether through open access or by database subscriptions are delivered directly to reader's workstations within a few seconds. Many digital publications put works in the hands of readers within a few months, sometimes within weeks. As the quantity of material available digitally exceeded the content of most conventional academic libraries, as the power of digital searching exceeded conventional indexing, and as a host of quality materials became instantaneously available at any workstation, the digital document took center stage from the published paper document as the standard medium of scholarly communication.

In 2007, *Ulrich's Periodicals Directory* listed more than 23,550 active, peer-reviewed, academic periodicals worldwide; 15,205 of them were available online.[5] In August 2007 Ulrich's listed 1673 current, refereed academic journals as open access, 7% of the total. *The Directory of Open Access Journals* listed 2821 open, quality controlled academic journals, including many titles not

Encyclopedia of Library and Information Sciences, Fourth Edition DOI: 10.1081/E-ELIS4-120044492

captured by Ulrich's.[6] Of course, journals differ in intellectual reputation. One hallmark of quality is evaluation by ISI's *Journal Citation Reports* (JCR), as discussed more fully below. Ulrich's listed 6875 current, refereed, academic journals as being evaluated by the JCR, 29% of the total. Of the journals evaluated by JCR, 94% are available digitally and 4% (265 titles) are available in the open, a significant start.

FROM DIGITAL TO OPEN PUBLISHING

Whether a digital document will be supported by subscription or made available by open access depends on the extent of its up-front costs, the acceptance of fees paid by authors and funds from third parties, and the possibility of Internet advertising. Indeed, publishing strategies range from an author posting her work as-is on a personal Web site, freely available to all without review, editing, or promotion, to formal periodicals with creative editors who winnow large numbers of submissions, commission works by leading authors, rewrite author's drafts to improve style, include extensive graphics to enhance readability, and develop reputations for sustained intellectual influence. Up-front editorial costs will range, then, from zero to many thousands of dollars per essay. Open access, that is publication without charge to readers and libraries, dominates when editing costs are low. In contrast, significant revenue streams must support the intensity of editorial effort seen, for example, in *The New England Journal of Medicine* (Nature uses only a full-time editorial staff, located in nine offices around the world, http://www.nature.com/nature/about/contact/editorial.html. The editorial staff at NEJM appears at http://content.nejm.org/misc/edboard./shtml). A central issue in the development of open access publications is how much editorial service can be sustained with revenue streams from sources other than subscriptions?

A second issue for open access is the role of copyright. Lawrence Lessig, professor at Stanford Law School, launched the Creative Commons in 2001 to reduce the restrictions imposed by copyrights.[7] Authors can retain the copyright to their own materials and grant limited rights of use to others instead of assigning all rights to a publisher. Many open access publications only require a nonexclusive right to publish materials. Authors may allow reuse, for example, by others for noncommercial purposes. The ready opportunity to reuse materials may promote more rapid intellectual advance much as Open Software makes significant progress by expansive collaboration.

E-PRINT SERVICES

Understanding the financial underpinning of open archives provides a basis for understanding the possibilities for open journals discussed below. Paul Ginsparg developed a database of e-prints, that is, works-in-progress as well as published works, in high-energy physics beginning in 1991 at Los Alamos Labs that has become the dominant vehicle for physicists to share their work worldwide.[8] ArXiv, now owned by the Cornell University Library, expanded to encompass most topics in physics, mathematics, quantitative biology, and statistics. The database includes about 500,000 essays, received nearly 5,000 new submissions in some months in 2007, and has upward of 500,000 connections per day (a measure of usage) at peak periods at the Cornell site with additional usage at several mirror sites around the world. Research Papers in Economics (RePEc) is a similar service that depends entirely on volunteer effort in 57 countries (The RePEc: Research Papers in Economics, (repec.org) holds 470,000 items with 12,700 users and 10,250 participating institutions in 2007).

ArXiv provides a minimal screen of its submission, far short of editing. Authors register with the site and submit their work in a prescribed format. They may subsequently publish posted work in edited journals and works published in edited journals may be posted when consistent with the journal's copyright policies. Most of the processing of work into arXiv is automated. Readers search the database and download materials without charge. Cornell with some grant funds sustains the cost of the hardware, software, and modest staff for the arXiv service at a cost of under $300,000 per year.

ArXiv, then, is an open access self-publishing service (i.e., the author posts the work in the open for anyone on the Internet to read). It is widely used and operates at modest cost per unit of service. Scholars in the relevant disciplines use arXiv to search for the latest work in their area. The processing provided by arXiv, primarily a cursory decentralized review, is designed to assure that submitted essays are within the subject scope of the service. The author's work appears as the author submits it, however authors may replace or withdraw their essays.

A similar service in economics and related fields is self-financed. Michael Jenson, an economist at the Harvard Business School founded the Social Science Research Network (SSRN) in 1994.[9] It is privately organized and self-financed through sale of abstracting journals and other ancillaries, however, access to all author-uploaded papers in the SSRN database is free. Its annual budget is in excess of $800,000, supporting a database of 50,000 essays with over 300,000 downloads per month.

SELF-ARCHIVING

The success of arXiv, SSRN, and similar open e-print publishing services along with the growth of the Internet led scholars in other disciplines to consider services that allow authors to post their drafts in the open and that also invite authors to post the articles they have published in edited journals in the open. The up-front costs across all disciplines might be shared among many universities. One method of sharing the mostly fixed cost of universal, open access e-print services is to have each campus archive the work of its scholars in formats that could be readily indexed across all campuses and disciplines. To this end, the Open Society Institute launched the Budapest Open Access Initiative in 2001.[10,11] Stevan Harnad, a research professor of Cognitive Science at Université du Québec à Montréal, is one of the leaders of the open access movement.[12,13] Posting published, peer-reviewed work in open archives other than through a published journal is called green open access.[14]

The Open Archive Initiative (OAI) propounded standards for metatags, that is, a method for labeling the author's name, the essay's title, subject, and date.[15] When materials that are tagged in compliance with the OAI standard are posted to a compliant digital archive, the tagged information can be harvested by indexing software that spans all of the participating archives. Documents with tagged fields support more precise searching. A reader can then search the universe of open archives of all of the participating institutions, also called institutional repositories, as though they were all under one roof and identify and retrieve a document wherever it is stored. In 2007, there were 687 registered archives in 60 countries participating in the OAI with a total of over 6 million documents.[16] DSpace, developed by MIT and Hewlett-Packard and released in 2002, is open source, OAI compliant software for managing digital archives.[17] Institutional repositories are typically not specific to discipline and do not generate the attention of the discipline specific arXiv and SSRN.

Self-archiving under the OAI makes significant quantities of published material available to readers without charge. Libraries encourage open archiving as an antidote to expensive journal subscriptions.[18] If all published material were available in this format, how would publishers generate revenue streams to support the editorial processes for their journals? The European Commission, the U.S. Congress, and the national legislatures of several other countries are considering laws to require that research that is funded by their governments be made available in open archives shortly after publication.[19] Such legislation is typically supported by libraries but opposed by many scholarly publishers. Former Congresswoman Patricia Scott Schroeder, President and Chief Executive Officer of the Association of American Publishers, leads publishers on the issue.

WIKIPEDIA

Open publications using many volunteers with modest philanthropic support can create substantial digital publications. Wikipedia, a collaborative online encyclopedia published in the open, gives a sense of the power and limits of open publication. Founded in 2001 by Jimmy Wales and Larry Singer, Wikipedia supported close to 2 million articles in the United States in 2007 with an annual budget of just over $1 million in philanthropic funds.[20] Requests for Wikipedia pages approach 30,000 pages per second at peak times. Although Wikipedia articles appear without authors' names, submissions go through a review process and conform to style guidelines that require entries be neutral in tone and based on peer-reviewed publications. Occasionally, articles appear that are biased, erroneous, or fraudulent (Virgil Griffith, a graduate student at CalTech, developed Wikipedia Scanner to identify the IP addresses of people editing Wikipedia entries. He found, for example, that negative information about WalMart and Diebold had been deleted by people located at these companies).[21,22] The "discussion" section on each article provides reader comments. Problems flagged by readers may be changed in time through new submissions.[23] In a sense, however, Wikipedia is permanently a work in progress. Some professors ban the citation of Wikipedia articles by their students, citing errors and biases, the lack of author attribution, and to give preference to primary sources.[24] Wikipedia continues to evolve. In 2005 it began requiring contributors to register and it has introduced a more thorough review for "featured articles." Wikipedia also continues to invest in developing improved search software.

Wikipedia is the dominant encyclopedia on the Internet. Even though entries are often anonymous, scholars contribute and edit Wikipedia articles. Proponents of open access scholarly publishing, and indeed more generally of collaborative, network-based ways of doing intellectual work, have in mind technological and financial relationships that are similar to Wikipedia.[25] Voluntary editorial effort, supported by modest levels of philanthropic or institutional funds, can sustain large-scale publications, freely available to all. The building blocks of such an environment in academia are open journals that require a formal review mechanism and post only attributed works.

OPEN JOURNALS

Open archives and Wikipedia provide limited mechanisms for supporting an editorial process. Careful review that assures relevance, quality, originality, and acknowledgment of related work is a hallmark of academic publication. If scholarship consisted only of archives of material that wasn't reliably reviewed, readers would be challenged to sort through large quantities of poorly differentiated materials in order to identify the most important ideas and to evaluate the quality of the content. Often even very creative scholars present their work poorly and important new ideas may be ignored until ratified by a distinguished editor. Effective editors provide the valuable service of identifying the most important ideas, verifying accuracy, and polishing presentations to make them accessible to the intended audience.

Academic publication typically means that an editor has evaluated an author's work, often with the counsel of other scholars knowledgeable in the specific subject matter of the work. Such peer review helps keep new work focused on a specific audience, makes it more likely that the work both relates well to established ideas and adds something new, and that the style of presentation conforms to academic norms. Quality assurance allows an academic to concentrate on reading works that are sophisticated, original, relevant, and well written. In fact, editors of many higher quality journals select for publication from among many well-crafted and original submissions. In 2006, the 64 academic journals in biology that were evaluated by the ISI JCR published 5783 articles.[26] A working biologist will choose carefully what to read among the torrent of new materials.

Fortunately, there are several ways beyond subscriptions to finance the editorial process that turns the authors' raw materials into journals of sufficient quality to be attractive to readers. One method involves institutional support for the hardware, software, and managing editor supplemented by a significant amount of volunteer effort by reviewers, that is, an arrangement much like Wikipedia. Historically, universities supported their presses to produce books and journals that help advance their campuses' intellectual reputations. Supporting an open journal can be less expensive.

Readily available software lowers the cost of managing the editorial process. The Public Knowledge Project, launched in 1998 at the University of British Columbia by John Wilinsky, Pacific Press Professor of Literacy Technology, created the Open Journal Systems software and makes it available for use on any campus without charge. It and similar software support a database environment that manages the flow of submissions to a journal, the process of review and editing, and the presentation of the digital journal online with full-text searching.[27] With such software installed locally, a university can support scholars in launching and sustaining a digital journal at modest cost. As of 2007, the Open Journal Systems software supported the back-office functions of more than 900 journals worldwide, some supported by subscriptions and some in the open (A list of the journals is at http://pkp.sfu.calojs-journals. Cornell University has developed alternative software. E-Journal, http://drupal.org/project/ejournal).

Theoretical Economics is an example of an open journal, launched in 2006 and managed with public domain software at the University of Toronto with a distinguished international editorial board.[28,29] Authors pay a $75 submission fee but may avoid a per page publication charge by putting their essays in a specific format for publication. The editors reach a decision on 90% of submissions within 90 days, a relatively short time for an academic peer-review process. The journal is available without charge via the Internet and sells its annual volume in print. Publishing in formally reviewed open journals is called gold open access publishing.

AUTHOR-FUNDED JOURNALS

A second strategy for open publication relies on publication charges to authors to finance the up-front and distribution costs. With the cost of distribution to another reader near zero, a zero price provides access to everyone on the Internet. If usage grows dramatically with the drop in price to the reader to zero, then the author-pays strategy may yield more generally useful publications than the reader-pays system. The likelihood of greater exposure for an author may make author-based finance more desirable than a reader-based financial strategy.

The shift from reader-pays to an author-pays regime is somewhat like the change in the charge for postage made in the 1850s. In the old policy, the recipient paid the postage in order to receive the mail, much as in a reader-pays regime for publications. After the 1850s, the U.S. Post Office introduced postage stamps and imposed the charge for delivery of mail on the sender.[30] The post office has much lower costs in selling stamps than in collecting from each recipient for each separate piece of mail. The post office avoided the expense of attempting delivery of mail only to have it rejected. The shift to a sender-pays system allowed advertisers to use the mails to push unsolicited materials to customers, a change not necessarily welcomed by all recipients.

The *Public Library of Science* (PLoS) offers high-quality author-paid journals. It produces open journals with a high level of editing. PLoS launched its journal-publishing venture in 2003, a venture led by Harold Varmus, Nobel Laureate in Medicine, former head of the National Institutes of Health, and President of the Memorial Sloan-Kettering Cancer Center. BioMed Central, a comparable venture, began publishing open journals in the United Kingdom in 1999.[31] Because the content of these journals is in the open, their articles are archived as part of the OAI and readily available to many Internet search engines. In 2007, the author fees were $2750 for the top journals at PLoS ($2410 at BioMed Central) per published article. Because dissemination of research results is an important part of grant supported research, the funding agencies often allow payment of author fees from grant funds. Because publications advance a scholar's reputation, salaries often increase with more publication. It is then in an author's interest to support payment when an article is published in a more widely cited journal. Universities gain intellectual reputation as their faculty publish, and it is then in the interest of universities to support author fees.

A university provost might compare the university's cost of a subscription journal plus the cost of tracking and processing the subscription through the library to the likely outlay of author publication fees of the university's faculty. If the expenditure on editing is the same per article, on average the net gain with the open journal with author fees arises from the smaller number of transactions with authors rather than with readers and the expanded readership with a zero price to readers. A university with a large number of faculty who publish in the journal might incur more cost with author fees, net of grant support for the author fees, than with subscriptions, net of the partial indirect cost recovery from grants based on library expenditures. Prestigious universities with highly productive faculty may, however, place a premium on the greater exposure their authors receive in open journals.

INFLUENCE OF OPEN JOURNALS

On their face, open journals look a little like vanity publishing, much as a hobbyist might publish a memoir for his family at his own expense. Many readers are less likely to read self-published works than those that have been reviewed and edited. On the other hand, open journals can be scrupulously edited and have more value by being more accessible.

One way of gauging the intellectual impact of a publication, that is, its value to readers, is to observe the frequency with which other writers cite it. A commonly used measure of a journal's intellectual value is the ISI Impact Factor as posted in the JCR.[32] The Impact Factor is the ratio of the number of times the articles are cited in academic journals in the first 2 years after publication as the numerator to the number of articles published in a journal in a given year as the denominator. The median Impact Factor for 103 journals in medicine evaluated by ISI was 1.21 in 2006. Twenty-eight of BioMed Central journals were evaluated by ISI (among 100 it publishes) with a median Impact Factor of 2.74. BioMed Central's journals have impact. PLoS has five journals scored of seven it offers in medicine and biology with a median Impact of 7.67, far above the norm. PLoS Biology at 14.01 has the highest impact of 64 rated journals in biology and PLoS Medicine at 13.75 is the fifth highest among 103 rated journals in medicine. PLoS had the advantage of significant philanthropic support for its launch that enabled it to achieve extraordinary impact quickly and to build a reputation that should allow it to be self-sustaining with author fees. The high level of impact of PLoS and BioMed Central's journals clearly establishes that open journals can achieve high levels of intellectual quality. Articles in open journals are more likely to be cited and thereby enhance their authors' reputations more than subscription journals, other things equal.

Some publishers offer hybrid journals, with articles in the open with a substantial author publication fee combined with other articles available only by subscription without an author fee. For example, Springer, a publisher of over 1900 academic journals, offers Open Choice, its program that charges a $3000 publication fee from authors to allow their article to be published in the open. Springer promises to adjust journal prices in light of the number of open choice articles published in the preceding year.[33] Springer's journal, *Economic Theory*, for example, had a library price of $1398 per year in 2007. It published about 120 articles per year with an Impact Factor of 0.50, compared to a median of 0.66 among 175 rated journals in economics.[32] Two of the most recent 17 issues are available in the open, but no other individual articles are in the open in the 2006 volume.[34]

A publisher is likely to prefer selling subscriptions to libraries instead of selling publication to authors. Journal quality, after all, depends on the quality of its authors and author fees could discourage them. Libraries show limited response to price increases; they tend to sustain their subscriptions. In contrast, authors are more likely to be influenced by author publication fees in selecting a journal. When demand is more responsive to price, suppliers find that setting price closer to marginal cost maximizes profit. A journal based on author fees is then likely to be less profitable than one based on subscription fees to libraries, other things equal. Self-financing publishers, whether for-profit or not-for-profit, may be more reluctant to move to author fees. They may then set author fees in hybrid journals well above the fees that might prevail when fully open journals are ready alternatives in a discipline. From the point of view of readers, a likely advantage of the growth of open publications is a reduction in the price of subscriptions for other journals. Authors must be persuaded of the higher probability of citation in open journals.

Another way to compare the intellectual impact of subscription with open journals is to consider the number of citations to articles published in the open to other articles in the same journal that are not in the open, while controlling statistically for the number of authors and the author's prior publication record and other attributes. One study compares citations to 212 openly published articles in the *PNAS*: *Proceedings of the National Academy of Sciences* to 1280 articles in same journal that are only available by subscription.[35] Articles published in the open had more than twice as many citations 4–10 months after publication and nearly three times as many 10–16 months after publication, other things equal. Open publication is more valuable, given the reputation of the journal.

SUBSCRIPTIONS

Subscriptions continue to provide the dominant revenue stream for the support of the publication of academic journals. The *American Economic Review* (AER), for example, goes to members of the American Economic Association. For $90, the 18,000 members each get three journals and about 4000 libraries subscribe to the three-journal bundle at $345 per year in 2007. The Association devotes about $1.5 million to producing the AER with about 185 articles per year including those in a proceedings issue, that's about $8000 per article.[36] This figure is about three times that of the PLoS author fee. The *New England Journal of Medicine* has 200,000 subscriptions at $149 for print and online, $99 for online only, $599 for libraries. It is generating about $50 million per year in revenue associated with the *Journal*, offering 300 or so articles per year in its weekly publication (Massachusetts Medical Society: Waltham, MA, "2005990-RET Returns" reports $106 million of total revenue for the year with expenditure of $63 million on publishing. It lists eight publications on its website, http://www.massmed.org, of which the *New England Journal of Medicine* is the most important. Although the society does not provide detailed information about its expenditures, it seems reasonable to assume that $50 million is spent publishing the journal). It is probably spending more than $150,000 per article, although how much of the revenue is spent specifically on the publication is unclear.[37] Although distribution costs for a weekly are significant, the cost of selecting about 300 articles from among 5000 submissions per year, two-thirds of which are from abroad, and editing those selected into more readable essays is substantial. Publishers, particularly of journals with a high level of editorial effort and a high volume of circulation, are likely to continue to depend on subscription revenue. Readers value quality editing and are willing to pay for it. Editors are readers' agents just as they are also author's agents.

High circulation publications can sustain relatively low-cost subscription rates because they spread their front-end costs among many readers. The gain to readers from offering the same content with a zero subscription fee may be less than for a publication with a high subscription rate. Subscriptions to some high circulation scholarly publications are likely to continue even as more open publications appear that are financed with author fees, philanthropy, and advertising. The boundary for scholarly publications is likely to continue to shift as technologies and reader tastes change just as the boundary may shift for popular newspapers and magazines. Some publications like the *New York Times* offered some digital content free with premium digital content available by subscription. In 2007, the *Times* shifted to an all-open format, viewing the gain in advertising revenue from general Internet access as more than sufficient to offset the loss in subscription revenue.[38] Typically academic publications eschew advertising to focus reader attention on scholarship.

The timing of availability is an important dimension for academic publishing. Newspapers and magazines obsolesce quickly. Academic journals have enduring value. ISI publishes a cited half-life for journals, an estimate of the number of years in which half of all citations that will ever occur have occurred. The median half-life for articles in 103 medical journals is more than 6 years; for history, it is over 10 years.[32] A subscription publisher may then choose to offer online access to its content with a delay. The publisher imposes an embargo on online access to the full text of its content by online services in order to avoid cannibalizing subscription revenue. In effect, subscription buys immediate access while less restrictive or open access to full text online comes with a delay. Embargoes of 12 months are common for access to journals, as discussed below.

SEARCH AND INDEXES

In addition to attracting strong authors and providing effective editing, the intellectual success of publications depends on appearing in indexes and finding aids. Although readers find items by browsing, many also look for materials on specific topics when an interest arises. Finding aids migrated from print to digital ahead of the publications themselves because digital searching is more convenient than searching a printed index.

Printed indexes typically covered journals and books within a discipline. Professional indexers scanned each item as it was published, noted author and title and assigned a subject category. The index then showed citations to articles listed under subject categories with an index to authors, aggregated by year or less frequently.

The leading professional society in each discipline typically published an index for its discipline. For example, *Chemical Abstracts* began publication in 1907 and became part of the American Chemical Society in 1956. It first offered an online service in 1980. Its database contained more than 27 million bibliographic records in 2007.[39]

A milestone in the launch of a new journal is when the appropriate indexing service includes the content of the new journal. For example, *Theoretical Economics*, an open journal launched in 2006, was indexed in *EconLit* from its first issue while the *International Journal of Economic Theory*, a subscription journal addressing a similar audience, was not indexed in *EconLit* even in its second year of publication.

With the digital revolution, the conventional indexes moved to digital media with search engines to provide faster, more comprehensive searching than can be achieved with print. Digital searching can identify materials by words in titles and abstracts and allow Boolean operators to control searches. With the success of the digital tools, the print version of indexes began to shrink and disappear. For example, the American Economic Association stopped publishing its *Index to Economic Articles* in 1996.

Other indexes have broader scope. The Institute for Scientific Information, for example, published the *Science Citation Index* beginning in 1961 to report the citations to prior works and now covers the content of more than 6400 journals in science and technology. Tracking references to other published literature allows building a bibliography that traces how ideas develop. It also provides a way to identify the importance of particular publications. The ISI Impact Factor, mentioned above, is a by-product of the *Citation Index*. The *Social Sciences Citation Index* indexes 1700 journals in the social sciences and the *Arts and Humanities Citation Index* tracks the contents of over 1000 journals.

The digital revolution made radical changes in indexing, epitomized by the founding of Google by Larry Page and Sergey Brin in 1998 while they were graduate students at Stanford University. Google, the largest search service on the Web, provides nearly 100 million searches daily.[40] It gained dominance because of the quality of its method for ranking Web pages in response to a search. By counting and evaluating the linkages from other pages to a given page, a process called dynamic indexing, Google identifies pages that are more likely to be sought and presents them first. Dynamic indexing is superior to static indexing, that is, searching based only on the words in the article, even when the word search encompasses the full text of a document. Google generates substantial revenue from the advertising it sells that appears as part of typical result-screens on basic Web searches.

In 2004, Google launched *Scholar*, its free service for searching a large part of the scholarly literature in a single database. *Scholar* encompasses many journals, books, working papers, and government reports. It applies Google's powerful dynamic indexing search engine to retrieve results. It reports a count of materials that cite the item at hand and will provide a list of them. When copyright allows, Scholar provides a link to the full-page images of the item, sometimes by linking through a local library's digital subscription. *Scholar* plays a key role in open access publishing by providing an open access index.

Critics of *Scholar* lament that *Scholar* uses a machine-created database that does not use systematic tagging of authors, titles, dates, and subjects.[41] (The American Economic Association attempted to replicate assignment of its subject codes to articles using software and achieved only a 50% success rate. Private communication from the Secretary of the Association.) As a consequence, the result of a *Scholar* search often includes more extraneous items than a search of a carefully structured data file. Critics also note that Google does not describe what materials are included in the *Scholar* database. Users cannot be sure what literature they have missed with a *Scholar* search. Because databases differ, a *Scholar* search typically complements other searches. Because *Scholar* is free and simple, it is often the starting point for searches. Another generation of open indexes may invite readers to set tags to indicate their assessment of quality that then influence the importance of an item in a search result.[42]

DATABASE INTEGRATORS

Another player in scholarly publishing is the database integrator, a firm that provides access to multiple databases with a common interface. A firm with suitable search software may license the use of databases from their publishers, for example the index databases of a number of scholarly societies, and, in turn, license an aggregation of the databases to libraries, using the integrator's common search software. Since the 1990s, a number of integrators began offering linkages to full text.

Ingenta, founded in 1998, launched a service called IngentaConnect in 2004 that provides access to the content of more then 31,000 publications with the full text of 8000 of them via the Internet, either by subscription through libraries or by direct pay-per-use. Ingenta reached agreement in 2004 to allow Google to index Ingenta's digital collection. Users can search Scholar for free and retrieve full text from Ingenta for a fee. In 2007, IngentaConnect processed 31 million sessions per month.

Also in 2004, Elsevier, publisher of 1900 academic journals, launched its latest search service, SCOPUS, as a digital service offered by subscription through libraries.[43] In 2007, SCOPUS indexed 15,000 academic journals with abstracts, including 1000 open journals, 30 million abstracts, and 21 million patents with links to the content of many journals in full text. It also alerts readers to new items appearing in the database that match the reader's standing search query. Elsevier developed a Web search engine, Scirus, to identify and index only science-oriented pages on the Web. Access to a Scirus search is open.[44] The SCOPUS subscription service includes the Scirus index of 275 million scientific Web pages.

Another major integrator is EBSCO. EBSCO markets its integration service to libraries, offering specific services by individual discipline. In 2007, its service for economics uses the American Economics Association *EconLit* index database to 1233 publications and provides links to the full text of 400 of them.[45] Of these, 11 had embargoes of 6 months and 227 had embargoes of 12 months.

The National Library of Medicine (NLM) plays a number of roles, including being an integrator of a number of databases relevant to medicine and medical research. It began publishing *Index Medicus*, an index to the medical literature in 1876.[46] It began creating a digital search and retrieval system in 1964 and put it online 1976. It made the MEDLINE service available in the open on the Internet in 1997. In 1996, it began offering links from the citations in MEDLINE to the full text of articles in PubMedCentral. These articles are then available in the open. MEDLINE abstracted about 5000 current journals in 2007 and contains more than 17 million citations. PubMed supports 3 million searches per day.[47] The NLM has given significant support to the growth of open scholarly publication.

Academic libraries themselves also act as database integrators. They provide links from varied search services that allow a campus searcher to click to the library's full-text service for the item. Open access services both compete with and complement subscription services (For example, the Exlibris Group, http://www.exlibris group.com/index.htm, offers to libraries software that integrates searches across disparate sources).

ADVERTISING

Although academic journals generally include few ads, database integrators have an opportunity to offer access to full-text academic journals in the open supported by advertising. In 2007, Elsevier launched OncologySTAT.com, an Internet portal with immediate open access to the current content of 100 of its own medical journals.[48] Elsevier expects to earn more from advertising than it loses in dropped subscriptions. OncologySTAT.com will include synopses of articles published outside Elsevier and will include the full text of such articles once their embargoes expire. Elsevier's initiative suggests that advertising may support significant quantities of open scholarly publications in some disciplines. Elsevier's move to open publication supported by advertising is a part of a widespread movement including the *New York Times* and other mass publications.[49]

BOOKS

Scholarly monographs have played a principal role in some disciplines, for example, history and the humanities, but the digital revolution is reshaping the place of books. The digital revolution for books began in 1971 in the early days of computing when Michael Hart invented e-Books and launched Project Gutenberg at the University of Illinois with the goal of making the full text of books freely available in digital format.[50] Gutenberg had mounted 20,000 items in 2007. The World Public Library, founded in 1996, offered 75,000 titles without charge in 2007 and more than 500,000 total for a modest annual membership fee.[51] The titles are generally old titles in the public domain rather than current publications. Producing digital books and making them available on the Internet either in the open or by subscription is technically no more difficult than offering digital journal articles. However, few people choose to read whole books online. Although several firms have marketed appliances for reading digital books that are nearly as portable as a conventional book, none to date have enjoyed wide appeal. For example, the Sony Reader System launched in January 2006.[52] Sony offers several thousand titles for its reader through http://ebooks.connect.com/. Making digital books in page turners, *Business Week*, September 3, 2007.[53]

Digital books appear to be successful in two other ways. First, digital access to the full text of a book allows the work to be readily searched, making the content discoverable by general Web searches. Led by its Director, Scott Lubeck, the National Academy of Sciences Press offered access to all its books in the open online in 1994 and sales of print increases.[54] In this case, the digital book was a complement to print.[55] In 2004, Google reached agreement with several large academic libraries to digitize large blocks of each library's holdings.[56] Materials out of copyright are made fully available in the open. For materials under copyright, Google's Book Search points to the work with links to libraries. Book Search is a very large and powerful book catalog available in the open.[57] The site includes both links to publishers and booksellers as well as advertising.

Second, digital books offer ways of presenting color, graphics, and even extend to animation, video, and sound. Rice University announced the reopening of its press in 2007 as a publisher of digital materials exclusively, particularly books.[58] Among other things, it intends to offer medical diagnostic books with rich color photographs and illustrations. Readers may read the works online in the open or buy print-on-demand copies.[59] Print-on-demand vendors use the digital file from the publisher and print books in a variety of formats, paper, color, and bindings. Authors who publish with the Rice University Press will submit works under the Creative Commons copyright policy, offering nonexclusive rights to the press to publish the work while allowing others to reuse the material under terms the authors specify.[60] Scholarly monographs can be published in the open with normal editorial review at less expense as digital products with print-on-demand available. In this manner, digital books may allow book-oriented disciplines to communicate more effectively with larger audiences than in paper-only formats.

LONG-TERM STORAGE AND RETRIEVAL

Scholarly publishing includes a commitment to long-term storage and retrieval so that the work of today's authors can influence the work of future generations. Works printed on acid-free paper, kept in climate-controlled conditions, and not subjected to vandalism can be used for hundreds of years. Libraries owned the physical artifacts and could maintain storage and access as long as the library maintained its facility. Digital products, in contrast, are often inherently volatile and rely on machines for use that quickly obsolesce. In addition, libraries sometimes license access to digital products. Under some contracts, the library loses all access when it stops paying the license fees and long-term access depends on the viability of the vendor rather than on the library.

The advantage of digital storage is that remote access is as convenient as local and therefore the cost of fixed long-term storage can be widely shared. William G. Bowen, President of the Andrew W. Mellon foundation, led the launch of JSTOR in 1995 to capitalize on this opportunity. Now a freestanding, not-for-profit, JSTOR seeks permission from publishers to digitize page images and create full-text files of the complete historic runs of journals. It then licenses access to libraries to its digital collection, with an embargo on recent years as stipulated by each publisher. Libraries pay an initial capital fee and a continuing annual license for access to more than 900 journals from 450 publishers in 2007 with more expected.[61] In 2007, 1900 libraries in the United States and its possessions and a similar number in 122 other countries subscribed to JSTOR, including academic, school, and other types of libraries. EBSCO and similar database integrators provide similar de facto shared digital storage services for their collections. JSTOR and similar organizations store their files at multiple sites, maintain off-site copies, and use formats that can more easily migrate to future technologies.

Long-term archiving of open access materials is another step. JSTOR is essentially a subscription service for storing and retrieving materials also originally published and paid for by subscription by libraries. One of JSTOR's criteria for deciding to include a journal in its collection is the number of institutional subscribers to a journal. Libraries justify participation in JSTOR, in part, on the ability to substitute a license to a remote digital archive for building more space to store old print journals. Open access journals do not involve library subscriptions and require no storage space. Will libraries pay for long-term archival storage of materials that are readily available without charge today on the Internet? Libraries have often purchased reprints and microform collections of historic materials. Library subscriptions to back files of open access journals seem well within the scope of traditional library collections just as JSTOR licenses sustain back files. Intellectually valuable open access publications are then likely to endure as part of library collections based on library license fees just as digital archives of subscription journals will. The Portico, spun off by JSTOR in 2005, archived 1.8 million articles by 2007 with funding from publishers and libraries.[62]

FRONTIERS

For scholarly journals, there are several frontiers at play between subscription and open publication. One frontier is the launch of new journals. A group of scholars or a publisher who intends to launch a new journal will decide whether to sell it by subscription or to offer it in the open. If in the open, the scholars might decide to depend on the good offices of a university and philanthropy to sustain the venture, relying primarily on volunteers as editors or they might rely on author fees to generate revenue flows to compensate editors. In 2007, Blackwell Publishing, a for-profit publisher, launched its first fully open access journal, *Archives of Drug Information* with author publication fees of $2600.[63] The fee is $2600 for up to 10 pages plus $250 for each page over 10. This new publication points to an expanding role for open journals through the launch of new journals. In contrast, the American Economic Association will launch four new journals in 2009 that will be offered by inexpensive subscriptions (Journal closings also influence the number of journals of each type. *Ulrich's Periodical Directory* lists 1679 referred academic journals as ceased; 535 of these had been available online but only 19 had been evaluated in JCR. Only 17 of the ceased journals were open access).

A second frontier arises in the selection of editors. For small-scale journals intended for specialists, an editor might serve as a volunteer, depending primarily on the good offices of his home campus. For large-scale journals that aim for wider intellectual impact that therefore must manage a larger flow of submissions, voluntary editors may not suffice. Among the distinguished scholars with the temperament and organizational skill needed to be successful editors, substantial financial inducements may be necessary to draw people into the role. Annual payment in excess of $100,000 plus support staff may be necessary to fill demanding editorships. Substantial author fees will be necessary to support editing of such journals when they are to be open. Subscription fees may be necessary for journals with high circulation to sustain the necessary level of editorial expertise. The ability to recruit appropriate editors is an important frontier for open journals.

A third frontier, the requirement of green archiving, involves the policy of research funding agencies in requiring results to be posted in the open. As mentioned above, governments might require open publication of publicly funded research. The policy might include an embargo, might limit open publication to prepublication versions, and limit posting to institutional repositories rather than in discipline-specific databases. Leading subscription-based journal publishers, particularly those with hybrid journals, can negotiate lower author payments with longer embargoes or limit the versions and location of postings. This frontier is one of political action and contract negotiation.

A fourth frontier is the critical one of authors choosing where to publish. Authors who focus on achieving substantial reputations can choose open publications with higher expected citation rates with their highest quality works appearing in journals with significant author fees. The support of funding agencies and universities for author fees will advance this frontier. Authors may also choose subscription journals with wide circulation.[64] For authors who publish works for narrower audiences, open journals with volunteer editors and modest or no author fees may dominate other choices.

A fifth and critical frontier is that of libraries who make decisions about support for relevant open publications and purchase of subscriptions. With modest effort, libraries can include reference to intellectually important open journals and other publications in their catalogs and other finding tools. Libraries can use their role as database integrators to include indexes that point to open materials, enhancing the frequency of use and value of open materials.

The libraries make decisions about subscriptions to databases. Some databases will be more valuable for some libraries than others in the way that a large set of medical journals is more valuable to a medical library. The better the fit of the database to a library, the more a vendor is likely to charge with database prices varying by type and size of library. The vendor will increase profit (or publisher's net in the case of not-for-profits) with prices high enough to nearly induce some libraries not to subscribe. For large databases taken to be very significant for a given category of library, the subscription rates can be quite large. The greater the extent and quality of open access alternatives, the more easily some libraries may choose not to subscribe. For smaller libraries and those for which a given database is less relevant, the vendor will offer lower prices in part because the library is more likely to find a given set of open materials to be sufficient. The vendors, in turn, seek to bundle materials into larger databases and to offer unique features to make their offerings more compelling. Open posting in institutional repositories with short embargoes narrow differences in service available in the open compared to the subscriptions.

A sixth frontier is that of readers in choosing to use open publications more often than subscription publications. Even on well-supported campuses, however, readers may turn first to open indexes and link more readily to digital full-text materials published in the open. As readers, for whatever reason, give precedence to open materials, authors, editors, publishers, and libraries will move toward open journals. Readers' willingness to tolerate advertising will also have influence. In 2007, conventional subscription journals hold sway.[65] Scholars invest in building their reputations by publishing in highly regarded journals. Most take the traditional system of subscription journals as given in deciding where to publish and this behavior gives existing patterns inertia.

The speed of development of open publication will vary across disciplines because these frontiers will differ. Disciplines with high levels of research funding, those where more new journals are being launched, where volunteer editors are more common, where authors accept publication fees more readily, and where library support is not as deep, are likely to move to open publication faster. Where high levels of editing produce polished publications that reach wide audiences subscriptions are more likely.

Online Public–Organizational

THE KNOWLEDGE BASE

The intellectual success and economic viability of open access archives, journals, and indexes creates the possibility of a universal, open access knowledge database, an intellectual commons.[66] The knowledge base could be universal in the sense of encompassing all disciplines, in being accessible to everyone on the Internet, and expanding with media beyond black text on white pages. As a large and increasing proportion of the workforce are college graduates, universal access to the knowledge base will make it more valuable. As countries around the world make larger commitments to higher education, scholarship will play a larger role in economic growth everywhere. Scholarship, when it is available in the open, will have more value than in the past.

The tragedy of the commons, the loss of value from congestion—making it more difficulty to identify the most important ideas, exploitation—pressing volunteers to undertake unreasonable efforts, and pollution—an overflow of extraneous materials, points to limitations of overreliance on sharing. The market place for ideas where intellectual property has dollar value can be an antidote to the excesses of the commons. Market forces focus effort on more important ideas, reward leading scholars who invest in becoming editors who promote the work of others, and encourage scholars to develop teaching materials and to put scholarship in forms useful beyond academia. Scholarship has value in training a more capable workforce and a better-informed citizenry. Subscription services may have particular value with high levels of editorial service, more structured and precise searching, and long-term archiving. Financial incentives tied to intellectual property from reputation, copyrights, and patents channel scholarly effort to more valuable roles in ways that may be difficult to achieve simply by sharing.

On the other hand, markets are seldom perfect. They can be frozen by monopoly. They can be overheated by pointless arms races. Dollars can give misleading signals of value. A report in 2007 by Ithaka, a not-for-profit committed to promoting innovation in higher education, urges an active role for universities and not-for-profits in developing digital publishing services.[67] It calls for new publishing models to offer immediate access, dynamically updated materials, and collaborative environments with a broad range of digital materials. New investments will be needed to support more sophisticated publishing operations. The extent to which universities and philanthropy will decide to support such ventures will influence whether such developments will be under not-for-profit and university control. Finally, by the nature of their investments, the universities will determine the extent of open access scholarly publishing.

REFERENCES

1. Van Orsdel, L.C.; Born, K. Serial wars. Libr. J. April 15, **2007**, *132* (7), 43–48.
2. Bergstrom, T.C. Free labor for costly journals? J. Econ. Perspect. Summer **2001**, *15* (3), 185–198.
3. Getz, M. Open access scholarly publishing. J. Libr. Admin. January **2005**, *42* (1), 1–39.
4. Ellison, G. Evolving standards for academic publishing: A q-r theory. J. Polit. Econ. October **2002**, *110* (5), 994–1034;

Ellison, G. The slowdown of the economics publishing process. J. Polit. Econ. October **2002**, *110* (5), 947–993.
5. *Ulrich's Periodicals Directory*; R. R. Bowker: New Providence, NJ, 2007. http://www.ulrichsweb.com/ulrichsweb/
6. Directory of Open Access Journals, http://www.doaj.org/
7. Creative Commons Wikipedia, September, 2007.
8. arXive, http://arxiv.org/
9. Social Science Research Network, http://www.ssrn.com/.
10. Budapest Open Archives Initiative, December 2001. http://www.soros.org/openaccess/.
11. The Berlin Declaration on Open Access to Knowledge in the Sciences and Humanities, October 2003. http://oa.mpg.de/openaccess-berlin/berlindeclaration.html.
12. Bailey, C.W., Jr. *Open Access Bibliography*; Association of Research Libraries: Washington, DC, 2005. http://www.escholarlypub.com/oab/oab.pdf.
13. Harnad, S. Fast-forward on the green road to open access: The case against mixing up green and gold. Ariande January **2005**, *42*, http://www.ariadne.ac.uk/issue42/harnad/.
14. Suber, P. Paying for green open access. *The SPARC Open Access Newsletter*; April 2, 2007; Vol. 108. http://www.earlham.edu/~peters/fos/newsletter/04-02-07.htm.
15. Consultative Committee for Space Data Systems, *Reference Model for Open Archival Information System* (OAIS), 2002, http://public.ccsds.org/publications/archive/650x0b1.pdf.
16. Open Archives. *Registered Data Providers*, August, 2007. http://www.openarchives.org/Register/BrowseSites.
17. DSpace, DSpace Foundation, http://www.dspace.org/. In 2007, over 200 institutions have adopted DSpace to manage digital archives.
18. Ober, J. Facilitating open access: Developing support for author control of copyright. Coll. Res. Libr. April **2006**, *67*(4). http://www.ala.org/ala/acrl/acrlpubs/crlnews/backissues2006/april06/facilitatingopenaccess.cfm.
19. http://openaccess.eprints.org/index.php?/archives/198-guid.html.
20. http://en.wikipedia.org/wiki/. Wikipedia Worldwide Wikipedia mounts 8 million articles in hundreds of languages with coordinate entities in several countries.
21. Montagne, R. Scanner tracks who's changing what on wikipedia, *National Public Radio*, August 16, 2007. http://www.npr.org/templates/story/story.php?storyId=12823729.
22. Encyclopedia Britannica, Fatally flawed: Refuting the recent study of encyclopedic accuracy by the journal *Nature*, March 2006, http://corporate.britannica.com/britannica_nature_response.pdf (suggests that Wikipedia is not as accurate as Britannica).
23. Viegas, F.B.; Wattenberg, M.; Dave, K.Studying cooperation and conflict between authors with history flow visualizations. CHI 2004 paper, http://alumni.media.mit.edu/~fviegas/papers/history_flow.pdf.
24. Cohen, N. A history department bans citing wikipedia as a research source. New York Times February 21, **2007**.
25. Willinsky, J. What open access research can do for wikipedia. FirstMonday February 12, **2007**, *12*(3), http://firstmonday.org/issues/issue12_3/willinsky/index.html.
26. ISI Web of Knowledge. *Journal Citation Reports*. Thomson Reuters.
27. Public Knowledge Project, University of British Columbia, *Open Journal Systems*, *http://pkp.sfu.ca/?q=ojs*.
28. http://www.econtheory.org/.
29. Getz, M. Incubating open journals in economics. Internet First University Press at Cornell http://hdl.handle.net/1813/2468 January, 2005, for a comparison of this open journal to a similar subscription journal.
30. Reebel, P.A. *United States Post Office: Current Issues and Historical Background*; Nova Science Publishers: Hauppauge, NY, 2003; 18.
31. Brynko, B. BioMed central opens doors for physics community. Inform. Today May **2007**, *XXIV* (5), 136 reports the BioMed will become profitable in 2007.
32. Institute of Scientific Information, *Journal Citation Reports*; Institute for Scientific Information: Philadelphia, PA.
33. http://www.springer.com/east/home/open+choice?SGWID=5-40359-12-115382-0&teaserId=55557&CENTER_ID=115391.
34. http://www.springer.com/west/home/economics?SGWID=4-165-70-1100472-0. Ulrich's does not count hybrid journals as open access.
35. Eysenbach, G. Citation advantage of open access articles. PLoS Biol. May 15, **2006**. Other studies draw similar conclusions, for example: Harnad, S.; Brody, T. Comparing the impact of open access (OA) vs. non-OA articles in the same journals. D-Lib Mag. **2004**, *10*.
36. American Economic Association, Statement of Financial Condition. Am. Econ. Rev. June **2006**, 917.
37. *New England Journal of Medicine website*, http://authors.nejm.org/Misc/AuthorFAQ.asp.
38. Pérez-Peña, R. Times to end charges on Website. *New York Times*, September 18, **2007**.
39. Chemical Abstract Services, http://www.cas.org/aboutcas/cas100/annivhistory.html.
40. SearchEngineWatch.com, http://searchenginewatch.com/showPage.html?page=2156461 reported 91 million searches on Google per day, April 20, 2006.
41. MacColl, J. Google challenges for academic libraries. Ariadne February **2006**, *46*, http://www.ariadne.ac.uk/issue46/maccoll/intro.html.
42. Penn Tags at the University of Pennsylvania Library, http://tags.library.upenn.edu/, is an example of social bookmarking.
43. Scopus, http://info.scopus.com/overview/what/.
44. Scirus, http://www.scirus.com/.
45. ISI Web of Knowledge. *Journal Citation Reports*; Thomson Reuters.
46. National Library of Medicine, http://www.nlm.nih.gov/about/nlmhistory.html.
47. PubMed Celebrates its 10th Anniversary. NLM Tech. Bull. September/October **2006**, http://www.nlm.nih.gov/pubs/techbull/so06/so06_pm_10.html.
48. Freudenheim, M. A medical publisher's unusual prescription: Online ads. *New York Times*, September 10, **2007**; C1.
49. Mulligan, T.S. *Wall Street Journal* online may become free, LATimes.com September 19, **2007**.
50. About Project Gutenberg, http://www.gutenberg.org/wiki/Gutenberg:About.
51. World Public Library, http://worldlibrary.net/public.htm (The Internet Archive, archive.org lists more than 250,000 text items freely available from various sources in 2007).

52. For example, the Sony Reader System launched in January 2006. http://www.sonystyle.com Sony offers several thousand titles for its reader through http://ebooks.connect.com/. Making digital books into page turners, *Business Week*, September 3, 2007.
53. http://www.businessweek.com/magazine/content/07_36/b4048065.htm?campaign_id=rss_daily.
54. Pope, B.K. National Academy Press: A case study. J. Electron. Publish. June **1999**, *IV*(4). http://www.press.umich.edu/jep/04-04/pope.html.
55. Jensen, M. Academic press gives away its secret of success. *Chronicle of Higher Education Review*, September 14, 2001.
56. Wyatt, E. Googling literature: The debate goes public. *New York Times*, November 19, 2005. Book publishers and authors challenged Google under the copyright law.
57. Google, http://books.google.com.
58. Rice University Press, http://ricepress.rice.edu/.
59. Ingram Books' Lightning source is an example of a print-on-demand vendor. https://www.lightningsource.com/.
60. Creative Commons, http://creativecommons.org/.
61. JSTOR, New York, http://www.jstor.org/about/.
62. Portico, *About Portico*, http://www.portico.org/.
63. Blackwell Publishing, Arch. Drug Inform., http://www.blackwellpublishing.com/journal.asp?ref=1753-5174&site=1.
64. University of California Office of Scholarly Communication and the California Digital Library eScholarship Program, *Faculty Attitudes and Behaviors Regarding Scholarly Communication: Survey Findings from the University of California*; Berkeley, CA, 2007; 31–44. http://osc.universityofcalifornia.edu/responses/materials/OSC-survey-full-20070828.pdf.
65. University of California Office of Scholarly Communication and the California Digital Library eScholarship Program, *Faculty Attitudes and Behaviors Regarding Scholarly Communication: Survey Findings from the University of California*; Berkeley, CA, 2007; 4. http://osc.universityofcalifornia.edu/responses/materials/OSC-survey-full-20070828.pdf.
66. Sunstein, C. *Infotopia: How Many Minds Produce Knowledge*; Oxford University Press: New York, 2006.
67. Brown, L.; Griffths, R.; Rascoff, M. University publishing in a digital age. *Ithaka Report*, July 23, 2007. http://www.ithaka.org/.

Open Archival Information System (OAIS) Reference Model

Christopher A. Lee
School of Information and Library Science, University of North Carolina at Chapel Hill, Chapel Hill, North Carolina, U.S.A.

Abstract
The Reference Model for an Open Archival Information System (OAIS) describes components and services required to develop and maintain archives, in order to support long-term access to and understanding of the information in those archives. This entry discusses the context in which the OAIS was initiated and provides a chronology of the OAIS development process, including its transformation from a space data standard into a document of much wider scope. The author explains the nature of reference models as a particular type of standard, and then describes the major components and concepts of the OAIS Reference Model. The primary mechanisms that the Reference Model uses to convey the aspects of an OAIS are its functional model and information model. The entry also summarizes numerous (completed, ongoing, and emerging) initiatives that have adopted and expanded on the OAIS. Finally, the author discusses major implications of the OAIS.

INTRODUCTION

The Reference Model for an Open Archival Information System (OAIS) describes components and services required to develop and maintain archives, in order to support long-term access to and understanding of the information in those archives.[1] The development of the OAIS took place within a standards development organization called the Consultative Committee for Space Data Systems (CCSDS), whose formal purview is the work of space agencies, but the effort reached far beyond the traditional CCSDS interests and stakeholders.[2] It has become a fundamental component of digital archive research and development in a variety of disciplines and sectors.

This entry discusses the context in which the OAIS was initiated and provides a chronology of the OAIS development process, including its transformation from a space data standard into a document of much wider scope. It then describes the major components and concepts of the OAIS Reference Model. The entry also summarizes numerous initiatives that have adopted and expanded on the OAIS. Finally, the author discusses major implications of the OAIS.

HISTORICAL CONTEXT

Digital preservation has long been an area of concern for those responsible for repositories of digital objects. Data mismanagement, technological dependency, media degradation, and technological obsolescence have all threatened the long-term accessibility of resources stored in digital formats. In the 1950s, 1960s, and 1970s, organizations began increasingly to rely on collections of computer-dependent data. Several streams of activity gradually emerged to address parts of the digital preservation problem (e.g., care and physical properties of physical storage media; hardware and software interoperability; management and provision of access to digital library collections), but there was often little communication or coordination across the streams. The streams of activity often developed their own distinct forums (journals, conferences, consortia) and sets of funding mechanisms (government budget areas, research agendas, foundation support).

Two trends that began in the 1960s and 1970s, but became much more prominent during the 1980s and early 1990s, were: 1) actors with long traditions of preserving physical artifacts (e.g., archivists, librarians, museum curators) increasingly recognizing that information which fell within the scope of their responsibility was now digital; and 2) actors with long traditions of managing computer-dependent data sets (e.g., scientific data center personnel, corporate information technology managers) increasingly recognizing that information which fell within the scope of their responsibility had long-term preservation value. The effort to develop the OAIS came at a time when the separate streams of activity were making important progress but they were only beginning to identify points of intersection between the streams. During the years immediately preceding and throughout the OAIS development effort, participants in digital preservation work increasingly recognized that they were addressing similar issues.

The 1990s were characterized by a broadening societal awareness of both the importance of standards in supporting the infrastructure that underlies various activities and the challenges of long-term digital preservation. Two

Encyclopedia of Library and Information Sciences, Fourth Edition DOI: 10.1081/E-ELIS4-120044377

closely connected factors were the development of widely distributed computer networks and an industry trend toward commercial off-the-shelf (COTS) equipment. Rather than depending on the compatibility of an entire suite of hardware and software from a single vendor, producers and consumers of computer equipment came to rely on conventions for interchange of data between a heterogeneous set of components. Both the International Organization for Standardization (ISO) and Internet Engineering Task Force (IETF) developed layered architectures to which hardware and software producers could conform in order to ensure that their products could interchange data with other products on the Internet. In the early 1990s, the adoption of the World Wide Web reflected and contributed to a dramatic growth in the base of consumers who had a stake in the interchange of data over computer networks. The Year 2000 (Y2K) conversion effort was one widely recognized example of dependence on a widespread assortment of hardware and software components that usually interoperated in ways invisible to most people, but could cause significant problems when they failed to interoperate. In 1994, the Commission on Preservation and Access (CPA) and Research Libraries Group (RLG) created a Task Force on Digital Archiving. The Task Force issued a report in 1996 called *Preserving Digital Information*, which was frequently cited by subsequent literature on digital preservation.[3] Two works that brought digital preservation to popular attention were a 1995 article by Jeff Rothenberg in *Scientific American* called "Ensuring the longevity of digital documents"[4] and a movie called *Into the Future*,[5] which was released in 1997 and shown on Public Broadcasting Service (PBS) across the United States in 1998.

Prior to the development of the OAIS, there had been numerous calls in professional literature for both development and adoption of open standards in support of long-term digital preservation. The most active standardization and consensus was associated with physical storage media and storage conditions. In other areas of digital preservation, most of the existing standards had served primarily to advance work within specific streams of activities, rather than spanning multiple professions.

OAIS DEVELOPMENT PROCESS

The historical context discussed in the previous section is essential to understanding the character and impact of the OAIS. The Reference Model was both a product of and an influential factor in the evolution of digital preservation activities in the mid- to late-1990s—reflecting preexisting notions and helping to define new notions. A major factor in the success of the OAIS was the timing of its development. Actors within several streams of activity related to digital preservation perceived the need for a high-level model but had not themselves developed one. At the same time, several actors now felt they had knowledge from their own recent digital archiving efforts, which could inform the development of the OAIS. Despite this growing body of practical experience and understanding of the functions associated with digital archiving, one essential element that was missing was a common vocabulary. Problems had often stemmed from terms—such as archives/archiving or metadata—that were used so widely and for so many different purposes that it was difficult to determine if they were being used in the same way by different actors. The combination of pressing need, available expertise, and inconsistent language meant the time was ripe for developing a reference model that could codify and support greater consistency in discussions of digital archives.

The development of the OAIS took place within the CCSDS, whose formal purview was specifically support for study of the terrestrial and space environments. However, the OAIS development effort took on a much wider scope than one may have reasonably predicted, given its CCSDS origins. The OAIS development process ultimately involved and gained visibility among a much broader set of stakeholders than simply members of the CCSDS. The word "Open" in the acronym OAIS—meant to indicate that the standard was "developed in open forums"—was a defining feature of its evolution. The leader of the OAIS development process was Don Sawyer, Computer Scientist and head of the U.S. National Aeronautics and Space Administration (NASA) Office of Standards and Technology (NOST) at the Goddard Space Flight Center (GSFC) in Greenbelt, Maryland. Sawyer indicated early and continued to reiterate that the process should be open and inclusive, in order to get sufficient input and buy-in. The core development team actively recruited commentary on the drafts of the document and gave dozens of public presentations about the Reference Model to a diverse range of professional groups.

The formal process began on April 5, 1994, when Gael Squibb of the Jet Propulsion Laboratory (JPL) proposed a New Work Item (NWI) related to "archiving space data" to ISO Technical Committee 20 (Aircraft and Space Vehicles), Subcommittee 14 (Space Systems and Operations). This proposal ultimately found a home in another subcommittee of ISO TC 20: Subcommittee 13 (Space Data and Information Transfer Systems). The formal Secretariat for TC 20/SC 13 is the American National Standards Institute (ANSI), and it is administered by NASA. The CCSDS is a liaison organization to TC 20/SC 13 (see Fig. 1). Sawyer made the case for this effort to NASA management. As the NASA representative, Sawyer also submitted a document to Panel 2 (Information Interchange Processes) of the CCSDS on April 25, 1995, proposing a new "work package." In May, Panel 2 created "WP [Work Package] 700 Archiving" with Sawyer as the leader and the initial subtask being "WP 710 Archiving Reference Model." Sawyer and Lou Reich, who worked under contract for

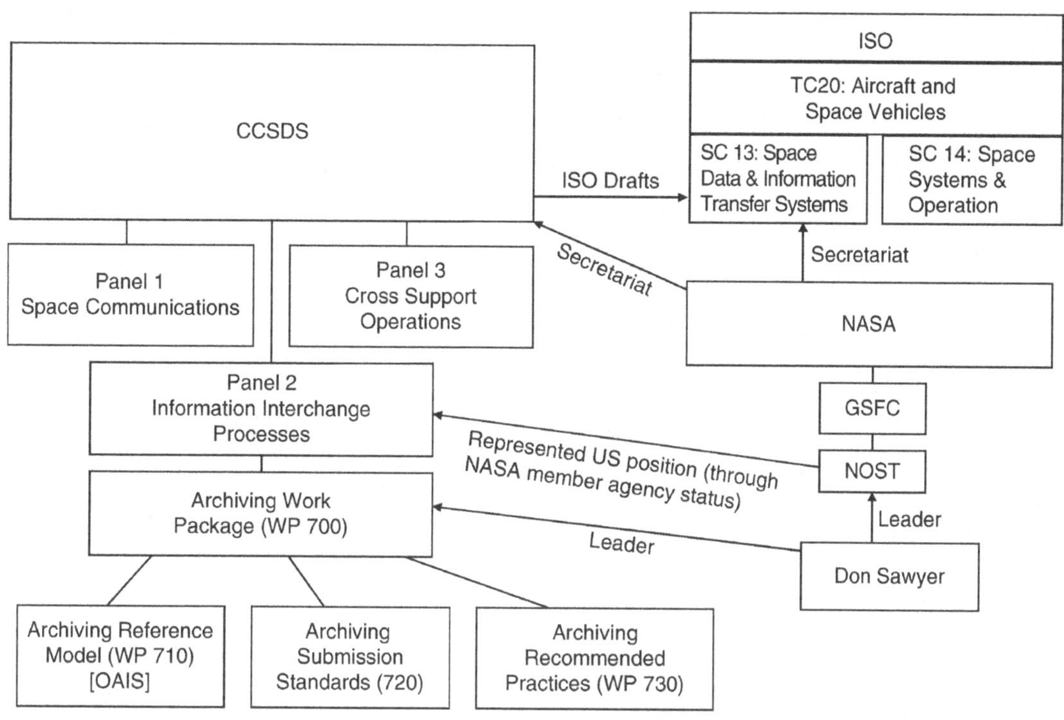

Fig. 1 Organizational context of OAIS development.
Source: Adapted from C. Lee, Defining *Digital Preservation Work: A Case Study of the Development of the Reference model for an Open Archival Information System.* Doctoral Dissertation, University of Michigan: Michigan, 2005.[2] CCSDS, Consultative Committee for Space Data Systems; GSFC, Goddard Space Flight Center; ISO, International Organization for Standardization; NASA, U.S. National Aeronautics and Space Administration; NOST, NASA Office of Standards and Technology.

the GSFC as Senior Consulting Engineer for the Computer Sciences Corporation, coauthored a preliminary discussion draft of a reference model document. Sawyer and Reich remained the primary authors and editors of later versions, but the process also increasingly drew from contributions (both text and figures) from other participants. John Garrett, who was a contractor for the NSSDC as Senior Analyst at Hughes STX (ST Systems Corporation), helped to set up the initial meeting, and he served as a significant source of administrative support and documentation throughout the OAIS development process.

Development of the OAIS was markedly different from the previous standards development efforts of the CCSDS by being both broader in scope and inclusive of a more diverse set of actors. In order to support this unusually inclusive effort, the leaders set up a unique meeting and decision-making structure. In addition to the well-established semiannual CCSDS meetings, the OAIS development effort also involved a set of 18 U.S. Workshops, devoted primarily to document development, and a set of more open meetings (one in France, two in the United Kingdom, and two in the United States), designed to gather input and review from a wider set of actors. Most of the U.S. Workshops took place at the Archives II facility of the U.S. National Archives and Records Administration (NARA); Bruce Ambacher, Archives Specialist at NARA, was one of the most active participants in the OAIS development process. The creation of the Reference Model involved a relatively small and stable set of core actors, but it also involved a much larger set of actors who had more limited Workshop participation. The latter played an extremely important role in the development, review, and visibility of the Reference Model. There were 306 individuals who participated in one or more of the Workshops.

Development of the OAIS involved negotiation over issues such as the scope of the Reference Model, its intended purpose, and the definition of basic terms. The development process also involved considerable borrowing and adaptation of ideas and documents already in existence. Over time, common notions about the content of the Reference Model became more established, and the number and extent of revisions to drafts of the Reference Model decreased.

After being requested to do so by CCSDS Panel 2, ISO SC 13 voted on May 22, 2000 to allow circulation of Red Book 1[6] as a Draft International Standard (DIS) to all ISO national member bodies. By releasing the Reference Model as a Red Book, the CCDS was indicating that the document was "technically mature and ready for extensive and formal review by appropriate technical organizations within each Member Agency." Comments received in response to Red Book 1 implied substantive changes to the document. SC 13 sent a request to the ISO in January

2001 to "reprocess" the DIS, meaning a revised document would be resubmitted to ISO member bodies for another vote. Red Book 1.1 (April 20, 2001), Red Book 1.2 (June 2001), and Red Book 2 (July 2001) were the result of efforts to address the comments received in response to Red Book 1. On October 23, 2001, SC 13 approved the submission of Red Book 2 for ISO vote. There were then a few minor editorial changes to the document before it was circulated (as the Blue Book)[6] to ISO member bodies for balloting. A Blue Book is a CCSDS Recommendation, which "reflects resolution of official comments from Member Agencies during formal reviews, and, as such, represents the consensus of appropriate implementing organizations within each Member Agency. Member Agency approval of a Blue Book implies an intent to reflect its provisions in future data systems standards developed through internal mechanisms." The ISO balloting process, which involved ISO national member bodies, ran from January 24 to April 5, 2002. There were eight affirmative votes, no negative votes, and two abstentions. The chair of SC 13 formally reported the results of voting on the Reference Model to ISO on August 20, 2002. On February 24, 2003, the Reference Model was finally published by ISO as an International Standard (ISO 14721:2003).[7] The Blue Book version, which is freely available from the CCSDS Web site, is identical in content to the International Standard, except that the current Blue Book version reflects a September 2007 "editorial correction," involving slight alterations to several figures to correct "display anomalies" (problems with encoding of line breaks had resulted in extraneous square blocks appearing next to some text elements) and a "typographical error" in one of the figures.

Many important activities in the development of the OAIS took place outside the context of formal ISO Archiving meetings and review processes. Teleconferencing, e-mail, and the Web greatly facilitated work on the OAIS and allowed review and use of the Reference Model drafts by those who were not necessarily able to attend the Workshops. Core members of the OAIS development effort gave dozens of presentations related to the Reference Model at conferences and other professional events. Several of the actors in the ISO Archiving Workshops also took part in mass storage systems and technologies (MSST) conferences, which served as forums for both the dissemination of information about the development of the Reference Model and recruitment of actors into the process. Individuals and organizations involved in initiatives that attempted to apply and test the Reference Model—e.g., CEDARS (CURL [Consortium of Research Libraries] Exemplars in Digital Archives) in the United Kingdom, NEDLIB (Networked European Deposit Library), British Library, and PANDORA (Preserving and Accessing Networked Documentary Resources of Australia)—played an essential role in the process. The archives certification work that built off of the Reference Model also provided important input into the development of the OAIS and demonstrated the Reference Model's potential value to a variety of stakeholders.

Development of the Reference Model drew from many other sources. These included concepts, terminology, models, and strings of text and images from guidelines, reports, and standards. In some cases—such as the "Z39.50 profile for access to digital collections" (PDC),[8] *Preserving Digital Information*, *Planetary Data System Data Preparation Workbook*,[9] and *IEEE Guide to the POSIX Open System Environment (OSE)*[10]—it is possible to identify specific terms or concepts that were incorporated into the Reference Model. Other sources were discussed during Workshops and provided varying degrees of conceptual background for the work on the Reference Model.

OAIS AS A REFERENCE MODEL

The OAIS is a reference model, which is a very particular type of standard. Carl Cargill provides a framework for describing standards, which distinguishes providers of information technology products and services from the users of those products and services. According to Cargill, these two groups have very different motivations and needs in the standardization process.

> On the provider side is the global model that describes all of the potentials that the IT industry will need to satisfy all users over a long time in nearly all situations, and that serves as a reference for all providers. This reference model, if it is correctly constructed, includes some present and future technologies, a road map function, and some of the methodologies of the thought processes that occurred when it was constructed. The time span covered is up to ten years, and the model is applicable to all technical disciplines that deal in this area. On the IT user side is a description of a solution implementation that is immediate and particular to that user's application problems (p. 1-11).[1]

As explained by Cargill above, reference models operate at a higher level of abstraction than other types of standards and are purposely designed to be "implementation-independent." The OAIS itself provides the following definition of reference model:

> A framework for understanding significant relationships among the entities of some environment, and for the development of consistent standards or specifications supporting that environment. A reference model is based on a small number of unifying concepts and may be used as a basis for education and explaining standards to a nonspecialist.[11]

Cargill explains that bridging the gap between reference models and application implementations requires a chain of standards at increasing levels of specificity (p. 1-12).[1] Within the arena of digital archives, this means that one would expect more specific standards to emerge, which indicate how to apply the concepts of the OAIS in more specific contexts. As explained later in the section on "OAIS Adoption, Extension, and Future Directions," such follow-on standardization has been taking place.

CONTENT OF THE OAIS

The OAIS is a 148-page document, composed of six sections and six annexes. Section 1 frames the content to follow, by providing discussions of purpose, scope, applicability, definitions, rationale, and conformance requirements. It also situates the document in a larger context by including a "road map for development of related standards." Section 2 lays out several core concepts that are then modeled in more detail in Section 4. These include archive; information (as distinct from data); interfaces between an archive, Producers, Consumers, and Management; and Information Package and its subtypes: Submission Information Package (SIP), Archival Information Package (AIP), and Dissemination Information Package (DIP). Section 3 discusses the responsibilities of an Open Archival Information System and "some examples of mechanisms to discharge these responsibilities." Section 4 presents a "more detailed model view" of the concepts previously laid out in the document. The section includes a functional model (including a high-level view and then unpacking of each entity and data flows between the entities) and an information model, which provides a hierarchical set of views and explanations for what logical elements should be stored and managed in association with a data object. Section 4 also provides an account of the "transformations, both logical and physical, of the Information Package and its associated objects as they follow a lifecycle from the Producer to the OAIS, and from the OAIS to the Consumer." Section 5 provides some discussion—intended to be implementation agnostic—of technical issues and strategies that an archive can potentially use to address changes in underlying hardware, software, formats, and access services. Section 6 discusses potential arrangements between multiple archives. The annexes that follow Section 6 are not considered part of the Reference Model's normative content but are instead "provided for the convenience of the reader." The annexes include a set of five "scenarios" that use OAIS terminology and concepts to describe specific existing archives; explanations of how the Reference Model relates to other standards and projects; a brief Unified Modeling Language (UML) tutorial; list of references; a layered model of how software could be used to support Representation Information; and a "composite diagram" that presents in one place the detailed interfaces between each of the entities in the functional model.

Fundamental Terms and Concepts

The Reference Model defines an OAIS as "an archive, consisting of an organization of people and systems, that has accepted the responsibility to preserve information and make it available for a Designated Community." Many of the requirements for an OAIS are based on the needs of its Designated Community, which is the set of one or more "user communities" that the OAIS is serving. An OAIS is responsible for digital information over the "long term," which is "long enough to be concerned with the impacts of changing technologies, including support for new media and data formats, or with a changing user community" (p. 1-11).[1] One of the fundamental challenges of an OAIS is to ensure that the digital information in its care is "independently understandable" to the Designated Community, which means that the Designated Community can understand it "without having to resort to special resources not widely available, including named individuals" (p. 1-10).[1] The Designated Community has a certain "knowledge base," which can change over time.

One of the most important insights embedded in the Reference Model is that the "Content Information" to be preserved by an archive is composed not only of a "set of bit sequences" (the "data object") but also associated sufficient "Representation Information" to allow the bits to be rendered, used, and understood.

> Since a key purpose of an OAIS is to preserve information for a Designated Community, the OAIS must understand the Knowledge Base of its Designated Community to understand the minimum Representation Information that must be maintained. The OAIS should then make a decision between maintaining the minimum Representation Information needed for its Designated Community, or maintaining a larger amount of Representation Information that may allow understanding by a larger Consumer community with a less specialized Knowledge Base. Over time, evolution of the Designated Community's Knowledge Base may require updates to the Representation Information to ensure continued understanding (p. 2-4).[1]

The three main roles played by the external entities with which an OAIS interacts are Producer, Consumer, and Management. Producers are "persons, or client systems, who provide the information to be preserved." Consumers are "persons, or client systems, who interact with OAIS services to find preserved information of interest and to access that information in detail." Management is "the role played by those who set overall OAIS policy as one component in a broader policy domain (p. 1–11)."[1]

A diversity of workflow and collaborative arrangements can be mapped to the Reference Model by representing "other OAISs" and "internal OAIS persons or systems" as Producers and Consumers (pp. 1–8, 1–12).[1] The Reference Model describes "four categories of archive association" based on "successively higher degrees of interaction":

- Independent—"no management or technical interaction."
- Cooperating—"potential common producers, common submission standards, and common dissemination standards, but no common finding aids."
- Federated—serve "both a Local Community (i.e., the original Designated Community served by the archive) and a Global community (i.e., an extended Designated Community) which has interests in the holdings of several OAIS archives and has influenced those archives to provide access to their holdings via one or more common finding aids."
- Shared resources—have agreed to share resources between the archives, which "requires various standards internal to the archive (such as ingest-storage and access-storage interface standards), but does not alter the user community's view of the archive" (p. 6–2).[1]

The primary mechanisms that the Reference Model uses to convey the aspects of an OAIS are its functional model and information model. Roughly speaking, the former indicates what an OAIS must do, and the latter indicates what the OAIS must have in its collections.

Functional Model

The functional model is composed of seven main functional entities and the interfaces between them: Access, Administration, Archival storage, Common Services, Data Management, Ingest, and Preservation Planning. The single figure from the Reference Model that has received the most attention in the digital preservation literature is a representation of six of the functional entities (see Fig. 2). Not directly represented in Fig. 2 are Common Services, which are the "supporting services" that must be in place for computer systems to operate and perform properly, including interprocess communication, name services, temporary storage allocation, exception handling, backup, directory services, as well as other aspects of operating system, network, and security services. Although Common Services are necessary for an OAIS, they are not a major focus of the Reference Model, because they are "assumed to be available" (p. 4–2).[1] As illustrated in Fig. 2, the OAIS functional model also identifies between Administration and management, but it does not elaborate any function within management itself.

Many aspects of the functional model rest on the distinction between SIPs, AIPs, and DIPs. SIPs are what the OAIS receives from Producers. AIPs are what the OAIS manages and preserves. DIPs are "derived from one or more AIPs, [and are] received by the Consumer in response to a request to the OAIS" (p. 1–10).[1]

Ingest is the entity that receives SIPs, performs quality assurance on the SIPs, generates AIPs, extracts Descriptive Information from AIPs, and coordinates updates to Archival Storage and Data Management. Archival Storage is responsible for "receiving AIPs from Ingest and adding them to permanent storage, managing the storage hierarchy, refreshing the media on which archive holdings are stored, performing routine and special error checking, providing disaster recovery capabilities, and providing AIPs to access to fulfill orders" (pp. 4–1, 4–2).[1] Data Management supports the populating, maintenance and accessing of both Descriptive Information and administrative data associated with the OAIS holdings; this includes database administration, database updates, performing queries on the data, and producing reports that result from the queries. Administration is responsible for "the overall

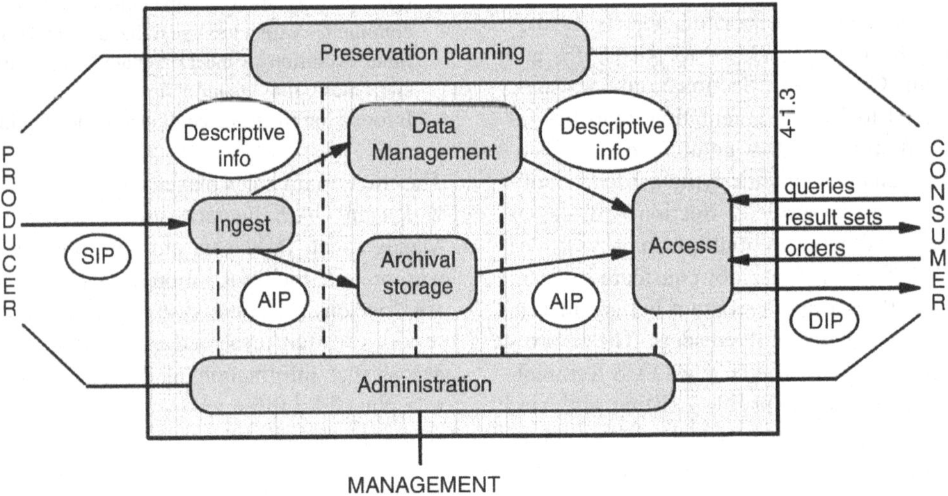

Fig. 2 OAIS Functional Entities.
Source: Reference model for an Open Archival Information System (OAIS); Consulative Committee for Space Data System: Washington, D.C, 2002; 4:1. [SIP = Submission Information Package; AIP = Archival Information Package; DIP = Dissemination Information Package].

operation of the archive system," which includes soliciting and negotiating submission agreements, auditing submissions, configuration management, system engineering, activating stored requests, and the establishment and maintenance of standards and policies (p. 4–2).[1] Preservation Planning monitors the environment for important changes in technology or the needs of the Designated Community; evaluates the implications of those changes to the archive's holdings; designs Information Package templates; "provides design assistance and review to specialize these templates into SIPs and AIPs for specific submissions"; "develops detailed Migration plans, software prototypes and test plans," and provides periodic recommendations for "archival information updates," standards and policies (p. 4–2).[1] Access both provides and appropriately restricts Consumers' ability to discover, request, and receive information from the archive, including DIPs, "result sets" and reports (p. 4–2).[1]

Information Model

The information model defines and describes "the types of information that are exchanged and managed within the OAIS" (p. 4–18).[1] It is based on the recognition that long-term preservation of digital information requires an archive to "store significantly more than the contents of the object it is expected to preserve" (p. 4–19).[1] The Reference Model uses the term "Information Package" to refer to the logical unit that includes both a digital object and the other types of information that should be associated with the digital object in order to preserve and provide meaningful access to it over time. AIPs are the information packages that are managed internally by the OAIS. An AIP can be either an Archival Information Collection (AIC), "whose Content Information is an aggregation of other Archival Information Packages" (p. 1–7),[1] or Archival Information Unit (AIU) "whose Content Information is not further broken down into other Content Information components."[24] Fig. 3 presents the main types of information that constitute and are associated with an AIP. The Package Description is information about an Information Package, which is used by Access Aids. An Access Aid is "a software program or document that allow[s] Consumers to locate, analyze, and order Archival Information Packages of interest" (p. 1–7).[1] Packaging Information, in contrast, is not intended for direct use by Consumer but is instead "used to bind and identify the components of an Information Package"

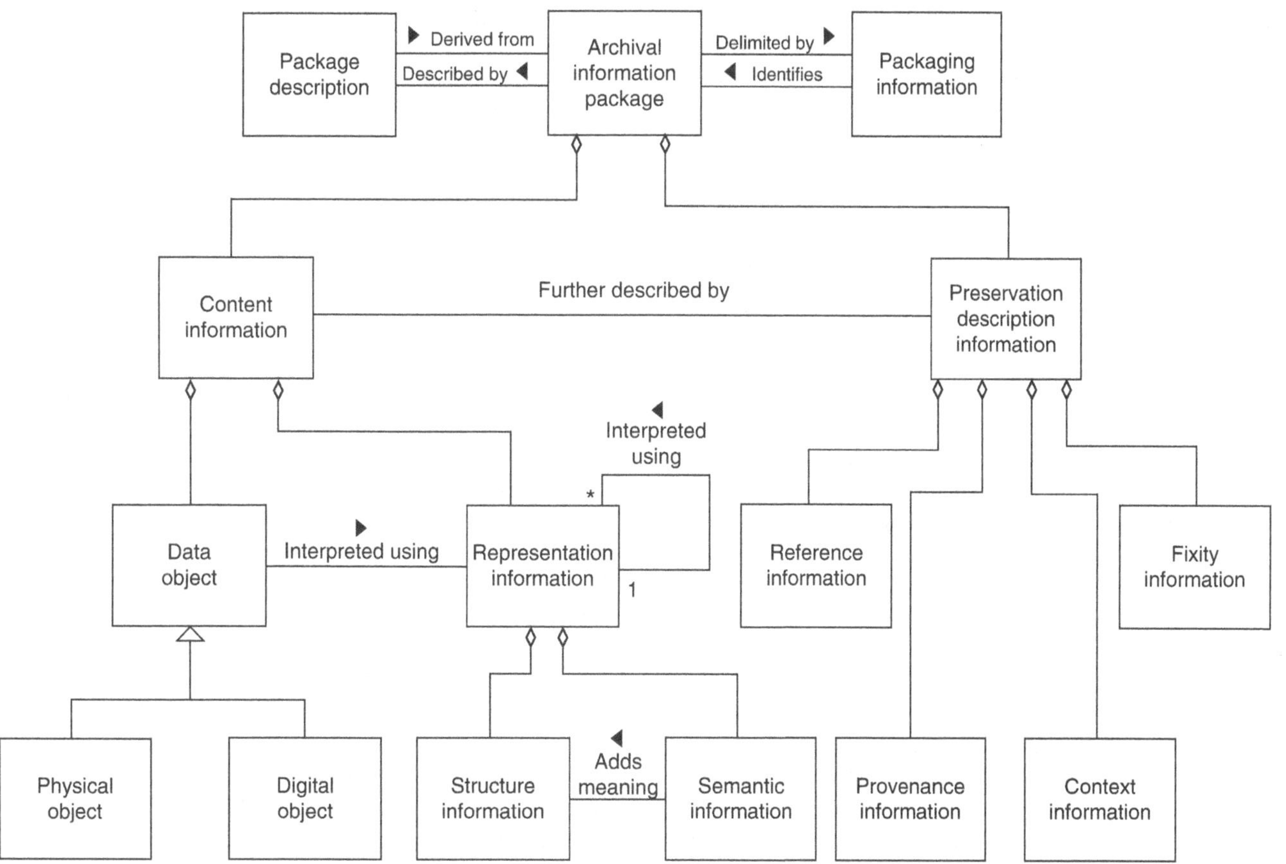

Fig. 3 Archival Information Package (Detailed view).
Source: Reference Model for an Open Archival Information System (OAIS); Consulative Committee for Space Data Systems: Washington, D.C, 2002-4-37.

(e.g., volumes and directory information for the components) (p. 1–12).[1]

The Content Information is the "the original target of preservation" (p. 1–8).[1] As described earlier, Content Information is composed of both the Data Object (for digital information, one or more sequences of bits) and Representation Information, which "allows for the full interpretation of the data into meaningful information" (p. 4–19).[1] Representation Information can be either Structure Information, which "imparts meaning about how other information is organized," such as mapping "bit streams to common computer types such as characters, numbers, and pixels and aggregations of those types such as character strings and arrays" (p. 1–13),[1] or Semantic Information, which indicates the meaning of language used in either the Structure Information or other parts of the Content Information.

Representation Information is often conveyed using Digital Objects, which then require their own Representation Information, resulting in what is called a Representation Network. For example, a string of bits (Digital Object) could represent an array of pixels, but a Consumer would also need information about the file format (Representation Information), in order to render and use that Digital Object as an image. If the image were encoded using Scalable Vector Graphics (SVG), which is based on Extensible Markup Language (XML), then rendering and using the image would require not only the SVG specification but also the specification for XML, as well as other specifications for character encoding and Uniform Resource Identifiers (URIs) upon which XML itself depends.

As illustrated in Fig. 3, Content Information is "further described by" Preservation Description Information (PDI), which "is necessary for adequate preservation of the Content Information." PDI is composed of:

- Reference Information—"identifies, and if necessary describes, one or more mechanisms used to provide assigned identifiers for the Content Information" and "provides identifiers that allow outside systems to refer, unambiguously, to a particular Content Information."[13]
- Provenance Information—"origin or source of the Content Information, any changes that may have taken place since it was originated, and who has had custody of it since it was originated" (p. 1–12).[1]
- Context Information—"documents the relationships of the Content Information to its environment" including "why the Content Information was created and how it relates to other Content Information objects" (p. 1–8).[1]
- Fixity Information—"documents the authentication mechanisms and provides authentication keys to ensure that the Content Information object has not been altered in an undocumented manner" (p. 1–10).[1]

PDI is an extension and elaboration of what *Preserving Digital Information* called the "features that determine information integrity and deserve attention for archival purposes": "content, fixity, reference, provenance, and context."[12]

OAIS ADOPTION, EXTENSIONS, AND FUTURE DIRECTIONS

Several years before it had reached formally approved status within the CCSDS or ISO, the OAIS was already receiving considerable attention from those engaged in digital preservation research and development. An extensive survey of the English-language literature up to April 2005 identified 335 sources that cite or discuss the OAIS, beginning in 1997 and increasing every year thereafter.[13] Over the past several years, the OAIS has come to be a widely assumed basis for research and development on digital archives, with conference papers, articles, and reports very often presenting their findings within the context of the OAIS.

The OAIS has become "the reference model of choice of those involved in digital preservation worldwide,"[14] serving as a "galvanizing force"[15] and a "major factor in the advancement of digital archiving efforts."[16] It has contributed "a common language and concepts for different professional groups involved in digital preservation and developing archiving systems."[17] "The reference model represented common ground upon which to consolidate understanding of the needs and requirements of digital preservation: an opportunity to gather the strands of isolated digital preservation activities, merging them into a shared (albeit highly conceptual) characterization of the problem's boundaries."[18]

A large number of research and development projects have either based their work directly on or claimed that their final products conform to the OAIS, many of which are listed in Table 1.

Professional development has also been strongly influenced by the OAIS. One of the earliest activities of the Digital Preservation Coalition (DPC) in the United Kingdom after its formation in 2001 was to develop, along with the British National Space Centre (BNSC), a seminar to discuss and "raise the profile of" the OAIS. The Cornell University Library offered a highly acclaimed workshop series from 2003 to 2006, and disseminated an associated tutorial, both called Digital Preservation Management: Implementing Short-Term Strategies for Long-Term Problems, which used the OAIS as a foundation.[19] In 2008, Inter-University Consortium for Political and Social Research (ICPSR) became the host of the Digital Preservation Management workshop and tutorial, which continue to be based heavily on the OAIS.

From its initial conception, the OAIS was intended to serve as the basis for further development of more specific digital archives standards, and the OAIS has indeed played that role. It has served as the basis for several very prominent digital preservation metadata initiatives, including

Table 1 Examples of research and development activities with stated OAIS influence or requirements.

Major institutions, organizations, and repositories	British Library
	Digital Curation Centre in the United Kingdom
	European Union
	French Archive Institute
	French National Archiving Center for University and Scientific Publications (CINES)
	Inter-University Consortium for Political and Social Research (ICPSR)
	JSTOR (Journal Storage)
	National Library of Australia
	National Library of France (BnF)
	National Library of New Zealand
	National Library of the Netherlands (KB)
	Online Computer Library Center (OCLC)
	Portico
	Project Euclid—Cornell University Library and Duke University Press
	U.S. Government Printing Office
	U.S. Library of Congress, National Library of China
	U.S. National Archives and Records Administration
	U.S. National Library of Medicine
	U.S. National Oceanic and Atmospheric Administration
	United Nations Educational, Scientific and Cultural Organization (UNESCO)
	Numerous university libraries and space agencies
Funding bodies emphasizing OAIS in solicitations and research agendas	U.S. National Science Foundation
	Joint Information Systems Committee (JISC)—United Kingdom
Digital collection management systems and preservation platforms	aDORe Archive—Los Alamos National Laboratory
	CONTENTdm—OCLC
	DSpace—Massachusetts Institute of Technology
	Flexible Extensible Digital Object and Repository Architecture (Fedora)
	Digital Information Archiving System (DIAS)—IBM
	LOCKSS (Lots of Copies Keep Stuff Safe)—Stanford University Libraries
	Integrated Rule-Oriented Data System (iRODS)—Data Intensive Cyber Environments (DICE) Group
	Preservation and Long-term Access through Networked Services (PLANETS) Testbed
	Securing a Hybrid Environment for Research Preservation and Access (SHERPA)
	Digital Preservation (DP) Service—Arts and Humanities Data Service (AHDS)

CEDARS, NEDLIB, and two joint Research Libraries Group (RLG)/Online Computer Library Center (OCLC) efforts—the Working Group on Preservation Metadata and then the Preservation Metadata Implementation Strategies (PREMIS) Working Group. The CCSDS also has been coordinating the development of follow-on standards based on the OAIS, which provide more detailed guidance related to parts of the OAIS functional and information models. The *Producer–Archive Interface Methodology Abstract Standard* (PAIMAS) "defines the methodology for the structure of actions that are required from the initial time of contact between the producer and the archive until the objects of information are received and validated by the archive."[20] PAIMAS was issued as a CCSDS Blue Book in May 2004 and was published as an ISO standard (ISO 20652) in 2006.[21] The *Producer–Archive Interface Specification* (PAIS) focuses on an even finer level of granulating, by presenting "a standard method to formally define the digital information objects to be transferred by an information Producer to an Archive and for effectively transferring these objects in the form of Submission Information Packages (SIPs)." As of the writing of this entry, the PAIS was in a tenth White Book version (April 2009), undergoing consideration for Red Book status. A White Book is "a preliminary draft of a planned CCSDS Recommendation or Report" that is "under development" and "not necessarily endorsed by any CCSDS Member or Observer Agency or given any CCSDS external distribution."[22]

RLG and NARA formed a Digital Repository Certification Task Force, whose efforts were explicitly tied to the OAIS. An initiative by the Center for Research Libraries (CRL) is extending the RLG/NARA certification work, with funding from the Andrew W. Mellon Foundation. A Birds of a Feather group is also attempting to develop an ISO standard for digital repository audit and certification, through the same channels as the OAIS, viz. ISO TC 20, SC 13, and the CCSDS.

The OAIS is currently undergoing a 5-years review within the CCSDS and then within the ISO. During the comment period, which ended in October 2006, the CCSDS received 11 separate documents containing comments. At a meeting on October 4, 2007, the Digital Archive Ingest (DAI) Working Group began reviewing the OAIS review comments, and identified several action items related to specific parts of the text. In 2003, the CCSDS underwent a major reorganization. The digital archives standardization activities that were previously part of Panel 2, including the OAIS, were moved into a new area called Mission Operations and Information Management Services (MOIMS). The DAI working group, is part of MOIMS. The DAI Working Group determined an initial set of responses to the comments, shared the potential responses with those who submitted the original comments, and then revised the OAIS document based on the comments and follow-on interchanges. On May 5, 2009, John Garrett (Chair) and David Giaretta (Deputy Chair) of the DAI Working Group disseminated a proposed draft of the revised OAIS Reference Model through several electronic mailing lists, "seeking primarily to identify errors" in preparation for submitting the revised Reference Model for ISO review and balloting.

CONCLUSION

The OAIS has been a focal point and foundation for discussion of digital preservation and digital curation across many professional boundaries. It is thus valuable for information professionals not only to understand the content of the document but also to learn lessons about how the Reference Model was developed and promulgated. A reference model is a very high-level, conceptual standard. Rather than providing detailed specifications of mandatory data elements or file formats, the OAIS has introduced a set of interrelated terms and concepts. Its development occurred during a period when many professional communities had a need for such a high-level standard but had not yet developed one themselves. There are various ways in which the Reference Model is able to provide detailed concepts, while still remaining relatively "implementation-independent": presentation of the functional model and information model in terms of high-level entities; extensive use of figures; and elaboration of implementation details in nonnormative appendices to the document, including several organization-specific "scenarios."

Much of the value of the Reference Model comes from its coherence, clarity, and synthesis of ideas. The Reference Model does define many new terms and introduces many original concepts, but its development has also been characterized by significant adaptation and reuse of preexisting sources.

Finally, the word "Open" in the acronym OAIS—meant to indicate that the standard was "developed in open forums"—was a defining feature of its evolution. The leaders of the effort presented draft products to many professional forums and actively recruited contributions and commentary. In addition to the traditional set of CCSDS stakeholders (space agencies and their contractors), many other organizations and individuals also contributed to the OAIS development process.

The OAIS is playing a major role in many current standardization, research, and development initiatives. Its impact on professional conversations surrounding digital preservation and digital curation continues to grow, 7 years after the Reference Model was approved as an International Standard.

ACKNOWLEDGMENTS

The author would like to thank Don Sawyer for sharing information about the OAIS five-year review process and the CCSDS for granting rights to use two of the figures from the OAIS.

REFERENCES

1. *Reference Model for an Open Archival Information System (OAIS)*, Consultative Committee for Space Data Systems: Washington, DC, 2002; CCSDS 650.0-B-1.
2. Lee, C.A. *Defining digital preservation work: A case study of the development of the reference model for an open archival information system*, University of Michigan: Michigan, 2005; Doctoral dissertation.
3. Waters, D.; Garrett, J. *Preserving Digital Information: Report of the Task Force on Archiving of Digital Information*, Commission on Preservation and Access and Research Libraries Group: Washington, DC, 1996.
4. Rothenberg, J. Ensuring the Longevity of Digital Documents. Sci. Am. **1995**, *272*(1), 42–47.
5. Sanders, T.; MacNeil, R. *Into the Future: On the Preservation of Knowledge in the Electronic Age*, Commission on Preservation and Access, and American Council of Learned Societies, 1997.
6. Procedures Manual for the Consultative Committee for Space Data Systems Consultative Committee for Space Data Systems: Washington, DC, 2003; November 1–4 CCSDS A00.0-Y-8.
7. *Space Data and Information Transfer Systems–Open Archival Information System–Reference Model*, International Organization for Standardization: Geneva, Switzerland, 2003; ISO 14721:2003.
8. *Z39.50 Profile for Access to Digital Collections*, Library of Congress: Washington, DC, 1996.
9. *Planetary Data System Data Preparation Workbook*, Jet Propulsion Laboratory, California Institute of Technology: Pasadena, CA, 1995.
10. *IEEE Guide to the POSIX Open System Environment (OSE)*, Institute of Electrical and Electronics Engineers: New York, NY, 1995.
11. Cargill, C.F. *Open Systems Standardization: A Business Approach*, Prentice Hall: Upper Saddle River, NJ, 1997; 90.
12. Waters, D.; Garrett, J. *Preserving Digital Information: Report of the Task Force on Archiving of Digital Information*, Commission on Preservation and Access and Research Libraries Group: Washington, DC, 1996; 12.
13. Lee, C.A. English-language literature citing or discussing the OAIS. *Defining Digital Preservation Work: A Case*

Study of the Development of the Reference Model for an Open Archival Information System, University of Michigan: Michigan, 2005; 227–253, Doctoral dissertation.

14. Greenstein, D.; Smith, A. Digital preservation in the United States: Survey of current research, practice, and common understandings. In *New-Model Scholarship: How Will It Survive?*; Smith, A., Ed.; Council on Library and Information Resources: Washington, DC, 2003; 40–48, 43.
15. Waters, D. Good archives make good scholars: Reflections on recent steps toward the archiving of digital information. *The State of Digital Preservation: An International Perspective*, Council on Library and Information Resources: Washington, DC, 2002; 78–95, 80.
16. Hodge, G.M. Digital Preservation: Overview of Current Developments. Inform. Serv. Use **2002**, *22*(2/3), 73–82.
17. Beagrie, N. *National Digital Preservation Initiatives: An Overview of Developments in Australia, France, the Netherlands, and the United Kingdom and of Related International Activity*, Council on Library and Information Resources and the Library of Congress: Washington, DC, 2003; 45.
18. Lavoie, B.F. *The Open Archival Information System Reference Model: Introductory Guide*, OCLC Online Computer Library Center and Digital Preservation Coalition: Dublin, OH, 2004; 2.
19. Kenney, A.R.; McGovern, N.Y.; Entlich, R.; Kehoe, W.R.; Olsen, E.; Buckley, E.; DeMello, C. *Digital Preservation Management: Implementing Short-Term Strategies for Long-Term Problems*, Cornell University Library: Ithaca, NY, 2005. Available at http://www.library.cornell.edu/iris/tutorial/dpm/ (accessed November 14, 2007).
20. *Producer–Archive Interface Methodology Abstract Standard*, Consultative Committee for Space Data Systems: Washington, DC, 2004; CCSDS 651.0-B-1.
21. *Space Data and Information Transfer Systems–Producer–Archive Interface–Methodology Abstract Standard*, International Organization for Standardization: Geneva, Switzerland, 2006; ISO 20652:2006.
22. Procedures Manual for the Consultative Committee for Space Data Systems Consultative Committee for Space Data Systems: Washington, DC, 2003; November 1–3 CCSDS A00.0-Y-8.

Open Source Software

Michael Tiemann
Open Source Initiative, Chapel Hill, North Carolina, U.S.A.

Abstract

Open Source software is distinguished not by programming language, operating environment, nor application domain, but rather by the license(s) that governs the use, distribution, and, most importantly, the rights to access and modify the software's source code. Together, software source code and open source licensing have dramatically changed many conventional assumptions about software and the software industry itself.

Open Source software is an important[1,2] and growing[3] class of software. Open Source software is distinguished not by programming language, operating environment, nor application domain, but rather by the license(s) that governs the use, distribution, and, most importantly, the rights to access and modify the software's source code. Together, software source code and open source licensing have dramatically changed many conventional assumptions about software and the software industry itself.

As of early 2009 there are roughly 70[4] licenses that are officially recognized as Open Source Licenses. These licenses govern software that spans the software gamut from operating systems (like Linux) and compilers (like GCC and G++) to Web servers and clients (like Apache and Firefox) to leading applications and technologies in bioinformatics, statistical display and analysis, 2-D and 3-D paint, illustration and animation software, databases, content management, customer relationship management, accounting, and geographic information systems. And even these categories encompass but a few of the 10,000 + open source software packages that are freely available for major Linux distributions such as Fedora,[5] Ubuntu,[6] and Red Hat Enterprise Linux.[7] In 2004 it was estimated that the Linux kernel, if it were to be developed using proprietary methods and private investment, would have cost more than $600M to create, and that the roughly 1000 packages typical in Linux distributions of the time would have cost more than $1B.[8] In 2005 an analysis of the Debian project estimated that its 230 million lines of source code (230M SLOC) would have required 60,000 person-years of development at a cost of more than $3B USD.[9] But these estimates speak to the possible cost, not the real cost of developing open source (which was far lower, most likely less than 1/20 the cost of developing proprietary software, for reasons discussed later in this entry). Nor does it consider the true value of open source, which has the potential to remedy as much as $1T USD per year in dead-loss write-offs of failed proprietary software implementations. (The $1T per year figure is extrapolated from the statistics that worldwide ICT is expected to top $3.4T USD in 2008[10] and because 18–30% of all ICT investments, predominantly based on proprietary software because that is the dominant model of the industry today, are dead-loss write-offs).[11,12] Open source software is thus an important topic because the financial implications to the global economy are potentially large.

Before explaining what is an open source license, and thus what is open source software, we will first give a brief history of the origins of open source principles and the success of the open source software model.

The two most important precursors to the idea of open source software as a movement unto itself were the Berkeley Systems Distribution of Unix (also known as BSD Unix) and Richard Stallman's Project GNU (GNU is a recursive acronym for "GNU's Not Unix!"). Both of these projects became known to the academic and entrepreneurial communities in the early 1980s. BSD was licensed under terms that permitted users to read, modify, and redistribute the software for research or commercial purposes, but without a requirement that the source code be made freely available to all who used any product that incorporated the operating system. Sun Microsystems successfully commercialized BSD as the basis of their SunOS operating system, and Sun chose to make their version of BSD—including access to the source code—proprietary to Sun, as permitted by the BSD license. The GNU project was covered by the General Public License (GPL), which permitted users the freedom to read, modify, and share (redistribute) the software, subject to the restriction that users who distribute modified or unmodified versions of the software must also distribute the source code from which those versions were created. These two licenses, one which made source available and sharing optional, one which made source availability and sharing both mandatory as a condition of redistribution, began a long and far-reaching experiment: what licensing model is best for what type of software project, in what contexts, and for whom?

The Free Software movement, founded by Richard Stallman and defined by his *GNU Manifesto*[13] argued

Encyclopedia of Library and Information Sciences, Fourth Edition DOI: 10.1081/E-ELIS4-120043730

that software freedom was an ethical issue of the highest importance, and that software hoarding was an unethical activity. Some programmers were swayed by this argument and joined the Free Software Foundation or made common cause with Stallman, but many more simply enjoyed the freedoms granted by the GPL to use what they considered to be better software than any proprietary alternative. And as more software developers used GNU software, more developers also naturally contributed to it (as they were free to do). Before long, despite the fact that many did not agree with Stallman's politics, they found his software to be unimpeachable and they found that contributing their changes to the GNU project was more economical than trying to maintain those changes themselves.

At the same time, the University of California at Berkeley provided a great institutional environment for software developers to learn, contribute, make a reputation, and then join the ranks of Silicon Valley startups to make millions. By the late 1980s, Sun Microsystems was one of the most powerful and respected companies in Silicon Valley. Their key technology asset, SunOS, was based on source code that Bill Joy wrote while a graduate student at Berkeley. But the fact that Sun did not share their code freely with the community began to irk many, and there were signs that for all its power, Sun's competitive position was vulnerable to the many projects that freely shared source code could produce, including versions of BSD that others chose to work on and commercialize.

Cygnus Support was the first company to make a business providing commercial support exclusively to software whose source code was freely available. The tagline of the company was "We make free software affordable," a joke about the fact that just because something is freely available doesn't make it cheap to use or manage. Although Cygnus Support was a successful company, growing fast enough to be profiled in FORTUNE[14] and earn a spot[15,16] on the Software 500 list of the world's largest software companies before its 10th anniversary, the mainstream business press focused so much on the paradox of making money on "free" software that it never could take seriously the multimillion dollar revenue streams that Cygnus generated year after year.

Moreover, the politics of "free software" was off-putting to many would-be entrepreneurs who wanted to focus their efforts on technology and business, not freedom *per se*. Thus, while GNU software was seriously challenging the core assumptions of proprietary software advantage (that somehow secret knowledge is superior to knowledge that is widely known and shared), and while GNU software was demonstrating just as clear and positive a return on investment as companies investing in proprietary software,[17] there was a distinct lack of critical mass around the idea of commercializing free software.

In 1997, Eric Raymond published a seminal essay, The Cathedral and The Bazaar.[18] This paper attempted to unravel how it was that a group of amateurs (doing software for the love of it), many of whom had not even met each other, could coordinate their activities and out-produce the best funded, most highly recruited programmers of Silicon Valley and the Pacific Northwest. Among the many insights in this paper, one of the most powerful (dubbed Linus's law) was the idea that the more widely available the source code is for public testing, scrutiny, and experimentation, the more rapidly all forms of bugs will be discovered. This was a remarkable repudiation of Brook's Law (discussed below), which argued that adding more developers to a late project only makes it later.[19] In the world of software, this insight was like finding a way to travel faster than the speed of light, and the only requirement, it seemed, was to abandon the model of proprietary software development.

In 1998, a group of individuals that included both Eric Raymond and the author advocated that the term "free software" be replaced by open source software (abbreviated OSS) as an expression which is less ambiguous and more comfortable for the corporate world.[18] In addition to creating the term "open source," the group attempted to codify the features and benefits they saw that derived from granting liberal rights with respect to software source code and software distribution. The group created the Open Source Definition (OSD)[19] which codifies how licenses must be written to provide these rights and thus deliver the benefits. The term "open source" became immediately popular, and the Open Source movement was born (Fig. 1)

The Open Source Initiative (OSI) was founded in 1998 as a California 501(c)3 nonprofit education and advocacy group for open source software. The OSI acts as the steward of the OSD and it judges whether licenses submitted to it do or do not meet the criteria set forth in the OSD. The GNU GPL and the BSD licenses were among the first to be approved as "open source licenses," but now there are dozens and dozens that have been approved. The license approval process developed from the time-honored tradition of scientific peer review. Namely, when a new theory (or in this case, license) makes a claim (or in this case, a license asserts that it is open source), it is up to the community to study the claim and attest to its validity or point out its flaws, and it is up to some formal authority to review the community's findings and make a judgment as to whether the claim is accepted into the canon of knowledge (or in this case the list of approved licenses). This consensus-based approach has been sufficiently transparent and fair that an increasing number of national governments are adopting the OSD and the OSI's rulings as a legitimate basis for determining whether software is open source for national policy purposes.[20]

We shall now turn our attention to the subject of software development, specifically to compare and contrast open source software development with some prominent

1. Free Redistribution

The license shall not restrict any party from selling or giving away the software as a component of an aggregate software distribution containing programs from several different sources. The license shall not require a royalty or other fee for such sale.

2. Source Code

The program must include source code, and must allow distribution in source code as well as compiled form. Where some form of a product is not distributed with source code, there must be a well-publicized means of obtaining the source code for no more than a reasonable reproduction cost preferably, downloading via the Internet without charge. The source code must be the preferred form in which a programmer would modify the program. Deliberately obfuscated source code is not allowed. Intermediate forms such as the output of a preprocessor or translator are not allowed.

3. Derived Works

The license must allow modifications and derived works, and must allow them to be distributed under the same terms as the license of the original software.

4. Integrity of The Author's Source Code

The license may restrict source-code from being distributed in modified form *only* if the license allows the distribution of "patch files" with the source code for the purpose of modifying the program at build time. The license must explicitly permit distribution of software built from modified source code. The license may require derived works to carry a different name or version number from the original software.

5. No Discrimination Against Persons or Groups

The license must not discriminate against any person or group of persons.

6. No Discrimination Against Fields of Endeavor

The license must not restrict anyone from making use of the program in a specific field of endeavor. For example, it may not restrict the program from being used in a business, or from being used for genetic research.

7. Distribution of License

The rights attached to the program must apply to all to whom the program is redistributed without the need for execution of an additional license by those parties.

8. License Must Not Be Specific to a Product

The rights attached to the program must not depend on the program's being part of a particular software distribution. If the program is extracted from that distribution and used or distributed within the terms of the program's license, all parties to whom the program is redistributed should have the same rights as those that are granted in conjunction with the original software distribution.

9. License Must Not Restrict Other Software

The license must not place restrictions on other software that is distributed along with the licensed software. For example, the license must not insist that all other programs distributed on the same medium must be open-source software.

10. License Must Be Technology-Neutral

No provision of the license may be predicated on any individual technology or style of interface.

Fig. 1 Text of the OSD.

examples of proprietary software projects and development models.

The documented failure of the industrial model of software development is almost as old as the software industry itself. IBM's OS 360 project, begun in 1961, was perhaps the most ambitious attempt to industrialize the development of software.[17] Fred Brooks, the IBM executive responsible for the project,[21] hired the best coders, managers, analysts—whatever it took. And IBM ended up spending more money to produce that operating system than the U.S. Government spent on the Manhattan Project to develop the first atomic weapon, a fact that greatly troubled IBM's CEO at the time, Thomas Watson Jr. The product shipped—barely—in 1965, and though the product was a great commercial success, IBM's CEO really wanted to understand how it was possible that the software part of the project was so much more difficult and costly than the hardware part. He put the question to Brooks, but Brooks himself did not have a ready answer. Ten years later Brooks answered the question in the form of a book titled *The Mythical Man Month.* The title comes from his insight that "it takes a woman nine months to have a child, no matter how many women are assigned the task." This was the first clue that the process of industrialization—breaking down tasks into simpler steps, optimizing the steps, and then managing the steps through production—had very significant limits when applied to software. Today, this book is often the first reference given to explain why multibillion dollar software projects like Microsoft's Vista slipped and slipped and slipped again, running wildly over budget and why, when it finally did ship, it did so without the very features that justified the project in the first place. Thus, more than 30 years later, we have the Gartner Group (who famously predicted the success of the Personal Computer in enterprise computing) making the only logical prediction that can be inferred from *The Mythical Man Month* and Microsoft's own experience:[22]

> Vista will be the last major release of Windows in its current form. The current, integrated architecture of Microsoft Windows is unsustainable—for enterprises and for Microsoft. Each new version integrates more functionality and features, adding to the scale and complexity of the operating system.

While IBM and others struggled to industrialize software, the mainstream industrial model itself was beginning to show weakness across the board. In the 1940s, Dr. W. Edward Deming properly identified serious problems with the model that focused on optimization in terms of measurable (but arbitrary) inputs and outputs as related to costs and production. Deming had no luck convincing American companies to focus on quality as defined by the customer, nor to recognize the value of people working in teams on a larger and transforming goal, nor to consider whether work gave people joy. However, Deming did find a receptive audience in Japan, and the transformation that resulted from his approach has set the standard for modern industry, lowering costs, accelerating innovation, reducing environmental impact, improving safety, and inspiring pride in workmanship.[23]

By the 1980s, Deming's work had reached even those still trying to industrialize software, in the context of the Software Engineering Institute (SEI) and their Capability Maturity Model (CMM) in a 1987 SEI Technical Report.[24] First adopted not in the United States, but offshore, in Chennai, India,[25] it was credited with dropping software defect density 98% while doubling profits. Though these first attempts have now been retired,[26] the urgent question remains: why is software quality so low?[27]

In 2005, Bill Gates gave a keynote speech at the RSA Security conference where he said "We spend over US$6 billion a year on research and development. I'd say that over a third of that is directly security-focused, and the other two-thirds all tie in and relate to that security work, all the new code being reviewed and going through the threat model, a pretty dramatic thing there."[28] Why is it that companies like Microsoft spend fully a third of their R&D budget correcting remedial security problems that should never have existed in the first place? As President of the OSI and Vice President of Open Source Affairs for Red Hat, I believe software quality is low because companies place a higher value on control than on innovation or quality or transparency or user participation. It is a failure to understand both the negative lessons that Brooks have taught, as well as the positive lessons that Deming taught. And perhaps it is because those who have achieved great status, wealth, and power are rarely willing to trade all three for a new system that requires accepting new, disruptive assumptions.

The most significant transformation in ICT has been the emergence of Free and Open Source Software (FOSS).

Consider the popular Internet as embodied by the World Wide Web. This vision was first published by Vannevar Bush in 1945,[29] and prior to 1990 there had been dozens of attempts to create such systems, the most popular being the French MiniTel system.[30] But none of these systems became truly ubiquitous until the underlying software was free as in freedom. The freedom to read, modify, and share Web server and client code led to an explosion of innovation, and to date the most popular product of that explosion, the Apache Web server, remains dominant in spite of considerable efforts by some powerful companies to take over that space.[31]

This came as no surprise to Tim Berners-Lee, creator of the World Wide Web, who explained his decision to make the original Web software free and open:[32]

> [H]ad the technology been proprietary, and in my total control, it would probably not have taken off. The decision to make the Web an open system was necessary for it to be universal. You can't propose that something be a universal space and at the same time keep control of it.

The popular Internet has created a dramatic new factor in the software industry equation, which is that developers and users represent a creative continuum, not distinct castes. Developers can be any people interested in a problem, not merely people employed to work on a specific problem. Free and Open Source software turns on its head the practice of optimizing software production by limiting the number of people working on a problem. Instead, those employed (producers), those annoyed (customers), and those who merely enjoy working on a problem (hackers)[33] can work together in a problem-specific, rather than organization-specific or property-specific way. In his book *Democratizing Innovation*, Eric Von Hippel presents several studies which, together, show that 85% of all quantum innovation (as opposed to incremental innovation) is user-driven.[34] The proprietary software model therefore limits innovation to one-sixth of its theoretical potential.

The democratization of innovation has also demonstrated a remarkable solution to the problem of *The Mythical Man Month*, thereby transcending the limits of conventional industrialization. For example, *sourceforge.net* is an open source development resource that hosts over 180,000 projects and has more than 1.9M registered users as of December 2008.[35] Extrapolating from the extensive Free, Libre, and Open Source Software (FLOSS) survey of 2002[36] (and updated in 2005)[37] there were over 490,000 *sourceforge.net* developers in 2006 (when the thesis of this section was first developed–Tiemann) who spend more than 10 hr a week or more tending their open source projects[38]—an aggregate effort of some 5 million person-hours per week. The three top reasons they list for their involvement is:

1. Because it's fun.
2. Because it improves their skills.
3. Because it is good for society.

Note that this does not include Linux developers (who use *kernel.org*, not *sourceforge.net*), nor Apache, nor the GNU project, nor many of the other larger and more heavily commercialized open source projects. To put these 5 million joy-filled person-hours per week into perspective (again, this does not include Linux, Apache, GNU, or many of the other "large" projects), let's look at the productivity potential of the most successful proprietary software company, Microsoft, in two ways (using numbers that were contemporaneous with the FLOSS survey data, October 2006):

1. If all 61,000 employees[39] wrote code, they would have to work over 80 hours per week.
2. If Microsoft's $6.6B per year R&D budget[40] were spent on programmers averaging just $25 per hour, they could pay for about 5 million person-hours of work per week.

Thus, the *sourceforge.net* Web site has equaled or exceeded Microsoft's productive potential using a social, not an industrial model. When we consider all the open source developers not included in the *sourceforge.net* numbers (numbers that are increasing exponentially), we see the clear emergence of a new software production capacity entirely outside the conventional limits of the industrial model. Moreover, we find precisely the kind of improvements that Deming would have predicted by taking a transformative approach: according to findings published by Coverity (references below), typical proprietary software has a defect density of 20–30 defects per 1000 lines of code (KLOC), a number relatively unchanged since the 1960s. When they measured the quality of the Linux kernel (and later, other open source software) they found the following results:

Online Public–Organizational

2004: 985 defects in 5.7 MLOC of Linux kernel source code, or 99.3% lower defect density than average (compared to 114,000–171,000 defects in the same amount of code).[41]

2005: While the Linux kernel grew 4.7% in overall code size, defect density decreased by 2.2%. Moreover, 100% of all "serious" defects identified were fixed within 6 months.[42]

2006: The survey was expanded to entire LAMP stack and an additional 32 OSS programs. No correlation found between size and defect density, implying OSS development methodology is not limited by scale (nor restricted to just Linux developers).[43]

What the top industrialists could not achieve with proprietary software and financial capital, free software has demonstrated with community development and intellectual capital.

But free and open source has done more than revolutionize the production or the quality of software. The open source model has opened innovation. Open source helped crack grand challenge science problems such as sequencing the human genome.[44] The world's largest public search engine, google.com, is built on open source.[45–47] Open source has become a fixture in tech-heavy disciplines such as financial services,[48] military intelligence,[49] online retailing,[50] and next-generation cellular telephones and base stations[51] and handsets, including the recently announced Google Android project/product.[52] And open source is helping to bridge the digital divide for millions of children who are literally off the grid.[53] The model has even informed the strategy of the Bill & Melinda Gates Foundation to better combat infectious diseases:[54]

> [On July 20, 2006] the Bill & Melinda Gates Foundation announced that it would require that any researcher who accepts its grant monies for HIV/AIDS research will have to agree to share their scientific findings. The Gates Foundation was apparently frustrated that two decades of secrecy and competition among AIDS researchers have impeded efforts to come up with an AIDS vaccine.

Clearly there is a bright future for those who embrace the open source model, whether as users, developers, or entrepreneurs. The best way to learn more about open source is to become involved in a project, first as a user, then as a person who reports bugs or tests releases, and then follow where interests or expertise leads. Different projects have different personalities and protocols, but almost all viable projects have a history of being inviting at some level, and almost all provide concrete rewards for participants of all kinds. And with open source software doubling in size and scope every 12.5 months,[3] there are more than enough examples to demonstrate why open source has become an increasingly preferred method of software development, procurement, and deployment, as the above references make clear.

REFERENCES

1. http://www.osor.eu/news/eu-ec-considers-study-on-migration-to-open-source/?searchterm=policy
2. http://www.fcw.com/online/news/151858–1.html
3. http://www.dirkriehle.org/publications/2008/the-total-growth-of-open-source/
4. http://opensource.org/licenses/alphabetical

5. http://fedoraproject.org/
6. http://www.ubuntu.com/
7. http://www.redhat.com/rhel/
8. http://www.dwheeler.com/sloc/
9. http://www.upgrade-cepis.org/issues/2005/3/up6–3Amor.pdf
10. http://blogs.techrepublic.com.com/tech-news/?p=1348
11. http://www.codinghorror.com/blog/archives/000588.html
12. http://people.redhat.com/tiemann/STS-Forum-Tiemann-2006.pdf
13. http://www.gnu.org/gnu/manifesto.html
14. http://money.cnn.com/magazines/fortune/fortune_archive/1993/09/27/78381/index.htm
15. http://oreilly.com/catalog/opensources/book/tiemans.html
16. http://en.wikipedia.org/wiki/The_Cathedral_and_the_Bazaar
17. http://en.wikipedia.org/wiki/The_Mythical_Man-Month
18. http://en.wikipedia.org/wiki/Open_source_software
19. http://opensource.org/docs/osd
20. http://www.csis.org/media/csis/pubs/070820_open_source_policies.pdf
21. http://www.cs.unc.edu/~brooks/FPB_BIO.CV.06.2006.pdf
22. http://www.telegraph.co.uk/finance/2803555/Microsofts-Vista-release-may-be-last-big-bang.html
23. http://deming.org/index.cfm?content=651
24. http://www.sei.cmu.edu/publications/documents/87.reports/87.tr.023.html
25. http://www.businessweek.com/1999/99_49/b3658020.htm
26. http://www.sei.cmu.edu/cmmi/adoption/migration.html
27. http://www.cio.com/archive/101501/wasting.html
28. http://www.microsoft.com/presspass/exec/billg/speeches/2005/02–15RSA05.aspx
29. http://www.theatlantic.com/doc/194507/bush
30. http://en.wikipedia.org/wiki/Minitel
31. http://news.netcraft.com/archives/web_server_survey.html
32. http://www.w3.org/People/Berners-Lee/FAQ.html#What2
33. http://www.ccil.org/jargon/jargon_23.html#TAG833
34. http://web.mit.edu/evhippel/www/democ1.htm
35. http://alexandria.wiki.sourceforge.net/What±is±SourceForge.net%3F
36. http://flossproject.org/floss1/stats_5.html
37. http://www.flosspols.org/research.php
38. http://flossproject.org/floss1/stats_7_2.html
39. http://finance.yahoo.com/q/pr?s=MSFT
40. http://finance.yahoo.com/q/is?s=MSFT&annual
41. http://www.eweek.com/c/a/Linux-and-Open-Source/Linux-Kernel-Review-Shows-Far-Fewer-Flaws/
42. http://www.internetnews.com/dev-news/article.php/3524911
43. http://www.internetnews.com/stats/article.php/3589361
44. http://www.ddj.com/184410424
45. http://www.eweek.com/c/a/Linux-and-Open-Source/Google-Opens-Up-About-Open-Source/
46. http://www.informationweek.com/news/software/open_source/showArticle.jhtml?articleID=187202790
47. http://www.informationweek.com/news/software/linux/showArticle.jhtml?articleID=192300293
48. http://www.eweek.com/c/a/Linux-and-Open-Source/Open-Source-Making-Inroads-on-Wall-Street/
49. http://www.nsa.gov/selinux/
50. http://oreilly.com/pub/a/oreilly/ask_tim/2004/amazon_0204.html
51. http://www.linuxdevices.com/news/NS2577652026.html
52. http://code.google.com/android/
53. http://laptop.org/en/
54. http://www.commonsdev.us/content.php?id=885

Oral History in Libraries and Archives

Debra Gold Hansen
School of Library and Information Science, San Jose State University, Yorba Linda, California, U.S.A.

Abstract
This entry reviews the development of oral history in the United States, covering its theory and method, major professional associations, and influential programs. It also describes how oral history collections are processed, cataloged, and made available for public use and concludes with a discussion of the international oral history movement.

INTRODUCTION

Oral history is an historical/archival method of recording the memories of individuals involved in a specific historical event or era. The term oral history encompasses both the creation of the interview as documentation in historical study and the processing and preservation of the recording in a library or archives. These historical/archival activities can occur together as a holistic project. In other instances, the interview is conducted solely for research purposes and afterwards it is deposited in an historical repository. Regardless of the interviews' origin or purpose, oral histories exhibit key characteristics which distinguish them from other forms of oral documentation such as folklore and oral tradition.

This entry will survey the origin and progress of the oral history movement, its theory and method, and the major functions of its professional infrastructure. It will also note the major oral history programs in the United States and trace how oral history collections and their administration have evolved since the 1950s. The entry covers recent theoretical trends and concludes with the emergence of an international oral history movement.

ORAL HISTORY DEFINED

Defining oral history begins with what it is not. Although humankind has preserved its cultural memory for centuries, oral history differs from oral tradition in several ways. Oral tradition is passed down from generation to generation and does not require that the narrator be a participant in or witness to the event being told. Oral tradition also requires a narrator to memorize and perform the story as opposed to critically describing observed events. Neither is oral history an oral memoir, although an oral history interview includes elements of a life review. The difference here is that a memoir is an uninterrupted, unproblematic personal narrative. Oral history, in contrast, requires the intervention of an interviewer, whose questions guide the narrator's reminiscences and probes for further reflection.

Oral history, then, is a structured conversation between a researcher and an individual who has witnessed or participated in an historic event. Its goal is to gather information that supplements and expands traditional primary source material such as personal papers and archival records. For some topics, oral history creates historical documentation where none other exists. Oral history is an audio form of historical evidence, though many oral history programs create verbatim transcripts for researchers' use.

HISTORY OF ORAL HISTORY

Although the present-day oral history movement originated following World War II, historians have made use of eye-witness accounts since ancient times. As early as the fifth century B.C.E. Herodotus used firsthand testimonies in his writing on the Persian Wars. There is evidence that personal narratives were recorded by scribes in China (1122–256 B.C.E.) and early modern Europe as well. Priests in colonial Latin America similarly preserved the stories of indigenous people, in this case to create a record of their declining civilizations.[1]

In the United States, the term "oral history" reportedly was first used in 1863 when Joe Gould recorded overheard conversations in New York City for a book he never actually wrote called "An Oral History of Our Time."[2] About this same time, historians and antiquarians began preserving pioneer reminiscences in more a systematic manner. A prolific collector was Lyman Copeland Draper. When he died in 1891, his interviews and papers collected from Revolutionary War veterans and other prominent individuals filled 486 volumes and were donated to the Wisconsin Historical Society.[3] On the West Coast, historian/publisher Hubert H. Bancroft also recorded pioneer reminiscences, which he called "Dictations." The resulting 125

Online Public–Organizational

Encyclopedia of Library and Information Sciences, Fourth Edition DOI: 10.1081/E-ELIS4-120044733

interviews with the state's leading Californios (i.e., pre-1848 inhabitants of Alta California) are now part of the University of California, Berkeley's Western Americana Collection.

Oral history fell into disfavor at the turn of the century as historians pursued what they believed to be a more objective means of understanding the past. Following the dictates of German historian, Leopold von Ranke, these so-called "scientific" historians preferred to ground their research in official written records and dismissed personal narratives as hearsay. However, as official and personal records gained ascendancy in historical writing, new forms of long-distance communication and modes of travel were causing them to disappear. The reel-to-reel tape recorder, invented in Germany in the 1930s, offered a solution by making it possible to permanently capture people's conversations.

The modern oral history movement began in the late 1940s, when Columbia University professor Allan Nevins employed several graduate students to interview important figures in New York politics and government. Nevins first raised concerns about the loss of primary sources in his 1938 book, *The Gateway to History*, proposing that historians make a "systematic attempt" to record the firsthand accounts of individuals important in contemporary society.[4] In 1948, Nevins secured an endowment from the university's Bancroft Fund and the Columbia Oral History Research Office was born.

Columbia's oral history program set the agenda for oral history projects during the movement's formative period. The program was largely funded through grants and contracts, which reinforced its initial focus on prominent individuals in government and industry. (Among Columbia's early projects were oral histories of prominent government officials as well as executives of major corporations like the Carnegie Corporation, Ford Motor Company, Weyerhaeuser Timber Company, and McDonnell Douglas Aircraft.) Columbia's interviews were recorded in longhand until the portable tape recorder became available in the early 1950s. Even after the interviews were recorded, they were still transcribed and the original tape destroyed or reused. Theoretically, early oral historians felt that the printed transcript—which included editorial corrections by the researcher and narrator—was the primary source of record, the tape being simply a conduit. Reusing tapes was also an economic measure, since the oral history method was expensive and funding scarce.

In 1958 Allan Nevins retired and turned over the administration of Columbia's program to his associate director, Louis Starr. Starr hired Elizabeth "Betty" Mason as his assistant, and together the two regularized and systematized the management of their growing oral history collection. They developed formal guidelines for conducting and processing interviews and arranged for formal deposit of the completed transcripts in the Special Collections Department at Columbia's Butler Library. They also established policies regarding access to and use of the transcripts, which set in place various protections governing the interests and rights of narrators. In 1964, the Columbia Oral History Research Office published its first catalog containing descriptions of the program's 1345 interviews.

During the 1950s and 1960s, Columbia's Oral History Research Office continued to function as an independent, self-funded entity on campus. When it decided to offer a class in oral history, it did so not through the university's history department but instead in its library science program. According to Betty Mason, these original oral history classes attracted 16–20 faculty and students from various disciplines across campus. "We saw oral history as something which could be used in lots of different ways," she recalled. "Louis [Starr], in his speeches, used to talk about it being more than a tool and less than a discipline."[5,6]

While Columbia University was developing oral history in the East, other programs were starting up in universities and government agencies throughout the country. In 1965, 89 different oral history centers were in operation; by 1971, 230 programs had begun with 90 more planned.[7] Oral history programs were in colleges and universities, historical societies, private foundations, museums, and government agencies. Their collections ranged from interviews with Jewish labor activists to the lives of American composers.

Driven by technological advance and popular culture, oral history expanded rapidly in the 1970s. The inexpensive portable cassette player (invented in 1963) made oral history activity feasible outside government and the academy. Best-selling oral history-based books published by Studs Terkel and Alex Haley popularized the oral history method among the general public, and the oral history work of Eliot Wigginton's high school students with Appalachian old-timers attracted nationwide praise. By the time Haley's "Roots" aired as a wildly popular TV miniseries in 1977 oral history had come of age.[8–10]

Key to oral history's development in the 1970s was a major theoretical shift from preserving the memories of prominent individuals to collecting the stories of everyday life. This new theoretical thrust was a by-product of changing lines of historical inquiry, most notably the emergence of the new social history. Often described as "history from below," social history documented the lives of nonelites—workers, women, and ethnic minorities—whose personal papers rarely found their way into the government archives or university library. It was an energizing time for oral historians, as Linda Shopes recalled. "I was excited by what I sensed to be oral history's potential for transforming that body of received wisdom called history, transforming it from the codifications of a few learned men to the experiences, attitudes, and perceptions of ordinary men and women."[11] The major projects inaugurated at this time reflected oral history's widening historiographical lens: Howard University's Civil Rights Documentation Project (now the Ralph J. Bunche Collection); Long Beach State University's Feminist Oral History Project; Radcliffe College's Black Women Oral History Project; Wayne State University's Autoworkers Oral History Project; and the Doris Duke American Indian Oral History Program to which many university's contributed interviews.[12]

By the end of the 1970s, oral history had become an established historical methodology with a growing body of practical and theoretical literature. Much of the early writing on oral history appeared in library science and archival journals. In fact, between 1968 and 1978, more than 110 articles were published. Most reported on new oral history projects and collections. Some, however, raised concerns regarding the value of oral history as historical documentation and the role archivists should play in its creation and administration.[13]

The 1970s saw the expansion of oral history books as well. Written by oral history pioneers, initially these texts focused on oral history methods. In 1969, Willa Baum, head of the University of California, Berkeley's Regional Oral History Office (ROHO), published one of the earliest manuals, *Oral History for the Local Historical Society*. A flurry of how-to guides appeared thereafter, including *A Guide for Oral History Programs* (1973), *Transcribing without Tears* (1976) and another text by ROHO's Baum, *Transcribing and Editing Oral History* (1977).[14–17]

Coincident with the publication of these practical guides, oral history writing moved in a more theoretical direction. The turning point came in 1975 when Ronald Grele put together a small volume of essays titled *Envelopes of Sound*. With contributions from historians, anthropologists, and popular writers, *Envelopes of Sound* asked some challenging questions regarding oral history method and use. In the introduction, historian Alice Kessler Harris compared oral history to more traditional archival sources created as a natural by-product of daily activity. "Unlike diaries, letters, and personal papers that were themselves responses to the event or period being studied," Kessler Harris observed, "interviews are created after the fact and reflect the participants' self-conscious attempts to preserve what they remember for the future."[18] In his essay "Movement without Aim," editor Grele also considered the authenticity of oral history as evidence, given the role played by the historian in its own creation. "The recorded conversations of oral history," Grele maintained, were "joint activities, organized and informed by the historical perspectives of both participants [narrator and interviewer]." They are not really autobiographies, he continued, but "conversational narratives." Their content must be understood within this unique framework.[19]

Subsequent writings on oral history continued this introspection concerning the meaning and value of oral history as primary source material, especially in light of criticisms coming from traditional documentary historians regarding the interviewees' faulty memories. David Henige, in *Oral Historiography* (1982), devoted several chapters to interpreting oral history evidence, stressing how the context of the interview's creation impacted the resulting content.[20] Other publications confronted the issue of historical accuracy of interviews, suggesting ways in which information should be authenticated. There was also a growing interest in how other disciplines might use oral histories in their research. Publications such as Daniel Bertaux's *Biography and Society: The Life History Approach in the Social Sciences* (1981), David Dunaway and Willa Baum's *Oral History: An Interdisciplinary Anthology* (1984), and David Stricklin and Rebecca Sharpless's *The Past Meets the Present: Essays on Oral History* (1988), considered how interviews can serve as documentation for not just historical study, but also for sociology, cultural anthropology, literary studies, linguistics, and more.[21]

This theoretical dialogue regarding oral history's creation and use came to full flower with Michael Frisch's 1990 book, *A Shared Authority: Essays on the Craft and Meaning of Oral and Public History*. A collection of his own ruminations of oral history theory and practice, Frisch explored how the interviewer, narrator, historian, and audience all play a part in constructing and interpreting the past. Frisch stressed that oral history is a socially constructed activity which not only reflects personal experience but also cultural forms and the context from which it emerges. An oral history interview, argued Frisch, is a mix of experience, memory, and cultural perspective. As such, it allows the researcher to "stand somewhat outside of cultural forms in order to observe their workings."[22]

Questions about memory and oral history did not diminish its value as a primary source, but became its strength, allowing scholars to not only learn about what happened in the past, but also to see how memory can be influenced by culture and time. Moreover, the increasingly international exchange among oral historians (see below) has deepened practitioners' appreciation of the field's sociocultural implications and its multiplicity of uses. As British oral historian Alistair Thomson explains, the interview provides "clues not only about the meanings of historical experience, but also about the relationships between past and present, between memory and personal identity, and between individual and collective memory."[23] Oral history has thus evolved from historians' desire to preserve the memories of powerful individuals into an important interdisciplinary tool for the study of society and culture.

ORAL HISTORY METHODS

Michael Frisch's concept of shared authority (that is, the redistribution of power between the historical actor and the historian) has particular resonance for understanding the theoretical underpinnings of oral history practice.[24] Typically oral history is not a single interview but a series of interviews to gain multiple perspectives on a given topic. The project director selects narrators based on their knowledge and representativeness of the community their story embodies. The interview itself is a dialogue between the interviewer, who has researched the topic extensively, and the narrator, who responds to a series of questions posed by the interviewer. While the interviewer prepares an outline of topics to cover, the narrator is encouraged to tell his or her story without interruption or contradiction. Oral historians typically ask open-ended, neutral questions. They listen patiently as the narrator reminiscences at length or stops and pauses to consider his or her answer. Once the narrator fully responds to a given question, the interviewer probes for further details and reflection. The interviewer is expected to be sensitive to the narrator's perspective and personal background, allowing the interviewee to determine what will be discussed and how it will be expressed. This give-and-take between the interviewer and interviewee, and attentiveness to the narrator's feelings and values, allows for an oral historian to discover not only what happened but, in the narrator's view, why it happened and what it meant.

Once an interview has been recorded, a verbatim transcript is prepared and returned to the narrator. The narrator has the opportunity to review what was said in the interview and correct or clarify material not accurately expressed. The narrator can delete passages that, upon reflection, he or she would prefer to be kept off the record. When controversial material has historical significance, the interview might be sealed for a number of years or until vulnerable parties are deceased. The power of the narrator to review and approve the transcript before depositing it in a library or archives is a core component in this collaborative process and serves as the backbone of ethical oral history practice.

For both ethical and legal reasons, oral history transcripts are carefully vetted to prevent unintended harm to those mentioned in or connected to the interview. As the Oral History Association Evaluation Guidelines warn: "Interviewers should guard against possible exploitation of interviewees and be sensitive to the ways in which their interviews might be used."[25] An oral history project will often employ editors to go through the transcript and identify material potentially injurious to the narrator, innocent parties, and the oral history program itself. Oral history programs can be held accountable for libelous or slanderous material contained in interviews subsequently published and distributed.[26]

Because oral history methodology emphasizes the narrator's right to voice and control his or her own story, other protections are part of standard practice. In addition to reviewing and approving the transcript, the narrator signs a legal agreement form that deeds the interview to a specific repository and outlines copyrights pertaining to its publication and future use. Before signing this release, the narrator is fully informed of his or her rights and told how the interview will be used. Because an oral history is a "coauthored" document, the interviewer signs a similar agreement form transferring his or her interest in the tape and transcript to the repository as well. Typically, a repository asks the narrator and the interviewer to transfer copyright to the institution so that the archives can control the interview's access and use. Without these signed release forms, an oral history collection cannot be made available to researchers and the public.

Although oral history methodology focuses on the recorded interview, the ultimate archival record includes collateral material in addition to the tape and transcript. In some programs, the interviewer prepares field notes about the interview experience that become part of the archival record. Oral history projects might accumulate other documentation, such as a narrator biographical form (to record personal and contact data about the interviewee), photographs, research files, and personal papers. Thus each interview in an oral history project generates a large body of documentary material in multiple formats. Once the project is completed, these materials are cataloged and shelved according to a system designed by the oral history program. Many oral history programs transfer completed projects to their institution's library or archives for curating.

CURATING ORAL HISTORY

Oral history curating refers to the administrative and archival activities surrounding the processing and management of oral history tapes and transcripts. It includes the paper trail that provides important context for researchers to understand the project's provenance and authenticity as a primary source. Curating also involves the management of legal rights as stipulated in the signed agreement forms. Finally, oral history curating requires the creation of various finding aids and access tools to promote oral history collection awareness and use.

For many years oral history curating was done by oral historians (as opposed to librarians and archivists) who focused on processing the interview. This included transcribing, editing, and indexing the recording. The standard text on oral history processing devoted a mere two paragraphs to the actual "curating" of a collection:

> With the deposit of the interview(s) and related materials in an appropriate depository, the processing phase of oral history is completed. But the work is not done. If the interviews are to serve their intended purpose, they must be properly preserved, serviced, publicized, and used.
>
> This passes over into the area of curatorship and involves such considerations as storage conditions for tapes, cataloging, publicity, dissemination of information about

> holdings to appropriate regional and national information networks, and encouraging users. But that is a subject of another book.[27]

As more and more historians conducted interviews in the course of their research, librarians and archivists had to consider oral history's place in an archives or manuscript repository. Some information professionals believed that oral histories were not true records, according to traditional definitions. Others pressed that archivists and curators collected documents created as a natural by-product of daily activity; to generate records themselves was both inauthentic and a conflict of interest. On a more pragmatic level, oral history collections—with their numerous interviews, legal forms, and multiple formats—did not fit into standard cataloging or other descriptive practices. Preserving reel-to-reel and cassette tapes, not to mention various generations of tape recorders to play them, presented problems as well.

On the other hand, historiographical developments in the 1970s and 1980s demanded that library and archival collections keep pace. Social history, in particular, called for new documentation strategies that would capture the histories of previously ignored groups and topics. Oral history provided an ideal opportunity for libraries and archives to expand their collecting areas and provide historical materials for an increasingly diverse clientele. In the 1980s, numerous articles appeared in the *Journal of Library History*, *American Archivist*, and other professional journals promoting the value of oral history collections. In 1983, the Society of American Archivists established its Oral History Section to coordinate and sustain the profession's growing interest in oral history materials.

A major obstacle in curating oral history collections was the dearth of cataloging models and standards. "In an age in which even artifact curators are moving toward a standardized format for information exchange," complained Bruce Bruemmer, archivist at the Charles Babbage Institute, "oral history remains steadfast in its reliance on the published guide."[28] Indeed, since Columbia published its first oral history catalog in 1964, many programs printed their own collection guides. Other oral history centers created in-house databases of their interview holdings. Some simply kept an on-going list of narrators and topics. When librarians and archivists did catalog oral histories, they treated the transcript as if it were a book. This item-level approach to cataloging oral history was expensive and time consuming and discouraged many libraries from fully processing their recorded and transcribed interviews. As a result of these cataloging problems, curators and librarians frequently resorted to what might be called the shoe-box method: they put their oral history tapes in a shoe box and stowed them away on a remote shelf.

In the early 1990s, several prominent archivists, including Bruce Bruemmer, Lila Goff, James Fogerty, Stephen Hearn, and Michael Fox, secured a grant from the National Historical Publications and Records Commission (NHPRC) to adapt standard cataloging rules for oral history collections. At the outset, they had to confront the uniqueness of the materials' origin and content:

> The oral history interview has developed as a distinct intellectual form, sharing some characteristics of deliberately created works, such as monographs, and some characteristics of unself-conscious accumulations, such as archival records. Oral histories are sometimes both produced and managed by separate oral history program units within larger repositories (usually libraries or archives). Small repositories often acquire oral histories created by individuals, schools, or community projects which don't have the resources to undertake long-term preservation and management of their products.[29]

The challenge, then, was to adapt descriptive cataloging rules and the MARC format to accommodate the full range of materials comprising an oral history collection.

The grant project was overseen by Marion Matters, who had previously worked on the Society of American Archivists' cataloging manual *Archives, Personal Papers, and Manuscripts* (1989). The resulting *Oral History Cataloging Manual*, published by the Society of American Archivists in 1995, was an important step in "mainstreaming" oral histories so that they could be included in online catalogs and bibliographic databases. Key was the decision to describe oral history as a collection or project. That is, oral history cataloging would take an archival rather than library materials approach so as to depict oral history as a group of materials related by provenance.

Another important step in oral history curating was the 1985 publication, *Oral History and the Law*. Written by history professor and municipal judge John Neuenschwander, this text provided authoritative discussion of laws, court cases, and legal precedents relating to the creation and use of oral histories. It provided sample legal forms and policy documents (i.e., release forms, deeds of gift, contracts, etc.) to guide curators in developing policies and procedures that met legal requirements. Successive editions have continued to keep oral historians informed of changing case law and how it affects oral history administration. (This guide is now in its third edition. See work by Neuenschwander).[30]

A third element in curating oral histories involves tricky preservation issues relating to the sound recording. For many years, audiotapes were not preserved, despite pleas from several prominent archivists and librarians.[31] (See, for example, speech by Louis Shores, Dean of Florida State University's School of Library and Information Science.) Ultimately changing oral history theory convinced oral historians of the recording's research value, so even when the tape is transcribed, it is now preserved as the primary source. As a consequence, librarians and archivists must contend with the vulnerability of audiotape, its gradual degradation over time, the loss of quality when copied, and the obsolescence of machines needed for playback. Oral historians initially debated the merits of reel-to-reel vs. cassette tapes as the best format for archival preservation. The debate then shifted to the feasibility and potential impact of videotaped interviews. When digital recording became commonplace in the 1980s, oral historians argued over the positive and negative aspects of replacing more stable analog tapes with compact disks. As with earlier debates over preserving audio recordings, the analog vs. digital controversy has been decided by the marketplace. Now that reel-to-reel and cassette recorders have all but disappeared, oral history curators are engaged in large-scale digitization projects to preserve their analog collections on CD and in other digital formats.

Responding to growing concern about the long-term viability of sound recordings, the U.S. Congress passed the National Recording Preservation Act in 2000. This legislation authorized the Library of Congress to establish the National Recording Preservation Board (NRPB) to develop a comprehensive program to preserve America's recorded heritage. Comprised of sound experts from the music, library, and archival fields, the NRPB commissioned a series of publications on audio preservation and digitization. Of particular importance was the 2006 report, *Capturing Analog Sound for Digital Preservation*, which established best practices for transferring analog recordings to digital format.[32]

Despite this progress in digitizing oral history collections, the transitory nature of digital technology makes long-term preservation increasingly elusive. As Kevin Bradley, curator of oral history and folklore at the National Library of Australia, observed in 2007, "The goal of a permanent media has been wrecked on the rocks of relentless progress. Even if any media could be claimed and trusted, as permanent, the quandary is that within a short period of time the storage system would be technically superseded by storage media exhibiting superior performance specifications, and manufacturers would no longer support the old technology."[33] Currently sound preservationists speak of "digital sustainability" rather than archival permanence and argue that the storage, access, and migration of sound recordings must become part of a broader and continuing digital assets management program.[34]

While posing troubling preservation issues, digitization has revolutionized how libraries and archives are making their oral history collections available to researchers and the general public. Initially, oral history programs prepared published directories containing brief annotations of the interviews in their collections. Once cataloging rules were developed, oral histories were added to large bibliographic utilities like OCLC and RLN as well as to more specialized primary source databases like Alexander Street Press's *Oral History Online*. Individual oral history programs are now placing transcribed and recorded interviews on their institutional Web sites, expanding access to their collections in ways unimaginable when many of the interviews were originally conducted.

More recently, libraries and archives have begun developing new indexing systems to enhance access to digitized audio files. For example, the Shoah Foundation's Visual History Archives enables online searching of its 52,000 testimonies of Holocaust victims by indexing the interview in 1-minute time segments and linking the index terms to the original recording. The Virtual Oral/Aural History Archive at California State University, Long Beach, provides online access to 1000 hours of its interviews by connecting segments of the voice recording to written synopses of the interview's content. At the University of North Carolina, the Southern Oral History Program partnered with the University Library to develop an ambitious oral history database which contains both the transcript and the audio file so users can move back and forth between the text and spoken word. Perhaps most promising is the software currently under development by Randforce Associates that will embed indexing terms and cross references directly into the audio file, making the interview itself fully searchable.[35]

These innovations in digital storage and access have profound implications for oral history methodology and practice. Digitization reemphasizes the aurality of oral documentation, allowing researchers to by-pass mediation imposed by transcribers, editors, and catalogers.[35] At the same time, putting unprocessed, digitized oral histories on the World Wide Web raises new theoretical, ethical, and legal concerns which the oral history profession assuredly will address in the near future.

ORAL HISTORY ASSOCIATIONS

The diverse oral history community is tied together by a network of national and regional professional associations. Through conferences, workshops, discussion lists, and publications, these organizations foster standards and ethics in oral history practice and help disseminate information regarding new programs and projects.

The Oral History Association (OHA) had its genesis in the First National Colloquium on Oral History held in September 1966 in Lake Arrowhead, California. Spearheaded by University of California, Los Angeles, special collections librarian James Mink, the conference attracted over 70 participants, including the movement's founder, Allan Nevins. The historians, archivists, librarians, folklorists, psychiatrists, and medical doctors in attendance debated how to define oral history and what constituted good interviewing technique. They also considered ethical issues involving funding arrangements and interview use. Conference organizer Jim Mink recalled that the "hottest and heaviest" topics were "keeping the tapes" and the editing the transcripts.[36]

It was not at this meeting, but at the second national oral history colloquium that the Oral History Association was officially established. Held in New York City in November 1967, the 145 oral historians present chose Columbia's Louis Starr as OHA's first president and crafted the organization's constitution. One of OHA's earliest priorities was to establish connections with library and archival groups to promote oral history as a documentary source. Oral History Association representatives spoke at American Library Association, Society of American Archivists, and other professional conferences and contributed articles about oral history to their publications.[37]

The OHA continued to host annual fall conferences, attracting a multidisciplinary audience interested in the conduct and use of oral history. From 1966 through 1972, the association recorded and transcribed conference proceedings and distributed them among its members. As the field matured, the OHA sought to expand its publication's coverage, and in 1973 began its journal, the *Oral History Review*. Under the founding editorship of Samuel Hand, the *Review* came out once a year. It continued to publish selected conference presentations and OHA board meeting minutes, but featured articles by leading oral history theorists and practitioners, and, after 1976, added book reviews. The publication of meeting minutes was dropped in 1981, making the journal a purely refereed periodical. The *Oral History Review* is now published twice a year, affiliated with a prominent university press, and continues as major source of professional and theoretical discourse for the field.

In addition to hosting conferences and publishing the *Oral History Review*, the OHA sponsors a helpful pamphlet series and other publications to codify and promote professional practice. The quarterly *Oral History Association Newsletter*, edited for many years by Baylor University historian Thomas Charlton, provides a window on current oral history issues and events. The pamphlet series addresses topics of general concern, such as "Using Oral History in Community Oral History Projects" and "Oral History Projects in Your Classroom."

The OHA also maintains an influential and highly regarded policy document called "Oral History Evaluation Guidelines." Available on the OHA Web site and reprinted in every oral history text, these guidelines were developed at the 1979 "Wingspread Conference" to define and describe ideals of oral history practice. (The Wingspread Conference was named after the conference center in Racine, Wisconsin, where the meeting was held.) Revised in 1989 and again in 2000, the current version sets forth oral historians' ethical and professional responsibilities to the interviewees, the public, the profession, and the sponsoring institution. In addition to establishing standards for oral history conduct, the Evaluation Guidelines also include best practices for oral history project design and implementation. Taken together, these guidelines and standards serve as a benchmark against which oral history work can be assessed.[38]

The oral history movement is also supported and sustained by a network of regional associations. These local groups are quite active, holding annual conferences, organizing workshops, and publishing newsletters. They also raise money for scholarships and give awards for significant oral history work in their regions. Presently there are seven active groups: Michigan Oral History Association, New England Association for Oral History, Northwest Oral History Association, OHMAR—Oral History Mid-Atlantic Region, Southwest Oral History Association, and Texas Oral History Association.

MAJOR ORAL HISTORY PROGRAMS

"Let us begin by disposing of the myth that I had anything to do with the founding of oral history," protested Allan Nevins at the first national meeting of oral historians in 1966. "It founded itself," he asserted, and "would have sprung into life in a dozen places, under any circumstances."[39] Although Columbia's Oral History Research Office is credited with launching the modern oral history movement in the United States, Nevins rightly recognized that other historians were beginning to record interviews about the same time.

Several government-funded projects predate Columbia's pioneering work. The Federal Writers' Project, a New Deal program sponsored by the Works Progress Administration between 1935 and 1943, employed over 6600 interviewers to collect the stories of Americans representing all walks of life. (These interviews are now available online through the Library of Congress's American Memory Historical Collections.) During World War II, the United States Army hired historians to accompany troops into battle and record their experiences as they were happening. The Army continued its oral history program after the war, and today over 1200 interviews with military men and women are available at the U.S. Army Center of Military History.

The U.S. Army is not the only government department to employ oral history. Since the 1960s all branches of the armed forces have sponsored oral history projects to supplement their documentary record.[40] One of the largest collections is housed at the Marine Corps Historical Center and includes interviews with nearly 6500 soldiers who served in Vietnam. The U.S. Senate Office also has an important oral history program dating back to 1976. Under the direction of Senate historian Donald Ritchie, hundreds of interviews have been conducted with senators and people associated with the Senate spanning half a century.

American presidential libraries were another significant player in the American oral history movement. The Roosevelt Presidential Library was the first to collect oral histories, contracting with the Columbia Oral History Office to interview individuals associated with Roosevelt's administration. The Truman, Hoover, Eisenhower, Kennedy, and Johnson presidential libraries also sponsored major oral history projects in the 1960s and 1970s, often hiring full-time oral historians to oversee the work. The Johnson Presidential Library, which interviewed people while Johnson was still in office, boasts the largest oral history collection, with over 1500 interviews in its archives. Presidential libraries established since the Carter Administration have not undertaken such large-scale oral history projects, but instead preserve exit interviews done with White House staff members leaving office.[41,42]

Other federal agencies and institutions have also used oral history to document their programs and activities. The National Institutes of Health, National Library of Medicine, Social Security Administration, NASA, and the National Parks Service have all conducted interviews since the late 1960s. Today the Smithsonian Institution has an ambitious oral history program dealing with the history of aeronautics, science, and technology. The Smithsonian also sponsors important oral history projects for the Archives of American Art and on the history of American jazz.

The most impressive government-funded oral history work is happening at the Library of Congress. Its American Memory Web site contains thousands of interviews recorded by federal employees or donated by the general public. The Library of Congress also sponsors the Veterans History Project which asks former military personnel to donate oral histories and documents relating to their wartime experiences. At this writing, the Veterans History Project contains more than 45,000 personal testimonies, making it one of the largest oral history collections in the world.

Much of the oral history activity in the United States takes place in colleges and universities. As more and more faculty used oral history in their research and teaching, they needed an institutional base to manage the expanding body of documentary materials, leading to the establishment of oral history programs on campus. California's universities provide a good case in point. In the early 1950s, James Hart and George Stewart, English professors at the University of California, Berkeley, were inspired by Bancroft's "Dictations" to hire graduate students to interview additional California pioneers. In 1954, the university established the Regional Oral History Office to coordinate this oral history effort. The University of California, Los Angeles, began its oral history program in 1959, the brainchild of British historian John S. Galbraith and University Librarian Lawrence Clark Powell. The University of California, Los Angeles (UCLA) oral history program was initially managed by faculty member Doyce Nunis and librarian Elizabeth Dixon, until Special Collections Librarian James Mink, who as a graduate student had earlier worked on the Berkeley oral histories, assumed responsibility in 1967. Claremont College's Oral History Program was founded in 1962 by history faculty members Douglass Adair and W. John Niven. Niven had been a student of Allan Nevins at Columbia University, and Nevins served as a consultant to Claremont's program in its founding years. Forty miles away, California State University, Fullerton, history faculty were also conducting interviews for their research and assigning oral history projects in their classes. The Cal State Fullerton oral history program was founded in 1968 by Gary Shumway and administered jointly by the history department and the university library.[43–45]

California has been a hotbed of oral history activity for over 40 years, which explains why the first national oral history meeting was held in that state. However, many other regional colleges and universities are equally productive and influential in the field. It is not possible to list every major academic program, but any count would have to include: the Oral History Institute at Baylor University; the Southern Oral History Program at the University of North Carolina, Chapel Hill; the Maine Folklife Center at the University of Maine, Orono; the Center for the Study of History and Memory at Indiana University; the Center for Oral History at the University of Connecticut, Storrs; the Oral History Program at the University of Alaska, Fairbanks; the University of Kentucky Oral History Program; and the University of Nevada, Reno Oral History Program. These programs are significant not only for their collections, but also for the leading role they take in conducting oral history institutes, publishing oral history manuals and texts, and making available other oral history products and services.

Although government and university-based projects dominate the American oral history movement, public libraries, historical societies, and museums have also successfully used oral history to enhance their historical projects, exhibits, and collections. The New York Public Library (NYPL), for instance, began its Oral History Project and Archive in 1974 to document the history of dance. A significant project within NYPL's dance archive are interviews with dancers afflicted with AIDS. Smaller libraries have also relied on oral history to document their distinctive communities. A good example is the "Front Porch Oral History Series" sponsored by the Way Public Library, in Perrysburg, Ohio, which videotapes and preserves conversations with longtime residents born before 1930.[46,47]

Oral history is also an important tool for preserving institutional memory, in both the for-profit and nonprofit sectors. The Forest History Society was, perhaps, the first organization to use oral history to document changes in its field of interest—forestry management and conservation—beginning its oral history collecting in the late1940s. Many other organizations have followed suit and developed important oral history projects to document the experiences of individuals in their organizations and communities. Among the most ambitious is the Shoah Visual History Foundation, founded by film director Steven Spielberg in 1994 to videotape the stories of holocaust survivors and witnesses. Nearly 52,000 interviews have been collected as a result of this project. They are now part of the Shoah Foundation Institute, established at the University of Southern California in 2006.[48]

INTERNATIONAL ORAL HISTORY MOVEMENT

Although oral historians have been active outside of the United States for 60 years, the oral history movement has been self-consciously international since the 1980s. The first International Conference on Oral History was held in England in 1979; the *International Review of Oral History* began publication the following year. Renamed the *International Annual of Oral History* in 1990, it merged with the European oral history journal *Life Stories* in 1992 to become the *International Yearbook of Oral History and Life Stories*. Interdisciplinary as well as international, each *Yearbook* addressed a different theme, such as memory and totalitarianism, cultural transmission between generations, and migration and identity. The *Yearbook* ceased publication in 1996 when the International Oral History Association was established. In addition to sponsoring biennial conferences, the association publishes the bilingual, *Words and Silences/Palabras y Silencias*, continuing the *Yearbook's* mission to promote dialog among oral historians throughout the world.

Oral history's internationalism has challenged accepted oral history methodologies and fostered new theoretical understanding and applications. For example, oral historians' experiences interviewing people in different cultures have better illuminated the extent to which memory, culture, and the telling of history are interconnected and grounded in social context. Interviewing techniques promulgated in one region or culture may be entirely inappropriate and counterproductive in another.

The international movement in oral history also shows that the motives behind and uses of oral history vary in different parts of the world. While in the United States oral history originally sought to document the experiences of political leaders, the oral history movement in England, led by sociology professor Paul Thompson, has focused more on nonelites as a means of empowering the lower classes. Oral history in Latin America has an openly political agenda and is tied to important social movements of the region. Oral historians in postapartheid South African have found in oral history a means to cultivate a new national identity that, to quote its Oral History Association, "encompasses all people, irrespective of race, culture, genders, sexual orientation and social status."[49] In New Zealand and Australia, capturing the history of aboriginal peoples has been among those regions' major oral history goals.

Finally, some of the most significant theoretical developments in oral history originated within this international setting, particularly in the work of Luisa Passerini and Alessandro Portelli. Passerini, in her studies of Italian women and the working class, uses sociological, psychological, and feminist theory to better understand the multiple "subjectivities" of oral history interviewees and the fluidity of their personal narratives depending on the interview's context and goals. [See, for example, *Fascism in Popular Memory: The Cultural Experience of the Turin Working Class* (1987) and *Memory and Utopia: The Primacy of Inter-Subjectivity* (2007).] Portelli, arguably the most influential contemporary oral history theoretician, writes about how communities create and popularize their own historical narratives, sometimes in opposition to what actually transpired. As Portelli explains in *What Makes Oral History Different?* oral history "tells us less about *events* than about their *meaning*." [As cited in work edited by Perks and Thomson.[50] Portelli's books include *The Order Has Been Carried Out: History, Memory, and Meaning of a Nazi Massacre in Rome* (2003); *The Battle of Valle Giulia: Oral History and the Art of Dialogue* (1997); and *The Death of Luigi Trastulli and Other Stories: Form and Meaning in Oral History* (1991).]

CONCLUSION

In this encyclopedia's original essay, Louis Starr defined oral history as "primary source material obtained by recording the spoken words—generally by means of planned, tape-recorded interviews—of persons deemed to harbor hitherto unavailable information worth preserving." These interviews, Starr elaborated, were not solely conducted for researchers' personal use, "but for libraries or other repositories to hold for the benefit of scholars of this and succeeding generations." Reflecting the status of oral history in 1977, Starr's entry focused on the strengths and weaknesses of oral history as historical documentation and chronicled the growing list of publications based on oral history interviews. Starr could already see social history's impact on oral history, noting that this historical methodology had the potential to "reflect the myriad interests of a pluralistic society." Starr was also enthusiastic about emerging technologies, most notably microforms, and their promise to extend oral history's reach beyond the originating institutions. Despite oral history's success and future prospects, Starr still bemoaned the fact that many historians continued to reject oral history as primary source material. He also criticized archival and educational institutions for not providing the financial support oral history programs sorely needed.[51] (See also work by Fogerty[52] for a similar comparison between Starr's early writings and contemporary oral history.)

While the spirit and substance of Starr's oral history remains much the same, there are important changes as well. Whereas Starr claimed that the vast majority of oral history producers and users preferred the typed transcript, today's interdisciplinary and theoretically attuned researchers rely as much on the audio as the printed document to do their work. Starr was impressed with the many books using oral histories in the 1970s. Today's important publications are as much about oral history as based upon its interviews. And while Starr complimented oral historians on their printed catalogs and openness to new technologies, contemporary curators look to digitization to make oral histories available to researchers and the public. The opportunities of the World Wide Web, unimagined in Starr's time, have raised new issues concerning narrator rights. So while Starr barely mentioned legal and ethical practice in 1977, today they are central to oral history curating.

Starr concluded his essay rather plaintively, stating that until more universities and research libraries "perceive the work as central to their purpose" the full impact of oral history would not be felt.[53] Today oral history enjoys wide acceptance, its value as both historical and cultural documentation is fully appreciated. Librarians and archivists are integrating oral history holdings into online catalogs and databases and developing exciting new ways of disseminating digitized tapes and transcripts on the World Wide Web. It appears that the days of shoe-box cataloging are coming to an end as oral history finds its rightful place in library and archival collections.

REFERENCES

1. Sharpless, R. The history of oral history. In *Handbook of Oral History*; Charlton, T.L., Myers, L.E., Sharpless, R., Eds.; AltaMira Press: Lanham, MD, 2006; 19–20.
2. Morrissey, C.T. Why call it "oral history"? Searching for early usage of a generic term. Oral Hist. Rev. **1980**, *8*, 20.
3. Conaway, C.W. Lyman Copeland Draper, father of American oral history. J. Libr. Hist. **1966**, *1*, 241.
4. Ritchie, D.A. *Doing Oral History: A Practical Guide*, 2nd Ed.; Oxford University Press: New York, 2003; 22.
5. Polsky, R. An interview with Elizabeth Mason. Oral Hist. Rev. **2000**, *27*(2), 168–175.
6. Pogue, F. Louis Starr, A remembrance. Oral Hist. Rev. **1980**, *8*, 93–97.
7. Shumway, G. *Oral History in the United States: A Directory*; Oral History Association: New York, 1971; 3.
8. Terkel, S. *Hard Times: An Oral History of the Great Depression*; Pantheon: New York, 1970.
9. Haley, A. *Roots: The Saga of an American Family*; Doubleday: Garden City, NY, 1976.
10. Wigginton, E., Ed. *The Foxfire Book*; Doubleday: Garden City, NY, 1972.
11. Shopes, L. Developing a critical dialogue about oral history: some notes based on an analysis of book reviews. Oral Hist. Rev. **1986**, *14*, 10.
12. Sharpless, R. The history of oral history. In *Handbook of Oral History*; Charlton, T.L., Myers, L.E., Sharpless, R., Eds.; AltaMira Press: Lanham, MD, 2006; 28–29.
13. Swain, E.D. Oral history in the archives: its documentary role in the twenty-first century. Am. Archivist **2003**, *66*, 143–149.
14. Baum, W.K. *Oral History for the Local Historical Society*; Conference of California Historical Societies: Stockton, CA, 1969.
15. Curtiss, R., Shumway, G., Stephenson, S., Eds. *A Guide for Oral History Programs*; California State University Fullerton, Oral History Program: Fullerton, CA, 1973.
16. Deering, M.J.; Pomeroy, B. *Transcribing without Tears: A Guide to Transcribing and Editing Oral History Interviews*; Oral History Program, George Washington University Library: Washington, DC, 1976.
17. Baum, W.K. *Transcribing and Editing Oral History*; American Association for State and Local History: Nashville, TN, 1977.
18. Kessler Harris, A. Introduction. In *Envelopes of Sound*; Grele, R., Ed.; Precedent Publishing: Chicago, IL, 1975; 5.
19. Grele, R. Movement without aim. In *Envelopes of Sound*; Grele, R., Ed.; Precedent Publishing: Chicago, IL, 1975; 135–136.
20. Henige, D. *Oral Historiography*; Longman: London, U.K., 1982.
21. Thomson, A. Four paradigm transformations in oral history. Oral Hist. Rev. **2007**, *34*(1), 61–65.
22. Frisch, M. *A Shared Authority: Essays on the Craft and Meaning of Oral and Public History*; State University of New York Press: Albany, NY, 1990; 13.
23. Thomson, A. Four paradigm transformations in oral history. Oral Hist. Rev. **2007**, *34*(1), 54.
24. Frisch, M. *A Shared Authority: Essays on the Craft and Meaning of Oral and Public History*; State University of New York Press: Albany, NY, 1990; xx.
25. Ritchie, D.A., Ed. *Doing Oral History: A Practical Guide*, 2nd Ed.; Oxford University Press: New York, 2003; 253 Principles and Standards of the Oral History Association. Reprinted in.
26. Neuenschwander, J. *Oral History and the Law*; Oral History Association: Carlisle, PA, 2002; 18–23.
27. Baum, W.K. *Transcribing and Editing Oral History*; AltaMira Press: Walnut Creek, CA, 1991; 121.
28. Bruemmer, B.H. Access to oral history: a national agenda. Am. Archivist **1991**, *54*, 495.
29. Matters, M.C. *Oral History Cataloging Manual*; Society of American Archivists: Chicago, IL, 1995; 1.
30. Neuenschwander, J. *Oral History and the Law*; Oral History Association: Carlisle, PA, 2002.
31. Oral History Association, In *Oral History at Arrowhead: Proceedings of the First National Colloquium on Oral History*; Dixon, E.I., Mink, J.V., Eds.; Oral History Association: Los Angeles, CA, 1967; 55.
32. Council on Library and Information Resources et al., *Capturing Analog Sound for Digital Preservation: Report of a Roundtable Discussion of Best Practices for Transferring Analog Discs and Tapes*, Council on Library and Information Resources and Library of Congress: Washington, DC, 2006.
33. Bradley, K. Defining digital sustainability. Libr. Trends **2007**, *56*(1), 153.

34. Bradley, K. Defining digital sustainability. Libr. Trends **2007**, *56*(1), 151.
35. Frisch, M. Oral history and the digital revolution. In *The Oral History Reader*, 2nd Ed.; Perks, R., Thomson, A., Eds.; Routledge: London, U.K., 2006; 102–114.
36. Treleven, D. An interview with James V. Mink. Oral Hist. Rev. **2000**, *27*(1), 132.
37. Starr, L.M. Oral history. In *Encyclopedia of Library and Information Science*, 1st Ed. Marcel Dekker, Inc.: New York, 1977; Vol. 20, 449–450.
38. http://alpha.dickinson.edu/oha/pub_eg.html Oral History Association. Evaluation guidelines.
39. Oral History Association, In *Oral History at Arrowhead: Proceedings of the First National Colloquium on Oral History*; Dixon, E., Mink, J., Eds.; Oral History Association: Los Angeles, CA, 1967; 35.
40. Ritchie, D.A. Oral history in the federal government. J. Am. Hist. **1987**, *74*(2), 590.
41. Ritchie, D.A. Oral history in the federal government. J. Am. Hist. **1987**, *74*(2), 587–595.
42. Greenwell, R. The oral history collections of the presidential libraries. J. Am. Hist. **1997**, *84*(2), 596–603.
43. K'Meyer, T.E. An interview with Willa K. Baum: A career at the Regional Oral History Office. Oral Hist. Rev. **1997**, *24*(1), 91–114.
44. Douglass, E.H. The initial development of oral history in California. In *A Guide for Oral History Programs*; Curtiss, R., Shumway, G., Stephenson, S., Eds.; California State University Fullerton Oral History Program: Fullerton, CA, 1973; 7–12.
45. Hansen, A. The Oral History Program collections. In *Very Special Collections: Essays on Library Holdings at California State University, Fullerton*; Vogeler, A.R., Hansen, A.A., Eds.; California State University Fullerton Patrons of the Library: Fullerton, CA, 1992; 99–122.
46. http://www.nypl.org/research/lpa/dan/background.htm New York Public Library for the Performing Arts. Oral History Project.
47. Baranowski, R.; Calderone, T. Reconnecting the past through oral history. Public Libr. **2004**, *43*(2), 109–112.
48. http://college.usc.edu/vhi/ University of Southern California Shoah Foundation Institute.
49. http://www.ohasa.org.za/index.php?option=comcontent&task=view&id=1 Oral History Association of South Africa.
50. Perks, R., Thomson, A., Eds. *Oral History Reader*; Routledge: New York, 1998; 67.
51. Starr, L. Oral history. In *Encyclopedia of Library and Information Science*, 1st Ed. Marcel Dekker, Inc.: New York, 1977; Vol. 20, 440–463.
52. Fogerty, J.E. Oral history: Prospects and a retrospective. In *Advances in Librarianship*; Nitecki, D., Abels, E., Eds.; Elsevier: New York, 2006; Vol. 30, 179–199.
53. Starr, L. Oral history. In *Encyclopedia of Library and Information Science*, 1st Ed. Marcel Dekker, Inc.: New York, 1977; Vol. 20, 458.

BIBLIOGRAPHY

1. Bradley, K. Defining digital sustainability. Libr. Trends **2007**, *56*(1), 148–163.
2. Charlton, T.L., Myers, L.E., Sharpless, R., Eds. *Handbook of Oral History*; AltaMira Press: Lanham, MD, 2006.
3. Council on Library and Information Resources et al., *Capturing Analog Sound for Digital Preservation: Report of a Roundtable Discussion of Best Practices for Transferring Analog Discs and Tapes*, Council on Library and Information Resources and Library of Congress: Washington, DC, 2006.
4. Fogerty, J.E. Oral history: Prospects and a retrospective. In *Advances in Librarianship*; Nitecki, D., Abels, E., Eds.; Elsevier: New York, 2006; Vol. 30, 179–199.
5. Frisch, M. *A Shared Authority: Essays on the Craft and Meaning of Oral and Public History*; State University of New York Press: Albany, NY, 1990.
6. Grele, R., Ed. *Envelopes of Sound*; Precedent Publishing: Chicago, IL, 1975.
7. Hamilton, P., Shopes, L., Eds. *Oral History and Public Memories*;; Temple University Press: Philadelphia, PA, 2008.
8. MacKay, N. *Curating Oral Histories: From Interview to Archive*; Left Coast Press: Walnut Creek, CA, 2007.
9. Matters, M.C. *Oral History Cataloging Manual*; Society of American Archivists: Chicago, IL, 1995.
10. Neuenschwander, J. *Oral History and the Law*; Oral History Association: Carlisle, PA, 2002.
11. Perks, R., Thomson, A., Eds. *Oral History Reader*, , 2nd Ed; Routledge: New York, 2006.
12. Portelli, A. *The Death of Luigi Trastulli and Other Stories: Form and Meaning in Oral History*; State University of New York: Albany, WY, 1991.
13. Portelli, B. *The Battle of Valle Giulia: Oral History and the Art of Dialogue*; University of Wisconsin Press: Madison, WI, 1997.
14. Ritchie, D.A. *Doing Oral History: A Practical Guide*, 2nd Ed.; Oxford University Press: New York, 2003.
15. Shopes, L. Making sense of oral history. *History Matters: The U.S. Survey Course on the Web*, Available at http://historymatters.gmu.edu/mse/oral/ (accessed February 2008).
16. Sommer, B.W.; Quinlan, M.K. *The Oral History Manual*; AltaMira Press: Walnut Creek, CA, 2002.
17. Thompson, P.R. *The Voice of the Past: Oral History*; Oxford University Press: New York, 1978.
18. Thomson, A. Fifty years on: an international perspective on oral history. J. Am. Hist. **1998**, *8*(2), 581–595.
19. Thomson, A. Four paradigm transformations in oral history. Oral Hist. Rev. **2007**, *34*(1), 49–70.
20. Yow, V. *Recording Oral History: A Guide for the Humanities and Social Sciences*, 2nd Ed.; AltaMira Press: Walnut Creek, CA, 2005.

ORCID

Laurel L. Haak
Open Researcher and Contributor ID, Inc. (ORCID), U.S.A.

Abstract

ORCID is a nonprofit organization dedicated to providing an open registry of unique person identifiers for researchers, and to working collaboratively with the research community to embed these identifiers in research workflows to connect researchers and research. Together, the registry and embedding of identifiers supports discoverability and ensures that researchers get credit for their work. This entry describes the ORCID mission and organizational structure, describes relationships with other identifier systems, and provides details on the use of technical tools to support adoption and embedding of ORCID identifiers in research systems.

ORCID (https://orcid.org) was founded in 2010, a product of conversations among commercial and association publishers, research funders, universities, repositories, researchers, and data providers, who together determined that to solve the name ambiguity problem in scholarly and research communication required an organization that represented the entire research community without proprietary interest. ORCID spans sectors, disciplines, organizations, and nations. It is a community-driven effort to implement a standard and persistent representation of an individual contributor's name, and to link that standard to others, such as document and dataset identifiers, research sample identifiers, grant identifiers, association membership, other person identifiers, and other research activities as determined by the community. Together these linkages support the unique identification of an individual connected with their research contributions.

WHAT IS AN ORCID ID?

The ORCID identifier is a 16-digit number, expressed as a URI, that is unique to an individual. The format of the ORCID iD is consistent with the ISNI ISO 277729 standard, and ISNI has set aside a block of numbers from its range for assignment through the ORCID registry. An example of an ORCID iD is https://0000-0001-5109-3700. Display guidelines are posted online at http://orcid.org/trademark-and-id-display-guidelines.

WHAT DISTINGUISHES ORCID FROM OTHER IDENTIFIERS FOR RESEARCHERS?

ORCID is different in three ways. First, ORCID is an open effort. ORCID code and APIs are available as open-source code (see https://orcid.org/blog/2013/02/21/orcid-open-source), and the identifier is not tied to any proprietary system. This means that an individual may use their ORCID identifier throughout their research career. Second, ORCID links to other identifiers, making it possible for researchers to connect their work between existing systems, whether they are disciplinary or organizational, without devaluing those systems. The ORCID registry supports identifier linkages and metadata exchange with many identifier systems including Scopus Author ID, Researcher ID, and ISNI. ORCID and ISNI are committed to interoperation (see https://orcid.org/blog/2013/04/22/orcid-and-isni-issue-joint-statement-interoperation-april-2013). Third, ORCID is a community-wide effort. It does not stop at providing a registry, but also works to ensure the identifier becomes part of the metadata on works and research activities at the time the work enters the public domain. This removes author ambiguity for new works and makes it possible to use metadata to link back with an individual's ORCID record and automate the update process. Together, ORCID makes a researcher's work more easily discoverable, regardless of the system used to search. In short, the goal of ORCID is interoperability through community collaboration.

THE ORCID REGISTRY

The ORCID registry is a hub for linking information between systems and sources. As such, to the extent possible, ORCID uses persistent identifiers, such as DOIs for publications and datasets, to establish a persistent connection between the ORCID record and the object. We capture metadata in addition to the object identifier but do not capture or store objects themselves.

The registry is researcher-driven. Located at https://orcid.org, an individual may register and obtain an identifier without fee or membership requirement, nor are there requirements to qualify as a researcher. To register,

Encyclopedia of Library and Information Sciences, Fourth Edition DOI: 10.1081/E-ELIS4-120050534

an individual must provide their name, e-mail address, create a password, and accept the ORCID privacy policy and terms of use. ORCID does not collect date of birth, financial, or government identification information. A user may augment their ORCID identifier by adding additional information such as other names they have published under (e.g., their married name or name expressed in different character sets), research area keywords, website URL, other e-mail addresses, and country in which they are currently employed. A user may also add information on their organizational affiliations, and search external databases through the ORCID registry to link their record to their existing research works, such as publications and datasets, and in some cases, push their ORCID identifier into these databases.

The ORCID iD is always public and may never be deleted. Individual users control the privacy of all other information in their record. A user may set each data field to either public, limited access, or private. Public data are searchable and viewable by anyone and are provided by ORCID to the public in an annual data snapshot under a CC0 waiver. This waiver means that ORCID makes no copyright, related, or neighboring rights claims to the aggregated data. Limited access data are only available for search or view by ORCID members that the user has specifically approved. Private data is only viewable by the user or their designated proxy.

Through adoption and embedding, ORCID is becoming a part of the metadata for publications and other works, making it possible to automatically update ORCID records with new research works metadata. ORCID iDs are being embedded in publisher workflows, grant application and reporting systems, university research information and personnel systems, repository submission systems, dataset management systems, and professional society member and meeting management systems. Each of these workflows supports a validated linkage between a researcher and their works.

COMMUNITY INVOLVEMENT AND GOVERNANCE

ORCID is governed by an elected board of directors, majority nonprofit, comprised of 11–15 members of the global scholarly research community https://orcid.org/about/team. Membership in the board of directors is drawn from and representative of ORCID member organizations. The board is responsible for establishing general policies for the governance of ORCID based on a set of core principles, among them openness and transparency. In addition to the board of directors, ORCID has several steering and working groups, open to the research community.

The ORCID community includes individual researchers, universities, national laboratories, commercial research organizations, research funders, publishers, national science agencies, data repositories, and international professional societies, all of whom have been critically affected by the lack of a central registry for researchers. Prior to the launch of ORCID, over 300 organizations had registered their support for ORCID, and 50 of these provided start-up financial support. Since launch, a number and variety of organizations are integrating ORCID identifiers into their research workflows, using the application programming interfaces (APIs) ORCID has made available. A list of ORCID members, sponsors, and partners is available on our community page, at https://orcid.org/about/community.

ORCID has established groups to guide and support the evolution and ongoing development of the ORCID system. These are structured to facilitate broad and open participation of interested community members, provide opportunities to participate with different levels of time commitment according to interest and expertise, and provide ORCID guidance on priorities and execution of specific plans. ORCID encourages and welcomes community involvement in our business, outreach, and technical activities, ad hoc working groups, and community groups.

Our principles of openness and transparency extend into how the registry is managed. Development is carried out with new features and bug fixes tracked in an open manner. In addition, ORCID has implemented tools for community technical input, both through an open code repository and a support forum, where users are encouraged to submit ideas for new features, and view and vote on existing submissions. Input from both channels feeds into the prioritization of development work.

ORCID staff include the executive director, technical and outreach directors, and internal and contract technical staff. ORCID maintains a distributed office, with a primary location in Bethesda, MD. ORCID Inc. maintains a governance relationship with its ORCID EU affiliate but is distinct from a financial and legal perspective.

DATA PRIVACY AND SECURITY

Confidence and trust are important to ORCID. We have put in place controls, policies, and practices (see https://orcid.org/about/trust) so that connections are controlled by researchers, and that the source of each connection is openly articulated.

Researcher privacy is important to ORCID. Following research community–sanctioned privacy practices is essential to the success of ORCID and the registry it operates. ORCID is committed to providing users with meaningful choices about privacy and the ability to control how information is used. The ORCID privacy policy is available online at http://about.orcid.org/privacy-policy.

A core ORCID principle is that users control the privacy settings of their own ORCID record data through various opt-in features. To that end, ORCID allows users the right to control how their information is published on and shared via the ORCID registry. Data marked as *public* is available to the public for viewing and use, including commercial use. Data marked as *limited access* may be viewed through the registry by the user, their designated proxy (if any), or the user may elect to share a field or specific data within a field with trusted parties. Data marked as *private* are viewable only by the user or their designated proxy.

To ensure the transparency of the registry, ORCID maintains an audit trail of when and by whom registry information has been deposited or changed and any changes to privacy settings. ORCID uses this information to assist users in addressing concerns about the provenance of data in the registry and questions about identity ambiguity or theft. ORCID reviews concerns about data in accordance our dispute resolution procedure (see http://about.orcid.org/content/orcid-dispute-procedures), which includes the provision to remove or hide from the registry and its servers any record data that violates the privacy, publicity, or other rights of any person.

ORCID is committed to protecting the registry and users from unauthorized access to or authorized alteration, disclosure, or destruction of personal information in the ORCID registry or which we otherwise hold. ORCID stores information in a data center with restricted access and uses a variety of technical security measures to secure data. We also use secure socket layer (SSLtechnology) and intrusion detection and virus protection software. Data are stored on servers that are not accessible directly via the Internet. We periodically review our information collection, storage, and processing practices, including physical security measures. We restrict access to information marked as private or limited access or which is otherwise not public. And, all passwords are hashed and are not visible to ORCID, its contractors, or agents.

ORCID may store and process personal information on servers or on a cloud located outside of the country where a user originally deposited the data. Regardless of where data are stored, ORCID takes steps to protect information, consistent with the principles set forth in the ORCID privacy policy, intended to comply with the Safe Harbor and Privacy Shield Principles issued by the U.S. Department of Commerce for data transfers from the European Union and Switzerland to the United States. As a not-for-profit organization, ORCID is not subject to the jurisdiction of the U.S. Federal Trade Commission, which oversees the implementation of Safe Harbor and Privacy Shield Principles. However, we adhere to the Principles in recognition of their importance in ensuring the protection of user information. We undergo an annual enterprise privacy certification review by an independent third party to verify our compliance with user data privacy management practices.

HOW IS ORCID SUPPORTED?

ORCID has many generous participants who have supported the start-up phase of ORCID: hundreds of volunteer hours from dozens of participants and board members, sponsorships and loans received from publishers; grants received from The Andrew W. Mellon Foundation, National Science Foundation, the European Commission, and the Alfred P. Sloan Foundation; the Leona M. and Harry B. Helmsley Charitable Trust, and a perpetual no-fee license of the Researcher ID code from Thomson Reuters.

Over the longer term, ORCID revenues are entirely derived from membership and subscriber fees from organizations that license the member API (see https://orcid.org/about/membership). In addition to a standard member and subscriber agreement, ORCID supports consortial membership and national membership. To support broad community adoption and use, ORCID provides fee-free access to a public API, including authentication and exchange of an ORCID identifier. Discounts are provided to nonprofit organizations, and to groups. Member policies are reevaluated regularly by the ORCID Board to ensure inclusiveness. Members and subscribers are listed on the ORCID website, at https://orcid.org/about/community/members.

EMBEDDING ORCID IDENTIFIERS

ORCID APIs

ORCID integration is entirely through APIs. There is no system to implement. As such, the technical work to embed ORCID identifiers into local systems involves mapping to the ORCID API. Maintenance involves monitoring the API documentation for updates and ensuring continued connectivity. ORCID APIs, software code, and documentation are posted in an open-source repository, and the community may obtain information on updates by registering for a mailing list.

ORCID provides two APIs. The public API, open for anyone to use, supports search of the public data in the registry. The member API is available only to those organizations that have accepted the terms of the ORCID member agreement. It supports authentication, search, read, write, and update. ORCID members may also serve as trusted parties, with the ability to read limited access data when approved by the user.

To support integration, ORCID provides a sandbox server for testing. Use of this server is free but requires registration and provision of a test token. It is the goal of ORCID, through provision of these tools and community resources to support not only integration of identifiers, but also the creation of tools and applications to interact with the registry itself. Third-party tools already created include sites that use the APIs to consume ORCID works data and generate publication usage statistics.

Other APIs and Data Exchange Standards

Fields to capture ORCID identifiers are being added to other data exchange standards. The widely used CERIF standard for data exchange with research information systems (CRIS) includes a field to capture the ORCID identifier, as does the VIVO ontology, another CRIS system used in the United States, Australia, and Europe. The National Library of Medicine (NLM) article and journal DTDs both provide a field to capture ORCID identifiers as do several publisher production systems that submit article metadata to NLM and CrossRef. CrossRef captures ORCID identifiers during the journal article deposition process, and DataCite is doing the same for datasets. This information can be used to trigger a process to update the ORCID registry.

ORCID identifiers are included in the Journal Publishing Tag Library NISO JATS Version 1.0 XML specification. ORCID identifiers are captured in the %contrib-id-type attribute on <contrib-id> as the full URI. For more on the standard, see https://orcid.org/blog/2013/03/22/orcid-how-more-specifying-orcid-ids-document-metadata.

<contrib-id>Contributor Identifier

One identifier for a person such as a contributor or principal investigator. This element will hold an ORCID, a trusted publisher's identifier, a JST (Japanese Science and Technology Agency) identifier, or an NII (National Individual Identifier).

Attributes

content-type Type of Content
contrib-id-type Contributor Identifier Type
specific-use Specific Use

Content Model

<!ELEMENT contrib-id %contrib-id-model; >

Expanded Content Model

(#PCDATA)

Description

Text, numbers, or special characters

This element may be contained in

<contrib>, <principal-award-recipient>, <principal-investigator>

Example

```
<contrib-group>
<contrib>
<contrib-id contrib-id-type="orcid">http://orcid.org/
0000-0002-1825-0097</contrib-id>
<name><surname>Carberry</surname>
<given-names>Josiah</given-names>
</name>
<degrees>BA, MA</degrees>
</contrib>
</contrib-group>
```

Use Cases

There are four basic steps for implementing ORCID identifiers, all of which require authentication as a core component. (1) **Collecting** validated ORCID iDs for individuals to ensure they're correctly associated with their affiliations and contributions. (2) **Displaying** iDs to signal to researchers that an information system is plumbed to support their use of ORCID. (3) **Connecting** information about affiliations and contributions to ORCID records, creating trusted assertions and enabling researchers to easily provide validated information to systems and profiles they use. And, (4) **Synchronizing** between research information systems to improve reporting speed and accuracy and reduce data entry burden for researchers and administrators alike (see https://members.orcid.org). Using these integration points, ORCID identifiers have been embedded in a number of different systems. Researchers are being asked to include their ORCID identifier when they submit a manuscript, dataset, or grant. Publication metadata repositories are ingesting ORCID identifiers and adding fields to search by ORCID identifier. Universities are providing faculty tools to link their local CRIS data with their ORCID record and the opportunity to synchronize data between the systems. Students are being asked to register for an ORCID identifier at the time of thesis submission. Data repositories have amended their metadata standards to include an ORCID identifier for dataset creators and contributors and are supporting linkages with ORCID records. Repositories are using ORCID identifiers as a means to maintain and update their holdings. External identifier systems are supporting cross-platform linkages between identifiers, supporting opportunities to review and validate algorithmically created name-based information clusters, and pass metadata between platforms. Altmetrics providers and research funders are leveraging ORCID registry data to support assessment of research impact. More detailed information on use cases is available at https://members.orcid.org.

CONCLUSION

The core issue underlying the ORCID initiative is the effective and appropriate identification of individuals who participate in the research community, and linking them with their research works, funding, and affiliations. Prior to the formation of ORCID, there were fragmented proprietary and discipline-based systems for uniquely identifying researchers, many of which are still operational today. In addition to providing a common identifier that can link existing researcher identifier systems, ORCID works with the community to ensure that the common identifier is embedded in research workflows and becomes part of the metadata associated with research works, funding, and affiliations. It is the combination of these two ORCID mission activities—common open identifier and linking—that gives the community cause to believe that ORCID is a key component of solving the name ambiguity problem in research and scholarly communications. Solving this problem makes individuals more discoverable, assisting researchers in finding resources and collaborators to support their work. Linking the common researcher identifier with works, funding, and affiliations extends interoperability and supports reporting. At the individual level, this means improved discoverability and less time entering data on forms such as grant applications and postaward reporting, and at the institutional level this means less time and more accuracy in identifying researchers and their works for workforce and outcomes evaluation reporting. Overall, the system interoperability supported by ORCID can lead to broader acknowledgment of research activities and the potential for expanding existing incentives.

ACKNOWLEDGMENTS

The author thanks Amy Brand, Rebecca Bryant, and Martin Fenner for comments on this entry.

Organization Theories

Evelyn Daniel
School of Information and Library Science, University of North Carolina at Chapel Hill, Chapel Hill, North Carolina, U.S.A.

Abstract
The dominant paradigm of organization theory based on bureaucracy, open systems, and contingency theory is described with concepts traced to their historical roots. Parallel developments in public administration are also presented. This entry concludes with a consideration of network theories that have emerged in the latter half of the twentieth century as researchers consider groups of organizations rather than individual units.

For many years, organization theory has had a dominant paradigm based on bureaucracy, structural analysis, systems and contingency theory. This theoretical paradigm, usually called functional or rational, despite criticism from interpretative theory and critical social theory[1] continues to be supported in schools and journals and to guide manager's decisions. Changes in the environment that reward speed and innovation have brought new networked organizational forms to the fore. These changes have affected both public and private sector organizations.

In this entry, I will take a more or less historical approach beginning as most organization texts do (Daft–Tsoukas[2–9] (among others)) with a description of classical organization theory and then contrasting newer networked organizations to the classical model.

I have attempted to include theoretical writings from public administration that sometimes parallel and sometimes diverge from writings about corporations in the for-profit sector. Another article could be written about applications of these theories to the library and information world. Certainly libraries as large bureaucratic organizations are often involved in competition for resources and even existence. They confront issues of power and control, and have concerns about how to choose an appropriate structure (physical and social), how to integrate technology, how to socialize workers (professionals and nonprofessionals, full-time and part-time, career and contract workers), and how, when, and whether to enter into strategic alliances and joint ventures beyond their organizational boundaries. Libraries and other information agencies are good laboratories to study the interplay of forces described and predicted in organizational theory. However, the exigencies of time and space leave this task to others.

One fairly inclusive and often quoted definition of an organization by Hall[10] is as follows: "An organization is a collectivity with a relatively identifiable boundary, a normative order, ranks of authority, communication systems, and member coordinating systems; this collectivity exists on a relatively continuous basis in an environment and engages in actions that are usually related to a goal or set of goals" (pp. 22–23). Some of the qualities that define organizations often referred to in the literature include that a pattern of interaction has developed that is enduring and resists change, that there is a dominant and definable culture, that there is a hierarchical power structure that ensures conformity and provides control such that certain behavior regularities are more likely to occur than others.[9] Over time, organization theory has come to embrace a fairly large domain. Lawrence and Lorsch[11] argue that the heart of organization theory is the task of integrating and coordinating the components and domains of an organization including its environment, its strategy and decision-making processing, its goals and values, its culture, its structure, its authority and power relationships, its tasks, its communication processes, its people—leaders, teams, groups, and their individual motivations, work attitudes and behaviors.

Since Adam Smith[12] first described the positive effects of work specialization and division of labor, organization theorists have wrestled with two primary opposing forces—differentiation and coordination. The more an organization divides labor into specialized tasks and separates departments, the greater the strain on communication and the greater the need for coordination or integrating mechanisms. As specialization increases and the complexity of the organization, so techniques of coordination must also increase. Even today with the potential of coordinating through electronic networks, the hierarchy continues as the dominant coordinating mechanism although there are signs that this is beginning to change.

Formal investigations of the organization qua organization began with Max Weber, who was born in 1864 and died in 1920. He wrote at a time when industrialization was affecting all facets of society and traditional authority structures were being challenged. Weber, a sociologist

Encyclopedia of Library and Information Sciences, Fourth Edition DOI: 10.1081/E-ELIS4-120044125

defined and described the bureaucracy and called it the "ideal model" for an organization.[13] He identified division of labor and the centralization of authority through hierarchy as two of its primary characteristics.

In fact, in one of the earliest of a continuing stream of criticism of Weberian bureaucracy, Merton in 1940[14] observed that specialization (division of labor) and an emphasis on adhering to rules can lead to *trained incapacity*, in which employees find difficulty in dealing with situations that do not fit the rules or changes in rules and routines. *Displacement of goals* can occur in which people focus so much on following rules or on pursuing the goals of a simple department that the larger organizational goals as a whole are ignored. Victor Thompson,[15] a public administration scholar in his book tellingly titled *Without Sympathy or Enthusiasm; the Problem of Administrative Compassion*, argued that Weberian bureaucracy can cause "bureaupathology" in its members who can become overly concerned with protecting the authority of their offices and too impersonal in their dealings with clients and other members of the organization.

Early writers on organizations built on Weber's definition of bureaucracy and focused on technical rationality as the principal objective of an organization. This early period of organization theorizing is often referred to as classical organization theory. For example, Henri Fayol,[16] a mining engineer, studied the problem of state public services and developed a theory appropriate to a wide range of organizations. He defined management as comprising five core functional elements: planning, organization, command, coordination, and control. He then outlined 14 fundamental principles of organization design, many of which are still considered valid today, are described below as tenets of classical organization theory. In 1937 Luther Gulick,[17] a public administration theorist used Fayol's theory and advocated dividing government work up into small specialized segments, allocating the work to those most skilled and coordinating it through supervision, clear task definition, instruction, and direction. Like Fayol, Gulick proposed a set of functions for the executive that form the acronym POSDCORB that, for some reason, has proved memorable to generations of management students. POSDCORB stands for planning, organizing, staffing, directing, coordinating, reporting, and budgeting.

By contrast, Mary Parker Follett,[18] a consultant to government and business organizations, suggested that the same principles that create strong social communities could be applied to creating successful organizations of all kinds. In a startlingly modern formulation, she proposed a cooperative participatory process for giving orders in which supervisors and subordinates develop a shared understanding of the situation and what is required. This "law of the situation" foreshadowed ideas of workplace democracy and nonhierarchical networks of self-governing groups.

At the turn of the twentieth century, professionalization and the scientific method emerged. Efficiency became the chief goal of both government and industry. Engineer and efficiency expert, Frederick W. Taylor[19] urged a "scientific management" approach in order to learn the "one best way" to perform each task in the organization. The primary goal of the organization, according to Taylor and other proponents of the "organization as machine" model, was efficiency gained through research and task analysis. Taylor's ideas met with bitter resistance on the grounds that work controls alienate workers and displace master craftsmen. Despite the furor, Henry Ford adopted Taylor's principles for the assembly of automobiles. Later developments of total quality management (TQM) and business process reengineering (BPR) are considered direct descendents of Taylor's ideas or Fordism, as it came to be known.

These ideas about organizations covered both public and private enterprises. Classic organization theory emphasizes rationality and efficiency, the importance of specialization and coordination, and asserts that the principles of classical organization theory are universal, "irrespective of the purpose of the enterprise, the personnel comprising it, or any constitutional, political or social theory underlying its creation" (p. 49).[20] Writers in the 1920s and 1930s found attractive the idea of a strong chief executive vested with power and authority operating through an organization structure characterized by unity of command, hierarchical authority, and a strict division of labor. Dwight Waldo, a well-known public administration theorist, wrote "Democracy, if it were to survive, could not afford to ignore the lessons of centralization, hierarchy and discipline" (p. 200).[21]

Woodrow Wilson, then a college professor, suggested in an often quoted paper[22] that public administration should follow the model of business and that a government should establish executive authority, a controlling hierarchical organization, and have as its goal the achievement of the most reliable and efficient operations possible. The notion of the business model for government and nonprofit agencies, including libraries, with the primary goal of efficiency and an assumption of rationality continues today as a dominant theme in the study of organizations.

Classical theory of organization deals almost exclusively with the structure and design of the formal organization. The principles of classical theory are prescriptive for the rational structuring of organizations. Drawing upon early ideas from Fayol, the *functional* principle asserts that labor must be divided as the organization grows and that the division should follow clear areas of specialization. This leads to *departmentation* and the grouping of like activities into departments. The *scalar* principle deals with vertical growth in the chain of command through the dynamics of delegation of authority and responsibility. *Unity of command* ensures that a subordinate is accountable to one supervisor only. No gaps or overlaps in authority jurisdictions among the positions in the chain of command should exist. The resulting shape of the organization structure becomes the familiar pyramid.

The *line-staff* principle addresses the proper relationship between specialists employed for their technical expertise and the people with central decision-making authority ("the line"). The distinction between line and staff comes from military organizations and dates back to antiquity. The potential of conflicting authority between line and staff is recognized in classical organization theory and resolved by stipulating that the staff may advise and facilitate line work but may never command the line; only those with formal legal authority may do so. We see this principle in public administration theory as well. The line-staff division is most clearly seen in the emphasis by Wilson on the distinction between politics and politicians (here equivalent to the line of command) and public administration and administrators (equivalent to staff support in an advisory capacity).[23]

Span of control refers to the number of subordinates a manager can effectively manage. When people are added to an organization the result can either be a wide span of control and a relatively flat structure or a short span of control and a tall structure. Classical theory favored close supervision and recommended that a supervisor have responsibility for no more than four to six direct reports. The more various the work, the fewer people are to be supervised and conversely, the more similar the work of those supervised, the more people a supervisor can oversee.

Today, the structural approach to organizations is still the aspect to which most space in organization texts is dedicated. Probably the most well-known and thorough description of the structure of an organization comes from Mintzberg[24] who provides a comprehensive review summarizing the structural alternatives that managers can choose among. Galbraith[25] also described strategic choices in organization design. Mintzberg's scheme for describing organizational structure identifies five major components: *the operating core* where members perform the basic work of the organization, the *strategic* apex where the top positions reside, *the middle line* for those managers who link the apex to the core through supervision and implementation (hence the term "middle managers") and two types of staff units: *the technostructure*, where analysts work to standardize work, output, and skills, and *the support staff* who provide support to the organization outside the work flow of the operating core, for example the mail room, food service, public relations, the library, legal services, and the like. Often these latter units are considered the first candidates for outsourcing as they are not essential to the work of the organization.

According to Mintzberg, organizations establish structures to divide and then coordinate work within and among these five components through the use of four different structural design tools:

1. *Positions* through the use of job specializations, behavior formalization, training, and indoctrination.
2. *Superstructure* or departmentation through unit groupings based on knowledge and skill, function, time, output, clients, or place. Grouping choices can follow workflow among departments or join people working on common processes or one can group by scale (large units need their own functional categories); groupings can even be created to facilitate social relations, morale, and cohesiveness.
3. *Lateral linkages* through performance-control systems, action-planning systems, and liaison devices.
4. *Decision-making systems* through decentralization either vertically by pushing decision-making authority down or horizontally by spreading decision-making authority out to staff analysts, experts, and other individuals involved in the work of the organization.

Mintzberg also proposed a typology of five kinds of organization structures based on their choice of these design elements. The five structures begin with *simple structures* for new and small entrepreneurial organizations with vertical and horizontal centralization and coordination by direct supervision at the apex. Mintzberg identified two types of machine *bureaucracies* that are elaborations of simple structures that have evolved through growth, age and/or external control. These organizations employ a standardizing technostructure for work processes, experts, and staff specialists. *Public machine bureaucracies* are required to standardize their operations for political reasons. *Professional machine bureaucracies* are those organizations where professionals dominate the operating core, decentralization is general, and coordination is via standardization of skills. These machine bureaucracies may further evolve to divisionalized forms with product-oriented subunits each with its own manufacturing and marketing units. The final kind, Mintzberg calls the *ad-hocracy*. It is organic, innovation oriented, greatly emphasizes fluid communication and flexibility and is decentralized into design teams. The ad-hocracy may be seen as a forerunner of some of the newer networked and virtual organizational forms to be described in the last section of the paper.

To return to the historical thread, in the 1930s a reaction to the dominant classical organization theory was provoked by some experiments performed at the Hawthorne plant of the Western Electric Company that demonstrated the importance of human motivation on the expenditure of effort in an organization and shifted the attention of theorists away from the structure and design of the organization to a focus on the employees within and relationships among them. Workers were more than "hands" but had "hearts" (feelings and attitudes that affected productivity). Norms or implicit rules of work groups affected productivity.

Charles Barnard,[26] an American industrialist and telecommunications executive, developed a theory of management and organization that he called a cooperative system. He observed that human physical, psychological, and social limitations forced people to enter a "cooperative contract" in order to achieve goals that they could not accomplish alone. Having agreed to cooperate, the range of individual freedom to act autonomously was reduced and the domain of joint action was enlarged. Independence was sacrificed (or traded off) for greater material and social satisfactions from the cooperative effort. Barnard saw the problem of maintaining the cooperative spirit once the cooperative contract was formalized as the primary task of the manager. His ideas echo those of Mary Parker Follett.[17]

Barnard asserted that the manager needs to develop a deeper understanding of the organization and its employees by drawing upon the behavioral sciences. Organizational rationality, he argued, results from the manager's conscious effort to create a cooperative system by continually maintaining an equilibrium between organizational goals and individual employee goals. Barnard's one book, *The Functions of the Executive*,[26] remains an influential work calling the manager's attention to the importance of social and psychological factors in motivating workers. Motivation and the culture of the organizations continue to be major topics within organizational theory.

Some examples of often cited early theorists who write about motivation include Maslow,[27] Hertzberg,[28,29] McGregor,[30] and McClelland.[31] Maslow's theory of human needs and motives first advanced in the mid-1950s may be the best known motivation theory. People continue to find the theory appealing even though research validation is lacking. Maslow held that needs and motives fall into a hierarchy ranging from lower order to higher order needs. *Physiological needs* (food, shelter) are lower order, followed in ascending steps by *safety and security*, *love and belonging*, *status and self-esteem* and at the highest level, *self-actualization*. The needs at each level, according to Maslow, dominate until satisfied and then the individual can focus on the next level of need.

Herzberg's two-factor theory of motivation,[28] distinguishes between what he terms *hygiene factors* that are extrinsic and cause dissatisfaction, like working conditions and rewards, and *motivating factors* that are intrinsic and relate to interest and enjoyment of the work itself accompanied by a sense of growth and achievement. Other researchers argued that the methods used to develop Herzberg's theory (self-report of events leading to satisfaction or dissatisfaction) may have skewed the findings because of a social desirability effect in which the participants may have provided what they felt were the most socially acceptable responses.

McGregor[30] divided managers into two types: Theory X and Theory Y. The theory X manager sees workers as passive requiring management and motivation and direction; theory Y managers take advantage of higher order needs and build on the worker's capacity for self-motivation and self-direction. Many current writers on motivation theory focus on theory Y concerns and advocate for a human investment philosophy.

One of the most enduring and well-supported theories on motivation is David McClelland's[31] grouping of people into three categories depending on what is the primary motivating factor: the need for *achievement* (to master one's environment and to successfully accomplish tasks based on one's own abilities), the need for *power* and control over oneself and others, and the need for *affiliation* (the desire for friendly relations with others). McClelland concludes that the most effective managers develop a high motivation for power but with an altruistic orientation and a concern for group goals. He adds that too strong a need for friendship (affiliation) can hinder a manager.

Current emphasis on work motivation emphasizes process more than content. Expectancy theory, for example, asserts that an individual performs a mental calculation summing up the desirability to him/her of all the outcomes that might result from an action with each outcome weighted by the probability of its actually happening. The rational individual will do what he/she perceives will most likely result in the most good and the least bad.[32] Social learning theory blends behavioral ideas from operant conditioning (positive and negative reinforcements provided on some schedule either fixed or variable) with cognitive processes like goal-setting and a sense of "self-efficacy" or personal effectiveness.[33,34]

The approach to organizations that focuses on motivation and uses social psychology is often called the human relations approach. Effectiveness is measured by the commitment, cohesion, and good morale of the employees. A strong focus is placed on participation, conflict resolution, and consensus building. Teams are emphasized and there is a belief that involvement leads to commitment.[35]

Leadership and group processes in organization have also received substantial theoretic attention in the study of organizations. Studies on the traits of effective leaders at Ohio State in the 1950s led to the observation that leadership behavior was more important than any particular trait. Two dimensions of leadership behavior have been singled out: *consideration* or a concern for people and *initiating structure* or a concern for production. Blake and Mouton[36] developed a managerial grid based on these two dimensions as an approach to improving management practice. They urged managers to strive for high levels on both factors.

In reaction to too great an emphasis on the qualitative aspects of the work in organizations, Herbert Simon[37] attacked these principles as too vague and contradictory. Simon followed up with a book, *Administrative Behavior*[38] focused on decision-making. Simon observes that managers are less rational than theorists assume. Decisions are limited by the number of variables our brains can handle, the time available, and our reasoning powers so that decisions are made under conditions of bounded rationality. Simon invented the term "satisficing" to describe administrative decision-making behavior in selecting the best available alternative after a limited search using simple heuristics or rules of thumb. Simon's work on bounded rationality and satisficing challenged the assumptions of the rational man economic theory and won him the Nobel Prize in economics in 1978. Cyert and March[39] provided evidence in support of Simon's observations in a study of business firms reported in *A Behavioral Theory of the Firm*. March and Simon's 1958 *Organizations*[40] book provided a more elaborate conceptual framework with hypotheses about behavior in organizations, especially about an individual's decision to join an organization and to participate actively within it.

Using this conceptual framework, the Tavistock Institute in Great Britain began conducting research on "sociotechnical systems" emphasizing the close relationship between technical and social factors in the workplace.[41] This ushered in a new model of the organization as an open system. It drew heavily on general systems theory as described by biologist Ludwig von Bertalanffy.[42] He envisioned an overarching theory that would govern all living phenomena from molecules and cells up to individuals, groups, and society. To generalize across all these elements he referred to each phenomenon as a system with mutually interrelated parts that affect each other and depend upon the whole. Kenneth Boulding,[43] an economist, outlined a hierarchy of systems from the simplest that he called *frameworks* (e.g., lists, indexes, anatomies) through nine levels to the *transcendental* (metaphors and esthetics). His level 4 included living things which he called "open systems." These were characterized by input of energy, throughput of materials, reproduction, and self-maintenance.

Open systems theory became popular in part due to the rapidly changing environment of the mid-1960s. Two aspects were key. First, each different part of the organization was seen as interdependent on the other parts, and second, the external environment affects the way an organization performs.[44] The open systems perspective for organization theory was most fully developed by Katz and Kahn[45] who used general systems theory as a broad framework for conceptualizing the organization as an open system with inputs, throughputs, and outputs. They stated that the organization has *equifinality*, that is, the same outcome can be achieved by different means. *Negative feedback* enables the organization to adapt and innovate in order to continue to acquire needed external resources. The internal regulatory mechanisms within an organization must be at least as diverse and complex as the environment in which it operates ("the law of requisite variety" appropriated from cybernetics.[46] In analyzing the processes in the throughput, Katz and Kahn distinguish three major subsystems—maintenance, adaptive, and managerial. The vision of the organization as an open system adapting to a variety of influences and imperatives suggests that the "fit" between the organization and its environment and between the organization structure and its dominant technology is central.

Burns and Stalker[47] argue that effective open systems organizations must adapt their structure to contingencies. They propose that successful organizations are either *organic* or *mechanistic*, depending on the environment in which they function. Successful mechanistic organizations operate under stable conditions with a high need for consistency and specificity and are bureaucratic. Organic institutions are more fluid and able to adapt to rapidly changing environmental or technological conditions. In the organic organization, greater emphasis is placed on networking and lateral communication rather than on hierarchy; superiors act as facilitators.

Formulating a contingency theory of organization structure, Lawrence and Lorsch[11] studied U.S. firms in three different industries where they confronted varying degrees of uncertainty, complexity, and change. More uncertainty and turbulence in the surrounding environment meant more differentiated internal structures (different goals, time frames, and work cultures). The more differentiated firms, as one might expect, also had more elaborate structures for integrating diverse units. Organizations in more stable environments showed less differentiation and integration.

James Thompson[48] further developed the contingency perspective drawing on Herbert Simon's ideas about bounded rationality and consistency. Thompson presented his work as a series of propositions about how the rational organization will use hierarchy, structure, and buffering units to isolate the technical core in order to provide stable conditions for the work of the organization. He suggested that the organization will group subunits based on its need for information exchange during the work process. When organizations confront a shifting unstable environment, Thompson hypothesized they will adopt a more decentralized structure with fewer rules and procedures. A decadc later, Mintzberg[49] echoed this proposition with his assertion that the more complex the structure, the more decentralized the structure, all things being equal.

One school of thought with the central thesis that organizations are limited in their power to adapt to their environments is called "population ecology."[50] Here the emphasis is on groups of organizations that are "selected" for survival on the basis of adaptation and "fit" between their structure and the environmental characteristics. In this theoretical framework, the environment is the determinant of effectiveness which explains why organizations in similar environments have similar structures. As the environment changes, different structural variants become more fitting and previously selected characters are selected out. The organizational environment has a saturation point beyond which it cannot support more organizations, so claim Hannan and Freeman.[51]

Robert Quinn[52] attempted to combine four of the main streams of organization theory into what he called a "competing values" framework. The four streams he selected were scientific management from Taylor in the late 1800s, administrative theory from the 1920s with Fayol and Weber's ideal bureaucracy. The third stream was the human relations school from the Hawthorne studies of the late 1920s and 1930s and Barnard's writings. The fourth stream was the decision-making school described by March and Simon in the late 1950s. In the Quinn framework there is no "one best way" to manage in all situations but effective leadership varies according to the particular situation. The two key dimensions that predict the appropriate managerial style are first, the continuum between flexibility (innovation) and control (prediction, order, stability) and second, the continuum between emphasis on the organization (concern for productivity, systems) and emphasis on people (concern for people).

Another primary concept of organization theory is the organization life cycle. Every organization seems to pass through the same stages on the way to maturity. Haire[53] suggested that a biological metaphor could be used, (see above for biological metaphors for open systems and for sets of organizations selected for survival). The life-cycle approach has some key assumptions. There are distinct stages through which an organization progresses; the stages follow a consistent pattern and the transitions from stage to stage are predictable. Based on age, size of the organization, and growth rate for the industry, Greiner[54] proposed five phases, each stage having a specific management, style, and a dominant problem whose solution initiates the next stage. Phase one is marked by *creativity*. The organization is young and has an energetically committed leadership and resourceful employees, all dedicated to the mission. Communication is frequent and face-to-face. A leadership crisis emerges because the owner-founder's competence is often technical rather than managerial. Phase two is marked by *direction* under the leadership of a capable business manager who creates a functional structure and reporting requirements, puts a hierarchy in place, and hires specialists. As things become more formal and systematized, a crisis of autonomy emerges. Lower level employees feel encrusted in red tape and want more initiative. This leads to *decentralization and delegation* allowing the organization to expand in many directions; this, in turn leads to a crisis of control and the need for coordination. The fourth coordination phase uses *formal systems* to promote integration often through databases and formal planning procedures. A proliferation of systems leads to a crisis of red tape solved by a fifth *collaborative* phase in which project teams are initiated, problem-solving task forces are created, and more collaboration is encouraged. Social control, personal responsibility, and self-managed teams tend to replace formal control systems. Greiner suggests the crisis at this stage may be "psychological saturation" or burnout and provides a few strategies to deal with it. The main message is that no solution is permanent as the characteristics of the solution often breed new problems.

Other life-cycle models are similar suggesting that an organization is formed, grows, matures, and then declines or possibly undergoes radical change and renews itself. Organizational learning is one way for the organization to move away from inevitable decline. Argyris and Schōn[55] define learning as the ability to detect and correct errors, which they define as a mismatch between intention and outcomes. They identify two kinds: single-loop learning (improving strategies to reach a goal) and double-loop learning (questioning the fundamental assumptions and values of the organization). They define organization learning as a preference for double-loop learning and the will to implement it.

W. Richard Scott[56] in summing up the changes in the field or organization studies asserts that the introduction of open system models provided the impetus for a search out into the environment to identify the determinants of organizational structure. Contingency theory predicts that the variation in the complexity and uncertainty of an organization's environment leads to "best fit" organization structures. Resource dependence theory also focuses on adapting organizational structure to the environment. It emphasizes political as well as economic dependencies based on the fact that an organization must exchange resources in order to survive and that, in the exchanges, power differences arise. Thus, managers must not only adapt their organizational structure to the environment but must try to act on the environment reducing dependencies in order to see advantages in power relationships.[57]

Network theory has also emerged as a powerful explanatory tool and methodology to measure the relationships of organizations within a network.[58] The location of an organization within a network and the structure of the network affect behavior and decisions within an organization.[59] Hannan and Freeman[60] argue that researchers should shift attention from the individual organization to a set, or population, of organizations of the same type, because, according to these theorists, fundamental change affects all organizations of the same type in an approximately equal way. Just as the life cycle approach to organizations (described above) follows the birth, growth, maturity, and decline (or renewal in a new form) of a single organization, so in the population ecology approach groups of organizations of the same type are examined over long periods of time in a similar way from birth, growth, maturity, and decline (or renewal as a new type of organization).[61]

Research in organizations today focuses on a set of similar organizations and their resource exchange partners as the appropriate unit of analysis. This allows concentration on resource dependence relations and organizational strategy by looking at exchange partners, funding sources, competition, and regulations.[62]

The shift to open systems and the emphasis on looking at populations of organization within their exchange environment reveals that the boundaries of organizations have become less stable and fixed. Organizations now employ more temporary, part-time, and contract employees so that the concept of membership in an organization is less meaningful. Individual firms merge or split off components; they enter into alliances and partnerships creating new, often temporary organizations.

In the past organizations tended to absorb environmental challenges through adding workers, technologies, and technical expertise as well as incorporating sources of inputs and marketing and distribution systems, thus growing in size and scope over time.[63] Today organizations have moved in the opposite direction shedding personnel and units and contracting out functions that were formerly performed in-house.[64]

Miles and Snow[65] describe the dynamic network—a group of organizations, partnerships, and/or individuals who subcontract their services to a "broker" core that provides coordination, supervision, and control of a given project. The networked organization keeps human relations and overhead low while increasing responsiveness to customers. They describe the network organization as "delayered, highly flexible, and controlled by market mechanisms rather than administrative procedures" (p. 4).

Galbraith[66,67] contends that all organizations today need to develop lateral capability, that is, ways of coordinating different functions with other functions that need to communicate with throughout the organization. He describes three types of lateral linkages: across functions, across business units in a diversified corporation, and across countries and regions for global firms. Horizontal structures are sometimes called *process structures* while network structures are *organic* and increase lateral capability.

Horizontal organizations are flat structures with minimal layers of management and self-managed, multidisciplinary teams organized around a core process. The primary goal is customer satisfaction, which is attained by reducing the boundaries with suppliers and customers and by empowering employees. Teams are the central organizational building block and they manage themselves. Members are rewarded for skill acquisition and team performance. The benefits include lower management costs, more widely shared communication and decision-making and greater employee involvement. Decision-making is more rapid. The disadvantage is figuring out how to define the numerous processes in most organizations. The design is most appropriate in companies with short product life and development cycles where customer satisfaction is the goal and the environment is uncertain.

Four major design features of the new organizational forms are: 1) *vertical disaggregation*—major functions like finance, product design, and manufacturing are performed by independent organizations and tied together in a network; 2) *brokers*, who facilitate linking, locate potential partners, and coordinate the separate aspects; 3) *market mechanisms*—work is by contract and payments are based on performance; (4) *full-disclosure information systems*, which become important in mutually and instantaneously verifying individual contributions.

Walter Powell[68] asserts that today's economy resembles a Web and not a hierarchy and "to force technologies that enhance 'networking' into a pyramidal form serves only to constrain their effectiveness" (p. 502).[69] He argues that the impact of the rapid growth of new information and communication technologies is changing the way work is constituted and the way organizations are structured. One big change is the shift in conceptualizing work from *jobs* to *projects*. Jobs have been the standard way to package work for the last two centuries and are suitable for situations where the same tasks are done repeatedly. The emerging form of work organization is a team or work group charged with responsibility for a project. The activities of the team are coordinated by iterated goal-setting as the group members learn through monitoring the partial results of their work.[70] The project form of work organization integrates design and production and rewards productivity rather than seniority. Thus, according to Powell, the conception of work has changed from a focus on specific tasks carried out by individuals and constrained by rules and standard operating procedures to a collective effort conducted by teams with diverse skills and considerable discretion who are judged by results.

The change in the organization of work causes the rise of the networked organization where the firm is "an intricate latticework of collaborations with outsiders" (p. 507)[71] thus blurring the boundaries of individual organizations. Harrison[72] states that the new networked firms have four key components: 1) a core-ring structure in which there is a group of highly paid, highly skilled employees and everyone else is relegated to a lower cost periphery; 2) new information technology is used to coordinate widely scattered activities for just-in-time production; 3) extensive use is made of subcontracting, especially across national boundaries for lowest cost work; and 4) the firm uses various measures to attempt to gain greater commitment from the most expensive-to-replace employees. Powell et al.[73] examined the biotechnology and pharmaceutical industries and concluded that centrality is key and that a firm grows by becoming a player and not vice versa. Speed is also important. Brown and Duguid[74] point out that the core task of organizations today is to access knowledge rapidly and turn it into tangible products.

The not-for-profit organizational side has also been affected by these deep structural changes although perhaps less so. Public and private organizations remain different in goals and operation, so the movement in the direction of post-bureaucracy is more limited. Traditional bureaucracies continue to exist in government and not-for-profit agencies, but we also see an array of public-private partnerships with many services that are contracted out.

The new public management movement has encouraged a shift toward government by network and government by market.[75,76] Fiscal authority measures and efforts to improve public productivity led to experimenting with alternative service delivery mechanisms in the public sector, including contracting out and privatization. These ideas were captured in Osborne and Gaebler's 1992 book, *Reinventing Government*.[77] These writers provided 10 principles for what they called "public entrepreneurs" to bring about massive governmental reform. These principles are at the core of what is called the "New Public Management," and include introducing competition among public, private, and nongovernmental service providers, injecting the concept of profit into the public realm through charges and fees for public services, using information technology and improved communications systems to decentralize government and shaping the environment to create a market.

Reinvented government praises competition, flexibility, employer empowerment, and customer service. Central control mechanisms are reformed and performance measures introduced. An ethos of innovation, experimentation, and cross-agency work replaces the ethos, according to one proponent of reinventing government.[78] Critics of the government by network call it a "hollow state,"[79] in which a government agency relies on others (firms, nonprofits, or other government agencies) to deliver public services jointly and no one knows how to manage these networks.

In government by market, the government uses state power to create a market that fulfills the public purpose. For example, in order to control pollution, one might require polluters to pay for their right to pollute. As in the private sector, we see decentralization and empowerment of individual government agencies (now called "business units") to create own objectives. Through the use of information and communication technology, the staff is controlled less by regulation and more by market and customer measures. Hierarchy and rule-based controls are replaced by such market-type mechanisms as benchmarking for best practice, setting targets, and using service-level agreements.

Critics of the network and market governance models[80] predict that these newer organizational forms that are intended to make government more flexible and responsive and less hierarchical may have unintended dysfunctional consequences. Growth in centralized monitoring can lead to a decline in trust and collegiality. Bureaucracies represent some positive values, such as impartial conduct, due process, separation between public and private, between the role and the person. Some of the restructuring of work described above can lead to problems on the human relations front. As boundaries become more permeable, roles more flexible, there will be fewer career paths and rewards for loyalty and conformity to standardized organizational obligations. The "portfolio" worker becomes reliant on his/her own human capital and knowledge and exists outside the corporate hierarchies. Post-bureaucratic theorists need to consider alternative ways of holding organizations together. Presumably cultural and other indirect means of cooperation replace rapidly disappearing middle management. Even within the organization, units are compelled to serve as customers in simulation of market disciplines.

Denhardt and Denhardt[81] have proposed an alternative to the new public management which they call the new public service. This alternative draws on more humanistic traditions, such as interpretive theory (phenomenology), critical social theory, and postmodernism. In this view, the individual is not seen as a customer but rather as a citizen who looks beyond self-interest to the larger public interest. Even as the rhetoric speaks to new networked organizations with responsibility devolving to self-managed teams, there is a counter trend that appears equally strong. In the fast food and retail industries and in call centers operations incorporate classic organizational processes. The service encounter is standardized and employees must learn scripted language and behavior. They work in continued high surveillance via technology and customer monitoring. Even in organizations embracing knowledge management, networks, and communities of practice, there is parallel work in codification, storing, and distributing the commodified knowledge and many rules for using these databases.

What does the future hold for theories of organization? The purely rational approach has been softened and added to by an understanding that decisions are made on the basis of human emotions and intuitions.

It is best to see the forms assumed by contemporary organizations as a series of hybrids often with hierarchy concealed behind more complex forms of coordination and control.

REFERENCES

1. In *Organization Theory and Postmodern Thought*; Linstead, S., Ed.; Sage: Thousand Oaks, CA, 2004.
2. Daft, R.L. *Organization Theory and Design*, 8th Ed. Thomson, Southwestern: Mason, OH, 2004.
3. Hall, R.H.; Tolbert, P.S. *Organizations: Structures, Processes, and Outcomes*, 9th Ed. Prentice Hall: Englewood Cliffs, NJ, 2005.
4. Hodge, B.J.; Anthony, W.P.; Gales, L.M. *Organization Theory; A Strategic Approach*, 6th Ed. Prentice Hall: Englewood Cliffs, NJ, 2003.
5. Jaffee, D. *Organization Theory: Tension and Change*, McGraw-Hill: New York, 2001.
6. Jones, G.R. *Organizational Theory, Design and Change*, 5th Ed. Prentice Hall: Englewood Cliffs, NJ, 2007.

7. Robbins, S.P. *Organization Theory: Structures, Designs and Applications*, 3rd Ed. Prentice Hall: Englewood Cliffs, NJ, 1990.
8. Scott, W.R.; Davis, G.F. *Organizations and Organizing: Rational, Natural and Open Systems Perspectives*, Prentice Hall: Englewood Cliffs, NJ, 2007.
9. In *The Oxford Handbook of Organization Theory*; Tsoukas, H., Knudsen, C., Eds.; Oxford University Press: Oxford, 2003.
10. Hall, R.W. *Organizations: Structure and Process*, 8th Ed. Prentice Hall: Upper Saddle River, NJ, 2002.
11. Lawrence, P.R.; Lorsch, J.W. *Organizations and Environment; Managing Differentiation and Integration*, Harvard Business School: Boston, MA, 1967.
12. Smith, A. *An Inquiry into the Nature and Causes of the Wealth of Nations*, Modern Library: New York, 1776/1937.
13. Weber, M.; Parsons, T. *The Theory of Social and Economic Organization*, Free Press: New York, 1964.
14. Merton, R.K. Bureaucratic structure and personality. Soc. Forces **1940**, *18*, 560–568.
15. Thompson, V.A. *Modern Organization*, University of Alabama Press: Tuscaloosa, AL, 1977.
16. Fayol, H. *General and Industrial Management*, Putnam: London, 1916/1949; Reprinted and translated from 1916 *Administrative industrielle et géneále*.
17. Gulick, L. Notes on the theory of organization. In *Papers on the Science of Administration*; Gulick, L., Urwick, L., Eds.; Institute of Public Administration, Columbia University: New York, 1937.
18. Follett, M.P. *The New State: Group Organization the Solution of Popular Government*, Longmans, Green and Co.: New York, 1923.
19. Taylor, F.W. *The Principles of Scientific Management*, Harper: New York, 1911.
20. Urwick, L. Organization as a technical problem. In *Papers on the Science of Administration*; Gulick, L., Urwick, L., Eds.; Institute of Public Administration: New York, 1937.
21. Waldo, D. *The Administrative State*, Ronald Press: New York, 1948.
22. Wilson, W. The Study of Administration. Polit. Sci. Quart. **1887**, *2* (June), *Classics of Public Administration*; Reprinted in Shafritz, J.M.; Hyde, A.C., Eds.; Dorsey Press: Chicago, IL, 1987.
23. Peters, B.G. *The Future of Governing*, 2nd Rev. Ed. University Press of Kansas: Kansas, 2001.
24. Mintzberg, H. *Structure in Fives: Designing Effective Organizations*, Prentice Hall: Englewood Cliffs, NJ, 1993.
25. Galbraith, J.R. *Organization Design*, Addison Wesley: Reading, MA, 1977.
26. Barnard, C. *The Functions of the Executive*, Harvard University Press: Boston, MA, 1938.
27. Maslow, A.H. *Motivation and Personality*, Harper Collins: New York, 1954.
28. Herzberg, F. *Job Attitudes: Review of Research on Organizations*, Psychological Services of Pittsburgh: Pittsburgh, PA, 1957.
29. Herzberg, F. One more time: How do you motivate employees?. Harvard Bus. Rev. **1968**, *46*(1), 36–44.
30. McGregor, D. *The Human Side of Enterprise*, McGraw-Hill: New York, 1960.
31. McClelland, D.C. *The Achieving Society*, Free Press: New York, 1961.
32. Rainey, H.G. Work motivation. In *Handbook of Organizational Behavior*; Golembiewski, R.T., Ed.; Dekker: New York, 1993.
33. Vroom, V.H. *Work and Motivation*, Wiley: New York, 1964.
34. Bandura, A. *Social Learning Theory*, Prentice-Hall: Upper Saddle River, NJ, 1978.
35. Pinder, C.C. *Work Motivation: Theory, Issues, and Applications*, Scott Foresman: Glenview, IL, 1984.
36. Blake, R.R.; Mouton, J.S. *The Managerial Grid; The Key to Leadership Excellence*, Gulf Publishing: Houston, TX, 1964.
37. Simon, H. The proverbs of administration. Public Admin. Rev. **1946**, *6* (Winter), 53–67.
38. Simon, H. *Administrative Behavior; A Study of Decision-Making Processes in Administrative Organizations*, Free Press: New York, 1948.
39. Cyert, R.M.; March, J.G. *A Behavioral Theory of the Firm*, Prentice-Hall: Englewood Cliffs, NJ, 1963.
40. March, J.G.; Simon, H.A. *Organizations*, Wiley: New York, 1958.
41. Emery, F.E.; Trist, E.L. Socio-technical systems. In *Management Science; Models and Techniques*; Churchman, C.W., Verhulst, M., Eds.; Pergamon Press: Oxford, 1946; Vol. 2.
42. Von Bertalanffy, L. *General Systems Theory: Foundations, Development, Applications*, George Braziller: New York, 1968.
43. Boulding, K. General system theory—the skeleton of science. Manage. Sci. **1956**, *2*, 197–208.
44. Katz, D.; Kahn, R.L. Organizations and the Systems Concept. In *Perspectives for Behavior in Organizations*; Hackman, J. H., Lawler, E., Porter, L.W., Eds.; McGraw-Hill: New York, 1983; 98–99.
45. Katz, D.; Kahn, R.L. *The Social Psychology of Organizations*, Wiley: New York, 1978.
46. Wiener, N.; Rustom, M. *Cybernetics, Science, and Society; Ethics, Aesthetics, and Literary Criticism*, MIT Press: Cambridge, MA, 1985.
47. Burns, T.; Stalker, G.M. *The Management of Innovation*, Tavistock: London, 1961.
48. Thompson, J.D. *Organization in Action*, McGraw-Hill: New York, 1967.
49. Mintzberg, H. Organization design; Fashion or fit?. Harvard Bus. Rev. **1981**, *59*(1), 103–116.
50. Aldrich, H. *Organizations and Environments*, Stanford Business Books: Stanford, CA, 1979.
51. Hannan, M.; Freeman, J. The population ecology of organization. Am. J. Sociol. **1977**, *82* (March), 929–964.
52. Quinn, R.E. *Beyond Rational Management*, Jossey-Bass: San Francisco, CA, 1988.
53. Haire, M. Biological models and empirical histories in the growth of organizations. In *Modern Organization Theory*; Haire, M., Ed.; Wiley: New York, 1959; 272–306.
54. Greiner, L.E. Evolution and revolution as organizations grow. Harvard Bus. Rev. **1972**, *50*(4), 37–46.
55. Argyris, C.; Schōn, D. *Organizational Learning*, Addison-Wesley: Reading, MA, 1978.
56. Scott, W.R. Reflections on a half-century of organizational sociology. Ann. Rev. Sociol. **2004**, *3* (August), 1–21.

57. Pfeffer, J.; Salencik, G.R. *The External Control of Organizations; A Resource Dependence Perspective*, 2nd Ed. Stanford University Press: Stanford, CA, 2003.
58. White, H.C. *Identity and control; A structural theory of social action*, Princeton University Press: Princeton, NJ, 1992.
59. Powell, W.W.; Koput, K.W.; Smith-Doerr, L. Interorganizational collaboration and the locus of innovation: Networks of learning in biotechnology. Admin. Sci. Quart. **1996**, *41*, 116–145.
60. Hannan, M.; Freeman, J. *Organizational Ecology*, Harvard University Press: Cambridge, MA, 1989.
61. Kalleburg, A.L. *Organizations in America: Analyzing Their Structures and Human Resource Practices*, Sage: Thousand Oaks, CA, 1996.
62. In *The Twenty-First Century Firm: Changing Economic Organization in International Perspective*; DiMaggio, P., Ed.; Princeton University Press: Princeton, NJ, 2001.
63. Chandler, A.D., Jr. *The Visible Hand; The Managerial Revolution in American Business*, Harvard University Press: Cambridge, MA, 1977.
64. Carroll, G.R.; Hannan, M.T. *The Demography of Corporations and Industries*, Princeton University Press: Princeton, NJ, 1999.
65. Miles, R.E.; Snow, C.C. The new network firm: A spherical structure built on a human investment philosophy. Organ. Dyn. **1995**, *23*(4), 5–18.
66. Galbraith, J.R. *Competing with Flexible Lateral Organizations*, Addison, Wesley: Reading, MA, 1994.
67. Galbraith, J.R.; Downey, D.; Kates, A. *Designing Dynamic Organizations*, AMACOM: New York, 2002.
68. Powell, W.W. The capitalist firm in the twenty-first century: Emerging patterns in western enterprise. In *The Sociology of Organizations: An Anthology of Contemporary Theory and Research*; Wharton, A.S., Ed.; Roxbury Publishing Company: Los Angeles, CA, 2007; 495–515.
69. Powell, W.W. The capitalist firm in the twenty-first century; Emerging patterns in western enterprise. In *The Sociology of organizations; An Anthology of contemporary theory and research*; Wharton, A.S., Ed.; Roxbury Publishing Company: Los Angeles, CA, 2007; 502.
70. Sabel, C.F. Learning by monitoring: The institutions of economic development. In *The Handbook of Economic Sociology*; Smelser, N.J., Swedberg, R., Eds.; Princeton University Press: Princeton, NJ, 2005; 137–165.
71. Powell, W.W. The capitalist firm in the twenty-first century; Emerging patterns in western enterprise. In *The Sociology of organizations; An Anthology of contemporary theory and research*; Wharton, A.S., Ed.; Roxbury Publishing Company: Los Angeles, CA, 2007; 507.
72. Harrison, B. *Lean and Mean: The Changing Landscape of Corporate Power in the Age of Flexibility*, Basic Books: New York, 1994.
73. Powell, W.W. Learning from collaboration: Knowledge and networks in the biotechnology and pharmaceutical industries. Calif. Manage. Rev. **1998**, *40*(3), 228–240.
74. Brown, J.S.; Duguid, P. *The Social Life of Information*, Harvard Business School Press: Boston, MA, 2000.
75. In *The New Public Management*; McLaughlin, K., Osborne, S.P., Ferlie, E., Eds.; Routledge: London, 2002.
76. Kamarck, E.C. *The End of Government... as we Know It; Making Public Policy Work*, Rienner Publications: Boulder, CO, 2007.
77. Osborne, D.; Gaebler, T. *Reinventing Government*, Addison-Wesley: Reading, MA, 1992.
78. Pinkerton, J.P. *What Comes Next; The End of Big Government and the New Paradigm Ahead*, Hyperion Press: New York, 1995.
79. Milward, B.; Keith, G.P. Governing the hollow state. J. Public Admin. Theory **2000**, *10*(2), 359.
80. In *The Values of Bureaucracy*; du Gay, P., Ed.; Oxford University Press: Oxford, 2005.
81. Denhardt, J.V.; Denhardt, R.B. *The New Public Service*, M.E. Sharpe: Armonk, NY, 2003.

Organizational Culture

Gunilla Widén-Wulff
Information Studies, Åbo Akademi University, Åbo, Finland

Abstract

The literature covering organizational culture is broad and there are many angles and perspectives, different fields of study, schools of thoughts, and theories covering the subject. In this entry, organizational culture is first described through the historical influences with some general definitions and categorizations. Furthermore, organizational culture is described from an information and knowledge perspective, giving information resources a cultural dimension. Finally organizational culture is presented in the library context and some reflections on the assessment of organizational culture are given.

INTRODUCTION

Organizations may be described from many different points of view, depending on what one chooses to emphasize. Organizations can be viewed from environmental, cultural, or social perspectives. The physical structures and the technology of an organization can be focused and there are different metaphors to use as a starting point. In his 1986 book, Gareth Morgan introduced a set of metaphors to describe different perspectives of organizations (e.g., as machines, organisms, political systems, and cultures).[1] These images have been valuable tools when talking about complex phenomena within organizations. The image of organizations as cultures can be used as an umbrella concept when approaching organizations from cultural and symbolic points of view. Organizational culture is a way of understanding an organization in all its richness and variation (p. 2)[2] but is at the same time very complex and includes subcultures, information cultures, etc.[3] Organizations consist first of all of individuals shaping together a unique context. This means that every organization has its own unique organizational culture. The culture of an organization is a mix of values, thoughts, and traditions of the people in the organization (p. 5)[3] and the organizational culture sets the framework for what is expected and how things are normally done, and supports the organizational goals and aims.[4] Organizational cultures carry systems of meanings shared to various degrees that help the members of the organization to collaborate without having to define or contextualize their action constantly (p. 2).[2] Using the organizational culture metaphor brings forward useful information on intangible assets and explains informal behavior and activities of an organization. On the other hand, this metaphor generates a fairly general picture, covering many aspects, and might become vague in its meaning.

The literature covering organizational culture is broad and there are many angles and perspectives, different fields of study, schools of thoughts, and theories covering the subject. While there are a wide range on meanings and perspectives, this entry starts by briefly looking at the historical influences on the organizational culture perspective and thereafter describe the information and knowledge perspectives within the organizational culture context, and how organizational culture perspectives are used within Library and Information Science.

INFLUENCES ON ORGANIZATION CULTURE

The development of studying organizational culture has its origin in many different perspectives and fields of study. In the 1980s, a shift from the more static and system-oriented perspectives toward the perspective of organization's as cultures[2,5] began to emerge from success stories of Japanese companies as well as big companies in the United States.[2] The main themes of this cultural perspective are based on anthropological studies and symbolic aspects,[6] the sociological perspective, and aspects of social construction of reality,[7] and the management perspective looking at the social psychology of organizing.[8]

Through the anthropological perspective, studies on organizational culture have been inspired to look at language, rituals, and social structures.[9] The symbolic cultural theory identifies culture as a system of common meaning and symbols. For example, a company culture consists of values, norms, and symbols shared by the employees in the company. These are shaped within the company's process of surviving external challenges and demands while striving to keep its internal stability. These values and norms are actively shared by the members of the company, shaping the culture that creates continuity and behavioral structures.[10]

The influence of organizational sociology is very broad and direct. According to the sociocultural perspective,

Encyclopedia of Library and Information Sciences, Fourth Edition DOI: 10.1081/E-ELIS4-120043702

culture is a component in the social system and relational and structural perspectives are highlighted. Organizational life has been studied through numerous sociological studies with the organizational culture as the basis.[9] Many researchers have described the organization as a microsociety where the structures and systems are the same as those existing in the society.[11] The sociological perspective has also been combined with social psychology, which is connected to cognitive viewpoints and organizational climate. Representatives of the cognitive viewpoint are, e.g., Witkin and Goodenough (p. 57)[12] and according to this theory, culture is a result of common processes of thoughts. Studying events, behaviors, and feelings of the organizational culture may be pictured and it gives a possibility to reveal whether everyone has the same way of thinking or if different subcultures can be identified. The difference between the social and cognitive perspective to organizational culture lies in the question whether culture is something an organization has, or what an organization is.[5,13] If organizational culture is a possession or a definition of the organization has also managerial implications. While culture has long been a strategic tool in business organizations it is important to clarify which perspective is more important for the particular organization.

Apart from the many existing theories concerning cultural influence, there are also several dimensions and layers of the culture to take into account. Culture is not an isolated variable affecting the organization. On the contrary, it is always integrated into many other areas of organizational understanding.[10] A way of mapping the understanding of organizational culture is to use schemes and dimensions. Quite a useful model and definition is the one by Schein[14] who says that culture is "a pattern of basic assumptions—invented, discovered, or developed by a given group as it learns to cope with its problems of external adaptation and internal integration—that has worked well enough to be considered valid and, therefore, to be taught to new members as the correct way to perceive, think, and feel in relation to those problems" (p. 9).[14] He then distinguishes three levels of culture. The first and most visible level is artifacts and creations including the written and spoken language and the behavioral patterns of the members of a group or organization. The second level is described through values reflecting the sense of how to deal with problems and unpredicted action. Most values are conscious and serve as the normative function, guiding members in how to deal with situations. The third level, basic underlying assumptions, is reached when a solution to a problem has worked several times and it becomes the pattern of how to deal with it. When something becomes this taken for granted there is little variation within the cultural unit (p. 14–18).[14] According to Schein's definition the underlying assumptions are at the core of organizational culture and communicated through values and artifacts. This definition is further developed by Hatch[15] who integrates dynamics of symbols and processes into organizational culture. This is done in order to obtain a more holistic picture of how culture is formed by assumptions, values, artifacts, symbols, and the processes that link them.

Another important way of categorizing organizational culture is through the dimensions introduced by Hofstede (p. 188).[16] Through a large research project across 20 organizational units in Denmark and the Netherlands in the 1980s, Hofstede identified six independent dimensions of practices which play a role in determining the organization's culture:

- Process-oriented versus result-oriented;
- Job-oriented versus employee-oriented;
- Professional versus parochial;
- Open systems versus closed systems;
- Tightly versus loosely controlled; and
- Pragmatic versus normative.

Identifying where an organization stands in these dimensions makes it easier to manage the organizational culture.

A third example of defining different kinds of organization cultures is Wallach's[17] identification of bureaucratic, innovative, and supportive cultures. The bureaucratic culture is based on systematic thinking, clear division of responsibility and power, with business activities based on long traditions. The innovative culture is alert to changes and flexibility, whereas the supportive company culture strives to create a safe environment for the personnel where there is no need to be afraid of changes.

These kinds of categorizations, dimensions, and layers of organizational culture are important managerial tools. Identifying and understanding the organization's culture makes it easier to adjust the organizational activities to change and respond to challenges, or other kinds of activities to fit the particular organization and its members.

DEFINING INFORMATION CULTURE AS A PART OF THE ORGANIZATIONAL CULTURE

During the 1990s there was a shift in the literature on organizational culture toward dynamic perspectives that underlined the individuals in a social context[18–20] targeting aspects of learning and knowledge creation,[18,20,21] with a further focus on innovation[4] and performance. Managing information and knowledge as important assets became important perspectives especially in information science research (p. 88).[3] In the following section, the role of organizational culture is discussed from an information management (IM) and knowledge management (KM) perspective.

When the concept information culture is discussed in the literature, we are often reminded of the fact that every company has its unique information culture. There are several factors affecting the information culture and several layers of information behavior to take into account. Wilson[22] shows that individual information behavior is affected by psychological, social, and environmental variables, and consequently the organizational information behavior is a result of constant interaction between individuals in a social and cultural context. Knowledge is created through human interaction which means it is a cultural product. In organizations, one finds networks of people interacting which are not visible on the organizational chart. It is therefore important to recognize these networks in order to manage knowledge effectively.[23]

The function of information culture is about having access to information as a resource for reaching organizational aims. Information culture is responsible for unwritten and tacit behavior and fills the gap between what has officially happened and what really happened (p. 24).[24] Its function is also to maintain the balance in the social system and create meaning and contents. The information culture focuses more specifically on cooperation, communication, and information behavior in general in the organization. Information culture can be defined in many ways. On a general level information culture could be defined as "... a context in which needed information is communicated so that the company has the greatest possible use of internal and external information. This culture consists of individuals, traditions, systems, and values. The aim is to show how these factors together create the context in which the information is regarded as an information resource for fulfilling corporate goals" (p. 32).[25] Information culture is often also defined from a more specific information technology perspective: "a culture in which the value and utility of information in achieving operational and strategic success is recognized, where information forms the basis of organizational decision making and Information Technology is readily exploited as an enabler for effective Information Systems" (p. 94).[26]

Different kinds of information cultures provide different solutions for handling quick changes and challenges in the information intensive society. In a study of the information culture in Finnish insurance businesses it was shown that information, as a resource in an organization, should be supported by an open and active information culture. While there are different kinds of information cultures among the insurance businesses and they adapt differently, it is important to know what kind of culture exists in the company in order to adjust the information work and planning accordingly. Open, changeable companies, where integration of processes and functions are working well, can more easily shape an active information culture. That means that the planning of processes like production and marketing is strongly integrated and a company is able to create overall solutions for the whole company. Because of the integration of the processes, a more active communication between the units is created[25] with effective knowledge-sharing as a goal.[27] Actual information use in the workplace is shaped by the organizational culture[25,27–29] through its influence on the organizational values. Knowledge about existing information culture and information infrastructure enables a more effective implementation of IM strategies and makes KM an important part of cultural management.[30,31]

As mentioned earlier the categorization of organizational cultures is a usable managerial tool. This has also been shown in the context of integrating KM practices into the organization. Among others Leidner, Alavi, and Kayworth[32] have examined how different kinds of cultures influence the KM practices. For example, a bureaucratic culture[17] favors an initial process approach to KM. An innovative culture[17] enables groups in organizations to develop KM practices useful to their group. Cooperative cultures[33] enable more process-oriented and practice-oriented KM activities as well as creation of different communities of practice around KM, while individualistic cultures[33] inhibit sharing, ownership, and reuse of knowledge.

An important premise of the knowledge-based view of the firm is that organizations exist to create, transfer, and transform knowledge into competitive advantage.[34] When a KM culture is the goal it is important to make knowledge sharing a norm in the organization. In reaching a KM culture it is important to encourage people to work together effectively and collaborate.[3,6] When people collaborate they try to clarify each other's knowledge, which means that they interpret codified information and vague perceptions of implicit knowledge, which eventually will correspond to one's expectations (p. 222).[35,36] This means collaboration is not always a very straightforward process and when aiming at effective knowledge sharing it is important to create a culture of trust, respect, recognition, reward, and interactivity (90–92).[3] Cultural enablers and barriers to knowledge sharing are however often invisible and difficult to grasp. The visible dimensions of culture such as values and missions, structures and stories, should then be balanced with the invisible dimensions of culture such as unspoken sets of core values. This means that the awareness of cultural dimensions and widely held core values helps to link knowledge sharing efforts with the common interest. Visible connections between knowledge sharing and practical goals are then possible to make and the holistic view of persons working closely, techniques, and technology is important.[28,37,38] In the end, overcoming the cultural barriers to sharing information and knowledge has more to do with how one designs and implements one's management efforts into the culture than with changing the culture.[28]

ASSESSMENT OF ORGANIZATIONAL CULTURE

Cultural analysis includes a variety of possible perspectives in a multidimensional context. Alvesson (p. 189–190)[2] suggests some principles for the productive use of the culture concept.

- The cultural concept should be related to specific events, situations, actions, and processes.
- Culture should be treated as a network of meaning guiding feeling, thinking, and acting rather that an external force. Meanings should be viewed as processual and situated, not as a fixed essence.
- Cultural interpretation should be sensitive to variation and contradiction.
- It is also important to relate the understanding of culture to power and how power operates in social relations.

These principles can be realized both theoretically and empirically. Theoretical studies of organizational culture include both macro- and micro-perspectives. When looking at organizational culture from a macro-perspective, culture is usually interpreted as a consequence of the needs of the firm. Rites and ceremonies are studied and different types of cultures and subcultures are identified (e.g., productive, bureaucratic, professional, closed, open). The micro-perspective is more concerned with the psychological point of view, attitudes, and behavior. Usually the studies look beyond the surface, and culture may be assessed from a psychoanalytical perspective going deeper into meaning and structures.[9]

Empirical studies of organizational culture can mainly be divided into three categories: holistic studies (ethnographic, observations), semiotic or language studies (focusing on language and symbolism), and quantitative studies. Often organizational studies involve a combination of both qualitative and quantitative techniques mentioned above.[9] Several methods are often needed when the aim is to study company values, practices, artifacts, and core tasks, finding underlying assumptions existing in the company.[39]

ORGANIZATIONAL CULTURE IN THE LIBRARY CONTEXT

Organizational culture has also become important when studying libraries and how they can meet challenges and changes in today's society. Challenges in libraries are anchored in the demands that the information society shapes where especially the technical development has been of critical importance.[40] The main goal for a library is to bring clarity into the information chaos and help the information users to find and use relevant information at the right time and place. Apart from the traditional information resources management issues there are aspects of user orientation which have also become important for libraries to manage. Collaborative and information sharing skills are highlighted. For example, sharing knowledge is important where librarians share desk duty and consistent service is required.[41] There is a growing trend of using libraries both locally and virtually giving them great potential for collecting new forms of user-produced information. The libraries need to reconstruct their role from being a physical location of information and knowledge, where the information professionals have all the keys to knowledge organization, to an organization where the users actively can take part in shaping the library and their information provision. The development of new electronic services, digital libraries, and new learning environments affect the structures and organizational culture within the library, and put great demands on their management.[42–46]

Cultural studies in library organizations are challenging. As public organizations the libraries are different from, e.g., private as far as their external environment and expectations are concerned. Public organizations are often more structured and rule-oriented. This often means that public organizations are not often accustomed to change management or aware of the role of organizational culture in practice.[47] The role of organizational culture in the context of change management has been underlined in some empirical library studies.[42,48] Cultural studies in the library context have also discussed different organizational challenges for different kinds of libraries, e.g., the importance of a cross-cultural approach in the leadership of university libraries which are situated in large organizations with a variety of subcultures.[49] Promoting cultural change and cultural awareness through training and leading by example has been showed to be effective when it comes to public organizations[47] and is probably true in library context as well.

CONCLUSIONS

It has been stated that organizational culture is a multidimensional concept with many meanings and definitions. We have seen that culture is significant for how the organization functions, what is valued, what it is aiming for, how the aims are reached, and how capable the organization is to change. How people's knowledge is created, interacted with, and used is crucial in this process (p. 2).[2] The company culture plays an important role in the company's ability to handle changes (e.g., new information technology), but also on a broader perspective, i.e., in the handling of information as a resource.[50,51] Although the whole company culture is difficult to picture, it provides an easier way to analyze the information culture in order to focus on the role of information as a resource. Studying information culture is concluded to be a useful where aspects of organizational culture and IM are combined. In these studies the understanding of networks, motives for sharing, and learning aspects are important.[52] IM and KM is about structure and management of information in organizations in order to shape better circumstances for organizational activities (p. ix).[53] Today, most organizations are a mix of traditional, digital, local, and global arenas making the information activities a great challenge. Naturally, these circumstances are shaped by environmental and cultural factors and IM should be adjusted to both internal and external specialties.

Studies into organizational culture today emphasize the individuals in a social context focusing on aspects of learning and knowledge creation. This is important while organizations in general and libraries in particular, face challenges in their organizational structures because of the technical development as well as the virtual and digital development, resulting in new tasks and services. The organization is not solely a physical entity which gives new perspectives on cultural issues in the organization. It is important to address these kinds of studies in the future.

REFERENCES

1. Morgan, G. *Images of Organization*; Sage: Beverly Hills, CA, 1986.
2. Alvesson, M. *Understanding Organizational Culture*; Sage: London, 2002.
3. du Plessis, M. *The Impact of Organisational Culture on Knowledge Management*; Chandos Publishing: Oxford, 2006.
4. Lemon, M.; Sahota, P.S. Organizational culture as a knowledge repository for increased innovative capacity. Technovation **2004**, *24*, 483–498.
5. Sinclair, A. Approaches to organizational culture and ethics. J. Bus. Ethics **1993**, *12*, 63–73.
6. Geertz, C. *The Interpretation of Cultures*; Basic Books: New York, 1973.
7. Berger, P.L.; Luckmann, T. *The Social Construction of Reality: A Treatise in the Sociology of Knowledge*; Penguin: Harmondsworth, 1991.
8. Weick, K.E. *The Social Psychology of Organizing*; McGraw-Hill: New York, 1979.
9. Ouchi, W.G.; Wilkins, A.L. Organizational culture. Ann. Rev. Sociol. **1985**, *11*, 457–483.
10. Suomi, R. Information technology and corporate culture—The uneasy symbiosis. Liiketaloudellinen aikakauskirja **1992**, *4*(1), 27–41.
11. Allaire, Y.; Firsirotu, M.E. Theories of organizational culture. Organ. Stud. **1984**, *5*(3), 193–226.
12. Witkin, H.A.; Goodenough, D.R. *Cognitive Styles: Essence and Origins*; International University Press: New York, 1981; Psychological Issues.
13. Meek, V.L. Organizational culture: Origins and weaknesses. Organ. Stud. **1988**, *9*(4), 453–473.
14. Schein, E.H. *Organizational Culture and Leadership*; Jossey-Bass: San Francisco, CA, 1985.
15. Hatch, M.J. The dynamics of organizational culture. Acad. Manag. Rev. **1993**, *18*(4), 657–693.
16. Hofstede, G. *Cultures and Organizations: Intercultural Cooperation and Its Importance for Survival*; Harper Collins: London, 1994.
17. Wallach, E.J. Individuals and organizations: The cultural match. Train. Develop. J. **1983**, *37*, 28–36.
18. Nonaka, I.; Takeuchi, H. *The Knowledge-Creating Company*; Oxford University Press: New York, 1995.
19. Morgan, G. *Images of Organization*; Sage: Thousand Oaks, CA, 1997.
20. Senge, P. *The Fifth Discipline: The Art and Practice of Learning Organization*; Currency Doubleday: New York, 1994.
21. Argyris, C. *On Organizational Learning*, 2nd Ed.; Blackwell Publishing: Malden, MA, 2002.
22. Wilson, T.D. Information behaviour: An interdisciplinary perspective. Inform. Process. Manag. **1997**, *33*(4), 551–572.
23. Bonaventura, M. The benefits of a knowledge culture. Aslib Proc. **1997**, *49*(4), 82–89.
24. Ginman, M. *De intellektuella resurstransformationerna: informationens roll i företagsvärlden*; Åbo Akademis förlag: Åbo, 1987.
25. Widén-Wulff, G. Business information culture: A qualitative study of the information culture in the Finnish insurance industry. In *Introducing Information Management: An Information Research reader*; Maceviciute, E., Wilson, T. D., Eds.; Facet: London, 2005; 31–42.
26. Curry, A.; Moore, C. Assessing information culture—An exploratory model. Intern. J. Inform. Manag. **2003**, *23*, 91–110.
27. Widén-Wulff, G.; Suomi, R. Utilization of information resources for business success: The knowledge sharing model. Inform. Resour. Manag. J. **2007**, *20*(1), 46–67.
28. McDermott, R.; O'Dell, C. Overcoming cultural barriers to knowledge sharing. J. Knowl. Manag. **2001**, *5*(1), 76–85.
29. Widén-Wulff, G. Information as a resource in the insurance business: The impact of structures and processes on organisation information behaviour. New Rev. Inform. Behav. Res. **2003**, *4*, 79–94.
30. Alvesson, M.; Kärreman, D. Odd couple: Making sense of the curious concept of knowledge management. J. Manag. Stud. **2001**, *38*(7), 995–1018.
31. McDermott, R. Why information technology inspired but cannot deliver knowledge management. Calif. Manag. Rev. **1999**, *41*(4), 103–117.
32. Leidner, D.; Alavi, M.; Kayworth, T. The role of culture in Knowledge Management: A case study of two global firms. Int. J. e-Collaboration **2006**, *2*(1), 17–40.
33. Earley, P.C. Self or group? Cultural effects of training on self-efficacy and performance. Admin. Sci. Q. **1994**, *39*, 89–117.
34. Kogut, B.; Zander, U. Knowledge of the firm, combinative capabilities, and the replication of technology. Organ. Sci. **1992**, *3*, 383–397.
35. Lang, J.C. Social context and social capital as enablers of knowledge integration. J. Knowl. Manag. **2004**, *8*(3), 89–105.
36. Baumard, P. *Tacit Knowledge in Organizations*; Sage: London, 2001.
37. Bhatt, G.D. Knowledge management in organizations: Examining the interaction between technologies, techniques, and people. J. Knowl. Manag. **2001**, *5*(1), 68–75.
38. Park, H.; Ribière, V.; Schulte, W.D.J. Critical attributes of organizational culture that promote knowledge management technology implementation success. J. Knowl. Manag. **2004**, *8*(3), 106–117.

39. Reiman, T.; Oedewald, P. *The Assessment of Organisational Culture: A Methodological Study*; VTT: Helsinki, 2002; VTT tiedotteita—Research notes, Vol. 2140.
40. Vaagan, R.W. LIS education—Repackaging infopreneurs or promoting value-based skills? New Libr. World **2003**, *104*(4/5), 156–163.
41. Lister, L.F. Reference service in the context of library culture and collegiality. Ref. Libr. **2003**, (83/84), 33–39.
42. Davis, H.L.; Somerville, M.M. Learning our way to change: Improved institutional alignment. New Libr. World **2006**, *107*(3/4), 127–140.
43. Davies, C. Organizational influences on the university electronic library. Inform. Process. Manag. **1997**, *33*(3), 377–392.
44. Travica, B. Organizational aspects of the virtual/digital library. *Proceedings of the 60th Annual Meeting of the American Society for Information Science*, Washington, DC, 1997.
45. Tam, L.W.H.; Robertson, A.C. Managing change: Libraries and information services in the digital age. Libr. Manag. **2002**, *23*(8/9), 369–377.
46. Lakos, A.; Phipps, S. Creating a culture of assessment: A catalyst for organizational change. Libr. Acad. **2004**, *4*(3), 345–361.
47. Schraeder, M.; Tears, R.S.; Jordan, M.H. Organizational culture in public sector organizations. Leadersh. Organ. Dev. J. **2005**, *26*(6), 492–502.
48. van der Sar, E.; Heijne, M. Changing culture—The experience of TU Delft Library. *IATUL Annual Conference Proceedings*, Krakow: Poland, 2004. Available at http://www.iatul.org/doclibrary/public/conf_proceedings/2004/Mariazo-Heine.pdf.
49. Dewey, B.I. Leadership and university libraries: Building to scale at the interface of cultures. J. Libr. Admin. **2005**, *42*(1), 41–50.
50. Koenig, M. *Information Driven Management Concepts and Themes*; Saur: München, 1998.
51. Owens, I.; Wilson, T.D. Information and business performance: A study of information systems and services in high-performing companies. J. Libr. Inform. Sci. **1997**, *29* (1), 19–28.
52. Kirk, J. Information in organizations: Directions for information management. In *Introducing Information Management: An Information Research Reader*; Maceviciute, E., Wilson, T.D., Eds.; Facet: London, 2005; 3–17.
53. Choo, C.W. *The Knowing Organization: How Organizations Use Information to Construct Meaning, Create Knowledge and Make Decisions*; Oxford University Press: New York, 1998.

Organizational Learning

Erica Wiseman
Graduate School of Library and Information Studies, McGill University, Montreal, Quebec, Canada

Abstract
Organizational learning (OL) is a growing field that studies the processes through which new knowledge is learned and used in an organization. OL involves the leveraging of organizational knowledge assets and the continued development of an organization's knowledge base. While OL has been studied since the mid-1960s, there are many aspects of the field for which researchers have yet to reach a consensus. Most notable is the lack of commonly accepted definition of OL. Additional aspects that remain unresolved include the appropriate theoretical perspective from which to view OL and the identification of the most appropriate agent of learning. This entry begins with a discussion of the various definitions of OL followed by a brief history that highlights key OL researchers and key OL journals. The following section reviews cognitive, behavioral, and social constructivist perspectives of OL; the individual, group, and organizational levels as agents of learning; the commonly accepted components of the OL process; and the types of learning that occur in organizations. This entry concludes with a discussion of the value of OL and a map of the conceptual landscape of OL research.

INTRODUCTION

Organizational learning (OL) is an evolving field that studies the processes through which new knowledge is learned and used in an organization. OL involves the leveraging of organizational knowledge assets and the continued development of an organization's knowledge base.[1–3] Knowledge assets can be viewed as the inputs, outputs, and moderating factors that are involved in the knowledge creating process, the sum of which forms the organization's knowledge base. While OL has been studied since the mid-1960s, there are many aspects of the field for which researchers have yet to reach a consensus.[4] Most notable is the lack of a commonly accepted definition of OL. Additional aspects that remain unresolved include an appropriate theoretical perspective from which to view OL as well as which elements of the organization are the learning agents.

This entry begins with a discussion of the various definitions of OL. This section is followed by a brief history that overviews some key individuals in the field and the leading journals that publish OL research. The following section reviews cognitive, behavioral, and social constructivist perspectives of OL; the individual, group, and organizational levels as agents of learning; the commonly accepted components of the OL process; and the types of learning that occur in organizations. This entry concludes with a discussion of the value of OL and a map of the conceptual landscape of OL research.

DEFINING OL

While the field of OL has already received numerous and extensive reviews, there remains multiple conceptualizations and inconsistencies in the terminologies used to define OL.[5] Distinguishing OL from other processes such as knowledge sharing, knowledge transfer, change management, and the learning organization, which are each sometimes confused with OL, is an appropriate first step in defining it.

The scope of OL extends beyond the processes of knowledge sharing and knowledge transfer to include processes through which new knowledge is understood, remembered, and embedded in the organizational level in a way that it can be easily reused in the future.[6] In addition, OL is a continuous ongoing dynamic process, as opposed to a specific episode of organizational change, that focuses on managing ongoing collective learning processes. While on the surface the cognitive and/or behavioral changes that result from OL may appear to be punctuated or disjointed episodes of change, they are actually the result of fluid and continuous underlying OL processes.[7] In this way, OL differs from traditional change management initiatives, which are generally conceived of as a process of various stages of freezing, changing, and refreezing.[8]

Last, the two terms OL and the "learning organization" (a concept that was popularized by Peter Senge's 1990 book *The Fifth Discipline*) are often used interchangeably.[9,10] However, the two domains focus on different research goals. Research on the *learning organization*

Encyclopedia of Library and Information Sciences, Fourth Edition DOI: 10.1081/E-ELIS4-120043075

focuses on prescriptive and practice-oriented theory building that deals with specific applications of best practices that an organization *should* follow in order to become an organization that learns. In essence, the *learning organization* domain tries to identify *what* characterizes organizations that learn effectively and productively. This differs from the descriptive theories of OL which focus on describing the processes through which learning occurs in an organization.[11,12]

When looking at explicit definitions of OL, one sees that the field is still saturated with an array of partially overlapping and sometimes contrasting definitions. Below are a few sample definitions:

> ...the ability of the institution as a whole to discover errors and correct them, and to change the organization's knowledge base and values so as to generate new problem-solving skills and new capacity for action. Organizational learning refers specifically to a change in organizational knowledge and values.[13]

> process in the organization through which members of the dominant coalition develop, over time, the ability to discover when organizational changes are required and what changes can be undertaken which they believe will succeed.[14]

> the process of improving action through better knowledge and understanding.[15]

> the acquiring, sustaining, or changing of subjective meanings through the artifactual vehicles of their expression and transmission and the collective actions of the group.[16]

> a dynamic process, occurring over time and across levels, that involves a tension between new and existing learning.[7]

> organizational learning as the process of change in thought and action—both individual and shared—embedded in and affected by the institutions of the organization.[5]

A thorough review of these and other definitions of OL reveals a number of common themes:

Organizational learning is

- a cyclical process;
- a response to changes in an organization's environment;
- based on experience and observation;

that involves

- knowledge acquisition and distribution;
- collective interpretation and sensemaking;

and results in

- cognitive and/or behavioural changes;
- increased understanding of action–outcome relationships; and
- the embedding of new routines and/or practices.[7,13,14,17–19]

Based on these common themes, an overarching definition of OL can be provided as follows:

> Organizational learning is a process through which knowledge is developed and shared, changes in cognition and/or behaviour occur, and new routines and practices are embedded in the organization.

HISTORY

Early research on OL was initiated in the late 1950s and early 1960s by March and Simon, and Cyert and March respectively.[19,20] Together with researchers such as Argyris and Schön,[21] Levitt and March,[22] Simon[23] and Huber,[24] these early OL researchers focused specifically on either the cognitive or behavioral aspects of OL. Until the 1990s much of the literature used the metaphor of knowledge acquisition to understand the process of OL.[21–24] This metaphor suggested that learning in an organization was a process of employees acquiring new knowledge (cognition) and then acting upon it (behavioral).[25] Research that has followed the knowledge acquisition metaphor has typically focused on the individual, who is separate from the organization, as the agent of learning.[26]

Beginning in the 1990s, authors such as Brown and Duguid,[27] Lave and Wenger,[28] Cook and Yanow[16] and Gherardi and Nicolini,[29] began exploring a more participatory perspective in which learning was viewed as a social process.[16,25,27–29] Within this social perspective, authors began to integrate individual learning with learning processes on the group, organizational, and interorganizational levels of analysis.[26]

The literature on OL has grown considerably since the 1990s with notable increases in the new millennium. The growth of interest in OL has been attributed to the emergence of the knowledge economy in which knowledge, knowledge management, and OL are cited as key factors in creating and sustaining competitive advantage.[4,30] Academically, journals such as *Management Learning* and *The Learning Organization* focus specifically on OL and the learning organization (with crossover between the two). Other popular journals for OL research include *Academy of Management Journal*, *Academy of Management Review*, *Administrative Science Quarterly*, *Human Relations*, *Management Science*, *Organization Science*, *Organization Studies*, *Sloan Management Review*, and *Strategic Management Journal*.[31]

THEORETICAL FOUNDATIONS

Organizational learning has been explored from a number of theoretical foundations including the cognitive, behavioral, and social constructivist perspectives.

Cognitive

Cognitive perspectives of OL focus on changes in the mental states of the individual within the organization. These sorts of cognitive changes can manifest themselves as modifications to the individual's knowledge base, conceptual frameworks, mental models, beliefs, or interpretations and do not require any sort of behavioral change to qualify as learning.[15,32] The organizational cognitive perspective incorporates the individual cognitive perspective, which emphasizes the ability of the individual to absorb and organize knowledge for later reuse, and extends this process in order to apply it at the level of the organization as a whole. The focus of inquiry in this approach is centered on individuals and the changes in their understanding of organizational knowledge.

Behavioral

Behavioral perspectives on OL view changes in an individual's observable behavior as a consequence of a stimulus–response occurrence. From this perspective, the internal cognitive processes of the individual are largely ignored, and it is the observable changes in behavior that are equated with learning. Behavioral theories of OL are based on three fundamental observations: 1) Organizational behaviors are based on routines where action reflects a sense of legitimacy rather than an understanding of action outcomes; 2) Routines are based on past experience more than on anticipation of the future environment. These routines include rules, procedures, strategies, belief, frameworks, culture etc...; and 3) Organizations are target-oriented and behavior is based on success or failure in attaining specific targets.[15] The focus of inquiry in this approach is thus centered on changes in routines which manifest as behavioral changes.

Social Constructivist

Finally, the social constructivist perspective examines the individual within the context of a social system and purports that people build their understanding of the world through constant sense making within their social systems.[33] Consequently social constructivism moves away from strictly cognitive notions of information acquisition, storage, and retrieval as well as behavioral conceptions of change that are viewed as the simple consequence of stimuli and response. Instead, OL is viewed as a social process with multiple actors interacting within an organizational environment. As individuals interact and converse, new knowledge is created and a shared social understanding of the world emerges. As people develop a common language and a shared knowledge base, organizational members begin to learn from their interactions with one another.[34] Organizational theorists who favor this view emphasize the importance of relationships in creating and sustaining successful organizational practices.[35] Consequently, the focus of inquiry shifts to studying learning in the context of organization-based social practices.[36]

LEARNING AGENTS

One of the more controversial elements of OL is determining whether individuals, groups, or organizations are the agents of learning. Some of the literature suggests that only individuals are capable of learning and not the organizations as a whole. At the individual level of analysis, individual learning is said to lead to changes in beliefs, schemas, and behaviors in the organization. Others propose that learning occurs at the group level where the focus is on integrating knowledge from different parts of the organization. It is suggested that group learning leads to shared beliefs and concerted actions. A third group proposes that OL at occurs the organizational level, where learning is a process of institutionalizing knowledge and routines that have been learned.[7]

Individuals

Individuals may be studied as the main agent of OL from both the cognitive and behavioral perspectives. Within the cognitive perspective, there are two main schools of thought about individuals as the agents of learning. The first views OL as a particular kind of individual learning that is simply occurring in an organizational context. The second suggest that it is possible to use individual learning theories to understand OL based on the similar capacities and capabilities that exist between individuals and organizations.[4] In contrast, the behavioral perspective views changes in individual behavior as the mechanism that permits the organization to learn.

Numerous authors however, have found weaknesses with viewing the individual as the main agent of OL.[4,16] Their arguments suggest that OL can not be studied by looking exclusively at individual learning because there is no evidence to suggest that an organization can learn through the same cognitive processes as individuals do. Others argue that focusing on individual behavioral responses fails to sufficiently take into account the social aspects of learning that are so critical to OL. Argyris and Schön argued that individual learning is a necessary but insufficient condition for OL.[21] While individuals are undoubtedly agents of learning in organizations, OL is not just the cumulative result of individual learning events repeated or captured on a larger scale. Many authors[6,13,17,37] argue that individuals' learning processes and behaviors cannot be used as an appropriate metaphor for the processes that permit OL[6,13,17,37] because the storage of and access to knowledge in the individual and the organization differ in dramatic ways. Individuals have access to personal knowledge that is rarely, if ever, accessible to organizations, while organizations can retain knowledge that has been forgotten or lost to individuals.[13,38] Similarly, OL is not simply the sum of individual learning because behaviour at the collective and organizational levels is often significantly different from those of the individuals in an organization.[13,23,37,38] Mob mentality or "group think" are examples of how collectives and groups of individuals can act in a manner that differs radically from how individuals might act on their own.

As these reviewed shortcomings emerged in the research field, many theorists began to look for a more appropriate agent of OL.

Groups

Social constructivism focuses on groups as the agent of learning in organizations. From a group level perspective, it is suggested that group learning leads to the development of shared beliefs and concerted actions which then results in OL.[6,7] Organizational groups which may consist of such groups as formal teams, departmental divisions, or informal gatherings of colleagues who share similar professional interests, are viewed as the agent of OL from the social constructivist perspective. This latter type of group is generally referred to as "communities of practice" and are often perceived as the bridge between individual and OL.[28,34] From a group level perspective, it is suggested that group learning leads to the development of shared beliefs and concerted actions which then results in OL.[6,7] The emphasis in this perspective shifts from individual knowing, to collectively made decisions and agreements. The sensemaking processes that are critical to learning are no longer attributed solely to the individual but are recognized as fundamentally social in nature.[34] The researchers who focus on groups as the agents of learning in OL view OL as a social process that constructs and situates knowledge within work practices.

For some authors though, even the group level perspective is insufficient for understanding how learning occurs in the organization.

Organizational

More recently there appears to be an evolution in OL research towards viewing OL as a process that occurs on all three levels of an organization (individual, group, and organizational).[31] This view argues that learning at the organizational level is a process that can only occur once knowledge at the individual and group levels have been collectively recognized, accepted, and used as organizational knowledge. Learning is thought to begin with individuals' cognitive and behavioral changes, followed by socially constructed interpretations of these changes and ultimately maintained by organizational adoption.[39] At the organizational level, learning is embedded in the organization's systems, structures, procedures, and strategies which are then available to all employees on an ongoing basis,[40,41] through a process that is referred to as "institutionalization" by Crossan, Lane, and White.[7]

ORGANIZATIONAL LEARNING PROCESSES

A tension exists between learning by exploring new possibilities and learning by exploiting known certainties. Exploration involves searching for new information, experimenting, playing, taking chances, discovering, and innovating. It is a process that helps overcome organizational inertia and institutional rituals but that can be confronted with internal political resistance.[42] Exploitation, on the other hand, involves refining existing knowledge, improving upon practices and procedures, and increasing efficiency. Exploration feeds new knowledge into the organization's knowledge base and exploitation feeds existing knowledge from the organization's core back to the individuals and groups who make daily use of it.[43] OL cycles are affected by a trade-off between exploration and exploitation as the organization attempts to address both short- and long-term goals.[44,45] There are a number of models that map out the various processes of OL which suggests that, while there is no single definitive model of OL processes, an underlying understanding of the processes is emerging.[7,35,46,47] The following section provides an integration of these various models by adopting the terminology developed by Crossan, Lane, and White[7] to describe four main OL processes: intuition, interpretation, integration, and institutionalization.

Intuition

Organizational learning is triggered by intuition. Intuition occurs when individuals identify and acquire knowledge that has potential use in their current work environment through pattern recognition (exploitation), or through making novel connections and identifying new possibilities (exploration) in the way they do their job. In many ways, intuition is seen as a preconscious process, in that the knowledge is hard to describe in concrete terms and often occurs as a result of observation, participation, or socialization.[7,46]

Interpretation

Interpretation is the process through which individuals verbalize or put into action their own intuitions. It is also the phase in which individuals develop personal cognitive maps of their knowledge. Metaphors, which describe a relatively unknown or unfamiliar domain in more familiar terms, are often used to help individuals interpret and share their insights and ideas with others. Finding the right words to describe intuitions is a critical part of the interpretation process. Interpretation involves individuals interacting with other organizational members in an effort to make sense of their own intuitions. Viewed in this way, interpretation can be seen as a social process that involves sensemaking activities between organizational members. At this stage, however, the process is still focused on making sense of the individual's ideas. Other authors have also used the terms exchange, distribution, or externalization to describe this process.[7,24,35,46,47]

Integration

As the understanding and value of the knowledge extends beyond the individual and is shared among group members, the process is said to be one of integration. Integration involves the collective development of a shared understanding of new ideas and of how to put them into action. This process occurs and has impacts on the group level in the organization. Through continued conversations, group members engage in mutually adjusting each other's understanding of new knowledge and through this, an agreed upon way of making use of the knowledge emerges. This new knowledge can impact how the group works in ways that are often different than those prescribed in the organization's standard operating procedures, rules, or guidelines.

This process has also been called combination, which is a process in which new knowledge is combined with existing knowledge; and objectification, which is the process in which knowledge; becomes common property and is accepted as being reliable, valuable, and useful by the organization's members.[7,35,46,47]

Institutionalization

Institutionalization involves a deliberate effort to embed knowledge at the organizational level so that it may persist and be available for future use. This new knowledge then becomes a norm or custom of the organization and can at that point, be viewed as having been added to the organizational knowledge base. It is through institutionalization that individual and group learning is leveraged and capitalized on in an organization.[7] In essence, institutionalization is the process through which knowledge that has been intuited by individuals, and interpreted and integrated on a group level, is finally internalized into the organization's systems, routines, structures, and culture and consequently, can be seen as evidence of OL. Transfield and Smith explained that "this embedding, or institutionalizing of new ways of working, is complete when old tacit routines are removed and replaced with new taken-for-granted ways of working".[48] Institutionalization is the process that distinguishes OL from individual and group learning as it is through institutionalization that ideas are transformed into institutions of the organization, which are then available to all employees on an ongoing basis.[40,47] Fig. 1 shows how these four processes of OL occur at the individual, group, and organizational levels.

These processes are affected by internal politics and the organization's culture. In order to take into account the political nature of organizations, some authors[40,42] have explored the influence that power has on OL processes. It has been argued that new ideas only have the opportunity to become institutionalized when they are championed by key players in the organization and when coalitions are formed to support the interpretation and continued development of the ideas. These can be seen as political activities in that champions will only support particular ideas at particular moments in time and coalitions will be instrumental in gaining resource allocation.[42] These champions and coalitions are also instrumental in the institutionalization of new knowledge by using their power to get senior management and the rest of the organization in line with the new knowledge. Power may be used to influence people to accept a chosen interpretation, to drive particular ideas to the top of the organizational agenda, to restrict alternate options, and to socialize and train organizational members into the new way of thinking or behaving.[40]

While these processes and the role of politics give the impression that OL is a particularly structured process, it is also appropriate to see it as a fluid and dynamic process that is greatly influenced by the organization's culture, identity, and ability to be self-reflective. An organization's culture, which includes its beliefs, values, and philosophies along with the artifacts and means through which they are transmitted across the organization, influences the way knowledge is interpreted, who will champion it, and when it can be integrated and institutionalized in the organization.[16,49] Organizations with rigid cultures struggle in the exploration phase of learning because they cannot see beyond their existing organizational configuration, or

	Individual	Group	Organizational	
Individual	Intuiting	Interpreting		
Group			Integrating	
Organizational				Institutionalizing

Fig. 1 4I framework of organizational learning.
Source: Adapted from Crossan et al.[7]

organizational identity, to envision ways to integrate new knowledge[50] To overcome such challenges, organizations need to be more actively reflexive and engage in improvisational learning and working. Improvisation has been used as a technique to support OL as it teaches the organization to quickly and dynamically interpret and process vague and incomplete information and to recombine past knowledge and experiences to create new solutions and directions for action.[49,51] Schön[52] refers to the activity of reflecting on past knowledge while acting as "reflection-in-action". As organizations embrace these learning behaviors, their capacity to identify new potential strategic directions, to engage in transformative learning, and to adapt their organizational culture and identity increases.[50]

TYPES OF OL

The processes of OL can be further characterized by three types of learning; single loop, double loop, and deutero-learning.[21]

Single-Loop Learning

Single-loop learning involves the detection and correction of errors in routine actions. When single-loop learning occurs, the actions and rules of the organization may change, but the values and norms behind the actions are not questioned.[53] In this type of OL, the focus is on improving specific techniques, routines, or work processes. New ways of carrying out routines can reach the organizational level (become institutionalized) without requiring any changes in organizational strategies, culture, or identity.

Double-Loop Learning

Double-loop learning occurs when the underlying causes of errors or poor performance are analyzed and altered.[54] The focus in this type of learning is on the adjustment of cultural values, norms, and strategies rather than specific activities and behaviors. Resulting changes in routines are thus based on new organizational goals and perspectives.[53] The results of double-loop learning may include the development of new organizational skills, cognitive frameworks, interpretive schemes and the unlearning of earlier, ineffective behaviors.[15]

Deutero-Learning

Deutero-learning is a "meta" process in which the learner reflects on his own learning (either single- or double-loop learning). From an organizational standpoint this involves reflecting on the way the organization thinks about and approaches learning opportunities. This type of learning can have an influence on the learning processes and culture that is already in place in an organization. Deutero-learning is actually less knowledge and skill dependent than double-loop learning as it can be a simple reflection on single-loop issues.[53]

VALUE OF OL

Organizational learning is an essential activity for organizations in a knowledge-based economy. The strategic management of OL and knowledge assets is most successful when these activities are linked to the organization's strategies, goals, and practices.[55,56] When organizations focus their learning on strategic issues, these issues will influence the firm's perception and interpretation of knowledge and this knowledge will in turn influence, and often renew, the organization's strategies, goals, and practices.[5] When learning is effectuated on the organizational level, the basic assumptions underlying organizational knowledge are reframed and can lead to changes in the strategic orientation of the organization.[57] Linking OL with strategic goals helps build the organization's ability to both discover new knowledge (exploration) and make the most out of the knowledge that it already has (exploitation).[5,56]

Organizational learning is also at the heart of an organization's ability to adapt and respond to a changing environment and can ultimately lead to improved business performance. Research has found that OL can enhance the survival and effectiveness of acquisitions, increase innovation, and facilitate the implementation of new information systems and business process reengineering.[31] OL has also been shown to reduce costs and to contribute to organizational success by reducing the number of repeated tasks and preventing individuals from repeating the mistakes of others.[58–60]

Organizational learning also contributes to sustainable competitive advantage by enabling organizations to learn faster and to deploy their knowledge assets more quickly than their competitors.[2] Furthermore, an organization's core competencies are typically the result of its collective and continuous learning and the ability to manage the knowledge assets that result from this learning.[2,61] Managing these processes and assets allow organizations to achieve greater flexibility and adaptability, and through that, increased competitive advantage.[17]

CONCLUSION

Organizational learning is a complex process that involves multiple learning agents, subprocesses, and types of learning and can be viewed from a variety of theoretical perspectives. The growing tendency in OL research is to integrate as many of these components as possible into a

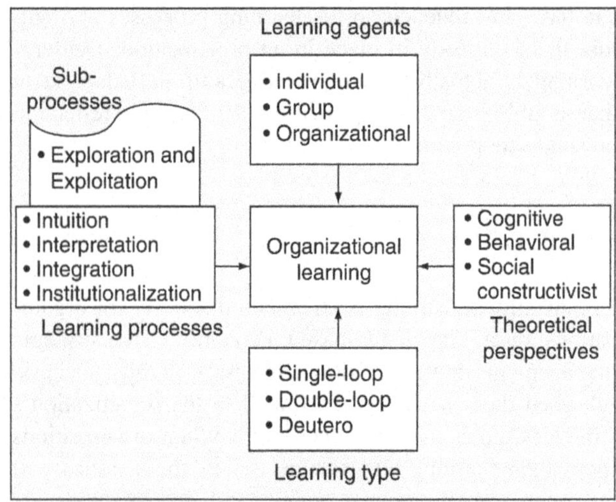

Fig. 2 A conceptual landscape of organizational learning.
Source: Reproduced by permission of Oxford University Press. From figure 3.2 in "A Conceptual Framework for the Management of Organizational Learning" from Chapter by Pawlowsky et al.[47]

single framework. This implies integrating cognitive, behavioral, and social perspectives on learning to develop comprehensive models that explore the OL process as a cycle that affects, and functions differently, on all levels of the organizations. The following diagram (Fig. 2) represents a mapping of this conceptual OL landscape, highlights components that are critical for a more in-depth understanding of OL and can serve as a foundation for further research and exploration in this area.

An improved understanding of these key aspects of OL is crucial for more effective strategic management of learning at the organizational level.

REFERENCES

1. Bogdanowicz, M.S.; Bailey, E.K. The value of knowledge and the values of the new knowledge worker: Generation X in the new economy. J. Eur. Ind. Train. **2002**, *26*, 125–129.
2. Pemberton, J.D.; Stonehouse, G.H. Organisational learning and knowledge assets—An essential partnership. Learn. Organ. **2000**, *7*, 184–193.
3. Nonaka, I.; Toyama, R.; Nagata, A. A firm as a knowledge creating entity: A new perspective on the theory of the firm. Ind. Corporate Change **2000**, *9*, 1–20.
4. Chiva, R.; Alegre, J. Organizational learning and organizational knowledge: Towards the integration of two approaches. Manage. Learn. **2005**, *36*(1), 49–68.
5. Dusya, V.; Crossan, M. Strategic leadership and organizational learning. Acad. Manage. Rev. **2004**, *29*(2), 222–240.
6. Chonko, L.B.; Dubinsky, A.J.; Jones, E.; Roberts, J.A. Organizational and individual learning in the sales force: An agenda for sales research. J. Bus. Res. **2003**, *56*(12), 935–946.
7. Crossan, M.; Lane, H.W.; White, R.E. An organizational learning framework: From intuition to institution. Acad. Manage. Rev. **1999**, *24*(3), 522–537.
8. Weick, K.E.; Quinn, R.E. Organizational change and development. Ann. Rev. Psychol. **1999**, *50*, 361–386.
9. Senge, P. *The Fifth Discipline—The Art and Practice of the Learning Organization*; Currency Doubleday: New York, 1990.
10. Dimitriades, Z.S. Creating strategic capabilities: Organizational learning and knowledge management in the new economy. Eur. Bus. Rev. **2005**, *17*(4), 314.
11. Yeo, R.K. Revisiting the roots of learning organization: A synthesis of the learning organization literature. Learn. Organ. **2005**, *12*(4), 368–382.
12. Tsang, E.W.K. Organizational learning and the learning organization: A dichotomy between descriptive and prescriptive research. Human Relat. **1997**, *50*(1), 73–89.
13. Probst, G.; Buchel, B. *Organizational Learning: The Competitive Advantage of the Future*; Prentice Hall: New York, 1997.
14. Duncan, R.; Weiss, A. Organizational learning: Implications for organizational design. Res. Organ. Behav. **1979**, *1*, 75–123.
15. Fiol, C.M.; Lyles, M.A. Organizational learning. Acad. Manage. Rev. **1985**, *10*(4), 803–813.
16. Cook, S.; Yanow, D. Culture and organizational learning. J. Manage. Inquiry **1993**, *2*, 373–390.
17. Edmondson, A.; Moingeon, B. When to learn how and when to learn why: Appropriate organizational learning processes as a source of competitive advantage. In *Organzational Learning and Competitive Advantage*; Moingeon, B., Edmondson, A., Eds.; Sage Publications: London, U.K., 1996; 17–37.
18. March, J.G.; Sproull, L.S.; Tamuz, M. Learning from samples of one or fewer. In *Organizational Learning*; Cohen, M.D., Sproull, L.S., Eds.; Sage: Thousand Oaks, CA, 1996; 1–19.
19. Cyert, R.M.; March, J.G. *A Behavioral Theory of the Firm*; Prentice-Hall: Englewood Cliffs, NJ, 1963.
20. March, J.; Simon, H. *Organizations;* Wiley: New York, 1958.
21. Argyris, C.; Schön, D.A. *Organizational Learning: A Theory of Action Perspective*; Addison-Wesley: Reading, MA, 1978.
22. Levitt, B.; March, J.G. Organizational learning. Ann. Rev. Sociol. **1988**, *14*, 319–340.
23. Simon, H. Bounded rationality and organizational learning. Organ. Sci. **1991**, *2*(1), 125–134.
24. Huber, G.P. Organizational learning: The contributing processes and the literatures. Organ. Sci. **1991**, *2*(1), 88–115.
25. Elkjaer, B. Organizational learning with a pragmatic slant. Int. J. Lifelong Educ. **2003**, *22*(5), 481–494.
26. Berson, Y.; Nemanich, L.A.; Waldman, D.A.; Gavin, B.M.; Keller, R.T. Leadership and organizational learning: A multiple level perspective. Leadership Quart. **2007**, *17*, 577–594.
27. Brown, J.S.; Duguid, P. Organizational learning and communities of practice: Toward a unified view of working, learning, and innovation. Organ. Sci. **1991**, *2*(1), 40–57.
28. Lave, J.; Wenger, E. *Situated Learning: Legitimate Peripheral Participation*; Cambridge University Press: New York, 1991.

29. Gherardi, S.; Nicolini, D. The organizational learning of safety in communities of practice. J. Manage. Inquiry **2000**, *9*(1), 7–18.
30. Berends, H.; Boersma, K.; Weggeman, M. The structuration of organizational learning. Human Relat. **2003**, *56*(9), 1035–1056.
31. Bapuji, H.; Crossan, M. From questions to answers: Reviewing organizational learning research. Manage. Learn. **2004**, *35*(4), 397–417.
32. Leroy, F.; Ramanantsoa, B. The cognitive and behavioral dimensions of organizational learning in a merger: An empirical study. J. Manage. Stud. **1997**, *34*(6), 871–894.
33. Easterby-Smith, M.; Crossan, M.; Nicolini, D. Organizational learning debates: Past, present and future. J. Manage. Stud. **2000**, *37*(6), 783–796.
34. Huysman, M.H. Organizational learning and communities of practice, a social constructivist perspective. Proceedings of the Third European Conference on organizational Knowledge, Learning and Capabilities, 2002; 1–16.
35. Huysman, M.; De Wit, D. *Knowledge Sharing in Practice*; Kluwer Academic Publishers: Dordrecht, the Netherlands, 2002.
36. Henriksson, K. *The Collective Dynamics of Organizational Learning: On Plurality and Multi-social Structuring*; Lund University Press: Lund, Sweden, 1999.
37. Bell, S.J.; Whitwell, G.J.; Lukas, B.A. Schools of thought in organizational learning 173. J. Acad. Market. Sci. **2002**, *30*(1), 70–86.
38. Spender, J.C. Organizational knowledge, learning and memory: Three concepts in search of a theory. J. Organ. Change Manage. **1996**, *9*(1), 63–78.
39. Dyck, B.; Starke, F.A.; Mischke, G.A.; Mauws, M. Learning to build a car: An empirical investigation of organizational learning. J. Manage. Stud. **2005**, *42*(2), 387–416.
40. Lawrence, T.B.; Mauws, M.K.; Dyck, B.; Kleysen, R.F. The politics of organizational learning: Integrating power into the 4I framework. Acad. Manage. Rev. **2005**, *30*(1), 180–191.
41. Crossan, M.; Bedrow, I. Organizational learning and strategic renewal. Strategic Manage. J. **2003**, *24*(11), 1087–1105.
42. Kleysen, R.F.; Dyck, B. Cumulating knowledge: An elaboration and extension of Crossan, Lane & White's framework for organizational learning. In *Organizational Learning and Knowledge Management: New Directions*, 4th International Conference Proceedings; Crossan, M., Olivera, F., Eds.; Richard Ivey School of Business: London, 2001; 383–394.
43. Lunnan, R.; Barth, T. Managing the exploration vs. exploitation dilemma in transnational "bridging teams". J. World Bus. **2003**, *38*, 110–126.
44. March, J. Exploration and exploitation in organizational learning. Organ. Sci. **1991**, *2*(1), 71–87.
45. Holmqvist, M. A dynamic model of intra- and interorganizational learning. Organ. Stud. **2003**, *24*(1), 95–123.
46. Nonaka, I.; Takeuchi, H. *The Knowledge-Creating Company 56*; Oxford University Press: New York, 1995.
47. Pawlowsky, P. The treatment of organizational learning in management science. In *Handbook of Organizational Learning and Knowledge*; Dierkes, M., Berthoin Antal, A., Child, J., Nonaka, I., Eds.; Oxford University Press: New York, 2001; 61–88.
48. Transfield, D.; Smith, S. The strategic regeneration of manufacturing by changing routines. Int. J. Oper. Prod. Manage. **1998**, *18*(2), 114–129.
49. Akgun, A.E.; Lynn, G.S.; Byrne, J.C. Organizational learning: A socio-cognitive framework. Human Relat. **2003**, *56* (7), 839–868.
50. Brown, A.D.; Starkey, K. Organizational identity and learning: A psychodynamic perspective. Acad. Manage. Rev. **2000**, *25*(1), 102–120.
51. Barrett, F.J. Coda: Creativity and improvisation in jazz and organizations: Implications for organizational learning. Organ. Sci. **1998**, *9*(5), 605–622.
52. Schön, D.A. *The Reflective Practitioner*; Basic Books: New York, 1983.
53. Argyris, C. A life full of learning. Organ. Stud. **2003**, *24*(7), 1178–1192.
54. Edmondson, A.C. The local and variegated nature of learning in organizations: A group-level perspective. Organ. Sci. **2002**, *13*(2), 128.
55. Teece, D.J.; Pisano, G.; Shuen, A. Dynamic capabilities and strategic management. Strategic Manage. J. **1997**, *18*(7), 509–533.
56. Thomas, J.B.; Sussman, S.W.; Henderson, J.C. Understanding "strategic learning": Linking organizational learning, knowledge management, and sensemaking. Organ. Sci. **2001**, *12*(3), 331–345.
57. Kuwanda, K. Strategic learning: The continuous side of discontinuous strategic change. Organ. Sci. **1998**, *9*, 719–736.
58. Marquardt, M.J. *The Learning Organization: Mastering the 5 Elements for Corporate Learning*; Davies-Black Publishing: Palo Alto, CA, 2002.
59. Husted, K.; Michailova, S. Diagnosing and fighting knowledge-sharing hostility. Organ. Dyn. **2002**, *31*(1), 60–73.
60. Ladd, D.A.; Ward, M.A. An investigation of environmental factors influencing knowledge transfer. J. Knowl. Manage. Practice **2002**, *3*(38). Available at http://www.tlainc.com/articl38.htm-.
61. Prahalad, C.K.; Hamel, G. The core competence of the corporation. Harvard Bus. Rev. **1990**, *68*(3), 79–91.

BIBLIOGRAPHY

1. Cohen, M., Sproull, L., Eds. *Organizational Learning*; Sage Publications: Thousand Oaks, CA, 1996.
2. Dierkes, M., Antal, A.B., Child, J., Nonaka, I., Eds. *Handbook of Organizational Learning and Knowledge*; Oxford University Press: Oxford, U.K., 2001.
3. Easterby-Smith, M., Lyles, M., Eds. *The Blackwell Handbook of Organizational Learning and Knowledge Management*; Blackwell Publishing: Oxford, U.K., 2005.

Organizational Memory

Maureen L. Hammer
Knowledge Management, Batelle Memorial Institute, Charlottesville, Virginia, U.S.A.

Abstract

Organizational memory (OM) has to do with an organization's ability to access and use the knowledge, expertise, and experience gained by its staff for the purpose of meeting its ongoing business needs. Across the literature, there is consensus that the primary repository of OM is the staff that carries out the work of that organization. This is increasingly important given the large wave of retirements expected across the private and public sectors in the near future as well as a change in employment tenure as workers increasingly change jobs every 3–5 year. This entry provides a high-level review of OM.

How can an organization remember? what does that mean? and why should we care? Organizational memory (OM) is about the accrual and preservation of knowledge held and shared by its employees paired with the organization's history and culture. Together, these contribute to its uniqueness, all of which leads to competitiveness and improved decision-making. Evidence of it may also be found in the organization's documents, systems, and processes. OM may be lost through resignations, retirements, and reorganizations, as well as through deliberate or unconscious suppression. Memory loss can be expensive as without the benefit of prior knowledge and experience, organizations may duplicate work and have to relearn lessons.[1] This entry provides a high-level review of OM. References at the end of this entry can be consulted by the reader wanting more detail or to further explore specific issues raised in the text.

As long ago as 1959, Penrose, in *The Theory of the Growth of the Firm*, recognized that an organization functions as a knowledge repository (as cited in Bontis).[2] What goes into the repository is the tacit (unwritten and uncaptured) knowledge of its employees. Tacit knowledge influences the attitudes of individuals and is a knowing that informs the individual about how to best accomplish a task; it is produced by the individual and changed by experience.[3,4] The knowledge is dynamic and can change frequently and take on new meaning as a result of new experiences.[5] It is impacted by the individual's personal way of interpreting it so the knowledge may be held and explained differently person to person. Memory is the application of this knowledge, impacted by further experience, and the sum of all employees' knowledge becomes the institution's OM.

This knowledge must be passed on to each generation to establish continuity and to allow each generation to contribute to and build upon the previous knowledge base so that it becomes an organizational asset.[6] Knowledge is further expanded and shared by the relationships in which employees participate (their networks), by use of explicit knowledge such as databases and paper files, and through organizational processes and procedures that have been refined through lessons learned.[7] Employees contribute to the dissemination of personal and organizational tacit knowledge; this is important because it ensures that the various interpretations can be heard, understood, and combined with the individual interpretations to build expertise. "From very early times, wise people have secured sustained succession by transferring in-depth knowledge to the next generation."[8]

Kransdorff and Williams break OM down into three time frames, short term (less than 5 year), medium term (up to 10 year), and long term (over 10 year).[1] It is the short- and medium-term memory that is most relevant to an organization's daily or core operations, while long-term memory impacts its strategy. Since OM is critical to an organization's ability to perform effectively (do the right thing) and efficiently (do things well) and much of this critical knowledge is held by individuals within the organization in tacit form, it is particularly at risk for loss in countries or sectors expecting a large number of long-term employees to retire. It is also increasingly impacted by the new trend of employees' tenure lasting five or less years and by outsourcing.

ORGANIZATIONAL MEMORY: DEFINITION AND OVERVIEW

In 2000, Olivera defined OM as the means of storing knowledge for future use by discussing OM as it relates to the complex environment of an organization that exists as multiple units and including networks of individuals, sophisticated computer-based technologies, and formal knowledge management initiatives. He discusses OM in

Encyclopedia of Library and Information Sciences, Fourth Edition DOI: 10.1081/E-ELIS4-120053481

this environment as dispersed among people and documents and integrated through mechanisms such as social networks and computer-based technologies.[9]

As important as individuals may be in creating the knowledge base, OM is more than just the addition of what individuals know or store in databases. The existence of an OM is what makes it possible for an organization to have a memory that is sustained even as individuals leave.[10] It is through sharing by individuals, according to Walsh and Ungson, that "organizational interpretation is made possible" and "through this process of sharing, the organizational interpretation system in part transcends the individual level. This is why an organization may preserve knowledge of the past even when key organizational members leave."[11] Walsh and Ungson identify five storage bins for OM: individuals, culture, transformations, structures, and ecology, and one external bin—external archives.[12]

Beazley, Beazley, and Harden identify seven types of operational knowledge:[6]

- *Cognitive knowledge*: Content knowledge that includes job-specific data and information and their sources.
- *Skills knowledge*: The skills and training necessary to perform well in the position.
- *Systems knowledge*: An understanding of the interplay of cause-and-effect relationships that is essential for sound decision-making.
- *Social network knowledge*: An understanding of the crucial social relationships that make it possible to get things done in the organization, including who can grease the wheels, provide inside information, clarify options, or offer reliable advice and counsel. When employees face an unfamiliar situation with which they feel unprepared to deal, they do not rely on databases or procedure manuals. They turn to their network of trusted colleagues for information, knowledge, and advice.
- *Process and procedural knowledge*: Knowledge of formal and informal organizational processes and procedures, which are often more effective for getting things done in an organization.
- *Heuristic knowledge*: Knowledge of shortcuts for accomplishing tasks, rules of thumb for decision-making, and quick fixes that have come to constitute best practices for the position. Heuristic knowledge includes procedures that modify or circumvent obsolete, ineffective, or cumbersome official procedures.
- *Cultural knowledge*: Knowledge of organizational norms, values, roles, and standards of conduct that govern interaction with colleagues and other stakeholders.

The importance of OM to an organization lies in its role in problem-solving, decision-making, strategic planning, and developing tactical approaches. In 2006, Feldman and Feldman note that "despite continued efforts to dismantle the concept's mystery, it has not lost its essentially baffling quality." They suggest that this baffling quality may be due to an approach that is too "narrow to capture the complex character . . . of organizational remembering." They suggest a shift from the term "'organizational memory' (an object) to 'organizational remembering' (a practice)" and discuss organizational remembering as "a collective, culture and time specific process and practice, hinged on the concept of tradition as the cradling framework of meaning."[13]

ORGANIZATIONAL MEMORY AND CULTURE

"Culture embodies past experience that can be useful for dealing with the future. It is, therefore, one of organizational memory's retention facilities. ... Because this information is transmitted over and over again, some of the detail and context of the various decisions are likely to be dropped or even altered to suit the telling."[14]

According to Adler, Goldoftas, and Levine, management's task is to create an environment that promotes interaction between the individual and the organization to share knowledge.[15] "Managers must accept the inevitability of employee turnover, and through an understanding of social networks, make structural changes to their organization which promotes the diffusion of knowledge before crucial information is lost."[16] Brief and Motowidlo state that leadership style and organizational climate affect prosocial organizational behavior.[17] Prosocial behavior supports knowledge sharing through encouraging interactions between employees. Leaders determine what activities are rewarded by role modeling and supporting wanted behavior such as networking. "Leaders have direct control over what activities are rewarded, what behaviors are encouraged, and how work will be valued in the organization. These factors all influence workers' motivation and ability to develop new knowledge."[18]

A knowledge sharing culture is one in which employees are encouraged to share and to ask questions, where experience and knowledge from other sources are included, and where mentoring is supported.[19] Awareness of and support for knowledge sharing networks and the individuals within is a critical function of leadership and management as the networks are used daily in the completion of work. "The traditional organization chart may show who reports to whom, but often who talks to whom is more important in getting work done and generating new ideas."[20]

Fahey and Prusak note that when management recognizes that knowledge is part of a process rather than an object, it will be recognized that it is affected by the organization's structure and systems.[21] Often knowledge sharing is confined to small groups of employees who have developed a trusting relationship over the years. "A great deal of knowledge in an organization is undocumented and therefore isn't easily available to everyone. It may be shared among a few individuals or within local groups, but rarely migrates outside those circles."[22] Organizational leaders and managers must create a culture that encourages sharing to these groups and beyond.

According to Choi and Lee, organizational knowledge management programs with a human orientation focus on the sharing of tacit knowledge. The human orientation is important in industries with high uncertainty or complexity because employees rely on the experience and knowledge within networking relationships.[23] It is also valuable within more stable environments to ensure that organizations continue to grow and innovate. The human orientation can be complemented by a technical orientation that captures the supporting explicit knowledge and makes it available through a knowledge repository such as a searchable database or a corporate intranet.

TOOLS AND APPROACHES TO PRESERVE ORGANIZATIONAL MEMORY

"Devising strategies to properly manage knowledge is imperative for many organizations due to its significance for attaining organizational outcomes."[24] In addition to being stored in people's memory or in databases, OM is embedded in processes, systems, services, and cultural norms. It is encoded in routines, in established policies and procedures, in products, in the way a business is organized, in the beliefs and routines in which employees are trained, and the cultural norms that guide how staff interact and share knowledge. And these things can, in turn, be impacted by "changing incentives, evaluation processes, or planning and budgeting processes."[25]

Knowledge sharing by individuals is fundamental to creating an organizational knowledge base—the foundation of OM. Walsh and Ungson note the important role of the individual in acquiring and sharing information. "This focus on individual cognitive activities as the central element in the organization's acquisition of information reflects an active construction of memory."[11] It is in the give and take among individuals combining their understanding and experience of how to accomplish work (tacit knowledge) with known information (explicit knowledge) in a specific context that new knowledge is created.[9,26–28] This creativity, in turn, allows an organization to more effectively exploit what it already knows if that new knowledge is transformed into organizational knowledge.[29–31] This suggests that the process of learning by individuals and sharing of information by them is an important step in creating an organizational knowledge base.[32,33] Networks among staff, in turn, are frequently identified as an important means of accumulating, accessing, and sharing knowledge.[34]

> As long-tenured staffs begin to leave, they take with them their knowledge, skills, and other valuable job-related information—components of the organization's memory that may become inaccessible to the organization. Additionally, this loss may disrupt OM systems as these components are part of organizational knowledge that may be dispersed across actors, systems, and interactions in organizations.[35]

Knowledge repositories—databases or document collections—are an important tool in storing and making accessible organizational knowledge, but they play a limited role. In practice, "people are about five times more likely to turn to friends or colleagues for answers than to other sources."[36] The U.S. Department of Defense identifies knowledge sharing as being 90% culture and 10% technology in its Knowledge Management Primer.[37] Aside from usage tendencies, there are issues related to inputting information in such a way that it is accessible to users. A report by the U.S. Federal Highway Administration on a 12-state survey of Quality Assurance databases ended up concluding that "Data Rich and Information Poor" best describes the current status of today's databases. The focus of many agencies is on entering data, not retrieving or analyzing the data.[38] "Briefly, individuals store their organization's memory in their own capacity to remember and articulate experience and in the cognitive orientations they employ to facilitate information processing. Moreover, individuals and organizations keep records and files as a memory aid."[39] Therefore, encouraging employees to share their knowledge and to capture elements that explain the "why" of actions and strategies in databases may act as a catalyst for remembering.

OM may be shared between members of a group for a specific purpose or it may be passed down through mentoring or apprenticeships.[26] Tacit knowledge originates with the individual and it is necessary for that knowledge to transfer from person to person to be useful to the organization. One way of transferring is described by Nonaka and Takeuchi as socialization, the sharing of experience to create shared mental models as through apprenticeships.[29] It might also be codified within organizational routines through rules and guidelines:[2]

> The organization, however, cannot dictate the rules of coordination and knowledge sharing. Since only a part of tacit knowledge is internalized by the organization, the other part is internalized by employees. Therefore, it becomes critical for management to find some kind of commonality between individual and organizational knowledge and provide necessary incentives to employees to share their knowledge and enhance the contents of the organizational knowledge base.[40]

Sharing is dependent on the levels of solidarity and employee buy-in to organizational goals.[41] Leadership is critical to garnering this buy-in and willingness to share. Management is critical to establishing the means to share both explicit and tacit knowledge.

"Blue-collar skills are predicated on available explicit knowledge; white-collar skills are predicated mainly on the less-than-visible tacit experience. Explicit knowledge can be taught while tacit knowledge is best learned.... Teaching is instruction *received*. Learning is instruction *acquired* out of an abstracted process of critical reflection, reasoned deduction, and applied action, the evidential base for which is OM."[42] "Learning as an integral part of working occurs when individuals adapt new tools to solve current problems, share success and failure stories, etc. Unlike individuals who are 'automatic' learners, OL (Organizational Learning) is a conscious activity in the organizational context and can be enhanced by an effective knowledge-management system."[43] Individuals develop knowledge based on personal experience, their personal values and beliefs, and the addition of new knowledge, thus determining what it is they remember.[13] Providing training and education will ensure the sharing of explicit knowledge. Creating networks, such as through communities of practice, will support sharing of tacit knowledge and provide access to those with expertise and experience.

Access to experts within the organization is important to problem-solving, building the knowledge base of employees and innovation in product construction or delivery. "The role of experts is important as they are ultimately the source of the innovations or knowledge that is being diffused. Consequently, they form local peaks in the knowledge distribution, and agents directly connected to them benefit, becoming second-order experts."[44] By sharing knowledge with others, the demand on the time of experts is lessened freeing the expert to focus on high-value projects. It also supports the redundancy of knowledge within the organization ensuring that knowledge does not walk out the door. Lesser and Prusak state that

> The research and experience at the Institute for Knowledge Management has shown that social networks play a critical role in helping people identify, share and work with corporate knowledge. Through such networks, individuals identify experts, provide referrals for those seeking answers and facilitate knowledge transfer among groups. Downsizing disrupts the structures and causes 'potholes' that impede and often block the flow of knowledge.[45]

The presence and support of networks within the organization supports knowledge sharing by creating opportunities for employees to exchange information and insight informally as well as formally. Access to different knowledge through interactions with others allows employees to update their knowledge banks.[42] The transfer requires that members of the network share a common framework to effectively share knowledge.[46] This can be accomplished through organizationally supported communities of practice to share lessons learned and after-action reviews. According to Swan et al., "knowledge has to be continuously negotiated through interactive social networking processes."[47] It is the organization's responsibility to establish a culture or environment that supports the forming of these networks, both loose and tight, to encourage the sharing of knowledge.[26,47]

Networking with external experts is also critical. Many of these networks are based on personal relationships. Creating an expert database to share these relationships can be helpful to other employees. "External memories are accessed through directories held in the mind of individual team members that identify existence, location, and mechanisms for retrieval of knowledge held by other team members or in various storage devices."[48] These connections may be direct or indirect.

> In the 1960s, an American psychologist named Stanley Milgram tried to form a picture of the web of interpersonal connections that link people into a community. To do so, he sent letters to a random selection of people living in Nebraska and Kansas, asking each of them to forward the letter to a stockbroker friend of his living in Boston, but he did not give them the address. To forward the letter, he asked them to send it only to someone they knew personally and who they thought might be socially 'closer' to the stockbroker. Most of the letters eventually made it to his friend in Boston. Far more startling, however, was how quickly they did so—not in hundreds of mailings but typically in just six or so.... Milgram's findings became famous and passed into popular folklore in the phrase' six degrees of separation.[49]

Often, the size of the organization influences how easily and readily employees share information. The smaller the organization, the more likely employees will share as they know and trust each other.[50,51] Sharing may also be affected by employee age and where they are in their career.[50] Sveiby and Simons found that senior people are more experienced in sharing knowledge than junior people due to larger networks and that investing time in assisting less experienced employees to build these networks in the first 3–5 year of employment is a profitable investment by the organization.[52] While this may not be practical now given the increasingly short tenure of employees, developing a mechanism to quickly acquaint them with expert networks will benefit the organization.

ORGANIZATIONAL FORGETTING

If organizations remember they also forget, either deliberately or through a lack of awareness of knowledge at risk because it has not been shared.

> Organizations that have been deeply concerned about organizational 'learning' have been oddly negligent about

> its opposite: corporate 'forgetting,' which occurs with every departing knowledge worker. What kind of organizational learning can take place if the knowledge base on which it relies is subject to continual degradation or if the organization itself cannot remember enough to pass on its knowledge and its secrets to the newcomer expected to carry the torch?[53]

However, strategic forgetting is also important. According to Bontis, much of the literature fails to acknowledge that while tacit knowledge can contribute to the competitiveness of an organization it can also limit its competitiveness if that knowledge does not fit the context of the desired industry.[2] At the same time, too much forgetting may impact employee ability to identify with the organization. Organizational forgetting may be by mistake or on purpose and it may be helpful or hurtful to the organization and therefore, organizations need to also pay attention to what and how they forget in a strategic way. Strategic forgetting may be employed to help employees learn and adapt to new circumstances. Nonpurposeful forgetting may hurt the organization when it loses the value of lessons learned that might be helpful to future events. Official and personal historical memories can omit or neutralize events and perspectives that contradict the approved history. This may be purposeful or unintentional. The emphasis on remembering and on forgetting impacts the actual history.[54]

It is necessary to strategically capture knowledge that the organization wishes to retain and embed it in procedures and the culture.[55] If the organization forgets critical knowledge, it must be relearned or created anew at great expense and can affect the competitiveness of an organization.[53] It can also be harmful as seen in the Challenger and Columbia disasters at the U.S. National Aeronautics and Space Administration where the focus was on the

> Quantitative measure 'experience base.' (In 1986 the Space Shuttle Challenger broke apart 73 sec into its flight. In 2003, the Space Shuttle Columbia broke apart on reentry over Texas). This measure abbreviates memory to a dangerously low level because it not only excludes qualitative data, but also arrests and reifies memory by excluding historical analysis of quantitative data relevant to safety and other organizational goals. In other words, a lack of memory was not only responsible for misunderstanding the level of risk on Columbia's last flight, but engineers also did not notice the accumulation of risk in the flight history preceding Challenger.[56]

Unfortunately, the organization may not be aware of its knowledge if it lacks awareness of employees' personal knowledge.

> Managers do not know the value of their own intellectual capital. They do not know if they have the people, resources, or business processes in place to make a success of a new strategy. They do not understand what know-how, management potential or creativity they have access to with their employees. Because they are devoid of such information, they are rightsizing, downsizing, and reengineering in a vacuum.[57]

As employees leave, they take the organizational knowledge with them, employee networks are disrupted, and documentation is lost or hidden.[58] According to Lesser and Prusak, when organizations downsize, it is often the most knowledgeable employees who leave first, resulting in a damaged critical social network and an increase in time needed for knowledge transfers.[45] This often occurs when organizations offer buyouts and early retirement incentives without considering the knowledge held by those designated as eligible. These knowledgeable employees have built and maintained extensive networks used to share knowledge. Trends such as rightsizing and reorganizations along with the pending retirements of long-term employees and the mobility of the new workforce destroyed or compromised tacit knowledge networks. The informal contract between the company and an employee moved from employment for life to employment for as long as there is mutual benefit.[59] As noted earlier, trust is a determining factor for knowledge sharing, and when organizations have a history of downsizing, trust is compromised and requires focused attention to reestablish.[60,61]

CONCLUSIONS AND RECOMMENDATIONS

OM is the accumulation of employees' knowledge and experience. It is the means through which an organization ensures that its historical knowledge, experience, and expertise are retained to support its future. While snippets of it may be captured for future use in databases, processes, and procedures, the richness of the knowledge is only realized in ensuring employees or provided with opportunities to share and discuss their personal knowledge. Focusing just on structure, like databases and processes, means we miss the activity happening between people. Leadership is required to ensure focus on its importance to the organization and to create a culture that values knowledge sharing. Management is required to ensure opportunities for sharing and learning are supported. Careful consideration is required to determine what should be remembered and retained for consistency and competitiveness versus what should be strategically forgotten to allow room for innovation and adaptability. Failure to consider this strategically may result in inaccurate remembering or loss of cultural knowledge when employees leave.

By building up knowledge sharing networks among staff, organizations are not just able to share information, but it becomes second nature when there is a need. This conclusion is supported by a 2006 study by Scalzo looking at midsized financial services organizations with approximately 2500 employees and that underwent radical change (a significant shift in values, behavior, and how the organization performs the work required to meet organizational need). Scalzo found that an organization can successfully manage the process in order to retain the wealth of information and knowledge that exists in the OM. The findings showed that the subject organization of this research study followed three key management practices throughout the entire change process (ongoing communications, senior management commitment, and planning) that enabled it to access, share, and retain its OM while undergoing radical change.[62]

REFERENCES

1. Kransdorff, A.; Williams, R. Managing organizational memory (OM): The new competitive imperative. Organ. Dev. J. **2000**, *18* (1), 107–117.
2. Bontis, N. Managing organizational knowledge by diagnosing intellectual capital: Framing and advancing the state of the field. Int. J. Technol. Manag. **1999**, *18*, 433–462.
3. Constant, D.; Kiesler, S.; Sproull, L. What's mine is ours, or is it? A study of attitudes about information sharing. Inform. Syst. Res. **1994**, *5*, 400–421.
4. Cook, S.D.N.; Brown, J.S. Bridging epistemologies: The generative dance between organizational knowledge and organizational knowing. Organ. Sci. **1999**, *10*, 381–400.
5. Davenport, T.H.; De Long, D.W.; Beers, M.C. Successful knowledge management projects. Sloan Manage. Rev. **1998**, *39*, 43–57.
6. Beazley, H.; Beazley, J.; Harden, D. *Continuity Management: Preserving Corporate Knowledge and Productivity When Employees Leave*; John Wiley & Sons, Inc.: New York, 2002.
7. Cross, R.; Baird, L. Technology is not enough: Improving performance by building organizational memory. Sloan Manage. Rev. **2000**, *41* (3), 69–78.
8. Wiig, K.M. Knowledge management: An introduction and perspective. J. Knowl. Manag. **1997**, *1*, 6–14.
9. Olivera, F. Memory systems in organizations: An empirical investigation of mechanisms for knowledge collections, storage and access. J. Manag. Stud. **2000**, *37* (6), 811–813.
10. Hedberg, B. How organizations learn and unlearn. In *Handbook of Organizational Design*; Nystrom, P.C., Starbuck, W.H., Eds.; Oxford University Press: Oxford, U.K., 1981; 3–27.
11. Walsh, J.P.; Ungson, G.R. Organizational memory. Acad. Manag. Rev. **1991**, *16* (1), 57–91. 61.
12. Walsh, J.P.; Ungson, G.R. Organizational memory. Acad. Manag. Rev. **1991**, *16* (1), 57–91.
13. Feldman, R.M.; Feldman, S.P. What links the chain: An essay on organizational remembering as practice. Organization **2006**, *13* (6), 861–887.
14. Walsh, J.P.; Ungson, G.R. Organizational memory. Acad. Manag. Rev. **1991**, *16* (1), 57–92. 64–65.
15. Adler, P.S.; Goldoftas, B.; Levine, D.I. Flexibility versus efficiency? A case study of model changeovers in the Toyota production system. Organ. Sci. **1999**, *10*, 43–68.
16. Droege, S.B.; Hoobler, J.M. Employee turnover and tacit knowledge diffusion: A network perspective. J. Manag. **2003**, *15* (1), 50–64. p. 59.
17. Brief, A.P.; Motowidlo, S.J. Prosocial organizational behaviors. Acad. Manag. Rev. **1986**, *11*, 710–725.
18. Bryant, S.E. The role of transformational and transactional leadership in creating, sharing and exploiting organizational knowledge. J. Leadersh. Org. Stud. **2003**, *9* (4), 32–44. p. 35.
19. Smith, H.A.; McKeen, J.D. *Instilling a Knowledge-Sharing Culture*. Unpublished manuscript; Queen's University: Kingston, Ontario, Canada, 2003. http://www.business.queenssu.ca (accessed October 2003).
20. Foster, F.; Falkowski, G. Organization network analysis: A tool for building a learning organization. Knowl. Process Manag. **1999**, *6*, 53–60. p. 53.
21. Fahey, L.; Prusak, L. The eleven deadliest sins of knowledge management. Calif. Manag. Rev. **1998**, *40*, 265–276.
22. Ruddy, T. Taking knowledge from heads and putting it into hands. Knowl. Process Manag. **2000**, *7*, 37–40. p. 38.
23. Choi, B.; Lee, H. An empirical investigation of KM styles and their effect on corporate performance. Inf. Manag. **2002**, *40*, 403–417.
24. Birasnav, M. Knowledge management and organizational performance in the service industry: The role of transformational leadership beyond the effects of transactional leadership. J. Bus. Res. **2014**, *67*, 163.
25. Cross, R.; Baird, L. Technology is not enough: Improving performance by building organizational memory. Sloan Manag. Rev. **2000**, *41* (3), 69–78. 72.
26. Droege, S.B.; Hoobler, J.M. Employee turnover and tacit knowledge diffusion: A network perspective. J. Manag. **Spring 2003**, *15* (1), 50–64. 53.
27. Gherardi, S.; Nicolini, D.; Odella, F. Toward a social understanding of how people learn in organizations. Manag. Learn. **1998**, *29*, 273–97.
28. Brown, J.S.; Duguid, P. Organizational learning and communities of practice: Toward a unified view of working, learning, and innovation. Organ. Sci. **1991**, *2*, 40–57.
29. Nonaka, I.; Takeuchi, H. *The Knowledge-Creating Company*; Oxford University Press: New York, 1995; 64–73.
30. Walsh, J.P.; Ungson, G.R. Organizational memory. Acad. Manag. Rev. **1991**, *16* (1), 57–92.
31. Von Krogh, G. Chapter 19: Knowledge sharing and the communal resource. In *The Blackwell Handbook of Organizational Learning and Knowledge Management*; Easterby-Smith, M., Lyles, M.A., Eds.; Blackwell Publishing Ltd.: Malden, MA, 2003; 372–392.
32. Bhatt, G.D. Management strategies for individual knowledge and organizational knowledge. J. Knowl. Manag. **2002**, *6* (1), 31–39.
33. Cross, R.; Bayrd, L. Technology is not enough: Improving performance by building organizational memory. Sloan Manag. Rev. **Spring 2000**, *41* (3), 69–79.
34. Olivera, F. Memory systems in organizations: An empirical investigation of mechanisms for knowledge collections, storage and access. J. Manag. Stud. **2000**, *37* (6), 815.
35. Scalzo, N.J. Memory loss? Corporate knowledge and radical change. J. Bus. Strategy **2006**, *24* (4), 60–69. p. 60.
36. Cross, R.; Baird, L. Technology is not enough: Improving performance by building organizational memory. Sloan Manag. Rev. **2000**, *41* (3), 69–78. p. 7.

37. US GAO, NASA. *Better Mechanisms Needed for Sharing Lessons Learned*; US General Accounting Office: Washington, DC, January 2002; 39, GAO-02-195.
38. FHWA TechBrief on Guidelines for Establishing and Maintaining Construction Quality Databases; US DOT: Federal Highway Administration: McLean VA, December 2006.
39. Walsh, J.P.; Ungson, G.R. Organizational memory. Acad. Manag. Rev. **1991**, *16* (1), 57–92. p. 63.
40. Bhatt, G.D. Management strategies for individual knowledge and organizational knowledge. J. Knowl. Manag. **2002**, *6* (1), 31–39. 34–35.
41. Jarvenpaa, S.L.; Staples, D.S. Exploring the perceptions of organizational ownership of information and expertise. J. Manag. Inf. Syst. **2001**, *18* (1), 151–183.
42. Kransdorff, A. Knowledge management: Begging for a bigger role: How organizational memory can help transient managers make better decisions, 2nd Ed.; Business Expert Press: New York, NY, 2009; 9.
43. Ozorhon, B.; Dikmen, I.; Birgonul, M.T. Organizational memory formation and its use in construction. Build. Res. Inf. **2005**, *33* (1), 67–79. p. 67.
44. Cowan, R.; Jonard, N. Network structure and the diffusion of knowledge. J. Econ. Dyn. Control **2003**, *28*, 1557–1575. p. 1568.
45. Lesser, E.; Prusak, L. Preserving knowledge in an uncertain world [Electronic version]. MIT Sloan Manag. Rev. **2001**, *43*, 101–102. See Damage to Social Networks Section. 38. Bhatt, G.D. Information dynamics, learning and knowledge creation in organizations [Electronic version]. Learn. Organ. **2000**, *7*, 89.
46. Augier, M.; Vendele, M.T. Networks, cognition and management of tacit knowledge. J. Knowl. Manag. **1999**, *3* (4), 252–261.
47. Swan, J.; Newell, S.; Scarbrough, H.; Hislop, D. Knowledge management and innovation: Networks and networking. J. Knowl. Manag. **1999**, *3*, 262–272.
48. Alavi, M.; Tiwana, A. *Knowledge Integration in Virtual Teams: The Potential Role of KMS.* (Goizueta Business School Paper Series); Emory University: Atlanta, GA, 2001; 11. http://gbspapers.library.emory.edu/archive/00000025/ (accessed September 5, 2008).
49. Buchanan, M. *Nexus: Small Worlds and the Groundbreaking Science of Networks*; W.W. Norton & Company: New York, 2002; 3.
50. Connelly, C.E.; Kelloway, E.K. Predictors of employees' perceptions of knowledge sharing cultures. Leadersh. Org. Dev. **2003**, *24*, 294–301.
51. Knowledge Management Working Group of the Federal Chief Information Officers Council. *Managing Knowledge at Work: An Overview of Knowledge Management*; CIO Council: Washington, DC, 2001. http://www.providersedge.com/docs/km_articles/Km_at_Work.pdf (accessed December 1, 2016).
52. Sveiby, K.E.; Simons, R. Collaborative climate and effectiveness of knowledge work—An empirical study. J. Knowl. Manag. **2002**, *6*, 430–433.
53. Beazley, H.; Beasley, J.; Harden, D. *Continuity Management: Preserving Corporate Knowledge and Productivity When Employees Leave*; John Wiley & Sons Inc.: New York, 2002; 14.
54. Anteby, M.; Molnar, V. Organizational Identity: Remembering to forget in a firm's rhetorical history. Acad. Manag. J. **2012**, *55* (3), 515–540.
55. de Holan, P.M.; Phillips, N.; Lawrence, T.B. Managing organizational forgetting. MIT Sloan Manag. Rev. **2004**, *45* (2), 45–51.
56. Feldman, S.P. The culture of objectivity: Quantification, uncertainty, and the evaluation of risk at NASA. Hum. Relat. **2004**, *57* (6), 691–718. p. 714.
57. Bontis, N. Managing organizational knowledge by diagnosing intellectual capital: Framing and advancing the state of the field. Int. J. Technol. Manag. **1999**, *18*, 433–462. p. 436.
58. American Productivity & Quality Center *Creating a Knowledge-Sharing Culture Consortium Benchmarking Study: Best-Practice Report* , Houston, TX, 1999.
59. Smith, E.A. The role of tacit and explicit knowledge in the workplace. J. Knowl. Manag. **2001**, *5*, 311–321.
60. DeLong, D.W.; Fahey, L. Diagnosing cultural barriers to knowledge management. Acad. Manag. Exec. **2000**, *14*, 113–127.
61. Ives, W.; Torrey, B.; Gordon, C. Knowledge management: An emerging discipline with a long history. J. Knowl. Manag. **1998**, *1*, 269–274.
62. Scalzo, N.J. Memory loss? Corporate knowledge and radical change. J. Bus. Strategy **2006**, *24* (4), 60–69. p. 64. 4094.

Pacific Islands Association of Libraries and Archives (PIALA)

Arlene Cohen
Pacific Islands Library Consultant, Seattle, Washington, U.S.A.

Abstract

The Pacific Islands Association of Libraries and Archives (PIALA) is a voluntary association established within the islands of Micronesia in the Western Pacific Ocean. Officially created in 1991, it has grown to be a stable association of librarians and archivists, holding annual conferences on different islands, supporting training opportunities, encouraging awareness and fostering resource sharing among libraries, archives, museums, and related institutions in the Pacific Islands.

INTRODUCTION

The Pacific Islands Association of Libraries and Archives (PIALA) is a regional association established in 1991 within the islands of Micronesia in the Western Pacific Ocean. The islands include the United States (US) Territory of Guam, and the former U.S. Trust Territory entities of the Commonwealth of the Northern Mariana Islands (CNMI); the Federated States of Micronesia (FSM) comprising the states of Chuuk, Kosrae, Pohnpei and Yap; the Republic of the Marshall Islands; and the Republic of Palau. The goals of PIALA are to promote knowledge of the functions, resources, services, and needs of regional collections of information resources; to develop and promote programs for the extension and improvement of information literacy and services in the region; and to provide an ongoing forum for people working in libraries, as well as archives and museums.

Regional Context

Micronesia, meaning "tiny islands," is composed of some 2200 volcanic and coral islands spread throughout 4,500,000 mi^2 of the vast Pacific Ocean (see Fig. 1).

Lying north of Australia, south of Japan, east of the Philippines, and west of Hawaii, these tropical islands cover an expanse of water almost as large as the mainland United States, yet the total landmass is less than 1200 mi^2, with a total population estimated at no more than 300,000 inhabitants.

The region has a history of foreign involvement dating back to 1521 when Fernando Magellan, sailing for Spain, landed on the island of Guam. Throughout the next several hundreds of years, the Micronesian islands have been at various times under Spanish, German, Japanese, Australian, British, New Zealand, and United States rule. After World War II, with the exceptions of Guam, Kiribati, and Nauru, all the islands were designated by the United Nations as a Trust Territory to be administered by the United States with the eventual goal of each achieving some type of self-government. Over the past 50 years, these U.S. affiliated islands have grouped together into five separate political entities (with one entity, the FSM, comprising four separate states). These political entities are reflected in the composition of PIALA. Although Kiribati and Nauru are geographically considered part of Micronesia, they were not included when establishing PIALA. Recently, representatives from the *Kiribati Library and Information Network (KLIN)*, the local Kiribati library association, have participated in PIALA conferences.

HISTORICAL BACKGROUND

The seeds for regional cooperation that grew into a regional association go back to the early days of the Trust Territory of the Pacific Islands administration and the work of Daniel Peacock, Director for Library Services for the Trust Territory. Through his efforts, Peacock established the foundation from which PIALA could emerge. In his insightful article, "Micronesian Library Services," Nicholas Goetzfridt[1] provides a context for understanding Micronesian library development and the significant role Peacock played in fostering this development.

In 1967, when the Trust Territory became eligible for the *Library Services and Construction Act* (LSCA) funds, Peacock wrote both the 1967, and later the 1972 state plans, providing funding for library projects in the region. Very early on, Peacock saw the need for regional networking and "The 1972 state plan called for increased bibliographic cooperation between the Trust Territory and 'the libraries of the neighboring Pacific area.'"[2] This is further discussed under the section "Resource Sharing" in this entry.

The 1978 *Commonwealth of the Northern Mariana Islands Pre-White House Governor's Conference on Library and Information Services*, held on Saipan, was a first attempt to bring regional librarians together, although

Encyclopedia of Library and Information Sciences, Fourth Edition DOI: 10.1081/E-ELIS4-120044118

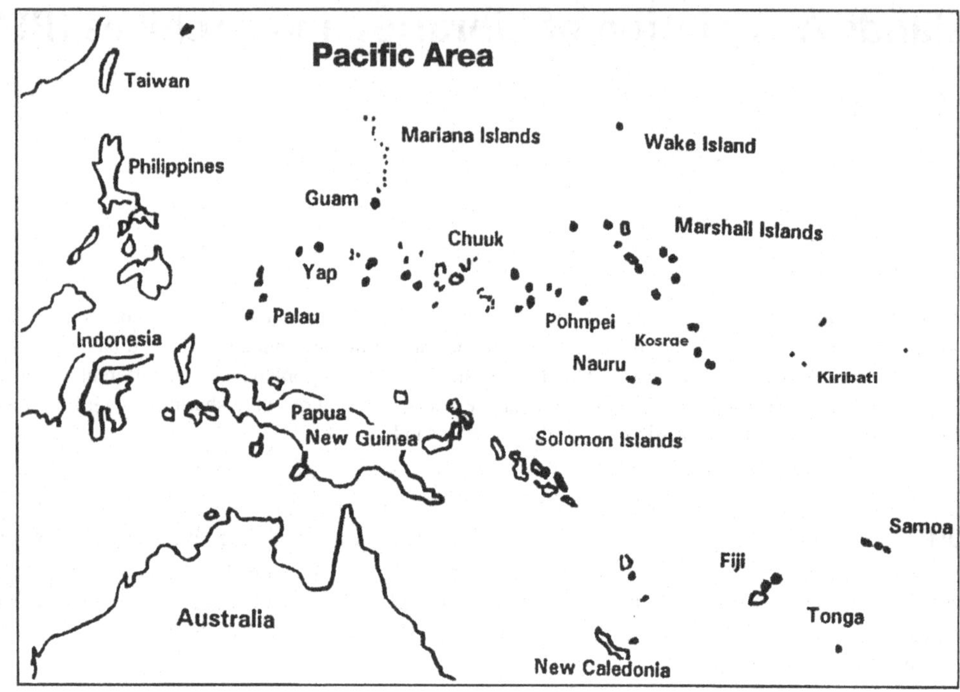

Fig. 1 Map of the Pacific Area. Created by Joanne T. Crotts.
Source: From Developing library and information services in Micronesia, by A. Cohen,; J.T. Crotts, I. Lovas, In *Libraries: Global Reach/Local Touch*, de la Pena Cook, K., Ford, B.J., Lippincott, K., Eds., American Library Association, Chicago, IL. 1998, 58. Revised for this entry by the author (Arlene Cohen) with permission of the creator.

no formal organization emerged from this gathering. Twelve years later, the 1990 *Commonwealth of the Northern Mariana Islands Pre-White House Governor's Conference on Library and Information Services*, held again in Saipan in October of that year, finally provided the impetus for the establishment of a regional association. Several participants and observers from outside CNMI were invited to attend and during the conference, an informal meeting was held to discuss establishing a regional library association. Minutes of the meeting were taken and the group called themselves the *Western Pacific Library and Archives Association.*

The 1990 *Guam Pre-White House Governor's Conference on Library and Information Services* was held the following month and the group met again informally in Guam. During this meeting, funding from the U.S. government was identified to hold an organizational meeting at the University of Guam in February 1991. With funding secured, two participants each from the Federated States of Micronesia, the Republic of Palau, the Republic of the Marshall Islands, the Commonwealth of the Northern Marianas Islands, and the Territory of Guam were invited to the organization meeting. At that meeting, a set of *By-Laws* was adopted, the Executive Board was elected and Palau was selected as the site of the first conference, planned for November 1991.

Soon after the organizational meeting, Margo Vitarelli, a prominent artist and educator in Micronesia designed the letterhead of PIALA using Micronesian art motifs. Her design is still being used today, incorporated into the *PIALA Newsletter*, announcements, brochures, and other publications.

Thus, PIALA was born. From the onset, people working in museums have been an integral part of PIALA. In 1991, at the first PIALA general meeting in Palau, there was an attempt to change the name of the association to the *Pacific Islands Association of Libraries, Archives and Museums* (PIALAM); however, the attempt failed and the name has remained PIALA.

Throughout the years, several publications about PIALA have appeared, many of which are listed at the end of this entry. One article worth noting came about during Barbara J. Ford's term as President (1997–1998) of the American Library Association (ALA). Under her leadership, *Libraries: Global Reach/Local Touch* was published, and includes a detailed description of the development of PIALA in the chapter on library services in Micronesia.[3]

In 1996, PIALA began submitting information to the Belgium-based *Union of International Organizations* (http://www.uia.be/), with updates submitted yearly.

As PIALA evolved, so did the materials documenting the association. Serving as a model for the importance of preserving historical materials, the permanent collection of PIALA archives was established and are housed in the Pacific Collection of the College of Micronesia—FSM

National Campus Learning Resources Center in Palikir, Pohnpei, Federated States of Micronesia.

GOVERNANCE

The *Pacific Islands Association of Libraries and Archives By-Laws* were adopted on February 28, 1991. Interestingly, the *PIALA Constitution* was not drafted until 1993, reflecting what was already in the *By-Laws*.

The original *By-Laws* included the purpose, duties of officers, composition of the Executive Board, voting, the committee structure, and dues. The group also decided that the venue of the annual meeting (including the annual conference) would rotate among all locations represented. By having the meetings on different islands, local librarians and archivists with little possibility to travel would have the opportunity to plan and attend a professional conference. Moreover, hosting a conference would also provide an excellent advocacy opportunity, focusing attention on the island's libraries, archives, and museums.

Purpose

The purpose of PIALA, as established in the *By-Laws* in Article II, Section A is

a. to foster awareness and encourage cooperation and resource sharing among the libraries, archives, museums, and related institutions of the Pacific Islands;
b. to promote knowledge of the functions, resources, services, and needs of regional collections;
c. to develop and promote programs for the extension and improvement of library, archival, museum, and related services in the region;
d. to improve a forum for discussing issues of interest to libraries, archives, museums and related institutions;
e. to provide a vehicle for the exchange of ideas and information to librarians, archivists, museum curators and related personnel; and
f. to offer continuing education experiences for library, archival, museum, and related personnel.[4]

By-Law changes

Although the purpose of PIALA has not changed over the years; other parts of the *By-Laws* have changed to reflect the development and changing needs of PIALA.

When PIALA was established, the *By-Laws* stated that "The Executive Board shall consist of the officers, shall represent all locations, and have no fewer than five members. Locations not represented by officers shall elect a representative."[5] Over time, the island states of Chuuk, Kosrae, Pohnpei, and Yap were considered locations in their own right and subsequently the *By-Laws* were changed to expand the Executive Board to no fewer than nine members. Other important changes included dropping the office of Executive Secretary; allowing all members to vote, including institutional members, instead of just individual members; voting at the annual meeting instead of by mail; and accepting proxy votes. Attesting to the stability of PIALA's governance structure, the last time the *By-Laws* were changed was November 1996.

PIALA Board Meetings

Soon after PIALA was established, the Executive Board attempted, with varying degrees of success, to hold monthly meetings and this effort continues. The PEACESAT (Pan-Pacific Education and Communication Experiments by Satellite) federally funded satellite network has been used since the beginning and remains the most economical means of voice communication. PEACESAT stations are on the major Micronesian islands; however, the system has limited channels, tight schedules, and frequent breakdowns, with few spare parts available locally and limited local expertise to carry out the repairs.

In 2007, an attempt to conduct PIALA Board meetings using an online collaboration and conferencing system was tested. After several unsuccessful attempts to bring the group online, it was abandoned. It became clear that any new communication system, no matter how extensive the documentation is, must be accompanied by hands-on, onsite training for most users.

Happily, in the past few years with e-mail becoming more widely available and less costly, much of the work of the PIALA Executive Board is handled this way, with monthly scheduled PEACESAT meetings held whenever possible.

FINANCIAL ORGANIZATION

When PIALA was established, a bank account was set up in the Commonwealth of the Northern Mariana Islands. A few years later, this became the PIALA Publications account and another account was set up for general income and expenses. There is usually an account also set up on the island where the conference will be held, sometimes in conjunction with the establishment of the local library association. These arrangements have worked well throughout the years. However, with the retirement of the author from the University of Guam, the PIALA Publications account has been closed.

Although not part of the *By-Laws*, to facilitate the planning of the annual conference, PIALA provides $500 as seed money to the island entity hosting the conference. Conference registration fees become part of the PIALA treasury, although any pre- or postconference fees remain with the hosting island.

MEMBERSHIP

PIALA members are divided into two categories: individual and institutional or corporate members. The membership fee was established with the founding of PIALA and to date, has never been increased. The fee for an individual member is $20 per year, and institutional or corporate membership is $50 per year.

Membership is not restricted to PIALA's geographical boundaries. In December 2007, PIALA had 63 currently paid members representing Micronesia, several other Pacific Islands and Hawaii. In the past, people have joined PIALA from Australia, New Zealand, the Philippines, Japan, Canada, Finland, Sweden, the United Kingdom, and the continental United States; however, it is difficult to collect membership fees on an ongoing basis. They are usually paid at the annual meeting. Many people from outside of Micronesia who have attended a PIALA Conference usually join at that time, but do not keep up their membership in succeeding years.

COMMUNICATIONS LINKS AND PUBLIC RELATIONS

Given the vast geographic area covered by PIALA, coupled with the reality of costly and unreliable telecommunication systems, one of the biggest challenges is maintaining membership and communication links within the PIALA and promoting the association throughout the world. PIALA uses several methods to communicate, as described below.

PIALA Newsletter

The *PIALA Newsletter* was born soon after PIALA was established, with the first issue published in June 1991. When first launched, it was hoped that the newsletter would be published quarterly. Although the publication has continued throughout the years, being a volunteer effort has made for an irregular publication pattern. All issues ever published appear on the PIALA WWW site (http://piala.org.googlepages.com/newsletter) (accessed September 2008).

As many parts of the world still have inadequate, costly, slow, and unreliable Internet access, paper copies of the *PIALA Newsletter* are mailed to all individuals and institutions that are or have been members in the recent past, or have participated in an annual conference. PIALA maintains a distribution list used for mailing the *PIALA Newsletter* throughout the region and the world. This has been an important way to keep people involved in the association, even if they may not have recently paid dues. As of October 2007, we had 393 addresses on our list. Although the last issue of the PIALA Newsletter was published in 2005, it is hoped future issues will appear.

PIALA Web page

The first PIALA Web page appeared in 1995 and was the result of the collaborative efforts of the author and Tom C. Gerhardt, an information scientist with an interest in the Pacific at Saarland University and State Library in Saarbruchen, Germany. The site was hosted on a server at Saarland University and remained there for several years. In 1998, the University of Guam offered to host the www page and it continued to reside on their server until early in 2008, when it was moved to (http://piala.org.googlepages.com/) (accessed September 2008).

PIALA Listserv

In 2000, an electronic mailing list for PIALA was established on the University of Guam Robert F. Kennedy Library server. A few years later, the list was moved to a server at the Secretariat of the Pacific Community in Noumea, New Caledonia, where it currently resides. This is an open list and anyone with an interest in PIALA or Pacific Island libraries, archives or museums may subscribe to it. As of the beginning of 2008, there were 132 subscribers and the number of messages posted varies between 15 and 50 per month. [Anyone with an interest in PIALA or the Pacific Islands can subscribe to the PIALA list at http://lists.spc.int/mailman/listinfo/piala_lists.spc.int (accessed September 2008). The PIALA list archives beginning from 2001 are available for public access at http://lyris.spc.int/read/?forum=piala (accessed September 2008). Archives beginning in August 2006 are also available at http://lists.spc.int/pipermail/piala_lists.spc.int/ (accessed September 2008).]

PIALA Proceedings

Beginning with the PIALA 1993 Conference held in Saipan, Commonwealth of the Northern Mariana Islands, the proceedings of most conferences have been published, with some exceptions. The PIALA 1999 Conference proceedings were never published, the PIALA 2001 Conference was cancelled, and the PIALA 2002 and PIALA 2003 Conference proceeding were not published as well. The PIALA 2004 and PIALA 2005 Conference proceedings were published as one volume, and the proceedings for the PIALA 2006 and PIALA 2007 Conferences are still in process.

Once published, the volume is submitted to ERIC (Educational Resources Information Center) in the United States and is available online in full text from the ERIC www site (http://www.eric.ed.gov/) (accessed September 2008), as well as the PIALA www page (http://piala.org.googlepages.com/proceedings> (accessed September 2008). They are also deposited with the United States Library of Congress and have ISBN numbers assigned.

One complimentary copy of each edition of the proceedings is deposited in every public and academic library throughout Micronesia. A complimentary copy is also given to each contributor included in the publication. They are also sold worldwide and the money received from the sale has been used to publish succeeding volumes. In the future, it appears that all new editions will be available only electronically, at no cost.

PIALA CONFERENCES

The traditional *bai* (a traditional Palauan men's hut or council house) on the grounds of the Belau National Museum was the venue of PIALA's first conference held in November 1991, with the theme *Preserving Knowledge for Tomorrow*. Over 40 participants from throughout Micronesia, Fiji, Hawaii, and the mainland United States gathered in the *bai* to hear presentations on resource sharing, preservation techniques for the tropics, serials and government documents, continuing education, and electronic telecommunications (see Fig. 2).

With each year, this eagerly awaited conference moves to another island with a new theme, and a continually growing number of local librarians and archivists participating and appearing on the conference program. Although the same general areas from the first gathering still are discussed, each year new topics are added to reflect the changing landscape of the field and new areas of interest.

A keynote speaker is selected for each conference. One memorable keynote speech was given by Norma Amenu-Kpodo, the Executive Secretary of the *Commonwealth Library Association*, coming all the way from the island of Jamaica for the PIALA 2000 Conference in Guam. She presented *Library Associations in Developing Countries: the Caribbean Islands as a Point of Comparison with Micronesia*,[6] conveying in her paper that no matter where in the world your library association resides, we all face an array of the same problems. At the PIALA 1995 Conference in Yap, Dr. Marcia Bates from the University of California at Los Angeles presented another important keynote speech, *"Learning About Your Users' Information Needs: A Key to Effective Service."*[7]

In 1996, at the Marshall Islands PIALA Conference in Majuro, the first PIALA resolution was passed,[8] addressing the need for cost-effective high performance Internet access to libraries and archives. In passing this resolution, the association took on an important advocacy role in fostering library development and information access in the region.

In addition to providing an opportunity to experience a professional conference for many who do not have the opportunity to travel, the PIALA conferences have served to promote libraries and library services to the host island communities. Local government officials are always invited to the opening session in hopes that they show their support for local libraries, and are encouraged to speak on behalf of their government, with their remarks being included in the *PIALA Proceedings*. Local newspapers usually report the event, along with local radio and television coverage. Usually banners announcing the conference appear at the airport to welcome participants and decorate the conference venue.

PIALA conferences are also used to exchange local resources. Local telephone books and college catalogs are among the most popular materials exchanged. There is also a time set aside for each island group to report on their activities during the year, providing for the exchange of new ideas between participants. Tours of local libraries, archives, and museums are always a part of the conference, providing local hosts the opportunity to proudly spotlight their facilities and for participants to become familiar with the islands' resources.

Fig. 2 Participants sitting in the Belau National Museum's traditional *bai* during a session at the first PIALA conference. Photograph by Arlene Cohen (the author).

Depending on the venue, the conference draws between 50 and 75 people, with about 40–50% of the participants representing the local island hosting the conference. Conference registration fees are usually determined by the local organizers, as well as pre- and postconference workshop fees. To promote the conference and raise local funds, PIALA T-shirts are usually sold during the conference.

Because conferences are planned by people on the hosting island, PIALA conferences have at times spurred the establishment or reawakening of local library associations. After PIALA met on Palau in 1991, the local librarians established the *Palau Library Association*. Soon after the 1992 conference, the Marshall Islands also established their own local library association. A library association was formed in Yap prior to the 1995 annual conference held there. Although Pohnpei has hosted PIALA Conferences from the beginning, it was in 2006 that the *Libraries, Archives, and Museums of Pohnpei (LAMP) Library Association* began to meet informally. The *By-Laws* and a charter are currently in draft form, almost ready to be formalized by the membership. Chuuk and Kosrae began working to revitalizing their library associations soon after the *Library Advocacy Workshop* held at the PIALA 2006 Conference in Palau. The *Guam Library Association* had been active for several years before PIALA was established and took an active part in the PIALA 1994 and PIALA 2000 Conferences held in Guam.

A *Chronology of PIALA Conferences* was published in the 2004/2005 *Proceedings*, including the conference theme, date, and conference venue.[9]

ADVOCACY

As in many parts of the world, Pacific Islands government officials, educators, and the public generally do not appreciate the role and value of libraries in our society. Given this reality, library associations must take an active role in influencing government decisions in such areas as basic funding for libraries, new emerging areas of information literacy, copyright, indigenous knowledge, training, and telecommunications technology. However, to have any impact, library association leaders must understand the role of library associations as pressure groups for political action and policy decisions, and must have the requisite skills in policy development and implementation, building effective advocacy campaigns and public relations.

To address this advocacy training need, at the PIALA 1997 Conference in Pohnpei, a postconference workshop on library advocacy was presented by Tuula Haavisto, then the Finnish Library Association Director General. The workshop was funded by the *International Federation of Library Associations and Federations (IFLA) Advancement of Librarianship in the Third World Programme* and brought local librarians from throughout Micronesia to Pohnpei. At the PIALA 1998 Conference in Kosrae the following year, several participants reported on their advocacy projects.

Several years later in 2005, another library advocacy workshop was proposed and funding was again obtained from the *IFLA Advancement of Librarianship in the Third World Programme*, as well as the *IFLA Management of Library Associations Section (MLAS)* and the ALA. At the PIALA 2006 Conference in Palau, the library advocacy workshop was held as a preconference and was presented by Keith Michael Fiels, the ALA Executive Director and Michael Dowling, the ALA International Relations Office Director.[10] This workshop also brought library association leaders from throughout Micronesia, as well as Papua New Guinea and Kiribati.

At the Palau advocacy workshop, the participants prioritized issues ripe for advocacy, which reflect the pressing needs in the region. Those areas were

> "Increased government funding for library materials and technology
> Funding and resources for school libraries and librarians
> Need for national libraries and archives
> Extension of services for un-served regions and islands and
> Increase public awareness of value and benefit of libraries."[11]

Participants created action plans for their islands and the following year, presented reports of their work at the PIALA 2007 Conference in Tinian. Most recently, stemming from the Palau advocacy workshop and the subsequent Tinian reports, Atarino Helieisar presented a paper on library advocacy in Micronesia at the 74th IFLA Conference in Quebec, Canada. http://www.ifla.org/IV/ifla74/papers/093-Helieisar-en.pdf (accessed September 2008).

Moreover, as a result of the advocacy training, several islands were able to obtain funding for projects, and local library associations in Chuuk, Yap, and Kosrae were refreshed.

Thanks to PIALA, librarians throughout the region are aware of each other's needs, issues, and challenges, and help to advocate for each other. Recently, a librarian from Guam worked to establish a school library in Kapingamarangi, an isolated atoll in the Federated States of Micronesia. In another instance, a terrible typhoon in 2004 completely devastated the Yap State Public Library and the Yap State Hospital Medical Library in the Federated States of Micronesia. The author of this entry, working with another Guam librarian wrote successful grants to help reestablish these libraries.

TRAINING INITIATIVES

The region faces a serious lack of professionally trained librarians, archivists, and museum curators. In a plea made by Jean Thoulag, Vice-President for Institutional Affairs at the College of Micronesia—FSM at the PIALA 2005 Conference in Kosrae, she said, "Please let us in PIALA and those of you from these [Pacific] institutions work together to find practical and affordable solutions to address the critical need for staff development training in the region."[12]

Currently, there is only one active library skills training program in Micronesia at Palau Community College. The only one certificate/diploma program in the rest of the Pacific Islands is provided through the University of the South Pacific. In the recent past, there was an undergraduate School Librarianship program at the University of Guam, however, due to lack of university support, it is now defunct. The closest campus offering a Master in Library Science is the University of Hawaii.

Beginning in 1994, PIALA began to actively address this critical problem by providing the first preconference 2 day workshop on collection development for small libraries, given by Dr. Harry Uyehara, a noted librarian in Guam. In 1995, another pre-conference workshop was presented by two noted archivists, Karin Brennan from the University of New South Wales in Sydney, Australia and John C. Wright from Honolulu, Hawaii. The 2 day workshop dealt with the practical care of books, preservation, and disaster preparedness and recovery. At the following year's conference, both pre- and postconference workshops were presented and now are an integral part of all PIALA conferences, covering a wide range of topics.

Although these PIALA pre- and postconference workshops attempt to fill a gap, there still remains the serious lack of opportunities for education and training leading up to a credential or professional degree.

RESOURCE SHARING

One of the purposes stated in PIALA's *By-Laws* is "To foster awareness and encourage cooperation and resource sharing."[4] In a 1998 paper, the authors observed that "perhaps the most important impact of PIALA has been the increase of networking and resource sharing among the members."[13] However, before one can do resource sharing, one must know who is out there and what they have. Given the geographical vastness and lack of easy communications, when PIALA was established, very few in the Pacific Islands knew who was out there and what resources were where.

To address this critical need, one of the first projects PIALA undertook was compiling a list of regional libraries and in 1993, the *Directory of Libraries, Archives, and Museums in Micronesia*[14] was published. This was the first comprehensive regional directory ever done. Subsequently, in 2003, the content became part of a bigger online project undertaken by the National Library of Australia, *Libraries of Asia and the Pacific Directory*http://www.nla.gov.au/lap (accessed September 2008). The online resource allows libraries to update and amend their own entries whenever needed. However, since many Pacific Islands do not have reliable, or in some cases, any Internet access, a print edition[15] was published, funded by IFLA from a grant submitted by PIALA, in cooperation with the National Library of Australia and the Secretariat of the Pacific Community.

The first attempt to compile a regional union catalog came about with the help of Daniel Peacock's LSCA funds when a bibliography of reports, surveys, and studies dealing with the Trust Territory was compiled and published.[16] Throughout the ensuing years, there were scattered lists of serial holdings throughout the region. The first attempt to draw these serials holdings together was in 1997 with the publication of the *Union List of Serials in Libraries in Guam and Micronesia*.[17] The collection of content for this publication was done with the support of PIALA members realizing the value of a union list for resource sharing. The latest edition published in 2002 and titled the *Union List of Serials in Pacific Islands Libraries*[18] was expanded and now contains the holdings of both the University of the South Pacific Library in Suva, Fiji, and the Secretariat of the Pacific Community Library.

LIBRARY ASSOCIATION LINKAGES OUTSIDE OF MICRONESIA

As Goetzfridt wrote when referring to meeting the needs of the public, "the Pacific Islands Association of Libraries and Archives (PIALA) established an organizational paradigm of unity for Micronesia."[19] As PIALA has matured that unity has expanded to include other library associations both inside and outside the Pacific Islands working toward meeting those needs, as discussed below.

International Federation of Library Associations and Institutions

In 1996, PIALA was first represented at the IFLA Conference in Beijing, China[20] and the following year, the author of this entry was elected as the PIALA representative to sit on the *IFLA Roundtable for the Management of Library Associations* (RTMLA), which later became *MLAS*. In 1998, the author became the RTMLA (then MLAS) Secretary and continued in that position until 2005.

In 2004, PIALA nominated Mark Perkins from New Caledonia to stand for election to the *Regional Standing Committee for Asia and Oceania*. He was elected with his term beginning in 2005. Then, in 2006, PIALA nominated three members to stand for election to IFLA Standing Committees and all were elected. Tamina Noddy from Papua New Guinea became a member of the *Management of Library Associations Standing Committee*; Libby Cass from Fiji was elected to the *Regional Standing Committee for Asia and Oceania*; and Mark Perkins was elected to the *Free Access to Information and Freedom of Expression Committee*, each with terms beginning in August 2007.

Throughout the years, PIALA has applied for and received several grants from IFLA for publications, workshops and attendance at both PIALA and IFLA conferences.

Swedish Library Association

For several years, PIALA's IFLA membership was supported by the *Swedish Library Association*, under the visionary leadership of their Secretary General Christina Stenberg. She hoped this would serve as a model within IFLA for library associations in developed countries to encourage library associations in developing areas to engage with IFLA. This arrangement allowed PIALA members to see the benefits of IFLA membership before the major financial decision to join IFLA was made by PIALA. In 2001, PIALA voted to become a self-supporting member of IFLA and has maintained their membership since.

Moreover, without the additional financial support of the *Swedish Library Association*, PIALA's participation in the *RTMLA* and later the *MLAS* meetings between 2000 and 2004 would not have been possible. This too was part of the *Swedish Library Association's* effort to model library associations in developed countries supporting the participation of officers on IFLA Sections from developing areas.

Hawaii Library Association

Throughout the years, participants from Hawaii have attended and participated in PIALA conferences, conducting workshops, presenting papers, and providing support.

In 1998, inspired by the *America Library Association* President Barbara Ford's theme *Global Reach, Local Touch*, the *Hawaii Library Association (HLA)* and the *Pacific Islands Association of Libraries and Archives* formed an international partnership. This relationship was formalized in a resolution passed on November 2, 1998 by the *HLA* Executive Board, followed by another resolution passed by the PIALA Executive Board on November 19, 1998. The ALA Chapter Relations Office was informed of the partnership and the resolutions appear on the PIALA www page http://piala.org.googlepages.com/history (accessed September 2008).

American Library Association

Although individual PIALA members were involved with ALA throughout the years, it was not until 2005 that ALA became actively involved with PIALA. At that time, ALA took on a leadership role in the *IFLA Management of Library Associations Section* and funded the author's participation as Secretary of the section at the 2005 meetings, much as was previously done by the *Swedish Library Association*.

Soon after, thanks to funding from IFLA and ALA, the *2006 Library Advocacy Workshop*, described elsewhere in this entry, was a pivotal event in bringing ALA to the Pacific Islands. Stemming from that involvement, in 2007, when judging was over for ALA's *Outstanding Reference Books* competition, ALA donated many of the reference books to the Palau Community College Library. Hopefully, this relationship will continue to the benefit of both associations.

Fiji Library Association

Several *Fiji Library Association* members have participated and presented papers at PIALA Conferences throughout the years. Recently, PIALA and the *Fiji Library Association* worked together to request the *Australian Library and Information Association* to develop a sponsorship program for Pacific Island librarians to attend the 2010 IFLA Conference in Brisbane, Australia.

OTHER LINKAGES

To foster greater unity between library associations, PIALA representatives have participated in many library conferences throughout the world. In addition to the many IFLA, HLA and ALA conferences where PIALA has participated as early as 1994, PIALA participated in the 1994 joint *New Zealand Library and Information Association and the Australia Library and Information Association Conference* in Wellington, New Zealand. PIALA also participated in both the *8th Interlending & Document Supply Conference* in 2003 in Canberra, Australia and the *10th Interlending and Document Supply Conference* in 2007 in Singapore.

Most recently, PIALA was invited to participate in the *11th Aboriginal and Torres Strait Islander Library Information and Resource Network (ATSILIRN) Conference* in Darwin Northern Territory, Australia in 2008. These events each broaden the network and increase awareness of PIALA and the issues faced in Micronesian libraries.

Pacific Resources for Education and Learning

Pacific Resources for Educational and Learning (PREL), an independent, nonprofit agency based in Honolulu and serving the educational communities in Micronesia, has been supportive of PIALA for many years. In 2000, PREL funded a librarian from the Solomon Islands to present a paper about the Forum Fisheries Agency Library at the PIALA 2000 Conference in Guam.[21] Throughout the years, PREL representatives have attended PIALA conferences and presented papers and workshops.

In the past several years, PREL has funded several training initiatives for librarians in the region. Most recently, a successful 3 day workshop on disaster preparedness, response and recovery was held in conjunction with the PIALA 2007 Conference in Tinian, Commonwealth of the Northern Mariana Islands. This workshop was the first to be presented with funding from a 3 year United States Institute of Museums and Library Services grant entitled *Leaders for Pacific Libraries*. The grant included three, 3 day subject-specific workshops held in conjunction with PIALA annual conferences, providing the opportunity for workshop participants to attend the PIALA Conference, as well.

OTHER NOTABLE EVENTS

The PIALA Lifetime Achievement Award

The PIALA Lifetime Achievement Award was created by a resolution passed by the PIALA Executive Board 1997 at the annual meeting in Pohnpei. This award was designed to "honor librarians and lay persons who have made a substantial and integral contribution to libraries and librarianship in the Western Pacific."[22]

In 1998, the award was first bestowed on Daniel J. Peacock, former Director of Library Services for the Trust Territory of the Pacific Islands. In 2006, Dr. Karen Peacock, the University of Hawaii Library Head of Special Collections and Pacific Collection Curator was the second recipient of the award. Most recently in 2007, the author, who was then the University of Guam Robert F. Kennedy Memorial Library Circulation and Interlibrary Loan Librarian, was presented the award.

Florence Nalezny Warpeha Memorial Books to Micronesian Libraries

The PIALA 1997 Conference in Pohnpei saw the beginning of the *Florence Nalezny Warpeha Memorial Books to Micronesian Libraries*. Every year, Rita Warpeha, formerly a librarian at the Pohnpei Public Library, would donate a selection of Micronesian and Pacific Island–related natural science children's books in memory of her mother. The donations continued until 2003 and the books found homes in local libraries on the island hosting the annual conference.

Dakio Syne Memorial

Dakio Syne, the Director of the College of Micronesia—FSM Learning Resources tragically passed away in 2002. He was a founding member of PIALA and PIALA's first President, as well as the first Micronesian to earn a master's degree in library science in 1976 from New York University. In his honor, the *Dakio Syne Memorial Fund* was set up to help fund a Micronesian librarian's first attendance to PIALA. Also, PIALA supported the publication of a book memorializing him and his work.[23]

CONCLUSION

The Pacific Islands Association of Libraries and Archives was established 17 years ago as a voluntary association of dedicated people sharing many hopes and challenges. Yvan Souares, a Pacific Islands epidemiologist summed up well the challenges when he wrote,

"These islands are scattered over 30 million square kilometers of the Pacific, an area almost four times that of Australia. Ninety-eight percent of that area is water, leaving a total land area only half that of the Northern Territory of Australia. For seven million Pacific people, the development of human networks in these conditions is both a challenge and a prerequisite to socio-economic development."[24]

Although he was writing about health care workers throughout the entire Pacific, these human networks are just as profoundly important to people working in libraries, archives, museums within Micronesia. With the establishment and growth of PIALA, in the face of the major economic, communication, and training challenges, the human networks are alive and thriving, expanding borders to throughout the Pacific Islands. As these networks continue to grow, we all benefit in access to the information and resources needed for socioeconomic development and personal well-being.

ACKNOWLEDGMENTS

A heartfelt thanks to Joanne Tarpley Crotts and Karen Peacock who helped give birth to PIALA; Iris Falcam for her willingness to share her wisdom; Mark Perkins, for his helpful insights; Elisabeth Newbold for her fresh look at the manuscript, Marcia Bates for her encouragement, and my husband Steve for his patience while I sat at my computer. They all had their part in making this piece come to life. And, to all who worked to grow PIALA these past 18 years, so this entry could exist.

REFERENCES

1. Goetzfridt, N.J. Micronesian library service. In *Encyclopedia of Library and Information Science*; Allen, K., Ed.; Marcel Dekker, Inc.: New York, 2000; Vol. 66, 217–230 Supplement 29.
2. Goetzfridt, N.J. Micronesian library service. In *Encyclopedia of Library and Information Science*; Allen, K., Ed.; Marcel Dekker, Inc.: New York, 2000; Vol. 66, 226 Supplement 29.

3. Cohen, A.; Crotts, J.T.; Lovas, I. Developing library and information services in Micronesia. In *Libraries: Global Reach/Local Touch*; de la Pena Cook, K., Ford, B.J., Lippincott, K., Eds.; American Library Association: Chicago, IL, 1998; 50–59.
4. Pacific Islands Association of Libraries and Archives, *By-Laws*, PIALA: Mangilao, Guam, 1991; February 28, 1991 1 Adopted.
5. Pacific Islands Association of Libraries and Archives, *By-Laws*, PIALA: Mangilao, Guam, 1991; February 28, 1991 3 Adopted.
6. Amenu-Kpodo, N. Library associations in developing countries: The Caribbean Islands as a point of comparison with Micronesia PIALA 2000—Libraries and Archives: Where Information and Language Literacy Begin, joint with the Annual Regional Language Arts Conference—Engaged Readers and Writers in Multicultural Island Communities; Cohen, A., Quan, C., Eds.; Pacific Islands Association of Libraries and Archives: Mangilao, Guam, 2004; 21–36 Selected Papers from the 10th Pacific Islands Association of Libraries and Archives Conference and the 13th Annual Regional Language Arts Conference; Tumon, Guam.
7. Bates, M. Learning about your users' information needs: A key to effective service PIALA '95: Preservation of Culture through Archives and Libraries; Cohen, A., Ed.; Pacific Islands Association of Libraries and Archives: Mangilao, Guam, 1996; 5–12 Selected Papers from the 5th Pacific Islands Association of Libraries and Archives Conference.
8. PIALA resolution on Internet access PIALA '96 Jaketo Jaketak Kobban Alele Eo– Identifying, Using and Sharing Local Resources; Cohen, A., Ed.; Pacific Islands Association of Libraries and Archives: Mangilao, Guam, 1997; 121 Papers from the 6th Pacific Islands Association of Libraries and Archives Conference.
9. Chronology of PIALA conferences PIALA 2004—14th Annual Conference Proceedings Maron In Read Im Jeje Ej Ad Kojatdikdik, Library Ko Rej Jikin Kakurmool Kojatdikdik In Im Jolet Eo Ad Ej Bwinnid/Literacy Our Hope, Libraries Our Scope and Heritage Our Property and the PIALA 2005—15th Annual Conference Proceedings Kasrpacsr Misenge Ac Etwack Lutu/Resources Today and Learning Tomorrow; Cohen, A., Ed.; Pacific Islands Association of Libraries and Archives: Mangilao, Guam, 2006; ix–x Selected papers from the 14th and 15th Pacific Islands Association of Libraries and Archives Annual Conferences.
10. Dowling, M. ALA brings advocacy workshop to Pacific. ALA Int. Leads **2007**, *21*(1), 1.
11. Cohen, A. Uppsala University Library: Sweden, 2007; March 3 Final Report on the *Workshop to Train Library Association Leaders in the Pacific Islands in Library Advocacy and Policy Development*; submitted to Birgitta Sandell, IFLA/ALP.
12. Thoulag, J. Three A's for PIALA PIALA 2004—14th Annual Conference Proceedings Maron In Read Im Jeje Ej Ad Kojatdikdik, Library Ko Rej Jikin Kakurmool Kojatdikdik In Im Jolet Eo Ad Ej Bwinnid/Literacy Our Hope, Libraries Our Scope and Heritage Our Property and the PIALA 2005—15th Annual Conference Proceedings Kasrpacsr Misenge Ac Etwack Lutu/Resources Today and Learning Tomorrow; Cohen, A., Ed.; Pacific Islands Association of Libraries and Archives: Mangilao, Guam, 2006; 81–88 Selected papers from the 14th and 15th Pacific Islands Association of Libraries and Archives Annual Conferences.
13. Cohen, A. Crotts, J.T. Lovas, I. Developing library and information services in Micronesia. In *Libraries: Global Reach/Local Touch*; de la Pena Cook, K., Ford, B.J., Lippincott, K., Eds.; American Library Association: Chicago, IL, 1998; 58.
14. Cohen, A. *Directory of Libraries, Archives and Museums in Micronesia*, University of Guam Micronesian Area Research Center: Mangilao, Guam, 1993; Comp.
15. *Directory of Libraries and Archives in the Pacific, Islands*, 2nd Ed.; Cohen, A., Henderson, S., Eds.; University of Guam: Mangilao, Guam, 2003.
16. Wright, G. *A Bibliography of Reports, Surveys, and Studies Prepared by, for, or about the Trust Territory of the Pacific Islands*, Department of Education, Trust Territory of the Pacific Islands: Saipan, Mariana Islands, 1969; compiled by Gordon Wright as part of the Union Catalog Project and Funded by the Library Services and Construction Act, Title III.
17. Crotts, J. *Union List of Serials in Libraries in Guam and Micronesia*, University of Guam: Mangilao, Guam, 1997; 3rd Rev.
18. Cohen, A., Yoshida, P., Eds. *Union List of Serials in Pacific Islands Libraries*; University of Guam: Mangilao, Guam, 2002; 5th rev.
19. Goetzfridt, N.J. Micronesian library service. In *Encyclopedia of Library and Information Science*; Allen, K., Ed.; Marcel Dekker, Inc.: New York, 2000; Vol. 66, 228 Supplement 29.
20. Cohen, A. Library associations in underdeveloped regions and their impact on library development Paper presented at the 62nd International Federation of Library Associations General Conference: Management of Library Associations Workshop Beijing, China August, 29, 1996 Unpublished.
21. Kwalea, N.D. Moving ahead in the Solomon Islands: Information access and dissemination in the Forum Fisheries Agency Library PIALA 2000—Libraries and Archives: Where Information and Language Literacy Begin, joint with the Annual Regional Language Arts Conference—Engaged Readers and Writers in Multicultural Island Communities; Cohen, A., Quan, C., Eds.; Pacific Islands Association of Libraries and Archives: Mangilao, Guam, 2004; 85–98 Selected Papers from the 10th Pacific Islands Association of Libraries and Archives Conference and the 13th Annual Regional Language Arts Conference.
22. Resolution passed. PIALA Newsl. **1998**, *7*(4), 2 http://piala.org.googlepages.com/PIALA_Vol7_4.pdf (accessed September 2008).
23. Falcam, I., Ed. *Tributes to Micronesia's Librarian Dakio Syne 1943–2002*; New Horizons Printing and Publishing Co.: Pohnpei, Federated States of Micronesia, 2002.
24. Souares, Y. PPHSN and PACNET: The Pacific Islands are now tuned into the 21st century. Pacific Health Dialog **1998**, *5*(1), 200.

BIBLIOGRAPHY

1. Cohen, A. The Pacific Islands Association of Libraries and Archives (PIALA) formed in the Pacific Islands. FID News Bull. **1992**, *42*(12), 285–6.
2. Cohen, A. The Pacific Islands Association of Libraries and Archives (PIALA). Pacific Health Dialog: J. Clin. Health Community Med. Pacific **1999**, *6*(1), 132–4.
3. Crotts, J.T. PIALA in Micronesia. InCite **1997**, *18*(12), 16.
4. Crotts, J.T.; Rungrad, I. Atolls in association. Nat. Libr. Aust. News **1997**, *7*(7), 9–11.
5. Lane, N. Library education needs in the Pacific Islands. *Research Into Practice*, Pacific Resources for Education and Learning: Honolulu, HI, 2004; http://www. prel.org/products/pr_/compendium04/Lane.pdf (accessed September 2008).
6. Newbold, E. Tyler, J. *Pacific Islands Association of Libraries and Archives*, San Jose State University: San Jose, CA, 2007; Team Project: Part I. Unpublished research paper submitted October 28, 2007.
7. Tarpley, J. Pacific Islands Association of Libraries and Archives Conference. Third World Libraries **1993**, *4*(1), 63–64 http://www.worlib.org/vol04no1/tarpley_v04n1.shtml (accessed February 2008).
8. Tarpley, J. Conference report: Pacific Islands Association of Libraries and Archives (PIALA). Third World Libr. **1995**, *5*(2), 76–7 1994 meeting, Tamuning, Guam, November 2–4, 1994.
9. Tarpley, J. Pacific Islands Association of Libraries and Archives: Training in the Islands. Associates The Electronic Library Support Staff Journal **1995**, *3*(1), http://associates.ucr.edu/395featur10.htm (accessed September 2008).
10. http://www.worlib.org/vol05no2/tarpley_v05n2.shtml (accessed September 2008).

Papyrology

Roger S. Bagnall
Institute for the Study of the Ancient World, New York University, New York, New York, U.S.A.

Abstract

Papyrology is the science of preserving, reading, and interpreting ancient texts written on papyrus. It includes texts written on other materials using ink. The majority of preserved papyri come from the first millennium B.C. and the first millennium A.D.; most are in Greek, but many texts in Egyptian and other languages also survive. They contribute to our knowledge of ancient literature and books, as well as practically every aspect of ancient history, including especially social, economic, and cultural history.

INTRODUCTION

Papyrology is the science of preserving, reading, and interpreting ancient texts written on papyrus. The field historically dealt particularly with those papyri written in Greek or Latin; those in other languages were often considered part of the domains of Egyptology and Semitic studies, but papyrology has increasingly included a wider range of languages and materials; studies of papyri in Demotic Egyptian, Coptic, and Arabic are now active parts of the discipline. This entry explains what papyrus is, how it was used in ancient times and is treated today, how the discipline of papyrology works with papyri and other ancient textual supports, where papyri are published, and what contributions the work of papyrologists has made to the study of literature, history, and language.

THE PLANT AND THE PAPER

The writing material is made from the fibers of the reed *Cyperus papyrus*; strips are cut from the stalks, laid side by side, first in one direction and then on top of these at a right angle. They are pressed together so that the natural juices of the plant flow, acting as a binding agent. After drying, the resultant pieces provide a smooth, flexible, light-colored, and durable writing surface. Typically, a number of such pieces would be glued end to end (with small overlaps) to make a roll, which was the standard form of papyrus for commerce and book production. For documents of smaller than roll size, pieces would then be cut from the roll to the desired dimensions.

Paper from papyrus was manufactured by the Egyptians as early as the fourth millennium B.C.; for various reasons (partly the circumstances of preservation), the papyri that have survived to modern times come largely from the first millennium B.C. and the first millennium of the present era, although there are some notable earlier literary, documentary, and funerary texts in Egyptian. Papyrus came to be used less and less after the Byzantine period, for reasons that are not fully understood (see "Contributions of Papyri: Literature," subsection "History of the Book"). Whether as cause or effect, the papyrus swamps in Egypt, which were the source of the raw material of the paper industry, gradually silted up and disappeared from Egypt so that the plant is now found growing wild only in an area 500 miles up the Nile in Ethiopia. It has been reintroduced in Egypt and elsewhere in modern times.

Papyrologists also deal with texts written on certain other materials: potsherds (*ostraka*), wood, waxed tablets, leather rolls, and parchment. Writing on stone and metal, on the other hand, is considered to belong to the province of epigraphy. The division between the two disciplines is sometimes indistinct.

THE REDISCOVERY OF PAPYRI

Although a certain number of papyri continued to be preserved in archives in Europe through the Medieval Period, the Western world lost awareness of papyri during this period, and not until the eighteenth century did papyri come back to the attention of Europe. In Herculaneum, in 1752, a villa was found in which numerous carbonized rolls of papyrus from a private philosophical library were preserved. When to the difficulty of unrolling the brittle texts was added the disappointment of the literary world at the failure of the rolls to contain famous lost works of literature, the papyri of Herculaneum receded from the public view. (The study of these papyri, mainly works of the Epicurean philosopher Philodemus, has had a notable resurgence in the last 30 years.) No less disappointing to scholars of the time was a papyrus roll brought back from Egypt in 1778 that turned out to be an account of laborers on irrigation works rather than a lost play of Sophocles or some such.

It was not until the middle of the next century that a few sizable collections of papyri in Europe were formed

Pacific–Philosophy

Encyclopedia of Library and Information Sciences, Fourth Edition DOI: 10.1081/E-ELIS4-120043964

and published, notably those of London, Leiden, Paris, and Turin. Then in the last quarter of the nineteenth century, numerous finds were made and a vast expansion of papyrus collections in Egypt, Europe, and North America was underway. Over the next 60 years, hundreds of thousands of texts, often fragmentary, were found, both literary and documentary, from organized or clandestine excavations. The largest number of papyri comes from Middle Egypt, particularly Oxyrhynchus (modern Bahnasa) and the Fayûm, a low-lying area to the southwest of Cairo, but other finds have ranged from the Nubian frontier in the northern Sudan to the Delta. Few papyri, however, have been excavated in the Delta and other regularly irrigated areas, because of the destructive effects of water on papyrus; desert areas (especially tombs) and once-cultivated but now dry regions have been the most productive. From Alexandria, the capital, we have only a small number of texts found in other areas (sometimes sent there as waste paper for wrapping mummies—cartonnage, as it is called).

Outside Egypt, significant finds of papyri have been made at Dura-Europos and elsewhere in the Euphrates valley in Syria (mostly from the third century of our era), from Nessana in the Negev (late Byzantine period), in the area of the Dead Sea, at Petra (Jordan, also Byzantine), and in Italy the carbonized papyri of Herculaneum already mentioned. A very early carbonized roll (fourth century B.C.) was found in a tomb at Derveni in Macedonia. Unsuitable climatic conditions have caused papyri to be destroyed in most areas, but more finds may yet be made in countries with desert regions similar to Egypt. Ostraka are found more widely, from North Africa to Iran, and parchment documents have been found from late antique Bactria and other parts of the Near East and Central Asia. Wooden tablets with ink texts have been excavated in England, at the Roman military camp at Vindolanda, where anaerobic conditions preserved them.

COLLECTIONS OF PAPYRI

There is no full census of collections and their contents available, for papyri are usually made known only when published in full, and the process of publication is slow. The largest collection is probably the Oxyrhynchus papyri (in the Sackler Library, Oxford, from Grenfell and Hunt's excavations a century ago), not yet fully inventoried, the next that in the National Library in Vienna, formed by the Archduke Rainer by purchases 75 to 100 years ago; its total number of objects, in many languages, is around 180,000. There are many collections in Germany, with the largest in Berlin, and others in Heidelberg, Cologne, Munich, Freiburg, Jena, Leipzig, and Trier. The principal French collections are those in Paris, Strasbourg, and Lille; in Italy in Milan, Florence, and the Vatican; in England in London, Oxford, and Manchester; and in Scandinavia at Oslo and Copenhagen. Egypt itself possesses one of the largest collections in the Egyptian Museum in Cairo and smaller ones in the Coptic Museum (Cairo) and Graeco-Roman Museum in Alexandria. In North America, the largest collection is at the University of Michigan, and smaller but important ones exist at Berkeley, Yale, Columbia, Duke, and Princeton. Still smaller but significant collections are at New York University, Washington University, Toronto, Pennsylvania, and others. Many American colleges have small groups of papyri distributed by the Egypt Exploration Fund in the early part of the century. There are also private collections in many countries, mostly small but occasionally (as with Martin Schøyen in Norway) quite large.

TREATMENT OF PAPYRI

Papyri are commonly in bad condition when found—torn, full of holes, wadded together, dirty, folded, and even charred. Relatively simple problems can be solved by humidifying the papyri and manipulating them in this condition, allowing them to dry only when clean and straightened. For cartonnage, a technique has been developed whereby a dilute solution of an enzyme is used to dissolve the adhesive between sheets within a few minutes. Papyri of any size are normally best preserved between thin sheets of glass, held together with clips or tape, although folded acid-free paper or blotting paper may be an acceptable short-term substitute for little-handled materials. Like other old paper materials, they benefit from storage out of the light and in controlled temperature and humidity conditions.

Various aids can be used in reading texts that are not clear to the naked eye: first, simple magnifiers, then if needed, more powerful microscopes. Photography by infrared or ultraviolet is sometimes helpful, and even conventional photography can on occasion, by long exposure time, make faint ink traces appear more clearly. Digital photography has largely displaced film; multispectral imaging allows more precise targeting of the wavelength of ink and sometimes the recovery of effaced or hidden ink.

RESEARCH AND RESEARCH FACILITIES

The beginning of the study of a treated papyrus is reading it. This is an easy or difficult task depending on the physical condition of the papyrus, the difficulty of the handwriting, the clarity or obscurity—and sometimes, the vulgarity—of the writer's language, the nature of the contents, and the skills of the reader. The papyrologist's task is not so much to read individual letters and words as to grasp the thought of the writer; once that is understood, the words can be read more easily. In a banal standardized document (e.g., a lease) this can often be very easy, while a very individual, private letter may resist all attempts at understanding. The reading of a text is thus inseparable from the work of translation and commentary, which sets forth the editor's understanding of the text. In the commentary to a papyrus one finds an explanation of its general import and contribution to our knowledge, as well as a detailed examination of problems in the language or contents.

The publication of the annotated and translated text is only the start, however. Because of the many difficulties of reading and understanding papyri, few texts are so perfect when published as not to need correction. And a published text may give rise to extensive studies of its literary, historical, juristic, economic, or social implications: studies that often finish by correcting the texts.

To carry on the various stages of this work, the papyrologist needs good light, a magnifying glass, and sometimes a microscope, but above all, a complete collection of the already-published papyri of other collections. These volumes (see section on "Publication"), together with the special lexica, grammars, prosopographies, indices, and monographs in the field, form the indispensable working library of the papyrologist. In the course of a few hours work, one may consult dozens of volumes to check references to possible parallels to a phrase or an institution, and only the assembly of the requisite books in one place for easy consultation can make serious papyrological research possible; such studies have flourished only where special working libraries could be created. Particularly good collections in North America of this sort exist at Michigan, Columbia, Duke, Toronto, and Yale—not surprisingly, the places where actively worked collections are found. The Greek documentary texts on papyrus have been digitized in the Duke Databank of Documentary Papyri, allowing scholars to find words and names relatively easily, and the Heidelberger Gesamtverzeichnis der griechischen Papyrusurkunden Ägyptens provides a typological catalog useful in finding parallel texts. Similar tools for other languages are at various stages of development and completeness. Many papyri are available on the Web in digital images. But the full editions, with commentary, are still available almost entirely in book form. That limitation may be expected to be removed in time, making it far easier to conduct research in places far removed from major libraries.

PUBLICATION

All modern editions of papyri follow, in essentials, the form outlined above: introduction, text, translation, and line-by-line commentary. These texts are published primarily in volumes uniting many papyri from one collection, provenance, or archive. Publications by the place of finding include notably the *Oxyrhynchus Papyri* (now 70 volumes with over 4800 texts) and the *Tebtunis Papyri* (5 volumes with over 1100 texts); specific archives are numerous, the largest being that of Zenon, an estate manager of the third century B.C., which is scattered in several collections and numbers around 2000. Other large collections published are the Michigan papyri, the collection of Florence, the Berlin papyri, and several series of volumes of Cairo papyri. Papyrologists have a standard set of abbreviations for these volumes (e.g., *P.Oxy.* = *The Oxyrhynchus Papyri*).

Many other texts are published for the first time in journals. These are periodically reprinted in the *Sammelbuch*, started by Fr. Preisigke, which indexes them as well. More than 20,000 texts (inscriptions as well as papyri) are printed and indexed in the 26 volumes that have appeared so far. Preisigke also started another publication that records, in more or less systematic fashion, conjectures and corrections to papyri and *ostraka*, scattered through the literature. More details on this and the other essential reference works of the subject are given in the bibliography.

CONTRIBUTIONS OF PAPYRI: LITERATURE

History of the Book

Papyri provide virtually all of our firsthand evidence about the form and character of ancient books. The usual form of the book was a roll of papyrus on which a succession of columns of writing was placed, so that the reader would start with the outer edge of the inside face, unrolling the papyrus as he went, rolling up again from the other side. (In Egyptian the texts on these rolls generally run from right to left, in Greek from left to right.) Practical considerations limited the amount that could be written on one roll, and the cumbersomeness of referring to a location inside a roll encouraged the habitual practice of giving references to other authors only by the "book" (i.e., roll), with no further precision.

About A.D. 100, we get the first examples of the codex, the forerunner of the modern book with pages created from folded sheets and opening from a common spine. The codex appears to have originated in Rome in imitation of notebooks of tablets. It was popular in the Christian community in the early centuries A.D. and was used for scriptural texts almost to the exclusion of the roll. Later, and gradually, it came into much wider use for all kinds of books and for some types of documentary records, perhaps under Roman influence. Increasingly, parchment was also used for making codices, perhaps because it resisted wear and tear along edges better than papyrus. But because parchment was more expensive than papyrus, parchment books remained luxury items.

Many examples of both types of books have been found, whether largely complete or (more commonly) badly damaged, among the papyri. They show us not only the form of the book but its characteristics, notably the handwriting (book-hands are normally neat, carefully written scripts) and the critical marks (full or partial accentuation of Greek appears for the first time in a few papyri, above all in educational contexts). From these, we are able to form a more accurate idea of the type of manuscript that lies behind the medieval ones through which most ancient literature is preserved.

Greek Authors

The range of literature in circulation in Hellenistic and Roman Egypt was much larger than what survives to our day in medieval manuscripts, and numerous discoveries, occasionally of complete or nearly complete works—but more often of scraps—have considerably enriched our store of Greek literature over the last 100 years. Among authors or works found in significant amounts are lyric poets, especially Bacchylides, Sappho, Archilochus, and Alcaeus; the Athenian orator Hyperides; the comic dramatist Menander (of whom previously only fragments had survived); the "Constitution of Athens" by Aristotle; Callimachus; the *Hellenica* from Oxyrhynchus by a historian of the fourth century B.C.; the Epicurean writings by Philodemus found at Herculaneum; Herodas; a satyr play by Sophocles; and the epigrams of Poseidippos. Some of the paraphernalia of ancient learning have also appeared to increase our knowledge, such as lists of initial lines of plays; lists of Homeric vocabulary, which was obscure already in ancient times; summaries of works; and the like. Through these we get valuable information about lost works and come to understand how the ancient reader approached texts.

The majority of the literary papyri discovered and identified give us texts from works already known; besides informing us on the character of ancient books, these give us an idea of the reading habits of the literate public in Hellenistic and Roman Egypt. The *Iliad* of Homer was by far the most popular work, with the *Odyssey* next. After Homer come Demosthenes, Euripides, Callimachus, Hesiod, Isocrates, Plato, Thucydides, Aeschylus, and Xenophon. Many more authors have more than one papyrus each, and another large group just one apiece. Well over 100 authors—to count only those identified—were read even in provincial Egypt. The literate Greeks of the period thus had available to them a considerably larger selection than survived the Middle Ages. At the same time, we see that very few works were *commonly* read that have not survived in medieval manuscripts.

Almost half of all literary fragments have not been assigned with certainty to a known author and work. Sometimes this results from our knowing too little about the works of authors whose books have not otherwise survived; the *Hellenica Oxyrhynchia*, of which we have a sizable amount but whose authorship is disputed, is an example. Most often, the fragment is very small and, in the absence of its discovery in a known work, the preserved material is so small as to make an attribution to an author (about whom little may be known) very difficult, even impossible. Many fragments have, however, been assigned to known authors in the past two decades since the corpus of classical Greek literature became available in digital form (the Thesaurus Linguae Graecae) and thus easily searchable even for brief sequences of letters.

Religious Literature

Numerous papyri have preserved parts of the texts of the Old and New Testaments, contributing considerably to the study of the earliest form of these texts. Many other Greek and Coptic papyri of theological or liturgical significance have been found, including many witnesses to the diversity of the early Christian tradition, in particular the *Sayings of Jesus* from Oxyrhynchus, and the Gospel of Thomas from the important find of Coptic Gnostic texts at Nag Hammadi and the Gospel of Judas from a separate discovery in Middle Egypt. Other apocryphal gospels have also been found. The history of the New Testament is further illuminated by early manuscripts of the gospels and by a fragment of Tatian's *Diatessaron*, giving an attempted harmonization of the four gospels (with some apocryphal material), found at Dura-Europos.

The early centuries of Christianity in Egypt are also illuminated by some outstanding discoveries, notably two major works of Origen and a large number of commentaries on the Old Testament by Didymus the Blind, found in the Tura quarries near Cairo.

Many aspects of other religions also gain from the papyri; those from Egypt provide much information on the life of Jews in Egypt, and the finds from the Dead Sea region in Palestine make a more direct contribution to the study of Judaism in the first two centuries. Major finds of Manichaean texts have transformed our knowledge of that religion. In pagan religion, there is a wealth of information varying from hymns to priestly practices to organizations of cultic associations. Magic and astrology are well represented in the papyri, with horoscopes and spells well known.

CONTRIBUTIONS OF PAPYRI: HISTORY

Political History

Most of the thousands of documents found concern affairs internal to Egypt and usually local in character. The history that they yield is largely the story of the otherwise unknown landowners, small farmers, businessmen, soldiers, and other ordinary people, a story entirely ignored by the "historical" writings that we have from antiquity. There are exceptions, cases in which the papyri provide us with important facts about the main course of politics, war, and diplomacy. It is, for example, from papyri that most of our information about the chronology of the Ptolemaic kings comes. From the archives of Zenon (see section on "Publication"), we hear of court intrigues, diplomacy with the Seleucids, and the government of the Ptolemaic empire. A report by Ptolemy III gives a narrative of part of the Syrian War of 246–241.

The several native revolts and civil wars of Ptolemaic Egypt are documented in the papyri, especially by repeated royal amnesty decrees such as the well-preserved edicts of 118 B.C. and by some correspondence from troubled periods. Typically, we get, from the papyri, not an overview but rather the effects that historical events had on some individuals.

From the Roman period, with its larger number of papyri, we derive correspondingly more abundant information. We learn the names and dates of the Roman governors of Egypt, and we have considerable information on the composition and activities of the garrisons they commanded. The political vicissitudes of Egypt in the turmoil of the later empire are reflected in the dating formulas used, giving us a degree of precision about shifts of allegiance difficult to come by in other provinces.

It is, however, more in the areas of institutions, social and economic aspects, and culture that the masses of papyri create for us, with a wealth of detail (but not always any generalizations!), a minutely detailed panorama of life. Particularly valuable are the surviving archives, groups of interrelated papyri, which taken together give us much greater insight than the individual documents could if isolated. Several examples are cited below.

Law and Institutions

We learn of the governing of Hellenistic and Roman Egypt, both in theory and in practice, from a considerable number of documents. Nearly a hundred Ptolemaic laws of various sorts are preserved in full or in extracts: city laws of Alexandria; royal decrees about subjects such as military service, slavery, taxes, police work, and judicial procedure; detailed regulations for the operation of the monopolized oil industry; and royal laws applicable to areas outside Egypt such as Syria and Phoenicia.

Under the Romans, we are no less richly benefited by legal texts on papyrus. The famous Gnomon of the Idios Logos (a collection of excerpts of imperial rulings and laws) gives the gist of the detailed and repressive code under which Roman administrators confiscated property, prohibited marriage between many groups, and enforced numerous aspects of Roman social policy. Imperial and prefectural edicts and responses to petitions set forth principles of law and their application, broad or narrow; some of the most famous are two edicts of Germanicus Caesar and some responses of Septimius Severus.

The detailed application of the law and the machinery through which it operated are revealed in numerous records of court proceedings and in a host of related documents. One of the most famous is the dossier recording the feud between a Greek soldier and some Egyptian priests of the dead about a house in Thebes in Upper Egypt. The extensive knowledge of judicial procedure gained from these texts has led to scores of monographs and many works of synthesis. It is fair to say that the study of Greek and Roman law has been profoundly influenced in the last century by the papyri.

The other aspects of royal and imperial administration—finances especially—are shown in great detail by surviving official correspondence, petitions, accounts, memoranda, and other records. One of the most interesting archives is that of Menches, a village scribe in a Fayûm hamlet in the late second century B.C., struggling to maintain royal revenues in a time of declining agricultural production—and, above all, to protect his own position. His counterpart 300 years later, Petaus, is barely able to sign his own name, but his scribe-written files give us much information on such problems as compulsory public service in his period.

Society and Economy

The papyri offer no economic laws and few obvious generalizations, but they do give us thousands of transactions—leasing land, renting a house, selling crops, buying a slave, apprenticing one's son or oneself, paying taxes, and much more. We see the major processes of the economy of Egypt from both the government's side and that of the individual. In the so-called Revenue Laws papyrus, we find the detailed instructions for the maintenance of the crown monopoly on the production and sale of edible oils; elsewhere, we hear about smuggled oil and violation of other regulations. We find Ptolemaic soldiers selling plots of land that belong to the king rather than to them; we also have the royal edicts prohibiting this practice.

The economy of Egypt rested predominantly on the grain crop, and so it is the grain crop about which we hear most—its sowing, cultivation, harvest, taxation, and ultimately its sale or dispatch abroad for Ptolemaic foreign trade or the Roman grain dole. But we learn also of other industries like papyrus, of trade in rarer items like spices, of the trade through the Red Sea ports to India. In many cases, the evidence allows the distillation of statistics, though their reliability is not always secure.

The society of Egypt that we see in the papyri was a mixture of Greek and Egyptian, but only to a limited extent a blend of them. We find Greeks living in groups in towns, Egyptians mostly farming the land. The Greeks preserved their culture by various institutions (see section on "Culture"). Some Egyptians sought self-advancement through learning Greek and rising in the bureaucracy (or the Roman army), and some Greeks married native women and were essentially absorbed by Egyptian society. In general, the vast mass of Egyptians was only slowly affected by any direct influence of Hellenism, but over time even such fundamental Egyptian habits as drinking beer gave way to the Greek preference for wine.

The Greek papyri, naturally, come predominantly from the part of society that could speak Greek, a group that included many Egyptians as time went on. The early Ptolemaic papyri reveal to us a still very Hellenic society, made up of immigrants and their children, but the more ambitious natives were added to it as time went on, and the Greek openness to the gods of their new country led to a growing adoption of personal names based on Egyptian deities. The longer the separation from the world of the Greek *polis* (city-state), the greater the tendency was to develop what we may call a Greco-Egyptian society, rather less centered on a privileged citizen body than the classical pattern and accepting many native customs. If more of our surviving documentation concerned the Greek cities, our view might be different, but it is the provincial towns and villages that are, above all, represented in the surviving texts.

Culture

The extent of literacy and reading among the Greeks in Egypt has already been discussed briefly. The Greeks sought to preserve a corporate and cultural identity by means of their educational institutions—schools, and especially the gymnasium, in which the young men of Greek families received the athletic training and other education to fit them for a place in Hellenic society. The gymnasium remained a center of community life for these men as adults, providing the focus for the athletic contests, which were such a prominent part of social activity. Fewer women received an education, but some were literate thanks to schooling whether at home or in a more formal school. Many papyri, ostraka, and tablets preserve examples of both teacher's models and student exercises from the schools of Egypt, allowing a detailed reconstruction of the process by which students learned to write and read, probably in that order.

A host of smaller private clubs existed among both Greeks and Egyptians to promote a congenial social atmosphere and to celebrate the cults of various gods. We find some evidence of Greek forms of entertainment in the papyri, such as flute players and comic actors, often hired for private parties.

Language

Fifty thousand Greek papyri and ostraka, together with thousands of texts in other languages, provide one of our major resources for understanding several ancient languages. The material is richest for the transformation of the language known in the classical Greek authors into that of modern Greece. There is still much to be done in the systematic study of this evidence, but already the trends that are visible have been described in sufficient detail for it to be clear that the *koine* Greek of the New Testament was not a special language concocted for it alone, nor yet a heavily "semitized" Greek from Palestine, but rather a type of Greek abundantly illustrated by documents and letters, very characteristic of the actual language of its time. Similar insight has been gained into the language used by many literary figures of postclassical Greek antiquity.

The tendencies of the period are heavily in the direction of simplification, in part no doubt because of the absorption of many non-Greek peoples into the body of Greek speakers. The perfect tenses and the optative mood become rarer, and many irregular forms give way to newly formed regular ones. The vocabulary too changes; many Homeric words were sufficiently unknown in Roman times that readers of Homer would have special glossaries at hand to help. The nature of papyrus texts has led to a knowledge of many classes of words connected to everyday life that literary sources do not use, thus broadening our knowledge of the language. Conversely, the papyri shun much of the elaborate vocabulary of classical Greek, especially of poetry.

The other languages found in the papyri were in some cases written mainly by trained professionals (as in the case of Demotic Egyptian) according to rules that changed far more slowly than did the spoken language. The last written form of Egyptian, Coptic, is recorded in many documents of everyday life that give a vivid sense of something closer to the spoken vernacular of the time, which had absorbed many Greek words. And early Arabic papyri show how the language was written at a time when the written form familiar today was not yet fully fixed.

CONCLUSION

Papyri are an important part of our written heritage and document several major steps in the development of human communication. Papyrus was a crucial element in the organization of one of the earliest complex societies, the first reasonably portable means for recording man's memory, the most convenient way of transporting information across distances, and the vehicle by which large portions of the ancient world came to have more than perfunctory literacy. In the papyri, we find, more than in any other source, the material for a direct understanding of the daily life of ordinary people in antiquity. Although papyrus gave way to parchment and paper after four millennia of use, the shape of books in paper remained the codex, one of those for which papyrus was employed, and only the invention of movable type changed significantly the style of communication that papyrus represents in the history of the Western world.

ACKNOWLEDGMENTS

The principal international organization in the field is the Association Internationale de Papyrologues, with headquarters in Brussels (http://www.ulb.ac.be/assoc/aip/). Its American affiliate is the American Society of Papyrologists (Department of Classics, University of Cincinnati, Cincinnati, OH 45221; http://classics.uc.edu/asp/). The International Association of Coptic Studies (http://rmcisadu.let.uniroma1.it/%7Eiacs/) and the International Society for Arabic Papyrology (http://www.ori.unizh.ch/isap.html) deal with specific parts of the field.

BIBLIOGRAPHY

1. Introduction: E.G. Turner, *Greek Papyri* (Clarendon, Oxford, 1968) is the standard introduction in English. O. Montevecchi, *La papirologia* (2nd ed., Vita e Pensiero, Milan, 1983) is useful for bibliography and lists.
2. The plant: N. Lewis, *Papyrus in Classical Antiquity* (Clarendon, Oxford, 1974), with a *Supplement* (Fondation Egyptologique Reine Elisabeth, Brussels, 1989) is the standard work on the plant, its uses, and the writing material. See also Richard Parkinson and Stephen Quirke, *Papyrus* (Austin, 1995). For *ostraka*, see U. Wilcken, *Griechische Ostraka aus Aegypten und Nubien* (München, 1899), Vol. 1. Many papyri are now available in digital images; see the Advanced Papyrological Information System. Available at http://www.columbia.edu/cu/lweb/projects/digital/apis/index.html, with other resources listed there.
3. Discoveries: A general survey of the history of papyrology is given by F.G. Kenyon, "Fifty Years of Papyrology," *Actes du Vc Congrès International de Papyrologie, 1937* (Brussels, 1938) 1–11. Chapter 2 of E.G. Turner, *Greek Papyri* (Clarendon, Oxford, 1968) is more detailed. A fuller survey is K. Preisendanz, *Papyrusfunde und Papyrusforschung* (Hiezsemann, Leipzig, 1933). For papyri from Dura-Europos: *Excavations at Dura-Europos, Final Report* V, Part I: *The Parchments and Papyri*, C.B. Welles, R.O. Fink, and J.F. Gilliam, eds. (Yale Univ. Press, New Haven, 1959). For Nessana, see *Excavations at Nessana*, H.D. Colt, L. Casson, E.L. Hettich, and C.J. Kraemer, Jr., eds. (Princeton Univ. Press, Princeton, 1950–1962, 3 vols.). For Petra see J. Frösén, A. Arjava, and M. Lehtinen, *The Petra Papyri* I (American Center of Oriental Research, Amman, 2002); additional volumes are forthcoming.
4. Collections: The most useful list of papyrus collections is now the *Leuven Homepage of Papyrus Collections*. Available at http://www.trismegistos.org/coll.php.
5. Treatment: See Jörg Graf, Myriam Krutzsch, *Ägypten lesbar machen—die klassische Konservierung/Restaurierung von Papyri und neuere Verfahren* (De Gruyter, 2008). For the extraction of papyri from cartonnage see J. Frösén, chapter on conservation in R.S. Bagnall, ed., *The Oxford Handbook of Papyrology* (Oxford U.P., New York, 2009). For formal standards for conservation generally, see Advanced Papyrological Information System, Guidelines for Conservation of Papyrus, Leyla Lau-Lamb, ed (University Library, University of Michigan, Jan. 2005) Available at http://www.lib.umich.edu/pap.conservation/guidelines.html.
6. Research and facilities: For an introduction to the work of reading a papyrus text, see H.C. Youtie, "The Papyrologist: Artificer of Fact," *Greek Roman and Byzantine Stud.*, **4**, 19–32 (1963); a more detailed exposition is found in his *Textual Criticism of Documentary Papyri* (Inst. Class. Stud., London, 1974). The other aspects of papyrology are adequately illustrated by the material cited under *Literature* and subsequent headings.
7. Publications: The standard list of papyrus editions, with usual abbreviations, is J.F. Oates et al., *A Checklist of Editions of Greek, Latin, Demotic, and Coptic Papyri, Ostraca, and Tablets* (5th ed., David Brown Book Company, Oakville, CT, 2001); an online version is kept current Available at http://odyssey.lib.duke.edu/papyrus/texts/clist.html. *The Oxyrhynchus Papyri* were edited first by A.S. Hunt and B.P. Grenfell, later by many other scholars; they are published by the Egypt Exploration Society (London) in its Graeco-Roman Memoirs. The volumes of the *Tebtunis Papyri*, edited by the same scholars and others, also appeared in this series. For the Zenon archive, see Cl. Préaux, *Les Grecs en Egypte* (Off. de Publicité, Brussels, 1947) and C. Orrieux, *Les papyrus de Zénon: l'horizon d'un grec en Egypte au IIIe siècle avant J.C.* (Macula, Paris, 1983). The other series of papyri are listed in the *Checklist.* Preisigke's collection of corrections is the *Berichtigungsliste der griechischen Papyrusurkunden* (now E.J. Brill, Leiden, 1915–), now in 11 volumes. The principal bibliography is M. Hombert, G. Nachtergael, and A. Martin, *Bibliographie Papyrologique*, available for 1932– (CD-ROM plus quarterly updates; Association Egyptologique Reine Elisabeth, Brussels). For Demotic, see M. Depauw, *A Companion to Demotic Studies* (Association Egyptologique Reine Elisabeth, Brussels, 1997).
8. Literature: The standard listing of literary texts is R.A. Pack, *The Greek and Latin Literary Texts from Graeco-Roman Egypt* (Michigan, Ann Arbor, 1965), now essentially replaced by a digital version prepared by P. Mertens et al ("Mertens-Pack3") Available at http://www.ulg.ac.be/facphl/services/cedopal/pages/mp3anglais.htm. A fuller online-only database of literary works is the Leuven Database of Ancient Books. Available at http://ldab.arts.kuleuven.be/ldab_text.php. On the history of the book, see F.G. Kenyon, *Books and Readers in Ancient Greece and Rome* (Clarendon, Oxford, 1951); W. Schubart, *Das Buch bei den Griechen und Römern* (Koehler und Amelang, Leipzig, 1961); C.H. Roberts, "The Codex," *Proc. Brit. Acad.*, **40**, (1954); W.A. Johnson, *Bookrolls and Scribes in Oxyrhynchus* (Toronto, Univ. of Toronto Press, 2004). The Tura papyri are mostly published in the series *Papyrologische Texte und Abhandlungen* (Habelt, Bonn, 1968). Texts concerning Jews in Egypt and elsewhere are collected by V. Tcherikover and A. Fuks, *Corpus Papyrorum Judaicarum* (Harvard, Cambridge, MA., 1957–1964, 3 vols.).
9. History: The information on Ptolemaic Egypt is in considerable part collected systematically in the *Prosopographia Ptolemaica* of W. Peremans, E. Van't Dack et al. (Publ.

Univ., Louvain, 1950, 10 vols. to date; on line. Available at http://prosptol.arts.kuleuven.ac.be/). A good series of case-studies can be found in N. Lewis, *Greeks in Ptolemaic Egypt* (Clarendon, Oxford, 1986). Works on Roman Egypt are numerous; see collections of documents on the army by S. Daris, *Documenti per la storia dell' esercito romano in Egitto* (Vita e Pensiero, Milan, 1964); and R.O. Fink, *Roman Military Records on Papyrus* (Amer. Phil. Assoc., Monograph 26, 1971), and the synthesis of N. Lewis, *Life in Egypt under Roman Rule* (Clarendon, Oxford, 1983). For history and the papyri see generally A.K. Bowman, *Egypt after the Pharaohs* (British Museum, London, 1986) and R.S. Bagnall, *Reading Papyri, Writing Ancient History* (Routledge, London, 1995), with bibliography. For the Demotic contribution, see Friedhelm Hoffmann, *Ägypten Kultur und Lebenswelt in griechisch-römischer Zeit: Eine Darstellung nach den demotischen Quellen* (Akademie Verlag, 2000). For Ptolemaic law see M.-Th. Lenger, *Corpus des ordonnances des Ptolémées* (Acad. Roy., Brussels, 1964); many of the important documents concerned with Roman law appear in V. Arangio-Ruiz, *Fontes Iuris Romani Anteiustiniani*, Vol. 3 (Barbéra, Florence, 1943). The trial of Hermias and the Priests is found in U. Wilcken, *Urkunden der Ptolemäerzeit* (de Gruyter, Leipzig, 1927–1957). The Gnomon of the Idios Logos is in *Aegyptische Urkunden aus den Staatlichen Museen zu Berlin, Griechische Urkunden*, Vol. 5, W. Schubart and W. Graf Uxkull-Gyllenband, eds. (Staat. Mus., Berlin, 1919–1934). The replies of Severus are in *Apokrimata*, W.L. Westermann and A.A. Schiller, eds. (Columbia, New York, 1956). Menches' papyri are in *The Tebtunis Papyri*, Vol. 1 (E.E.S., London, 1902), those of Petaus in *Das Archiv von Petaus*, U. Hagedorn, D. Hagedorn, L.C. Youtie, and H.C. Youtie, eds. (Westdeutscher Verlag, Cologne/Opladen, 1969). A.C. Johnson, *Roman Egypt*, in T. Frank et al., *An Economic Survey of Ancient Rome* (Hopkins, Baltimore, 1936), gives a mass of documents in translation with commentary. More recent sourcebooks include J. Rowlandson, ed., *Women and Society in Greek and Roman Egypt* (Cambridge U.P., Cambridge, 1998); R.S. Bagnall and P.S. Derow, *The Hellenistic Period* (Historical Sources in Translation; Blackwell, Oxford, 2004); and R.S. Bagnall and R. Cribiore, *Women's Letters from Ancient Egypt, 300 BC-AD 800* (Univ. of Michigan, Ann Arbor, 2006). For schools, see R. Cribiore, *Gymnastics of the Mind: Greek Education in Hellenistic and Roman Egypt* (Princeton U.P., 2001).

10. Language: The Duke Databank of Documentary Papyri provides a full-text database of the documentary Greek papyri. A CD-ROM version up to 1995 was published by the Packard Humanities Institute; an online version with more recently published texts is available at http://www.papyri.info. The lexicon of the papyri is F. Preisigke et al., *Wörterbuch der griechischen Papyrusurkunden* (Author, 1924): Vols. 1–2, dictionary; Vol. 3, special lists of kings, officials, taxes, etc.; Vol. 4, a supplement in form of dictionary, 5 fascicles to date. Three Supplements (1969–2000) give references only for texts from 1941 to 1988. For later publications, the online *Wörterlisten*. Available at http://www.zaw.uni-heidelberg.de/hps/pap/WL/WL.html may be consulted. For personal names, F. Preisigke, *Namenbuch* (Author, Heidelberg, 1922); and D. Foraboschi, *Onomasticon Alterum Papyrologicum* (Cisalpino, Milan, 1967–1971). E. Mayser, *Grammatik der griechischen Papyri der Ptolemäerzeit* (de Gruyter, Berlin/Leipzig, 1906, 2 vols., in several parts) is the standard work on grammar, but he does not treat the Roman papyri. A treatment of phonology and morphology of papyri of Roman and Byzantine times is given by F.T. Gignac, *A Grammar of the Greek Papyri of the Roman and Byzantine Periods*, 2 vols. (Cisalpino, Milan, 1976–1981).
11. Conclusion: Besides works cited above, note the general introduction to the field and selection of texts in the fundamental work of U. Wilcken and L. Mitteis, *Grundzüge and Chrestomathie der Papyruskunde* (Teubner, Leipzig, 1912, 4 vols.). A selection of documents is translated in the Loeb Classical Library *Select Papyri* (Heinemann, London, 1932–1934, 2 vols.), by C.C. Edgar and A.S. Hunt; a volume of literary papyri (poetry only) by D.L. Page (Heinemann, London, 1941) has also appeared.

Patents and Patent Searching

Michael J. White
Engineering and Science Library, Queen's University, Kingston, Ontario, Canada

Abstract

Patents are limited monopoly rights granted by governments that allow inventors to prevent others from making, using, or selling their inventions for up to 20 years. In exchange, inventors must disclose details about their inventions. Patent documents are a valuable open source of scientific and technical information, some of which does not appear in other types of publications. For more than 200 years patent offices have disseminated patent information to the public in order to promote awareness of patent rights and to further technological development. During that time patent documents have evolved from handwritten manuscripts to printed documents to electronic text. Print-based search tools such as indexes and patent classification manuals have given way to online databases and hyperlinked documents. Today, patent searchers can search and retrieve millions of patent documents from numerous free Web-based databases hosted by patent offices and independent organizations.

PATENT INFORMATION

Patent literature is one of the oldest and most interesting forms of technical literature in the universe of sci-tech information. Patents first appeared in Europe in the fifteenth century as a special privilege granted by monarchs. The World Intellectual Property Organization (WIPO) predicts that in 2008 more than 2 million patent applications will be filed and 750,000 patents granted worldwide. China, Japan, and the United States are the countries with the highest growth.[1]

Simply stated, a patent is a monopoly right granted by a government to an inventor for a limited time, generally 20 years, that allows the inventor to exclude others from making, using, or selling his or her invention. Modern patent law is based in part on the concept of novelty. That is to say, in order to obtain a patent, an inventor must prove that his or her invention has never before been published, used, or sold in public. This requirement is not limited by geography or time. The inventor must also fully disclose the nature of the invention he wishes to protect. This exchange of information for monopoly rights is at the heart of the patent system.

Of course, patent information is most useful to patent owners and inventors wishing to apply for patent protection. It is always a good idea to conduct a patentability search before applying for a patent. Patents are also a valuable source of business information and competitive intelligence.[2,3]

Patents are an important source of historical information about technological development, geographic regions, culture, and social trends.[4–6] Patent documents can be used for genealogical research or to identify the date of an antique. Patents can be used to teach students at all levels about science, engineering, inventiveness, and problem solving.[7,8] Patents are an important source of technical information that is not published in scientific journals.[9,10] Increasingly, patent information is a window into industrial and academic research conducted in developing countries.

In order to understand patent information and patent searching, it is necessary to understand how patent information and search tools and techniques have evolved over the last 200 years.

HISTORY OF PATENT INFORMATION

1790–1870: Early Beginnings

Prior to the 1870s, patent information was difficult, costly, and at times impossible for the average citizen to obtain. Printing was expensive, communications were slow and public access to government documents limited. In many countries, patent laws were administered in a haphazard and decentralized fashion. For example, in the United Kingdom prior to 1852, patents were registered by three separate offices located in England, Scotland, and Ireland. In North America, colonial assemblies granted their own patents, a practice that was continued by U.S. state legislatures after the American Revolution. In Canada, the patent office moved no fewer than six times from 1824 to 1857 as the colonial capital moved to Kingston, Montreal, Toronto and, finally, Ottawa.

In the United States, the Patent Act of 1790, the first federal patent statute, provided no means for printing patent documents or publishing information about granted patents.[11] It did, however, authorize the secretary of state, who was responsible for administering patent

Encyclopedia of Library and Information Sciences, Fourth Edition DOI: 10.1081/E-ELIS4-120043653

records, to provide copies of specifications upon request for a small fee. In 1791, Secretary of State Thomas Jefferson proposed patent reform legislation that would require inventors to publish information about their patents in federal district court gazettes. Furthermore, Jefferson proposed that copies of patents, printed at the government's expense, be made available to the public upon the expiration of the 14 year patent term.[12] However, no such provisions were included in the Patent Act of 1793, although it did allow the public to request copies of patents at the rate of 20¢ per 100 words and $2 for drawings.[13] Patent applications were confidential and, therefore, not permitted to be copied.

The Patent Act of 1793 was in force until 1836. During most of this time the patent system was administered by one man, Dr. William Thornton, who served as the superintendent of patents from 1802 until his death in March 1828. Thornton understood and appreciated the value of patents as records of scientific progress and human ingenuity. When the British captured Washington, D.C. during the War of 1812, Thornton's appeals to the officer in charge of burning government buildings saved the Patent Office from being put to the torch.[14]

Having saved patents for posterity, Thornton, however, was less enthusiastic about providing copies of patents to his fellow citizens. He frequently rejected such requests on the grounds that he did not have the authority or resources to do so. The latter was certainly true. Burdened with an increasing workload and lacking sufficient staff, Thornton often enlisted his wife to help write out patents.[15] Thornton also wanted to protect the patent rights of inventors, believing that easy access to patents would only encourage piracy. In 1825, the Franklin Institute of Philadelphia sued Thornton after he refused to provide copies of patents which it wanted to abstract in its journal. After a lengthy court battle, the matter eventually was put before Secretary of State Henry Clay (Thornton's boss), who decided that patents were indeed public documents.[15]

The Patent Act of 1836 clarified and affirmed the public's right to access patent documents.[16] It also reduced the fee for copying patents to 10¢ per 100 words. In order to meet the demand for patent copies, the Patent Office hired temporary employees, most of them women working in their own homes, to transcribe documents on a piecework basis. In the 1850s the Patent Office was the first government office to hire women as full-time clerks. Clara Barton, founder of the American Red Cross, worked as a patent copyist and clerk from 1855 to 1857 and 1860 to 1865.[17] When printed patents reduced the need for copyists, women were employed in the production of patent documents and the *Official Gazette*.

On December 15, 1836, fire destroyed the Patent Office and all its records and models. After the smoke cleared, Congress quickly appropriated funds to restore the files.[18] But of the approximately 10,000 patents issued from 1790 through 1836, only about 2,700 were recovered. Of these, 70% issued after 1830, 23% issued from 1810 through 1830 and 7% prior to 1810. Only six of the 67 patents issued under the Act of 1793 exist today. Occasionally, persistent patent researchers discover copies of missing pre-1836 patents in libraries, archives, and courthouses.[19]

The Patent Office Fire of 1836 was a huge disaster for patent information, but not everything was lost. Lists of patentees and patented inventions had been published from time to time by the Patent Office and private companies. For example, S. Alfred Eliott, a Washington, D.C. printer of directories and guidebooks, published a list of granted patents from 1790 forward, updated annually, throughout the 1820s. Other publishers soon took notice of the public's increasing interest in patent information. The *Scientific American*, a weekly periodical established in 1845 to chronicle developments in American science and technology, also published claims of newly issued patents. Prior to the establishment of the *Official Gazette of the Patent Office* in 1872, it was the only reliable and timely source of information on new patents. The Patent Office even purchased extra copies of each issue for the use of patent examiners and in the preparation of its annual reports.[20]

Lists of granted patents were included in the superintendent of patent's annual report to Congress from 1810 forward; however, it was published regularly only after 1836. During the 1840s the annual report was expanded to include alphabetical and classified lists of expired patents, a classified list of issued patents, alphabetical list of patentees and the claims of issued patents, miscellaneous reports and statistics, and other information related to agriculture. The latter was discontinued in 1862 upon the creation of the Department of Agriculture. Latter years included patent drawings. During this period the annual report was printed in huge quantities; for example, 135,000 copies of the 1847 report were produced, the bulk of which was delivered to members of Congress.[21] Two especially useful guides to early U.S. patent documents include *A List of Patents for Inventions and Designs, Issued by the United States from 1790 to 1847*[22] and the three-volume *Subject Matter Index of Patents for Inventions Issued by the United States Patent Office from 1790 to 1873, Inclusive*.[23]

1870–1970: The First Golden Age of Patent Information

Three developments in the early 1870s ushered in a golden age of patent information: the printing of patent specifications and drawings, the establishment of a weekly *Official Gazette* containing abstracts of issued patents, and the distribution of patents to public libraries. Advances in printing technology in the mid-1800s greatly reduced the cost of printing, making it feasible for the first time to produce large quantities of patent documents quickly and relatively inexpensively. The invention of photolithographic printing in the 1850s revolutionized the reproduction of technical drawings. Previously, patent drawings had to be hand-drawn by a skilled draftsman or engraved on metal plates at great expense. Photolithography also allowed drawings to be reproduced in different scales without the loss of details. The adoption of wood pulp papermaking techniques in the 1870s and the invention of the linotype automatic printing press in the 1880s further decreased the cost of printed patents.

In 1861, Congress first authorized the printing of patent specifications and drawings, but very little progress was made toward this goal during the Civil War. In 1871, a new Patent Commissioner, General Mortimer D. Leggett, was appointed and Congress again directed that copies of patents be printed for sale to the public and free distribution to libraries. Commissioner Leggett undertook this task with energy and initiative. He ordered that copies of all patents, including patents recovered after the fire of 1836, be transcribed and printed. The weekly publication and distribution of new patents would continue for over a century. By the 1960s, the Patent Office had amassed an archive of 100 million printed patents stored in vaults beneath the Department of Commerce Building on Pennsylvania Avenue.[24]

In 1870 the Patent Office began publishing a weekly pamphlet containing claims of issued patents. This publication evolved into the *Official Gazette of the United States Patent Office*, which officially debuted on January 3, 1872. The *Official Gazette*, or OG as it became known, contained one or more patent claims with a representative drawing for each patent, in addition to summaries of the Decisions of the Commissioner of Patents, Patent Office statistics, and official notices. The OG greatly expanded the distribution of patent information. The $6 yearly subscription fee was affordable to most individuals and organizations. Numerous patent attorneys, inventors, libraries, and foreign patent offices subscribed. A week's worth of patents occupied a thin volume; an entire year could fit easily on a bookshelf. The publishers of the *Scientific American* enthusiastically proclaimed that the OG would end the need for costly patent examination and litigation, as every applicant could consult the OG prior to filing their application.[25] The success of the OG inspired other countries to follow suite with their own patent journals. The *Canadian Patent Office Record* was first published in 1873. The British Patent Office established its *Official Journal (Patents)* in 1884.

The third development in the 1870s that greatly enhanced the public's access to patent information was the decision by Congress and the Commissioner of Patents to distribute copies of patents to libraries. The Patent Act of 1836 required the Patent Commissioner to grant the public access to the patent models and records stored in the Patent Office. About 20 libraries, mostly located in the industrial cities of the northeast and midwest, were initially selected to receive copies of patents. This network of patent depository libraries would remain relatively stable until the mid-1970s when the U.S. Patent and Trademark Office (USPTO) launched a program to recruit more libraries into the program. There are currently 83 designated Patent and Trademark Depository Libraries (PTDL).[26] Of course, many non-PTDL libraries can and do provide patent information to the public.[27]

Patent information dissemination became international. The 1870s and 1880s was a time of increasing international trade and capital investment and closer cooperation among countries on matters related to intellectual property protection. In 1883, 10 countries, including France and the United Kingdom, signed the Paris Convention for the Protection of Industrial Property, the first international intellectual property agreement. Article 12 of the Convention requires member states to establish a central office for disseminating patents to the public and to publish an official periodical journal containing information on granted patents and registered trademarks. Although countries had exchanged patent documents as early as the 1850s, the Paris Convention set the first international standard for disseminating patent information.

The dissemination of patent information remained unchanged for 100 years. The Patent Office continued to print and distribute copies of patents for a small fee to individuals and designated patent depository libraries. Those who did not want or could not afford to purchase patent copies, could subscribe instead to the *Official Gazette*.

1970–2008: Patents Go Digital

The arrival of digital computers in the 1950s promised to revolutionize how patent information was produced, stored, searched, and disseminated. As early as 1950, the Patent Office had conducted pilot projects using IBM punch card machines to store and retrieve patent information.[28] In 1955 the U.S. Patent Office established the Office of Research and Development (ORD) to study the possibility of developing mechanical and, later, hybrid mechanical–digital patent search systems.[29] In 1962, the Patent Office joined with other national and regional patent offices in the International Committee for Information Retrieval among Examining Offices (ICIREPAT) to study the possibility of an international patent search system. During the 1960s, ORD tested a number of experimental patent search systems based on index cards, inverted files, and microforms.

Little progress was made in digital search systems until 1970 when the Patent Office awarded its first contract for transcribing the full text of allowed patent applications onto magnetic tape. The tapes were used on a Linotron machine at the Government Printing Office to compose patents for printing; the first patents printed from electronic text issued on August 4, 1970.[30] Afterward, the

Patent Office retained the tapes to create a full-text patent database. In the meantime, the Patent Office continued to test and deploy computer-operated microfilm search and retrieval systems. In 1980 the USPTO started distributing to libraries copies of patents on microfilm, thus ending more than a century of paper distribution.

In September 1981, the Patent and Trademark Office awarded a contract to a private firm to develop and deploy to patent depository libraries a Classification and Search Support Information System (CASSIS). Using CASSIS, users could, among other things, search words in U.S. Patent Classification (USPC) class and subclass titles and display all patent numbers assigned to a specific subclass. CASSIS was the first online patent search system available to the public. In 1987, the USPTO established a pilot project to evaluate the potential for a CD-ROM-based patent search tool as a replacement for CASSIS. The project was a success and in 1989 the first CASSIS/CD-ROM discs were released to patent depository libraries. The CASSIS series expanded in the early 1990s to include CD-ROMs containing searchable patent bibliographic, classification and assignment data, and full-text patent manuals.[31] In the mid-1990s, a second CD-ROM product called *USAPat* was released. *USAPat* contained the facsimile images of patent documents and by the end of the decade replaced patents on microfilm.

In the early 1980s, Congress ordered the USPTO to develop an in-house patent search system for patent examiners. The Automated Patent System (APS) was operational by the end of the decade. APS was a full-text database with powerful search functions. Beginning in 1991, APS was offered at select patent depository libraries. APS was replaced by the WEST and EAST search tools in 1999, which were extended to all patent depository libraries in 2003.

The development of the World Wide Web in the early 1990s ushered in a new age in the dissemination of patent information.[32] In 1994, the USPTO in cooperation with the Center for Networked Information Discovery and Retrieval (CNIDR) mounted its first patent database on the Web, the International AIDS Patent Database, a full-text collection of European, Japanese, and U.S. patents related to AIDS/HIV. In November 1995, the USPTO released a database of bibliographic data from patents granted from January 1976 forward. By October 1, 2000, the USPTO patent database contained full-text patents from 1976 forward and images from 1790 forward. In March 2001, the USPTO launched a second database for published applications.

Other patent offices quickly followed suit with their own Internet patent databases. In addition, a number of free unofficial patent databases appeared in the late 1990s. First were the EDS Shadow Patent Office, which offered free browsing of the current 52 weeks of U.S. patent titles and numbers, and IBM Patent Search, a free database of U.S. patents from 1971 forward. EDS and IBM are no longer operational, but in their place have appeared Google Patents, Patent Lens, FreePatentsOnline, and others.

The rise of powerful computer technology and universal Internet access radically changed patent dissemination in a very short time. Most patent offices discontinued print gazettes. The print version of the USPTO OG was discontinued in 2002 in favor of Web-based and CD-ROM versions. In 2003, paper patent search files were removed from examiner work areas and the Public Search Facility. Also in 2003, the USPTO launched Public PAIR, an online repository for case files for published applications and issued patents.

Of course, these rapid changes also presented challenges. The patent information industry, which earned large sums from patent search tools and document delivery services, was angered by what it saw as unfair competition from the patent offices. Its representatives argued that patent offices were exceeding their mandates in providing free Internet access to patent data.[33,34] At times the relationship between patent offices, which supply patent data, and patent information companies has become tense and confrontational.[35] Although there has been some consolidation in the patent information industry since 2000, free patent databases have also inspired new products and services.

Librarians at patent depository libraries were also concerned that Internet patent databases might put them out of the patent information business.[36,37] To date this has not happened. There are currently 83 patent depositories in the United States, four more than in 1995. And in Europe, the PATLIB network of patent information centers has expanded four more than 320 sites in 83 nations. Librarians at non-depository libraries, especially librarians at universities, may be working with patent information more in response to increasing interest among instructors and students.[38]

PATENT DOCUMENTS

Historically speaking, patent offices have published patent documents in a variety of formats that reflect their own national customs, patent laws, and publication requirements. During the last few decades, however, the patent offices of the world, under the auspices of WIPO and various intergovernmental working groups, have established a number of standards governing the format of patent information in order to facilitate the exchange, storage, and use of electronic patent data. The international movement toward harmonization and increasing cooperation between patent offices has also led to greater standardization in patent documents.

Patent documents consist of three parts: the *front page*, *drawing*, and *specification*. The term *Letters Patent* refers to the grant, drawing, and specification. The *grant* is the certificate issued to the inventor. The *front page* contains bibliographic information describing the patent document and may also include an abstract, the name of a patent attorney/agent, list of references, and/or representative drawing. Common bibliographic data include patent number, date of issue, publication number, date of publication, application number, date of application, name of inventor, name of applicant or assignee, patent classification, and title of invention.

The *drawing* consists of one or more pages of numbered figures that illustrate the invention. It may appear after the front page or at the end of the patent document. Patent offices have specific requirements on what constitutes an acceptable drawing. In general, drawings must be rendered in black and white and show enough detail to enable the reader to understand the invention. Color drawings and photographs are generally not acceptable, except for U.S. plant patents, and black and white photographs are only permitted in limited circumstances where black and white drawings would not adequately illustrate the invention. Drawings are not required in patent documents that describe a process or method of doing something, such as a method of synthesizing a new chemical compound.

The *specification*, which is also known as the description, contains a description of the invention. At the end of the specification are the claims. The specification may start with a description of the background of the invention and a discussion of the prior art related to it. The claims describe, in legal terms, the scope of the invention.

A patent document may be of any length ranging from a few to several hundred pages depending on the complexity of the claimed invention. A few exceptionally long patent documents have page counts in the thousands.

INID Codes

INID is an acronym that stands for "Internationally Agreed Numbers for the Identification of (bibliographic) Data." INID codes, which are described in WIPO Standard ST.9, identify bibliographic data printed on the front page of a patent document. See the table below for selected INID codes. (see Table 1) INID codes are printed in circles or parentheses.[39]

Table 1 Selected INID codes

10	Patent number
12	Type of document
21	Application number
22	Filing date
43	Issue date
45	Publication date
51	International Patent Classification
54	Title
57	Abstract
71	Applicant
72	Inventor
73	Assignee

Document Kind Codes

Document kind codes distinguish between types of published patent documents as defined under WIPO Standard ST.16.[40] While most major patent offices began including kind codes on their patent documents in the 1970s and 1980s, the USPTO began doing so only recently on January 2, 2001. (see Table 2) Kind codes are usually printed near the patent or published application number on the front page of a patent document and may be enclosed in a circle or parentheses. In general, kind codes A, B, and C are used on documents related to patent applications; P for plant patents (US); S for design patents (US); T for translations; and U, Y, and Z for utility models.

Utility Patents

Utility patents protect new and useful processes, machines, products, and compositions of matter or improvements of any of the above. The type of subject matter eligible for patent protection may differ from country to country. For example, patent protection for some applications of computer software, medical therapies, and genetically modified living organisms is allowed in the United States but not in many other countries. Some countries severely restrict patents for pharmaceuticals and medical treatments. Inventions deemed harmful to public safety and national security may be denied patent protection. For example, inventions that facilitate criminal or immoral activity, e.g., a letter bomb, cannot be patented in most countries. In the United States, the Atomic Energy Act of 1954 specifically prohibits the patenting of inventions related to nuclear weapons.

In most countries, utility patent applications are published 18 months after filing. The United States adopted 18 month publication only in 2001. The term of a utility patent is 20 years from the date of application and

Table 2 Kind codes applied to U.S. patent documents as of January 2, 2001

Code	Document type
A1	Utility application, first publication
A2	Utility application, second or subsequent publication
A9	Utility application, correction
B1	Utility patent, no pregrant publication
B2	Utility patent, with pregrant publication
C	Rexamination certificate (C1, C2, C3, etc.)
E	Reissue patent
H	Statutory invention registration
P1	Plant patent application, first publication
P2	Plant patent, no pregrant publication
P3	Plant patent, with pregrant publication
P4	Plant patent application, second or subsequent publication
P9	Plant patent application, correction
S	Design patent

most countries require the payment of maintenance fees during the life of a patent. About 7.5 million patents have been granted in the United States since 1790; 1.9 million utility and plant patent applications have been published since 2001.

Since 1995, applicants have been able to file in the United States a provisional application for a plant or utility patent. Provisional applications are not examined and applicants have one year from the date of filing to file a regular, or non-provisional, application based on their provisional. The requirements for a provisional application include a written description and drawing, if necessary to understand the invention. Provisional applications are not published but are included in the file wrapper of any subsequently field non-provisional application.

Utility Models

Utility models are a weaker form of protection for innovations that do not meet the criteria for a patent. They are granted in a few countries, including Australia, China, Germany, Japan, and Mexico. Application fees are less expensive and the examination process is much less rigorous than for patents. The term of a utility model is much shorter than a patent, generally 5–10 years. Utility model applications may be assigned International Patent Classification (IPC) codes.

Design Patents

Design patents, or industrial designs as they are known in some countries, protect new, original, and ornamental designs applied to a product. For example, the ornamental design of a lamp or the shape of a food storage container may qualify for design patent protection. In the U.S. design patents have a term of 14 years from the date of issue. In Canada, the term for industrial designs is 10 years. Design patents were first granted in 1842 in the U. S. and in 1849 in Canada. The specification of a design patent is short, generally limited to a brief description and one claim. As of July 2008, approximately 560,000 design patents have been granted in the U.S. The WIPO-administered Hague System for the International Registration of Industrial Designs provides for the international registration of designs. The U.S. and Canada are not members of the Hague System. The Locarno Classification system provides for the classification of designs; approximately 49 countries, including the U.S. but not Canada, apply Locarno classifications to their industrial designs.

Plant Patents

Plant patents are unique to the U.S. They were established in 1930 for the protection of distinct and new varieties of asexually propagated plants, which includes plants that are reproduced by means other than seeds. Like utility patent applications, plant patent applications are published 18 months after filing. The first plant patent was granted in 1931. The term of a plant patent is 20 years from the date of filing and maintenance fees must be paid as for utility patents. Plant patent specifications must provide a complete description of the plant but only one claim is allowed. Where color is a distinctive feature of a plant, color drawings or photographs must be provided. Plant patents are classified in the USPC in Class PLT. As of July 2008, approximately 18,000 plant patents have been granted.

Reissue Patents

An inventor who has claimed less then he or she is entitled to in a patent may apply for a reissue patent. Reissue patent applications are examined like regular patents. The term of a reissue patent does not extend beyond the term of the original issued patent. The first reissue patent was granted in 1838 and about 39,000 reissue patents have been granted since.

Additional Improvement (AI) Patents

The Patent Act of 1836 permitted inventors to apply for AIs to their patented inventions within 2 years of issue. From 1837 through 1861 the Patent Office granted approximately 300 AIs.[41] AI patents were assigned a unique serial number for identification purposes but were considered integral to the original patent specification. The Patent Act of 1861 abolished AI patents and instead required inventors to obtain separate patents for subsequent improvements. AI patents are included in the USPTO database and may be retrieved by number, date of issue, and current classification.

Defensive Publications and Statutory Invention Registrations (SIRs)

In 1968 the USPTO enacted a new rule permitting applicants to request publication of unexamined patent applications. The intent of the rule, which was known as defensive publication, was to give applicants a means of protecting their inventions when obtaining a patent was not practicable. Defensive publication documents include only bibliographic information and an abstract. The entire application may be obtained by requesting the appropriate file from the USPTO. Defensive publications are identified by a unique number consisting of the prefix T (for technical disclosure) followed by the *Official Gazette* volume number and a serial number ranging from 1 to 999. Approximately 5,000 defensive publications were published from May 1, 1968 through July 5, 1988.

In 1985 defensive publications were replaced by statutory invention registrations (SIRs). SIRs never exceeded 200 in any given year and have steadily decreased in number since 2001 when the USPTO began publishing utility and plant patent applications.

Reexamination Certificates

Reexamination certificates are issued upon completion of a reexamination proceeding. Reexamination proceedings were introduced in 1980 as a means of allowing third parties to challenge the validity of claims in a granted patent based on new prior art. Approximately 9,300 reexamination certificates have been issued since 1981. Reexamination certificates are attached to the original patent and can only be retrieved in the USPTO's Web-based patent databases by searching the appropriate document number.

Certificates of Correction, Disclaimers, and Dedications

The USPTO does not republish patents that contain minor typographical errors. Instead, the USPTO may at the request of the patent owner issue a certificate of correction that contains the corrected material. A copy of the certificate is then attached to the original patent. Certificates of correction have been issued since the late 1800s. (See patent no. 200,709.) Lists of patent numbers that have been issued certificates of correction are published weekly in the *Official Gazette*. In recent years, it is not uncommon for the USPTO to issue several hundred certificates of correction in any given week. The USPTO publishes data on the number of issued certificates of correction in its annual report. Since 2003, the USPTO has issued approximately 137,000 certificates of correction.

A disclaimer is formal statement made by the applicant or owner of a patent that disavows one or more claims in an issued patent or allowed application that have been found to be invalid. A patent owner may also file a terminal disclaimer that dedicates to the public the entire term or any part of the term of a patent or allowed application.

The Certificate of Correction Branch in the Office of Patent Publication is responsible for issuing certificates of corrections and disclaimers. Electronic copies of certificates of correction and disclaimers may be accessed in the USPTO's Patent Application Information Retrieval (PAIR) system and PatFT patent database (but they are not searchable) several weeks prior to their publication in the *Official Gazette*.

Trial Voluntary Protest Program (TVPP) Publications

In the mid-1970s, the PTO conducted two trial voluntary protest programs (TVPP) to assess the effectiveness of allowing the public to comment on pending patent applications. The intent was to elicit from the public prior art information not cited by the examiner which could impact the patentability of the claims. About 650 applications were partially published (abstract, drawing, and cited references). These documents were designated with a B prefix before the application serial number. The PTO concluded that TVPP was not effective and plans for a permanent program were abandoned.[42]

Alien Property Custodian (APC) Documents

During World War II the U.S. government seized approximately 4,700 patent applications assigned to nationals of enemy and enemy-occupied countries. The Office of the Alien Property Custodian, the agency responsible for managing seized property, published the applications in order to promote their use by American industry.[43,44] These documents became known as APC documents; they are identified by the prefix "APC" followed by the application serial number and date of publication. APC documents are not included in the USPTO patent database.

PATENT CLASSIFICATION SYSTEMS

Patent offices created patent classification systems to organize patent documents and, in some cases, non-patent literature (NPL) into searchable collections based on related subject matter. The two principal patent classification systems in use today are the USPC, which is used by the USPTO, and the IPC, which is used by more than 100 countries worldwide. Many countries that once maintained their own national patent classification systems have in recent years switched to the IPC. For example, the Canadian Intellectual Property Office phased out the Canadian Patent Classification (CPC) in the early 1990s and the U.K. Patent Classification, which was established in 1888, was discontinued in July 2007. The IPC has inspired two regional versions, the European Classification (ECLA) system used by the European Patent Office (EPO) and the File Index (FI) system used by the Japan Patent Office (JPO). These will be discussed in the context of the IPC.

USPC

The USPC was officially established in 1898, although its origins can be traced back to the 1870s.[29] Originally consisting of some 200 classes, the USPC today consists of approximately 450 classes and 150,000 subclasses.[45] The range of subject matter classified in the USPC is immense, ranging from apparel in Class 2 to genetically engineered animals in Class 800. It also includes one class for plant patents (PLT) and 33 classes for design patents (D1-D30, D32, D34, and D99). In this respect, the USPC is unique: no other patent classification system in use today encompasses inventions, designs, and plants.

The USPC also includes seven cross-reference art collection classes for subject matter that falls into multiple classes.

USPC classes are organized under one of four principals: 1) Industry or Use; 2) Proximate Function; 3) Effect or Product; and 4) Structure. An excellent starting point for learning about the USPC is *The Examiner's Handbook to the U.S. Patent Classification System.*[46]

The USPTO assigns patent classifications to utility, design, plant and reissue patents, published utility and plant applications, SIRs, and defensive publications. Between 1979 and 1995, the USPTO classified foreign patents in the USPC.

The base unit of the USPC is the class/subclass, which is often referred to as a classification code, classification symbol or, simply, a classification. Each class/subclass pair is a unique identifier. For example, the classification "482/140" represents "Class 482, Exercise Devices," and "subclass 140, Sit Up Device." The USPC is a flat taxonomy. That is to say, classes are arranged in numerical order and not by subject matter. In a few cases one class has been expanded to multiple classes in order to accommodate an exceptionally large amount of subject matter. For example, classes 600, 601, 602, 604, 606, and 607 are considered to be integral to Class 128, Surgery.

The principal document of the USPC is the *Manual of Classification*, which includes class schedules for all 450 classes. A class schedule is a listing of all subclasses arranged as a hierarchy. The *Manual of Classification* is supported by *Index to the U.S. Patent Classification System*, an alphabetical listing of common terms and trademarks corresponding to individual classifications. Users can consult the *Index to the USPC* in order to determine their initial classification. Definitions are provided for all utility and plant subclasses and most design subclasses.

Revisions to the USPC are handled by reclassification projects, the end product being a classification order. Classification orders contain information on abolished and established classes and subclasses, indent changes, position changes, title changes, and changes to the definitions and USPC-IPC concordance. Orders are issued on the first Tuesday of every month. Since 1947 there have been approximately 1886 classification orders. Classification orders issued since November 2003 are available in PDF format on the USPTO Web site. In addition, a *Classification Orders Index*, which is updated quarterly on the USPTO Web site, contains all changes to the USPC from 1976 forward.

IPC

The IPC is administered by the WIPO in consultation with a Committee of Experts representing members of the Strasbourg Agreement. More than 100 countries apply

Table 3 IPC hierarchy

Section	A	Human necessities
Class	A62	Life saving, fire-fighting
Subclass	A62C	Fire-fighting
Group	A62C 11/00	Portable extinguishers with manually operated pumps

IPC codes to their patent documents. It is estimated that almost 95% of the 2 million patent documents published annually are assigned IPC codes. The United States began using the IPC in 1969 and Canada in 1978. The IPC is a hierarchical system that is divided into four subdivisions: sections, classes, subclasses, and groups. (see Table 3) There are 70,000 groups, of which 10% are main groups and the rest subgroups. Each subdivision is identified by a unique code and title. The eight top-level sections are identified by letter codes ranging from A, Human Necessities, through H, Electricity.

In January 2006, a new reformed version, the 8th edition, of the IPC was implemented. Prior to 2006, the IPC was revised and updated every 5 years. The 7th edition was in force from January 1, 2001 to January 1, 2005. The 8th edition is divided into two levels, the core and the advanced. The core level contains 18,000 classifications and is intended for use by smaller patent offices that issue fewer patents. Revisions to the core level occur every three years. The advanced level contains the full 70,000 classifications. Changes to the advanced level are made quarterly.

The EPO maintains the European Classification (ECLA), an extension of the IPC that includes, about 134,000 groups. ECLA's structure is very similar to IPC. In fact, many of the classifications are identical to corresponding IPC codes. For example, A01M 23/10 is the code for animal traps with rotating turnstiles or cylinders in both IPC and ECLA. The EPO classifies documents that are published in English, French, and German, German utility models, and documents published by Belgium, the Netherlands, and Luxembourg. About 30 million documents in esp@cenet have ECLA codes. ECLA is updated on an ongoing basis.

The JPO also maintains a version of the IPC called FI. Like ECLA, the FI is more detailed than the IPC.

PUBLIC PATENT DATABASES ON THE INTERNET

An in-depth discussion of all the public patent databases and search tools available on the Internet is beyond the scope of this entry. Therefore, only the most important resources will be discussed. The proliferation of Web-based public patent databases in the last decade has been both a boon and a challenge for public access to patent information. The public now enjoys better access to patents than at any other time in history. Anyone with a laptop computer and a connection to the Internet can search dozens of free or semifree patent databases (from both patent offices and independent organizations) containing millions of patent documents. However, this wealth of information may also confuse and mislead novice searchers. When considering which patent database to use, the patent searcher must balance functionality and ease-of-use with currency and comprehensiveness.

CIPO

The CIPO launched its Canadian Patents Database (CPD) in October 1998. Today, the database includes patent bibliographic data from 1869 to the present and full-text data for abstracts and claims from August 15, 1978 forward. Images of patent documents in PDF and GIF formats are available for patents issued from January 1, 1920 to the present and laid-open applications published from October 1, 1989 to the present. As of July 2008, the database contains approximately 1.9 million records. It is updated weekly. As Canada has two official languages, English and French, patent applications may be written in either.

Since its launch, the CPD has undergone numerous improvements and enhancements. In August 2003 administrative status data became available for withdrawn applications and patents that have been reissued, reexamined, or expired. Maintenance fee payments and status data was added in April 2004. In May 2006 bibliographic data for patents issued from 1869 to 1920 was added. Searchable fields include title, abstract, claims, inventor, owner, applicant, Patent Cooperation Treaty (PCT) filing number, international publication number, and IPC and Canadian Patent Classification (CPC) codes. The CPC was discontinued in the early 1990s and is not included on patent documents published after this time.

USPTO

The USPTO Web site hosts four significant patent information systems: two patent document databases, a patent assignment database, and a patent application file search system. Additional patent status information is also published in the front sections of the *Official Gazette* which is available on the USPTO Web site from 1995 to the present.

USPTO Patent Databases

The Patent Full-Text and Image Database (PatFT) is one of the largest and oldest public patent databases on the Internet. It can trace its history back to November 1995 when the USPTO launched PatBib, its first comprehensive Internet-based patent database containing bibliographic data for patents issued from 1986 through 1995. The USPTO maintained a small database of AIDs-related patents from December 1994 through April 1999. PatBib was expanded a few months later to include bibliographic data from January 1976 forward. Full-text data was added in November 1998, followed in March 1999 by images of patent documents in TIFF format. In October 2000, the USPTO again expanded PatFT by adding number and current classification data and TIFF images for patents back to 1790. Also in 2000, the USPTO added an integrated patent classification search tool that allowed searchers to retrieve patents in any given subclass. In April 2006, the date of issue for all patents from 1790 through 1975 was added.

PatFT currently contains data and images for approximately 8 million issued patents and related documents. It is updated every Tuesday when new patents are issued. Patent classification data for all patents is updated approximately bimonthly. In addition to searching full-text, users may also search separate fields including title, abstract, name of inventor, name of assignee, date of issue, patent number, date of application, application number, current classification, etc. Patents issued from 1790 through 1975 may only be retrieved by number, date of issue, and current classification. Certificates of correction, disclaimers, and dedications are not searchable, but are attached to the end of the patent document image.

In early 2001, the USPTO launched a second database called AppFT containing full-text data and images of published utility and plant patent applications, which are also known as pregrant publications. Since November 1999, all utility and plant patent applications have been eligible for publication 18 months after their effective filing date. The first pregrant publication was published on March 15, 2001. Searchable fields include many found in PatFT and Kind Code, etc. AppFT is updated on Thursdays when new applications are published. AppFT currently contains full-text data and images for approximately two million pregrant publications.

USPTO Assignment Database

Assignments on the Web, launched in December 2003, consists of two databases, one for patent assignments and one for trademark assignments. The Patent Assignment database contains all recorded assignment information for patents and published applications from August 1980 to the present; data is updated daily. Assignment records are searchable by patent number, publication number, assignor name, assignee name, and microfilm reel/frame number. Assignment records display the title of the patent, inventors' (assignor) names, assignee name, application number, date of application, date of execution, and date of recordation. Assignment records are linked to the PAIR system.

PAIR

The USPTO launched the PAIR system in mid-2003 using software acquired from the EPO. The system is divided into two components: Private PAIR and Public PAIR. Private PAIR provides secure access to current patent application status. Only registered patent attorneys/agents, independent inventors, and persons granted limited recognition who have a valid USPTO customer number and digital public key infrastructure (PKI) certificate may access Private PAIR.

Public PAIR, which may be accessed by anyone, contains application bibliographic data for patents and published applications from about 1989 to the present. The system has very limited search capabilities. PAIR records may be retrieved by application number, patent number, publication number, PCT, application number, and control number (for *ex parte* and *inter partes* reexamination proceedings). In addition to application data, PAIR contains transaction history, patent term extension history, maintenance fee payments, applicant address, patent attorney/agent, parent/child application data and supplemental content, such as computer program listings and nucleotide/amino acid sequences.

PAIR also provides access to application file wrapper documents in PDF format for applications pending on or filed after June 30, 2003. File wrapper contents include all correspondence between the USPTO and applicant, application worksheets, copies of cited foreign patent documents, examiner search strategies, information disclosure statements, related provisional patent applications, etc. Copies of cited NPL, such as journal articles, are not available due to copyright restrictions.

The USPTO does not disclose the current number of file wrappers available in Public PAIR, but 1.5 million is a plausible estimate. In the first year after the launch of PAIR the USPTO digitized more than half a million pending applications. Since July 2003, the USPTO has published approximately 1.2 million applications and issued some 762,000 patents.

EPO

The EPO's public patent database is esp@cenet. Launched in 1998, esp@cenet contains more than 60 million patent documents, including utility models, from approximately 70 countries and 1 million references to NPL.[47] The data is current for most patent offices. Patent documents are stored in PDF format and may be printed one page at a time. Documents with fewer than 100 pages may be downloaded and printed. Up to 100 documents may be stored in the My Patents list. Machine translation is available for several languages including German, Spanish, and French.

Documents may be retrieved by application, publication, or priority number, or NPL reference number. The Advanced Search allows users to search terms in the title, title and abstract, inventor and applicant, publication date, European Classification, and IPC. No date range search is available, but up to 4 years may be entered into the publication date field in order to limit a search. Searches may also be limited by country by entering up to four country codes in the publication number field, e.g., CA, US, WO. Search results are displayed in accession order and may not be re-sorted.

Individual patent records are linked to INPADOC legal status and patent family data, and citing references. Cited references are provided for WO and EP documents.

Register Plus is the EPO's equivalent of the USPTO's PAIR system. It contains bibliographic and procedural data for published EP applications and international applications in which the EPO or one or more of its member states are designated. Legal status is available only for published EP applications. Patent family information is also available. One of the most useful features of Register Plus is that it provides access to all documents in an EP application case history, also known as a file wrapper. Users may retrieve documents by application or publication numbers, date of filing, date of publication, priority number, priority date, inventor, applicant, representative, opponent, and IPC classification. Users may register with the WebRegMT e-mail alert service to monitor changes in the status of EP applications; up to 1000 applications may be monitored per e-mail address.

The EPO's third free patent database is ESPACE EP, which was launched in May 2008. Unlike esp@cent and Register Plus, users must register with the EPO in order to access the system. ESPACE EP runs on MIMOSA, a powerful full-text search engine. Users may search the most recent 4 weeks of EP published applications and patents. Users may also customize display, printing, and download options.

JPO

The JPO's Intellectual Property Digital Library (IPDL) contains Japanese patent and utility model data and images from 1922 to the present. IPDL offers several access points. Users may retrieve documents from the Patent and Utility Model Gazette Database by kind code and document number. Prior to January 2000, Japanese patent and utility model documents numbers were prefixed by the imperial year. For example, H12-123456, is the number of a document that was published in the 12th year (2000) of the reign of Emperor Akihito (1989-), also known as the Heisei period. After January 2000, the JPO adopted western years, e.g., 2000-123456, as prefixes.

Users may search the *Patent Abstracts of Japan* (PAJ) by document number, word in the title, applicant or abstract fields, date of publication, and IPC code. PAJ contains data from 1976 forward and is updated monthly. Utility models are not included in PAJ. Recent documents are automatically machine translated into English. PAJ contains legal status data from January 1990 forward; it is updated biweekly. Users may also conduct an FI/F-term classification search or browse the FI/F-term system using the Patent Map Guidance. An FI/F-term search will retrieve patents and utilities models back to 1885. Users may limit an FI/F-term search by publication date range and document type.

WIPO

WIPO's PatentScope Web portal, which was launched in mid-2005, provides access to bibliographic and full-text data and document images for 1.3 million PCT international patent applications published from 1978 to the present. The database is updated weekly (usually on Thursdays) when new international applications are published. PatentScope is the successor to the WIPO's electronic *PCT Gazette*, which went online in October 1998. The print and digital versions of the *PCT Gazette* was discontinued in April 2006.

PatentScope supports more than 25 searchable fields, including title and abstract in English or French, applicant and inventor name, address and country of residence, publication, application and priority number, IPC code, etc. The language of filing and publication may be searched by the full name or abbreviation of the language, e.g., "German" or "DE." Approximately 650,000 PCT applications are available in English, German 139,000, and Japanese 130,000.

PatentScope supports a number of advanced features not found in other patent office databases. Users may register for a free account where they can store search queries in between sessions. Search results may be sorted by date or relevance and search result displays customized. In late 2006, WIPO added RSS feeds for updated searches and graphical views of search results. Users may generate graphs displaying search results by year of publication, country of publication, applicant name, and IPC code.

The WIPO Web site also hosts the Hague Express Database of internationally registered industrial designs. Records are searchable by registration number, owner, international registration date, Locarno classification, indication of products, priority date, publication date, and contracting parties. No information is provided on coverage and update frequency.

FreePatentsOnline

FreePatentsOnline is a free patent database supported in part by paid advertising. Since its launch in 2004 it has become one of the more popular independent patent databases on the Internet. It contains searchable full-text patent documents from the United States (1976–), Europe (1978–), WIPO/PCT (1978–), and Japanese abstracts from 1976 forward. PDF images of U.S. patent documents are available from 1790 forward. Data and images for U.S. withdrawn patents are available back to the mid-1980s. Certificates of correction and reexamination certificates are attached to the original patent.

There are 26 searchable fields, many of which are identical to the search fields found in the USPTO patent database. The Advanced Search mode allows complicated search queries using field codes, Boolean operators, proximity operators, term weighing and wildcards. Users who register for a free account may store up to 10,000 records in 20 folders. Saved references (up to 250 at a time) may be downloaded in spreadsheet format. Citations may be exported in BibTex and EndNote formats. Other tools include a Google Toolbar plugin and RSS feeds for new patents and published applications organized by category or USPC class.

FreePatentsOnline recently introduced a chemical structure search based on SureChem's normalized database of chemical names and structures. It is the first free patent database to offer chemical structure searching. Chemical structure, substructure, and similarity searches may be searched using SMILES (a chemical notation system that allows two-dimensional chemical structures to be represented by a linear string of characters) or a graphically drawn structure. Structure data is updated about week after new patents are published.

Google Patents

Google Patents was launched in June 2006. It contains OCRed full text of U.S. patents and published applications from 1790 forward. It is not clear how frequently the data is updated, but the online FAQ indicates that coverage includes patents issued in the past few months. Documents are stored in PDF format and may be easily printed or downloaded. Certificates of correction and reexamination certificates are attached to the original patent.

The Advanced Search option allows users to search by patent number (but not by published application number), words in title, inventor name, assignee name, USPC code, and IPC code. Searches may be limited by document status (issued patent or published application), type of patent (utility, design, plant, etc.), issue date, and filing date. Search results are automatically ranked by relevancy and may be sorted by date. Records are linked to records in the USPTO patent database.

Google Patent's principal weaknesses are its lack of current USPC classification data and erratic classification search results. Its reliance on optical character recognition (OCR) full text also produces unreliable and erratic search results.

Patent Lens

Patent Lens, launched in early 2006, is the brainchild of a group of life science researchers in Australia who want to make the patent system more transparent and patent searching easier for nonprofessionals. It contains almost 9 million full-text patent documents from Australia (1998–), the United States (1976–), Europe (1980–), and WIPO/PCT (1978–). Data is current for US, EP, and WIPO/PCT documents. AU documents may be several weeks behind.

Search modes include Quick, Structured, and Expert. Searchable fields include full-text, frontpage, title, abstract, inventor, assignee/applicant, agent, references, claims, and description. Expert search allows complicated search queries using field codes, Boolean operators, and wildcards. Searches may be limited by publication or filing date, and U.S. patent predicted expiry date and lapsed date. Patent documents may be saved and previous searches reused. Patent family and status data is provided where available. Patent families may be displayed as graphical trees in PDF format. RSS search alerts may be created.

Patent Lens is the only free patent database that supports gene sequence searching. It uses the National Center for Biotechnology Information's BLAST software to find DNA and protein sequences that are listed in U.S. patents and published applications.

The greatest disadvantage of the system is the inability to search current USPCs or IPCs. This is not an oversight. The designers of Patent Lens believe that patent classification is too complicated for their intended users. It is possible to do a crude approximation of a classification search by searching USPC or IPC codes in the frontpage. However, search results should be treated with caution.

SELECTED WEB SITES

1. Canadian Intellectual Property Office—http://www.cipo.gc.ca
2. European Patent Office—http://www.epo.org
3. FreePatentsOnline—http://www.freepatentsonline.com
4. Google Patents—http://www.google.com/patents/
5. Japan Patent Office—http://www.jpo.go.jp
6. Patent Lens—http://www.patentlens.com
7. State Intellectual Property Office of the People's Republic of China—http://www.sipo.gov.cn/
8. U.S. Patent and Trademark Office—http://www.uspto.gov
9. World Intellectual Property Organization—http://www.wipo.org

REFERENCES

1. World Intellectual Property Organization, *World Patent Report: a Statistical Review*; WIPO Publication No. 931 (E); WIPO: Geneva, Switzerland, 2008. http://www.wipo.int/ipstats/en/statistics/patents/wipo_pub_931.html (accessed August 2008).
2. Singh, V.K. Patents: A tool for technological intelligence; IPFrontline.com 2006, http://www.ipfrontline.com/ (accessed June 2008).
3. Wolff, T. Freedom-to-operate patent searching: my six basic rules. Searcher **2008**, *16* (5), 34–39.
4. Hertel, K. Idaho ghost towns: Patents as a key to the past. Intellectual Property (IP) J. Patent Trademark Deposit. Libr. Assoc. **2003**, *3* (1), 29–40. http://www.ptdla.org/journal/2003hertel (accessed February 2008).
5. Melvin, T.C. Not just for inventors: Using patents for historical research. DttP **2002**, *30* (3/4), 22–27.
6. Rohan, D. Inventing a patent database: Lessons learned while creating the Wyoming Inventors Database. Intellectual Property (IP) J. Patent Trademark Deposit. Libr. Assoc. **2003**, *1* (1/2), 1–0. http://www.ptdla.org/journal/2003rohan (accessed April 2008).
7. Garris, C.A. The United States patent systems: An essential role in engineering design education. J. Eng. Educ. **2001**, *90* (2), 239–246.
8. MacMillan, M.; Shaw, L. Teaching chemistry students how to use patent databases and glean patent information. J. Chem. Educ. **2008**, *85* (7), 997–999.
9. Kruse, G.A. Patent literature in university libraries: A special form of "grey literature". INSPEL **1989**, *23* (4), 199–240.
10. Walker, R.D. Patents as information—an unused resource. IFLA J. **1984**, *10* (2), 175–181.
11. United States, *Patent Act of 1790*, http://ipmall.info/hosted_resources/lipa/patents/Patent_Act_of_1790.pdf (accessed July 2008).
12. Walterscheid, E.C. Thomas Jefferson and the Patent Act of 1793. Essays Hist **1998**, *50*, http://historyofideas.org/journals/EH/EH40/walter40.html (accessed August 2008).
13. United States, *Patent Act of 1793*, http://ipmall.info/hosted_resources/lipa/patents/Patent_Act_of_1793.pdf (accessed July 2008).
14. Dobyns, K.W. *The Patent Office Pony: A History of the Early Patent Office*; Sergeant Kirkland's Museum: Fredericksburg, VA, 1997.
15. Preston, D. The administration and reform of the U.S. Patent Office, 1790–1836. J. Early Republ. **1985**, *5* (3), 331–335.
16. United States, *Patent Act of 1836*, http://ipmall.info/hosted_resources/lipa/patents/Patent_Act_of_1836.pdf (accessed July 2008).
17. United States, *The Story of the United States Patent and Trademark Office*; Government Printing Office: Washington, DC, 1981.
18. Federico, P.J. The patent office in 1837: The restoration of records. J. Patent Off. Soc. **1937**, *19* (12), 954–965.
19. Chartrand, S. Patents: The earliest U.S. patents went up in smoke; but a few are still being recovered, even 168 years after the fire. New York Times August 9, **2004**, http://www.nytimes.com/ (accessed May 2004).
20. Anonymous, Patent office printing. Sci. Am. **1874**, *30* (3), 32.
21. United States, *Report of the Commissioner of Patents*; Patent Office: Washington, DC, 1852.
22. United States, *A List of Patents for Inventions and Designs, Issued by the United States from 1790 to 1847*; Patent Office: Washington, DC, 1847.

23. United States, *Subject Matter Index of Patents for Inventions Issued by the United States Patent Office from 1790 to 1873, Inclusive*; Patent Office: Washington, DC, 1873.
24. Jones, S.V. *The Patent Office*, 1st Ed.; Praeger: New York, 1971.
25. Anonymous, Publication of the patents. Sci. Am. **1872**, *26* (10), 151.
26. United States Patent and Trademark Office. List of PTDLs by State, Sept. 9, 2008, http://www.uspto.gov/go/ptdl/ptdlib_1.html (accessed July 2008).
27. Thomas, D.R. Out of the fire and into the frying pan: Hope for patent reference service in a non-patent depository library. Ref. Libr. **1991**, *32*, 125–138.
28. Munafo, G.A. Modern systems of information retrieval at the U.S. Patent Office. J. Patent Off. Soc. **1966**, *48*, 500–528.
29. Rotkin, I.; Dood, K.J. *A History of Patent Classification in the United States Patent and Trademark Office*; Patent Documentation Society: Arlington, VA, 1999.
30. United States, *Commissioner of Patents Annual Report*; Patent Office: Washington, DC, 1971.
31. Melvin, T.C. Patent information on compact disc: A review of four products. Sci. Technol. Libr. **1991**, *12*, 35–54.
32. Morehead, J.A. A patent saga: From print to CD-ROM to the internet. Ref. Libr. **1997**, *58*, 107–119.
33. Ebersole, J.L. Competition, jobs, and information policy: The case for private-sector information services for U.S. patents. World Pat. Inform. **1994**, *21* (2), 83–104.
34. Ebersole, J.L. Patent information dissemination by patent offices: Striking the balance. World Pat. Inform. **2003**, *25* (1), 5–10.
35. Poynder, R. Viscious circle: The current state of the patent information industry. Inform. Today **2004**, *21* (5), 24.
36. Crawford, J. Obsolescence or opportunity? Patent and trademark librarians in the internet age. World Pat. Inform. **1999**, *21* (4), 267–269.
37. Newton, D.A. The patent library: an obituary. IP Matters **2003**, http://scientific.thomsonreuters.com/free/ipmatters/ (accessed January 2008).
38. MacMillan, D. Patently obvious: The place for patents in information literacy in the sciences. Res. Strat. **2005**, *20* (3), 149–161.
39. World Intellectual Property Organization. *Standard ST.9—Bibliographic Data On and Relating to Patents and SPCs*; WIPO: Geneva, Switzerland, 2008.
40. World Intellectual Property Organization. *Standard ST.16—Identification of Different Kinds of Patent Documents*; WIPO: Geneva, Switzerland, 1997.
41. Paulauskas, J.A. *Additional Improvement Patents, 1837–1861*; National Archives and Records Service: Washington, DC, 1977.
42. United States Results of the trial voluntary protest program; Official Gazette of the U.S. Patent and Trademark Office, 1977; Vol. 956, 2.
43. White, M. US Alien Property Custodian patent documents: A legacy prior art collection from World War II—Part 1. History. World Pat. Inform. **2007**, *29* (4), 339–345.
44. White, M. US Alien Property Custodian patent documents: A legacy prior art collection from World War II—Part 2. Statistics. World Pat. Inform. **2008**, *30* (1), 34–42.
45. United States. *Manual of Classification*; U.S. Patent and Trademark Office: Washington, DC, 2003. http://www.uspto.gov/go/classification/ (accessed August 2008).
46. United States Patent and Trademark Office. *Examiner's Handbook to the U.S. Patent Classification System*; USPTO: Alexandria, VA, 2003. http://www.uspto.gov/web/offices/pac/dapp/sir/co/examhbk/ (accessed August 2008).
47. White, M. esp@cenet: Europe's network of patent databases. Issues Sci. Technol. Libr. **2006**, *47*, http://www.istl.org/06-summer/electronic3.html (accessed July 2008).

BIBLIOGRAPHY

1. Adams, S.R. *Sources of Information in Patents*, 2nd Ed.; K. G. Saur: Munich, Germany, 2006.
2. Caraher, V. The evolution of the patent information world over the next 10 years: A Thomson Scientific perspective. World Pat. Inform. **2008**, *30* (2), 150–152.
3. Carr, F.K. *Patents Handbook: A Guide for Inventors and Researchers Searching Patent Documents and Preparing and Making an Application*; McFarland: Jefferson, NC, 2009.
4. European Patent Office, *New Patent Information Policy Promises "Barrier-free" Access for All*; EPO: Vienna, Austria, 2007, http://www.epo.org/topics/news/2007/20071018.html (accessed April 2008).
5. Hitchcock, D. *Patent Searching Made Easy: How to Do Patent Searches on the Internet and in the Library*, 5th Ed.; Nolo Press: Berkeley, CA, 2008.
6. Hunt, D.; Nguyen, L.; Rodgers, M. *Patent Searching: Tools & Techniques*; Wiley: Hoboken, NJ, 2007.
7. Newby, F. *How to Find Out About Patents*, 1st Ed.; Pergamon: London, U.K., 1967.
8. United States Patent Office. *How to Obtain Information from United States Patents*; U.S. Department of Commerce: Washington, DC, 1962.
9. Walker, R.D. *Patents as Scientific and Technical Literature*; Scarecrow Press: Metuchen, NJ, 1995.
10. Weber, G.A. *The Patent Office: Its History, Activities and Organization*, 1st Ed.; Johns Hopkins Press: Baltimore, MA, 1924.
11. Wherry, T.L. *Patent Searching for Librarians and Inventors*; American Library Association: Chicago, IL, 1995.
12. World Intellectual Property Organization. *Inventing the Future: An Introduction to Patents for Small and Medium-sized Enterprises*; WIPO Publication No. 917(E); WIPO: Geneva, Switzerland, 2006.
13. World Intellectual Property Organization. *Looking Good: An Introduction to Industrial Designs for Small and Medium-sized Enterprises*; WIPO Publication No. 498(E); WIPO: Geneva, Switzerland, 2006.

People with Disabilities

Amelia Koford
Blumberg Memorial Library, Texas Lutheran University, Seguin, Texas, U.S.A.

Abstract

This entry discusses people with disabilities in relation to libraries and other information institutions. It briefly summarizes the social category of disability, the disability rights movement, relevant laws, and the history of disability in the literature and practice of information studies. It focuses largely on libraries, with some discussion of archives, museums, and for-profit information professions. The United States is the primary geographical focus, although other countries and international bodies are discussed. In addition to addressing accessibility of physical spaces, print resources, and electronic resources, the entry discusses disability as subject matter, library staff members with disabilities, and outreach. The entry emphasizes the importance of involving people with disabilities, both in scholarly research that concerns them and in accessibility evaluation and planning.

INTRODUCTION

Disability is a part of the human experience. Approximately 15% of people around the world have physical or cognitive impairments that limit their ability to perform one or more important functions.[1] The interaction between these impairments and barriers in the environment is defined as disability.[2] Disability is a category that anyone can enter as life circumstances change; some activists highlight this fact by referring to people without disabilities as "temporarily able-bodied."[3] People with disabilities are almost certainly present in any community served by libraries or other information institutions.

In recent decades, people with disabilities have made important gains in asserting their right to live, work, and play alongside others in their communities. Laws in many countries have affirmed the idea that social institutions and public spaces should be accessible to all. However, people with disabilities are still socially and economically marginalized. They face barriers to full participation in education, public life, and the workforce. Libraries, museums, websites, and other sources of organized information can be empowering resources for this underserved group; they also have the potential to contain barriers to access, reinforcing marginalization and isolation. Most information institutions contain a combination of enabling and disabling features. Information professionals need not wait until our institutions are perfect before cultivating relationships with the disability community.

Information professionals believe strongly in equity of access. The notion that resources should be available to everyone in a community is a core ethical principle of information professions. In practice, however, institutions often fall short of the accessibility ideal for a variety of reasons: finances, competing priorities for time and attention, attitudinal barriers, and lack of awareness. Many dedicated information professionals have worked for decades to promote empowering and fair services for people with disabilities. In becoming allies with people with disabilities, information professionals enter a mutually beneficial relationship with a large, diverse sector of the community.

DISABILITY AS A SOCIAL CATEGORY

The meaning and scope of the category of disability varies among cultures and countries. A given set of physical or cognitive characteristics might be considered a disability in one context, but thought of as simple human variation in another context. Although the context-dependent nature of the term disability makes it difficult to quantify, the World Health Organization estimates that 15% of people worldwide have a disability.[1]

The contemporary understanding of disability is that it is a social phenomenon. The social model of disability represents a shift from the previous conception of disability as an individual problem. Historically, the responsibility for disabled individuals' quality of life lay with the individuals and their families. Institutions that made accommodations for people with disabilities did so out of charity. In the second half of the twentieth century, due largely to activism and organizing by people with disabilities, a social model of disability emerged. The social model contests the idea that individuals and families should bear the burden of conforming to a nondisabled world. Under the social model, society is responsible for building its institutions in ways that include all citizens. The social model calls attention to the way that disability results from the interaction between a person's impairment and their environment.

Encyclopedia of Library and Information Sciences, Fourth Edition DOI: 10.1081/E-EISA-120053103

There are many different kinds of disability. Some broad categories of disability are

- Mobility disabilities
- Sensory disabilities
- Cognitive disabilities
- Learning disabilities
- Mental illness

Many disabilities change in severity and expression over time. Some people experience multiple disabilities. Many disabilities are "invisible"; arthritis, epilepsy, learning disabilities, and many more are not apparent to an outside observer. In most cases, information professionals do not need to know the details of our users' medical diagnoses; the important thing to understand what they need to effectively use information resources. In many cases, the best way to learn about what people need is to ask. A great deal of the current literature on accessibility of information institutions emphasizes the importance of consulting with people with disabilities.

The disability rights movement, which began after the end of WWII and continues today,[3] focuses on the rights of disabled people to make their homes outside of institutions and to participate in all aspects of society. Some histories of the disability rights movement are Shapiro's *No Pity: People with Disabilities Forging a New Civil Rights Movement*[4] and Fleischer and Zames's *The Disability Rights Movement: From Charity to Confrontation*.[5] The academic field of disability studies, which is closely aligned with the disability rights movement, developed in the 1980s.[6] The *Disability Studies Reader*, a good introduction to the field, is periodically updated with new editions.[7] The major professional organization in the field is the Society for Disability Studies, which publishes the journal *Disability Studies Quarterly*.

Print Disabilities

The category of print disabilities is convenient when discussing disability in relation to libraries and information. Print disabilities are any disabilities that affect a person's ability to read standard print and can include blindness, low vision, some learning disabilities, and some cognitive disabilities. The category includes people who have difficulty holding a book or turning pages. The term "print disabled" was coined by George Kerscher in the late 1980s.[8] Ways for print-disabled people to access books and articles include magnification, change in font, text-to-speech technologies, audiobooks, and Braille.

Language

Among people with disabilities, as among many historically marginalized groups, language and labels are taken seriously. Words are understood as vehicles for social power that can either enforce or subvert oppressive structures. Historically, people with disabilities have been given many labels, many of which strike the modern reader as dehumanizing: invalids, cripples, freaks, and the insane. In the 1980s, the people-first language movement grew out of a concern about the dehumanizing nature of much of the language used to describe people with disabilities.[9] Advocates of people-first language promoted the use of words and phrases that emphasize the person rather than the disability. The American Psychology Association's "Guidelines for Non-Handicapping Language in APA Journals"[10] explains key principles of people-first language. Examples of preferred language include "blind people" rather than "the blind"; "people who have epilepsy" rather than "epileptics"; and "people with disabilities" rather than "disabled people." Terms with superfluous negative overtones, like "a victim of...," "afflicted by...," or "confined to a wheelchair," are discouraged.

Person-first language is not universally embraced; there is ongoing debate about it within the disability community. Especially in the United Kingdom, writers and activists tend to use "disabled people" rather than "people with disabilities." Many in the autistic and blind communities also embrace identity-first language. Those who use identity-first language often view it as less linguistically cumbersome and as a way to assert their social and political identity (Schur et al.,[11] p. 7). Both people-first and identify-first language are used in this encyclopedia entry.

In another example of the significance of language, many Deaf people capitalize the term to denote Deafness as a culture, while the term deafness with a lowercase "d" describes the physical condition. Hard-of-hearing is often used to describe the condition of partial hearing loss.[12]

Some writers reject the term "hearing impaired": Harlan Lane writes, "The label has embedded within it the infirmity model that legitimates that establishment; and it exists only in opposition to hearing; in this it is like 'non-men' as a label for women, 'non-white' as a label for people of color, or 'sexually impaired' as a label for gays" (Lane,[13] p. 89). Others, in contrast, find "impairment" a useful term. Lennard Davis writes, "An impairment involves a loss or diminution of sight, hearing, mobility, mental ability, and so on. But an impairment only becomes a disability when the ambient society creates environments with barriers—affective, sensory, cognitive, or architectural" (Davis,[14] p. 41).

As cataloging and metadata librarians are well aware, language norms are culturally relative and change over time. The most important policy for information professionals is to speak respectfully, be willing to ask people about their preferred language, and be open to changing language after receiving new information.

LEGISLATION

In 1990, the United States passed the Americans with Disabilities Act (ADA), a major piece of legislation addressing the civil rights of people with disabilities. Among other provisions, the ADA requires that employers make reasonable accommodations for workers with disabilities and that public buildings offer ramps, accessible parking, and accessible bathrooms. Several other countries also passed major civil rights legislation in the 1990s, including Australia (Disability Discrimination Act of 1992) and the United Kingdom (Disability Discrimination Act of 1995).

Another relevant law in the United States is the Rehabilitation Act, which prohibits discrimination on the basis of disability by the federal government. Section 508 of the Rehabilitation Act requires that websites and other information technologies used by the government be accessible to people with disabilities.

The United Nations Convention on the Rights of Persons with Disabilities, an international treaty obliging countries to protect the human rights of people with disabilities, was adopted by the UN General Assembly in 2006. As of this writing, 158 countries had signed the convention and 149 had ratified it. The United States is not among the countries that have ratified the convention.

NONLIBRARY INFORMATION INSTITUTIONS

While this entry focuses primarily on libraries, information needs and perspectives of people with disabilities are highly relevant to all information-focused institutions. Many of the entry's statements about libraries hold true for other types of institutions.

For-Profit Sector

Many information professionals are employed by for-profit companies, working in fields such as usability, information architecture, and database management. Accessibility of electronic resources is an important aspect of these fields. A 2007 special issue of the Information Society provides a multidisciplinary analysis of disability in information technology, addressing questions about how to align accessibility with the profitability goals of corporations.[15]

Museums

In museum studies, there are ongoing conversations about ways to design exhibits with accessibility in mind. Strategies for enhancing the museum experience for disabled people include tactile exhibits, touch-tours, audio description of visual works, and closed captioning of audio works. A 2013 special issue of *Disability Studies Quarterly* focuses on museum experience and blindness, featuring best practices, curators' perspectives, and personal accounts of museum experiences.[16] Designing for accessibility can be a creative endeavor: Cachia, an art curator and chair of the Dwarf Artist Coalition of the Little People of America, calls on museums to "think about how access can move beyond a mere practical conundrum, often added as an afterthought once an exhibition has been installed, to use as a dynamic, critical and creative tool in art-making and curating" (Cachia,[17] p. 259).

A few museums focus on disability as subject matter. The June 2014 issue of the *Journal of American History* features exhibition reviews of several brick-and-mortar museums: the Museum of disABILITY History in Buffalo, New York; the Oregon State Hospital Museum of Mental Health; and the Museum of the American Printing House for the Blind.[18] Several online museums and exhibits document disability history. The Smithsonian's National Museum of American History hosts EveryBody: An Artifact History of Disability in America, which launched in 2013, as well as an ongoing web version of their 2000–2001 exhibit the Disability Rights Movement. The University of Leeds maintains the online Disability Archive UK. Another major online museum is the Disability History Museum maintained by Straight Ahead Pictures. Laurie Block, founder of the Disability History Museum, discussed the challenges of collecting and describing artifacts for the online museum in a 2007 article.[19]

Representing disability in museums is complicated by historical traditions of exploitative, dehumanizing presentations of disabled bodies. Sandell, Delin, Dodd, and Gay discuss this topic in their article "In the Shadow of the Freakshow."[20]

Archives

The archival record of disability experience, like the archival record for many historically disenfranchised groups, is fragmented. Some archives, such as the University of Toledo Archives, have proactively sought to find and preserve historical materials by partnering with community organizations.[21] The Bancroft Library at the University of California, Berkeley, has a substantial collection of records from the disability rights and independent living movements. Articles in the archives literature have addressed finding aid accessibility[22] and people with disabilities as archives employees.[23]

HISTORY

Libraries began addressing the needs of people with disabilities long before the passage of the ADA. Throughout the 1960s, 1970s, and 1980s, a variety of books and articles discussed library services for disabled patrons, particularly those with visual and mobility disabilities.

In the United States, the Boston Public Library established the first collection of embossed books for blind people in 1868, followed closely by the Library of Congress Reading Room for the Blind.[24] In 1931, Congress passed the Pratt-Smoot Act (Act to Provide Books for the Blind), establishing what is now the National Library Service for the Blind and Physically Handicapped (NLS). The NLS produces Braille materials and audiobooks—also known as talking books—and distributes them by postage-free mail to borrowers' homes. They recently began offering online access to talking books and Braille books (digital Braille books can be downloaded and printed using embossing hardware). The NLS operates through a national network of libraries in each state.

Before the independent living movement of the mid-twentieth century, many people with disabilities lived in institutions. A few authors have explored the histories of libraries patients' libraries in hospitals and mental institutions.[25,26]

After the ADA was passed in 1990, many libraries made changes to come into compliance with its requirements for physical spaces. In a 1991 *American Libraries* article, Gunde describes efforts by the library profession to respond to the ADA. He describes brochures and conference programs sponsored by Association of Special and Cooperative Library Agencies (ASCLA). In colorful language, he calls on libraries to do more to make their programs and services inclusive: "Many citizens with disabilities will come to question the sincerity of our commitment to the professional principles that we so eloquently proclaim at our overcrowded conferences and in our bombastic Association resolutions" (Gunde,[27] p. 809).

In 1994, Scheimann studied ADA compliance among Ohio public libraries.[28] Although the study's scope is limited, it provides a useful glimpse into a point in time shortly after the passage of the ADA. Libraries reported relatively high levels of physical accessibility and provision of alternative formats—87% had accessible parking, 71% had appropriate aisle width, and 95% provided large print, for example. Most libraries had not solicited significant patron input—only 7% had done so, with some including patrons with disabilities on an ADA evaluation committee, some distributing evaluation forms, and one inviting members of the local Handicapped Society to tour the building and offer suggestions. Many libraries had neglected to perform the self-evaluation that public entities were legally mandated to perform in 1993. Survey respondents expressed concerns about the cost of modifications, and several stated a perception that their service community did not include people with disabilities.

Perry's 2014 study of information services for older adults showed that many, but not all, libraries were in compliance with ADA guidelines.[29] Perry surveyed libraries in suburban counties, receiving 91 responses. Over 90% of responding libraries provided large print and audiobooks, 87.9% of buildings met ADA guidelines, and 81.3% of library websites were ADA compliant. In a variety of other categories, including assistive technologies, large-print brochures, and visible and high-contrast signage, between 35% and 45% of libraries provided accommodations.

The ASCLA, a division of the American Library Association, has done substantial work promoting improved library services to people with disabilities. The ASCLA maintains a series of library accessibility tip sheets that provide brief, readable introductions to topics such as assistive technology, service animals, and various categories of disability.[30] In 2001, the ASCLA was instrumental in adding a section on Library Services for People with Disabilities to the policy manual of the American Library Association.[31]

The International Federation of Library Associations and Institutions (IFLA) is another long-time player in the field. What is now IFLA's section on Library Services to People with Special Needs was founded in 1931 as the Sub-Committee on Hospital Libraries. From 1981 to 2008, it was called the Section for Libraries Serving Disadvantaged Persons.[32] During the section's long history, it has facilitated international cooperation among libraries serving people with disabilities and has published many sets of standards, guidelines, bibliographies, and resource lists. In 2005, it published the Access to Libraries for Persons with Disabilities Checklist, which is used internationally to evaluate and improve services.

In a content analysis of disability and accessibility in the library and information science literature from 2000 to 2010, Hill found a strong emphasis on accessibility of electronic resources and on visual disabilities.[33] A comparatively small amount of research has focused on information behavior or on attitudinal and social barriers to access. Thirty-six percent of the research articles Hill examined involved participation by people with disabilities, and she states that increasing this proportion would benefit the field.

In the United Kingdom, the now-defunct Museums, Libraries, and Archives Council produced several tools and documents related to people with disabilities, including a database launched in 2005 of disability trainers and consultants with an interest in working with heritage organizations.[34] The Museums, Libraries, and Archives Council was closed in May 2012 as part of government restructuring. Some of the Council's responsibilities were taken over by Arts Council England and the National Archives, but the Disability Experts database appears to no longer be maintained.

PHYSICAL RESOURCE ACCESSIBILITY

Space

Accessibility of physical spaces is an essential aspect of library services to people with disabilities. People who use wheelchairs, walkers, or scooters need wide enough pathways to navigate library buildings. Some physical space considerations, such as signage, also affect people with visual and cognitive disabilities. The ADA mandates that any new construction or renovation of a public space follow accessibility standards. Institutions that do not follow these standards are open to lawsuits. The ADA Standards for Accessible Design were updated in 2010, replacing the 1991 Standards.

The practice of designing spaces to be inherently accessible to all, including elderly and disabled people, can be called universal design, accessible design, barrier-free design, or inclusive design. Universal design from the beginning of a project is easier than retrofitting non-accessible spaces, and it is more inclusive than making only certain areas accessible. William Sannwald's *Checklist of Library Building Design Considerations* includes a chapter on ADA considerations and is periodically updated to keep pace with current standards and technologies.[35] Several libraries have successfully obtained grant or government funding for ADA compliance construction projects (Vincent,[36] p. 51).

There are many ways for libraries to improve their physical accessibility without undergoing new construction or renovation. They can provide plenty of seating, good lighting, and large and high-contrast signs. They can make sure that aisles, workstations, and handrails are kept clear. Tables can be raised or purchased at an appropriate height for wheelchairs. Vincent's *Making the Library Accessible for All* has a clear and concise chapter on architectural and environmental accessibility.[36]

Physical Books and Media

Physical books present inherent accessibility challenges to many people with visual disabilities, learning disabilities, and mobility disabilities. Libraries have a long history of collecting large-print books, which facilitate access by people with low vision. Another way to increase accessibility of physical books is to offer assistive technology that magnifies printed text, such as closed-circuit televisions. Many libraries arrange accommodations such as extended borrowing periods, proxy borrowers, renewal by phone, or extended reference help to facilitate access by disabled patrons. Communicating directly with patrons is the most effective way to learn what accommodations might help them use the library's books.

Under the 1996 Chafee Amendment, the NLS has permission to convert print materials to accessible formats, such as audio and Braille, without being subject to copyright law. Materials converted under the Chafee Amendment can only be distributed to eligible borrowers with a documented disability. These materials represent only a small fraction of the books published in any given year.

Standard type can often be made accessible through scanning. Scans can be run through optical character recognition programs to produce text that can be converted to audio, Braille, more readable font, or large print. In 2013, the University of California, Berkeley, library announced that it will scan materials on demand for students with disabilities as part of an out-of-court settlement following structured negotiations with four students.[37]

Deaf and hard-of-hearing patrons can access a much larger proportion of a library's holdings than visually disabled patrons, but videos may present an accessibility challenge. Many DVDs and Blu-Rays include captioning. Some libraries lend audio-described videos, which provide narration of the film's action for blind viewers.[36]

Services and Programming

Libraries offer a wide range of programs, classes, book clubs, and other events. One way to avoid excluding people with disabilities from events is to publicize the fact that sign language interpretation or other accommodations are available if the library is notified a certain number of days in advance. Providing reasonable accommodations so that people with disabilities can participate in library programs is not only ethical, but likely falls under the ADA's provision that no individual should "be denied the benefits of the services, programs, or activities of a public entity."[38]

Staff delivering presentations can increase accessibility by making sure slides and visual aids are clear and readable, with large text. White text on a dark background is easier to read by people with low vision.[36]

Libraries increasingly produce video tutorials. An article by Oud offers guidance for creating accessible screencasts.[39] She recommends Captivate or Camtasia for creating accessible videos. Best practices for accessibility include captioning, keyboard alternatives to mouse clicks, avoiding videos that start automatically, and including either alt text or spoken narration that describes what is happening onscreen. She writes that closed captioning (hidden by default) is preferred over open captioning (visible by default) because open captioning has been shown to be distracting to nondisabled users.

Many libraries provide programs specifically geared for people with disabilities. The Seattle Public Library, for example, hosts a book club conducted in American Sign Language. Several books and websites offer suggestions for programming for children and youth on the autism spectrum.[40,41]

There is a long tradition of programs that deliver library materials directly to people's homes, historically called "homebound" or "housebound" services. These programs serve people who have difficulty getting to the library for a variety of reasons, including age, illness, and disability. In a 2004 study of home library service in the United Kingdom, Ryder found that libraries provide home library service to over 120,000 people and that volunteers—often in combination with paid staff—support programs in over half of responding libraries. Only 62% of responding libraries publicize their home library service, partly due to fear of not being able to cope with demand, which may make them legally vulnerable under the UK's Disability Discrimination Act.[42]

ELECTRONIC RESOURCE ACCESSIBILITY

Born-digital electronic resources have the potential to be more inherently accessible than print since assistive technology can modify text in a variety of ways to make it possible for people with disabilities to access. Assistive technology can change font size, style, or color; convert print to spoken word; or convert print to Braille. Other types of assistive technology allow users to use speech for text input or to navigate resources using a keyboard, mouth stick, or head wand. Unfortunately, many websites and electronic resources contain features that make them difficult or impossible to navigate using assistive technology.

Nina McHale provides a concise overview of web accessibility guidelines.[43] Accessible web design is defined by two major sets of guidelines: the Web Content Accessibility Guidelines (WCAG), which are produced by the World Wide Web Consortium (W3C) and followed voluntarily, and the guidelines of Section 508 of the Rehabilitation Act, which are mandatory for federal agencies.

Many web accessibility guidelines are related to website performance on assistive technologies such as screen readers, while some, such as the recommendation to provide text transcripts of videos, address accessibility needs that are not related to screen readers.

Tatomir and Durrance developed a 10-point checklist, the Tatomir Accessibility Checklist, which provides a quick overview of some key components of accessibility. The checklist was inspired by a combination of the WCAG guidelines, Section 508 guidelines, and personal experience.[44] The 10 elements of the Tatomir Accessibility Checklist are

1. Accessible versions of PDF web pages and documents
2. Skip navigation and jump-to links
3. Clearly labeled page elements
4. Text captions for tables, images, graphics, graphs, and charts
5. Limited use of incompatible programming languages and scripts
6. The absence of identically named page elements
7. Text transcripts of videos, animations, and podcasts
8. Logical and consistent page organization
9. Absence of timed responses
10. Digital forms and functionalities accessible and usable with adaptive technologies[44]

Accessibility often goes hand in hand with usability. Accessible websites tend to be well-structured, quick to load on slow connections, compliant with web authoring standards, optimized for search engines (due to semantic markup), and easy to view on mobile devices.[36]

Accessibility of electronic resources is relatively well covered in the library literature, although gaps still exist in many areas, such as usability testing by people with disabilities.[33] Schmetzke edited special accessibility issues of Library Hi Tech in 2002[45,46] and 2007.[47] In 2012, Booth edited a special accessibility issue of Library Technology Reports.[48]

Vendor Databases

One of the more troubling findings in the literature on electronic accessibility is that many vendor-supplied databases, to which large portions of library budgets are dedicated every year, do not meet accessibility standards. Tatomir and Durrance studied 32 vendor databases and found only 9 to be moderately accessible; most were either marginally accessible or inaccessible.[44] Tatomir and Durrance gave relatively high marks to government websites, Google Scholar and Google Books, JSTOR, ProQuest, and OCLC World Cat. They noted that as of 2010 important accessibility elements were missing from databases produced by Gale, Lexis-Nexis, and Elsevier Science Direct. EBSCO databases were marginally accessible. Through a questionnaire directed at database vendors, Dermody and Majekodunmi found that most vendors did not work with people with disabilities to conduct usability tests.[49]

The ASCLA maintains an online toolkit entitled Think Accessible Before You Buy, which provides checklists and questions to ask when evaluating electronic resources for accessibility.[50] Libraries can require that potential vendors submit a Voluntary Product Accessibility Template (VPAT), a standardized document for reporting a product's compliance with accessibility standards. Many federally funded projects require a VPAT.[51]

The Universal Accessibility Interest Group of the Association of College and Research Libraries maintains an online guide to resources on web accessibility, which as of this writing included information on vendor databases and LibGuides in addition to websites.[52] Mulliken compiled a list of statements from vendors on their products' accessibility or lack thereof, which is no longer being maintained but remains informative.[53]

Library Websites

Website accessibility may be a new field for many managers of "homegrown" library websites, and even for some professional web designers. Several websites and books outline small changes that can make a big difference for accessibility.[36,54,55]

Comeaux and Schmetzke have collected longitudinal data on accessibility of North American academic library websites since 2002. In both 2010 and 2012, approximately 60% of websites were approved by Bobby 3.1.1, an automated checking tool.[56] Maatta Smith used another checking tool, the WebAIM Accessibility Evaluator, for a 2014 study of 127 urban public libraries in the United States. She found that all websites contained some errors, with the most common being contrast errors (low contrast between text and background), missing alt text (no text alternative to images or video), and missing form labels (no navigational aids to help users identify and fill out forms).[57]

Circulating Equipment

Increasingly, libraries circulate electronic equipment such as e-readers. Some e-readers are accessible to people with print disabilities, and some are not. The Free Library of Philadelphia and the Sacramento Public Library have both been sued for loaning inaccessible e-readers.[58] The Department of Justice and Department of Education issued a Dear Colleague letter in 2010 stating any e-readers used by colleges and universities should offer text-to-speech functionality.[59]

Assistive Technology

Many libraries provide assistive technology, also known as adaptive technology, for patrons' use. Vincent's book *Implementing Cost-Effective Assistive Computer Technology* provides an overview of options and considerations.[60] Decisions about what technology to offer should be based on assessment of local needs.

STAFF TRAINING

One of the most important accessibility resources a library can offer is quality public service. All public services staff should know the library's accommodation procedures and the basics of using assistive technology within the library, including what is available through operating systems, browsers, and Microsoft Office. Accessibility information can be compiled in a staff manual easily accessible from service points. Training can be provided in-house, with outside trainers, through webinars, or through attendance at conferences.[36]

In a qualitative study of library access, Clayton Copeland quotes from interviews with several people with disabilities. One of the participants, Nate, offers his impression of library staff attitudes:

> ...librarians are among the people who are most interested in helping people...their whole job is to help you find the book that you want and maybe even the book that you didn't even know you wanted. And I think that tends to carry over into how they treat people with disabilities. Now in a modern situation where all jobs are getting more and more duties put on top of them, and cutting back on how many staff there are...If anybody comes along and needs a little extra work [deep sigh], that can be a problem. And certainly, you know, I think they catch their breath before they take on a whole new area. But I don't find a lot of resistance (Copeland,[61] p. 235).

As Nate observes, the vast majority of library staff are friendly and willing to help, but many are unsure and hesitant when it comes to disability issues. Clear policies and staff training on effective communication with people with disabilities can increase the quality of service and decrease staff uncertainty and anxiety.

The tipsheets provided by the ASCLA present a good overview of best practices and etiquette. For example

> Staff should ask, "What's the best way I can help you?" when a patron requests assistance. Let the person guide you.
>
> After offering assistance, wait for acceptance; don't be afraid to ask questions if you aren't sure about something.
>
> Respect the patron's privacy. Do not ask questions about his or her disability or its cause.
>
> Understand that the adaptive equipment of a person with a disability is an extension of his or her body—this is true for adults and children. Ask for the person's permission before touching or moving the equipment.
>
> Always speak directly to a person with a disability—not the person's companion, aide, or sign-language interpreter.[62]
>
> Use normal language. "See you later" will not offend visually impaired persons.[63]

Written library policies can include statements that affirm the institution's commitment to the ADA and to providing access to all patrons. Policies and procedures can also outline the steps a library will take if it receives a complaint or request. Some libraries might write transition plans for changes that are not yet financially or logistically feasible.[64]

Library Staff with Disabilities

People with disabilities are underrepresented in librarianship and library work. As the library profession works to increase diversity in its ranks, disability is one of the areas targeted. The ALA Century Scholarship is provided annually to support a library school student with disabilities. Few empirical studies of librarians with disabilities have been conducted. A study of academic library managers in the Republic of Ireland found that they were aware of the need to accommodate disabilities, but that one-third of their libraries did not have procedures in place to address requests for reasonable accommodation.[65]

In the title of a 1995 opinion piece in American Libraries, Barlow exhorted, "Don't Just Serve People with Disabilities—Hire Them." She recounts the struggles and successes of several library employees with disabilities, gathered from a listserv query. Marilyn McLean, then head of science reference at Boston Public library, who has spina bifida, stated, "I frequently have had students writing paper or other people call about disabilities or birth defects, and I can often lend a personal touch to the reference encounter" (Barlow,[66] p. 722).

Fran Ziglar, a wheelchair user, wrote about her 31-year career at the Nashville Public Library in a 2006 Tennessee Libraries article. She writes, "There have been a few issues about accessibility: what to do when the elevator broke; early accessible bathroom stalls with curtains rather than doors, etc. Overall, I think that a sense of humor, concerned supervisors, and supportive co-workers have made the way successful and meaningful."[67]

OUTREACH

Community members with disabilities might not know that the library has resources for them. Especially if they have had negative experiences with libraries in the past, the prospect of going to a library without knowing whether they will be able to carry out simple tasks could be daunting. Outreach is an important part of an accessibility strategy. Used here, outreach refers to communication with community members who may not be library users and includes both informing people about what the library offers and asking them about what they need. Outreach might be conducted through partnerships with disability organizations, schools, or senior centers. Outreach could include co-hosted events or inclusion of library information in outside organizations' marketing materials.

In *Making the Library Accessible for All*, Vincent recommends that every library recruit a group of "accessibility resource people." This advisory group would provide ongoing feedback on local needs and accessibility issues. Accessibility resource people could provide information either through in-person meetings or electronic communication; she recommends SurveyMonkey as the most accessible of the free online survey tools. Vincent's book includes a sample list of questions for initial information-gathering. She quotes Alan Bern of the Berkeley Public Library: "There is, perhaps, nothing more important than a focus group—or, better, an ongoing Advisory Group—to discuss accessibility issues at your library. You WILL get requests you cannot meet—and even off-base questions and requests—but the number of spot-on questions and requests AND unexpected, fantastic ideas far outweighs any negative outcomes" (Vincent,[36] p. 3).

Once people with disabilities feel welcome in the library, they are often enthusiastic and active patrons. Vincent quotes computer accessibility expert Marc Sutton: "There are many books and magazines available through online library databases that would otherwise not be accessible to print-impaired persons. Often, a patron just needs a little help finding these items and then a whole new world of knowledge opens up" (Vincent,[36] p. xii).

DISABILITY AS SUBJECT MATTER

Discussions of disability and libraries often focus solely on the accessibility of resources and services. Another important aspect of disability, however, is disability as subject matter. Materials related to disability culture, art, and politics, as well as materials created by people with disabilities, are of interest to library users with and without disabilities. Strong collections will include materials that reflect the intersections of disability with other aspects of diversity, including class, race, gender, and sexual orientation.

Collection development in the disability field may involve turning to some specialized reference sources or small publishers. Many mainstream depictions of disability, especially in film, continue to rely on stereotypes, portraying people with disabilities either as villains or as one-dimensionally inspirational or tragic figures.[68] The Schneider Family Book Awards, administered by the ALA, are given yearly to children's and young adult books about the disability experience. A bibliographic essay by Cole, focusing on disability studies, also contains useful references to materials on disability history, culture, and memoir.[69] An annotated bibliography by Klauber, although out of date, lists categories of books providing practical information about aspects of living with a disability: College and Careers; Easier Living; House and Garden; Recreation and Travel; and Love, Marriage, Baby Carriage.[70]

Cataloging and Indexing

Because the terminology used to describe disability has historically reflected discriminatory cultural attitudes, library catalogs can contain archaic or insensitive words. The word "handicapped," for example, is commonly found in indexes despite not being in general use. Emmett and Catherine Davis discussed subject access to disability materials in the 1980s *Mainstreaming Library Service for Disabled People*, where they critiqued then-current Library of Congress headings such as *Idiocy* and *Castration of Criminals and Defectives*.[71] In a 2013 study of award-winning books about disability for youth, Kaney found that catalog terms failed to adequately represent many important disability issues.[72] In a 2014 article, Koford interviewed nine disability studies scholars about their impressions of subject headings, finding that they often encounter and use nonpreferred language when searching.[73]

Catalogers and indexers continuously change standards to reflect changes in society and language. Drabinski argues that problematic subject access terms can be used as pedagogical tools, helping library users better understand historical and social aspects of information.[74] In the *Disability Studies Reader*, disability studies scholar Lennard Davis recounts a meeting between the Committee on Academics with Disabilities and a bibliographer from the MLA Bibliography. He writes, "an article on 'crippled saints' could not be searched by computer because the word 'crippled' was disallowed by MLA regulations as constituting discriminatory language. The bibliographer therefore filed the article under 'saints' thus rendering it unretrievable by anyone with an interest in disability" (Davis,[7] p. xvii). This story illustrates the idea that access structures cannot be fixed by replacing terminology; rather, structures serve as evidence of history, struggle, and change. In practical terms, the variety of words historically used to describe disability means that searching for disability information is challenging and might require extra time and creativity.

CONCLUSIONS

Access to information, both about disability and about other topics, is essential for people with disabilities. Many disabled people have had positive experiences finding information through websites, databases, museums, archives, and libraries; at the same time, many have encountered barriers that prevented them from accessing the full range of information available to nondisabled people. Awareness of some disability issues, such as the importance of large-print books, is high within the library profession, while awareness of other issues, such as the poor accessibility record of many vendor-supplied databases, is low. There are many gaps in the library and information science literature on disability, and more studies that include disabled people as participants are needed. Some key principles that emerge in the literature are

- People with disabilities should be involved in the accessibility evaluation and planning process.
- Universal design, when it is possible, is more efficient and equitable than retrofitting nonaccessible structures or building alternate versions. This principle applies both to physical spaces and to electronic resources.
- Designing for accessibility often leads to usability. For example, large and clear signs benefit not only people with low vision or cognitive disabilities, but also nondisabled library users. Websites designed for accessibility tend to perform well not only on screen readers, but also on slow connections and mobile devices.

Providing equitable access to information for all people, including those with disabilities, is an ongoing process. Asking questions and opening lines of communication is essential to improving library services to people with disabilities.

REFERENCES

1. WHO. World report on disability summary, 2011. http://whqlibdoc.who.int/hq/2011/WHO_NMH_VIP_11.01_eng.pdf?ua=1 (accessed September 2014).
2. UN convention on the rights of persons with disabilities and optional protocol, 2006. http://www.un.org/disabilities/documents/convention/convoptprot-e.pdf (accessed August 2014).
3. Longmore, P. Disability rights movement. In *Dictionary of American History*; Kutler, S., Ed.; Charles Scribner's Sons: New York, 2003; 32–33.
4. Shapiro, J.P. *No Pity: People with Disabilities Forging a New Civil Rights Movement*; Three Rivers Press: New York, 1993.
5. Fleischer, D.Z.; Zames, F. *The Disability Rights Movement: From Charity to Confrontation*; Temple University Press: Philadelphia, PA, 2001.
6. Snyder, S.L. Disability studies. In *Encyclopedia of Disability*; Albrecht, G.L., Ed.; Sage Reference: Thousand Oaks, CA, 2006; 478–490.
7. Davis, L.J., Ed. *The Disability Studies Reader*, 3rd Ed.; Routledge: New York, 2010.
8. Reading Rights Coalition. The definition of "print disabled." http://www.readingrights.org/definition-print-disabled (accessed September 2014).
9. Disability is Natural. About Kathie Snow. http://www.disabilityisnatural.com/about/about-kathie-snow (accessed September 2014).
10. American Psychological Association. Guidelines for non-handicapping language in APA journals, 1992. http://www.apastyle.org/disabilities.html (accessed September 2014).
11. Schur, L.; Kruse, D.; Blanck, P.D. *People with Disabilities: Sidelined or Mainstreamed?*; Cambridge University Press: New York, 2013.
12. National Association of the Deaf, Community and Culture. Frequently asked questions. http://nad.org/issues/american-sign-language/community-and-culture-faq (accessed September 2014).
13. Lane, H. *The Mask of Benevolence: Disabling the Deaf Community*; Knopf: New York, 1992.
14. Davis, L.J. *Bending Over Backwards: Disability, Dismodernism, and Other Difficult Positions*; New York University Press: New York, 2002.
15. Annable, G.; Goggin, G.; Stienstra, D. Accessibility, disability, and inclusion in information technologies: Introduction. Inf. Soc. **2007**, *23* (3). 145–147. doi:10.1080/01972240701323523.
16. Levent, N.; Kleege, G.; Pursley, J.M. Museum experience and blindness. Disabil. Stud. Q. **2013**, *33* (3). http://dsq-sds.org/article/view/3751/3252 (accessed July 2014).
17. Cachia, A. "Disabling" the museum: curator as infrastructural activist. J. Visual Art Pract. **2013**, *12* (3), 257–289. doi:10.1386/jvap.12.3.257_1.

18. Horrigan, B.; Franz, K. Museum of disABILITY history. J. Am. Hist. **2014**, *101* (1), 200.
19. Block, L. "An invented archive": the disability history museum. RBM **2007**, *8* (2), 141–154.
20. Sandell, R.; Delin, A.; Dodd, J.; Gay, J. In the shadow of the freakshow: the impact of freakshow tradition on the display and understanding of disability history in museums. Disabil. Stud. Q. **2005**, *25* (4), http://dsq-sds.org/article/view/614 (accessed July 2014).
21. Britton, D.F.; Floyd, B.; Murphy, P.A. Overcoming another obstacle: archiving a community's disabled history. Radic. Hist. Rev. **2006**, *94*, 211–227.
22. Southwell, K.L.; Slater, J. An evaluation of finding aid accessibility for screen readers. Inf. Technol. Libr. **2013**, *32* (3), 34–46.
23. Waddington, N. The employment of people with disabilities as archivists, records managers, conservators and assistants. J. Soc. Arch. **2004**, *25* (2), 173–188. doi:10.1080/0037981042000271493.
24. Caulton, J.; Prine, S. Blind and physically handicapped: library services. In *Encyclopedia of Library and Information Sciences*; Bates, M., Maack, M., Ed.; Taylor & Francis: New York, 2010; 221–232.
25. Older, P. Patient libraries in hospitals for the insane in the United States, 1810–1861. Libr. Cult. **1991**, *26* (3), 511–531.
26. Panella, N.M. The patients' library movement: an overview of early efforts in the United States to establish organized libraries for hospital patients. Bull. Med. Libr. Assoc. **1996**, *84* (1), 52–62.
27. Gunde, M.G. What every librarian should know about the Americans with Disabilities Act. Am. Libr. **1991**, *22* (8), 806.
28. Scheimann, A. *ADA compliance: What are we doing?*; Thesis, Kent State University: Kent, OH, 1994.
29. Perry, C.A. Information services to older adults: initial findings from a survey of suburban libraries. Libr. Q. **2014**, *84* (3), 348–386.
30. Association of Specialized and Cooperative Library Agencies. Library accessibility—What you need to know, 2010. http://www.ala.org/ascla/asclaprotools/accessibility tipsheets (accessed July 2014).
31. Association of Specialized and Cooperative Library Agencies. Library services for people with disabilities policy, 2001. http://www.ala.org/ascla/asclaissues/libraryservices (accessed September 2014).
32. Panella, N. The library services to people with special needs section of IFLA: An historical overview. IFLA J. **2009**, *35* (3), 258–271. doi:10.1177/0340035209346213.
33. Hill, H. Disability and accessibility in the library and information science literature: a content analysis. Libr. Inf. Sci. Res. **2013**, *35* (2), 137–142. doi:10.1016/j.lisr.2012.11.002.
34. MLA launches disability experts database. http://ifacca.org/international_news/2005/03/21/mla-launches-disability-experts-database/ (accessed September 2014).
35. Sannwald, W.W. *Checklist of Library Building Design Considerations*, 5th Ed.; ALA Editions: Chicago, IL, 2008.
36. Vincent, J. *Making the Library Accessible for All: A Practical Guide for Librarians*; Rowman & Littlefield: Lanham, MD, 2014.
37. Schwartz, M. Settlement expands access at UC-Berkeley. Libr. J. **2013**, *138* (11), 20.
38. United States Department of Justice. Americans with Disabilities Act of 1990, as amended, 2009. http://www.ada.gov/pubs/adastatute08.htm (accessed September 2014).
39. Oud, J. Improving screencast accessibility for people with disabilities: guidelines and techniques. Internet Ref. Serv. Q. **2011**, *16* (3), 129–144. doi:10.1080/10875301.2011.602304.
40. Farmer, L.S.J. *Library Services for Youth with Autism Spectrum Disorders*; ALA Editions: Chicago, IL, 2013.
41. Libraries and Autism: We're Connected. Libraries and autism. http://www.librariesandautism.org/index.htm (accessed September 2014).
42. Ryder, J. Can't get to the library? Then we'll come to you. A survey of library services to people in their own homes in the United Kingdom. Health Inf. Libr. J. **2004**, *21*, 5–13. doi:10.1111/j.1740-3324.2004.00515.x.
43. McHale, N. An introduction to web accessibility, web standards, and web standards makers. J. Web Librariansh. **2011**, *5* (2), 152–160.
44. Tatomir, J.; Durrance, J.C. Overcoming the information gap: measuring the accessibility of library databases to adaptive technology users. Libr. Hi Tech **2010**, *28* (4), 577–594.
45. Schmetzke, A. Accessibility of web-based information resources for people with disabilities. Libr. Hi Tech **2002**, *20* (2), 135–136.
46. Schmetzke, A. Accessibility of web-based information resources for people with disabilities (part two). Libr. Hi Tech **2002**, *20* (4), 397–398.
47. Schmetzke, A. Introduction: accessibility of electronic information resources for all. Libr. Hi Tech **2007**, *25* (4), 454–456.
48. Booth, C. Why accessibility? Libr. Technol. Rep. **2012**, *48* (7), 5–6.
49. Schmetzke, A.; Greifeneder, E.; Byerley, S.L.; Beth Chambers, M.; Thohira, M. Accessibility of web-based library databases: the vendors' perspectives in 2007. Libr. Hi Tech **2007**, *25* (4), 509–527. doi:10.1108/07378830710840473.
50. Association of Specialized and Cooperative Library Agencies. Think accessible before you buy. http://www.ala.org/ascla/asclaprotools/thinkaccessible/default (accessed September 2014).
51. Tatomir, J.N.; Tatomir, J.C. Collection accessibility: a best practices guide for libraries and librarians. Libr. Technol. Rep. **2012**, *48* (7), 36–42.
52. Mulliken, A. Introductory resources for web accessibility, 2015. http://connect.ala.org/node/79199 (accessed September 2014).
53. Association of Specialized and Cooperative Library Agencies. Accessibility to library databases and other online library resources for people with disabilities, 2014. http://ascla.ala.org/toolkit/index.php?title=Accessibility_to_Library_Databases_and_Other_Online_Library_Resources_for_People_with_Disabilities (accessed September 2014).
54. Utah State University Center for Persons with Disabilities. Web accessibility in mind. http://webaim.org/ (accessed September 2014).
55. Williams, S. Web Accessibility. http://hr.umich.edu/webaccess/ (accessed September 2014).

56. Comeaux, D.; Schmetzke, A. Accessibility of academic library web sites in North America: current status and trends (2002-2012). Libr. Hi Tech **2013**, *31* (1), 8–33. doi:10.1108/07378831311303903.
57. Maatta Smith, S.L. Web accessibility assessment of urban public library websites. Public Libr. Q. **2014**, *33* (3), 187–204. doi:10.1080/01616846.2014.937207.
58. Enis, M. FLP settles Nook accessibility suit. Libr. J. **2012**, *137* (19), 12.
59. US Department of Justice; US Department of Education. Joint "Dear Colleague" letter: Electronic book readers, 2010. http://www2.ed.gov/about/offices/list/ocr/letters/colleague-20100629.html (accessed July 2014).
60. Vincent, J. *Implementing Cost-Effective Assistive Computer Technology: A How-to-Do-It Manual for Librarians*; Neal-Schuman: New York, 2012.
61. Copeland, C.A. Library and information center accessibility: the differently-able patron's perspective. Tech. Serv. Q. **2011**, *28* (2), 223–241. doi:10.1080/07317131.2011.546281.
62. Association of Specialized and Cooperative Library Agencies. People with mobility impairments: what you need to know, 2010. http://www.ala.org/ascla/sites/ala.org.ascla/files/content/asclaprotools/accessibilitytipsheets/tipsheets/4-Mobility_Impairmen.pdf (accessed September 2014).
63. Association of Specialized and Cooperative Library Agencies. People with multiple disabilities: What you need to know, 2010. http://www.ala.org/ascla/sites/ala.org.ascla/files/content/asclaprotools/accessibilitytipsheets/tipsheets/12-Multiple_Disabili.pdf (accessed September 2014).
64. Association of Specialized and Cooperative Library Agencies. The ADA library kit, 1994. http://www.ala.org/ascla/asclaissues/adalibrarykit (accessed September 2014).
65. O'Neill, A.-M.; Urquhart, C. Accommodating employees with disabilities: perceptions of Irish academic library managers. N. Rev. Acad. Librariansh. **2011**, *17* (2), 234–258. doi:10.1080/13614533.2011.593852.
66. Barlow, C. Don't just serve people with disabilities—hire them. Am. Libr. **1995**, *26* (8), 772–773.
67. Ziglar, F. My point of view? Tenn. Libr. *56*(1), 2006. http://www.tnla.org/associations/5700/files/tl561ziglarbio.pdf (accessed July 2014).
68. Nelson, J. Broken images: portrayals of those with disabilities in American media. In *The Disabled, the Media, and the Information Age*; Nelson, J., Ed.; Greenwood Press: Westport, CT, 1994; 1–24.
69. Cole, K.L. Disability studies: an evolving discipline and its literature. Choice **2012**, *49* (11), 1999–2007. doi:10.5860/CHOICE.49.11.1999.
70. Klauber, J. An enabling collection for people with disabilities. Libr. J. **1996**, *121* (6), 53–56.
71. Davis, E.A.; Davis, C.M. *Mainstreaming Library Service for Disabled People*; Scarecrow Press: Metuchen, NJ, 1980.
72. Kaney, P. *Representations of disability in youth literature: a discourse analysis of award winning books*; Dissertation, Emporia State University, 2013.
73. Koford, A. How disability studies scholars interact with subject headings. Catalog. Classif. Q. **2014**, *52* (4), 388–411. doi:10.1080/01639374.2014.891288.
74. Drabinski, E. Queering the catalog: Queer theory and the politics of correction. Libr. Q. **2013**, *83* (2), 94–111.

Personal Information Management

William Jones
Information School, University of Washington, Seattle, Washington, USA

Jesse David Dinneen
School of Information Studies, McGill University, Montreal, Quebec, Canada

Robert Capra
School of Information and Library Science, University of North Carolina, Chapel Hill, North Carolina, USA

Anne R. Diekema
Gerald R. Sherratt Library, Southern Utah University, Cedar City, Utah, USA

Manuel A. Pérez-Quiñones
Department of Software and Information Systems, University of North Carolina, Charlotte, North Carolina, USA

Abstract

Personal information management (PIM) refers to the practice and the study of the activities a person performs in order to acquire or create, store, organize, maintain, retrieve, use, and distribute information in each of its many forms (paper and digital, in e-mails, files, web pages, text messages, tweets, posts, etc.) as needed to meet life's many goals (everyday and long term, work related and not) and to fulfill life's many roles and responsibilities (as parent, spouse, friend, employee, member of community, etc.). PIM activities are an effort to establish, use, and maintain a mapping between information and need. Activities of finding (and refinding) move from a current need toward information, while activities of keeping move from encountered information toward anticipated need. Meta-level activities such as maintaining, organizing, and managing the flow of information focus on the mapping itself. Tools and techniques of PIM can promote information integration with benefits for each kind of PIM activity and across the life cycle of personal information. Understanding how best to accomplish this integration without inadvertently creating problems along the way is a key challenge of PIM.

INTRODUCTION

Personal information management (PIM) refers to the practice and the study of the activities a person performs in order to acquire or create, store, organize, maintain, retrieve, use, and distribute information in each of its many forms (paper and digital, in e-mails, files, web pages, text messages, tweets, posts, etc.) as needed to meet life's many goals (everyday and long term, work related and not) and to fulfill life's many roles and responsibilities (as parent, spouse, friend, employee, member of community, etc.) or, to paraphrase, *PIM is the art of getting things done in our individual lives through information.*[1] PIM places special emphasis on the organization and maintenance of personal information collections (PICs) in which information items, such as paper documents, electronic documents, e-mail messages, digital photographs, web page references, and handwritten notes, are stored for later use and repeated reuse.[2]

PIM provides a productive meeting ground for several disciplines including cognitive psychology and cognitive science; human–computer interaction, information science, and human-information behavior; and the fields of data, information, and knowledge management. In a world increasingly defined by the information we receive, send, and share, the ability to manage this information is one of life's essential skills.

One ideal of PIM is to always have the right information in the right place, in the right form, and of sufficient completeness and quality to meet the current need. This ideal is far from reality for most people. In practice, people do not always find the right information in time to meet their needs. It may be that the necessary information is not found or may arrive too late to be useful. Or information may arrive too soon and then be misplaced or forgotten entirely before opportunities for its application arrive. People forget to use information even when (or sometimes because) they have taken pains to keep it stored somewhere for future use.

To better "keep found things found,"[3] people may store their information in multiple locations and in multiple applications, using organizational schemes that are roughly comparable but still inconsistent (often in

Pacific–Philosophy

Encyclopedia of Library and Information Sciences, Fourth Edition DOI: 10.1081/E-ELIS4-120053695

important ways). The result is *information fragmentation*[4]—the information people need is scattered widely, making activities of PIM more difficult:

- *Maintaining and organizing* personal information is more difficult when so many separate stores of information must be considered. Are organizations the same or at least consistent? Which version of a document is current? Is information getting backed up?
- *Managing for privacy, security, and the overall flow of information* (incoming and outgoing) is more difficult when a person's information is so widely scattered. What have people shared and with whom? [5] Is there an "Achilles heel" in a person's data protection efforts?
- Information fragmentation makes more difficult even the basic, every-minute activities of *keeping* and *finding*. Where/how to keep an important file, reference, or reminder when there are so many alternatives to choose from? And where among these alternatives should people later look for this information?

Information fragmentation is manifest in the many sources of information a person must consult to make even simple decisions. The decision to accept a dinner invitation, for example, may depend upon the information to be found in digital calendars, paper calendars (e.g., a shared household calendar), web pages, and e-mail exchanges. PIM activities in general take longer and are more prone to error when information is scattered.

While new applications, tools, and devices often increase information fragmentation, this does not have to be the case. Some tools and techniques of PIM promote information integration, which can simplify PIM activities and have benefits across the life cycle of personal information. Tools can also simplify the sharing and exchange of information across devices and people, and can help users to see unified views of their information spaces.

In the following sections, we provide

- A brief history of PIM
- An analysis of PIM including the several senses in which information can be "personal" and major kinds of PIM activity
- A selective review of PIM research especially as this relates to major kinds of PIM activity
- Concluding notes on some of the significant challenges and opportunities for the PIM field of study in the years ahead

A BRIEF HISTORY OF PIM

PIM is a new field with ancient roots. When the oral rather than the written word dominated, human memory was the primary means for information preservation.[6] As information was increasingly rendered in paper form, tools were developed over time to meet the growing challenges of management. For example, the vertical filing cabinet, now a standard feature of home and workplace offices, was first commercially available in 1893.[7]

The modern dialog on PIM is often traced to the publication of "As We May Think" by Vannevar Bush at the close of World War II.[8] Bush expressed a hope that technology might be used to extend our collective ability to handle information and to break down barriers impeding the productive exchange of information.

The 1940s also saw the development of Shannon's theory of communication that laid the groundwork for a quantitative assessment of information.[9] Key to this theory is the notion that the information content of a message can be measured for its capacity to reduce uncertainty.

To understand information exclusively as the reduction of uncertainty can be seen as overly restrictive.[10] As Buckland notes, "sometimes information increases uncertainty,"[11] p. 351. Nevertheless, even as we search for complementary, qualitative characterizations of information (e.g., Dinneen and Brauner[12]), a larger point in Shannon's work endures: The value of information is not absolute, but relative to a context that includes the intentions of the sender, method of delivery, and the current state of a recipient's knowledge. This holds true even when the sender and the recipient are the same person albeit separated in time, for example, when people place "appointments" in their calendars a week from today as a reminder to do something (e.g., "book plane tickets").

With the increasing availability of computers in the 1950s came an interest in the computer as a source of metaphors and a test bed for efforts to understand the human ability to process information and to solve problems. Newell and Simon pioneered the computer's use as a tool to model human thought.[13,14] They produced "The Logic Theorist," generally thought to be the first running artificial intelligence program. The computer of the 1950s was also an inspiration for the development of an *information processing approach* to human behavior and performance.[15]

After research in the 1950s showed that the computer, as a symbol processor, could "think" (to varying degrees of fidelity) like people do, the 1960s saw an increasing interest in the use of the computer to help people to think better and to process information more effectively. Working with Andries van Dam and others, Ted Nelson, who coined the word "hypertext,"[16] developed one of the first hypertext systems, the Hypertext Editing System, in 1968.[17] That same year, Douglas Engelbart also completed work on a hypertext system called NLS (oN-Line System).[18] Engelbart advanced the notion that the computer could be used to augment the human intellect.[19,20] As heralded by the publication of Ulric Neisser's book *Cognitive Psychology*,[21] the 1960s also saw the emergence of cognitive psychology as a discipline that focused primarily on a better understanding of the human ability to think, learn, and remember.

The computer as an aide to the individual, rather than a remote number cruncher in a refrigerated room, gained further validity from work in the late 1970s and through the 1980s to produce personal computers of increasing power and portability (for more on the history of the personal computer, see Refs.[22–24]). These trends continue. Computational power roughly equivalent to that of a desktop computer of a decade ago can now be found in devices that fit into the palm of a hand (see Jones,[25] Chapter 4, for discussion on the present and future of information "always at hand" via devices).

The phrase "personal information management" was itself apparently first used in the 1980s[26] in the midst of general excitement over the potential of the personal computer to greatly enhance the human ability to process and manage information. The 1980s also saw the advent of so-called "PIM tools" that provided limited support for the management of such things as appointments and scheduling, to-do lists, phone numbers, and addresses. And a community dedicated to the study and improvement of human–computer interaction also emerged in the 1980s.[27,28]

As befits the "information" focus of PIM, PIM-relevant research of the 1980s and 1990s extended beyond the study of a particular device or application toward larger ecosystems of information management to include the organization of the physical office[29] and the management of paperwork.[30] Malone[31] characterized personal organization strategies as "neat" or "messy" and described "filing" and "piling" approaches to the organization of information. Other studies showed that people vary their methods for keeping information according to anticipated uses of that information in the future.[32] Studies explored the practical implications that human memory research might carry in the design of, for example, personal filing systems[33–35] or information retrieval systems.[36] Studies demonstrated a preference for navigation (browsing, "location-based finding") in the return to personal files,[37] a preference that endures today notwithstanding significant improvements in search support[38–41] and an increasing use of search as the preferred method of return to e-mails.[42]

PIM, as a contemporary field of inquiry with a self-identified community of researchers, traces its origins to a special interest group session on PIM at the CHI 2004 conference[43] and to a special National Science Foundation–sponsored workshop held in Seattle in 2005.[44] (Since 2005, PIM workshops have been held roughly every 18–24 months, see: http://pimworkshop.org/.)

AN ANALYSIS OF PIM

A deeper understanding of what PIM *is* begins with definitions of associated concepts and the description of a conceptual framework in which to interrelate key kinds of PIM activity.

The Information Item and Its Form

Information sent and received takes many *information forms* in accordance with a growing list of communication modes, supporting tools, and people's customs, habits, and expectations. People still send paper-based letters, birthday cards, and thank you notes. But ever more so, people communicate using digital forms of information including e-mails, documents shared (as attachments or via a service such as Dropbox), and "tweets," text messages, blog posts, Facebook updates, and personal web pages.

Across forms, it is useful to speak of an *information item* as a packaging of information. An item encapsulates information in a persistent form that can be managed. An information item can be created, stored, moved, given a name and other properties, copied, distributed, and deleted.

The concepts of information item and information form are helpful abstractions for considering aspects of PIM. For example, an e-mail message, as an item, packages together information such as a sender, receiver, subject, body text, and date sent. All e-mails, as befits their form, share common characteristics such as the expectation of a timely delivery (i.e., in seconds not days) and a timely response (i.e., within a day or two, not a month later). An e-mail message can be *transformed,* i.e., it can be copied to create a new information item of a different form. For example, a user may print the e-mail and view it in a paper form. Each form is associated with a distinct set of tools, techniques, habits, and expectations for interacting with and managing the information.

Personal Information

There are several senses in which information can be personal. Each represents a different relationship between the information and the person: Information can be owned by, about, directed toward, sent by, experienced by, or relevant to "me." (See Table 1.) This definition and the several relationships captured in Table 1 form an inclusive definition of personal information. Prior work in PIM has at times limited the definition of PIM by not including some of these relationships.

Clearly, the senses in which information can be personal are not mutually exclusive. In many cases, the same information may be personal in several senses. For example, a folder of photos taken last Thanksgiving is information about the friends and family at the dinner—and about "me" (P2). The photos are owned by "me" (P1), and these represent events experienced by "me" (P5). The owner can also elect to share the photos with others via a service like Dropbox (P4).

Table 1 Information can be personal in any of several relationships to a person

	Relation to "me"	Examples	Issues
P1	Controlled by/owned by me	E-mail messages in our e-mail accounts; paper documents in a home office; computer files on a hard drive or in a web cloud service.	Security against break-ins, virus protection, backups to prevent data loss, etc. What to share and with whom? These questions apply both for paper filing cabinets and for folders in a service like Dropbox.
P2	About me	Credit history, medical records, web search history, records of library books checked out.	Who sees what, when, and under what circumstances? How is information corrected or updated? Does it ever go away?
P3	Directed toward me	E-mails, phone calls, drop-ins, TV ads, web ads, pop-ups. Also, invitations to join a share of a cloud service. Facebook posts. Tweets "@" you.	How to stay focused long enough to complete a task? "When I'm not interrupted by others, I interrupt myself! I worked nonstop today, but what did I accomplish?"
P4	Sent/posted/ shared by me	Sent e-mail, personal websites, published reports and articles, folders shared via a cloud service like Dropbox.	Who sees what when? Did the message get through? Am I making the "right" impression? Am I sharing the right information for our teamwork?
P5	For things experienced by me	Web history, photos (taken by others as well as by me), handwritten notes, full-motion videos from head-mounted cameras.[45]	How to get back to information again later? How to pick up where I left off (i.e., with a task, a book or episodes of a drama on Netflix)? How much history do I really need?
P6	Potentially relevant/ useful to me	Somewhere "out there" is the perfect vacation, house, job, lifelong mate. If only I could find the right information!	If only I knew (had some idea of) what I don't know. But also... how to filter out information we don't wish to see? (How to do likewise for our children?)

A Personal Space of Information

Each person has a single unique personal space of information (PSI) defined by the union of personal information in each of its six senses as depicted in Table 1. A PSI affects the way its owner views and interacts with the rest of the world. A PSI also affects the way its owner is seen, categorized, and treated by others.

At its center, a person's PSI includes all the information items that are, at least nominally, under that person's control. At its periphery, the PSI includes information that the person might like to know about and control, but that is under the control of others. Included is information about the person that others keep. Also included is information in public spaces, such as a local library or the web, which might be relevant to the person.

Personal Information Collections

Personal information collections, referred to as PICs or simply collections, are personally managed subsets of a PSI. PICs are "islands" in a PSI where people have made some conscious effort to control both the information that goes in and how this information is organized. PICs can vary greatly with respect to the number, form, and content coherence of their items. Examples of a PIC include

- The papers in an office and their organization, including the layout of piles on a desktop and the folders inside filing cabinets
- A collection of projects each represented by a folder stored in a cloud storage service and accessed from different devices
- A collection of information items related to a specific project that are initially "dumped" into a folder on a person's notebook computer and then organized over time as the project takes shape
- A reference collection of articles in digital format, organized for repeated use across projects
- Digital songs managed through a laptop computer or smartphone
- A collection of media (TV shows, movies, music) stored in a streaming service under a personal account, organized by some preference and including information such as ratings, watched/unwatched, and other notes

A PIC includes not only a set of information items but also their organizing representations, including spatial layout, containing folders, properties, and tags.

Activities of PIM

PIM activities are an effort *to establish, use, and maintain a mapping between information and need*, whether actual, perceived, or anticipated. Fig. 1 depicts a mapping between information and need as well as the activities of PIM that work with this mapping.

Information can arrive as aural comments from a friend, a billboard seen on the way to work, letters in

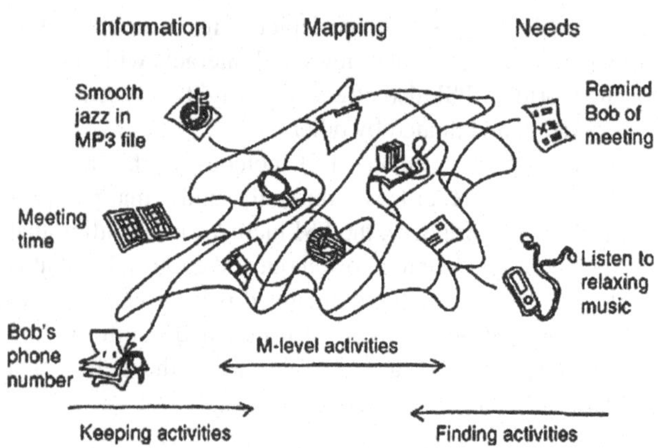

Fig. 1 PIM activities viewed as an effort to establish, use, and maintain a mapping between needs and information. Keeping and finding activities are interrupt driven (as prompted by incoming information or a need). M-level (meta-level) activities are broader in focus and more strategic in nature.

surface mail, or any number of digital items including e-documents, e-mail messages, Web pages, text messages, and tweets.

Needs can arise from internal or external sources. A person may recall, for example, that she needs to make plane reservations for an upcoming trip. The need may arise from the question posed by a colleague in the hallway or a manager's request during a meeting. External needs can also evoked by an information item, such as an e-mail message or a web-based form.

Connecting between need and information is a mapping. Only small portions of the mapping have an observable external representation. Much of the mapping has only a hypothesized existence in the memories of an individual. Large portions of the mapping are potential and not realized in any form, external or internal. A sort function or a search facility, for example, has the potential to guide from a need to the desired information.

However, parts of the mapping can be observed and manipulated. The folders of a filing system (whether for paper or digital information), the layout of a desktop (physical or virtual), and the choice of names, keywords, and other properties for information items all form parts of an observable fabric helping to knit need to information.

Activities of PIM can be grouped and interrelated with reference to Fig. 1 as follows:

- **Keeping activities** map from encountered information to need (immediate or anticipated). This grouping includes decisions concerning whether to attend to information in the first place and, then, whether to make any effort to keep the information. Some information—the time on a clock or a sports score, for example—is "consumed" immediately with no need to keep the information for later access. Much of the information people encounter is simply ignored. For the subset of encountered information to be kept for later use, questions arise regarding how the information should be kept. Should information items be piled (where?), filed (which folder?), tagged (with which tags?), or committed to memory?
- **Finding/refinding activities** map from need to information. This grouping includes explicit search queries as posted to a web-based search service or to a computer desktop–based search facility. The grouping also includes various activities of sorting, navigation, and "nosing around" that people use to get back to information for reuse.
- **Meta-level activities** focus on the mapping itself as a way of connecting together information and need. Meta-level activities include efforts to maintain (through backups, periodic cleanups, updates, and corrections) and organize (via schemes of piling, filing, or tagging) information; manage privacy, security, and the flow of information (e.g., through subscriptions, friendships, policies of disclosure, firewalls, virus protection); measure and evaluate (how are supporting tools and strategies working?); and make sense of and use of personal information ("What is the information telling me? What should I do?").

PIM RESEARCH

PIM research can be organized according to PIM activity as follows:

Finding/Refinding: From Need to Information

The focus of a finding/refinding activity can be on information in a public space such as a physical library or the web, or focus can be on the information a person owns in a private space such as an office filing cabinet, the hard drive of a personal computer, or a cloud storage service.

A large body of information seeking and information retrieval research applies especially to finding public information.[46–50] There is a strong personal component even in efforts to find new information, never before experienced, from a public store such as the web. For example, efforts to find information may be directed by a personally created outline or a to-do list. In addition, information inside a person's PSI can be used to support a more targeted, personalized search of the web.[51]

The search for information is often a sequence of interactions rather than a single transaction. Bates[52] describes a "berry picking" model of searching in which needed information is gathered in bits and pieces through a series of interactions, and during this time, the user's expression of need, as reflected in the current query, evolves. Teevan et al.[53] note that users often favor a stepwise approach even in cases where the user might have sufficient knowledge to access the information more quickly and more directly via a well-formed query. The stepwise approach may preserve a greater sense of control and context over the search process and may also reduce the cognitive burden associated with query formulation. For frequent information needs, users may well-trod paths of access, whereas for less common needs, search may be more likely to play a role.[54]

People may find (rather than refind) information even when this information is ostensibly under their control. For example, items may be "pushed" into the PSI (e.g., via the inbox, automated downloads, web cookies, the installation of new software, etc.), and a person may have no memory or awareness of these items. If these items are ever retrieved, it is through an act of finding, not refinding. Memories of a previous encounter with an information item may also fade so that its retrieval is more properly regarded as an act of finding rather than refinding.[55] While searching for information, one might come across information that, though not relevant to the current search, is relevant to another project. Or one may find information that is incorrectly filed or is in a "download" folder awaiting more proper organization (e.g., as part of "spring cleaning").

Lansdale[26] characterized the retrieval of information as a two-step process involving interplay between recall and recognition. The steps of recall and recognition can iterate to progressively narrow the search for the desired information—for example, when people move through a folder hierarchy to a desired file or e-mail message or navigate through a website to a desired page.

But a successful outcome in a refinding effort depends upon the completion of another step preceding recall: A person must remember to look. A person may know exactly where an item is and still forget to look for the item. It is also useful to consider a final "repeat?" step. Failure to collect a complete set of information (e.g., all potential conflicting commitments before accepting a proposed meeting time) can mean failure for the entire finding episode.

Refinding, then, is a four-step process with a possibility to fail at each step:

Step 1. Remember (to look). Many opportunities to refind and reuse information are missed for the simple reason that people forget to look. This failure occurs across information forms. In a study by Whittaker and Sidner,[56] for example, participants reported that they forgot to look in "to do" folders containing actionable e-mail messages. Because of mistrust in their ability to remember to look, people then elected to leave actionable e-mail messages in an already overloaded inbox.

Web information is also forgotten. In one study of web use, participants complained that they encountered web bookmarks; in the course of a "spring cleaning," for example, that would have been very useful for a project whose time had now passed.[57] In a study where participants were cued to return to a web page for which they had a web bookmark, the bookmark was used on less than 50% of the trials.[58] Marshall and Bly[59] report a similar failure to look for paper information (newspaper clippings).

Remembering to look depends, in part, upon the effective use of *attentional spaces*[3], such as the surface of a physical desktop, a computer desktop, or the visible region of an inbox's display.

Steps 2 and 3. Recall and recognize. Recall and recognition can be considered together as two sides of a dialog between people and their PSIs. A person types a search word (recall) and then scans through a list of results (recognition). A person's recall is often partial. For example, a person may have some sense that the e-mail message was sent by a person whose name starts with an "S" ("Sally?"). As prompted by this partial recall, she might then sort e-mail messages by sender and then scan through the "s" section of this sorted list.

Though any act of retrieval involves a combination of recall and recognition, their relative importance can vary with method. Recall is typically more important in a search, i.e., a person initially recalls the keywords to be used in a search query (though, of course, the person might have recognized these words from a web page previously viewed and simply copied them into the query). Recognition is typically more important in what is alternately referred to as location-based finding, orienteering, browsing, or, simply, *navigation*.[37,53,60]

Many PIM studies have determined that users prefer to return to information, most notably the information kept in personal digital files, by navigating rather than searching.[37–39,41,53,60–62] This may be surprising; the use of navigation often depends on remembering or recognizing a specific path to the folder in which the item was stored, while a search is more flexible insofar as users can specify in their query any attribute they happen to remember about the information item. Fertig et al. argued back in 1996[63] that an observed preference for navigation over search was due to the limitations in the search technologies at the time and that improvement in search would inevitably lead to a shift from navigation to search as the preferred method of return. Commercial PIM search engines have indeed improved dramatically. However, the combined results of a large-scale study and a longitudinal study[39] indicated that the availability of new and improved search facilities (such as Mac Spotlight) did not result in more search than was observed for older and slower search facilities (such as Sherlock). Search was apparently used only as last resort on those occasions when participants could not remember the location of the files they sought. This finding gains further support from a recent log study indicating that participants used search in only 4.2% of their retrievals.[64]

One explanation for a preference for navigation over search in the return to personal information derives from a persistent, general finding in cognitive psychology literature that people are better able to recognize than to recall information previously encountered (see Neisser[21]). As noted previously, in the interplay between recognition and recall, recognition is more dominant in navigation and recall is more dominant in search.

"Navigation" to digital files and other information is, of course, done in a computing environment that is much less rich in sensory experience than the physical environments people navigate through on a daily basis. But perhaps digital and physical navigation engage, at some level, some of the same processes. In support of this intuition is a recent, innovative fMRI study[65] demonstrating that, when people use navigation as a means to retrieve their own personal files, they are using some of the same brain structures as when navigating in the physical world (i.e., the posterior limbic regions). In contrast, search activates Broca's area, commonly observed in linguistic processing.

Another recent study asked people either to navigate to or search for a target file. As people did so, a list of words was read to them in the background. People were later better able to remember these words, presumably a linguistic task, when navigating rather than searching.[66]

The argument for the observed preference for navigation to search in the retrieval of personal information would then appear to be very strong indeed. Navigation places higher reliance on recognition, which people are usually better at than recall. Navigation to digital information engages some of the same neural structures as are engaged in physical navigation, which is a highly practiced skill in people. Furthermore, navigation places fewer demands than search on linguistic processing and the regions of the brain involved in linguistic processing, thus freeing this capacity for use elsewhere in a person's computing interactions.

But the discussion continues. Just as navigation vs. search and the use of supporting tools appear to engage different facilities and different areas of the human brain, there is reason to suppose that other activities, too, as done through the computer and computer-based tools, will vary qualitatively in the nature of processing demands placed upon the user. Studies done in the 1980s, for example, suggested a significant shift in processing demands with the advent of support for full-screen, WYSIWYG text editing.[67–69]

A more recent study suggests that the now-standard support for fast, indexed "desktop" search may be having some impact, not on the preferred method for return to personal digital files, which remains navigation, but on another form of personal information: e-mail.[42] Consistent with this is the finding that people are less inclined to invest in the organization of e-mails into folders electing instead, for example, to leave information in a single larger folder or even the inbox.[70]

How, then, to account for this apparent disparity—that even as preference may be shifting toward search as a primary method for return to e-mails (i.e., those that aren't readily available in the current inbox display)—people persist in navigating to digital files? And why is this despite the fact that essentially the same fast, indexed search support can be applied to both e-mails and files?

We consider one last explanation that relates to the well-established *primacy* effect of psychology research:[21] Under a *first-impressions* hypothesis,[42] people's first choice of return aligns with their initial experience with the encountered information. Given adequate search support, people might naturally prefer to retrieve an e-mail via a search on the sender or subject since this information is often an initial focus of attention (and is used as a basis for deciding whether to attend to the e-mail). Likewise, since people must initially place a file into a folder (unless they accept a "My Documents" default), navigation to the folder is a first choice of return to the file. Given better, more universal support for tagging, for example, people might be more likely to prefer search (on tags) as a preferred method of return to documents and other files. (But see the section on keeping for its discussion of folders vs. tags). Conversely, were people first to create and exchange e-mails "in place," in the context of a project (folder) they are working on, they might prefer navigation as a method of return (see, e.g., work on the Project Planner/Planz representing one attempt to situate e-mail by project.[71,72])

Habits change slowly and desktop search support continues to improve. Desktop search is increasingly integrative and ever closer to an ideal where anything that can be remembered about an information item or the circumstances surrounding encounters with it (e.g., time of last use or nearby events) can be used to help find this item.[35,73,74]

Search vs. navigation? Since many circumstances of real-world information retrieval are likely to involve a little of both,[53] a challenge in our tool-building efforts toward better PIM is to support artful ways of combining and seamlessly switching between these two general methods of information retrieval. Toward this goal is recent work that explores ways to integrate search and navigation by highlighting certain navigational pathways based upon the results of a background search.[75]

Step 4. Repeat? In many instances, information need is not for a single information item but, rather, for a set of items whose members may be scattered in different forms within different organizations. If the likelihood of successful retrieval of each item is strictly independent from the others, then the chances of successful retrieval of all relevant items go down as their number increases. So even if the likelihood of success for each of four items is high, the retrieval of all four items is presumably much lower.

However, in situations of *output interference*, items retrieved first interfere with the retrieval of later items so that chances of successful retrieval of the whole set are worse than predicted by a strict independence of individual retrievals.[76] The effect can be explained with reference to interference paradigms of human memory retrieval such as the basic *spreading activation model*.[77] As a useful simplification, think of items in a simple set as primarily indexed and accessed through a single node such as "People in my book club." In this case, during a retrieval attempt, each item in the set competes with other items for a limited amount of activation. Moreover, the successful retrieval of initial items strengthens their connections to the access node at the expense of later items not yet retrieved, e.g., as "Susan" is retrieved, the corresponding link to "People in my book club" is strengthened at the expense of, say, the link to "Jonathan" (not yet retrieved).

The chances of successfully retrieving all members of a set can also be much better than predicted by independence. Certainly, retrieval is better if all items are in the same larger unit—a folder or a pile, for example. Retrieval may also be better if items of a set have an internal organization or are interconnected to one another so that the retrieval of one item actually facilitates the retrieval of other items.[78] By one explanation, activation sent to one item can be "shared" with other items through these interconnections.[79]

Keeping: From Information to Need

Many events of daily life are roughly the converse of finding events: People encounter information and try to determine what, if anything, they should do with this information, i.e., people must match the information to current or anticipated needs. Decisions and actions relating to encountered information are collectively referred to as *keeping* activities.

The ability to effectively handle information that is encountered by happenstance may be essential to a person's ability to discover new material and make new connections.[80] People also keep information that they have actively sought but do not have time to process currently. A search on the web, for example, often produces much more information than can be consumed in the current session. Both the decision to keep this information for later use and the steps to do so are keeping activities.[57]

Keeping activities are also triggered when people are interrupted in the midst of a current task and look for ways of preserving the current state so that work can be quickly resumed later.[81] For example, people keep appointments by entering reminders into a calendar and keep good ideas or "things to pick up at the grocery store" by writing down a few cryptic lines on a loose piece of paper.

People *keep* not only to ensure they have some particular information later, but also to build in a reminder to look for and use that information. Failure to remember to use information later is one kind of prospective memory failure.[82–84] People may, for example, self-e-mail a web page reference in addition to or instead of making a bookmark because the e-mail message with the reference appears in the inbox where it is more likely to be noticed and used.[57]

Research relating to keeping points to several conclusions: 1) keeping is difficult and error-prone; 2) keeping "right" has gotten harder as the diversity of information forms and supporting tools has increased; and 3) some costs of keeping "wrong" in the digital realm have gone away due to advanced search capabilities, but challenges remain.

Keeping is difficult and error-prone. The keeping decision is multifaceted. Is the information useful? If so, do special steps need to be taken to keep it for later use? How should the information be kept? Where? On what device? In what form should the information be kept? The keeping decision can be characterized as a signal detection task subject to errors of two kinds: 1) an incorrect rejection ("miss") when information is ignored that, as time tells, should have been kept (e.g., those paper receipts that are needed now that the tax return is being audited) and 2) a false positive when information kept as useful ("signal") turns out not never to be used later. The physical and digital clutter in our lives is often evidence for false positive decisions.

Filing information items—whether paper documents, e-documents, or e-mail messages—correctly is a cognitively difficult and error-prone activity.[26,31,56] Difficulty arises in part because the definition or purpose of a folder or tag is often unclear from its label (e.g., "stuff") and then may change in significant ways over time.[56,85] Filing and tagging difficulties increase if people do not recall the folders or tags they have created previously and then create new folders or tags rather than reusing those already created.[56]

But placing (or leaving) information items in piles, as an alternative to filing, has its own problems. In Malone's study,[31] participants indicated that they had increasing difficulty keeping track of the contents of different piles as the number of piles increased. Experiments by Jones and Dumais[86] suggest that the ability to track information by location alone is quite limited. Moreover, the extent to which piles are supported for different forms of information is variable, limited, and poorly understood.[87]

Kwasnik[32] identified a large number of dimensions that might potentially influence the placement and organization of paper-based mail and documents in an office. Overall, a document's classification was heavily influenced by the document's intended (anticipated) use—a finding subsequently reproduced by Barreau.[88] Similarly, Jones et al.[57] observed that the choice of method for keeping web information for later use was influenced by a range of considerations or functions. Marshall and Bly[59] also note that the reasons for keeping information vary and are not necessarily task related or even consciously purposeful.

Keeping "right" is harder when information is more fragmented. An act of keeping might be likened to throwing a ball into the air toward a point where we expect to be at some future point in time and space. The ongoing proliferation of information forms and supporting tools and gadgets makes keeping activities even harder. The information people need may be at home when they are at work or vice versa. It may be on the wrong device. Information may be "here" but locked away in an application or in the wrong format so that the hassles associated with its extraction outweigh the benefits of its use. Users employ a variety of methods to ensure that information is in the "right" place when it is needed and methods may require additional, manual work to transfer and synchronize information across devices and locations. Personally imposed and employer-imposed information boundaries may further fragment the information owned by or under the control of the user (P1—see Table 1) with significant impact on activities to maintain and organize and also to manage the flow of information.[89] Considerations for these and other *meta-level activities* are further described later in this section.

People must contend with the organization of e-documents, e-mail messages, web pages (or references to these), and possibly also a number of additional forms of digital information including phone messages, digitized photographs, music, and videos—each with its own special-purpose tool support.[90] The number of keeping considerations further increases if a person has different e-mail accounts, uses separate computers for home and work, or uses any of a number of special-purpose PIM tools.

Keep less, keep nothing, keep more, keep everything, or keep "smarter"? With respect to some forms of information, people may elect to adopt a "keep less" (or even a "keep nothing") approach. For example, people can rely on "do nothing" methods of return to web pages—such as searching, auto-completion, inspection of browsing history, or navigating from another website—that require no explicit keeping activity.[58]

On the other hand, experiencing difficulty in refinding can motivate people toward a "keep more" approach. After a failure to refind a useful website, for example, teachers were reported to have shifted toward a more aggressive strategy of bookmarking "anything" that looked at all useful.[91] But conscious keeping is costly in time, distraction, and the potential clutter of new items, especially when these end up to be "false positives," i.e., information judged to be useful but never in fact used.[4]

Digital memory research (e.g., Tan et al.[92]) explores an automated "keep everything" or "total capture" approach manifest in one extreme by a full-motion, line-of-sight video recording of daily experiences, second by second.[45] But the utility of such an approach can be questioned on grounds both practical (e.g., how to selectively access just a portion of the continuous stream?) and psychological (the recording alone does not compare to human memory, and its ability to evoke a person's actual memory for events may decline with time),[93] Chapter 6.[94] Automated keeping also points to a dilemma identified by Lansdale:[26] without some engagement in the keeping process, people may be much more likely to forget about the information later. Alternatives to "keep everything," "keep nothing," and "keep automatically" approaches are ones that help people to "keep smarter," i.e., to make better decisions concerning future uses of current information.[4] If people have prepared a clear plan, for example, they are often more effective at keeping relevant information (including a recognition of its relevance) even when the plan and its goal are not the current focus of attention.[95]

Folders or Tags?

The demise of folders and the file system is a recurrent theme in discussions on the future of information management (e.g., Economist,[96] Seltzer and Murphy;[97] see also Jones,[98] Chapters 6 and 7). There are good reasons for such predictions. A strict folder hierarchy does not readily allow for the flexible classification of information even though, in a person's mind, an information item might fit in several different categories.[99] For example, pictures from a conference in Copenhagen can be stored under "Pictures," "Trips," "Conferences," or "Copenhagen." Why not then, instead of placement in a single folder, allow people to tag these items, i.e., with a tag for each of the categories?

Tagging models of information storage would seem to align more closely with the way people think and might wish to represent their information. Toward the exploration of this possibility, a number of tag-related prototypes for PIM have been developed over the years (e.g., Refs.[100–103]). A tagging approach has also been embraced in commercial systems, most notably Gmail (as "labels").

The verdict? The success of tags so far is at best mixed. In one study, Bergman et al.[104] found that users, when provided with (and informed of) both options to use folders and tags, preferred folders to tags (for both their files and e-mails), and even when using tags, they typically refrained from adding more than a single tag per information item (also a finding in[105]). Even Gmail, though fundamentally architected to support tagging, has added support for "folders," http://googlesystem.blogspot.com/2009/02/gmail-adds-folders-by-improving-label.html.

Why isn't the case for tagging more compelling (so far)? Support for the tagging (annotating, labeling) of information items remains basic and fragmented. Many design questions remain. One study, for example, found that users performing tagging had more persistent memories about their information, but that nuanced interaction design was necessary to alleviate the cognitive demand entailed by creating and recalling tags.[106]

But more fundamental limitations may also apply. Civan et al.[105] through an engagement of participants in critical, comparative observation of both tagging and the use of folders (through the use of Gmail and Hotmail for the organization of e-mails), were able to elicit some limitations of tagging not previously discussed openly in comparisons between tagging and the use of folders. For example, once a user decides to use multiple tags, it becomes important to continue doing so. A tag such as "Copenhagen", when not consistently used, becomes much less useful later as a retrieval cue. Conversely, critical discussion can reveal advantages in the use of folders that are not always apparent, for example, that a folder structure can serve as an informal task decomposition and a simple kind of reminder for task completion.[107]

Just as the answer for the finding (retrieval) of information may be neither navigation nor search but tools that support an artful combination of both, so to the answer toward better keeping may be neither purely tagging nor use of folders but a tool that artfully combines the best of both.

The Meta-Level: Mapping between Need and Information

Meta-level activity operates broadly upon collections of information (PICs) within the PSI, on the configuration and effective use of supporting information tools, and on the mapping that connects need to information. The daily actions of keeping and finding are largely reactive (i.e., faced with a need, find the information to meet this need; faced with information, identify if and what need it might meet). In contrast, meta-level activity is more proactive. Thus, meta-level activity focuses not on the need or information immediately at hand but on a larger consideration of information collections, supporting tools, and the overall mapping. Alternatively, meta-level activity can be seen to move to a more strategic level in a person efforts to manage their information.

One factorization of meta-level activity makes the simplification that the PSI is one big store to be maintained and organized, and for which, input and output should be managed. People might also benefit from an ability to take measurements in support of various evaluations of the store (e.g., does it have the right information in the right forms, sufficiently current and complete?). This approach leads to the following overlapping kinds of meta-level activities: *maintain and organize; manage privacy, security, and the flow of information* (incoming and outgoing); and *measure and evaluate*. Implicit in each of these activity types is an effort to *make sense of and use* the available information. This section takes a close look at each of these meta-level activity types.

But first, note the following:

- Actual PIM behavior we would wish to observe and analyze is likely a combination of meta-level activity, keeping, and finding. The sharing and synchronization of information in a cloud service, such as Dropbox, has elements of *maintenance and organization* (i.e., information is automatically backed up) and *managing for privacy, security, and information flow* (can people trust that their information is secure and safe from snooping? With whom should people share what?). The meta-activity types we consider here might be thought of as vectors—independent but not necessarily orthogonal from one another—forming a basis for the description of a "point" of actual PIM behavior (in a large space of possibilities).
- A consideration of meta-level activity makes clear the point that information is not an end in itself but rather a means to an end. Going back to the definition of PIM at this article's outset, PIM is about managing information to realize life's goals and roles. Further, information provides people with a way of managing their limited resources. Here we can consider "META" as an acronym for money, energy, time, and attention. Each of these resources must be managed if people are to be effective in the realization of their goals and the fulfillment of their roles and responsibilities. But people don't "touch" (manage) these resources directly. People manage via their information. Financial statements tell people whether their expenses are under control and whether they are on track for retirement. Their calendars help them to manage their time. The use of open windows and the tabs of a web browser can be considered as a way of managing attention.
- Further and especially as people's information is increasingly in digital form, people don't "touch" (manage) their information directly either but rather via their information tools. Even for information in paper form, people use tools, of course, including staplers, filing cabinets, and their own hands. An investment to select, configure, and learn to use information tools is a critical component of each kind of PIM activity. This holds especially for meta-level activity.
- Finally, as another sense of "meta," meta-level activity is the "after" activity. Actions at this level such as "spring cleaning" or "cleanup," notwithstanding their overall importance, are seldom urgent and so easily postponed and avoided.

Patterns of postponement and avoidance are in evidence as we further explore meta-level activity in the remainder of this section.

Maintaining and organizing

Differences between people are especially apparent in their approaches to the maintenance and organization of information. Malone[31] distinguished between "neat" and "messy" organizations of paper documents. "Messy" people had more piles in their offices and appeared to invest less effort than "neat" people in filing information. Comparable differences have been observed in the ways people approach e-mail,[56,108–110] e-documents,[58,62] and web bookmarks.[62,111]

Across information forms, differences in approaches to organization correlate with differences in keeping strategy. For example, people who have a more elaborate folder organization—whether for paper documents, e-documents, e-mail messages, or web bookmarks—tend to file sooner and more often.[62] However, people are often selective in their maintenance of different organizations. Boardman and Sasse,[62] for example, classified 14 of 31 participants in their study as "pro-organizing" with respect to e-mail and e-documents but not with respect to bookmarks; 7 of 31 participants only took the trouble to organize their e-documents.

Diekema and Olsen[91] found that spring cleaning of information by teachers mostly pertained to physical information rather than digital information. Organization behaviors may also vary based on context. In a study by Capra et al.[112] university employees reported having more folders for their work e-mail accounts than for their personal accounts.

Several studies have now looked at how the same person manages across different forms of information.[62,107,113] The following composite emerges:

- People do not generally take time out of a busy day to assess their organizations or their PIM practice in general.
- People complain about the need to maintain so many separate organizations of information and people complain about the fragmentation of information that results. People struggle to organize their information so that they can keep their focus of attention and avoid "getting lost."[114–116]
- Even within the same PIC, competing organizational schemes may suffer an uneasy coexistence with each other. People may apply one scheme on one day and another scheme the day after.
- Several participants in one study reported making a special effort to consolidate information in their PICs,[57] for example, by saving web page references and e-mail messages into a file folder organization or by sending e-documents and web page references in e-mail messages.
- People don't, in general, have reliable, sustainable (i.e., automatic) plans for backing up their information.[117,118]

Even if digital forms of information can be integrated, people must still contend with paper forms of information. Paper documents and books remain an important part of the average person's PSI.[85] The integration of paper and digital forms of information can be troublesome. In a study of elementary and secondary teachers, for example, Diekema and Olsen[91] found that the teachers' dualistic system of digital and physical information was especially challenging; while some teachers tried to standardize their organization schemes across material type, some teachers resorted to digitizing all materials. Others printed out their digital materials so they could be filed with the rest of the paper files.

Managing privacy, security, and the flow of information

We continue with the useful simplification that a person's PSI is one large store. If maintenance and organization activities are concerned with the store itself and its contents, the activities to manage privacy, security, and, more generally, the flow of information are concerned with the input and output to the store. What do people let in? What do people let out?

Letting the wrong things (information, data) into a PSI or letting the wrong tools access or modify a PSI can, at minimum, be a major hassle (e.g., a need for "disinfection"). At worst, the computer may be hijacked to nefarious ends, and all its data corrupted. Indeed, problems of malware ("viruses," "Trojans," "worms") are endemic. By some estimates, 30% or more of the computers in the United States are infected.[119] Letting the wrong information out to the wrong people can also be a costly source of trouble—e.g., if credit cards are compromised or worse a person's identify is stolen.

And yet, the exchange of information, incoming and outgoing, and increasingly in digital forms, is an essential part of living in the modern world. To order goods and services online, people must be prepared to "let out" their credit card information. To try out a potentially useful, new information tool, people may need to "let in" a download that could potentially make unwelcome changes to the web browser or the desktop. Providing for adequate control over the information, coming into and out of a PSI, is a major challenge. Even more challenging is the user interface to make clear the implications for various choices in privacy control and in clicking the "Accept" button for use of services such as Facebook.[120–128]

Also of relevance are the daily challenges associated with sharing information with others in various social situations ranging from the home, to school, to work, to play, and "at large" (e.g., via open-ended discussion boards on the web). These challenges are further discussed in the section "GIM and the Social Fabric of PIM."

Measuring and evaluating

Choices are made in support of all the activities described so far. Schemes of organization are selected; strategies, policies, and procedures are adopted; and supporting tools are put in place. People then need to ask, at least occasionally, "Is it (the resulting mapping between information and need) working? Is it helping me to make the best use of my limited resources (money, energy, time, attention) toward meeting my goals and fulfilling my roles and responsibilities? Can it work even better? If so, what should change?"

These questions depend both upon the measurements that can be made and also on the evaluations people must make in cases where measurements (and the underlying objectives they reflect) are in competition with one another.

Actions of measuring and evaluating are often high level and qualitative. For example, as people are driving home from work much later than they'd planned for and with no time nor energy to exercise at the gym, they may reflect on a day of nonstop meetings and interruptions as they ask themselves "What did I _really_ accomplish?"

But increasingly evaluations can be based upon numerical data. Questions such a "where does the money go?" or "where did the time go today?" needn't be only rhetorical.

Increasingly detailed, consolidated data is becoming available to answer these and other questions concerning not only how people manage their resources but also how effectively they're living the lives they wish to live. Detailed financial data can tell people "where" the money is going. Calendars consolidated with activity logs can tell people "where" the time went and much more besides. On which devices? Which applications? Relating to which people or which projects? Involving physical activity as well? Or, conversely, the intake of calories (e.g., a business lunch)? How did physical measures of heart rate, blood pressure, blood sugar levels, etc., vary during these activities?

People's every actions can be tracked, and a digital trace formed. The nearly constant use of computational devices (even as people sleep) creates opportunities to capture additional data about people and their environment for purposes of correlation and, potentially, deeper understanding. Associated issues of privacy are enormous and beyond the scope of this article to address (but see Refs.[129–131]).

On a more positive side, how can measurements be used to a person's advantage?

The increasing capture (by intention or incidentally) and availability of data in digital form to measure everything from heart beats to gaze duration to affective response give rise to notions of the *quantified self* and *personal informatics*.[132–137] Definitions of personal informatics (PI) vary. Some would tightly connect PI to enabling devices and applications for tracking (e.g., Li et al.[138]). But self-efforts to track personal activity—the better to understand and make adaptive changes in behavior—are not new (see, e.g., the description of Benjamin Franklin's efforts at self-observation in Jones,[139]). Rapp and Cena provide a more flexible definition: "**Personal Informatics** (PI), also known as Quantified Self (QS), is a school of thought which aims to use technology for acquiring and collecting data on different aspects of the daily lives of people,"[140] p. 613.

PI applications are often affiliated with health information and many times have a dedicated hardware device, such as the FitBit, http://www.fitbit.com/. But some examples also include systems that collect personal information over time from a variety of sources to provide upon request more integrative summaries of the many scattered events happening that relate to a person in one way or another. A popular example of this second variety is Mint.com, which collects information from all of one's financial accounts (checking, saving, credit cards, etc.) and summarizes this data into an integrated dashboard.

Personal informatics is properly regarded as a subset of PIM where special focus is given to activities of measuring and evaluating and also to making sense of and using the data collected. For example, Li et al.[141] decompose a personal informatics system into five stages: 1) preparation; 2) collection; 3) integration; 4) reflection; and 5) action. The first three stages fit well under the more general activity of measuring and evaluating while the last two stages fit well under the more general activity of making sense of and using information. Not surprisingly, users of PI systems also face challenges to manage for privacy and information flow and to maintain and organize the large amounts of data collected. According to Li et al.,[142] users face information fragmentation problems comparable to those already discussed in the introduction to this article. More recent work in personal informatics seems to acknowledge a need to think more broadly and to place efforts at "self-tracking" in the larger context of an overall PIM practice.[134,143,144]

Making sense of and using information

Making sense of information represents another set of meta-level activities operating on personal information and the mapping between information and need. People must often assemble and analyze a larger collection of information in order to decide what to do next. For example, among the choices available in new automobiles (new laptops, new employees, etc.), which will best meet a person's needs? Which treatments to select in the aftermath to surgery for cancer? Does radiation therapy "make sense"? Making sense of and using information means more than just retrieval and comprehension of the information "at hand." A person may look up a budget number and understand that it reads "42" but may conclude that the number doesn't "make sense" (and is possibly a pop culture reference, https://en.wikipedia.org/wiki/42_(number)) if all other budget numbers are 9-digit numbers beginning with "11-."

Making sense of information is "meta" not only for its broader perspective but also because it permeates most PIM activity even when the primary purpose may be ostensibly something else. For example, people organize information in folders ostensibly to insure its subsequent retrieval but then also as a way of categorizing and so making sense of the information. In the Jones et al. study,[107] folder hierarchies developed for a project often resembled a project plan or partial problem decomposition in which subfolders stood for project-related goals and also for the tasks and subprojects associated with the achievement of these goals. Similarly, some teachers organize their files by utilizing the structure as established in their curriculum standards.[91]

Barsalou[145,146] has long argued that many of a person's internal categories arise to accomplish goals. His research demonstrates an ability of people to group together seemingly dissimilar items according to their applicability to a common goal. For example, weight-watchers might form a category "foods to eat on a diet." Rice cakes, carrot sticks, and sugar-free soda are all members of the category, even though they differ considerably in other ways.

Folders and tags (and piles, properties/value combinations, views, etc.) can form an important part of external representations, which, in turn, can complement and combine with internal representations ("in our heads") to form an integrated cognitive system.[147,148] Finding the right external representation can help in *sense-making*,[149,150] i.e., in efforts to understand the information. For example, the right diagram can allow one to make inferences more quickly.[151] The way information is externally represented can produce huge differences in a person's ability to use this information in short-duration, problem-solving exercises.[152] Different kinds of representations, like matrices and hierarchies, are useful in different types of problems.[153–155]

But the effects of an external representation on longer-term efforts to plan and complete a multiweek or multimonth project are less well understood. Mumford et al.[156] note that, more generally, the study of planning has proceeded in "fits and starts" over the past 50 years and remains underdeveloped. Of special relevance to the study of PIM is the possibility that better support of planning might also, as a by-product, lead to better organizations of the information needed to complete a project.

GIM and the Social Fabric of PIM

Group information management (*GIM*) as a natural extension to PIM has been written about elsewhere.[157,158] The study of GIM, in turn, has clear relevance to the study of Computer Supported Collaborative Work (CSCW).[159]

In legal contexts, it may be useful to treat a corporation as an entity—a "person"—in its own right. A corporation or other organization may have policies, procedures, habits, history, and routines that further give it a collective identity as an entity in its own right.

But in many situations, there really is no group entity operating on its own behalf to manage information toward realization of goals and fulfillment of roles. Rather, there is a collection of individuals. Members of a group may hold in common (more or less) certain goals (whether implicit or explicitly expressed in a charter or mission statement). Members may apportion group roles (e.g., treasurer, secretary, president, etc.), but each member operates as an individual and according to personal interest. In keeping with this article's topic, therefore, focus is more appropriately on what might be called the *social fabric of* PIM,[160] Chapter 10. The needs of the individual must be met in any group situation, for example, when engineers need their own private space for working drafts, they are not yet ready to share with a larger team.[161] On the other hand, group and social considerations frequently enter into a person's PIM strategy, for example, when one member of a household "keeps" medical test results by passing these on another member of the household who has agreed to maintain and organize medical information for all household members. (And perhaps there is a reciprocal arrangement for financial information.)

Although a collaborative "divide and conquer" approach, where responsibilities are apportioned among the members of a group, can reduce the burdens of PIM, the opposite is frequently the case when people seek to share information collections. People may vary greatly in their approaches, especially to keeping and maintaining and organizing information.[162] Working together through these issues often entails a delicate negotiation process,[89,163] as categorization affects each member of the shared space, and the tools used to perform such activities provide no preexisting conventions for tasks like organizing a project's files and folders.[164] Some users may customize shared information spaces to meet their own needs, but at the cost of decreasing the intelligibility of that space for others.[165] These challenges later affect refinding information in shared spaces, where attempts to retrieve information from a shared collection are more likely to fail than when retrieving from a PIC that is not shared.[166]

As further studies aim to better understand the challenges of sharing and managing information in group contexts, improved software may help to alleviate some of these challenges and facilitate the relevant activities.[5] Prototypes of such software have attempted to support GIM, for example, by analyzing group activities;[167] a "silver bullet" solution has yet to be found, however. When faced with the limitations of current software, users often prefer more traditional, ad hoc methods of sharing information, such as the use of e-mail attachments,[168] to more sophisticated methods supported by tools more explicitly designed to support collaborative work such as the use of web services that support shared folders.[166,169] In some cases, people will circumvent group-centered approaches even when they are institutionalized.[170] Therefore, the need for understanding and improving collaborative information tasks is clearly great, and work remains to be done.

The Interplay between PIM Activities

We noted in the previous section that the senses in which information can be personal (i.e., owned by, about, directed toward, sent/shared by, experienced by, or relevant to "me") don't provide for groupings of information that are cleanly separated from one another. Rather, these are better seen as different perspectives on one large PSI.

Likewise, activities of PIM can be seen as different vectors of approach, we might say, to a person's PSI and to the creation, use, and maintenance of a mapping (between need and information) for this space. Any actual action of PIM is likely to be a mixture of each. The interplay between activities of finding and keeping was noted in the previous section. An act of keeping, for example, often engenders acts of finding (e.g., the effort to find a folder where the encountered information should be kept). Likewise, an act of finding frequently engenders ancillary acts of keeping. In the effort to retrieve a file from a personal store, for example, the person may move ("re-keep") other files after noticing these are in the wrong folder. And certainly, newly found information beyond simple look-ups (e.g., the weather report or a sports score) must often be kept pending the proper time and place for more careful study.

Interplay is in further evidence as the meta-level of PIM activity is considered. Any actual activity of PIM observed or reported is likely to resist clean categorization as solely one or another kind of activity. People may elect to place project-related files, web references, and even e-mails into a single folder named for the project[71,171,172] and may elect to keep this folder under a larger folder synced with a service such as Dropbox. The folder may then be shared with others also involved in the completion of the project. Keeping activity? Maintaining and organizing? Making sense of and using information? Managing for the flow of information (and privacy/security)? Yes: all four. And since a cloud service such as Dropbox maintains a log of activity in the folder, we can add measurement and evaluation.

CONCLUSION: CHALLENGES AND OPPORTUNITIES

To summarize, the practice of PIM involves finding, keeping, and several kinds of meta-level activities in an effort to establish, maintain, and use a mapping between information and need. Challenges arise with respect to each kind of activity:

Finding is a multistep process. First, people must *remember* to look. An item is retrieved through variations and combinations of searching and navigation. Navigation and searching each involve an iterative interplay between basic actions of *recall* and *recognition*. Finally, in many situations of information need, people must *repeat* the finding activity several times in order to "re-collect" a complete set of information items in order then to make sense of and use the information at hand.

Keeping is multifaceted. Certainly keeping, like finding, can involve several steps. But the essential challenge of keeping stems from the multifaceted nature of the decisions about information needs. Is the information useful? Do special actions need to be taken to keep it for later use? Where? When? In what form? On what device? With no crystal ball to see into the future, answering these questions is difficult and error prone. Caution is warranted with regard to tool support to "keep everything" or "keep automatically." The approach can lead to the collection and storage of information that overwhelms even as it falls far short of providing a true "external memory."

Meta-level activities are important but easily overlooked. Meta-level activities are critical to a successful PIM practice, but rarely urgent. There are few events in a typical day that direct a person's attention to meta-level activity involving considerations of maintenance and organization, managing privacy, security and the flow of information, measuring and evaluating, or making sense of and using information in a larger collection. As a result, meta-level activities can easily become afterthoughts.

Researchers also face several challenges in their efforts to develop PIM as a field of study:

Integration to counter fragmentation. In their daily practices of PIM, people must overcome problems of both information overload and information fragmentation. Problems of information fragmentation are often introduced by the very computer-based tools that are meant to help with PIM. The study of PIM itself is often fragmented in similar ways. Many excellent studies focus, for example, on e-mail, other studies on the web, or the management of special forms of digital information (such as digitally encoded songs or photographs). There is a need for integrative approaches both in the study of PIM and in the design and evaluation of supporting tools. The "I" in "PIM" should be for information in all its many forms, paper based and digital, and for a larger perspective that considers the life cycle and impact of information as it is communicated from one person to the next.

Toward more practical methodologies with more practical implications. PIM requires the study of people, with a diversity of backgrounds and needs, over time as they work in many different situations, with different forms of information and different tools of information management. This scope of PIM inquiry brings a need for practical, cost-effective methodologies that can scale. Furthermore, there is a need not only for *descriptive* studies aimed at better understanding how people currently practice PIM (e.g., [173]) but also for *prescriptive* studies aimed both at evaluation [174] and also toward the recommendation of proposed solutions in the form of new, improved tools, techniques, and strategies of PIM.

A kind of "checkbox" methodology—call it "*six by six* (*6 × 6*)"—can be devised from the framework described in this article (first described in Jones[139] and subsequently updated[1]) with its provision for six senses in which information can be personal 1) controlled by/owned by, 2) about, 3) directed toward, 4) sent/posted/shared by, 5) for things experienced by, and 6) potentially relevant/useful to "me") and its six-part factorization of PIM activity 1) keeping; 2) finding; 3) maintaining and organizing; 4) managing privacy, security, and the flow of information; 5) measuring and evaluating; 6) making sense of and using information).

For any tool, technique, or larger strategy of PIM, real or proposed, it is important to consider the likely impact on personal information in each of its senses. For example, a "cool new tool" (desktop or web based) that promises to deliver information potentially "relevant to me" (P6, the "6th sense" in which information is personal) may do so only at the cost of a distracting increase in the information "directed to me" (P3) and by keeping too much personal information "about me" (P2) in a place not under the person's control. Similarly, a tool, technique, or strategy of PIM can be considered for its impact on PIM activity. Tools of personal informatics and digital tracking, for example, may do a great deal to improve "measuring," but if such improvements are accompanied by extra hassles in maintaining and organizing or in managing privacy, security, and the flow information, then the trade-offs may not be worth it.

This 6 × 6 methodology is not the only approach toward a more thoughtful, systematic design of PIM tools. Bergman, for example, reports good success in the application of a *user-subjective approach* in PIM system design.[175] The user-subjective approach advances three design principles. In brief, the design should allow the following: 1) all project-related items no matter their form (or format) are to be organized together (the *subjective project classification principle*); 2) the importance of information (to the user) should determine its visual salience and accessibility (the *subjective importance principle*); and 3) information should be retrieved and used by the user in the same context as it was previously used in (the *subjective context principle)*. The approach may suggest design principles that serve not only in evaluating and improving existing systems but also in creating new implementations. For example, according to the *demotion principle*, information items of lower subjective importance should be demoted (i.e., by making them less visible) so as not to distract the user but be kept within their original context just in case they are needed. The principle has been applied in the creation of several interesting prototypes.[176–178]

In a similar vein is the research by E. Jones[179] identifying five factors that determine whether a promising new system (tool, technique, and strategy) of PIM will be successfully adopted:

1. *Visibility*—More generally, do users notice the system and remember to use it?
2. *Integration*—Does the system connect and work well with what the user already has in place?
3. *Co-adoption*—Is it necessary for others to use the system as well? (Lack of co-adoption is a major source for failure in CSCW applications.[180])
4. *Scalability*—Will the system still work over time and especially as the amount of information continues to increase?
5. *Return on investment* (*ROI*)—After the hopeful enthusiasm with which a system is initially embraced has waned, the system has to prove its value and that the costs of its use are more than compensated for by benefits.

The trouble with the adoption of PIM systems is twofold: 1) some may be discarded prematurely before the daily habit of their use has been established (e.g., for lack of visibility or integration); and 2) the problems with other systems (e.g., lack of scalability or ROI) are apparent only much later after a system has been deeply embedded in a person's overall practice of PIM, making its removal a costly hassle. Consider, for example, a "perfect" folder organization that turns out to be too much trouble to maintain but can't be undone without many hours of reorganization.

More recently, the notion has been advanced that tools, techniques, and strategies of PIM might be assessed for their ability to increase or reduce the "clerical tax" people pay as they manage their information.[93] What is the impact on the time spent in clerical, mechanical actions of PIM (think filing paper documents in a vertical filing cabinet), and how much time remains for the more fun, creative aspects of working with information? The utility of such an approach will depend upon the development of more detailed methods for reliably, effectively "assessing" the clerical tax.

Finally, are efforts to engage the user in active discussions (possibly mediated by the web) directed toward the evaluation and even the design of PIM systems? The use of participant observation is well established in fields such as sociology and anthropology (see, e.g., Jorgensen[181]). But here we might talk instead about the *observant participation,* i.e., explicitly tasking a participant to reflect upon a PIM system, the good and the bad, either in a single session or over an extended period of time. The use of diary methods of data gathering is well established (e.g., Czerwinski et al.[81]), though motivating people to consistently record their thoughts can prove challenging and reminders can prove intrusive or, worse, impact the data gathered.[182]

Two recent efforts of *observant participation* are worthy of further mention. Civan et al.[105] engaged users in a within-subjects comparison of tagging (labeling) vs. the use of folders as a means of organizing e-mails. Participants experienced each condition (via actual web-based versions of Hotmail and Gmail as these were offered in 2007/2008) in an ordering counterbalanced across participants. After each condition (each lasting for 5 days), participants were interviewed using an open-ended set of questions to assess their experiences of and reflections on the condition just experienced (i.e., use of folders vs. tags for organization of information). The study provided a very useful set of considerations and some unexpected drawbacks in the use of tags (e.g., with the freedom to tag items in several ways comes the potential tedium of then consistently using multiple tags for _every_new item). A second method—following a Delphi approach[183]—shows great promise for better understanding various current practices of PIM and assessing which to "recommend" and "advise against."[184]

Observant participation relates to but is distinct from approaches in *participatory design*[185,186] wherein that attempt to "actively involve all stakeholders (e.g., employees, partners, customers, citizens, end users) in the design process to help ensure the result meets their needs and is usable," http://en.wikipedia.org/wiki/Participatory_design. Methods of observant participation such as those described previously are best seen as exploratory heuristics to gather pros and cons and considerations in the use of one tool, technique, system, or strategy of PIM vs. another. The participant observer approach to PIM can be traced at least back to Malone's[31] work (with only 10 participants). In his "methodological note," Malone writes, "Sometimes... carefully controlled studies or more extensive naturalistic observations are suggested by the insights obtained from exploratory observation, and these are certainly worth performing. In other cases, the needs for designing systems (or time and budget constraints) do not justify other studies" (p. 101).

How to protect the privacy and security of personal information? The more complete the digital records of personal information, the more completely a person's identity can be stolen. New PIM tools—especially those aimed at information capture—must be accompanied by new levels of information security and privacy.[127]

Other questions arise for PIM-related tools and technologies:

How to keep e-mail from being spoiled by its own success? E-mail messages are easy and free to send—good for us; good for spammers too. E-mail is used for tracking tasks, storing documents, and saving contact information. It was designed for none of these. People may feel like they are "living" in their inbox.[187] But are they doing the things they really want to be doing? Why should all incoming correspondence go into one undifferentiated inbox? E-mail filters to sort have their own problems (e.g., that people forget to look in the sorting folders later). Research efforts have explored ways to better situate e-mails and other correspondence in larger contexts involving tasks, projects, and "places" of collaboration (e. g., Refs.[188–190]). People are also making ad hoc use of alternatives to e-mail such as Facebook groups.[191]

How can search get more personal? Search has application to PIM both as an interaction and as an underlying technology. Search as an interaction supports finding and refinding and also other PIM activities such keeping, maintaining, and organizing. Search as technology, including the analysis and indexing of information, can be seen more broadly as a way of "mining" a PSI toward a wide range of personalized support.[51,98,192,193]

How can information convergence bring information integration? Information tools increasingly let people work with their information anytime and anywhere. This has increased the amount and diversity of information collected. Thoughts of laptops, smartphones, or tablets as a point of convergence for information and practices of PIM are inspired by the ongoing rapid pace of technical developments in hardware capacity, miniaturization, and integration.

Thoughts of the web as a point of convergence are also inspired by hardware advances supporting, for example, increases in bandwidth (especially along the "last mile" to private homes) and storage capacity. But equally, the web is a point of convergence for its basic ability to connect, nearly instantaneously, person to person and person to information, no matter where these are in the real world, no matter what the physical distances. But convergence does not equal integration. Web-based and portable computing are still in their infancy, and new opportunities for convergence and integration are still being created (e.g., watches, wearables). The field of PIM has a special opportunity to guide development in these new areas.

As researchers study and strive to improve PIM, it is important never to lose sight of the "personal" in PIM. People manage information neither for its own sake nor for the joy of managing. PIM is a means to an end. A person manages information in many forms, ranging from appointments of a digital calendar to paper checks of a check book, in order to manage life's resources—money, energy, attention, and, especially, time. A person manages information as a means toward the fulfillment of a life's important goals and precious roles.

REFERENCES

1. Jones, W. *The Future of Personal Information Management, Part 1: Our Information, Always and Forever*; San Rafael, Calif.: Morgan & Claypool Publishers, 2012, Retrieved from http://www.morganclaypool.com/doi/abs/10.2200/S00411ED1V01Y201203ICR021.
2. Jones, W. Personal information management. Annu. Rev. Inf. Sci. Technol. ARIST **2007**, *41*, 453–504.
3. Jones, W. *Keeping Found Things Found: The Study and Practice of Personal Information Management*, Chapter 4, 1st Ed.; Morgan Kaufmann: Amsterdam, the Netherlands; Boston, MA, 2007.
4. Jones, W. Finders, keepers? The present and future perfect in support of personal information management. First Monday, 2004 httpwwwfirstmondaydkissuesissue93jonesindex html.
5. Voida, S.; Edwards, W.K.; Newman, M.W.; Grinter, R.E.; Ducheneaut, N. Share and share alike: exploring the user interface affordances of file sharing. Human Factors in Computing Systems. Proceedings of the SIGCHI Conference, Montral, Quebec, Canada, 2006; 221–230.
6. Yates, F.A. *The Art of Memory*; University of Chicago Press: Chicago, IL, 1966.
7. Yates, J. *Control through Communication: The Rise of System in American Management*; Johns Hopkins University Press: Baltimore, MD, 1989.
8. Bush, V. As we may think. The Atlantic Monthly **1945**, *176* (1), 641–649.
9. Shannon, C.E. A mathematical theory of communication. Bell Syst. Tech. J. **1948**, *27*, 379–426, 623–656.
10. Howard, R.A. Information value theory. IEEE Trans. Syst. Sci. Cybern. **Aug 1966**, *2* (1), 22–26.
11. Buckland, M.K. Information as thing. J. Am. Soc. Inf. Sci. **1991**, *42*, 351–360.

12. Dinneen, J.D.; Brauner, C. Practical and philosophical considerations for defining information as well-formed, meaningful data in the Information Sciences. Libr. Trends, *63* (3), 378–400.
13. Newell, A.; Simon, H.A. *Human Problem Solving*; Prentice-Hall: Englewood Cliffs, NJ, 1972.
14. Simon, H.A.; Newell, A. Heuristic problem solving: The next advance in operations research. Oper. Res. **1958**, *6*, 1–10.
15. Broadbent, D.E. *Perception and Communication*; Pergamon Press: London, U.K., 1958.
16. Nelson, T.H. File structure for the complex, the changing, and the indeterminate. Proceedings of the 1965 20th ACM/CSC-ER National Conference, Cleveland, OH, 1965; 84–100.
17. Carmody, S.; Gross, W.; Nelson, T.; Rice, D.; Van Dam, A. A hypertext editing system for the/360. *Pertinent Concepts in Computer Graphics*; University of Illinois Press: Urbana, IL, 1969; 291–330.
18. Engelbart, D.C.; English, W.K. A research center for augmenting human intellect. Proceedings of the Fall Joint Computer Conference, Part I, New York, December 9–11, 1968; 395–410.
19. Engelbart, D. Augmenting human intellect: A conceptual framework. *SRI Rep.* 1962, http://www.dougengelbart.org/pubs/papers/scanned/Doug_Engelbart-AugmentingHuman Intellect.pdf.
20. Engelbart, D.C. Special considerations of the individual as a user, generator and retriever of information. Am. Doc. **1961**, *12* (2), 121–125.
21. Neisser, U. *Cognitive Psychology*; Appleton-Century Crofts: New York, 1967.
22. Farwell, M.P. *A Short History of the Personal Computer*. CreateSpace Independent Publishing Platform: San Rafael, CA, 2013.
23. Nicholson, M. *When Computing Got Personal: A History of the Desktop Computer*, 1st Ed.; Matt Publishing: Chelmsford, U.K., 2014.
24. Swaine, M.; Freiberger, P. *Fire in the Valley: The Birth and Death of the Personal Computer*, 3rd Ed.; Pragmatic Bookshelf: Dallas, TX, 2014.
25. Jones, W. *he Future of Personal Information Management, Part I: Our Information, Always and Forever*; Morgan & Claypool Publishers: San Rafael, CA, 2012. Retrieved from http://www.morganclaypool.com/doi/abs/10.2200/S00411ED1V01Y201203ICR021.
26. Lansdale, M. The psychology of personal information management. Appl Ergon. **1988**, *19* (1), 55–66.
27. Card, S.K.; Moran, T.P.; Newell, A. *The Psychology Of Human-Computer Interaction*; Lawrence Erlbaum Associates: Hillsdale, NJ, 1983.
28. Norman, D.A. *The Psychology of Everyday Things*; Basic Books: New York, 1988.
29. Cole, I. Human aspects of office filing: Implications for the electronic office. Proceedings of the Human Factors Society 26th Annual Meeting, Seattle, WA, 1982; 59–63.
30. Case, D.O. Collection and organization of written information by social scientists and humanists: A review and exploratory study. J. Inf. Sci. **1986**, *12* (3), 97–104.
31. Malone, T.W. How do people organize their desks: implications for the design of office information-systems. ACM Trans. Off. Inf. Syst. **1983**, *1* (1), 99–112.
32. Kwasnik, B.H. How a personal document's intended use or purpose affects its classification in an office. Research and Development in Information Retrieval Proceedings of the 12th Annual ACM SIGIR Conference (SIGIR 1989), Cambridge, MA, 1989; Vol. 23, 207–210.
33. Jones, W.P. The memory extender personal filing system. *Human Factors in Computing Systems*. Proceedings of the SIGCHI Conference, New York, 1986; 298–305.
34. Jones, W.P. On the applied use of human memory models: The memory extender personal filing system. Int. J. Man-Mach. Stud. **Aug 1986**, *25* (2), 191–228.
35. Lansdale, M.; Edmonds, E. Using memory for events in the design of personal filing systems. Int. J. Man-Mach. Stud. **1992**, *36*, 97–126.
36. Case, D.O. Conceptual organization and retrieval of text by historians—The role of memory and metaphor. J. Am. Soc. Inf. Sci. **1991**, *42* (9), 657–668.
37. Barreau, D.; Nardi, B.A. Finding and reminding: File organization from the desktop. SIGCHI Bull. **1995**, *27* (3), 39–43.
38. Barreau, D. The persistence of behavior and form in the organization of personal information. J. Am. Soc. Inf. Sci. Technol. **2008**, *59* (2), 307–317.
39. Bergman, O.; Beyth-Marom, R.; Nachmias, R.; Gradovitch, N.; Whittaker, S. Improved search engines and navigation preference in personal information management. ACM Trans. Inf. Syst. **2008**, *26* (4), 1–24.
40. Bergman, O.; Whittaker, S.; Sanderson, M.; Nachmias, R.; Ramamoorthy, A. The effect of folder structure on personal file navigation. J. Am. Soc. Inf. Sci. Technol. **2010**, *61* (12), 2426–2441.
41. Bergman, O.; Whittaker, S.; Sanderson, M.; Nachmias, R.; Ramamoorthy, A. How do we find personal files?: The effect of OS, presentation & depth on file navigation. *Human Factors in Computing Systems*. Proceedings of the 2012 ACM Annual Conference, New York, 2012; 2977–2980.
42. Jones, W.; Wenning, A.; Bruce, H. How do people re-find files, Emails and Web pages? iConference 2014 Proceedings, Berlin, Germany, 2014.
43. Bergman, O.; Boardman, R.; Gwizdka, J.; Jones, W. Personal information management. In CHI '04 Extended Abstracts on Human Factors in Computing Systems, ACM: New York, NY, 2004; 1598–1599. https://doi.org/10.1145/985921.986164.
44. Jones, W.; Bruce, H. A report on the NSF-sponsored workshop on personal information management, Seattle, WA, 2005. Personal Information Management 2005: A Special Workshop Sponsored by the National Science Foundation, Seattle, WA, 2005.
45. Mann, S.; Sehgal, A.; Fung, J. Continuous lifelong capture of personal experience using eyetap. *Continuous Archival and Retrieval of Personal Experiences Proceedings of the First ACM Workshop (CARPE'04)*, New York, 2004; 1–21.
46. Case, D.O. *Looking for Information: A Survey of Research on Information Seeking, Needs and Behavior*; Emerald Group Publishing: Bingley, U.K., 2012.
47. Julien, H.; O'Brien, M. Information behaviour research: Where have we been, where are we going?/La recherche en comportement informationnel: D'où nous venons, vers quoi nous nous dirigeons? Can. J. Inf. Libr. Sci. **2014**, *38* (4), 239–250.

48. Marchionini, G. *Information Seeking in Electronic Environments*; Cambridge University Press: Cambridge, U.K., 1995.
49. Rouse, W.B.; Rouse, S.H. Human information seeking and design of information systems. Inf. Process. Manag. **1984**, *20*, 129–138.
50. Urquhart, C. Meta-synthesis of research on information seeking behaviour. Inf. Res. **2011**, *16* (1), 7.
51. Teevan, J.; Dumais, S.T.; Horvitz, E. Personalizing search via automated analysis of interests and activities. Proceedings of the SIGIR 2005, Salvador, Brazil, 2005; 449–456.
52. Bates, M.J. The design of browsing and berrypicking techniques for the online search interface. Online Rev. **1989**, *13*, 407–424.
53. Teevan, J.; Alvarado, C.; Ackerman, M.S.; Karger, D.R. The perfect search engine Is not enough: A study of orienteering behavior in directed search. *Human Factors in Computing Systems*. Proceedings of the ACM SIGCHI Conference (CHI 2004), Vienna, Austria, 2004; 415–422.
54. Capra III, R.G.; Manuel, A.P.; Using web search engines to find and refind information. Computer **2005**, *10*, 36–42.
55. Foster, A.; Ford, N. Serendipity and information seeking: An empirical study. J. Doc. **Jun 2003**, *59* (3), 321–340.
56. Whittaker, S.; Sidner, C. Email overload: Exploring personal information management of email. In Proceedings of the SIGCHI Conference on Human Factors in Computing Systems. Vancouver, British Columbia, Canada. ACM, New York, 1996; 276–283. DOI=http://dx.doi.org/10.1145/238386.238530.
57. Jones, W.; Dumais, S.; Bruce, H. Once found, what then? : A study of "keeping" behaviors in the personal use of web information. Proceedings of the 65th Annual Meeting of the American Society for Information Science and Technology (ASIST 2002), Philadelphia, PA, 2002.
58. Bruce, H.; Jones, W.; Dumais, S. Information behavior that keeps found things found. Inf. Res. **2004**, *10*(1).
59. Marshall, C.C.; Bly, S. Saving and using encountered information: Implications for electronic periodicals. Human Factors in Computing Systems. Proceedings of the SIGCHI Conference, Portland, OR, 2005; 111–120.
60. O'Day, V.; Jeffries, R. Orienteering in an information landscape: How information seekers get from here to there. *Human Factors in Computing Systems*. Proceedings of the ACM SIGCHI Conference (CHI 1993), Amsterdam, the Netherlands, 1993; 438–445.
61. Whittaker, S.; Bergman, O.; Clough, P. Easy on that trigger dad: A study of long term family photo retrieval. Pers. Ubiquit. Comput. **Jan 2010**, *14* (1), 31–43.
62. Boardman, R.; Sasse, M.A. "Stuff goes into the computer and doesn't come out" A cross-tool study of personal information management. Human Factors in Computing Systems. Proceedings of the ACM SIGCHI Conference (CHI 2004), Vienna, Austria, 2004.
63. Fertig, S.; Freeman, E.; Gelernter, D. Finding and reminding reconsidered. SIGCHI Bull. **1996**, *28* (1), 7.
64. Fitchett, S.; Cockburn, A. An empirical characterisation of file retrieval. Int. J. Hum.-Comput. Stud. **Feb 2015**, *74*, 1–13.
65. Benn, Y.; Bergman, O.; Glazer, L.; Arent, P.; Wilkinson, I.D.; Varley, R.; Whittaker, S. Navigating through digital folders uses the same brain structures as real world navigation. Sci. Rep. **Oct 2015**, *5*, 1–8.
66. Bergman, O.; Tene-Rubinstein, M.; Shalom, J. The use of attention resources in navigation versus search. Pers. Ubiquitous Comput. **Apr 2012**, *17* (3), 583–590.
67. Egan, D.E.; Gomez, L.M. Assaying, isolating, and accommodating individual differences in learning a complex skill. Individ. Differ. Cogn. **1985**, *2*, 173–217.
68. Gomez, L.M.; Egan, D.E.; Bowers, C. Learning to use a text editor: Some learner characteristics that predict success. Hum.-Comput. Interact. **Mar 1986**, *2* (1), 1–23.
69. Gomez, L.M.; Egan, D.E.; Wheeler, E.A.; Sharma, D.K.; Gruchacz, A.M. How interface design determines who has difficulty learning to use a text editor. *Human Factors in Computing Systems*. Proceedings of the SIGCHI Conference, New York, 1983; 176–181.
70. Whittaker, S.; Matthews, T.; Cerruti, J.; Badenes, H.; Tang, J. Am I wasting my time organizing email?: A study of email refinding. *Human Factors in Computing Systems*. Proceedings of the SIGCHI Conference, New York, 2011; 3449–3458.
71. Jones, W.; Klasnja, P.; Civan, A.; Adcock, M. The personal project planner: Planning to organize personal information. *Human Factors in Computing Systems*. Proceedings of the ACM SIGCHI Conference (CHI 2008), Florence, Italy, 2008; 681–684.
72. Jones, W.; Hou, D.; Sethanandha, B.D.; Bi, S.; Gemmell, J. Planz to put our digital information in its place. *Human Factors in Computing Systems*. Proceedings of the CHI'10 Extended Abstracts, New York, 2010; 2803–2812.
73. Cutrell, E.; Dumais, S.; Teevan, J. Searching to eliminate personal information management. Commun. ACM **2006**, *49* (1), 58–64.
74. Lansdale, M. Remembering about documents: Memory for appearance, format, and location. Ergonomics **1991**, *34* (8), 1161–1178.
75. Fitchett, S.; Cockburn, A.; Gutwin, C. Improving navigation-based file retrieval. *Human Factors in Computing Systems*. Proceedings of the SIGCHI Conference, New York, 2013; 2329–2338.
76. Rundus, D. Analysis of rehearsal processes in free recall. J. Exp. Psychol. **1971**, *89*, 63–77.
77. Anderson, J.R. *Language, Memory, and Thought*; Erlbaum: Hillsdale, NJ, 1976.
78. Jones, W.; Ross, B. Human cognition and personal information management. In *Handbook of Applied Cognition*. Nickerson, R.S.; Dumais, S.T.; Lewandowsky, S.; Perfect, T.J. Eds.; John Wiley & Sons: Chichester, UK, 2006.
79. Jones, W.; Anderson, J.R. Short vs. long term memory retrieval: A comparison of the effects of information load and relatedness. J. Exp. Psychol. Gen. **1987**, *116*, 137–153.
80. Erdelez, S.; Rioux, K. Sharing information encountered for others on the Web. New Rev. Inf. Behav. Res. **2000**, *1*, 219–233.
81. Czerwinski, M.; Horvitz, E.; Wilhite, S. A diary study of task switching and interruptions. *Human Factors in Computing Systems*. Proceedings of the SIGCHI Conference, Vienna, Austria, 2004; 175–182.
82. Ellis, J.; Kvavilashvili, L. Prospective memory in 2000: Past, present and future directions. Appl. Cogn. Psychol. **2000**, *14*, 1–9.
83. O'Connail, B.; Frohlich, D. Timespace in the workplace: Dealing with interruptions. *Human Factors in Computing*

Systems. Proceedings of the ACM SIGCHI Conference, Extended Abstracts (CHI 1995), Denver, CO, 1995; 262–263.
84. Sellen, A.J.; Louie, G.; Harris, J.E.; Wilkins, A.J. What brings intentions to mind? An in situ study of prospective memory. Mem. Cognit. **1996**, *5* (4), 483–507.
85. Whittaker, S.; Hirschberg, J. The character, value and management of personal paper archives. ACM Trans. Comput.-Hum. Interact. **2001**, *8* (2), 150–170.
86. Jones, W.; Dumais, S. The spatial metaphor for user interfaces—Experimental tests of reference by location versus name. ACM Trans. Off. Inf. Syst. **1986**, *4* (1), 42–63.
87. Mander, R.; Salomon, G.; Wong, Y.Y. A "pile" metaphor for supporting casual organization of information. *Human Factors in Computing Systems* Proceedings of the CHI 92: ACM SIGCHI Conference, Monterey, CA, 1992; 627–634.
88. Barreau, D.K. Context as a factor in personal information management systems. J. Am. Soc. Inf. Sci. **1995**, *46* (5), 327–339.
89. Capra, R.; Vardell, E.; Brennan, K. File synchronization and sharing: User practices and challenges. 77th ASIS&T Annual Meeting, Seattle, WA, Oct 31–Nov 5, 2014.
90. Brinegar, J.; Capra, R. Managing music across multiple devices and computers. Proceedings of the 2011 iConference, Seattle, Washington DC, 2011; 489–495.
91. Diekema, A.R.; Olsen, M.W. Teacher Personal information management (PIM) practices: Finding, keeping, and Re-Finding information. J. Assoc. Inf. Sci. Technol. **Nov 2014**, *65* (11), 2261–2277.
92. Tan, D.; Berry, E.; Czerwinski, M.; Bell, G.; Gemmell, J.; Hodges, S.; Kapur, N.; Save everything: Supporting human memory with a personal digital lifetime store. *Personal Information Management*, University of Washington Press: Seattle, WA, 2007.
93. Jones, W. *Transforming Technologies to Manage Our Information: The Future of Personal Information Management, Part 2*, Chapter 9. Morgan & Claypool Publishers: San Rafael, CA, 2013. Retrieved from http://www.morganclaypool.com/doi/abs/10.2200/S00532ED1V 01Y201308ICR028.
94. Sellen, A.J.; Whittaker, S. Beyond total capture: A constructive critique of lifelogging. Commun. ACM **2010**, *53* (5), 70–77.
95. Seifert, C.M.; Patalano, A.L. Opportunism in memory: Preparing for chance encounters. Curr. Dir. Psychol. Sci. **2001**, *10* (6), 198–201.
96. The Economist. Death to folders! The Economist Technology Quarterly, September 15, 2005, Q3, 30–33.
97. Seltzer, M.; Murphy, N. Hierarchical File Systems Are Dead. *Hot Topics in Operating Systems*. Proceedings of the 12th Conference, Berkeley, CA, 2009; 1.
98. Jones, W. *Transforming Technologies to Manage Our Information: The Future of Personal Information Management, Part 2*, Morgan & Claypool Publishers: San Rafael, CA, 2013. Retrieved from http://www.morganclaypool.com/doi/abs/10.2200/S00532ED1V01Y2 01308ICR028.
99. Dourish, P.; Edwards, W.K.; LaMarca, A.; Lamping, J.; Petersen, K.; Salisbury, M.; Terry, D.B.; Thornton, J. Extending document management systems with user-specific active properties. ACM Trans. Inf. Syst. **2000**, *18* (2), 140–170.
100. Cutrell, E.; Robbins, D.; Dumais, S.; Sarin, R. Fast, flexible filtering with phlat. *Human Factors in Computing Systems*. Proceedings of the SIGCHI Conference, New York, 2006; 261–270.
101. Bloehdorn, S.; Görlitz, O.; Schenk, S.; Sarin, R.; Völkel, M.; et al. Tagfs-tag semantics for hierarchical file systems. *Knowledge Management*. Proceedings of the Sixth International Conference (I-KNOW 06), Graz, Austria, **2006**, *8*.
102. Voit, K.; Andrews, K.; Slany, W. Tagging might not be slower than filing in folders. *Human Factors in Computing Systems Extended Abstracts*. Proceedings of the 2012 ACM Annual Conference Extended Abstracts, New York, 2012; 2063–2068.
103. Dourish, P.; Edwards, W.K.; LaMarca, A.; Salisbury, M. Presto: An experimental architecture for fluid interactive document spaces. ACM Trans. Comput.-Hum. Interact. **1999**, *6* (2), 133–161.
104. Bergman, O.; Gradovitch, N.; Bar-Ilan, J.; Beyth-Marom, R. Folder versus tag preference in personal information management. J. Am. Soc. Inf. Sci. Technol. **2013**; N/A.
105. Civan, A.; Jones, W.; Klasnja, P.; Bruce, H. Better to organize personal information by folders or by tags?: The devil is in the details. 68th Annual Meeting of the American Society for Information Science and Technology (ASIST 2008), Columbus, OH, 2008.
106. Gao, Q. An empirical study of tagging for personal information organization: Performance, workload, memory, and consistency. Int. J. Hum. Comput. Interact. **2011**, *27* (9), 821–863.
107. Jones, W.; Phuwanartnurak, A.J.; Gill, R.; Bruce, H. Don't take my folders away! Organizing personal information to get things done. *Human Factors in Computing Systems*. Proceedings of the ACM SIGCHI Conference (CHI 2005), Portland, OR, 2005, *2005*, 1505–1508.
108. Bälter, O. Strategies for organising email messages. Proceedings of the Twelfth Conference of the British Computer Society Human Computer Interaction Specialist Group—People and Computers XII, Springer, Bristol, UK, 1997; 21–38.
109. Gwizdka, J.; Chignell, M. Individual Differences. In *Personal Information Management,* Jones, W.; Teevan, J., Eds.; University of Washington Press: Seattle, WA, 2007.
110. Mackay, W.E. More than just a communication system: Diversity in the use of electronic mail. *Computer-Supported Cooperative Work*. Proceedings of the 1988 ACM Conference, New York, 1988; 344–353.
111. Abrams, D.; Baecker, R.; Chignell, M. Information archiving with bookmarks: Personal web space construction and organization. *Human Factors in Computing Systems*. Proceedings of the ACM SIGCHI Conference (CHI 1998), Los Angeles, CA, 1998; 41–48.
112. Capra, R.; Khanova, J.; Ramdeen, S. Work and personal e-mail use by university employees: PIM practices across domain boundaries. J. Am. Soc. Inf. Sci. Technol. **2013**, *64* (5), 1029–1044.
113. Ravasio, P.; Schär, S.G.; Krueger, H. In pursuit of desktop evolution: User problems and practices with modern desktop systems. ACM Trans. Comput. Hum. Interact. **2004**, *11* (2), 156–180.
114. Hanrahan, B.V. *Getting lost in email: How and why users spend more time in email than intended*, Doctoral

dissertation. Virginia Tech, Department of Computer Science. Blacksburg, VA, 2014.

115. Hanrahan, B.V.; Pérez-Quiñones, M.A.; Martin, D. Attending to email. Interact. Comput. **2016**, *28* (3), 253–272.
116. Hanrahan, W.; Pérez-Quiñones, M.A. Lost in email: Pulling Users Down a Path of Interaction. Proceedings of the 33rd Annual ACM Conference on Human Factors in Computing Systems (CHI 2005), Seoul, Korea. ACM, 2015; 3981–3984.
117. Marshall, C.C.; Bly, S.; Brun-Cottan, F. The long term fate of our digital belongings: Toward a service model for personal archives. In Archiving Conference. Society for Imaging Science and Technology, 2006; Vol. 2006, 25–30. Retrieved from http://www.ingentaconnect.com/content/ist/ac/2006/00002006/00000001/art00007.
118. Marshall, C.C.; McCown, F.; Nelson, M.L. Evaluating personal archiving strategies for Internet-based information. In Archiving Conference. Society for Imaging Science and Technology 2007; Vol. 2007, 151–156. Retrieved from http://www.ingentaconnect.com/content/ist/ac/2007/00002007/00000001/art00036.
119. Samson, T. Malware infects 30 percent of computers in U.S. InfoWorld, Aug 08, 2012, http://www.infoworld.com/article/2618043/cyber-crime/malware-infects-30-percent-of-computers-in-u-s-.html (accessed Mar 06, 2015).
120. Ackerman, M.S.; Cranor, L. Privacy critics: UI components to safeguard users' privacy. *Human Factors in Computing Systems*. Proceedings of the CHI'99 Extended Abstracts, Pittsburgh, PA, 1999; 258–259.
121. Bauer, L.; Cranor, L.F.; Reeder, R.W.; Reiter, M.K.; Vaniea, K. Real life challenges in access-control management. *Human Factors in Computing Systems*. Proceedings of the 27th International Conference, Boston, MA, 2009; 899–908.
122. Bos, N.; Karahalios, K.; Musgrove-Chvez, M.; Poole, E.S.; Thomas, J.C.; Yardi, S. Research ethics in the Facebook era: Privacy, anonymity. *Human Factors in Computing Systems*. Proceedings of the 27th International Conference Extended Abstracts, Boston, MA, 2009; 2767–2770.
123. Boyd, D.; Hargittai, E. Facebook privacy settings: Who cares? *First Monday* **2010**, *15*(8).
124. Egelman, S.; Tsai, J.; Cranor, L.F.; Acquisti, A. Timing is everything?: The effects of timing and placement of online privacy indicators. *Human Factors in Computing Systems*. Proceedings of the 27th International Conference, Boston, MA, 2009; 319–328.
125. Hoofnagle, C.J. Beyond Google and evil: How policy makers, journalists and consumers should talk differently about Google and privacy. 2009, http://firstmonday.org/htbin/cgiwrap/bin/ojs/index.php/fm/article/view/2326/2156.
126. Iachello, G.; Hong, J. End-user privacy in human-computer interaction. Found. Trends Hum.-Comput. Interact. **2007**, *1* (1), 1–137.
127. Karat, C.-M.; Brodie, C.; Karat, J. Management of personal information disclosure: The interdependence of privacy, security and trust. *Personal Information Management*; University of Washington Press: Seattle, WA, 2007.
128. Al-Shakhouri , N.-S.; Mahmood, A. Privacy in the digital world: Towards international legislation. 2009, http://firstmonday.org/htbin/cgiwrap/bin/ojs/index.php/fm/article/view/2146/2153.
129. Moore, A.D. *Privacy Rights: Moral and Legal Foundations*; Penn State Press: University Park, PA, 2010.
130. Moore, A.D. Privacy, security, and government surveillance: Wikileaks and the new accountability. Public Affairs Quarterly, **2011**, *25* (2), 141–156.
131. Tunick, M. Privacy and Punishment. Soc. Theory Pract. **2013**, *39* (4), 643–668.
132. Choe, E.K.; Lee, N.B.; Lee, B.; Pratt, W.; Kientz, J.A. Understanding quantified-selfers' practices in collecting and exploring personal data. *Human Factors in Computing Systems*. Proceedings of the SIGCHI Conference, New York, 2014; 1143–1152.
133. Elsden, C.; Kirk, D.S. A quantified past: Remembering with personal informatics. *Designing Interactive Systems*. Proceedings of the 2014 Companion Publication, New York, 2014; 45–48.
134. Froehlich, J.E.; Kay, M.; Larsen, J.E.; Thomaz, E. Disasters in personal informatics: The unpublished stories of failure and lessons learned. *Pervasive and Ubiquitous Computing: Adjunct Publication*. Proceedings of the 2014 ACM International Joint Conference, New York, 2014; 673–678.
135. Gurrin, C.; Smeaton, A.F.; Doherty, A.R. LifeLogging: Personal big data. Found. Trends Inf. Retr. **Jun 2014**, *8* (1), 1–125.
136. Rooksby, J.; Rost, M.; Morrison, A.; Chalmers, M.C. Personal tracking as lived informatics. *Human Factors in Computing Systems*. Proceedings of the 32nd Annual ACM Conference, New York, 2014; 1163–1172.
137. The Economist The quantified self: Counting every moment. The Economist, 2012. From the print edition: Technology Quarterly.
138. Li, I.; Medynskiy, Y.; Froehlich, J.; Larsen, J. Personal informatics in practice: Improving quality of life through data. *Human Factors in Computing Systems*. Proceedings of the CHI'12 Extended Abstracts, 2012; 2799–2802.
139. Jones, W. *Keeping Found Things Found: The Study and Practice of Personal Information Management*; Chapter 8, Morgan Kaufmann Publishers: San Francisco, CA, 2007.
140. Rapp, A.; Cena, F. Self-monitoring and yechnology: Challenges and open issues in personal informatics. In *Universal Access in Human-Computer Interaction. Design for All and Accessibility Practice*. UAHCI 2014. Stephanidis, C.; Antona, M. Eds.; Lecture Notes in Computer Science, Springer, Cham. Vol. 8516, 613–622.
141. Li, I.; Dey, A.; Forlizzi, J. A stage-based model of personal informatics systems. *Human Factors in Computing Systems*. Proceedings of the SIGCHI Conference, New York, 2010; 557–566.
142. Li, I.; Dey, A.; Forlizzi, J. Understanding my data, myself: Supporting self-reflection with ubicomp technologies. *Ubiquitous Computing*. Proceedings of the 13th International Conference, Beijing, China, 2011; 405–414.
143. Burns, P.J.; Lueg, C.; Berkovsky, S. Using personal informatics to motivate physical activity: could we be doing it wrong? In Chi 2012 Workshop, Austin, TX, 2012; 1–4. Retrieved from http://ecite.utas.edu.au/81716.
144. Khovanskaya, V.; Baumer, E.P.; Cosley, D.; Voida, S.; Gay, G. Everybody knows what you're doing: A critical design approach to personal informatics. *Human Factors*

in Computing Systems. Proceedings of the SIGCHI Conference, Paris, France, 2013; 3403–3412.
145. Barsalou, L.W. Ad hoc categories. Mem. Cognit. **1983**, *11* (3), 211–227.
146. Barsalou, L.W. Deriving categories to achieve goals. Psychol. Learn. Motiv. Academic Press: New York, 1991.
147. Hutchins, E. *Cognition in the Wild*; MIT Press: Cambridge, MA, 1994.
148. Kirsh, D. A few thoughts in cognitive overload. Intellectica **2000**, *30* (1), 19–51.
149. Dervin, B. From the mind's eye of the user: The sense-making qualitative-quantitative methodologyQualitative Research in Information Management **1992**; *9*, 61–84.
150. Russell, D.M.; Stefik, M.J.; Pirolli, P.; Card, S.K. The cost structure of sensemaking; 1993.
151. Larkin, J.H.; Simon, H.A. Why a diagram is (sometimes) worth ten thousand words. Cogn. Sci. **1987**, *11*, 65–99.
152. Kotovsky, K.; Hayes, J.R.; Simon, H.A. Why are some problems hard? Evidence from Tower of Hanoi. Cognit. Psychol. **1985**, *17* (2), 248–294.
153. Cheng, P.C.-H. Electrifying diagrams for learning: Principles for complex representational systems. Cogn. Sci. **2002**, *26* (6), 685–736.
154. Novick, L.R. Representational transfer in problem solving. Psychol. Sci. **1990**, *1* (2), 128–132.
155. Novick, L.R.; Hurley, S.M.; Francis, M. Evidence for abstract, schematic knowledge of three spatial diagram representations. Mem. Cognit. **1999**, *27* (2), 288–308.
156. Mumford, M.D.; Schultz, R.A.; Van Doorn, J.R. Performance in planning: Processes, requirements and errors. Rev. Gen. Psychol. **2001**, *5* (3), 213–240.
157. Erickson, T. From PIM to GIM: Personal information management in group contexts. Commun. ACM **Jan 2006**, *49* (1), 74–75.
158. Lutters, W.G.; Ackerman, M.S.; Zhou, X. Group information management. In *Personal Information Management*. Jones, W.; Teevan, J. Eds.; University of Washington Press: Seattle, WA, 2007.
159. Schmidt, K.; Simonee, C. Coordination mechanisms: Towards a conceptual foundation of CSCW systems design. Comput. Support. Coop. Work CSCW **1996**, *5* (2–3), 155–200.
160. Jones, W. *Building a Better World with our Information: The Future of Personal Information Management, Part 3*; Morgan & Claypool Publishers: San Rafael, CA, 2015 Retrieved from http://www.morganclaypool.com/doi/10.2200/S00653ED1V01Y201506ICR042.
161. Hicks, B.J.; Dong, A.; Palmer, R.; Mcalpine, H.C. Organizing and managing personal electronic files: A mechanical engineer's perspective. ACM Trans. Inf. Syst. **2008**, *26* (4), 1–40.
162. Berlin, L.M.; Jeffries, R.; O'Day, V.L.; Paepcke, A.; Wharton, C. Where did you put it?: Issues in the design and use of group memory. *Human Factors and Computing Systems*. Proceedings of the Conference INTERACT'93 and CHI'93, Amsterdam, the Netherlands, 1993; 23–30.
163. Wulf, V. Storing and retrieving documents in a shared workspace: Experiences from the political administration. Human-Computer Interaction Proceeding of the Conference INTERACT'97, 1997; 469–476.
164. Mark, G.; Prinz, W. What happened to our document in the shared workspace? The need for Groupware conventions. Human-Computer Interaction Proceeding of the Conference INTERACT'97, 1997; 413–420.
165. Dourish, P.; Lamping, J.; Rodden, T. Building bridges: Customisation and mutual intelligibility in shared category management. Supporting Group Work. Proceeding of the International ACM SIGGROUP Conference, 1999; 11–20.
166. Bergman, O.; Whittaker, S.; Falk, N. Shared files: The retrieval perspective. J. Assoc. Inf. Sci. Technol. **2014.**
167. Prinz, W.; Zaman, B. Proactive support for the organization of shared workspaces using activity patterns and content analysis. Supporting Group Work. Proceeding of the 2005 International ACM SIGGROUP Conference, 1999; 11–20.
168. Capra, R.; Marchionini, G.; Velasco-Martin, J.; Muller, K. Tools-at-hand and learning in multi-session, collaborative search. *Human Factors in Computing Systems*. Proceedings of the SIGCHI Conference, New York, 2010; 951–960.
169. Marshall, C.; Tang, J.C. That syncing feeling: Early user experiences with the cloud. Proceedings of the Designing Interactive Systems Conference, New York, 2012; 544–553.
170. Johnson, M.L.; Bellovin, S.M.; Reeder, R.W.; Schechter, S.E. Laissez-faire file sharing: Access control designed for individuals at the endpoints. New Security Paradigms Workshop. Proceedings of the of the 2009 Workshop, 2009; 1–10.
171. Bergman, O.; Beyth-Marom, R.; Nachmias, R. The project fragmentation problem in personal information management. *Human Factors in Computing Systems*. Proceedings of the SIGCHI Conference , Montreal, Quebec, Canada, 2006; 271–274.
172. Jones, W.; Bruce, H.; Foxley, A. Project contexts to situate personal information. Proceedings of the SIGIR 2006, Seattle, WA, 2006.
173. Naumer, C.M.; Fisher, K.E. Naturalistic approaches for understanding PIM. Personal Information Management, Jones, W.; Teevan, J. Eds.; University of Washington Press: Seattle, WA, 2007.
174. Kelly, D.; Teevan, J. Understanding what works: Evaluating PIM tools. Personal Information Management, Jones, W.; Teevan, J. Eds.; University of Washington Press: Seattle, WA, 2007.
175. Bergman, O.; Beyth-Marom, R.; Nachmias, R.; Whittaker, S. The user-subjective approach: A new direction for pim systems design. PIM 2008: Proceedings of the Third International Workshop on Personal Information Management, Florence, Italy, 2008.
176. Bergman, O.; Tucker, S.; Beyth-Marom, R.; Cutrell, E.; Whittaker, S. It's not that important: demoting personal information of low subjective importance using GrayArea. *Human Factors in Computing Systems*. Proceedings of the 27th international Conference, Boston, MA, 2009; 269–278.
177. Bergman, O.; Komninos, A.; Liarokapis, D.; Clarke, J. You never call: Demoting unused contacts on mobile phones using DMTR. Pers. Ubiquit. Comput. **2012**, *16* (6), 757–766.

178. Bergman, O.; Elyada, O.; Dvir, N.; Vaitzman, Y.; Ami, A. B. Spotting the latest version of a file with old'n gray. Interact. Comput. 2014; iwu018.
179. Jones, E.; Bruce, H.; Klasnja, P.; Jones, W. "I Give Up!" five factors that contribute to the abandonment of information management strategies. Presented at the 68th Annual Meeting of the American Society for Information Science and Technology (ASIST 2008), Columbus, OH, 2008.
180. Grudin, J. *Why CSCW applications fail: Problems in the design and evaluation of organization of organizational interfaces*, 1988.
181. Jorgensen, D.L. *Participant Observation: A Methodology for Human Studies*; Sage: Thousand Oaks, CA, 1989.
182. Bolger, N.; Davis, A.; Rafaeli, E. Diary methods: Capturing life as it is lived. Annu. Rev. Psychol. **2003**, *54* (1), 579–616.
183. Linstone, H.A.; Turoff, M. *The Delphi Method: Techniques and Applications*; Addison-Wesley: Reading, MA, **1975**, *29*.
184. Jones, W.; Capra, R.; Diekema, A.; Teevan, J.; Pérez-Quiñones, M.; Dinneen, J.; Hemminger, B. "For Telling" the present: Using the Delphi method to understand personal information management practices. Proceedings of the CHI 2015, Seoul, Korea, 2015.
185. Muller, M.J. Participatory design: The third space in HCI. Hum.-Comput. Interact. Dev. Process. **2003**, *4235*.
186. Schuler, D.; Namioka, A. *Participatory Design: Principles and Practices*; L. Erlbaum Associates Inc.: Hillsdale, NJ, 1993.
187. Ducheneaut, N.; Bellotti, V. E-mail as habitat. Interactions **2001**, *8* (5), 30–38.
188. Bellotti, V.; Ducheneaut, N.; Howard, M.; Smith, I. Taking email to task: The design and evaluation of a task management centered email tool. *Human Factors in Computing Systems*. Proceedings of the ACM SIGCHI Conference (CHI 2003), Ft. Lauderdale, FL, 2003; 345–352.
189. Jones, W.; Hou, D.; Sethanandha, B.D.; Bi, S.; Gemmell, J. Planz to put our digital information in its place. *Human Factors in Computing Systems*. Proceedings of the 28th of the International Conference Extended Abstracts, Atlanta, GA, 2010; 2803–2812.
190. Whittaker, S.; Bellotti, V.M.E.; Gwizdka, J. Email as PIM. *Personal Information Management*, University of Washington Press: Seattle, WA, 2007.
191. Rockquemore, K.A. Essay on how academics can gain control of their e-mail and their time @insidehighered. https://www.insidehighered.com/advice/2015/02/25/essay-how-academics-can-gain-control-their-e-mail-and-their-time (accessed Mar 06, 2015).
192. Jones, W.P. *Keeping Found Things Found the Study and Practice of Personal Information Management*; Chapter 11, Morgan Kaufmann Publishers: Amsterdam, the Netherlands; Boston, MA, 2008.
193. Russell, D.M.; Lawrence, S. Search everything. *Personal Information Management*, University of Washington Press: Seattle, WA, 2007.

Peru: Libraries and Library Science

Sergio Chaparro-Univazo
Graduate School of Library and Information Science, Simmons College, Boston, Massachusetts, U.S.A.

Abstract

Libraries in Peru have been the subject of tremendous evolution. The Spanish influence brought the concept of libraries and the printing press, but it was not until the twentieth century when librarianship in Peru was established as a discipline and profession. Library education has grown rapidly and the post-Internet times have produced a very dynamic information society that still requires more consistent library services.

INTRODUCTION

Located on the western rim of South America, Peru is bordered on the north by Colombia and Ecuador, on the east by Brazil, on the southeast by Bolivia, on the south by Chile, and on the west by the Pacific Ocean. Its geography varies from the arid plains on coast to the spectacular Andes Mountains and the lush tropical forests of the Amazon Basin. Estimated at 29,180,900 (July 2008), the population of Peru is multiethnic: Amerindian 45%; mestizo (mixed Amerindian and white) 37%; white 15%, black, Japanese, Chinese, and other 3%. The government is a representative democratic republic divided into 25 regions (Fig. 1).

HISTORICAL BACKGROUND

Libraries in Perú have a long history that started with the Spanish conquest and the introduction of the printing press in the sixteenth century. During the Spanish domination there was a strong impetus to create private and monastic collections, intended mostly to indoctrinate the indigenous populations. The Inca and Pre-Inca cultures did not have an alphabet, but that did not preclude them from achieving extraordinary development. Based on oral traditions and quipus as a way of translating words, they built up one of the most important cultures in the southern hemisphere. The Inca Empire also gave birth to the most important and wealthiest Spanish possession in the Americas—Peru. During the period when Peru was a colony of Spain (from 1535 to 1824) monastic and private collections were developed to instruct the Indians with Christian doctrine. The Franciscan Monastery of our Lady of Ocopa was a good example of a large monastic collection of around 20,000 volumes.

Some of the Spanish conquerors carried personal libraries with them, and during the expansion of the Spanish viceroyalty reading spread among clergyman, lawyers, and a growing student population. The book trade also developed, but most works were imported from Europe. However, the sixteenth century was critical for the development of a book culture and printing thanks to Antonio Ricardo and his printing Press in Lima. The Jesuits gave a space to Antonio Ricardo at the Colegio de San Pablo to install his printing press which was set up as early as 1584. Ricardo's first book was the *Doctrina Christiana* and it was published in three languages: Spanish, Quechua, and Aymara.

The Inquisition also played an important role in its censorship role of heretic literature. The Holy Office of the Inquisition in Spain controlled the importation and publishing of books. Efforts to counteract that control were sometimes made by individuals who collected private libraries that then emerged as a sort of "counter culture" space because they held materials that were listed as banned in the *Index Librorum Prohibitorum*. However, the owners of these private libraries that contained banned materials risked being prosecuted. The French Enlightment and the Bourbon dynasty of 1701 brought new impetus to those private collections.

Special mention needs to be made here about the important role that universities played in the creation of library collections, encouraging reading and developing the culture of the viceroyalty of Peru. The Universidad Nacional Mayor de San Marcos (UNMSM) was founded in 1551. When the Jesuits were driven out of Peru in 1768 their major collections at the Colegio de San Pablo were given to UNMSM. Around this time we find the first attempts to promote some sort of public librarianship. Around 1778 UNMSM suggested that rooms at the Colegio de San Pablo be offered to the public for public reading.

It was mainly during the independence period of 1821–1824 that the concept of public libraries emerged in the new republic. The National Library was created by Don José de San Martín on September 17 of 1822. At the time of its inauguration, the library held around 112,256 volumes. Most of its holdings came from citizens' donations, from the University of San Marcos, and even the private collection of Don José de San Martín. During the Pacific

Encyclopedia of Library and Information Sciences, Fourth Edition DOI: 10.1081/E-ELIS4-120044837

Fig. 1 Map of Peru.
Source: CIA World Factbook. https://www.cia.gov/library/publications/the-world-factbook/geos/pe.html

War in 1881 the National Library was invaded and decimated by the Chilean army and its collections ransacked. Of the 56,000 volumes only 738 remained after the Chileans left. Ricardo Palma, a writer and scholar, who was later famous for his *Tradiciones Peruanas*, rebuilt the National Library from the ruins. Palma's task was monumental and symbolizes perhaps one of the most challenging reconstruction tasks of a library in world history. When assigned to the job by President Iglesias, he asked the president if he was going to be a "mendicant librarian," the President's answer was yes. He then got the nickname *the mendicant librarian* (el bibliotecario mendigo). International donations were essential, and many donations were received through Palma's contacts in the South American region. Palma even asked the President of Chile for the restitution of some collections. Contrary to what we might think, his wishes were acknowledged. The National Library reopened on July 28, 1884.

RECENT HISTORY: THE POST-WAR YEARS

Library education and professionalism in Peru were given an impetus by the events that happened around 1943. The library profession itself took its first major step with the appointment of Jorge Basadre (1905–1980) to rebuild the Biblioteca Nacional (National Library) devastated by a fire in 1943, and the foundation on June 23 of the same year of the Escuela Nacional de Bibliotecarios (National School of Librarians). Basadre had been exposed to international librarianship and had a strong interest in building and strengthening the library profession. For example, he participated in professional exchanges with North American advising committees such as the American mission of 1943, which included Dr. Keyes D. Metcalf, Director of Harvard libraries and President of ALA; Lewis Hanke, Director of the Spanish Foundation of the Library of Congress; and Wilmarth S. Lewis, Director of Yale University Libraries. Basadre's push brought a new wave of library publications. Important library publications of those years were the *Boletín de la Biblioteca Nacional*, *Fénix*, and the publication of the *Anuario Bibliográfico Peruano* in 1945. Basadre's influence was also noticeable in the new conceptualization of public libraries and their role in society. He was responsible for the promotion of the popular libraries and the decree of May 25, 1947, Law 10847 that supported taxation for public libraries.

Basadre's interest in public librarianship later stimulated the development of some important public libraries like the Ricardo Palma in the district of Miraflores and the ones in Surco and San Isidro. The post–World War II era saw an increasing concern in society about the need to strengthen and solidify municipal and public libraries, two institutions that targeted similar kind of patrons. Municipal libraries are administered by the municipal government, and by 2004 there were 1080 municipal libraries in Peru. Even though such libraries are numerous, their work is very much limited by the lack of an adequate funding, and their overall development has been hindered by the lack of a coherent vision concerning their role in society. One of the oldest municipal library is the *Callao Municipal Pilot Library* founded in 1936. The first bookmobile in Perú was inaugurated in 1957.

School libraries are present in most private schools, but their quality varies depending on their funding and administration, which is based on tuition and the school policies. The earliest academic libraries in Peru date from the sixteenth century around the time of the founding of the oldest University in the Americas, the *Universidad Nacional Mayor de San Marcos* on May 12 of 1551 by decree of Charles V. Numerous new academic institutions have proliferated since then. Among the oldest public academic institutions are the *Universidad San Antonio Abad* (1692, Cuzco), and the *Universidad Nacional de Trujillo* (1827), and the *Universidad de San Agustín* (1827, Arequipa). There are around 98 public and private universities in Peru, and most of them have academic collections. The quality of their collections however is very uneven. Some recent efforts toward more digital collections have been made and academic libraries were among the first institutions that developed digital resources and supported widespread use of the Internet. One of the leaders in this area was the *Universidad Peruana de Ciencias Aplicadas*, which began to develop digital resources in the mid-1990s. In terms of collections (print and online), among the most important are the collections from the UNMSM (public) and the Peruvian Pontifical Catholic University (private), Cayetano Heredia, and the Pacific University (private).

Other important libraries that are not necessarily public in terms of access but contain important collections are those of foreign institutes such as the Alliance Francaise, the Instituto Británico and the Instituto Cultural Peruano Norteamericano (ICPNA). The library of the Lima Art Museum, the *Manuel Solari Swayne Library*, holds around 10,000 volumes, and was created in 1986. The Getty foundation has supported its acquisitions program.

LIBRARY EDUCATION AND PROFESSIONAL ASSOCIATIONS

The *Escuela Nacional de Bibliotecarios* was transferred to the UNMSM as a university program, and its name changed to *Escuela Académico Profesional de Bibliotecología y Ciencias de la Información.* This national school and the Library School at the Peruvian Pontifical Catholic University (PUCP), established under the sponsorship of the British Council in 1990, are the only library schools in Peru.

In recent years research in library and information science has developed, as is evident in the production of professional journals such as *Alexandría*, *Bibliodocencia*, *Biblios*, *Bibliotecólogos*, and *Infobib*. Some of these journals are peer reviewed and reflect the interest of an increasing professional and research community to improve professional knowledge. The existence of associations is also another sign of the interest of professional librarians in expanding their knowledge and professional expertise. Among the most important associations are the *Colegio de Bibliotecologos del Perú* that followed the *Asociación Peruana de Bibliotecarios* created in 1945.

THE NATIONAL LIBRARY

On March 27, 2006, the Peruvian National Library inaugurated a new building, which also houses the *Centro Bibliográfico Nacional*, which is in charge of national bibliographic control through legal deposit (the current Legal Deposit Law 26905 was passed in 1997). The national bibliographic center also carries out other tasks such as the registration of all bibliographic materials at the national library, implementation of technical processing of Peruvian materials, and the creation of bibliographies of important Peruvian authors. The National Library is a member of the *Asociación de Bibliotecas Nacionales de Iberoamérica.* In many ways, the move to a new building has also enhanced the visibility of the National Library in Peruvian society, but much more work around public librarianship needs to be done.

MODERN CHALLENGES

The modern challenges are related to building a stronger municipal/public library system with adequate funding, the improvement of the public library system that still is administered by the National Library, and the provision of Internet access in broadband to the academic and special library sector. In addition, environmental concerns and the importance of the indigenous population in Peru have prompted discussions about librarianship that are centered around enhancing the development of library services for underserved populations and on the implementation of projects that target their information needs. Some projects revolved around The *Centro de Documentación e Información del Instituto de Investigación de la Amazonía Peruana* (IIAP) and the "*Red de bibliotecas fluviales del Alto Marañón.*" Rural librarianship and its growth is also another area that librarianship needs to integrate more consistently into the progress and development of the indigenous information needs.

Academic libraries in Peru are now facing important changes and challenges with regard to database access, use of open access software, design of OPACS, and the integration of their services. Most academic libraries utilize closed stacks and that affects the circulation and the characteristics of the services they provide.

Special libraries, such as the ESAN (Escuela Superior de Administración de Negocios) or Inrena (Instituto Nacional de Recursos naturales), are important examples of the diversity of information resources available now. Peru has a tremendous diversity of natural resources and land, and given the current interest on environmental issues, has paid attention to creating information networks and virtual libraries concerning natural and agricultural resources. For example, Rebiape is a portal of agricultural information. The *Biblioteca Agrícola Nacional* is located at the *Universidad Agraria* in la Molina, a district of Lima. Public health has also been an important focus for the development of information services in Peru. With regard to public health, special mention needs to be made of REPEBIS, *Red Peruana de Bibliotecas en Salud*, which also produces the *Biblioteca Virtual en Salud*.

Librarians in Peru began to participate in the trend toward the development and promotion of Internet use for education, scientific information, and libraries when Red Científica Peruana (RCP, the Peruvian Scientific Network) was created in 1991 as a nonprofit organization. RCP developed an innovative way of offering Internet access to citizens using public computer terminals. RCP was innovative in many other ways as well, implementing the first satellite connection to the Internet, the first use of listservs, the first Web site, and the first electronic newspaper, all without government subsidies. In many ways the RCP introduced the value of the Internet as an educational tool to Peruvian society.

CONCLUSION

In summary, librarians in Peru are currently working

- To improve the access and quality of their collections, particularly in academic areas.
- To design and implement innovative efforts to build up information resources for indigenous populations.
- To expand special libraries.
- To strengthen rural librarianship.
- To provide better access services through broadband.

Libraries will not be able to evolve without dependable electronic access services and discounted access rates that need to be discussed in the context of wider information policies. For that reason, advocacy on the part of the library world is necessary as is awareness and education about ways to advocate for library funding and tools. Another challenge comes from the lack of a coherent and supportive policy on the part of the government regarding the book trade and publishing, since this is still the main source supplying materials in library collections. High costs and widespread piracy are factors that make the production of books in Peru difficult.

Libraries are still working hard to find a permanent space in the every day life of the Peruvian citizen. Funding and professional expertise remain a challenge for most of the small public/municipal and academic libraries that survive on donations and small budgets. The last 10 years of post-Internet development have stressed the importance of the library, but the improvement of the quality and promotion of the services is a major task yet to be done.

BIBLIOGRAPHY

1. Aliaga, C.C. Library services for Latin American indigenous populations. IFLA J. **2004**, *30*(2), 134–140.
2. Benrubi, D. Un regard sur le livre et les bibliotheques au Perou. Bulletin des Bibliotheques de France **2008**, *53*(3), 84–92.
3. Dearden, C.D. Global connections: private healers. Bookbird **2002**, *40*(3), 24–33.
4. Guerrero, J.C.O. La produccion del libro en el Peru 1960–2002. Book production in Peru, 1960–2002. Revista Interamericana De Bibliotecologia **2003**, *26*(1), 153–167.
5. Hampe-Martínez, T. The diffusion of books and ideas in colonial Peru: A study of private libraries in the sixteenth and seventeenth centuries. Hisp. Am. Hist. Rev. **1993**, *73*(2), 211–233.
6. Heery, S. Rural libraries, Cajamarca province, Peru. Focus Int. Comp. Libr. **2001**, *32*(2), 63–65.
7. Henriod, G.V.B. The Manuel Solari Swayne library at the museum of art of Lima. Art Libr. J. **2005**, *30*(3), 16–19.
8. Ibarra, A. Education for cataloging and related areas in Peru. Catalog. Classif. Quart. **2006**, *41*(3/4), 389–406.
9. Martinez-Arellano, F.F. The state of bibliographic control in Latin America. Int. Catalog. Bibliogr. Control **2005**, *34* (1), 3–7.
10. Morgan de Goni, P.; Goni, P.M.D.; de Goni, P.M. The experience of Peru in planning a development-oriented approach to information. UNESCO J. Inform. Sci. Librariansh. Archiv. Admin. **1981**, *3*(2), 125–131.
11. Nehmad, A. The Sala de Investigaciones—Fondo Reservado of the University of San Marcos Central Library, Lima, Peru. RBM **2005**, *6*(2), 108–123.
12. Nehmad, A.L. The sala de investigaciones fondo reservado of the university of San Marcos central library, Lima, Peru. RBM J. Rare Books Manuscr. Cult. Herit. **2005**, *6*(2), 108–123.
13. Olaya Guerrero, J. La Produccion del Libro en el Peru 1960–2002. Revista Interamericana de Bibliotecologia **2003**, *26*(1), 153–167.
14. Revilla, V. El bibliotecario mendigo: a bookman's response to the sacking of the Peruvian national library in 1881. Libri **1993**, *43*(1), 19–38.
15. Rojas, A.C. El mercado laboral de los bibliotecarios en el Peru: Una aproximacion a su estudio. An approach to the librarian labor market in Peru. Investigacion Bibliotecologica: Archivonomia, Bibliotecologia, e Informacion **2003**, *17*(35), 113–141.
16. Talavera Ibarra, A.M. Education for cataloging and related areas in Peru. Catalog. Classif. Quart. **2005**, *41*(3/4), np.
17. Torres, P.A. Parliamentary library and information services as instruments for democratic development. Inspel **2000**, *34*(2), 115–122. Available at http://www.csa.com.
18. Vichez Roman, C. Habitos de Lectura de los Adolescentes Peruanos: Nuevas Perspectivas. Revista Interamericana de Bibliotecologia **2003**, *26*(2), 57–71.
19. Villanueva, E. Accidental open access and the hazards involved: preliminary experiences on Internet-based publishing in a Peruvian university. First Monday **2006**, *11*(6), 1 (Online).
20. Zaidman, L. Keeping the oral tradition alive. Bookbird **2001**, *39*(1), 43–45.

Philosophy and the Information Sciences

Jonathan Furner
Department of Information Studies University of California, Los Angeles, Los Angeles, California, U.S.A.

Abstract
Philosophy and the information sciences intersect in various ways. Philosophical approaches to the study of information and information-related phenomena focus on metaphysical, epistemological, and ethical questions; philosophical approaches to the study of the information sciences focus on methodological issues. Metaphilosophical questions may also be asked about philosophy of information and about philosophy of the information sciences.

INTRODUCTION

There are several scholarly activities or practices that coalesce at the intersection of, on the one hand, philosophy, and on the other, the information sciences. The aim of this entry is to distinguish among some of these practices, and to assess their significance, both for philosophy and for the information sciences. In particular, a distinction is drawn between philosophical questions asked *in* the information sciences and philosophical questions asked *about* the information sciences, and the goals and subject matter of *philosophy of information* and *philosophy of the information sciences* are described. This distinction is made in the spirit of conceptual clarity, rather than to reflect a division that is rigorously respected in actual scholarly practice: people interested in philosophy are likely to be interested in questions of all of these kinds.

To some who work in the information sciences, the questions that are posed in philosophy may seem like "meta-questions," in the vague sense that they are after, later, beside, beyond, or above other questions to which answers are required more immediately, directly, or pressingly. Since categories of meta-questions are commonly identified as forming core components of the contents of fields at the intersection of philosophy and the information sciences, it is worth taking some care to clarify several different conceptions of the qualities that distinguish meta-questions from their non-meta counterparts.

Philosophy of Information as a Meta-Field

Encountering the information sciences for the first time, we might wonder what they are all about. We might want to ask, for example, What is this thing they call "information"? In what way does it exist? What kind of thing is it? Of what fundamental category of things is it an instance? What is its essence? What are its properties? What are the necessary and the sufficient conditions some thing must satisfy for it to be counted as information? Questions about the mode of existence and the basic nature of different kinds of things are questions that are asked in the branch of philosophy known as *metaphysics*, i.e., philosophy of being. They might be treated as meta-questions simply because they are foundational questions about the fundamental nature of the things in which we are interested. The simple form of questions of this sort belies the difficulty of providing answers that survive all challenges.

The questions just listed are questions about a phenomenon—information—that is a core component of the subject matter of the information sciences, and they are questions that are commonly addressed both in introductory texts[1] and in more advanced treatises[2] in the information sciences. Their philosophical nature (of which more will be said below) and their focus on the phenomenon of information are individually necessary and jointly sufficient conditions of their also being considered part of a branch of philosophy known as philosophy of information, and they are questions that are commonly addressed both in introductory texts[3] and in more advanced treatises[4] in that field, too. Philosophy of information is discussed in a seperate section below (headed "Philosophy of Information").

Meta-Questions about the Information Sciences

We may distinguish questions that are raised *by* or *in* a discipline or field of inquiry, or in a group of fields like the information sciences, from questions that are *about* that field or group of fields. Questions of the second kind might include questions about the subject matter of the field, its scope, its purposes and/or goals, its methods, its relationships to other fields and to other activities, and its usefulness, worth, or value. These are meta-questions about the field *as a field*, i.e., questions that are raised by studies *of* the field, rather than by studies *in* the field.

Sometimes it is considered that it is worth keeping the second-order questions that relate to a given field separate

Pacific–Philosophy

Encyclopedia of Library and Information Sciences, Fourth Edition DOI: 10.1081/E-ELIS4-120043239

from their first-order cousins, and treating the second-order questions collectively as a discrete "meta-field." Sometimes such meta-questions are identified as being philosophical questions simply in virtue of their second-order status, and the aggregate of such questions is what is construed as the philosophy of field *x*—even though it might be unclear as to what is strictly *philosophical* about any given meta-question. More commonly, however, the history, sociology, and politics of any given field *x* are identified as meta-fields that are distinguishable from the philosophy of field *x*. Meta-questions about the who, what, where, when, and why of the information sciences are the kinds of questions that are asked by sociologists, historians, and political theorists: What is the subject matter of the information sciences as they have been practiced at different points in history, and in different social contexts? What are the characteristics of the social groups whose members work on the information sciences? What motivations have people had for devoting time and other resources to the study of information and related phenomena? Why ought people to be interested in information?

Philosophy of the information sciences may then be distinguished from the history, sociology, and politics of the information sciences as the meta-field in which distinctively philosophical questions are posed (and philosophical answers attempted) about the information sciences. We might ask, for example, What is the nature of the information sciences? In what essential respects do they differ from other areas of inquiry? Questions of this kind are different from questions of the kind asked in Philosophy of Information (as defined above), in the sense that they do not arise *in* the information sciences and are not answerable by doing information science. Indeed, philosophy of the information sciences—like, for instance, philosophy of the biological sciences—may readily be construed as a branch of philosophy of science. Philosophy of the information sciences is discussed in a seperate section below (headed "Philosophy of the Information Sciences").

Philosophy of Philosophy as a Meta-Field

There is another, narrower sense in which a field of inquiry may be identified as a meta-field. This is the sense in which philosophy of philosophy (also known as *metaphilosophy*) is considered a meta-field. One important characteristic of metaphilosophy is its reflexivity. A *reflexive* meta-field is one that comprises the *x*-like study of *x*—for example, the philosophical study of philosophy;[5] or the information-scientific study of the information sciences.[6] Indeed, it is possible to ask philosophical questions about philosophy of information and about philosophy of the information sciences: about, for instance, how they ought to be done. Again, questions of this kind are different from questions of the kind mentioned in the previous paragraph, in the sense that they are questions *about* philosophy of those particular kinds, rather than questions that arise *in* philosophy of those kinds or that are answerable by doing philosophy of those kinds. The possibility of a productive metaphilosophy of information and of the information sciences is briefly revisited in the section below on "Meta-Questions about Philosophy."

The Information Sciences as Meta-Fields

Sometimes the information sciences themselves are taken to form a group of fields of inquiry that are each, in a unique and significant way, concerned to answer meta-questions about other fields.[7] In one important sense, much of the subject matter of library and information science, for instance, consists of other fields of inquiry: the objects of inquiry are those other fields. Studies of the structural relationships among and within different fields (for example, studies of the frequency with which, and the ways in which, authors in field *x* cite authors in field *y*), of the information needs and uses of people working in and between different fields, of the processes by which information is produced, organized, retrieved, communicated, and applied in different fields—these can all be considered as exemplifying a meta-field, in the sense that the subject matter of that field is made up of other fields. Other fields of inquiry that are regularly identified on this basis as meta-fields are education and, indeed, philosophy of science. Introductory characterizations of the information sciences and of philosophy are respectively provided in sections below on "The Information Sciences" and "Philosophy."

Information Meta-Studies as a Meta-Field

Sometimes it is enough that a particular study involves or requires comparative evaluations of alternative theories, models, or conceptual frameworks, or simply that it consists of an overview or summary of multiple sets of previously published data, findings, or conclusions, for it to be categorized as a meta-study. Examples certainly exist of named meta-fields that are devoted to classifying and assessing theoretical frameworks: recently emerging subfields of philosophy include meta-ethics, metaontology, and metametaphysics. By analogy, we might imagine a field called "information meta-studies" that comprises comparative evaluations of alternative theories in the information sciences. Such work is not considered further in this entry.

Personal/Professional Philosophies of Information Work

Similarly, one sense of "philosophy" that will not be covered further in this entry is the one that people mean when they talk about their (or their institution's) personal or professional "philosophy" of information work, scholarship, or research. It is in this sense that people sometimes talk about *having* a philosophy, which is different from the sense in which philosophers *do* philosophy. Talk about the philosophy that one has, in this sense, is typically equivalent to a statement of one's long-term or fundamental goals or mission, or a statement of one's basic or most strongly held values. Having a knowledge of professional ethics is not a necessary prerequisite for making statements of goals or values. Nevertheless, study of professional ethics can provide suggestions of values to hold that are in line with others', and can provide knowledge of ethical principles that can aid choice among values. Information ethics is commonly construed as a branch of philosophy of information, but mere statements of values (which may or may not result from the study of information ethics) are not usually conceived as contributions to philosophy—at least, not in the strict sense of "philosophy" used by most philosophers.

THE INFORMATION SCIENCES

Before embarking on any further examination of the intersections between them, it would be useful to be able to draw on characterizations both of philosophy and of the information sciences—ideally by considering suggestions of the necessary and sufficient conditions which must be satisfied before identifying any given work as a contribution to either philosophy or the information sciences. Some would say that to define either field would itself be to engage in philosophy; so maybe if we briefly indulge in an attempt to define the information sciences, it will become partially clear, through example, what philosophy of the information sciences is.

The goals of people engaged in any field of inquiry typically include not just fame, fortune, and happiness, but also the production of knowledge about (or, perhaps, the shedding of light on, or the making of sense of) a particular part or aspect of the world, through the construction of theories and explanations and the interpretation of meanings and understandings, and the application of that knowledge in a way that changes the world for the better in some respect. What is the particular part or aspect of the world with which the information sciences, especially, are concerned? In other words, what is the subject matter of the information sciences? What are they *about*?

The simplest answer, of course, would be that the information sciences are about information. Perhaps this answer could be extended relatively uncontroversially to include, as the subject matter of the information sciences, certain phenomena that are thought to be closely related to information, and the ways in which people interact with information and with information-related phenomena. Even taking this short step, however, would likely dismay some who would prefer to treat an emphasis on people's interactions with information as merely one example of a range of approaches that may possibly be taken to the study of information, each of which is associated with a number of presuppositions about the nature of information and its role in the world. In any case, such a barely extended answer would require augmentation in several respects before it could provide real insight into the nature of the information sciences. Helpful additions would include: a definition of information; enumeration and description of information-related phenomena, and indication of the respects in which and strengths with which they are related; and enumeration and description of ways in which people interact with information and with information-related phenomena.

Definitions of Information

Different conceptions of information have attracted consensus to different degrees in different communities. The multiplicity of current conceptions partly reflects the lack of agreement among communities on a prioritization of the desiderata that a conception should satisfy. In particular, the outlook for those who would hold out for a "one size fits all," transdisciplinary definition of information is not promising. It is possible, nevertheless, to identify a number of general categories or families of conceptions of information that have proven useful in relatively broad ranges of contexts.

1. A *semiotic* family. In conceptions in this group, distinctions are typically made on the one hand between: 1) real-world states, facts, or situations; 2) mental representations of those situations; and 3) linguistic expressions of those representations, and on the other between tokens and types, of situations, representations, and expressions—forming a model (of the relationships between reality, thought, and language) of the kind roughly depicted in Fig. 1.[8] Each distinct conception of information in this family equates information with the content of a different cell in the model. For many, the crucial decision will be to choose between a conception of information-as-signal (Buckland's "information-as-thing"), and one of information-as-message (Buckland's "information-as-knowledge"), but conceptions of information as the stuff of which real-world states are actually composed are not rare.[9–11] *Objectivist* versions of the popular view of information-as-message assert that information resources (texts, sentences, words, characters, bits) "contain" information, that information resources "have" meanings, that "the" meaning of an information resource is discoverable by all, and that whether a given information resource has a given meaning is an objective matter. *Subjectivist* versions recognize, in contrast, that information resources do not "have" meanings, but that different meanings are assigned to the same resource by different people at different

	Real-world situations: Information as reality	Mental representations: Information as message, meaning, knowledge, image	Linguistic expressions: Information as signal, vehicle, data, document, thing
Tokens / Particulars	States of affairs	Thoughts	Utterances
Types / Universals		Propositions	Sentences

Fig. 1 A semiotic model of the relationships between reality, thought, and language.

times, and that "the" conventional meaning of a given resource is a matter of intersubjective consensus.[12]

2. A *sociocognitive* family. In conceptions in this group, the emphasis is on action and process, and especially on processes by which people become informed or inform others. Information is conceived either as the act that causes a change in a person's mental state or internal "knowledge structure," or as the event in which such change takes place.[13,14] Different theorists have different views about the respective strengths of different kinds of influence on the effects of the informing act. Adherents to a *physical*, systems-oriented paradigm that is based on a literal reading of Shannon's mathematical theory of communication[15] ascribe no role to the intentions of the individual person, whereas proponents of the *cognitive*, user-oriented viewpoint allow that the nature of the change wrought on an individual's mental model or image of the world by a given informative act depends at least partly on the prior state of that individual model. The main theme of the *sociological*, community-oriented paradigm is that individuals' images of the world are shaped at least partly by those individuals' understandings of others' views, while the *cultural*, discourse-oriented paradigm derives from a recognition that the world itself is socially constructed in a strong sense, i.e. as a direct result of people talking about it.[16]
3. An *epistemic* family. Conceptions of information in this group are developed with the aim of providing an account of the properties that an information resource must have if the beliefs that are generated upon interpreting the content of that resource may be said to be justified. These are conceptions of information-as-*evidence*.[17] On the relatively few occasions on which information is taken seriously in the philosophical literature as a category to be distinguished carefully from knowledge, it is typical for "information" to be equated roughly with "evidence," and for the primary question about information to be understood as the question about what the evidence must be like to justify a given belief-that-*p*, and thus to qualify that belief (if it is one that is true) as knowledge. Theories of *semantic information* (also known as informational semantics) have been developed that propose probabilistic methods of evaluating the informativeness of evidence as the degree to which it provides warrant or grounds for believing-that-*p*. Such methods typically involve calculating the unexpectedness of the observed evidence given the probabilities of occurrence of all the possible alternatives. In this sense, they derive from Shannon's "information theory" (i.e., the mathematical theory of communication), and form the core of the branch of philosophy of knowledge known as *information-theoretic epistemology*.[15,18] The project that Floridi calls "Philosophy of Information" (PI) is a major contribution to this subfield.[19]

Information-Related Phenomena

Different kinds of phenomena may be considered to be "related" to information (howsoever information is defined) in different ways. Some phenomena may be seen to be related in virtue of their being the same kinds of things as information. Conceptions of information-as-message, for example, tend to be held at the same time as conceptions of knowledge-as-message, in which case knowledge and information are said to be related in the sense of their being identical. On the other hand, in such conceptions, information is distinguishable from data on the basis that information is the content or meaning of data: here, information and data are related, not in virtue of a conceptual identity, but in virtue of one (information) being a kind of property of the other (data). Similarly, authors, indexers, and searchers are related to information in respect of their being agents that are involved in the creation, representation, and seeking of information resources; libraries, archives, and museums are related to information in respect of their being institutions that are involved in the preservation and provision of access to collections of information resources; aboutness and relevance are related to information in respect of their being relations that structure networks of information resources; and so on.

Kinds of Human–Information Interaction

Lists of information-related phenomena are necessarily endless, and of limited utility: what is potentially more interesting from a philosophical perspective is the structure of fundamental categories of phenomena (e.g., objects, properties, relations, agents) developed by the listmaker. Similarly, no list of the kinds of things that we might imagine people wanting to do to, with, or through information could be exhaustive, no matter what definition of information is accepted. But taxonomists of information-related actions or events commonly adopt a framework that is loosely based on the notion of an information life cycle, whereby information resources (if not the meanings attributed to those resources) are assumed to have a concrete existence in space–time, and to be subject to change and to processes of cause and effect. Within such a framework, distinctions are often made between the following categories of actions or events: production, creation, and generation; reproduction; preservation and storage; representation, description, cataloging, registration, and documentation; organization, arrangement, and classification; transfer, communication, retrieval, and provision of access; search, discovery, and seeking; evaluation and appraisal; use and application; and destruction.

The Scope of the Information Sciences

The aggregate scope of the fields collectively labeled "the information sciences" or "information studies" is very broad. Any precise delineation of that scope will depend partly on the sense in which "information" is understood. Different authors, working with different conceptions of information, continue to define the scope of the information sciences in very different ways. There nonetheless appears to be a reasonably stable consensus about the identity of those areas of concern that collectively form a central core, in contrast to other areas that are typically recognized as more peripheral. One formulation of the goals of projects associated with this core might run as follows:

1. Understanding the nature of information, of information-related phenomena, and of human–information interaction.
2. Understanding the identities, purposes, motivations, intentions, needs, desires, and actions of people engaged in interaction with information.
3. Designing and building systems, services, and structures that help people to meet their goals when interacting with information.
4. Developing and administering policies and institutions that enable and/or constrain people's interactions with information.

Within this framework, it is possible also to distinguish between a conception of the information sciences (or of some of its components) as essentially descriptive, devoted to the construction of theories that explain how information-related events actually do occur in the real world and why real people actually do act and think in the ways that they do, and a conception of the field as essentially prescriptive or normative, devoted to the specification of the ways in which things should happen and the ways in which people should act.

In pursuing projects of these kinds, information scientists draw on theories and practices developed in many overlapping fields of inquiry, not least of which is philosophy and its various branches. Understandings of the nature of information and of information-related phenomena are constructed in the light of developments in metaphysics, epistemology, ethics, and logic, as well as in the humanistic fields of art theory, literary theory, semiotics, linguistics, and history. Understandings of the activities of information users build on the behavioral and cognitive models developed in the life sciences: biology, psychology, cognitive science. Information systems design is informed by work done in engineering, technology, and design fields, including computer science; while information policy development and institutional management rely on insights generated by the social sciences and related applied fields: sociology, anthropology, political science, economics, public policy, business administration, and law. Notwithstanding one's readiness to accept the particular formulation of the core of the information sciences presented above, the extent to which the content of the information sciences overlaps with that of "other" fields should be clear.

PHILOSOPHY

The question "What is philosophy?" is a meta-question about philosophy. It is one that arises in philosophy of philosophy (a.k.a. metaphilosophy). Answers of many different kinds have been proposed since the original identification of philosophy as a discrete field in the ancient era. These proposals may be categorized on the basis of the kinds of criteria on which each proposal distinguishes philosophy from other fields. For example, one proposal might be to distinguish philosophy from other fields by pointing to differences between the kinds of *phenomena* that form the subject matter of philosophy and those of other fields; another might point to differences in the kinds of *questions* that are asked in philosophy and in the other fields; another might point to differences in the kinds of *methods* that are used to answer the questions that arise in philosophy and in the other fields; while yet another might point to differences in the kinds of *goals* or purposes that motivate people to engage in philosophy and in the other fields.

Different kinds of proposals have attracted varying levels of consensus at different times and in different places. It is important, yet difficult, to avoid misleading overgeneralization when characterizing the state of philosophy, even when the scope of the exercise is deliberately restricted to whatever is called "philosophy" by those who claim to practice it in a particular culture, such as the academy in the "western" world of the early twenty-first century. A simple caricature of the nature of philosophy at this point in its history might emphasize its concern with the most basic, fundamental, or foundational of phenomena (such as action, beauty, belief, being, causation, consciousness, evidence, existence, experience, goodness, identity, intentionality, justice, knowledge, meaning, necessity, rationality, reality, representation, responsibility, rightness, thought, time, truth, value, and virtue); its concern to ask the most basic of questions (such as "What is *x*?," "How do we know that *p*?," and "Why ought we do *a*?"); its promotion of, and reliance upon, the most basic of methods in answering such questions (such as analysis of the very concepts that are used in expressing the questions, analysis of the logical form of arguments, and analysis of the mental processes by which we interpret our worlds); and its pursuit of the most basic of goals (such as truth, happiness, justice, peace, authenticity, power, and an understanding of the meaning of life). Such a caricature would fail to represent several significant respects in which metaphilosophy inspires ongoing debate:

1. The ways in which contemporary "western" philosophy is similar to and different from philosophy as practiced in "other" contemporary cultures, and from philosophy as practiced in earlier eras.
2. The ways in which philosophy as traditionally practiced is infected with systemic biases deriving from its domination by old, white, middle-class, heterosexual males.
3. The ways in which twentieth-century "analytic" philosophy (also known, somewhat misleadingly, as Anglophone or Anglo-American philosophy) is similar to and different from twentieth-century "continental" philosophy (also known, again somewhat misleadingly, as European philosophy).
4. The ways in which several historically specific "turns" or transdisciplinary shifts in emphasis (such as "the cognitive turn," "the linguistic turn," and "the cultural turn") have affected different groups' understanding of the nature of inquiry in general and the proper purpose of philosophy in particular.
5. The extent to which philosophy is conceived as having: 1) a normative or prescriptive rather than merely descriptive purpose, on account of which conclusions are drawn about how the world *ought* to be, as well as or instead of about how the world *is*; and 2) an "applied" as well as a "pure" function, in which real-world decision-making is informed by insights derived from philosophical analysis.
6. The ways in which different communities of philosophical practice emphasize different criteria for evaluating the results of philosophical analysis: e.g., truth, correspondence with external reality, internal coherence, power, utility for producing testable theory, utility for controlling future events, richness of coverage, simplicity, and elegance.
7. The ways in which the methods and goals of philosophy are similar to and different from those of the empirical or natural sciences, and the ways in which, historically, the pendulum of dominant opinion has swung between rationalism (very roughly, the view that a priori knowledge is possible) and empiricism (which denies the possibility of any kind of justification for knowledge other than experience).
8. The ways in which philosophy may be divided into discrete branches or subfields.

At the most general level, it has become conventional to distinguish between, on the one hand, a small number of long-standing subfields such as metaphysics (which focuses on questions to do with being and existence), epistemology (knowledge and belief), ethics (goodness), aesthetics (beauty), phenomenology (experience), and philosophical logic (truth), and on the other, a much larger number of subfields with (in most cases) shorter histories, whose names typically take the form "philosophy of *x*." There are branches of philosophy that are concerned with the fundamental ways in which human beings relate to their selves, to one another, and to their environments: philosophy of mind, philosophy of language, and philosophy of action. And there are branches of philosophy that are concerned with particular intellectual, creative, spiritual, social, and physical pursuits: philosophy of education, philosophy of art, philosophy of technology, philosophy of religion, political philosophy, and philosophy of sport. There are branches of philosophy that are concerned with particular disciplines, fields, professions, and practices: philosophy of science (including philosophy of physics, of mathematics, of psychology, of the social sciences, of the information sciences, etc.), philosophy of history, and philosophy of law. And there are branches of philosophy concerned with particular phenomena: philosophy of time, philosophy of race, and philosophy of information.

These branches of philosophy are themselves social constructs. Their boundaries are entirely arbitrary and far from definite. Insights derived from any one are regularly applied in (or, just as regularly, contradicted by) work done in another. Both philosophy of information and philosophy of the information sciences, for instance, are informed by many findings, claims, and proposals originating in other of the branches of philosophy listed above. That the findings, claims, and proposals that originate in philosophy of information and philosophy of the information sciences likewise inform the work done in those other branches is a claim that warrants further investigation (see "Conclusion," below).

PHILOSOPHY OF INFORMATION

Some of the questions asked *in* the information sciences are philosophical questions and it is in this sense that philosophy and the information sciences overlap.

Metaphysics

Some of these philosophical questions are *metaphysical* questions, in that they are motivated by a desire to understand the essential nature of information-related phenomena, and the roles or positions of those phenomena within the totality of phenomena. For instance, we may ask: What is information? What are documents, data, records, metadata? What are works, texts, editions, versions, copies? What are representations, reproductions, images? What are information sources, information structures? What is relevance, aboutness, authorship? What are subjects? What are authors, indexers, searchers? What is information production, reproduction, representation, preservation, storage, organization, access, seeking, transfer, retrieval, evaluation, use, destruction? The basic motivation for attending to questions of these kinds is the prediction that our answers—developed by carrying out careful analysis of the concepts or categories that we construct and use to think about real-world substances and properties—will help us to clarify our thoughts, strengthen our arguments, and improve the quality of the decisions and actions taken on the basis of the conclusions of those arguments.

Some of these metaphysical questions can be construed as *ontological* questions. Ontology is the branch of metaphysics that is concerned to identify and understand the fundamental categories or kinds of things that exist in the world. For any of the phenomena listed above, we may ask, What kind of thing is it? An abstract thing or a concrete thing? A universal or a particular? A substance or a property? An object or an event? A set or an element? One of the tasks of ontology is to identify and characterize these different categories.[20] It may sometimes be helpful to distinguish between "pure" ontology in that sense and the "applied" ontology that is being done when information-related phenomena are being fitted into any predefined categorical structure.[21] (Another sense of applied ontology is that which is used to encompass work on modeling the kinds of entities and relationships about which information is to be stored in databases.[22]) In virtue of its focus on human-created artifacts that are the objects of human interpretation, ontology of information is closely related both to ontology of art (including ontology of literature) and to projects with metaphysical ramifications in philosophy of language and representation and in semiotics.[23,24]

Epistemology

Some of the philosophical questions that are asked in the information sciences are *epistemological* questions, in that they are motivated by a desire to understand the ways in which information and other information-related phenomena are involved in the processes by which belief can become knowledge.

In the information sciences, just as there is no standard conception of information, there is no standard conception of knowledge. The two main rival views are those of knowledge as true information (or information about the facts, i.e., information about the way the world really is), and knowledge as internalized information (i. e., the content of individuals' mental images or representations of the world). These both differ from the theory of knowledge that is traditionally provided by epistemology, which is that knowledge is justified true belief. In other words, for any one of our beliefs to count as knowledge, it must be both 1) one that is true, and 2) one for which justification can be provided. Different forms of the traditional theory give different accounts of what it means for a belief to be evaluated as true, how the truth-value of a belief may be determined, how justifications of different kinds may be supplied, what degree of certainty is required of a justification, and so on.

For the information scientist, there is a dual motivation for studying and contributing to epistemology. In the first place, we may learn about potentially productive methods of generating information-scientific knowledge (see the section below on "Philosophy of the Information Sciences"). In the second place, if we accept the idea that there is some sort of conceptual relationship between information and knowledge, we are only a short step away from accepting that what we say about the nature of knowledge and about how it is acquired will influence what we say both about the nature of information and about how we collect, organize, and provide access to the content of information sources (i.e., recorded knowledge). An understanding of epistemology thus helps us to determine what our information structures, systems, services, policies, and institutions ought to be like, and what they ought to do, if the processes by which we interact with information are to result in the satisfaction of our "epistemic objectives"—e.g., the rapid, cheap, and easy acquisition of all and only those beliefs that are justified, true, and relevant.[25]

Historically, there have been two main points of intersection between epistemology and the information sciences. Firstly, and as already mentioned above in the section on "Definitions of Information", some accounts of justification rely on a particular conception of *information-as-evidence*. Secondly, library scientists were among the first to express and address the idea that the processes by which knowledge is acquired are significantly *social* in several respects. Margaret Egan and Jesse Shera were the first authors to use the term "social epistemology" in print, and focused on demonstrating how an understanding of the ways in which social groups (as well as individuals) acquire knowledge can be applied in the design of information services to those groups.[26–28] More recently, epistemologists such as Alvin Goldman have been concerned to give an account of the conditions under which social processes such as the provision and receipt of testimony can result in the acquisition of knowledge, and a number of philosophical analyses have been undertaken of trust, reputation, authority, reliability, and other criteria for evaluating the likelihood that information sources of various kinds will be productive of epistemically valuable beliefs.[29–31]

Ethics

Several branches of philosophy deal with questions of value or goodness, and with claims about the kinds of things that ought to be done in given situations. Social and political philosophy, for example, are concerned with the evaluation of public policy, and governmental activity, and group interaction, and with the analysis of socially valuable states such as justice and freedom. Aesthetics is concerned to establish criteria upon which works of art may be evaluated. Ethics is concerned with the rightness of actions in general. Within ethics, some fairly fuzzy boundaries may be drawn between ethical theory, meta-ethics, and applied ethics. Ethical theories propose criteria for distinguishing between right and wrong actions; meta-ethics categorizes ethical theories and analyzes the concepts and assumptions on which they are based; and projects in applied ethics demonstrate the consequences of applying particular ethical theories as guides to action in particular situations.

As we approach the end of the first decade of the twenty-first century, information ethics is the most visible of subfields of philosophy of information. This is a field which already has its own international association, its own journals, and its own handbooks.[32] "Information ethics" is typically understood to include "computer ethics," and to emphasize questions about the ethical implementation and use of information technologies, but rarely to the exclusion of more general questions about the ethical provision and use of information services (online or off-line; computerized or not). For the information policymaker, systems developer, or service provider, the fundamental ethical question is: Who should have what level of access to what information? The issues that tend to arise in the evaluation of rival answers to this question include equity of access to information; intellectual freedom; information privacy and confidentiality; and intellectual property.[33] The literature on each of these issues is large and straddles the boundaries between ethical theory, meta-ethics, and applied ethics. Further research on meta-ethical categories and concepts can only raise the profile of information ethics within mainstream philosophy circles even higher.

Other Branches

Other branches of philosophy upon which work in the information sciences has touched more than momentarily include philosophies of action, art, communication, education, history, language, law, logic, mathematics, mind, representation, science, and technology, as well as critical theory, hermeneutics, and phenomenology. A comprehensive review would require more space than allotted here. In an attempt to succinctly demonstrate the diversity of philosophical approaches that may potentially be taken in the information sciences, in this section a particular object of information-scientific study is selected, and a number of specific issues highlighted as ones that could be productively addressed from various, overlapping, philosophically informed perspectives. The selected object of study is the design of a service for the effective provision of access to relevant information resources or documents (i.e., a document retrieval or resource discovery system).

- What are documents? What kinds of things are they?—Metaphysics.
- What is the nature of the relationship between a document and the work that it instantiates? What is the nature of the relationships between a document and the classes of similar documents of which it is a member?—Philosophy of art; Philosophy of logic; Philosophy of mathematics.
- What do documents do? How do they "mean"? How do they inform?—Philosophy of representation; Philosophy of language; Philosophy of mind; Epistemology.
- How do documents serve as evidence? How does the informational value of a document relate to its evidential value?—Epistemology; Philosophy of science; Philosophy of history; Philosophy of law.
- What is the nature of people's conscious experience of interacting with documents, with information, with information services?—Phenomenology; Hermeneutics; Philosophy of mind.
- What is information? What is the difference between information, education, and entertainment? What kinds of motivation do people have for choosing to engage with information, education, and entertainment services? How do we evaluate these interactions?—Metaphysics; Philosophy of action; Philosophy of education; Philosophy of communication; Philosophy of language; Philosophy of value.
- What is effectiveness? How do we determine how effective information services are?—Philosophy of value; Philosophy of technology; Epistemology.
- What is relevance? How does relevance relate to other epistemic values? How do we determine how relevant a document is?—Philosophy of logic; Philosophy of value; Philosophy of mind; Epistemology.

- What is access? How does access relate to other socially important objectives, such as preservation? In what ways are information services socially valuable? How should access to information resources be distributed among members of a given social group? How should resources be represented and organized so that access is optimized?—Social and political philosophy; Ethics; Critical theory.

PHILOSOPHY OF THE INFORMATION SCIENCES

Some of the questions asked *about* the information sciences are philosophical questions. The aggregate of these questions forms the field of *philosophy of the information sciences*. On a strict view, philosophy and the information sciences do not literally overlap in this sense, since philosophy of the information sciences is a branch only of philosophy (specifically, of philosophy of science), not of the information sciences.

The goals of philosophy of the information sciences may be stated as follows:

- To locate and illuminate the position of the information sciences as a group of fields in the universe of inquiry, i.e., to understand their role in interpreting and changing the world, their internal structure, and their relationships with other fields.
- To provide justifications for any decision to engage in information-scientific research.
- To provide orientations toward and directions for information-scientific practice by identifying the kinds of problems that are most significant, the kinds of questions that are most relevant, the kinds of methodologies that are most reliable, and the kinds of answers that are most acceptable.

There are two general approaches to philosophy of the information sciences. One is more descriptive, passive, and sociohistorical: the emphasis is on giving an explanatory account of what information scientists actually do, and what they have actually done, to locate themselves in the academic universe, justify their decisions, and orient their practices. Another flavor of philosophy of the information sciences is more prescriptive, active, normative, and (it might be argued) genuinely philosophical: the assumption is that philosophy of the information sciences should determine what the information sciences should be about, now and in the future.

Some of the questions asked in philosophy of the information sciences are *metaphysical* questions. For example: Do the information sciences share a distinctive ontology, or a distinctive view of the kinds of things that exist in the world? The short answer here appears to be "No." Any acceptance, explicit or implicit, of a proposition that a given category of things exists is an ontological commitment. Different theories in the information sciences, constructed by scholars working in different subfields, have different ontological commitments. Often, however, the precise nature of a theory's ontological commitments will not be made clear at the time of the theory's presentation, even though it may well be recognized that any evaluation of the theory will depend partly on an evaluation of those commitments.

Many of the philosophical questions that are asked about the information sciences are *epistemological* questions, in that they are motivated by a concern to understand the various kinds of knowledge that are produced, and the various processes by which knowledge is producible, in the information sciences. Even more specifically, such questions are normative, methodological questions about the ways in which research in the information sciences ought to be carried out—about the ways in which hypotheses should be tested, results interpreted, and theories constructed. Again, we might ask: Do the information sciences share a distinctive methodology, or a distinctive view of how knowledge claims might be generated and defended? And again the answer appears to be "No."

One common way of distinguishing among fields of inquiry or communities of inquirers is to locate the fields or communities somewhere between two opposite poles according to their methodological assumptions. Kuhn,[34] for instance, distinguishes between those academic communities whose members generally find themselves in agreement about the kinds of question that they ought to be asking (and about the kinds of method that they ought to be using to arrive at answers), and those "preparadigmatic" communities that presently lack such consensus (but that continue to strive toward it). Becher[35] develops a two-dimensional model that distinguishes between the "hard pure" (natural sciences and mathematics), "hard applied" (science-based professions, such as engineering), "soft applied" (social professions, such as education and law), and "soft pure" (social sciences and humanities). In Becher's model and others like it, the hard–soft dimension roughly corresponds to a scientific–humanistic distinction. "Hard" fields are restricted in scope, studying a clearly delineated range of physical phenomena with a limited range of tried-and-tested methods, with the positivist goal of establishing general, deterministic laws of cause and effect that can each be used to explain the occurrence of large numbers of discrete events. Members of "hard" communities tend to make objectivist assumptions about the nature of reality, of truth, and of knowledge: scientists typically proceed, for example, on the basis that it is possible to acquire knowledge of "the" truth about "the" real world. "Soft" fields, in contrast, are more open to the study of complex, messy, lumpy problems, using a wide range of exploratory methods to come to interpretative understandings, both of the unique constellations of factors that produce particular events, and of the meanings those events have for individuals and for groups. Members of "soft" communities typically allow that our knowledge of the world (if not the world itself) is both socially constructed, in the sense that our beliefs are shaped not only by the ways in which we interpret others' beliefs about the world, and perspectival or relative, in the sense that the "truth" (or goodness) of our beliefs may be evaluated differently depending on the evaluator's present point of view.

Several communities of inquirers who have self-identified with a focus on information and information-related phenomena have a long tradition of soul-searching when it comes to locating themselves among the four quadrants of the Becherian model. Many commentators have drawn attention, in more or less exasperated tones, to the positivist nature of much of the research in the information sciences,[36,37] and such observations have usually been accompanied by impassioned calls for a "softening" (in the Becherian sense) of information research. These days, we are more likely to read about information studies' hospitality to a plurality of approaches, the implication being that each of its different subfields can be comfortably located in different quadrants, or even that each of its topics or problem sets can be explored using multiple methods originating in different quadrants. Bates,[11] for instance, distinguishes nomothetic (hard, scientific, universal) from idiographic (soft, humanistic, particular) approaches, and describes 13 separate approaches to library and information science that can be located along the nomothetic–idiographic spectrum.

Humanistically oriented scholars are more likely to emphasize questions about the relations between information and the following (among other phenomena): conscious experience and the human condition; interpretation and sensemaking; meaning, language, and discourse; ideology, race, class, and gender; identity and diversity; preservation and cultural heritage; remembering and forgetting; narratives and stories; and aesthetic and moral value. Several attempts have been made to develop complete epistemological frameworks for such research, based variously on phenomenology, hermeneutics, critical theory, and discourse analysis. An understanding of philosophy of representation, itself a diffuse area, would appear to be a quality shared by proponents of the emergent view that the information sciences are properly about the relation between people and (not technology, nor even information, but) *reality*.[38]

Comparative evaluation of the propriety of rival approaches to the information sciences is a difficult task. We could choose to ignore that the issue exists, or at least to deny that it is important (other than perhaps from a sociohistorical perspective), given that the bundling up of questions and methods to form more or less distinct fields is essentially arbitrary and varies historically and culturally according to how phenomena are perceived rather than according to how the phenomena change in themselves. A more productive approach might be to focus on establishing the criteria (truth, power, utility, etc.) upon which different approaches may be evaluated, and the methods by which an approach's "performance" against such criteria may be measured.

META-QUESTIONS ABOUT PHILOSOPHY

Just as there are meta-questions (philosophical, historical, sociological, and political) to be asked about the information sciences, there are meta-questions that may be asked both about Philosophy of Information and about philosophy of the information sciences. These include questions about when, where, and how philosophy of these kinds has been done, who it has been done by, and what motivations people have had for doing it. Such questions are asked by historians and sociologists of philosophy.

It is relatively easy to trace the histories of a few well-defined branches of philosophy of information: information ethics, information-theoretic epistemology, and social epistemology come to mind. But, taken as wholes, both philosophy of information and philosophy of the information sciences are diffuse, unbounded fields that lack scholarly associations, journals, textbooks, and reputations. The high-quality work that exists remains scattered, infrequently cited, and (one sometimes suspects) unread. The appearance in the early 2000s of several special issues of journals devoted to topics in philosophy of information demonstrates that the field is gradually attaining some degree of respectability within the information sciences (if not within philosophy); but, given the field's lack of a clearly expressed identity, it is probably too early to expect any significant contributions to an understanding of its historical development. When that history is written, it will assuredly be of great interest to scholars wishing to see how the kinds of philosophical questions asked in the information sciences, and the kinds of answers offered, have changed over the years, which long-standing assumptions and beliefs (if any) have been challenged by the various paradigm shifts that have been identified in the broader academy, and how social factors have played a role in those developments.

Some of the meta-questions about philosophy of information and philosophy of the information sciences are themselves philosophical questions. For instance, we may ask what kinds of questions ought to form the content of each field, and how each kind of philosophy ought to be done. Contributions to the general field of metaphilosophy, which examine the nature of philosophy and the nature of motivations to engage in philosophical thinking, may serve as provocative resources in this regard.

CONCLUSION

The intent of this entry has been to examine the influence of philosophy on the information sciences. As part of any general quest to understand the interdisciplinary nature of information studies,[39] we may well wish to look in the opposite direction and ask, To what extent do the information sciences contribute to "mainstream" philosophy? The short answer here is... well, "Hardly at all." The "trade deficit" produced by the imbalance between intellectual imports (from philosophy to information studies) and exports (to philosophy from information studies) could doubtless be demonstrated bibliometrically (see, e.g., Cronin and Meho[40] for a description of the kinds of method that might be used). Certainly, the frequency with which contributions to the literature of the information sciences are cited in the literature of philosophy is vanishingly low. Moreover, the respective statuses within the general philosophical community of philosophy of information (in the broader, pre-Floridian sense) and philosophy of the information sciences sometimes seem to be roughly on a par with that of the philosophy of pasta. Things may change in the future as increasing numbers of philosophers first find inspiration in information-related phenomena and subsequently become aware of the existence of an entire field that, for one reason and another, has often struggled to attract the academic respect for which it has yearned. The most philosophically interesting of contributions to the information sciences—those with the highest potential value for philosophy, if only they were to be disseminated appropriately—include the following:

- Marcia Bates's definitions of fundamental forms of information.[2]
- David Blair's analysis of the implications of contemporary philosophy of language for our understanding of information retrieval as a linguistic process.[41,42]
- Brien Brothman's deconstruction of conceptions of record and evidence in archival discourse.[43]
- John Budd's evaluation of the prospects for a phenomenological approach to information studies.[44]
- Rafael Capurro's assessment of the significance of intercultural information ethics.[45]
- Ron Day's critical-theoretic analysis of the discourse and rhetoric of the information society.[46]
- Don Fallis's development of epistemic value theory as an approach to the evaluation of information services.[25]
- Luciano Floridi's and Kay Mathiesen's analyses of the moral value of information.[47,48]
- Bernd Frohmann's discourse-analytic reformulation of traditional epistemological frameworks for the study of scholars' information behavior.[49]
- Kenneth Einar Himma's meta-analysis of justifications for the legal protection of intellectual property rights.[50]
- Birger Hjørland's examination of the epistemological assumptions underlying the practice of library and information science.[51]
- Allen Renear's examination of the metaphysical assumptions underlying the design of data models for library and museum catalogs.[52]
- Keith van Rijsbergen's (and colleagues') demonstration of the utility of mathematical logic (including nonclassical systems of logic) for modeling the process of information retrieval.[53]
- Patrick Wilson's and Elaine Svenonius's incomparable explications of the philosophical foundations of bibliographic description and organization.[54,55]

REFERENCES

1. Case, D.O. The concept of information. In *Looking for Information: A Survey of Research on Information Seeking, Needs, and Behavior*; 2nd Ed.; Academic Press: London, U.K., 2007; 40–67.
2. Bates, M.J. Fundamental forms of information. J. Am. Soc. Inform. Sci. Technol. **2006**, *57* (8), 1033–1045.
3. Floridi, L. Information. In *The Blackwell Guide to the Philosophy of Computing and Information*; Floridi, L., Ed.; Blackwell: Oxford, U.K., 2003; 40–61.
4. Floridi, L. Is information meaningful data? Philos. Phenomenol. Res. **2005**, *70* (2), 351–370.
5. Williamson, T. *The Philosophy of Philosophy*; Blackwell: Oxford, U.K., 2007.
6. White, H.D.; McCain, K.W. Visualizing a discipline: An author co-citation analysis of information science, 1972–1995. J. Am. Soc. Inform. Sci. **1998**, *49* (4), 327–355.
7. Bates, M.J. The invisible substrate of information science. J. Am. Soc. Inform. Sci. **1999**, *50* (12), 1043–1050.
8. Furner, J. Information studies without information. Libr. Trends **2004**, *52* (3), 427–446.
9. Buckland, M. Information as thing. J. Am. Soc. Inform. Sci. **1991**, *42* (5), 351–360.
10. Floridi, L. Open problems in the philosophy of information. Metaphilosophy **2004**, *35* (4), 554–582.
11. Bates, M.J. An introduction to metatheories, theories, and models. In *Theories of Information Behavior*; Fisher, K.E.; Erdelez, S.; McKechnie, L., Eds.; Information Today: Medford, NJ, 2005; 1–24.
12. Hjørland, B. The concept of "subject" in information science. J. Doc. **1992**, *48* (2), 172–200.
13. Brookes, B.C. The foundations of information science, Part I: Philosophical aspects. J. Inform. Sci. **1980**, *2* (3/4), 125–133.
14. Belkin, N.J. The cognitive viewpoint in information science. J. Inform. Sci. **1990**, *16* (1), 11–15.
15. Shannon, C.E. A mathematical theory of communication. Bell Syst. Tech. J. **1948**, *27*, 379–423. 623–656.
16. Talja, S.; Tuominen, K.; Savolainen, R. "Isms" in information science: Constructivism, collectivism and constructionism. J. Doc. **2005**, *61* (1), 79–101.
17. Furner, J. Conceptual analysis: A method for understanding information as evidence, and evidence as information. Archiv. Sci. **2004**, *4* (3/4), 233–265.
18. Dretske, F.I. *Knowledge and the Flow of Information*; MIT Press: Cambridge, MA, 1981.

19. Floridi, L. What is the philosophy of information? Metaphilosophy **2002**, *33* (1/2), 123–145.
20. Lowe, E.J. *The Four-Category Ontology: A Metaphysical Foundation for Natural Science*; Oxford University Press: Oxford, U.K., 2006.
21. Smith, B. Ontology. In *The Blackwell Guide to the Philosophy of Computing and Information*; Floridi, L., Ed.; Blackwell: Oxford, U.K., 2003; 155–166.
22. Le Boeuf, P. FRBR: Hype or cure-all? Introd. Catalog. Classif. Q. **2005**, *39* (3/4), 1–13.
23. Thomasson, A.I. The ontology of art. In *The Blackwell Guide to Aesthetics*; Kivy, P., Ed.; Blackwell: Oxford, U.K., 2003; 78–92.
24. Mai, J.-E. Semiotics and indexing: An analysis of the subject indexing process. J. Doc. **2001**, *57* (5), 591–622.
25. Fallis, D. Social epistemology and information science. In *Annual Review of Information Science and Technology*; Cronin, B., Ed.; Information Today: Medford, NJ, 2006; Vol. 40, 475–519.
26. Egan, M.E.; Shera, J.H. Foundations of a theory of bibliography. Libr. Q. **1952**, *22* (2), 125–137.
27. Furner, J. Shera's social epistemology recast as psychological bibliology. Soc. Epistemol. **2002**, *16* (1), 5–22.
28. Furner, J. "A brilliant mind": Margaret Egan and social epistemology. Libr. Trends **2004**, *52* (4), 792–809.
29. Goldman, A.I. *Knowledge in a Social World*; Oxford University Press: Oxford, 1999.
30. Goldman, A.I. Social epistemology. In *Stanford Encyclopedia of Philosophy*; Zalta, E.N., Ed.; Metaphysics Research Lab, Center for the Study of Language and Information, Stanford University: Stanford, CA, 2006.
31. Wilson, P. *Second-Hand Knowledge: An Inquiry into Cognitive Authority*; Greenwood: Westport, CT, 1983.
32. Himma, K.E.; Tavani, H.T., Eds. *The Handbook of Information and Computer Ethics*; Wiley: Hoboken, NJ, 2008.
33. Fallis, D. Information ethics for 21st century library professionals. Libr. Hi Tech. **2007**, *25* (1), 23–36.
34. Kuhn, T.S. *The Structure of Scientific Revolutions*; University of Chicago Press: Chicago, IL, 1962.
35. Becher, T. The significance of disciplinary differences. Stud. High. Educ. **1994**, *19* (2), 151–161.
36. Ellis, D. Theory and explanation in information retrieval research. J. Inform. Sci. **1984**, *8* (1), 25–38.
37. Harris, M.J. The dialectic of defeat: Antimonies [sic] in research in library and information science. Libr. Trends **1986**, *34* (3), 515–531.
38. Borgmann, A. *Holding on to Reality: The Nature of Information at the Turn of the Millennium*; University of Chicago Press: Chicago, IL, 1999.
39. Smith, L.C. Interdisciplinarity: Approaches to understanding library and information science as an interdisciplinary field. In *Conceptions of Library and Information Science: Historical, Empirical and Theoretical Perspectives*; Vakkari, P., Cronin, B., Eds.; Taylor Graham: London, U.K., 1992; 253–267.
40. Cronin, B.; Meho, L.I. The shifting balance of intellectual trade in information studies. J. Am. Soc. Inform. Sci. Technol. **2008**, *59* (4), 551–564.
41. Blair, D.C. Information retrieval and the philosophy of language. In *Annual Review of Information Science and Technology*; Cronin, B., Ed.; Information Today: Medford, NJ, 2002; Vol. 37, 3–50.
42. Blair, D.C. *Wittgenstein, Language, and Information: "Back to the Rough Ground!"*; Springer: Dordrecht, the Netherlands, 2006.
43. Brothman, B. Afterglow: Conceptions of record and evidence in archival discourse. Archiv. Sci. **2002**, *2* (3/4), 311–342.
44. Budd, J.M. Phenomenology and information studies. J. Doc. **2005**, *61* (1), 44–59.
45. Capurro, R. Intercultural information ethics. In *The Handbook of Information and Computer Ethics*; Himma, K.E., Tavani, H.T., Eds.; Wiley: Hoboken, NJ, 2008; 639–665.
46. Day, R.E. *The Modern Invention of Information: Discourse, History, and Power*; Southern Illinois University Press: Carbondale, IL, 2001.
47. Floridi, L. On the intrinsic value of information objects and the infosphere. Ethics Inform. Technol. **2002**, *4* (4), 287–304.
48. Mathiesen, K.K. What is information ethics? ACM SIGCAS Comput. Soc. **2004**, *34*(1).
49. Frohmann, B. *Deflating Information: From Science Studies to Documentation*; University of Toronto Press: Toronto, Ontario, Canada, 2004.
50. Himma, K.E. The justification of intellectual property: Contemporary philosophical disputes. J. Am. Soc. Inform. Sci. Technol. **2008**, *59* (7), 1143–1161.
51. Hjørland, B. Empiricism, rationalism and positivism in library and information science. J. Doc. **2005**, *61* (1), 130–155.
52. Renear, A.H.; Dubin, D. Three of the four FRBR Group 1 entity types are roles, not types. Proceedings of the 70th ASIS&T *Annual Meeting*, Milwaukee, WI, Oct, 19–24, 2007; Grove, A., Rorissa, A.Information Today: Medford, NJ, 2007.
53. van Rijsbergen, C.J. Another look at the logical uncertainty principle. Inform. Retriev. **2000**, *2* (1), 17–26.
54. Svenonius, E. *The Intellectual Foundation of Information Organization*; MIT Press: Cambridge, MA, 2000.
55. Wilson, P. *Two Kinds of Power: An Essay on Bibliographic Control*; University of California Press: Berkeley, CA, 1968.
56. Budd, J.M. *Knowledge and Knowing in Library and Information Science: A Philosophical Framework*; Scarecrow: Lanham, MD, 2001.
57. Capurro, R.; Hjørland, B. The concept of information. In *Annual Review of Information Science and Technology*; Cronin, B., Ed.; Information Today: Medford, NJ, 2002; Vol. 37, 343–411.
58. Cornelius, I.V. *Meaning and Method in Information Studies*; Ablex: Norwood, NJ, 1996.
59. Cornelius, I.V. Theorizing information for information science. In *Annual Review of Information Science and Technology*; Cronin, B., Ed.; Information Today: Medford, NJ, 2002; Vol. 36, 393–425.
60. Day, R.E. Poststructuralism and information studies. In *Annual Review of Information Science and Technology*; Cronin, B., Ed.; Information Today: Medford, NJ, 2005; Vol. 39, 575–609.
61. Hjørland, B. *Information Seeking and Subject Representation: An Activity-Theoretical Approach to Information Science*; Greenwood: Westport, CT, 1997.

BIBLIOGRAPHY

In philosophy, the standard encyclopedic sources are the 10-volume *Routledge Encyclopedia of Philosophy* (Craig, E., Ed; Routledge, 1998), and the continuously updated, online *Stanford Encyclopedia of Philosophy* (Zalta, E.N., Ed.; Metaphysics Research Lab, Center for the Study of Language and Information, Stanford University: Stanford, CA, 1997–). The standard bibliographic database is *The Philosopher's Index* (Philosopher's Information Center: Bowling Green, OH, 1967–). Leading publishers include Blackwell, Cambridge University Press, Oxford University Press, Routledge, and Springer. Useful series of collections of introductory essays to various branches of philosophy include the Blackwell Philosophy Guides, the Oxford Handbooks in Philosophy, and the Routledge Philosophy Companions. *The Blackwell Guide to the Philosophy of Computing and Information* (Floridi, L., Ed.; Blackwell: Oxford, 2003) is a title in the first of these series; Luciano Floridi's earlier monograph, *Philosophy and Computing* (Routledge: London, 1999) covers similar ground. *The Handbook of Information and Computer Ethics* (Himma, K.E., Tavani, H.T., Eds.; Wiley: Hoboken, NJ, 2008) is a comprehensive introduction to information ethics. The leading journals in philosophy include *Analysis, Journal of Philosophy, Mind, Noûs, Philosophical Quarterly, Philosophical Review, and Philosophical Studies*. There is no journal that is devoted exclusively to philosophy and information, but several titles cover areas of specialist interest: *Episteme* and *Social Epistemology* in epistemology; *Applied Ontology* and *Axiomathes* in ontology; *Ethics and Information Technology, International Review of Information Ethics, Journal of Information, Communication and Ethics in Society* and *Journal of Information Ethics* in ethics; etc.

In the information sciences, the standard encyclopedic source is, of course, the one you are reading. The cumulative volumes of the *Annual Review of Information Science and Technology* (ARIST; Information Today: Medford, NJ, 1966–) are equally indispensable. There are several bibliographic databases that cover different portions of the field: one with good international coverage is *Library and Information Science Abstracts* (LISA; ProQuest: San Diego, CA, 1969–). The environment for scholarly publishing in the information sciences is very diverse, and different subfields are represented well by different publishers (e.g., information retrieval by Cambridge University Press; digital libraries by MIT Press; museum studies by Routledge). There is no single text that provides a comprehensive overview of philosophical concerns in the information sciences, but monographs by Blair,[42] Budd,[56] Cornelius, Day,[46] Frohmann,[49] Hjørland,[61] Svenonius,[55] and Wilson[54] serve as philosophically sophisticated introductions to their respective areas, as do chapters in ARIST by Blair,[41] Capurro and Hjørland,[57] Cornelius,[59] Day,[60] and Fallis[25] (all listed in "References," above) Journals in the information sciences that carry philosophically informed articles on more than a very occasional basis include *Archival Science, Archivaria, Journal of the American Society for Information Science and Technology, Journal of Documentation, Library Quarterly, and Library Trends.* The Special Interest Group on the History and Foundations of Information Science (SIG/HFIS) of the American Society for Information Science and Technology (ASIS&T) regularly sponsors sessions of philosophical interest at annual meetings of ASIS&T, and the Conceptions of Library and Information Science (CoLIS) conference series is similarly receptive to philosophically themed papers.

Philosophy of Science *[ELIS Classic]*

Paul Evan Peters
University of Pittsburgh, Pittsburgh, Pennsylvania, U.S.A.

Abstract

The author notes: "...although a scientist may understand a science to the extent that he or she *does* science, a second level of understanding, that of understanding his or her understanding, may be absent." Philosophy of science is about that second level of understanding. That philosophy forms the basis of how and why a scientist conducts research, and conditions the judgments a scientist forms about the value and validity of the results of that research. Peters also addresses implications for library and information science.

—***ELIS Classic***, *from 1977*

INTRODUCTION

The philosophy of science is of fairly recent vintage as far as philosophical specializations go. Harré[1] calls our attention to this fact by noting that the idea that the systematic sciences presuppose styles of inquiry different from those of the ordinary commerce of the mind did not really take root until the early nineteenth century. Before this time, what we have by way of a literature are the records of the methodological deliberations of scientists and the technical developments of epistemologists (philosophers of knowledge). It seems quite natural that at some point efforts would have been made to marry these two, in many ways different, literatures.

The courtship preceding the marriage began in the nineteenth century, but the wedding has not been an easy one to arrange. Representatives of the two families involved, that is, philosophy and science, have sometimes traded harsh words. It is not difficult to find scientists who resent the "intrusion" of philosophers who never have had to face the demands of empirical research. Philosophers can be found, moreover, who retort that scientists can be likened to clumsy bears wandering about in a woods with no concept of, or even a desire for a concept of, the geography of the forest. Ackermann[2] illustrates this familial rivalry by calling attention to the awkwardness of the situation in which a philosopher is placed when queried by a scientist (particularly a physicist): Tell me something you've learned recently about science. The situation can be balanced by the philosopher reversing the initiative and questioning: Tell me something you've learned recently about philosophy. Socially, however, scientists seem to win the day, because, on the whole, it is philosophers who have declared an interest in science and not scientists in philosophy.

Such rebuffs and retorts may seem to be so much dirt in the laundry of the philosophy of science. In fact, however, they are diagnostic of a most stubborn impasse in the foundation of a philosophy of science. This impasse, as phrased by Danto,[3] is the attitudinal predisposition of philosophers and scientists alike that competent works in the philosophy of science are philosophic, for the former, or scientific, for the latter. It is the case, nevertheless, that since the nineteenth century, we can find not only individuals who are known for their philosophy but produced scientific works, such as René Descartes, or who are known for their science but produced philosophic works, such as Francis Bacon, but also individuals who refer to their works as the philosophy of science.

Some of these individuals, moreover, have produced "introductory" treatments and, consequently, have provided a resource from which we can derive a general appreciation for the scope of philosophies of science:

1. Hanson—exploration of the internal structure of scientific thinking.[4]
2. Churchman and Ackoff—explication of the systemic presuppositions of inquiry.[5]
3. Ackermann—explication of general, problem-independent principles of scientific practice.[2]
4. Frank—systematic approach to the understanding of the tactics and strategies of science.[6]
5. Harré—exposition of the principles operative in science that enable the acquisition of knowledge about the world and the things in it.[1]
6. Lambert and Brittan—analysis of conceptual and methodological issues in science and exploration of how science, as an experience, relates to human activity in general.[7]

An attempt to synthesize these six statements (among others) concerning the scope of philosophies of science results in a statement to the effect that a philosophy of

Encyclopedia of Library and Information Sciences, Fourth Edition DOI: 10.1081/E-ELIS4-120009002

science constitutes a critical understanding of science. The word "critical" in this statement is important in that it implies that the ways in which science is understood are themselves subjects for examination and understanding. Consequently, although a scientist may understand a science to the extent that he or she *does* science, a second level of understanding, that of understanding his or her understanding, may be absent. The degree to which this second level (and an infinite number of other levels defined similarly) is missing in the thinking of science (or a science) is the degree to which science's (or that science's philosophy) is undeveloped.

In discussing the critical understanding of science attempted by the philosophy of science, it is important for us to keep in mind that its understanding is just one such of a number possible. Others have come, recently, to be subsumed under the umbrella descriptor of "sciences of science." The closest of these to the philosophy of science is probably that of the history of science. Whereas, however, history of science inquiries usually result in descriptive expositions (as is characteristic of history), those of the philosophy of science result in prescriptive developments (as is characteristic of philosophy). These sciences of science will occupy our attention again in the final section of this article.

ORGANIZATION

Our objectives for this article are two: *a*) we want to conduct a survey of some of the thinking that has been done in the name of the philosophy of science and *b*) we want to open discussion of how this thinking can be said to apply to the work of library and information scientists. The "applications" aspect of this article is included more for crystallizing the material around familiar seeds than for any other reason. It is hoped that each reader will be able to think through her or his own applications, given the material of the survey.

It is evident that a survey can take any of a number of forms. Some surveys are organized around people, others around eras, and still others around issues. The organization of the present survey is that of "-isms." Other authors who have employed this style are Churchman and Ackoff,[5] Churchman,[8] Pepper,[9] and Turner.[10] (What we understand by "-ism," others have called "school.") It is possible to overwork the notion of an "-ism." consequently, before we identify those we will cover, we do well to take steps to clarify our intentions. (Our development in this area is related to Ackermann's discussion of scientific theories.)

When discussing the genetic constitution of an organism, it is convenient to make a distinction between "genotypical" and "phenotypical" characteristics. Genotypical characteristics are those said to be encoded in the organism's genetic makeup, while phenotypical characteristics are the result of the interaction between this makeup and a specific environment. Insofar as an organism is always in an environment, we can observe only phenotypical characteristics and, by examination of a number of "similar" organisms, infer genotypical characteristics. Since genotypical characteristics are inferred, they stand as idealizations and, as a result, no one expects to be able to observe them directly.

As we discuss the characteristics of philosophy of science "-isms," we will be dealing with the genotypical. This is to say that when we outline an "-ism" in terms of the way in which an "-ist" views the world, the "-ist" does not actually exist. Nevertheless, we will name historical personages and label them as an "-ist" of one type or another. It should be understood from here forward, however, that when we do this, we mean to say that the person involved is more of this type of "-ist" (has more of the characteristics of this "-ism") than he or she is of any other.

With these cautionary comments in mind, we can turn to identifying the "-isms" of our survey. This identification has been accomplished by grouping orientations assumed by philosophers of science as they have considered the following two questions:

How should scientists conduct their inquiry?
What should be our attitude toward the products of scientific inquiry?

These questions are not the only ones asked by philosophers of science. Nevertheless, they can be said to account for much of that which philosophers of science have debated among themselves. We shall refer to the first of these questions as the "how" question and the second as the "what" question.

Given these two questions of interest, we note that it is possible to find philosophers of science who agree in their orientations toward one and disagree on the other. Consequently, we have at our disposal a two-dimensional classification of philosophy of science thought. This classification is represented by the matrix shown in Fig. 1. Therein the "-isms" associated with orientations toward the how questions are displayed as rows, while those associated with orientations toward the what question are given as columns. Some "-isms," moreover, are presented in parentheses. These are "-isms" that we will develop as "modern" variants of traditional approaches.

The matrix in Fig. 1 expresses exactly the way in which we will organize our survey. Our first concern will be that of orientations toward the how question. This discussion will be followed by one centering around orientations toward the what question. As mentioned at the start of this section, the material of these survey sections will be focused through a perusal of what the philosophy of science might be said to have to do with the work of library and information scientists. After that, the article will

	What question	
How question	**Conventionalism**	**Realism**
Rationalism (speculativism)		
Empiricism (positivism)		
Criticism (pragmatism)		

Fig. 1 Two-dimensional classification of philosophy of science thought.

conclude with an articulation of some of the present and future issues in the philosophy of science.

ORIENTATIONS TOWARD THE HOW QUESTION

All vital questions raised by philosophers seem to attract a great deal of attention directed at stating them precisely and clearly. Authors can be observed to begin discussions so directed with the query: What is it that we are really asking? Answers to such second-order questions usually lead directly to answers for the original question.

The two questions that we have chosen are philosophically vital in the above sense. For this reason, we can say that it is according to the way in which an author formulates the how or the what question that we will class him or her as an "-ist" of one type or another. Authors can be said to subscribe to the same "-ism" by virtue of the similarity of their statement of questions.

Applying this reasoning to the how question leads to three main "-isms": rationalism, empiricism, and criticism. Each of these had reached a high degree of sophistication prior to the nineteenth century. Consequently, each has had an opportunity to undergo growth sufficient to allow identification of "modern" variants. These contemporary counterparts are known as speculativism, positivism, and pragmatism, respectively.

In this section, our primary concerns will be those of the traditional "-isms." This is the case for two reasons: *a*) due to their place in history, the traditional "-isms" appear more "stable" than their modern versions and *b*) we have provided for a section dealing with "current and future issues" in this article and can focus upon the modern there rather than here. Consequently, our immediate plan is one of laying out the traditional and discussing the modern only insofar as they can be said to carry on certain lines of thought.

We can convey a quick notion of who the people involved were, how they formulated the question under discussion, and what answers they provided. Some of the principal proponents of each "-ism" were:

Rationalism—Leibniz (1646–1716),[11] Descartes (1596–1650),[12] and Spinoza (1632–1677)[13]
Empiricism—Locke (1632–1704),[14] Berkeley (1685–1753),[15] and Hume (1711–1776)[16]
Criticism—Kant (1724–1804)[17,18]

These people can be said to have formulated our how question as follows:

Rationalism—What are the simplest ideas which: *a*) can be had by a scientist and *b*) are sufficiently "powerful" as to make their correctness unquestionable?
Empiricism—What are the simplest sensations which: *a*) can be had by the scientist and *b*) are sufficiently "clear" as to make their existence unquestionable?
Criticism—What capabilities must a scientist have prior to an inquiry in order to make judgments about the experience represented by that inquiry?

These formulations, in turn, lead to the following answers:

Rationalism—Scientists should conduct their inquiry so that it is guided by theory.

Empiricism—Scientists should conduct their inquiry so that it is guided by data.
Criticism—Scientists should conduct their inquiry so that it is guided by both theory and data.

Rationalism and empiricism were, and are, diametrically opposed positions that became synthesized with the advent of criticism. Such a synthesis was required because both rationalism and empiricism, taken separately or together, were, in one degree or another, inadequate for the explanation of certain notions judged basic to science. The explication of the areas of adequacy and inadequacy of both rationalism and empiricism will be our first concern.

For both rationalists and empiricists, the component of science requiring the most explanation is the ability of its practitioners to make any "sense" out of the flows of perceptions that arise from interactions between the human sensorium and the energies of the universe. Characteristically, a rationalist looks to the world of sensory experience and finds no permanence, no order, no intelligence; in short, he or she finds a world of appearance. Rationalistic reasoning led to the conclusion that the fact that there is any stability in human perception is due to the existence of certain simple concepts. These concepts were said to be used by the scientific *mind* to recognize the things contained in the chaos of sensation. Scientists come to make sense of the world, rationalists proposed, when they come to see instances of concepts.

Let us illustrate the rationalist program to the extent that we have presented it. In the world of everyday experience there are familiar objects that we call "chairs." None of us would claim that we have seen or will see all chairs. We know that chairs are manufactured according to different designs and are fabricated from different materials. Yet none of us feel particularly stressed when applying the term "chair" to an object we have never seen, manufactured by a design we have never seen, and fabricated from materials we have never seen. Rationalists concluded that this state of affairs is possible only because there exists a concept of "chair" that is common to all human reasoning and that can be employed by each of us to recognize, without hesitation, that each of a number of sensually dissimilar things is, in fact, an instance of this concept.

Rationalism received its justification from the "force" of the double-edged proposition that God exists and is good. From this basis, rationalists proceeded to conclude that a good God would not construct an unintelligible universe. Consequently, as we have said in the above, it was asserted that the flux of reality was deceptive. The problems of science were proposed to be: *a*) the discovery of the simplest of ideas and *b*) the combination of these ideas to develop other ideas. The methods appropriate to science were claimed to be intuition, for discovery, and deduction, for combination. The correctness of the products of intuition was debated according to the "principle of contradiction," which required that for an idea to be judged correct, it must be impossible for the universe to be otherwise. The products of deduction, moreover, had their correctness assessed according to the demands of logic wherein the principle of contradiction also played a role in that a combination of ideas would be judged to be incorrect if it could be shown that it asserted the opposite of other ideas that were already accepted as correct.

The twentieth-century mind, in general, has not been sympathetic to the rationalist program. It somehow seems incredible that philosophers and scientists would have proposed that intuition was the primary method of discovery appropriate to science. Although we will soon have much more to say on this, it seems important to itemize, at this point, some of the contributions to science made by scientists who ascribed to rationalism. First of all, Leibniz was a rationalist, and he, with Newton, added integral calculus to the armamentum of science. Descartes, to whom we owe gratitude for the Cartesian coordinate system, was also a rationalist. Finally, almost all of mathematics, in particular, and logic, in general, can be said to be motivated by rationalistic considerations.

It is much, therefore, that science can be said to have gained as a result of the efforts of individuals who believed deeply in a rationalistic philosophy. The fact remains, however, that the rationalist program was, in a sense, lopsided. Rationalism could always talk with more confidence and precision about deduction than it could intuition. The question of discovery of simple ideas and the associated validity of the entire rationalistic program loomed large. This was particularly the case because empiricism submitted that the notion of "simple ideas" was confused altogether.

It is difficult to imagine how two systems of belief could be more fundamentally opposed than those of rationalism and empiricism. Whereas, as we have discussed, rationalists viewed the products of sensation as intelligible only when based in thought, empiricists viewed the products of thought as intelligible only when based in sensation. Empiricists located the responsibility for the flux and chaos of experience in the mind. The world as we see it, the empiricists submitted, is simple and clear. It is the influence of undisciplined operations of the mind that introduces confusion. Whereas the existence and goodness of God is a matter of mere opinion, the clear and distinct sense impressions of a crisp, juicy, sweet, and red apple are undeniable facts. It was the proposition of the empiricists that scientists come to make sense of the world when they begin to notice the similarity of certain simple sensations among a number of objects.

Empiricists have always been quick to call attention to the superfluity of rationalistic beliefs when compared to theirs. As an example of this, consider the experience of pain. For an empiricist, pain is understood to be simply and distinctly forceful in its influence of the mind of man. There is no need to assume, with the rationalists, that a concept of pain is needed for the experience of pain. As children, each painful experience we encounter is unique. With time, we come to associate the similarity of all painful experiences and to develop a general notion of pain together with a system of types (such as dull, sharp, shooting, and the like). It is the sensation of pain that enables the recognition of a concept of pain. If it were otherwise, then children would have to be assumed to partake of the same experience as adults. For an empiricist, this implication of rationalism was decidingly absurd.

The justification of the empiricistic attitude was one of common sense (almost taken literally). Empiricists challenged scientists to admit that colors and shapes of things are trustworthy, while their naming of things was error prone. From this framework, the problems of science that empiricists recommended were observation and induction. The products of observation, that is, the simplest sensations, were verified by the agreement (consensus) of scientists performing the observation (either together or separately over time). The ideas admitted by induction, moreover, were said to be judged according to the "sufficiency of evidence" invoked in the induction.

Previously, we commented that the twentieth-century mind has not been, in general, sympathetic to rationalistic science. This is, in part, demonstrated by the fact that for most of us, our basic image of science is one of controlled observation of the world through experimentation, an image of empiricistic origin. All "good" scientific investigations must be replicable. All "good" scientific theories must fit the "facts." It is easy to recognize the empiricistic program as it enters our daily lives through social values and customs. Logical thinking is also a scientific value, and we still turn to rationalists to give us assistance in this area. Yet we refer to them as "logicians" instead of "scientists."

Rationalism was challenged by empiricists to explicate the origins of simple ideas. Such an explication, the argument was made, was the whole point of science. The program of empiricism proposed an explication, as we have discussed, involving a notion of simple sensations and induction in contrast to the simple ideas and deduction of rationalism. It is important to note, however, that the observations of simple sensations are "guaranteed," so to speak, by the trustworthiness of consensual agreement. The execution of induction, furthermore, is guaranteed by a belief in the principle of sufficiency of evidence. Rationalists challenged empiricists to explicate exactly how the principle of sufficiency of evidence could *itself* be verified. Using this approach, rationalists argued that empiricism was at fault due to circularity of reasoning.

As might be expected, adherents to rationalistic and empiricistic orientations toward our how question did not find much ground for thoughtful communication. There was one rationalist, however, who, late in his life, heeded the arguments of an empiricist and proceeded to define a new orientation. The rationalist was Immanuel Kant. The empiricist was David Hume. The emergent philosophy of science "-ism" was criticism.

The message that Hume[16] sent from England to Germany (which, incidentally, was the direction of most empiricistic critiques of rationalism) was contained in a revolutionary account of the scientific use of the notion of "causality." Hume had believed in the empiricistic proposition that we come to awareness of the cause of somehting, say B, by observing that it is always preceded by another thing, say A. It is said that while playing billiards one evening, Hume, by observing the interaction of the balls on the table, recognized that all one could correctly say is that "B succeeds A." He concluded that the notion of causality made no sense or was, at least, superfluous when viewed strictly from an empiricistic vantage point. The situation was no better, he discovered, in the rationalistic camp. In order for a rationalist to state that "A causes B" it would have to be assumed that the concepts of A and B "provided" for their causal relationship. Otherwise, the concept of A causing B could not be deduced from their individual concepts. But this would require our concepts of everything to include provisions for their relationship to everything else. This, Hume concluded, would result in our concepts being "unworkably" broad. Hume thus argued that the notion of causality was not scientific and that it should be abandoned.

Kant[17] accepted Hume's devastating thesis, announced that the notion of causality had to be "saved," and set about the task. Evidently, the only way that this salvation could have been accomplished was by formulating a new orientation. This is what Kant attempted and his approach was one of synthesis of rationalism and empiricism. As mentioned in the above, the synthesis he devised came to be known as "criticism."

The fundamental premise of the criticistic orientation was that the products of scientific inquiry originate neither *exclusively* in the world nor the mind. Rather, these products are the result of a process of cooperation between thinking and sensing. For a criticist, simple sensations or simple ideas simply do not exist. Instead, there are actions of judgment that are made possible when the mind structures reality as presented through the senses. A criticist would regard our how question as directed to the problem of a scientist deciding exactly how to conduct her or his observation. When asked how a scientist should conduct inquiry, criticists think of the structure of the world that must be assumed in order for observation to be possible.

The criticistic program called for the senses to provide the contents of our scientific judgments while the mind provided their form. As examples of what criticists meant by "form," we cite space, time, and a number of "categories of the understanding." One of these categories Kant defined "as to Relation" and it included, among substance and community, cause. Herein Kant's proposed solution of the Humean problem can be found. Whereas the senses inform us as to what needs to be related, the mind performs the relation. One such category of performance results in the judgment that A causes B. We find causality neither in the world nor in our concepts, suggested Kant, not because there is no causality but because it is contained in the *operation* of the mind.

Over time, the details of Kant's philosophy have been shown to be in error by developments in science itself. For instance, Kant accepted the Newtonian treatments of space and time as basic to the operation of the mind. Einstein and his followers have taught us that it is logically possible to think otherwise and that it is empirically mandated in certain situations to do so. Nevertheless, the criticistic orientation toward our how question deserves a place alongside of its parents, rationalism and empiricism. Rationalistically oriented scientists have given us logic, empiricistically oriented scientists have given us experimentation, and criticistically oriented scientists have given us motivation to temper our logics with experiments and our experiments with logics.

With the articulation of criticism, the divisions between orientations toward our how question have become progressively less distinguishable. It would be admitted now by almost all scientists and philosophers of science that scientific theories do not occur in the minds of people without some provocation, brought to bear by data from experimentation, as to what it is that needs to be theorized. Observation in the name of science, moreover, is generally accepted to require some theoretical deliberation if only to define the extremes that can be measured by the instruments to be used. The issues of debate among interested parties in the twentieth century seem to have become those of "degree" (the degree to which intuition is important and the degree to which observation is important), with speculativism emphasizing intuition and positivism, observation.

As we have mentioned in one way or another a number of times in this section, it is speculativism, the modern version of rationalism, that is on the defensive in contemporary discourse. The speculativist program claims that certain sciences, particularly those dealing with life and society, are intrinsically intuitionally based. This is to say that important components of the conceptual frameworks associated with these sciences will never be able to be expressed in terms that enable observation. Consequently, speculativists reason, there will always be a central place in science for intuition. Realizing this, a number of speculativists, Husserl,[19] for example, have devoted attention to the development of well-circumscribed intuitional methods.

Positivists, on the other hand, have responded to speculativistic arguments by acknowledging that unobservable concepts may be required by science, but the extent to which they are required is the extent to which the body of knowledge involved is prescientific. The demand of positivists is that scientific knowledge be "positive" in the sense that it make assertions about things that are observable. The meaning of *scientific* terms, argue the positivists, is nothing more and nothing less than the operations required to observe the terms' referents. Terms for which such operations cannot be specified are said to be nonscientific. The fact that there are other types of meanings than those scientific should not influence the scientist. As well, positivists regard the analysis of the language(s) of science as one of the most important tasks to be performed by philosophers of science.

Two individuals who have done the most with the positivistic orientation as we have discussed it are Carnap[20,21] and Bridgman.[22] Other individuals involved in the speculativism–positivism debates are:

Speculativism—Whitehead (1861–1948)[23] and Bergson (1859–1941)[24]
Positivism—Mach (1838–1916),[25] Wittgenstein (1889–1951),[26] and Ayer (1910–)[27]

It seems important to note that the positions of both speculativism and positivism can be said to be reasonable. Scientific knowledge, as we have come to understand it, must be based on publicly available information. Positivists have concluded that this requires that scientific knowledge be based on observation even though at some point some of the components of that knowledge may have been little more than very private, and very tentative, intuitions of some scientists. Speculativists complain that the labeling of the products of intuition as nonscientific or prescientific is an arbitrary and dangerous limitation of the scope of science. To them, it seems warranted that whatever influences, the development of scientific knowledge be considered to be part of science.

Speculativism and positivism can be said to have arrived at the same sort of communication impasse as their forebears, rationalism and empiricism. Criticism, we have seen, attempted to break this barrier by demonstrating how the scientific mind could be both rationalistic and empiricistic at the same time. Although criticistic arguments seem to have succeeded in this demonstration, the resurgence of rationalism and empiricism can be interpreted as an indication that the criticistic thrust did not cut deep enough. Pragmatism can be viewed as the modern version of criticism in that it attempts to demonstrate how a philosophy of science can harmonize speculativism and positivism.

The basic component of the pragmatic orientation as we shall discuss it is that a *science* can be both speculativistic and positivistic at the same time. Pragmatists bring to the surface of contemporary debates the fact that at any given time a science involves a number of different individuals at different stages of understanding of different (types of) problems (phenomena). Some of these individuals may be speculativistic in their outlooks, while others may be positivistic. Pragmatists regard as unnecessary the classification of concepts as nonscientific simply because they are speculativistically based. The classification of fields of inquiry as nonscientific simply because their practitioners are predominantly speculativistic is similarly viewed.

For pragmatists, science as an activity is not as separable from other forms of human activity as other philosophers of science seem to view it. The relations among sciences, that is, physics, biology, etc., moreover, are not as cut-and-dried as many would have it. The question of what psychology has to say to physics, or what art has to say to physics for that matter, is meaningless to a pragmatist unless a problem has been defined. Once a problem has been specified, the importance of a solution to the problem assessed, and an inventory of available knowledge accomplished, a pragmatist will accept anything as scientific that contributes to the attainment of a state of knowledge that is appropriate to the importance of the problem.

Pragmatism, then, attempts its synthesis of speculativism, positivism, and the other orientations we have covered in this section by focusing upon the inquiry of science rather than of individual scientists. Some of the people who have enunciated a pragmatic philosophy of science are James (1842–1910),[28] Dewey (1859–1952),[29] and Singer (1873–1954).[30] It should be noted, as we complete this discussion of pragmatism, that pragmatic thinking has not received the same recognition from speculativism and positivism as did criticism from rationalism and empiricism. Some additional remarks will be made on this point when we turn to the current and future issues in a later section.

It has been our goal in this section to expose some of the main currents in the thoughts that philosophers of science have given to the question of how scientists should conduct inquiry. This we have done by discussing the tenets of orientations to the question that we obtained by grouping the efforts of individuals who can be said to have formulated the question similarly. Although this survey has focused on the "-isms" so defined, it is important to recognize the issues involved to be basically those of the relative contributions to be made to science by intuition versus observation and deduction versus induction.

ORIENTATION TOWARD THE WHAT QUESTION

The second question that we selected for the survey of this and the preceding section was: What should be our attitude toward the products of scientific inquiry? In comparison to our first question, the meaning of this second query is less obvious. Its history, moreover, is considerably less extensive in that it has only been an active area for debate since the middle of the nineteenth century. Nevertheless, deliberations in its name have become increasingly commonplace in recent times.

Before proceeding much further, we had best be clear about our understanding of the question. First of all, we acknowledge that the products of scientific inquiry are manyfold. The specific class of products that we are addressing with the question, however, is that of "theories." Generally, we want to avoid the question of what the structure of a theory might be said to be [see Campbell[31] or Braithwaite[32] for expositions of widely accepted views]. The question that we do want to raise is that of the *function* of scientific theories. The debate that we want to survey has been concerned with the correctness of supposing that we can do certain things with theories.

To illustrate the form of this debate, we appeal, for the moment, to what is probably the most prevalent opinion on the subject. For many of us, scientific knowledge in the form of theories constitutes the "safest" and most "useful" knowledge that we humans can achieve. It is "safe" in the sense that it is dependably error-free. It is "useful" in the sense that it is tailored to provide solutions to problems of survival. No matter how strongly we might argue that the cost of scientific knowledge is excessive or that the methods by which it is obtained are inhumane, scientific theories have the advantage that they "work." They have provided direction for handsome material development, they have enabled us to reach for the stars, and they have justified utopian visions of disease-free societies. In sum, scientific theories enable us to predict, explain, and control the events of our world with precision.

The view of scientific knowledge that we have just articulated can be analyzed to expose an orientation toward our what question. For instance, we note that the viewpoint assumes: a) that a world of physical objects and processes exists independent of the scientific mind; b) that the nature of these objects and processes are (in principle) knowable; and c) that scientific theories are the most precise form of such knowledge attainable. Debates on the merits of the third part of this characterization usually occur between scientists and nonscientists, and even though they are fascinating, we have omitted any record of them from this article. There has been debate in philosophers' circles, moreover, on the appropriateness of the assumption that a world exists independent of the mind, but we will also leave that discussion to another place and another time. What we will take up for discussion are the thoughts of those scientists and philosophers of science who have found themselves more in agreement than not when comparing attitudes toward questions about the existence of a physical world and the precision of scientific knowledge relative to other forms of human knowledge but, all the same, disagree radically on the issue of the knowability of the physical world.

The orientation that holds that scientific knowledge does constitute an understanding of the nature of things in the physical world has come to be called realism. Two of the individuals who have thought through realistic positions are Moore[33] and Ryle.[34,35] Most of the rationalists and empiricists whom we cited in the previous section can be said to have been realists to one degree or another. In addition, a number of psychologists have attempted to develop theories of sense perception that are overtly realistic ["Gestalt" theorists, such as Köhler,[36] for instance, postulate that the contents of reality and those of the mind are "isomorphic," i.e., are in a one-to-one correspondence]. Turner[37] can be cited as a contemporary, philosophically minded psychologist who openly discusses his commitment to realism.

Realists are opposed by a number of points of view that agree to the extent that they all emphasize the strongly *conventional* rather than *real* character of scientific knowledge. Individuals of this orientation frequently refer to certain events in the history of science in order to convey an appreciation for why they have brought the realistic thesis under examination. Inventories of these events always include the "revolutions" of Copernicus and Einstein whereby complete systems of scientific knowledge, those of Ptolemy and Newton, respectively, were summarily replaced.[38–40] Mention is also made of developments in modern physics (in the form of quantum mechanics) that have led to the conclusion that there are limits to the ability of the human mind to know in real terms.[41] Even the world of mathematics, the contents of which lie beyond the perceptive powers of most of us, has been the scene of similar developments.[42–44] It is noted, moreover, that astrologers and alchemists once laid an unchallenged claim to being scientists; and ether, phlogiston, and humors once laid a similar claim to being scientific, realistic concepts. In no small way, the history of science can be said to be littered with the decaying parts of discarded theories and concepts.

It is not the case that realists ignore the dramatic events itemized in the previous paragraph. Rather, they don't accept the conclusions that "conventionalists," as we will call them, can be said to draw from the study of the history of science. Realists claim that it is to be expected that science's movement toward *real* theories should exhibit progress whereby concepts and theories are refined. Events such as the replacement of Ptolemy by Copernicus and Newton by Einstein should be viewed as nothing more than "growing pains." The assertion that scientific theories are realistic *in principle* cannot be rejected simply because we haven't yet achieved perfect science.

Conventionalistic response to realistic arguments can be said to have appeared in two major forms. First of all, there are those who have held that science doesn't need to assume a realistic attitude. This tactic has been most forcefully adopted by psychologists of a behavioristic bent[45,46] and has come to be known popularly as the "stimulus-response," "black-box," or "input-output" view of things. It has also influenced philosophic treatments of cybernetics [that of Craik,[47] for example]. Essentially, this strain of conventionalism, which has also been called "instrumentalism," holds that science need only record the correlations of actions performed by scientists and results observed. Introduction of any additional material into scientific theories is said to be unnecessary.

A second conventionalistically motivated response to realism can be found in the writings of Mach,[25] Poincaré,[48] and Duhem.[49] The suggestion of these authors, among others, is that the realistic attitude is inappropriate. It is their assertion that the reality of a theory cannot be assessed on *scientific* grounds. How could such an assessment be performed, they ask, without a comparison of the contents of the theory with those of reality itself. Obviously, such a comparison is impossible because it presupposes knowledge of that which is unknown. These conventionalists acknowledge that one theory can be said to be unrealistic in comparison to another in the sense that it does not account for observations as adequately. But, they are quick to remind us, science has experienced in its history the "unfortunate" co-occurrence of theories that account for the same observations to the same degree of accuracy. To say that one such theory became ascendant because it was more *real*, they conclude, is to postulate an impossible decision-making capability.

In the place of a realistic orientation, conventionalists of the form we are discussing would substitute an orientation that views scientific theories as "languages" by which scientists can communicate results of observation unambiguously and economically. It is not to be denied that the contents of these languages are provoked by reality as observed, but it is to be contested that they tell us about that reality as it is unobserved. If Duhem's program is followed,[49] it is held that the relationships among the contents of a theory, on the one hand, and the relationships among the contents of reality, on the other, move toward a coherence over time, but beyond this "natural classification," little more of the realistic attitude toward scientific theories can be interjected.

The survey of conventionalistic critiques of realism that we've conducted to this point hopefully engenders an appreciation for why the assumption of "in-principle knowability of reality" has come under examination. Without introducing considerable additional detail, it would be difficult to take the discussion much further. It has been our intention in going this far to demonstrate how quickly the deceptively simple question "What should be our attitude toward the products of scientific inquiry?" becomes complicated when investigated critically. As with the previous section, it is important to keep in mind the issues that have structured debate about the question. For our what question, these issues can be said to be those of the (in)appropriateness, (un)necessity, and (im)possibility of the attitude toward scientific theories as constituting real versus conventional knowledge of the world.

APPLICATION TO LIBRARY AND INFORMATION SCIENCES

At the start of this article, the promise was made that our survey of philosophy of science thinking would be applied to the problems of the library and information sciences. To produce such an application in the full form possible would be to develop a philosophy of library and information sciences. This we cannot do within the scope of a single article, but we hope to sketch out the components and promise of such a philosophy.

If we recall, for a moment, the definition of "philosophy of science" that we introduced for our discussion, we will be able to develop precisely what function a philosophy of library and information science might have. This definition stated that a philosophy of science constitutes a critical understanding of science where the word "critical" implies that the means by which the science is understood are themselves subjects for examination and understanding. People who dedicate thought to the philosophy of science, or to the philosophy of a science, therefore function, through the results of their work, to enable scientists to be more selective, more conscious about what they do and the ways they do it than they might be otherwise. This is the case, that is, if there exist open lines of communication between the two groups of scholars (those concentrating on the science, on the one hand, and those concentrating on the philosophy, on the other).

Stated in familiar terms, those who work upon a philosophy of a science assist those who work in that science in conceptualizing design options and interpreting situations. The options available to an individual approaching a system or an experimental design task can be categorized, given sufficient work, along the lines we followed in discussing our how question in previous sections. This is to say that a design task essentially raises questions about how something should be done and, philosophers of science assert, answers to such questions, upon examination, can be said to contain rationalistic, empiricistic, and criticistic orientations. It follows that a scientist who is able to recognize and analyze the strengths and weaknesses of these orientations is better equipped to formulate and evaluate design alternatives than one who is not.

Library and information scientists, for instance, face daily the problem of representing the contents of documents. Whether the mode of representation is that of classifying, abstracting, or indexing, to cite three, the problem remains to be one of developing a "substitute (surrogate)" for a document that enables that document to be related to other documents for purposes of storage and retrieval. We solve this problem by using classification and indexing systems. The designs of these systems have evolved over time and can be viewed to demonstrate the philosophy of science orientations we have discussed. The approach to classification adopted by Dewey, for example, relied heavily upon a conceptualization of the universe of knowledge, while that of the Library of Congress is based more upon the actual contents of documents themselves. In this respect, the Dewey decimal classification, oriented toward the ideational, can be said to be predominantly rationalistic while the Library of Congress classification can be said to be predominantly empiricistic because it is oriented toward the observable. S.R. Ranganathan, moreover, with his colon classification, can be recognized to have assumed a criticistic orientation. This is by virtue of his use of the process-matter-energy-space-time formula in the context that *every* document contains something about each of these facets (an ideational assertion), but what is contained has to be determined by continual surveillance of published literature (an observational assertion).

The point of discussing how library and information scientists have gone about designing systems for representing the contents of documents, however, is not to claim that the designers involved used philosophy of science thought to guide their work. Rather, this brief exposition stands as evidence for the proposition that philosophers of science do serve to help the practicing scientist understand more fully the ways things have been done in the past and the ways they could be done in the future. Faced with a problem of design and equipped with a comprehension of philosophy of science, scientists could explore, at the outset of work on the problem, the rationalistic, empiricistic, and criticistic viewpoints to the problem. Such an exploration would result in a preliminary inventory of subproblems, subtasks, associated with the theory that has to be invoked relevant to the problem (rationalistic), the data that has to be collected relevant to the problem (empiricistic), and the means by which the theory and the data can be matched to evaluate the effectiveness of the design (criticistic). This inventory, in turn, can function to clarify what the design could do and, after consideration of the practical, what it can do. It is in this latter category, that of what is practical for a design, that the inventory is again very useful because it enables an understanding of what the design is not doing. Thus, the task of explaining design failures, after a system is implemented or an experiment is conducted, becomes more systematic and less ad hoc than it is otherwise.

In some ways the above may be read as an articulation of the "systems approach" or the procedure of "systems analysis." This is not by accident. A number of contemporary philosophers of science have also contributed to the "systems" literature. A partial list of authors in this category includes Ackoff,[50,51] Churchman,[5,8,54,55] Helmer,[56] and Rescher.[57,58] The work of Mitroff[59] is particularly interesting in this respect, especially his effort with Williams and Rathswohl,[60] because it is frequently applied to information science topics.

Beyond the functioning of philosophy of science thought as an aid for the conceptualization of design issues and options, which is a function it has for all science, there are a number of possibilities for the direct application of philosophy of science developments to the problem spaces of library and information sciences. The concept of "user," for instance, is one that library and information scientists have discovered needs increasing precision. Library and information workers are frequently encouraged to actively consider and involve the "user" in the design of services first and in the delivery of services over time. Indeed, the attention that the concept of "user" has attracted in recent years can be said to account for the metamorphosis of the library and information sciences into the behavioral and social realms. To date, however, the language that the library and information profession has developed for discussing this concept is predominantly anecdotal in tone and descriptive in approach.

The concept of "user" can probably be said to have begun its ascendance as people who work with information endeavored to make scientific sense of the associated concept of "relevance." On both intuitional and evidential grounds, it is clear that the relevance of an item of information is a judgment made by a recipient of that item. The proposition is offered, then, that relevant items of information transform a passive recipient of information into an active user. A design objective that is consistent with this reasoning is that information delivery systems should strive for making *users* out of the *recipients* of their services. The manner in which these systems might do this, to come full circle, is to deliver highly relevant items of information.

In an article summarizing conclusions made from experimentation with relevance, Saracevic[61] notes that comparisons of relevance judgments have been made among users, nonusers, experts, and nonexperts. The remark we want to make at this point is that such comparisons are quite obviously based upon a typology of recipients of information. This is to say that considering the degree of subject specialization of a recipient or the conditions of reception, an individual is typed, for purposes of analysis, as a user, nonuser, expert, or nonexpert. Referring back to our previous comment about the language that library and information scientists have for discussing the concept of user, we can now see exactly what that language is.

The hint of an alternative language, that is, an alternative typology, for discussing recipients and users of information can be recognized to reside in the philosophy of science thought we have surveyed. Assuming that library and information work will be concerned with scientific and technical communication for years to come, which is certainly true in part, the ways in which philosophers of science have come to discuss orientations assumed by scientists toward their work could be explored as a base for similar discussions among library and information scientists. This is to say that we would come to state information requirements and judgmental criteria of groups of recipients of information in terms of the degrees to which they could be said to be rationalistic, empiricistic, and criticistic in their orientations. Although statements of this type are premature given current levels of development, we can suggest for purposes of illustration that the differential relevance of items of information could be systematically approached by assessing the rationalistic, empiricistic, and criticistic influence at work in the author and recipient.

Insofar as philosophies of science provide theories of science and of scientists, then, they allow two major areas of application to the library and information sciences to be pursued. Both of these have been discussed in the above. First of all, in summary, philosophies of science as theories of science help to make library and information scientists more aware of the constellation of approaches available for the execution of any given inquiry. Second, as theories of scientists, they contain characterizations of recipients and users of information to the extent that the information involved is that of scientific and technical communication. It is not to be concluded, however, that the philosophy of science is completely ready to be applied in these ways. There remains much work to be done by both philosophers and scientists.

SOME PRESENT AND FUTURE ISSUES

That which one regards as an "issue" in a field is that which is regarded as the problematic. It is the case, moreover, that the perception of the problematic is something that varies greatly from individual to individual. Everything we have said in this article pays tribute to this fact: what a rationalist takes for granted, an empiricist questions and vice versa. It has to be understood, therefore, that as we state some current and future issues in the following, these statements have to be interpreted, more than those of any other section of this article, in the light of the author's point of view. Obviously, this point of view is not that of a philosopher of science per se; rather, it is that of an information scientist who has found material in the literature of the philosophy of science that provokes thought about and adds perspective to his work. In addition, the point of view of the author tends to be criticistic, that is, he favors the examination of the interaction of concepts and observations over the examination of concepts or observations by themselves.

Within this framework, it can be stated, preliminarily, that the major present and future issues of the philosophy of science are at the "fringes" of the field instead of at its core. In truth, it has to be acknowledged that this entire article has been on the fringes. Such "core issues" as laws versus empirical generalizations, the (a)symmetry of explanation and prediction, the structure of theories, and the explication of terms have occupied little space in the preceding. These core topics can be said to be focused on the *products* of science. Our focus can be said to have been that of the *processes* attendant with the science. This consideration of processes attendant with science, moreover, is still a fringe concern for philosophers of science.

It is not fringe, however, for a number of other groups of scholars that we reference through the descriptor of the "sciences of science." Such scholars have come to understand that a full treatment of the processes of science will require *at least* a politics, sociology, and psychology of science and scientists. Seminal works in this respect are those of Price[62] and Maslow.[63] Crane[64] published a related effort, as has Mitroff.[65] The monumental study by Freidson[66] is also of interest, as are those of Hanson.[4,38]

It is the case that many philosophers of science in modern times have systematically excluded the psychological from their sphere of inquiry. As he begins his milestone treatise on probability as inductive logic, Rudolf Carnap[67] remarks at length on how it is inappropriate for a logician to attempt to speak to the point of the ways in which scientists actually do or even should reason. Logic and, so it seems, philosophy of science in this widespread conception should be neutral as to the actual practice of science. The core issues raised in this context are associated with the development of objective knowledge and the formulation of universal hypotheses and laws from time-bound experimentation. As is the situation with mathematics, the results of such research are presented as declarations of possibilities rather than imperatives for action.

In a certain sense, this attempt to define the core of the philosophy of science is similar to what some authors have tried to do with the issue of relevance in library and information science. Cooper,[68] referencing Wilson,[69] for instance, states clearly that his concern is that of *logical* relevance (topic-relatedness) rather than utility. King[70] has also seen value in separating the psychological aspects of relevance from other aspects that could be considered. The main group of philosophers of science have placed such logical matters at the center of their specialization, as many library and information scientists can be said to have done with relevance.

The formal or "logico-mathematico" vein of philosophy of science has spawned a richly substantial literature. Recently, moreover, it has developed along lines that bring it into proximity with the library and information sciences. Some of the work in this class has been done by Kemeny,[71] Watanabe,[72] Hintikka and Suppes,[73,74] and Suppes and Atkinson.[75] The common ground involved here is bounded by inductive inference and information theory wherein information theory provides a "calculus" for certain measurement of language tasks associated with the procedures of inductive logic.

The neutrality of this style of philosophy of science can be said to be responsible for both its strength and its weakness. It has been strong because scholars devoted to it and working within it have been able to push forward without being constrained at every step by speaking to the actualities of science and scientists. Note that this state of affairs, wherein philosophers of science have excluded behavioral and social inquiry from their approach, is symptomatic of a rationalistic frame of mind. This is the case even when the philosophers involved have been extolling the virtues of empiricism. But it is important to recognize that philosophers of science *do* philosophy and not science and, consequently, it is not inconsistent for them to use rationalistic arguments in philosophy for empiricistic conclusions in science.

There are those who are not convinced by this reasoning, and it is these that we have referred to as the fringe of the philosophy of science. We are at a point now from which we can understand clearly their position and the present author's conception of the future. The fringe of the philosophy of science is constituted by those individuals who have adopted empirical methods for developing their philosophies. Evidently, they believe such philosophies are possible even though it can be expected that philosophy, psychology, and sociology may be radically transformed in the process. This is the area, the "empiricizing" of philosophy, in which interesting future issues will develop. It is the area in which interesting present issues have crystallized. The projected result is that the core of philosophy of science will itself transform to something that is more directly approachable and appropriate to scientists than that which is currently the case. Whether or not this transformation will also result in a philosophy that is too "vulgar" to attract the attention of competent philosophers is something that is difficult to decide.

Possibly the first and foremost group on this fringe of which we have made so much is that of the pragmatists. The reasons for this are not hard to guess. Philosophies can be characterized, as we have in the preceding to a limited extent, by their "unit of analysis." Rationalism, for instance, analyzes things in terms of ideas, while empiricism uses sensations. Criticism's interest is in the act of judgment and thus its emphasis is on the relation of idea and sense. The unit of analysis of pragmatism, which we have presented as the modern variant of criticism, is that of human action in general [see Mead,[76] for instance] For pragmatists more than any other philosophers of science, therefore, the demand has been for an action-directed philosophy of science.

In addition to the push pragmatists have provided from the fringe, certain developments in the study of "objectivity" have set off some minor eruptions in the core itself. Primarily, it would seem, most of the problems are associated with the social sciences. Therein the appropriateness or even possibility of an objective comprehension of human and social behavior has been strongly questioned. Basically, the issue has come to be known as that of the "value-(non-) freedom" of the social sciences. Krimerman's anthology[77] contains an excellent sampling of opinions on this subject. The biases that a social scientist can introduce into an experiment have been the subject of study by Rosenthal,[78–80] among others. To make the situation complicated many times again, moreover, it has been determined that the objectivity of social science research is in question due to biases introduced by *subjects* themselves. The classic case in point in this regard is that of the "Hawthorne Program" [which provided the material for a book by Roethlisberger and Dickson[81,82]], wherein it was concluded that an improvement in industrial worker productivity and satisfaction could be traced to the workers' participation in an announced experiment rather than to any alteration of the working environment.

No doubt to some, the problem of objectivity in the social sciences represents no less than a diagnosis of their inadequacy as sciences. Things, however, are not that simple. Astronomy, for instance, is certainly an "acceptable" science and yet astronomers have struggled for years (indeed, centuries) with the problem of consistency in observation. Such consistency would be, in principle, possible if objectivity of observation and reporting were operative. Physics, as viewed by Heisenberg,[41] has evolved to a state of uncertainty in this respect as well. In an almost poetic chapter,[41] Heisenberg outlines the dilemma of the physicist historically an expert in the realms of the obviously real (levers, inclined planes, pendula, etc.), approaching the atom and the awareness that with things atomic there is a world of "potentialities or possibilities rather than one of things or facts." When the language of the physical sciences moves toward a potential or possible or probable calculus, it begins to sound similar to the dispositional or expectational or probable one of the social sciences.

So we find that the concept of objectivity, at the center of logico-mathematico strains of philosophy of science, is in a position of change of outlook. Modern physical science and modern social science have furnished evidence to the effect that objectivity is in the process of being replaced by intersubjectivity. Intersubjectivity, moreover, seems radically less a logical matter than one empirical insofar as the "inter-" of the concept requires attention be given to at least two things acting together rather than the solitary "ego" that can be found in so much of what we understand as logic. This is the major issue, though, that we have identified with the present and future of the philosophy of science. For purposes of summary, we again state that this issue, and all attendant issues, are those associated with the development of empirical techniques of philosophy in general and philosophy of science in particular.

CONCLUSION

The bibliographical sources for this article are extensive, and, thus, it may be of use to cite some works for purposes of general reference. The author's personal favorites, which is to say the ones that he consults most often, are those of Hanson,[4,38] Turner,[10] Churchman,[8] Duhem,[49] Kuhn,[39,40] and Pepper.[9] These are listed according to some measure of increasing difficulty. In the area of collections, the author favors those of Krimerman[77] and Brody.[83] It can be noted that all of those references are from the twentieth century; it is the author's opinion that it is best to start with these rather than the original, classic sources from which they draw.

Individuals who have not received citation in the preceding discussion but who have played influential roles in the development of contemporary philosophy of science thought are: Broad,[84] Crombie,[85] Eddington,[86] Feigl,[87] Feyerabend,[88,89] Kaplan,[90] Merleau-Ponty,[91] Merton,[92] Mill,[93] Neurath,[94] Pascal,[95] Pearson,[96] Popper,[97,98] Quine,[99] Reichenbach,[100] Russell,[101–103] Schlick,[104] and Scriven.[105] This list, however, should not be regarded as being exhaustive, for it reflects the scope of study of its author. The references given throughout this article also need not in every case be the most representative of an author although the attempt has been consciously made to meet such a condition for the majority.

ACKNOWLEDGMENT

The opportunity to prepare this article was extended to me by Ian I. Mitroff, University of Pittsburgh. Dr. Mitroff has been my philosophy of science mentor and I gratefully acknowledge his influence on my thinking.

REFERENCES

1. Harré, R. Philosophy of Science, History of. In *The Encyclopedia of Philosophy*; Macmillan and the Free Press: New York, 1967; 8 vols.
2. Ackermann, R.J. *Philosophy of Science: An Introduction*; Pegasus: New York, 1970.
3. Danto, A. Philosophy of Science, Problems of. In *The Encyclopedia of Philosophy*; Macmillan and the Free Press: New York, 1967; 8 vols.
4. Hanson, N.R. *Perception and Discovery: An Introduction to Scientific Inquiry*; Freeman, Cooper, and Co.: San Francisco, CA, 1969.
5. Churchman, C.W.; Ackoff, R.L. *Methods of Inquiry: An Introduction to Philosophy and Scientific Method*; Educational Publishers: Saint Louis, MO, 1950.
6. Frank, P. *Modern Science and Its Philosophy*; Collier: New York, 1961.
7. Lambert, L.; Brittan, G.G. *An Introduction to the Philosophy of Science*; Prentice-Hall: Englewood Cliffs, NJ.
8. Churchman, C.W. *The Design of Inquiring Systems: Basic Concepts of Systems and Organization*; Basic Books: New York, 1971.

9. Pepper, S.C. *World Hypotheses: A Study in Evidence*; Univ. of California Press: Los Angeles, CA, 1942.
10. Turner, M.B. *Philosophy and the Science of Behavior*; Appleton-Century-Crofts: New York, 1967.
11. Leibniz, G.W. *Monadology and Other Philosophical Essays*; Bobbs-Merrill: Indianapolis, IN, 1965.
12. Descartes, R. *Discourse on Method, and Meditations*; Liberal Arts Press: New York, 1960.
13. de Spinoza, B. *Ethics*; J. M. Bent: London, U.K., 1910.
14. Locke, J. *An Essay Concerning Human Understanding*; Clarendon Press: Oxford, U.K., 1924.
15. Berkeley, G. *A Treatise Concerning the Principles of Human Knowledge*; Bobbs-Merrill: Indianapolis, IN, 1957.
16. Hume, D. *Enquiries Concerning Human Understanding and Concerning the Principles of Morals*; Clarendon Press: Oxford, U.K., 1957.
17. Kant, I. *Prolegomena to Any Future Metaphysics That Will Be Able to Present Itself as a Science*; Manchester Univ. Press: Manchester, U.K., 1953.
18. Kant, I. *Critique of Pure Reason*; St. Martin's Press: New York, 1963.
19. Husserl, E. *Ideas: General Introduction to Pure Phenomenology*; Macmillan: New York, 1931.
20. Carnap, R. *Philosophical Foundations of Physics: An Introduction to the Philosophy of Science*; Basic Books: New York, 1966.
21. Carnap, R. *The Logical Structure of the World: Pseudoproblems in Philosophy*; Univ. of California Press: Berkeley, CA, 1967.
22. Bridgman, P.W. *The Nature of Physical Theory*; Princeton Univ. Press: Princeton, NJ, 1936.
23. Whitehead, A.N. *Science and Philosophy*; Philosophical Library: New York, 1948.
24. Bergson, H.L. *Creative Evolution*; Modern Library: New York, 1944.
25. Mach, E. *The Analysis of Sensations and the Relation of the Physical to the Psychical*; Dover: New York, 1959.
26. Wittginstein, L. *Tractatus Logico-Philosophicus*; Routledge and K. Paul: London, U.K., 1955.
27. Ayer, A.J. *Language, Truth, and Logic*; Dover: New York, 1952.
28. James, W. *Pragmatism, A New Name for Some Old Ways of Thinking: Popular Lectures in Philosophy*; Longmans, Green, and Co.: New York, 1907.
29. Dewey, J. *Logic: The Theory of Inquiry*; Holt: New York, 1938.
30. Singer, E.A., Jr. *Experience and Reflection*; Univ. of Pennsylvania Press: Philadelphia, PA, 1959.
31. Campbell, N.R. *Foundations of Science: The Philosophy of Theory and Experiment*; Dover: New York, 1957.
32. Braithwaite, R.B. *Scientific Explanation: A Study of the Function of Theory, Probability, and Law in Science*; Cambridge Univ. Press: Cambridge, U.K., 1953.
33. Moore, G.E. *Some Main Problems of Philosophy*; Collier: New York, 1962.
34. Ryle, G. *Dilemmas*; Cambridge Univ. Press: Cambridge, U.K., 1954.
35. Ryle, G. *The Concept of Mind*; Hutchison's Univ. Library: New York, 1949.
36. Köhler, W. *The Place of Value in a World of Facts*; Liveright: New York, 1938.
37. Turner, M.B. *Realism and the Explanation of Behavior*; Appleton-Century-Crofts: New York, 1971.
38. Hanson, N.R. *Patterns of Discovery: An Inquiry into the Conceptual Foundations of Science*; Cambridge Univ. Press: Cambridge, U.K., 1958.
39. Kuhn, T.S. *The Copernican Revolution: Planetary Astronomy in the Development of Western Thought*; Harvard Univ. Press: Cambridge, MA, 1957.
40. Kuhn, T.S. *The Structure of Scientific Revolutions*; Univ. of Chicago Press: Chicago, IL, 1970.
41. Heisenberg, W. *Physics and Philosophy: The Revolution in Modern Science*; Harper: New York, 1958.
42. Gödel, K. *On Formally Undecidable Propositions of Principia Mathematica and Related Systems*; Oliver and Boyd: Edinburgh, U.K., 1962.
43. Nagel, E.; Newman, J.R. *Gödel's Proof*; New York Univ. Press: New York, 1958.
44. Rosser, B. An informal exposition of proofs of Gödel's and Church's theories. J. Symb. Logic **1939**, *4*, 53–60.
45. Watson, J.B. *Behaviorism*; Norton: New York, 1930.
46. Skinner, B.F. *The Behavior of Organisms: An Experimental Analysis*; Appleton-Century-Crofts: New York, 1938.
47. Craik, K.J.W. *The Nature of Explanation*; Cambridge Univ. Press: Cambridge, U.K., 1967.
48. Poincaré, H. *Science and Method*; Dover: New York, 1952.
49. Duhem, P.M.M. *The Aim and Structure of Physical Theory*; Princeton Univ. Press: Princeton, NJ, 1954.
50. Ackoff, R.L.; Emery, F.E. *On Purposeful Systems*; Aldine-Atherton: Chicago, IL, 1972.
51. Ackoff, R.L. Towards a behavioral theory of communication. Manage. Sci. **1958**, *4*, 218–234.
52. Ackoff, R.L. Management mis-information systems. Manage. Sci. December **1967**, *14* (4), 147–156.
53. Ackoff, R.L.; Gupta, S.K.; Minas, J.S. *Scientific Method: Optimizing Applied Research Decisions*; Wiley: New York, 1962.
54. Churchman, C.W. *Challenge to Reason*; McGraw-Hill: New York, 1968.
55. Churchman, C.W.; Ackoff, R.L.; Arnoff, E.L.; Edie, L.C.; et al., *Introduction to Operations Research*; Wiley: New York, 1957.
56. Helmer-Hirschberg, O. *The Application of Cost-Effectiveness to Non-Military Government Problems*; The Rand Corp.: Santa Monica, CA, 1966.
57. Helmer-Hirschberg, O.; Rescher, N. On the epistemology of the inexact sciences. Manage. Sci. **1960**, *6*, 25–52.
58. Rescher, N. *The Coherence Theory of Truth*; Clarendon Press: Oxford, U.K., 1973.
59. Mitroff, I.I. A communication model of dialectical inquiring systems: A strategy for strategic planning. Manage. Sci. June **1971**, *17*(10).
60. Mitroff, I.I.; Williams, J.G.; Rathswohl, E. Dialectical inquiring systems: A new methodology for information science. J. Am. Soc. Inf. Sci. November/December **1972**, *23* (6), 365–378.
61. Saracevic, T. Ten years of relevance experimentation. Proc. Am. Soc. Inf. Sci. **1970**, *7*, 33–36.
62. de Solla Price, D.J. *Little Science, Big Science*; Columbia Univ. Press: New York, 1963.
63. Maslow, A.H. *The Psychology of Science: A Reconnaissance*; Harper and Row: New York, 1968.

64. Crane, D. *Invisible Colleges: Diffusion of Knowledge in Scientific Communities*; Univ. of Chicago Press: Chicago, IL, 1972.
65. Mitroff, I.I. *The Subjective Side of Science: A Philosophical Inquiry into the Psychology of the Apollo Moon Scientists*; Elsevier: Amsterdam, the Netherlands, 1974.
66. Freidson, E. *Profession of Medicine: A Study of the Sociology of Applied Knowledge*; Dodd Mead: New York, 1970.
67. Carnap, R. *Logical Foundations of Probability*; Univ. of Chicago Press: Chicago, IL, 1962.
68. Cooper, W.S. A definition of relevance for information storage and retrieval. Inf. Storage Retr. June **1971**, *7* (1), 19–37.
69. Wilson, P. *Two Kinds of Power: An Essay on Bibliographic Control*; Univ. of California Press: Berkeley, CA, 1968.
70. King, D.W. Design and evaluation of information systems. Ann. Rev. Inf. Sci. Tech. **1968**, *3*, 61–104.
71. Kemeny, J.G. A logical measure function. J. Symb. Logic. December **1953**, *18* (4), 289–308.
72. Watanake, S. *Knowing and Guessing: A Quantitative Study of Inference and Information*; Wiley: New York, 1969.
73. *Information and Inference*; Hintikka, K.J.J.; Suppes, P., Eds.; Dordrecht, the Netherlands, 1970.
74. *Aspects of Inductive Logic*, Hintikka, K.J.J.; Suppes, P., Eds.; North-Holland: Amsterdam, the Netherlands, 1966.
75. Suppes, P.C.; Atkinson, R.C. *Markov Learning Models for Multiperson Interactions*; Stanford Univ. Press: Stanford, CA, 1960.
76. Mead, G.H. *The Philosophy of the Act*; Univ. of Chicago Press: Chicago, IL, 1938.
77. *The Nature and Scope of Social Science: A Critical Anthology*, Krimerman, L.I., Ed.; Appleton-Century-Crofts: New York, 1969.
78. Rosenthal, R. *Experimenter Effects in Behavioral Research*; Appleton-Century-Crofts: New York, 1966.
79. Rosenthal, R. Experimenter outcome-orientation and the results of psychological experimentation. Psychol. Bull. **1964**, *61* (6), 405–412.
80. Rosenthal, R. On the social-psychology of the psychology experiment: The experimenter's hypothesis as unintended determinant of experimental results. Am. Sci. **1963**, *51*, 268–283.
81. Roethlisberger, F.J.; Dickson, W.J. *Management and the Worker: Technical versus Social Organization in an Industrial Plant*; Harvard Univ. Press, Graduate School of Business Administration, Bureau of Business Research: Boston, MA, 1934.
82. Roethlisberger, F.J. *Management and Morale*; Harvard Univ. Press: Cambridge, MA, 1941.
83. *Readings in the Philosophy of Science*, Brody, B.A., Ed.; Prentice-Hall: Englewood Cliffs, NJ, 1970.
84. Broad, C.D. *The Mind and Its Place in Nature*; Routledge and K. Paul: London, U.K., 1951.
85. Crombie, A.C. *Medieval and Early Modern Science*; Harvard Univ. Press: Cambridge, MA, 1961.
86. Eddington, A.S. *The Nature of the Physical World*; Macmillan: New York, 1928.
87. Feigl, H. Logical Empiricism. In *Twentieth Century Philosophy: Living Schools of Thought*; Runes, D.D., Ed.; Philosophical Library: New York, 1943.
88. Feyerabend, P.K. Explanation, Reduction, and Empirium. In *Scientific Explanation, Space, and Time*; Feigl, H., Maxwell, G., Eds.; Minnesota Studies in the Philosophyof Science; Univ. of Minnesota Press: Minneapolis, MN, 1962; Vol. 3.
89. Feyerabend, P.K. Problems of microphysics. In *Frontiers of Science and Philosophy*; Colodny, R.G., Ed.; University of Pittsburgh Series in the Philosophy of Science; Univ. of Pittsburgh Press: Pittsburgh, PA, 1963; Vol. 1.
90. Kaplan, A. *The Conduct of Inquiry: Methodology for Behavioral Science*; Chandler: San Francisco, CA, 1964.
91. Merleau-Ponty, M. *The Structure of Behavior*; Beacon Press: Boston, MA, 1963.
92. Merton, R.K. *Social Theory and Social Structure*; Free Press: New York, 1968.
93. Mill, J.S. *A System of Logic, Ratiocinative and Inductive: Being a Connected View of the Principles of Evidence and the Methods of Scientific Investigation*; Longmans: New York, 1916.
94. Neurath, O. *Foundations of the Social Sciences*; Univ. of Chicago Press: Chicago, IL, 1944.
95. Pascal, B. *Pensees*; Pantheon: New York, 1950.
96. Pearson, K. *The Grammar of Science*; Meridian: New York, 1957.
97. Popper, K.R. *The Logic of Scientific Discovery*; Harper and Row: New York, 1968.
98. Popper, K.R. *Conjectures and Refutations: The Growth of Scientific Knowledge*; Routledge and K. Paul: London, U. K., 1969.
99. Quine, W.V.O. *Methods of Logic*; Holt: New York, 1959.
100. Reichenbach, H. *Experience and Prediction: An Analysis of the Foundations and the Structure of Knowledge*; Univ. of Chicago Press: Chicago, IL, 1938.
101. Russell, B. *The Problems of Philosophy*; Holt: New York, 1912.
102. Russell, B. *Our Knowledge of the External World*; Norton: New York, 1929.
103. Russell, B. *On the Philosophy of Science*; Bobbs-Merrill: Indianapolis, IN, 1965.
104. Schlick, M. *General Theory of Knowledge*; Springer-Verlag: New York, 1974.
105. Scrivan, M. Definition, Explanation and Theories. In *Concept, Theories and the Mind-Body Problem*; Feigl, H., Scriven, M., Maxwell, G., Eds.; Minnesota Studies in the Philosophy of Science; Univ. of Minnesota Press: Minneapolis, MN, 1968; Vol. 2.

Index

C

D

E

G

I

J

K

O

P

S

U

X

Y